# THE HOLSTEIN PAPERS

### THE MEMOIRS, DIARIES AND
### CORRESPONDENCE OF
### FRIEDRICH VON HOLSTEIN
### 1837–1909

## IV

# CORRESPONDENCE

## 1897–1909

D0171156

HOLSTEIN IN 1906

# THE
# HOLSTEIN PAPERS

EDITED BY
NORMAN RICH & M. H. FISHER

VOLUME IV
★
## CORRESPONDENCE

1897–1909

CAMBRIDGE
AT THE UNIVERSITY PRESS
1963

PUBLISHED BY
THE SYNDICS OF THE CAMBRIDGE UNIVERSITY PRESS

Bentley House, 200 Euston Road, London N.W.1
American Branch: 32 East 57th Street, New York, 22, N.Y.
West African Office: P.O. Box 33, Ibadan, Nigeria

©

CAMBRIDGE UNIVERSITY PRESS
1963

The editors and publishers wish to record their gratitude to Michigan State University for a generous grant assisting the publication of the Holstein *Correspondence*

*Printed in Great Britain by*
*Robert MacLehose and Company Limited*
*The University Press, Glasgow*

# CONTENTS

## CORRESPONDENCE

| | | | |
|---|---|---|---|
| 1897 | *page* 1 | 1904 | 277 |
| 1898 | 62 | 1905 | 323 |
| 1899 | 103 | 1906 | 379 |
| 1900 | 175 | 1907 | 452 |
| 1901 | 217 | 1908 | 513 |
| 1902 | 244 | 1909 | 611 |
| 1903 | 274 | | |

*Index to Correspondence 1861–1909 ( two volumes )*     *page* 623

# PLATES

Holstein in 1906            *frontispiece*

Holstein in 1906            *facing page* 1

HOLSTEIN IN 1906

# 1897

592.   Holstein to Hugo von Radolin[1]

Berlin, 10 January 1897

Dear Radolin,

Muraviev as the director of Russian foreign policy—that is not a brilliant result for H.M.'s efforts during the past few years to make himself agreeable to the Tsar. Without Breslau[2] and without Darmstadt[3] things might perhaps be better.

Muraviev will probably have to be regarded as the personal enemy of H.M., because Muraviev knows that it was H.M. himself who had him removed from Berlin.

I nevertheless don't believe that a revision of the Treaty of Frankfurt is imminent because the flow of the Far Eastern Question, whether fast or slow, cannot be halted and will absorb the attention of Russia as well as her energies. Therefore we don't have to worry.

In view of Muraviev's servile nature, I do not think it would be a good idea for you to make any sort of advances to him. Put yourself on good terms with as many Grand Dukes and influential people as possible, then he too will come around. By that I don't mean the Vladimirs, because they are apparently unfriendly *de parti pris*. If I were you I would not go beyond the conventional requirements in my relations with them.

Is old Michael[4] a person with whom you could get on closer personal terms? A lonely old man is often very responsive to invitations *en petit comité* with the right people. Perhaps he would talk more freely at an Ambassador's than he does among Russians. In any case you must bestir yourself, because you will have no support in Mur. H[erbert] B[ismarck] will see to that.

With kindest regards
Your old

H

---

[1] From the Radolin Papers.

[2] See vol. III, p. 652, , note 3.

[3] After his enthusiastic reception in Paris from 5–9 October 1896, the Tsar returned to Germany and stayed in Darmstadt from 11–29 October. On 19 October the Kaiser visited the Tsar in Darmstadt. Waldersee wrote: 'There is no question that the Tsar had no desire whatever to meet our Kaiser again, and it is really deplorable that the latter absolutely runs after him. The meeting was arranged with a vast amount of trouble by having our Kaiser go to Darmstadt and having the Tsar repay the visit on the following day in Wiesbaden. The Kaiserin did not accompany her husband to Darmstadt, nor did the Tsarina come to Wiesbaden, a proof of how cool the relationship is and that the two empresses did not get along together at all well at Breslau and Görlitz.' (Waldersee, *Denkwürdigkeiten*, vol. II, pp. 373–4.)

[4] Michael Nicholaivich, Grand Duke of Russia. Brother of Tsar Alexander II.

### 593. Philipp zu Eulenburg to Holstein

Vienna, 13 January 1897

Dear friend,

Hülsen had nothing to do with Goluchowski's visit during the festival of the Order.[1] During the visit H.M. paid to Szögyéni some time ago, the former told him of Goluchowski's projected visit, and subsequently H.M. issued an invitation that he should come to the festival of the Order, which was at once accepted and reported in Vienna.

I would now like to tell you the following about my last talk with Goluchowski before he arrives [in Berlin.] He had come directly from Kaiser Franz Joseph and had apparently discussed politics in general with him. I asked if he had received any news about the proposed appointment of Muraviev as Minister. He replied in the negative. I said that this man who was wholly dependent upon the Empress Mother was not a pleasant prospect. The memories they had of him in Berlin were also not especially good. He was just one of those Russians who made use of *all* methods. Goluchowski replied: 'Yes, you will still experience many surprises in Russia! I simply do not *understand* your attitude. You (P. Eulenberg) are always full of distrust. This does not seem to be the case in Berlin.' I said that my opinion was identical with that of Berlin. My Government also regarded the vacillation shown in St Petersburg with mistrust. But to make this opinion the starting-point for an inimical policy towards an Empire from which we were not divided by any interests that ran counter to ours would be madness, *especially with regard to Austria* to whom we still hoped to render *valuable* service through our friendly relations in critical days.

Goluchowski remarked how regrettable it was that our views, for example on the subject of an occupation of Constantinople, were *so far* apart.

I replied that every Power like every individual formulated its views academically and expressed them to its friends. Austria also had her own particular ideas on various questions and was nevertheless our loyal friend. And so did we. We would be there in the hour of need, but what would happen if we suddenly tipped the scales against Russia? The nervousness of the French would not stand that, and in a twinkling of an eye we would be faced with a European war. The Count acquiesced in these views and throughout the remainder of our conversation he maintained this reassured attitude. I also told him with reference to Constantinople that he should please not draw conclusions about a lack of loyalty on our part to our treaty obligations from our divergent views about the good or evil effects of an occupation by Russia. He surely did not intend to beat the same drum as those people who thought themselves justified by the *Hamburger* 'revelations'[2] in doubting our loyalty? The Count strongly denied any such intention and acknowledged that

---

[1] Count Goluchowski was in Berlin from 16–19 January. (See *Grosse Politik*, vol. XIIi, nos. 2933, 3114–15, pp. 72–4, 275–9.)

[2] See above, vol. III, p. 652, note 2.

one might discuss Constantinople *in a perfectly friendly manner* without necessarily quarrelling about it.

Finally he broke into a very academic lament. 'Bismarck caused the whole trouble when he turned down Gambetta's serious suggestion of an alliance with Germany.[1] He touched us with the plague-spot of the republic and prevented that ideal of all alliances: Germany, France, Austria. The value of such an alliance was *so great* that he should have joined it even at the cost of a neutralisation of the imperial provinces. I worked my fingers to the bone at that time in Paris in order to make propaganda for this idea here and indirectly in Berlin. Now naturally there is no longer any talk of it—but we will all live to see what Russia will do to us *with* France. I simply do not understand how one can fail to look upon Russia as the *common hereditary foe* of all western civilized States.'

You can see Goluchowski's ideas very clearly from the course of this conversation. If I was successful this time in pacifying him, his fanatical hatred of the Russians will always break out again and arouse the wish to involve us. If we *remain calm* however that is unimportant. I prefer that to the opposite, especially now with Muraviev on the scene, for he may make determined efforts to separate Austria from us. It therefore seems to me that Goluchowski's attitude to Russia is a great advantage for us. For his ideas about an alliance with France are *also* completely incapable of realisation in view of his opposition to Russia.

If you think it would be useful to put this letter into the form of a secret report, you may easily do so. I did not want to do so here.

But that is enough for to-day!

With kindest regards
Your faithful
PEulenburg.

Please be so kind as to send the [enclosed] two letters to Their Majesties to the Palace as quickly as possible. Although they contain nothing of importance, they are urgent. I asked H.M. (as a postscript) not to talk about Constantinople with Goluchowski and to show *little enthusiasm* if he brought up the subject.

## 594. Alfred von Kiderlen-Wächter to Holstein

15 January 1897

Dear friend,

About Muraviev we are surely of the same opinion. As a character he is a swine! There is no doubt about that. I hope to tell you shortly in an official gossip report what they think of him here[2] and about the influences here that played a part in his appointment. To-day I only want to direct your personal attention to one point. Muraviev is *not* a friend of France. He has no political convictions of any kind. Only he thinks the English disgusting and he has a fanatical hatred of the Poles. Both sentiments are perfectly agreeable to us.

---

[1] See *Grosse Politik*, vol. III, no. 654, p. 387.　　　　[2] In Copenhagen.

He will *only* conduct a policy which he believes will make him most popular in St Petersburg. He will do only what the person in power at the moment—the Tsar or Maria Feodorovna[1]—tells him to do, but he will do that with finesse. He is full of the most petty and ridiculous vanity, and I have never seen anything to compare with the way he licks the boots of everything connected with the Court! It was ludicrous and was ridiculed here by *everybody*, especially by the Danes, how he crawled in the meanest and most undignified way into Imperial, Royal and Grand Ducal bottoms. At the same time he always boasted here of how well he was liked at our Court. *'L'empereur m'a dit cela', 'Lorsque j'étais à un thé intime de l'Impératrice Augusta'*, etc. Now he knows, however, that he was rejected at the time as possible Russian Ambassador to Berlin. That offended him deeply. He has often spoken to me about it. I told him straight out that this was not the work of the Foreign Ministry. Whether anything was ever said, I did not know. Perhaps it was only a *Russian* intrigue against him! On this point, therefore, it would be wise to be cautious. At the same time I think that it would be *extraordinarily useful* to praise him in the Press and as much as possible officially for his service in Berlin— which up to now had been his pride—and to treat him like an 'old Berliner'. He is *so conceited* that this certainly will flatter him, and after all Christmas comes but once a year.

He doesn't like Osten-Sacken. Perhaps he will wring his neck as soon as he feels himself to be sufficiently firmly in the saddle. As I already said, his political attitude will depend to a large extent on how much he has to depend on the support of Maria Feodorovna and how much support he thinks she will give him. To regard him as an out-and-out foe of Germany would be to overestimate him!

*D'avoir une bonne presse* is for him the highest good. He was ecstatic when he was mentioned in the *Danebrog* here. The more you have people write about him, the more he will be amenable to one thing or another.

You are probably already better informed than I am, but I nevertheless wanted to write this to you. I only hope that he will not immediately be regarded and treated as an enemy of Germany just because he was a cad in Berlin. *cf.* Shuvalov : *'C'est un si petit caractère!'*

Always your faithfully devoted

Kiderlen

### 595.  Edmund von Heyking[2] to Holstein

Peking, 17 January 1897

My dear Herr von Holstein,

[…] I would like to permit myself to raise a point which is familiar to you, my dear Herr von Holstein, but the consequences of which may be more obvious here on the spot. We are completely isolated in China;

---

[1] The Empress Mother.

[2] Consul-General in Calcutta, 1889–93, in Cairo, 1893–5; Minister in Tangier, 1895–6, in Peking, 1896–9, in Belgrade, 1904–6; frequently a member of the Foreign Ministry staff in Berlin.

there is no Triple Alliance to back up our position in China. The Italians are at the moment represented by a twenty-four year old interpreter and play a sorry role in Peking; the Austrians intend to accredit a Minister here in the near future, but they have neither interest nor influence in China.

Our isolated position has its favourable side; out here we do not have to consider our allies and our hands are free to take care of the interests of Germany, which are more extensive than those of her two allies.

If it were therefore possible to reach an understanding with Russia beforehand to the effect that we would like to acquire a naval base in southern China outside the Russian sphere of influence, the Russians might be quite happy to see us establish ourselves there to weaken the hitherto predominant English influence, whereas the English at the moment feel so threatened in China that they would let us establish ourselves here wherever we liked because they would hope that in the end we would provide a counterweight to Russian influence. I don't think that the Russians in that case would proceed with annexations of their own because this would be in complete contradiction to their previous policy of waiting and slow absorbtion. The Russians simply can afford to wait, they have plenty of time and are confident that the Chinese inheritance will fall to them. We, however, are not in this position. We can't wait, because our warships can't swim about here forever like homeless waifs, and we run the risk of losing prestige because we have expressed wishes without pushing them through. A success in Far Eastern waters would certainly stand our fleet in good stead, for the public by and large after all has most understanding and sympathy for a concrete proof of the utility of the naval budget.

You, my dear Herr von Holstein, have exercised an influence on the policy of Germany and the efforts to protect her from the dangers that surround her which no German will forget who knows anything about the inner history of our policies. In grateful memory of the long years in which I was allowed to work as your pupil, I venture to ask you to take into consideration that for the preservation and strengthening of Germany a strong maritime force is a vital necessity, and that our fleet cannot do without the firm support of a naval base in overseas territories. [...]

Always yours most obediently<br>Heyking

## 596.  Hugo von Radolin to Holstein

St Petersburg, 18 January 1897

My dear friend,

What you write me[1] about the new man may well be true and it is very regrettable that something happened at the time to betray the antipathy of a certain person[2] to him. Just one more sign of how dangerous this

---

[1] In the letter of 10 January. See above.  [2] The Kaiser.

personal intervention is. But I think he will be clever enough to take things as they are and to reckon with the given factors abroad. *Il ne cassera pas les vitres*, of that I am convinced. He is far too concerned to maintain himself in office to go to extremes. Please read my first report about him and his friendly behaviour.[1] He was so natural and easy that I received a good impression. Certainly L[obanov] never behaved as warmly towards me as he did. He complained at length to my Austrian colleague about the irresponsibility of the Press in picturing him as anti-German; he had lived far too long in Germany to be anything of the sort. I will not run after him but continue to deal with him in a natural and friendly manner, as we have always dealt with each other and as we did in our present meetings. He came to see me at once before going to anyone else, stayed for a long time and chatted very comfortably about old times. I told him I hoped he would dine with me before returning to Copenhagen, to which he very willingly consented. [...] We will be able to trust this new man just as little as we were able to trust his former chief, Shishkin, or Shuvalov, etc. Our attitude towards him will depend on his conduct of policy. I will watch him without a preconceived opinion. I am convinced, however, that his policy will be the same as that of anyone else they might have selected. I doubt whether Kapnist would have been better. He too had connections with H[erbert] B[ismarck], and he has besides a whole rat's nest of relatives behind him who swear only by Paris. Would Nelidov have been better? I don't know about that either. Every Russian Minister of the present era will conduct a Russian policy and will try to be on good terms with whatever Power seems useful. He will at all events be careful and not attempt any adventurous *coups*. His position in the country is not secure enough for that, for he has the greater part of Society against him and only the Empress Mother for him—and her influence after all can't remain omnipotent in the long run. I regard his coming to power with great equanimity and tell myself that none of the other candidates was a dependable friend of ours. The Eastern Question will take up a good deal more of his time because he knows nothing about the East. And he can hardly behave more falsely towards me than L[obanov].

I have just returned from Muraviev's first reception and could only report about it briefly because the courier is leaving immediately. I can only say that I am very satisfied by this first official visit. Just as are my colleagues. He couldn't have been more friendly, and what was especially encouraging was that he placed himself entirely at our disposal and of his own accord told us of information he had received, whereas Lob. never did this and in his arrogance replied condescendingly to the questions *tant bien que mal* which one put to him. In the Eastern Question he has taken the view of his predecessor, i.e., not to put too much pressure on the Sultan and thus make it impossible for him, out of regard for his Mohammedan subjects, to carry out what is demanded of him. One has to

[1] Radolin reported on 16 January that Muraviev had informed him that it would be his earnest endeavour to cultivate good and friendly relations between the two Governments. (From the Foreign Ministry files.)

consider his domestic difficulties and not demand the impossible. He was very well satisfied with the concessions the Sultan had made or had promised.[1] The choice of Lamsdorff[2] as *adjoint* is *very good*. He is an upright and decent man. Kapnist (of the Asiatic Department) is furious and is resigning. He is *no* loss. Charikov,[3] from Sofia, has been designated as his successor. Muraviev has the reputation of being energetic and they say he will put new life into the Foreign Ministry. Actually, the stagnation in the Foreign Ministry is indescribable. Everybody is asleep.

Lob. wanted to introduce reforms but in the end he lacked the courage to do so. I cannot help it. I think I will have a pleasant official relationship with Muraviev. He may be false but he has good manners and after all I want nothing from him. He will be easier to deal with on the Constantinople question than his predecessor, and politically he will not differ from any other Russian statesman in his conduct of affairs. Of that I am convinced. [...]

You wrote that I should try to seek the support of some of the Grand Dukes as *contre poids* to Muraviev; that isn't possible; for *no Grand Duke* has any influence whatever or a dominant position. I am on very good terms with Michael and Constantine and with the Constantine ladies. With the exception of old Grand Duke C, *ils n'ont in politicis pas voix au chapitre*. I am on very good terms with Pobedonostsev. That is not unimportant. La Vladimir also has no political influence. She plays a role only among the *fast set*[4] which is very much *in discredit*[4] at the Tsarist Court. In this Vladimir *set*[4] they do nothing but tell dirty stories and there is no discussion of serious matters. This is what I am told by everyone who belongs to it. I will find out more from the people with whom I am on good terms—for example the Mistress of the Imperial Household, the ladies in waiting of the young and the old Empresses, the more serious people like Pobedonoszev, and a number of old and important dignitaries like Richter—than I would from the Grand Dukes. [...]

Everyone sends you warmest regards,

Your sincerely devoted Hugo.

Ask Frau von Lebbin, to whom we send our kindest regards, to read this letter aloud to you. Forgive this scrawl. I have no time to write more carefully.

597.   Holstein to Hugo von Radolin[5]

19 January 1897

Dear Radolin,

The instruction concerning Muraviev[6]—which you may show to the

---

[1] In his dispatch about Muraviev's reception, Radolin stated that Muraviev had heard from Constantinople that the Sultan had yielded to the pressure of the Ambassadors and promised a number of reforms. (From the Foreign Ministry files.)

[2] Vladimir Nicholaievich, Count Lamsdorff. On the staff of the Russian Foreign Ministry, 1885–97; Assistant to the Foreign Minister, 1897–1900; Foreign Minister, 1900–6.

[3] N. W. Charikov. Consul-General in Sofia, 1896–1907; Third Delegate to the Second Hague Peace Conference, 1907; Assistant to the Foreign Minister, 1908–9.

[4] In English in the original.

[5] From the Radolin Papers.             [6] Not found.

Princess but otherwise to *nobody*—had to be sent as a private letter; the part concerning H.M. could not be sent through official channels.

They say that Muraviev doesn't like Osten-Sacken. Try to keep him if you can, because we know what we have but we don't know what we may get. O.S. is not an intriguer.

That H.M.'s interference makes our work infinitely more difficult is something to make one cry out to heaven.[1] Though I am tough, I am gradually losing my nerve. The international situation in itself is not at all unfavourable for us, for the reasons described in Hohenlohe's letter.[2] But to turn them to advantage one must know how to wait. This is something H.M. doesn't know how to do at all.

Now farewell. Remember me to your ladies.

Your weary<br>H.

## 598.   Philipp zu Eulenburg to Holstein

Vienna, 1 February 1897

Dear friend,

[...] Your exceedingly interesting letter[3] about the consequences of a free passage for the Russians from the Black Sea into the Mediterranean is not only instructive for me personally but also valuable in another way.

Whenever my conversations with Goluchowski touched in academic fashion on the Mediterranean, I was always careful to point out to him the advantages of a free *débouché* for the Russians. He invariably listened to me attentively, did not have any special objection to raise, but then—like a woman who does not allow herself to be convinced—always returned in the end to the argument 'that Constantinople and the Dardanelles in Russian hands would be the death-blow for Austrian policy, whose centre of gravity lay in the *East*.'

Your letter was far too valuable a weapon for me not to make use of it. Quite apart from the impressive argument pointing out the advantages of a free *débouché* into the Mediterranean for the Russians, your letter contained certain subtle ideas about a sensible course for Austrian policy which determined me to communicate its contents to Goluchowski.

I also thought that Szögyényi would not be able to repeat his conversation with you *so exactly* as would your letter.

Goluchowski found its contents 'extremely interesting'. He shrugged his shoulders regretfully when I remarked: 'Herr von Holstein is my superior in argument—but otherwise you can see that we are pulling on

---

[1] The Kaiser informed Hohenlohe in a letter of 15 January that he had questioned the English Military Attaché about his suspicion that England was negotiating secretly with Russia about exchanging Constantinople for Egypt. The English official had pointed out that since the other Powers would not fight for Constantinople, England could not do so alone. The Kaiser had then expressed the hope that England would not act behind the backs of the interested Powers. (*Grosse Politik*, vol. XIIi, no. 2932, p. 71.)

[2] In his reply to the Kaiser on 16 January, Hohenlohe argued that the occupation of the Straits by Russia would not necessarily be harmful to Germany. (*Grosse Politik*, vol. XIIi, no. 2933, pp. 72–4.)

[3] Of 22 January. (*Grosse Politik*, vol. XIIi, no. 3116, pp. 279–82.)

the same oar.' This shrugging of the shoulders expressed Count Goluchowski's renewed regret that he was unable to convince us how *unthinkable* it was that Constantinople and the Dardanelles should be in Russian hands. He may have been annoyed that he was unable to accomplish anything in this regard in Berlin. He did not show it to be sure—but there was a hint of it in certain casual remarks of Count Welsersheimb.[1] Another indication of this feeling was his avoidance of any detailed discussion of the contents of your letter.

Count Goluchowski protested against one remark; that was 'an agreement with France even at the cost of the neutralisation of Alsace-Lorraine'. He maintained that he did not have the slightest sympathy for this idea—but I must nevertheless repeat in strictest confidence that at the time he said : 'An infinite number of things could have been accomplished and an infinite number of things avoided by accepting Gambetta's proposals. This should have been done at that time even at the cost of the neutralisation of the imperial provinces'. Those were the words almost exactly.[2] But please do not make any further use of this but let his *dementi* pass. We have too much to be grateful for to this sincere friend not to spare him in every way. [...]

With kindest regards
Your faithful
PEulenburg.

### 599.   Holstein to Philipp zu Eulenburg[3]

3 February 1897

Dear friend,

It was not precisely my intention that you should read my letter[4] directly to Goluchowski, and I find this somewhat disagreeable on account of two points—one of them being Szögényi's shaking his head about Goluchowski's neutralisation idea. In considering the chances of producing a favourable effect with what I write, I count to a large extent on your extraordinarily skilful interpretation. [...]

Salisbury's anger that Austria too is now beginning to see through him (cf. report from London no. 63)[5] and his effort to pull us into the maelstrom by offering us a bit of Morocco is not without its humourous aspect.

---

[1] Rudolf, Count Welsersheimb. Senior Department Head in the Austro-Hungarian Foreign Ministry, 1895–1900; First Austrian Delegate to the First Hague Peace Conference, 1899.

[2] See above, Eulenburg's letter of 13 January 1897.

[3] From the Papers of Baroness von der Heydt. Only a typewritten copy of this document was available to the editors. Partly printed in Haller, *Eulenburg*, pp. 224–5.

[4] Of 22 January. (See p. 8, note 3, and Eulenburg's letter to Holstein of 1 February 1897.)

[5] Of 29 January. (*Grosse Politik*, vol. XIIi, nos. 2935, 3106, pp. 76, 264.) The section of Hatzfeldt's report dealing with Morocco (not printed in *Die Grosse Politik*) stated : 'Almost abruptly the Minister then turned to the Mediterranean Question, which he described as very boring. He then quite casually and almost in a whisper let fall the remark : "Isn't there anything you want there? There is always Morocco." I looked at him in astonishment and said : "Morocco? You have already apportioned the choicest morcels to yourselves, like Tangier for instance." He replied that he did not lay claim to either Tangier or Cape Yubi,

There is less humour and much that is sad in the Imperial marginalia to the report from London no. 38[1] which is being sent to you via this dispatch bag. Here H.M. emphasizes that 'it is our duty to establish closer relations with Gaul' and 'to aid [Gaul] in its task as a main bulwark of European culture against the barbaric preponderance of the East.' So here we have the third foreign policy programme within six months: first, closer relations with Russia and France to protect our colonies against England;[2] then, the cession of our colonies to that same England with the sole exception of East Africa;[3] now, after the Darmstadt fiasco[4] and the refusal regarding the Jubilee,[5] both Russia and England are over and done with and we are to seek our salvation with Gaul. We are simply dealing with a sensitive character who gives vent to *personal* displeasure in *practical* affairs. What material these three programmes in six months would have afforded a Bismarck for handing in his resignation!

That the Hohenlohe regime will hold firmly to its previous course in foreign affairs as long as it remains in its power to do so need hardly be said. I can tell you with absolute certainty that the views of which you approved in my letter of 22 January[6] were completely identical with those of the Chancellor. The letter was submitted to him before it was sent off. Hence we will not run after France but wait until France approaches us. And the moment H.M. already sees approaching when France will seek our alliance as a *substitute* for the alliance with Russia—that moment is still a long way off so far as human reckoning can judge. Before that time comes—if it ever does—we will have to get around a good many sharp corners. H.M. is only harming himself by speaking about this possibility with politicians at this early date. I do not suppose that you will disagree with any of the foregoing.

If you could at some time insert a word in a letter to H.M. to the effect that we must wait until the French approach us, you would be doing not only the present regime but the German Reich a service. The political situation to-day is more simple than it has been for a long time for anyone who has eyes to see. The Eastern Question compels Russia as well as England and France to reckon with us; but calm and caution are in order in dealing with the empty phrases of these three. The attitude of a wealthy uncle towards three dissolute nephews who want to pump him for money seems to me to be the best example of what our attitude should be.

but that he would to be sure lay claim to some other point. When I replied laughingly that the point in question was one from which he could if necessary stretch out his hand to Gibraltar to close the Mediterranean, the Minister did not in any way deny this. We dropped the subject after I emphasized once again that, as he knew, we wanted no extension of territory in the Mediterranean.' (From the Foreign Ministry files.)

[1] Of 20 January. (*Grosse Politik*, vol. XIIi, no. 3104, pp. 260–3.)

[2] See *Grosse Politik*, vol. XIII, no. 3396, pp. 3–4.

[3] See *Grosse Politik*, vol. XIII, no. 3399, pp. 7–8.          [4] See p. 1, note 3.

[5] The Kaiser had written to Queen Victoria on 2 January 1897 asking whether he should attend her Diamond Jubilee. In view of the animosity still felt in England towards the Kaiser on account of the Krüger telegram, the Queen had advised against his doing so.

[6] See p. 8, note 3.

The Chancellor just told me that the Kaiser came to see him a short time ago. I saw traces of His Maj.'s presence in the form of large sheets of paper on which pictures of squadrons had been drawn. These were graphic surveys of the naval strength of the various Great Powers. The Kaiser had brought these to the Chancellor to convince him of the unavoidable necessity of increasing our fleet more rapidly and on a larger scale than had been done heretofore. As the Chancellor said, this was the reemergence, unchanged and undiminished, of the old 'unlimited' fleet programme. The Kaiser added that this plan must be implemented energetically next autumn. Admiral Hollmann was not the man for the job. He must therefore be replaced in the meanwhile by a sailor of outstanding energy.[1]

It is a well-known fact that a Reichstag gets more and more stingy with its appropriations the closer it gets to an election period. The Ministers were already saying last winter that they could notice from the timidity of the Reichstag people that elections were to be held in the summer of 1898. This timidity will increase this coming winter and *that* is the time the Kaiser has chosen to approach the Reichstag with the most unpopular of all demands, the 'unlimited fleet programme'. The Chancellor told me a little while ago: 'If the voters so much as suspect that the dreaded "unlimited fleet programme" is in prospect, this will have a quite fatal influence on the elections.' Either the Kaiser has not considered this, or he has considered it and is steering towards a coup d'état. In other words, a coup d'état in the interests of an anti-revolutionary law and a gigantic fleet. Which of the German Princes do you think will stand by the Kaiser in all this, now that the Kaiser has accidentally or intentionally been snubbing them since the previous autumn? The Saxons were so badly treated at the manoeuvres that Prince Georg neither stayed for the formal conclusion of the manoeuvres nor appeared here this year for the Kaiser's birthday. The Bavarians and even the gentle Grand Duke of Baden are outraged about the manner and the form in which the Prussian War Minister sent them directives on his own initiative on the subject of the military courts-martial law and the cockade,[2] and that he completely ignored the diplomatic channels. Whether after such a prelude and introduction the German Princes will be in the mood to follow the Kaiser in dubious undertakings with the certain prospect of thereby seriously endangering their relations with their own subjects—this is something that you can judge just as well as I, if not better. Just ask Monts what they are saying about the Kaiser in Munich.

To tell the truth, I think that the anti-revolutionary law is more of a pretext and that the gigantic fleet is the real goal for which the Kaiser is willing to stake the peace and one might even say the existence of the Reich. In Kiel he has now once again been so fired up that he can't wait for the time to come to strike.

I recently heard from a thoroughly reliable source that your cousin

[1] See Hohenlohe, *Denkwürdigkeiten der Reichskanzlerzeit*, pp. 295–6.
[2] See vol. III, p. 658, note 1.

11

Botho is looked upon by the entire imperial entourage as the man who is to be made Chancellor for the purpose of initiating those two hopeless tasks : the anti-revolutionary law and the gigantic fleet. The 'entourage' visualizes the sequence of festivities as follows : a change of Chancellors, then a dissolution of the Reichstag, then the summoning of the German Princes to Berlin *ad audiendum verbum* to be told what is expected of them. This sequence is in itself enough to guarantee the defeat of the Kaiser, as I already told you last summer. Because for the Kaiser the *emergency* will begin the moment he parts with Prince Hohenlohe. As soon as the reason for the dismissal is known, the Reichstag will reject all Government demands through fear of the voters, and the new Reichstag elected under these auspices will be worse than its predecessor. And at the very moment that the German people has shown that the majority of its voters is against the Government, the Kaiser expects the peace-loving, fearful, and hard-pressed German Princes to collaborate in a campaign against their own subjects which might have to be conducted not only by political but perhaps by violent means. Under these circumstances the defeat of the Kaiser is certain. The Princes will concede the Kaiser *one* dissolution, but he will not get the necessary majority in the Bundesrat for a second. And even if he got it, a minority including Saxony, Bavaria, Baden, and perhaps *Hesse*, would have an incredible importance in a vote that would mean civil war. For that reason I am to-day more convinced than ever that the era of the coup d'état, if it is inaugurated as things stand now, will only be a short interlude and that within a few months the Kaiser will be compelled to yield to the inevitable and to look realities in the face.

I know that you have always done your best to forestall crises which threaten to begin under unfavourable auspices for H.M. And perhaps the present crisis will also be postponed *ad diem incertum*; who can tell ? But *one* thing I would like to tell you now in your own interest so that you can do something about it while there is still time. Prevent your cousin Botho from coming to power, for otherwise *you* will be made responsible for Hohenlohe's removal as surely as I am sitting here! Anyone else, civilian or soldier, would be better for you, and perhaps also for the country, because from all I hear Botho is in a very poor state of health. The extent to which all the newspapers, liberal as well as Fronde publications, were trying to hang something on you was something I was able to see when we were trying to restore to its proper proportions that business about the Order which had been so tendentiously exaggerated by Tausch.[1] With several papers the most we could do was to see that they kept quiet. No, they couldn't say something favourable, they already had too much material proving the contrary.

My dear Eulenburg, will you think back and try to recall what I told you in the *summer of 1890*? I told you or wrote you something like this : 'Beware of your relatives. You won your position with the Kaiser all by yourself. If your family comes along it can only endanger your position, for there is always something repellent about a clique.'

[1] See Haller *Eulenburg*, pp. 215–18.

This prophecy has not yet been fulfilled so far as the Kaiser is concerned, but it has proved all the more true with regard to the whole of German public opinion. The Press has been manipulated with much skill during the past years, with the result that *you* are regarded as the instigator of *everything* that the clan and its cohorts have started. If the appointment of His Excellency Botho to Strasbourg in October '94 had not luckily been prevented, you would have experienced something in the way of calumnies then. If Botho now comes into power, *your* official career will probably end with *his* fiasco. After the defeat, the Kaiser will hardly have the power or the desire to keep you. You know that I will go if Hohenlohe and Marschall go, so to me personally their successors are a matter of indifference. But I think it would be an absolute misfortune for the Kaiser if you too were broken on this occasion. I would like to suggest whether, if the worst came to the worst—that is, if Botho actually took office—it would not be best for you to ask for a leave of absence from official duties for six months for reasons of health, and also to be allowed to withdraw from attendance on the Kaiser. If you don't do so, you will be held up to the nation as the man who advised the Kaiser to embark on the campaign which—of this there can even now be no doubt—ended in a political Jena.

I think I can say in all conscience that for almost eleven years now I have often given you good and never bad advice—please refresh my memory if I am mistaken on this point. I can also say of you that you have at all times been a loyal comrade to me. So if I warn you to-day of the greatest danger of your life, I only do what is natural in view of our relationship. In this I am following my instinct, which is what I am doing in dealing personally [eigenhändig] with the 'Eulenburg Question'.

In old friendship
Your faithful
Holstein[1]

## 600.   Holstein to Bernhard von Bülow[2]

5 February 1897

First of all, my dear Bülow, many thanks for your letter, interesting as always, which came to-day.[3] [...]

*Ad vocem* the Kaiser's foreign policy, I must tell you that at yesterday's Court Ball he said to the representative of the Transvaal who had come here from Amsterdam: 'You may depend on me. I understand how difficult it is for a person who fights with honourable against dishonourable methods.' I would be surprised if this remark of the Kaiser's will pass unnoticed. I asked Mühlberg who has connections with Blokland[4] to tell him emphatically that to use this remark in the Press would be tantamount to disloyalty. I did not know what else could be done.

[1] Holstein submitted these same arguments to Bernhard von Bülow in a letter of 4 February. (From the Bülow Papers.)

[2] From the Bülow Papers. Only a typewritten copy of this document was available to the editors.

[3] Not found.

[4] Beelaerts van Blokland. Minister of the South African Republic to the Hague and Berlin.

The 5th, evening.

The Reichstag debate to-day ended in a tremendous triumph for Marschall.

Now good-bye. Remember me to your wife and Donna Laura.

In old friendship
Holstein.

### 601.  Philipp zu Eulenburg to Holstein[1]

Vienna, 7 February 1897

Dear friend,

Your kind letter of 3 February gave me much food for thought. I am replying without really knowing *what* I should say. For I can neither modify the facts nor your views. I would like to modify the latter in one respect, and that only because I have already sent off my yesterday's report about my conversation with Wolkenstein.[2] You will have observed from this that I *immediately* took steps in the way you advised and I would add that I will continue to do so along private channels. *Even so* I don't take the marginal comments too seriously because there is a profound difference between such comments and serious action. On the occasions when H.M. showed France a good many attentions, I have heard the question of an *alliance* discussed and I have *joined* in the *discussion*—but it was always regarded as a vision of the future, though H.M. dealt with it with his characteristic lively interest. I therefore *cannot* see in this the *intention* to introduce a new programme—though I agree it would be good to present counter-arguments. And they will certainly not fail in their effect. [...]

As for the unlimited fleet programme, you have to take into consideration that in an era of petty bargaining a king must *demand a great deal* in order to get *something*. But there is no doubt that a good deal of inflammatory material has been left behind which I find anything but reassuring. I would in particular *deeply* regret the loss of the excellent Hollmann. In his place I would *only* want Senden, because within a month he would get *so* badly stuck that not even a god could help him out of the mire.

I was deeply moved by what you wrote at the end of your letter. It breathes a friendship which I—perhaps have in some measure earned, but for which I would like to thank you *from the heart*.

You know what I think about a certain possibility. I have no more lost my objectivity to-day than I ever have in the past.

With kindest regards

Your faithful
PEulenburg

---

[1] Partly printed in Haller, *Eulenburg*, p. 226. See also Hohenlohe, *Denkwürdigkeiten der Reichskanzlerzeit*, pp. 297–8.

[2] According to Eulenburg's report, Wolkenstein had told him that Hanotaux was trying to pursue a policy agreeable to Russia in the Eastern Question without offending the protagonists of French interests in the Mediterranean. With respect to Franco-Russian relations Wolkenstein said: 'For the time being France has accepted the role of a satellite and Hanotaux has to reckon with the fact, as do we all.' (From the Foreign Ministry files.)

## 602. Paul von Hatzfeldt to Holstein

London, 8 February 1897

Dear friend,

If it is true that the Ambassadors in Constantinople will finish their work in the course of this week and that the communication to the Sultan can therefore be submitted soon afterwards—if the Governments can agree among themselves about the wretched document—then we may soon be faced with a crisis and cannot keep our eyes open wide enough.[1] I have therefore taken the liberty of expressing my humble views on the subject in a lengthy report.[2]

The thing that makes an estimate of the situation infinitely more difficult is that neither here nor in Paris or St Petersburg do they seem to know what they really want. The French have sung to the English in every key that they would never embark on anything serious with regard to Egypt, which has naturally only encouraged the English to press on further. People assume that the Russians, despite the rebuff,[3] have no intention of undertaking anything in Egypt, which would in any case be very difficult. What is left for them to do, unless they want to swallow the insult, than to revenge themselves in Constantinople?

But this too has its difficulties unless they simply disavow the solution which was chiefly worked out by Nelidov and adopt an entirely different attitude.

But how is that to be brought into conformity with the constant assertion that the Russians want neither Constantinople nor anything else?

I don't think the Dardanelles question is so dangerous at the moment, and am almost inclined to believe that England would prefer to make certain small treaty concessions in this regard than to risk her newly-built and freshly-lacquered ships in unfriendly conflicts.

I hardly bother to read Saurma's reports any more; because they might just as well have been written by Philip Currie, and he obviously knows nothing about the one question I would like to have answered, namely whether the Sultan would accept the concessions demanded of him in this manner, or whether he will reject them at any cost. The Turk here[4] declares, as I am reliably assured, that he will definitely reject proposals made to him in this insulting manner. Quite apart from the manner, I think that this is very likely because, as I understand matters there, he is compelled in the interests of his own security to place the greatest emphasis on publicly proving to the Turks that he only gave in to physical force.

The new uproar in Crete,[5] which has obviously been artificially

---

[1] The reform programme of the Ambassadors was never submitted to the Sultan.

[2] In his report Hatzfeldt expressed the opinion that Lord Salisbury would only take up the cudgels in the event of a serious Russo-French action against England's position in Egypt. (From the Foreign Ministry files.)

[3] At the beginning of the year French and Russian representatives sent a protest to the Khedive against the advance of £500,000 made by England for the expenses of the Dongola campaign. The protest did not lead to any result.

[4] Costaki Anthropulo Pasha. Turkish Ambassador in London, 1896–1903.

[5] The Cretan insurrection had flared up again in January 1897. On 6 February the leaders of the revolution in Crete proclaimed the union of Crete with Greece. (See *Grosse Politik*, vol. XIIii, chapter LXXX.)

inspired, is completely incomprehensible to me. It would have been terribly easy to prevent all that, and it would still be easy if the Powers were only in agreement. As it is it will only mean another loss of face for them. [...]

With kindest regards<br>
Always yours<br>
PH.

### 603. Philipp zu Eulenburg to Holstein

Vienna, 14 February 1897

Dear friend,

I hope that my reports about Goluchowski's present attitude will have pacified you.[1] I also wrote a letter yesterday to Marschall[2] in clarification. If there is anyone who wants to maintain peace it is Goluchowski—and now even more than formerly because he knows our reserve in Eastern Questions and has nothing definite to expect from the English. Only *no initiative* can now be expected from him. He has found too many flies in the ointment.

Your last telegram about our attitude regarding the integrity of the Ottoman Empire and withdrawal from participation if this were infringed upon[3] aroused my liveliest interest. *That is undoubtedly the right move on the chess-board*; strongest pressure in regard to the maintenance of peace and an absolutely free hand if war comes. I must express my admiration to you. [...]

In old friendship<br>
PE.

You must have an appalling amount of work!

### 604. Paul von Hatzfeldt to Holstein

London, 15 February 1897

Dear friend,

This afternoon I worked on Lord Salisbury to the best of my ability. His attitude was not unfavourable on the whole, but he twisted and turned on the question of what was ultimately to be regarded as an act of aggression.[4] I tried to convince him that it was also to his own best advantage to leave the decision to the captains of the ships[5] because in that case his, Salisbury's, responsibility would be considerably lowered in

---

[1] See *Grosse Politik*, vol. XIIi, no. 2982, pp. 138–9. On 12 February Eulenburg telegraphed that Goluchowski had informed the King of Greece that Austria like the other Great Powers could not approve of Greek intervention in the Cretan revolution. On the same day Eulenburg elucidated this report in a further telegram in which he expressed the opinion that Goluchowski had only one aim—the maintenance of peace in the Near East. (From the Foreign Ministry files.)

[2] Not found.

[3] See *Grosse Politik*, vol. XIIii, no. 3144, pp. 319–20.

[4] On 10 February Prince George of Greece, the second son of the King, sailed to Crete with four torpedo boats. He arrived off Canea on 12 February, but left the next day. (See *Grosse Politik*, vol. XIIii, nos. 3137, 3150–1, pp. 313, 325–6.)

[5] The warships of the Powers that had sailed to Crete when the insurrection once again broke out on the island.

the eyes of public opinion. He seemed to agree with this, but commented that I perhaps did not know how many influences were being brought to bear here in favour of the Greeks which would make firing on Greek ships a great deal more difficult. Among other things the future Queen was a Danish Princess, and he could tell me in strictest confidence that hardly a day went by in which the Princess of Wales didn't send an urgent telegram to the Queen in the cause of the Greeks.[1]

I am very happy to see that you and I have once again come up with the same idea, namely that everything should be blamed on the ships' captains. That is in my opinion the only way to save Europe from another loss of face and may perhaps bring about some common action which would frustrate the Greek intentions. I still regret that we only have one ship down there, if only because more ships would give us a more influential voice in the council of the naval captains. Since the Russians as well as the French and the English will be reluctant to fire on Greek ships, the next best thing in my opinion would be that the joint occupation of the four cities as proposed by the Consuls were carried out as soon as possible.[2] This action would be enough to convince the Greeks that they had nothing to hope for, and would presumably also put an end to intrigues in Belgrade, Sofia, etc. We won't be spared the fun in Macedonia in any case, and it seems to me to be most important that we clean up the business in Crete *beforehand* in order to put something of a damper on Greek ardour.

I am very pleased about the decision taken by the naval commanders on the Russian flagship which I have just reported by telegram.[3] Even though it certainly isn't everything one might have desired, it nevertheless proves that something can be accomplished by this policy and that it should not be abandoned. If we had been represented in this council by one or two energetic sea captains, it may be assumed that they would have accomplished even more that would have been in line with our wishes. As things stand now it would be desirable if the Captain of the *Augusta*[4] could count on the support of the Austrians and the Italians if the need should arise. Would it not be possible to persuade Vienna and Rome to send a telegraphic instruction to their respective commanders?

Good-bye for to-day, dear friend. It was so late when I was at last able to see Salisbury that there was no time left to write.

Many thanks for your last letter and with kind regards

Always yours
PHatzfeldt.

*Postcript.*
Enclosed please find the original of Thomas Sanderson's letter.

---

[1] King George I of Greece was the son of King Christian IX of Denmark and the brother of the Princess of Wales.

[2] The Consuls of the Great Powers in Canea had suggested the provisional occupation of Canea, Candia, and Rethymnon by a force composed of men drawn from the crews of the foreign ships of war. (See *Grosse Politik*, vol. XIIii, no. 3143, pp. 318–19.) On 15 February Canea was occupied by European troops with Turkey's consent.

[3] See Postscript.

[4] Captain Koellner.

Thomas Sanderson to Paul von Hatzfeldt[1]
Private

15 February 1897

My dear Ambassador,

In reply to the enquiries you made of me whether any agreement had been come to between the naval commanders of the Great Powers in Cretan waters as to the measures which they should take in pursuance of their instructions to prevent aggressive action on the part of Greece, Lord Salisbury desires me to say that he has just received a telegraphic report of a Naval Council held on board the Russian flagship, at which it was agreed that the following acts should be opposed—if necessary by force
1. Bombardment of towns.
2. Disembarcation of troops, arms or munitions from Greek ships of war.
3. Disembarcation of regular forces from Greek merchant ships.
4. Attacks on Turkish ships of war or merchant ships by Greek ships of war.

Lord Salisbury has made no objection to this decision.

Believe me,
Yours very sincerely
Th. Sanderson.

605.    Holstein to Bernhard von Bülow[2]

Berlin, 17 February 1897

Dear Bülow,

I don't remember whether I already wrote to you, or only Ph. E[ulenburg], about his Maj.'s table-talk at Miquel's dinner. To be on the safe side I will at worst repeat myself.

Well, at Miquel's H.M. spoke to the Deputies who were present about the necessity of reviving the old cartel of 'national' Parties in order not to be dependent any longer on the Centre for the granting of credits, especially for the navy. H.M. also mentioned the possibility of dissolving the Reichstag for refusing money for the navy. While these remarks were made, several members of the Centre Party, for instance Heeremann,[3] were present, listening quietly.

You can imagine the results. Hollmann, a splendid and courageous man, told the Kaiser straight out that as a result of this All-Highest table-talk, the chances of securing passage of this year's naval appropriations are as good as ruined. Moreover it was to be feared that in the course of the debate the fact would be brought out that the charts sent directly from H.M. to the Reichstag which are intended to show the strength of the various European fleets are inaccurate. For H.M. omitted from the list all German ships he did not consider modern

---

[1] In English in the original.

[2] From the Bülow Papers. Only a typewritten copy of this document was available to the editors.

[3] Klemens, Baron von Heeremann von Zuydwyk. Member of the Reichstag.

enough, even though they were still usable, whereas for the French and English fleets he included everything, even the most ancient barges.

The day before yesterday H.M. called on the Chancellor with the proposal of sending an imperial message to the Reichstag exposing our dangerous international position. This would naturally lead to a demand for several hundred millions for the speedy construction of ships, and perhaps the Chancellor would be willing to put this demand to a vote of confidence. I don't think the Chancellor saw the matter in the same light; at any rate he dropped the idea of an imperial message. I believe this business might be connected with the cool tone permeating the imperial congratulations for the Golden Wedding.[1] It is no *boutade* but tragically serious when I say that to-day the value of a person for H.M. depends on his willingness or usefulness to co-operate directly or indirectly in increasing our supply of ships. Whether it be coup d'état, anti-revolutionary law, or a change of the electoral law, it all amounts to the same thing: to get a Reichstag willing to grant appropriations. H.M. makes no secret of the fact; the German Princes and the German voters now know that they will have to go through the antics and the dangers of a coup d'état campaign *in order* to enjoy the satisfaction of granting money for the gigantic fleet.

The Kaiser's character contains two very great dangers to himself: as long as things are going well, he believes everything he wants to believe without any reasonable justification; then, when things begin to look threatening, he overestimates the danger.

We are still in the first phase. H.M. has no doubt whatever—and in this opinion he is probably supported by Senden and Co.—that it is only due to the ineptitude, ill-will and lack of interest on the part of his Government that the money for the gigantic fleet hasn't yet been granted, or that the first steps have not yet been taken to secure the appropriations —for instance, a coup d'état, change of the constitution, etc. Hence the imperial bad mood against the Government that is aired in nasty marginal comments. I don't think things can go on much longer this way. At the same time it cannot be denied that the position of the Government in its totality is steadily growing stronger in the country as well as in the Reichstag, and for the very reason that people know that individual members of the Government, e.g. Hohenlohe, Marschall, Hollmann, occasionally put through their own views independently of the views of H.M. The imperial entourage will of course not tell the Kaiser this, nor will that grab-bag of Frondist ideas, the *Wedekind Korrespondenz*. But on the day after the change of Governments the Kaiser's eyes will be rudely opened. The Kaiser's lessons will begin at the hour Hohenlohe departs.

I would only like to add with respect to H.M.'s treatment of foreign affairs that the Ambassadors already know—one of them told me so

[1] Prince Hohenlohe's golden wedding was celebrated on 16 February. The Kaiser's congratulations are printed in Schulthess, *Europäischer Geschichtskalender*, 1897, p. 41.

yesterday—that in every conversation H.M. is trying to warn the Russians against the English and the English against the Russians.

What do you think that will accomplish in the long run?

With best wishes

Your head-shaking

Holstein

## 606.   Philipp zu Eulenburg to Holstein[1]

Vienna, 25 February 1897

Dear friend,

It is easier to write unfriendly telegrams than to answer them in a friendly way.

I am doing my best in telling you quite calmly that the demands being made by the Foreign Ministry at the moment occasionally remind one of the procedure adopted by old Bismarck and son Herbert to get rid of undesirable diplomats. I would like to know what people were thinking about when they didn't telegraph me *a single word* about H.M.'s proposal —which was telegraphed here by Szögyényi, who received an immediate reply from Goluchowski,[2] but made *me* responsible for the fact that Goluchowski's reply didn't happen to be exactly what the For. Min. desired.[3]

How do people think I can influence Goluchowski to make the desired answer conform to the idea of going ahead without England or Italy[4] when the wish [to include England] had *previously* been very emphatically expressed to Szögyényi, who immediately telegraphs here to this effect, and now Goluchowski comes to see me all excited and with preconceived opinions which can then of course no longer be changed, etc.

In view of the fact that a certain nervousness on the part of the For. Min. towards Goluchowski was communicated to him via Szögyényi and made him angry, I have for some time regarded it as my task to do everything possible to keep Goluchowski *amenable*. Thank goodness I have been successful. But this would *not* have been so easy if he had not felt such a great personal admiration for H.M.

Quite apart from that, it is just as difficult to persuade Goluchowski to give up certain opinions as Visconti Venosta[5]—despite the Triple

---

[1] Printed in part in Haller, *Eulenburg*, p. 227; see also Hohenlohe, *Denkwürdigkeiten der Reichskanzlerzeit*, pp. 308–9.

[2] On 14 February Kaiser Wilhelm II proposed to the English, Russian and Austrian Ambassadors a joint naval blockade of the Piraeus. On 15 February Goluchowski read Szögyényi's report of this conversation to Eulenburg. From the documents it appears that Hohenlohe himself had not been informed of the Kaiser's proposal until after it had been made. Hohenlohe dispatched an official proposal for the joint blockade of the Greek ports to Eulenburg on 17 February. (See *Grosse Politik*, vol. XIIii, nos. 3152–4, pp. 326–30.)

[3] There is no evidence that Eulenburg was held responsible, although the Kaiser made unfavourable marginal comments on Goluchowski's reply. (See *Grosse Politik*, vol. XIIii, no. 3163, pp. 338–40.)

[4] Hohenlohe had made this request in a telegram of 21 February. (*Grosse Politik*, vol.XIIii, no. 3167, pp. 345–6.)

[5] Emilio, Marquis di Visconti-Venosta. Italian Foreign Minister, 1896–8, 1899–1900; Italian delegate to the Conference of Algeciras, 1906.

Alliance. You will therefore have to leave him in the Merino sheep farm.[1]

Incidentally, in case the Foreign Ministry wants to send me to the farm *too*, I would be *very happy* to go since my stall would be in *Liebenberg*. The only question is whether the For. Min. would so easily find another such good-natured and useful sheep as I am.

Finally I assure you that I am neither offended nor angry. Thank goodness I am not one of those people who bear grudges. But I will *always* say what I think.

In old friendship your<br>
PEulenburg.

## 607.  Philipp zu Eulenburg to Holstein[2]

1 April 1897

Dear good Holstein,

I received your dear lines when I was about to depart and was still overwhelmed with business.

I will *of course* do my utmost.

These lines are *only* to tell you that I was deeply moved by the tone of old and faithful friendship in which you wrote, and that I *bitterly reproached* myself for having saddened you in the midst of all the work and trouble with which you are burdened! But I was *really very* run down—I *still am* —and may therefore very possibly have been made more nervous by the matter than was justifiable. I can only say to you to-day (for I am *very* tired and run down) that we will both do our duty to the utmost limits of the possible—but that the centre of gravity of our friendship rests in a sphere 'far away' from the Service and politics.

I feel that it is *on account of this 'far away'* that you have become fond of me—and *you* feel that I am able to understand and love you because I *sought* and *found* you too in this 'far away'.

Take my hand as usual for that reason, and let us remember that friendship smiles even though the grey clouds of politics can assume forms that prefigure retirement from the Service. [...]

Adieu, my dear good friend,

Your old<br>
Philipp E.  [...]

## 608.  Holstein to Paul von Hatzfeldt[3]

Berlin, 12 April 1897

Dear friend,

Some days ago the Director of the Wolff Bureau came to me late in the evening with the news, which has meanwhile been denied, of the occupation of the island of Inhaca (Delagoa Bay) by English ships. The Consul in Lourenco Marques[4] and the Consul-General in Cape Town[5] report all

---

[1] Holstein had telegraphed to Eulenburg on 15 February: 'Could you not make use of your friend Goluchowski in the Merino sheep farm at Liebenberg?' (Haller, *Eulenburg*, p. 227.)

[2] See Eulenburg's correspondence with Holstein in February and March 1897 which is printed by Haller, *Eulenburg*, pp. 228–31.

[3] From the London Embassy files.          [4] Count Pfeil.          [5] Herr Schuckmann.

sorts of signs which—if that were still necessary—confirm the view that a South African crisis is in preparation and that the news of the occupation of the island of Inhaca was certainly only the shade of things to come.

What is our attitude towards all this? Or more important, what will our attitude be if in a week, or six weeks, the Cape Colony makes an advance, whether it be against the Dutch or against the Portuguese? It is my firm conviction that we must get out of the position in which the Krüger Telegram placed us. For what practical results can we expect from the Krüger Telegram policy? No sensible person can expect Germany to establish herself in Delagoa Bay or its vicinity, with Madagascar on one side and the Cape Colony on the other. But if we don't want that, what business have we to be there at all? We can't burden ourselves with the luxury of England's antipathy simply for the sake of the Boers, who like all Dutchmen are full of mistrustful antagonism towards Germany.

I admit that I agreed last year to the Krüger Telegram and that I knew of its contents before it was dispatched. I remained silent because Marschall told me on his return from the conference with the Kaiser, Chancellor, and various military and naval officers: 'You have no idea what proposals were made there, this is still the mildest.' At that moment I did not suspect *how* harmful the effect of that telegram would be for what I regard as German interests. But I still remember very well that during the following six weeks I passed more than one sleepless night when I noticed that Courcel (with Hanotaux as his unofficial confidant and adviser) was tastefully playing Salisbury a theme with variations on the subject that 'France has only one enemy and that is Germany. England can frame her policy accordingly'. If the English had really made a move at that time it might perhaps have been possible, in view of the situation then prevailing with Lobanov not yet dead[1] and the Cretan Question not yet born, to have found an opportunity to revise the Peace of Frankfurt.

So when the news of the occupation of Inhaca came in recently, I wrote to the Chancellor[2] that in view of the possibility that the Kaiser might come along with all kinds of proposals, I must urgently advise that His Highness resist all proposals whether for forcible action or for a mere demonstration with the *utmost determination*. The Chancellor told me on the following day that His Majesty had not been there, but that he—the Chancellor—fully shared my views and would energetically defend them in case of necessity. But, dear friend, this standpoint—the prevention of further disasters—will not get us out of the South African blind alley. We must do more than this. Do you belive that England, i.e. Salisbury, would be amenable to the idea of compensating us if we agree not to place any further obstacles in England's way in South Africa? At present we could exploit a concession on England's part with regard to Chinese territory more easily than heretofore since we are now certain that Russia

[1] Lobanov had died on 30 August 1896.

[2] This letter, undated, is printed in Hohenlohe, *Denkwürdigkeiten der Reichskanzlerzeit,* p. 327–8.

will not make any difficulties for us but rather that she will afford us her *appui moral*. If we have Russia and England on our side, France alone will not risk any protest so long as we do not tread directly on her corns. The distances between the points in the triangle Berlin–St Petersburg–Paris are to-day different from what they were a year ago. At least that is my impression. Present-day Russia, that is the Government, has, I think, realized that France is less useful and Germany not so useless as Lobanov seems to have thought. France knows to-day that she will hardly be able to count on Russia if she adopts an aggressive policy towards us, at least not from the outset, whereas they are telling themselves in St Petersburg that after all even Germany sometimes has her good points. That is why, *quod erat demonstrandum*, we need only an agreement or a simple talk with Salisbury in order to be able to pocket a bit of China without any fuss. England could in this case still 'voluntarily' give the assurance that she had no intention of completely crushing the Boers, but that everything would remain within the framework of the Conventions of the '80's,[1] and that our unconditional most-favoured-nation position for the whole of South Africa would be guaranteed. Obviously this opportunity should also be used to settle once and for all the difficulties over Walvis Bay *and Samoa*. After an agreement of this kind between ourselves and England, the South African Question would be left as a trial of strength between the Boers and the English. This would perhaps be further postponed by the fact that France would place herself on the side of the Boers more than she now does as soon as she saw that *we* were disinterested and that there was no longer any hope of a revision of the Peace of Frankfurt with English help via the Transvaal.

England interpreted the Krüger Telegram in all seriousness as a military challenge. All signs point to that. At that time London made an enquiry in Copenhagen as to whether they could count on Danish co-operation in the event of a war with Germany. Gutschmid quite recently reported that during the acute period of the Transvaal crisis England had enquired whether Japan would immediately give England a couple of warships which had just been completed in England? Japan could determine the price.[2] I would suspect from these indications (though there are people who think otherwise) that Salisbury would greet the above-mentioned compensation proposal with a deep sigh of relief. The difficulties connected with carrying out this project do not lie in England but here, in the person of our Imperial Sovereign. To him the Krüger Telegram was not a prelude to war—at most he thought of a war on land in South Africa in which the fleets would be onlookers!—but as an argument for bringing the German Navy up to the strength of the English. This is still the Kaiser's guiding political idea which takes precedence over all others, and it is not impossible that he will be afraid that his plans

[1] The Treaty of Pretoria of 5 April 1881 and the Convention of London of 27 February 1884 defined the relations between the South African Republic and Great Britain.

[2] Report from Tokyo of 5 March 1897. The information came from the Japanese Navy Minister, Marquis Saigo, who added that Japan had flatly refused the unreasonable English request. (From the Foreign Ministry files.)

for the fleet will lose in urgency the moment our relations with England are again somewhat better. However, 'money talks'. A political offer— that is, a casual remark by Lord Salisbury that, for example, he would have no objection to an occupation of Amoy and its hinterland—would in my opinion still be very effective. Moreover the Kaiser, despite his naval hobby-horse, is too open-minded not to see how greatly Germany's political power would be increased if we, without sacrificing our good relations with Russia, were to restore our relations with England in such a way as to make it more feasible than it is at present to operate *à cheval* between Russia and England. We would thereby have attained the very goal that Hanotaux is obviously striving towards, perhaps recently not without success.

The Chinese plan with which I have dealt in this presentation of my views might also have a psychological effect. If France puts out feelers in search of support from Russia or England against our establishing our-selves in the Far East, and if she fails to find such support, the relations of France to those two Powers will thereby necessarily be forced out of the sphere of active friendship and into that of conventional courtesy.

It all depends on our Kaiser, i.e. everything depends on how this plan is presented to him. This very morning the report to the Kaiser about the representation of the German Navy at the English Jubilee festivities was returned with the marginal comment: 'Yes, provided we do not come to blows about the Transvaal.'[1]

There are two other possibilities of danger that I must emphasize.

First, in case England seized Portuguese territory, for instance Delagoa Bay, our chauvinists would make a furious attack on any policy by which Germany received compensation only in China and not in the Portuguese African possessions as well. This would mean particularly the territory bordering German Southwest Africa on the north, with Walvis Bay and Mossamedes. As you may remember from previous negotiations which used up a great deal of paper,[2] the stealing of territory in this fashion (*quia nominor leo*) is not much to my liking. In my opinion the possibility of our annexing Portuguese territory would not come into question until she had showed herself incapable or unwilling to contest her right to Delagoa Bay with the English. The Portuguese could not do so with their own forces, to be sure, but it could be done if they appealed for outside assistance. If they fail to make such an appeal, it will be necessary to conclude that this was a case of *tacitus consensus*, not necessarily on the part of Portugal but on the part of certain leaders, which is all the same thing to world opinion. But so long as England leaves Portuguese possessions alone and only expands or intensifies her power at the ex-pense of the Transvaal, I can see no half-way plausible excuse for us to

---

[1] In English in the original. On the report of 11 April the Kaiser made the further marginal comment: 'My battle-cruiser *König Wilhelm* flying the flag of Rear-Admiral Prince Heinrich of Prussia is to represent the Navy of the German Reich in Spithead. It was built thirty-two years ago in England for Abdul Medjid and the English will be delighted to see the old thing again. At all events it will unquestionably be the oldest ship in the squadron there'. (From the London Embassy files.)

[2] See vol. III, pp.493–4.

annex Portuguese territory. The idea of compensation would thus fall into two stages in the process of realization: first stage, compensation in China for allowing England to subordinate further the Dutch elements in South Africa to her influence; second stage, a piece of Portugal, if England for her part violates the integrity of Portuguese territory. In that case our annexation of Portuguese territory could be characterized as an act of self-defence by which we intended to prevent the area seized by us from also falling under English control.

As the second possibility of danger I must bring up the fact that there are people here who think that English animosity towards Germany is due only to a minor extent to colonial rivalry and that the main reason for it is commercial competition. For this reason England is systematically trying to bring about a situation in which it can fall upon the German merchant fleet and destroy it. All navy enthusiasts think this is the case. Even if you should share this view, it would in my humble opinion be useful to approach Lord Salisbury about the compensation question, to which you with your light touch could give any nuance you desired, because in doing so you could judge with fair certainty whether Lord Salisbury felt it was possible or desirable to restore good political relations with Germany. I need hardly draw your attention to the danger that Lord S., as soon as he sees what you are driving at, will try to *draw you out*[1] in order to make use of your remarks elsewhere.

Now, while Lord Salisbury is away, think over quietly whether, after considering the question from all sides, you think it would be more useful than dangerous or more dangerous than useful to broach the question of compensation—entirely on your own initiative, of course. In broad outline, I should think that you could open the conversation with an expression of regret about the feelings of irritation on both sides and with an allusion to the influential colonial-chauvinistic elements in Germany who can make their displeasure felt in Parliament, so that it is a matter of importance to the Government to satisfy them. Something like that, only much nicer. At the very outset somebody who knows Salisbury as well as you do will be able to form an opinion about his attitude.

*But before you make a single move or say a single word, let me know your opinion.* You know what confidence I have in your instinct.

With kind regards<br>
Holstein.

Shortly before the post was to go off, Marschall came in. I asked that the above be read to him. He agrees in principle. So now please write me what you think—privately or officially.

609.  Paul von Hatzfeldt to Holstein[2]

London, 14 April 1897

Copy

Dear friend,

I hope I am in agreement with you in regarding the detailed telegram of the State Secretary as a directive by which I can guide my own activities

---

[1] In English in the original.      [2] From the London Embassy files.

if the need should arise.[1] I was as you know brought up to be well disciplined and do not feel justified in arguing further with a superior after he has expressed his opinion so definitely. I can tell you completely confidentially, however, that my anxieties about the future development of events—if nothing is done about the situation—remain the same, though I would naturally be very happy if they should prove to be unfounded.

Here the stoppage of official business which I foresaw has now in fact occurred,[2] and my activity and that of Count Deym is now necessarily restricted to asking Sanderson every other day if and whether there is any news. Even the task of keeping an eye on Courcel and his intrigues here will now be at an end because he is returning to France to-day or to-morrow and won't be coming back here until the end of the month, allegedly to present his letters of recall.[3] Lord Salisbury is expected back at the same time, around the 28th of this month, and Courcel will then have an opportunity to intrigue with him further. Courcel adopted a rather changed attitude towards me this time. When we met in the waiting room of the Foreign Office, he attacked me in the presence of Deym and Ferrero in an almost contemptuous tone for our non-participation.[4] As you can imagine—and as you can see from my short official telegram on the subject[5]—I did not hold back with my reply. Since then I haven't seen him again, although he informed the Austrian Ambassador in my presence of his intention to call on him.

The worst thing of all, however, is the reserve of Russia, which can also be seen from the fact that Staal,[6] who to be sure is very badly informed, hardly ever appears at the Foreign Office. Neither Deym nor I have seen him for a week.

Two days ago I went to call on the Turkish Ambassador and was told that he was in the country. Quite frankly, I am rather doubtful as to whether it is still advisable to advise the Sultan to sit still under all circumstances. It almost seems to me that the best and quickest way to

[1] Irregular Greek troops under Greek regular officers had crossed the Thessalonian border on 10 and 11 April and had thus begun the war against Turkey. In a telegram to Marschall on 11 April Hatzfeldt argued that a blockade of the Greek coast remained the only effective means of exercising pressure on the Greeks, and advised sending another German naval vessel to show where Germany stood in the matter and also to allay suspicions of German policy in Austria and Russia. (*Grosse Politik*, vol. XIIii, no 3219, pp. 398–400.) In a telegram of 12 April Marschall expressed doubts whether a naval blockade could still bring effective pressure to bear on Greece, especially since the Greeks knew that some of the Powers were opposed to the use of force. He therefore decided against involving Germany further in the affair. (*Grosse Politik*, vol. XIIii, no. 3220, pp. 401–3.)

[2] On account of the forthcoming Easter holidays.

[3] Courcel had intended to retire for some time, but actually stayed on until 1898.

[4] In the projected blockade of the Greek coast. (See Hatzfeldt's report to Hohenlohe of 14 April, *Grosse Politik*, vol. XIIii, no. 3222, pp. 404–7.)

[5] The telegram in question was no. 103 of 10 April which was summarized in the London Embassy's document catalogue as follows: 'Conversation with French Ambassador. France wants to compel us either to send more ships to Crete or through our refusal to place us in opposition to both Russia and England.' The telegram was not found in the Foreign Ministry files.

[6] Russian Ambassador in London, 1884–1903; First Russian Delegate at the First Hague Peace Conference, 1899.

put an end to the whole business would be for the Turks to use the next clear-cut provocation to put the Greeks to rout. The influential Russian newspapers seem to assume that this will be done in any case. Only then, as things stand now, do I see any possibility of the Powers reaching some agreement about intervention.

Meanwhile I have a very definite feeling that behind our backs very secret negotiations are going on between Hanotaux, Salisbury, Copenhagen, Athens, and perhaps also St Petersburg, which will possibly result in the proposal of a plan concerted with Greece; for example, to hold free elections for the Governor-General by the Cretans. What will we do then? I only see two ways out for us: either the outbreak of war between the Turks and the Greeks which would put an end to all such intrigues, or we withdraw from the affair and at the same time order back the *Augusta*. But all that is only the first act in the drama, and we must be prepared for a second act which will be far more dangerous and will follow shortly: a proposal by the English that the question of reform in Turkey be taken up again and the Sultan be compelled by force to give way.

Right now we have the holidays before us and pretty well everything here will be at a stand-still. The Ministers and individual Ambassadors will be away. Even Deym will go to the country for a few days at the beginning of next week.

Good-bye for to-day, dear friend. Naturally this letter is only for you and I do not in any way expect you to make use of it if it could cause you the least embarrassment.

With kindest regards<br>Always yours

## 610.   Holstein to Paul von Hatzfeldt[1]

Berlin, 14 April 1897

Dear friend,

I was very pleased about your recent telegraphic correspondence with His Excellency[2] because it will have shown you one doesn't have an easy time of it here. No one.

With the Kaiser, the Navy Question now takes precedence over everything. Senden is said to dominate him completely. After the negative attitude of the Reichstag—which after all granted 58 of the 70 million that were demanded—H.M. refuses to send any ships anywhere. For that reason His Excellency tried to avoid an audience by which he feared he would accomplish nothing.

The imperial marginalia which you will receive to-day will serve to show you what the situation is. The greatest bitterness all around against the Centre, which voted against the naval appropriations; against England, which has the greatest naval strength; and as opposed to that, an inclination to reach an understanding with France.

---

[1] From the London Embassy files.
[2] State Secretary Marschall. See p. 26, note 1.

You will see from the marginal comments on your report that you are in H.M.'s good books.[1]

All these marginal comments are excessively excited and vibrant. The internal situation is very depressing. The Kaiser wants a fleet like that of England—with twenty-eight first-class battleships—and wants to direct his entire domestic policy to that end, i.e. to a fight. Yet the King of Saxony said here recently: 'The German Princes would under no circumstances follow *this* Kaiser into a fight because they would run the risk that he would change his mind in the middle of it, he is too unstable.'

The Conservatives for their part have declared through their executive committees: 'They would not support a coup d'état policy, whether with or without the naval programme, and in fact they would not support any measures intended to increase the power of *this* Kaiser in the Reich or in Prussia.'

I believe that the Kaiser has recently been informed of all this indirectly. But I doubt whether he believes it. He is made impervious to sober, practical considerations by the incense strewn by the 'entourage', as for example: 'Compared to Your Maj., Frederick the Great was only a silly boy.'

As far as the colonial compensation question is concerned, it is important to reach a decision soon. As soon as I get your views I will get to work here on a memorandum. I don't know whether Marschall, on whom the entire burden will fall later on in Parliament, will be very enthusiastic. He is after all chiefly a Parliamentary Minister, and he feels isolated. But he is still the only sensible and energetic person here.

I hope I will hear from you soon about the Transvaal by letter or telegram. A pleasant quiet holiday is the wish for you of your old *compagnon de chaine*.

Holstein. [...][2]

## 611. Philipp zu Eulenburg to Holstein

Vienna, 18 April 1897

Dear friend,

Only a short word of greeting to-day to report that I am back. [...]

I am entirely of your opinion with regard to policy. Please be quite calm about that, dear friend. You will be completely satisfied with me.

In old friendship—but physically much tormented.

Yours
PE.

[1] The report in question was dated 8 April and dealt with the Eastern Question. The Kaiser wrote in the margin at the close of the report: 'Superbly written and a completely correct point of view.' (From the Foreign Ministry files.)

[2] On 15 April Holstein telegraphed to Hatzfeldt: 'Private. Since an English advance in South Africa does not now appear to be imminent, it might be advisable to postpone the enquiry recommended in my letter which arrives tomorrow in order not to make Russia mistrustful of us at this moment without pressing necessity. But your judgment as to the possible raising of the issue *later* in the sense of my proposal will be of the greatest value. (From the London Embassy files.)

### 612.    Paul von Hatzfeldt to Holstein[1]

Copy

London, 22 April 1897

Dear friend,

In accordance with your wishes I am sending to-day by courier and even under special cover a detailed report about the Transvaal Question to Baron Marschall.[2] I have left it up to him to use it in any way that still seems desirable under the present circumstances.

Meanwhile I have just received a report from the Reuter Bureau that English ships have appeared before Delagoa Bay and have sailed up the river. If this is confirmed—something I probably won't be able to find out until tomorrow—my report will be useless, for with that the crisis will have begun, whereas an agreement would have had to be concluded *beforehand.*

What will be His Majesty's attitude if the report is confirmed and the affair proves to have been an intentional demonstration against the Republic? My own view that we have nothing to gain from a conflict between England and the Transvaal will naturally not be changed thereby. If Hohenlohe shares this view, as I am led to hope by your letter, then he will have to take a very firm stand against new Krüger Telegrams or worse. Take my word for it: if Chamberlain, with Salisbury's approval, has now actually decided on aggressive action, no protest on our part and no dispatch of auxiliary troops from our colony would prevent it from being carried out. The sole result of such steps would be a conflict between England and ourselves, in which we could do absolutely nothing against the English; whereas they could take Heligoland away from us again and perhaps bombard Hamburg. To desire to intervene under such circumstances would therefore be sheer madness. Who knows whether all this has not already been discussed in Paris between Salisbury and Hanotaux, and received the latter's approval!

In my opinion there is only one thing to do if the report is confirmed: I must be sent telegraphic instructions to say here that we did not doubt Lord Salisbury's repeated assurances that he did not wish to change the status quo in South Africa and that the English ships had received no instructions which would conflict with these assurances. If this later proves to have been the case after all, the only thing that would be left for us to do if we did not wish to get engaged in a senseless conflict would be to broach the question of compensation and to apply the necessary pressure for *that.* That is, I would then tell Salisbury confidentially and nicely but also firmly that he only had a choice between two things: *either* he must give us compensation, which was the only thing by which we could calm down our public opinion; *or* he would have to reckon with the fact, as I could definitely assure him, that from now on and in every question, no matter what it might be, we would under all circumstances take the side of the enemies of England and employ our entire influence in

---

[1] From the London Embassy files.
[2] Report of 22 April. ( *Grosse Politik,* vol. XIII, no. 3404, pp. 16–21.)

Europe to oppose English interests. All efforts on the part of Russia or other Powers to push England out of the Mediterranean, and out of Egypt in particular, to harm her position in Asia (China, etc.), and to prevent her further expansion wherever it might be, would from now on receive our determined and if necessary our active support.

I must end this letter because it is almost time for the courier to leave, but tomorrow evening I will have another safe means of sending a letter because Gutschmid[1] is going directly to Berlin. I will finish this letter then.[2] By that time we will probably be able to see more clearly whether and how much of the Wolff[3] report was true.

With kind regards
Always your

### 613.   Paul von Hatzfeldt to Holstein[4]
Copy

London, 23 April 1897

Dear friend,

According to what Sanderson says and the statement in the *Standard*, which I have just reported by telegram,[5] it appears that the report of a definite action on the part of the English is still premature, which of course by no means proves that some sort of action is not being prepared with Chamberlain and Rhodes behind the scenes. Every suspicion is permissable in this matter and what makes me personally more suspicious than anything else is the prolonged absence of Lord Salisbury, whose idiosyncrasies I know exactly. If he has let himself be bullied into doing what Mr Chamberlain wishes, then it would be very typical of him to arrange for everything to happen during his absence so that he could not be immediately called to account, and could afterwards speak of a *fait accompli* about which he could no longer do anything.

In my letter yesterday I already stated what in my opinion should be done and said here to keep the way open for negotiations about compensation, without getting involved in a conflict in which we would certainly not play *le beau rôle*. I am now waiting to see what is decided about this in Berlin, and would only like to repeat once more: for Heaven's sake no new Krüger Telegrams, no threats of colonial troops, and, above all, nothing whatever which could bring about a conflict and render further negotiations impossible.

I must now return again to my letter of yesterday and complete it, for I had no time to explain the reasons which guided me in writing my report no. 200.[6]

---

[1] The German Minister in Tokyo.          [2] See below.

[3] The report came from the Reuters, not the Wolff news agency.

[4] From the London Embassy files.

[5] Hatzfeldt reported in his telegram that Sir Thomas Sanderson had told him that the English Government did not contemplate a move against the Transvaal from Delagoa Bay. A statement in the *Standard* declared that the English squadron in Delagoa Bay had no special orders. (From the Foreign Ministry files.)

[6] See p. 29, note 2.

I of course completely share your opinion about the political damage caused by the Krüger Telegram. I was not asked to give my opinion at the time, which would surely have been advisable since I alone could tell what effect such an exceptional step would produce not only on the Government but above all on English public opinion as a whole—an effect which has not even yet been fully obliterated. Instead I received instructions to demand my passports,[1] if need be, and the consequences would have been incalculable if I had not at that time secured an assurance from Salisbury to do his utmost to persuade the Jameson gang to return.[2]

The political consequences which I then foresaw have been realised: public opinion in England, which at that time was not unfavourable towards us as the result of years of endeavour, changed overnight to our disadvantage; Lord Salisbury, deeply hurt and suspicious, told himself that he would have to leave German friendship out of his political calculations and seek for means to break off the spearhead of the threatening coalition between Russia and France. This to a large extent explains his efforts to cultivate now Russia, now France. Although these efforts have fortunately met with no success in St Petersburg, I am for the present not at all convinced that this will be the case in Paris in the long run, for there they are obviously beginning to realize that no reliance can be placed on Russia unless one is prepared to go with her through thick and thin, even in the Mediterranean, and all this without demanding any particular favours from St Petersburg in return.

It is certainly not in our interest to permit even a temporary rapprochement to take place between Paris and London. If we have supported the English in Egypt for years, this was done above all in the hope that the schism between the two Western Powers would thereby become steadily greater and more unbridgeable.

From *this* standpoint I have enthusiastically welcomed your idea of making an attempt here to reach an understanding over the Transvaal Question,[3] and have expressed myself definitely in favour of the idea in the report which was sent off yesterday in which I had to leave many things unsaid which I can say here in confidence. But I cannot conceal from you, dear friend, that my hope of success in this regard is at present very small. I fear above all, as you do also, that it will be very difficult if not impossible to obtain His Majesty's agreement to it. The same people who at the time agitated for the Krüger Telegram would undoubtedly raise another howl for war and make the Kaiser believe it was another insult to himself if any sort of action were taken here against the Transvaal. They will convince him that it only needs a strong *quos ego* on his part to strike fear and terror into everyone and to induce the English to retreat. Do you believe that in such circumstances—to which must be added the general irritation of His Majesty with England—it will be easy to induce him to negotiate on the basis of *do ut des*? If you are convinced of this, then you are right to go ahead, and my yesterday's report can

[1] *Grosse Politik*, vol. XI, no. 2590, p. 19.
[2] See Hatzfeldt's telegram of 1 January 1896. (*Grosse Politik*, vol. XI, no. 2596, p. 24.)
[3] See above, Holstein's letter to Hatzfeldt of 12 April 1897.

perhaps be of service in this connection. If on the other hand the Kaiser's feelings towards England are such that the attempt is hopeless, then my report won't do any good either and he will simply be angry with me for this official proposal.[1]

In addition I also regard it as my duty to say here plainly what I only hinted at in my report: that I am by no means certain whether Lord Salisbury would enter into a negotiation of that kind. Apart from personal resentment which—do not let us forget—has again been stirred up by the latest affair in Zanzibar,[2] it is not impossible that he will say to himself: 'Why should I make sacrifices to do something which nobody can prevent me from doing, and what advantage would it bring me if I nevertheless agreed to such a solution? I am not being offered material advantages and therefore it can only be a question of a political benefit in the future. Where would this advantage be, now that Germany has already gone over to the Russian camp and put herself at the side of the Russians at every opportunity wherever a difference existed between Russia and England (China, Crete, Dardanelles, etc)?' As I know Salisbury, a further difficulty will be his fear that if he entered into any such agreement he might come into conflict with public opinion which is hostile to us and would therefore have even less understanding for a transaction in which there was no perceptible advantage, but would on the contrary, from the English point of view, require sacrifices. Furthermore it is at present impossible to see whether Salisbury has not already committed himself too far to France to be able to offend France by an agreement with us.

Although I am bringing up all these difficulties which make me doubt the possibility of success, I by no means intend to imply that the attempt had better not be made. Quite the contrary, I am of the opinion that it must be made if you can procure the consent of the Kaiser for doing so, and if you have sufficient confidence in me to let me choose the time and the method. Only then would it perhaps be possible for me to bring up the matter in such a way that Salisbury would not know for certain whether I was acting under orders and so be able to compromise us with our proposal if he did not wish to consider it. First I would like to wait for a time when he was being frank and open with me, which is not always the case and which I alone can judge. At such times I can discuss any question with him, and he has for years been so accustomed to hear me express my own ideas that he will not be astonished by anything I might say to him half in jest.

---

[1] The Kaiser wrote 'Yes' at the head of Hatzfeldt's report of 22 April and at the end: 'Absolutely right. I agree. W.' Hohenlohe sent Hatzfeldt the Kaiser's marginal comments in a telegram of 2 May. (*Grosse Politik*, vol.XIII, no. 3405, p. 21. See also below, Holstein's letter to Hatzfeldt of 4 May.)

[2] The Sultan of Zanzibar died suddenly on 25 August 1896 and a relative, Said Kalid, proclaimed himself his successor. The British denounced Kalid as an usurper, sent him an ultimatum to leave the Palace, and when he refused took military action against him. Said Kalid fled to the German Consulate. The German Consul refused to surrender him to the British and on 2 October placed him on the German warship *Seeadler* which took him to German territory.

Finally I feel it is my duty to point out also that we must not demand *too much* if we want to succeed, if only because Salisbury, though otherwise favourable, would see in such demands new reason to fear that public opinion would not forgive him for making so many and such great concessions without anything palpable in return. At the moment I think the Chinese business is thoroughly practicable, as well as the assurance that everything should remain within the framework of the Conventions, and also our most-favoured-nation status. On the other hand Walvis Bay and *especially* Samoa seem to me to be extremely dubious and I don't think he would have the courage to defend these concessions here. But these are in my opinion merely secondary questions for the time being, and the immediate problem is to get some idea as to whether they would be at all inclined to make such an agreement here. Once we entered into unobtrusive and confidential discussions of the subject, this would be revealed very quickly.

If Salisbury has no desire to do so or other reasons for not wanting to, he will immediately point out to me that we had long been in agreement about the preservation of the status quo in South Africa and that he for his part, whatever Mr Rhodes and his friends might say, had no intention whatever of abandoning this policy. The Under Secretary of State just told me exactly that when we began talking about the sensational report of Reuters yesterday about English ships in Delagoa Bay. He said in this connection that he thought he could assure me that here they demanded only the preservation of the status quo, but on this they would insist. There were of course people who maintained that such a correct attitude did not exist everywhere. When I urged him to tell me what he meant by that, he finally said that many people here believed that the Transvaal Government intended to embark on a policy of territorial expansion and that they for their part were getting ready for action. I replied that I did *not* believe this, if only because President Krüger would not be foolish enough to provoke a conflict with England in his own right. I have no time before the post goes to report about this officially.

Finally, as far as Portuguese territory in South Africa is concerned, I do not doubt for a moment that Salisbury will emphatically deny that he has any intention of seizing part of it. So, providing the people here want to enter into negotiations at all, we can only deal with this matter by making an agreement about a possible partition in the event that Portugal evinces a desire to cede the colony or can't hold it any longer. As you know, I once tried to make such an agreement with Lord Kimberley;[1] the effort failed at that time because Kimberley demanded the southern and larger half of the colony, *including Delagoa Bay*.

In concluding this letter, which you may of course use in any way you see fit, I await your further instructions and will naturally refrain from any initiative in the matter until I receive them.

With kindest regards
Your
Hatzfeldt

[1] See vol. III, p. 493, note 5.

### 614. Holstein to Hugo von Radolin[1]

Berlin, 23 April 1897

Dear Radolin,

I thank you most sincerely for having eased my entry into my sixth decade by this proof of friendship. Probably this is the last birthday I shall celebrate in office. We can both look back on many difficult days in our lives which we survived by standing loyally shoulder to shoulder. On this, probably my last birthday in office, I remember these days with particular satisfaction.

The attempted assassination yesterday[2] is grist to the mill of those who clamour for a 'policy of force'. And so the attempt will probably be made. Defeat remains as certain as it was before; absolutely certain.

But I can do nothing about it. I will withdraw *beforehand* to the role of a spectator. By beforehand, I mean as soon as the policy of force is initiated by the departure of my two superiors.

In certain circumstances that may happen quickly. No theory of probabilities exists.

Farewell, most affectionately
I am not signing this letter because it is going abroad.

### 615. Alfred von Kiderlen-Wächter to Holstein

Karlsruhe, 25 April 1897

Dear friend,

I would like to sum up the situation in general as follows :

H.M. is afraid to drop Marschall without any reason, but is *very* annoyed with him and would gladly make use of any excuse to get rid of him. Yet H.M. will not get rid of Hohenlohe in the foreseeable future just because he fears the bad impression it would make. Hohenlohe therefore has it in his power to retain Marschall if he declares his solidarity with him, which he can easily do by pointing to the parliamentary situation. H.M. will not make up his mind to replace Marschall by someone else at the cost of Hohenlohe's departure. [...]

Always yours<br>Kiderlen.

### 616. Holstein to Paul von Hatzfeldt[3]

Berlin, 4 May 1897

Dear friend,

I sent your report no. 200[4] on its journey to Court with an accompanying letter to Kiderlen[5] which said much the same thing as my letter to you of 12 April.[6] I only omitted Samoa and Walvis Bay in accordance with your view, but sharply emphasised that the Kaiser needed some sort of

---

[1] From the Radolin Papers.
[2] On 22 April an unsuccessful attempt was made to assassinate King Umberto of Italy.
[3] From the London Embassy files.    [4] See p. 29, note 2.
[5] Not found.    [6] See above.

success in foreign affairs to strengthen his popularity at home. (On reaching this point in the letter, the Kaiser said to Kiderlen: 'Well really, I have a certain amount of that already.')

The Kaiser at first had some objections to the idea of a rapprochement with England. But he quickly accustomed himself to the idea. To Kiderlen he said: 'Hatzfeldt is indeed a clever man, he will see whether he can do anything and what he can do'. On the following day the Kaiser again spoke of the matter to the Chancellor and was keen on the idea.

*Consensu omnium* who are concerned with the plan is that the chief danger in carrying it out now lies in the possibility that H.M., upon receiving an interesting report from you, will have the horses harnessed and drive off to the English Ambassador. This might easily lead to discord because it is not certain whether you and H.M. would be playing in the same key, the same tempo, and the same rhythm. In order to avoid unpleasantness in this regard, it would be a lucky coincidence if your reports on the compensation question were to arrive here when the Kaiser is away. He will be away, as you know, most of the time during the coming months, Kiderlen will be with him until the 18th of this month, afterwards there will be Philipp Eulenburg during the week at Prökelwitz, provided that the latter, who is at present quite run down, has sufficiently recovered by that time.

As for Crete, I am more and more convinced that this question will make for great complications if the Greeks get an armistice before they have formally, that is to say in writing, agreed to renounce Crete and other aggrandizements.[1] The letter of the Queen of England to the Tsar containing the proposal that the three guarantor Powers should now take over the job of settling the Greek affair[2] will not exactly improve the relations between England and Austria, not to mention the Italians, though they are more accustomed to bad treatment.

There is nothing new in internal affairs, everything is completely obscure, but the feeling in the country is unmistakably turning more and more against H.M. as a result of the well-known telegram from the Kaiser to Prince Heinrich.[3] I regret this whole unnecessary complication so very much because I am firmly convinced that it will finally end with a powerful landslide to the Left, into democracy.

With kindest regards,
Holstein.

---

[1] Turkey declared war on Greece on 18 April, and had already inflicted a series of decisive defeats on the Greek Army.

[2] On 25 April Queen Victoria telegraphed to the Tsar: 'I most earnestly appeal to you to use all your powerful influence to bring about an armistice and terminate this disastrous war which, I am sure, must distress you as much as it does me. I earnestly trust that you will be able to agree to Lord Salisbury's proposal for joint action with you and France.' (*Letters of Queen Victoria*, Third Series, vol. III, p. 154.)

[3] Prince Heinrich had read aloud to his ship's company a telegram which he said came from his brother the Kaiser in which the Reichstag deputies who cut the naval estimates were referred to as 'unpatriotic rascals' and 'scoundrels'. Hohenlohe succeeded in obtaining an official *dementi* on 29 April. (See Hohenlohe, *Denkwürdigkeiten der Reichskanzlerzeit*, p. 332.)

### 617. Paul von Hatzfeldt to Holstein[1]
Copy

London, 12 May 1897

Dear friend,

From my long report to-day[2] you will see how Lord Salisbury feels about the business. On the one hand he would like to, on the other hand he would not like to. In other words, he doesn't love us and hasn't forgiven us for the Krüger Telegram, but he would nevertheless like to see relations improved for political reasons if it doesn't cost anything. With respect to the Transvaal, he assumes that Krüger will now be as amenable as necessary for English purposes, and he therefore sees no reason why he should make concessions to us. There remains only Amoy, and even that is doubtful.

I hope that after this you will agree with me that I should not say a word more until Salisbury himself raises the subject and [shows] a desire to be conciliatory.

In my opinion we should now continue for the time being to range ourselves on the side of the opponents of England at every opportunity. Perhaps they will then grow mellower. But for heaven's sake see to it that H.M. doesn't talk to Lascelles about the matter. The fiction must be maintained that H.M. and the Foreign Ministry have given me neither authority nor instructions and that they know nothing whatever about what I have said.

I am very glad about the instructions to Saurma[3] and hope that we will hold firmly to them, if only because in doing so we will be opposing English wishes and intentions.

It is time for the courier and therefore I must say farewell to you for to-day.

With kind regards
Yours
[...]


### 618. Paul von Hatzfeldt to Holstein[4]
By Post. In Cipher

London, 20 May 1897

Private

If, as you recently seemed to assume, we can count on the support or at least the approval of Russia in this matter, I see no reason why we should not act now in regard to Amoy even without previous agreement with England.[5] I have in general always been of the opinion that in dealing with the English in colonial questions it was a mistaken policy either to

---

[1] From the London Embassy files.

[2] *Grosse Politik*, vol. XIII, no. 3407, pp. 23–7.

[3] On 8 May the German Ambassador in Constantinople was instructed not to participate in any mediatory action so long as Greece did not follow the advice of the Powers and recognize Cretan autonomy. (From the Foreign Ministry files.)

[4] From the London Embassy files.

[5] See above, Holstein's letter to Hatzfeldt of 12 April 1897.

demand the cession of English possessions and to quarrel with them about it, or to make intended acquisitions on our part dependent on their previous consent. I would always have thought it far more advisable to have presented them with a *fait accompli*, and this seems to me to be all the more indicated in the present case because the people here probably have little desire at present to get involved in the Far East, at least not while the English Government is still uncertain that it may not yet be involved in difficulties in the Near East (Constantinople). I have the impression that they are somewhat at a loss about this question at the moment here, because the hope is steadily dwindling of being able to incite the Continental Powers against each other in the Near East while they themselves look on, with the proviso of eventually acquiring a juicy morcel by means of their overwhelming sea power.

The feeling here against us, as you will have seen from the cuttings from the English Press, is again very strong, no longer on account of the Transvaal alone, but because of our policy in the Greek question which, no matter how justifiable, brought us into definite opposition to English policy and especially to public opinion here. I therefore believe that Salisbury, even if he wanted to, would not try to reach an agreement with us for fear of public opinion, especially if he had to give us territorial compensation to obtain it. There remains therefore only the question whether he would intervene in the event of a *fait accompli* in Amoy, something I consider doubtful to say the least. I think it far more likely that he himself would then demand a territorial concession on the Chinese coast which, if I am not mistaken, would be unwelcome to the Russians and, since this would not serve to improve Anglo-Russian relations, could only be welcome to ourselves. [...]

PH

619.  Holstein to Bernhard von Bülow[1]

Berlin, 22 May 1897

Dear Bülow,

I am curious about the final outcome of the Cretan Question. If the affair should end a second time in a futile demonstration by the European Powers, I would—if I had anything to say in the matter—cast my vote in favour of our withdrawing from the game altogether. The one thing which prevents me from advising such a drastic course this very day is the *possibility*—unhappily it is nothing more than that—of securing better terms for our Greek creditors—that is to say, for thousands of school-teachers, peasants, porters and clerks. But the moment I see that nothing can be done, that is, when the majority of the Powers take this matter lightly, then I would advise that we leave the other Great Powers to their own devices and go home with our much maligned *Kaiserin Augusta*.

My views in this matter are not the result of anger but of cool reflection. In the first place, the annexation of Crete by Greece would be a

---

[1] From the Bülow Papers. Only a typewritten copy of the document was available to the editors.

blow to the prestige of so-called Europe, and secondly it would involve a very considerable risk of war; for I do not need to tell you that Bulgaria and Serbia are anything but quiet. The two of them simply maintain that if Greece gets something, they also want to have something. We can assume that Montenegro is *dans les mêmes idées*, and—let us not deceive ourselves—Montenegro has power behind the 'idea'; because for Italy she is a relationship,[1] and for Russia she is the old and only friend.

I hear from a reliable source—not Saurma—that the Turks got their worst fright of the whole war when fourteen Albanian battalions mutinied. The reason for the mutiny—one could call it a military *strike*[2]—was that they had hoped to conquer Serbia. They felt no friendship whatever for the Greeks, but they hated them less.

The Porte has since then put 80,000 men into Albania, so that for the present the Albanians will hardly want to break loose, at least not until these 80,000 men have found something to do elsewhere.

Mention of Albania brings me to Goluchowski's latest diplomatic arrangement—the treaty concluded during the visit to Russia.[3] I would suppose that after this achievement Italy is in fact—to use the language of the railway companies—uncoupled from the Triple Alliance. For the Italians had gradually 'imagined themselves' into Albania, and I can never forget how my old friend Launay, a most unacquisitive person, could not for the life of him be talked out of the fact that one could see the coast of Albania from Italy *au moyen d'une bonne longue-vue*.[4] That shows the power of this idea. Goluchowski burst this idea like a soap-bubble when he made the 'independence' of Albania into an Austro-Russian axiom. I asked Szögyéni whether they will inform Rome of the agreement. He was somewhat disconcerted and asked in turn what we would advise? I replied that we had nothing to advise in this matter, but that we for our part would say nothing about it since the secret was not our affair.

It is the same with this treaty as with the German-Russian treaty of 1890 which was resurrected from the grave by last year's 'revelations'.[5] Russia in the one case *has*, and in the other *had*, gained the power over the co-signatory of destroying its relations with a third party at any chosen moment, just as at the beginning of a war one blows up a bridge.

Nevertheless I regard the Albanian Question as a secondary con-

---

[1] On 24 October 1896 the Crown Prince of Italy (the later King Victor Emanuel III) had married Elena, a daughter of Prince Nicholas of Montenegro.

[2] In English in the original.

[3] An Austro-Russian agreement of 30 April 1897, arranged during a visit of Kaiser Franz Joseph and Goluchowski to St Petersburg, by which the two Powers agreed to maintain the status quo in the Balkans. If partition were to become inevitable, the partition was to be made by the Balkan States themselves in so far as this would not affect existing treaty rights of the Great Powers, and an independent state of Albania was to be created. It was also recognized that the question of Constantinople and the Straits, because of its 'eminently European character' was not of a nature to be made the object of a separate understanding between Austria-Hungary and Russia. This informal agreement was summarized in a note by Goluchowski of 8 May and modified in a note by Muraviev on 17 May. (Pribram, *Secret Treaties*, vol. I, pp. 184–95.)

[4] See *Memoirs*, p. 105.

[5] Bismarck's 'revelations' of the Reinsurance Treaty with Russia in the *Hamburger Nachrichten* of 24 October 1896. (See *Memoirs*, p. 131, and vol. III, p. 652, note 2.)

sideration in comparison with other conditions of this treaty, whereby the Straits Question with Constantinople and the rest is excluded from the terms of the agreement as a 'European Question'. In other words, the nerve-centre of Byzantium, which is the only thing in the entire Balkans that can still make Russia's nerves vibrate, is to be reserved for consultation with French and English *princes de la science*. This stamps the treaty as provisional. The disparity in its results for the two signatories lies in the fact that Russia knows even more accurately than formerly *what* Austria does *not* want. Austria, however, does not know what Russia wants. I will not presume to tell you what this is; but I can say that the article of this treaty concerning the Straits fits in perfectly with confidential remarks made by the Russian Minister Witte some weeks ago: 'Russia must now hold aloof from all European, and especially Turkish, complications, and get everything ready for a conflict with England. After about five years, railway construction in Asia will have progressed far enough to permit us at last to attack England on land in India.'

At the very moment when the Russians were wondering how they could gain time for this undeniably grandiose project—the repetition of Alexander's march to India—Goluchowski appeared with his draft treaty and helped them out of their difficulty.

If I wanted to speak of internal affairs I would only be able to repeat what you will find in all the newspapers, namely that unfortunately the Kaiser's position is growing weaker every day.

With kind regards<br>Holstein.

620.    Paul von Hatzfeldt to Holstein[1]
        Copy

London, 22 May 1897

Dear friend,

Salisbury has not been visible for some days and Sanderson, on whom I called yesterday, assured me that there was nothing new. My colleagues are in the same state of ignorance, and each waits for news about the further progress of the peace negotiations. Under these circumstances I am to-day completely without material for an official report and I hope you will not be astonished by my silence.

When I last saw Salisbury some days ago, I had the impression, as you will see from my letter in cipher,[2] that he was pretty much at a loss as to what should now be done. I think he was fairly certain about only two things: first, that for the sake of his own position he could not completely drop the Greeks despite the fact that he does not like them, and, second, that he neither wishes nor hopes for an understanding with us as to how the affair is to be dealt with. He will try to do this in Paris, in Vienna, or in St Petersburg, and if he finds a majority which he can join in opposing our views he will not be at all reluctant to do so.

---

[1] From the London Embassy files.          [2] Of 20 May.

Now that they have apparently decided that the Turks are to get only a strategical rectification of the frontier, they will probably make great exertions here to reduce Turkish war indemnity claims as far as possible. Lord Salisbury's whole *raisonnement* on this point was in this respect significant. He emphasized with obvious intention that the Sultan had the unqualified right to demand the payment of the war indemnity in cash. The Greeks unfortunately had no money, and even the establishment of an international financial control would not afford the possibility of obtaining a corresponding loan for Greece. Since the people here will not consent to any acquisition of territory by Turkey, and are just as little disposed to leave Thessaly in Turkish hands for a long time as a pledge, it is easy to draw the conclusion that they will try to reduce the indemnity to a minimum.

From the telegrams communicated to me I have seen without any surprise that the tendency still predominates in Athens to avoid the consequences of the defeat they have suffered, that is to say, not to pay anything, and to save all available money for a war of *revanche*, while at the same time leaving instructions with the insurgents in Crete that will make an honest effort at autonomy impossible and insure the reversion of the island to Greece after the departure of the international military forces. Under these circumstances Prince Hohenlohe's view that pressure by the Powers is less necessary in Constantinople than in Athens is certainly and unquestionably correct.[1] I only hope that Vienna and St Petersburg share this opinion, and that Calice and the unreliable Nelidov will be instructed to express themselves in this sense. If this is done, it seems to me that the manner which the Powers should exert pressure in Athens is very simple. It would I think be a mistake to become involved in discussions with the Greeks over individual points, and it would be enough to point out that Greece had appealed to the decision of the Powers and that it was therefore up to her simply to accept the bases for peace arranged by the Powers without discussion. In my opinion we must hold firmly to this standpoint, as also to the condition that the negotiations over the details arising out of these bases must be carried on between Greek and Turkish plenipotentiaries, but with the assistance of the Powers.

Good-bye for to-day, dear friend. You will certainly have received my letter in cipher, and I hope you will soon let me know what you think of it.[2]

With kind regards

Yours

[1] In a telegram on 16 May Hatzfeldt was informed that Saurma had been instructed not to participate for the time being in steps to bring about an armistice. In the interests of European peace it was not desirable to be too hasty in inducing Turkey to renounce her most effective means of pressure on Greece. The suitable moment for bringing about an armistice would only come if Greece expressed herself ready to accept the advice of the Powers. (From the Foreign Ministry files.)

[2] No reply from Holstein has been found.

## 621. Paul von Hatzfeldt to Holstein[1]
Copy

London, 18 June 1897

Dear friend,

Here they can think of nothing but the Jubilee,[2] and therefore I have no material for reports for to-day's courier. But since you have perhaps seen from the English newspapers that I have at last had another opportunity of speaking with Salisbury, it will surely interest you to hear that our conversation, though brief, was more friendly than it had been for many weeks past. There was hardly any mention of Greeks and Turks, and he passed fleetingly over that subject by simply telling me the latest news as, for example, that the former President of Switzerland has refused to allow himself to be made Governor-General of Crete—which you, of course, have known for a long time. We then passed on quickly to the relations between England and Germany, and I threw in the remark that the English newspapers were assiduously pursuing their campaign of agitation against us. And when in this connection I let fall the remark that it was not a good thing that this state of mutual irritation should continue too long, Salisbury readily agreed. His whole attitude towards me was easier and more friendly than it has been for months.

If I confine myself to informing you in this manner of this impression, based on a short general conversation, the reason is that I have more than once experienced such changes on the part of Salisbury, and am by no means convinced that the mood in which I found him this time will be a lasting one from which one could expect concrete results. I did not therefore consider myself justified—indeed I would have regarded it as a great imprudence—to allow myself to look upon this conversation as the 'suitable occasion' foreseen in dispatch no. 851 and to act upon it.[3] An official report, no matter how cautiously phrased, might, contrary to my intentions, give the impression that the people here have become more conciliatory than is in fact the case, and that I 'should have made use' of this opportunity. But I ask that you believe my assurance that reserve was urgently necessary in this instance. It is *possible* that Salisbury for the moment is not wholly content with the Russians and the French and therefore remembers our existence. It is equally possible however that I will meet with an entirely different attitude on the occasion of our next meeting. At all events I believe I must wait and see whether the present mood lasts and whether I get the impression that I can proceed without danger. Up to now I only believe that they would be quite happy to have our friendship again if they did not have to do *anything* to get it, and that is not enough.

[1] From the London Embassy files.

[2] The celebrations for the 60th anniversary of Queen Victoria's accession to the throne. These lasted from 19 June to the beginning of July 1897.

[3] In his report of 12 May (see p. 36, note 2), Hatzfeldt said that he did not have the impression that Salisbury 'would accede to our wishes in China without more ado', and he asked whether he should return to this question 'at a suitable opportunity'. Hatzfeldt was informed in dispatch no. 851 of 5 June that the Kaiser had written 'Yes' opposite 'suitable opportunity'. (*Grosse Politik*, vol. XIII, no. 3408, p. 28.)

Good-bye for to-day, dear friend. It is a long time since I last heard from you and I would be very glad to have news of you.

With kind regards<br>Yours<br>P. Hatzfeldt.

## 622. Philipp zu Eulenburg to Holstein

Vienna, 18 June 1897

Dear Holstein,

Many thanks for your information. You have summed up the situation with your accustomed tact and have evolved a plan that is much more important than even you yourself think. Since then I have been much more at ease.[1]

I know very well how good an effect this will have on H.M. who will never make M[iquel] Chancellor, but who is very receptive to the idea of according him a certain recognition and of 'pushing him into the foreground'. [...]

Your loyal<br>PE.

## 623. Philipp zu Eulenburg to Holstein

Vienna, 22 June 1897

Dear friend,

The summoning of our friend as Deputy State Secretary[2] has greatly surprised and shocked me because I regard his vacation as a necessity before he goes to Berlin.

Did H.M. say anything about this to the Chancellor?

The poor little lady[3] is in floods of tears—naturally.

I am very anxious to hear what Miquel will do in the end. From the statements in the newspapers there does not seem to be anything definite about this. Your last telegram also ended only with: 'M. will almost certainly agree'[4]. I am off tomorrow. [...]

Affectionately, your old faithful<br>PEulenburg.

[1] To meet the Kaiser's desire to dismiss Bötticher and Marschall, Holstein proposed to Hohenlohe on 10 June that Miquel replace Bötticher as State Secretary of the Ministry of the Interior. In Holstein's opinion Miquel was also the best man to replace Marschall as the spokesman for the Government in the Reichstag. (See Hohenlohe, *Denkwürdigkeiten der Reichskanzlerzeit*, pp. 352–3; Haller, *Eulenburg*, pp. 247–9; see below, Holstein's letter to Radolin of 5 July 1897.)

[2] Marschall had requested and been granted a long leave of absence. Bernhard von Bülow was recalled to Berlin on 21 June. The appointment of Bülow as Deputy State Secretary of the Foreign Ministry was announced on 28 June. His official appointment as Deputy State Secretary was not made until 6 August. On 20 October he was appointed permanent State Secretary in succession to Marschall.

[3] The wife of Bernhard von Bülow.

[4] Miquel did not want to take over Bötticher's position as State Secretary of the Reich Ministry of the Interior, which the Kaiser demanded. He finally succeeded in restricting his position to that of Vice President of the Prussian Ministry of State.

### 624. Holstein to Bernhard von Bülow
Copy

B[erlin], 24 June 1897

Dear Bülow,

Since I see that it will be difficult for someone with your kindly nature to cut the cable, I have done it myself. I have just handed the Chancellor my resignation, naturally without saying that I had already sent a copy to you. The contents are identical, except for the addition that the present moment seems specially suitable because during the summer holiday season the changes rendered necessary by my departure can be undertaken without confusion. To the Chancellor's query as to whether there had been any differences between you and me, [I] replied emphatically: 'absolutely none'. I added that in addition to my eye trouble I had also taken into consideration the fact that the Kaiser's displeasure with me continued—and so, as the Service was able to do without me and I without the Service, I saw no reason for continuing to serve.[1]

Sincerely yours

H.

### 625. Alfred von Kiderlen-Wächter to Holstein

Kiel, 1 July 1897

Dear friend,

I had a long talk yesterday evening with Lucanus, from which I communicate to you the following. If I say 'talk' it is not really accurate, for I merely played the part of listener.

(1) As you know, Hohenlohe had asked to be allowed to date Bötticher's dismissal as from 3 July in order that B., who is badly off, would still be able to draw his salary on 1 July. Lucanus seized on this to make a violent attack on Bött. It was a scandal to bother the Kaiser with such an item when greater things were at stake. If he had been in B's place he would rather have borrowed the money from the Jews—(!). Such things must give the Kaiser an increasingly poor opinion of the highest Civil Servants if they put their petty private interests in the foreground at a time of far-reaching changes. By doing so Bött. could so discredit himself with the Kaiser that H.M. might not even make him head of a provincial administration. And a man was certainly not fitted for the headship of a provincial administration who was without money on the first of the month like any student, because the head of a provincial administration must after all be a superior man who could fill a representative role, etc. These remarks, together with a casual remark made by L. on another occasion that 'The men of the New Course were already trembling because they saw that politics were once again to be conducted along Bismarckian lines',

---

[1] In a letter to Hohenlohe of 17 June Holstein threatened to resign if anyone were appointed temporary head of the Foreign Ministry before 1 October, because such an appointment would be regarded as a sign of the Kaiser's want of confidence in himself. (Hohenlohe, *Denkwürdigkeiten der Reichskanzlerzeit*, pp. 355–6.)

seems to me a sure indication that L. is now working to prevent B. from getting the headship of a provincial administration. I leave it to you as to whether and how you make use of this information.

(2) I will tell you what he said about Marschall in a separate letter[1] because I promised Bülow to write to him if I heard anything interesting. Since I don't want now to write everything twice, I will ask you to send the other letter to Bülow—*this* one is *only for you*.

On the subject of Marschall, apart from what is in the other letter, Luc. said that the Kaiser would probably send him to Constant-[inople]. (I also put this in the other letter.) Please do *not oppose* this. If the Foreign Ministry again immediately thwarts H.M.'s wishes, particularly in a personnel question, it will only hurt the chances of carrying out our wishes in *policy* questions. With regard to what you told me when we parted, I want to emphasize that I will be quite happy in my present post for some time to come, and believe that I can be more useful in serving our interests there than in a diplomatically more important post if I were to be given such a post as a candidate virtually imposed by H.M. Let things run their course—Bülow will see to it that Engelbrecht does not become his successor. I suspect that he would prefer a successor who could be easily disposed of and who would as it were be only his *locum tenens*, such as Saurma. I believe you will agree with this opinion.

(3) You will see from my other letter that Lucanus is heart and soul with Miquel, and Luc. has made this clear to me in the most varied ways. (I observe here that my very long conversation with Lucanus yesterday evening took place between eleven and one o'clock; he had returned from a great dinner; I had eaten a beefsteak *solo* and drunk half a bottle of wine with mineral water— I merely listened, only throwing in a cautious question here and there in order to learn as much as possible, although I would have liked best to box the fellow's ears. For example when he said: 'The whole so-called crisis was prepared months ago; I must arrange something like that, only one must be very cautious. I won't say a word to the Kaiser either, for he immediately blurts everything out and spoils things for one.' ! ! ! ! ! ! *In vino veritas*, one could certainly hardly be more frank—whether you tell this to His Highness [Hohenlohe] I leave to your discretion—I will *cautiously* tell Ph. E[ulenburg] about it in conversation and also tell Bülow after my return; but I will *write* such things to *nobody*, one becomes cautious with time!—pardon, I did not mean to say that you are 'nobody'—you know what I meant!

Hence Luc. and Miquel are a pair *nobile fratrum* and work *with* Friedrichsruh—probably more out of fear than love.

*Continued on 3 July*

---

[1] Not found.

That Lucanus spoke so frankly shows how firm and secure he feels his position to be; he is really simply the executant of every imperial whim, and if one of these meets with opposition from anyone, he appears as the man who 'puts everything in order'.

To-day the new Ministers and State Secretaries will be received in audience, together with the departing Bötticher; they will then dine with H.M. on board the *Meteor*—quite the suitable place for a ministerial audience!

Lucanus is fortunately away and will therefore not be able to greet his friend Miquel here.

It has—*hélas*—been decided that I am to go along to St Petersburg.[1] In personnel matters, Bülow was quite ready to arrange the whole business in principle with H.M. right away, during the first washing-up in Kiel: Krauel, Tokyo; Raschdau, Rio; Henckel or Ratibor, Weimar; Gutschmid for the present on half-pay. His Highness upset this by expressing the urgent personal wish that Holleben should go to Japan— what does the Old Man have in mind? Please tell Pourtalès about this too, in case Bülow has not already told you everything.

Otherwise nothing new except that the important occupation of yachting leaves no time for the secondary affairs of state.

Always yours<br>Kiderlen.

Plessen also arrived to-day in order to report on England—and naturally acts frightfully important!

Marschall's demand that Wolff justify the Kiel telegram is interesting![2] (see *Badenser Zeitung*). That, together with what is in my other letter, characterises this snake we have nourished in our bosoms!

I have neither pointed up nor underlined by commentary the facts contained in my other letter because I would like you to send it to Bülow. You can imagine what kind of marginal comments I would have made! For example on Lucanus's remark made quite as a matter of course: 'I had the documents sent to me!'. That also says a lot about our Courts—that they send the documents about a pending trial to the Civil Secretariate![3]
[...]

The Ministers dined to-day on board the *Meteor* with the Kaiser. Only Plessen and Senden were present owing to lack of room! The conversation turned among other things on the navy. Posadowsky said that it was possible to get credits for the navy from this Reichstag. Miquel then said: 'I ask in that case to be allowed to join in the debate'!!

Next the conversation turned on universal suffrage and its pernicious effects. A Boeotian thought that the Catholic Church, by its very nature,

---

[1] The Kaiser and Kaiserin paid a visit of state to Russia from 7–10 August 1897.

[2] On 28 June the Wolff News Bureau had reported from Kiel that Marschall was to be replaced by Bülow as State Secretary in the Foreign Ministry. This news was apparently released prematurely, hence Marschall's demand for an explanation.

[3] The reference is to the Tausch trial. (See Hohenlohe, *Denkwürdigkeiten der Reichskanzlerzeit*, p. 342.)

would assist in getting rid of it! Then Miquel intervened: Universal suffrage was introduced as a liberal institution, but was now exploited by the Catholic Church which had made an about-face in this regard.

My confidant (Plessen) took it that Miquel's ulterior motive in making his lengthy statement was: 'Don't be surprised if I go with the Centre.' I was not there, and cannot therefore judge, otherwise I would say that Miquel's ulterior motive was: 'Universal suffrage has ceased to be a liberal institution, therefore don't be astonished if I back up H.M. in demanding that the *Reich* Government attack universal suffrage'. What do you think?

Yours<br>K.

## 626.  Holstein to Hugo von Radolin[1]

Berlin, 5 July 1897

Dear Radolin,

Since Mumm has been wandering about the world for weeks, I have a great deal to do and consequently ask you to excuse my silence. Moreover it was difficult to write anything about the domestic situation since the picture changed every few days.

Much that has happened recently can be explained by the fact that Marschall for some time past has urgently desired to exchange his post here for an embassy, for reasons of health if for nothing else. In addition, Lucanus and Köller, the former Minister, have both contributed their share in doing everything possible to bring on the crisis. I told Hohenlohe that if he went I would go with him. Whether he is doing the right thing by staying on, the results will show. To-day I refrain from expressing a judgment.

Bülow will have a very difficult time. A great deal depends on who will be Secretary of the Treasury[2] for it will be his responsibility even more than that of the State Secretary of the Foreign Ministry to oppose attempts which will undoubtedly be made to interpret certain articles of the commercial treaties as infractions of other treaties. The commercial treaties are undoubtedly bad and need revision. This is especially true of the Austrian, Italian, and Swiss. But while they are in force they must be observed if one does not want to be considered guilty of treaty violation. If the new Secretary of the Treasury does not support Bülow in this matter I cannot see how he will pull through.

From a monarchist standpoint I regard the latest turn of events, which makes peaceful co-operation between Government and Parliament more difficult, as a misfortune. The Kaiser has adopted a course which will bring him disappointments and perhaps humiliations. The forces over which he disposes are hardly sufficient for what he would like to carry through. For seven long years one has done one's utmost to keep him out of a position of constraint. Our success has resulted in his no longer

---

[1] From the Radolin Papers.
[2] On 10 August Baron von Thielmann, the former Ambassador in Washington, was appointed to this post.

believing in the possibility of such a position, and now he is steering directly towards it. The constraint, that is to say the surrender of the imperial freedom of decision, can come in two ways : either the Kaiser will retreat before the 'movement to the Left', which will make itself felt with unprecedented intensity at the next elections (summer 1898 if not sooner); or the Kaiser will give himself up to a terrorist with a war-programme for both domestic and foreign affairs. This programme will probably prove a failure, for apart from the German electorate, the German Princes will not support it either, so far as one can tell. The move to the Left would then take place after all, and by that time with redoubled strength.

You can imagine under these circumstances I find my work discouraging.

Foreign affairs take their peaceful course. Why does Muraviev not put forward a candidate for Crete?

Please give my regards to the Princess.

In old friendship<br>Holstein.

On your report 'from a good source' that the Russians would refuse a visit by Faure,[1] H.M. commented : 'This time the source has failed'. Who was it?

## 627.   Alfred von Kiderlen-Wächter to Holstein

Göteborg, 7 July 1897

Dear friend,

Immediately after this I am writing you another letter[2] in which I explain that Hohenlohe *cannot* be kept. I am sorry for the old man and for the cause. But since the Chancellor has dug his own grave *against* your and our advice *I see no reason why you should go with Hohenlohe.*[3] Bear that in mind. That is the *urgent* request in old and *loyal* friendship, of

Yours<br>Kiderlen.

## 628.   Note by Chlodwig zu Hohenlohe

Berlin, 3 August 1897

The telegrams on official matters, which *Geheimrat* von Holstein has for a number of years been in a position to address as private telegrams to Ambassadors and other members of the Foreign Service, were expressly approved by me because I am convinced of their necessity in the interests of the Service.

Prince Hohenlohe<br>Chancellor.

[1] President Faure of France paid a visit of state to Russia from 23–26 August 1897.

[2] Not found.

[3] Hohenlohe had released a statement about the military courts-martial question that was published on 2 July 1897 in the *Norddeutsche Allgemeine Zeitung*. The statement said in conclusion: 'We believe, however, that we can give the assurance that the Chancellor and Minister-President will not agree to any draft which is irreconcilable with the declaration which he made in the Reichstag last year.' (Hohenlohe, *Denkwürdigkeiten der Reichskanzlerzeit*, pp. 365–6.)

### 629. Bernhard von Bülow to Holstein

Semmering, 26 September 1897

Dear Holstein,

[...] In Homburg I found Visconti less pro-English than formerly.[1] The gross mistakes of English policy in the Greek Question have cooled off even Visconti and Goluchowski. But naturally they both desire an improvement in our relations with England if only because neither would like to come into direct opposition to Albion. I believe—are you not also of this opinion?—that we should not be on worse terms with England than is Russia. The sudden revulsion of the Russians to the proposal for a signing *à cinq*,[2] certain remarks which appeared at the same time in the Russian Press about the alleged irreconcilable opposition between Germany and England, and (*last not least*[3]) the attempts by the French immediately afterwards to seek a rapprochement with England (Tunisian commercial agreement)[4]—all this gives food for thought. Naturally we should not run after the English. H.M. will not pay a visit to Balmoral. [...]

I am deeply distressed by what you tell me about the condition of your eyes. Nobody can admire the stoicism with which you bear your sufferings more than I. I am convinced, however, that you see the future too blackly. I know of many cases—it is in fact the rule—in which the ability to work was preserved even after a double operation. You can of course arrange matters in the Ministry with regard to work by dictating, being read to, and in any way it suits you. We will all—with myself in the lead —endeavour to make everything easy for you. My wife sends you the most affectionate greetings. She is upset by parting from her mother, who has gone back to Italy in company with Blaserna. Blaserna intends to visit you and us in the winter. I am thinking of coming to Berlin in the first days of October. Once again best wishes. Always in loyal friendship and attachment

Yours

B.

### 630. Holstein to Paul von Hatzfeldt[5]

Berlin, 13 November 1897

Dear friend,

To-day I find it necessary to send you a commentary on certain

---

[1] Visconti-Venosta accompanied the King and Queen of Italy on a visit to the Kaiser in Homburg on 3 September when the King took part in the manoeuvres. (See Bülow, *Denkwürdigkeiten*, vol. I, p. 134.)

[2] A Russian proposal that the continental Great Powers should sign the preliminaries of peace in the war between Greece and Turkey without the participation of England if England refused to accept the text of the treaty. (See *Grosse Politik*, vol. XIIii, no. 3249, pp. 432–3.) Later Muraviev told Radolin he did not think all the Continental Powers would agree to the exclusion of England. (*Grosse Politik*, vol. XIIii, no. 3251, pp. 435–6.)

[3] In English in the original.

[4] A treaty of 15 September 1897 whereby the English gave up their rights in Tunis based on a treaty of 1875 in exchange for preferential tariffs for English woollen goods in Tunis.

[5] From the London Embassy files.

information which you will be receiving at the same time through official channels.[1]

You know that our navy for a long time past has been longing to seize something in the Far East. The affair was put off by the fact that on the one hand Marschall was of the opinion that forcible action without China's agreement (which incidentally he hoped to obtain) would injure German-Chinese trade, and on the other, and above all, by the fact that the navy was not unanimous as to the place that was to be occupied. The chief instigator of action at any price was, as you can probably guess, Senden.

During recent weeks, as we have since heard, Senden was often at the High Command of the Navy to ask whether no report about Kiaochow Bay had been received from Admiral Diederichs, who is in command of the Far East squadron. The expected report, which was probably ordered by Senden, finally arrived, written at great length, very detailed, and arguing in favour of the occupation of Kiaochow Bay and its hinterland.[2]

The Kaiser was greatly excited by this report and expressed himself to Bülow at his last audience on the 4th of this month very indignantly about the flaccid policy of the Foreign Ministry which had not understood how to exploit the favourable opportunities which had repeatedly presented themselves in recent years[3] (as I said, the chief obstacle to any action was the fact that the navy had not decided where it was to take place). But when, by an act of fate, the news of the murder of German missionaries in Shantung[4] arrived here on the day after the audience, restraint was no longer possible. The Kaiser telegraphed to the Chancellor that the hypercautious policy of the Foreign Ministry was to come to an end and that action must be taken immediately—against Kiaochow.[5]

The Chancellor replied that on the occasion of the visit to Peterhof the two Emperors had agreed that a prolonged stay by our ships in Kiaochow would be dependent upon obtaining the prior consent of Russia. Therefore either this consent would have to be obtained at once, or the projected action would have to take place at some other point on the Chinese coast, for instance at Hangchow (not far from Chusan).[6] The Kaiser at once telegraphed directly to the Tsar, who replied in a telegram of which the principal sentence ran: 'Can neither approve or disapprove, Kiaochow having only been temporarily ours from 1895 to 1896'.[7]

The Tsar's reply took the wind out of the sails of the opposition which we had up to then been offering to the occupation of Kiaochow. This opposition was based simply on a look at the map. The inner Yellow Sea,

---

[1] See *Grosse Politik*, vol. XIVi, no. 3698, pp. 81–3.

[2] The report was one from Diederichs dated 21 August 1897, a copy of which was sent to the Foreign Ministry on 27 October by the High Command of the Navy. (From the Foreign Ministry files.)

[3] See *Grosse Politik*, vol. XIVi, no. 3690, pp. 69–71.

[4] On 4 November two German Catholic missionaries were murdered in South Shantung.

[5] *Grosse Politik*, vol. XIVi, no. 3686, p. 67.

[6] *Grosse Politik*, vol. XIVi, no. 3688, p. 68.

[7] *Grosse Politik*, vol. XIVi, no. 3689, p. 69. The quoted sentence is in English in the original.

which together with the Gulfs of Chihli and Liaotung, is regarded by the Russians as a Russian lake, is bordered at its outward opening by two strips of land which, with a touch of imagination, can be regarded as the upper and lower jaw of an open mouth. On the upper jaw stands Port Arthur, on the lower, Kiaochow. It therefore obviously belongs to the district which the Russians regard as their future sphere of interest. It is only natural that for the present and as long as the affair is not yet ripe, they will not unnecessarily trumpet their intentions and claims with regard to Kiaochow. Nevertheless, Muraviev's remark, which you will find in Bülow's 'Memorandum',[1] namely 'that Russia does not intend to establish herself in Kiaochow but cannot yet determine the date when she will withdraw completely from Kiaochow' is a sufficiently clear hint that she will never withdraw from there. At least that is the way I understood the matter up to the moment when the Tsar telegraphed to the Kaiser that Russia was not interested in Kiaochow. Even then the affair seemed fishy to me, as can be seen from a letter which I wrote on that same day to Bülow. But I must admit I was not prepared for the brutal manner of the refusal by the Russians which came on Tuesday, the 9th, after Muraviev had had an audience of the Tsar.[2] Our squadron had meanwhile received orders to leave for Kiaochow, and Senden, who was present at Naval Headquarters when the Head of our Chinese Department informed them of the Russian answer, exclaimed: 'Everything now depends on the Diplomatic Service which must surely have a thousand trumps in their hands to play against Russia.' I referred to this remark in conversation yesterday with Captain Jeschke, Chief of the Naval General Staff, and said to him: 'The only really valuable trump against Russia, namely the possibility of entering into closer relations with England, has been taken out of our hands by the navy with its continuous agitation against England.' I think that this opinion will now make itself felt with such elemental force that at least a certain effect upon our Kaiser's intentions can be expected. To what extent and at what time these intentions can be directed into more favourable and propitious channels will depend in the first place on England, and consequently also upon you. I received telegrams yesterday and to-day from Bülow and Philipp Eulenburg in which both say: 'Things cannot go on this way any longer, we must try to reestablish our connection with England.' Radolin was the first who at my request, and later at the repeated request of Bülow, told the Kaiser in Wiesbaden in the presence of Bülow and P. Eulenburg that our position with regard to Russia was weakened by our bad relations with England.

These are possibilities for the future. Let us now return to the concrete case. While I am writing this the German squadron has been anchored for about twenty-four hours in Kiaochow Bay. We found out *yesterday* that the Admiral had been ordered to proclaim the occupation

---

[1] The London Embassy files show that the document in question was Bülow's telegram from St Petersburg to the Foreign Ministry of 11 August. (*Grosse Politik*, vol. XIVi, no. 3679, pp. 58–9.)

[2] *Grosse Politik*, vol. XIVi, no. 3693, pp. 73–4.

of the province of East Shantung. We learned this from the Chief of the Imperial Naval Office, Admiral Tirpitz,[1] who came to the Chancellor and told him that he (Tirpitz is just back from China) regarded a war with China as unavoidable if such a programme were carried out. The Chancellor, after securing Imperial consent in general, thereupon forced the High Command to alter the instructions to Admiral Diederichs in the sense that he is to restrict himself to such measures as will not commit us for the future. It now remains to be seen whether the proclamation was not already issued before this telegram arrives.

It is difficult to prophecy how the immediate future will turn out. It will depend upon the attitude of the Russians and also upon how far our Admiral has already gone. I can already perceive that an opinion is forming, which Bülow seems to share, that we should exchange Kiaochow for another port farther removed from the Russian sphere. But, if we get farther away from the Russians, we get closer to the English, and the question which you will have to ask yourself first is: how will the English take it if we occupy Hangchow, for example? (I can surely assume that you have a good map of China; if not, this would certainly be the time to procure one at the Reich's expense). To be sure, among the points which the navy indicates as acceptable, Hangchow comes very nearly in the last place; the Chusan Islands or Wusung are higher on the list. But do you think it conceivable that England would renounce these if we were to offer the English compensation?

Questions like these really need years of observation and feeling out the ground; but time is precisely what we do not have. Do you think it conceivable and possible that you could exert your magnetism upon Lord Salisbury in the sense that he would gain a more sympathetic view of Germany's usefulness for England's more immediate and also more distant future than he has had heretofore?

We have learned from confidential information passed on by Parisians to bankers here that while the French and English are quarrelling in public over the Niger, Hanotaux is secretly beginning to support English policy towards the Transvaal Government, ostensibly only out of regard for French financial interests. The actual fact of co-operation, however, is of course designed to promote better feeling. Could we do something similar in South Africa or elsewhere? Could you perhaps use the occasion of similar co-operation, even though it were of little importance, to make Salisbury see the light? Do not be astonished at the dilettante nature of my questions. They must necessarily correspond to the whole dilettante development of our present situation.

In moments of depression I am filled with the fear that the English, as soon as they perceive that we will retreat from Kiaochow in face of the Russian uproar, will for their part summon up the courage to keep us out of places which might be uncomfortable for England if they were in the

---

[1] Alfred von Tirpitz. German Admiral. Commander of the Cruiser Squadron in the Far East, 1896–7; State Secretary of the Reich Naval Office, 1897–1916.

hands of Germany. It seems to me that tendencies of this kind could be effectively countered, or better still prevented, by an insinuation that it would not be difficult for Germany to come to an understanding with Russia, but that Germany up to now did not want to pay the required price. This insinuation rests on a foundation of truth. On the occasion of the manouevres in Homburg, the Chief of the General Staff of the Russian Army, General Obrutshev, at Muraviev's orders, brought Bülow the proposal that Germany might ally herself with Russia and France against England for three to five years; the specific conditions were reserved for further agreement.[1] Bülow refused on the grounds that if this were Russia's opinion, he could only be astonished that she had not made use of the several occasions during the past year when an understanding between Continental Powers without England's participation would have been of direct practical utility for the interests of European peace.

The *possibility* of an understanding with Russia is therefore present. The Kaiser emphasised this in a telegram the day before yesterday which said: 'The Russians will demand a high price for Kiaochow but it will not be impossible to pay it.'[2] This 'high price' appears sinister to me, perhaps also to you. For the sake of an agreement with England, I would prefer another usable Chinese port to an agreement with Russia over Kiaochow. There is a wide gulf between this idea and its realisation. Nevertheless, consider thoroughly and quickly what can be done. The question is well worth the trouble of an examination. A fiasco before the eyes of a watching world would be fatal, for it would give courage to our enemies. But to agree to certain conditions which Russia may propose would be almost equally bad.

Could you not give Salisbury the idea that this would be a psychological moment to bring the Kaiser back within earshot of England by means of a relatively worthless concession?

As to the brusque but at the same time cunning attitude of the Russians, two interpretations are possible: the most obvious is that they wanted to frighten us off; the other is that they wanted to get us to pay a 'high price' in the sense of Obrutshev's proposal.

Rotenhan, who has read this letter up to this point, expressed the fear that Salisbury would regard every friendly remark on your part as a sign of Germany's intimidation and would therefore be less inclined than ever to meet us half-way. If you with your keen intuition have the same feeling, then do not speak about it at all to Salisbury, but merely send us your own impressions in your reply to to-day's dispatch.[3]

Is it possible that Salisbury already knows of the whole situation, that is to say, of the brusque Russian communication? Through All-

---

[1] See *Grosse Politik*, vol. XIII, no. 3451, pp. 88–9.

[2] *Grosse Politik*, vol. XIVi, no. 3695, pp. 77–8.

[3] Hatzfeldt telegraphed on 16 November that in his opinion the Russian price for Kiaochow would be too high and he advised that Germany try to obtain Amoy instead. He intended to speak with Salisbury on the subject and wondered what compensation Germany should offer England. (*Grosse Politik*, vol. XIVi, no. 3703, pp. 87–8.)

Highest feminine channels perhaps? In that case I can well believe that he is laughing a little maliciously—but mistakenly, because for a high price an understanding with Russia may still be possible (at least H.M. thinks so).

In the hope that you are as well as possible<br>
and with kindest regards<br>
Holstein.

## 631.   Philipp zu Eulenburg to Holstein

Vienna, 13 November 1897

Dear friend,

Many thanks for keeping me so will informed.

I am completely in agreement with your statement to Osten-Saken.[1] Muraviev's attitude is *unheard of*. Goluchowski may be right when he says to me every time I meet him: 'I do not like Hanotaux—he makes policy in Russia and has Muraviev in tow.'

H.M.'s statement[2] corresponds with your view that above all one must not show fear. In my opinion too this is a necessity. But it is *equally* necessary not to embark on any *warlike* action.

*How right you are* to point out that we would thereby inflict an almost fatal blow on our trade with the Far East.

Muraviev's statement is too great a contradiction of the Tsar's telegram not to allow one to hope that a middle-way will yet be found. But what? Tirpitz should be very competent to deal with the matter since he has just come back from the Far East. The purchase of Kiaochow would be difficult and would not be very popular in Germany. The German inclines more to taking than to paying. Moreover the amount to be paid would not be small, as H. M. thinks, but *very large*. I am more in favour of *another* port because I have been told by very influential people that Kiaochow is *unsuitable*. At all events opinions are *much divided* on the subject.

Goluchowski's ill-humour with Hanotaux is just what I could wish for at this moment. I admit that Russia makes me uneasy. So for heaven's sake let us move as far as possible towards England! [...]

Kindest regards!

What would Bülow do without you now! The poor man *really* needs a little peace in Rome. I found him *terribly* run down and depressed in Berlin. He will in any case be back in a week. I am worried that H.M. will suddenly summon him!

Your faithful<br>
PEulenburg.

---

[1] The Russian Ambassador was told that the Kiaochow problem had been openly and loyally discussed, and that Muraviev, in suddenly opposing the German action, probably did not know of the Tsar's telegram to the Kaiser in which he had disclaimed Russian rights there. (*Grosse Politik*, vol. XIVi, no. 3697, pp. 79–81.)

[2] In a marginal comment on the document cited above.

Vienna, 13 November 1897

I most respectfully report to Your Imperial and Royal Majesty that His Majesty Kaiser Franz Joseph accorded me an audience to-day in the Palace and entrusted me with the most affectionate greetings for Your Majesty.

The Kaiser looked well and was in good spirits so long as the conversation did not touch upon the internal situation. The Cretan Question was discussed and the Kaiser declared that it did not seem to him to be at all possible, in case the proposal for a provisional Governor were dropped—which is what Russia and France probably intended—to give the Sultan's refusal as the reason for doing so. For the Sultan would then have a refusal ready for *every* question and everything would be at a stand-still. Austria had no interest whatsoever in Herr Schäfer.[1] If a permanent Governor were now proposed, then Austria would simply agree as soon as the other Powers had reached agreement.

The Kaiser then made some pointed remarks about M. Hanotaux, who maintained that Count Goluchowski had launched Herr Schäfer. That was simply a lie.

I replied that Your Majesty too had taken the standpoint in this Schäfer question of not showing any initiative *in rebus orientalibus*, but that you also regarded Herr Schäfer as being little suited to the post. The question now seemed to be entering a new phase, and it would soon be seen what Russia and France intended to do about the new developments and whether a fresh candidate would be put up.

The increased desire for action on the part of those two boon companions, Muraviev and Hanotaux, about which Count Goluchowski informed me is disquieting, but I was reassured to know that Count Goluchowski was keeping his eyes open. It is imperatively necessary to be on the alert. Count Muraviev had first of all to pacify the Triple Alliance Powers which had shown little friendliness towards him. But he would show his true face as soon as he felt himself to be firmly in the saddle; that is, as soon as he thought he could *lead* the Tsar.

The Kaiser agreed with me and replied that his mind was not made up about Muraviev, but that it was the duty of the friendly Governments to maintain the greatest watchfulness.

The conversation soon turned to the gloomy internal situation. The Kaiser looked worried. 'One does not know how one is to get out of this dilemma', he said. 'The misfortune is that we need *votes* in order to arrive at a legal settlement of the *indispensable* questions. One must therefore work with a machine which refuses to work. The difficulty here in Austria lies in the fact that we cannot, as in Hungary, *make* the elections. Of course this is not an entirely honourable method—but at least one knows where one stands. Here one has no influence—and we are faced with a mob of people on whose account one must feel ashamed

---

[1] On 23 October the Powers proposed to nominate Colonel Schäfer, a native of Luxemburg, as provisional Governor-General of Crete. His name was subsequently withdrawn.

before all Europe! We certainly want to show consideration for the Germans—but why do the moderate elements among them behave *so* weakly? It is as if that horrible group of Radicals had deprived the better Germans of all courage!—and with these people nothing can be done!

'The way the German Government handled the agitation that has spread into Germany is *very* pleasing to me—I thank you most particularly for this. We will at all events exercise reciprocity in such questions.[1]

'The Hungarian Government is very correct. Baron Bánffy,[2] who has a good many social snags to overcome, is proving his worth more and more. He is reliable and keeps his promises. I have confidence in him. The Opposition in Hungary has also become much more tractable. They no longer demand the impossible but keep within limits. [...]

Three things stand out fairly clearly from this conversation: the intention to come to an understanding with Parliament, confidence in Count Badeni!,[3] and satisfaction with Hungary. It is not easy to see how His Majesty will reconcile the latter two in the long run. Influential people who know the Kaiser well maintain that one of these days he will drop Count Badeni with surprising suddenness when nobody expects it. For him to do that, however, the situation will have to become even *more* difficult. Though how this is possible I do not know.

Nevertheless, the situation by and large does not seem to be by any means so serious as the liberal Press likes to declare. In this confusion it is easier to believe that the Crown forms the immovable object, whereas the Parliament gets weaker. This is due to the circumstances that the Kaiser is always in the position of seeking the support of another *race* when the support of the last one has broken down. At the moment *Hungary* has placed the bolster under the feet of its King.

Socially everything is dead here. The weather is cold and windy.

Your Majesty's *brilliant* bag has caused me only relative pleasure. 1235 pheasants in one day are a strain despite a light non-recoiling gun.


### 633.   Holstein to Paul von Hatzfeldt[4]

TELEGRAM

Berlin, 18 November 1897

Private.

It was to be foreseen that Lord Salisbury would have no objections about Kiaochow and would in fact be at pains to push us into the Russian sphere.[5] His attitude is the more conducive to make us think more

---

[1] Marginal comment by Eulenburg: 'This seems to me to be a phrase inspired by Count Goluchowski which is perhaps intended to convey the idea: we will keep our hand on Polish propaganda *if* you remain firm.'

[2] Desiderius, Baron Bánffy zu Losoncz. Hungarian Minister-President, 1895–9.

[3] In the unprinted part of this conversation, Kaiser Franz Joseph had expressed his satisfaction that Badeni had emerged unscathed from a duel with a Deputy named Wolff.

[4] From the London Embassy files.

[5] See *Grosse Politik*, vol. XIVi, nos. 3708–9, pp. 92–5.

seriously of an understanding with Russia at any price, because there also seems to be no prospect of a German-English agreement over any other item which would serve as a sign of improving German-English relations and thereby lessen Russian self-confidence.

Holstein.

## 634.   Holstein to Paul von Hatzfeldt[1]

Berlin, 25 November 1897

Dear Hatzfeldt,

[...] The news that the French have captured Nikki[2] after a bloody battle with the English came in an hour ago and helped to hasten Zimmerman's[3] journey.[4] For it is possible that this event—which London and Paris will of course treat as a mere incident and misunderstanding—is for us a psychological moment. It is at any rate conceivable that the English will thereby become more conciliatory towards us. This event again shows that Germany's position is less serious than pessimists often imagine. The world's stock-pile of hatred is more equally divided than one sometimes thinks. We must bear lightly the share allotted to us. [...]

May things go as well for you as is wished for you by

Holstein.

## 635.   Holstein to Paul von Hatzfeldt[5]

2 December 1897

Dear friend,

You will find in Bülow's letter,[6] in more cautious form, what I would otherwise have written to you.

The chief question now is: how do we avoid a definite treaty with Russia?[7] What arguments can be used against it *if* the Russians actually come up with one? My hope is that they will not risk putting the French in a bad temper by the actuality of a German-Russian agreement. But it is after all possible and we must be prepared for it.

Please let me have your views.

Kind regards<br>H. [...]

## 636.   Bernhard von Bülow to Hatzfeldt[8]

Berlin, 2 December 1897

My dear Count,

The courier is being sent to-day in order to bring you the necessary

---

[1] From the London Embassy files.

[2] The report of an Anglo-French conflict at Nikki in the hinterland of Togoland proved to be unfounded.

[3] Dr Alfred Zimmermann. Assistant in the Foreign Ministry; *Vortragender Rat*, 1905–10; later Under State Secretary and State Secretary.

[4] Dr Zimmermann was being sent to London to assist Hatzfeldt in negotiations over the delimitation of a neutral zone in the hinterland of Togoland. (See *Grosse Politik*, vol. XIII, no. 3420, pp. 43–4, and vol. XIVi, no. 3721, pp. 108–10.)

[5] From the London Embassy files.          [6] See below.

[7] Holstein refers to the possibility of a treaty with Russia over Kiaochow.

[8] From the London Embassy files.

information about the present phase of the Russo-German talks over Kiaochow.[1] The indications up to now indicate that with the failure of Muraviev's first attempt at intimidation he would now like to come to terms.[2] This may not be easy for him, however, for apparently, in his first transport of arrogance and driven on by Hanotaux, he said all sorts of things which will now be difficult for him to carry out.

We will not leave Kiaochow under any circumstances. The reasons against doing so are: (1) the insolent tone adopted by the Russians at the outset; (2) the will of the Kaiser, to which he himself has already given unequivocal expression; (3) the attitude of England, which would welcome Germany as a neighbour with at least the same degree of dislike as does Russia. I understand that it might have been possible earlier to have considered an occupation further to the south. But I do not believe in the desirability of a move, for instance from Kiaochow to Amoy, brought about by Russian pressure; we would leave too much of our prestige hanging on the thorns by the wayside.

All observations up to now indicate that the Russians will not make war on us at present. In fact, this would be a greater risk for Russia than Muraviev's nerves could stand. For a war of Germany against Russia and France would be the signal in London, Vienna, Rome, and Tokyo, for the simultaneous pursuit of their individual interests, with or without treaties of alliance. It is beyond the discernment of the wise to see to-day who would in the last result emerge the winner from this colourful confusion, but from what I know of Muraviev I do not believe that he would like to sail into this gloomy mist-enveloped future at 'full steam ahead'.

A war against Great Powers is therefore at present improbable; but not a war against China in the spring. The latter depends largely on Franco-Russian agitation or on unforeseen incidents on the spot.

The Kiaochow question has up to now been handled by the Press both here and in Russia with the greatest caution. Attempts have indeed been made in quarters inimical to the Government to exploit in the Press certain information about Russo-German tension which may have come from the Palace in Darmstadt[3] in order to make things more difficult for the Government. Up to the present, however, this agitation had not been taken up by our Press, which has so far behaved most tactfully.

Our previous exchange of ideas with St Petersburg falls into two periods. In the first period, Muraviev's attempt at intimidation was answered according to the maxim 'rudeness must be met with rudeness'. During the second period, which is not yet over, there has only been talk of expediency, compensation, and the like.[4] You will observe that we

[1] The courier brought Hatzfeldt the three documents mentioned in *Die Grosse Politik*, vol. XIVi, pp. 104–5, note *. The conversation with Witte was not conducted by Radolin, as stated there, but by Tschirschky.

[2] See *Grosse Politik*, vol. XIVi, nos. 3693, 3697, 3699, 3700, pp. 73–4, 79–81, 83–4, 84.

[3] On 19 October the Kaiser visited the Tsar in Darmstadt to return the call the Tsar had made on him the previous day in Wiesbaden. No record of a political conversation between the two monarchs has been found in the files of the Foreign Ministry. (See *Grosse Politik*, vol. XIII, p. 89, note ***.)

[4] See *Grosse Politik*, vol. XIVi, nos. 3707, 3711, 3717, 3719, pp. 90–1, 97–8, 102–6, 107.

have treated the problem of the future collaboration of two Powers entirely as one arising from our community of interests and that we have played down the question of a treaty.

I hear from naval quarters that they are in anything but a light-hearted mood there, and are disposed to take the possibility of complications with China seriously. We can only welcome the possibility that the navy too will not neglect the *suaviter in modo*. [...]

In sincere esteem

Your very devoted

B. von Bülow.

### 637.   Paul von Hatzfeldt to Holstein[1]

TELEGRAM

London, 5 December 1897

Secret

Private

It was to be expected that St Petersburg would begin to put out feelers to find out whether and what high price they could get for permitting what has already happened. You will know better than I whether Witte, despite his quarrel with Muraviev, is to be regarded as the representative of Russian policy in this matter and whether we can trust him despite his former unfriendly attitude—especially in the matter of the Chinese loan.[2] In my opinion the greatest danger now is that the Russians will demand written agreements, and I am afraid that consideration for France will not prevent them from doing so. If the agreement in question is only a matter of mutual support in the *Far East* and not a general treaty of alliance, they are not yet likely to fear that the French will desert them, no matter how much they may dislike the business, and leave us alone with the Russians. It seems to me, therefore, that it would be our task to awaken and encourage this fear in the Russians in case they become too insistent about the written agreement. We can do this all the more easily because the possibility of the French leaving the Russian camp is actually not out of the question under certain circumstances. What practical value would Russian friendship retain for France if Russia concluded a treaty of friendship with us as well, and therefore definitely had to renounce her support for France's anti-German purposes? In addition to this, however, is the fact that the conclusion of a treaty between ourselves and Russia might have more far-reaching effects than St Petersburg seems to suspect. So far as English policy is concerned, such a treaty would be tantamount to the conclusion of an anti-English coalition between Russia, France and Germany which they would have to prevent at any price. It is not difficult to assume that in this case they would make every effort here to facilitate the negotiations in Paris by greater conciliation and that they would try to reach an agreement with the French which could be extended politically and give both parties a useful counterweight against

---

[1] From the London Embassy files.       [2] See above, vol. III, pp.529–30.

Russia. This danger for Russia would disappear if Russia, instead of demanding treaties, were content to accept the actual community of interests existing between us in the *Far East* and our assurances of loyalty in this regard. It is my conviction that everything depends on making these considerations clear to the Russians in an appropriate and *skilful* manner if the need should arise.

At the same time I would point out to Witte that the danger he mentioned of a break with China could be removed easily if Russia, instead of agitating in Peking with the French, were to give China the firm advice to reach an agreement with us about the cession of Kiaochow in the form of a long-term lease.

Japan will probably remain quiet as well if she sees that no trouble is to be expected between Russia, Germany, and France, and that no effective support is to be expected from England.

I will make this the subject of my next official report, but thought that I should not delay in replying to your question since time is probably short. Please submit the foregoing to Herr von Bülow, with my sincere thanks for his private letter.[1]

PH.

### 638.   Adolf Marschall von Bieberstein to Holstein

Pera, 25 December 1897

Dear friend,

I feel I must send you my best wishes for the New Year, and once again express my deepest thanks for all the loyal and really friendly support which you have given me during many years, especially during the difficult years that have just passed. I will never forget it, and even if Fate has separated us in space, I still retain the same feelings which united us throughout so many years of loyal collaboration. May the New Year bring you pleasant days and no more unpleasantness than is inevitably bound up with human existence and your responsible position.

Things are going very well for me. My health is excellent, as is that of my wife and family. The post here suits me, as does the life here. [...]

My appointment[2] created a great sensation here, so that I feel I should keep to myself for the time being and try to counter the belief that I was chosen to inaugurate a new and sensational German Near Eastern policy. Even if that were the case I would behave in the same way, because I doubt whether it is right to start off by proclaiming *urbi et orbi* that one intends to do something big. [...]

With best compliments and greetings to the State Secretary and best wishes for the New Year to all old friends,

With all regard
Your very devoted
Marschall

My wife sends you her best wishes.

[1] Of 2 December. See above.        [2] As Ambassador to Turkey.

### 639. Extract from a very confidential private letter from Hugo von Radolin[1]

St Petersburg, 28 December 1897

I have the definite impression here that our entire procedure in Kiaochow has gone against the grain with the Russians. They found it very disconcerting that we should have occupied Kiaochow, that they have lost this harbour for winter quarters,[2] and that they will be compelled to look for something else. They have made *bonne mine à mauvais jeu* in order not to quarrel with us *now*. I am convinced, as I already said at the time in Berlin, that Tsar Nicholas will bear a grudge against us for this affair.[3] He feels that he has been taken by surprise and will {hold it against us despite all the telegrams and greetings. He will}[4] be strengthened in this feeling by many people here. The hand-in-hand policy, as Tsar Nicholas himself called it, will in my opinion only last as long as it suits the Russians.[5] Typical is a remark made yesterday by Witte {which I will not include in an official report in order not to make bad blood.}[4] He said to me: 'Count M[uraviev] is a man who only thinks of himself. Just as he made an about-face on the question of Greece to please the Empress-mother, so will he change his policy in the Far East if complications arise. He wanted to go to Port Arthur out of vanity. If big difficulties arise he may well give up this port. It is impossible to trust him. I tell you that in confidence.'[6] In addition, I feel that Muraviev does not feel at all friendly towards our activity in China. His statement yesterday that he must first obtain the Tsar's orders in order to be able to support our policy on Kiaochow in *Peking*[7] proves to me that even if he does support it he will do so *lukewarmedly*. He also told me yesterday when I mentioned this point and he wanted to put me off with something that he had advised the Chinese Minister to settle the matter with us in a friendly way (I wrote this in a report to-day);[8] he had moreover given the Chinese the soothing assurance that *if ever China asked for our good offices, not only in dealing with Germany but also in her relations with* other Powers *with which we maintain friendly relations, we would always be ready to do so.*[9] That surely means that Russia does not wish to burn her fingers in Peking on our account.[10] Now as to the *financial* action in China, I am convinced that it would be most unwelcome to the Russians if we took part in it. Herr Witte

[1] From the Foreign Ministry files. The files do not make it clear whether the letter was addressed to Holstein or to Bülow.

[2] Marginal comment by Wilhelm II: 'Nonsense! They never intended to go there'.

[3] Marginal comment by Wilhelm II: 'Most certainly not!'

[4] The sections enclosed in brackets were omitted from the version of this letter submitted to the Kaiser.

[5] Marginal comment by Wilhelm II: 'And ourselves.'

[6] The quotation is in French in the original. Marginal comment by Wilhelm II: '*rien de nouveau. nous le savions déjà!*'

[7] See *Grosse Politik*, vol. XIVi, p. 133, note *.

[8] See *Grosse Politik*, vol. XIVi, no. 3742, p. 133.

[9] In French in the original.

[10] Marginal comment by Wilhelm II: 'No! But rather that she thinks she already has her fingers completely in the Peking pie!'

expressly told me that he had found out that China was looking for money not only in France and England *but also in Germany*. He would however only take over the loan if China could not get money anywhere (thus not in *Germany, either*). At all events he did not say a word to me about the German syndicate being asked to keep the Russian leaders informed. This phase reminds me very much of the loan question in the summer of 1895 when in the beginning Witte never told me the truth or the *whole truth*,[1] and Lobanov assured me that he *knew nothing* about the *financial question*. That was a matter for financiers and the Minister of Finance, but not for the Foreign Minister. Yesterday when I spoke to Muraviev of the sixteen million loan, he told me that '*he knew absolutely nothing about it*'.

I have come to the conclusion that we can *only* depend on ourselves and only count in a restricted degree on Russian support.[2]

I do not know whether Witte is right when he advises us to secure only our commercial advantages in Kiaochow and to use the harbour as a commercial 'but not as a naval port.' At all events he very warmly advocated this (I have written about it.) It may of course be possible that we would not be in a position to hold the *fortified* harbour against British superiority *at sea*, whereas a commercial port is not so much an object for attack. I must moreover say that Witte is very sincerely in favour of our *commercial* interests in China and does not begrudge these to us. I believe we have *a friend* in him *at the moment*—which does not prevent him from preferring to handle the financial business *alone*.

### 640. Chlodwig zu Hohenlohe to Holstein

31 December 1897

I have told His Majesty everything we talked about and met with understanding. He read Radolin's dispatch with interest.[3] The idea of suggesting to the Russians a possible withdrawal from the Near East and an independent advance in the Far East met with his approval, which he summed up by saying that one should tread on Muraviev's corns. I did not risk attempting to dissuade him from sending a drawing done by himself to Tsar Nicholas, because he expected that it would make a good impression.[4]

CH.

[1] Wilhelm II: 'Dear Rado! no impossible demands! No Russian has ever done that!'
[2] Wilhelm II: 'We knew that from the beginning, Rado! You are too honourable! and you are always astonished if another person is not so honourable! In addition somewhat optimistic and also again somewhat too pessimistic.'
[3] See *Grosse Politik*, vol. XIVi, no. 3742, p. 133. The part of the telegram not printed in *Die Grosse Politik* stated that Muraviev advocated an understanding between Russia, Germany, and possibly France, over the measures necessary to force Japan to evacuate Weihaiwei. After an understanding had been reached, the Chinese should be given a loan which would make it possible for them to get the Japanese out of Weihaiwei quickly. In a report to the Kaiser on the same day Bülow expressed the opinion that Muraviev's attempt to secure Germany's support against Japan should be rejected. To this the Kaiser made the marginal comment 'Yes'. (From the Foreign Ministry files.)
[4] The drawing shows a European wearing a sword, carrying an immense cross before him, and leading a Chinaman by the hand.

# 1898

### 641.   Bernhard von Bülow to Paul von Hatzfeldt[1]

Berlin, 17 January 1898

Dear Count,

In your report no. 31 you indicated the possibility of an English occupation of Crete.[2] If this occupation—complete or partial—were to become a fact, I would regard it as one of the most favourable events for Germany which has happened since the capture of Paris. I see four advantages for Germany:

(1) Germany will have pushed through her programme that Crete should not go to Greece. Successful trial of strength.

(2) Russian-French friendship will come to an end. To bring this about it will be sufficient for France to deny Russia her support in the Cretan question, not to mention Syria, which, because of the Holy Places, plays the same sort of part in Russia's dreams for the future regarding the Mediterranean as the Shantung Peninsula may well have done in the Far East, only to a far greater extent.

(3) Germany makes use of the moment when England has really established herself in Crete and everyone is distrustfully watching everyone else to acquire some new territory for herself somewhere outside Europe; this would have to be at a point which is not more important for England than Crete (Delagoa Bay, for example?) or of far-reaching significance for French colonization plans. But one can think of quite a number of valuable territories which do not possess either of these draw-backs. *Germany would take possession without any prior understanding or agreement*, whether with England or anyone else. If therefore Lord Salisbury, as is probable, sounds you out suspiciously, you can reply without difficulty on the good conscience of your Government that we are neither aiming at compensation nor planning some surprise which would be unpleasant for England.[3]

(4) The solution of the Cretan question in this manner, with its accompanying features, would furnish proof that Germany holds the

---

[1] From the London Embassy files.

[2] Hatzfeldt reported on 13 January that Salisbury had asked him: 'But what will be said if all the Powers gradually withdraw *and England alone remains in Crete?*' (*Grosse Politik*, vol. XIIii, no. 3263, pp. 457–8.) The report was received in the Foreign Ministry on 15 January. Holstein thereupon drew up a memorandum, the first part of which was sent almost verbatim as a dispatch to London on 17 January. (See p. 63, note 3.) The second part of the memorandum was used by Bülow, again practically verbatim, for the above letter. (From the Foreign Ministry files.)

[3] This sentence was not in Holstein's memorandum.

deciding position among the European Powers, because the present state of national interests precludes a grouping of Powers which would be strong enough to dare fight a world war against or even without Germany.[1]

The final result of this analysis leads to the thought that Germany has less need to seek support abroad than other Powers. It is far more true that, provided German policy is correctly conducted, she will always find this support ready made, because the other Powers need us more than we need them, either because our opposition or our mere non-participation would represent too great a threat or hindrance to them in the execution of their own plans. Thus, for example, Germany was the *decisive* factor in the Far Eastern intervention of 1895, the cement which bound Russia and France together in this action. Prince Lobanov, who owes his reputation to this action, had an interest, just as M. Hanotaux did, in hiding and distorting this fact. But the world will realize it at the very moment when the 'irresistible Dual Alliance' will be called upon to act *without* Germany, be it in the Far East or because of Crete. The sooner such a sobering event occurs, the better it will be for Germany and the peace of the world. *For that reason* it is advisable to examine closely, but with caution, this remark of Lord Salisbury's which might perhaps lead to something further.

In sincere devotion
Ever your
B. von Bülow

## 642.   Holstein to Paul von Hatzfeldt[2]

Berlin, 17 January 1898

Dear friend,

My own ideas are sufficiently well expressed in what you are receiving to-day on Crete (English occupation) in the form of dispatch[3] and letter[4] to make further scribbling superfluous. If you succeed in giving Salisbury the conviction that Germany is not setting a trap for him but really intends to remain honestly neutral, I do believe it possible that he will go in [to Crete]. For I do not think I am mistaken if I

---

[1] At this point in Holstein's memorandum there followed two paragraphs which Bülow did not use:

'Germany can maintain this powerful position as long as she uses it with moderation. In spite of the family relationship between the royal houses, the Russian-English hostility will grow stronger as Russia slides nearer to the Indian border and does so in greater strength. The Franco-Russian friendship is burdened by the fact that France cannot rely on Russia against Germany, and Russia cannot rely on France against England. England and France are both too greedy by nature to get on well together in the long run; they have tried it repeatedly, but it never lasted for long.

'All these are favourable factors for Germany's future, provided that she does not by the immoderateness of her acquisitive urge cause this self-same fault of the others to be forgotten, thus driving them to unite, just as the countries on the shores of the Baltic, injured by the Peace of Westphalia to the advantage of Sweden, finally united against Charles XII to put an end to Sweden's domination in the Treaty of Nystadt.'

[2] From the London Embassy files.        [3] *Grosse Politik*, vol. XIIii, no. 3267, pp. 466–9.

[4] See above, Bülow's letter to Hatzfeldt of 17 January.

assume that a foreign success would be urgently desirable to the English Government at this very moment. The Russians too sense something, as is apparent from the enclosed cutting from the *Nord*,[1] which has set itself the task of frightening England with the *Triplice*; a naive idea, for Goluchowski and Visconti are only too ready to go with England through thick and thin and only feel embarrassed with Germany.

One more thing to which I would especially like to draw attention. The Austrian Ambassador just now told Bülow that it was not impossible that Muraviev would have the Cretans advised to proclaim the annexation to Greece in the very near future.[2] You will perhaps be able to make use of this information *to persuade Salisbury to hurry*, that is if you have reason to suppose that he is really serious about an English Crete. And herewith good hunting.

Ever your<br>H.[3]

I don't think that England will ever again find a more favourable moment for a *coup de main*, for such a cowardly Russian Minister as Muraviev and such a trimming Frenchman will not soon again be in office simultaneously.

But of course—the main point is that Salisbury must be *hungry*; otherwise it doesn't matter what one puts before him. After your report no. 31 I assume, however, that you believe in the existence of this pre-condition. That is why I took so much trouble with the matter.[6]

### 643.   Holstein to Paul von Hatzfeldt[4]

TELEGRAM

Berlin, 25 March 1898

Private

China officially settled by to-day's telegram.[5] That you should speak with Mr Chamberlain in the sense suggested by you about neutral zone

---

[1] On 14 January 1898 the paper *Le Nord* had published a report on alleged intrigues in Crete designed to produce a demand from the leaders of the insurgents for the protection of a certain Great Power. The paper pointed out that neither Russia nor France would permit the establishment of a regime in Crete similar to the one obtaining in Cyprus, and that France and Russia had already reached agreement with the Triple Alliance Powers on that point.

[2] Bülow summarized Szögényi's statement of his Government's view on this question as follows: 'Count Goluchowski is concerned because the Cretan question is threatening to become bogged down, and that the Russians, should Prince George's candidature fail, would demonstratively withdraw from Cretan matters and let it be understood that under the circumstances they would no longer have any objection to an annexation movement by the Cretans.' (*Grosse Politik*, vol. XIIii, no. 3265, pp. 461–4.)

[3] See Hatzfeldt's telegram of 19 January (*Ibid*, vol. XIIii, no. 3269, pp. 471–2), and Bülow's reply (drafted by Holstein) of 20 January (*Ibid*, vol. XIIii, no. 3270, p. 472).

[4] From the London Embassy files.

[5] Bülow had instructed Hatzfeldt by telegram to tell the British Ministers that, as far as Hatzfeldt knew, Germany had carried through her action in China without having undertaken any fixed obligations towards other Powers in case of a war. The fact that Germany had chosen Kiaochow instead of a port farther south, near the British sphere of influence, showed that she wished to avoid conflict with Britain. (*Grosse Politik*, vol. XIVi, no. 3780, pp. 194–5.)

is certainly right.[1] It is very important that you get under way with Chamberlain on this occasion.

Holstein

### 644. Paul von Hatzfeldt to Holstein[2]

TELEGRAM

London, 26 March 1898

Private

I will also try to meet Chamberlain in the next few days, but would like to point out that my approaching any one of the other Ministers would *not* have been advisable until now, because Salisbury and I had agreed—this being a pre-condition of our confidential relations—that I would establish contact on business matters with other Ministers only in special cases and with his express approval. You can also be sure that Chamberlain will do nothing for us unless he expects some political advantage from us in England's present critical situation.

I have postponed my going on leave for a few days, necessary though a change of air would be to me after a heavy cold.

### 645. Bernhard von Bülow to Paul von Hatzfeldt[3]

TELEGRAM

Berlin, 27 March 1898

Private

With reference to telegram no. 80.[4]

I leave it to Your Excellency whether to tell Mr Balfour[5] at your next meeting quite academically and as your personal view—the Imperial Government must be completely left out of it: Italy seemed to feel a bit lonely now as regards Crete after Germany and Austria had withdrawn; perhaps this was the psychological moment to make up in some way for the incorrect and excessively harsh treatment which Italy had been forced to endure on the Abyssinnian question, and once again to strengthen somewhat Italy's trust in England. To you *personally* it seemed to lie more in Germany's interest if, in questions which did not

---

[1] Hatzfeldt had telegraphed on 24 March that Alfred Rothschild had asked him to meet some English Cabinet Ministers, and that he believed a confidential attempt at a rapprochement would be made. Hatzfeldt thought he might tell the English Ministers that in his opinion they were acting unwisely in opposing German policy in China and were thereby driving Germany onto the other side. 'I would also make it quite clear to Mr Chamberlain, should we meet, that, in order to recommend a rapprochement in Berlin at all, I would first of all have to be convinced that we could expect greater consideration to be shown to us by him in certain colonial questions, e.g. neutral zone [in the hinterland of Togo]'. (*Grosse Politik*, vol. XIVi, no. 3779, pp. 193–4.)

[2] From the London Embassy files.          [3] From the Foreign Ministry files.

[4] By this telegram of the same day, the Foreign Ministry had transmitted a telegram from Rome according to which Italy would not give up her independent policy in the Cretan question in spite of the withdrawal of the Austrian forces from Crete. (From the Foreign Ministry files.)

[5] Arthur James Balfour. First Lord of the Treasury, 1895–1902; Prime Minister, 1902–5.

concern the Triple Alliance, Italy kept closer to England than to France!

Your Excellency might possibly also find an opportunity on this occasion to add something about England's habit of exploiting her friends. The military means of action, guns and rifles, had been repeatedly modified in the whole of Europe, not excluding England. But her diplomatic means of action, i.e. the tactic of pushing others to the front whilst herself remaining in the rear, was still used by England. But with the passage of time this had become generally known and therefore ineffective. Thus only a few days ago the Japanese Military Attaché in St Petersburg[1] had remarked that Japan would take care not to advance alone, because she would then be by no means certain that England would follow. Germany wanted to see the peace maintained everywhere and was therefore pleased at Japan's prudence; but for England this remark was proof that her policy was incorrect. I also leave it to Your Excellency whether to answer the above by a private telegram or letter.

[Bülow]

### 646. Paul von Hatzfeldt to Bernhard von Bülow[2]
Copy

London, 28 March 1898

Dear Herr von Bülow,

I am making use of to-day's courier to thank you for the private telegram of yesterday.[3] I particularly wanted to get to know your point of view concerning the questions dealt with, and I will naturally not fail to express myself in that sense at the next opportunity. I presume that you know that I for my part have not shrunk from any exertion during the last few years in order to persuade the English of the necessity to assure themselves of the trust and support of the Italians. The failure of these efforts was due to two causes; first, the fact that England was asked to cede a port in English possession,[4] something which was regarded here as quite unjustified and which it was believed could not be defended in the House or before public opinion; secondly, and by no means least important, the concern of the English lest by favouring the Italians they might provoke French anger and bring unpleasantness upon themselves.

It is unfortunately to be feared that this consideration for the French will remain decisive here as long as the English go on wanting to keep the door open for an understanding with the French in order to separate them from the Russians, if the latter should ever show signs of becoming seriously unpleasant towards England. True, to-day the situation is the opposite one, and the assumption that the English wish to draw closer to

---

[1] Colonel Outchijama Kojiro.    [2] From the London Embassy files.
[3] See above.
[4] Hatzfeldt refers to Italy's desire for the port of Zeila in British Somaliland.

Russia so as to isolate the French in China is not without foundation. But it is certainly not impossible, particularly if the effort in St Petersburg fails, that the former game with the French will be resumed here.

As regards the second point in Your Excellency's private telegram—the English habit of pushing others to the front whilst herself remaining in the rear—I have been telling the English, especially Lord Salisbury, home truths in a friendly way for years. Unfortunately, however, that is quite hopeless, and I am convinced that there will only be a change if another Power steps on England's feet so hard that there is no alternative but to fight. But the probability of this happening seems pretty small to me, for, unless I am completely mistaken, the French in their heart of hearts certainly don't want a war with England, and Russia, which even before Crete carefully avoided everything which might have provoked an intervention by the English Mediterranean fleet, will, I feel, *for the moment* be satisfied in China too with whatever she can get without a war against England, and that after all is still quite a big mouthful.

Lord Salisbury's vacillating policy in the Chinese question has not failed to affect his position in the country and in his own party, and the attacks on him would be even sharper if he had not fallen ill and since then been forced to surrender the leadership of affairs. Certainly the feeling is fairly general here that England cut a sorry figure in the affair. But, if the affair is drawn out and finally some sort of arrangement is reached—which, as usual, will take Russia a big step further—I feel that this will not prevent a large part of the nation in the end from regarding the preservation of peace as a heroic deed by the Cabinet. One should, however, never try to prophecy here, and if national pride is too deeply wounded, the danger that public opinion would force the Government into statements or other demonstrations which would seriously prejudice any agreement is not to be excluded.

Finally I would like to add that I do not believe in Lord Salisbury's alleged intention to retire for one moment. He himself specifically told the Under Secretary of State that he would allow himself one more week of rest, but that in Beaulieu he would once again want to see and decide everything. Another fact in favour of this is that Lord Salisbury has taken a secretary with him and that a second one is supposed to follow him in the next few days. Thus in the meantime the only question here will be whether Mr Balfour will carry on foreign affairs in the Prime Minister's sense, as I believe he will, or whether he will run into difficulties in this with the other Ministers. For my part I do not believe that Mr Chamberlain could now already think of becoming the head of the Ministry, even if Lord Salisbury were to retire voluntarily, something he certainly doesn't think of doing for the time being.

With sincere respect I remain

Your Excellency's<br>most devoted

### 647. Holstein to Paul von Hatzfeldt[1]

TELEGRAM

Berlin, 28 March 1898

Private

All right, don't do anything with Chamberlain; perhaps it is better because of the relationship with Balfour.

Holstein.

### 648. Holstein to Paul von Hatzfeldt[2]

Berlin, 3 April 1898

Dear friend,

If Chamberlain is the sort of man you have always described him to be —clever and unscrupulous—he will already have told himself that the purpose of compromising Germany towards Russia irretrievably will be achieved at the very moment when a German-English draft treaty is *submitted* to Parliament.[3]

I think the idea is very clever and therefore do not believe it impossible that at a later date, under changed circumstances, they will actually try to conclude a treaty. But for the present I believe that neither Parliament nor Chamberlain himself have been softened up sufficiently to accept the idea of a treaty, which is instinctively detested by the English. I think it more probable that this solicitation was nothing more than a novel method—Chamberlain's patent—by which England could cross her arms and take cover behind Germany. The thought that Chamberlain deliberately wants to do us in is not so sharply expressed in Bülow's letter,[4] which in my opinion contains nothing from beginning to end that is unsuitable for passing on to Chamberlain. For our purposes, the possibility that he has miscalculated suffices. Furthermore one argument which the English, particularly Chamberlain, now love to use has been reversed, i.e. expressed correctly. Chamberlain says: 'I will make no concessions to you in specific questions, e.g. Togo; all concessions will be saved up for the big treaty.'[5] Balfour's reply in the Chinese railway question seems inspired by the same, in this case unexpressed, basic idea.[6] Our reply is: 'The irritation of the German people with England must be reckoned among the factors which make the conclusion

[1] From the London Embassy files.　　　　[2] From the London Embassy files.

[3] In a talk with Hatzfeldt on 29 March 1898, Chamberlain admitted that England could no longer maintain her policy of isolation and suggested the possibility of an Anglo-German alliance, which would in effect be equivalent to England's adherence to the Triple Alliance. (*Grosse Politik*, vol. XIVi, no. 3782, pp. 196–9.) Holstein telegraphed to Hatzfeldt on 31 March: 'Under certain circumstances the mention of the possibility of a Treaty by Act of Parliament could be abused in St Petersburg. But you are a careful man.' (From the Foreign Ministry files.)

[4] Of 3 April. *Grosse Politik*, vol. XIVi, no. 3785, pp. 204–7.

[5] Hatzfeldt reported Chamberlain as saying 'that any small colonial differences which might exist could be settled if an understanding on major political interests were achieved *simultaneously*.' (See above, note 3.)

[6] Britain had objected to the priority granted to German interests in the Shantung railways by the Sino-German treaty on Kiaochow of 6 March 1898. On 25 March Hatzfeldt asked Balfour the reason for England's unfriendly attitude towards Germany on this subject.

of a treaty difficult. Petty chicanery, as for instance in Togo or in the Chinese railway question, keeps this dislike alive and strong. If therefore England is thinking of possibly having Germany fight by her side, she must avoid these minor examples of inconsiderateness.' The question now is what choice England has if Germany for the present, *rebus sic stantibus*, refuses. She can then only try to come to terms with France *or* Russia—to come to terms with both would be too expensive— either on a general basis or on specific problems. Judging by Chamberlain's attitude, Russia is given up as hopeless;[1] but there are quite a number of sure indications that the aim still is to bring about a *modus vivendi* with France. These efforts will fail because France will probably be prepared to come to terms on *particular problems* but not on a *general basis*, that is, France will not say, at least not yet: 'This is the price for which I will cut loose from Russia, leave Russia to her fate, turn against Russia.' That they won't say. On the other hand France will be prepared in certain circumstances to state the price for which she is prepared to be friends with England once again in specific, concrete cases. But the good friendship will then apply only to specific questions and will not change the solidarity of the Franco-Russian grouping. In other words everything that England may concede to France is thrown out the window. But we cannot ask the English to take our word for that, they will have to experiment and find out. After having experimented and found that being nice to France is a waste of time, they will probably strike a different tune, and, as Germany won't come running at the first whistle, experience and reflection will lead them to use other political forces for their purposes which, while not equivalent to Germany, are not to be despised for all that. I am thinking here first of all of Italy and Islam. Italy is despised, the Sultan maltreated. You know all this better than I do. Could you not, as your personal opinion, point out to Chamberlain or Balfour how completely England is playing the Russian game by kicking the Sultan into Russia's arms? I tend to believe that Salisbury's anger at the Sultan for failing to ratify the Drummond-Wolff concession [sic] in the past is still a contributory factor in that.[2] But whatever the cause, it is senseless to act in this way.

I would like to emphasize here that *very recently* the English seem to have acted more sensibly in Crete, i.e. they have paid more attention to the Turks. Could you not, with your great skill and delicate touch, and taking as a starting point the major world problem on which you are negotiating with Chamberlain, use Crete in particular as an example to demonstrate the stupidity of an English policy hostile to Turkey. I think such considerations would have little success with Balfour, who,

'Mr Balfour throughout our whole conversation confined himself to advocating better relations between us, without formulating any proposal, particularly with regard to China.' (*Grosse Politik*, vol. XIVi, no. 3781, pp. 195–6.)

[1] See Hatzfeldt's report on his conversation with Chamberlain of 1 April. (*Grosse Politik*, vol. XIVi, no. 3784, pp. 202–4.)

[2] A Convention drawn up between Britain and Turkey on 22 May 1887, which provided for the provisional evacuation of Egypt by Britain in three years. France and Russia persuaded the Sultan not to ratify the Convention because of its provisional character.

presumably, would tend to defend his uncle's anger.[1] But Chamberlain's behaviour seems now to be pretty close to that of a Prime Minister. If the English should suddenly become pro-Turkish once again, this would not only be a victory for sound common sense, but would also present quite a number of other advantages. As long as Salisbury has something to say, this question doesn't arise at all. But his health must, I think, now be very bad, for *The Times* already writes him off as a 'has been', and pious respect for Salisbury's views is probably the least of Chamberlain's faults.

To summarize briefly all that has been written to-day, I think you should say to Chamberlain: For the time being Germany cannot be had for an alliance for these and these reasons; but things are in flux, and for Germany's future decisions only Germany's interests will continue to be the key factor; if the latter change, the former will change too. England cannot avoid the struggle for her existence and must prepare for it, trying first of all to reach an understanding with France concerning a common attitude towards Russia. If, as is to be expected, such an understanding cannot be reached, England will have to seek friends elsewhere, that is in Italy and Turkey. If Chamberlain knows of something better he needn't bother to go on asking. Naturally Italy and Turkey cannot be mentioned as the main points, but *en passant*, according to the principle that *every little helps*.[2]

With best regards and best wishes for your health

Holstein

649.    Paul von Hatzfeldt to Bernhard von Bülow[3]
Copy

London, 20 April 1898

[...] Finally I would like to be permitted to remark in strict confidence that His Majesty, in a comment to one of my reports, has set me a very difficult task, for His Majesty expects me to preserve the feeling that exists in responsible circles here for the purpose of a possible later rapprochement with us.[4] Your Excellency knows how much that accords with my own view, and I need therefore hardly say that I will do my best in this direction. For the moment one must wait and see what effect our negative attitude has had on Lord Salisbury and also on Mr Chamberlain, whom I have not yet seen again because of the intervening holidays.[5] As Your Excellency knows, I think there can be little doubt

[1] Balfour was Lord Salisbury's nephew.                     [2] In English in the original.
[3] From the London Embassy files.
[4] See Wilhelm II's telegram to the Foreign Ministry of 10 April (*Grosse Politik*, vol. XIVi, no. 3790, pp. 217–18.)
[5] Bülow had stated Germany's objections to an alliance with Britain in a telegram to Hatzfeldt on 30 March: 'Résumé: We cannot conclude a treaty with England without ratification by the English Parliament, because it would be a *negotium claudicans*, i.e. it would bind us, but not England.' (*Grosse Politik*, vol. XIVi, no. 3783, pp. 199–202.) Bülow reviewed the situation more fully in a private letter to Hatzfeldt of 3 April in which he stated: 'The German Government cannot, *as long as the situation remains the same as it is now*, give an assurance to the English Government.' (*Grosse Politik*, vol. XIVi, no. 3785, pp. 204–7.)

that Lord Salisbury will take over affairs again completely after his return, and we will therefore have to continue to reckon with him. I shall only be able to judge after his return to what extent he was in agreement with me and what impression our reserve has left on him. In view of Chamberlain's character it would not surprise me for a moment if a certain degree of irritation had been the outcome, which might possibly find expression in a renewed attempt at a rapprochement with France. Your Excellency knows that I have never regarded such a rapprochement as completely out of the question and impossible, difficult though it may appear. I hear from a good source that Lord Rothschild[1], who is in Paris, has written from there that the chances of an understanding concerning West Africa have once again improved considerably. The dominant thought of the statesmen here still is to break the threatening Russo-French coalition against England, and I fear that Chamberlain and others, if forced to renounce Germany, would continue to believe that it would still be easier to satisfy the French in West Africa than to satisfy Russia, with whom England must be prepared for differences and conflicts almost everywhere: in India, in China, in Persia, and on the Bosporus. It was this realization which in my opinion brought the English to the bitter decision to seek the alliance of Germany and her friends. On the other hand, without wishing to anticipate Count Münster, I cannot overcome my concern that the French have not the least intention of risking a fight with England over Africa, in which they could by no means be sure of Russian support. I must leave it open whether there are not already a lot of people in France who have no further expectations regarding the Russian alliance. I certainly believe that we must keep the more or less remote possibility of an Anglo-French rapprochement in mind, in which Mr Chamberlain's statement to me: 'Colonial concessions if there is an alliance, without an alliance none',[2] would be applied, with the modification that France's neutrality would have to take the place of the alliance demanded from us in the event of a Russo-English conflict.

By that I certainly don't want to say that people here are thinking of provoking a conflict with Russia in case France were prepared to come to such an understanding. On the contrary I am still convinced that, at least so long as Lord Salisbury is in power, the English Government will leave nothing untried to avoid any warlike complication in which England would have to participate directly. This thought was also, in my opinion, decisive when Weihaiwei was occupied. England counted with certainty and with justification on the fact that Russia would not make this into a *casus belli*, if only because her military preparations on the Chinese frontier are not yet completed.

I think the situation would have been a totally different one if Mr

[1] Baron Alfred de Rothschild. Member of the London banking house.
[2] Chamberlain had informed Hatzfeldt on 29 March 'that Germany's and England's interests are identical apart from the commercial rivalry, which should only be a peaceful one, and minor colonial differences, which could probably be settled simultaneously with the understanding over political interests.' (*Grosse Politik*, vol. XIVi, no. 3782, pp. 196–9.)

Chamberlain's efforts to make an alliance with the Triple Alliance had succeeded. In that case I really believe that he would, as he openly stated, have done everything to persuade the Cabinet to take far more decisive action, such as a landing at Talienwan, which he hinted at and which would still have been possible at that time, and which presumably would have resulted in an immediate conflict with Russia.[1] Little though I trust Mr Chamberlain on the whole, I do believe and feel obliged to state openly to Your Excellency that it would be a mistake to attribute to him in this instance the secret plan of involving us in difficulties with Russia while he himself stood aloof. His calculations did not go so far as that and, unless I am totally mistaken, his basic idea was that Russia would have had to eat humble pie in the face of an alliance between England and the Triple Alliance, or that, if there had been a fight after all, she would have been defeated; in either case, however, Mr Chamberlain would inevitably have been recognized as the greatest statesman in England and as future Prime Minister after such a success.

If in these circumstances I ask myself how I can execute the task set me by His Majesty to preserve the existing desire for friendly relations for the purpose of a possible later rapprochement, I come to the following conclusion, which Your Excellency will, I trust, allow me to state quite openly in this confidential form. First of all I must aim, without, however, taking on even the semblance of a future obligation, to create the impression in my conversations with English statesmen that our refusal is not a final one, valid for all time, and that conditions could arise which would make a political rapprochement with England desirable to us because of our own interests. I cannot yet judge to-day how far it will be possible to keep that hope alive in them and thus deter them from steps which would bind England in another direction which would be undesirable to us. If I succeed in this, my main effort will be directed to persuading Lord Salisbury and his colleagues of the necessity of paying more attention to relations with Austria and Italy on the one hand, and on the other of showing more consideration towards us in any minor question that might arise and thereby prepare our public opinion as well for the establishment of amicable relations. To inform Your Excellency fully about the situation, I must, however, point out at this stage that, knowing Salisbury as I do from long and intimate experience, I will definitely fail with him because of one point unless I use the greatest caution. Your Excellency will see at once what I mean if I tell you briefly part of a conversation I had with Lord Salisbury shortly after Prince Bismarck's retirement. When I asked him in the course of a very confidential and frank discussion whether he could tell me openly what he really thought of the political suggestions which the Prince had made heretofore, the Prime Minister replied: 'I will tell you personally and quite frankly that nothing that you told me at the Prince's instructions during the past years affected my view of our policy, because I had to tell myself and recognized clearly that his whole object was to involve

---

[1] Chamberlain mentioned this possibility in his talk with Hatzfeldt on 29 March.

England in a war with France without taking part in it himself.' Your Excellency will see from this that I must maintain the greatest caution in my efforts to make clear to the statesmen here that they would do well to reach an understanding with Russia over China and let things come to a struggle against France alone, if I don't want to run the danger of reawakening and reviving the old suspicions of our intentions. I would therefore regard it as advisable to present my arguments along the lines that as long as we cannot abandon our reserve, English policy must aim first of all at securing the support of Austria and Italy, whose political interests more or less coincide with those of England and whose obligations towards us represent no obstacle in this respect. It is then only a short step to the hint—without any obligation being assumed on our part—that in the event of a fight in which our allies were engaged, public opinion in Germany, as far as can be humanly foreseen, would almost certainly be opposed to leaving our friends in the lurch. It would be of the greatest value to me if I could be informed whether H.M. shares my view of the attitude I should assume here, and whether Your Excellency as well as the Chancellor also agree. In that case, however, I think I must also stress at this point that I can probably press success-fully for greater consideration for ourselves in any minor questions which might arise only if, with the support of the Imperial Government, I can indicate the same friendly treatment of such questions for the English. I permit myself here to remind you of Mr Balfour's personal request to authorize, in the interests of the security of the English colony, a punitive expedition against a robber chief in the neutral zone [of Togo] which would retire again immediately after the completion of its task. The curt refusal of this request disappointed people here greatly, and I almost believe that Mr Balfour for his part would have been more flexible regarding the last sentence of the statement on Kiaochow which we requested from England if his personal request had been met. Without wishing to pass judgment, I am almost led to the conclusion that it would have been possible to avoid such a brusque refusal without injury to our local interests, perhaps by the offer of a common expedition against the chief in question. Similar occasions will no doubt recur, and my task of demanding friendly treatment in cases where our interest is involved would undoubtedly be rendered much more difficult if I could not concede the same when English interests are in question. Finally I might also mention […] that the attitude of the German Press towards England is followed here with very particular attention, and that every Press statement which can be regarded as insulting to England is exploited by the papers which are hostile to us with special satisfaction. This applies particularly to those German papers which are assumed here to be close to the Government or in-spired by it. It is felt to be particularly insulting if these papers break out into yells of triumph—as, unless I am mistaken, the *Hamburger Korrespondenz* did the other day—at the fact that England at last has realized her isolation and weakness, and has come crawling to Germany,

73

which doesn't think of giving up her friendship with Russia on that account. Such articles in allegedly inspired newspapers also have an unfortunate effect on the Queen, and I would therefore urgently request that my task here be facilitated by instructions to those newspapers connected with the Government to write in the present circumstances in a way which spares susceptibilities here and leaves the way open for a rapprochement. I hope I can count on Your Excellency's kind forebearance with me for having taken up your valuable time with such a lengthy piece and for having chosen the form of a private letter. If you think it suitable, I leave it entirely to you whether to submit it to H.M. I could not speak as openly and without reservations in an official report as I could permit myself to do here, trusting in Your Excellency's forebearance and our agreement regarding the most vital aims of our foreign policy.

With sincere respect I have the honour to remain

Your Excellency's
most devoted
PH.[1]

650.   Philipp zu Eulenburg to Holstein

Vienna, 30 April 1898

My dear old Holstein,

I must confess to you that a tear came to my eyes when I received your dear letter.

As I have followed all my life the principle to bother neither one's friends nor others with one's own private worries—for after all every human being has enough to bear with his own troubles—I 'circumvented' you, as you say, and only talked to Bülow, with whom for various reasons I had already considered and discussed my sorrow.[2]

Moreover I was so terribly depressed that even the sight of many faces in the Ministry would have been painful.

But now, after you have placed your friendly hand so simply and faithfully in mine, I must first of all tell you that you have done me *a lot of good*, and secondly that I will ask you to meet me somewhere the next time I am in Berlin (before Whitsun).

We won't talk a lot about myself, but I don't want to miss the joy of telling you how I feel towards you and how deeply I felt your words of sympathy.

Physically I am in dreadful shape as a result of mental pressure. I would *definitely resign* if that were not a bad mistake at this moment.

Your grateful
PEulenburg.

[1] No direct reply to this letter has been found. (See Bülow's telegram to Hatzfeldt of 24 April 1898. (*Grosse Politik*, vol. XIVi, no. 3792, pp. 218–21.)
[2] In the course of the divorce case of Eulenburg's brother Friedrich, it had been discovered that the latter had unnatural sexual tendencies. (See Bülow, *Denkwürdigkeiten*, vol. I, p. 224.)

## 651.   Holstein to Paul von Hatzfeldt[1]

Dear friend,

I am truly pleased that in your laborious conversation with Chamberlain you have at least achieved one thing, namely that His Majesty is satisfied. I cannot deny that his marginal comments make good sense to me. Thus I too believe that for the present, as long as she is alone, England will not reach an agreement with Russia,[2] but that if Chamberlain's idea of an English adherence to the Triple Alliance were realized the Russians *then* would indeed offer a very high price to England to persuade her to stand by quietly while Russia and France settled accounts with us. Italy could probably also be bought, she would join the side which promised her Albania. If Austria—on which one cannot absolutely count in view of the Slavic movement—stood faithfully by us, we would then end up with the alignment: Germany and Austria against Russia, France and Italy? Do you fancy that? I don't. Perhaps you will think that my mistrust is exaggerated, but as of now I still do not believe that Chamberlain really intends to make England participate in a war. His remark the other day that England could manage Russia alone, but that Russia and France together were too much for England,[3] seems an empty boast when one considers that France would not lift a finger—not even for the sake of Russia—as long as Germany remained neutral. It would be easy for the English to assure themselves of Germany's neutrality. If they really thought as Chamberlain talks, they could thus tackle Russia with complete peace of mind. But that is just it, they think differently; as always they are only thinking of how they can send the Triple Alliance into the fight and stay out themselves.

It also seemed very suspicious to me that Chamberlain is not inclined to support Turkey as a concession to Austria.[4] Perhaps he wants to use Turkey, i.e. the Straits, as compensation for Russia at the last moment. This, to be sure, would be a miscalculation, for the Russians are prevented from occupying the Straits not by anxiety about England but by the fear of annoying the French badly if they did so.

I am not afraid of the agreement with France with which we have often been threatened. Do you believe that England would throw away

---

[1] From the London Embassy files.

[2] At the end of Hatzfeldt's report of 26 April on his conversation with Chamberlain the Kaiser wrote: 'For the moment the Russian has not reached for his gun, but has reserved this for later. John Bull is beginning to realize this and wants to have someone who'll help him out of the predicament! I certainly won't do that merely on the basis of promises by Chamberlain! We shall see what will happen later.' (*Grosse Politik*, vol. XIVi, no. 3793, pp. 221–7, note 20.)

[3] Evidently an error on the part of Holstein. Chamberlain had said that England could manage France alone (*Grosse Politik*, vol. XIVi, nos. 3784, 3789, pp. 202–4; 212–16), but there is no record of his having stated that England could manage Russia. In fact, he told Hatzfeldt that England could not oppose Russia by herself. (*Grosse Politik*, vol. XIVi, no. 3793, pp. 221–7.)

[4] Chamberlain told Hatzfeldt in his conversation with him on 25 April that English public opinion would never tolerate English support for the Sultan, and that if the Government tried to do so it would be risking its life. (*Grosse Politik*, vol. XIVi, no. 3793, pp. 221–7.)

Egypt to the French unless France in return undertook to fight against Russia? But that is something no French Government would risk to-day because of public opinion. And England will probably not decide in favour of any important concessions because of the danger that France—morally and materially strengthened by England's compliance—could nonetheless be awkward in the next war and lean to the side of Russia. If England really only wants the lists kept free for a duel with Russia, she doesn't need to make any concessions to France; France will remain neutral if Germany remains neutral. As long as England shows no understanding of this clear state of affairs, I shall go on believing that she doesn't want to fight herself, but only wishes to push others to the front. [...]

> With best regards
> Ever your
> Holstein.

### 652.   Holstein to Paul von Hatzfeldt[1]

Sunday, 15 May 1898

Dear friend,

I don't want to dictate what follows:

Consul Krüger[2] in Manila—the not very able but pushing son of the late Hamburg Minister—telegraphed three days ago:

'Spanish rule over the Philippines at an end as far as can be judged. Bloody reckoning with natives imminent. Natives incline towards monarchy under German prince.'[3]

Such a telegram can have the same effect to-day as a burning match thrown into a straw-rick. The telegram is going to-day to H.M. with a long report for him[4] and a private letter from the State Secretary.[5] You will find the main points in the copy of my memorandum which I enclose, but which because of its dry brevity is unsuitable for direct use.[6]

I am sending this to you for once *without* the State Secretary's knowledge. He wants *first of all* to inform H.M. and get his decision.

I would regret it deeply if we were to disturb the growth of the opposition now developing between St Petersburg and London on the one hand, between Washington and Paris on the other, by our premature grabbing. Pointing to the embarrassments which France is laying up

---

[1] From the London Embassy files.

[2] Friedrich von Krüger. Consul in Manila, 1897–1903.

[3] This is a paraphrase. For the actual text of the telegram, see *Grosse Politik*, vol. XV, no. 4145, pp. 33–8.

[4] See the document cited in note 3 above.

[5] Not found in the Foreign Ministry files.

[6] In his undated memorandum Holstein discussed the possibilities of a protectorate, the partition, or the neutralization of the Philippines and concluded: 'As opposed to these, the idea, suggested or transmitted by Consul Krüger, of placing the Philippines under a king of German descent should be turned down as unpractical, because the plan would have the rare quality of opposing the interests of *all* the other seapowers to German interests.' (From the London Embassy files.)

for herself would, I believe, have a special effect on the Kaiser and persuade him—*if anything can*—to wait.

As for Salisbury, he will apparently never change, i.e. he doesn't want to move at all. As long as he is in power, England will not work with or against anyone, but, as the Berliner says, move 'slow and steady-like', with the intention of letting others get into a mess. I think that there is no reason why you shouldn't tell him so, i.e. that that is the view of your Government. But you know better than I what you have to do.

In my opinion we should not hesitate at the moment to tell the English that we regard their apparent leaning towards us merely as a strategic manoeuvre and a clever move whose only purpose is to compromise us with Russia and France, and that the move is not in any way based on the conviction that an alliance treaty would actually be approved of by the English Parliament.

There is one other point moreover on which you can speak quite freely, and that is that we have no agreement of any sort with Russia—*up to the present*—which would prevent us from reaching an understanding with England in so far as this would otherwise appear useful to us.

I am very sorry that your leave was interrupted.

As ever

H.

## 653.   Paul von Hatzfeldt to Holstein[1]
Copy

London, 17 May 1898

Dear friend,

Many thanks for your letter. I whole-heartedly agree with the first part of it and hope that Herr von Bülow will successfully oppose any undue haste.

But I cannot completely share the views transmitted to me from Berlin on some not absolutely unimportant points concerning the situation here, which will of course not prevent me from doing exactly what I am ordered to do. The first of these points is the supposition that Lord Salisbury's sudden mistrust of Austrian policy[2] is based on premises invented by him and hides ulterior motives.[3] The *Frankfurter Zeitung* has quickly furnished us with the proof that the cause was in fact a Russian intrigue, to which the information which Salisbury received must no doubt also be attributed.[4] I know Salisbury from long experience and was therefore personally in no doubt from the very start that his obvious irritation was not feigned. Thus, believe me, it is of the

---

[1] From the London Embassy files.

[2] In a conversation with Hatzfeldt on 11 May, Salisbury had referred to an Austro-Russian treaty of May 1897 on Balkan questions (Pribram, *Secret Treaties*, vol. I, pp. 184–95) to disparage the value of Austria and Italy as alliance partners for England. (*Grosse Politik*, vol. XIVi, p. 230, note *.)

[3] Bülow had assumed this in a dispatch to Hatzfeldt of 15 May. (*Grosse Politik*, vol. XIVi, no. 3796, pp. 230–3.)

[4] On May 16 the *Frankfurter Zeitung* had published details of a secret treaty between Russia and Austria-Hungary.

utmost importance that Goluchowski should lose no time in persuading the English that there are no secret agreements with Russia and that he would therefore still be in a position to make common cause with them on the basis of the Treaty of Berlin.[1]

Now as regards Salisbury personally, you are unfortunately right on this, *qu'il a baissé beaucoup depuis quelques années*. But I cannot go so far as to agree that he would be incapable of any energetic action no matter what the circumstances, particularly if it were clear to him that he would thereby lose touch with the country or the majority of his colleagues. Assume for example the case that Chamberlain were able to get up in the Cabinet and say : 'I know for certain that the Triple Alliance is prepared to conclude a defensive alliance with England. That is what we need and I and my friends demand that the treaty be concluded and submitted to Parliament.' Believe me, Salisbury would not think of opposing this. All he could do would be to resign and he would then probably be replaced by Chamberlain. True, the question remains how the decision would go in Parliament, and *that* in my humble opinion is, if not the only, yet the main reason why we must observe great caution.

I think Chamberlain's diplomatic virtuosity is being very much over-estimated if it is believed that he only wants to lure us into a mess. Quite apart from his burning personal ambition, which naturally plays a part, he is completely and honestly convinced of two things. First, that England must now adopt a more energetic policy towards Russia, possibly also towards France. Second, that England cannot do this without a strong alliance, which it needs in any case for its future security, and that only the Triple Alliance, more particularly Germany, can give England the necessary support. Moreover I don't doubt that in that case he would be fully prepared to make us not inconsiderable colonial concessions.

This view is shared by many Englishmen, and from everything I hear it is pretty generally thought that his statements in Birmingham are to be interpreted as an invitation to Germany to conclude an alliance.[2]

I have not yet seen Salisbury since Chamberlain's speech, and will probably not be able to judge before tomorrow where he stands on this. But I already have no doubt that Chamberlain would not have dared act like this if by and large he had not been sure of the approval of his colleagues *and of Salisbury*. The latter may differ on points of detail or prefer a slower tempo, but on the major issue he is certainly in agreement with Chamberlain.

Incidentally, up to the present only the Spanish Ambassador[3] has questioned him on the Colonial Secretary's speech. He regarded it as a taking of sides for America, a view which Salisbury described as mis-

[1] In the Foreign Affairs Committee of the Hungarian Delegation Count Goluchowski stated on 17 May that the article in the *Frankfurter Zeitung* was a clumsy invention.

[2] In a speech in Birmingham on 13 May Chamberlain pointed to the danger of a war with Russia over China and the need for an alliance with those Powers whose interests most closely approximated those of England.

[3] Juan Antonio, Conde de Rascón. Spanish Ambassador in London, 1898–1902.

taken. To Count Rascón's further remark that probably all the foreign diplomats would ask him what Mr Chamberlain really meant, Salisbury is said to have replied that in that case he could suggest that Rascón ask Mr Chamberlain himself.

If you, dear friend, should wonder why I am informing you in this form of my views, which differ somewhat on certain nuances of the situation here, instead of expressing them officially, I would beg you to remember that I was brought up and have grown old under good discipline. I therefore do not regard it as fitting to argue, and confine myself to carrying out to the best of my ability what I am told to do. In this it is a small consolation to me, which I trust you will not grudge me, *de confier mes soucis à votre amitié éprouvée.*

With best regards
Ever yours
Hatzfeldt [...]

## 654. Paul von Hatzfeldt to the Foreign Ministry[1]

TELEGRAM

London, 22 May 1898

No. 137

With reference to my report no. 411 of 20 May.[2]

The Austrian Ambassador has told me that in a confidential conversation with him Lord Salisbury had not contradicted the view that Chamberlain's speech had been a *ballon d'essai.* At the same time he had described as unfounded the widely spread assumption that the conclusion of alliances ran counter to English traditions, and had cited the alliance with France at the time of the Crimean War in support of this.[3] Count Deym did not seem disinclined to regard this as a hint that such an alliance might once more be concluded with France at the present time.[4]

From another good source Count Deym claims to know that great concern is felt here that we would pose excessive conditions for our friendship, particularly as regards colonies.[5] People here were thinking of suggesting to us a cession of English possessions in Borneo,[6] in return for which we should have to grant compensation to England in Africa.[7] Count Deym did not know any details of this.[8]

Hatzfeldt

---

[1] From the Foreign Ministry files. (See *Grosse Politik*, vol. XIVi, p. 239, note *.)

[2] *Grosse Politik*, vol. XIVi, no. 3798, pp. 235–8.

[3] Marginal comment by Kaiser Wilhelm II: 'Here he is directly contradicting all the statements he made to us at the end of the eighties and beginning of the nineties, when we were trying to persuade him to join the Triple Alliance, or rather to draw closer to Italy! Thus England must find the situation sticky now.'

[4] Wilhelm II: 'What does Russia say to that?'

[5] Wilhelm II: 'But we haven't been properly asked yet, or received a request.'

[6] Wilhelm II: 'Not enough! Samoa, Carolines, and one of the Philippine Islands—(if possible)—'

[7] Wilhelm II: 'What sort.'

[8] Wilhelm II: 'Why is something like this said to Deym and not to Hatzfeldt or to me by Lascelles?!'

### 655. Holstein to Paul von Hatzfeldt[1]

Berlin, 31 May 1898

Dear friend,

Yesterday evening a letter from our Kaiser to the Tsar[2] was dispatched by courier which stated : 'I am faced with a momentous decision. England has offered me an alliance, a famous politician offered it to my Ambassador actually twice, before and after Easter; now recently for a third time with a definite time limit for my answer, and with tremendous prospects for the future. I am informing you of this and am asking you quite openly what you think of it and what you suggest. Do give me a clear answer, so that I can consider what should be done in the interests of my country and of peace.'

The trend of thought which is briefly expressed in the above was naturally inspired by family influence. In what proportion the wish to profit and concern at suffering harm are mixed in this I can't decide. But evidently this concern has been played on, i.e. by the hint that if she could not become our ally England would decide in favour of active hostility and destroy our trade. Even Lascelles is remarking to all and sundry : 'We (England) need a row with someone or other.' This fear of a naval duel with England—unknown before the Krüger Telegram— is not without effect and probably played some part in the drafting of the above mentioned letter.

I don't take this letter too seriously. Our Kaiser is a talented but impulsive man who has already accustomed his relatives to surprises and unexpected conclusions. Naturally it is not impossible that the letter merely aimed at shaking the Russians out of their role of indolent spectators; on the other hand I certainly do not doubt that, if not the text, at least the contents of the letter will be transmitted to England by the normal channel, and that it will then be said that H.M. has taken Chamberlain's auctioneering methods as a model and now intends to receive and consider Russian as well as English offers. No matter what the Russian reply may be, I regard it as out of the question that the Kaiser will really wish to bind himself by a treaty directed against Russia. I fear far more that the transmission of the contents of the Kaiser's letter will lead to irritation and agitation between ourselves *and* England, and that thereby the prospects of an understanding between Germany and England in the future, which after all would be pretty welcome to us all, will be postponed still further than is already the case. The State Secretary therefore requests you to keep a particular eye open for this danger and to work against it. It would already have a favourable effect if you could state—*in good conscience naturally*—that the danger of a sudden English attack at sea need not be taken into consideration. Actually I am astonished that it is still necessary to describe this fear as unfounded. In the present world situation it seems to me out of the question that England should attack Germany with Russia and

---

[1] From the London Embassy files.
[2] Letter of 30 May. (See *Briefe Wilhelms II an den Zaren*, pp. 309–11.)

France watching. But there are people who hold a different view. The removal of this fear would lead to the disappearance of the inclination towards a closer relationship with Russia, a result which would please me. Up till now we have fortunately been able to avoid the fixing of our policy towards Russia, and I continue to believe in the possibility that we shall remain on good, decent neighbourly terms with Russia even without such a tie.

The question would appear more serious to me if H.M. were to ask officially in England what were the 'tremendous offers' which have presumably been foreshadowed by some completely irresponsible member of the family. The answer to this might perhaps be such that the result would be an indescribable deterioration in any relations with England. To prevent this unpleasant outcome it would, I tend to think, be desirable to treat the question of a German-English rapprochement dilatorily, i.e. to report—and this as a cautionary measure, *before* this query of the Kaiser's arrives—that visible efforts were being made to accustom English public opinion to the idea of a rapprochement with Germany, and that the idea of purchasing a treaty relationship with Germany by substantial concessions will perhaps become popular in England in the not distant future, but that the moment for this, as both Balfour and Lord Salisbury have hinted, has not yet come.

I would sum up in brief that this letter by the Kaiser—which also mentioned that the Queen, through a confidential intermediary, had asked the English Press to refrain from its attacks on Germany[1]—could conceivably cause trouble, and this less with Russia than with England. This could best be prevented by toning down, unostentatiously but rapidly, the fear of an English attack as well as the expectation of 'tremendous' English concessions.

With best regards<br>Holstein.

### 656.   Holstein to Paul von Hatzfeldt[2]

31 May [1898]

Dear friend,

As Willisch is on leave I would like to add something in my own hand.

Somehow I have the notion that Kaiserin Friedrich is involved in the affair.[3] I also know that the remark had been made by that side—i.e. the family: *Count Hatzfeldt is informed of everything.* Without knowing exactly the significance and meaning of this remark, I have known *you* long enough to be certain that you have not been working against the Ministry.

The Kaiser has been afraid for some time that the English might

[1] The Kaiser had written: 'In the beginning of April the attacks on my country and person till then showered on us by the British Press and people, suddenly fell off, and there was, as you will have perceived, a momentary lull. This rather astonished us at home and we were at a loss for an explanation. In a private inquiry I found out that H.M. the Queen herself through a friend of hers, had sent word to the British Papers that she wished this unnoble and false game to cease. This is the land of the "free Press"!' (In English in the original.)

[2] From the London Embassy files.

[3] The English alliance offer. See below, Kaiser Wilhelm's letter to his mother of 1 June.

suddenly attack us one day; Tirpitz shares this fear, and in his case I understand it, for this fear is the most effective argument in favour of either giving up our colonies *or* increasing our fleet.

As I have said I am only imperfectly aware of the causes of the excitement which the Kaiser suddenly demonstrated yesterday, but one effect of it for example was that H.M. felt the impulse to request the Tsar for a meeting in Alexandrovo. The 'request' was later dropped, and only the 'preparedness' for such a meeting was expressed in a postscript. In the course of the day the Kaiser wrote several short memoranda. I quote the following short sentence from one : 'At the beginning of the next century we would have a battle fleet which, with *others* which will also have grown, could represent a real danger to England's fleet. Hence the intention either to force us into an alliance or to destroy us before we have become strong, like Holland in times past.'[1]

But now at the end one important point. Since you have not been informed officially from here that this fear of an English attack exists, you must avoid exposing yourself to the suspicion that what you say on this score is a put-up job. It would therefore perhaps be best if you did not mention the possibility of such an attack directly.

I have written many pages without discussing the problem of a German-English alliance on its merits. I have not done this for the simple reason that I regard it as an inescapable problem of the future but not one for the present. It does not look much like 'tremendous concessions' if Lord Salisbury voices the fear that we would sell our friendship at too high a price.[2] On the other hand a move towards England and a corresponding move away from Russia would create a storm in public opinion in Germany *to-day*. That is why the best method of treatment seemed to me 'friendly and dilatory'. That has now been made more difficult by the sudden greater swing of the pendulum. I fear that the pendulum will jar on both sides.

Still I hope that this difficulty too, just like some others which looked dangerous in the last twelve months, will be surmounted without too much damage. If, against my present expectation, there should be a change in personnel, there is little doubt that Holleben would be considered first, then Radowitz. But we are not that far yet.

Good hunting
H.[3]

### 657.  Kaiser Wilhelm II to Kaiserin Friedrich[4]
Draft

1 June 1898

D[ear] M[ama]

I hasten to thank you for your two kind letters[5] which I received and

---

[1] See *Grosse Politik*, vol. XIVi, no. 3799, pp. 239–40.

[2] See *Grosse Politik*, vol. XIVi, p. 230, note *.

[3] Holstein added : 'I have already closed my letter. But I want to add that Bülow has read *everything*.'

[4] From the Foreign Ministry files. In English in the original. The original spelling has been retained.

[5] Not found.

which have interested and I may say fascinated me very much. The idea of an Alliance of the Anglo-Saxon race is not new, the accession of Germany to it however *is so*, as far at least as the English government is concerned. Let me make a short sketch of our relations in the first six years of my reign. I tried to the very utmost of my powers by letter, conversation, and persuasion to elicit from L[ord] S[alisbury] a word implying the approval of the idea of an Anglo-German cooperation and Convention. But it was utterly without any result, as he invariably allways ended in the same refrain : 'An English government cannot and never will form an alliance with any *Continental Power* for the simple reason, that Parliament would hardly ever ratify such an instrument and because England prefers to keep its *liberty of action*, therefore I am unable to fullfill your wishes.' ! ! So I let the matter drop and with a heavy heart gave up a task, which was a difficult one, though dear to me, seeing that I worked on the same lines dear Papa and Grandpapa (Consort) had shaped. In numerous phases of Foreign Affairs, notably in the Siamese Imbroglio (under the Liberal government of L[ord] Rosebery) I staunchly stood by England and volunteered my help L.R. so warmly begged for with Grandma's consent at Osborne in 1894! But instead of thanks or of help in our colonising enterprises I got nothing whatever, and for the last 3 years have been abused, ill-treated and a butt to any bad joke any musikhall singer or fishmonger or press-man thought fit to let fly at me. Notwithstanding all this two years ago I tried to have L.S. help to give us a coaling station in China, he flatly refused in a language that only Hatzfeldt knew how to interpret so that no serious action came out of it![1] So pushed back, ill-treated and riled by Great Britain and her Prime Minister instead from them I got from Russia in a few conversations with the Emperor all I wanted and even more than I ever hoped for! This as 'eine kleine Orientierung'. Now with respect to what you wrote about the Alliance of England-Amerika and Germany, this has very much interested me. The idea has been ventilated in the papers since 2 months and also sundry allusions and suggestions from Mr Ch[amberlain] have been wafted over here by the spring breezes. But as they were not officially transmitted as coming from the government or Prime Minister nobody very much heeded them as they seemed to be merely a repetition of the articles in the Press. By your letter I see for the first time that the thing is ment in earnest, and purports to be an overture, at least so it was ment by Mr Ch. If that is the case and if as I gather there is a certain speed wished in the treatment of this question, then why in the name of all that is diplomatic use and sense, does not the *Prime Minister* make a *real proposal*? Why does Cabinet not make real propositions to serve as base for pourparlers? Why does the Cabinet not empower L.S. or L.S. Mr Ch. under his authority to expound the terms of a treaty to me? Private conversations and even statements before others are all very well, but do not represent the right way to a Treaty of Alliance! Besides if even Mr Ch. and as it

[1] See *Grosse Politik*, vol. XIVi, no. 3685, pp. 62–4, note *.

seems part of the Cabinet are in earnest and begin to treat with me in the above informal manner, who will ever guard me against a sudden desaveu in the House of Lords by the Premier or in Parliament by Balfour, if they found popular feeling not in the lines they expected, as long as L.S. is in such a bad way with Mr Ch. and has not implicitly bound himself to this affair by officially authorising his ministers to enter into negotiations? England would not feel anything, but a *miscarried try* at an Alliance with her brings Russia and France down on my head and over my frontier on the same day!? These are some of the difficulties which have cropped up in my mind since I have given your letters serious attention, and are the consequences of the treatment I have gone through at the hands of the British Government and notably of L.S., and the result of the experience I had in the ten years of my reign of British Foreign Politics. Should Government wish to get out of the 'splendid isolation', promote the idea of a 'rapprochement' to me and the formation of an Alliance, then let the British Premier speak out openly and manly and officially as it is *'d'usage'* among Great Powers, and I will with pleasure listen and consider. But he can never expect me to 'slip in by the back door' like a thief at night whom one does not like to own before ones richer friends. I will be most thankful if I can have any information how the things are going on.

### 658.   Paul von Hatzfeldt to Holstein[1]

TELEGRAM

London, 2 June 1898

Private.

Received letters;[2] you can imagine the impression they made. For the time being, to lose no time, I am sending off telegram no. 150,[3] which will suit you I hope, and will write tomorrow by courier in the desired sense.

I have seen no symptom of these 'tremendous' advantages. The feared naval attack is even more improbable. As far as can be humanly foreseen it could only take place if we ourselves first took up a hostile attitude. I have heard in a roundabout way but from a reliable source that the most important members of the Cabinet still feel as urgently as ever the desire for a rapprochement with us, but that some disappointment is setting in because of our cool attitude.[4] I am definitely assured that Mr Chamberlain was annoyed at my reserve in our last conversa-

---

[1] From the London Embassy files.      [2] Of 31 May. See above.

[3] Hatzfeldt telegraphed that he had had a confidential conversation with Lord Salisbury. 'The whole conversation gave me the impression that the Prime Minister [ . . .] wishes to cultivate good relations with us and is reserving the possibility of suggesting a formal understanding with us if the political situation becomes more tense and makes it desirable. But in that case, I believe, Lord Salisbury would choose a quite different basis from Chamberlain's, designating as the purpose of the understanding the maintenance of peace and possible common defence in some clearly defined instances.' (*Grosse Politik*, vol. XIVi, no. 3800, pp. 240–1.)

[4] See *Grosse Politik*, vol. XIVi, no. 3801, pp. 241–8.

tion,[1] and that Salisbury too, when questioned by members of the Cabinet on the position of the question, has attributed the standstill in the negotiations to my reserve.

It is beyond any human calculation what effect will be created here when it is learned from St Petersburg what our communications to that address contained, but it will certainly be very unfavourable, objectively as well.

PH.

### 659.  Bernhard von Bülow to Paul von Hatzfeldt[2]

TELEGRAM

Berlin, 3 June 1898

Private.

Our wish would be to improve our relations with England as far as possible, certainly not to worsen them, but maintaining the independence enjoyed hitherto on both sides.

Bülow.

### 660.  Holstein to Paul von Hatzfeldt[3]

Berlin, 3 June 1898

Private.

Lord Salisbury's view that alliances should be conducted not for the future but to answer existing needs is shared here. That is why we do not want to ally ourselves with England immediately; but we will try to avoid everything which could hinder the possibility of such an alliance at a later time.

Holstein

### 661.  Kaiserin Friedrich to Kaiser Wilhelm II[4]

Schloss Friedrichshof, Cronberg (Taunus), 3 June 1898

Dearest Willy,

So many thanks for writing to me, and giving me your *Auffassung* of the situation. For fear of your having misunderstood what I said, pray let me explain that the *whole object* of my letter was to *prepare* you for what I *hope* is coming, though I *do not* know! ! The rumours that reached me, showed me, that something was *'in der Luft'*, and this in itself seemed *so* important that I thought I ought to acquaint you with what I had heard! Though I am only in the position of a simple outsider now. In *no* way did I say or intend to imply that you should 'slip in by the back door', in so important a matter no one I think could dream of entertaining such an idea!

I quite understand your *'griefs'* against English expressions of public opinion etc. etc. . . . but I also know that on the other side of the water

---

[1] Of 25 April. See *Grosse Politik*, vol. XIVi, no. 3793, pp. 221–7.
[2] From the London Embassy files.      [3] From the London Embassy files.
[3] From the Foreign Ministry files. In English in the original.

they also received impressions which created *distrust* and that it will take time before the belief again takes root that German intentions can be trusted. But these are, I hope *passing* shadows, and I wish with all my heart that the idea floating in people's minds of an Alliance may take *shape* and *form* and be brought forward in an official and decided way; *Whether* and *when* this would be of course *I* cannot know, only official people could; till then naturally there is no other course than to watch events and avoid so good an idea being nipped in the bud; I trust nothing may happen on either side of the water to prevent its maturing. I do not think that England can be long before taking a decided line, and though events have not been so precipitate as they seemed likely a short while ago, yet the situation and open questions remain the same, and there is no time for very long deliberation.

Goodbye dearest Willy, with many thanks for writing and best love from both sisters

Ever

Yr. devoted

Mama

V.

Should I hear anything again which could be of interest to you, I will instantly tell you.

### 662. Paul von Hatzfeldt to Holstein[1]

Copy

London, 8 June 1898

Dear friend,

I have again had word from a good source a few days ago that Chamberlain was irritated by my reserve at our last meeting[2] and is representing this in the following light: I am supposed to have been friendly and interested during the whole of our conversation, but suddenly to have shown a certain coolness when we separated. I have informed him via the same source that he is quite mistaken in this assumption; the good-byes had taken place in the ante-room and I therefore had had to confine myself to the expression of the hope that we would have occasion to meet again and could then resume our conversation. I told Salisbury this to-day in confidence. He was visibly amused by Chamberlain's alleged dissatisfaction and seized the opportunity with pleasure to poke fun at Chamberlain's diplomatic ability in the treatment of the difficult alliance question.

I don't have to tell you that I would much regret any interference by outside parties—be their position great or small—in this matter, particularly because of the effect on the outcome, for any such interference can only do harm. As for me, I herewith repeat my definite assurance that I am in no way involved. To anyone who knows me this assurance is practically superfluous, for I have proved during my career of almost thirty years that it is not my way to start on mysterious

---

[1] From the London Embassy files.　　　　[2] See p. 85, note 1.

machinations behind the Foreign Ministry's back. Here as always I follow a straight road, reporting everything I know and learn to Berlin and trying to the best of my ability to carry out the instructions I receive. As you know, I have also expressed quite openly my personal opinion on this question. It is and remains the same and can be summarized in a few words: I believe that the idea as such is a good one and that probably a time will come when it will be to our advantage to take it up in greater detail; but that at the moment this would be premature for a number of reasons, and that therefore we must treat the question dilatorily while at the same time trying to keep open the possibility of a future understanding. Judging by everything I have received from Berlin up till now that is also the view of H.M. and the Foreign Ministry, and I shall therefore carry on along this line undisturbed as long as I don't receive different instructions. I regard this policy as all the more correct and indicated because I am convinced—as you know—that Lord Salisbury, on whom in the last resort the decision depends for as long as he is Prime Minister, still holds to the idea that the conclusion of an alliance at this time would be premature and that one should confine oneself to preparing for it gradually.[1] Hence, as I would like to remark in this connection, I regard it as quite out of the question that the Prime Minister should be thinking of offering us great colonial and other advantages or of having them offered to us by others in order to tempt us into a premature agreement.

The latest speech by Chaplin—who, after all, as a member of the Cabinet is a man of some standing—furnishes one more proof that there are quite a number of people here who have warmed to the idea of an alliance with Germany, and this in contrast to their past sympathies. I also have some indications, which you probably will not have missed either, that a certain change has taken place as regards the Prince of Wales, and that he regards both a personal and political rapprochement as desirable now. So far I have not been able to discover whether he suggested insinuating this to H.M., or whether he participated in doing so. But, knowing him as I do, it seems to me beyond doubt that he confined himself to general wishes and certainly did not think of authorizing anybody to transmit more farreaching messages.

If such messages have been transmitted, they would be quite valueless without Lord Salisbury's prior approval, and as I have already said, I am in no doubt that he has had nothing to do with them and for the time being would not do so.

I hope that you will let me know by the courier who arrives the day after to-morrow whether my last long report[2] suited Herr von Bülow and yourself. All I can say is that I took the greatest pains to bring in unobtrusively the two points which really mattered.[3] I can't tell whether and to what extent I succeeded in this. But, as you can imagine,

---

[1] See p. 84, note 3.    [2] Of 3 June. ( *Grosse Politik*, vol. XIVi, pp. 241–8. )
[3] The price England was willing to pay ( colonial concessions ) and the sincerity of English statesmen ( Salisbury and Chamberlain ) in wanting an alliance with Germany.

it would be of the greatest value to me to learn as soon as possible what sort of reception the unexpected news had in St Petersburg. You know of my fear that the repercussions here will be unpleasant. As regards this I am thinking least of all of my own person, but rather of the objective disadvantages. If it should come to the point, I shall be able to defend my personal position. [...]

With best regards<br>
Ever yours<br>
H.

### 663.    Paul von Hatzfeldt to Holstein[1]
Copy

London, 17 June 1898

Dear friend,

I would ask you to honour my detailed report of to-day[2] with a glance, although the telegraphic instructions I have just received[3] have rendered it out of date, for you will see from it the extent to which I have to struggle here with lack of understanding, greed, ill-will and weakness in colonial questions.

One thing I did not say in my report, which I add here *in confidence* for Herr von Bülow and you, is that in my last conversation with Lord Salisbury, when I pointed to the bad impression which the disregarding of our wishes concerning the Portuguese colonies would create in Berlin, I also added that he would thereby render my task of preparing a political understanding in the future much more difficult, if not impossible. When Salisbury thereupon remarked that we would then probably reach an understanding with Russia, I replied that I had simply wanted to say that many of our people would seize the occasion with satisfaction to point out to H.M. that this incident once again showed where he should seek his friends. In truth the fact could not be denied that the Russians had not created the least difficulty for us in China, whereas here people begrudged us every trifle. He did not answer anything, until later in the conversation he came out again with the ominous remark: *'Vous demandez trop pour votre amitié.'*[4]

[1] From the London Embassy files.

[2] Hatzfeldt refers to a report of 14 June on his conversation with Salisbury. Hatzfeldt had already reported the same day by telegram. (See *Grosse Politik*, vol. XIVi, no. 3807, pp. 261–3.)

[3] On 15 June Hatzfeldt telegraphed that Salisbury had raised the question of a loan to Portugal, and requested permission to negotiate with Salisbury on the future of the Portuguese colonies. 'If it were to become apparent that Lord Salisbury is generally inclined to take up this idea—a point on which I am by no means certain yet—I would *then*, to make it easier for him and representing it as a *valuable concession* on our part, express to him our preparedness to declare ourselves satisfied with the customs revenue of Angola as security, leaving the same security regarding Delagoa Bay to England.' (*Grosse Politik*, vol. XIVi, no. 3808, pp. 263–4.) Bülow replied on 17 June that only in the recognition of German interests not only in Angola—or at least the southern districts of that province—but also in the remainder of Portuguese East Africa, i.e. North Mozambique to the Zambesi-Schire, could Germany see adequate compensation for conceding Delagoa Bay (with the southern part of Portuguese East Africa belonging to it) to England as security. (*Grosse Politik*, vol. XIVi, no. 3809, p. 264.)

See *Grosse Politik*, vol. XIVi, pp. 230–1, note *.

It is not yet clear whether the purpose of this attitude is to lower our demands, or whether it should be concluded that the idea of a political understanding has been given up altogether here because there is no desire to pay a big colonial price for it, but this will probably soon become apparent.

In the meantime may I ask for a few more days time to answer the questions put in dispatch no. 513[1] as to which colonial concessions I regard as possibly obtainable. The answer depends above all on the sentiment here in this respect, which, as you see, is not a very favourable one at the moment. Late this afternoon I am to see Salisbury on the Portuguese question and it will then become apparent whether and to what extent a show of consideration is to be reckoned with.[2]

I would like to take this opportunity to pose the question whether we could not use the fall of Manila, which seems imminent,[3] simply to occupy the Sulu-Archipelago and the Carolines. I don't see what objections the Americans could have to that, and for the moment have not yet got the impression that one would get particularly excited about it here. Out of good will we left the Carolines to the Spaniards in the past, but that is hardly a reason why we should make a present of them to a third party if the Spaniards can't hold them. We could occupy them temporarily as a pledge until the Philippine question has been settled to our satisfaction, and perhaps reach agreement on them with the Spaniards, who, in return for our not having let these islands fall into American hands, would probably cede some of them to us, or at least some valuable stations.

If I am to make this suggestion officially, please send a telegram.[4]

### 664.   Holstein to Philipp zu Eulenburg
Copy

Berlin, 4 August 1898

Dear Eulenburg,

It would seem in your interest as much as in my own if I were to summarize briefly the main points of our last conversation in the following :

For the first time after a long interval you mentioned the Henckel-affair[5] again and told me that Count Guido Henckel would soon be celebrating a jubilee and had the intention of donating one million marks to the province of Silesia for charitable purposes on this occasion. As a result of this the old Henckel-affair had once again been raised by persons who are interested in this donation. Moreover some members of His Majesty's entourage held the view that the army was disturbed by the difference of opinion between an Adjutant-General and an Aide-de-

---

[1] Of 8 June, *Grosse Politik*, vol. XIVi, no. 3806, pp. 259–60.

[2] See *Grosse Politik*, vol. XIVi, no. 3817, pp. 270–1, *et seq.*

[3] Manila did not fall until 13 August 1898.

[4] No such telegram appears to have been sent.

[5] See above, Holstein's letter to Count Guido Henckel of 31 March 1894, and the Holstein-Bissing correspondence for that year.

Camp which had arisen as a result of this affair. Thus the matter had once again been brought before His Majesty the Kaiser.

At this stage you asked how I now viewed the matter.

I replied that the matter could be brought to my attention *only* through my erstwhile second, General Baron von Bissing, if only because I was quite ignorant regarding the procedure in affairs of honour and their after-effects. Entirely on my own I could perhaps see this or that possibility, but was unable to express any binding opinion. At this stage I had a definite personal opinion on only two specific points.

First, I would utterly reject the idea—if this should be mooted—that now after four years the dispute should once again be made the subject of an examination, no matter by what authority, for by accepting this idea I would open up the possibility—since no human decision can be predicted for certain in advance—that Our Most Gracious Lord, who, as you know better than anyone, at that time generously and in a clearly recognizable way took my side, might now stand corrected.

Secondly, the introduction of His Majesty's name among the motives of any possible step taken by Henckel's side would render it impossible for me to discuss any such step.

As I've said, on these points I already hold firm views, quite independent of the views of General Baron von Bissing, with which I am not acquainted at the present time. It is natural that this whole affair, which had no definite outcome, should gradually have lost in interest.

You agreed with my opinion concerning the two specific points outlined above, and then asked me whether perhaps I would take an opportunity to discuss the matter with my State Secretary. I refused to do so as I had no reason for my part to take any initiative in order to change the existing state of affairs.

These, dear friend, are in short the main points with which our conversation dealt.

With best regards.[1]

665.   Moritz von Bissing to Holstein

Freiburg, 12 August 1898

Dear Herr von Holstein,

I was informed some time ago by an acquaintance of mine that the affair of honour *contra* Count Henckel, whose conduct you entrusted to me at the time, would be revived, and that it was hoped in influential circles that a conclusion satisfactory to all parties would be reached. I had no reason to react in any way to this information as it is useless in most instances to proffer uncalled-for advice and help; I was also of the opinion that you would be in no doubt that I was at your disposal in all matters at any time. However, to-day I have received a letter from Count Waldersee in which he suggested to me that I pass on certain information to you, as he had been told that you would conduct any

---

[1] A note by Eulenburg on the copy of this letter in the Eulenburg Papers states: 'This letter sent on 5 August to August Eulenburg with the request that it be communicated to Waldersee, but without telling him I was the intermediary.'

negotiations concerning the Henckel-affair only through me and intended to rely solely on my advice.

I hope that the new information will excuse my uncalled-for intervention; all the same I feel obliged to intervene because Count Waldersee also told me the following:

He had met Henckel after Bismarck's death, and in the course of the conversation Count Henckel had expressed the hope that you would gradually have reached the conviction that your accusation against him had been groundless. As a Christian and a man of honour he would openly admit it even to-day if he were conscious of having wronged you. He would be very happy if you, who had also been close to Prince Bismarck for many years, could agree with him to regard the whole episode, which had been the result of misunderstandings, as never having happened.

By expressing these wishes Count Henckel is showing a desire to meet you half-way which, in my opinion, should not be rebuffed out of hand. Several years have passed, during which Count Henckel, whether he was one of the guilty parties or not, has done penance in many respects, and has certainly refrained from all open or secret attacks on you. This, taken together with the words of your opponent which express a wish for reconciliation, might make you feel conciliatory even if you do not choose to believe in the misunderstandings. Certainly the most punctilious judge of affairs of honour will understand and appreciate it if you do not rebuff Count Henckel's advances. But we are both of us no friends of half-measures, and I therefore believe myself to be in agreement with you if I were to oppose a renewed negotiation on the affair of honour, and to state that if it is to be settled it must be done once and for all and in a dignified manner. It also seems to me illogical to accept Count Henckel's advance in any way and to uphold and maintain at the same time the serious insult contained in the letter to Count Henckel,[1] which you addressed to Count Henckel on your own responsibility before I entered into the affair of honour and which as I already told you at the time ran counter to the code of honour. That this insult remained unavenged is in my view the worst reproach to be levelled against Count Henckel.

Even now this letter has not been touched upon, at least with me, and no conditions have been posed regarding it. It would be all the more high-minded therefore if you, who voiced the insult, were to declare in this case that you would consider the letter as never having been written, that is provided that you are prepared to accept a *modus vivendi*, a *compromise*. [...][2]

With the expression of my particular respect I remain

Your truly devoted
Baron von Bissing
Lieutenant-General

[1] The letter of 31 March 1894.

[2] Bissing concluded with the draft of a written statement which he would hand to Count Waldersee for transmission to Count Henckel. Holstein replied on 15 August that he saw no reason to make a written statement since he had received none, but authorized Bissing to make an oral statement. (See below, Holstein's letter of 3 September 1898.)

### 666.  Holstein to Paul von Hatzfeldt[1]

TELEGRAM

Private                                                        Berlin, 19 August 1898

What do you say about the American move in China?[2] Is the understanding with England of which we spoke in our dispatch no. 603[3] actually coming into being already?

We cannot retreat in the face of the Americans. Should we first of all merely apply pressure on the Chinese or should we simultaneously speak calmly and clearly to the Americans? The latter seems the better method to me. Second, who is to speak? Herr von Holleben with the President,[4] the Under State Secretary with the Ambassador here,[5] or you with Hay?[6] If Hay is still in London, this would appear to me to be the correct channel.

Do you think that the English would support the Americans in a naval war against Germany? If they do, England would expose herself to the danger that Russia and France would take advantage of the opportunity, though not out of love for Germany. If they don't, that is if America remained alone, we would probably finish off their fleet fairly quickly and kill off the desire for war by ravishing their big ports. It is unavoidable that with our present expansionist colonial policy we should sometimes get into sticky situations. A retreat would be the signal for the conduct of a general campaign of humiliation against us.

This report from China has created a new situation. Do you think that by renouncing Timor[7] and accepting the English proposals concerning South Africa[8] we would obtain a free hand against America?

Holstein.

### 667.  Paul von Hatzfeldt to Holstein[9]

TELEGRAM

London, 19 August 1898

Private

Reply to the telegram of this afternoon.

I share your view that we should not confine ourselves to the requisite pressure on the Chinese, but must simultaneously talk to the Americans

---

[1] From the London Embassy files.

[2] The German Minister in Peking had telegraphed that day: 'American Minister has demanded from the Tsungli-Yamen the Tientsin-Chinkiang railway concession through Shantung for American capital in conjunction with Jungwing, giving as reason that the Americans had not been granted any railway concessions by China up till then, and that America did not recognize German *secret* agreements concerning special privileges in Shantung. (From the Foreign Ministry files.)

[3] Of 6 July. (*Grosse Politik*, vol. XV, no. 4154, pp. 47–52.)

[4] William McKinley. President of the United States, 1897–1901.

[5] Andrew D. White. U.S. Ambassador in Berlin, 1897–1902.

[6] John Hay. U.S. Ambassador in London, 1897–8; Secretary of State, 1898–1905.

[7] In the negotiations with Britain on the Portuguese colonies. Richthofen telegraphed Hatzfeldt the same day that an agreement which did not grant Timor to Germany would be unacceptable. (*Grosse Politik*, vol. XIVi, no. 3854, pp. 321–2.)

[8] See *Grosse Politik*, vol. XIVi, no. 3842, pp. 307–10, *et seq.*

[9] From the London Embassy files.

in a friendly but firm way. But I would regard it as best if the Under State Secretary were to speak with the Ambassador in Berlin, for this direct and official step will undoubtedly create a greater impression in Washington than any statement which reaches Washington by detour via London, in which case the Americans might even doubt whether the authority of my Government was backing me. However, naturally I am ready to talk to Hay, who has little sympathy for us and hasn't even been polite, as he has shown no sign of life since my visit to him. He is in the country, but is said to come into town almost every morning for a few hours.

The question whether England would support the Americans in a naval war against Germany cannot be answered off-hand. This is especially true if our negotiations here about Portugal should be broken off and leave behind, as seems inevitable to me, a feeling of irritation in both Governments. A defeat of the American navy which in certain circumstances is expected here, would, even though there is as yet no treaty, certainly not suit the English very well, and for this reason it is impossible to predict whether they would not try to prevent such an eventuality even at the risk of Russia and France seizing the opportunity to harm England.

I have just asked Bertie[1] in a confidential conversation whether he had heard anything of American demands concerning railway concessions in China. He answered, 'no', but added the remark that such an event would be neither remarkable nor unexpected. When I remarked jokingly that the only reason why he found it so pleasant was because the Americans, with whom England was now on such intimate terms, were involved, he did not deny it and pointed to the fact that nowadays the factor of common race played a big part in politics. In reply to my remark that with such strong navies as those of England and America combined a great deal could be done, but after all, without a correspond-ingly strong army, not everything, he said that this was certainly true, and then added that the situation would be much better for all concerned if England, America and *Germany* were to work together. But even the mere joining of the two navies would already present the inestimable advantage that the home shores of the partners would be absolutely protected for quite some time to come against attacks by third parties.

If we assume that Bertie was indiscreet and that America's help is being reckoned with here to protect the English coast if need be, it follows from this that the people here would be very unwilling to permit the defeat of the American navy.

In view of the report from China and the possibility of difficulties with America, I think that we should not handle the Portuguese question here too brusquely at this moment, and leave open the *possibility* of reaching an agreement even without Timor. Though we probably could not at once get the assurance that we would be given a free hand against

[1] Sir Francis Leveson Bertie. British Assistant Under Secretary in the Foreign Office, 1894–1903; Ambassador in Rome, 1903–5, in Paris, 1905–18.

America in return—this seems doubtful to me for the reasons stated above—the English might perhaps decide to use their influence in Washington to ensure that the Americans created no difficulties for us in Shantung. This would be in England's own interest, for a conflict between ourselves and America can definitely not be desired by them.

PH.

668.   Holstein to Moritz von Bissing
        Copy

Kissingen, 3 September 1898

Dear General,

I have had the honour to receive Your Excellency's letter of the 29th of last month. I see from it that two additions to the statement Your Excellency made the other day in my name are still expected on the part of Count Guido Henckel.[1] One of these additions I regard as unobjectionable and, if only so that Your Excellency should not have written in vain, I want to empower Your Excellency to expand the recent statement accordingly. This would thus now read :

'After Count Guido Henckel has stated to Herr von Holstein, with Colonel-General Count Waldersee and myself acting as intermediaries, that he would to-day still regard it as his duty as a gentleman and Christian to admit openly if he were aware of ever having committed an injustice against Herr von Holstein, Herr von Holstein takes account of this statement with satisfaction and on that basis states that he now no longer holds to his former belief that Count Henckel was concerned in the Press articles in question, that he also no longer stands by the letter written to Count Henckel at that time as a result of this belief, and that he regards the matter as settled.'

On the other hand I do not intend that the second additional statement be made. 'That I desire my former opponent to regard the actions resulting from my former suspicions as never having occured.'

This would be equivalent to an expression of regret for which I see no reason, for I am still firmly convinced to-day that in the situation then obtaining I had to act as I did. I feel that I have now gone as far as I possibly can, *and I will not go any further*.

If Your Excellency should then assure me that the affair of honour has thus been correctly settled, this will be the decisive thing for me, and as compared with that any statements coming from the other side will [not] be of any importance to me.

---

[1] Bissing had written on 29 August : 'Count Waldersee wrote me to-day that although Count Henckel had taken note with great satisfaction of my statement made with your approval, he still hoped that you would now be prepared to state that in view of Count Henckel's assurances you now no longer believed that he had been involved in the newspaper attacks in question and that you would wish that your former opponent should regard the actions resulting from your former suspicions as never having occurred. After such a reassurance Count Henckel for his part would state that he recognizes the affair as having been fully settled.'

Together with the renewed expression of my sincere gratitude I would like to add my fervent wish that Your Excellency will now be spared any further annoyance arising out of this unpleasant affair, and remain

Most respectfully,

### 669. Moritz von Bissing to Holstein

Freiburg, 22 September 1898

Dear Herr von Holstein,

Your Excellency must have thought me tardy for not having replied earlier to your last letter and not having reported to you sooner what decision your former opponent had taken after the latest statement which you sent me. After having only just returned from manoeuvres I now have to report as follows :

I transmitted your final statement to me to Count Waldersee on 6 September with the comment that you had neither cause nor inclination to go any further and that I regarded the affair of honour satisfactorily settled as a result of this statement and the terms of Count Henckel's statement to you.

On 10 September Count Waldersee wrote to me that he now entirely shared my view, that he had informed Count Henckel of this, and he enclosed at the same time the draft of a report addressed to His Majesty the Kaiser and King, in which he develops his view on the settlement of the affair of honour. I immediately did so too, explaining in particular the point of view you had adopted in the matter and the factors which had led to the final compromise. In so doing I anticipated an order from His Majesty which reached me a few days later while I was on manoeuvres. Yesterday I received the following communication from the Chief of the Military Cabinet : 'His Majesty the Kaiser and King was pleased to take note with satisfaction of Your Excellency's report to Him of the 15th according to which the affair of honour between *Wirklicher Geheimer Legationsrat* von Holstein and Count Guido Henckel von Donnersmarck has now been settled.'

Thereby the matter has been concluded satisfactorily in every way, and the affair of honour is to be regarded as settled for all time. It only remained for me to inform Count von Waldersee, who probably will have received a similar letter from the Military Cabinet, of the receipt of the letter addressed to me, adding that I would inform you as indicated. Count Waldersee will not delay in taking similar steps towards Count Henckel.

I have the honour to remain most respectfully

Your Excellency's
very devoted
Baron von Bissing

## 670. Holstein to Bernhard von Bülow
Copy

2 October 1898

Dear Bülow,

Your news about the *Hamburger Korrespondenz*[1] struck me all the more as it is not the only symptom of the fact that people are working against you behind the scenes. Almost simultaneously Fischer,[2] who is at the moment travelling around the western provinces, wrote to me that he was surprised to notice more and more to what extent your person was being pushed into the background as compared to the Kaiser and Chancellor when foreign policy was being discussed; the successes of the past year are attributed to them, and both had risen considerably in estimation as a result, whereas you were regarded more in the light of a courtier. Fischer, who without saying so seems to believe that public opinion is being systematically influenced, would like to report his observations to you personally after his return. Furthermore I have to tell you that some weeks ago—I was still in Berlin—the Minister of War in a private conversation let slip the remark that a plan existed to make Langenburg[3] Chancellor in succession to our Hohenlohe; it was hoped to win over the Kaiser by suggesting that Prince Adolf von Schaumburg[4] should become Governor [of Alsace-Lorraine]. All these symptoms point to the fact that a concerted move is in progress to lessen your position and push you out. If you should harbour the idea of requesting the next embassy that becomes vacant you can be fairly indifferent concerning the world's estimate of your achievements—though I do not know for how long you would be left in quiet enjoyment of your embassy by your opponents once they were on top. That is therefore all the more reason for you not to let things run on as they are now if you are envisaging the possibility of a protracted stay in Berlin. To a certain extent you yourself have helped to produce the view now held by the public by allowing first of all a political beginner[5] and then a generally recognized cypher[6] to deputize for you during your unusually long leave. As a result the public believes itself justified in assuming that the direction of foreign policy lies not with the State Secretary but with the Chancellor and H.M. I have therefore been asking myself after the event—unfortunately not in time—whether Richthofen may not have been inspired from outside *dans cet ordre d'idées* when he suggested Derenthall, without himself sensing the purpose. What has given me this idea is the fact that Prince Bismarck—who also occasionally liked to demonstrate that beside him the State Secretary was only the fifth wheel—called on Derenthall to deputize when Berchem went on leave and before Herb. Bismarck had returned. But Herb. B. resented this

---

[1] Not found.

[2] Dr Franz Fischer of the *Kölnische Zeitung*.

[3] Hermann, Prince zu Hohenlohe-Langenburg. Governor of Alsace-Lorraine, 1894–1907.

[4] Adolf, Prince zu Schaumburg-Lippe. Regent of Lippe-Detmold, 1895–7.

[5] Oswald, Baron von Richthofen.

[6] Eduard von Derenthall.

measure, stated openly that the position of the State Secretary was being lessened by D. acting as deputy, refused to allow it again in the future and treated D. abominably. It is just this that gives me reason to think, especially as we know that the use of incapable men at a suitable moment is one of the means employed. Think back to the attempt made with Stirum in 1880.[1] The question now is this: 'How can one meet a *continuation of harmful influences?*' At the moment I only see one means, and that is that during your next absence, which will moreover be of a quite abnormal nature,[2] you appoint someone to deputize for you who is neither a beginner nor a cypher, thus Brincken[3] for example. Richthofen, to be sure, will see in this a setback of his plan of gradually moving into the State Secretaryship and will scream loudly at being insulted. The answer to this would be that the Colonial Division now required the greatest attention, that he was being counted on for that, that the formal duties of the State Secretary and the actual duties of the Chancellor would in fact pass to him, R., but that he would then have neither the necessary time nor strength left for high policy. It is up to you how you persuade the Chancellor to agree to this scheme; you'll find a way. As regards H.M., he will see in Brincken's appointment a vote of no confidence in me. Do you think that will influence him against the idea? I hardly think so, I shall easily reach an understanding with my old friend Brincken, who is very sensitive, and will help him where I can. On the other hand I absolutely refuse to accept an interim solution like the one with Richthofen last summer, and if it should be adopted I will do what is certainly medically highly advisable, i.e. I shall devote the coming two months to giving my bad eye rest and treatment. You have the right to say to me at this stage: 'But I only recently offered to have you made Under State Secretary, so what are you complaining about?'

My dear Bülow, that is something I remember with gratitude, but *in the first place,* I stated in 1890 that I would refuse any promotion in the future; *secondly,* it is true that the simple instruction that I should also sign all drafts coming from the Political Division would have pretty well the same effect as my appointment as Under State Secretary. But it is only human that the present older generation of political *Räte*—even including the sensitive but touchy Lindenau—would regard such an innovation as a *capitis diminutio,* and I don't want to estrange old comrades yet again; that has been my lot often enough in the past. *Thirdly* and finally, my coming into greater prominence at this *very* moment would do nothing for *your* position, perhaps rather the contrary.

Thus I see at present only one means to preserve you and myself from harm, and that is the temporary bringing in of Brincken. As regards the *treatment* of this question, I believe it would be best to get H.M.'s approval for summoning Brincken by emphasizing the abnormal

[1] See, *Memoirs*, pp. 64–6.

[2] Bülow was to accompany the Kaiser on his trip to Italy, Constantinople and Palestine, 12 October–26 November 1898.

[3] Egon, Baron von der Brincken. Minister at the Hague, 1895–9.

character of the imminent absence, then to talk to the Chancellor, and finally to Richthofen.[1] [...]

Your H.

## 671. Memorandum by Holstein
Copy

12 November 1898

Lord Salisbury's Guildhall speech[2] has disappointed and confused the English public. The proclamation of the protectorate over Egypt had been expected; this did not take place, on the contrary the Prime Minister expressed the hope that there would be no necessity for any changes in Egypt's position. Nevertheless Lord Salisbury did give his speech a bellicose undertone, especially in the passage dealing with the inheritance of the dying states.[3]

The general public is puzzled at the secret thoughts of the speaker, but these are clear enough to all who know the South African agreement.[4] Germany is bound to support England in a war over South Africa—but only then. As a sensible Englishman Lord Salisbury is therefore trying to ensure that the war, if it should come, should break out over Delagoa Bay, not over Egypt or China. Once the struggle is in progress all pending questions will be settled simultaneously.

England has lately been trying to boast of her relations with Germany as of those with America; these are represented as part of England's military strength. The practical Americans have already sensed that this display of their friendship could in certain circumstances be inconvenient to them. The important American newspapers have therefore remarked recently: 'There are as yet no United States of Europe and Asia'. This is meant to criticize Lord Salisbury's statement 'that America's entry into world policy is not a pacifying factor, but one favourable to English interests'. Germany too is for her part most interested in not leaving the representation of German-English relations

---

[1] In fact Richthofen did deputize for Bülow as State Secretary.

[2] Of 9 November.

[3] Salisbury said: 'It is the first year in which the mighty force of the American Republic has been introduced among the nations whose dominion is expanding, and whose instruments to a certain extent are war. I am not implying the slightest blame. Far from it. I am not refusing sympathy to the American Republic in the difficulties through which it has passed, but no one can deny that their appearance among the factors of Asiatic, at all events, and possibly of European diplomacy is a grave and serious event, which may not conduce to the interests of peace, though I think, in any event, they are likely to conduce to the interests of Great Britain. But what has been impressed upon us as the subject matter of war is terribly prevalent on all sides. You see nations who are decaying, whose Government is so bad that they can neither maintain the power of self-defence nor the affection of their subjects. You see this on all sides, and you also see that when that phenomenon takes place there are always neighbours who are impelled by some motive or other—it may be from the highest philanthropy, it may be from the natural desire of empire—are always inclined or disposed to contest with each other as to who shall be the heir of the nation that is falling away from its position. And that is the cause of war.'

[4] The Secret Convention of 30 August 1898 on the Portuguese colonies, in which **Great Britain** and Germany agreed jointly to oppose the intervention of any third **Power** in the provinces of Mozambique, Angola, and in Portuguese Timor. (*Grosse Politik*, vol. XIVi, no. 3872, pp. 347–55.)

uncritically to the English, for the results of a misunderstanding could be much more serious for us than America, because our situation is more exposed.

Germany was able to bind herself towards England on South Africa without breaking with the policy she has pursued hitherto, because we had ascertained beforehand that Russia had no interests in South Africa. And the risk we took because of this obligation was infinitesimal, for we were able to prevent France from ever making the South African Question into a question of war; we would only need to make it clear to the Paris and St Petersburg Cabinets that we were bound to support England on this question, but *only* on this one. It is on this very assumption, that under *these* circumstances France would not start any serious action over South Africa, that the hope of a favourable outcome of our South African undertaking rested.

The precondition of a favourable outcome—the information that our agreement with England does not extend beyond the Portuguese colonies—does not seem to be available as yet, for France is beginning to act as if she would seriously oppose our Portuguese plans. France is retreating or advancing depending on the way St Petersburg pulls the strings. Russia might *possibly* have advised her to stand firm on Fashoda,[1] but she would *never* have agreed to any action concerning South Africa if she had been certain that Germany would go with England only on the latter question but in no other. France's attitude in the Fashoda as in the Delagoa Question thus represents a not undeserved setback for German policy.

Still, it would even now not be too late to let the French know via Hatzfeldt-Courcel that *only* South Africa represents a German-English *casus foederis*. But this would have to be done soon, for the more determined the French become in this matter, the more humiliating and therefore difficult a retreat would be for them.

As regards Russia, we have *artificially* induced the belief in her that our agreement with England was not a special agreement on South Africa, but a general one. A Russian Foreign Minister is thus faced with two alternatives. He can either say: 'It doesn't matter on which question we fight the German-English group. Since these two co-operate *everywhere*'; or he can tell the French: 'England states, without contradiction from the German side, that she is reckoning with German support in case of an attack. How would it be if we tackled the matter from the opposite end, and started by going for Germany instead of England if a suitable opportunity should present itself? Let us first of all sound out whether England would unhesitatingly come to Germany's assistance in such a case.'

What would be the result of such Franco-Russian diplomatic soundings? If the lessons of the past mean anything at all, we should prepare ourselves to face the fact that England would give the reply best suited

[1] On 3 November 1898 the French yielded to British pressure and ordered the evacuation of Fashoda on the upper Nile which had been occupied by French forces in July.

to producing a continental war and assisting England to regain at the end of the century the position of power to which Pitt and Nelson raised her one hundred years earlier. England will reserve her freedom of action to come in or stay out at the psychological moment. Whether she came in or not, after a continental war weakening the Continental Powers, she would once more be the decisive factor in Europe. Because of Germany's faulty policy England's prospects would become infinitely more favourable than could have been foreseen by English statesmen who six months ago offered us a general alliance with England and great compensations. At that time the Kaiser commented that the whole English navy would be of no use to him in the defence of East Prussia.[1] The general alliance was therefore refused because the dangers outweighed the advantages. And to-day we are supposed to take upon ourselves the same danger *without* the advantages by deliberately creating the belief that a *general* alliance between England and ourselves existed, which in fact it does not.

The Tsar is a peace-loving man. We have seen in the Kiaochow question that he allows quite a lot to be done as long as he believes that Germany is not one of Russia's inveterate opponents. But this legend of the English alliance—about whose effect you and I were agreed from the moment when Lascelles brought it into being—could, together with some aspects of the Palestine trip, produce in the mind of the Russian ruler 'patriotic concern' similar to that which in the four years from 1866 to 1870 was quietly preparing the ground for the French war.

We are now playing with fire. We can avert the danger of war from the German Reich with one word, by correcting the tendentious English legend. If we don't do that, if we drift onto the rocks fully aware of what is happening and with folded arms, then everything that Bismarck has ever said of the force of English influences will be as nothing compared to what will be said of *this* policy in the future.

As said above, there is probably still time, though very little time, to prevent Germany from becoming involved in England's wars by letting it be known in confidence that the German-English agreement extends neither to Egypt nor to Asia. If this is not made known, then the possibility of an Anglo-German war against Russia and France, though serious enough, is still less frightening than the chance that the two will now yield for the second time, but with the intention of having their revenge on Germany at the first opportunity when she is isolated. This plan would be nipped in the bud if Russia were to learn in time that England and Germany had not reached agreement on a single question concerning the *Russian* sphere of interests. Then it wouldn't really matter about the *French* sphere of interests.

H.

672. Philipp zu Eulenburg to Holstein

Vienna, 11 December 1898

Dear friend,

Your letter gave me real and great pleasure. I was very worried at

[1] See *Grosse Politik*, vol. XIVi, p. 216, note 15.

your shrouding yourself so *completely* in silence. I thought you were ill and would have liked somehow to have shown you my sympathy and offered my help—but it was *absolutely* impossible to discover your address.

You are right to concern yourself with the situation here. I have reported at length[1] and written to Bülow. The situation is very serious and a wrong course is being steered here. All ears are closed to my attempts to influence the situation which I am making to the limits of what is possible. They don't *want* to see that a continuing development of internal affairs *must* inevitably affect foreign relations. There's an element of fate in Kaiser Franz Joseph's rule. It seems that the old man must really end in revolution, just as he started.

The difficulty for us is that our friends, the Hungarians, seem to be weakening at the decisive moment—because of internal disputes and conflict.

I shall soon write more. To-day I can't. I must see Bánffy.

Faithfully as ever
Your
PEulenburg

## 673. Holstein to Paul von Hatzfeldt[2]

TELEGRAM

Berlin, 22 December 1898

Private

[...] As the State Secretary gathered from the conversation on the day before yesterday, the Kaiser does not at present think of expanding the South African agreement[3] into a possible alliance—two against two. His Majesty sees clearly the advantages to us of abandoning our position as spectator as late as possible.

Holstein[4]

## 674. Adolf Marschall von Bieberstein to Holstein

Pera, 30 December 1898

Dear Holstein,

Receive to-day my best wishes for the New Year; I hope above all that your health will remain good, your eyes will grow stronger, and also that your work in the Ministry will afford you continued satisfaction. There will of course be grounds for annoyances, but on the whole I do have the impression that matters are going very well as regards foreign policy, and internally certainly much better than in the last years of my ministerial activity.

---

[1] See *Grosse Politik*, vol. XIII, no. 3480, pp. 126–8.
[2] From the London Embassy files.      [3] See p. 98, note 4.
[4] Hatzfeldt replied by telegram on the same day that the Queen was not yet thinking in terms of an actual alliance with Germany. 'Lord Salisbury too has not yet reached the stage of thinking that he requires our help; moreover he regards any complications in the near future as out of the question. In my opinion we must wait quietly until these arise.' (From the London Embassy files.)

I cannot praise the way things are going here as highly. The decision on everything is being concentrated more and more in one person, and what the Ministers may think of some affair is by now only of importance insofar as if they work against something they can harm it. Positive support by the Foreign Minister[1] or the Ministers of other departments is completely valueless. After one has discussed some matter with the Foreign Minister, he produces a watered down report for the First Secretary who adapts it even further *ad usum* of the Master. Naturally there is no result. The most effective method is a personal talk with Effendi and therefore I fixed a time for an audience the other day, three days before the Selamsis, in order to press the questions of the cable and the Port of Haidar-Pasa. Since then the matter has been moving and I am now pretty certain that I shall have both problems settled before the start of the Ramadan—13 January.

Our opponents here blamed us for the existing state of affairs in the palace. The Sultan wants to decide everything himself and refuses to listen to anyone because we flattered him too much and thus made him conceited. The Kaiser's visit and the honour shown to him then were the last straw and have made the Master completely intractable. That of course is nonsense; it has long been the case that the Sultan decided everything alone, and the fact that the decision is nearly always to do nothing or to do nothing for the time being is an old Turkish national habit. I think much rather that the development of the Turkish Question which has led all Mohammedans to be extremely bitter is the real cause of the present mental outlook of the Master. [...]

In friendship as ever

Your

Marschall.

[1] Ahmed Tewfik Pasha.

# 1899

675. Holstein to Castell Rüdenhausen[1]

Berlin, 24 February 1899

Dear Count,

I would like in the following to tell you something about German-Italian relations to make up for the fact that unfortunately we did not have a talk.

You will find that the Triple Alliance is looked upon with indifference in Italy. It has not fulfilled Italian expectations. This is not a matter of to-day or yesterday, but is due to a basic difference of views. For us as for Austria the alliance is an insurance for mutual protection; the Italians envisaged it as a profit-making concern. Both the Italian people and Government were furious when Count Corti returned empty-handed from the Congress of Berlin instead of having extended their territorial possessions, as England and Austria had done. The fury grew when shortly afterwards France acquired Tunis, and England gained control of Egypt. After that the Italians sought to join the Triple Alliance, but their aim—there were plenty of indications for this—was profit, not preservation. Even my late friend Launay, a calm diplomat of the old school, thought of acquiring Albania, 'which after all you could see on clear days from the Italian coast through a telescope'.

Crispi and Blanc with their ever-present acquisitive desires were the most difficult to deal with. When Crispi accompanied King Umberto to Berlin in the summer of 1889, he discovered that Prince Bismarck was not prepared to extend the Triple Alliance to cover an acquisitive policy, and was most displeased.[2] Shortly afterwards, i.e. still in the summer of 1889, he sent a confidant, Cucchi,[3] to Varzin, and from the hints which the latter dropped to me on the way there, I could see that Crispi's concern was to determine in advance what territory Italy would acquire in case of the expected catastrophe in the Balkans. Cucchi avoided Berlin on the return journey, and I did not learn what had been discussed in Varzin.[4]

I might remark here that Crispi, as an old conspirator, has a deep-rooted antipathy for professional diplomats. He always prefers a consul

[1] First Secretary in the German Embassy in Rome, 1899–1901.
[2] King Umberto and Crispi visited Berlin 21–26 May 1889.
[3] Francesco Cucchi. Italian Deputy.
[4] Crispi repeatedly expressed his fears of a French attack on Italy to Solms in July 1889. He feared that such an attack would take place with the Pope's support, and sent Cucchi to Germany for personal discussions. After a talk with Herbert von Bismarck in Berlin on 18 July, Cucchi went to Varzin, where the Chancellor told him that he did not believe that France

to an ambassador as a confidant, and an old Garibaldian is naturally best of all. He has a certain amount of confidence in me, because we met in the year 1870 under extraordinary circumstances.[1] When I saw him the last time in 1889 he told me: 'If you have something special to tell me, write to me direct and I will reply.' When I replied that Count Launay had earned the complete confidence of the German Government, Crispi was silent and displeased. Crispi had always inclined towards Germany because he was convinced that Germany, in her own interest, would have to defend the Italian Kingdom against France even without a treaty. For that very reason he regarded a *defensive* Triple Alliance as superfluous, an unnecessary burden on Italy, and I think it safe to assume that Crispi, had he been in power when the treaty came up for renewal the last time, would never have agreed to its renewal *without change.*

In the summer of 1890, shortly before his retirement, Crispi made the last, and for us most awkward, attempt to interpret the Triple Alliance Treaty as a profit-making concern. He suddenly informed London and Vienna that he had been informed that France had a short time previously concluded a Treaty of Devolution with the Bey of Tunis, according to which France would simply gain possession of Tunis after the Bey's death. Under these circumstances the Italian Government had to ascertain immediately what attitude her allies, Germany and Austria, would take in view of such flagrant disregard for Italy's rights and interests.[2] I believe and, until the contrary is proved, will continue to do so, that the story of the Treaty of Devolution was a tendentious fraud; I believe this if only because the Resident-General, the official representative of French policy, was on leave in France at the time when the apocryphal treaty was supposed to have been concluded and signed. Moreover nothing has ever leaked out concerning such an agreement from that day to this. But the more difficult it seemed to assign a motive to Crispi's action, the more worrying were the conclusions to which it was bound to give rise. Crispi had wanted to give clear expression to his contempt for the worth of a *defensive* Triple Alliance. On the other hand it was impossible for Germany as well as for Austria to pursue an aggresive policy towards France—and this without any visible justification—merely in order to secure Tunis for Italy. Because of the basic differences between the two points of view the Triple Alliance was in danger of being shattered, and this outcome was prevented only by our drawing England into the question. Count Hatzfeldt was instructed to inform Lord Salisbury of the affair, and the latter soon realized the danger which might arise for England if after the shattering of the Triple Alliance Italy were to draw closer to France. Thus Salisbury allowed himself to be persuaded by Hatzfeldt to write a personal letter to Crispi, in which, whilst not giving any definite assurances, he admit-

had aggressive intentions; above all he did not believe in the co-operation of the Curia in such plans. Neither the files of the Foreign Ministry nor Cucchi's letters to Crispi of 21 and 24 July 1889 on his conversations in Germany (*Memoirs of Crispi*, vol. II, pp. 407–16) give any indication whether Cucchi discussed Italian plans for aggrandizement in the Balkans.

  [1] See *Memoirs*, pp. 42–6.                              [2] See *Ibid.*, pp. 151–6.

ted all the same that under certain circumstances Italy might have to defend well-founded interests in Tunis.[1] Crispi declared himself satisfied by this letter and stated, though without conviction or explanation to the Ambassador, Count Solms, that the whole matter was settled.

I have treated this past episode in such detail because it touches on a point which is still of decisive importance for Italy's policy to-day, and that is Italy's position towards England.

When Count Cavour[2] was preparing for his policy of action in the later 1850's, he asked the English Minister, Sir Charles Hudson, a friend of his, whether he could count on English support in the pursuit of his aims. The Englishman replied: 'As an honest man I must tell you, sympathy yes, support no'. Count Cavour replied: 'Sympathy alone isn't enough', and from then on he conducted his policy with Napoleon. This story, which someone close to Cavour told me in Turin in 1860, illustrates a point of view, which, I believe, you will find many Italians still hold to-day. In the opinion of many, Italy needs France, at least economically. The non-republican Italian admires France and yet has a feeling of timidity towards her, whereas republicans and non-republicans alike have a feeling of admiration and sympathy for England.

For that reason the indifference concerning the existence of the Triple Alliance will hardly assume practical importance as long as England is on better terms with Germany than with France, as is the case now. I would therefore recommend that if Italy's relations to the Triple Alliance and France are touched upon, you should take the following line :

'The Triple Alliance is not topical, as one cannot say at the moment that the existence of any one of the three allies is threatened from outside. Since world policy has become the order of the day, i.e. since the end of the Chinese-Japanese war, the areas of conflict between the great European nations lie outside Europe. If by an unforeseen turn of events Italy were to be threatened in Europe, the Triple Alliance would do its duty without any doubts or hesitation. As regards Germany I know this, and I believe it of Austria-Hungary. No one will object to an economic rapprochement between Italy and France, least of all Germany, whose own economic relations with France are excellent. As for a *political* rapprochement between Italy and France, it lies in the nature of things that Italy should keep in touch on this point with England.

'As my personal opinion I would like to state that Germany will follow any political steps taken by Italy with calm, satisfaction, good-will, sympathy (you can chose the nuance there, dear Count), as long as these do not disturb Italian-English relations. This limitation results from Germany's interest in Italy's existence, and this would, in view of the fact that Italy is a peninsula, be greatly threatened if the English fleet were no longer to fight for, possibly even against, Italy.'

To the rejoinder that England and France are well on the way to reaching an understanding and that a renewal of the Crimean War

[1] Letter of 4 August 1890. ( *Memoirs of Crispi*, vol. II, pp. 454–5).
[2] Camillo, Count Cavour. Head of the Sardinian Government, 1852–9, 1860–1.

group (England, France, Italy, Austria) is perhaps not too far away, the answer is dictated by the circumstances : 'At the time of the Crimean War world policy in to-day's sense did not exist, the areas of conflict between nations were different ones. England and France can reach a partial and temporary agreement at any time, but not a general understanding which would remove distrust for at least a generation. An understanding of the latter kind might perhaps be reached with less difficulty between France and Germany than between France and England, for in comparison with the conflicting interests between France and England the object of dispute between France and Germany is fairly insignificant. In any case for the time being all this lies in the future, and one could argue a long time about it. So let us wait and see.' And this, dear Count, brings me to a close, for I feel that I have taken up enough of your time.

Naturally I leave it to you whether you wish to show this letter to your Chief, should he be interested in it.

With best wishes for your future, both in official and private life, I remain

Your devoted
Holstein

676.    Holstein to Hugo von Radolin[1]

Berlin, 9 March 1899

Dear Radolin,

[...] During the last week the Conference Question[2] gave you all sorts of trouble. I think the telegram, which Pourtalès is working on now, will bring the discussion on the question of participation to an end.[3] The attitude we have adopted is hostile to no one, on the contrary its purpose is to keep us out of hostilities as far as that is possible. We state from the outset that we will only participate in the consultation if all the Great Powers of Europe are represented. If one Power does not participate or drops out, we too will not participate or drop out, not because we are identifying ourselves with the non-participating Powers or a certain point of view, but because the non-participation of one Power would disturb the balance of forces. Under any circumstances this Conference is a risky undertaking, and I doubt whether our Kaiser, who has regarded the question with misgivings from the start, would have agreed if the initiative had come from anywhere other than St Petersburg. But doubtlessly the Tsar is guided by the noblest motives and it was this consideration which decisively influenced our Most Gracious Master, though he was not blind to the fact that we are venturing into unknown territory. It is generally easier to risk a forecast on the result of deliberations in which only the Great Powers take part. But in the case under discussion any forecast is made quite im-

---

[1] From the Radolin Papers.

[2] The First Hague Conference, initiated by the Tsar in a communication circulated to the representatives of foreign Powers at St Petersburg on 24 August 1898. (See *Grosse Politik*, vol. XV, no. 4215, pp. 141–3.)

[3] *Grosse Politik*, vol. XV, no. 4246, pp. 179–80.

possible by the participation of the medium-sized States and of America. As long as all the Powers are there, the course of the discussions will to a certain extent be dominated by their mutual existing relations. But if all the Great Powers do not participate the question becomes incalculable, and it would then probably be best for the peace of the world if the Conference came to an end as quickly as possible, in order perhaps to be revived under more favourable auspices. For I certainly believe that the idea of disarmament will not die out.

I don't think the Russian-English disputes over China are serious.[1] Those two will bark at each other, but not bite. After all we saw last autumn how Salisbury gave way after a determined start. But now I don't want to strain your eyesight any more.

I was very pleased to see your family in Dresden. They were in the best of health.

> With best regards
> Your
> Holstein [...]

## 677. Philipp zu Eulenburg to Holstein

Vienna, 8 April 1899

My dear friend,

I haven't written to you for quite a long time. I wanted to send you Easter greetings, but first of all I got a dreadful attack of influenza, and then my dear boys came on holiday, proving absorbing both to me and my time. [...]

When we last met you said that, now that people were becoming preoccupied with world policy, Austria was no more than a *quantité négligeable*. In my opinion domestic problems, which sooner or later could lead to more serious changes, have brought Austria once again into the limelight—in a most unpleasant way at that. This forces us to all sorts of serious reflections and actions.

But all this is very general and nothing new. [...]

> Your old faithful
> PEulenburg.

## 678. Georg zu Münster to Holstein

Paris, 12 April 1899

Holograph and confidential
My dear Herr von Holstein,

I haven't heard from you directly for a long time but presume you are now back in Berlin. I am glad that His Majesty has designated me for the Hague Conference, a sign of Our Gracious Master's confidence. But I do not overlook the difficulty and thanklessness of the task. We

---

[1] Over spheres of influence for railway concessions. Negotiations between England and Russia, begun in February 1899, ended in an exchange of notes of 28 April 1899 by which Russia recognized British interests north of the Great Wall. (See *British Documents on the Origins of the War, 1898–1914*, edited by G. P. Gooch and Harold Temperley, (London), vol. I, no. 61, pp. 40–1.)

will have to give the appearance of accepting the proposals and recognize the Russian Tsar's initiative as noble and humane for political reasons and because of the Tsar's personal identification with the proposals. But we must not accept anything which would limit or impair our military strength and Germany's independence.

That will be my guide. The great difficulty will be to formulate meaningless resolutions and find a cloak with which we can cover the inevitable fiasco. It will be a question of a few rules and interpretations, in the most general terms possible, of international law and additional regulations concerning the Geneva Red Cross.

The arbitration problem may be more dangerous, but there too we cannot accept anything which might in any way limit our political independence.

Though I am decidedly of the opinion that we must avoid anything at the Conference which might hurt the Tsar or lead to a deterioration of our relations with Russia, we can say, *strictly amongst ourselves*, that the whole affair is a really dirty advertising stunt which the Russians are running for their young Tsar, whom they want to make into the Prince of Peace. It is not better than and no different from advertising malt-extract, Schweitzer pills or Menier [sic] chocolates, the only difference being that it is the stupidity of the European nations rather than that of the buying public which is being counted upon. [...]

In friendship as ever

Yours sincerely
Münster.

P.S. I am counting on your influence to get rid of Stengel.[1] *One Professor Zorn*[2] is enough. I would prefer a sensible diplomat as second delegate.

### 679.   Paul von Hatzfeldt to Holstein[3]

London, 28 April 1899

Dear friend,

As you already know from my personal telegram of last Wednesday,[4] nothing happened in my conversation with Salisbury which I could have reported officially. But, *c'est le ton qui fait la chanson*, and therefore I sent you a personal telegram so that you and Herr von Bülow should know immediately on what basis Salisbury and I resumed relations after his return. I would only like to add that I went to see him with the deliberate intention to show indifference and avoid anything which might have been interpreted as an attempt on my part to achieve something or to

[1] Karl, Baron von Stengel. Professor of International Law at the University of Munich; Second Delegate to the First Hague Peace Conference, 1899.

[2] Philipp Zorn. Professor of International Law at the University of Königsberg; Member of the German Delegation at the First Hague Peace Conference.

[3] Hatzfeldt's letter to Holstein of 15 April 1899 is printed in *Die Grosse Politik*, vol. XIVii, no. 4067, pp. 606–9. Kaiser Wilhelm II wrote the following comment on a copy of the letter in the Foreign Ministry files: 'Excellently written! and confirms my view that in future too I cannot consider co-operation with England, at least as long as Salisbury is in office.'

[4] In this telegram of 26 April Hatzfeldt had given a brief account of his conversation with Salisbury on that day which is here described in detail. (From the Foreign Ministry files.)

convert him to a friendlier attitude towards us. He for his part was gay and talkative and acted as if nothing had happened. But then in the course of the conversation he did drop the remark—as though it were a very funny joke—that I presumably had not always had a very amusing time with Sanderson, Balfour and others (he did not mention Chamberlain, nor, naturally, did I.) I made use of this observation in order to tell him that it did in all truth give me no pleasure to watch here how my determined efforts over many years to bring about a better German-English understanding had been ruined because of a miserable object like Samoa.[1] Apart from that I had no *personal* complaints about anybody during his absence. I had had a slight clash only with Sanderson, who, as was known, occasionally got a rush of blood to the head, and then really wasn't aware of what he was saying. On that occasion he had wanted to hold me responsible for a statement on Samoa made in some German newspaper, and had followed this up with the strange assertion that the *lies* about England printed in that paper must have been *inspired*. Though I was normally very calm, that had gone beyond a joke, and I gave him a very firm reply. I had not reported the incident so as not to pour oil on the flames, and I had no personal resentment for I knew his idiosyncracies and was certain that his intentions were really of the best. Salisbury laughed heartily at my description of the incident, and, without going into the matter, reminded me that in days past I had had quite a few little verbal battles with Currie, then Under Secretary of State, who had been even touchier.

I can only conclude from Salisbury's attitude on this occasion—he clearly wanted to place things on a friendly footing—that for the time being he wants to wait and see how the situation in Samoa will develop, especially as regards the Commission's activities,[2] and that until then at least he wants to avoid new differences with us. My opinion, which I continue to stand by, is that his final attitude to the question will depend primarily on America's attitude towards us. He has noticed long ago that the Americans, fully occupied elsewhere, have little desire to let matters come to a break with us over Samoa for England's sake. Salisbury himself does not place great expectations on America's friendship, and this has already caused him to calm down. I can't judge as yet to what extent Salisbury's joking remark—mentioned in my personal telegram —that the commission might do best to divide the cake into three parts, as equal as possible in size, for which lots should be drawn, is to be taken seriously. But I incline to the belief that if all else fails he sees this as a way out, enabling him to accept even Sawaii as the English share. You may already have heard from Washington whether this idea has been mooted there too. In the meantime it is certainly in our interest to

[1] Civil war had again broken out in Samoa in 1898 after the death on 22 August of Malietoa, who had been recognized as King in 1889 by the supervisory Powers, Germany, Britain and the United States. The conflicting interests of the supervisory Powers gave rise to considerable tension between them in the early months of 1899.

[2] A tripartite commission to investigate rival claims in Samoa arrived at Apia on 13 May 1899.

co-operate with the Americans as far as possible so as to isolate England as regards Samoa, and I hope sincerely that Sternburg[1] will not lose sight of this point for a single moment.

The statement by Postmaster-General Smith, allegedly a close friend of the President's, which is reported in to-day's *Standard*, that America does not want any sort of alliance and has no intention of helping England in China, seems pretty significant to me.

I shall keep a watch on Spanish-English relations as far as possible. Yesterday Drummond Wolff[2] came to see me, but he told me little that was new and that I could have reported. He remains of the opinion that the syndicate which has advanced Don Carlos[3] £60,000 is not made up of business men who wish to speculate, but consists of fanatical legitimists like Lord Ashburnham, who is still dreaming of a Stuart restoration, although there are no more Stuarts, and who every year places wreaths at the statue of Charles I. I should say that Drummond Wolff is right, if only because of the small sum advanced, and I don't think it probable that Don Carlos will be able to do much with it. Apart from that Wolff spoke with much sympathy of the present Spanish Ministry, thought that Silvela[4] had realized that it would be an advantage to be rid of Cuba and the Philippines, and that he planned serious internal reforms. If these should succeed, it was not impossible for the country to recover and become once again a factor in European politics. I have had an impression for some time that this possibility is being reckoned with here. Moreover the danger to England which would result from an overthrow of the Spanish monarchy is recognized; since Portugal is not strong enough to stand on its own, this would mean that the whole republican peninsula would be driven into France's arms. Not so long ago a number of remarks by Salisbury indicated his lively concern about this, and in part this was the cause of his very restrained steps in Lisbon on the colonial question. For that very reason I just cannot imagine that intentions concerning Ceuta or Gibraltar which might shake the monarchy will be made public here. However, the situation would be quite different if indications were to be observed here that the Spanish Government were prepared for a *friendly* cession, possibly in return for cash compensation. That is one point which, I believe, Radowitz will have to watch closely, for I am not convinced that the Spaniards, in their need, would withstand the temptation of a large sum. I certainly have the impression that events in Spain are being followed with great attention here; and Drummond Wolff, who had a conversation with Salisbury a short time ago, is in quite a hurry to return to his post.

I cannot completely share the view that Salisbury wants to cut loose

[1] Hermann, Baron von Speck von Sternburg. First Secretary in the German Embassy in Washington, 1898–1900; German representative on the Samoa commission; Consul-General in Calcutta, 1900–3; Minister on special mission to Washington, 1903; Ambassador in Washington, 1903–8.

[2] Sir Henry Drummond Charles Wolff. British Ambassador in Madrid, 1892–1900.

[3] Pretender to the throne of Spain.

[4] Francisco Silvela y de la Vielleuze. Spanish Minister-President and Foreign Minister, 1899–1900; Minister-President, 1902–3.

from our Portuguese agreement, though I have realized from the beginning that Balfour conceded more to us than Salisbury would have wished. Salisbury is by no means in a hurry to implement the treaty, and possibly is quietly pleased that we are cross at the delay imposed on our desires in that direction. But that is certainly not the only reason for his attitude in Lisbon, and I believe he is really afraid to damage the monarchy there, which he regards as a friend and ally of England's, by pressure and harsh treatment. Furthermore he tells himself—I know him well enough—that now that England has concluded the treaty with us, she can await developments without any danger, for sooner or later she is bound to get that portion of the Portuguese colonies which we have conceded to her. This policy of wait-and-see and allowing things to ripen is in accord with Lord Salisbury's most basic views and habits. Naturally he couldn't care less if the Portuguese in the meantime grant valuable concessions in our share. But until proof to the contrary is forthcoming I don't believe that he wants either to break or evade the treaty by arranging, for example, to obtain Delagoa Bay or something else without allowing us our share. He knows us too well not to realize that he would then meet with determined contradiction and opposition from us. Similarly I do not think it probable that he helped the Portuguese pay the interest, if only because he could hardly have found the money for it here without it becoming known. And I also remind you of a remark of Chamberlain's, who suspected President Krüger of having given financial help to the Portuguese. I think Chamberlain seriously held this suspicion, and it cannot be assumed that Salisbury lent the Portuguese money without Chamberlain's knowledge. Naturally I will continue to watch the matter, but I would like to suggest that enquiries also be made in Lisbon to discover whether Portugal, as has happened so often in Spain, found temporary means at home by smallish transactions, concessions etc. and usurious loans from private individuals.

By the above I naturally don't want to say that the Portuguese treaty would be adhered to here if Samoa, for example, had produced a break. In that case I don't believe that England would have confined herself to dividing Samoa with America, but would have expected with certainty that she would have damaged our colonial interests everywhere, including a separate agreement with Portugal concerning Delagoa.

If you have received indications from America that Hay returned from here with great colonial projects, I can naturally do nothing else but accept this. Until now it was my impression that such a calm and coolly calculating man as Hay would not believe it possible to make further far-reaching colonial projects, apart from Cuba and the Philippines, acceptable to his compatriots. And when saying this I disregard the fact that the Philippines alone have already turned out to be a hard nut to crack, thus cooling the desire for expansion. For I don't even believe that Hay entered into great partition projects with Salisbury before his departure, i.e. before the setback in the Philippines, and that Salisbury has had an opportunity to reach an understanding with him.

111

What Salisbury certainly did attempt, and unfortunately he has been successful for the moment, was to ensure America's agreement to make our position in Samoa as difficult and unpleasant as could be, to push us out if possible, and at the same time to humble our pride.

Even though I do not assume that England will suddenly undertake great things, whether alone or together with America, it is nevertheless quite clear, and I want to state this explicitly here and now, that a situation can arise at any moment which will cause England to decide on a sudden advance. Two possibilities in particular lead me to this opinion: (1) The as yet I hope distant prospect of an internal catastrophe in Spain, (2) a collapse in Morocco.[1] In the latter case I have no doubt whatsoever that the English fleet would immediately occupy certain points on the Moroccan coast, and that these would not be surrendered again. Objections and reclamations on our part would, I fear, do precious little good; and I think it equally improbable, particularly with our relations in their present state, that we could reach an agreement with England *in advance* on a fair partition. We would then be faced with two alternatives: either we state here in advance, firmly and categorically, that should England occupy Tangier, for instance, we would claim other specified points and would not permit England to occupy these: or—this would be even better—we would in turn occupy these by raising the flag, and notify everyone, England in particular, of our occupation. Naturally we need ships in order to do this, but not many, for we couldn't get anywhere by the use of force against the English fleet, and would have to assume that England would prefer to avoid a break. Another question, one that lies in the more distant future I hope, is what we should do if the Spanish monarchy collapses and certain Spanish possessions become ownerless. In that case, it seems to me, France would have quite a say, and, if England did not want to show us sufficient consideration, we would be in a position to co-operate with France against England on such an issue.

To prevent this letter reaching infinite lengths, I only want to add now that I was delighted to see from your letter that by and large you share my views on the importance of our relations with Holland. The marriage question naturally stands out, and on this I would like to say that any direct persuasion by us in The Hague would be dangerous.[2] The young Queen is supposed to be very obstinate and prefers to do whatever people try to prevent her from doing. Persuasion would therefore have to come not from us, but, if we have no clever aunt at our disposal, for example from the Dutch Press, without any appearance of our being involved. Preparations might possibly be made here in London. As I already mentioned in my last letter, the achievement of lasting contractual relations, with all the advantages this would entail

[1] In 1894 Abdul Aziz, a boy of thirteen, became Sultan of Morocco. He was unable to control domestic conflicts or the forces of European penetration, and the country was in a state of chronic disorder.

[2] The marriage of Wilhelmine, Queen of the Netherlands since 1890. On 7 February 1901 she married Heinrich, Duke of Mecklenburg-Schwerin.

for both sides in the future, seems to me much more important than the marriage question.[1] But here too it is a prerequisite that the initiative does not come from us, and that Holland should make the advances. The crux of the matter lies in how this is to be accomplished. I may go into this question in greater detail when the next courier goes.

With best regards
Your
PHatzfeldt [...]

## 680.  Paul von Hatzfeldt to Holstein

London, 4 May 1899

Dear friend,

I have just sent off a telegram to you on Chamberlain's strange démarche,[2] and, as I don't want to deal with the matter officially, I am now enclosing a copy of his hand-written and most illegible letter[3] to Eckardstein.[4] I will not discuss the significance of this step here and now, as we shall see this evening, i.e. before this letter goes, whether it is of any practical importance and whether it will bear the interpretation that people here want to improve relations. In this connection it seems to me worth noting that Salisbury was more talkative and conciliatory yesterday than he has been with me for some time past. Symptomatic for this, so it seemed to me, were his remarks—the importance of these, however, must not be overestimated—when I drew his attention to the continuing aggressive attitude of the English in Samoa, basing my arguments on the material available to me. I did this by starting out with the remark, that, according to telegrams printed in yesterday's newspapers, the English agents had at last received instructions to keep quiet. If this were correct, it might now be hoped that affairs there would take a turn for the better. But these telegrams also showed that the English

---

[1] In a section of his letter to Holstein of 22 April 1899, not printed in *Die Grosse Politik*, (vol. XIVii, no. 4071, pp. 611–13) Hatzfeldt wrote: 'Finally, dear friend, I just want to touch on a subject which occupies me a great deal and which I propose to treat in greater detail in the near future. I am referring to our relations with Holland, more particularly at this time the marriage of the young Queen. It seems to me that it cannot be a matter of indifference to us if the marriage with young Teck, as English as they come, materializes, and we should try to prevent it, naturally without our part in this becoming apparent. On the other hand I have been assured that Dutch trade and commerce is decreasing, and that the Dutch, particularly the wealthy and trading classes, especially in Amsterdam, would to-day no longer oppose a customs-union with Germany, possibly even more far-reaching agreements, provided their national independence is safe-guarded. I am also told that the Dutch are worried because England and America are said to harbour plans concerning the Dutch colonies (Curaçao in particular) and that this worry is not without cause.
'This then seems, in my opinion, to merit serious consideration, though it may still appear to concern a far distant future. But one can certainly say that the German statesman who succeeds in establishing a firm contractual relationship between Holland and Germany will one day have an honoured place in history.' (From the Foreign Ministry files.)
[2] Not found.  [3] See enclosure I.
[4] Hermann, Baron von Eckardstein. Diplomatically active with the German Embassy in London, although not in Government service; granted the title of Counsellor of Legation, 1898; First Secretary in the London Embassy, December 1899–1902. (See his *Lebenserinnerungen und Politische Denkwürdigkeiten*, 3 vols., (Leipzig, 1919–21), vol. II, pp. 17 *et seq.*)

Government's instructions to keep quiet now and await the arrival of the commission had provoked very great dissatisfaction and indignation in English circles. Lord Salisbury remarked spontaneously at this point that this did not astonish him. The probable explanation was that people had hoped to create a *fait accompli* in accordance with English desires by continuing the struggle. When I replied that it was very regrettable all the same that the English had behaved so unpleasantly to the Germans during the latest fighting—for example they had refused to issue passes to anyone German, something the Americans had not done—Salisbury said that this was probably the result of Captain Sturdie's[1] obstinacy and prejudice. He seemed to be completely fanatical in this question. Salisbury then again complained about the lack of telegraphic communications which made everything difficult and impossible. In particular, agreeable co-operation between the three Powers was prevented thereby, and if this were to be achieved, telegraphic communications would just have to be established. He then also spoke of the Protestant missions in Samoa, whose fanaticism and influence was responsible for quite a number of things.

I hope the State Secretary will approve of my not, or at least not yet, reporting officially these confidential remarks of Lord Salisbury's about his own men, made in a confidential conversation.[2] Everything can change again by to-morrow if something crops up, and I therefore want to avoid the danger of the above remarks, if they appear in a dispatch, assuming an official character and being interpreted in Berlin as an *official surrender* on the part of England. We haven't reached that stage yet, and I am only bringing the matter up because it appears to me as a minor and as yet not very clear symptom indicating that Salisbury does not wish to maintain the differences with us in an acute stage. In the meantime this has brought with it an advantage. Our personal relations are more or less back at a point where we chat quite easily,[3] and this gives me the opportunity to bring up various points informally and humourously and to see what sort of face he pulls. Let me give you the following example :

While we were talking about colonial acquisitions, especially by England, I said laughingly that England's excellent appetite in this connection was a universally accepted fact, and they could therefore not be surprised if they were suspected of having plans for taking over everything, even places of very moderate value. When he replied that this was really exaggerated, he didn't want to take anything but would like to know to what I referred, I said that he was after all well acquainted with my views concerning his future plans for Morocco. I had expressed it to him more than once. I for one didn't doubt for a single moment that, should a crisis arise there, he would at once seize Tangier and other points along the Moroccan coast. Some Englishmen perhaps regarded Ceuta as a desirable possession as well. Salisbury interjected

---

[1] Commander of H.M.S. *Porpoise*, stationed off Samoa.
[2] Marginal Comment by Bülow : 'Yes'.          [3] Bülow : 'Very pleasing'.

that Ceuta, which moreover belonged to Spain, would be a most expensive possession for England; considerable sums would have to be spent to complete the fortifications (which does prove that the question has been made the subject of military study here). In connection with this I dropped the remark that poor Spain did in fact still have some possessions which might lead others into temptation, Minorca for example. At this stage Lord Salisbury became somewhat pensive and then said that Minorca was indeed a beautiful possession. It wasn't really too long ago since it had belonged to England, and the English admiral who had lost it had been shot because of it.[1] I now dropped the subject, while adding that naturally I could only speak of my personal impression as I wasn't the Chancellor and thus had no influence over our policy. If I were in that position and all these beautiful places were to be distributed one day, I would certainly defend the view that we should also have a word to say on these matters.

Here Salisbury suddenly asked me whether we would now buy the Carolines from Spain. I answered that I had heard nothing about it. Should the Spaniards decide to sell, I believed that we should close the deal, for we had special interests in the Carolines, as I had already told him earlier. Furthermore I had understood his remark on that subject at the time to mean that, should the case arise, no English interests would be affected thereby. He confirmed this again yesterday.[2]

For a moment I had the impression that this sudden question on the Philippines was meant to be a hint to us. England would give us a free hand in this respect, if we were ready to do the same for England's acquisition of other Spanish colonies. Is it not conceivable that the Spaniards in their financial straits might be persuaded to sell Ceuta or even Minorca for a large sum in cash, and that this is the aim being pursued here?[3]

I informed you yesterday by telegram of what Salisbury had said about the Russian agreement.[4] It wasn't much and consisted in part of humourous remarks about Lord Charles Beresford[5] and his disappointment on the 'open door' question. Radolin will perhaps be able to ascertain whether what he says is true, that is that no negotiations are now going on in St Petersburg on other questions. Certainly no negotiations are in progress here, if only because Staal has already left for St Petersburg, or rather The Hague. More than one great subject for differences between the two countries survives, and therefore I don't attach excessive importance to Lord Salisbury's assertion that he regards the danger of war as averted following the agreement. Even if people here are prepared to let Constantinople go, that doesn't mean that once

[1] Admiral Byng, executed after being condemned to death by court-martial in March 1757.
[2] See *Grosse Politik*, vol. XV, chapter XCVIII.       [3] Bülow: 'Hardly'.
[4] According to Hatzfeldt's telegram Salisbury had stated that the agreement now reached between England and Russia (see p. 107, note 1.) averted the danger of war. No further negotiations with Russia were taking place. (From the London Embassy files.)
[5] British naval officer; Conservative Member of Parliament, 1897–1900, 1902–3, 1910–16; Chief in command of the Channel Squadron, 1903; Commander-in-Chief in the Mediterranean, 1905; Admiral, 1906; Commander-in-Chief of the Channel fleet, 1907–9.

Russia wants to advance things will go smoothly there between England and Russia. We know from all the statements Russia has made and it lies in the very nature of things that St Petersburg wishes to exercise sole control over the Dardanelles and doesn't want to open them to anyone else.[1] That was what Alexander I had asked of Napoleon. Lord Salisbury on the contrary has, for as long as I have known him, always stated firmly that Russia might possibly be allowed free passage, but that one would then have to insist that the fleets of other nations, the English included, were given the same right. I doubt very much that he could concede this point even if he wanted to.[2] And that after all is not the only tricky point at issue between the two countries. Furthermore I have gained the impression that the wish to draw closer to Turkey again and reestablish the position there is current here. Yesterday, quite *en passant*, he also remarked that the English were now enjoying slightly better treatment in Constantinople than formerly. When I jokingly replied it could hardly have caused surprise that the Sultan did not repay the infamous treatment to which he had been subjected by special friendliness, Salisbury said this was true enough, but it had all been the fault of old Gladstone. He thereby conveniently forgets that he treated the Sultan just as badly afterwards. But the remark does not imply *qu'on veut se désintéresser ici de la Turquie*.

Under these circumstances I still fail to see why we should be in a great hurry[3] to conclude an agreement on the Near East with the Russians. We would thereby alienate our allies, Austria in particular, without gaining a new ally in return, for all that Russia offers is a free hand economically in Asia Minor, and this without disarming or immobilizing France, i.e. without guaranteeing our security.

I think I also ought to mention here some remarks of Rothschild's and Chamberlain's which are not without interest concerning the agreement between England and Russia. The former naturally looks at it from a financial point of view and told me in the strictest confidence that the Russians had concluded the agreement due to Witte's influence and only in order to obtain at long last the loan here which they need so badly. How much importance they would attach to the agreement once this object had been achieved was an open question. But no one here would think of lending them money which would be used for armaments directed against England, and he regarded it as certain that all the efforts by Witte and his local agents in the city would remain unsuccessful.

If I can rely on other sources in the city, it seems doubtful whether this prophecy by Rothschild will turn out to be correct; it is partly attributable to the anti-Russian feeling of his family because of the Jewish question. I have been told on the contrary that a number of other big city houses with whom the Russian agents are negotiating are not disinclined to float a Russian loan, if need be without the Rothschilds. As regards Chamberlain, he talked to Eckardstein yesterday as if only very small importance was to be attached to the agreement with Russia.

[1] Bülow: 'Yes'.  [2] Bülow: '*Tout est là*'.  [3] Bülow: 'No'.

In this connection I would add that when Lord Salisbury accidentally met Rothschild, he spoke to him along similar lines, emphasizing that too great importance should not be attached to this agreement.

I would like to repeat that as far as I am concerned, the main significance of the agreement for us does not lie in the rapprochement between England and Russia, which strikes me as temporary and insecure, but in the fact that, as Salisbury himself had to admit to me, the theory of the 'open door' has in reality been set aside and abandoned.[1] We must take the consequences of this fact into account, for they must soon become obvious and as far as the human eye can see will now lead everyone, England included, to plan the greatest possible extension and strengthening of their spheres of interest in China. It would lead too far to take into consideration now all the possibilities to which this could give rise, also as regards future Anglo-Russian relations, and I therefore confine myself to expressing the hope that we shall get our fair share when the distribution takes place.

Through my telegram you already know of Chamberlain's strange communication via Eckardstein—it was naturally meant for me. Whether it is to be regarded as nothing more than an outbreak of rage because we have dared for once to oppose English ambitions and interests, or, as Eckardstein believes, as a means to improve relations, I cannot determine as yet. That remains to be seen. Yet it certainly is remarkable that Salisbury, who clearly had received the relevant reports from Brussels[2] two days ago and probably informed the Cabinet at the meeting in the morning, not only didn't mention them to me at all, but proved more talkative and willing to go into details during our conversation than normally. It is of course not impossible that our delegate (it is supposed to be Göhring)[3] made careless remarks to colleagues about deliberate antagonism towards England, and no doubt you will investigate this and rectify it if necessary. If the matter is brought to my attention again here, I shall stick to the view—I presume I have the State Secretary's approval for this[4]—that there can be no question of deliberate antagonism on principle, and that our representative's only task is to defend our material interest as we see it, without consideration for other matters.

And now farewell, dear friend. This letter, which Eckardstein was supposed to take with him to-day, the 5th, will unfortunately be delayed, for due to family reasons he had to postpone his departure till to-morrow. He says he is going to Berlin to see whether he can get into the Reichstag. I would be grateful if the State Secretary and you were to receive him, so that he could give you some information on conditions and personalities here, which he knows well because of his own and Maple's[5] connections. Incidentally I might say that I have no intention, as you

---

[1] Bülow: 'Quite correct'.　　　　　　　　[2] See enclosure II.

[3] Delegate to the International Africa Alcohol Conference in Brussels, 1899.

[4] Bülow: 'Certainly'.

[5] Eckardstein had married the daughter of Sir John Blundell Maple, a leading English industrialist.

seem to think, of pushing him, personally, into the foreground. I don't even think that he has ambitious plans for a career. But as his intimate standing with Chamberlain, Rhodes, Cameron[1] and many others shows, he is decidedly useful to us here, both in the collection of information and also occasionally in order to establish connections and exercise influence behind the scenes. This is very important here, and quite objectively I would regard it as unjustifiable if we did not make use of this possibility for our purposes. If in the end he were to receive some recompense, a decoration or something else, this would be no more than fair, and I couldn't look on it as a disaster.

With best regards

Yours as ever
PHatzfeldt.

P.S. I am enclosing at the last minute a copy of the letter which Eckard-stein sent to Chamberlain to-day.[2] I would be very grateful for a copy of my last long letter to you.[3]

ENCLOSURE I

Joseph Chamberlain to Hermann von Eckardstein[4]

Private

Colonial Office, 3 May 1899

My dear Baron Eckardstein,

Would it be possible for you to see me at the House of Commons to-morrow at any time between 4.30 p.m. and 6.30 p.m. ?

A serious matter has arisen which is illustrative of the difficulties connected with Anglo-German relations and which I should like to submit to you. It is not a question to be treated formally and therefore I do not ask to see Count Hatzfeldt although I have no objection to any-thing I say being reported to him if you think desirable.

Pray forgive me for troubling you, it is only because I know you share my interest in the establishment of good relations between our two countries,—and also my contempt for the 'tracasseries' which some people are always anxious to encourage.

My general principle is—let us agree after full discussion—and if we can—on great questions involving large interests. If we can't agree let

---

[1] Sir Ewen Cameron. Director of the English Hongkong-Shanghai Bank.

[2] See enclosure II.

[3] Bülow commented at the end of this letter: 'For numerous reasons (feeling of H.M., German public opinion, German dogmatism and sentimentality) the further development of the Samoa affair will prove decisive for future relations between Germany and England for many years to come.

'If the English bully and outvote us, any co-operation with England will be out of the question in the forseeable future and *nolens volens—par la nature des choses*—we shall have to draw closer to Russia and even to France.

'If England shows herself prepared for a fair settlement of the Samoa affair, we will be able to pursue our present independent policy *du juste milieu*.

'If the English are sufficiently intelligent to make concessions to us either in Samoa or in return for it, they would thereby render true co-operation with and support for England possible for the future.' (See Bülow's instruction to Hatzfeldt of 6 May, *Grosse Politik*, vol. XIVii, no. 4072, pp. 613–14.)

[4] In English in the original.

us fight—loyally but to the best of our abilities—but for Heaven's sake do not let us quarrel like two old women over petty questions which are not worth 'a twopenny down' for either of us.

Yours very truly
J. Chamberlain.

ENCLOSURE II

Hermann von Eckardstein to Joseph Chamberlain[1]

London, 5 May 1899

Dear Mr Chamberlain,

I have seen Count Hatzfeldt with reference to our conversation of yesterday. Count Hatzfeldt does not think for a moment, that Mr Göhring has been instructed by the German Government to obstruct the English proposal at the Brussel's Liquor Conference simply in order to annoy England. On the contrary he is perfectly convinced that Mr Göhring has been instructed to act at the Conference only according to real German interests as they are understood to be in Germany.

Count Hatzfeldt is now as before desirous of maintaining good relations between the two countries, based of course on real reciprocity.

Count Hatzfeldt says he is no friend at all of pin-pricks and will if you wish be glad to discuss at any time matters with you openly and loyally.

I am leaving for Berlin to-morrow morning and hope to be back in a week's time.

With kind regards etc.
Eckardstein.

681.   Paul von Hatzfeldt to Holstein[2]

TELEGRAM

London, 7 June 1899

Private

To-day, after having first of all expressed his satisfaction at the suspension of the Consuls by the Samoa-Commission, Salisbury made use of our strictly confidential conversation to tell me that His Majesty the Kaiser had complained of him, Lord Salisbury, in several letters to the Queen, and had described him as an inveterate opponent,[3] so much so that he had to justify himself to the Queen.[4] His Majesty had similarly expressed himself to the Duke of Connaught a short time ago, and the latter had spread this about everywhere. Lord Salisbury then went on to say that he regretted most deeply that His Majesty should hold this opinion, which he believed to be unjustified, and that he was quite incapable of understanding how he could have given rise to it; he was

---

[1] In English n the original.        [2] From the London Embassy files.

[3] See *Grosse Politik*, vol. XIVii, no. 4074, pp. 615–19.

[4] *Grosse Politik*, vol. XIVii, no. 4076, enclosure, pp. 621–3. By a personal telegram of 21 June Hatzfeldt informed Holstein: 'Lord Salisbury told me to-day he was afraid that the Queen's latest letter would not create a pleasant impression. When pressed he added in strict confidence that in it the Queen had taken the attack on her Prime Minister as being contrary to her dignity and had treated it as such.' (From the London Embassy files.)

certainly not an inveterate opponent and could assure us that no sort of ill-will had ever guided or influenced his political attitude towards us. When I countered by saying that English behaviour towards us in Samoa had surely not been friendly, and that he therefore should not be surprised if His Majesty and public opinion in Germany as well had attributed this to the unfriendly intentions of the leading statesmen. Lord Salisbury replied that it was unjust to saddle him with responsibility for all the actions taken by British officials in Samoa. He had by no means always approved of these or desired them, but had been unable to prevent them because of the distance and lack of telegraphic communication. And surely he had proved his desire to draw closer to us once again by accepting the unanimity rule in spite of opposition by Chamberlain and others.[1] The English in Samoa and people here were furious with him on that count. I answered that to our way of thinking it was difficult to understand how the English officials in Samoa had been left without instructions in the past, thus enabling them to work against us. And in any case Samoa was not everything and I was forced to remind him that we had simultaneously met here with definite unwillingness to reach an understanding with us on other questions lying further in the future. This had been bound to strengthen the impression that we were faced with a definite decision to turn away from us. When he asked me what I was referring to, as he couldn't remember, I replied that I would like to cite Morocco, merely as an example and naturally not on instructions.[2] He answered that this was a question which wasn't ripe yet and for that reason it would be difficult [to conclude] an *agreement* on it. Moreover if an understanding had been reached, we might possibly have demanded *common action forthwith* to speed the matter, and this would not be regarded as advisable here. I said that this view was quite wrong, for at the time I had not envisaged a formal treaty nor speedy action but merely a confidential understanding concerning division and possible mutual support in such a case. Lord Salisbury seemed to be struck by this and remarked that under these circumstances the question might possibly be taken up. I advised him on leaving to think it over again seriously, and he agreed to do this.

Make use of this if you wish. I have the impression that people here are getting softer.

PH.

682.   Paul von Hatzfeldt to Holstein

London, 13 June 1899

Dear friend,

Many thanks for your last letter and the preceding ones, which I

[1] Salisbury had agreed to the German proposal for a tripartite commission to investigate rival claims in Samoa only on condition that differences of opinion be settled by majority vote. (*Grosse Politik*, vol. XIVii, no. 4055, p. 594.) Salisbury finally agreed to the unanimity rule only after Germany had exerted considerable pressure. (See Bülow's telegram to Hatzfeldt of 13 April 1899, *Grosse Politik*, vol. XIVii, no. 4066, pp. 605–6.)

[2] See Hatzfeldt's letter to Bülow of 8 February 1899. (*Grosse Politik*, vol. XVII, no. 5152, pp. 295–6.)

could not answer before now due to the lack of opportunity for safe transmission.

First of all let me take up one point in your last letter which seems to me to be of extraordinary importance. You say that Morocco can wait, Samoa can not, particularly the question of war reparations.[1] Against this I would like to make the point that the inclination, lately apparent and possibly transitory, to negotiate on Morocco is, I feel, largely due to the desire to make concessions on *one* problem, because they believe themselves unable to do all that we wish on the *other* one. There is no way of telling how long this inclination will last, and I would therefore regret deeply if I were not in a position to seize the next opportunity which might occur and say: 'This is what I must have, now tell me your demands and let us see if we can't square the two.' If instead of that we want to make the one dependent on the other, that is, to throw Morocco and Samoa together and to discuss Morocco only after England has agreed to compensation for the Germans, I am firmly convinced that we would run the greatest risk of not getting either. I am sure that is so because to the best of my judgment and after mature reflection I don't see the slightest chance that people here will agree voluntarily to recognize England's *obligation* to compensate the Germans in Samoa unless threatened by concrete and immediate dangers. I don't think I need assure you that I have not left anything untried, neither attempts at persuasion nor hidden threats, to win over Salisbury to this course, but I have met such unyielding resistance that I am unable to entertain any illusions as to the hoplessness of the matter. If his only motive were ill-will, it might be possible to overcome it, but what is much worse and cannot be dealt with is his fear that if he were to recognize the obligation, public opinion as well as a large number of his colleagues would not support him. His prestige in his own party as the maker of foreign policy is by now badly shaken, and I believe that he would sooner risk a serious quarrel with us on this question than run the danger of accepting an obligation which would also involve official admittance of the fact that England's position towards the disturbances in Samoa had been wrong all along, and of having to say *pater peccavi* now. It was clearly for this reason that he suggested arbitration, which makes it possible for him to risk being condemned to pay compensation without people here being able to reproach him with a shameful retreat in the face of Germany.

In saying this I don't want to imply that it would under all circumstances be wrong for us to stick to our demands if His Majesty regards this as advisable in view of the feeling in Germany. In that case I would be prepared at any time to fight through our demands with utter ruthlessness and determination. But it is my inescapable duty not to deceive my own Government about the fact that in the present situation, i.e. without some overwhelming pressure in the background, the demand is a hopeless one, which no arguments, whatever they may be, will make

[1] For the damage inflicted on German property in Samoa by Anglo-American military action during the early months of 1899.

acceptable here. Thus all you have to do is to order me in the instruction you promised[1] to pose a categoric demand and to fight it through, and Bülow as well as you can be quite certain that this will be done with the ruthless energy of which I believe I have given proof on various occasions during my official career. In this connection I would, however, like to draw attention to the fact that such a step would not really harmonize with the line I was instructed to adhere to in dispatch no. K55,[1] and I would especially ask you to read my report of to-day's date[1] on that subject.

In any case I see no reason why we should not in the meantime use an opportunity, if one presents itself, to advance the Moroccan question and possibly reach a provisional understanding about it. Should Salisbury again show himself inclined to follow me on this path, we could then go a step further and sound out England's attitude towards German action in Muscat (consulate, coaling station) etc. Already the other day, when he asked me on what subjects an understanding might be reached, I was tempted to bring this up, but finally decided it would be more prudent to make a start with Morocco, which is less tricky.

You know from a telegram of mine[2] that Salisbury is depressed, partly because of his wife's health, partly also for other reasons. His depression is being generally noticed, and it may now be due primarily to the worries and difficulties which the Transvaal question occasions him and to the resultant differences of opinion with the quarrelsome Chamberlain. Added to this, in my opinion, must be his realization that many of his supporters are dissatisfied with his [lack of] success and would be easily consoled if he were to disappear from the scene to-morrow. Moreover his health leaves quite a lot to be desired and it does not seem impossible that he should collapse one of these days. It is hard to say who would succeed him; certainly not Chamberlain, rather Balfour, perhaps under the nominal Premiership of someone else, as for example the completely senile Devonshire.[3] That would not be the worst solution for us by any means.

Incidentally, His Majesty's letters to the Queen about Salisbury[4] did make some impression on the latter. He was annoyed, there is no doubt about that, but on further reflection he has realized that it would be better to show a bit more amiability, also because of the Queen. At first, in his anger, he said to me: 'I don't know what they want of me, *je ne l'aime pas et je ne le déteste pas'*. I took the occasion to tell him off properly, also because of his own personal behaviour towards the Kaiser. We also talked again about Cowes where he had allowed the Kaiser to wait for two hours, and I proved to him that it had been this lack of consideration which had brought about the estrangement.[5] Relations had been excellent prior to that. He did not deny this but brought up

---

[1] Not found.
[2] Hatzfeldt's telegram to Bülow of 9 June 1899. (From the London Embassy files.)
[3] Lord President of the Privy Council.
[4] See *Grosse Politik*, vol. XIVii, no. 4074, pp. 615–19.
[5] See Kiderlen's letter to Holstein of 7 August 1895.

again the old excuses for his failure to put in an appearance on that occasion. He said in particular that he had only received an oral message from a footman in Osborne asking him to come aboard the *Hohenzollern*, and had been unable to assume that His Majesty should have wished to invite *him* in *this* way. I replied that it wasn't our fault if the sole means of communication with Osborne consisted of one telephone installed in the billiard room and attended, as I knew from experience, by a footman. He certainly did not have the least justification for the belief that His Majesty's suite, which had been instructed to transmit the invitation, had intended to show a lack of the respect due to him by using the telephone.

I expect to see Goschen in the next few days, but do not think that anything much will come of the conversation. I know him well and am certain in advance that he will ask a lot of questions, and apart from that will listen and avoid any compromising statements.

My conversation with Walter[1] in the near future will perhaps prove more interesting and I shall write a report on it.

Incidentally, dear friend, as always your wishes are my commands, and I would like to report obediently that I shall give the first fairly large luncheon party, for Englishmen and diplomats, next week after Ascot, and will continue to do so regularly.

I am sorry for poor Toni,[2] if only because he has gone soft in the head. That can happen to anyone, and I am happy to add in all modesty that I have not yet discovered any symptoms in myself, though otherwise my health leaves much to be desired. Ah well, we are getting older and there is nothing to be done about *'des ans l'irréparable outrage.'* But, as Brandenburg[3] once told me many years ago, a general always makes the best representative abroad, and in view of that I should neither be surprised nor complain if I suffered the same fate as poor Toni, although I achieved a hardly to be hoped for success only last year,[4] have on the whole had some success during my life-time, and am in good shape mentally. For the sake of the Service I could then only wish for a successor here who would know conditions here as well as I do, be equally good at dealing with the people here, and execute Herr von Bülow's intentions and yours as conscientiously as I believe I have done.

With best regards,
Yours as ever,
PHatzfeldt [...]

683.   Phillip Zorn to Holstein

Scheveningen, 13 June 1899

Your Excellency,

Your Excellency gave me permission to write privately should I

---

[1] Arthur Frazer Walter. Chief Proprietor of *The Times*. No report on such a conversation was found in the Foreign Ministry files.

[2] The reference is presumably to Anton von Saurma, who was replaced as Ambassador in Rome by Karl von Wedel in October 1899.

[3] Probably Friedrich Wilhelm, Count Brandenburg, bastard son of King Friedrich Wilhelm II of Prussia. Minister-President of Prussia, 1848–50.

[4] The agreement on the Portuguese Colonies.

believe this to be necessary, and I am making use of this gracious permission to-day, for I do not know whether the responsibility I am bearing at this moment is not too heavy for a poor professor, who is neither diplomat nor statesman. [...]

The situation in the arbitration question has now become tricky and delicate.[1] It was not surprising that the small [Powers] took up this question with wild enthusiasm and wanted nothing more than to set up a compulsory permanent World Court. The original Russian proposal[2] was reasonable enough, but Sir Julian Pauncefote's[3] intervention and the pressure of the small [Powers] also drove the Russians further.[4] It was in fact impossible to oppose this trend successfully. Neither Austria nor France were prepared to do so. Under these circumstances my aim was to demand and defend such clauses and palliatives as were *attainable*, while completely reserving every *decision* for my Government.

In the sub-committee, at whose meetings von Staal, Count Nigra, Sir Julian Pauncefote, and Bourgeois[5] participated, *soi-disant* compulsory arbitration for certain non-political matters, and a *soi-disant* permanent tribunal were decided on.[6] But the clauses are drawn up in such loose and general terms that I can see no danger. In any case all the decisions taken here by us are purely theoretical, for the home Governments will examine everything very closely before taking the final decisions. The arbitration agreement will surely suffer the same fate as the Brussels Declaration of 1874;[7] twenty-five years later it has still not been ratified.

But public opinion is excited about this issue at this moment; big words are used to discuss 'the big idea'. I don't know to what extent the representatives of the Great Powers believe that something practical will come of it. As for me, the object is not yet in sight. If, with all due respect, I might say so: To me it seems like a political toy, not to be taken seriously. The astonished remark by one Englishman: '*He takes it serious* [sic]!' has become a household word.

But if a toy is suddenly taken from a child or broken, the child may in turn break a mirror or a window; that is something I am frequently

[1] The discussions concerning an International Court of Arbitration. It was proposed to make arbitration compulsory for certain international disputes of minor importance. (See *Conférence Internationale de la Paix* (La Haye, 1899, part 4.)

[2] *Conférence Internationale de la Paix*, part 4, pp. 201–16. See also *Grosse Politik*, vol. XV p. 233, note *.

[3] British Ambassador in Washington, 1883–1902; senior British delegate at the First Hague Peace Conference. Pauncefote proposed the setting up of a permanent Tribunal of International Arbitration. (*Conférence Internationale de la Paix*, part 4, pp. 4; 217–20.)

[4] For Russia's amplification of the Pauncefote proposal, see *Conférence Internationale de la Paix*, part 4, pp. 221–3; *Grosse Politik*, vol. XV, pp. 243, note *.

[5] Léon Bourgeois, French Minister-President, 1895–6; Foreign Minister in the Sarrien Cabinet, 1906; senior delegate at the First and Second Hague Peace Conferences.

[6] *Conférence Internationale de la Paix*, part 4, pp. 128–31. The final resolution of the conference is printed in part 1, pp. 224–34.

[7] Following a Russian proposal, an International Conference of all the European States met in Brussels, 27 July–28 August 1874, to discuss the problem of international law in time of war. The Conference drew up a 'Draft for an International Declaration concerning the laws and customs of war' which was submitted to all Governments for further consideration.

thinking of now. In all conscience I cannot take either 'obligatory' arbitration or the 'permanent' tribunal seriously.

But the mood of the Russian Tsar and the mood of the nations as a whole do deserve *close* attention. In my opinion these should not be spoiled by breaking the favourite toy of the moment. As of now my personal position in the committee is a very pleasant one. I am treated most courteously, particularly by Bourgeois and Martens.[1] As yet the mood has not been spoiled, and I would feel it to be a matter of the gravest importance if this were to happen. Only yesterday evening Martens explained to me how very interested the Tsar was in this particular question, that on the other hand it was a very long way from our deliberations to a realization in practice. He earnestly desired that *no* great differences in our views should become apparent. Article 10—cases falling under so-called 'obligatory' arbitration—is to be debated in second reading by the committee on Friday. If in accordance with my instructions[2] I must again propose the deletion of the complete article, I shall be isolated when the vote is taken. Neither Count Welsersheimb nor Count Nigra will support me—and the atmosphere will deteriorate considerably, all the more since these matters always reach the public at once, usually by way of the English Press.

I submit these considerations in all obedience to Your Excellency's kind consideration and would be grateful if any statements by us could be postponed till the committee or possibly even the plenary assembly meet.

Trusting Your Excellency will permit the expression of my deep respect, I remain

Your Excellency's most obedient,

Zorn.

## 684. Georg zu Münster to Holstein

Scheveningen, 14 June 1899

My dear Herr von Holstein,

[...] On the whole, in spite of this Conference, international law will remain what it was. The Russian influence will lose more than it gains, and that is the good thing about it. Our influence will win out after all. Disarmament and all regulations in regard to equipment etc. will be turned down; the Russian case for them is badly put. In private conversation they admit themselves that the military part of Muraviev's famous programme[3] was silly, a tilting at windmills.

The Red Cross is only being discussed with reference to the application of its rules at sea. The relevant decisions are sensible, and we shall be able to accept them.

The real difficulty lies in the question whether the Court of Arbitration should be permanent or not.

[1] Official of the Russian Foreign Ministry; delegate at the First Hague Peace Conference.
[2] See *Grosse Politik*, vol. XV, no. 4302, pp. 273–4; p. 278, note *.
[3] Muraviev's circular of 11 January 1899.

On this question nearly all the delegates fail to see the wood for the trees. If the Conference does not result in some sort of Court Arbitration, they will consider themselves dishonoured in the eyes of public opinion. They regard this question as the sheet-anchor, which can keep the sinking Conference afloat. Being sensible, we are pretty well isolated (Rumania apart). We shall soon be in a position where we shall have to accept some utterly worthless compromise proposal or else be looked upon as the rock on which the good ship 'Conference' foundered.

At first sight the permanent Court of Arbitration, as suggested by the English and accepted by the Russians (if not in part inspired by them behind the scenes), is harmless enough, for each state can utilize the Court or not, use it or not as it pleases. On the other hand a certain danger does lie in the existence of such an institution which is nothing but will always want to become something. Only men of the third or fourth rank will appear on the list [of judges] and these *world* arbitrators will do damage. It will not be a completely harmless toy.

Zorn, who was sent here because of the arbitration question, has worked very zealously, wants to achieve some sort of result, and is beside himself because he could not be given a free hand.

The question for us will be simple : do we accept this bad Court of Arbitration out of consideration for Russia and public opinion artificially roused by her, and later refuse to ratify the Conference decisions; or do we stick to a completely negative attitude?

I can hardly wait to learn what the wise men in Berlin are deciding ? ! !
[...]

> In friendship
> Yours as ever
> Münster

### 685.   Georg zu Münster to Holstein

Scheveningen, 16 June [1899]

My dear Herr von Holstein,

In politics one should not break windows unless this is *absolutely* necessary. The statement which was sent to me yesterday would have been an example of doing so unnecessarily.[1] Surely we do not want to take responsibility needlessly for the failure of the Conference or to spoil our relations with the other Powers, but on the other hand we do not want to allow our independence as a powerful nation to be limited.
[...]

Please make use of all your influence to ensure that we don't force matters too soon, and that we try to make arbitration—which has made all the delegations go quite mad—definitely optional and thereby less harmful. First of all the problem should be cast in a form which would in

---

[1] By a telegram of 15 June, drafted by Holstein, Bülow had instructed Münster to make a statement refusing a permanent Court of Arbitration. (*Grosse Politik*, vol. XV, no. 4308, pp. 281–3.)

the last resort be acceptable to us. In my opinion that involved that *no one* can be forced to submit a question to the Court of Arbitration. The permanent office can then be turned into [...][1] by the delegate here.

In friendship as ever

Münster [...]

### 685a.   Holstein to Paul von Metternich[2]

Berlin, 22 June, 1899

Dear Metternich,

The purpose of this is to bid you farewell. My resignation petition has just been sent in. I asked to be excused from drafting a report to His Majesty recommending that he agree to a loose and indefinite establishment of the permanent arbitration commission. I expressed the view, in complete agreement with the Legal Division, that this new institution, even in loose and qualified form, is not without danger, because it will gradually grow in scope and significance like a Heligoland stage. Bülow used to share my view, but he has suddenly been taken in by Münster. The latter, who finds it uncomfortable to swim against the current, suddenly sent Zorn here to present the view that if we did not agree to the permanent institution—whether it is to be a tribunal or a board makes little difference—the Conference would break up and Germany would be exposed to serious complications. Münster telegraphed and wrote in this sense even before Zorn got here in order to prepare the way for him. Zorn nevertheless had to admit in the conference we had with him that there was no possibility of a break-up of the Peace Conference, but that at most the work of Commission III for arbitration might come to a halt. As for the complications threatened by Münster, I ask myself in vain where they could come from. Read the reports from Teheran which you must have received yesterday or today, and then ask yourself if it is conceivable that Russia and England, together or individually, will clash with Germany because she fails to participate right from the beginning in the permanent arbitration commission, but wishes instead to reserve her participation. Hellewig and Frantzius[3] by the way have put in writing their technical objections to the permanent arbitration commission, and since this memorandum will probably be enclosed with the report to the Kaiser, which is now to be drawn up by Klehmet, I will not go into it further. The decision of the Kaiser will have no effect on my going or staying in office. I intend to leave in any case because I am tired of constant fighting. You know what sort of existence I have led for years. In former times one also had annoyances, but one at least knew one had the Kaiser's confidence. When the *Kladderadatsch* campaign was at its height, old Schlözer once said to somebody: 'All that won't do any good; even if Caprivi is done

---

[1] Words illegible.

[2] From the Metternich Papers. The first part of this letter was dictated by Holstein presumably to *Hofrat* Willisch (see below, no. 694a).

[3] Officials in the Legal Division in the German Foreign Ministry.

in you won't get rid of Holstein, his position with the Kaiser is firm as a rock.' This rock may well have been a stumbling block, and various people have gotten together to remove it. Among these I do not reckon Philipp Eulenburg. I know that he has shown the Kaiser letters of mine that were written in a harsh tone. But he was justified in doing so because I had repeatedly empowered him in writing and orally to submit to the Kaiser everything that came from me that in his opinion might be useful, *without* considering whether it would injure me. So Eulenburg was behaving correctly. On the other hand I know by intimation that someone I will not name has unloaded on me almost everything for which *he* has been blamed, according to the tried and true principle that baggage is lightest when you let other people carry it.

I have mentioned these past events because they will explain to you why I am today bringing my official life to a close for a relatively insignificant reason. When I found out two years ago that the Kaiser had turned against me, I nevertheless remained in the service because Bülow urgently requested me to do so and because I myself believed that I was still useful to the Kaiser and the Reich. But there is not much usefulness left if the opinions of an irresponsible and egotistical old boy like Münster are preferred to mine. In addition I can see the question of the German-Russian Straits Convention looming up behind the Conference question. Osten-Sacken, who was in Vienna to attend a Russian wedding, told Eulenburg there that the danger of an understanding between Russia and England was imminent if Germany did not conclude the treaty with Russia over the Straits. So there can be no doubt that Osten-Sacken will constantly revert to the subject.

The Russians need a *written* statement that our Kaiser will give them a free hand with the Straits. With this piece of paper they would be able to destroy in five minutes the entire influence the Kaiser now has on the Sultan and in the Moslem world. That is one purpose. The other is that by hinting at this treaty they may intimidate England and that *then* they may actually succeed in getting England to make concessions to them in Persia, i.e. on the south coast, which England doesn't think of doing today. In that respect the above-mentioned reports from Rex[1] are very interesting because they show the cat and dog relationship of the English and Russians in Persia. So long as the English believe that we we will remain neutral in a conflict between England and Russia, they will show us a little consideration; least of all perhaps Salisbury, who all his life—already when I came to London in 1864—had the reputation of a despicable character. But Salisbury's health and also his political position are now on the decline, and in the not too distant future he will be replaced by younger elements. Balfour is not at all anti-German and Curzon, the Vice-King of India, is even less so. His official newspaper, *The Times* of India, makes a big distinction between Russia and France on the one hand and Germany on the other; the first two had but the one idea to drive the English out of India, whereas the German government

---

[1] German Minister in Teheran, 1898–1906; in Peking, 1906–11.

had no intention of doing so, on the contrary Germany was *in favour of* maintaining English control of India. Therefore Germany could also be allowed to draw closer to the Indian border than either of the other two.

So long as Salisbury is at the helm the opinion of Curzon will hardly come to the fore, but Salisbury's time is almost up. We would provide grist for his mill, however, if he were in a position to show that Germany had a secret treaty with Russia. Then there would be no more *tolerari posse* for German colonial acquisitions in Morocco or anywhere else, because this would provide the excuse to oppose us and give us the cold shoulder everywhere.

Although I know that you think very much as I do, I wanted to conclude by bringing up this point again. I would consider our giving in on this matter far more dangerous than the question of the permanent arbitration commission. As for myself, however, I am weary of strife because I know that whatever else may come as a result of these struggles there will certainly be some unpleasantness for me.[1]

This letter, my dear Metternich, is intended exclusively for *you*. If it has some influence here and there on *your* views, I will be pleased. Any communication of the letter to anyone else, however, would be regarded by me as a *breach of confidence*. I am, therefore, also sending the letter off half a day after the report for the Kaiser so that the decision of His Majesty will already have been made when it arrives. Should the dissenting opinion of the Legal Division not be included—I don't know— may I ask you *not* to telegraph or write to Berlin for it. I am tired of playing providence in matters that don't concern me, or rather things for which I at least am not responsible. Doing so has brought me all the unpleasantness I have had in life, and I have never had any thanks for it.

With best wishes and with old regard

Yours,
Holstein

It has done me good to write myself out.

I motivated my resignation solely on the basis of my eyes, which unfortunately is not altogether untrue. Bülow of course will not want to let me go because I am a convenient old work horse.

I forgot one thing more. Ambassador Wedel told me a few days ago: 'Apparently the Kaiser is considering sending Metternich to London when Hatzfeldt is completely finished. Metternich to be sure is on cat and dog terms with the Prince of Wales. Whether that is a recommendation for the position might be doubted.'

Wedel is an intimate friend of Herbert Bismarck. You probably know that he and also his wife are burning for the London post. The insinuation about the Prince of Wales may well come from that quarter. Could you not get on better terms with the Prince of Wales again? Hatzfeldt after all will not be removed tomorrow, so you have ample time. The Prince too will perhaps be quite happy to let bygones be bygones. Of course I don't know what happened between you.

---

[1] After this point the letter is in Holstein's hand.

### 686.  Bernhard von Bülow to Holstein

22 June 1899

Dear friend,

Two years ago to-day, on 22 June, I arrived in Berlin much against my will with a heavy heart. When at that time I finally decided to answer the call I had received, I did so in the certain expectation that I would not lack your support. Your withdrawal of the same makes my set task more difficult, and I cannot simply accept this.[1] No one knows better than I how dutifully and successfully you have stood by my side in spite of the poor state of your health. I am firmly convinced that successful conduct of our foreign policy in the future would be impossible without you, and I therefore refuse to forward your resignation.

Faithfully yours as ever

Bern. Bülow

### 687.  Holstein to Bernhard von Bülow
Draft

Berlin, 23 June 1899

Dear Bülow,

Your objection to the forwarding of my resignation request, caused I feel by friendly sentiments, only confirms the thoughts I have repeatedly expressed to you. Therefore you will understand my wishing to put an end to an undignified situation. If you should not forward my request, I shall have to submit it to the Chancellor to-morrow, and then it might conceivably be said that we have had a row. I think that should be prevented. So let fate run its course.

Your sincerely devoted

Holstein

### 688.  Holstein to Chlodwig zu Hohenlohe[2]
Draft

B[erlin], 24 June 1899

I regret that I must request Your Highness to accept my resignation, as the state of my one good eye requires attention. I have chosen the present time for my request, as the changes made necessary by my leaving can be considered without any need for hurry during the summer holiday period.

Holstein.
*Wirklicher Geheimer Rat*

### 689.  Holstein to Bernhard von Bülow
Draft

B[erlin], 24 June 1899

Dear Bülow,

I have heard that you have had a long conversation with the Chancellor,

[1] Holstein had handed in his resignation because he refused to draft a report to the Kaiser (*Grosse Politik*, vol. XV, no. 4320, pp. 300–6) recommending acceptance of a permanent Court of Arbitration. (See Rogge, *Friedrich von Holstein*, pp. 194–5.)

[2] From the Foreign Ministry files.

and the thought obtrudes itself that the question of my resignation is to be settled over my head, and that I am to be calmed down again, for example by a decoration. That is not the point, dear friend. Under these circumstances I will tell you what I didn't tell the Chancellor and would have preferred not to tell you either, namely that after my observations during the past weeks—since the Wiesbaden trip[1]—I am no longer certain that you would stand firm in a difficult situation. A plan is agreed, its execution is begun, but as counter-pressure gradually becomes noticeable you suddenly show a tendency to yield—I would call it political seasickness. That is what happened on the arbitration question, where we yielded at the precise moment when the position we had originally adopted was being understood and approved in the most varied quarters.[2] Probably this will also in the end happen in the Straits question, which as I gathered from a remark made by Sacken yesterday is to be pursued.[3]

Your tendency to yield is particularly noticeable where Russia is concerned, actually only there. I attribute this to an influence which, without concern for the development of the world, continues to work with old methods.[4] Though I do not believe all the boasts, I think that this influence undoubtedly exists, and I therefore vacate the field as there is no possibility of agreement, even on questions of fact. I regard the return to the maxims of pre-Kiaochow days as much out of the question as a return to the muzzle-loader. But, of course, a different opinion may be held. In a team of horses the pull exerted by any one horse is less important than the fact that the whole team should pull together. I have recently convinced myself that in our team this pulling together is no longer as it should be. That is the reason why I want to be taken out of harness. In place of me you could take Tschirschky[5] or Below;[6] they just occur to me. Both of them still remember the crack of

[1] On 18 May the Kaiser had toasted the Tsar in Wiesbaden and drunk to the success of the Conference which the Tsar had initiated.

[2] Actually there was considerable opposition to the German point of view. (See above, Münster's letter to Holstein of 16 June 1899, and Grosse Politik, vol. XV, nos. 4312–15, pp. 285–92.) Radolin telegraphed on 19 June : 'Now that the creation of a permanent Court of Arbitration is the main point under discussion at The Hague, and the particular attention of the Conference is focussed thereon, and now that the establishment of a permanent Court of Arbitration is generally regarded—also by Russia—as the only possible result of any value, it is quite clear to me that if this result is not achieved because of German opposition— irrespectively of whether it will prove harmful or not in the future—Russia will place the responsibility and the odium for the failure of the Conference on us alone.' (Grosse Politik, vol. XV, no. 4317, pp. 296–8.)

[3] See Grosse Politik, vol. XIVii, chapter XCV.

[4] Holstein presumably refers to the influence on Bülow of Herbert von Bismarck, whom Holstein had accused of pursuing a Russophile policy while in office.

[5] Heinrich von Tschirschky and Bögendorff. Temporarily employed in the Foreign Ministry, 1885–7; Secretary of Legation in Athens, 1888–90, in Bern 1890–2; First Secretary in the Embassy in Constantinople, 1893, in St Petersburg, 1894–1900; Minister in Luxembourg, 1900–2; several times Foreign Ministry representative in the Kaiser's retinue; State Secretary in the Foreign Ministry, 1906–7; Ambassador in Vienna, 1907–16.

[6] Paul von Below-Schlatau. Temporarily employed in the Foreign Ministry, 1888–90; First Secretary in the Embassy in Paris, 1897–9; Vortragender Rat in the Foreign Ministry, 1904–7.

the old whip, and will obey it from *metus reverentialis*, without asking themselves whether it may not be only an empty sound, a fairy-tale of long ago. On the other hand, were I to remain, I would fear that the present unimportant though unpleasant personal crisis would recur, and that the relapse would as always be more serious. For that reason, dear Bülow, it is right that we should separate *now*.

I am writing this without any bitterness. We *two* have done nothing to each other which could embitter. I only want to prevent future bitterness.

With best wishes for you and your task I remain as always

Your truly devoted<br>Holstein.

### 690.   Bernhard von Bülow to Holstein

Saturday evening, [24 June 1899]

Dear friend,

Don't torture me any longer. I *can*not reconcile it with my conscience, whether as a Government servant or a patriot, to let you go. That you should want to leave *me* in the lurch is not very nice of you; but you *must* not abandon the Ministry, policy-making, the nation.

There is the added point that I am firmly convinced that without your long-accustomed, painful, thankless, but so very useful and (you will interject, when I did not interfere with you) successful work, you will not be happy. And that too is something I do not want, because, quite apart from my admiration for your political genius, I love you much more as a human being than your stony scepticism will allow you to believe.

At least do give me, the Foreign Ministry, and the fatherland a period of grace, so that we may continue to try and preserve them from so heavy a blow as your resignation would be.

With best regards<br>Yours<br>B.

Your letter which I have just received[1] only strengthens my conviction. The premises from which you depart are completely unfounded, the conclusions you draw completely mistaken. After your return I shall be able to prove this to you with ease, even with my debating skill (which is inferior to yours). But it does hurt me that you should estimate both my political judgment and my political temperament so unfavourably, for I grew up in your school. Until now I imagined that in the Samoa Question as in the Kiaochow Question and other campaigns we fought together—and finally in my life as a whole—I did not show such obvious weakness.

---

[1] Of 24 June. See above.

## 691.   Paul von Metternich to Holstein

Kiel, 24 June 1899
H.M.Y. *Hohenzollern*

Dear Holstein,

Ever since yesterday evening I have been under the impression of your letter of 22 June, which I opened after a lengthy sail on the *Meteor*. In the bustle of Court life I did not find a moment's peace to write a few lines to you until this afternoon.

I remember very clearly the occasion on which we met for the first time and lunched together in a *bistro* opposite the *Palais Bourbon*. You were a Secretary of Embassy and my attention was devoted to anything rather than politics. The fact that in your zeal for the cause you honoured a young inexperienced man by a drawn-out political conversation made a lasting impression on me. When later on I entered the Foreign Ministry and you admitted me to your stimulating company on walks and at other times, you became my mentor, you introduced me to and enlightened me on the business of politics. My most pleasant memory of those days is the contact with you and Hatzfeldt. Since then our relations have always remained the same. In Brussels, London, Cairo, in your office in Berlin, your refreshing conversation, oral and written, has always been a sheer joy to me and a valuable guide, which in the many wastes of a diplomat's calling pointed the way to the bubbling springs of political wisdom. Also in my present position I shall feel in future the lack of your advice and your instruction as a personal loss. A number of events have brought us together again and again in the past, and I am grateful to you for the trust you have shown me in the most important questions. Your leaving makes me feel alone and I therefore needed this retrospect of what you have meant and mean in my political life.

But personal feelings and reflections must be secondary when I think of the cause we have both served, you in a big way and I in my little one, and at the loss which the absence of your experience and your skill involve. I am therefore still hoping that a compromise will be found and you will remain.

That you should have thought of me at such an important moment of your life, and not only with a few lines, has truly touched me. I regard your letter as a political testament and an invaluable treasure, and I shall treat and keep it accordingly.

Whatever the outcome of the present situation should be, whether I see you again as a private individual or whether I still shall have the pleasure of seeing you stay, I firmly expect that whatever happens you will let me know your address and that we shall still while away many an hour in conversation.

Yours as ever
Paul Metternich.

### 692.   Chlodwig zu Hohenlohe to Kaiser Wilhelm II[1]
Draft

Berlin, 26 June 1899

Your Imperial and Royal Majesty : Enclosed I submit most respectfully the resignation of *Wirklicher Geheimer Rat* von Holstein, *Vortragender Rat* in the Foreign Ministry.

I sincerely regret the loss of this experienced and meritorious official, but believe that I cannot fail to advocate acceptance of his request because this is motivated by a reference to severe illness. I must refrain from an application for the granting of an Imperial decoration to the above-named, for only a few months ago he was granted the title of *Wirklicher Geheimer Rat*[2]

In case Your Majesty should grant the request, I most respectfully submit the document of dismissal for *Wirklicher Geheimer Rat* von Holstein and the draft of the necessary order for signature by Your Majesty.

H[ohenlohe]

### 693.   Holstein to Bernhard von Bülow

B[erlin], 26 June 1899

Dear Bülow,

Many thanks for your kind letter.[3] You have the right to an explanation as to why I am nevertheless going through with my resignation. Two years ago I remained in the service despite the fact that I knew that my sovereign master was dissatisfied with me, because I could calm my conscience with the thought that I was needed to introduce you to the realm of affairs here, which was new to you. This cause of yesteryear would to-day be no more than a pretext. You are used to the work and well enough acquainted with the staff to find the men to do the work.

If I were to continue to cling to my position, I would simply be hanging on, and in my own view—which is a matter of considerable importance to me—I would no longer be a gentleman. Therefore don't be angry with me, dear friend—I can do no other.

Ever your truly devoted
Holstein.

### 694.   Holstein to Bernhard von Bülow
Draft

B[erlin], 30 June 1899

Dear Bülow,

I am filled with gratitude for your kind efforts and regret the difficulties I created for you.

My resignation was caused by my relationship to His Majesty and concern on political issues. In regard to the former His Majesty's

---

[1] From the Foreign Ministry files. (See Hohenlohe's letter to Bülow of 26 [June 1899]. Hohenlohe, *Denkwürdigkeiten der Reichskanzlerzeit*, pp. 509–10.)
[2] On 2 January 1899.          [3] Of 24 June. See above.

statements, obtained and transmitted by you, preserve the decencies.[1] But I am still not free from my concern on political issues. From the German point of view the acceptance of a permanent arbitration authority[2] is a world historical mistake, which will lead sooner or later to unfortunate consequences, probably quite soon. Why should this case remain the only instance of sudden retreat? There is no reason to assume this. Have you read the recent statement[3] by Colonel Schwarzhoff?[4] He talked of disarmament in the way in which we talked of the permanent arbitration authority before the policy change brought about by Münster. Naturally certain circles will again proclaim: 'Dashing soldier, feeble civilians.'

I am particularly sensitive to this reproach, perhaps all the more so because I have never been a soldier. I also believe that the public will most easily put up with a policy of occasional retreat if it is carried out by men like yourself and Richthofen, who have risked their necks for the fatherland.

Therefore it would be advisable for you to give Richthofen a free hand during the summer so that he can recruit—provisionally at first—those men whom he considers suitable for the Political Division. When you return you will soon see what suits you and what you might still want changed. In this way you would certainly avoid any internal friction; hence this is the best advice of which I am capable at the moment.

## 694a.   Holstein to Paul von Metternich[5]

Berlin, 30 June, 1899

Dear Metternich,

Nobody besides the absolutely discreet Willisch knows that I wrote to you, and nobody will find it out from me.

My resignation was occasioned by my relations with the Kaiser and by political reservations. In the one case the proprieties have now been preserved, but I still have the reservations. The concession of the permanent arbitration board is from the German standpoint a mistake of world-historical significance. You will feel this before you are ten years older, either through constant bickering over petty non-political matters which will be brought before the arbitration tribunal against our will, or perhaps by one single serious case. Nothing more can be done about this. The question is only whether one should expose oneself in future to the danger of such things happening again—that is, whether I should?

---

[1] In an official communication of 29 June 1899, Bülow informed Holstein that the Kaiser had not seen fit to accept Holstein's resignation. As confirmation of his benevolence, the Kaiser had instructed Bülow to present Holstein with a signed and inscribed portrait of His Majesty. (From the Foreign Ministry files. Printed in Friedrich von Trotha, *Fritz von Holstein als Mensch und Politiker* (Berlin, 1931), pp. 74–5.)

[2] Holstein's original wording reads: 'By accepting a permanent arbitration authority you have—from the German point of view [committed] . . .'

[3] Of 26 June. See *Grosse Politik*, vol. XV, no. 4259, pp. 200–3.

[4] Gross von Schwarzhoff. Special delegate to the First Hague Conference; Chief of Staff of the China Expeditionary Corps, 1900–1.

[5] From the Metternich Papers.

That is what I will think over during my coming lengthy leave of absence. I will also put my superiors *au courant* about my attitude.

Farewell. With old regard,

Holstein.

### 695.   Hugo von Radolin to Holstein

St Petersburg, 30 June 1899

My dear friend,

[...] Please read my report on Asia Minor, dispatched to-day.[1] I was somewhat surprised at the difference in the views concerning the treaty or agreement desired by Russia. Count M[uraviev] spoke in a manner somewhat reminiscent of Lobanov, represented the matter as if we were receiving a sort of favour, and emphasized simultaneously that if we did not want to meet Russian wishes, England would do so on still more favourable terms. No doubt he thought he would impress and intimidate me. I did not give him this pleasure, on the contrary I made it fairly apparent that we were in no way intimidated thereby. Let him try whether the English will simply allow the Russians to mess around on the Bosporus. The Russians will take care not to allow the English a free hand in the Persian Gulf and in eastern Asia Minor. 'We don't frighten easy' and in the end result we shall be able to carry through our affairs in Asia Minor, if need be without Russian support and permission. I naturally emphasized constantly that we were only pursuing economic interests on the Euphrates and in Asia Minor. The regrettable expedition of Major Morgen[2] does not square with this. As Count Muraviev emphasized, he has been very busy as instructor of the Turkish troops in Erzerum and as explorer. Mur. said, not unjustly : 'Your projects look suspicious when the military agent of your Embassy wanders about exploring our frontiers. For me this proves the opposite of what you assure me concerning the exclusively commercial nature of your interests.'[3] The Russians apparently regard this gentleman as a political intriguer and seem greatly incensed against him. At any rate his present appearance on the frontier does not facilitate my task of negotiating in a conciliatory manner concerning this matter of our operation in Asia Minor. Tsar N[icholas] is supposedly much annoyed at this incident and full of unmistakable distrust.[4] I only want to add that Mur.'s view of the treaty he wishes to conclude with us is quite different from that which Count Osten-Sacken seemingly holds,[5] for the latter represents it as advantageous to both parties and as a friendly bond. Mur. regards it

[1] Muraviev had told Radolin that the time had come for Russia and Germany to reach an understanding about their respective spheres of interest in the Turkish Empire in order to avoid possible conflict in the future. (*Grosse Politik*, vol. XIVii, no. 4022, pp. 549–54.)

[2] Military Attaché at the German Embassy in Constantinople.

[3] In French in the original.

[4] On 28 June Muraviev complained to Radolin that Morgen and another Prussian officer had inspected Turkish troops on the Russian-Turkish frontier near Erzerum, and had participated in exercises there just as if they were Turkish officers. (*Grosse Politik*, vol. XIVii, no. 4023, p. 555.)

[5] See *Grosse Politik*, vol. XIVii, nos. 4020–1, pp. 546–9.

as a simple business deal. The one who poses better conditions gets the bonus. I have heard from a reliable source that at the moment Mur. is in high favour with the Tsar and his position has gained much in esteem.

He will have to be reckoned with more than hitherto. I would not like to leave unmentioned that the Tsar in his full confidence shows him all letters and telegrams of political content. I believe I can say that he knows all the letters which our Most Gracious Master writes to Tsar Nicholas. *Avis au lecteur*.

I am pleased to tell you that my new Austrian colleague, Baron Aehrenthal, is seeking in a most pleasant way to establish close contact with me. I think that the departure of his predecessor, Liechtenstein, is no loss to us. During his stay the aim was to carry on negotiations between Vienna and St Petersburg without Berlin. I believe Vienna is now convinced, or at least feels, that this method will not lead to the goal, that no progress is to be made by it. The definite tendency is to lay the road to St Petersburg via Berlin. [...]

Your faithful

Hugo

### 696.    Paul von Hatzfeldt to Holstein[1]

TELEGRAM

London, 30 June 1899

Private.

Brought up Morocco in strictly confidential conversation to-day, but so far without noticeable success. Lord Salisbury made all sorts of objections to any agreement, particularly that England already had agreements with Spain and Italy concerning maintenance of the status quo in Morocco which would conflict with partition plan,[2] that the matter wasn't ripe yet, that the collapse might not come for a long time, finally, that he was not sufficiently prepared for my question and had not expected me to press for a definite answer already at this stage. After refuting his objections and stressing that we wished the status quo to be maintained and that I was prepared to advocate a statement by ourselves to this effect in an agreement, I made the point[3] that one should not wait till the catastrophe occurred before reaching agreement. Moreover I could give him no sort of guarantee that other Powers would not make acceptable proposals to us—as had happened in the Niger Question[4]— if England refused agreement with us, or delayed it. As for me, my one aim was improvement of our relations, compromised by Samoa, and I was discussing the matter on my own responsibility and without instructions. My personal view was that the basis of discussion between

---

[1] From the Foreign Ministry files.

[2] The First Mediterranean Agreement between England and Italy, 12 February 1887, adhered to by Austria 24 March 1887, and by Spain 4 May 1887, which provided for the maintenance of the status quo in the Mediterranean.

[3] Marginal comment by Bülow: 'Very good.'

[4] See *Grosse Politik*, vol. XIII, no. 3463–7, pp. 101–5.

us should be the possible partition of the Atlantic Coast (the North for England, the South for Germany). Regarding possible satisfaction for France, Spain, and Italy I expressed the sense of your letter[1] as my personal view. Lord Salisbury objected that Spain would demand greater advantages in Morocco, and that Italy too would surely not be satisfied with Tripoli. He did not go into any detail regarding French claims, only remarking that the fate of the oases was a matter of indifference to him. Altogether England's concern with Morocco did not involve the acquisition of territories, but of important places on the coast.

After long discussion Lord Salisbury finally said that he would have to reflect before giving a definite reply to so serious a question, and would also have to ascertain the opinion of the Intelligence Department as to whether it regarded an agreement concerning the Atlantic coast advisable as of now, and which places on the coast England would then have to claim.

My impression at the moment is that people here don't want territories, but certain places along the whole of the Atlantic coast, also further to the south, and that therefore they will not be satisfied with the northern half. This assumption is backed by the fact that Lord Salisbury to-day again made the well-known remark: 'You demand too high a price for your friendship.'

Should the State Secretary think it advisable, you may make use of the above.

Hatzfeldt.

697.   Hugo von Radolin to Holstein

St Petersburg, 1 July 1899

My dear friend,

Shortly before the departure of the courier, Director Rothstein, Witte's well-known adviser, was announced, and in the course of conversation he told me that Persia is trying to raise a loan in St Petersburg through the mediation of the International Bank. After Herr Rothstein had refused, the Persians took their request to Paris. Paris inquired here whether such a loan was advisable. After a negative reply the loan question is for the time being at a standstill. But Herr Rothstein is of the opinion that a loan for Persia will in the end be raised jointly in St Petersburg (Paris) and London, that agreement thereon will be reached by St Petersburg and London, and that Persia will pledge the customs duties on the Persian Gulf to England and those on the northern shore of the Caspian Sea to Russia. Herr Rothstein told me on this occasion that an understanding between England and Russia on all points is being carefully considered, and that he, Rothstein, had been instructed by Witte not to create difficulties for the English in any financial operations. I have heard that Witte once again needs a lot of money (probably for the Manchurian Railway) and is trying to get it in England. As he probably will not get any there, he will try to get German and Dutch

[1] Not found.

banks to give him the money he needs (about 200 million) via a loan which will be floated in London. True, he will get no English money this way, but he will create the impression that he has succeeded in doing so and that the loan has been subscribed in England. He has successfully carried out such a manoeuvre once before. I see from this and other indications that the Russian Government is trying hard to establish friendly relations with England in every field. But it seems doubtful to me whether a lasting alliance will eventuate. Naturally I am watching carefully and will take note of every symptom.

The courier is leaving and I can't make this letter any longer. I did not cast its contents into the form of a report, for the news is still too incomplete and I did not have the time to have it copied as a report.

With best regards
Your truly devoted
Radolin.

## 698. Paul von Hatzfeldt to Holstein[1]

TELEGRAM

London, 3 July 1899

Private

My *impression* still remains that there will be *no* war,[2] because *neither* side has the inclination. But nobody can say so with certainty, and it is sure that even the best informed people here are still in doubt on this point. Mr Chamberlain has been allowed to advance so far in public that the Government now *must* insist on certain minimum concessions if it is not to run the danger of being accused here of a shameful retreat. Moreover the possibility remains, which however cannot be calculated here, that disorders will break out in Johannesburg. Military intervention against them and reports of alleged mistreatment of foreigners would, in the present situation, result in mobilizing the Press and public opinion here in favour of using force and silence those who have opposed this hitherto, including members of the Cabinet.

Probably this situation will not change as long as reports arriving here—which seem contradictory—can still give rise to the opinion that there is a chance that President Krüger will yield and peaceful agreement can thus be reached. But the decision cannot be long postponed.

Naturally I fully agree with your view that if it comes to the point we should envisage all sorts of possibilities. But I regard it as highly advisable that we should stick for the time being to the impartial attitude we have maintained hitherto and *appear* to avoid most carefully anything which might arouse the suspicion here that a change in our attitude is possibly to be feared. I am already firmly convinced, without however being able to cite supporting facts, that the strong ill-feeling against England observed in Germany has contributed considerably to

---

[1] From the Foreign Ministry files.
[2] Between Great Britain and the South African Republic.

strengthen the dislike of Lord Salisbury and his supporters in the Cabinet for warlike entanglements in South Africa.

Can I perhaps report and telegraph privately also to Herr von Bülow during your absence? Probably instances will constantly recur here when I have something important to report, but I will be unable to judge whether the State Secretary would find official use appropriate or even down right harmful.

Hatzfeldt.

### 699. Paul von Hatzfeldt to Holstein[1]
Letter in code

London, 8 July 1899

Private.

Received your letters[2] and would like to remark first of all re 1) Reparations Question :[3] As you know arbitration was *suggested* here, and I was empowered to take up the idea only under the clearly expressed reserve that His Majesty disliked the idea in principle. Later, however, I was instructed to insist on a definite obligation for reparations being accepted here. The result was Lord Salisbury's unsatisfactory reply, reported in telegram no. 152.[4] Whereupon I was left without reply or instruction till now and therefore had to let the matter rest. At the next opportunity I will again suggest arbitration, but must be prepared for the objection that we had not accepted the proposal when first made, and that the situation had changed due to the decisions reached by the commission since that date.

Re 2) Meeting.[5] I too had the same idea, and already introduced it in our last conversation by saying, jokingly, that if I had anything to say I would lock up the two ringleaders and thus force them to talk things over. Salisbury laughed and didn't say no, but on the other hand didn't follow it up. Now I shall have to wait a *little while*, for he has by no means yet got over the personal attacks, and though he feigns indifference, some of his remarks show that deep down he still feels irritated. When I mentioned the *personal* annoyance over Samoa again, he said that I ought to know as well as he did that the real cause of this annoyance was to be sought not so much in the Samoa Question but in the Queen's behaviour in *personal* matters, which he, Salisbury, could not influence, either officially or personally.

Our political discussion which followed our talk about Morocco was a pretty lively, not to say sharp, one. As regards Morocco I reported by telegram.[6] But I had serious scruples about sending an official report on Salisbury's statements in the conversation that followed. These are due to his present personal irritation, and reporting them would have poured oil on the flames. I would feel a report to be indicated and justified only if the State Secretary demands it, all the more since Salisbury has had

---

[1] From the London Embassy files.    [2] Not found.    [3] See p. 121, note 1.
[4] Not found.    [5] Between Kaiser Wilhelm II and Salisbury.
[6] On 30 June. See above.

similar moods before which in the end have passed. For my part I did not fail to issue friendly but *very definite* warnings concerning a change of course such as no one else could have risked here. When Salisbury showed a certain scepticism as to alternative groupings, I told him that as an example I could tell him from personal experience that some time ago his friend Courcel had offered me French support if only we agreed to include Egypt in the list of reclamations to be made here. I had refused.[1] But, France apart, there were others making *constant* efforts to reach an understanding with us, most probably at England's expense. The other day his colleague Goschen had objected that we could not desire a serious weakening of England, and I had replied that this was true *provided* that our lawful interests met with their due respect here. But I could not conceal from him that the danger of such combinations was *always* present as long as we were badly treated by England and our interests were shown neither appreciation nor accommodation. What then? Powerful though the English fleet might be, it seemed impossible to me to dispute the possibility that certain, after all possible, combinations might create an uncomfortable situation for England which could definitely be avoided by a somewhat more accommodating attitude towards us.

Salisbury, who was evidently not very enthusiastic about my conversation with Goschen and the latter's remark, did not enter into a closer discussion of future political possibilities. When I pressed him by pointing to the uncertain future, he said that in certain circumstances England would have to act in accordance with the motto: *Dieu et mon droit,* and only added that he did not in the least doubt the friendly intentions behind *my* statements. His *personal* irritation came out very clearly this time over Morocco. After turning and twisting for quite a time to avoid any sort of detailed statement, he said he had to admit to me that for him the main reason against an agreement on that subject was his decided dislike of *all* treaties which divided the possessions of living owners in advance. When I objected that he had done just that with the colonies of England's friend Portugal, he replied heatedly that that had been done by Balfour, whom he did not want to blame for it; he himself would not have concluded the agreement. When I immediately and strongly objected that I had negotiated and fixed the main part of the agreement with him in person, he shrugged his shoulders and repeated that *he* would not have concluded it.[2] When I made the further point that it was important to restore the relations impaired by Samoa and that consideration for our interests in Morocco was the way of doing it, he replied with some bitterness: 'You want to please your Kaiser and I am to help you.'

The State Secretary and you will, I hope, agree with me that such irritated, personal remarks, of which I could cite more, are not suitable for inclusion in official reports, for, things being what they are, they

[1] See *Grosse Politik*, vol. XI, no. 2739, pp. 195–8; vol. XIII, no. 3398, pp. 5–7.
[2] See *Grosse Politik*, vol. XIVi, chapter XCII; *British Documents*, vol. I, Chapter II.

would do the greatest harm. I feel that it is not impossible that this irritated mood will pass, as has happened before, and will give way to a calmer and more objective estimate of the political situation. I need hardly add that I will leave nothing undone in order to bring about this change as soon as possible. But this takes a bit of time and my view, based on lengthy experience, is that I must keep absolutely quiet for the time being and avoid the impression that we are running after England's friendship in spite of everything. For this reason I did not go and see Salisbury last Wednesday, but will do so next Wednesday if he is receiving visitors. How long he will stay here and when he will go on leave depends solely on the state of his wife's health, which is again unsatisfactory. Perhaps it will be easier to get along with Balfour, who as of now is supposed to deputize for him.

P.H.

700. Holstein to Bernhard von Bülow
Copy

B[erlin], 20 July 1899

Dear Bülow,

As days may perhaps count in the Bear Island Question,[1] but a few hours don't, I prefer to reply to your telegram of yesterday[2] by letter; for a telegram always passes through a number of hands.

That Radolin should share the consequences if the Bear Question misfires corresponds with diplomatic usage. But he does not share the guilt, for it was not his idea, he was not consulted in the execution and is not responsible for the noticeably more arrogant attitude which the Russian Government has recently adopted towards us. If Muraviev now speaks to the German Government, directed by you, in the same tone as Lobanov used to do, the fault is not Radolin's but yours. The Russians know that you wish to obtain Russian good-will *at any price*, and act and talk accordingly. Prince Bismarck also desired good relations, but not at any price, and the Russians knew it. That is the difference. From his conversations with the Kaiser Osten-Sacken knows that His Majesty does not incline towards humility, but the Ambassador is counting on your influence in successfully persuading the Kaiser to sanction a policy of humility towards Russia. I too believe that you will succeed in doing so if you try it, although the Kaiser's comments on your report on the Straits agreement don't give that impression.[3] But probably the Kaiser will for once not follow his instincts, for he tells himself that up till now you have brought off everything. Though when he comes to see later just what he has let himself in for, the reaction will be as speedy as it will

---

[1] See *Memoirs*, p. 176, note 2.

[2] Bülow had telegraphed from Semmering that, in view of his urgent need for rest, he expected the Foreign Ministry and Radolin to deal with the Bear Island Question without any help from him. He hoped that it would be possible to avoid serious difficulties with Russia, since both the Kaiser and public opinion would not think these worth while for such a minor cause. (From the Foreign Ministry files.)

[3] Report to the Kaiser of 4 July 1899. (*Grosse Politik*, vol. XIVii, no. 4025, pp. 558–60.)

be violent, just as after the 'unfortunate Krüger Telegram' (that is what *he* called it afterwards), and he will then naturally try to make it obvious that the responsibility for the mistake that was made was not *his*.

For you the difficulty of the present moment lies in the fact that the Russians no longer believe that the Kaiser, as long as you are his adviser, will stick to an idea of which Russia disapproves. Unless you wish to abandon an independent Great Power policy altogether, you must rid the Russians of that belief. His Majesty however demands this independent Great Power policy, *recognized as such by all sides*, even though he will let you have your way occasionally over some issue or other—because, and for as long as, you have the lucky touch. But no one who *fixes* German policy along anti-English lines will be his Minister for long. His Majesty will soon shake off both the responsibility and the Ministers, after having perhaps taken up the idea in the beginning in a momentary burst of feeling. I am more firmly convinced of this than ever after having just seen how strongly he is reacting to Salisbury's friendlier attitude.[1] His rages against England are always only *dépit amoureux*. If you don't want to miscalculate, you must take that into account.

To come to the question on the agenda : what is to be done, and who must do something? Radolin *by himself* can't do anything. For how can an Ambassador—let it even be Hatzfeldt—make an impression on a Minister, who knows or believes that the Ambassador has nothing to back him, nothing and no one. I fear that even you would not really frighten the Russians to-day. They are probably convinced that your policy approaches more closely that of Bismarck *fils* than of Bismarck *père*. Thus the only possible means of exercising pressure is the Kaiser. The first thing to do is to wait and see His Majesty's comments on the reports on Bear Island now reaching him from St Petersburg, and whether he attaches greater weight to the good-will of the Russians or to Bear Island; he can choose between these alternatives. If he decides in favour of the former, we will simply say that the Bear escapade was just private fun, and the matter is closed. But if the Kaiser sticks by Bear Island, *he* will have to pull it out of the fire; there is no other way. Richthofen must read suitable remarks by the Kaiser verbatim to Sacken 'in strictest confidence *et sans qu'on le sache*', and while doing so hint that the English, Salisbury in particular, have lately repeatedly shown us signs of consideration (Chambers, arbitration).[2] Muraviev and his

---

[1] Bülow telegraphed to the Kaiser on 13 July : 'Count Hatzfeldt has just telegraphed to me that Lord Salisbury told him that in case of a visit to England by Your Majesty he would be happy 'to be able to remove the misunderstandings which had unfortunately arisen in a personal conversation, as nothing was further removed from his mind than the adoption of a policy hostile to Your Majesty's well-founded interests'. (*Grosse Politik*, vol. XIVii, no. 4077, p. 623.)

[2] In the above-cited telegram Bülow stated: 'At the same time Lord Salisbury not only agreed to the dismissal of Chambers, but in addition agreed that the so very difficult reparations question on Samoa (in accordance with Article II, section 2 of the Samoa Act) be settled by the arbitration of the King of Sweden.'

Judge Chambers, an American who held office under the provision of the Samoa Act of

master immediately become scared when they notice that the other side is not frightened nor especially considerate—Kiaochow taught us that lesson. But Richthofen must on *no account* mention the invitation question[1]—neither Cowes, nor Scotland, otherwise the Russians will immediately interfere in it. You must instruct Richthofen to pass on the Kaiser's remarks to Sacken in such a way that, provided H.M.'s intentions are *not* identical with the Russian desire, Sacken is left in no doubt concerning the Kaiser's determination. That is the only way for *you* to avoid finding yourself between the upper and the nether millstones later.

Don't hesitate, dear friend; arrange the matter so that everything further will be settled between H.M., the Under State Secretary and the Russians. But you must *order* the Under State Secretary—who will certainly not like doing it—to give the Russian *full and authentic* information on H.M.'s view—naturally all this only if H.M. does *not* retreat.

I wish this could be a more pleasant letter, but at least it is well meant.

With best regards
Yours
H.

When asked I said nothing on Samoa arbitration. As the matter now stands, you did not consider it opportune to follow up the idea because H.M. opposed it in the past.

### 701. Holstein to Hugo von Radolin[2]

Berlin, 26 July 1899

Dear Radolin,

You know the Kaiser's marginal comments on your detailed Straits report;[3] they were, I think, sent to you on the 17th of this month by courier. H.M. expressed agreement wherever you took a strong line, remained silent about the somewhat weak ending, and did not put his normal 'correct' or 'good' at the end. Thus the slightly anxious tenor of the last paragraph, which moreover does not fit in with the rest of the report, did not please him. I have also heard indirectly that he did not read your long report on the conversation concerning Bear Island[4] through to the end, apparently because he disapproved of the tone, but on the other hand was more satisfied with the contents of your telegram 133.[5]

1889, had rejected the election of Mataafa, the German candidate, as King of Samoa early in January 1899. Thereafter he had remained one of the principal opponents of German policy in the islands.

[1] See above, Hatzfeldt's letter of 8 July 1899.

[2] From the Radolin Papers.

[3] Of 29 June. See *Grosse Politik*, vol. XIVii, nos. 4022, 4026, pp. 549–54, 561.

[4] Report of 15 July, according to which Witte and Muraviev had expressed to Radolin the concern, widely felt in Court and Government circles, regarding German action with respect to Bear Island. (From the Foreign Ministry files.)

[5] Of 21 July. Radolin had reported Muraviev's assurances that the captain of the Russian warship sent to Bear Island had received strict instructions to avoid all friction with German nationals. On 23 July Eulenburg telegraphed to the Foreign Ministry that the Kaiser was so

From this it is clear that the Kaiser expects you to speak and act firmly. That is no reason for your relations with Muraviev to deteriorate. On the contrary, I would hoist him with his own petard, appear full of *well-meant warnings*, and tell him: 'Don't be mistaken about one thing; if you fail our Master, he is quite capable of doing something as a result of which good relations between Germany and Russia might be *permanently* impaired. Therefore think twice before doing something which the Master might look upon or interpret as lacking in consideration. Let me give you a piece of advice; if you think I am exaggerating, why don't you let the Russian Chargé d'Affaires in Berlin raise the matter (thus e.g. Bear Island) there so as to find out what the Berlin view is.' If Muraviev then returns to the question a few days or weeks later and tells you: 'In Berlin they have said such and such, Russia has no objection to *this* statement'—you simply pass on this remark as it stands, yet adding, in order to make things quite clear in Berlin, that it would in future be hopeless for you to defend a different point of view from that which has been given to the Russian Chargé d'Affairs as the point of view of the German Government.

The Bear Island Question is in somewhat of a mess. Too many agencies took a hand in it, Ministry of the Interior, Admiralty; for that reason there may still be friction—I mean with the Russian Government. You must prevent *your* becoming the scapegoat whose weakness and lack of influence are to be blamed for the possibly unsatisfactory result. Remember that the Kaiser is the decisive factor, and that he wants us to use *firm* language to the Russians and indeed to every one. Incidentally it is hardly to your advantage that you allowed yourself to be used to force the Kaiser's acquiescence to the Hague permanent Court of Arbitration;[1] he was strongly opposed to it, and I do believe that one day at a critical moment the matter may turn out badly for Germany. But Bülow was influenced by the authority of that unscrupulous old idiot Münster, and *you* appear as the decisive factor which caused H.M. to reverse himself.

For this reason I would like to warn you to be [...][2] *careful about yielding*. If you and Muraviev should have a difference of opinion, you should tell him in the friendliest way: 'Don't think that I am acting with *trop de zèle*; do me a personal favour and sound out Berlin, where the views of my Kaiser must be known directly from their source; then tell me afterwards what you have found out.'

Muraviev has no nerves for a conflict. He only appears to be getting bigger recently because we appear to be getting smaller. He will soon be brought back to his right size if he sees that we are serious—friendly but serious—and this is a task for which our Most Gracious Master is particularly fitted. An occasional remark by *him* would have a useful

sensitive in this question that he had refused to take cognizance of Radolin's report of 15 July (see above, note 4). However, telegram no. 133 had met with his approval. (From the Foreign Ministry files.)

[1] See Radolin's telegram of 19 July 1899. (*Grosse Politik*, vol. XV, no. 4317, pp. 296–8.)

[2] One word illegible.

effect. But there is no need that you alone and exclusively should transmit these [remarks]; from time to time that can also be done in Berlin. And if they don't feel inclined to do so in Berlin, you simply write, as I said before : 'The Russian Chargé d'Affaires has reported such and such.'

Marshal Marmont wrote in his memoirs :[1] 'Russia's natural policy is : *menacer souvent, frapper rarement.'* Alexander III acted according to this principle of the permanent frown towards Bulgaria; Muraviev is now doing the same with Serbia and is trying it with Germany. But matters won't go beyond a frown, expecially not because of Muraviev's timidity. Three causes have led to the deterioration of Russia's general situation : the need for money is getting worse; the hostile position towards England is becoming more and more marked by *objective* grounds for opposition which are independent of the will or ability of this or that person; and German-English relations have improved so considerably in the last six weeks that I now regard the possibility—did it ever exist ?— of England making substantial sacrifices to buy Russian good-will as a *fata morgana* pure and simple. Anyway, judging by your report 333[2]— if I remember the number correctly—you answered Muraviev's fibs on that subject very well, quite undisturbed, and genial at the same time.

Don't show this letter to *anybody*, please, except possibly the Princess, to whom please give my very best regards.

As always
Your
Holstein.

I have been on leave for weeks, am staying here only temporarily but do not know for how long. Thus it is uncertain whether a letter will now reach me.

702.   Hermann von Eckardstein to Paul von Hatzfeldt

Cowes, 31 July 1899

Your Excellency,

I have the honour to report the following.

The Prince of Wales, who had announced his intention to dine with me yesterday evening with the Duke of York, took me aside after the meal and told me he was particularly pleased that at long last there was a chance that the existing misunderstandings with H.M. the Kaiser might be finally removed.[3] The Queen had been very pleased at the Kaiser's cordial telegram,[4] and he *hoped* that the Kaiser's visit to Windsor

---

[1] *Mémoires du Duc de Raguse de 1792 à 1832,* 9 vols. (Paris, 1857).

[2] Of 15 July. Radolin had reported that Muraviev had tried in conversation to represent Russia's relations with Britain as excellent, but that he had not been convincing. (From the Foreign Ministry files.)

[3] See Eckardstein, *Lebenserinnerungen,* vol. II, p. 27.

[4] On 22 July the Kaiser telegraphed his regret at being unable to take advantage of the Queen's invitation to Osborne because of an accident to the Kaiserin, but he expressed the hope that a visit would be convenient in the autumn. (*Letters of Queen Victoria,* Third Series, vol. III, p. 388.)

in the autumn would materialize. He added that he had written to Your Excellency only a few hours earlier.

In the further course of the conversation the Prince said that *he* personally had been particularly pleased that Your Excellency had gone to see him and told him quite openly all the reasons why Berlin had been so irritated with England. He himself would do everything that lay in his powers to remove all misunderstandings, both of a personal and political nature. In this connection, however, he mentioned that a certain person in the entourage of H.M. the Kaiser, i.e. Admiral von Senden, had stood between him and the Kaiser and had contributed considerably to deepen existing misunderstandings. Without saying so directly, the Prince let it be understood that it would be better if Admiral von Senden did *not* come to England.

Admiral von Eisendecher,[1] who is here on the *Meteor*[2] and whom the Prince of Wales treated with special consideration at my dinner-party, will talk to the Kaiser about Admiral von Senden when announcing his return to His Majesty. In fact Admiral von Senden did intend to come to Cowes at the end of this week, but Eisendecher prevented it.

The attitude of the Duke of York has also changed completely, and he wants to go out sailing on the *Meteor* one day this week.

I remain as always,

Your Excellency's most obedient
Hermann von Eckardstein.

703.   Paul von Hatzfeldt to Holstein

London, 6 August 1899

Dear friend,

It was unfortunate that I had to become ill just now, but it can't be helped. I have a bad bronchitis, which hasn't happened to me for years, and my two doctors were in full agreement yesterday that I should not be allowed to leave my room for the next ten or twelve days. The harm is not as great as it might seem at first sight, for in the next few days no one of importance will be in town and thus not much could be done even if I could get out. Moreover I am in constant touch with Rothschild whose own financial interests lead him to keep himself as well informed as possible, particularly on French intrigues in St Petersburg. But as yet, as I have ascertained, he knows absolutely nothing about that, and according to him the Paris Rothschilds know just as little about the purpose of Delcassé's trip.[3] At the moment Rothschild is spending the holidays at his country house, and I got my son to accept an invitation to stay there until to-morrow in order to stay as much as possible *au courant* of Rothschild's news. Furthermore Eckardstein at my request

---

[1] Karl von Eisendecher, the Prussian Minister in Karlsruhe. Eisendecher was a Vice-Admiral *à la suite* and in 1899 had been placed in charge of the Imperial Yacht *Meteor*.

[2] The Kaiser's yacht was in Cowes to compete for the Queen's Cup.

[3] Delcassé paid a surprise visit to St Petersburg from 4–9 August during which modifications of the Franco-Russian treaties of 1891 and 1892 were agreed to by an exchange of notes on 9 August.

has announced himself there for to-morrow or the day after, and I'll get him moving at once, also on the Press publication[1] you want, which can best be arranged by him.

I am sending you to-day under separate cover Eckardstein's last letter from Cowes on events there.[2] Please send it back soon. I would like to take this opportunity to remark that presumably it was a mistake of yours when you assumed that I could recall Eckardstein.[3] His relationship to me is no longer an official one in any way, and I therefore have to rely on his good will, which incidentally he certainly does not fail to show.

As far as can be seen there will be nothing new to report from here in the Transvaal Question during the next few days. This is not due to me or to lack of information but to the facts of the situation. Please do make this clear to the State Secretary. Obviously one will have to wait here to see whether, how far, and in what form President Krüger will take up Chamberlain's proposals,[4] and future decisions here will depend on that. If, in spite of the influence which the Afrikanders of the Cape and the Orange Republic are now clearly bringing to bear in Pretoria, the reply is a completely negative one and unacceptable in the view of people here (which I don't believe for the moment), my feeling is that we shall first of all enter a new phase. During that period the English Government will mount troop concentrations in South Africa more openly than hitherto in order to increase the pressure. This phase too will take some time, and it will then become clear whether the expectations here—that President Krüger wants to wait for this pressure in order to be able to justify greater concessions before his own people—will prove well founded. In any case, as I have emphasized before, the real centre of decision for the time being does not lie here, but in Pretoria, and I have no means of keeping myself informed except by the, in my opinion pretty unreliable, news which Herr Goerz[5] sends me on this subject.

As far as the Transvaal Question is concerned I regard Delcassé's trip as a most welcome event. For it will obviously strengthen the impression here, especially in the case of Salisbury, that one must be prepared for unpleasantness if matters in South Africa are allowed to lead to war-like complications. It may therefore probably be assumed that Salisbury will operate carefully and will not allow himself to be dragged further

[1] Note by Holstein: 'An article that a renewed attempt on Milan's life is being talked of as probable in St Petersburg.'

[2] In his letter to Hatzfeldt of 2 August, Eckardstein described the pleasure with which the English greeted the victory of the *Meteor* in the Queen's Cup, and the corresponding anger when the Kaiser replied to the English telegram of congratulation by saying that the handicap placed on his yacht was 'simply appalling'. (Eckardstein, *Lebenserinnerungen*, vol. II, pp. 27–30.)

[3] Holstein had advised Hatzfeldt to do so in a telegram of 3 August. (From the London Embassy files.)

[4] On 24 July the British Cabinet approved a dispatch drawn up by Chamberlain calling for a joint enquiry by British and Boer delegations for the purpose of reaching a satisfactory agreement on the franchise, and for a subsequent personal conference between President Krüger and the British High Commissioner to discuss remaining issues. (See J. L. Garvin, *The Life of Joseph Chamberlain* (London, 1934), vol. III, pp. 422–3.)

[5] Proprietor of the Goerz Commercial firm in London, which had branches in Berlin and Johannesburg.

than he can help by Chamberlain in the Transvaal Question. True, the danger to the preservation of peace lies in this reserve. As I have often stressed, we must never forget that it is not always the national interest which is decisive here but personal or party interests. Thus a decidedly negative or completely unacceptable reply by the Transvaal Government would have as a consequence that Chamberlain, by advocating energetic action, could then appear before public opinion here as the real defender of England's honour, and that is a role which Salisbury cannot allow him to play without serious damage to himself and his party. It is at the very least doubtful whether he will not subordinate his better judgment of the political situation to this consideration. Thus, if my assumption is correct, we always come back to the conclusion that the decision on the further development of events now lies in Pretoria and not here, and that everything will depend on that.

Another advantage of Delcassé's trip in my opinion lies in the fact that it must work to our benefit here. Whatever faults Lord Salisbury may have, he is too intelligent a statesman not to know very well that France cannot engage itself à fonds against England without being sure of at least our tolerance. Thus this is a further reason for him to show us consideration and to continue on the path of a friendly rapprochement which has been initiated. Furthermore I do not believe that, even if he allows Scott[1] to continue his friendly relations with Muraviev, he seriously envisages a rapprochement with Russia, nor that he believes in its feasibility. Quite apart from statements to the contrary which I shall cite hereafter, I do not see anything on which an understanding can be reached. In regard to China the situation is such that an understanding on railway questions can be reached, and Lord Salisbury does not happen to attach particular importance to these. But that is all. An understanding regarding the Persian Gulf appears to me to be wholly out of the question. As regards Turkey, it is well known in St Petersburg that public opinion here would not allow the Government to protect the Sultan against Russian attacks; but that does not apply to the Dardanelles, and it seems to me extremely doubtful whether the English Government could and would agree to accept the Russian claim to close the Dardanelles and thus the Black Sea to an English fleet. It is obvious that England herself would thereby give the Russian Government the means to prepare a mighty Russian fleet not only in the Black Sea but also in the Golden Horn and the Sea of Marmara, which could pass the Dardanelles whenever the convenient moment had come and in conjunction with the French fleet place English supremacy in the Mediterranean in jeopardy. Is it conceivable that England would voluntarily expose herself to such a danger? If this question must be answered in the negative, the question as to which important points an understanding between the two Powers could now be reached seems to me a difficult one to resolve.

As regards the above-mentioned statements by Lord Salisbury, I have

[1] Sir Charles Stewart Scott. British Ambassador in St Petersburg, 1898–1904.

this to say: In our last conversation we again came to speak of the Sino-Japanese war. I let fall a remark about how much I had regretted at that time that the English Government had been unable to decide to take up the attitude adopted by us towards Japan together with Russia and France. England might then perhaps have been in a position to exercise a moderating influence on Russia's territorial demands on China. Lord Salisbury replied with a certain emphasis and not without some excitement that he had not been in office then and thus was not responsible for the attitude of the English Government. Had he been in power he would for a start not have allowed the war at all. *Should that have proved impossible, he would under no circumstances have permitted the demand on Japan to give up the Liaotung Peninsula in Russia's favour, thereby making it possible for the latter to establish herself at Port Arthur.*

Finally I feel I must also mention a remark by Sir Frank Lascelles. During our last conversation on the day of his departure I repeatedly pointed out that greater consideration would have to be shown to us here if friendly relations were to be established. When he countered with the question as to the points on which I regarded an understanding possible and desirable, I replied that I had to rely on my own judgment in this respect, for instructions on this point would as yet clearly be premature. With this reservation I could only say that for the time being I could see two issues on which I regarded an understanding between us as urgently desirable. The first was the Moroccan question, the second our railways in Asia Minor, to which we were forced to attach great value for economic reasons. It appeared to me that a great mistake would be made here by opposing us in this question, for it was clear that we could not pursue any political objectives there and merely had our economic interests in view. For this reason it might perhaps be desirable for us to establish a few consulates for the protection of our interests. Sir Frank Lascelles replied that he completely shared my point of view to the extent that it would not run counter to English interests if English goods were transported by German railways as far as Basra. He had expressed himself in London in this sense. I therefore intend to raise this point with Lord Salisbury when a suitable occasion arises.

In the further course of our conversation I had the opportunity to remark that in regard to the general European situation our position was a thoroughly favourable one, as we could quietly await future developments. Whatever form these might take, I was convinced that the time would come when the decision would depend on which side of the scales His Majesty the Kaiser would choose to throw his weight and possibly his sword. Sir Frank Lascelles replied that he could not dispute for one moment the justice of this view.

Finally I would only like to add that Russia's obvious reluctance to allow us to join their alliance with France appears to me very characteristic, and in my humble opinion demands the exercise of the greatest caution by us.[1] They want to make sure of us direct, at the same time

---

[1] See *Grosse Politik*, vol. XIVii, no. 4020, pp. 546–8.

keep France on the leash, but prevent any agreement between us because they want to retain the means of unleashing the French against us if need be. Thus I think that we can never set any store by Russia's honesty as long as they are not prepared to assure us of their most absolute neutrality in case of a war between ourselves and France.

A warm farewell for to-day. In my present condition, when I can hardly talk, I did not find it easy to dictate the above letter. Naturally I leave it entirely to you whether you want to show it to the State Secretary and possibly also His Majesty.

With best regards
Your
PHatzfeldt.

## 704. Paul von Hatzfeldt to Holstein

London, 27 August 1899

Dear friend,

I have only a few minutes before the courier leaves and I must therefore be brief.

With regard to the last sentence of my report to the Kaiser about the Queen[1] I would like to add *only for you and the State Secretary*: The situation is this; some time ago, i.e. before the invitation to Windsor, the Queen was deeply suspicious, or had been made so, that H.M.'s aim was to involve her in a war with France and Russia, while she is particularly anxious that the end of her reign should be peaceful. I naturally could not say this in my report, but it does merit to be taken into account.

Even to-day I still don't believe in war unless they have gone mad in Pretoria. Salisbury certainly doesn't want the war if he can avoid it, but he will be dragged along if Krüger insists that England must expressly renounce suzerainty.[2] By doing so he would be doing Chamberlain the greatest favour; if Krüger yields on this point, Chamberlain will take a fall. The Boers should be satisfied with the tacit continuation of the existing treaties, possibly with the proviso that differences of opinion which might arise should be settled by a *judiciary* court of arbitration. My feeling is that Chamberlain will not keep quiet in any case, even if an agreement is reached, and will start again with a different pretext, until he has achieved his aim. But to-day the odds are that the Transvaal would definitely be beaten and then lose everything. An agreement would gain time, and no one can know how the European situation will develop in the meantime and whether a coalition against England might not then be formed. [...]

With best regards
Your
PHatzfeldt

---

[1] Of 27 August. See *Grosse Politik*, vol. XV, no. 4374, pp. 385–90.

[2] That is, British suzerainty over the Transvaal as laid down in the Pretoria Convention of 5 April 1881. Disagreement over this issue was one of the main causes of the breakdown in the negotiations between Krüger and the British Government. (See Garvin. *Chamberlain*, vol. III, chapter LXVI.)

### 705. Paul von Hatzfeldt to Holstein

London, 31 August 1899

Dear friend,

That the Samoa Question must be settled definitely right now before the visit came as a surprise to me.[1] As H.M. is impatient about it, this will naturally have to be done. I only hope that H.M. is informed of the fact that it was not my fault that the Question was not taken up again earlier.

From my private telegram yesterday[2] you will already have seen that I regret the impatience in the interest of the cause itself, and the reason why I do so. The more impatience we show, the less we will be offered. My idea was to prepare the ground here for the compensation question, and reserve definitive agreement on it until the State Secretary and Salisbury have their conversation. But if this is impossible I will naturally do what I can, and I hardly need assure you that I will not fail to show the necessary forcefulness. But success is something I can't promise you; on the contrary I must not conceal from you that I regard it as extraordinarily doubtful. I think I can even forecast to you pretty accurately his reply. He will say: 'You demanded the commission,[3] and I accepted it to do you a favour. I entirely share their view that in the long run things won't work with three of us there, and I therefore suggested the drawing of lots, as earlier negotiations had already shown that we would not be able to agree to a partition. The part which you are offering to us, Sawaii, is in our opinion of much less value than the part you want to keep. If the question is one of compensation, with America being satisfied with Pago Pago and England or Germany getting the rest, the facts of the matter are that you have been offering us the Tonga Islands now for many years and that we have always refused these as inadequate. Moreover you are thereby giving away things, which though neutral, do not belong to you, while on the contrary you demand from us as compensation things which are in our undisputed possession.' Finally he will make the point that if we estimate our share so highly that we demand Zanzibar, British New Guinea or the Solomon Islands in return, the English share of Samoa is equally valuable, and England could thus demand compensation of equal importance for her leaving.

I add here that Salisbury once hinted to me that perhaps the German

---

[1] Bülow telegraphed to Hatzfeldt on 29 August: 'It seems absolutely necessary that the Samoa affair be definitively settled on a basis acceptable to the Imperial Government before the visit of His Majesty the Kaiser to England which is planned for the autumn. The English Government too, if only because of the critical situation now obtaining in South Africa, will surely be anxious to settle this dispute between us at long last.' (*Grosse Politik*, vol. XIVii, no. 4081, pp. 627–8.)

[2] Hatzfeldt had telegraphed: 'I regret the impatience in this matter because, if a compensation deal is accepted here at all, we will be offered less if we show impatience instead of demonstrating that we can wait. May I talk this over with Chamberlain if I find an opportunity to do so without taking any chances? Perhaps he is more inclined to a compensation deal and he could then exercise his influence on Salisbury.' (From the London Embassy files.)

[3] See p. 109, notes 1 and 2, and p. 120, note 1.

share of New Guinea might possibly represent adequate compensation for Samoa, which would also be acceptable to Australia. As far as I can judge I believe that I can foretell almost with certainty that if he is prepared to accept the idea of compensation at all—which he rejected during our last conversation as impracticable—he will certainly demand *nothing less* for England.

I don't think I need emphasize that with respect to the drawing of lots I am in full agreement with you that that proposal is unacceptable to us. I have already explicitly said this when the idea was first mooted. If I allowed Salisbury to talk about it in our last conversation, I did so because I myself could as yet make no proposal, and I hoped to hear— without compromising myself—what his attitude to the idea of compensation might possibly be. But I think you are mistaken in one respect, and that is if you believe that Salisbury is aware of the frivolity of his proposal and its unacceptability for us. I believe that he is on the contrary, and probably not without justification, convinced that people here would find it quite natural to toss for Samoa, and that no one would reproach him if England lost the toss and had to give up Samoa. Starting out from this premise he does not understand that we hold quite different views and that the German public would level reproaches against the Government because of this gamble, particularly if the Government were to lose.

That the State Secretary and you should under these circumstances be annoyed with England is something I fully understand and I too feel that way. You don't know with what difficulty I have sometimes withstood the temptation here to get disgustingly rude and to tell people that things couldn't go on like this. I told myself again and again on these occasions that feelings, no matter how justified they may be, have nothing to do with politics, and that in so far as I can judge, our correct policy lies in quietly waiting without premature engagements towards any side. As you know I am far from advocating that we should render friendly services and favours to the English unless they do exactly the same for us. This is the case now and will probably remain so for the present, as I said on purpose in my report to the Kaiser.[1] A real change in this respect is to be expected only if the English get into difficulties which is bound to happen sooner or later. But while I too fully agree that we should render neither friendly services nor favours to England and remain cool, I still do not really understand why we must seek a rapprochement with the other side because England isn't showing us the requisite consideration. I feel that our position in the world is now so great that for the time being we can make our way alone, without having to lean to any side, whichever one it may be. It further seems to me that this attitude best answers our interests, for sooner or later the time must come when the Great Powers will need us and, if we know how to wait, the decision will then lie in our hands.

As regards Lourenço Marques I already gave you a brief hint as to

[1] See p. 151, note 1.

153

my views yesterday.[1] The more I think about it, the more probable it seems to me that the English will not take full possession, if only so as not to give us any cause for complaint or encourage us to take analogous steps. Moreover there is no urgent reason to take possession, for they have the Portuguese in their pockets and thus need not fear that the latter will create any sort of difficulties in case of a war there. But should a *temporary* occupation be really deemed necessary here, an appeal will probably be made to the first paragraph of our secret note of last year,[2] which does not exclude the possibility of acquisitions of an occasional nature. Perhaps we will also receive a statement that the occupation will end immediately after the war. In any case we must be prepared for action to be taken here along these lines; for I think there cannot be the slightest doubt that people here are most anxious to prevent any occupation by us, and therefore they would be extremely upset and annoyed if this were to come about. There is the additional consideration that the Portuguese would naturally start a tremendous row and, appealing to the treaties, demand help and salvation from England. I beg you not to draw the conclusion from the above that I would be necessarily opposed to our seizing a pledge for the honest execution of our secret treaty in case England took possession of Lourenço Marques. Should England occupy Lourenço Marques without previously or simultaneously giving us the most definite guarantee that it would be evacuated immediately after the war, no one can blame us if we seek to obtain our own guarantees to prevent our being swindled. It would have to be done at once, before any explanations of the English move could be made here. If these come *after* we have seized our pledge the answer would be very simple : we will evacuate after England for her part has done the same. The situation would be a difficult one only if England had the time to offer us the guarantee of her future evacuation before we could act.

We must be quite clear that should we act along the lines sketched out above the annoyance here, as far as human foresight can judge, will be very considerable. But if the failure to reach an understanding on Samoa does lead to mutual annoyance and to the adoption of an anti-English attitude by us which will inevitably lead to further estrangement, there is then no reason why we should show particular consideration at this juncture for English feelings about the Portuguese colonies in South Africa. The visit, which I used all my strength and all my influence to bring about, will then probably fall through also.

I only add with regard to the execution of my instructions re Samoa that I have already requested a conversation with Salisbury, but have not yet received a reply. It is not impossible that he will not come to town yet for the time being. In that case I shall ask you to let me know whether I am to write to him so as not to lose time; the written ex-

---

[1] In the telegram cited on p. 152, note 2, Hatzfeldt had reported that he regarded an English occupation of Lourenço-Marques as improbable. If it did take place it would be represented as a temporary measure.

[2] See p. 98, note 4.

ecution of my instructions seems to be by no means unobjectionable, however.

With best regards<br>
Your<br>
PHatzfeldt.

### 706.   Holstein to Paul von Hatzfeldt[1]

TELEGRAM

Berlin, 12 September 1899

Private.  Secret

You will see from the Kaiser's rejection of your proposals,[2] that under no circumstances is the Kaiser willing to take the risk of being fobbed off, for example with Savaii, without some other full compensation; moreover, that the matter is to be decided *before* the date for which his visit to England is planned.  A private telegram from the State Secretary, just received,[3] confirms that the Kaiser looks on this question as the acid test for our attitude towards England.  If a satisfactory solution is not reached—the possible patching up of the Samoa-Protocol would only be regarded as a miserable makeshift—a change of system can be expected with certainty.

I did try to get a less sharp reply, but must say that I can understand the Kaiser finally losing his patience.  Lord Salisbury plays with him as if he were a little boy.  Perhaps it was a mistake to take up the question of a visit with Lord Salisbury.  His presumption has been further increased, and *this presumption* will finally make possible our shift to the East.

Your difficulty now is that after the advances in the question of the visit, the English will not feel inclined to believe that the Kaiser is now really serious. After the State Secretary's reports, I on the other hand am convinced that, if the current negotiations should not lead to a satisfactory result, the Kaiser will give some recognizable expression to his annoyance.

Holstein.

### 707.   Paul von Hatzfeldt to Holstein

[London], 14 September 1899

Dear friend,

Some remarks by my son gave me the impression that he wanted to hide something from me, and so I pressed him until he admitted that he had received a letter from you.  But don't be cross with him because of

---

[1] From the London Embassy files.

[2] On 8 September Hatzfeldt had telegraphed that he thought Lord Salisbury might agree to arbitration concerning the allocation of Savaii and Upolu. (*Grosse Politik*, vol. XIVii, no. 4082, pp. 628–30.) Bülow informed the Foreign Ministry on 11 September that the Kaiser considered the relinquishing of Upolu and Apia as an impossibility. Bülow thought, however, that the Kaiser would give up Germany's Samoan claims in return for adequate compensation. (*Grosse Politik*, vol. XIVii, no. 4083, p. 630.)

[3] Not found in the Foreign Ministry files.

this. I am truly grateful to you for the consideration which you intended to show for the state of my health; please be convinced of that. But on the one hand I am really a bit better now, on the other my emotions as regards some things are getting blunted. It has become a regular occurence now that at intervals of two or three months [one hears] one is to be dismissed because something is unattainable here, no matter how hard one may try and in spite of all sorts of results achieved in other directions. *Cela ne compte pour rien* in the beloved fatherland if everything doesn't go according to desire. But how I can be held responsible for the fact that Salisbury will not simply give up Upolu is really quite beyond me. And it is surely understandable if in the end one gets dulled towards such imaginary responsibilities and finally tires of the feeling of always sitting on a powder-keg if one has always well and truly done one's duty, as I have. Should His Majesty believe that Eulenburg or Herbert Bismarck or anyone else would understand affairs and conditions here better, I can only advise him to act on that belief. Experience will show who was right.

As regards the state of the question itself, it is, as is also apparent from my telegram of yesterday,[1] simply this: Salisbury is turning and twisting like an eel in the face of everything one suggests to him. He is anxious not to make any proposals himself and at the same time not to let the thread of the negotiations break. I admit quite openly that I am not completely clear as the motives guiding him in this and why he is above all trying to gain time. To a certain extent I believe that he is really afraid of his people, particularly in Australia and New Zealand, and is spinning out the matter in order to rouse our appetite and thereby gain greater advantages of which he can then boast there. But at the same time I have the suspicion that he wants to wait and see how the Transvaal affair will develop, so that he can then act according to circumstances, i.e. grant us more if it comes to a war, less if peace is preserved and there is thus no reason here to fear that we might possibly stage something unpleasant against the English in agreement with the Russians and the French. In any case this must soon become apparent, for the decision whether there will be a war or not cannot be delayed for very long.

In the meantime the question is how we shall treat the Samoa problem here, i.e. do we continue to negotiate or do we, in accordance with the impatience of H.M., insist on the immediate settlement of the question? If this impatience did not exist, I would say from a purely business point of view that we still have two months until H.M.'s visit, and by that time we shall know where we are. But if energetic action is to be taken, I am prepared to do so with pleasure as soon as I get clear instructions in that sense. In the meantime I am doing everything I can do in order to bring about a decision. As you already know, I wrote to Salisbury to-day,[2] privately and very urgently, and have also already taken steps

[1] *Grosse Politik*, vol. XIVii, no. 4085, pp. 632–3.
[2] On the same day Hatzfeldt had telegraphed privately to Holstein: 'I have just written a strictly confidential letter to Salisbury in which I explicitly drew his attention to the fact that

for a meeting with Chamberlain, providing that he is coming to town and he himself feels inclined that way. At the moment he is still in Birmingham, and no one knows when he is coming back here. But it seems he wants to see Eckardstein so as to find out from him something about the feeling in Berlin concerning the Transvaal. Eckardstein expects to hear from him to-day or to-morrow[1] and will tell him then that I would regard an unadvertised meeting between us as highly desirable.

Going by conditions on the continent one might believe that at such a critical time all the Ministers would be at their posts and overloaded with work. Instead Salisbury is at Hatfield, Chamberlain in Birmingham, Goschen is absent, Balfour at a Scottish sea-resort where he devotes all his time to golf and wants to hear nothing of business. Anyone who is objective will admit that under such conditions it is impossible to produce rapid decisions here. [...]

With best regards<br>Yours<br>PHatzfeldt.

P.S. In your last letter you said that it was *perhaps* a mistake to suggest the visit.[2] In my humble opinion it was a bad mistake in every way, which is now making itself felt in the Samoa question as well. I worked for it here with all my strength, you know that, and it was really no easy task. But our pushing the matter could obviously be interpreted in only one way, that we were placing the very greatest value on an invitation. In view of the already existing tendency towards conceit here, it was inevitable that the view would be taken that we have been shown a favour thereby and that there is no reason to grant us *concrete* advantages if we attach so enormous a value to such external signs of friendship as the invitation.

### 708.   Hugo Radolin to Holstein

St Petersburg, 29 September 1899

Dear friend,

[...] The bad aspect of all this[3] and many questions with the Russians is that *we* always *want* something from them, and *they* only want to be *left in peace*. They are *inconsiderate* in everything, indolent, and easy-going. That becomes apparent in this as in other matters. Thus the Russian Tsar is quite unconcerned whether our Kaiser pays him a visit in St Petersburg or not (he even prefers not to have to receive such visits); therefore he also finds it annoying if our Kaiser expects courtesy from

---

in view of the feeling in Berlin it was now a question of bend or break, and that if the former alternative were not taken, the latter would undoubtedly take place according to the information I had.' (From the London Embassy files.)

[1] Chamberlain wrote to Eckardstein on 14 September. (See *Grosse Politik*, vol. XV, no. 4382, p. 394.)

[2] See above, Holstein's telegram of 12 September.

[3] In the earlier part of this letter Radolin had expressed the fear that the Tsar would return to Russia from his family visit in Darmstadt without paying his respects to the Kaiser.

him and gets him into the unpleasant situation of having to make an official visit. It is exactly the same with all things we desire from the Russians. In most cases *we* demand something and the Russians are on the defensive. It is seldom that *they* demand something of us. The consequence is that we can hardly ever take reprisals against them or refuse their wishes. [...]

Your faithful
HR

### 709.   Paul von Hatzfeldt to Holstein[1]

TELEGRAM

London, 3 October 1899

Private

According to to-day's newspaper reports attack by the Boers appears imminent, and then war will be inevitable. I am convinced this is the suitable moment for our negotiations here[2] and I therefore instructed Baron von Eckardstein to talk to Mr Chamberlain as soon as he arrives.[3] Depending on the outcome of this conversation I shall resume negotiations with Lord Salisbury. I have as yet no clear indication as to English intentions concerning Delagoa Bay, but, though I don't believe it, I naturally cannot guarantee that a surprise move will not be made there. I hope that we are prepared for this eventuality.[4]

Hatzfeldt.

### 710.   Holstein to Paul von Hatzfeldt[5]

TELEGRAM

Berlin, 4 October 1899

Private

Only after having thought it over again during the night am I now coming to the conclusion which I hesitated to express at first because it seemed too harsh, namely that in view of Lord Salisbury's lack of consideration the correct thing for us to do is to *refuse* to protect English interests in the Transvaal.[6] *Acceptance* would, if only to a small extent,

---

[1] From the Foreign Ministry files.                     [2] Concerning Samoa.

[3] See Hatzfeldt's telegram of 30 September. (*Grosse Politik*, vol. XIVii, no. 4097, pp. 647–8.)

[4] Holstein telegraphed Hatzfeldt the same day: 'Have just received your last telegram, according to which war appears inevitable. In that case surely Chamberlain will gain the upper hand over Salisbury, i.e. we will be granted acceptable conditions. In the meantime we must make use of everything which can further our aims.' Salisbury's treatment of the Kaiser, Holstein continued, was similar to his treatment of the Sultan. 'He hates the one as much as the other, and I am sure that we shall get something acceptable only through Chamberlain. Our interest now is that Chamberlain's position should be strengthened. If for example the Boers now start the war it would be useful to point to the fact that Salisbury is solely responsible for the delay in English armaments.' (From the Foreign Ministry files.)

[5] From the London Embassy files.

[6] Derenthall, acting State Secretary in the Foreign Ministry, had telegraphed Hatzfeldt on 3 October: 'The English Ambassador on the instructions of Lord Salisbury has just enquired in writing whether the Imperial Government would be prepared to order the German

bind German policy, and would certainly strengthen Lord Salisbury's position, furnishing proof of the correctness of his policy towards Germany in the past.

The refusal would have to be officially motivated by the fact that we have just an ordinary consul in the Transvaal, whose position would not be equal to such a task. At the same time Chamberlain—and perhaps also the well-intentioned Ambassador here—should be given to understand that the refusal is an example of honesty in the face of Salisbury's mistreatment.

You don't need to hold back with your opinion, for all the telegrams, also the official one,[1] are by me. The view I expressed in the latter was an act of self-control, which, after further reflection, I do not think is indicated.

Why don't the English make use of their American cousins? Perhaps because Lord Salisbury wants to demonstrate to the English people that Germany eats out of his hand.

I suggest that you express your official view with a certain reserve and telegraph me privately as well.

Holstein.[2]

711.  Holstein to Paul von Hatzfeldt[3]

TELEGRAM

Berlin, 7 October 1899

Private

My first impression upon reading your telegram[4] is that Lord Salisbury's real attitude towards our wishes is a negative one, but that formally he does not want to turn them down now, but instead achieve the same result by delay.

Evidently Lord Salisbury can be influenced right now only from the *English* side, not by foreign political considerations, for in the foreign sphere he seems prepared for any sacrifice merely to avoid making any concessions to our Kaiser. His hatred of the Sultan misled him politically some years ago, just as his hatred of the Kaiser is doing now.

But it is very characteristic that on this, unlike on all previous occasions, Lord Salisbury is not hiding behind his colleagues' failure to give their consent. This seems to indicate that the latter would not agree with his opinion after his senseless resistance. This would appear

representative in Pretoria to protect British interests in case it should become necessary to withdraw the British agent from Pretoria following hostile Boer measures against British territory. Before submitting this enquiry to His Majesty I would like to know your view. I regard an affirmative reply as indicated, although this will receive little applause in Germany.' (*Grosse Politik*, vol. XIVii, no. 4099, p. 649.)

[1] See p. 158, note 6.

[2] Hatzfeldt telegraphed the Foreign Ministry on 4 October that owing to the negotiations in progress over Samoa, an affirmative reply could hardly be avoided. (*Grosse Politik*, vol. XIVii, no. 4100, p. 649.) Bülow informed Hatzfeldt on 8 October that the unfriendly attitude of the English Government forced Germany to abandon any idea of protecting English interests in the Transvaal. (*Grosse Politik*, vol. XIVii, no. 4103, pp. 653–4.)

[3] From the Foreign Ministry files.

[4] See *Grosse Politik*, vol. XIVii, no. 4102, pp. 651–2.

to be your means of taking action—not directly, but through intermediaries like Rothschild or Baron von Eckardstein; would Lord Lansdowne[1] and Chamberlain also hold the view that a small island in the Pacific Ocean is of greater significance to England than the development of the Sea of Marmara, opposite the Suez Canal, into a Russian naval base? Could not Baron von Eckardstein, possibly also by way of Cecil Rhodes' London Representative, mobilize a number of grands seigneurs who are working with Rhodes against Salisbury? Doesn't Rothschild know anyone who could present the matter to the Queen in all its enormity: giving up of the Straits in order not to allow the Kaiser to get the tiny island of Apia? I suppose it would not be indicated for you to talk with the Prince of Wales?[2] Finally another thought: you know how influential Chirol of *The Times* is. When a few years ago the King of Belguim made that Treaty on Bahr-el-Ghazal,[3] Chirol, at that time *The Times* correspondent here, went so far as to write an article against his own Government, and the yielding of the Government was probably at least partially brought about by this article. After the Krüger telegram Chirol and I naturally drifted apart, as each of us defended his Government. But as I have heard recently he has repeatedly expressed his regret at the estrangement and a desire to reestablish closer relations with me, I wrote him a few friendly lines last summer to which he sent a correspondingly friendly reply.[4]

To be continued.[5]

Holstein.

712.　Holstein to Paul von Hatzfeldt[6]

TELEGRAM

Berlin, 10 October 1899

Private

State Secretary agrees that you should not see Lord Salisbury for the time being.[7]

Just now at lunch the State Secretary told me that the Kaiser had said to him in Karlsruhe that he would never abandon Samoa by a treaty disliked by the German people, but would rather take the risk of England pushing him out. If he accepted a bad treaty, Germany could levy reproaches against him, but if he were pushed out, *he* could reproach the German people for not having granted him the necessary power for resistance soon enough.

---

[1] Henry Charles Keith Petty-Fitzmaurice, fifth Marquess of Lansdowne. Secretary of State for War, 1895–1900; Foreign Secretary, 1900–5; from 1903 leader of the Conservatives in the House of Lords.

[2] See *Grosse Politik*, vol. XIVii, p. 653, note *.

[3] The Congo Treaty of 12 May 1894 between Britain and the Congo State, by which Leopold II, King of the Belgians, secured the lease of the Bahr-el-Ghazal region of the Upper Nile, and Britain secured the lease of a corridor 25 kilometers wide from Lake Tanganyika to Lake Albert Edward. German protests forced the abandonment of the lease on 22 June.

[4] Not found.　　　　[5] Not printed.　　　　[6] From the London Embassy files.

[7] Hatzfeldt telegraphed to Holstein on 10 October: 'I hope you agree that, until my negotiations with Chamberlain reach some sort of conclusion, I entirely refrain from visiting Salisbury.' (From the Foreign Ministry files.)

The State Secretary believes that, rather than accept an *unpopular* treaty, the Kaiser will risk having Germany pushed out of Samoa *by force*. This, however, would then dictate the direction for Germany's policy at least for the next period of history.

If the English thus really want to negotiate only on the basis of our renouncing the Samoa-group entirely, they will certainly have to offer compensations of a sort which will be regarded as fully equivalent here. Otherwise everything will remain as it is, except that the pressure of the German people for an adherence to the Dual Alliance will increase.

I cannot tell you to-day what compensations would prove *acceptable*. Right now the Admiralty has been asked for a secret memorandum on this subject.[1]

I regard your suspicion, expressed in your last telegram, that the English Ministers are aiming at an understanding with Russia,[2] as very probably true, but don't consider an actual understanding likely. For first of all Russia will not cut herself loose from France under any circumstances, and to buy the whole Dual Alliance would after all be very expensive; secondly, the wishes of Russia and France are diametrically opposed in some questions, e.g. in the Straits Question, in which Russia, by prolongation of an English offer, would sacrifice her friendship with France. The reason why Russia during the last decade has until now halted before the Straits was presumably less because of fear of England than out of consideration for France. Would it not be useful if Eckardstein on occasion explained the diplomatic connection to Chamberlain?
[...]

Holstein.

713.   Paul von Hatzfeldt to Holstein[3]

TELEGRAM

London, 12 October 1899

Private.

Reply[4]

Eckardstein is now trying to see Chamberlain and will do all he can. But he said again just now after the arrival of your telegram that Chamberlain in their last conversation had told him firmly and categorically that if we were stupid enough to chose no. II[5] he would not

---

[1] See *Grosse Politik*, vol. XIVii, no. 4107, pp. 660–2.

[2] In the telegram of 10 October, cited above.

[3] From the London Embassy files.

[4] Holstein had telegraphed on 12 October at 12:13 p.m.: 'I hope you do not count amongst the unattainable concessions by Mr Chamberlain that *he* should take on the fight with Salisbury. He must do this if he wants to settle the matter at all, for he has the necessary means of pressure at his disposal as well as the requisite brutality in the use of same. Herr Tirpitz wrote a really passionate memorandum against renunciation of Samoa.' (See above note 1.) (From the London Embassy files.)

[5] In his talk with Eckardstein on 10 October, Chamberlain had presented two possible solutions to the colonial differences between Germany and England. 'Mr Chamberlain made the following remarks on this: we had to choose between the two proposals of which the first was a business-like one, more in accord with our real interests, while the second proposal

interfere in *anything* and would definitely confine himself to agreeing with Salisbury in case his opinion were asked.

If our foreign policy depends on the views of Herr Tirpitz we will not go far in the world. I am prepared to give him a signed and sealed statement that by his method we will *never* acquire Samoa nor such compensations as have been offered as long as England is not involved in a great European war, faced with imminent ruin, and therefore desirous of winning us at any price. Moreover in my humble opinion our public opinion could well be educated to realize that the cession of the important English Solomon-Islands, Savage Islands, and the great Volta Delta offers almost inestimable advantages, with which the purely sentimental value of Samoa just cannot be compared at all. I had held such valuable concessions barely possible, and they have been achieved *only* by drawing in Chamberlain. Obstinately though he sticks to once-taken decisions, he has a far broader view than Salisbury, and apart from that does sincerely want a lasting, and complete colonial settlement corresponding to the interests of both sides, and a friendship with us based on this.

I think as you do that people here are absolutely clear on the probable relations between England and Germany if nothing is achieved. But because of this I believe that this eventuality has already been reckoned with and they have therefore determined how far they can and will go to preserve our friendship. Also they certainly have the idea at the back of their minds to buy the Russians and thus prevent the transformation of the Dual into a Triple Alliance should we become unpleasant. As regards this, I unfortunately do not share your conviction that the Russians would allow themselves to be restrained from an advance in the Dardanelles by French opposition, and also doubt very much whether the French, unpleasant though they would find this, would sever themselves from the Russian alliance because of it.

H.[1]

714. Paul von Hatzfeldt to Holstein

London, 14 October 1899

Dear friend,

I cannot tell you how pleased I was at the news that the Colonial Council has been called and Eckardstein summoned to Berlin.[2] If that won't help, we shall have done what we could and can console ourselves with that.

would only accord with a certain sentimental interest shown by our public for Samoa. For his part he preferred the first proposal for the simple reason that it would settle at one blow all outstanding colonial difficulties between us.' (*Grosse Politik*, vol. XIVii, no. 4106, pp. 658–60.)

[1] Holstein telegraphed on 12 October at 9:17 p.m.: 'After Admiralty and Naval Staff, Woermann, and all the other persons who were asked have expressed themselves against total abandonment of Samoa, I regard it as certain that the Kaiser too will hold to his view that he would rather be pushed out by force. Personally I have no preference for either alternative, but think that the German Government and you have no interest in bringing about a decision which will be *so* unpopular as complete renunciation of Samoa would have been.' (From the London Embassy files.)

[2] See Eckardstein, *Lebenserinnerungen*, vol. II, p. 39 *et seq.*

I can swear that, exactly like you, I have no sort of preference for any one of the conceivable combinations, just as long as an agreement is somehow achieved. But I regard that as a *political* necessity, and as a patriot I would therefore most deeply regret the failure of the negotiations with all the ensuing consequences.

What I don't quite understand in view of this is the enormous value which we are attributing to the opinion of experts in this question. I am convinced that this matter is not primarily one of naval, commercial or even colonial interests, but above all a question of the greatest political importance, which will have decisive influence on our whole future. Naturally the chiefs of our navy have only naval interests in view, while people like Herr Woermann,[1] who is certainly a sound chap, consider only commercial or colonial interests, and none of them have the least idea whether or how their imagined ideal can be realized.

It is due to these people and their one-sided views if His Majesty yields to the belief that he would do better to 'allow' himself to be pushed out of Samoa. But that eventuality will probably not materialize even if the negotiations fail. In that case agreement will be reached on some inferior *modus vivendi* concerning the future tripartite administration in Samoa, and that can last for an indefinite period, for here there is at the moment no desire at all to provoke a serious quarrel with us. But it could happen if the people here succeed in securing an agreement in the Near East with Russia by concessions and then believe that they need show us no further consideration. In the meantime out of the purest sentimentality we would have lost the best and perhaps only chance to close a good deal here and simultaneously establish good political relations, which would be of great value in the future to us as well. I don't doubt for a moment that Chamberlain and his friends share this wish. But they necessarily have had to count up how much they can offer, and how they can justify their actions afterwards. Between you and me, knowing the country and people here as I do, I am not at all clear how Chamberlain will later justify his concessions to us in the House and before public opinion if he cannot say that he thereby wanted to buy our friendship. The motive underlying his offers can thus only be to establish good relations with us if at all possible.

I don't want to trouble you any further with these outpourings, though quite a lot could still be said on the subject. But the present situation reminds me vividly of your memorandum to the State Secretary some time ago in which you said so very truly that as far as could be foreseen we would never again have such a favourable opportunity to close a good deal with England. Farewell for to-day, dear friend. I do hope that all is well with your health. I am so overworked and feel so unwell that I must under all circumstances have a period of peace and rest in fresh air, as soon as the question pending here has been definitely decided.

With best regards

Your

PHatzfeldt.

[1] Adolf Woermann. Partner in the firm C. Woermann in Hamburg.

### 715. Holstein to Paul von Hatzfeldt[1]

TELEGRAM

Berlin, 19 October 1899

Private

You will know best what instructions to give Eckardstein for the conversation to-morrow.[2] It would after all be very useful to let the English know the view held here on the Straits Question. You might best pass this on to Rothschild, who, if he himself is convinced, can then pass it on to the English Ministers.

Basic idea: If England wants to reach an understanding with Russia she must sacrifice the Persian Gulf or make concessions in the Far East. An English-Russian agreement in which England merely gives up the Straits has only this advantage for Russia, that the Sultan is thereby made into a Russian tool and puts his influence over the Mohammedans in Asia and Africa at the service of Russia. Russia will try to get the treaty, but only in order to exploit the *document* against England.

Germany too could very recently have concluded such an agreement, and in this case too Russia presumably had the basic idea of exploiting the document. Germany refused, but England can try and see what the outcome of the matter will be; *we* don't mind.

Holstein.

### 716. Paul von Hatzfeldt to Holstein

London, 5 November 1899

Dear friend,

What was humanly possible has been done here to overcome all difficulties and to reach a decision at last. All the same I cannot as yet tell you with any degree of certainty whether I will be able to report a definite result to you on Tuesday evening. I will not shrink from any exertion to achieve this, you and the State Secretary can be sure of that, and as a last resort, if we can not as yet agree on the final text, I will concentrate my efforts on getting Salisbury at least to initial the proposal on seven points.[3]

As regards the cancellation,[4] naturally I cannot judge when it will be necessary and how long it can be postponed. I can therefore only repeat the request to postpone it to the very last minute, not only because this would mean the failure of the Samoa Question, but because the effect which the cancellation will have here is absolutely clear and beyond doubt. It will cause a tremendous sensation, hurt the Queen and all the rest of the family deeply, and be taken and regarded by public opinion as

---

[1] From the Foreign Ministry files.

[2] Hatzfeldt's instructions for Eckardstein's talk with Chamberlain are printed in Eckardstein, *Lebenserinnerungen*, vol. II, pp. 62–4; see also *Grosse Politik*, vol. XIVii, no. 4110, pp. 664–6.

[3] The Samoa agreement was finally signed on 14 November 1899. See *Grosse Politik*, vol. XIVii, p. 675, note *. The text of the agreement is published in the *Reichs- und Staatsanzeiger* of 23 November 1899.

[4] Of the Kaiser's visit to England. See *Grosse Politik*, vol. XV, p. 410, note *.

a deliberate show of lack of consideration and as an insult, and it would also serve as a direct notice of the ending of our friendly relations.

If this is necessary and unavoidable in view of our situation and circumstances it will naturally have to be borne. But even then I hope that we will not allow ourselves to be caught by the Russians, but that we continue independently along our path, as this corresponds to our interests in every way.

Farewell for to-day. I have had to work from morning to night during the past days and am exhausted.

With best regards<br>Your<br>PHatzfeldt

## 717.   Holstein to Paul von Hatzfeldt[1]

TELEGRAM

Berlin, 9 November 1899

Private

Finally I too send my congratulations.[2] I am very pleased about the material and also about your personal success. Yesterday at the Russian dinner, the Kaiser said to the Chancellor and several other people: 'Count Hatzfeldt has once again done his job superbly.' Take a bit of rest now and in the meanwhile think over what is to come.

I would first of all pose for your consideration that you do not negotiate on a single important question with Lord Salisbury; as Samoa has shown, it is no disadvantage if he sees that things can also be done without him; secondly, that the Moroccan Question is discussed again with Chamberlain only if he brings it up, i.e. when *he* is really in a hurry with it, for he will not make any [  ][3] that can be discussed before then; thirdly that under no circumstances should there be negotiations concerning Moroccan interests separate from African-Portuguese ones. Our presence in the Portuguese Colonial Question is awkward for the English because they believe that here too they can get along without us. But in the Moroccan Question they need us badly. Together with Germany they can hope *perhaps* to solve this question without war; without Germany they would have to wage war or remain satisfied with very unfavourable partitions. Lord Salisbury, whose only desire now probably is to postpone matters for a few more years, is no good for this. But Mr Chamberlain understands the question and certainly also understands that England's prospects—as Mr Chirol told Count Pückler[4] the other day—will deteriorate as soon as the French Exhibition and Russia's temporary financial difficulties are over. A note in the *Birmingham Post*, reprinted as a London report of yesterday in last night's *Frankfurter Zeitung*, leads me to assume that Mr Chamberlain has by no

---

[1] From the London Embassy files.          [2] On the Samoa Treaty.
[3] One word missing in the decoding.
[4] Karl, Count Pückler. First Secretary in the Embassy in Rome, December 1895–8, in London, January–December 1899, in Vienna, 1899–1900, in St Petersburg, August 1900–November 1901.

means forgotten the Italian factor either. For it says that complete agreement has already been reached on certain Mediterranean questions between England and Italy.

So, rest and reflect.

Holstein.

### 718.   Memorandum[1]

Berlin, 17 November 1899

In the conversations with the English Ministers one will have to adopt the point of view from the beginning that circumstances might develop in the near future which would make co-operation between Germany and England useful to both parties. Before such co-operation takes place, the obligations of both parties must naturally be fixed by treaty.

Germany's service in the alliance can consist in fighting alongside [England], or else, by remaining neutral, in preventing another Power from coming to the assistance of England's enemies. Both these services are equally valuable and deserve reciprocity from England, especially since in the present situation one can predict with certainty that the next big war will be caused by English rather than by German policy.

The English will presumably point out that Germany in her own interest cannot stand by and see England's power annihilated or crippled, because then the counter-weight to the Dual Alliance would be missing for Germany.

The reply to that is that there is no need to fear the annihilation of English power, for England, which can count with fair certainty on America covering her rear as long as McKinley is in office, can defend herself successfully against any diminution of her power *at sea*, and will only possibly find herself unable to prevent an increase in the power of the Dual Alliance on land through the acquisition of great territories in Asia and Africa, thereby restricting the English colonial empire. Moreover it can also be assumed that if England finds no firm support, she will simply maintain her power and territorial status as it now stands, and will quietly observe the expansion of the Dual Alliance Powers and the states co-operating with them. In that case the present balance of weight and counter-weight on the globe would remain more or less unchanged.

Germany, now that the agitation for *revanche* has lost its immediate political importance, faces no visible danger of war from any direction, and would endanger her peaceful security and make her own position worse if she undertook to support England, whether by participation in war or by alert neutrality. England's counter-service must correspond to this service. Service and counter-service will have to be carefully

---

[1] This unsigned memorandum from the Holstein Papers, written in an unidentified hand, was prepared by Holstein for the forthcoming trip of the Kaiser and Bülow to England, 20–28 November. A copy signed by Holstein was found in the Bülow Papers.

considered and therefore reserved for diplomatic negotiation. But it must be said in advance that, as long as Germany's relations with Russia remain unchanged, she will not accept an agreement which is visibly directed against Russia. On the other hand we do not assume that French and Russian interests are everywhere identical and that Russia will be obliged to support France in a *policy of aggrandizement*. On the contrary, after the information we have been given on the nature of the Dual Alliance, we are justified in regarding the Dual Alliance as a *pacte conservatoire*, which, just like the Triple Alliance, is by no means intended to cover *all* the interests of the contracting parties, but only to maintain their present territorial possessions. Therefore we are also justified in differentiating between Russian and French interests where a policy of aggrandizement is concerned, and to select the objects of our colonial policy from that point of view.

### 719.   Paul von Hatzfeldt to Holstein[1]

TELEGRAM

London, 25 November 1899

Absolutely confidential
Private.

Returned yesterday afternoon from Windsor. The Kaiser in a lengthy conversation with me was extremely kind and agreed with me in everything. The Kaiser is evidently highly satisfied with his visit, particularly with the sincere welcome of the whole family including the Prince of Wales. On the other hand His Majesty demonstrated his great displeasure with the instigators of the Press campaign in Germany opposing his visit.

I have reached complete agreement concerning future treatment of affairs here with Count Bülow.[2] In his conversations with the statesmen here he expressed the view, which I think is the only correct one, that our only purpose here was to remove the causes of friction by reaching an understanding on questions as they arise. We had no further positive wishes, because these would make for difficulties not only for England but also for ourselves. Apart from that he would with complete confidence leave it to me to deal with all questions as they might arise and to discuss any forthcoming suggestings.

H.

### 720.   Bernhard von Bülow to Holstein[3]

TELEGRAM

Sheerness, 28 November 1899

Secret.

Your conception of the parliamentary situation has much to be said for it.[4] On principle, however, I very much dislike interfering in

[1] From the London Embassy files.    [2] See *Grosse Politik*, vol. XV, no. 4398, pp. 413–20.
[3] From the Papers of Baroness von der Heydt. Only a typewritten copy of this document was available to the editors.
[4] The document containing Holstein's opinions to which Bülow replies in this telegram has not been found. In a letter to Bülow of 22 November, Holstein advised that if the Reichstag

internal problems when I see that the Chancellor is once again zealously at work on the great affairs of state, which, I am happy to see, now seems to be the case. In my opinion it is primarily the business of His Highness to explain to our Most Gracious Master what he believes are the factual and personal objections to the acceptance of the Navy Bill. Perhaps it would be desirable if the Chancellor assured himself of the support of the State Secretary of the Reich Naval Office in this connection. I thoroughly share the opinion that the concessions, which can be made and are essential, should be made at once and with good grace.

With all due modesty, I was nevertheless astonished that you believed me capable of intending to inaugurate an irresponsible and aggressive anti-English policy as soon as we were a little stronger at sea than we are to-day. I deserve this accusation all the less, because ever since my banishment to Berlin I have done all I could gradually to improve relations [with England] which were not exactly happy when I took office. What you write me with your usual political perspicacity about the strength of the English position as a world power and about the uncertainty of co-operation with France was something that I too had realized as a result of the Transvaal campaign of 1896.

My remark at the close of my very hasty note[1] meant only that right now we should pursue a doubly cautious policy towards England, for on the one hand our Press is constantly antagonizing and challenging England, whereas on the other hand, if things got serious, we are not even strong enough at sea to deal with England defensively, and would be at England's mercy like butter under a knife.

In strictest confidence I will add that the Prince of Wales wanted to persuade me, directly and indirectly, to go from Sandringham to Hatfield, which is seven hours away, in order to pay my respects to Salisbury there. I declined this presumptuous request in the friendliest manner by saying that this would be an indiscreet imposition on the English Prime Minister, who is heavily burdened by the death of his wife and by an attack of influenza. The visit to England went off without complications of any sort.

B.

721.  Hermann von Eckardstein to Holstein

London, 2 December 1899

Your Excellency,

I have the honour to submit a copy of a letter which I have just

rejected the Navy Bill, the Kaiser should adopt the attitude of Bismarck in his later years when his bills were rejected, namely that he was now absolved of all responsibility on the question and that the responsibility devolved on the Reichstag and the German electorate. Holstein thought the Kaiser might make a statement of *désintéressement* concerning the Navy Bill in a public speech. In a memorandum prepared for Bülow of 26 November, Holstein suggested that a change in the local election laws and the repeal of the law against association would help win the support of the Centre and Liberal Parties for the Government, and that the dismissal of Miquel was also very necessary if the Government's parliamentary position were to be strengthened. (From the Bülow Papers.)

[1] Not found.

received from Mr Chamberlain in the belief that the passage concerning the Kaiser and Count Bülow would be of interest to Your Excellency.[1]

Chamberlain is a firebrand by nature and in his sympathies and antipathies has always gone to extremes. That explains his speech in Leicester of the day before yesterday.[2] In spite of all the criticism to which Chamberlain is repeatedly subject among the Upper Ten Thousand, he is nevertheless at the moment the most important man in England, for he has the great masses behind him. Moreover he is now the focal point of the Cabinet, as the most important nucleus of it—i.e. Balfour, Devonshire, Lansdowne, Goschen, Chaplin etc.—are entirely on his side. The relationship between him and Salisbury also has improved very considerably lately through the mediation of Balfour, and the Prime Minister, who is becoming more and more easy-going and indolent, now more or less lets Chamberlain do whatever he likes. Hicks-Beach,[3] the Chancellor of the Exchequer, is and remains Chamberlain's chief enemy in the Cabinet. He hates Chamberlain personally and therefore intrigues against him constantly. But until now all these intrigues have been unsuccessful and moreover in the near future have little prospect of any sort of success. Chamberlain is not a diplomat in any way, but only a politician and people's tribune. But if one has him on one's side, one has also the support of the great masses in England. Diplomats on the continental model are few and far between in England, as the earth revolves quite differently when viewed from England rather than from the continent.

Though Chamberlain's speech was perhaps a trifle too sanguine and may have been a bit awkward for Count Bülow and German diplomacy, at least for the moment, I believe all the same that Chamberlain should be kept in a good frame of mind—even if cautiously—for the future. On the one hand he will be of great use to us in any future negotiations, as for example over Morocco, even though the negotiations will be conducted officially only with Salisbury and Balfour, and on the other hand England, under the aegis of Chamberlain, will in the next few years drift into a war with France and perhaps also with Russia which would seriously weaken both warring sides, and from which Germany would emerge as the arbiter of Europe. I am firmly convinced that Chamber-

[1] Chamberlain wrote to Eckardstein on 1 December : 'I had two lengthy conversations with the Emperor which confirmed my previous impressions of his extraordinary ability and grasp of European politics.

'I hope that in all respects His visit was a great success.

'Count v. Bülow, whose acquaintance I was delighted to make, also greatly impressed me.

'He expressed a wish that I might be able to say something as to the mutual interests which bound the United States to a triple understanding with Germany as well as Great Britain.

'Hence my speech yesterday which I hope will be not unsatisfactory to him.' (In English in the original.)

[2] In his speech in Leicester on 30 November, Chamberlain advocated the 'natural alliance' between Germany and Britain.

[3] Sir Michael Edward Hicks Beach, Bt. From 1864 Conservative Member of Parliament; Chief Secretary for Ireland, 1874–8; Colonial Secretary, 1878–80; Chancellor of the Exchequer, 1885–6; Irish Secretary, 1886–7; President of the Board of Trade, 1888–92; Chancellor of the Exchequer, 1895–1902.

lain already harbours the idea of a war by England and Japan against France and Russia, in which England would naturally need Germany's benevolent neutrality. Of course Chamberlain would only allow such a war to develop as long as he is convinced that he is on good terms with Germany.

As Your Excellency has already long been aware, the Kaiser's visit to England, so far as the latter is concerned, was a decisive success. If the Kaiser had *not* come to England after having been expected here, all the hatred of a nation at war—and made doubly sensitive on that account, as England is at the moment—would have been directed against Germany, and we would have been held responsible for the anti-English Press statements on the Continent. Now the odium falls on France and Russia, particularly on the former.

According to what the Duke of Devonshire told me yesterday, not only Chamberlain but also Balfour expressed himself highly satisfied about his audience with the Kaiser and his talk with Count Bülow.[1]

Great irritation is felt here in the most important circles against Herbert Bismarck, who is held responsible for all German Press attacks against England. Even Rosebery made some very derogatory remarks about his friend Herbert to me.

I visited the Ambassador in Brighton the day before yesterday and unfortunately found him in bed with a heavy cold. But I have heard to-day that he is very much better, and he will come to London again in the next few days.

Hoping that these lines may find Your Excellency in the best of health I sign as ever

Your Excellency's most obedient
Hermann v. Eckardstein.

722.   Bernhard von Bülow to Paul von Hatzfeldt[2]

TELEGRAM

Berlin, 14 December 1899

Private.

As Your Excellency is aware, groups envious of His Majesty the Kaiser's Government have for a number of years, one can say since the conclusion of the Zanzibar Convention in 1890, kept the suspicion alive in Germany that this Government inclines towards secret understandings with England in which German interests are always sacrificed to English ones. By constant repetition these insinuations had gradually acquired a certain weight, and a large part of the public regarded the Government's attitude in this respect with mistrust which was heightened by a number of newspapers and which repeatedly found expression in the Reichstag. The speech I made on Monday[3] was calculated to remove the grounds for this suspicion. All the same I found myself

---

[1] See *Grosse Politik*, vol. XV, no. 4398, pp. 413–20.
[2] From the London Embassy files.
[3] Speech of 11 December. See *Memoirs*, p. 182.

compelled on the following day, faced by an insinuation of Count Stirum's, to state once again quite explicitly that the Samoa agreement has no secret clause attached to it.

During my visit to England I was able to confirm that Your Excellency's view coincided with mine that German antagonism towards England has been fed by many aspects of English policy—I need only recall the events concerning Samoa this spring—and, until very recently, by statements in the great English papers, as for example the welcome-article in *The Times* of 20th of last month.[1] In this way the anti-English agitation has been helped along.

Yet I am too convinced an adherent of permanently friendly and confidential relations between the Cabinets in Berlin and London not to wish to avoid new misunderstandings between ourselves and England which might be produced by the tendentious and utterly warped interpretation which the Franco-Russian Press is trying to give to my speech. To this end I empower Your Excellency, should you regard it as necessary, to convey in strict confidence to the Prime Minister and possibly also to Mr Balfour either personally or through intermediaries, the verbal assurance that, provided naturally that England show consideration for German interests, His Majesty the Kaiser's Government will abstain from any continental grouping directed against England as well as from any collective action which might embarrass England. The English Government can count on this with certainty. I am anxious that complete clarity should reign between the two Governments concerning the state of their relations to each other, especially now when the situation of the English in South Africa is a difficult one.[2]

Bülow.

### 723.    Hermann von Eckardstein to Holstein[3]

London, 21 December 1899

Your Excellency,

I have received your kind letter of the 7th of this month,[4] and have immediately taken steps to revive unobtrusively my social contacts with the Liberal Party.[5] I have always been on very good terms with Rosebery[6] and my relations with him are such that I can go and see him at any time, whether in London or in the country. But, as I have said, I have now resumed closer contact with the other leaders of the Liberal Party.

I have read with great interest a letter of Prince Münster from Paris which was forwarded to the Embassy, and in which he deals with English politics and forecasts the fall of the present Ministry in the very

---

[1] The article assumed that a general agreement between Britain and Germany had been negotiated in the autumn of 1898, by which both countries undertook to regard certain ambitions as legitimate on either side and mutually to abstain from interference.

[2] Hatzfeldt reported in a telegram of 16 December that Count Pückler had spoken in the above sense to Balfour, who had expressed his thanks for the assurances given.

[3] See Eckardstein, *Lebenserinnerungen*, vol. II, pp. 133; 140–3.

[4] See *Lebenserinnerungen*, vol. II, pp. 132–3.

[5] Marginal note by Bülow: 'Very good'.           [6] Bülow: '*Bene*'.

near future.[1]  With all due respect for Prince Münster's great experience, I very much regret that I cannot share his view.  In spite of the great failures hitherto in the South African theatre of war, I regard the fall of the present Ministry as out of the question, at least for the duration of the war and the ensuing negotiations.[2]  As soon as Parliament re-assembles, the Liberals will certainly try to accuse the present Ministry of negligence in the administration of the army, but the Ministry will forestall this by coming out with a proposal to recognize and enlarge the land army *the moment* Parliament opens, and by reminding the Opposition on this occasion that they themselves always opposed a reorganization of the army.

If the Ministry were to fall at some later stage, this will hardly happen as a result of external or colonial questions but because of internal questions, as for example the Church question, the beer question or other internal matters.  Moreover the Liberal Party is still in a completely disorganized state.  Its official leader, Campbell-Bannerman,[3] is utterly insignificant, and the really able heads of the party, men like Sir Edward Grey,[4] Asquith,[5] etc. are in part adherents of Sir William Harcourt,[6] in part of Rosebery.  These two personalities, both momentarily standing outside the Party, watch each other most keenly, and when one appears to place himself again at the head of the party, the other intervenes at once in order to prevent it.

As regards the South African question, I have been trying for years to formulate as objective a judgment as possible on it by cultivating relations both with Cecil Rhodes and with Krüger's adherents.  I am saying this straightaway, so that Your Excellency should not perhaps think that I see this question only through English spectacles.  I have long held the view that the mines and the *uitlanders* are not the main issue, but that it has always been a question (already since Majuba Hill in '81[7]) of whether England would remain the predominant power in South Africa or whether she would be simply thrown out by the

---

[1] In his letter of 18 December, extracts from which were sent to the Embassy in London, Münster had expressed his great pessimism concerning English prospects in the war and the future of the Salisbury Cabinet. (From the Foreign Ministry files.)

[2] Marginal note by Bülow : 'Judging by continental standards this appears very improbable, but Eckardstein must be able to judge this better on the spot.'

[3] Sir Henry Campbell-Bannerman. From 1868 Liberal Member of Parliament; Chief Secretary for Ireland, 1884–5; Secretary for War, 1886, 1892–5; leader of the Liberal Party in the House of Commons, 1899; Prime Minister, December 1905–8.

[4] Sir Edward Grey. From 1885 Liberal Member of Parliament. Under Secretary of State for Foreign Affairs, 1892–5; Foreign Secretary, December 1905–16.

[5] Herbert Henry Asquith. From 1886 Liberal Member of Parliament; Home Secretary, 1892–5; Chancellor of the Exchequer, December 1905–8; Prime Minister, 1908–16.

[6] Liberal Member of Parliament, 1868–1904; Chancellor of the Exchequer, 1886, 1892–5; leader of the Liberal Party, 1896–8.

[7] On 30 December 1880 the Transvaal Boers revolted against English rule and proclaimed the Transvaal a republic.  The British force sent against the Boers was defeated on 27 February 1881 at Majuba Hill and its commander, Sir George Calley, was killed.  On 5 April 1881 the British Government concluded the Treaty of Pretoria with the Boers, by which the Transvaal Republic was granted its independence, but under the suzerainty of Great Britain.

Afrikanders and an Afrikander republic would be set up.[1] I have therefore always believed in the inevitability of a war, and I am now firmly
convinced that England started it only at the twelfth hour.

I am convinced that England will master this problem in the end,[2] but
that if she had waited only one more year to fight this war, she would
have been simply thrown out of South Africa. In that case we would
have seen an Afrikander republic in South Africa which would have
become far more democratic than the United States of America, and
would have created a kind of Monroe Doctrine for the whole of the
South Africa continent, to which both our German colonies as well as the
Portuguese colonies would inevitably have fallen victims. I am firmly
convinced that within a very short time Germany would have lost her
best colony, i.e. Southwest Africa, without being capable of the least
resistance, and moreover our agreement on the Portuguese colonies
would have become quite useless. If England were to be decisively
beaten, Germany would have to count with these eventualities.[3] If
England were to win, the danger could arise for us that with England
annexing the South African republics, a large part of the refractory Boer
population, encouraged by German public opinion, would emigrate to
German Southwest Africa and from there continue to intrigue constantly against England.[4] Taking the pro-Boer attitude in Germany
into account, our Government would after all probably find it very
difficult to prevent this.

To anyone who understands Count Bülow's difficult position in the
face of public opinion in Germany, his speech can of course only appear
masterly and most felicitous.[5] Here in England the great mass of the
people saw in it no sharpness or coolness towards England, but on the
other hand I have had to face for a few days the assaults of newspaper
proprietors, Cabinet Ministers, the Rothschilds, as well as of the Royal
family.[6] I calmed down all of them, even Chamberlain, who momentarily tended to see in the speech a cold douche for himself.[7] He is now
quite satisfied, especially after the State Secretary's *confidential* statement on the German Government's attitude—and now he has only one
small wish which he would like to have transmitted to the State Secretary when an occasion arises, but there is no hurry.[8]

Your Excellency will already have heard from the Ambassador, whom
I visited yesterday in Brighton, of the danger that the Delagoa Bay
question may be raised.[9] The Cabinet is very much afraid of this ques-

[1] Marginal note by Bülow: 'Surely it is in our interest that Boers and English should
balance each other in South Africa, neither one completely driving out the other.'
[2] Bülow: 'that after all (apart from England's military, strategic and tactical capacity)
depends on whether no European Power intervenes or makes itself unpleasant to England
somewhere else.'
[3] Bülow: 'Yes'.                              [4] Bülow: 'By no means improbable'.
[5] In his Reichstag speech of 11 December, Bülow had rejected the idea of an alliance with
England, and had spoken of building a fleet strong enough to resist English attack.
[6] Marginal note by Bülow: 'But English Ministers also reckon with *their* public opinion.'
[7] Bülow: 'That was by no means intended.'
[8] Bülow: '*Je suis à ses ordres.*'
[9] See *Grosse Politik*, vol. XV, no. 4404, pp. 428–9.

tion, but it looks as though it will be driven to it by public opinion against its own will.[1] I can already imagine the storm of indignation which the raising of this question would arouse in Germany, and still have the hope that this rock will be circumnavigated.[2]

Wishing Your Excellency a merry Christmas,

I remain as ever Your Excellency's
most obedient
Hermann von Eckardstein.

P.S. Rothschild received a telegram from Paris yesterday according to which Dr Leyds[3] is supposed to have requested Prince Münster as well as Delcassé to initiate peace negotiations under certain specific conditions. If there is any truth in it, Your Excellency will no doubt know of this by now. The Cabinet here was informed of it through Rothschild.[4]

## 724.   Philipp zu Eulenburg to Holstein

Vienna, 23 December 1899

Dear friend,

We have not seen each other or written for an eternity. I was *very* sorry that I did not succeed in meeting you in the autumn. The end of the year at the turn of the century invites one to look backwards as no previous year has done. When I look back on all the struggles and pain which I have suffered, your picture always appears to me, counselling, fighting and suffering by my side.

I always feel as if I belonged to you, and even if we should temporarily hold different views on a question, this should never act as a *separating* factor. I am anxious to express this to you very warmly. I cling to my old friends with great tenacity and loyalty—particularly to you.

With this Christmas greeting I close,

Your old faithful
Philipp Eulenburg.

[1] Marginal note by Bülow : 'I hope not.'

[2] Bülow : 'This is a *very* serious rock for German-English relations.'

[3] Minister of the South African Republic in The Hague, Berlin, and Paris, 1898–1902.

[4] Bülow noted at the end of Eckardstein's letter : 'We must after all wish that the English are neither pushed out of South Africa completely nor that they lose their position as a Great Power, but also that they do not swallow up the two South African republics. Thus, if possible, maintenance of the *status quo ante bellum*, after heavy English losses, which would make the English more modest towards us, and in the meantime make use of the momentarily so favourable situation for the Bagdad railway, coaling station on the Red Sea, and other things.'

# 1900

725.  Hermann von Eckardstein to Holstein

London, 23 January 1900

Your Excellency,

I have the honour to report the following :

A close acquaintance of mine, an old and intimate friend of Rosebery's, tells me that Rosebery, with whom he stayed for a few weeks in the country recently, received a long letter from Herbert Bismarck a short while ago.  In it the latter complained bitterly of the treatment he had received at the hands of the Kaiser as well as of the measures taken against him by his personal enemies, who were doing everything in order to undermine the political position in Germany which is his due. He insinuates further that at heart he is no enemy of England's as is said to be the case by his personal enemies in that country.

I gather from further remarks by my absolutely reliable informant that Rosebery actually has a very low opinion of the ability of his friend Herbert, but that he would not dislike to see him once again and soon in a responsible position, whether in Germany or as Ambassador in London.  Rosebery feels himself so superior to his friend Herbert that he believes he would be able to use him as a willing tool for his own plans.

To-day's courier is also bringing an unofficial report to the State Secretary on statements by Lord Salisbury concerning Russian intentions in Persia.[1]

The Bagdad railway question worries me.  I fear that our hot-headed businessmen will not be satisfied to act only as good carriers, but will try to establish themselves firmly in every way in Asia Minor.  The time may then easily come when Germany will be forced to opt either for England or for Russia in the Persian Gulf question so as not to fall between two stools.  I am firmly convinced that the English will do everything to *try* and involve us in the question of the Persian Gulf and to use us to get England's chestnuts out of the fire.  Co-operation with England in *this* question, however, would surely be very dangerous for us.  [...]

In the hope that these lines may find Your Excellency in good health, I remain

Your Excellency's always obedient
Hermann v. Eckardstein

[1] *Grosse Politik,* vol. XVII, no. 5212, pp. 372–4.

## 726. Holstein to Maximilian von Brandt[1]

B[erlin], 23 February 1900

Your Excellency,

Since 19 January I have been out of touch with the Ministry. I went there once, a fortnight ago, but then suffered a relapse. I intend to take up my work again to-morrow.

An article along the lines of Wichmann's[2] ideas is not to be objected to on principle, but it would have to be written in a somewhat different manner.

England's astonishment at Germany's bitterness[3] can in turn only be regarded here with the greatest astonishment. Is English astonishment real? If yes, a slap in the face must have a different meaning in England than it does in Germany. Just a year ago we received more than one slap in the face over Samoa. The worst was the bombardment of Apia.[4] The conduct of policy like the waging of war must vary according to whether England is dealing with an Indian Prince or with a Great Power whose good will or resentment could under certain circumstances be of importance. The German people has for a long time failed to observe that England makes this differentiation, and now inclines to the view that it cannot expect *reciprocal* consideration from England—without which satisfactory relations between Great Powers cannot be maintained—as a general rule but only in exceptional cases, and that England's political leadership still dreams of 'splendid isolation' as the ideal, with the corresponding lack of consideration for others in foreign affairs. There was in fact sufficient material to justify the popular belief that England regarded the break with Germany with equanimity, if not with pleasure, and that therefore Germany also would have to seek closer relations elsewhere in time. The German Government, whose task it is not to allow itself to be influenced by momentary trends, followed a policy of soberly pursuing its interests, and by its perseverance and patience gave the English Government every conceivable opportunity of improving relations. That the German Government exercised this patience and the English Government finally became more conciliatory must be regarded as a favourable outcome for both sides. In view of our territorial sacrifices, not to mention well-known earlier events, Germany had no cause for the demonstrative gratitude demanded by some English publicists. Yet for all those who share the opinions of the author of these lines, and their number in Germany is no small one, the Samoa Treaty offers a satisfactory prospect for the future

---

[1] From the Brandt Papers.

[2] Karl Wichmann. Representative of the German high explosives industry; member of the syndicate of the German Southwest Africa colonial society.

[3] At the stopping of the German mail steamer *Bundesrath* and other German ships in December 1899 and January 1900 by the British, who suspected them of carrying contraband to the Boers. On 16 January 1900 the British promised to release the ships and pay an indemnity. (See *Grosse Politik*, vol. XV, chapter CII.)

[4] British and United States warships bombarded Apia on 15 March 1899 as a move to depose the German-supported Mataafa, who had been successful in the civil war for the Samoan succession. (See p. 109, note 1, and p. 143, note 2.)

because as a result of it Germany is no longer under the immediate necessity of joining an Anti-English grouping. I also believe that the temporary calm brought about by the Samoa Treaty will be permanent, for I assume that the sober considerations which governed the attitude of the German Government will lead English politicians to the conviction that Germany's role in England's (near) future is by no means at an end, and that Germany's neutrality in the elemental developments which lie ahead is not a matter of indifference. From the moment that *reciprocal* consideration is recognized in principle and practised in fact, not only by the Governments but also by subordinate agencies, further friction can be regarded as impossible.

. . . . . . . . . . .

The short draft above can stand a bit of watering down in developing the arguments; in its present concentration it is too strong. But something along these lines will have to be said, for on the one hand the German public would not stand for England being petted and favoured by Germany, on the other I believe that the English would understand the matter most easily if they were told: well, you certainly behaved badly, but let's forget about it for *both* our sakes—or do you really think that it is not in your interest to be on good terms with us, that situations similar to those of the last three months will not recur, that there will be peace and quiet?

Something like that, only much better! And then one could talk good sense to the Germans, too. England of course has her good points. But it is inevitable that I am now more familiar with English shortcomings than with her inherent merit; thus I am thinking of the difference between our practice of neutrality, as demonstrated after the search of the mail steamers, and England's neutrality in 1870, when the French took delivery of completely equipped batteries. But I do not know whether this is the time to sow this particular dragon's tooth—and even less whether it would fit into the general framework.

Now, good-night Your Excellency. It is almost twelve.

Ever your sincerely devoted
Holstein.

The episode in 1864[1] also differed from Wichmann's account. According to our information Palmerston had taken the initiative to suggest intervention in Denmark's favour in Paris. Napoleon, as was his habit, thereupon talked of compensation: Rhine, Belgium, something or other; whereupon Palmerston, Belgium's protector, dropped the matter like a hot potato. Napoleon for his part took the opportunity to inform Berlin that *he* had scotched the English proposal for intervention. I was told this at the time by Clermont-Tonnerre[2] when we were out riding between Kolding and Fridericia. The English had better not bring up '64; that was the time they got the first black mark in our book.

[1] During the conflict of Austria and Prussia against Denmark.
[2] The French Military Attaché in Berlin.

But I doubt whether it is of any use to fetch out this particular set of chestnuts now; I see no reason for it. At the most you could set Wichmann right in private. But I don't attach any value to it.

## 727.   Bernhard von Bülow to Holstein

136 Königgrätzer Strasse
9 April [1900]

In spite of considerable scepticism and manifold experiences, I had not expected that after almost three years of our working together you would reproach me because people were saying in Berlin pubs 'and elsewhere' that I let 'everything slide'. Is this unfavourable estimate of my work and my qualifications due to a desire on your part to replace me with Kiderlen? You know that I don't stick. But when I do go, I hardly think K. will be my successor, much though I would wish it because of his virile and healthy ambition.

You yourself don't expect me to take seriously the minor points you raised, for these intrinsically trivial matters were clearly cited only as evidence on which to base your overall opinion of my fitness for my present post.

B.

## 728.   Holstein to Pietro Blaserna
Draft

Berlin, 11 April 1900

Dear friend,

Unfortunately I must inform you that—quite unexpectedly—I have landed myself in a conflict with Bülow which cannot remain without consequences.

Most of our official exchanges of views take place in writing—between the Ministry and his villa—by means of very concise notes, in which I try only to express fully what I have to say irrespective of form. I assumed as a matter of course that this would not be taken amiss. But it seems I deceived myself with this assumption.

The day before yesterday I sent a note of this kind warning Bülow not to allow the negligence of two subordinate officials to pass without reprimand because of the impression which would be created on all the other officials by letting the matter slide. (Normally Bülow is good-natured and doesn't like to hurt anyone. Nor am I vicious towards subordinates, but discipline must be maintained.)

To my complete amazement I received an immediate answer in which B. not only commented in great irritation on the tone of my communication and disputed the factual justification of my warning, but added that presumably I found so much to criticize in him only because I wanted to see Kiderlen in his place.

K. is Minister in Bucharest, about twenty years younger than I am, and for certain definite reasons I would leave the Ministry within the hour if he became its head.

As I read this I said to myself: '*Ce n'est pas sérieux*', and wandered over to the villa. There I found *visage de bois*. For that reason and because B. left without a personal discussion with me, it looks as if this affair is not just a short-lived outburst.

If only he had written me: 'The matters you raise are of no importance and I find your tone rude', I would have replied: 'Having drawn your attention to these matters, they are done with so far as I am concerned; as regards the tone I am no judge; when writing these notes—intended only for you—I don't weigh my words.'

That could have settled the affair, without the remark about Kiderlen. But from the latter one can see that I was already under suspicion, whereas I thought I enjoyed full trust. The existence of this suspicion makes it impossible for me to remain.

For Bülow in cold blood to regard the Kiderlen scheme as conceivable seems to me so improbable that I believe in the existence of another motive, which would, however, lead to the same ultimate outcome—separation. I am a lonely man, have no supporters, but a number of personal enemies who would rather see someone else in my place. The Kaiser too, who favoured me in the past, is now prejudiced against me, since—sometimes with my approval—he received knowledge of letters in which I criticized some of his actions with the sharpness natural to me. It could thus easily be imagined that Bülow's relations to certain persons would be improved and his position with the Kaiser eased if I disappeared. During the past years I have repeatedly drawn B.'s attention to this, orally and in writing; the last time I did so was barely a fortnight ago. His reaction, this last time too, was always entirely negative, but in view of the explosion of two days ago the question arises whether he has not meanwhile become more familiar with the thought that my person renders his life's task more difficult. In that case, however, I would have preferred it if he had treated the matter as openly and simply as I have done.

As regards future developments, I don't think we ought to furnish the Berlin public the spectacle of a row. Thus for the moment nothing will happen. I shall go on leave at the beginning of the summer and not return. I had a very bad winter, couldn't work at all for five weeks, so there are plausible reasons of health. At the age of sixty-three and with half an eye, one can retire without attracting attention. Some literary activity and walks on easy paths will fill my life satisfactorily. After all I bade a voluntary farewell to pomp and circumstance long ago.

The painless separation will take place without the exchange of a single word on the subject between B. and myself. Meanwhile everything will go on as if nothing had happened.

Secure in the knowledge of your sincere sympathy for both parties—naturally *à des degrés divers*—I wanted to inform you of what had happened while the impressions were still fresh.

Ever your devoted<br>H.

*Strictly confidential, only for you.*

P.S. I can hear you ask, dear friend: 'Who has been agitating?' The answer is, many people. Lindenau, whom you know, is one who has added one more sad experience to my life. He has a lot to thank me for. I was responsible for his dispensation from the examination for the diplomatic corps at the time. At his request and due to my intervention he was later transferred to the Foreign Ministry, because his dislike of society, particularly female society, made his social duties in posts abroad unpleasant for him. He is quite talented, but doesn't know how to work, and whenever possible passes on his work to others. Naturally this did not remain unnoticed in the Ministry and his position has become an artificial one. He feels this, and is no exception to the rule that character deteriorates in someone who holds down a position he cannot fill.

For years I was Lindenau's sole support in the Ministry, and he my devoted adherent. That changed when Bülow, with whom Lindenau had already been on close terms long ago in Paris, arrived. Amongst the Foreign Ministry staff it is now Lindenau and Lichnowsky who are most intimate with the State Secretary. But Lichnowsky plays no part in all this. As far as I can judge at present, he is completely decent and reliable, though impulsive and easily influenced. He does no damage, on the contrary. The same cannot be said of Lindenau. The State Secretary listens particularly to *his* views on *personalia*, while the *actual* work which falls to Lindenau's department is usually handed to other officials.

I don't merely assume, I *know*, that Lindenau has tried to make my already difficult position more difficult. But I can't name the absolutely reliable persons through whom I have found out about this.

As for me, you know that since Bülow has been State Secretary I have avoided everything which might have looked like boot-licking. I have always kept our relations on a sober, official basis, have never taken any part in social life either at Bülow's house or at the Chancellor's. But I did believe that Bülow valued my political advice (and on the whole he did not do badly with it), and the feeling of being useful satisfied me. Lately, however, I thought I noticed—this was also hinted to me—that Lindenau disagreed with some of the steps taken. It seems to me that Lindenau is pursuing a line which is too exclusively agrarian. Because of this he had a violent argument with Mühlberg a few weeks ago. Mühlberg was formerly in charge of one of the important Economic Divisions. Since then they face each other like *chiens de faïence*. I don't know enough about economic policy to be able to judge. But naturally I don't want us to face the rest of the world *à couteaux tirés*, a prospect which extreme agrarians face with equanimity. A difference of opinion on these matters may be contributing to Lindenau's attitude, but I believe only in small part. The main causes are faults of character to be found in men who want to have influence without doing any work.

Well, Bülow will find out how far he will get with advisers as conscientious as that. But I want to leave before that, in peace and quiet. Were I to remain, another incident would soon occur, for there are many who agitate: Herbert Bismarck, Countess Guido Henckel and heaven knows who else, not to mention Philipp Eulenburg. And Bülow is impressionable, though he tries not to show it. Finally I return to the beginning, those two notes. Mine was based on the intention to save the recipient from harm; the answer I have in front of me shows the nervous impulse to wound the recipient. That characterizes the situation.

Do you know how I got the idea to use the free morning for this long letter? I happened to look at the photograph showing you feeding the pigeons in St Mark's Square; it is framed and hangs here.

With a firm shake of the hand, old friend.

H.

### 729.   Pietro Blaserna to Holstein

Rome, 15 April 1900

Dear, esteemed friend,

I received your serious letter last night after returning from an outing to Tivoli. You are certainly right to look on me as the mutual friend whose life's task has always been to mediate and not to irritate. Hence I believe myself justified in sending the first part of your letter to Baveno this very day.

But even without awaiting the reply, I can assure you that Count B[ülow] always had and still has a very high opinion of your political integrity. I deeply regret this conflict, about which I can form no opinion because too many factors are unknown to me. But I do hope that a break will be avoided. When a poor Minister for once loses patience, do remember how great and how numerous are the difficulties of every kind which he must combat. A Ministry should be like a family, where one can rest and gather one's strength for the coming day. And it is the duty of a good friend to ensure and secure this rest. I do hope that the assurance, to which you give such friendly expression in your letter, will help to minimize the scope of the conflict.

In accordance with your wish I kept the second half of your letter to myself. But I can say that I have never heard Lindenau referred to as *other than your man*. It is possible that he has greater ambitions; but I wouldn't mind betting that you overestimate his role. Allow me, dear friend, to speak openly to you, as in the good old days at Pontresina. I have often told you, and I will risk repeating it, that you are much too suspicious in personal matters. True, you have enemies; who hasn't? But your greatest enemy is—Baron Holstein. I am convinced that were I to live in Berlin and have the honour of living with you on terms of constant intimacy, I would be able to eliminate much unpleasantness. Given your recognized efficiency and unselfishness you could enjoy a quite exceptional position above all parties if you were less suspicious. Just what the role of the agrarians and its importance will be in our future economic policy is a question of great moment. Italy and half the world are concerned, and as always you have hit the nail on the head in my opinion. Compared to that Lindenau is a mere atom, which will hardly tip the scales on one side or the other.

181

Your good opinion of Lichnowsky pleases me. He is a thoroughly honourable, healthy, independent character.

You see, dear friend, how frankly I talk to you, and I hope that you will regard my frankness as the best proof of my sincere friendship for you. *Entre nous*, my friend and your enemy von Holstein has a suspicious and jealous nature, and we must all of us unite to fight against it.

Thank you for the confidence which you have shown me by your letter. There is something to be said for the pigeons in the Piazza San Marco after all.

With best regards
Your old friend
Blaserna.

## 730.   Bernhard von Bülow to Holstein

Baveno, 20 April 1900

Dear friend,

In view of the absolute trust I have always had in you, the frequent demonstrations of my respect for you, and finally the affectionate consideration I have always shown you, you will understand that I was bound to feel deeply hurt when I saw you pass so unfavourable a judgment on my official work as you suddenly seemed to do.

This was bound to kindle the thought in me that you would consider a change in the position of State Secretary for Foreign Affairs and my departure from Berlin as not undesirable. No one knows better than you how little I want to stay in my present position, which I made no effort to attain. But as long as I am in this position, I want to fill it as well and with as much dignity as possible.

I see from your letter to Blaserna, which he forwarded to me, that you had not intended to insult me, and I therefore hope, indeed I am convinced, that our future co-operation will be as untroubled as heretofore.

Ever faithfully
Your
Bernhard Bülow.

## 731.   Holstein to Helene von Hatzfeldt[1]
Copy

Berlin, 1 May 1900

Dear Countess,

I am writing to you to Sommerberg because I don't know where you are staying at the present time.

You doubtless know that I had to advise your husband to confine himself to announcing from London the *fait accompli* of his return to work, instead of first asking when he should return. This hint undoubtedly already alerted your feminine instinct. In fact, I cannot hide from you that Hatzfeldt's position has become as weak as his health. The

---

[1] In French in the original.

Emperor, in speaking about the reports of Metternich, said recently: 'It's good to have a representative who can go out walking with people.' This was because Metternich had written on several occasions that he had gone out walking with this or that English statesman. My poor friend Hatzfeldt can't go out walking, he is living a little on the capital of his past services, and I hope he continues to do so as long as possible— that's why I'm now writing you these lines on my own initiative.

Recently the reports of Hatzfeldt have been limited for the most part to quoting every fortnight certain colourless words of Salisbury. This does not satisfy the Emperor who knows a lot of people in England and who wants to know what these people think. So if Hatzfeldt is to be kept at his post, if you do not want to risk having his mission end suddenly before the end of the year, *it is absolutely necessary that the reports from the Embassy should be fuller, that they should present a more complete picture than formerly about political life in England and the opinion of the leading men.* It matters little whether the information is collected by the Ambassador personally or by a member of the Embassy; the information—that is the essential thing. For this purpose Eckardstein would be a valuable collaborator. I hesitate to say this crudely to the sick Hatzfeldt, and am therefore addressing myself to you. Talk it over with your son and see what can be done. The danger of which I am warning you now I have seen developing for several years. To-day it is great and imminent.

If Hatzfeldt were forced to leave, Metternich would be the best qualified person to succeed him, and I think he would have the best chance. But I think that there is no hurry and that Hatzfeldt might well stay on for a while. The Foreign Ministry and his direct superior, I should emphasize, have done everything possible to support and keep Hatzfeldt; otherwise Hatzfeldt would have disappeared during the troubles of the summer of '97. So his fall—as I found out later—had been envisaged for a long time, but Bülow resisted. I need hardly tell you, however, that it hasn't been possible to resist the undermining activity, and the slogan that we need 'fresh blood' has lost nothing of its appeal. There is only one means to parry these underground attacks; Hatzfeldt has this means at hand in the person of Eckardstein, he has only to use him, that is, to put him to work. If he fails to do so, I fear that the consequences of this omission won't take long in making themselves felt.

I find it painful to tell you all this, but as things now stand it is the duty of a friend to be frank. I hope that my advice may prove useful, because Hatzfeldt's health, according to what I have heard indirectly, has improved significantly. So he would be able to direct the work of Eckardstein.

It is something like thirty years since Hatzfeldt and I began to work together at Versailles. I haven't forgotten this, and would like to do more for him to make his life easy. But at the moment the Foreign Ministry can't do much. The only person who can effectively help Hatzfeldt is Hatzfeldt himself.

### 732.    Holstein to Paul von Hatzfeldt

Copy

Berlin, 13 June 1900

Dear friend,

To-day I am abandoning my principle of not worrying you with letters as far as possible. First of all I want to say how pleased I am that you are back at work, and, as I have heard on several occasions, that your health has greatly improved. Secondly I want to say a few things in a letter, which, since I don't think they are supported by sufficiently good evidence, I did not want to include in a dispatch.

Reports from different sources show that the present French Government is under suspicion by the St Petersburg Cabinet—a few pro-English phrases in Delcassé's speeches may have contributed to this—and that therefore the Russians would quite like to see new men in power in Paris. Because of these suspicions, Petersburg is watching the activities of M. Waldeck-Rousseau and Delcassé particularly closely. As I do not think the latter has the nerve to conclude an important agreement directed against Russia or behind her back with England, I as yet do not believe that such an agreement exists, in spite of Salisbury's efforts. We have heard from St Petersburg that Salisbury's attempts to reach an agreement with France on a major question, Morocco or something else, are no secret there. Muraviev once mentioned not long ago that not only part of the French Press but also members of the Paris Municipal Council had been bought by England. Muraviev added: 'However, this tendency is not the dominant one in France.' I share this opinion and feel that any Russian Foreign Minister must do everything he can to prevent a major Franco-English agreement, at least until such time as Russia too has settled some of the vital problems with England. Do you believe this to be conceivable, possible, probable? Our friend Radowitz thinks 'yes' because there is room for everybody in China. I incline towards 'no' because apart from the concrete problem, *imponderabilia* do play a part in politics.

*A propos*, are you of the opinion that a flirtation with Russia might help to bring Lord Salisbury to repentance? I am an honourable man and don't favour such devious methods, but there is no rule without an exception. A flirtation with Russia would be a less transparent method than a flirtation with France, which latter I regard as useless because its purpose would be obvious.

Actually, I place fewer hopes on flirtation than on naked self-interest. Economically England's need for Delagoa Bay will now be greater than ever. I therefore expect that someone or other—perhaps Rhodes or one of his followers—will raise the question of a partial implementation of the German-English agreement, and then we will see. In this connection I have just remembered that the State Secretary has called a conference on Soveral's recent suggestion of a trade agreement with Portugal. Now that the Reichstag has adjourned, this should take place to-day or to-morrow. Thus I can give only my personal opinion to-day, which is that I consider the suggestion by the blue monkey[1] to be nothing more than an effort to invalidate our agreement and replace it by a new one. In the present mood of your amiable friend Salisbury this would be less favourable to us than the one which you wheedled out of honest Balfour in the past. But, as I have said, for the time being that is only my own opinion. And I do believe that if the first agreement remains in force, it should be implemented soon.

After all Chamberlain cautiously hinted at the problem of implementation when war broke out or soon after.[2] But in view of public opinion, no conscientious adviser of the Kaiser could recommend to him that the treaty be implemented then. I think that even if—*par impossible*—we had acquired Zanzibar, the outcry at the blood of the betrayed Boers would have been considerable. But to-day the situation has changed. A nation of soldiers like Germany was bound to be and was sobered by the manner in which the Boers have behaved since Cronje's capitulation.[3] The State Secretary tells me that yesterday's sensational speech by Liebermann von Sonnenberg against the Kaiser[4] was received without any acclaim. Three months ago it would surely have been different. Thus the taking up of an English suggestion to implement the treaty would no longer meet with the former objections.

> With best regards etc.
> Yours
> Holstein.

733.　Paul von Hatzfeldt to Holstein

19 June 1900

Dear friend,

I am using the mysterious summoning of Eckardstein[5] to send you greetings and also to thank you for your last letter.

The situation here is that there is tremendous distrust of Russo-French plans in China in the Foreign Office, particularly amongst the Under Secretaries and Counsellors, while Salisbury, whom I saw as recently as this afternoon, speaks of the matter with the greatest indifference. To-day he cracked poor jokes about the strange impracticable suggestion of the English Press that England should depose the Empress Mother and introduce a better government in China. In any case his

---

[1] The Marquis of Soveral is meant.

[2] In order to close Delagoa Bay for the transport of munitions to the Transvaal. (See *Grosse Politik*, vol. XV, nos. 4404; 4406; 4409, pp. 428–9; 431–2; 434–5.) On 14 October Britain had already concluded a treaty with Portugal whereby Britain guaranteed Portuguese territory, and Portugal undertook not to allow munitions to pass through Delagoa Bay to the Transvaal. (*British Documents*, vol. I, chapter II, part III.)

[3] On 18 February the Boer general, Piet Arnoldus Cronje, was defeated at Paardeberg. He was forced to surrender on 27 February. In the following weeks the British continued to inflict severe defeats on the Boers, who resorted increasingly to guerilla warfare.

[4] Liebermann von Sonnenberg had criticized the Kaiser for offending German national feeling, which was sympathetic to the Boers, by his telegrams of congratulations at British victories. (See *Stenographische Berichte über die Verhandlungen des Reichstages*, 1898–1900, vol. VII, p. 6038.)

[5] See Eckardstein, *Lebenserinnerungen*, vol. II, pp. 176–7.

remarks did not imply any keenness on his part to embark on a conflict with Russia if the latter should use more troops to restore order in China than England is capable of supplying. My impression therefore is that for the moment he will quietly wait and see whether the Russians will in fact take action, and whether in that case others may not be found who will feel inclined to pull England's chestnuts out of the fire. However, this waiting attitude may be considerably modified as a result of one factor which cannot be foreseen with any degree of accuracy: that is English public opinion, which is extraordinarily suspicious of Russia and might be most resentful if it appeared that Lord Salisbury intended to watch Russia's action in China with his hands in his lap. This could become all the more dangerous for Lord Salisbury's position and that of his Cabinet because the demand for strong anti-Russian measures in China comes particularly from Government supporters. Yet it is difficult to judge just how dangerous to the Government this might be, and I therefore raised this question in the strictest confidence in a conversation with Lord Rosebery. He replied that the afore-mentioned danger to the Ministry would only become serious if the right statesman were found to exploit it against the Cabinet. Evidently he wished to imply that even then the Ministry would have no cause for alarm as long as he, Rosebery, did not wish to seize the opportunity to bring it down.

As for me, I should think that as yet a conflict with Russia is not to be feared, for, unless I am utterly mistaken, Tsar Nicholas does not at the moment think of bringing about a conflict with England. All the less because, whatever the Russian Press and Russian public opinion may say, he must realize that Japan will fight if England is seriously involved, and that American abstention could then not be reckoned with.

Eckardstein will tell you, with respect to the Portuguese agreement with England, that I am of the opinion that we must await the further development of the situation. The time will come when England will need us much more urgently than Portugal, and will therefore be inclined to exert the necessary pressure in Lisbon. I could recommend in any case that we do not raise the matter again here directly, but leave that to other interested parties. Rhodes for example could do it; he is supposed to be inclining strongly that way. As Eckardstein will tell you, people here think that Balfour ceded an important port on the West Coast of Africa to me which would be surrendered unwillingly. That is said to be the main reason why people here hesitate to implement the treaty. I see no reason why we should make a concession over that.

As regards the development of the internal situation in England, I cannot with the best will in the world raise your hopes of getting rid of our friend Salisbury soon. I regard it as probable that new elections will be held in October, and, unless something unforeseen occurs, it seems beyond doubt that the Government will win an enormous majority. Some people maintain that Salisbury would then resign and be succeeded by Balfour, which would certainly not be undesirable from our point of view. But I shall only believe in Salisbury's retirement when I see it. He is fitter and more cheerful than ever, and I don't believe for a moment that he will voluntarily retire to private life. We can't do anything about it, least of all by flirting with Russia (this in answer to your question). Such a flirtation would not change his attitude, but apart from that it would do great harm. Contrary to the indications furnished by a certain agent, who still supplies reports to the Foreign Ministry, I believe I may state that as a result of our attitude during the Transvaal crisis a feeling of respect and almost gratitude is to be found here, particularly in parliamentary circles. Even Salisbury does not deny that we have thereby earned a right to gratitude. A flirtation with Russia would spoil this feeling without converting Salisbury to a friendlier attitude. His aversion is primarily due to personal motives. And he will turn towards us and will have to do so just as soon as it becomes apparent that England can't do without us.

The above naturally is also for the State Secretary and he may use it if he wishes.

Farewell for to-day, dear friend. Touch wood, my health is considerably improved. I therefore close with the wish Prince Bismarck once expressed to me: 'I hope we will still do great things together.' But if it should be thought that someone else might improve on my performance, all I can say is : so be it.

With best regards
Yours
PHatzfeldt

734.    Paul von Hatzfeldt to Holstein

London, 2 July 1900

Dear friend,

[...] I was very glad to get the telegraphic instruction concerning Portugal's colonies in South Africa,[1] particularly as I am not tied down as to time and can choose ways and means according to circumstances. Thus I first of all want to wait and see what Rhodes' agent, Mr Davis, has brought back from Lisbon—he has just returned from there—and whether he is inclined to suggest here in Rhodes' name that the question be settled. Perhaps it will in this way be possible to get things moving again without giving Salisbury the impression that we took the initiative. If it doesn't work, the only thing to be done will be to make another discreet attempt with Chamberlain and Balfour. But one thing is already absolutely certain in my opinion, we must avoid any direct approach to Salisbury.

If the other Powers in China want to wait for people here to make energetic proposals for the protection of foreigners and the restoration

---

[1] On 30 June Bülow instructed Hatzfeldt to sound out the responsible people in England through a suitable, possibly private, person on the question of Britain's attitude on the implementation of the Anglo-German Treaty concerning the Portuguese Colonies. 'We aim at the total implementation of the treaty; but we are in no hurry and aren't pressing. It does, however, seem to us worth knowing how the problem is regarded there now.' (*Grosse Politik*, vol. XVII, no. 5169, pp. 323–4.)

of order, they will, I fear, have a long wait.[1] When Salisbury and I recently discussed the theoretical question as to whether a state of war existed with China, he said to me: 'No, certainly not a state of war—that is not until our war in South Africa has come to an end.' At the same time he described as mad the demands in the Press here for a deposition of the Empress Mother and the introduction of a better government. It was impossible to think of taking over the administration of such an enormous country, no matter by what method. In the end there would be no alternative to an understanding and reconciliation with the Empress. It seems to me that this point of view of Lord Salisbury's is getting very close to the opinions of the Russian Press, as far as I can judge these from here; which naturally didn't prevent Lord Salisbury from acceding with pleasure to the Japanese request to support in St Petersburg and Berlin the proposal that they should intervene in China on the basis of a European mandate.[2] I know he will not have been so naïve as to expect acceptance of the proposal in St Petersburg. But if contrary to expectations it had succeeded, he would thereby have thrown a spanner into the Russian works without having taken any risk, as he had carefully refrained from promising Japan English protection in case of Russian dissatisfaction. If it failed, as now appears to be the case,[3] nothing would have been lost, and he could point out in Tokyo that he did everything possible to help the Japanese. [...]

The news just sent to you by telegram that they believe here that they have exact information concerning French intentions for concentrating the fleet at Cherbourg etc., sounds strange, I know, but I had to pass it on, as it came from an apparently very good source. Personally I do not believe in English bellicose intentions towards France, and even less that such plans are thought of in Paris. What is possible is that Paris got scared and thought it necessary to take security measures against an English attack, which might have been the final outcome of a break between England and Russia in China. Unfortunately I don't share this concern. As you know, my fear on the contrary is that Salisbury may incline towards an understanding with France.

This letter, which I naturally would like to be submitted to the State Secretary with my compliments, is already pretty long. I don't want to make it longer still by entering on a discussion of the question of what our policy should be if the Americans really break into Shantung and occupy a point there. If, as I see from the latest documents received from Berlin, we *must* in that case draw close to Russia and France, I will obviously raise no objections. I presume that there are irrefutable political arguments which would make this necessary. But I would regret it, though not because I am an adherent of friendship with England *à tout prix*. That I am not, as I believe to have proved repeatedly.

[1] Towards the end of 1899 and during the early months of 1900 the anti-foreign Boxer movement in China assumed violent form. On 20 June the murder of the German Minister, Baron von Ketteler, opened the siege of the Legations in Peking by the Boxers.

[2] See *Grosse Politik*, vol. XVI, no. 4532, pp. 20–1.

[3] See *Grosse Politik*, vol. XVI, nos. 4535, 4541, 4542, pp. 22–3, 28–9.

What I do believe is that our position in the world is incalculably powerful and great as long as we have no firm engagements towards *any* side whatever. If there really should be a conflict in China between England and her possible supporters on the one hand and Russia and her friends on the other, we could in my modest opinion lay down the law to both sides if we have remained uncommitted. Anyway we would then have the choice of which side we wanted to join and could pose our conditions accordingly. There seems no doubt that England, whose position without us would be pretty difficult, would have to grant us great advantages. The English are good enough shopkeepers to understand this and act upon it.

With best regards<br>
Ever yours<br>
PHatzfeldt [...]

735.    Holstein to Hugo von Radolin[1]

Berlin, 30 July 1900

Dear Radolin,

I have little time in which to write, but did want to tell you that your recent reports have been most praiseworthy. Carry on like that. Unfortunately the situation will continue to be critical.

Even for those who, like me, used to be attacked by the Bismarckian Press as 'Englishmen', Salisbury's attitude is discouraging. It can be said without exaggeration that every proposal of the English Government is a trap designed to set us at odds with Russia. In order to avoid any dubious situation we shall side with Russia to a greater extent than heretofore in all questions that arise, particularly the Yangtze question. The instruction of two evenings ago was dictated by me.[2]

I leave it to you whether you want to tell Scott that according to your news from Berlin, Berlin was becoming more and more convinced that Lord Salisbury's policy was completely dominated by his hatred of our Kaiser. Naturally this conviction was gradually leading the German Government to seek closer relations, in so far as Germany needed those at all, elsewhere. It would be useful if this reached English Court circles, with which I think Scott has had contacts ever since Gotha.

With best regards and my respects to the Princess.

Yours<br>
Holstein.

736.    Holstein to Bernhard von Bülow
        Draft

TELEGRAM

Berlin, 30 July 1900

State Secretary
Heligoland

About thirty-six years ago an English police inspector who had grown

---

[1] From the Radolin Papers.

[2] A telegram from the Foreign Ministry of 28 July informed Radolin of Hatzfeldt's opinion that the British Government would claim exclusive control over the Yangtze area. Radolin

old in the service told me: 'Whenever a crime which appeals to the imagination becomes known I prepare for repetitions; the urge to imitate is a strong one.' Remembering this statement caused me to send you this communication.

I don't need to tell you twenty-four hours after the assassination of the King of Italy what my quotation means.[1] At a time like this it is essential to subdue the waves of emotion and to concern oneself only with practical questions.

In practice the matter stands thus: until to-day our Kaiser has lived in security because he declared ten and a half years ago: 'I cannot start my reign by giving orders to fire on my own subjects.' At that time it was he who prohibited the use of force against the rebels, and that is held in his favour. The Social Democrats tell themselves: 'We may not approve of the present structure of the state, but we will never get a juster Kaiser.' I am convinced, and I am not alone in this, that that has been the Kaiser's safeguard until to-day. In the ten and a half years of the Kaiser's reign two tremendous developments have occurred: (1) The Power of the monarchy, or rather the personal power of the Kaiser, has reached[2] heights which were considered unattainable even at the height of Bismarck's rule. I consider this to be the most important phenomenon of the present day. (2) Social Democracy, left in peace, has become fat and lethargic. Although companies still pay high enough dividends, workers' wages have risen. The Social Democratic leaders, Liebknecht,[3] Bebel,[4] Vollmar,[5] Auer,[6] are to-day comfortably-off bourgeois. Neither these men nor their followers represent a threat to the life of the Kaiser. They say, just as they did ten years ago: 'We are not really imperialist, but if we have to have a Kaiser, we have the best one possible.' This thought is a talisman protecting the life of our Most Gracious Master.

I have brought up this question because I am convinced that many approaches will be made to the Kaiser to-day and in the next few days in an effort to persuade him to take the lead in a great international civil war against Social Democracy. Capitalists in all walks of life will urge this. Anything done in this direction will be directed against strikes, i.e. against attempts to gain higher wages—for how else can one lay hold of the Social Democrats? Social Democracy is much too vague a term, and apart from some insolence in the Press, to which no one pays attention any more, and possible riots in case of strikes, nothing illegal is done. But strikes are primarily a question of wages and dividends. Big capital

was instructed to ascertain Russia's attitude, and, if possible, what Russia knew of the United States' attitude towards this barely concealed British claim to incorporate the Yangtze basin in the British sphere of influence. (*Grosse Politik*, vol. XVI, no. 4702, pp. 202–3.)

[1] On 29 July 1900 King Umberto was assassinated at Monza by an anarchist.

[2] At this point in the draft Holstein crossed out the words: 'practically undisputed.'

[3] Wilhelm Liebknecht. Social Democratic Member of the Reichstag. From 1890 editor of the *Vorwärts*.

[4] August Bebel. Leader of the Social Democratic Party; Member of the Reichstag, 1867–1881; 1881–1913.

[5] Georg von Vollmar. Social Democratic Member of the Reichstag, 1881–7; 1890–1918.

[6] Ignaz Auer. From 1877 Social Democratic Member of the Reichstag; an influential member of the party leadership.

has a concrete interest to defend, but the Kaiser has to bear the consequences, the hatred and the danger, and these disadvantages are in fact borne by the whole country, which suffers under conditions of unrest and insecurity which are unavoidable if whole strata of the population are filled with a bitterness personally directed against the ruler.

Let us pose the question as it actually stands : what must be protected? Law and Order? They are not threatened anywhere in Germany, and whoever wanted to threaten them would be immediately crushed by that large steam-roller, the state. The personal security of the Kaiser? That has been secured until now by the memory of the Labour Conference of 1890, in spite of our insufficient police force. It is known that the Kaiser will suppress any disorder, yet the workers have been convinced until now that the Kaiser has no particular hostility towards them; on the contrary, older workers remember that he used to be called the Worker's Kaiser. The maintenance of order in the state would thus not be furthered by possible measures against the Social Democrats, measures which would in effect merely mean a harrying of the working class, and harm the Kaiser by creating the impression that in contrast to the early years of his reign he was now conducting a class policy instead of showing equal consideration to all classes of society.

My conviction, and it is at one with my conscience, is that the personal situation of the ruler can be secured only by a reorganization of the police, not by legislative measures; *international* legislation is out of the question anyhow, as England, America, and—in spite of the murder of Carnot[1]—republican France would not participate. It would thus not be difficult for enemies of the Kaiser and German power to represent *him* as the instigator of a campaign of suppression which would in any case be foredoomed to failure. Clearly every patriot must want to avoid such a situation.

Could you not possibly arrange for Hinzpeter to be consulted on this question? I have never met him, but believe him to be someone who sees clearly, and think that he is as attached to the Kaiser as a person, as I am to him as an idea. I would be surprised if Hinzpeter too were not to advise that we should allow our Social Democrats to continue the process of erosion they are undergoing, while the anarchists—for the most part individual fanatics or very small, barely discernible groups—should be supervised by an improved police force, at whose head some particularly able person should be placed. I know of no candidate, but one would be found. The present circumstances urgently demand the transformation of the police force from an ornamental into an effective institution.

H.

### 737.   Chlodwig zu Hohenlohe to Holstein

Werki, 3 August 1900

Dear Baron,

In the courier's bag of yesterday evening I received a letter from

[1] On 24 June 1894 President Sadi Carnot of France had been stabbed to death at Lyons by an Italian anarchist.

Prince Ph. Eulenburg,[1] which I am attaching as enclosure I. I have drafted a reply,[2] but do not want to send it off without having consulted you. The matter is too delicate for me to settle independently without consultation. The part of the letter in which Eulenburg writes that His Majesty the Kaiser told him he *would be* pleased to grant the money at first led me to believe that E. still laid claim to the 60,000 Marks. However, I think I can take the last part of the letter as a renunciation, as I have stated in my letter.

I have not talked to Lindenau, who without doubt is *not* in the picture. I won't write to Eulenburg until I have your reply.

With best regards
Your most devoted
CHohenlohe.

ENCLOSURE I

Philipp zu Eulenburg to Chlodwig zu Hohenlohe
Copy

Aboard *Hohenzollern*
29 July 1900

Secret
Your Highness,

May I inform you of the following : His Majesty the Kaiser had told me he would be pleased, at Your Highness' suggestion, to make me a grant of 60,000 marks from the secret funds in order to compensate me for the great expenses arising out of my frequent transfers and consequent moves. I presume that it was an error on the part of Your Highness to submit an application for such a sum to be paid to me, citing difficulties allegedly arising out of my private affairs. It can only be a question of compensation for expenses incurred in the course of my *duties*, expenses which I can prove by submitting my accounts.

In any case the private matter, which worried me some years ago and which I mentioned to Your Highness—as well as to His Majesty—in friendly *confidence*, has long ago been settled. The person who used the relationship of a lady to myself for purposes of dastardly blackmail has died.

I have long ago overcome the difficulties in which I found myself for some time, which had arisen suddenly due to my frequent transfers, and my financial situation is now excellent. An appeal to the Treasury would therefore be nothing less than frivolous.

I have told His Majesty that I cannot accept Government funds which others need more urgently than I do at a time when I have hired four new footmen and have bought all of Lanza's plate on his departure. I would therefore request Your Highness not to revert to a matter which I regard as settled.

I am, as always, most respectfully,

---

[1] See Haller, *Eulenburg*, pp. 339–41.
[2] See Enclosure II.

Chlodwig zu Hohenlohe to Philipp zu Eulenburg
Draft

Werki

Your Highness,

I am in receipt of your communication of the 24th of last month, and would like to thank you for the information contained therein. From it I see that the private matter we discussed some years ago is now settled. Your Highness has referred with some emphasis to the friendly and confidential nature of that discussion, and I may say that I never looked on it in any other light. But that could not prevent me from carefully hinting to His Majesty at the private matter which at that time weighed upon you. I could only and indeed had to tell His Majesty the truth, which was all the more necessary as it now appears that Your Highness yourself informed His Majesty of this private matter.

Finally I am happy to be able to send Your Highness my sincere congratulations at the satisfactory conclusion of the affair.

With the assurance of my deepest respect,

I am Your Highness

CH

## 738. Bernhard von Bülow to Holstein

136 Königgrätzer Strasse, [6 August 1900]

Dear friend,

His Majesty has just wired me that the Tsar has agreed in a most friendly manner[1] and has accepted Waldersee.[2] Everything now depends on getting the agreement of the other Powers. A failure in the Commander-in-Chief question when it is so close to success would leave His Majesty most ill-disposed towards the Foreign Ministry; a failure due to English opposition would cause grave harm to our relations to England (and to Hatzfeldt's position). Can you come to the Ministry at once? You will find Klehmet and the Tsar's telegram. I regard it as of the utmost importance that the telegram for London, Paris, Washington, Tokyo, Rome, Vienna go out at once.[3]

Best regards.

B.

## 739. Hugo von Radolin to Holstein

St Petersburg, 9 August 1900

My dear friend,

When I informed Count Lamsdorff the other day of Tsar N's approval of the choice of Count Wald[ersee], he confirmed this and added that he

[1] *Grosse Politik*, vol. XVI, no. 4602, pp. 83–4.

[2] As Commander-in-Chief of an international expeditionary force to suppress the Boxer movement and to relieve the Peking Legations. (See *Grosse Politik*, vol. XVI, no. 4603–4, pp. 84–6.)

[3] For the telegram to London see *Grosse Politik*, vol. XVI, no. 4604, pp. 84–6. On 7 August telegrams were dispatched to the other above-mentioned missions informing them of the Tsar's agreement and requesting them to obtain the formal agreement of the Governments to which they were accredited. (From the Foreign Ministry files.)

did not think the other Powers would object to the choice of a German Commander-in-Chief, especially of so well-tried a general. He added that he *believed* that France also would not object, but said that he had not been in touch with France on that point.

Now the War Minister[1] tells me how desirable it would be if the same query or proposal were sent from Berlin to the other Cabinets, that is also to France; he is afraid France's feelings might be hurt.[2] He hinted that Russia did not want to enter on an agreement which might create the impression in Paris that Germany and Russia had concluded an agreement to the exclusion of France. Count Lamsdorff had dropped *no* hint to show that he expected Berlin to take the initiative *vis-à-vis* the other cabinets. General Kuropatkin had no hesitation in stating this clearly. It seems to me that one is not inclined here to take the first step in *advocating* our proposal in France.

If I may give voice to my personal feelings and impressions, these are that here one is not at all inclined to go as far as we appear to have intended. Certainly there is no wish to take the initiative for an advance on Peking. If Germany wants to do it, they will be pleased to leave *us* with this responsibility so as to have a scape-goat. But one thing is clear to me. People here and other Cabinets would like to push *us* alone to Peking. Deep in their hearts all the Cabinets would prefer to let us deal with the Chinese before Peking by ourselves. I do believe that the military here and the War Minister are loyal to a certain degree, in that, if only because of the question of *military honour*, they incline towards a serious advance against Peking (with us). But in political circles such an advance is not popular. Nasty remarks can be heard that *we* were agitating and trying to involve the others because *our* representative had been murdered,[3] and *we* wanted to exact revenge. Personally I would have preferred it if a *Russian* had become Commander-in-Chief. I certainly wouldn't like to be in Count Waldersee's shoes, no matter how much glory he may garner. [...]

Now farewell. Hurriedly

Your faithful
Hugo

740. Chlodwig zu Hohenlohe to Holstein

Werki, 10 August 1900

Dear Baron,

Once again you have proved yourself the old, true, and careful friend, and I thank you with all my heart and will follow your advice not to answer now and to await a possible further hint.[4] In that case I will let you know beforehand. Apart from you, Bülow, and at the time, Rotenhan, no one knows of the affair. Lindenau, it seems to me, doesn't. I won't tell him anyway.

[1] Alexei Kuropatkin.
[2] See *Grosse Politik*, vol., XVI, no. 4605, pp. 86–7.
[3] See p. 188, note 1.
[4] See above, Hohenlohe's letter of 3 August 1900 and enclosures.

Is it true that Waldersee is going to China? He will have a difficult task to master.

Once again many thanks and best regards

Your most devoted
C. Hohenlohe

## 741.   Holstein to Paul von Hatzfeldt[1]

Berlin, 23 August 1900

Dear friend,

Your letter,[2] interesting as always, goes to the State Secretary to-day. The only point on which you start out from different premises to mine is your belief in the possibility that the question of compensating Germany elsewhere for the inclusion of the Yangtze in the English sphere of influence could arise.[3] I, on the other hand, believe in the necessity of preventing an English monopoly of the Yangtze because of the impossibility of attaining anything like equivalent compensation for ourselves. Or rather I believe that the attainment of this compensation would be more difficult than a prevention of English domination of the Yangtze, provided that a group of Powers co-operate to achieve this, as seems to be the case at present.  In spite of my mistrust of England's insatiable policy, I do regard it as not impossible that England's only reason for wanting to lay her hands on the Yangtze is the fear that Germany will do so if she doesn't.  During the last two months all sorts of written and spoken statements have been made which might give rise to this suspicion.  I don't only mean His Majesty,[4] but also lesser mortals, such as Eugen Wolff,[5] and Hasse,[6] the Pan-German Member of the Reichstag. If I were an Englishman such statements would make me most suspicious.  I am saying this to justify my belief that the English might *possibly* be satisfied for the moment if the Kaiser were to proclaim Germany's disinterestedness regarding the Yangtze and his preparedness to co-operate in an 'open-door' policy in that area.[7]  But even if the English don't like it, we shall continue to treat the Yangtze question under all circumstances as a problem of common interest to all trading nations.

In yesterday's conversation His Majesty told the English some things which might just as well have been left unsaid.  I refer to the

[1] From the Papers of Baroness von der Heydt. Only a typewritten copy of this document was available to the editors.

[2] Not found.          [3] See p. 189, note 2.

[4] Bülow had telegraphed to the Foreign Ministry on 29 June 1900 : 'The Yangtze-question dominates everything else for His Majesty.  His Majesty continually reverts to his statement that he expects our diplomacy to avert the great damage threatening our economic and political interests in this question.' ( *Grosse Politik*, vol. XVI, p. 206, note *.)

[5] German explorer.

[6] Ernst Hasse. Chairman of the Pan-German League; Member of the Reichstag (National Liberal Party.)

[7] Kaiser Wilhelm II had informed the Prince of Wales on 22 August that in the Yangtze area Germany only aimed at equal trading rights for all nations. ( *Grosse Politik*, vol. XVI, no. 4712, pp. 212–13.)

emphasis he placed on our differences with Russia.[1] It is true that the Russians have until now been more brutal and inconsiderate in their behaviour than the other Powers. Minister von Brandt, who has just returned from a brief trip to St Petersburg, tells me that the hatred of us is once again very lively there. Other sources confirm this. Witte, the Minister, is most furious of all, for he fears that the Russian finances cannot stand up to the trials of strength in the Far East. This consideration will probably leave you and me cold. You might even try to get an article into the English Press stating that a visit to Paris by the Tsar has once again recently been widely discussed in connection with plans for a loan, and that Minister Witte is shortly going to Paris to study the money market. You might at the same time also insert that the more intimate Court circles in St Petersburg are devoting their interests to the question of a marriage between Prince Louis Napoleon, who commands one of the Uhlan Guards regiments, and the Grand Duchess Helene, daughter of Grand Duke Vladimir.

We are hated in Russia and in England as well. Where aren't we hated? Love alone of course doesn't turn the trick, only a sensible policy. Let us hope for the best as regards that.

If Russia now grabs Manchuria, it will be difficult to prevent the other Powers from descending on China. Thus if England does not desire a partition of China, she will have to make Russia leave Manchuria. I would presume that the Americans would not be disinclined to participate in exercising diplomatic pressure on Russia. Holleben told me yesterday that anti-English sentiment was growing in the United States, and that this was making the position of Secretary of State Hay so unpleasant that he was thinking of resigning. The Americans want gradually to gain control of the China trade, and for this reason they are strongly opposed to any partition of China. They would therefore pursue a policy identical to that of England as regards Manchuria.

The Russians, so I believe, could get the support of Japan if they made concessions in Korea. But in my opinion they will only make these concessions if they are hard pressed.

As regards Germany, our Most Serene Master has expressed himself repeatedly in the last few days in favour of China's integrity.[2] I hope this view will last, for if we undertake to expand our territory in Shantung to any considerable extent—this being the obvious place—we run the risk on the one hand that America will make herself unpleasant, on the other that England will seriously advance on the Yangtze. Yet amongst the noisier political elements there are many supporters of territorial expansion.

Looking at the situation objectively it seems to me that the conflict of

[1] In his conversation with the Prince of Wales and Lascelles, the Kaiser expressed his displeasure at Russia's efforts to conclude a quick peace with China without regard for the interests of other Powers, after Russia had attained her own aims by the occupation of northern Manchuria. (*Grosse Politik*, vol. XVI, no. 4617, pp. 97–8; *British Documents*, vol. II, no. 8, pp. 7–9.)

[2] For instance in a speech in mid-August to German officers leaving for China, according to an article in the *Berliner Lokalanzeiger*.

interests—with respect to China—between ourselves and England could be resolved more easily than the one between ourselves and Russia. England will think twice before seriously tackling the Yangtze-question, for she would be opposed not only by Germany but also by France, America, and even Japan. On the other hand it will be very difficult for Russia to refrain from taking possession of Manchuria now. Because of its repercussions, such an occupation would be harmful to German interests. Germany would be able to defend her overseas interests far less decisively and would be a less desirable ally to-day than in four or five years' time, when we shall have a large navy. It would therefore be useful to us if England and America, perhaps with Japan as the third partner, were to face up to Russia over the Niuchwang question. In order to further this, the idea that Russia cannot and will not make war, because this would involve the collapse of Witte's whole financial system, must be widely publicized in the English Press. Can you unobtrusively get something along these lines into the Press? I don't even know whether a dispatch was forwarded to you in which Radolin reported that Witte lost all self-control when talking about the expenditure caused by Far Eastern adventures and enterprises.[1] If need be I'll arrange for you to get the dispatch now, and you will have to see whether it might suitably be shown to Rothschild as proof that the Russians won't risk a war even over Niuchwang. Neither England nor Russia want war. The only problem is always who is better at scaring the other. I could imagine that right now with the elections in sight, a diplomatic success over Russia would be most welcome to the English Government, provided it is certain that there is little risk involved.

Do consider what can be done. Naturally the Russians mustn't find out, at least they mustn't get any evidence against us. The problem is to feed the right arguments to the right people through the right channels. I think the arguments are pretty conclusive :

1. Russia has no money. Witte, at the moment the most influential personage, wants to avoid war under *any* circumstances.
2. Judging by the excited tone of the French Press, France will certainly not risk a great war in order to secure Manchuria for Russia.

Finally you should consider whether the English will take a tougher line with Russia if they are sure of our attitude regarding the Yangtze. A Yangtze-agreement, binding both sides to respect freedom of trade, would be completely unobjectionable to us, as it would not be directed against Russia. Now farewell.

I will send the copies next time. There was no time for it to-day.

With best regards<br>Yours<br>Holstein.

Naturally you can continue to avoid the F.O. as long as *you* think it advisable; after all you have other channels.

[1] Radolin to the Foreign Ministry of 12 July 1900. (*Grosse Politik*, vol. XVI, no. 4567, pp. 51–2.)

### 742. Paul von Hatzfeldt to Holstein[1]

TELEGRAM

London, 25 August 1900

Private

[...] As you know I have always warned against hurrying into definitive agreements with Russia. But in my opinion it is not in our interest now for people here to believe in possible cooler relations between ourselves and Russia concerning the Chinese question. The stronger this belief became, the more our friendship would lose in value. In this respect I feel that the unfriendly attitude towards us of part of the Russian Press, which is studied with attention here, has already done harm. I have therefore always expressed the view in confidential conversations that if people here step on our toes, we have it in our power by joining the others to create at any time the German-Russian-French Triplice against England. [...][2]

H.

### 743. Hugo von Radolin to Holstein

25 August 1900

My dear friend,

[...] No Russian wants war against China except for the military who want to collect military laurels. The move against Peking is most unpopular.[3] The only purpose the Russians pursued was to save the Minister by as pacific a method as possible (and they wouldn't have done that had they not been dragged along by the others and had it not been too outrageous not to join the relief column). If the Minister had been *dead already*, I am certain the Russians would *not* have joined in the move against Peking.

The one purpose is to acquire the Manchurian Railway *peacefully* in co-operation with the Chinese Government, thereby naturally conquering Manchuria *de facto*, whilst at all times maintaining the fiction of China's territorial integrity. Germany's energetic intervention in China was by no means welcome to the Russians and they don't conceal their feeling that if Germany wants to send an expedition to exact vengeance for the murder of the Minister she can do so at her *own* risk, but they are strongly opposed to the idea of Russia being dragged in. *Si l'Allemagne veut s'emballer dans cette aventure, qu'elle le fasse, cela ne nous regarde pas. Quant à nous, nous n'avons pas de ministre et de missionaire à venger.* One hears constantly something along these lines. I have

---

[1] From the London Embassy files.

[2] Holstein replied the same evening: 'I understand your point of view, and also think it superfluous to emphasize possible differences between ourselves and Russia. It may be assumed that it is known that should we agree to the creation of the Triplice of '95, we would be fulfilling the deep-felt wishes of the Russian and French Governments.' (From the London Embassy files.)

[3] On 21 August the news arrived in Berlin that, with the capture of Peking, the Tsar considered the war against China at an end. (*Grosse Politik*, vol. XVI, nos. 4614–15, pp. 94–6.)

reported it frequently and openly. It is *absolutely true* that the Russians (that means of course Russians in high society who have French sympathies and don't like the Germans) will be glad to see Germany get *deeply involved* in China and as a result rendered harmless elsewhere, and they agitate as much as possible to this end. These people regard *our* co-operation with the *Franco-Russian* grouping as undesirable. They do not want us to make the *third* in the *alliance*. That was something we already noticed when we joined them in China five years ago.

Their feelings of suspicion at our *disinterestedness* has increased further since we took Kiaochow. They are convinced that our keen interest in the settlement of the Chinese problem and our wish to go hand in hand with France and Russia are due to our desire for a 'second' Kiaochow or an extension of German territory. Our opponents hope we shall become sufficiently *deeply involved* so that we bleed to death. The way in which the Press *glorifies the triumphal march* of the Commander-in-Chief *before* any success has been achieved creates the *worst possible impression* even in circles which do not hate us. It strengthens the impression here that the general wants to win his spurs at the expense of others. His farewell speech, in which he hinted at future complications, has caused much worried shaking of heads.[1] It is said that the person concerned wants to influence his master's impulsive character and to involve him further than intended. One hears repeatedly that he is fighting on his own behalf with his *pen* at least as much as he *will* fight for Germany's honour arms in hand. Certainly the excited state of [our] *Press* harms our prestige in the eyes of *all* foreigners. [...]

The Russians absolutely *refuse to accept* the assertion now being made that the initiative for the appointment of the Commander-in-Chief *came from Tsar Nicholas*, and this *must* and will infuriate Russian statesmen and the Tsar *against the Supreme Command*.[2] I regret the fact that you did not reply to *my* query on this point.[3]

The more noise that is made by our Press concerning Count W[aldersee's] expedition, the cooler and more negative will be the judgment of this mission in Russian official circles and the general public. I cannot help feeling that this is a dangerous game and that we may easily lose the sympathies of the whole outside world. Many important people will certainly be pleased if we burn our fingers. [...]

Your most faithfully devoted

Hugo. [...]

[1] When Waldersee took leave of the Kaiser on 18 August, he thanked him for giving him the opportunity to show his gratitude for past imperial favours by deeds.

[2] The Kaiser had induced the Tsar to agree to the appointment of Waldersee as Commander-in-Chief of the international expeditionary force against China. (See p. 193, note 2.) The Tsar's assent was then communicated to the other Powers as a Russian proposal. (*Grosse Politik*, vol. XVI, nos. 4601; 4602; 4604; 4608; 4610, pp. 81–4; 84–6; 88–90; 91.)

[3] Radolin had telegraphed to Holstein on 23 August 1900: 'The censored Russian news agency when reporting Kaiser's address to Count Waldersee in Wilhelmshöhe simply substituted "agreement of the Tsar" [to Waldersee's appointment] for the phrase "on the initiative and wish of the Russian Tsar" as reported in the German Press.' Radolin was instructed by a telegram of 25 August to avoid all polemics, but to describe the German text as correct if forced to do so. (From the Foreign Ministry files.)

## 744.   Holstein to Bernhard von Bülow
Copy

27 August 1900

Radolin writes privately that Russian bitterness and jealousy over the Supreme Command are constantly growing because of all the noise about Waldersee. Also people are irritated by the Kaiser's statement that the Tsar 'suggested' W's appointment; evidently they believe that the object was to drive a wedge between Russia and France.

I am pessimistic concerning the future developments and complications of the Chinese question, for I do not believe in lasting 'luck', but do believe that in the long run the difference between 'sensible' and 'not sensible' remains decisive. The Kaiser is now arousing distrust and jealousy everywhere, *jealousy* in the Tsar and Salisbury, who are thereby being brought closer than would otherwise be the case, distrust in just about everybody. Holleben the other day expressed this in the formula: 'The triumphal march *before* victory has been won seems dangerous.' Holleben expresses the deepest sentiments of the German observer, whether he be prominent or unknown.

I can understand, dear Bülow, why you have gone along until now and agreed whenever it has been at all possible, for I know the reasons. But the time has come it seems to me when, notwithstanding your continuing devotion to the Kaiser, you must quietly give expression to some Cassandra-like warnings: for example you must carefully express the thought that the rulers and nations whose sensibilities His Majesty is trampling underfoot are still unconquered—therein lies the difference with Attila[1]—and will remain unconquered if the Kaiser continues to unite them in a common hatred of himself.

I think it will be best for *your* future if you can make him understand: 'I can see the dangers of your actions earlier than you can, but I am a faithful subject and therefore sacrifice my convictions. My duty lies only in smoothing as far as possible the rough edges; yet in the long run this will not suffice to keep misfortune from you.' The Kaiser must at a later stage have the feeling that you can justify yourself if you wish, and that on the whole he does better not to disregard your warnings.

One of the points you must make clear to the Kaiser, both in your own interest and that of your subordinates, is that Imperial intervention limits the scope of German diplomacy. Whether Salisbury can be persuaded depends on the impression created by the Kaiser's remarks as reported by Lascelles, not on what Hatzfeldt transmits in London after the battle.

H.

---

[1] According to an unofficial version of his speech on 27 July to German troops leaving for the Far East, the Kaiser had said: 'If you meet the enemy, you will beat him! There will be no pardon! Prisoners will not be taken! Your captives shall be in your power! A thousand years ago the Huns under their King Attila made a name for themselves which in history and legend still stands for power. May your actions ensure that the word German is similarly looked upon in China for a thousand years so that never again will a Chinese even dare to look insultingly at a German.'

745.　Hugo von Radolin to Holstein

St Petersburg, 31 August 1900

My dear friend,

What I have always reported and could be foreseen has happened. Governing circles here co-operated only *unwillingly* in the march on Peking, and then only in order to provide an escort to bring the freed Minister to safety, not in an expedition of revenge. The Tsar even opposed this and had given the order not to advance further. The local commander[1] went too fast, and the Tsar has disapproved of the steps taken. (The Minister of War and the military naturally do not share this view.) Now the order has been given to evacuate Peking. Though the Tsar has said he wants to act in concert with the other Powers, he does what he likes on his own. At any rate he is leaving *us* in Peking by ourselves. Things will turn out as I always assumed they would. After we had taken the initiative so strongly in China, all the others will gradually leave us in the lurch, and we can then conduct an expedition of revenge to Peking *alone*. Here they are skilfully backing out and rubbing their hands. *Our* Press has done us a great deal of harm. The stupid newspaper articles on Count W[aldersee's] triumphal progress have also done the latter a lot of harm. People tell themselves that Russia has no reason to burn her fingers in order to satisfy the ambition of a foreign general for cheap laurels. [...]

The restoration of order in Manchuria seems to be easier than was at first thought. To deprive us of every excuse for possible expansion in Shantung, I am being given ostentatious assurances that Russia does not want one square foot of territory and will withdraw from Niuchwang as soon as order has been restored and the railroad secured. *When* that will be is another question. It can be dragged out *indefinitely*, and this will surely be done.

I was very happy to see our dear old Prince[2] in Werki. He was so kind and visibly pleased to have us with him. I must say in confidence that he is hurt at his treatment as *quantité négligeable*, no one thinking it worth the trouble to keep him *au courant* of events—if only *pro forma*. He is sent only routine matters and *newspaper clippings*. He feels this deeply and told me that if you and Count B[ülow] had not persuaded him to stay he would regard it as more *dignified* to retire than to stay on in these circumstances. He was, thank goodness, very well both *mentally* and *physically* and takes a keen interest in everything. May the Lord preserve this good man for a long time.

I am sending you these lines by to-day's courier. Johanna sends her best regards.

Your faithful

Hugo. [...]

746.　Bernhard von Bülow to Holstein

Norderney, Villa Mathilde, 10 September 1900

Cordial thanks, dear friend, for your kind and important letter, pro-

---

[1] General Linevich. Russian Commander-in-Chief in China.　　[2] Prince Hohenlohe.

viding welcome proof that you are following the course of events with your normal attention and acuteness, even during the short vacation you are allowing yourself. I immediately instructed the Ministry in accordance with your suggestion. I quite see how important it is that the Russians should not draw the Japanese over to their side, which would be greatly facilitated for them if they could persuade the Japanese that we might join an anti-Japanese grouping in the Korea question.[1] The fact that Leyden received a telegram from Aoki[2] via Inouye,[3] seeking to discover our attitude towards the Korea question shows that you judged the Japanese attitude correctly. Aoki's telegram stated that Japan did not want to act outside the concert of Powers in China, but regarded the Korean question as a matter concerning Japan and Russia alone.

In the meantime the French have stated that they will evacuate Peking together with the Russians. It seems as if the Americans will follow suit. Sir Claude MacDonald[4] has come out very strongly against evacuation (secret private communication from Graf Hatzfeldt to me).[5] Thereupon Salisbury told the Russians that he could not evacuate Peking for the moment, but did not thereby wish to bind himself for the future.

At times an English desire has become apparent to make use of us against Russia, and in particular to estrange us from Russia by making us force the Russians to withdraw from the Taku-Tientsin-Peking railway. Hatzfeldt has very skilfully blocked these English attempts to exploit our present precarious situation (which the English exaggerate) and the present deterioration of our relations with Russia (which the English equally over-estimate) for English purposes. On the other hand Radolin is successfully working to prevent our estrangement with Russia from getting worse. If our two most important Ambassadors continue to work in this manner, they will not only do well by the country, but also afford me the opportunity to keep them in their positions *contre vent et marée* and bring them to higher honour.

With the best will in the world we cannot rectify the mistakes made without and against us. But it is to be hoped that we will succeed to some extent in saving face in China and thereby also our future. That requires that the other Powers do not reach agreement with China before Waldersee's arrival and do not withdraw their troops from the German Supreme Command, Prince Ching,[6] the English protégé, has arrived in Peking; the Russians apparently want to get their man, Li Hung-chang, to Tientsin. [...]

Your faithful

B.

[1] In March 1900 Russia secured a lease of land at Masampo, on the southern tip of Korea, for a coal depot and naval station. The control of Masampo, one of the finest natural harbours in the Far East, gave Russia command of the Tsu-shima Strait. The Russian move led to lasting tension with Japan over Korea.

[2] Japanese Minister in Berlin, 1892–8; Foreign Minister in the Yamagata Cabinet, 1898–1900.

[3] Katsunoske Inouye. Japanese Minister in Berlin, 1898–1907.

[4] British Minister in Peking, 1896–1900; in Tokyo, 1900–12.

[5] See *Grosse Politik*, vol. XVI, no. 4638, p. 126.

[6] President of the Tsingli-Yamen.

747.    Maximilian von Brandt to Holstein

Weimar, 21 September 1900

Your Excellency,

[...] As regards China I entirely share the views expressed in the State Secretary's circular.[1] The punishment of the chief culprits is the pre-condition for the prevention of the recurrence of incidents similar to the ones which occurred this year, and thus the pre-condition for the opening of negotiations with the Chinese Government. It is doubtful whether the surrender [of the culprits] can in all cases be secured, but their execution by the Chinese, i.e. beheading in the presence of German troops, would after all also answer the object we aim at. I shall write tomorrow to Lo Feng-luh,[2] the Chinese Minister in London, who is Li's man and whom I have known well for years, and I shall make it clear to him that in my view the fulfilment of Germany's demands, whether these are agreed to by all the Powers or not, is the *conditio sine qua non* for the restoration of relations with Germany, and that non-fulfilment might have dire consequences which China would do well to avoid. I shall also ensure that *my* view reaches Li.

I was pleased to gather from your letter and hints in the Press that we are not inclined to draw the Empress Dowager into the discussion.[3] Therein lies in my opinion the real danger for the present and future and I am sorry to see that people in England are apparently allowing themselves to be pushed in this direction through the intrigue of missionaries and a few newspaper correspondents, who are backing the dreamers and intriguers of the so-called Chinese Reform Party and acting as its mouthpiece. The only man in China is the Empress Dowager; whether she has been pushed by others into the xenophobe policy of the last few months, or whether she considered this to be a necessary defence against foreign aggression and inaugurated it herself is a question I want to leave open. But her removal would make of the Emperor a plaything for all intriguers—presumably the purpose of the measure—and would thus in no way be in our interests. I don't know whether the newspaper reports of German protests against Li and other allegedly xenophobe delegates are correct; I would regret it, for Li is the cleverest of all the

---

[1] Of 17 September. Bülow wrote: 'His Majesty's Government regards the surrender of the persons who have been identified as the instigators of the offences against international law committed in Peking as a precondition for the resumption of diplomatic relations with the Chinese Government.' (*Grosse Politik*, vol. XVI, no. 4643, pp. 130–2.)

In his letter to Brandt of 20 September Holstein expressed the hope that Brandt approved of the present German demand. 'If I were Foreign Minister', Holstein continued, 'I would fight this question through no matter what the consequences, if only because unless *a few* of the chief culprits are punished—and especially as long as they continue to bask in the sun of Imperial favour—any agreement concerning guarantees is nothing more than a farce. Once this question has been settled, however, I should be more than reasonable concerning compensation, etc.' (From the Brandt Papers.)

[2] Chinese Minister in London, 1897–1901.

[3] In his letter of 20 September (see above note 1) Holstein wrote: 'I do not believe that a tender conscience will prevent the Empress from agreeing to the surrender as soon as she is persuaded of its necessity and advisability. The decisive point therefore is to demonstrate the necessity to her. Reasons for the surrender can then be found; reasons are not hard to come by in China, either.'

Chinese and the only one who can afford the luxury of holding opinions of his own. The man who signed the Treaty of Shimonoseki and rendered it acceptable to his Government is still the only one who can do the same for the treaty now to be concluded. Prince Ching is not so clever as Li, nor does he possess the latter's courage and influence. The presence of so-called xenophobe delegates at the negotiations may make these negotiations more difficult but can hardly affect the outcome. Moreover the outside world has an interest in seeing that the odium of the satisfaction which it demands and receives should not fall exclusively on the few negotiators who are at least to some extent pro-foreign in their views; in part the odium should also fall on the others, thereby robbing them of both pretext and means for future accusations and intrigues. [...]

Once negotiations with China are opened, I consider it advisable in the interests of the outside world, in view of present circumstances and their future development, that China should not be placed in too disadvantageous a position, and in particular that the conditions to be imposed regarding trade and transport should not compare too unfavourably with those granted to China's Asiatic neighbour. Future troubles can only be avoided on condition that the real and to a certain extent the imaginary interests of the population are taken into consideration. The decision must be in favour of educational and therefore patient measures.

I do hope that we shall be spared the acquisition of any territory in Shantung and the colonial army which would inevitably go with it. I would then regard our future in China in the nature of an *expédition de Mexique*, from which the Lord preserve us.

Please forgive me for having spread myself like this, but if the heart is full the pen overfloweth.

With best regards and wishes I remain as ever Your Excellency's truly devoted

M. von Brandt [...]

748.   Maximilian von Brandt to Holstein

Weimar, 22 September 1900

Your Excellency,

I am enclosing the letter I am addressing to Lo Feng-luh, which, if it meets with your approval, can be posted at once in Berlin. Should you want me to alter anything in it, I will gladly do so. I thought it might after all be better if I submitted it before dispatch, as I am only most imperfectly acquainted with reactions abroad to our circular note and also not sure whether we are determined to stand by our demands embodied in it.[1] Sternburg's statement as reported in the Press has frightened me off somewhat.

I remain as ever Your Excellency's

truly devoted
M. v. Brandt

[1] A note to the Great Powers stating the German conditions for resuming diplomatic relations with China. All Powers except the United States expressed their agreement with the German terms.

## Maximilian von Brandt to Lo Feng-luh[1]

Weimar, 22 September 1900

Confidential

My dear Sir Chichen,

It is a long while since we have met, but I have heard a great deal of You since You were accredited to the Court of St James and You may have heard, by accident, of me too. I would not write to You to-day if it was not for the fact that I know You to be a faithful adherent of my old friend Li Hung-chang, who is coming forward so pluckily at this moment to do another and greater service than ever before to his country.

You know the Circular addressed by Count von Bülow to the other Powers interested in the Chinese question; the demand for the delivery of those persons who are to blame for the murder of Baron von Ketteler[2] and so many missionaries and the attack upon the foreign legations, i.e. the instigators of these misdeeds, is an eminently just and merciful one as it admits of a speedy settlement of the pending question by the punishment of a few really culpable persons. But what I wish You to understand and what I would like H.E. Li Hung-chang and H.H. Prince Ching to understand is that, as far as I am able to judge the German Government has fully made up its mind to carry this point, together with the other powers, and alone if necessary. This is of course my personal impression, but from what I know of the temper of the persons at the head of affairs, and of the whole nation, I am fully convinced that the only way to avoid greater calamities is for China to satisfy this demand of the German Government with as little delay as possible.

There is no intention as far as I can see of meddling with the internal affairs of China especially with the relations between H.M. the Empress-Regent and H.M. the Emperor but what is not the case to-day may become so, if the demand put forward by the German Government does not meet with a prompt and satisfactory response by the Chinese Government.

The situation is indeed a serious one and I should be glad if my old friends in China could be made to understand, that it is not one to be met by procrastination and tergiversation. You must have found out lately how far other persons, I need only mention Mr Morrison,[3] go in their denunciations and I can only add how sorry I would be to see the Chinese Government give any colour to such statements by the way they meet the demands of the German Government.

In the hope that this will find You in good health I am with kindest regards

my dear Sir Chichen,
Yours very truly
v. Brandt.

[1] In English in the original.
[2] Klemens, Baron von Ketteler. German Minister in Peking, 1899–1900.
[3] G. E. Morrison. Correspondent of *The Times* in the Far East.

## 749.    Paul von Hatzfeldt to Holstein[1]

TELEGRAM

London, 26 September 1900

Private.

Am pleased that you are back again. This will, I hope, in future prevent my not getting the opportunity to comment in advance on the chances here of such far-reaching matters as the extradition demand; otherwise I would have said straightaway that it would not be accepted here in its present form.

Naturally the reasons brought forward by Salisbury[2] are in part pretexts, but on the other hand the assumption that he does not want us to gain a diplomatic success is not wholly correct.[3] The real and main reason for his objections is distrust of our future intentions. He thinks that we would be perfectly satisfied if the Chinese turned down our demand for extradition, giving rise to new difficulties and the prolongation of the state of war, *so that Waldersee, in accord with His Majesty's wishes, would still find a situation favourable to military action and the opportunity for military and political successes.* Salisbury evidently fears that we would drag him into the complications arising therefrom. I have no doubt that this was Lord Salisbury's guiding consideration.

Salisbury's intention to ask the Englishmen on the spot has gained a bit of time. Please consider in the meanwhile whether some compromise is not possible, perhaps along the lines of the idea of an Imperial edict announcing actual penalties for the six culprits. Chamberlain, Balfour and Rothschild as well are absent. But Devonshire's recent remarks (telegram no. 604) unfortunately raise little hope of our finding support amongst Salisbury's colleagues in this instance.

P.H.

## 750.    Paul von Hatzfeldt to Holstein

London, 29 September 1900

Dear friend,

Events are moving fast and written communications usually arrive too late at this juncture. But I did want to use the opportunity to-day to tell how happy I am that we are once again at one in our opinion that we should try to reach an understanding on the basis of the proposals made here.[4] I purposely did not say 'Salisbury's proposals' for I am absolutely convinced that he would not have made such a different and more extensive proposal without prior consultation with the most important

---

[1] From the London Embassy files.

[2] See *Grosse Politik*, vol. XVI, nos. 4648; 4651, pp. 135–6; 140–1.

[3] Holstein had telegraphed to Hatzfeldt on 24 September: 'Am back again. Although I should have expected it of Lord Salisbury, I am surprised that he wants to hinder our extradition demand, so favourable to England, merely to prevent Germany from gaining a success.' (From the London Embassy files.)

[4] Salisbury had informed Hatzfeldt on 25 September that the German proposal for a Yangtze Treaty (*Grosse Politik*, vol. XVI, no. 4721, pp. 222–4) did not go far enough, and that the open door principle should not only apply to the 'Yangtze, its tributaries and basin', but also to 'the ports and littoral of China'. (*Grosse Politik*, vol. XVI, no. 4722, pp. 224–5.)

members of the Cabinet. In accordance with your telegraphed suggestion[1] I have just now expressed my opinion in an official telegram,[2] and I hope that this, suitably supported by you, will be of some help.

You just cannot imagine with what intensity Russians and Americans have lately been working against us here. We know for certain that the American Chargé d'Affaires originated the report launched by the Press Association, according to which Salisbury gave me a clearly negative answer in the extradition question during our last conversation. I have even been assured that in response to pressure by the American Chargé d'Affaires, Salisbury promised him the day before to give me the negative answer desired by the Americans during the above-mentioned conversation. I am therefore doubly pleased that I did everything in order to gain at least a delay. Only thus was it possible to deny this Press report, designed to expose our discomfiture to the whole world. The Russians too have not neglected to do everything they could against us, both in the Foreign Office and in Press circles. The English were told in every possible way that we were unreliable and dangerous people with whom they should have no dealings. Above all it was untrue that Tsar Nicholas had suggested or had been pleased with the German Supreme Command; he had only been unable to prevent the *fait accompli* presented by us. Germany had the most dangerous plans in China. Not only would Waldersee's actions make for new complications and render the conclusion of peace impossible or delay it, but we also had secret designs on Chinese ports, with which we would come out when the time was ripe. If England were to deal with us, she would become involved in all these complications.

Under these circumstances it is almost a miracle that at the last moment I got Salisbury not to refuse as yet, and to make the refusal dependent on enquiries with the English in Peking and further discussion with me after that. But we must not assume too readily that we have gained a lot of time and that the final decision will be altered to any extent. I don't even regard it as impossible that he will already give me

Hatzfeldt telegraphed Salisbury's proposals to Berlin on 27 September (*Grosse Politik*, vol. XVI, no. 4723, pp. 225–6. See also *British Documents*, vol. II, no. 14, pp. 12–13.)

Hatzfeldt telegraphed to Richthofen on 28 September : 'If we can objectively take this point of view into account without thereby getting into undesirable opposition to Russia, perhaps by following Lord Salisbury's suggestion to exclude the ports in the Amur area from the delimitation in question, I am of the opinion that we should try to gain English acceptance for a compromise proposal.' (From the London Embassy files.) Holstein replied on the same day : 'After carefully considering your telegram [to Richthofen] I have forwarded it to Bülow with detailed recommendation for acceptance of the English version concerning the Yangtze. As Russia again officially disclaims any intention of annexation, the expanded English version is not directed against Russia if the Amur is excluded. Perhaps also Port Arthur could be specifically mentioned with the Amur, as it has not been formally permanently separated from the Chinese Empire. You might answer yesterday's query by the Under State Secretary [*Grosse Politik*, vol. XVI, no. 4725, p. 227] along these lines without actual reference to the query. I have not shown your telegram to me [*Grosse Politik*, vol. XVI, no. 4726, pp. 227–8] to anyone in the Ministry.' (From the London Embassy files.)

[1] See p. 206, note 4.

[2] Telegram no. 617 of 29 September. The contents were in accord with Holstein's suggestion. (See p. 206, note 4.) (From the Foreign Ministry files.)

a negative answer next Tuesday based on alleged replies from Peking. Even then I would of course try to gain time. But it would be of the utmost importance that I should be able to make definite proposals on Tuesday concerning both points, open door and extradition,[1] so as to nullify Russian and American intrigues. I do therefore particularly ask you to do everything you can to enable me to do this.

Finally I want to mention a remark Salisbury just threw out which is not without interest as regards the peace negotiations between China and the Powers and negotiations between themselves. I had once again mentioned that our Chinese policy was only directed towards achieving the punishment of the culprits for the past and guarantees for the future when Salisbury interrupted me with the question how I envisaged these guarantees. When I replied that it seemed as yet too early to think about that, he remarked that he would think it best if forts were constructed in Tientsin and Taku in such a way that each of the interested countries, England, Germany, etc. would have its own fort manned by its own troops. I don't know whether this is a good idea as it stands. But it is certainly a good thing to know about it, because knowing Salisbury, it will certainly be brought up again in future negotiations.

From my telegrams you will have gathered that it is absolutely impossible now to get hold of anyone important here. London is completely deserted. The Ministers travel around and make election speeches. Of the Ambassadors only old Staal is here, and naturally I cannot look to him for either information or support just now. Salisbury is at Hatfield and does not come to town regularly. But he did promise me personally that he would make the trip up if I had to talk to him. Naturally, however, I can only make use of this if I have a really urgent and valid reason.

With best regards

Yours

PHatzfeldt [...]


751.    Holstein to Maximilian von Brandt[2]

Berlin, 1 October 1900

Your Excellency,

I sent on your letter to the Chinese Minister in London immediately, on the 23rd or 24th of last month.[3] I sent a copy of it to Count Bülow together with your two letters to me. Bülow sent his best thanks for the interesting news.

I find it impossible to foretell what will happen in the Chinese question, for too many factors are involved. The pressure is such that if a proposal is launched by one party or another, it is at once squeezed out of all shape, so that the originator can hardly recognize it.

I remain respectfully,

Your Excellency's most devoted

Holstein.

---

[1] See p. 203, note 1.        [2] From the Brandt Papers.
[3] See above, Brandt's letter to Holstein of 22 September.

## 752. Holstein to Paul von Hatzfeldt[1]

TELEGRAM

Berlin, 9 October 1900

Private.

I can hardly believe that Lord Salisbury really intended to achieve an explicit and active alliance with us for a war against Russia by means of this agreement.[2] For *this* we would certainly ask for different compensations and services. It is true that the eventuality may arise—that is my honest opinion—, but Lord Salisbury's unyielding attitude continuously provides new grounds for bitterness towards England, whereas he could, right now when the Kaiser and public opinion are cool towards Russia, use the agreement to switch the points in a favourable direction in preparation for the future. Does nobody in England understand this?

Holstein.

## 753. Holstein to Paul von Hatzfeldt[3]

TELEGRAM

Berlin, 12 October 1900

Private.

The Under State Secretary created difficulties concerning the drafts[4] by stressing again and again that Russia would feel insulted by the agreement. That will suit me fine. Actually our new version of Article I[5] could more easily be regarded as anti-Russian than Lord Salisbury's version. Equally your version of Article III concerning protection of interests is not one which will please the Russians. I regard the agreement as it now stands as the second step along the road of the Portuguese Treaty. This road we must follow if we do not want to give up the idea of extra-European acquisitions. By this agreement we get once again within calling distance of England, and—through your version of Article III—have the *possibility*, though not the *duty*, to reach an understanding with England concerning the results of the Russian Far Eastern policy.

To be continued.[6]

Holstein.

## 754. Paul von Hatzfeldt to Holstein[7]

TELEGRAM

London, 13 October 1900

Private.

The concluding part of your private telegram of yesterday helped me considerably to push through acceptance of the final version of Article

---

[1] From the London Embassy files.

[2] The reference is to the Anglo-German Yangtze agreement, signed on 16 October 1900, which provided for the maintenance of the Open Door in China.

[3] From the London Embassy files.      [4] Of the Yangtze Treaty.

[5] On keeping open to international trade the ports on the Chinese rivers and littoral. (See *Grosse Politik*, vol. XVI, no. 4741, pp. 245–6.)

[6] Holstein continued on the same day: 'It *cannot* be proved that the agreement is directed against Russia, as the Russian Government itself disclaims any intention of annexation. [...]'

[7] From the London Embassy files.

III. Salisbury actually expressed his concern that England's hands would be completely bound by it, and only yielded when I explained to him that the Article did not oblige the two Powers to reach an understanding concerning the results of Russian Far Eastern policy but left open the possibility that they should do so.

My feeling is that Salisbury is now very anxious to sign and especially to publish. I think it would be best if we could give him a certain time limit, say twelve days, during which secrecy would be preserved. If a longer time is set, an indiscretion somewhere or other must always be feared.

PH.

### 755. Chlodwig zu Hohenlohe to Holstein

Baden-Baden, 20 October 1900

Dear friend,

In view of the large number of letters, some of which I must reply to at once, I can only write a few words.[1] But I cannot omit thanking you sincerely for your kind letter[2] which both honoured and pleased me.

At the same time I thank you sincerely for the many proofs of your friendly feelings, which have always remained constant throughout the long years we worked together and in many a difficult situation.

I regret that you did not take the step mentioned in your letter,[3] but do hope that our country will continue to enjoy your services.

In true friendship<br>Your most devoted<br>CHohenlohe.

### 756. Karl von Wedel to Holstein

[Rome], 5 November 1900

Dear Herr von Holstein,

Following my report[4] on my audience with the young King[5] yesterday, I would like to mention to you an impression, which, just because it is merely an impression, I could hardly express officially. Thus when the King mentioned that his greatest desire was a speedy end of the complications in China, I replied that we entirely shared this desire. Thereupon he made a remark which seemed to mean, if not directly at least implicitly, that he believed that the Kaiser did not attach any importance to a speedy conclusion of the war. I felt also that his questions concerning our alleged acquisition of coaling stations in the Red Sea and on the Guatemalan coast[6] had certain overtones, but there I am

[1] Hohenlohe had resigned from his position as Reich Chancellor on 16 October. He was succeeded by Count Bernhard von Bülow.

[2] Of 19 October. See Hohenlohe, *Denkwürdigkeiten der Reichskanzlerzeit*, pp. 594–5.

[3] Holstein wrote that he had been offered the possibility of high office, but that he had decided to remain in his present position, if only because he would otherwise have been obliged to change his way of life completely.

[4] The main points of Wedel's report of 5 November are brought out below. (From the Foreign Ministry files.)

[5] Victor Emmanuel III, King of Italy, 1900–46.

[6] See *Memoirs*, pp. 177–8.

perhaps mistaken as this may only have been the after-taste left by his remark on China. Naturally my reply to the King was short and academic. I pointed to our cautious and honest policy, which will be carried on and is firmly guaranteed by our new Chancellor.

I have informed you of this remark merely for further clarification of the lines of thought of the new King. I am not reporting a fact but only following my flair. This tells me that Victor Emanuel mistrusts to a certain extent the ambition and enterprise of our Serene Master. The next few years will show whether my assumption was mistaken. I do not think the new King will embark on any adventures, and this after all is in our interest since we are opposed to any dispersal of Italy's power and any unnecessary demands made on her financial capacity. But all the same I believe that in order to keep the King's sincere friendship we must try to avoid completely giving the impression of our exercising undue political influence or of acting as political guardians. You will know what I mean without my explaining it in greater detail.

With best regards I remain respectfully

Your most devoted
Ct. Wedel

## 757.    Paul von Hatzfeldt to Holstein[1]

TELEGRAM

London, 5 November 1900

Private.

[...] I don't think I can be suspected of exaggerated sympathy for Russia. On the other hand I don't think that we ought to provoke Russian enmity unnecessarily, nor that we should support the English beyond the limits to which they are willing to go. If they want us to do more, particularly if we are to draw Russian enmity upon us, they must grant us far more in return than they did in our latest agreement.[2] I myself told Salisbury a short while ago—naturally after the conclusion of the agreement: 'I don't know whether you are aware of the fact that about two years ago some of your most important colleagues offered me a formal alliance, to be sanctioned by Parliament, in return for support of English policy in China.[3] At the time the idea was premature and therefore difficulties arose on both sides. But you will understand that were you to ask me to-day for general support of English policy in China, I would, were we to agree to it at all, have to pose conditions quite different from the ones you agreed to in the existing draft of our agreement. Lord Salisbury was astonished and remained silent, and so did I. My object was merely to make it clear to him that to-day's agreement only applies to specific points, and that if at a later stage England were to ask us to back her all the way in China, she would have to grant us something quite different in return.

[1] From the London Embassy files.

[2] The Anglo-German Yangtze agreement of 16 October 1900. (See *Grosse Politik*, vol. XVI, no. 4744, pp. 248–50.)

[3] In April 1898. See *Grosse Politik*, vol. XIVi, no. 3784, pp. 202–4.

This is still my opinion as of now, and I think we would do well to act accordingly, which, however, does not hinder energetic action on the part of Waldersee.[1] [...]

## 758. Hugo von Radolin to Holstein

Jarotschin, 14 November 1900

My dear friend,

Your letter of July[2] forced me to assume that our aim remained to work hand in hand with Russia and that an understanding with England could not be reached. How desirable the latter would be, provided it does not disturb our good relations with Russia, is clear. I took the contents of your letter as my guide. Now, suddenly, came the agreement with England,[3] of which I knew and learnt nothing until I read about it in the Press. The Russians must have known of it in advance, *before* I did; for as I reported at the time, I was told by important people that *we were following an English policy in China, peut-être sans le vouloir*, and that our differences with Russia were constantly increasing, in spite of our continuous assurances of collaboration. It would have been of value to the German Ambassador in St Petersburg to be informed in time of the new trend in our policy in order to abandon the *old* track and switch to the *new* one. The Russians must have thought me very badly informed when I continued to advocate our collaboration while they already knew that we were going to work with England. I must say I had not thought it possible that we would reach agreement with England so soon, after the recent very blunt letter to the Prince of Wales,[4] and after I had told Scott what I thought of Lord Salisbury's spitefulness. Until now I had always firmly believed that the friendly relations between Germany and Russia, based on solid mutual *trust*, formed the firm basis of Germany's policy, and that we would come to an agreement with England, which we had until now never regarded as reliable as an ally, only on specific issues. How can we now trust England whilst pursuing, as we aim to do, a comprehensive world-policy? It would of course be nice if it were possible and could last. [...]

As far as I am informed Germany and England demand the *open door for the trade of all nations along the whole coast of China and all the river-banks*, etc. Russia replies: We welcome with pleasure *that all Chinese sea- and river-ports in areas where England and Germany exert influence* should remain free and open to the trade of all nations.[5] I think the difference is very clear and obvious. Thus the Russians *will not let any*

[1] In the first part of this telegram Hatzfeldt had advised such energetic action.

[2] See above, Holstein's letter to Radolin of 30 July 1900.

[3] See p. 211, note 2.

[4] The reference is apparently to the Kaiser's letter to the Prince of Wales of 31 July, which was communicated to Radolin at the Kaiser's orders. In the letter the Kaiser complained about the lack of understanding shown by the British Government for Germany's China policy. (From the Foreign Ministry files.)

[5] For the Russian reply to the Anglo-German Yangtze agreement, see *Grosse Politik*, vol. XVI, no. 4747, p. 253.

*other Power into Manchuria,* which incidentally has in the meanwhile been divided into seven military districts, each under a general (naturally only to ensure winter quarters for the troops and the safety of the railroad construction!). This is in exact accord with Russia's old programme (about which I have reported sufficiently often in the past).

I regard it as my duty to inform you even from here of my *well-founded* observations. I am the first to welcome joyfully our *good* relations with England. But I think that these should *never go so far* as to *anger the Russians* and thus produce a coolness in Russo-German relations, which is becoming more and more noticeable. [...]

I pray to God that we shall regain close contact with Russia; for England will never compensate us for what we have lost in Russia. What I have written is based not on assumptions but on actual observation. After six years I do believe I know Russia. I regard it as my duty to write quite openly and without rose-coloured spectacles. I hope to come to Berlin soon. On my arrival here I found so much to do and important things to settle that I could not come to Berlin earlier.

Your faithful<br>Radolin.

## 759.   Holstein to Paul von Hatzfeldt[1]

TELEGRAM

London, 22 November 1900

Private.

In confidential discussion of the latest speeches in the Reichstag, you might point out the conventional character of the spoken word, in contrast to the German Government's acts which always aim to emphasize those points on which community of interests with England can be assumed. Thus it is questionable whether present Russian policy, which regards most of Asia as an object for acquisition, can be described as 'well-conducted' in the sense of Bülow's speech.[2] But on the other hand the point of view you are already maintaining towards Lord Salisbury—that we have no reasonable cause for war against Russia—must be adhered to. *Perhaps* you might let it become apparent that in a war of England against Russia and France, we would not remain spectators until the end, and that probably France would make no move anyway as long as Germany was watching with shouldered arms. These political laws of nature will remain valid, in spite of speeches in Parliament and [pro-]Boer demonstrations.

This is known in Russia too, and under present circumstances she will not risk a war against England, even if England were to take a very firm line in the Far East.

Naturally all of this must be adopted to the personalities involved.

Holstein.

---

[1] From the London Embassy files.

[2] Bülow had praised Russian foreign policy in a Reichstag speech of 19 November.

### 760. Holstein to Paul von Hatzfeldt[1]

TELEGRAM

Berlin, 3 December 1900

[...] For a number of years already I have argued with Herr von Brandt that nothing can be done with *all* the Powers—in that case action and counter-action neutralize each other—but that a smaller group must be formed in order to achieve anything. Our latest experiences seem to confirm this.

A grouping of England and the Triple Alliance would easily attain every just objective. France would probably not work with us, but neither would she work against us, for Delcassé keenly desires to pull out of China unmolested.

If England fails us now, we shall know, also for future reference, that no combinations can be based on her because England does not want to defend her own interests herself, but wants to leave this to others while remaining in the background.

The present Chinese problem, which turns on the question of punishment,[2] involves no immediate advantage but rather the decision as to who is stronger. And as regards prestige, England has more to lose in Asia than we have.

What would be the views of the Duke of Devonshire and Balfour on this question?

Holstein

### 761. Paul von Hatzfeldt to Holstein[3]

TELEGRAM

London, 5 December 1900

Private.

[...] And now finally a word or two concerning your telegram of the 3rd of this month and the view propounded to Herr von Brandt on a closer grouping between the Triple Alliance and England. As you know from all my earlier statements, I am in entire and absolute agreement, *provided*, as I've said repeatedly, that we can *wait* until the English see the value of this arrangement for themselves and offer us acceptable conditions for it. So far their difficulties have not been great enough for them to do this. Thus for the time being I can use the idea of an understanding on specific issues between two friendly nations only as an argument in favour of similar treatment of issues that may arise. Were I to advocate a new Triple Alliance-England grouping to Lansdowne, I would have to be prepared for the rejoinder that this would, in present circumstances, be equivalent to an alliance, and that I should pose our conditions for same. This presupposes that people here incline towards an alliance, which is by no means proven, as even Chamberlain, the standard-bearer of this idea, is supposed to have given it up. But is it

---

[1] From the London Embassy files.
[2] Of the main culprits in the Boxer rebellion.
[3] From the London Embassy files.

advisable for us to take up this idea already at this time? This would seem rather doubtful to me. But without an alliance of some sort, i.e. without binding commitments as they exist between members of the Triple Alliance, I don't really see the possibility of a closer grouping between the latter and England.

*Strictly confidential*

One great difficulty I face with several persons here is the belief that what I say here is not always in accord with what is said in the Wilhelmstrasse. I have not yet been able to discover whether that is due to Lascelles' dispatches.

PH.

762.   Paul von Hatzfeldt to Holstein[1]

TELEGRAM

London, 13 December 1900

Private.

[...] I regard it as an advantage whose importance can hardly be over-estimated that latest developments have enabled us to bring about a slight cooling-off of Anglo-American relations over the death penalty question.[2] I believe we would do well to further this coolness unostentatiously by showing as much friendliness and consideration for Lansdowne as possible.[3]

PH.

763.   Holstein to Paul von Hatzfeldt[4]

TELEGRAM

Berlin, 14 December 1900

Private. With reference to your telegram no. 831.[5]

The alleged *new* Anglo-Portuguese alliance[6] is being much exploited here against the German Government as providing proof that England deceived us with German-English Africa agreement, which was aimed at keeping us neutral during the Boer War.

Personally I believe the statement of the Under Secretary of State in telegram no. 831 to be true, but the Chancellor said to me on Tuesday with great bitterness that this English demonstration made his position, which was already difficult enough, even more difficult. I think that the Chancellor would have shown England greater consideration in Wednesday's speech without this *contretemps*.

You might get Lord Lansdowne to confirm the statement of the Under

---

[1] From the London Embassy files.

[2] For the main culprits in the Boxer risings.

[3] Holstein replied on 14 December: 'Agree re England and America.' (From the London Embassy files.)

[4] From the London Embassy files.

[5] By this telegram of 13 December Hatzfeldt reported the assurance of the Under Secretary of State that no Anglo-Portuguese agreement concerning Delagoa Bay had been concluded during the celebrations occasioned by the British fleet's visit to Lisbon, and that the British Government regarded itself as firmly bound by the Anglo-German treaty. (From the Foreign Ministry files.)

[6] See p. 185, note 2.

Secretary of State at the next suitable opportunity, and then take official cognisance of it. What do you think?[1]

Holstein

764.　Holstein to Bernhard von Bülow
　　　Copy

B[erlin], 26 December 1900

Dear Bülow,

Our long-distance communications are becoming as unsatisfactory as possible. If things go on like this we shall soon surely be at odds. As I have recently gained the impression that neither of us intends this, I have been pondering how this situation can be remedied.

I certainly do not under-estimate the value of one minute of the Chancellor's time, but since the preservation of our relations also has a certain value, I would like to suggest that you receive me once a week and always on the same day. In the meantime I will note down the points to be brought up, and thus we shall prevent the accumulation of mouldy misunderstandings. The law of nature, *les absents ont toujours tort*, is also valid in your case, dear friend. This is the only request I permit myself, and I therefore ask that you receive me to-morrow, the 27th, for the holidays are behind us and the Reichstag is still to come.

Your truly devoted
H.

[1] Eckardstein telegraphed on 15 December that he was firmly convinced that the Under Secretary of State had spoken the truth. On 1 January 1901 he telegraphed: 'Under Secretary of State yesterday again assured me that no agreement of any kind had been concluded between England and Portugal.' (From the London Embassy files.)

# 1901

765.   Paul von Metternich to Bernhard von Bülow[1]

Osborne,[2] 22 January 1901

Strictly private

Your telegram of yesterday to H.M.[3] and me[4] arrived after H.M. had already had long conversations with the Prince of Wales, the Duke of York, the Duke of Connaught and also female members of the royal family, that is at least with Princess Louise.[5]

To-night H.M. told me a lot about these. He talked to his relatives mainly about policy on China, the ill-feeling between Russia and France and the fact that it was now a tempting task for English policy to drive deeper the wedge between the two and draw the French wholly from Russia's side. H.M. then pointed to the rapprochement between America and Russia and America's drawing away from England. On the one hand disregard of the Hay-Pauncefote Treaty,[6] on the other the placing of the American troops in China under Russian command in Shanhai-kwan (latest report from Waldersee). America and Russia were fast drawing closer because both were hostile to Europe. Russia especially wished to drive *all* Europeans from China. Grand Duke Vladimir had made it clear only a few days ago in Berlin that his mission was to persuade us to withdraw our troops from China. H.M. had answered: only when the Chinese had fulfilled all our demands. The Russians should help to achieve this instead of withdrawing. Then our troops would also leave China more quickly. Generally H.M. seems to have emphasized strongly to the Prince of Wales Russia's perfidy towards Count Waldersee and in the Chinese question.

I replied to H.M. that the English were in a mess and therefore felt the desire for a rapprochement.[7] As yet, however, this was only seen at the top and not yet among the people. England, weakened in its prestige

[1] From the Foreign Ministry files.
[2] The Kaiser had travelled to England on 19 January after receiving the news of Queen Victoria's severe illness. Queen Victoria died on 22 January.
[3] *Grosse Politik*, vol. XVII, no. 4983, pp. 20–1.
[4] The telegram instructed Metternich to draw the Kaiser's attention to the danger that anything he might say in an anti-Russian sense to members of the English royal family, and especially to the Prince of Wales, would be used by them to render our relations with Russia worse, shift Russian opposition from England onto Germany, and in this way improve Anglo-Russian relations. (From the Foreign Ministry files.)
[5] Fourth daughter of Queen Victoria; married to the Marquis of Lorne.
[6] In the first Hay-Pauncefote treaty of 5 February 1900, England renounced the right to joint construction and ownership of the Panama Canal. The treaty was never ratified. A second Hay-Pauncefote treaty was signed in November 1901.
[7] Marginal comment by Bülow: ' Correct'.

and power by an inglorious war, was a weak friend, while Russia could become a strong enemy. The pretence of Anglo-Russian fraternization was utter sham. On the contrary English respect for us grew as our differences with Russia declined.[1] We should neither lend the Russians our money nor the English our soldiers.

As H.M. is strongly influenced by the charm of the Prince of Wales and his family here, and General Plessen was present at the conversation, I could not, without exceeding the limits of the permissible towards H.M., bring up the question of probable indiscretion to-night. It would, moreover, have been too late, as the conversations with the Prince of Wales etc. had already taken place. But the next time I am alone with H.M., I will draw His attention to the danger of indiscretions.

I would certainly assume that in his conversations with English statesmen H.M. will express himself more cautiously and in no circumstances will bind himself politically. [...]

Ever your faithfully devoted
Metternich [...]

766.    Holstein to Paul von Hatzfeldt[2]

TELEGRAM

Berlin, 14 February 1901

Private.

I regard it as self-evident that we should not run after the English with proposals for a rapprochement.[3] I now envisage the order of events as follows: The English and Japanese representatives deliver a statement in the sense outlined in your telegram no. 124 in Peking.[4] Following that the German representative in Peking also delivers the statement whose content is already known to you and the English.[5] If everything then moves smoothly and this slight pressure brings things in China—that is to say the question of concessions and acquisitions—into the desired form, the English will not feel the need for German support on a definite basis. The question of a rapprochement between England and Germany can then rest for the present. If things do not go absolutely smoothly, the English will soon enough look to us again. We can wait. Lord Lansdowne must on no account get the impression that you want to intimidate him so as to get something for Germany. It will also be easier for you to negotiate once England and Japan have really started their action. Therefore it seems to me that you should skate lightly over this matter to-morrow. Naturally you will have to avoid awakening

---

[1] Bülow: 'Naturally'.          [2] From the London Embassy files.

[3] In a telegram of the same day Hatzfeldt had advised leaving the initiative on the question of Anglo-German co-operation against Russia to England.

[4] On 7 February Lord Lansdowne had informed Hatzfeldt of a Japanese proposal for a joint démarche concerning Russian moves in China in general and the imminent ratification of the Russian-Chinese agreement on Manchuria in particular. Hatzfeldt sent this information to Berlin in telegram no. 124. (*Grosse Politik*, vol. XVI, no. 4808, pp. 311–14.)

[5] Holstein's draft of this statement (*Grosse Politik*, vol. XVI, no. 4810, pp. 315–16) was transmitted to Hatzfeldt by Bülow on 11 February. (*Grosse Politik*, vol. XVI, no. 4812, pp. 317–18.)

premature hopes just as much as premature fears. But you find the border line for all that by instinct better than anyone else.

Holstein.

### 767.   Holstein to Hermann von Eckardstein[1]

TELEGRAM

Berlin, 2 March 1901

Private.

As long as Lord Salisbury remains the decisive factor, we must be especially careful, for—obstinate as he is—his policy will never change from the one he has pursued hitherto, the policy of a confidence trickster which has led to England's present isolation. Perhaps he will yet succeed in a grand finale to drive Japan into Russia's arms. Then England would gradually achieve the status of an object of compensation from which the other Powers take their cut, just as happened in Germany one hundred years ago with the territories of the ecclesiastical rulers. Perhaps America will make the first move; for you surely do not believe that America would leave the English in possession of the Yangtze basin in case England and Russia reached an agreement with that in view. England and Lord Salisbury have both gone into a decline. They suit each other, no one else.

Holstein.

### 768.   Bernhard von Bülow to Holstein[2]

31 March 1901

Dear friend,

I had hoped to see you before my departure, but I hear that you are no longer at the office.

I would especially recommend the Chinese compensation question to you.[3] I place its political conduct into your hands with complete confidence. It is of absolutely vital importance that we should succeed in saving face in this question.

I will give your regards to Donna Laura and Blaserna, and with best wishes for a happy Easter remain as ever.

Your truly devoted
B.

### 769.   Hermann von Eckardstein to Holstein[4]

London, 31 March 1901

Your Excellency will have already learned from a telegram that I have submitted my resignation. First of all I don't want to omit expressing to Your Excellency my most sincere and deeply-felt gratitude for the great kindness which Your Excellency has always shown me. I naturally found it very difficult to decide on this step. But it was a

---

[1] From the London Embassy files.     [2] From the Bülow Papers.
[3] See *Grosse Politik*, vol. XVI, chapter CVII.
[4] See Eckardstein, *Lebenserinnerungen*, vol. II, pp. 291–2; 327–8.

decision which I would have had to take sooner or later. The Ambassador naturally knows of it. I visited him the other day in Brighton and am going there to see him again on Tuesday. He is *very much better* and plans to come to London after Easter. I just cannot express how terribly sorry I am that I must leave the Ambassador whom I respect so very much.

Stübel's[1] mission has unfortunately failed and, as I see from Your Excellency's letter, certain consequences and changes in personnel are imminent. I got on very well with Dr Stübel, who is really a very charming person. We did everything we could to get something through fast, but nothing can be achieved here in a hurry.

In my next letter, which I will send by courier, I shall write to Your Excellency on a number of matters concerning English politics. Moreover, I hope to be able to come to Berlin very soon and will not fail then to call on Your Excellency.

All indications point to Lord Salisbury's going soon, and my friend Devonshire will succeed him. But the latter too is by no means easy to 'take'. One must understand him in order to get on with him.

In the hope that these lines will find Your Excellency very well.

I remain as ever
Your Excellency's
gratefully devoted
Hermann von Eckardstein.

## 770.  Karl von Wedel to Holstein

Rome, 12 April 1901

Dear Herr von Holstein,

First of all I want to thank you most sincerely for your kind and interesting letter of the 14th of last month. As you will have gathered from my reports, I have recently undertaken a pretty candid examination of Italian policy and conditions here, without, however, allowing myself to be guided in this by any conscious or unconscious animosity. I am convinced now as before that Italy is useful and necessary for us, but we must be content with a passive role from her. I have held it to be my duty to leave no doubt that any demand for more than this belongs to the realm of illusions.

I believe I can claim that I do not tailor my reports to suit certain quarters. Such opportunism—which I do encounter from time to time in other quarters—is contrary to my character, quite apart from the fact that, judging quite objectively, I would regard this under present circumstances as positively and seriously dangerous. If, however, I cannot see my way to writing something which is contrary to my opinion, even though perhaps it might be well received, I would consider a

---

[1] Oskar Wilhelm Stübel. Director of the Colonial Division of the Foreign Ministry, 1900–5. Stübel had gone to London to discuss means by which China might pay the compensation demanded by Germany, and claims arising out of the South African War. (See *Grosse Politik*, vol. XVI, no. 4889, pp. 399–400; vol. XVII, p. 100, note **.)

certain reserve in the judgment of some matters or even complete silence quite permissible. Thus if you were to be of the opinion that I could serve our cause in this respect by greater reserve on my part, I would be gladly prepared to take this into account if need be.

The festivities in Toulon[1] are to-day happily reaching their end, after having finally after all exceeded the limits of a simple exchange of courtesies. This was to be expected. What causes me most concern in all this is the undoubtedly increasing megalomania in certain Italian circles. France's wooing strengthens the Italians' consciousness of their own importance and of the great value of Italian friendship. Even if at least the serious-minded circles certainly don't think of granting this friendship to the highest bidder, the danger does exist that people here will think they can claim a special premium for the continuation of this friendship.

But the awakening will not fail to come in this matter too, and I would assert that even the present Cabinet, and Signor Prinetti[2] *en tête*, would not hesitate to renew the alliance without any difficulty, provided, however, that we and Austria don't hurt the Italians too much economically. [...]

Could we not cautiously try to influence England to pay more attention again—in her very own interests—to her old Italian protégé? An Italy that knows that her position in the Mediterranean is secure would be safe from any tendency towards France.

Unfortunately I can't really make out the King yet. He is certainly not an enthusiastic friend of ours—as his father was—and I am beginning to have doubts concerning his determination, of which so far he has furnished no proof whatsoever. On the contrary he is said to be very frightened of attempts on his life. [...]

With best wishes
Your very devoted
Count Wedel

## 771.   Paul von Hatzfeldt to Holstein[3]

London, 20 April 1901

Private.

The Russian proposal[4] pleases me *tremendously* for I think it well suited to make people here finally see the light.[5] I do not for a moment

---

[1] An Italian squadron, commanded by the Duke of Genoa, visited Toulon from 8–13 April. The Duke paid a visit to President Loubet at the Préfecture de la Marine, and on the following day the President visited the Italian cruiser *Lepanto*.

[2] Giulio, Marchese Prinetti. Italian Foreign Minister in the Zanardelli Cabinet, 1901–3.

[3] From the London Embassy files.

[4] Bülow informed Hatzfeldt on 20 April that Osten-Sacken had suggested that Germany, France, and Russia should together guarantee a Chinese loan equal to the sum which the three Powers would demand as compensation from China. (*Grosse Politik*, vol. XVI, no. 4899, pp. 408–9.)

[5] Holstein had just telegraphed: 'How do you like the proposed collection guarantee? In this way the Far Eastern Triple Alliance is to be brought together again and Russia is to be given the chance to raise a loan of £17 million on favourable terms by involving the credit of France and Germany.' (From the London Embassy files.)

believe that it will actually be realized so far as Russian finances are concerned, and probably neither does Witte. But from Russia's point of view that would be a minor matter—badly though they need money in St Petersburg—if only the *political* aim could be achieved by gaining our agreement to the reactivation of the 1895 Triple Alliance. This Triple Alliance would have quite another meaning for England now than formerly, it would be absolutely disastrous both for English interests in China and for England's prestige in the whole world. Even Salisbury will hardly be able to close his eyes to this fact, and it therefore remains to be seen what attitude he will adopt when Lansdowne and his friends point out to the Prime Minister on his return that something must be done to prevent a definite change of course by Germany and to ensure German friendship for England instead.

In these circumstances the further development of events will largely depend on whether we handle the matter correctly. Provided that Lord Salisbury is still determined even now to avoid any understanding with us, there is hardly another way open to him except a direct agreement with Russia, obtained by great sacrifices. But would the other Ministers, such as Lansdowne and his friends, follow him without question along this path to-day? This danger—which, as you know, I myself have drawn attention to repeatedly—seems to me to have decreased now, provided that for the time being we keep quite still and do not give our political opponents here any pretext to arouse ill-feeling and distrust against us, whether within or outside the Cabinet. By that I naturally do not mean that we should make any extra concessions in any one question or hide or water down any divergence of views. But it must be done in a manner which will meet with understanding here. And above all we must hold firmly to the rule of letting the English come to us regarding their political decisions for the future, without showing any anxiety, impatience, or annoyance. This is of the greatest importance.

It is almost equally important, I think, that, without undertaking any obligations, we should not break the thread which Russia is now spinning. This is the best and most effective means of pressure on the political decisions of the English Government at our disposal, and therefore we must not surrender it. I can see no disadvantage if the English were to believe for the time being that we were considering whether the Russian proposal might not have advantages for someone who needs their money and has found no support here.

All activity will be at a full stop here to-morrow, as Lansdowne and the Under Secretary of State will be away. The former does not return until Wednesday or Thursday.

PH.

772.   Paul von Hatzfeldt to Holstein

London, 4 May 1901

Dear friend,

Eckardstein, whom you will presumably see to-morrow, will give you a report and also tell you how I am. On the whole I am much better, but the last attack weakened me so much that for a short time I must still avoid any effort for I am not to risk a relapse.

I have postponed sending the private letter I intended for the Chancellor mainly because this is a time when we must sit back and wait, and there is hardly anything to be said that has not been said often and at length before. Clearly they cannot make up their minds here yet on what path to follow in world policy and so, with their well-known indolence, they are awaiting developments in the hope that a favourable turn of events will save the English Government from the effort of reaching a decision. This does not mean that the situation has changed to our disadvantage, and our friends in the Cabinet—whose names you know—still want to reach an understanding with the Triple Alliance. As Eckardstein reported to you, this desire was, however, momentarily in abeyance at the time of Stübel's mission, which without exception was taken very much amiss in Government circles here.[1] This was not in any way due to the choice of this particular official, but because the impression obtained that the mission itself, without prior agreement with the English Government, showed a lack of consideration.[2] Eckardstein will probably tell you that the Duchess of Devonshire—you know how influential her position is—expressed herself quite heatedly in this sense not very long ago. But I think it can be assumed that the ill-feeling over this incident has already abated considerably, and will soon be forgotten if nothing else crops up. But as far as possible care should be taken that no new friction and misunderstandings occur.[3]

In the meantime we can regard it as a reassuring factor that at the moment there is no indication in favour of the assumption that the plan of a direct understanding with Russia or France is being seriously considered here. The Austrian, who is usually not ill-informed, to-day expressed to me the firm conviction that up till now no negotiation of any sort between England on the one hand and Russia and France on the other had taken place or was envisaged. But equally Count Deym shared my view that they will wait here until the last minute before taking a decision at all, and will only decide in favour of a definite rapprochement with the Triple Alliance when the danger of serious complications and losses has become graver and more imminent for England.

As you will remember from my private letter some time ago,[4] I had the impression that the proposal of a financial arrangement *à trois* in China made to us by the Russians would precipitate the decision here. It was clear that Lansdowne was very excited and frightened by this incident and this seemed to justify my expectation. I do not know what happened later in this matter, as I have received no further news from Berlin on the progress of the negotiations in question. Thus I also don't know what news or assurances have in the meantime calmed Lansdowne's

[1] Marginal comment by Bülow: 'Why?'
[2] Bülow: '*Ça c'est un comble.*'
[3] Bülow: 'As if that depended only on us and not also on England.'
[4] Not found. See above, Hatzfeldt's private telegram to Holstein of 20 April.

fears of the Russian attempt to revive a Triple Alliance in the Far East.[1]

Now it remains to be seen whether the Russians will keep quiet or end up by doing something or other which would be regarded as a serious threat here. My personal view, which as you know I have held for some time, is that the Russians have no intention of starting a war now if they can somehow decently avoid it, and the probability that they might allow themselves to be tempted after all would only increase if Witte were to succeed in raising a sizeable loan.[2] It is not easy to see how, even with the best will in the world, the French will find the necessary money, as they have already invested too much money in Russian bonds.[3] But if Rothschild considers it possible, then it probably is possible.[4] If the loan is raised it is bound to become clear whether this will make the Russians more aggressive and to what extent this will be suffered here without an attempt being made to find support.

I regard as the greatest danger to the further development of the situation, particularly here, the by no means impossible case that the Japanese should one day get tired of being fobbed off by the English with fair words and would prefer an understanding with Russia, which St Petersburg certainly wants.[5] I probably do not need to add that, were I to see any possibility of persuading the English to greater consideration towards Japan or at least to help her financially, I would decidedly advocate and work for such a course. But unfortunately the English are incorrigible in this respect[6] and still cannot understand that one sometimes must bring sacrifices if one is to find friends.[7]

For the moment peace will presumably reign here in the foreign political field, if only because Lansdowne is confined to bed with a cold. And even more important in this respect is the fact that Salisbury does not seem in any hurry to return. After his return had at first been fixed for the 3rd of this month and then postponed to the 11th, I hear to-day that he will probably not keep to this date either. But as he follows foreign policy as attentively as ever and is anxious to prevent Lansdowne from straying in any way from his, Salisbury's policy, it may be assumed that for as long as he remains in the South nothing special is in the offing.

Farewell for to-day, dear friend. I hope that your health remains good.

With best regards

Your

PHatzfeldt.

### 773. Bernhard von Bülow to Holstein

77 Wilhelmstrasse, [16 May 1901]

Dear friend,

I am longing for a political talk with you to-day like a child for the

---

[1] Marginal comment by Bülow: 'Perhaps the fact that from the very start we met this Russian proposal with *mine grise*?'

[2] Bülow: '*Il est en train.*'

[3] Bülow: 'This is the general view, not shared, however, by some bankers ([illegible], Mendelssohn).'

[4] Bülow: 'Yes'.         [5] Bülow: 'Quite true'.         [6] Bülow: 'True'.

[7] Bülow: 'cf. English policy towards Italy.'

breast, but I can fully understand that on Ascension Day you went for a walk in the country. Richthofen will transmit to you my ideas on the pending important questions. I know I am at one with you in wanting to settle the Chinese question as soon and as decently as possible and in not letting the possibility of an alliance with England founder.

With very best regards from

Your truly devoted

B.

## 774.  Paul von Hatzfeldt to Holstein

London, 26 May 1901

Dear friend,

First of all thank you once again for your sympathy which did me good.[1] If my health had not improved so very much I might perhaps not have been able to withstand the blow.

I want to use the opportunity for safe transmission afforded by Herr Spies' trip to write you a few words on personal and highly confidential matters. And I ask you at the same time to regard what I say as absolutely confidential and *destined only for you personally*, even though it is seemingly connected with official matters. When you have read this letter you will easily see the reasons for this and be persuaded that I am not guided by any consideration of my personal interests in this.

You will probably have wondered yesterday already that I did not deal with yesterday's exchange with Lansdowne (the memorandum which he asked for) officially, but merely informed you privately.[2] You will understand the reason at once by looking at the enclosed copy of Lansdowne's private letter, in particular the passage which shows Lansdowne demanding the fulfilment of *a promise which had been made to him*.[3] I trust I don't need to say that this was not made by me or on my instructions, nor that this promise could hardly facilitate my task of bargaining with Lansdowne on the basis of a treaty with the Triple Alliance in our conversation of the 23rd.[4] As you know I had called on Lord Lansdowne at the Foreign Office already on the 20th of this month to discuss the question, and, as I reported officially,[5] it was then agreed that the Minister would visit me here for a detailed conversation after his return from the country. In the meantime Eckardstein for his part returned from the country on Tuesday, looked at the files and went to the Foreign Office the following day. There he also discussed the alliance

---

[1] On the death of Hatzfeldt's daughter Nelly.

[2] Hatzfeldt informed Holstein in a private telegram of 25 May that Lansdowne had requested a confidential memorandum on the alliance question in a private letter to Eckardstein. (See *Grosse Politik*, vol. XVII, p. 67, note ***.)

[3] In his letter to Eckardstein of 24 May, Lansdowne requested 'the memorandum which you were good enough to promise me.' (*British Documents*, vol. II, no. 84, p. 66.) Hatzfeldt wrote to Lansdowne on 25 May that he knew nothing about such a memorandum and hoped that the matter could wait until Lansdowne was able to inform him personally of what it was all about. (*British Documents*, vol. II, no. 87, enclosure 2, p. 70.)

[4] See *Grosse Politik*, vol. XVII, no. 5010, pp. 65–7; *British Documents*, vol. II, no. 82, enclosure, pp. 64–5.

[5] In a telegram to Bülow of 20 May. (From the Foreign Ministry files.)

question with Lord Lansdowne,[1] although he knew that I was supposed to have a conversation with the Minister on the following day. From his own statements I must conclude that he raised no particular objection to Lansdowne's wishes, which he thinks by no means unjustified. After this conversation on Wednesday, Eckardstein came to me to impress upon me that as I was in mourning, Lansdowne was not sure whether he should come and see me the next day. It would therefore probably be better to postpone my conversation with the Minister altogether. He offered three times to write to Lansdowne in this sense and I firmly refused this offer three times, leaving it open whether I would do so myself. As you know Lansdowne then turned out to be very grateful when I received him the following day for a lengthy conversation.

I could tell you much more, for I know exactly what happened. For quite some time I have been warned in this respect from various quarters. All agreed that the object was not to *deputize* for me during my illness but to *replace* me to one's own advantage. Until now I have refused to believe this, not because I am too naive to believe something like this possible in a case where gratitude is due to me, but because, the situation being what it is, such a move would be too silly in the person's own interests. Eckardstein's interest, properly understood, would be to keep me here. My health requires care, and therefore he can earn some laurels serving under me, while any successor of mine would at once prohibit any interference and confine him to the execution of his duties as a Secretary.

It is not my purpose in giving you the above hints in strict confidence to make a complaint or to ask you for any sort of intervention. Because of this I have asked you to treat this communication as a strictly personal one. As you know from experience I am not the person to damage other people's careers if it can be avoided, nor even if, as far as I am concerned, they deserve it from every point of view. I also assume that it is a question of lack of understanding and tact rather than ill-will. Moreover I am prepared to accept as an excuse that the independent handling of affairs here, made possible by my long illness, had a certain intoxicating effect and may have given rise to the idea that after my removal he might succeed. Admittedly the idea is absurd, for the job requires somewhat more knowledge and experience, and it is not enough to be Maple's son-in-law and keep open house for Press-men and others.

The purpose of this letter is simply to prepare you personally, so that you will not be surprised if I should eventually be forced to intervene more forcibly. At the moment I do believe that he has gathered from my actions in the last few days that things cannot go on as at present. But this is not certain. Perhaps he believes himself clever enough to pursue his own policies both here and especially in Berlin without my noticing it. If I were to reach this conclusion, something I would regret in the interests of the cause more than in my own, I would intervene

---

[1] See Eckardstein, *Lebenserinnerungen*, vol. II, pp. 352–3; *British Documents*, vol. II, no. 82, pp. 64–5.

very energetically and bring the matter to an end at once. An attempt to hide behind the idea of personal favouritism would then not stop me from action, just as the fear of personal disadvantage would not. That is something I would have to risk. But I think that at my age, in my position, and with my past, I enjoy sufficient confidence at home for people to believe in me without question in this instance.

Let us hope that none of this will become necessary. I am quite satisfied that you are now informed.

I am very grateful for your letter to my wife, a further proof that I can count on your old friendship. I hope to be fit enough in the next few days to ask the King for an audience when he comes to London. The only handicap from which I still suffer is that my legs are so weak after such a long time in bed that I would find it very difficult to walk through a number of rooms, as I would have to do for an audience. To strengthen my legs they are being massaged one day and receiving electrical treatment the next.

I received an extremely kind and gracious telegram from His Majesty on the death of my daughter. Bülow, too, sent a telegram full of friendly feeling.

Hoping, dear friend, that you are completely well again, with best regards and in friendship as ever

Your
PHatzfeldt.

775.    Holstein to Paul von Hatzfeldt
        Copy

Monday, 7:30 p.m.
[27 May 1901]

Hurriedly these few lines in answer to your letter which I have just received. I'll plunge straight in.

E[ckardstein] is in no doubt whatever that your leaving would mean a change for the worse for him. Everything I know of his activities tends to show that he wants to help you. Thus, during the long time when you were completely out of action, he did not say a single word about your condition in the Ministry here, not even to me. It came out later through some naive persons. It is natural that during that time he should have grown used to a certain independence. Now it is up to you to emphasize that you want to take over the conduct of affairs again.

There can be no question of a *written* memorandum for the present, that is, not until we are agreed on the *basic principles*. You would have to be specifically empowered from here before such a memorandum could be handed over. On that there can be no doubt after yesterday's official telegram.[1]

Actually E. has hitherto also been of use to you in that, had he, E., not been present, the Kaiser would by now have sent someone else to London to take over, either provisionally or definitively. Both the Chancellor and someone else have told me the Kaiser had stated that E.

[1] *Grosse Politik*, vol. XVII, no. 5011, pp. 67–8.

still lacked some qualifications for the post, but that if only because of his connections he was better able to carry on for a while than many another.

After everything I have heard—particularly from the Chancellor—I must warn you most definitely against breaking with E., for I am forced to assume that such a step would lead immediately to far-reaching personal changes. Things will perhaps take a different course when you can *walk* once more. No one has doubted your mental capacity, but there has been doubt of your ability to overcome your state of physical immobility. And as the Chancellor said to me the other day, King Edward is supposed to be getting impatient at this, or to be so already.

To the best of my knowledge I can say that two things are certain:

the first is that His Majesty, and I believe also the Chancellor, regard E. as the necessary official complement in view of your physical immobility;

the second, that there is no prospect whatever of making your son Counsellor of Embassy in London in the foreseeable future. As your friend I cannot hide from you that the long duration of your withdrawal from official activity has greatly affected the strength of your position. This was achieved slowly but surely by a number of visitors—official and unofficial ones.

But I have by no means given up hope that, if your health really improves, matters will right themselves again. Your past is such that I don't think this is an exaggerated hope. But—keep the peace. You cannot start off, when taking over your post again, by quarrelling with the official who, in the opinion of the Kaiser and the Chancellor, kept everything going in the meantime. Tell E. quietly and without irritation what you want of him; he'll obey.

In friendship as ever and very hurriedly
Your
Holstein.

776.    Holstein to Helene von Hatzfeldt[1]
Copy

B[erlin], 6 June 1901

Dear Countess,

You will recall that I told you: 'The ball is rolling already, and a counter-movement from London or at least from England will be needed to stop it.' Well, this counter-movement failed to materialize, and feelings in high places are such as to make it useless to struggle further. There is nothing more to be done than to try to see that the small pension is doubled, or more if possible.

It seems that at Court—in London as here—they heard about everything that happened in Brighton,[2] and that was the reason why the

---

[1] In French in the original.

[2] Although Hatzfeldt was officially divorced from his wife, he had asked her to come to Brighton, where he had gone to recuperate, to help take care of him. (See below, Hatzfeldt's letter of 8 June.)

Emperor absolutely refused to distinguish H[atzfeldt] with a decoration or even with an audience after his stay in London. I need not tell you how sorry I am, but I have exhausted my resources.

E[ckardstein] has had nothing to do with all this,[1] the moving force came from much higher up, and I know that this wind has now been blowing for many years.

Health is the formal reason.

I will do all I can about the pension. It is the only thing I can still do.

Believe me . . . .

### 777.    Paul von Hatzfeldt to Holstein

London, 8 June 1901

Dear friend,

I received the news in question through my son,[2] and first of all I do want to tell you that I have never for a moment doubted your friendship. I am sure you did everything you could and will go on doing so now to bring the matter to as satisfactory a conclusion as possible.

You know me well enough to be certain that I don't fight the inevitable. Also, I do believe that it isn't worth while crying over spilt milk. I therefore merely want to add very briefly that of all the reasons which I have heard until now, I can only recognize one as in part justified; that is that my health—which, incidentally, I ruined in the course of duty, particularly here—no longer permits me to fulfill the social part of my duties. But, as I have achieved a number of things which others would not have done, this can hardly be regarded as a disadvantage. The insinuations concerning Brighton, made by the intriguers here and in Berlin, are simply ridiculous if one considers my age and the state of my health in the past years. Moreover, it appears to have been forgotten that I have asked for years that I should be allowed to bring my wife here to give me a house and care, and that this was prevented by Countess Brockdorff[3] and other noble souls, although Chancellor Hohenlohe had stated that, also as a relative of ours, he would definitely insist on it.

Also, it does now seem to become apparent that the ruler here, who allegedly started it all, played a far smaller part than was supposed. At least Lansdowne, who I don't think is a liar, yesterday gave me the positive assurance that he knew nothing of this.[4] He, Lansdowne, had first mentioned the matter to the King as a rumour which he had heard by chance, and if the King had really made such a request of the Kaiser, he certainly would have told him, Lansdowne. He promised to tell me more about this.

Now the main thing is to fix the method by which the decision which has been taken is to be executed, so that I too should know what I must

---

[1] In letters to Holstein of 1 and 4 June, Countess Hatzfeldt had said that she suspected Eckardstein of undermining her husband's position.

[2] Hermann, Count von Hatzfeldt-Wildenburg.

[3] Countess Therese Brockdorff. Mistress of the Robes.

[4] See Lansdowne's letter to Lascelles of 9 June. (*British Documents*, vol. II, no. 89, pp. 71–2.)

do.  As far as I can see—but I am not clear on this point—it is wished that I should first of all take three months' leave and then, towards the end of it, hand in the requisite [resignation] request.  Is that right, and *when* should I go on leave?  I trust I need hardly say that after a stay of many years there are a number of things I must arrange and settle before my departure, and, moreover, in the state of my health, I cannot foretell for certain when I shall be fit to travel.  But if in spite of that they are in a great hurry in Berlin they need only tell me.  I would then quietly move to a hotel while my successor moved into the Embassy.

But, as you know very well and can learn from my son, the greatest difficulty is the financial question; not because I have special claims for myself, but because the question will be whether the granted amount might not be decreased by claims from another quarter to such an extent that the remainder would be insufficient for even the most modest existence in Germany.  As I said, please discuss this with my son, who can give you all possible information on the subject.

Finally, I would like to hear from you confidentially how official matters are to be dealt with during the presumably short time I shall still be here.  For my part I have not the least objection to Baron Eckardstein, who had already taken a grip on almost everything, handling things here for that short time with me merely furnishing my name.  Probably nothing very important will crop up until then, for Lansdowne yesterday already avoided any mention of the alliance question with me, although my last letter to him was mentioned in the conversation.

Before closing this letter I only want to mention one fact concerning Eckardstein's behaviour towards me personally which seems to me to be of decisive importance.  He himself told my wife, to whom he wanted to explain his actions, that he has been negotiating about my position with the King *for months*, partly direct, partly through others.  When asked why he had not informed me of this, thus giving me the opportunity to meet the threatening difficulties in that quarter with the means at my disposal, he did not reply.  He merely, so I was assured, talked generally about instructions which he had received in this matter.  If one were to assume that this is due to stupidity, as I am quite prepared to believe, it shows at least a quite uncommon degree of stupidity which would seem to show that the person concerned is hardly fitted for a diplomatic career.  In my opinion there is no possible excuse for any decent and thinking man to keep his Chief—to whom moreover he has personal cause to be grateful—in ignorance of events which are of the highest importance for the latter's position and livelihood.

And now, dear friend, all the very best for to-day and thank you for your friendship, on which I count also for the future.  Incidentally I am conceited enough to think that it will be a loss for you too not to have me here any more, though Metternich is certainly the best choice that could be made in the circumstances.  But we, you and I, understood each other in everything politically, and you could count on my unchanging co-operation here, while I knew that you would not leave me in the lurch in Berlin.

My wife, unfortunately, is not very well. Nelly's loss was a heavy blow and she is very sad. This present blow has naturally not improved matters and I am worried how she will get through the return journey, on Tuesday or Wednesday. It was certainly not very noble of those who planned this coup not even to leave us a little time to overcome our first grief at our loss.

With best regards
Ever your
PH.

## 778.    Hermann von Eckardstein to Holstein

8 June 1901

Your Excellency,

I am sending this news by to-day's courier. I could not have sent it except by this safe channel.

With regard to the sad affair :[1] Immediately after my return from Berlin I told the son, while emphasizing that I had no direct instructions, that my advice was for him to go to Berlin to inform himself on the situation which had become unbearable due to the influence of London and Berlin Court circles. I had also told him that the King had refused to take any further steps. I purposely said very little about the incident concerning the alliance question, but he seems to sense that there too something had happened.[2] The son very sensibly at once understood the situation and gradually prepared his father. The poor Ambassador, who now appears to have given up the struggle to keep his post, has calmed down again. But the Countess is still terribly upset.

Naturally the sad events of the recent past depress me very much. I would have continued to do everything possible as hitherto to keep the poor Ambassador in his post here. But the sudden forcing of the alliance question had become so dangerous for us, with consequences which were incalculable, that unfortunately it could no longer be done.

In the disastrous conversation with Lord Lansdowne on 24 [sic][2] May, the Ambassador in his morbid, nervous state had made the following statements to him :

If an alliance treaty were not concluded now it would never be concluded, and in the latter case Germany would immediately ally herself with Russia, being in a position to anticipate England in this respect. Moreover his own position as Ambassador in London depended on it, and his successor, whoever he might be, would be unable to maintain the friendly relations with England. Mr Barrington[3]—who continues to be the main confidant of Lord Salisbury and an intermediary between him and Lord Lansdowne—told me in confidence that the Ambassador's above statement has been noted in the secret files of the Foreign Office.[4]

---

[1] The coming dismissal of Hatzfeldt.

[2] The reference is to Hatzfeldt's conversation with Lord Lansdowne of 23 May (see p. 225, note 4.)

[3] Sir Bernard Barrington.  Private Secretary to Lord Salisbury, 1895–1900, to Lord Lansdowne, 1900–5.

[4] See *British Documents*, vol. II, no. 82, enclosure, pp. 64–5.

According to Mr Barrington, Lord Salisbury is supposed to have commented that he refused to negotiate at pistol-point.

Lord Lansdowne, to whom immediately after my return I made the statement which the Chancellor had asked me to make,[1] is acting very considerately in the whole matter. He has talked to Lord Salisbury, pointing out to him that the remarks by the Ambassador were due to his morbid, nervous state. He has even offered, should this be desired in Berlin, to make a written statement to the effect that no German alliance proposal had been made and that until now only purely academic exchanges on both sides had taken place.

Naturally I have not touched again on the alliance question up till now, but have confined myself to waiting. But Lord Lansdowne said to me yesterday that he wanted to talk to me about it on Monday.

I must close as the courier is leaving.

Ever, Your Excellency's most obedient and devoted<br>Hermann von Eckardstein.

### 779.   Holstein to Hugo von Radolin[2]

Berlin, 21 June 1901

Dear Radolin,

The Spaniard's[3] insistence is putting you in a by no means easy situation. Be very amiable, but don't agree to anything positive, e.g. a discussion of the Moroccan question. That is one point of our policy on which the French and Spaniards want to see clearly, but we have no reason to allow ourselves to be interviewed on it. If the Spaniard asks again, I would tell him something like this: 'I have transmitted your very interesting remarks to my Government, including the fact that at present the French Government can not yet publicly avow its express recognition of the situation created by the Peace of Frankfurt, but that it has no aggressive intentions against Germany and wishes to co-operate with Germany if an opportunity were to present itself. I was told in reply that the co-operation of Germany and France through her representative in Peking had considerably facilitated the settlement of the Chinese question.[4] The German Government therefore reserves the possibility of suggesting co-operation between the two Governments in future when the occasion offers, i.e. if questions should arise in which Germany and France are equally interested.'

Your—difficult—task is to express yourself in such a way that a raising of the Moroccan question is avoided for the present, without, however, robbing the French of the prospect of a later understanding on specific questions. This is one of many instances where the rule

---

[1] It is not clear to what Eckardstein is referring here. No instructions from Bülow were found in the Foreign Ministry files.

[2] From the Radolin Papers. Radolin had recently been appointed German Ambassador in Paris.

[3] Marquis del Muni Leon y Castillo. Spanish Ambassador in Paris, 1897–1910. (See *Grosse Politik*, vol. XVIIIii, nos. 5868–70, pp. 772–7.)

[4] The Chinese compensation question.

*glissez, n'apuyez pas* applies, meaning don't let yourself be driven to any definite statement, while overflowing with good intentions and wishes for a rapprochement, like the other side.

Now farewell and best regards, also to the Princess.

Your Holstein

If the Spaniard replies—as would seem obvious for him: 'But I think that there is no question on which an exchange of ideas with Germany seems so strongly indicated as in the Moroccan one,' you could reply more or less: 'I don't know to what extent Berlin is interested in Morocco, but—*vous m'y faites penser*—it was not mentioned in my instructions.'

As regards Noailles,[1] he is supposed to be already somewhat *ramolli*. If his recall should at some time become necessary, Cambon would probably be the best successor.

### 780.   Alexander zu Hohenlohe to Holstein

Ragaz, 8 July 1901

Dear Baron,

I know only too well that your thoughts have been here during the last few days and so will not leave this place, which now has so many painful and sad memories for me, without writing a few words to you.[2] For many years, in many difficult situations in my father's official career, you were a true friend, a tried collaborator and adviser to him. It is therefore, in this sad hour, more than just an obvious duty to thank you for everything you did for the deceased. [...]

Most respectfully and with sincere regard

Your most devoted
Alexander Hohenlohe.

### 781.   Paul von Hatzfeldt to Holstein

London, 10 July 1901

Dear friend,

Many thanks for your letter. [...]

In view of the uncertainty regarding what will happen after my return,[3] I think that for the time being I should not discuss the question of official relations in the Embassy here in detail. I only want to say this much here. The present condition is completely untenable, and if only for this reason I have not the slightest desire, though this is apparently assumed in Berlin, to prolong my stay here at this time unnecessarily. His Majesty's protégé[4] (so at least I must assume) has not found it meet to come and report to me since his return from Berlin, i.e. for over a month. He deals with all matters, political and others, independently, negotiates with the Foreign Office, reports to Berlin, all this without consulting me. Naturally I would not stand this for a single day if I

---

[1] Emmanuel Henri Victurien, Marquis de Noailles. French Ambassador in Berlin, 1896–1902.

[2] Prince Chlodwig zu Hohenlohe had died on 6 July.

[3] Hatzfeldt had been granted a leave of absence on account of his ill-health.

[4] Hermann von Eckardstein.

were to stay on here permanently, no matter whose protection the person in question enjoyed in Berlin.

Ever your<br>PHatzfeldt.

### 782. Alexander zu Hohenlohe to Holstein

Kolmar, 27 July 1901

Dear Baron,

Please forgive me for not answering your kind letter of 18 July until to-day; but since my return here I have been so overloaded with affairs that with the best will in the world I could not have replied to it sooner. What you told me concerning the memoranda is of *great* value to me, and I shall follow your advice exactly. I have already started putting the papers in order, and I think that the man I have chosen to help me will meet my requirements in *every* way. I want to thank you for having written to me so openly about this matter, for you have considerably strengthened my resolve to carry out my plan.[1] You are quite right, my father must take his place among the so-called founders of the Empire and the place in history which he deserves. Because in his high-minded modesty he stayed in the background all his life, I am now in honour bound to see that after his death he will take *the* place he merits, and this duty I will fulfill. You can be sure that I will not be too faint-hearted in this task, for I am not a coward, though naturally I will proceed with the necessary *discernement*. [...]

With old regard,<br>Yours most sincerely,<br>A. Hohenlohe.

### 783. Holstein to Bernhard von Bülow
Copy

4 August 1901

Dear Bülow,

This is a letter I prefer to write myself.

The news about Egypt you sent me yesterday causes me to inform you of something which perhaps has some hidden connection with it.[2]

An intimate of Ballin's,[3] who is known in the Ministry, told Esternaux[4] that not long ago Ballin walked round the deck for two hours with the Kaiser and had felt quite crushed as a result of it. For two hours the Kaiser had spoken of all sorts of things, and Ballin had gained the con-

---

[1] The publication of Prince Hohenlohe's papers.

[2] Bülow had telegraphed to Holstein on 3 August: 'My brother Alfred wrote to me from Berne on the 1st of the month: "Felix Müller, who is here at the moment, has just told me under the seal of secrecy that, according to a confidential private letter he had received from Egypt, a number of letters had awaited Count Waldersee in Port Said. All had been from his wife except one whose address had been in the handwriting of the retired Minister Raschdau. Later Count Waldersee had mentioned *en passant* that a good friend, whose letter he had just received, had told him that there were serious differences between His Majesty and the Chancellor." Bülow.'

[3] Albert Ballin. Managing Director of the Hamburg-America Paketfahrt Aktiengesellschaft (Hapag), 1900–18. A personal friend of the Kaiser.

[4] Temporary assistant in the Foreign Ministry, 1899–1903.

viction that the Chancellor's position with the Kaiser was no longer what it was. The Kaiser was much too intelligent not to have noticed gradually that the Chancellor always agreed with him to his face, but then managed behind his back to get *his* way, either by acting through the Parties or by other methods. The Kaiser was firmly determined to uphold the commercial treaties.[1] The moment these were threatened, Bülow would fall. Could Ballin be the 'old friend' mentioned in your telegram yesterday? I would think so. Thus the connection becomes clear. I take Ballin's statement to be true.

When did Ballin last talk to the Kaiser? Kiel week? Or was Ballin on the *Viktoria Augusta* (or *Luise*) at the meeting the other day in Norway? You will be able to find out.

For the 'explanation' of the way you work, our friend P. E[ulenburg] is probably responsible. Ballin only repeated what the Kaiser had said to him.

In my opinion you must do something to neutralize this acid in the Kaiser's soul. You know best how you must treat him. But in your situation the best would be to admit straightaway and at the first opportunity having done what P.E. or whoever else reproaches you with. 'The worst that could happen to me with Your Majesty would be that Your Majesty imagined I invented airy and impractical theories in my ivory tower. That is why, if at all possible, I arrange matters in such a way that between my report and your decision Your Majesty has time and opportunity to observe how important forces at home and abroad regard the matter under discussion, whether they are for or against. This is a system I shall stick to, for experience has taught me that in these cases Your Majesty follows quietly, but attentively, all visible indications and allows them to take effect. On this basis I, contrary to the opinion of some Ministers, worked for a publication of the complete tariff. Now Your Majesty—and I, too—have the opportunity of observing how the discussion at home and abroad will develop. In two months' time it will be easier to reach a decision than it would be to-day; for on every individual problem we will know who is for and who against us, and also at what point the opposition will set in.'

Something like this, but nicer. The best thing about this interpretation is the fact that it has *un fond d'incontestable vérité*.

Don't lose any time. Mistrust spreads like a spot of oil. [...]

Good hunting<br>
Holstein.

784.  Bernhard von Bülow to Holstein

TELEGRAM

Homburg v.d.H., 5 August 1901

Strictly secret.

I talked to His Majesty at length in the sense of the memorandum AS

---

[1] The commercial treaties concluded during Caprivi's Chancellorship. These had reduced agricultural duties and favoured German industry, and were consequently attacked by agrarian interests.

1096 of the 2nd of this month[1] and he agreed unreservedly with the point of view I presented to him. Anyhow the atmosphere was friendlier towards Russia than towards England.

His Majesty agrees to the inclusion of the Russian element in the Bagdad group.[2] Obviously, however, anything which might look like a retreat, or worse, a defeat for German policy in Asia Minor must be carefully avoided in this. On the contrary the matter should be dressed up as renewed proof of the skill with which the men in charge of our foreign policy furthered Germany's world interests without endangering our good relations to our neighbours. I myself will first tell the Russian Ambassador of Russia's admission to the Bagdad group during my coming stay in Berlin in the near future. Count von der Osten-Sacken is only going on leave after having seen me.

When I informed His Majesty in broad outline of the present state of the negotiations concerning an agreement with England, His Majesty was strongly of the opinion that such an agreement was possible only between the Triple Alliance and England, not between ourselves alone and England. Even in the former case England had a greater interest in such an alliance than we have.

No decision concerning the future Foreign Ministry representative with His Majesty could be reached because of the uncertainty of all plans in view of the condition of Kaiserin Friedrich.[3]

Bülow.

785.   Paul von Metternich to Bernhard von Bülow[4]

London, 19 November 1901

Dear Bülow,

[...] The German protest meetings with their immoderate accusations of every kind against England's conduct of the war have aroused great bitterness in all circles here, including those in which Chamberlain's statement was regarded as uncalled for.[5] It is taken as another symptom of the fact that hostility to England is deeper-rooted in the German people than among other nations; this tremendous storm of indignation had only broken loose in Germany, not in Russia, Austria and France who had also been affected by Chamberlain's statement. When I was staying two days last week with King Edward at Frogmore, the present Prince of Wales, visibly upset, showed me an English newspaper which had published a resolution of the Protestant clergy in the Rhineland, full of violent insults against the English army. He then

---

[1] *Grosse Politik*, vol. XVII, no. 5022, pp. 92–4.

[2] For building a railway from Konia to Bagdad, for which a concession had been granted to a German syndicate.

[3] The Kaiser had gone to the deathbed of his mother, Kaiserin Friedrich, who died on 5 August 1901.

[4] From the London Embassy files. See *Grosse Politik*, vol. XVII, no. 5073, pp. 194–5.

[5] In a speech in Edinburgh on 25 October, Chamberlain had replied to foreign, especially German, criticism of the conduct of English soldiers in the Boer War by pointing out that the conduct of other armies in time of war, the German army included, was not above criticism.

asked why official steps could not be taken against such infamous conduct. I answered that it was not up to the Reich Government to reply to private resolutions and newspaper articles.

Naturally I do not permit myself to judge to what extent you regard it necessary to contradict publicly Chamberlain's statements in view of the excited and misguided state of German public opinion. But I assume that you want me to draw your attention to the effect which, as I firmly believe, a public rejoinder to Chamberlain's statement by you would have in England. As you know, Chamberlain was in favour of an Anglo-German rapprochement. Probably due to his misunderstanding of his conversation with you in Windsor,[1] he made his well-known Leicester speech,[2] which was received very coolly by us. This irritated him greatly. If you should be forced to contradict his latest statements in the Reichstag, thereby implicitly making an accusation against English methods of war, you will make him into a personal enemy and also an opponent of German policy, and this he will probably remain. For the moment he is still the most important politician in England. He has most influences and the masses behind him. This would probably change if the war were to go on for a long time and have an outcome unfavourable to England. Your action would be severely felt in official and unofficial circles in England, and in spite of your hitherto so anglophile policy you would no longer be regarded as a friend of England. Many people here in England look on Chamberlain's remark as clumsy and tactless, but there is hardly anyone here who would not take his part immediately if you take on the role of a champion of German public opinion, thereby, in the present state of feeling in the two countries, implying that English methods of war are less humane than those of Germany. [...]

M.

786.    Valentine Chirol to Holstein[3]

London, 23 November 1901

Private.

My dear Baron Holstein,

I don't think I have to add much to my telegrams[4] from which I hope you have gathered that though I cannot recognize your arguments I fully appreciate the spirit in which you have stated them. I do wish you had spoken to me about Chamberlain's speech when I was in Berlin.[5] It might then have been possible to arrange some frank and *spontaneous*

---

[1] In November 1899. See p. 169, note 1.    [2] See p. 169, note 2.

[3] From the Papers of Baroness von der Heydt. Only a typewritten copy of this document was available to the editors. The letter is in English in the original.

[4] They dealt with the bitterness in Germany occasioned by Chamberlain's speech of 25 October. (See p. 236, note 5.) The Chirol-Holstein telegrams are printed in *History of The Times* (London, 1947), vol. III, pp. 337–40.

[5] Holstein saw Chirol in Berlin on 31 October. His summary of the conversation is printed in *Grosse Politik*, vol. XVII, no. 5026, pp. 101–6; see also Chirol, *Fifty Years in a Changing World* (London, 1927), pp. 288–9; Holstein prepared a memorandum for a second talk with Chirol on 1 November (*Grosse Politik*, vol. XVII, no. 5027, pp. 106–9.) It is not known whether the second conversation took place, or if the memorandum was only prepared for the subsequent talk between Bülow and Chirol. (See *History of The Times*, vol. III, pp. 332, 810–19.)

explanation which would have removed all possibility of misconstruction. But now even if I personally were disposed to admit that there was anything that could rightly give offence in his speech—an admission I am *not* prepared to make—it would, I fear, be too late to do anything as it would involve the appearance of yielding to an outcry in Germany which has been characterised by the most undisguised bitterness towards England. We too have our feelings. Take for instance *The Times* office, and imagine the cumulative effect produced by the steady stream of insult and abuse which has poured in, without exaggeration, by every single day's post from Germany for the last two years : insulting letters, some anonymous, many of them signed apparently by people of fairly good position, not a few of an absolutely disgusting and obscene character, cuttings of all the most rabid articles in the German papers, with marginal notes : *Saubande, Hundsfott*, etc. etc. etc., unspeakable cartoons, one for instance representing the late Queen 'decorating the youngest soldier in the British army for having, although only 15 years old, already raped a number of Boer maidens'. Nothing of the kind comes to us from other countries, but only from Germany. Consider the atmosphere of resentment which this creates, and how enormously it adds to the difficulties of those who want to prevent at least any widening of the breach. Of course you deplore all this as sincerely as I do, and condemn it as strongly. But I cannot altogether acquit your official world of some responsibility for it. I have been too long in Berlin not to be aware of the splendid machinery the German Government disposes of for guiding and instructing the Press, especially as to foreign affairs. Of late I have noticed with great satisfaction that efforts have been made to curb the most outrageous manifestations of Anglophobia. But I cannot help thinking the curb might and ought to have been applied at an earlier stage. Now of course the agitation has acquired such proportions that it is becoming more and more difficult to stem it. And on this side too the resentment is growing proportionately deeper and stronger, and amongst all our national faults national pride is by no means the least— if it be a fault.

I confess I look forward with some anxiety in these circumstances to what the Chancellor will say in answer to the reported interpellation in the Reichstag.[1] If he could only take the opportunity of saying something in condemnation of the outrageous charges brought against the British army, any moderate criticism he might make of Mr Chamberlain's language as having been open to a misconstruction which was doubtless very foreign to his intentions, would, in my opinion at any rate, be accepted here as a legitimate and not necessarily unfriendly expression of opinion.

As you see I am writing to you with the greatest frankness because I fully believe that, though our opinion may differ, our intentions are the same.

Believe me,
dear Baron Holstein,
Yours sincerely
Valentine Chirol

[1] See below, p. 244, note 3.

## 787.　Bernhard von Bülow to Holstein

25 November [1901]

Many thanks! Much of what Chirol writes is undoubtedly correct, but much can also be said on the other side. If German newspapers are in many cases attacking the English Royal House with great vulgarity, the English attacks against His Majesty in '96–97 also transgressed all limits. At that time H.M. was ridiculed in all the London theatres, music halls, etc. As late as 1898, H.M. showed me a number of vulgar letters, some anonymous, some signed by alleged students, officers, etc., attacking him because of our Kiaochow expedition. While we have carefully avoided everything which might irritate English public opinion since the Krüger Telegram, the English have faced us in rapid succession and without good cause with the bombardment of Samoa,[1] the seizure of the liners,[2] and now Chamberlain's sally. True, the latter wasn't ill-intentioned, but it was incredibly clumsy. No doubt we shall nevertheless be able to pass over this incident without damage to Anglo-German relations or compromising the future if the English are fair enough and intelligent enough to realize that a German Minister, too, must reckon with public opinion in his own country, and must stand particularly firm in questions affecting military honour. Nothing could be more stupid than the English request for repression of the anti-English trend from above. Quite apart from the fact that the English have never condescended to act in this way in a similar situation, we would only be pouring oil on the flames here. If any statement of mine in the Reichstag were not to satisfy national sentiment, the only result would be to increase anti-English feeling in Germany.

B.

## 788.　Holstein to Valentine Chirol[3]

Berlin, 28 November [1901]

Dear Mr Chirol,

Of course I do not share your views in so far as you maintain that King Ive[4] can do, has done, no wrong. This I cannot be expected to admit. Further, I cannot accept the reproach that I did not turn your attention to Mr Chamberlain's speech while you were here. I quite clearly remember having said 'that new speech of Chamberlain is very unfortunate', but you scouted the idea that it could have any consequences. To be sure, I myself at the time did not foresee what a row there would be. On the other hand I consider it rather favourable that for some days the extreme party (or groups rather) had it mostly their own way, for that brought on the reaction which at present is working steadily and visibly gains ground. The Emperor has been calm and self-possessed all through.

---

[1] See p. 176, note 4.　　　　　　[2] See p. 176, note 3.

[3] From the Papers of Baroness von der Heydt. Only a typewritten copy of this document was available to the editors. The letter is in English in the original.

[4] The reference is presumably to Chamberlain.

The mortality of children in the camps of refuge[1] is a bad feature, and is being exploited to the utmost by the anti-English groups in all countries.

Well, let us continue to do our best.

Yours very sincerely

Holstein.

### 789. Holstein to Valentine Chirol[2]

Berlin, 11 December 1901

Dear Mr Chirol,

A slight indisposition keeping me at home, I will *carpere diem* to answer your letter of Nov. 30th.

The 'Chamberlain affair' is losing its attraction but as I said already, the bad impression produced on public opinion generally by the concentration camps remains, and the groups who look round for anti-English material find it there.

I read with much interest your allusion to the insinuations that were being spread against our Emperor from a Northern Capital. Well, all I can say is, that the Northern Capital had better keep quiet for if it came to emptying letter boxes, we should have the best of it by a very long chalk. If the insinuation, as I must infer, hinted that the Emperor promised to aid any anti-English enterprise, it was simply a lie. The Emperor has repeatedly shown, that even in mere diplomatic action he does not mean to side with the anti-English group. These are facts which could be proved any day, but I do not believe that indiscretions do any good. There are cases where they may be necessary in self defence, but as a rule they merely ruin diplomatic intercourse. And this brings back to my memory a story that I heard some months ago. It seems that at the last meeting of the two sovereigns[3] ours made reproaches to yours, because the British Government had communicated to an interested third party some strictly private and confidential information concerning the financial embarrassments of Japan, which had been given by the Japanese Government in hopes of finding relief in London. The king of course had no hand in the matter. The Japanese subsequently learnt that their secret had been let out, and expressed themselves very bitterly about it; that was how we came to know the matter. Your king must be a very attractive man when he chooses for our Emperor is now full of his praise, which was not always the case, as I well remember.

The question of the hour for us is the Polish question. It seems to come up at fixed intervals of 30–40 years and always has the same effect of bringing about an instinctive rapprochement between Russia and ourselves for the time being. *Russia* does not mean to allow the re-

---

[1] In order to combat the guerilla tactics of the Boers, Lord Kitchener, early in 1901, determined to lay waste the area of military operations and introduced a system of concentration camps in which non-combatants were interned.

[2] From the Papers of Baroness von der Heydt. Only a typewritten copy of this document was available to the editors. The letter is in English in the original.

[3] At Wilhelmshöhe on 23 August. (See *Grosse Politik*, vol. XVII, no. 5023, pp. 94–8; *British Documents*, vol. II, no. 90, p. 73.)

establishment of the Kingdom of Poland, which would cut off Russia from Europe. *We* cannot allow that restoration either, for reasons which force themselves upon any one who looks at a map of Central Europe as it was in the middle of the 18th Century, with the Polish frontier about three infantry days marches from Berlin. As for half measures or concessions of any kind, they only encourage the Poles to ask for more. The great risings of 1830 and 1861 were prepared and rendered possible—unintentionally I think—by Russian concessions. The Russians coquetted with the Poles, and when the latter came well out into the open, they were beaten down for a generation in the way that you know. But the beating down would have been very difficult indeed, if the western neighbour had not recognized the solidarity of interests and acted accordingly. That Russia knows.

On our side of the frontier we have always followed the preventive regime and have consequently only had one insignificant rising in 47. But our regime is odious to the Poles precisely because it has been tolerably effective. At present a rising is out of the question, with an army massed on each side of our eastern frontier. The Polish clergy, which instigated the row, was in hopes that the question of 'coercion' might be brought before the Reichstag, where they hoped to get a respectable no! [sic] minority with the smaller part of the Centre, the Suabian democrats, the Alsations and the social democrats. But the constitution is clearly on the side of the Government which treats the question as exclusively Prussian. [...]

Hoping that you are well, I remain,<br>
dear Mr Chirol,<br>
Yours very sincerely<br>
Holstein. [...]

## 790.    Holstein to Hugo von Radolin[1]

Berlin, 12 December 1901

Dear Radolin,

I am sending the courier to-day so that you can send him back in time for the next one to go on the 22nd. I regard the Christmas courier as a time-honoured institution.

Your latest reports came closer to that lively style which H.M. likes. After all, he is very 'personal' and likes the personal element in reports. Wangenheim's[2] report on the marriage of Sultan Murad's daughters was praised by the Kaiser as no report had been praised for a long time. It reported what the Princesses *are supposed* to look like, what political motives guided the Sultan when he decided upon the marriages, etc.

Your report about the King and the celebrations at the Ritz was too involved and too cautious.[3] The Kaiser—incidentally he read the report

[1] From the Radolin Papers.

[2] Hans, Baron von Wangenheim. First Secretary at the Embassy in Constantinople, 1899–1904; Minister to Mexico, 1904–8; Chargé d'Affaires in Tangier, 1908; Minister in Athens 1909–12; Ambassador in Constantinople, 1912–15.

[3] A 'gossip' report of Radolin's of 18 November, in which he criticized the behaviour of royal personages, but without mentioning any names. (From the Foreign Ministry files.)

with interest—reads too quickly to stop and ask himself: who is this, who is that? I would have given the names and facts, *crûment*, without criticism. That way you would have run no risk. My advice therefore is to carry on along these lines, but in particular not to bury the spicy anecdotes in private letters, where they do you no good, *but to include them in the official reports*, like raisins in a cake. Believe me, this admixture is the secret of success.

One thing I want to tell you in the *strictest confidence* (i.e. you can tell the Princess), is that H.M. has been making some very unfavourable marginal comments about Prince Eulenburg because the latter did not act decisively enough in the matter of the Lemberg riots.[1] Ph.E. will presumably keep his position as a pleasant companion, but H.M. does not think much of him as a politician. It is not the first time that I have noticed this. [...]

With best regards<br>
As ever<br>
Yours<br>
Holstein.

Did I ever tell you that it is advisable to write, or date, reports only *the day before* the courier leaves. H.M. is cross if he gets a report with an earlier date on it. [...]

791.  Valentine Chirol to Holstein[2]

London, 28 December 1901

My dear Baron Holstein,

I will not let the year draw to a close without sending you my good wishes for 1902, which will, I hope, prove more conducive than recent ones to friendly relations between our two countries. I have taken every opportunity since I was in Berlin to broach in conversation with people whose opinion was worth having the question of a permanent and stable agreement with England and Germany on the lines you sketched forth,[3] and I confess I have been surprised at the almost universal concensus of opinion that, in the present state of public feeling on both sides, the idea was quite futile. Many who are disposed to favour it in principle seem convinced that the German Government would certainly have nothing to say to it, and it is of course impossible for me, with a due regard for discretion to do more than express my personal dissent from that proposition. The chief argument with which I am most frequently met is that, whatever may be the sentiments of the German Government, none of its authorised mouthpieces has ever attempted to check the prevailing anglophobia by any public utterance and that even such an act of filial

[1] On 29 November Eulenburg had reported on a conversation with Goluchowski in which he had brought up the anti-Prussian demonstrations in Lemberg. In marginal comments Wilhelm II criticized Eulenburg's timid attitude, and expressed the view that he was not prepared to buy good relations with Austria at the price of concessions to the Poles in Prussia. (From the Foreign Ministry files.)

[2] From the Papers of Baroness von der Heydt. Only a typewritten copy of this document was available to the editors. The letter is in English in the original.

[3] See p. 237, note 5.

piety as the Emperor's visit to England at the time of the Queen's death was subjected to misconstruction of which the significance could not be ignored. The action of diplomacy is buried away in secret archives and the 'man in the street' who has perhaps too large a share in ruling this country is influenced by what he sees and hears. The hostility of the German people may not have been greater than of other continental nations, but they have shown more ingenuity in driving it home to us. Illustrated postcards of the most odious character have been showered upon people whose names and addresses happen to have been known in Germany either through business connections or through having their children educated there. In some cases it looks as if there must be some organisation in Germany which takes the trouble to study books of reference in order to bombard people whose names and addresses can be obtained in that way, with German war literature of the most offensive Pro-Boer type. One of the leading London clubs has, as a matter of historical interest, made a large collection of this kind of literature from all parts of the continent since that war broke out, and both in volume and in virulence the German section is *facile princeps*. All this sort of thing, coupled with the language of a large part of the German Press, has unquestionably created the impression that Germany is the country where we are best hated and that, however little the German Government may share that feeling, it is bound to take it into account.

I am reluctantly driven to the conclusion in these circumstances that all one can hope to do for the present is to avoid anything which should widen the breach, and to trust to time and the logic of events to heal it. I must say it is a great pity that the German Press should have selected Mr Chamberlain of all men as its *tête de Turc*. There was no more zealous, if not always very discreet, champion of an Anglo-German understanding than he used to be, and he would be more than human if his zeal were not to some extent abated by the vinegar douches which have been poured on to him with a quite too lavish hand.

I am afraid this is not a very cheerful or a very amiable new year's letter, but I do not think you would have me write more pleasant platitudes because they are supposed to be just now *de saison*. Believe me nevertheless to remain

Very sincerely yours
Valentine Chirol.

# 1902

## 792.  Diary Entry[1]

11 January 1902

To-day Sch.[2] told me with sincere regret that he regarded Bülow's speech against Chamberlain as B.'s greatest mistake.[3]  So do I.  I don't know what caused B. to let fly against all the advice he had received from Richthofen, Hammann,[4] Fischer, and myself.  Perhaps he thought that by doing so a rapprochement with England would be rendered impossible for the time being.  About fifteen months ago, I think it was in the autumn of 1900, Metternich said to me in these very words : 'As long as Bülow is around there'll never be a rapprochement with England.'  True, Metternich too is a strange person, not easy to see through.  He remained on good terms with Bülow until the moment he was appointed to London.  But shortly afterwards M. made a solemn farewell speech in Hamburg in which he described the attacks on England, now prevalent in Germany, as 'the policy of adolescence'; and Bülow, a few days later, launched his speech against Chamberlain.  The difference between the two men was thus marked.  That is why Richthofen advised the Chancellor to use the opportunity—while refuting Liebermann von Sonnenberg's positively revolting attacks on England two days ago[5]—to state that no difference obtained between himself and Mett.  Bülow did so, but the difference naturally remained.  I had seen it coming—it wasn't

---

[1] A number of diary entries for the years 1901–2 were found among the Holstein Papers. (See *Memoirs*, p. xxv.)  They are much more fragmentary than the earlier diaries and consist largely of political jottings.  Since they lack all continuity in themselves, they have not been published as a body, but, in so far as they are of historical interest, are printed here under the appropriate dates.

[2] The reference may be to the banker Paul von Schwabach, who maintained close contact with English banking circles.

[3] Replying to a question in the Reichstag on 8 January concerning Chamberlain's speech of 25 October in which he had criticized the conduct of German troops in the Franco-Prussian war (see above, p. 236, note 5), Bülow said : 'I think we are all agreed, and all sensible people in England will also agree with us, that if a Minister is forced to justify his policy—and that can happen—he would do well to leave foreign countries out of it.  If he should nevertheless wish to draw on foreign examples, it is advisable to use the greatest care, otherwise one not only runs the danger of being misunderstood, but also of offending foreign sensibilities without wishing to do so—as I would assume in the case in question, and must assume after all the assurances I have received from the other side.'  Regarding the attitude to be taken in Germany in case of attacks on the German army, Bülow quoted the words of Frederick the Great : 'Let the man be and don't get excited, he's biting on granite.'

[4] Otto Hammann.  *Vortragender Rat* in the Foreign Ministry, 1894–1916; in charge of the Press Department.

[5] In a speech in the Reichstag on 10 January, Liebermann von Sonnenberg had used expressions such as: 'This Chamberlain, who dares to attack the German army, is the most villainous knave on God's earth.', and 'The English army in South Africa is barely more than a mob of thieves and robbers.'  In reply, Bülow said : 'I believe I am in accord with the vast

difficult—and therefore barred my door to Mett. when he was here recently. Bülow thus can't say that it was I who inspired M.'s 'the policy of adolescence.' Bülow at all times is uncritically suspicious of everybody, but apart from that he is a very amiable and easy superior. In his youth he read but didn't digest Machiavelli; the teachings of this professor of intrigue often lead him astray and lessen his reliability in his relations with others. Because of this peculiar trait of his I have received nobody from London in the last few months, including Eckardstein and even Zimmermann. If some crisis between London and Berlin should be brewing I shall stay out of it. This is my urgent desire after all my experiences.

In some ways I feel sorry for Bülow. He is not a strong character, and up till now has achieved everything by amiability and his cleverness in taking people. But this by itself is not enough in the face of H.M.'s constantly growing awareness of his position as ruler. From time to time H.M. disregards the Chancellor, perhaps *in order* to demonstrate who is master. The other day the Chancellor proposed that, should the Government of Venezuela fail to meet certain fairly large German claims,[1] action should be taken against it—blockade, occupation of customs-houses in the ports, etc. The Kaiser kept the Chancellor's report to him[2] for quite a while; finally, two days ago, he got the Commanding Admiral, Diederichs, to write to the State Secretary in the Foreign Ministry—not to the Chancellor—that he regarded the use of force by naval vessels as inappropriate and unnecessary.[3] H.M. decided on refusal after hearing a report from the Commanding Admiral. Senden and Plessen were present and both spoke against the action. But the chief opponent was Tirpitz. The Commanding Admiral thinks that he had previously talked to the Kaiser. Tirpitz has no stomach for a fight. At the time of Kiaochow he was in favour of yielding. When Bülow arrived, in December 1897, the first thing he heard was Tirpitz saying : 'We shall probably have to get out of Kiaochow.' For my part I told Bülow : 'By getting out of Kiaochow we would demonstrate to the world that we yield to threats. In that case we are not very far from a revision of the Peace of Frankfurt.' Well, we stayed. When some time later a small punitive expedition into the interior, very close to Kiaochow, was proposed—the Minister in Peking and the Governor of Kiaochow had proposed it—it was again Tirpitz who opposed it with all his might. But the expedition took place and went off quite harmlessly. Tirpitz has shown a similar lack of nerve on other occasions.

Now I wonder whether the Chancellor will let the Venezuela matter

majority of this House when expressing the hope that it should not become the custom to insult foreign Ministers from the tribune of the Reichstag. [. . .] I am equally bound to express my deep regret at the manner in which the previous speaker referred to the army of a nation with which we live in peace and friendship.'

[1] As a result of damage to the property of German nationals during the recent revolutionary disturbances. (See *Grosse Politik*, vol. XVII, chapter CXII.)

[2] Of 31 December 1901. (From the Foreign Ministry files.)

[3] On 8 January 1902. Wilhelm II had decided against a blockade since its success was not assured. (From the Foreign Ministry files.)

ride, or whether he will defend his report to the Kaiser. I do believe that he has on occasion dissuaded the Kaiser from doing something, but has never directly opposed H.M. Firmness is not one of B's distinguishing characteristics, nor is his persistence very great. That is why I asked to-day that the imminent negotiations with Italy on the Triple Alliance[1] be dealt with by the official in charge of Near Eastern affairs. For I am afraid that Bülow will be, or rather is already, inclined to agree to Prinetti's new demands,[2] inspired by the French Ambassador, Barrère. They must be turned down at all costs. Whether Bülow will allow himself to be dissuaded is doubtful. If I dealt with these negotiations the result would be a row.

793.   Valentine Chirol to Holstein[3]

London, 12 January 1902

Dear Baron Holstein,

I wish I had answered your two letters[4] before the Chancellor's speech. For if I were not to answer them at all, I should be guilty of discourtesy towards you and you might misconstrue my silence, whilst it is difficult after what has happened to write to you with the frankness which marks our relations without running the risk of giving you offence. I will only say that its omissions made the Chancellor's first speech[5] and its expressions made his second speech[6] exactly [what] I had told you in one of my former letters I hoped his utterances would *not* be. They have certainly destroyed for the present the hopes and rendered futile the endeavours of those who looked to a narrowing rather than to a broadening of the estrangement between the two countries. I do not imagine that, absorbed as you are by the loftier and more practical aspects of diplomacy, you realize the sentimental effect produced by the torrents of abuse which have been poured out upon us in Germany for the last two years. Perhaps you are not even aware of what that abuse has been. But sentiment plays a much larger part over here than foreigners are inclined to allow to the British character, and there is no disguising the fact that the sentiment which Germany has aroused is growing intense. Nor can I honestly deny that it is to a great extent natural and even legitimate. Was it really too much to expect from the Minister of a friendly Power that, when a leading statesman of a foreign Government is publicly branded as a scoundrel, he should find some less equivocal

---

[1] For the renewal of the Triple Alliance. (See *Grosse Politik*, vol. XVIIIii, chapter CXXII.)

[2] Prinetti had informed Wedel on 4 January that he was ready to renew the Triple Alliance as soon as Italo-German trade relations had been settled. 'He had a completely free hand. He had merely made M. Barrère the promise that the treaty would contain no aggressive feature directed against France.' At this point Holstein commented in the margin of Wedel's report: 'According to yesterday's telegram from Rome, Signor Prinetti said: "nothing inimical".' (*Grosse Politik*, vol. XVIIIii, no. 5711, pp. 512–15.)

[3] From the Papers of Baroness von der Heydt. Only a typewritten copy of this document was available to the editors. The letter is in English in the original.

[4] Of 3 January (*British Documents*, vol. II, no. 96, pp. 84–6), and 5 January. A copy of the latter was found among the Heydt transcripts. In it Holstein related the opinions of a doctor, recently returned from South Africa, on the peace negotiations between England and the Boers.

[5] See p. 244, note 3.          [6] See p. 244, note 5.

formula or condemnation than the request 'not to make a practice' of such behaviour,—a sort of suggestion that 'in this case it was excusable, only don't do it too often'—or that when an interpellation has been so framed as to convey an insult to the army of a friendly power, his answer should not deliberately ignore that insult and give it the implied endorsement of his silence?

However a discussion of this kind in writing must necessarily be unsatisfactory to both parties, and though recent developments drive us once more into an appearance of antagonism, I should like to think that, when the storm blows over, our mutual good will shall remain undiminished as I remain

Yours very sincerely<br>
Valentine Chirol

## 794. Diary Entry

14 January 1902

Bülow's speech against Chamberlain[1] is the Krüger Telegram on a small scale. Internal reasons, i.e. popularity, made Bülow do it. Externally the speech does harm; I only hope that the internal repercussions, that is on the Kaiser, will not also end up by being unfavourable once H.M. is affected by these repercussions, for example if the English visits cease.

## 795. Diary Entry

15 January 1902

On Sunday I wrote to Bülow:

'The Italian passage of your speech yesterday[2] has given you an excellent starting point so that you can have Lanza summoned—as soon as possible—and tell him: "You see, I am making *la position aussi belle que possible* for Signor Prinetti, but there are certain limits beyond which I cannot go. I cannot risk M. Barrère saying at his next gala speech: 'Thanks to the changes made at my request in the wording of the Triple Alliance Treaty, thanks also to the separate agreement I have concluded with Italy, the Triple Alliance has ceased to be objectionable from the point of view of French policy.' That is something which I, Bülow cannot risk, because the reproach that I had allowed the Triple Alliance Treaty to become a *marché de dupes* could then be levelled against me. For this reason I can only extend the treaty on two conditions: First, there can be *no* changes, secondly, Italy must make an authentic

---

[1] See p. 244, note 3.

[2] In his speech to the Reichstag of 11 January, Bülow denied that any suspicion of Germany was felt by the other members of the Triple Alliance. He said Prinetti had just told the German Ambassador in Rome that there was not a single word in Bülow's speech on foreign affairs of 8 January to which he did not subscribe. During that speech Bülow had assured the Reichstag that the Triple Alliance still enjoyed the best of health and that he saw no reason for alarm in the increasingly cordial relations between Italy and France. 'In a happy marriage the fact that the wife has an innocent extra dance with someone else is no reason for the husband to lose his temper.' (See *Grosse Politik*, vol. XVIIIii, chapter CXXV.)

declaration to the effect that no other agreement exists which could affect the full defensive effectiveness of the Triple Alliance Treaty." '

I added : 'The odds are five to one on Prinetti giving in. If he doesn't and the negotiations come to a stop, get a question asked in the Reichstag. You will definitely get a majority in favour of these two demands, while in Italy Rudini and Luzzatti[1] will probably take the opportunity to overthrow Prinetti. For the majority of Italians want to bargain and flirt with France, but certainly not be left alone with her.'

I have not received an affirmative reply to this letter from Bülow, although Lich[nowsky] told me that he had Lanza summoned immediately on its receipt.[2] On the other hand Richthofen told me that B. had said to him in Hammann's presence—he confirmed it afterwards—that he wanted a renewal of the treaty with or without alterations above all *for internal reasons.*

'For internal reasons' means on the grounds of popularity. True, B. made this remark before receiving my letter of Sunday, but since I did not get an affirmative reply to this letter, I requested on Monday that the work on the Triple Alliance, etc. be given to the Near Eastern Section. If B. is going to conduct a policy with which I don't agree, at least I don't want to execute it, like Abeken,[3] who was reproached by Bismarck—I myself have heard Bismarck say so repeatedly—for having defended a policy of firmness before Olmütz,[4] and after Olmütz a policy of yielding. I can't dictate policy to the Chancellor, but I don't wish to help in the execution of a measure which I think dangerous.

### 796. Karl von Wedel to Holstein[5]

Rome, 15 January 1902

Dear Herr von Holstein,

Please accept my best thanks for your kind letter of the 10th of this month, which I found a most valuable supplement to the dispatch.[6] It needs no mention that I shall follow the line prescribed to me most scrupulously and conscientiously. Nevertheless I harbour both the hope and conviction that we will continue to remain within the well-tried framework of the Triple Alliance. There is no lack of good intentions here even though the young kingdom unfortunately tends to overestimate its own importance. For this very reason I welcomed the Chan-

---

[1] Luigi Luzzatti. Italian Finance Minister in the Giolitti Cabinet, 1903–5, in the Sonnino Cabinet, February–May 1906.

[2] See Bülow's memorandum of 12 January 1902, according to which he spoke to Lanza along the lines suggested by Holstein. (*Grosse Politik*, vol. XVIIIii, nos. 5715, 5850, pp. 523–4, 746–7.)

[3] Heinrich Abeken. In the Prussian Foreign Ministry from 1848; *Vortragender Rat*, 1853–71. (See *Memoirs*, p. 54.)

[4] To avert the war that threatened in November 1850 between Prussia and Austria, Friedrich Wilhelm IV commissioned Otto von Manteuffel to negotiate with Austria. By the Punctation of Olmütz of 29 November 1850, Prussia renounced her claims to the leadership of Germany within the Prussian (Erfurt) Union and recognized the existing Federal Diet in Frankfurt, which was substantially controlled by Austria.

[5] From the Foreign Ministry files.

[6] Of 9 January. *Grosse Politik*, vol. XVIIIii, no. 5712, pp. 515–18.

cellor's speech[1] as a clear *avis au lecteur* with great satisfaction. It is good for the Italians to know that they have more reason to run after us than we after them. But what is good for one is after all also good for the other, and I would think that if we let Rome come to us, we will not play the game the other way round with St Petersburg.

I certainly agree—and this without reservation—with our soldiers that we can*not* expect *much* of Italy's military capacity. But the instincts of self-preservation and aggrandizement will in the end cause our ally not to remain completely passive. And moreover the positive service we expect of Italy is that it should not attack Austria's rear, yet tie down part of the French army on the Alpine frontier. I can understand the reasoning of our agrarians and the Centre Party from their specific point of view, but not from a general standpoint.

For my part I firmly believe that our trade agreement with Italy could be renewed without any difficulty. Italy's exports to Germany consist for the most part of raw materials such as silk, hemp, sulphur, marble, which we need for our industry. If these are subtracted from Italy's exports to Germany, the balance of payments is favourable to us. [...][2] We do not produce vegetables and flowers, or only at times when there is no question of Italian competition. If our agrarians therefore were to campaign against these imports they would only harm the German consumer, without being able to speak as producers themselves, and any customs duty would take effect not as a protective but as a fiscal one, which can hardly be our intention.

And as regards the Roman Question, it cannot be the task of Protestant Germany to act as the protector of the Pontifex. After all we shall never be able to meet the greedy demands of the Centre Party as long as the German Imperial House remains *non-Catholic*. Italy, however, will have to realize that even a statement by us merely to the effect that we were not interested in the Roman Question could be disastrous to her. But I would not dare assert that she already completely appreciates this.

Incidentally, I think that there is another side to the whole question which we will have to consider seriously in reaching our decision. The turbulent elements in this country are, one might say, 'tamed and supervised' by the Triple Alliance. Were Italy to abandon the present treaty relationship, these elements would be set free. In that case would not the nationalist and chauvenist interests give free rein to their irredentist aims and desires for aggrandizement in other directions, thus piling up much dangerously inflammable material? I not only fear this, I believe it would happen. And would not Socialists, Republicans, and Radicals—whose revolutionary activities have been indirectly furthered by Signor Gioletti's[3] system of *laissez-aller* and who are spreading their influence more widely and intensely also in parts of the rural areas— easily come out on top if the young Italian monarchy is deprived of its support from the powerful Central European monarchies? The throne

[1] Of 8 January. See p. 247, note 2.　　　　　　[2] One word illegible.
[3] Giovanni Giolitti. Italian Minister of the Interior in the Zanardelli Cabinet, 1901–3; Minister-President and Minister of the Interior, 1903–5, 1906–9.

in Spain wobbles from time to time, and here too its foundations are as yet anything but safe. In Italy Blacks and Reds would presumably ally themselves temporarily to overthrow the throne together, though they would start fighting immediately afterwards. But can it be in our interest that the whole of South-West Europe should consist of republics?

True, I too do not expect that for the time being England will do anything for Italy. The South African war has not stopped England's boasting, but it does prevent her from taking any serious initiative in other fields. For the present then the roar of the British lion cannot be counted on as a compensatory factor. Nevertheless the Moroccan agreement[1] will make Lord Salisbury think. [...]

If Italy should leave the Triple Alliance—I hope that we shall continue to stand firmly by Austria—we would not lose much as regards material power, but, in my opinion, the moral effect would be fairly considerable. Italy is looked upon as a Great Power and its weight, thrown into the other side of the scales, would definitely, if only theoretically, disturb the European balance, now so fortunately achieved, thus giving new encouragement to the longings of *revanche*.

As for Prinetti, I still think that he is an honest man. Certainly he talks a bit too much and is always glancing at the Monte Citoria, which does somewhat affect his quality as a Minister, but to accuse him of being an opponent of the Triple Alliance is unjust. I think that his over-estimate of his own country's worth is due to some extent to his lack of experience. A plain girl, suddenly being ardently wooed by a brilliant lover, finally comes to believe that she must be more beautiful than she had thought hitherto. Up till now Prinetti has always met me with frankness, and I believe that I am one of those in whom he has full confidence, a merit which I attribute not to myself but to the country I represent. [...]

16 January

[...] The Chancellor's speeches came at the right time and Rudini's statements show that they were understood here. I have not seen Prinetti during the last few days; he was away. After receiving to-day the telegrams on Bülow's conversations with Lanza,[2] I am firmly convinced that people here will do everything in order to restore the Triple Alliance situation as quickly as possible. I was delighted by B's statement. It is superbly adapted to the situation here. [...]

Yours very sincerely
Wedel

797.    Holstein to Johanna von Radolin[3]

Berlin, 31 January 1902, 11–12 p.m.

Dear Princess,

First of all the appropriate wishes for the New Year. What can one wish you? That everything should remain as it is. That is what I wish and hope for with all my heart. There is an old saying which goes

---

[1] The reference is probably to the French Agreement with Morocco of 20 July 1901 which gave France considerable control of the police on the frontier.
[2] See p. 248, note 2.      [3] From the Radolin Papers.

'What is envied by others is enjoyed most'—something like that. That is what you must tell yourself if you hear now and then that Tom, Dick, or Harry think themselves particularly fitted to become Ambassador in Paris. For the moment I see no danger, at least as long as the present regime lasts, and that still seems to stand quite firm.

Prince Heinrich's visit to America,[1] which I regard as a fairly useful pleasure trip, has at least until now not been a source of pure joy to our Ambassador there. Before the matter even got under way, he heard some unpleasant things from H.M. because he had not given a definite enough answer to a query from H.M. 'That's not the way to reply to me.' But the one who is coming off worst is Phili.[2] H.M. is constantly remarking on his failings in official business, not only in marginal comments,[3] but also orally, yesterday for example to Richthofen. Tschirschky is telling people that in Vienna the question is beginning to be asked: 'Does P.E. still have his old position with the Kaiser?' That he certainly hasn't got, but probably H.M. doesn't know where else to put him; I wouldn't know either. As far as possible the more important exchanges with Austria must be handled here. That is already being done, but it adds further to the work. [...]

Now I kiss your hand and commend myself to your favour.

Holstein.

798.   Memorandum by Holstein
       Copy

9 February 1902

Vienna report no. 40[4] confirms the supposition that Vienna and Rome have discussed the matter on the basis of your statements to Lanza[5] and Szögyényi.[6] As a result Prinetti will allow his whole scheme to be changed and will only come out with proposals for quite insignificant alterations, just sufficient to enable him and Barrère to say afterwards: 'We did achieve an alteration'—even though this might be one of three unimportant words.'

1.  An alteration, even the smallest one, would be regarded by the world as a German concession to France and Italy, would therefore raise the prestige of the Franco-Italian group at the expense of Germany.

2.  Any alteration concerning Tripoli would destroy the *Sultan's* confidence in Germany. It is not impossible that *that* is what France is *working for*. And naturally the Austrians too would be delighted at any loss of prestige suffered by Germany in Constantinople. That is why Count Goluchowski has 'no objection' to the Tripoli question being touched upon. Goluchowski started by removing *Balkan* questions,

---

[1] On 11 January the Kaiser had telegraphed President Roosevelt his decision to send Prince Heinrich to the United States to be present at the launching of the Kaiser's new yacht by the daughter of the President. Prince Heinrich sailed on 15 February and returned to Germany on 18 March.

[2] Philipp zu Eulenburg.                [3] Not found.

[4] Of 5 February. (*Grosse Politik*, vol. XVIIIii, no. 5723, pp. 537–8.)

[5] See p. 248, note 2.

[6] See *Grosse Politik*, vol. XVIIIii, no. 5698, p. 493.

dangerous for Austria, from the agenda. Prinetti's and Barrère's self-esteem can therefore now only be satisfied at Germany's expense. Quite apart from the Tripoli clause, any *alteration as such* harms only Germany. It is to the profit of Austria if Germany's prestige and the confidence which we enjoy in Russia on the one hand, with the Sultan on the other, were to be diminished.

In view of this situation I would like to submit for consideration whether you should not get the Austrians to work on the Italians by telling Szögyényi:

'Any alteration of the Triple Alliance Treaty would arouse mistrust of the aims of the Triple Alliance in those Powers whose friendship and trust we value even though we are not allied to them. This mistrust would be further increased if it were learnt that the alterations were made after pressure from Italy, because it is suspected that the latter wishes to follow a policy of aggrandizement. And public opinion *inside* Germany too would not understand the reason for any alteration in a treaty as well tried as this one. We would therefore refuse *any* alteration, and would of course have to reckon with Italy's defection.

'To compensate for the loss of strength to Germany and Austria which might result, we should have to consider a special agreement with Russia, in which—protecting Austria-Hungary's interests in every possible way and after consultation with the Vienna Cabinet—we would take our stand regarding the future of certain Turkish territories in the, perhaps still remote, eventuality of Turkey's collapse or disintegration.'

Austria's fright at the opening up of this perspective will soon be transmitted to Rome and from there probably also to Paris, and will presumably cause the French to stop their intrigues against the Triple Alliance.[1]

H.

### 799.  Paul von Metternich to Bernhard von Bülow[2]

London, 21 February 1902

Dear Bülow,

Italy's conduct towards France seems after all to have enlivened the phlegmatic approach to things here. Mr Chamberlain made use of the Maltese language question[3] to say something pleasant in Parliament about the Italians,[4] and this seems to have fallen on fruitful soil over there. The Italian lesson may have contributed to advancing the efforts of Marquis Ito[5] and producing the Anglo-Japanese agreement.[6] After

[1] See Bülow's memorandum of 14 February. (*Grosse Politik*, vol. XVIIIii, no. 5724, pp. 538–9.)

[2] From the London Embassy files.

[3] On 28 January Chamberlain announced the withdrawal of the proclamation of 1899 which had provided for the eventual suppression of the official status of the Italian language in Malta.

[4] In his statement Chamberlain said that he regretted any pain or apprehension which the Maltese affair might have caused in Italy. He praised the beauty of the Italian language and stressed the friendship and many mutual interests binding England and Italy.

[5] Japanese Minister-President, 1892–6, 1900–1. Ito was on a visit to England at the time.

[6] Signed on 30 January 1902. *British Documents*, vol. II, nos. 124–5, pp. 113–20.

the Italian lesson the English Government probably did not fancy running the risk of reading one day in the newspapers that Japan had reached an understanding with Russia over England's head. Actually people in England are still astounded at their own courage in venturing into the field of entangling alliances, but they feel uplifted and happy to have come out of their isolation. The many unnecessary questions in Parliament alone show how pride is affecting the politicians here.

As far as we are concerned I do not look upon the Anglo–Japanese agreement as an unmixed blessing. It is of advantage to us that the Anglo-Russian attempts at a rapprochement are being pushed into the background. But a time could come one day when the English–Japanese group might oppose our aims in the Far East. I am convinced that right now the English Government attaches importance to our friendship and does not want to do us harm. But a judgment on the effect of the English-Japanese alliance on our interests will depend on how German-English relations develop in the future.

When the Cabinet decided to inform us of the agreement in confidence before its publication, they also considered asking us whether we wanted to join the agreement. I have been informed of this in confidence by one of the less important members of the Cabinet. On the day that Lord Lansdowne had asked me to call in order to inform me of the agreement,[1] Lord Salisbury and Mr Chamberlain had been to see him immediately before my visit, and I believe that it was only at this meeting that it was decided not to suggest to us that we should join. In accordance with your instructions I have in the meantime left Lord Lansdowne in no doubt that the present moment was not favourable to an agreement between Germany and England, and that our attitude is clearly defined by the German-English agreement on China.

Mr Chamberlain's power has increased enormously, and there are people who see in him the next Prime Minister. Right now he is supposed to be very angry with us. I myself have not talked to him; at the moment nothing would come of it; and he has not taken any steps to see me. [...]

When talking over the development of German-English relations with politician friends, I find nearly everywhere the opinion that while a good deal of irritation with Germany was the predominant feeling at present, this was only skin-deep and would disappear again. Amongst the English people there was no real hostility towards us. On the other hand I do find a strongly-marked anti-German trend in all political publications, newspapers and reviews. Wherever something can be found which can be interpreted to the disadvantage of Germany or as a weakening of her alliance system, it is being joyfully exploited, as if there could be no greater political boon for England than a weakening of Germany. And these attacks in the Press are particularly directed against your person. [...]

[1] See *British Documents*, vol. II, p. 122, and Metternich's telegram to the Foreign Ministry of 3 February 1902, *Grosse Politik*, vol. XVII, no. 5043, pp. 145–6.

The only thing which to some extent still preserves the much loosened bond between Germany and England is the person of H.M. the Kaiser. If the force of circumstances should ever make H.M. oppose England publicly on some issue at dispute, I am firmly convinced that the last bond would be broken. We would have to reckon with England's declared enmity for a generation. England for her part would not consider at all the question whether we could inflict more damage on England than she could on us. For the moment I would summarize the general situation by the saying: I wouldn't give twopence for Anglo-German relations. I hope that I shall be able to give you a more cheerful report on this subject in a few months.

I have been frank, as you desired it.

Your<br>M.

800.    Holstein to Bernhard von Bülow
        Copy

[26? February 1902]

Prinetti's reply[1] is definitely welcome: openly directed against Russia (I am getting out my old French memorandum). Moreover the senseless demand for a declaration of *désintéressement* on Tripoli. Since Article 9 of the existing treaty already promises more than simple *désintéressement*, to wit German support (*l'Allemagne s'engage à appuyer l'Italie en toute action sous la forme d'occupation ou autre prise de garantie etc.*), some secret thought *must* underlie the innovation. Article 9 of the present treaty is based on the pre-condition 'that Germany and Italy, after careful consideration, have become convinced that the status quo is untenable'. Probably the Italians now find this *pre-condition* a hindrance. Presumably we are now to undertake to help the Italians somehow—for example diplomatically in Constantinople—even if they take immediate action against the Sultan.

The whole effort shows a considerable narrowness of view and facilitates your task. That the *père cycliste*[2] should describe himself as dying is good news.

Now we should, however, consider whether it wouldn't be a good thing if you or I wrote briefly to Donna Laura[3] at this stage. Rudini is the father of Article 9 on Tripoli and is hardly likely to be enthusiastic at the thought that in Prinetti's opinion Italy's interests are not adequately safeguarded by the article. The only question is how openly one can hint at this. That depends on the man; you know him, I don't.

H.

[1] To the German conditions for the renewal of the Triple Alliance, transmitted to Wedel by a telegram of 24 February. (*Grosse Politik*, vol. XVIIIii, no. 5727, pp. 543–5.) Wedel telegraphed Prinetti's reply on 26 February. (*Grosse Politik*, vol. XVIIIii, no. 5728, pp. 545–6.) The actual text of the modifications desired by Italy in the treaty was handed to Richthofen on 1 March. (*Grosse Politik*, vol. XVIIIii, no. 5729, pp. 547–9.)
[2] Prinetti.
[3] Donna Laura Minghetti, Bülow's mother-in-law.

## 801. Holstein to Hugo von Radolin[1]

24 March 1902

Dear Radolin,

Just a few words, but those in friendship. I have a *great deal* to do. [...]

You can rest assured that Isidor[2] won't get an Embassy. He'll fail like many another light weight. Phili is the striking example of this. He'll stay in Vienna because otherwise he would have nothing to live on, but his influence will probably be more or less at an end.

Two groups are now facing each other in the Far East.[3] Presumably the Franco-Russians want us to take their side by undertaking not to abandon our neutrality during a war in the Far East. As far as one can see at present, we have no reason to give up our policy of the free hand. For whom and for what?

Please give my respectful regards to the Princess.

Your very old
Holstein.

## 802. Paul von Metternich to Bernhard von Bülow[4]
Draft

London, 20 July 1902

Dear Bülow,

[...] The other day I visited old Salisbury on the occasion of his retirement.[5] When I remarked by the way in the course of the conversation that he had not apparently left any very acute immediate problem in the world for his successor to deal with, he replied with a smile, characteristic of him when he wants to stimulate one's thoughts without wishing to go into detail: 'Might not someone or other be seeking to obtain a stretch of Morocco? Though this would probably be an even more difficult military task than the war against the Boers.' I asked in the same tone of voice to whom he attributed such bad intentions? And furthermore, judging by Lord Lansdowne's latest statements in the House of Lords, it appeared that he had friends in the Mediterranean. Whereupon Lord Salisbury: 'Where are our friends in the Mediterranean? I don't know them.' I did not think it meet during a farewell visit to remind the old gentleman that it was due to his policy that Italy had been practically lost. Altogether I would not attach too much importance to the above remarks. But they do show that, as regards England, he attaches special importance to the future of Morocco and that he does not believe the official reassurances that friendship with Italy has been restored.

He prepared his resignation, which seems somewhat strange so short a time before the coronation, in the greatest secrecy, and left even old and trusty Party members in ignorance of the date. Also, he did it on a

---

[1] From the Radolin Papers.          [2] Not identified.

[3] Russia and France against England and Japan, the latter group having agreed to maintain the status quo in the Far East in their treaty of 30 January 1902. (See p. 252, note 6.)

[4] From the London Embassy files.

[5] Lord Salisbury had resigned on 11 July 1902.

Sunday, when there is always little news, so that it wasn't until Monday that Parliament and people were faced by the accomplished fact of Mr Balfour's Premiership. The silence and speed with which the change was made were explained to me as due to the fact that the time during which Mr Chamberlain was in hospital was regarded as favourable to curb his ambition for first place in the Cabinet.

It is clear from a number of questions in Parliament and the replies thereto, in particular from Lord Lansdowne's speech of a few days ago in the House of Lords, that a feeling that Italy's friendship is useful has been awakened in England. According to Italian newspaper reactions, reported in the last few days by the *Times* correspondent, it would seem that Lord Lansdowne's assurances of friendship have not found the echo in Italy which might have been expected. Perhaps Italian opinion is also expressing its disappointment that England should merely want to maintain the *status quo*, whereas Italy wants Tripolitania and other things, i.e. not the *status quo*.

It is noteworthy that Lord Lansdowne did not mention the renewal of the Triple Alliance in his speech which touched on many issues. In years gone by the event was welcomed joyfully by English Ministers and the English Press. I have not the slightest doubt that Lord Lansdowne wants the Triple Alliance to remain solid and endure. But in view of the feeling towards Germany now current here, he apparently thought it inopportune to speak on this subject. One thing is as a rule forgotten or not believed on the Continent when judging the English. They are taken to be unsentimental businessmen, more or less immune to emotional impulses, and it is not realized that public opinion here is not only guided by logic and interests, but also by emotions. The English people were greatly excited by the abuse from Germany, which has now ceased. An Englishman takes a long time to assimilate something, but then it sticks for a long time. The average Englishman is convinced that in recent years the enmity and hatred of England apparent in Germany has been greater than in other countries, and now he makes his plans on the basis of this feeling. The neutrality observed by the German Government weighs less with him at this time than the daily screaming. How long this attutude will last is something neither I, nor probably anybody else, can foresee.

I know from remarks made to me by Lord Lansdowne that he attaches great importance to England's position in the Mediterranean and that he wants to tie Italy to England. If we could do something in Rome to help increase the Italian Government's confidence in Mr Balfour, we would in my opinion in this roundabout way regain contact with the English Government in international questions. This contact has been lost in the last few years, at least as far as Europe is concerned, due to the force of circumstances. With Lord Salisbury the great sceptic on Italy has gone, and conditions are thus favourable to a renewed rapprochement between Italy and England, unless Italy has already committed herself too far and too firmly with France. But Italy seems to have a big heart which can accommodate everybody.

Lord Lansdowne is very interested in Chinese questions. If I were put in a position to inform him from time to time of the course of the negotiations and our views—without thereby harming our interests—he would be grateful for it. [...]

With best regards<br>
Your<br>
P.M.

803.    Holstein to Bernhard von Bülow
         Copy

Berlin, 29 July 1902

Dear Bülow,

In accordance with your wishes I have tried to do something about England. As nothing could be done now with Chirol, I arranged for Rothschild to get some notes via Schwabach, some of which I had dictated to the latter. The point stressed was that at the moment Germany did not need England nor vice versa, and that this period of calm was therefore a suitable time to consider how the continuing newspaper war might be brought to an end.

Since Salisbury's departure Rothschild can once again be used in political matters. He is on good terms with Balfour and Chamberlain; Salisbury used to cut him.

Rothschild has telegraphed Schwabach that he has received the letter and hopes to be able to answer soon. Presumably we shall see from the answer where the English shoe pinches. I think that it would not be advisable to send a dispatch treating all the pending questions in detail to London *before* that. I would rather suggest that the Prince[1] should use his fluent pen to draft an answer to Metternich,[2] an easy task for him especially if he uses your marginal comments.[3]

Metternich's letter contains nothing new excepting Morocco. Klehmet said that it was indeed difficult to make up a dispatch with such scribblings.

I would not advise following up the hint on Morocco now. Hatzfeldt tried that after hints from Salisbury.[4] Nothing came of it, and I can't help suspecting that Salisbury allowed something about these talks to leak to the French in order to increase the French inclination towards that North African agreement with England which so shocked the Italians.[5] The present moment, one of suspicious irritation, would be the most unsuitable imaginable to break into the English house by way of the Moroccan door. [...]

In my opinion—and I am not the only one to hold it—the efforts now being made to represent England as irreconcilable and a demonstrative conciliatory gesture by the Kaiser as necessary *are aimed against you.* Hammann told me repeatedly in the last few weeks and again an hour

[1] Prince Lichnowsky.
[2] See above, Metternich's letter of 20 July. For the reply, see below, Bülow's letter to Metternich of 2 August.
[3] A copy of Metternich's letter bearing Bülow's marginal comments has not been found.
[4] See p. 120.
[5] The Anglo-French agreement of 21 March 1899.

before his departure that this campaign was in the main directed against you. I for my part would speak up without hesitation if I saw the least danger from England. On the contrary, however, I think that all this 'crying wolf' and all these so-called 'warnings' are utter nonsense. Those who originated these warnings don't believe them themselves; it is all designed to work on the excitable nature of the Kaiser.

'Meeting them half-way' is not going to achieve anything. Berchem's letter,[1] for example, had a bad effect in England and has increased English pride. I talked to Schiemann,[2] who has long been on good terms with Berchem, about the letter, and he praised it afterwards in the *Wochenschau*. But a few days later, on Saturday, he said : 'Berchem did go too far. I see it now, the effect was a bad one.' That can serve as a warning to us. *Nothing demonstrative, everything must be done quietly and gradually.*

Do you really want to mediate between Italy and England before knowing what sort of 'proof of friendship' Italy expects of England? If Prinetti thinks that this should consist in England advising the Sultan in favour of an immediate cession of Tripoli, any mediation in England would be hopeless. The whole English Press—I am enclosing the anti-Turkish Gladstone paper *Daily News*—follows the slogan 'Maintenance of the status quo in Tripoli'. There is also a report from Metternich according to which Lansdowne spoke along the same lines. He said something like : 'After all the Italians can't ask that Tripoli be presented to them on a platter.'[3] This English attitude is in no way due to friendship for the Sultan. On the contrary, right now the English are maltreating the Sultan in the Persian Gulf, and doing so to a greater extent than is advisable in their own interests—in view of the Mohammedans in India. As regards Tripoli, the sole decisive point is that the English are convinced that the French are only waiting for Italian action in Tripoli in order to follow it up with an immediate invasion of Morocco. This connection between Italian and French action has been expressed with naive frankness in Press articles, apparently inspired by Prinetti—three days ago, for example, in a piece in the Vienna *Information*, which praised Prinetti to the skies. French action in Morocco would not suit the English, and I don't think that they could possibly be persuaded to favour an immediate Italian acquisition of Tripoli.

I do hope you will not offer to mediate. But you must consider already at this stage your reply to Prinetti, if the latter should *ask* you to mediate with the Sultan and England. Perhaps he will do so during the Berlin talks.[4] It is desirable not only for German policy but also for you

[1] Not found.

[2] Theodor Schiemann. Professor of Eastern European history at the University of Berlin, 1892–1900; publicist, who enjoyed close relations with Kaiser Wilhelm II.

[3] Apart from Metternich's report printed in *Grosse Politik* (vol. XVIIIii, no. 5853, pp. 750–1), the Foreign Ministry files contain only a telegram from Metternich of 19 March according to which Lord Lansdowne had merely repeated to Metternich personally his statements contained in the above-mentioned report.

[4] Holstein referred to military conversations scheduled for later that summer. (See *Grosse Politik*, vol. XVIIIii, no. 5825, pp. 702–3.) According to the Foreign Ministry files no Italian request for German mediation was made.

personally that you should stay out of an affair in which England would, for the first time in ages, take the side of the Sultan (and in return would probably obtain from the latter all sorts of concessions in the Persian Gulf). From this point of view it would be best if you were to tell Prinetti: 'Germany is not a Mediterranean Power. France on the other hand, as a Mediterranean Power, has concluded agreements concerning North Africa with both Italy and England, and is therefore the obvious mediator between the two. Moreover relations between France and England are right now not as delicate as relations between Germany and England. Therefore turn to France. Barrère is the man for this, he will do it for you. If you have England and Russia on your side, the two Powers which the Sultan fears most, I think it possible that the Sultan will yield without war.'

If Prinetti then approaches the French and they wriggle out of mediation, Prinetti will become somewhat cooler towards France. If on the other hand the French approach the English and the latter refuse— and you could bet pretty heavily that they will refuse—Franco-English relations will in turn deteriorate.

In my opinion nothing should be said concerning Tripoli in Prince Lichnowsky's letter to Metternich.[1] On Morocco all that should be said is that the English hoodwinked us some time ago on this, and that therefore, at the present juncture, the Moroccan question cannot be discussed by us except in response to an *unequivocal* English initiative.

Marschall is convincing proof for you that it makes no difference to me in official matters whether I like someone or not. Marschall is capable. Metternich does not possess Marschall's gifts, but I do believe that it should be possible to raise the present standard of his work. In the opinion of the Foreign Ministry it is pretty well zero. I would like to know what old Prince Bismarck or your father would have said if an Ambassador, after a lengthy silence, had produced such a muddled mixture in which a number of important questions are thrown together or else dismissed separately in one or two sentences. The significant point about separating various subjects is not that it facilitates filing, but that it forces the writer of the report to treat a subject in somewhat greater detail than Metternich does. I would therefore suggest for your consideration whether you should request Metternich to correspond with you by way of the traditional reports, using private letters only in exceptional cases, not as the normal method of reporting. I believe that official business *s'en trouverait bien*. But—it isn't essential. We can do without diplomatic reports from England more easily than from other countries—unless as important a man as Hatzfeldt is there. The general situation and feeling become apparent in the Press and public speeches, and any negotiations can be conducted at this end. Richthofen will do this well, and, now that he no longer has to adapt himself to Salisbury's rudeness, Lascelles will also become less pessimistic. The other day Metternich was sent a pretty important query concerning Siam; the

<hr />

[1] See above, p. 257, note 2.

reply, not quite a page, furnished proof that it is better not to disturb him in his hypochondriac inertia but to seek other channels through which to transact business. If things go on as they are, Metternich's task will in the main be limited to social representation and to the gaining of friends for Germany by correctly attuned politeness. [...]

For obvious reasons I have written this letter in my own hand, but, because of my eye, it has been a hard job.

May Poseidon and Aeolus favour you in the coming weeks.

Ever yours very sincerely
von Holstein.

## 804.    Bernhard von Bülow to Holstein

Norderney, 1 August 1902

Secret.

Dear friend,

Many thanks for your long letter, rich in content.[1] I only regret that you wrote it yourself, and I sincerely hope that this had no bad effects on you. Please don't hesitate to dictate secret matters also; I have full confidence in those officials to whom you give it.

I am glad that you have chosen to use the channel Schwabach-Rothschild, which I regard as safe and useful. I find your explanation for this approach excellent. [...]

The thought that there might be friction between England and ourselves has actually been expressed repeatedly by Eckardstein, but to my knowledge never by Metternich. When you point out the faults of some of our Ambassadors, I would like to remind you of the reply which Montezuma gave to his general and fellow-sufferer on the red-hot gridiron when he bewailed his fate: Am I not the one who suffers most from these faults? But, it is my nature to try to make the best of any situation and to achieve the best possible results under given, unalterable circumstances. M. is one of those representatives abroad whom H.M. will keep for a very long time, and at the post which he now occupies.

Why do you think that the English attempts at intimidation are directed against me personally? Do you think that the English want to awaken distrust of me in H.M. by this method? They won't succeed. There is no doubt that some English circles would prefer another Chancellor for a variety of reasons, particularly a Chancellor who did not possess H.M.'s confidence in such high measure and thus would have less opportunity to conduct German policy independently. If you share this view, please arrange through Esternaux to have this raised in the Press, naturally most carefully and tactfully; perhaps by saying that the repeated personal attacks on me in the *Times* and other anti-German English papers—normally aided and abetted by the equally anti-German *Temps*—proved how inconvenient an independent German Chancellor was to our intimate enemies in Europe. Occasional hints of this sort can only have a good effect.

[1] Of 29 July. See above.

I do not think that H.M. is planning any demonstrative act towards England, and completely share your view that an improvement of our relations to England must take place calmly and gradually. [...]

With best wishes, also from my wife,

Your truly devoted
Bülow

805.    Bernhard von Bülow to Paul von Metternich[1]

Norderney, 2 August 1902

Dear Metternich,

I too do not doubt that Lansdowne wishes to see the Triple Alliance remain solid and endure, nor do I doubt his friendship for us and regard the change which has taken place in the leading position in London as an advantage. We must leave it to time to calm excited minds and above all we must take a stand against the insane and equally malicious view, which unfortunately seems to have adherents in England and is probably not sufficiently strongly opposed by Lascelles, that we intend to attack England after having increased our fleet. At the moment neither of us needs the other, neither Germany nor England, and it seems to me that this period of calm in foreign policy is a suitable one in which to consider how to bring about an end of the continuing Press war. It is wrong to assume that greater enmity and hatred have been shown on our side during the last few years than in other countries. In fact people here only cursed; no action hostile to England was taken or *even attempted*, and the attitude of all decisive German circles was much more friendly towards England than was the case in Russia or France. It is only necessary to call to mind the negative attitude we took up in regard to the various Russian-supported mediation proposals, and also in the case of President Krüger's visit, not to mention the granting of the Order of the Black Eagle to Lord Roberts[2] and H.M.'s lengthy stay in London when Queen Victoria died. It is a positive act of ingratitude for the English to forget these facts because of the Press polemics on both sides and to leave out of consideration that in most continental wars public opinion in England took its stand on the side of the so-called underdog.

I would not advise taking up the Moroccan suggestion *now*. The present moment, one of suspicious irritation, would not be a favourable one to break into the British house by way of the Moroccan door. Having been lured into the net by the English in the past, and Hatzfeldt, encouraged by Salisbury's hints, having vainly tried to reach an understanding with England on this point, it is out of the question for us at present, in view of the obtaining situation, to do so without an *unequivocal English initiative*.

I would be pleased if the feeling that Italy's friendship is useful were really to become stronger in England. The English have disappointed Italy too often in the last few years, have treated her too superciliously.

[1] From the London Embassy files.
[2] Commander-in-Chief of the British forces in South Africa from 1900; victor over the Boers.

Currie's behaviour in Rome certainly contributed to an estrangement between the two nations and helped to drive the Italians into the arms of the Russians and the French. Do England's leading statesmen seriously want to see the maintenance of the *status quo* in Tripoli, thereby playing the part of the Sultan's protector? Why, do you think, do they want it? Would it be in order to prevent a simultaneous opening up of the Moroccan question in the belief that the French would take the opportunity to march into Morocco? Or is it because they expect some concessions from the Sultan in return, perhaps in the Persian Gulf?

The importance which, in your opinion, Lansdowne places on England's position in the Mediterranean and his wish to bind Italy to England are good news. In this respect also Salisbury's retirement should represent an improvement. I shall be very happy to work for a rapprochement in Rome. I do not think that Italy has already gone too far with or tied herself too strongly to France to draw closer to England. The great majority of the Italian people continues to want to go with England, to which they are tied by historical memories and for whom they have strong sympathies. But England must treat the Italians with greater friendship and trust than Salisbury and Currie used to do. [...]

> With best regards
> ever your faithfully devoted
> Bülow

806.   Holstein to Oswald von Richthofen
       Copy

16 September 1902

Dear Richthofen,

You were quite right not to send a learned scribe as a messenger, for what I have to say does not require lengthy exposition.

You regard the internal danger as greater than the external one in regard to the China question. That settles the matter. Let it rest.

Delcassé will naturally handle the English in China with velvet gloves if he sees any chance of bringing Morocco under French protection.

In every one of these colonial questions the decisive point is always Chamberlain's mood. The question is whether he is really sufficiently furious with Germany to be prepared to leave Morocco to the French in order to get on good terms with them, *without* at the same time getting Tangier for England. The narrow neutral coastal strip around Tangier would of course also gradually become French.

If Eckardstein were less talkative you could call him over for two days some time and talk to him. But that can't be done for reasons of which you are aware. I therefore suggest that you write him a friendly letter, asking him to inform you personally and privately of his view. News had been received here (no source, naturally!) that England was negotiating with France concerning Morocco. The whole of Morocco— apart from a narrow neutralized coastal strip around Tangier—is supposed to become a French protectorate; in return England is to obtain concessions in Siam. Did he, Eckardstein, believe that the English

Government could face the English public with such a treaty—which would mean that Tangier would also be lost to England?

Furthermore, what did he, Eckardstein, think regarding Chamberlain's mood? Did he really think that Chamberlain would be capable of placing Tangier within reach of France's grasp, thereby closing England's access to the Mediterranean, for England would then neither be able nor want to hold the narrow coastal strip near Tangier with the French so close to it. On this Eckardstein should write to you, absolutely frankly —and hence privately.

From E.'s reply you will see whether it is worth while to take any sort of initiative in London. That is why it is advisable not to give instructions for a renewed enquiry there immediately, but to await E's letter first.[1]

Of all concerned, Japan is the Power for whom an Anglo–French understanding would be most disastrous. What has Arco[2] reported? Could Eckardstein possibly find out something from the Japanese representative in London, Hayashi?[3] This is another question which I think should not be put to Eckardstein officially, but in a private letter. [...]

That, my dear friend, is all I have to say at the moment. And at that the most important idea, to use Eckardstein, is yours.

With best regards

Your sincerely devoted

H.

Do you want to go so far as to ask Eckardstein directly how, in his view, Chamberlain might be brought to a better and more trusting frame of mind towards Germany? I think it might be better if you saved this direct question for a later letter.


807.    Memorandum by Holstein[4]

Berlin, 1 October 1902

For the first time since 1871 we are engaged in a direct exchange of political ideas with France on the question of the evacuation of Shanghai[5] and on Siam.[6] It was with particular interest, therefore, that immediately after my return I turned to the latest dispatches in order to get some impression about France's attitude as well as what we could expect in dealing with M. Delcassé. The impression was not favourable. The attitude of France is one of watching and waiting, as though they were trying to lure us into statements that might be exploited elsewhere,

[1] See Richthofen's letter to Eckardstein of 25 September 1902, and Eckardstein's reply of 4 October. (*Grosse Politik*, vol. XVII, nos. 5189–90, pp. 345–6.)

[2] Emmerich, Count von Arco-Valley. German Minister in Tokyo, 1901–6.

[3] Tadusa Hayashi. Japanese Minister in London, 1900–6; Foreign Minister, 1906–8.

[4] From the Bülow Papers. Only a typewritten copy of this document was available to the editors.

[5] Occupied since the summer of 1900 by French, German, and British troops to protect foreigners and foreign interests against the type of violence that had occurred in Peking. On this question, see *Grosse Politik*, vol. XVI, chapter CVIII.

[6] See *Grosse Politik*, vol. XVIIIii, chapter CXXVI.

particularly in London. With respect to the evacuation of Shanghai they are not giving us the same answer to the same question that they are giving to London or Tokyo.

After these experiences it does not seem advisable for us to continue to negotiate directly with France, also because, as the incoming telegrams show, Delcassé says not a word about our very substantial suggestions concerning methods of evacuation and simply presents his French programme to the other Powers. Delcassé did exactly the same thing two years ago at the beginning of the Ministerial Conference in Peking.[1] At that time too he tried, though without success, to make the negotiations follow the pattern of his French programme and to ignore the German suggestions.

If we continue confidential negotiations with Delcassé about the evacuation of Shanghai, we not only risk his ignoring our proposals in dealing with others, but that he might spice them with a nice anti-English flavour and then communicate them confidentially to London. Because this entire behaviour of Delcassé can leave no doubt that he at present regards a Franco-English understanding as the main goal of his policy. It would be unfortunate if this understanding were brought about just because Delcassé was given the opportunity to present Germany to the English as the villain in the piece.

The machinations of Delcassé will be undercut the moment we communicate our proposals—which do not have to fear the light of day—simultaneously to all the Governments involved, that is to say, to the three other occupying Powers, to China, and, to avoid misrepresentation, to Washington for purposes of information. By proposing guarantees to avoid the acquisition of special rights in the Yangtze Basin by any Power, we show that we are merely trying to give practical form to the principle of the Open Door. It is still too early and her fleet is still too weak to enable America to take over the exposed position of a *primary Power* in China. And the Japanese will be clever enough to realize that they are not powerful enough to hope for special rights in the Yangtze Basin. One may therefore assume that neither America nor Japan will raise objections to our proposals, but will treat them as a logical consequence of the principle of the Open Door.

As for the Franco-English rapprochement, it is certain that England will get every desired concession from the French in the Yangtze question and in many others besides if she will give up Morocco to France. But in the present world situation in which the existence of England is not threatened, there is no English Government that would dare to come before Parliament with the statement that, with the exception of a narrow coastal strip around Tangier, all of Morocco had been conceded to the French and that France therefore had the right to build arsenals and to collect troops behind that narrow coastal strip. That would leave it up to the French to select the time for annexing Tangier and for acquiring therewith domination over the western entrance of the Mediterranean. Before John Bull would concede that, he

[1] See *Grosse Politik*, vol. XVII, chapter CIV.

would have to feel much smaller than he does to-day, for now after the conclusion of the Boer War he again *feels* very *big*. Recently *The Times* correspondent in Morocco[1] told the German representative[2] that England was in the process of ceding all of Morocco to France with the exception of that narrow strip of neutralized territory around Tangier. Didn't the German Government want to ask questions about this in London? This was no more than a crude attempt, like many others on the part of Kaid Maclean,[3] to draw Germany into the Morocco question. Eckardstein too, who is trying to picture the attitude in England with black on black—and is doing as much as possible to contribute towards it—has telegraphed to-day after returning from a visit to Lord Lansdowne in the country: 'I found my earlier belief confirmed that Cambon, for whom Morocco is a hobby-horse, is constantly coming forward with propositions on this question, on the other hand I have also gained the distinct impression that up till now these have been treated dilatorily, to say the least, or even rejected outright.'[4] Tangier is a question of life and death for England's position as a Great Power. England will not expose Tangier simply out of anger against Germany.

Our next task therefore is to safeguard our programme for the evacuation of Shanghai from misinterpretation by communicating it to the five Powers involved simultaneously.

H.


808.   Bernhard von Bülow to Holstein

4 October 1902

Dear friend,

[...] The tendency you emphasize is in fact undoubtedly to be found in H.M. But towards me it is modified—or it might be better to say not applied—because of H.M.'s great personal generosity and friendship. H.M. does not want to lessen my personal standing, far from it. On the contrary he wants to help, support and back me. All the distinctions which I have received from H.M. came straight from him without being suggested by any one else, especially not by me. On more than one occasion I have prevented him from granting me a distinction because I did not want it. But it is certainly true that as soon as a Chancellor in regard to whom no personal feelings were involved came into office, the above-mentioned tendency would once more become as strongly apparent as it was before my nomination. [...]

As regards the customs tariff,[5] the main thing is that we get it through if at all possible; in any case the responsibility must not fall on the Government should it not succeed. Under no circumstances must a situation

---

[1] Walter B. Harris.

[2] Friedrich, Baron von Mentzingen. Minister in Tangier, 1899–1904.

[3] General Sir Harry Kaid Maclean. British Agent to the Sultan of Morocco.

[4] Published in Eckardstein, *Lebenserinnerungen*, vol. II, p. 402.

[5] In December 1901 Bülow had brought before the Reichstag a tariff bill which was chiefly concerned with the protection of agrarian interests.

like that of 1892 over the School Law[1] and 1899 over the Canal Bill[2] be allowed to arise. In case of a crisis a shift to the Right is likely, for H.M. is understandably very bitter about the incredibly stupid attitude of the Liberal Press over the Löhning case[3] and the exchange of telegrams.[4] A year ago that same Liberal Press staged a similar concentric attack on H.M. and myself because of the now dead and forgotten City Counsellor Kaufmann and the fairy-tale fountain.[5] Then H.M., under the impact of these attacks, said to me in Hubertusstock: 'I don't always agree with the Conservatives in economic matters, but they are after all the only ones with whom one can govern. The Liberals just aren't gentlemen.' Now the feeling is much the same, perhaps even more intense.

Do write or telegraph me what you think would be the best solution of the problem concerning the Boer visit from our point of view.[6]

With the very best regards and wishes

Your

B.

## 809.   Holstein to Hugo von Radolin[7]

Berlin, 3 November 1902

Dear Radolin,

[...] I no longer understand French Near Eastern policy as conducted by M. Delcassé. For some time he has been doing everything he can to destroy the Sultan's authority—the most important factor still holding Turkey together. It was also noteworthy that he pointed out Albania to the Italians as an Italian sphere of influence in his conversation with Ojetti,

---

[1] The Prussian School Law of 1892 (see vol. III, p. 400 et seq.) with its strong emphasis on religious education had brought the Government into conflict with a number of parties and resulted in a serious ministerial crisis in March 1892.

[2] On 19 August 1899 a bill providing for two new canals to furnish better transport between the Ruhr and the Rhine and the Rhine and the Elbe was defeated on third reading in the Prussian Chamber of Deputies. The agrarians had been largely instrumental in defeating the bill, which they felt would primarily benefit industry. The issue not only created a split between the Government and the Conservatives, but brought on a conflict of principles when the Government took punitive action against civil servants, who as deputies had voted against the bill.

[3] In July 1902, Löhning, the provincial tax director in Posen, had been pensioned off because, according to the *Norddeutsche Allgemeine Zeitung*, he had opposed the Government's policy towards the Poles. Löhning maintained that his dismissal was due to the fact that he had married the daughter of a Sergeant-major. The liberal and clerical Press bitterly attacked the Government, citing the case as an example of the way the caste system was pervading Posen.

[4] Of 10 and 11 August between the Kaiser and Prince Regent Luitpold of Bavaria. The Kaiser had expressed his indignation that the Bavarian Landtag had refused funds requested by the Prince Regent for artistic purposes. The liberal and clerical Press criticized the Kaiser for interfering in Bavarian affairs and needlessly incensing the Centre Party.

[5] On 11 July it had been decided not to confirm the election of City Counsellor Kaufmann as Lord Mayor of Berlin. The progressive Press maintained that confirmation was withheld because twenty years earlier Kaufmann had been obliged to resign his reserve commission on account of his progressive views. On 12 September the Kaiser for the second time refused to confirm Kaufmann's appointment. At the same time he objected on artistic grounds to a plan put forward by the City of Berlin to erect a fairy-tale fountain in the Friedrichshain.

[6] See below, Holstein's diary entry of 7 November 1902.

[7] From the Radolin Papers.

the correspondent of the *Giornale di Roma*,[1] in January. His hint at that time that Russia was in agreement with his policy was nonsense as far as official Russian policy is concerned. At no time has the Russian Government worked so energetically for quiet in the Balkan peninsula. Delcassé's treatment of the status quo in Turkey as *quantité négligeable* leads to the conclusion that a rapprochement with England rather than an understanding with Russia is being sought. The Italians too are taking very energetic action against the Turks in the Red Sea, and I doubt whether Prinetti would risk this if he were not sure of French support. He is hardly sufficiently naive to count on English support. Do ask your friend the Spanish Ambassador[2] sometime in conversation and without emphasis what in fact he thinks of Delcassé's Mediterranean and Near East policy.

Much work this last month. My health is going downhill.

In friendship as ever

Your

Holstein.

## 810.    Holstein to Hugo von Radolin[3]

Berlin, 6 November [1902]

Dear Radolin,

Please forgive the pencil. I am at home with 'flu', have a headache, and won't go to the Ministry till the afternoon.

I regard it as my duty to write to you that the Chancellor told me H.M. had commented unfavourably on your reporting, describing it as long-winded and saying: 'I hope that Radolin won't spoil his position in Paris as he previously did in St Petersburg.'

When I asked myself on what his statement—which grieved me greatly—could be based, I came to the conclusion that possibly your reporting is somewhat one-sided. At the moment you are completely gripped by the idea of bringing about a rapprochement between ourselves and France. Because of this *fata morgana*, you are neglecting what should be your primary duty, which is to observe and report on events in the political sphere. All your reports deal with German-French relations, and if a report occasionally deals with something else it is sure to end up with a phrase from which one can see that it too is designed to further the idea of a rapprochement. As far as I can remember, your reports do not show that Delcassé or other diplomats have talked to you about politics —apart from the semi-official rapprochement proposals by the Spaniard.[4] Naturally you must not run after these people with questions à la Baladzy,[5] but in view of your great natural tact that is unthinkable anyway.

[1] Should read : *Giornale d'Italia.*    [2] *Leon y Castillo.*    [3] From the Radolin Papers.
[4] See Radolin's report to Bülow of 15 October 1902. (*Grosse Politik*, vol. XVIIIii, no. 5884, pp. 797–9.)
[5] In a report to the Foreign Ministry of 2 June 1902, Radolin described Baladzy as a political agent of 'jesuitical-nationalist' persuasion. (*Grosse Politik*, vol. XVIIIii, p. 829, note ***.) In a letter to Holstein of 1 April 1903, Radolin wrote : 'Since the beginning of my stay here, [Baladzy] has either sent me memoranda on the political situation here or else

Also, the Kaiser loves stories which have a personal point to them, e.g. about friction between a General and a Minister, or news of what goes on in the salons; I might best say, a slight admixture of the gossip-column. H.M. is very taken with Schlözer's[1] reports.

As regards the Chancellor, I had the impression that he liked [?] the idea of visiting Paris, but that the discovery that Baladzy had talked to you about the return of Metz (and Urville) to France frightened him. It frightened me even much more. The Kaiser doesn't know a thing about it, else there would be a blow-up.

Baladzy's statement that the minimum demanded by Germany's best friends in France was a retreat to the language frontier was tactless but at the same time enlightening. As long as this view obtains—and you and I will hardly live long enough to see a change—all talk of a rapprochement is pointless. There is no need for you to shout this from the roof-tops, but you can take it as axiomatic. If we were ever to lose a war we should lose Metz and a great deal more besides.

But without a lost war Wilhelm II will not surrender anything acquired by Wilhelm I. He has said this repeatedly. On the other hand the chance of Russia and France going to war against us grows less to the extent that the Near Eastern Question and France's need to rebuild her former prestige on the Bosporus revive once more. It is laughable that a political windbag like Baladzy should try to intimidate us. Our situation is securer to-day than it was ten years ago, for in the meantime Russia has realized that the stronger France becomes, the stronger is the French bolt on the Straits. But Russia cannot openly avow this view; she needs French money.

Enough politics. Don't take the above to heart, don't talk about it—except with the Princess—and think over what can be done in practice. The practical requirement is to obtain more material for reports, partly from the salons, partly from socially unimportant people in political circles proper.

Now, best wishes to you and I kiss the Princess' hand

Your old
Holstein.

The Chancellor wondered for a long time how he could let you know most considerately that his view differed from yours. Finally he decided on a private letter—a thought I had thrown out in conversation. The private letter is not being circulated.

811.  Diary Entry

7 November [1902]
Nearly ten months have passed since the last entry. The Triple

communicated his views to me orally. In return he has for a number of years been receiving 500 francs a month. I have been growing more convinced the longer I have been here that this 'sensational information'—which usually proves to be wrong—is of no value to the Embassy, and certainly bears no relation to the 6000 francs we pay out every year. I would therefore like to ease this gentleman gradually out of the Embassy.'

[1] Karl von Schlözer. First Secretary of the Embassy in Constantinople, 1897–9, in Paris, 1899–1902; Minister at the Hague, 1902–7.

Alliance was renewed without alteration.[1] That I managed to force through, but there was nearly a break between Bülow and myself. He, pushed by Wedel, wanted to accept some 'harmless' alterations in the treaty to please Prinetti. I opposed this to the utmost and finally achieved my object after a great deal of annoyance. Wedel had done everything possible to ensure the realization of *his* idea. And I don't think it impossible that Wedel, Herbert Bismarck's friend, worked against me on purpose in order to eliminate me if he could.

At best the Triple Alliance is not worth much; but if we had allowed it to be altered—to please the French—we would have been disgraced before the whole world.

The Chamberlain speech[2] has in the meantime borne fruit. Already in the summer, before going on leave, I wrote to Bülow that there were indications that the English were engaged in a systematic campaign against him with H.M. In spite of my warning he made the foolish mistake—at Richthofen's suggestion[3]—of suggesting to the Kaiser[4] that the latter should receive in audience the three touring Boer generals DeWet, Botha and Delarey.[5] The Kaiser accepted the proposal—without any enthusiasm—but immediately posed the condition that the audience would have to be arranged by the English Ambassador.[6] The English Press went wild at the news of the audience and Eckardstein—who happened to be Chargé d'Affaires at the time—wrote a number of reports advising the Kaiser to give up his planned English visit in case the audience was held. Moreover he predicted war with England. The Kaiser, deeply impressed, wrote on a report by Eckardstein: 'It is only my person which prevents the English from attacking us. The audience will not take place.'[7] Fortunately the Boers had stated a short time beforehand that they could not take the first step, the Kaiser would have to invite them.[8] I had returned from leave a few days before this statement was made and had been watching the course of events with much displeasure. At this statement by the Boers I took action, got Richthofen to do the same, and telegraphed to The Hague that the statement by the Boers had closed the question of an audience. Now an audience was out of the question. The *Norddeutsche* made the same statement that day. The Kaiser's marginal note, saying that the audience should not take place, only arrived the following morning. Thus the face of the Chancellor and the Ministry had been saved. Bülow afterwards expressed his great gratitude to me for having got him out of the hole.

The acute crisis had in fact been overcome, but the agitation against

---

[1] On 28 June 1902.  [2] See p. 244, note 3.

[3] Telegram of 15 September. (*Grosse Politik*, vol. XVII, no. 5092, pp. 218–19.)

[4] On 17 September. (*Grosse Politik*, vol. XVII, no. 5093, pp. 219–20.)

[5] The Boer Generals had been received by King Edward VII on 17 August. They arrived in Holland on 19 August, and proposed to go on to Germany, France and other countries to raise money for needy Boers.

[6] See Eckardstein's telegram of 30 September. (*Grosse Politik*, vol. XVII, no. 5096, pp. 226.)

[7] See Eckardstein's report of 4 October. (*Grosse Politik*, vol. XVII, no. 5101, pp. 229–31.)

[8] See *Grosse Politik*, vol. XVII, no. 5102, pp. 231–3.

Bülow continued and still continues. Eckardstein came to Berlin and told the Kaiser and anyone else who wanted to hear it that the English would attack us some time within the next five years.[1] The Kaiser came to Berlin and Potsdam and stayed for a week without seeing Bülow. This caused general astonishment, shared by the Bülow ladies. Finally Bülow asked for an audience. It was very lively. The Kaiser complained that he was misunderstood by the German people as well as by the English, and that nothing was being done in the German Press to enlighten the two nations. In short, he was dissatisfied with the guidance of the semi-official Press and with the conduct of affairs in general. Whereupon Bülow told him a story put about by Eckardstein : 'In Kiel this summer, the Kaiser had gone aboard an American yacht. Believing that all present were American, he had collected all the gentlemen on board and said to them : England was the common enemy, against which America and Germany had to stand together. But there had also been an Englishman aboard who had sat down and reported the Kaiser's speech by letter to the Foreign Office. There the letter was kept. After this incident, Eckardstein had come to the conclusion that it was useless to go on struggling against the flood of English bitterness, hence he was leaving.'

The Kaiser got furious when he heard this story, denied everything, but was much quieter and less assertive afterwards. Bülow described it as the decisive stage in the conversation, which appears to have been unpleasant up till then.

At that time—about a fortnight ago—the usual crisis rumours were current once more, though not in connection with foreign policy but because of the tariff debates.[2] In these the Kaiser was wholly on the side of the Government. To show this, he invited himself and the Kaiserin to dinner with the Chancellor on the 26th, the Sunday, and two days later he had a meal alone with Richthofen in the latter's house.

It now remains to be seen what sort of results the Kaiser's visit to England will show. Bülow boasted mightily of H.M.'s affection of him, but he is nervous for he feels that he is regarded, sometimes even specifically described, in England as the main obstacle to a German-English rapprochement. At the same time he remains convinced that he is creating a secure place for himself in the hearts of the German people if he is painted as an enemy of England. Richthofen and Hammann to-day disillusioned him on that score in my presence. They told him that, apart from the Pan-Germans who counted for little, the German people were now deeply concerned lest the tension with England should grow even further; and that the bad effects were beginning to make themselves felt in business. Examples were given for the latter. I do not believe that Bülow was convinced. Hermann Arnim[3] and Hasse are his prophets and will probably remain so. Nor do I believe that the Kaiser will dismiss Bülow; the Kaiser finds him convenient because of his tracta-

[1] See Eckardstein, *Lebenserinnerungen*, vol. II, pp. 399–400.
[2] See p. 265, note 5.
[3] Hermann, Count von Arnim-Boitzenburg, Lord of Muskau.

bility. But Bülow's influence in foreign affairs will be still further circumscribed.

Rosen to-day told me the following curious story. Lascelles had told Rosen that he, Lascelles, had complained to the Kaiser that I did not receive him. The Kaiser replied: 'He doesn't come to see me either. When I granted him an order recently, I thought he would thank me, but no.'

The fact that worries me about this story is that Lascelles will probably have somehow hinted to the Kaiser that the people with whom he, the Ambassador, has to discuss policy were not the ones that mattered. I told this story to Bülow on purpose as a warning and without any comment. He evidently didn't like it at all. It would in any case be impossible for me to receive Lascelles. He would naturally immediately contrast my views and Bülow's.

Undoubtedly Bülow has allowed himself to be 'done' by the Bismarck-group. First, the Bismarcks have contributed greatly since 1890 to the anti-English agitation. That was old Bismarck's vengeance on Kaiserin Friedrich. Shortly before his fall the aged Prince had driven to see her and had asked her to act as mediator for him with the Kaiser. She had refused, as she had no influence. When the Prince had left, she said: 'It is his fault that I have no influence.' He, however, then began the great Press campaign against England. Lord Salisbury's policy, the Krüger Telegram, the South African war, Samoa, all these helped to increase the fury and the excitement against England. Bülow realized this and thought: 'If I were to make a speech against Chamberlain now, I'd become popular.' We—the Political Division—advised him against it—but Arnim-Muskau and Hasse pushed hard. Bülow had hardly made his speech and committed himself when Herbert Bismarck quietly went over to the English side. He frequently visits Lascelles. When the Boer leaders were here he treated them kindly, but advised them to reach an understanding with Balfour and Chamberlain; both were easy to get on with. When the Kaiser learned of this by way of a newspaper article, he commented in the margin: 'Cleverly calculated to appeal to His Majesty King Edward, who wishes him well.' Bülow is very nervous. He will now commit another error by allowing the English to realize that he is scared.

812.  Diary Entry

11 November [1902]

To-day a number of foreign policy questions—in connection with the evacuation of Shanghai—had to be decided.[1] The English Press had grossly misrepresented our attitude, the point therefore was to correct this. Bülow, however, could not be persuaded to publish corrections, but kept repeating that the English would then say to the Kaiser that his

[1] In a note of 11 October Britain suggested that the four Powers occupying Shanghai should withdraw their troops on the understanding that this would be done without demanding rights or concessions from China. Germany wished for more specific guarantees that other Powers would not later claim special rights. (See *Grosse Politik*, vol. XVI, chapter CVIII.)

Foreign Ministry was disturbing H.M.'s work of conciliation by boorish articles. Needless to say, the proposed article had presented the German point of view calmly and objectively without any discourtesy. But Bülow has lost his nerve. He has only now realized how completely he has failed to persuade the Kaiser to take an anti-English line, and he has finally seen what he has done with his Chamberlain speech. For the first time he seems to fear that he is becoming estranged from the Kaiser. That is why he is keeping absolutely still. He allows the Press to say whatever it pleases, and is only concerned with what might annoy the Kaiser.

Little Klehmet, the official in charge of Chinese affairs,—who is very efficient—sees all his drafts being turned down. This evening, after a long consultation, he said to me : 'Things have never been as bad for us before.' He was referring to the Chancellor's indecision.

The Centre Party, the Party which the Chancellor prefers, is fully aware of his inconstancy. That is why they are persisting in hounding him to allow Reichstag Members to be paid in order to help the customs tariff's passage. Last night they—Spahn,[1] Arenberg etc.—went to work on him again, and to-day he was soft as butter. Already before I arrived, Richthofen had talked to him for a long time in an attempt to make him stand firm. I said : 'If the Reichstag now shows itself unable to settle the tariff question, it'll be a defeat for the Reichstag. But if you now make some sort of concession, Member's pay or whatever it may be, you still can't be sure that the tariff will be accepted. If it is turned down then, it'll be a personal defeat for you, which, incidentally, it will also be if the tariff should in fact be accepted at the last minute as a result of some concession by you. For until now you have most definitely refused any concession. If you make one now in spite of that, no one will any longer believe in your determination.'

Richthofen supported my view. When Bülow said : 'But Arenberg says too that it can't be done without pay for Members', Richthofen replied : 'I don't understand how a personal friend can give Your Excellency such advice.'

Bülow finally stated : 'All right, no pay for Members'. But who knows whether they won't finally persuade him otherwise. Richthofen said to me afterwards that Bülow had evidently had a moral hangover to-day; he, Richthofen, also had one now, for he was convinced that the Centre Party, having seen how weak Bülow was, would maintain its opposition all the more strongly in the hope that Bülow would yield at the last moment.

813.   Diary Entry

13 November [1902]

[...] The Kaiser[2] sent Bülow a long telegram to-day[3] in which he

---

[1] Peter Spahn. Centre Party Member of the Reichstag; he belonged to the strongly conservative wing of the Party.

[2] The Kaiser had gone to England on 6 November.

[3] Of 12 November. (*Grosse Politik*, vol. XVII, no. 5031, pp. 115–17.)

says : 'I have been well received, am being well treated; a difference is being drawn between myself and the German Government. Chamberlain is most incensed against Your Excellency and the Ministers in general; he is not to be pacified; we will have to let time do so. The main point now is to avoid everything which might give the English cause or pretext for war.'

According to this, H.M. has been strongly intimidated by Chamberlain.

# 1903

### 814. Hugo von Radolin to Holstein

Paris, 1 April 1903

My dear Holstein,

[...] To-day, when Delcassé received me I found him noticeably pre-occupied and serious. He must be labouring under some difficulties. His position is not an easy one. It is always the same old story. He is envied because of his position and must defend himself against all sides. Morocco causes him much concern. He told me that anarchy is rife there, but he, Delcassé, is seeking to avoid any intervention. But if the wild Moroccans should continue to attack French troops on the border, as happened shortly when a number of soldiers were killed, the Minister will have no alternative but to use strong language. Until now, he said, he had made no use of the *droit de suite*, but one could not know whether he would not be forced to do so. [...]

In faithful friendship,
Your
Hugo.

### 815. Bernhard von Bülow to Holstein

15 May [1903]

I have discussed Eckardstein's memorandum[1] with Metternich. As he has been away from England for four weeks, he is reserving detailed comment until after his return to London.[2] For the moment his view can be summed up as follows. (1) Lansdowne, Balfour and a large number of English politicians do not desire a break with us and are not blind to the danger threatening England from Russia and France, even though they are for the present taking anti-German public opinion in England into account. (2) The English have long been inclined to reach an arrangement with the Russians (whom they fear), if only the latter's demands weren't too high. In all attempts to achieve a rapprochement between Russia and England hitherto, England has always been courting a recalcitrant Russia. The obstacle to an Anglo-Russian understanding has always lain in St Petersburg. (3) The Russians are intriguing in London, but Eckardstein overestimates both the significance and the success of these mining operations. [...]

Do you think the English might incite the Japanese to soften up the Russians and make them more desirous of an arrangement with England?

B.

[1] Of 10 May. (*Grosse Politik*, vol. XVII, no. 5369, pp. 567–70.)
[2] See *Grosse Politik*, vol. XVII, no. 5376, pp. 590–4.

## 816.  Bernhard von Bülow to Holstein

77 Wilhelmstrasse,
16 May [1903]

Many thanks for your kind letter. I think I can guarantee that H.M. will not take any unsuitable decisions in that particular direction. The expression of the fears in question will probably only reach the highest authority accompanied by commentary from me. Anyway, in the present situation H.M. will not do anything without having consulted me beforehand.

Seckendorff[1] yesterday supplemented his statement to me as follows: (1) Dislike of us in England was very great, but this was due more to commercial envy than to bitterness at the attitude of our public opinion during the Boer war; (2) No one in England thinks of attacking us; (3) but there is a strong tendency in England to reach an understanding with France and in particular with Russia—partly due to fear, especially of the latter Power, partly also because England feels the need of an ally but does not want us as an ally at this stage, being cross with us. Like Metternich, Seckendorff has the impression that in the Anglo-Russian flirtation, it is England who is doing the courting while Russia is reserved.

In the report for H.M. accompanying Eckardstein's memorandum[2] it should also be stressed that—according to verbal statements by Eckardstein—the fact that the *haute finance* has drawn closer to France and Russia is largely due to the allegedly discourteous treatment of the London Rothschilds by H.M. Or should I tell H.M. this in person? Eckardstein asserts that Lonsdale,[3] furious because the Rothschilds don't want to lend him any more money, has blackened their name with H.M. Alfred Rothschild, who is influential, was incensed particularly because H.M.'s suite during his latest visit to England[4] had at the behest of Lonsdale refused an invitation of his.

Altogether I entirely agree with you that we should first of all await the comments of the three Ambassadors who have been asked to report.[5]

B.

## 817.  Holstein to Bernhard von Bülow

Copy

B[erlin], 21 November 1903

After considerable thought, I advise a refusal or prevention of any debate on foreign policy questions. Such a debate must only take place either when some major successes have been achieved or major mistakes

[1] Götz von Seckendorff.
[2] Of 20 May. (*Grosse Politik*, vol. XVII, no. 5375, pp. 588–90.)
[3] Hugh Cecil Lowther, Earl of Lonsdale. A friend of the Kaiser.
[4] From 8–20 November 1902.
[5] The German Ambassadors in Paris and St Petersburg and the Chargé d'Affaires in London were asked to comment on the view expressed by Eckardstein in his memorandum of 10 May (see p. 274, note 1) that Germany would soon have to reckon with the possibility of an Anglo-French-Russian understanding. (*Grosse Politik*, vol. XVII, no. 5370, pp. 570–2.) For the replies, see *Grosse Politik*, vol. XVII, nos. 5371–3, pp. 573–80.

must be justified. Neither is the case to-day. One would only be able to tell the world of everyday happenings now.

To go into detail concerning Morocco it would not be possible at this time to foreshadow a German participation in a partition. Moreover, the mere intimation that Germany was interested in Morocco would be designed to bring France and England closer together than they are at present. (Cf. the question and reply during the last session of the French Chamber of Deputies, on Tangier.)[1]

Furthermore, if German and French ecclesiastical policy were to be compared, the former could not be defended without criticizing the latter. Even if you only said that the aims of French policy should be awaited. Coming from you this would represent criticism.

Regarding the 'extra dance',[2] if necessary one should say: 'This remark was the considered expression of a conviction which I expressed before you earlier in a different form, that is that the Triple Alliance is useful and welcome to Germany, but in view of the present changed world situation no longer necessary, so that we can face any eventuality with complete calm.' But would you please anyone with this statement? Hence it would be better to avoid it.

Regarding Austria-Hungary one could only say: 'We regret the quarrel,[3] but we also believe that interference by a third party in a marital dispute is a bad thing.'

But that also should be avoided if possible.

Stick fast by Bismarck's negative point of view. Foreign policy, like photographic development, cannot stand the light of day.

v.H.

[1] In the session of 19 November the desire was expressed for closer relations with Britain and the preservation of French preponderance in Morocco.

[2] See p. 247, note 2.

[3] With Italy, due to Italian irredentist agitation in the Austro-Hungarian Empire.

# 1904

### 818.  Bernhard von Bülow to Holstein

16 January [1904]

1.  All in all, do you think it would be better for us if there were a war in the Far East than if the storm were to pass?

2.  Do you think it is completely impossible that in the latter case the Russians would for the time being act with more caution in the Far East, and instead pay more intensive attention to their European policy than they have done in the last few years?

3.  Do you believe that the Franco-Russian alliance would survive a war in the Far East?

4.  Do you not believe that the war must definitely lead to a sharpening of the conflict between Russia on the one hand and England-America on the other, while if peace is maintained, Russia might be tempted to cultivate her relations with England-America, and even Japan, more carefully in the future?

5.  What strikes me is that our most irreconcilable and by and large most intelligent enemy in the world—Delcassé—is doing everything possible to maintain peace, and is being so assiduously supported in this by the *Revue Nationale* set. However, Tirpitz did say to me that he would regard the outbreak of war as a misfortune, because the English would then be able to seize the Yangtze.

From the point of view of our internal politics and to counteract the general dissatisfaction in Germany, it would of course be a good thing if 'somewhere far away' the nations came to blows.

Thank you very much in advance for kind reply.

B.


### 819.  Holstein to Bernhard von Bülow

Copy

Berlin, 17 January 1904

Following your instruction of the day before yesterday[1] concerning the attitude to be adopted by us towards any propositions which may be put forward by the Russians, I have just now put up a long memorandum through official channels.[2] This also answers most of the enclosed questions.[3] I would only like briefly to add the following:

The Far Eastern question can be postponed, the Balkan question can not. The latter rests on popular sentiment, the former does not.

A Russian-English understanding is out of the question, because

---

[1] Actually of 16 January. (*Grosse Politik*, vol. XIXi, no. 5943, p. 34.)
[2] *Grosse Politik*, vol. XIXi, no. 5944, pp. 35–8.    [3] Of 16 January. See above.

America has taken an anti-Russian stand, and England will and must remain on the same side as America.

If Russia were to pause in the Far East, she cannot but take up the Balkans question, whether she wants to or not.

The question whether Russia, once events start moving, will finally take possession of her own 'door-key' or will once more allow it to pass into other hands will then become more and more acute. As this question is of major interest to Vienna and Bucharest, our calming influence and mediation in those two centres will be of great importance to Russia. In my opinion this would suffice to enable us to ask for something in return.

The Dual Alliance will probably survive a war in the Far East, but not a war in the Balkans. It is by no means sure, but it is probable, that the two wars will come simultaneously.

If Delcassé should really wish to save the Russians from war, the most obvious reason for this might be that the owners of 10,000 million worth of Russian securities would suffer a bad scare and, should they wish to sell, heavy losses. But I am not sure whether Delcassé's London mediation proposal[1] was due to any plan other than that of satisfying a Russian wish. Perhaps he also knew that the Tsar was determined to avoid war under any circumstances, with or without mediation. But the retreat will not solve the Far East question, merely postpone it. The Japanese know this, and therefore, if war is avoided for now, they may use the opportunity of the next Balkan war to complete their present partial success.

One can truly say that during the whole of its existence the Russian Empire has never had so many enemies at once as now. Germany would shoulder no easy task if she were to take over all these enemies. In fact it is impossible to give a diplomatic opinion without basing it on military and naval appreciations of the power position.

To come back to Delcassé, I would tend to think that he, like the whole civilian government in Paris, is not a great believer in war, but hopes to achieve his aims through diplomatic pressure by an irresistible group of Powers. If, as appears to be the case now, Russia were to retreat in the face of Japanese and American diplomatic pressure, this would be a policy after the heart of Delcassé. He may try to go on working with this method.

Apart from the naval power problem, which I cannot judge, I find the greatest drawback of our going with Russia in the fact that we would draw further away from America, which could revenge itself on us in some way or other, even without war. Roosevelt[2] has always been anti-Russian but now the cautious Hay has become so too.

820.   Holstein to Hugo von Radolin[3]

Berlin, 27 January 1904

Dear Radolin,

[...] *Quoad politicam.* Delcassé has enquired in London whether

---

[1] See *Grosse Politik*, vol. XIXi, no. 5941, pp. 30–3.
[2] Theodore Roosevelt. President of the United States, 1901–9.
[3] From the Radolin Papers.

England together with France did not wish to work for peace in the Far East.[1] The English have given him the cold shoulder, for Japan does not want mediation, except possibly if the mediators were to *guarantee* the agreement. Naturally the English have no desire to do that, for it might possibly mean war against Russia. Nobody approached us with such a proposal, for it is known from former official statements that Manchuria could never become a *casus belli* for Germany. We haven't the least intention of guaranteeing anything. In conversation you can follow this line.

The Russians are in a very embarrassing situation because they see that they are isolated. France is quietly remaining neutral. As the Dual Alliance allegedly only applies to Europe, the Russians in 1901 suggested a Far East agreement designed to extend the Dual Alliance to the Far East. But—as we have now heard from St Petersburg—France at that time refused to accept the Russian formulation, and the only outcome was a loosely drafted Far East agreement (March 1902)[2] by which France does not regard herself obligated to come to Russia's assistance in the present conflict. It is possible that the Russians may have harboured illusions on that score. But now they are showing themselves very pliant. There is tremendous bitterness against the English in St Petersburg right now, because they have been inciting the Japanese ever since it became certain that France will not take part at Russia's side.

Incidentally, the *Novoye Vremya* said a few days ago that the Franco-English *entente cordiale* had become a *refroidissement cordial*. If there's a grain of truth in this at all, it could only refer to Morocco. During the last few weeks a movement opposed to the abandonment of Morocco to the French has been growing in England. The *Morning Post* is the chief mouthpiece of that party. In view of this the Government may hesitate to make any positive concessions to the French. Delcassé, who is evidently hoping to make a name for himself in French history through Morocco, may well be aggrieved at this. But it won't change his leaning towards the English.

I have spent a few days at home ill, but had to produce a memorandum on the situations in the Far and Near East, their connection and repercussions, for H.M. during that time.[3] Now I am better again. [...]

Farewell. In a rush<br>Your<br>H.

## 821. Holstein to Hugo von Radolin[4]

19 February 1904

Dear Radolin,

By suggesting the idea of a meeting[5] you have staked your diplomatic existence on one card—which outdoes Monte Carlo. As you might

[1] See p. 278, note 1.
[2] *Documents Diplomatiques Français*, Deuxième Série, vol. II, no. 145, pp. 177–8.
[3] Of 23 January. *Grosse Politik*, vol. XIXi, no. 5951, pp. 48–52.
[4] From the Radolin Papers.
[5] Radolin wrote to Bülow on 4 February that the Prince of Monaco had informed him of President Loubet's desire to meet the German Kaiser. (*Grosse Politik*, vol. XXi, no. 6431, pp. 105–6.)

have expected, the responsibility for a possible failure will be yours; and I think this is quite in order, for as you are on the spot you must be able to judge men and things better than would be possible from here.

Thus your problem will now probably be how to get decently out of the affair. I would emphasize the following for the purpose: 'Since I wrote my letter on the 4th of the month, war has broken out.[1] France would like to remain neutral, but as Russia's ally she is all the more anxiously concerned to preserve appearances. Since in the view of all Frenchmen the Dual Alliance was primarily concluded against Germany, a meeting with the Kaiser at this particular moment would in their eyes be an indication that the French Government no longer took the Dual Alliance seriously. This is a reproach which the Government cannot afford to have levelled against it, for it would lose the support not only of the nationalists but of wider circles. I have reached this conclusion after a careful study of the French Press since the outbreak of war. They don't want to join in the fight and feel that this reserve is a disappointment for the ally. They therefore want to avoid all the more anything which might offend or annoy him. For that reason any conciliatory or friendly action towards Germany would be more sharply and more universally criticized than in normal times. In this situation the possibility of a meeting in the not too distant future can best be kept alive by definitely preventing any discussion of the idea at the present moment. I could, for example, tell the Prince of Monaco that I had enquired about H.M.'s travel plans and had learned that these could not after all be adapted so as to render a realization of the idea of a meeting possible, etc. etc.'

There, that is what I think of the matter.

Hurriedly<br>Your<br>H.

I advise especially to emphasize and explain how since the 10th of the month the French Press is indicating more and more clearly that the French Government may have awakened expectations in Russia which were now being disappointed by French neutrality, and that therefore the French Government should now devote particular attention to a cultivation of the relations with Russia.

19 February, evening

I would also advise you to answer the Chancellor's letter[2] *as soon as possible*.

822.   Hugo von Radolin to Holstein

Paris, 21 February 1904

Please burn.

Secret.

My dear friend,

First of all my heartfelt thanks for your letter[3] and telegram.[4] You

---

[1] War between Russia and Japan was declared on 10 February, but hostilities had begun several days earlier.

[2] Of 18 February. (*Grosse Politik*, vol. XXi, no. 6432, pp. 106–7.) Radolin replied on 22 February. (*Grosse Politik*, vol. XXi, no. 6433, pp. 108–10.)

[3] Of 19 February. See above.     [4] Not found.

really speak my language, and I entirely agree with your view of the situation. I must, however, say at the outset that I did nothing on my own initiative. This is *strictly confidential*. If you have learned of the letter of 4 February,[1] which, on first reading—certainly must have seemed strange to you, I must assume that you also know how it *came to be written* and what caused me to send it to the recipient in such *secrecy* and *privacy*. I almost fear that you are not fully informed and I regard it as my duty to tell you of the genesis and development of the matter, naturally under the seal of the most absolute secrecy.

The evening before my departure (I left next morning), I had dinner with our friend H.[2] She will remember that after dinner our host[3] took me to his study, where I remained alone with him for quite a while. There he confided to me something which, he said, only he and I should know, namely that an *accidental* meeting in M[onaco] would not be unwelcome. He instructed me to suggest the idea to the P[rince] of M[onaco]—as coming *from me* and accidentally—whether a happy coincidence might not bring about a meeting. Under no circumstances was the impression to arise that I was acting on orders or that anything of all this was known in certain quarters. M. might sound out the *master here*[4] as on his own initiative. I was then to report the result in a private letter.[5]

Delicate though this instruction appeared to me, I wrote it down word for word at my host's desk in order that I would not say one word too much or too little.

After my return here, when I saw M[onaco], I first of all told him quite categorically that his invitation could not be accepted for obvious reasons. He regretted this, but resigned himself to it. In the course of the conversation which dealt with a number of things, e.g. his travels, his museum etc., I threw out a remark, in accordance with my instructions, regretting the fact that the 'two' did not know each other. I personally would be happy if they were to meet somewhere some day, but it seemed to me that this was a dream which could not be realized. Thereupon I dropped the *sujet*. Soon after this, M., who in the meantime had seen the master here (when he said good-bye to him before leaving for his estate), told me what I reproduced in my letter of the 4th. I confined myself to listening and put on a face from which he could see that I did not really believe that his plan would be realized. Since then he has left and I have heard nothing further about it.

If in my letter of the 4th I acted as if I had originated the matter, as if I were reporting something new, I did so in order not to mention the instruction I had received for fear of a possible indiscretion. But I did assume that the recipient would know what my private letter referred to, all the more since I normally send him private letters only on the rarest occasions. If I am disavowed, there is nothing I can do about it. I

[1] See p. 279, note 5.     [2] Probably Frau Helene von Lebbin.
[3] Bernhard von Bülow.
[4] Emile Loubet. President of the French Republic, 1899–1906.
[5] The letter to Bülow of 4 February. (See p. 279, note 5.)

believed that I was doing my duty conscientiously without compromising anybody. In the meantime circumstances have altered. While the matter didn't seem very promising to me already at the end of January, it has in my opinion become completely hopeless since 8 February, and I entirely share your view that considerations towards third parties are now decisive and cannot be overcome.

The fact that I remarked to our sovereign in Jarotschin last summer— on the occasion of the visit you know of—'that I would not like to be the Ambassador here if ever a visit to this place were to be made; I would not be able to shoulder such a responsibility'—will have afforded sufficient proof that I don't harbour any great illusions about the *sincerity* of the rapprochement, though externally relations are as good as they could be.

I gracefully accept the great friendliness with which I personally am met in all circles here, but I accept it *à sa juste valeur*, and am able to differentiate very accurately between the attainable and the non-attainable. The chasm is still a big one and only years of patience, and good *procédés* from both sides, can change that.

I am writing to the Chancellor by the same courier. Once more my heartfelt thanks for your good and faithful advice, which I am following exactly, as always.[1] [...]

Farewell for to-day

823.   Memorandum[2]

Berlin, 22 February 1904

The object of dispute in the Far East war is 'China as a market'— hence the recognition of [China's] integrity by certain countries—and Russia's real opponents are America and England, who are using the Japanese to pull their chestnuts out of the fire. The aim of the war is mainly an economic one—the object is to make dollars and guineas—and the destruction of Russia's predominance and prestige in Asia is secondary to this.

In view of this Admiral Alexeiev's[3] plan of campaign, as hinted at in the newspapers, with which the transfer of the headquarters to Harbin would seem to accord, appears questionable, although it may be sound from a purely military point of view. For it is thought that Alexeiev wants to allow the bulk of the Japanese forces to move into Manchuria before destroying them with one powerful blow. Yet the abandonment of a large part of Manchuria would be misunderstood not only in China, but also in Russia herself. The Chinese might regard this as an encouragement to attack, and the Russians as a mistake in the conduct of the war for which they could render the *Tsar* responsible. On the other

---

[1] Holstein replied on 24 February: 'I knew nothing of the original suggestion. But why didn't you drop off and see me when you drove to the station? Five minutes would have been enough.' (From the Radolin Papers.)

[2] This unsigned document may be a copy of a memorandum prepared by Holstein for Wilhelm II.

[3] Eugene Ivanovich Alexeiev. Russian Governor General in the Far East.

hand it is by no means impossible, it should rather be taken as certain, that America and England would intervene in Japan's favour as soon as Alexeiev prepares for his powerful blow. Russia would then have lost the greater part of Manchuria and her prestige. *That* would be the psychological moment for the outbreak of a world war, which must be avoided at all costs.

The disaster could be avoided by means which would also be of advantage to the Russians, to wit if the latter were to conduct the campaign against Japan as a side-show—i.e. without large-scale mobilization —fighting merely with their peace time army, preserving their finances, and bleeding the Japanese white *financially* by careful, purely defensive strategy, standing fast and defending every inch of Manchuria.

Every day and every degree of frost favours the Russians. Only in this way does it appear possible for actual possession to be transformed into legal possession and to avoid a world war.

And what could possibly cause Germany to stand by Russia and endanger herself? One can admire the bravery and other great qualities of the Russian army and navy, and one can understand, when reading the English report of the naval battle of Chemulpo, that His Majesty is proud to be Admiral of the Russian fleet. But if Germany were to take sides, her world trade would be endangered. If one tickles the tiger ('Meeting with Loubet'),[1] one must expect him to use his claws. Time will probably show whether and to what degree there is a causal connexion between the Herero revolt [2] and the 'key to the Baltic'.[3] If he were to use his claws again he might do so more violently, perhaps *too* violently. Are we in fact capable of taking on the English and the Americans? Late in the 1850's a Russian man-of-war sailed up the Swine, saluted the flag fluttering on the citadel, received no acknowledgement and went on firing with live ammunition until the salute was returned. The Russian Government's complaint was settled through diplomatic channels. The investigation showed that the key of the powder-magazine had been mislaid. Is the key to be found in its place in Wilhelmshaven, which would appear to be primarily threatened?

It is becoming fashionable to attack without warning—without a prior declaration of war.[4] Public opinion overlooked the Japanese breach of international law without great difficulty—an added reason for countries with well-known and perfidious enemies to be on their guard. The Russian had come alone and with peaceful intentions. But what would happen if an English naval squadron suddenly appeared at the mouth of the Jade? Would it be fired on by the coastal battery and met at least by the torpedo-boat flotillas? Or would it be able to get unhindered into the basin and to bombard the ships in the naval station? It is not very honourable for a hero to receive a mortal blow in bed.

[1] See p. 279, note 5.

[2] Early in January 1904 a revolt of the native Hereros had broken out in South-West Africa which many Germans believed to have been instigated by the British.

[3] At the time it was being considered that Germany and Russia should guarantee Denmark's neutrality, since Denmark, controlling the entrance to the Baltic, was not sufficiently powerful to preserve it unaided. (See *Grosse Politik*, vol. XIXi, chapter CXXIX.)

[4] Japan had attacked the Russians at Port Arthur before war was officially declared.

Cannot something be done for the security of the German North Sea fleet?

### 824. Memorandum[1]

Berlin, 8 March 1904

Bizerta,[2] French desires for revenge, Russian intrigues in the Near East and threats against Germany can probably be regarded as the reasons why the Triple Alliance was concluded, with the maintenance of peace and the status quo as its aim. Egypt was left to the English. The predominant object was : assistance in case a foreign Power *attacked* one of the signatories.

Regarding the Austrian and Italian desire for expansion, the late Chancellor held the view that Germany had no territorial interests in the Near East and would therefore agree to everything on which Russia, Austria, and Italy would agree. While Austria has remained conservative, Italy, not having achieved anything by way of the Triple Alliance and unable to do so, will now try to make progress with French assistance. The question thus is whether this will change Italy's situation, or whether the Triple Alliance, including Italy, would still serve a purpose, if for example the latter concluded a separate treaty with France. In the past Germany too had a separate treaty with Russia *besides* the Triple Alliance, Italy an agreement with England to which Germany did not object. Although the premises which were decisive when the Triple Alliance was concluded have long since lost their validity, it would still be regarded as advantageous to allow the Triple Alliance to remain in being, because Italy would then not be able to conclude an alliance directed *against* Germany.

In all probability Albania will give the Italians indigestion, but a long time could pass before that happens, and, as long as the Triple Alliance exists, Italy will not have a completely free hand, while France will hardly make any concessions concerning territorial possessions in the Near East without Russia's approval.

It could therefore hardly be counted a mistake if one allowed the Italians to carry on.

### 825. Anton von Monts to Holstein

Rome, 18 March 1904

Dear Baron,

The Loubet affair[3] did not come as a complete surprise to me, since

[1] The memorandum, probably a copy of a Holstein draft, is unsigned. No copy was found in the Foreign Ministry files.

[2] On 30 April 1881, a French naval force seized Bizerta, while land forces invaded Tunis from Algeria. By the Treaty of Bardo of 12 May the French obliged the Bey of Tunis to accept a French protectorate.

[3] The possibility of a meeting between the Kaiser and President Loubet. Monts mentioned to Tittoni that the Kaiser's present travel plans would take him past Naples at the very time that President Loubet would be arriving there for his visit to the King of Italy, and that the Kaiser could perhaps stop there once again. (See p. 285, note 2.) According to Monts' telegram of 17 March, Tittoni at once seized on this idea. (*Grosse Politik*, vol. XXi, no. 6436, p. 113.)

that ambassador of the future, Chelius,[1] has for a long time and repeatedly spoken of such a possibility as being desired by His Majesty.
When, however, Berlin used 'heavy artillery' in regard to the reception
here of the President, I regarded the matter as finished.[2] The suddenly
so much milder tone in telegram no. 85[3] drew my attention once again to
the atmosphere at Court, all the more since it would have been better not
to let the Italians off the hook so quickly.[4] Undoubtedly my very restrained comments on Lanza's telegrams—which incidentally were completely objective—created a deep impression.[5] I think that in an
emergency Giolitti would not have hesitated even to arrange a small
revolution in Naples. Such an unscrupulous Renaissance character would
do anything. Thus he has already suddenly allowed the work in Spezia
to be partially halted, although the difficulties had long been settled, in
order to use the unavoidable failure to complete the battleship *Regina
Elena*, which was to have been launched by Loubet, as an excuse in Paris.
The Italians are weird people, they are all liars, but they are also scared,
an outstanding national characteristic. Since they suddenly find us to be
*bons enfants*, their fear of us will certainly lessen somewhat. And my
position cannot be said to have been improved by the rapid withdrawal.[6]

I arranged a meeting with Tittoni[7] for yesterday afternoon, in order to
have a further consultation on Loubet's reception etc. on the basis of my
latest milder instruction and the reports which have in the meantime
arrived from Lanza.[8] But at lunch-time the express courier from the
Wilhelmstrasse arrived with the Chancellor's letter and your most
valuable comments.[9] My first impression was, don't touch the matter.
But what if His Majesty, under the influence of the blue skies of *la bella
Napoli*, should suddenly surprise his Italian colleague by expressing the
desire for another meeting on the siren-shore on the occasion of the
worthy Loubet's departure? The dates coincide to the hour, and probably the decision to stick by the return from the Adriatic to Genoa was
adhered to for some good reason, although the Court was advised from
here to disembark in Trieste or Venice. Or, what if in Naples His
Majesty were to order me to arrange the matter? That would have
produced a major disaster. I therefore decided that during my session

---

[1] Oskar von Chelius. Aide-de-Camp and friend of the Kaiser; Military Attaché in Rome.

[2] According to Monts' report of 28 February 1904, the Italians had planned a far greater
programme for the visit of the French President than for the visit of the German Kaiser, who
had proposed a stop in Naples to see the King of Italy in the latter part of March during the
course of his Mediterranean cruise. (See *Grosse Politik*, vol. XXi, p. 37, note *.) For the
'heavy artillery' from Berlin, see *Grosse Politik*, vol. XXi, nos. 6389, 6391, pp. 39–42.

[3] Of 15 March. (*Grosse Politik*, vol. XXi, no. 6395, p. 45.)

[4] Marginal comment by Bülow: 'That is what he warned against.' (See *Grosse Politik*,
vol. XXi, no. 6395, p. 45.)

[5] See *Grosse Politik*, vol. XXi, no. 6396, p. 45.

[6] Marginal comment by Bülow: 'He himself advocated to "take it easy".' (See above,
notes 3 and 4.)

[7] Tommaso Tittoni. Italian Foreign Minister in the Cabinets of Giolitti and Fortis,
1903–5, in the Giolitti Cabinet, 1906–9.

[8] See *Grosse Politik*, vol. XXi, nos. 6396, 6436, pp. 45, 113.

[9] Not found.

with Tittoni I would drop the hint that the Kaiser would sail past Naples on 28 April, which would make things more complicated; this might perhaps provide an opportunity to suggest the meeting *à trois* to the Italian Minister.

My session with Tittoni was a very long one : reading of Lanza's reports together, query from here about the naval review, the toast in Naples, Tittoni's coming along on 26 March. I kept on reverting to the not yet completely removed danger to the Triple Alliance and made use of popular ill-feeling in Germany. Then I went on to say that the meeting of the monarchs would presumably not be very gay, especially since Gianotti,[1]—he is the local Eulenburg—had (actually) said to me that the fact that the Kaiser's and Loubet's departure from Italy were fixed for the same day was gravely embarrassing the King and the Court. Tittoni now enquired about the travelling arrangements. I went into detail, finishing up with the Kaiser sailing past the Gulf of Naples. But he did not understand until I finally said that the Kaiser would see the fleets from his ship, would get angry, or possibly would regret not being present at the beautiful spectacle. Now the light went on in the Minister; he said that they would get out of the whole very nasty situation to which the lack of political understanding of the previous era had brought them if His Majesty were to have another meeting with King Victor Emmanuel on 28 April. That would rob the Italo-French naval meeting of its otherwise unavoidable embarrassing character. I replied that as a friend of Italy and as his personal friend I could only congratulate him on this idea. But it seemed very doubtful to me whether the Chancellor for one would agree to the solution. If he succeeded in persuading the Chancellor through Count Lanza, the Kaiser's agreement would, it seemed to me, be obtained more easily. Naturally it was a pre-condition that Italy was sure of France's agreement. Our interest in this whole matter was in any case not a direct one. We would of course be pleased to see the sour tone which the Loubet visit had brought into the harmony of the Triple Alliance eliminated.[2] I once again warned that the matter should not be taken too lightly, that the celebrations should be as limited as possible for even at best it would be a long time until the ill-feeling in Berlin disappeared.

That's how the matter now stands. Perhaps Tittoni started thinking about my remarks afterwards. But at first he showed himself completely taken with the possibility of getting out of the mess, while simultaneously affording prestige to his King and himself. In fact the scheme must be tempting to an ambitious Italian Minister, and Tittoni is that, and Victor Emmanuel too will probably be enthusiastic about it.[3] Obviously I shall not refer to it again, but I will probably see Tittoni before leaving for Naples on the 22nd.

If I had worked through an intermediary—since Nigra is absent, the only possibility would have been Visconti Venosta—I would have

---

[1] Italian Master of Ceremonies.
[2] Marginal comment by Bülow : 'It was a mistake to say that.'
[3] Bülow : 'Vederemo' [sic].

immediately exposed myself and thereby our Government. For Visconti is very clever, and, provided he would have agreed to take on the delicate mission, would have made the matter clear to Tittoni and the King at once. Moreover he is not aware of the background of our threats, on which I based my action and which in fact rendered it possible.

Now, as regards France, that is outside my competence. Barrère, whose voice will certainly carry much weight, is not really an enemy of Germany. As the French representative in Rome he was bound to conduct a policy directed against the Triple Alliance, as he did, and which did nearly lead to the desired end; it was really a question of weeks, and an Austrian-Italian conflict would have broken out. Barrère has never looked with sympathy on the Russian alliance. He said to me a few days ago that he now wanted to leave here in order to go to London, possibly also to Berlin, but never to the Neva. It was only a pity that you couldn't conduct policy with the completely incalculable Kaiser. In 1885 Bismarck had been very close to a reconciliation, which would definitely have been the greatest boon for the two pace-setting *Kulturvölker* in Europe.[1] He then sang the praises of Loubet and of the completely peaceful direction which the latter had given to French policy.

Although it is really self-evident, I would finally like to emphasize that the Chancellor should allow himself as much time as possible before meeting Lanza's request. It would be easy to nail down Italy as the initiator, provided the Chancellor told the Ambassador that he could only pass on a formal request by Tittoni to His Majesty, and that only if Italy had secured French agreement. I am more worried about the future than about this problem.[2] Though, presuming the meeting takes place, the Kaiser will be satisfied for the moment with the results achieved, he will soon wish to harvest further fruits from the meeting and will have us running after France. That to my mind is the danger which could retard for years the better relationship with France which time alone is slowly producing.

In gratitude and respect

Your Excellency's most devoted servant
A. Monts.

826.   Holstein to Oswald von Richthofen

Copy

Berlin, 28 March 1904

Dear Richthofen,

Do you want to ask Radowitz whether and how he envisages the possibility of an acquisition of Port Mahon?[3]

[1] Marginal comment by Holstein: 'The debacle over China—the triumph of Courcel.' (See *Memoirs*, pp. 107–10.)

[2] Holstein: 'It's still too early for that.'

[3] In a memorandum of 22 March, dictated during his Mediterranean cruise, the Kaiser had asked Bülow to investigate the possibility of leasing Port Mahon from Spain as a coaling station. Rosen reported from Rome on 30 March that the Kaiser had again spoken in this sense. To overcome British objections, Britain might possibly be granted the right of using

Do you want to ask Alvensleben—perhaps by private letter—whether he believes it possible that Russia would support our claim for acquiring something of the west coast of Morocco, or rather what counter-demands she would probably make of us ?[1]

I do not believe in success regarding Port Mahon, because our position there would be a direct threat to France's southern coast and French Mediterranean trade.

I also expect nothing of Russia in regard to Morocco because the Russians will not want to lose France now, which is in a very strong position between England and Italy.

Finally I believe that Germany, if it were to make any demands and these were sharply refused, would beat a hasty retreat.

But you could perhaps ask the two Ambassadors for their opinion. It can do no harm, even if it does no good. I do not, however, believe that foreign Governments, even friendly ones, will keep quiet about any enquiries after the experiences which we had over Denmark's neutralization.[2]

Most sincerely<br>
Your<br>
Holstein.

### 827.   Memorandum by Holstein[3]

9 April 1904

[...] The return journey via the Adriatic would invalidate the rumours that H.M. is seeking a meeting with the French.[4] To arrange such a meeting seems more impossible than ever at the present moment when France's self-confidence has been raised by the coincidence in time of the English treaty[5] and the Italian trip. But an unsuccessful attempt, even the mere suspicion that one might have been made, would produce general malicious satisfaction abroad and lively displeasure in Germany, directed not only against the Kaiser but also against the Government.

P.S. I had finished dictating the above when I saw a telegram no. 16

the station. Radowitz, requested to report on the matter on 30 March, explained in a report of 8 April the great difficulties which a German attempt to establish herself in the Mediterranean would meet. As far as can be seen the Kaiser's suggestion was not followed up. (From the Foreign Ministry files. See also *Grosse Politik*, vol. XXi, no. 6481, pp. 169–70.)

[1] The enquiry suggested by Holstein was not made. (See *Grosse Politik*, vol. XXi, nos. 6512–13, pp. 197–201.)

[2] See p. 283, note 3.

[3] The original of this document is in the files of the Foreign Ministry. In a private letter to Bülow of 6 April, Monts had proposed that the Kaiser should return either via Trieste or incognito via Genoa. On 9 April Bülow pronounced against both these suggestions and asked Holstein for his opinion. (From the Foreign Ministry files.)

[4] In the earlier part of the memorandum Holstein had argued against the proposed return of the Kaiser from his Mediterranean tour via Genoa and Piedmont. 'I would presume that it would not be difficult to arrange a small French counter-demonstration with *Evviva la Francia, Evviva Loubet*, if the French desired something like this.' Holstein argued that it would be safest for the Kaiser to return via Fiume.

[5] The Anglo-French agreement of 8 April. (*British Documents*, vol. II, no 417, pp. 373–407.)

from Genoa,[1] which opened the prospect that the arrival of His Majesty there might coincide with the presence of the French fleet, or with the preparations for its reception. This would significantly increase the possibility, already mentioned above, of French counter-demonstrations or other incidents.

828.    Holstein to Bernhard von Bülow
        Draft

In Hospital[2] Johannisstrasse 11
Berlin, 25 June 1904

Dear Bülow,

The cause of this letter is the enclosed notice in the *Lokal Anzeiger*: 'At the Chancellor's request, the State Secretary in the Foreign Ministry, Freiherr von Richthofen and his staff, have also left for Kiel.'[3] As Richthofen repeatedly stated last week that you insisted on his presence in Kiel, the presumption that the above news item is attributable to him is justified.[4]

When you and I talked over the Kiel matter with Hammann last time, we were all agreed that—although no political Minister was accompanying the English—your presence there could be satisfactorily explained by pointing out that you had also been in Kiel in previous years. This could naturally not be done if the State Secretary and staff accompanied you, and I was under the impression that on this point too we were agreed, but that Richthofen on the other hand had made clear his strong desire to be permitted to go to Kiel. In order to further as far as possible the point of view which I believed to be correct, I for my part told Richthofen straight out at the time: 'You must consider whether it would not be quite disproportionate if you too were to go to Kiel, while the English are only sending their Tirpitz.' The fact that Richthofen succeeded in pushing through his presence at Kiel marks a victory for his determined individualism over the courtesy which prevented you from refusing his request. But if it is said, as in the enclosure, that the State Secretary in the Foreign Ministry and staff have travelled to Kiel at your request, the whole world is told that the German Government, not put off by England's reserve, wants to push through something or other. Thereby we are just asking to be slapped down by the English Press, and it won't be our doing if we aren't. That is something which I cannot pass over in silence.

The way in which Richthofen regards his official task has already on a number of occasions run counter to tradition: the irregularity of his

[1] By this telegram of 8 April the German Consul in Genoa passed on an enquiry from the Mayor as to when the Kaiser would arrive in Genoa, so that the necessary preparations could be made. (From the Foreign Ministry files.)

[2] On 23 June Holstein had undergone an operation for cataract on his right eye.

[3] On 21 June the Kaiser had gone to Kiel to take part in the Elbe regatta. He was joined there on 25 June by the King of England. (See *Grosse Politik*, vol. XIXi, nos. 6038–40, pp. 186–90.)

[4] On this incident, see Otto Hammann, *Zur Vorgeschichte des Weltkrieges. Erinnerungen aus den Jahren 1897–1906* (Berlin, 1918), pp. 196–9.

work, above all the way in which documents destined for the Kaiser are delayed. The Foreign Ministry had to stand for the Kaiser speaking of 'the swine in the Foreign Ministry' in front of three members of the Foreign Ministry and numerous bystanders, because Richthofen had allowed the answers to the letters of condolence from the Princes on the death of Prince Heinrich's little boy to lie around for days.[1] At the time I let it go in silence; it is not a matter about which it is pleasant to talk. But as in the meantime other things have happened, I permit myself herewith to submit that a change, be it *in modo*, be it *in persona*, is desirable in order to cure these three main failings: irregularity of work, sloppiness, and the emphasis on personal rather than objective factors.

You said the other day that I was always objective in my judgment. I believe that I am also being so to-day. Certainly any wish to save myself personal unpleasantness is far from my intention, and I therefore leave it up to you whether you want to bring my view, expressed above and for which I take full responsibility, in its entirety to Richthofen's knowledge.

A newspaper item read to me states that Schoen[2] is also now present in Kiel. Don't you want to have a look at him to see whether you think him fit for the post of State Secretary? His Francophil wife is a drawback, but there is always some sort of snag. It is pretty doubtful whether I would get on with him, at least in the long run, but if the State Secretary himself knows something about high policy and has once acquired some experience, it will probably be possible to dispense with me. And I am old enough to know that only very few can tell whether a job is being done better or worse. For the public at large, and not only for them, the only criterion of the work done is the final result.

If you want to keep open the possibility of a change in the direction of the Foreign Ministry—but also if you don't envisage this at the present moment—it is of the utmost importance to you that the successor of Konrad, who I hear is the designated successor of Sternenberg, is really up to his job.[3] For Richthofen probably had some justice on his side when he replied to occasional reproaches: 'Yes, but where am I always to find the time; I am also Head of the Reich Chancellery and have other things to do besides.'

It seems probable that the clique in the Ministry of Agriculture, to which the Heads of the Reich Chancellery have belonged in the last decade, will again try to fill the gap by co-option, by a procedure analogous to that being followed on the board of the *Kreuzzeitung*. This procedure is, however, in my opinion not to be recommended. For one thing the last choice was not a happy one, and furthermore it will make a great difference for you whether the person concerned knows that you yourself chose him, or whether he is told that he was brought in by

---

[1] The third son of Prince Heinrich had died on 26 February 1904.

[2] Wilhelm von Schoen, Baron from 1909. Minister in Copenhagen, 1900–5; Ambassador in St Petersburg, 1905–7; frequently representative of the Foreign Ministry in the Kaiser's retinue; State Secretary in the Foreign Ministry, 1907–10.

[3] Dr von Konrad, Chief of the Reich Chancellery, succeeded Sternenberg as State Secretary in the Prussian Ministry for Agriculture. Konrad was succeeded by Friedrich Wilhelm von Loebell, Chief of the Reich Chancellery, 1904–9.

the Podbielski[1]-group. I would not have emphasized this difficulty if I did not believe that I could suggest a means to overcome it. The man who, as I presume, is closest to you in the whole of the official inner circle is your intimate friend [Duzbruder] and school-companion Wentzel[2] in Hanover; he is moreover a man who is thoroughly experienced in dealing with people on an official level and who must be aware that in many ways his welfare is closely linked with yours. I would write to him straight away from Kiel, briefly and to the point: 'I need a Head of the Reich Chancellery. Naturally he must not be a free trader, he must have agricultural interests at heart. But there are agrarians and agrarians, supporters of a maximum and a minimum tariff. I have no use for the maximum, and even if I wanted to I could not get H.M. to agree. Also he should (if possible) have these particular qualities. Can you suggest some one to me? Think it over and then write, or better come yourself to Berlin or Norderney so that we can talk.'

That's all I have got to say.

I have tried to further the Egyptian matter[3] in the only way I could by instructing Schwabach, who was going to Kiel, to ask Lansdowne— whom I don't know—from me, how an improvement in relations with England was to be rendered possible if the Kaiser and the German people were made to feel that [the English] were positively ashamed of the preparations for better relations with Germany. Schwabach is also to throw out the idea that the reception in Hamburg, to which Lascelles probably attaches great importance, would be very much warmer if the English agreement with Germany concerning Egypt were made public one or two days beforehand.

Metternich left a trifle early, but he may well have thought that minor difficulties would be smoothed over more easily in Kiel than in London.

I am well. The doctors say that the recovery is proceeding apace. I shall probably be allowed to go home already in the next few days. It is a novel feeling to have a right eye again which is of use.

With very best wishes, personal and political

Your
Holstein.

I very much hope that your conversation with King Edward will, as usual, have a beneficial effect. Whether this will last is of course questionable, but right now even a momentary, somehow generally recognizable success, would be very important.

829.   Bernhard von Bülow to Holstein

H.M. Yacht *Hohenzollern*
Kiel, 29 June 1904.

Dear friend,

The police enquiries, for which I gave immediate and secret orders,

---

[1] Viktor von Podbielski. Prussian Minister for Agriculture, 1901–6.

[2] Head of the Administration in Hanover.

[3] The Germans wanted the English to make specific provisions for German interests in Egypt following the Anglo-French settlement on Egypt of 8 April. (See *Grosse Politik*, vol. XXi, chapter CXLIII.)

show that the item in the *Lokalanzeiger* to which you drew my attention was based on a communication which reached that paper by express mail. An addition, suppressed by the editor, spoke among other things of the mobilization of a strong contingent, but that nevertheless no important world political decisions would be reached [at Kiel]. This addition leaves no doubt that the article in question was not inspired by any of the persons you named.

I doubt whether in case of a change in the post of State Secretary His Majesty would in fact pick Schoen as a successor. I believe H.M. has other persons in mind. I also believe that a change of State Secretary would greatly increase H.M.'s desire to bring about a reformation in the Foreign Ministry, not only *in capite* but also *in membris*. I would under any circumstances only be able to accept a State Secretary if he were indubitably capable of representing his Ministry in Parliament both independently and successfully.

The English visit passed off well. King Edward gave me the honour of repeated and lengthy conversations and met me with kindness and confidence. My general impression is that relations with England could improve in time, but that this cannot be achieved overnight, but only by patience and great tact.

I am so very happy that your operation went so successfully, praise the Lord. May your recovery now be a speedy one. You know that the heartfelt wishes of myself and my wife are with you in your convalescence.

Your

B.

830.    Holstein to Bernhard von Bülow
        Copy

Berlin, 1 July 1904

I request Your Excellency to be good enough to initiate my retirement with pension.

Holstein
*Wirklicher Geheimer Rat*

831.    Holstein to Marie von Bülow
        Copy

In hospital, Johannisstrasse 11
Berlin, 1 July 1904

Dear Countess,

First of all my heartfelt thanks for your kind enquiry. I am well.

Secondly, I want to say good-bye to you. I am resigning.

Already a little while ago I had spoken to you of my wish to leave. Recent events have strengthened this feeling and I have submitted my resignation to-day.

## 832. Otto Hammann to Holstein

1 July 1904

Dear Baron,

I would have come round to see you again if the discussion had not been prolonged until 7 :30.

The Chancellor immediately spoke of your to-day's resignation request, and I told him that you had informed me of the exchange of letters.[1] He was very angry and hurt. There were no grounds for the [resignation] request, his letter to you had been anything but unfriendly, and in fact he had always and particularly recently proved his friendship for and confidence in you. He had described the situation absolutely correctly in his letter, a change in the Foreign Ministry would certainly not be confined to the post of State Secretary. You were doing R[icht-hofen] an all the greater injustice as he had also spoken with great sympathy of your operation in Kiel.

My impression which I stated and which he confirmed was :

(1) that the Chancellor had not in any way intended to separate himself from you on his initiative;

(2) that in view of the difficulties with H.M. he wants to maintain R. in his position, and that therefore, should you no longer wish to work with R. and uphold your resignation request he would grant it.

I would also like to mention that he would not admit your objection regarding lack of support, and referred to the fact that only a fortnight ago he had expressed his full agreement with your proposals concerning Morocco.[2]

In spite of that I don't want to believe in a separation and I continue to hope that some other way out will be found.

As ever respectfully

Your

Hammann

## 833. Bernhard von Bülow to Holstein

Berlin, 2 July 1904

Dear Holstein,

I have received your communication.[3] I cannot separate myself over-night from such an old friend, who is so close to me, either politically or personally. I must therefore reserve the right not to deal with your resignation until the next time I am in Berlin, which will probably be some time this month.

I had looked forward to visiting you in hospital and bringing you my wife's best wishes. But in view of the abrupt manner you showed towards me I must refrain from doing so and also fear that I would not be welcome.

For my part, as ever

Your

B.

[1] Holstein's letter to Bülow of 25 June and Bülow's reply of 29 June. See above.

[2] Probably Holstein's memorandum of 3 June 1904. (*Grosse Politik*, vol. XXi, no. 6521, pp. 207–9.)

[3] Of 1 July. See above.

### 834. Marie von Bülow to Holstein

Norderney, 4 July [1904]

My dear friend,

Your letter[1] made me *very sad*, and astonished me. I do not understand how you could suddenly reach such a vital decision, and although I
am not an *official* personage, I believe that—due to self-inflicted pain—
you wanted to hurt us by leaving!!

I can say one thing to you in all sincerity—Bernhard has felt the
truest friendship for you since I have known him. Think of one thing,
we all love you and respect you. If my mother were here, she would say
the same to you.

In true friendship
Marie Bülow.

### 835. Holstein to Marie von Bülow
Copy

B[erlin], 5 July 1904

Dear Countess,

Your kind letter grieved me, for it renders the inevitable harder for
me.

The events in question are briefly the following. Richthofen is sloppy
in his work and leaves matters lying around too long. Thus, in the
spring he left fifty letters addressed to Princes which had to be signed by
the Kaiser lying around in his place, and they only reached the Kaiser on
the day of his departure for the Mediterranean. He was absolutely livid
about this, wrote a terribly rude marginal note and later said on board:
'Those swine in the Foreign Ministry gave me a few hours work on the
very day of departure.'

Klehmet, Rosen,[2] Reischach,[3] Redern[4] and a number of others were
present when the Kaiser made this remark. And all of us had the good
Richthofen to thank for this unpleasantness. Such remarks are well
designed to spoil one's job for one. But in addition I myself had
difficulties with Richthofen because of his lack of punctuality. He only
came to the Ministry irregularly, some days not at all, but screamed if
urgent matters, for example an 'immediate' enquiry by the Chancellor,
were settled by Hammann and myself without him, Richthofen. I
finally wrote to the Chancellor and explained to him the inefficiency
resulting from Richthofen's irresponsibility and sloppiness. Please, ask
to be shown my letter of 25 June—dictated in hospital.

I had expected that Bülow would say something to Richthofen, such
as: 'Please ensure that such unpleasantness with the Kaiser does not
recur. Do your work a bit more conscientiously, and there'll no longer be

---

[1] Of 1 July. See above.

[2] Friedrich Rosen. *Vortragender Rat* in the Foreign Ministry, 1901–5; Minister in Tangier, 1905–10.

[3] Hugo, Baron von Reischach. Court Marshal to Kaiserin Friedrich; Master of the Horse to Wilhelm II from 1905.

[4] Count Wilhelm von Redern, the diplomat, now on indefinite leave of absence.

any friction between you and Holstein. If—contrary to expectations—this should not turn out to be the case, tell me about it.'

Instead of that Bülow in his reply to me has passed over in complete silence the shortcomings in the Ministry and the considerable unpleasantness which has already sprung therefrom. He censures me for my complaint, and says that if I can't work with Richthofen there is no way out but my resignation, and that moreover the Kaiser would like to make some changes of personnel in the Foreign Ministry.

After that I shall of course leave. It is a glorious victory for Richthofen over myself; when at the time of the renewal of the Triple Alliance I had a dispute with Bülow on a matter of official business, Lichnowsky said to me one day: 'As you know, I am not a tell-tale, but I can't say that of everybody in the Ministry.' And some time later the Prince again said something similar.

Of you, dear Countess, I shall always think, also after the separation, with warm regard.

Your devoted servant,
Holstein.

836.    Holstein to Otto Hammann[1]
Copy

Berlin, 6 July 1904

Dear Colleague,

Your letter with the Chancellor's message[2] was posted on the 2nd, but only reached me on the evening of the 4th after a detour via the hospital. Yesterday I expected you in vain, and I am therefore answering now in writing to prevent further delay.

The point which stands out both in the message you transmitted and in the other statements by the Chancellor is that Count Bülow passes over in silence the disorderly and dilatory way of transacting business in the Foreign Ministry, which was the main subject of the letter I addressed to the Chancellor on 25 June. Yet it was precisely this dilatoriness which earned the Ministry a rebuke from the Kaiser of such severity that the person or persons bound to feel themselves affected by it could well think of resigning. It might have been expected that after receiving my letter the Chancellor would have said to the State Secretary who was just then present in Kiel: 'A repetition of such rebukes from the Kaiser as that concerning the fifty replies which were delayed must be prevented. Why don't you clear your desk every day, as I do, and stick more or less to office hours. Then there'll be no more friction between you and Holstein; if there should be any nevertheless, tell me about it.'

There is no hint in the various statements by the Chancellor that he has occupied himself at all with the objective problem. He has not said

[1] Published in Hammann, *Bilder aus der letzten Kaiserzeit* (Berlin, 1922), pp. 31–2. On the same day Holstein wrote to Hammann: 'My letter to you of this morning is the reply to a message from the Chancellor [of 1 July] which you transmitted and should therefore be forwarded to him. At this psychological moment I believe that loyalty demands complete frankness.' (Hammann, *Bilder*, p. 32.)

[2] Of 1 July. See above.

either that the dilatoriness has been exaggerated or that the matter is to be examined. All that is said is that if I could not work with Richthofen, I would have to go; furthermore, that the Kaiser would like to make a number of changes in the Foreign Ministry, which means that he would also like to see someone else take my place. On this latter point I would like to say a few words. For more than a quarter of a century I have sat in my office, have not gone to Court or sought to push myself forward. If, as the Chancellor has hinted, His Majesty should have been pre-judiced against me, Count Bülow could undoubtedly have influenced him in my favour during the past seven years. During this time I have had to produce untold major pieces of work, which could perhaps have brought H.M. to the view that I was a useful member of the Foreign Ministry. But what happened to all the memoranda prepared by myself and my colleagues on pending political problems? Only rarely and in excep-tional cases was one of them sent as a direct report to the Kaiser. A few others perhaps were used in private letters from the Chancellor to His Majesty. But the great majority wandered into the files. No wonder that the Kaiser has gradually got used to the idea regarding this un-productive Foreign Ministry with its present staff as an ossified structure, which the Chancellor is stupidly dragging along with him like a ball and chain.

Since the Chancellor has completely ignored the objective aspect of my representations, I will in a few days time take up again the matter of my resignation of 1 July, unless it has been settled in the meantime. Under the given circumstances there is no doubt that it will be accepted. There is equally no doubt of the attacks and suspicious speculations which will be directed against me from the well-known hostile quarters on the occasion of my sudden leaving. I shall then defend myself as best I can with all the means at my disposal. There will be no need to take personal considerations into account; there is no need to mention that I will not endanger any state secrets. In any case these latter are not involved in this dispute.

With sincere respect, dear colleague<br>Your very devoted<br>H.

837.   Arthur von Huhn[1] to Holstein

[July 1904]

Your Excellency,

I must inform you that Hammann is in a great quandary as to whether he should send on your letter[2] to the Chancellor, as he is not clear as to its impression and success, and on the whole thinks that it will produce an unfavourable impression. In particular he is worried about the passage which reproaches the Chancellor with an unjustified omission because he failed to submit the work of the *Räte*.

[1] Berlin representative of the *Kölnische Zeitung*.
[2] Holstein's first letter to Hammann of 6 July. See above.

Could this passage possibly be left out?

Could Your Excellency reach an agreement on this point with Herr Hammann *direct*, also on whether the letter—with or without omission —should be sent on by him to the Chancellor. Without being *specifically* empowered and instructed to do so he does not want to take the responsibility. I did actually tell him that it was obvious that you wished the letter to be transmitted to the Chancellor, but he is still concerned— evidently because he fears that by transmitting it he will not do good, but harm.

Respectfully as ever<br>
Your Excellency's most devoted<br>
Huhn.

## 838. Holstein to Bernhard von Bülow
Copy

Berlin, 10 July 1904

In view of imminent departure I request Your Excellency to deal quickly with my resignation, dated 1 July.

Holstein<br>
*Wirklicher Geheimer Rat*

## 839. Otto Hammann to Holstein

11 July 1904

Dear Baron,

I was very sorry to have missed you. But probably I would not have been able to change your mind either. More's the pity! Your express letter leads me to believe this.[1] This is an unhappy situation, in which I do not know what to advise. Huhn informed you of the official parts of the last letter of the Chancellor. In order to prevent any unnecessary bitterness I would like to cite the one personal passage word for word: 'No one is more willing than I to acknowledge H.'s great qualities, achievements and deserts. There are not many people who wish him better, and certainly very few who have held him in such sincere friendship.' There follows a complaint that these feelings are not recognized. I do believe he really means this.

Your 'farewell' touches me deeply. Whatever may happen, I do hope that the connection won't be completely broken and that you will preserve your, often proven, friendly sentiments towards me.

Respectfully as ever<br>
Your<br>
Hammann.

[1] In a letter to Hammann of 11 July Holstein wrote:

'I have been told that you were here. In order to save both parties unnecessary trouble, I would like to tell you the following:

'The present acute incident has its good sides. For reasons into which I do not want to enter here Germany's prestige has shrunk in the last few years, while our opponents and rivals are on the point of encircling us. Difficult situations must therefore be expected to arise for which I would prefer not to take the share of moral responsibility which every collaborator bears. That's why I am saying farewell to you.' (Hammann, *Bilder*, p. 33.)

### 840. Holstein to Hugo von Radolin[1]

Berlin, 5 August 1904

Dear Radolin,

I was sorry to hear yesterday that you intend to sail on a cruise from Cherbourg, so that it is quite uncertain when you'll be coming. Under these circumstances I must tell you something which I had hitherto kept from you in order not to spoil your trip. I got angry at something, have submitted my resignation and will go my way. By the time you arrive, my problem, delayed by H.M.'s absence, will already have been decided. There is no doubt that H.M. will accept my resignation, for evidently several people have been working on him against me. I therefore regard the matter as settled.[2] [...]

Best regards [...]

### 841. Holstein to Otto von Mühlberg
Copy

Berlin, 11 August 1904

Dear Mühlberg,

To-day I am sending off a reminder about my resignation. Please let the matter take its course. I would finally like to thank you very sincerely for the friendly sentiments of which you have repeatedly given proof in regard to my resignation. I am saying farewell to you in writing to save us both a useless discussion.

I wish you a happy holiday,

In friendship as ever,
Holstein.

---

[1] From the Radolin Papers.

[2] On 13 August Radolin had a conversation with Kaiser Wilhelm II at Wilhelmshöhe. In a memorandum on this conversation Radolin wrote: 'I then remarked: "Your Majesty probably already knows that poor Holstein had an operation for cataract. It was successful, but unfortunately he wants to resign." The Kaiser replied: "I thought he had left a long time ago, that he had retired at seventy. I have not heard his name for the past six years." I mentioned that he was only sixty-six and very fit. He was after all the political soul of the Ministry. He lived only for that and saw only very few people. He had heard a long time ago, under former Chancellors, not now, and it had been suggested to him, that his superiors would not like it if he appeared at Court because it would create difficulties for them if he saw H.M. Holstein had also decided not to meet the Ambassadors any more, in order not to embarrass his superiors. He had so submerged himself in his work that he did not even own a dress suit any more. He, Radolin, was telling His Majesty all this because he had heard that H.M. had taken umbrage because Holstein had never come to see the Kaiser. But if Holstein now resigned, it would, he believed, make him very happy to be received by His Majesty, if only to afford him the opportunity to give proof of his loyal affection and to disprove the insinuations that this was a matter of indifference to him. H.M. had in him a servant faithful as few were, and he would not be easily replaced in the Ministry. The Kaiser replied: "I hadn't heard anything about all this, but I will write to tell Bülow that he should not be allowed to leave after his operation." When he asked why Holstein wanted to leave, I replied that the reason was that he no longer felt he was trusted as heretofore and that younger officials were preferred to him when it came to dealing with confidential matters. His status had been lowered, and if he did not meet with confidence he felt insulted.'

In another memorandum on his conversation with the Kaiser, Radolin wrote: 'I also remarked that Tschirschky too had heard that Holstein was being dropped because the Kaiser

842. Holstein to Bernhard von Bülow
Copy

Berlin 11 August 1904

May I request Your Excellency once again to deal with my resignation, dated 1 July.

Holstein.

843. Holstein to Otto von Mühlberg
Copy

Berlin, 15 August 1904

Dear Mühlberg,

I am truly sorry that I am making your life so difficult, for your sake, not mine.

Two points have in the meantime been clarified :

(1) that the Kaiser had had no intention of pushing me out, for he could barely be persuaded not to write to the Chancellor himself that my eye-operation was no reason to let me go.

(2) that the Kaiser will receive me, even after I have left, if I request an audience. I shall then be able to submit to him the brief and unambiguous correspondence which led to my going.

At my age there is not much difference whether I go to-day or in two years' time. But the knowledge as to whether I left because of Richthofen or because of my Kaiser's displeasure does make a tremendous difference to me. It is natural that I should wish to clarify this point, it is actually a duty towards myself. So you can see, I won't escape the dress suit.[1]

With best wishes for your leave and all the future, and my regards,

Your old comrade

Holstein.

no longer took any interest in him. Whereupon the Kaiser replied : "But, my dear Radolin, you know me well enough to be aware that Holstein could always have come to see me; I no longer heard of his existence." Whereupon the Kaiser called Tschirschky to join us and asked : "What's all this about Holstein; why does he want to go? I have nothing to do with this." Tschirschky replied : "No, of course not. The reason probably is that he feels that his superiors, i.e. the Chancellor, no longer regard him as an essential prop as in former times." "That's something I can do nothing about", said H.M., "what actually is his position in the Ministry?" "Well, he is a *Vortragender Rat*, like Klehmet, nothing more." I intervened and said : "But he has an exceptional position as *homme de confiance* and as the best mind." Whereupon Tschirschky remarked : "He has in fact a first-class mind and he produces all the memoranda. But it is the Chancellor who finds him wanting, I myself have the greatest respect for him." The Kaiser then said : "Well, I shall write to Bülow that Holstein is not to go yet. But in the last resort it is up to the Chancellor to keep his people or let them go." Whereupon H.M. shook hands with me and left.

'Tschirschky said to me that there was nothing to be done with Bülow. All he knew was how to talk with H.M. Policy varied constantly. [...] Bülow hadn't said anything yet about Holstein; but in the long run things wouldn't work any more between him and Holstein. He did not always approve of his policy and his advice and overrode them.' (From the Radolin Papers. Published in Friedrich Thimme, 'Aus dem Nachlass des Fürsten Radolin. Fürst Radolin, Holstein, und Friedrich Rosen,' *Berliner Monatshefte*, vol. XV, 1937, pp. 751–3.)

[1] Holstein had heretofore always refused invitations to Court on the grounds that he owned no dress suit.

844.   Bernhard von Bülow to Holstein

Norderney, 18 August 1904

Dear friend,

From your letter of the 13th of this month,[1] submitted to me by Mühlberg, I see to my regret that you are sticking to your idea as regards leaving.  I cannot regard the reasons which you have given me through Mühlberg and Hammann for your resignation as valid.  I still do not want to give up hope that you will, after quiet reflection, make it possible for me to preserve your distinguished service to the Reich in the future.  At any rate, before dealing with your resignation I would like to have a conversation with you, as would seem to me natural and indicated in view of our long-standing good and close relations.  I hope to see you in October, and I shall then try to find a solution to the conflict in a form which leaves no scars on any side.

My wife and I wish you with all our hearts continued convalescence and a good recovery.  I am, as ever

Your

B.


845.   Holstein to Bernhard von Bülow
Copy

Berlin, 19 August 1904

Dear Bülow,

I had the honour of receiving your letter of yesterday.

The earlier letter,[2] which you sent to me in hospital a few days after the operation and in which I was informed that the Kaiser would wish to get rid of me when an opportunity offered, leaves a gentleman no alternative but to interpret it as a *consilium abeundi*.

But apart from that the unpleasant conditions in the Ministry, whose improvement cannot be expected, which on the contrary I see getting even more unpleasant in the future, would have caused me to leave.

I would therefore ask you to pass on my resignation.

Most sincerely
Your
Holstein.


846.   Holstein to Bernhard von Bülow
Copy

Berlin, 19 August 1904

I must report to Your Excellency that the condition of my eye prevents me from undertaking any official activity during the interval until my resignation has been dealt with.  I am therefore leaving for a lengthy stay in a holiday resort.

Holstein.

[1] Not found.  Holstein's letter to Mühlberg of 15 August may be meant.
[2] Of 29 June.  See above.

847.   Holstein to Friedrich von Pourtalès
       Draft

Berlin, 20 August 1904

Dear Pourtalès,

You have in times past stood by me as a friend in difficult circumstances and you can therefore expect that now too I should take your advice seriously.

My attitude regarding my resignation is not attributable to a single cause. Quite a number of things came together. Have you in fact read the letter which Hammann wrote to me on the Chancellor's instructions?[1] I think not and therefore enclose a copy. What would you do if such a message were delivered to you in such a form. I think I can guess.[2]

I leave it to you, no matter whether my affair has been settled or not by the time you arrive in Norderney, whether you want to mention this point to the Chancellor if he touches upon the matter with you.

Best regards

H.


848.   Holstein to Hugo von Radolin[3]

Sunday, [21 August 1904][4]

Dear Radolin,

Thank you most sincerely for your offer to undertake the ungrateful task of a mediator. You would, however, thereby act directly contrary to my intentions. Evidently you and the Princess have no idea *how* unpleasant my job has been made for quite some time now. And the last incident broke the camel's back. I don't want a patched-up peace, I would rather go. You needn't think that I am overwrought. On the contrary, I am absolutely calm and looking at things as they really are. Why should I expose myself to the possible recurrence of this incredibly undignified treatment just to remain two or three more years in the service?

If Bülow really wants to remedy matters, my last letter[5] left it open for him to do so; it actually hinted where the shoe was pinching. But I doubt whether Bülow is serious, and in that case it would be much better not to enter into *pourparlers* at all. [...]

Holstein.


849.   Bernhard von Bülow to Holstein

Norderney, 23 August 1904

Dear Holstein,

Many thanks for your letter of the 19th of this month. From it I see

---

[1] Of 1 July. See above.

[2] At this point in his draft Holstein crossed out the words: 'You can also tell this to the Chancellor if the matter hasn't been decided by then and he starts to talk about it.'

[3] From the Radolin Papers.

[4] Thimme in *Berliner Monatshefte*, 1937, p. 754, dates this letter 14 August, but the envelope shows the date to be 21 August.

[5] Of 19 August.

that you misunderstood my letter from Kiel.[1] My letter did not contain anything about His Majesty wishing to remove you. I had merely pointed out that as sudden a change in the post of State Secretary as you had demanded from me could lead to simultaneous changes in the composition of the Foreign Ministry, which for objective reasons I regarded as undesirable. This statement was in no way a *consilium abeundi*, but a friendly request *quieta non movere*.

As regards the second part of your letter, I am convinced that an objective and calm approach could restore the same peaceful co-operation in the Foreign Ministry as existed, thank goodness, until recently.

I continue to hope that the differences of opinion which now exist will be settled by verbal discussion after my return. With sincere wishes from myself and my wife for complete recovery, I am

Your sincerely devoted

B.

850.    Friedrich von Pourtalès to Holstein

Berlin, 28 August 1904

Dear friend,

[...] I had really secretly hoped to find you still here when I returned from Norderney on Wednesday. But on Thursday I was told at your flat that you had already left on Monday. Since then I have been intending to write to you every day. I already told you the other day that it was my intention to tell the Chancellor that I had the impression that the sentence in his Kiel letter regarding possible changes in the Foreign Ministry *'in capite et membris'* had hurt you especially. I did so when the opportunity offered. Bülow did not hesitate a moment before stating that you had completely misunderstood this sentence. He had never even thought of hinting to you that H.M. would like to remove you. He had actually merely wanted to point out that if there was a change in the post of State Secretary, the Kaiser might easily get the idea of 'bringing fresh blood' into the Foreign Ministry, i.e. of introducing undesirable elements. If, as I assume, Bülow has made this statement to you, you would in my opinion be wrong in continuing to refuse the offered discussion. Such a discussion would not hinder you from finally taking that decision which seemed best to you. Thus, if I may permit myself a piece of advice which I hope you will regard as friendly and well meant, it is that you should not *now* insist on your resignation being accepted, but that you should accept the proposal to discuss the matter with the Chancellor in October.

I have now offered my car for sale, so that at least until next spring this need not be a separating factor between us.

I forgot to mention that Countess Bülow repeatedly asked me to give you her best regards, in case I should still meet you here.

With best wishes for a good holiday in the Harz.

Your most sincerely devoted

F. Pourtalès

[1] Of 29 June. See above.

851.   Holstein to Friedrich von Pourtalès
       Copy

Dammhaus, 29 August 1904

Dear Pourtalès,

Your letter, just received, surprised me, for I had thought that matters had moved further. But I, to whom once you gave such good advice, am not going to end up by causing you any unpleasantness. Thus I will not insist any more, but for the present will keep completely quiet. But I am looking on the situation without any illusions.

First of all, I have not received the communication from the Chancellor of which you write. I therefore cannot make any comment. Please under all circumstances submit the copy of Hammann's letter to me,[1] which you have, to the Chancellor. As a man of the world, he must understand what impression *that* letter, as an *interpretatio authentica* of his letter, made on me. After that, a definition of *caput et membra* is unavoidable if I am to remain in the Service. Otherwise I would have to be ashamed of myself, and that is something I do not intend.

But this is the easy part of the task, for the Chancellor can, if he in fact wants to, give a quite clear and yet informal interpretation, without in any way losing any of his dignity. Much more difficult is a settlement of the official situation. When Bülow became Chancellor, he intended to conduct high policy with my assistance, and what has become of that to-day? He confides everything to Richthofen and Hammann and I sit in a corner. It is already a great deal if I am called in as the third, fourth, or fifth. I am too old to be pushed aside like that. Nobody has ever been able to say, unless he was lying, that at any time of my life I was after anybody else's position. But on the other hand I don't want to be the suffering lamb that puts up with everything, and when I see that that is what it comes to, I shall make the irrevocable break, be it in six days', be it in six months' time. In Kiel it was being said—I know this *definitely* —: 'Holstein is leaving, he is through.' Whoever said that was in a sense right.

With a cordial handshake
Holstein.

852.   Holstein to Johanna von Radolin[2]

Dammhaus, 30 August 1904

Dear Princess,

As my eye is paining me, I will only write briefly. Many, many thanks for your generous good-will which has once again found expression in your letter to-day.

Pourtalès wrote to tell me that Bülow wants to negotiate further.[3] A registered letter from the Chancellor arrived at my flat yesterday, but went back because my address was not known. In view of this change in the situation I have held back a letter to you, which was all ready to go and stamped, because in it I had treated the matter as settled.

---

[1] Of 1 July. See above.     [2] From the Radolin Papers.
[3] Letter of 28 August. See above.

Now we have to wait. After the experiences I have had I am awaiting a decision calmly and without illusions, may it go one way or the other. [...]

I kiss your hand,<br>
Respectfully<br>
Holstein.

It would be better not to talk of my affair except with Radolin.

### 853.  Friedrich von Pourtalès to Holstein

Berlin, 31 August 1904

Dear friend,

Thank you for your letters of the 29th and 30th of this month and two telegrams which I have received.

Unfortunately I must confess to you that I have left the copy of Hammann's letter, which was sent on to me to Munich, securely locked in my desk. I had locked up this document so as not to leave it lying around, and intended to take it with me when I left. My departure from Munich, immediately after Lichnowsky's wedding reception,[1] had to be in a great rush, and thus I unfortunately forgot to take the letter with me. But I had memorized the contents thoroughly, and did mention the letter to the Chancellor in Norderney.

Now, permit me to express to you once again my opinion that as far as you are concerned the situation has been changed by Bülow's statement that with 'changes in *capite et membris*' he had not meant what you read into it. The Chancellor is standing by his proposal that you should discuss the matter in October, and in my opinion you have no reason to turn down such a discussion.

I would think it best if you accepted the Chancellor's proposal and reserved yourself the right to bring up your various *gravamina* during this discussion. I must admit openly that it would not seem indicated to me if you were now to make all sorts of written requests concerning the work arrangements of the Ministry. Probably Bülow would not like to make any new work arrangements, etc., in the Ministry without having consulted the State Secretary, and that is something for which *au fond* you cannot blame him. I have the impression that Bülow honestly wishes to keep you in the Ministry. In my opinion you should not make it too difficult for him to find a solution to the existing difficulties. If it should not be possible to arrive at a result satisfactory to you at the discussion in October, there will still be time enough for you to say : I don't like this any more, I prefer to insist on my resignation. I would therefore advise against pressing the Chancellor to any decisions now. As regards my mediation, in my opinion this had to be confined to my pointing out to the Chancellor that you had felt deeply hurt by some phrase in his letter from Kiel[2] and that, should you possibly have

---

[1] Prince Lichnowsky was married to Mechtilde, Countess von Arco-Zinneberg, on 22 August in Munich.

[2] Of 29 June.

misinterpreted this phrase, it would perhaps be advisable to clear up the misunderstanding which had arisen. But I would like to submit to your consideration whether, as regards your further wishes, it would not be better to submit these to the Chancellor direct and by word of mouth in October, rather than through myself, as I am only temporarily working in the Foreign Ministry. I hope you will be in no doubt that I am raising this question only in your own interests.

If you do insist on it, I am of course ready to submit your letters to me to the Chancellor, but I do think that the method of dealing with the matter which I have suggested is preferable. [...]

> With best regards
> Most sincerely
> Your
> F. Pourtalès

854. Holstein to Bernhard von Bülow
    Copy

Dammhaus bei Clausthal, 5 September 1904

Dear Bülow,

It was kind of you to come back once again to the question of my staying, and I am grateful, no matter how it will all end.

I would like to say, merely as a correction, that I never demanded Richthofen's removal, but merely posed the question whether a change *in modo* or *in persona* would not be advisable. I don't remember the actual wording, but I do remember the sense of my letter exactly. We were in any case faced with this alternative of a change *in modo* or *in persona*—that is, my person. For the Kiel incident did not change anything in the situation in one way, namely in that it was clear to me, already before I went to hospital, that I would bring the question of my staying or leaving to a decision this autumn. My official position is an abnormal one. It is undefined, unrecognized, and therefore difficult to defend. Yet I am absolutely determined not to allow myself to be brought down in my old age to the official level of young men like Rosen and Kriege,[1] as has been attempted with noticeable effort particularly since this spring.

In Kiel it was being said—I know this definitely—: 'Holstein is leaving, he is through.' The man who said that was in a sense right. It had been my intention to have my operation for cataract at the start of my normal leave period, in the second half of August, but following some particularly insulting incident I reported myself sick already at the end of June, firmly determined to settle the matter in the autumn.

If I don't want to pursue the matter further now, it is not only because of my eye, but also because I share your belief that it may perhaps be easier for us to understand each other and reach agreement in a verbal discussion. If that doesn't prove successful, I shall in any case only leave eighteen months earlier than I had intended, for I wasn't going to

---

[1] Johannes Kriege. *Vortragender Rat* in the Foreign Ministry, 1900–11.

stay after I was over seventy anyway. One should not wait until *others* think the time has come.

Thus I am at your disposal from October onwards, and I would be particularly grateful if you would let me know *the day before* by a note from your office—which could possibly be forwarded to me by telegram from my flat—when you will receive me. I would not refuse a discussion *à trois*, although I could not foretell how that would go.

Please express my humble gratitude to the Princess, who was kind enough to send me her regards also through Pourtalès.

In the hope that your holiday will fulfill its purpose in spite of the somewhat frequent interruptions,

I remain

Your completely devoted

H.

855.    Holstein to Hugo von Radolin[1]

Dammhaus über Klaustal

Monday morning, 5 September 1904

Dear Radolin,

[...] The letter from B[ülow] finally arrived.[2] B. says that I misunderstood the passage concerning H.M., it had been meant in such and such a way. Then he again suggests that we should discuss the difficulties on official matters in October.

I have thought over the matter for a few days in peace and quiet, and have replied to-day. The letter has just left, I have agreed to the proposed discussion. Apart from that I merely hinted briefly that I cannot accept the situation in the Ministry as it has recently developed. I have not mentioned the earlier statement concerning H.M. any more.

I will now await the result of the discussion in complete calm, as it is after all only a matter of eighteen months. But I shall always be grateful to you and the Princess for your heartfelt sympathy. [...]

Now, as regards Tsch[irschky],[3] it is quite possible that he made a timid attempt and that H.M. possibly replied: 'First of all the chap can come to report to me in person, I am certainly not going to run after him.' The remark: 'You know that I am there if someone wants to see me', sounded a bit like that. It is not really to be expected that H.M. should now be particularly cordial after I have always avoided him. And naturally there will have been plenty of people to agitate. Now that B. has given a different interpretation to the sentence I objected to, one can decently wait and see how the discussion will go for a start.

There is nothing to report about my lonely existence. I am reading one newspaper and try to discover from it what goes on in politics. I don't think that our future is going to become easier, standing between England, France, and Japan—a group united by a common hatred of Germany.

---

[1] From the Radolin Papers.    [2] Of 23 August. See above.
[3] See p. 298, note 2.

Now, cheerio. Best regards to the Princess. The eye starts watering rather easily and still requires care. It will definitely stay weaker than the other one.

In friendship as ever,
Your
Holstein.

Yesterday afternoon I walked for six hours, uphill, downhill, without food, drink, or a rest. I wasn't really tired afterwards but had a twinge of lumbago. Somehow old age will make itself felt. [...]

## 856.   Bernhard von Bülow to Holstein

Homburg v.d.H.,
17 September 1904

Dear Holstein,

I have one particular objection to your letter of the 5th of this month, and that is that you have not told us how you are. That was the first question which my wife asked me when I gave her your kind regards. I do hope from my heart that your silence on this point is a good sign.

I am now convinced that I misunderstood the letter you sent to Kiel,[1] just as you interpreted some phrases in my reply[2] other than I had meant them.

I hope that now the personal misunderstanding has been cleared up and that a verbal discussion will lead to agreement, which I desire if only in the interests of the Service. In any case I shall inform you of my arrival before my final return to Berlin.

With our best wishes, in which Donna Laura, who arrived here yesterday, joins wholeheartedly,

Your sincerely devoted
B.

## 857.   Holstein to Bernhard von Bülow
    Copy

Dammhaus bei Claustal, 19 September 1904

Dear Bülow,

Many thanks for your kind enquiry. I received your letter in the evening after returning from the Brocken, which means nine to ten hours solid walking. I had already been up there three times in these last weeks. The view isn't worth the effort, but the various routes there are strangely beautiful, and also I am walking as much as possible in order to read little. The new eye is becoming usable, but it is weaker than the other one and waters easily. Probably the doctor who operated is to blame because he did not insist on sufficient care immediately after the operation. I then prescribed this care for myself when I saw how things were going. [...]

As regards the matter which has hitherto formed the subject of our correspondence, we can now presumably regard the personal aspect as

---

[1] Of 25 June.          [2] Of 29 June.

clarified. But I am under no illusions regarding the difficulty of settling the objective question, on which one will be met with a determined *parti pris*. Richthofen's—authentic—remark to someone who had expressed his regrets at my leaving : 'Well, if Holstein had died business would still have to carry on', pictures the situation. And the realization that I am unwelcome and in the way to more than one person is not designed to increase my desire to stay.

With best regards
Your very devoted
H.

### 858.   Holstein to Hugo von Radolin[1]

Dammhaus, 20 September 1904

Dear Radolin,

[...] Please don't mention anything of the above[2] to anyone. A letter from a journalist which I received four days ago leads me to assume that the Richthofen side would like to know exactly how matters stand between Bülow and myself. B., when passing through, only told Hammann that he had written to me repeatedly, that I had harked back to my resignation and that his hopes rested on the discussion. In fact the situation as it now stands is that after his written interpretation of this critical passage in his letter of 29 June the only point of difference between Bülow and myself may be regarded as settled. That only leaves the official causes of friction with Richthofen. The latter will object to any changes. I for my part will demand only small changes, but insist on those. But there is no need for the opposition—to which Hammann and, I feel, also Tschirschky belong—to know all this. Therefore silence in the Ministry. I shall be in Berlin on the 29th. A bow to the Princess.

Your old
H. [...]

### 859.   Bernhard von Bülow to Holstein[3]

[October, 1904]

Yesterday's conversation with R[ichthofen] was difficult. It was not because R. is hostile to you—I can truthfully assure you that not a single unfriendly word about you passed his lips—but because he regarded the possibility that some of the responsibility for the signature of political documents should be taken from him as so great a *capitis diminutio* that he stated he would then not be able to stay on. I had been right in thinking that his satisfaction with his present position was not as complete as is widely assumed, and his desire for a quiet and independent post is much greater than I had believed. Even my mention of his sons did not make any very deep impression, for R. believes that Schoen,

---

[1] From the Radolin Papers.

[2] In the earlier part of this letter Holstein had summarized Bülow's letter of 17 September and his own of 19 September.

[3] This undated extract of a letter from Bülow in the Holstein Papers is headed : 'Copy of the personal part'. The original has not been found. Bülow's talk with Richthofen took place in Homburg after his discussion with Holstein. (See below, p. 311, note 1.)

Tschirschky or Schlözer—with whom he is on good terms personally—would not treat his descendents any worse than he would himself. After a long and difficult discussion I finally succeeded in obtaining the assurance that R. would stay in the Service, even if I authorized you to sign certain outgoing documents; that he would be forthcoming with regard to the number and importance of these documents; but he requested that Mühlberg's agreement should be obtained beforehand, as he did not want to offend. R. stated most definitely that he wanted you to remain and that he would gladly work with you in a friendly manner; it was far from his mind to create difficulties for you. How would it be if you were to arrange the matter *à trois* with Mühlberg and R.? But I am convinced that you could now also reach an understanding with R. direct in half an hour, if, with the tact and intelligence which are always, and your kindness which is sometimes such a feature of yours, you avoid anything which would humiliate R. before the Ministry and the public. It would be a great satisfaction to me if future co-operation between yourself and R. could be achieved, which I regard not only as possible but even as not particularly difficult, and at the same time useful to the Ministry as to the country.

Your visit to Homburg was a real joy to us. We often think back to our beautiful walks and interesting conversation and only regret that you did not stay longer.

With the kindest regards from my wife and Donna Laura and our best wishes for your health I am

Your truly devoted

860.    Holstein to Bernhard von Bülow
        Copy

Berlin, 15 October 1904

Dear Bülow,

[...] Richthofen will become reasonable and stop playing the wild man as soon as he understands that by leaving the post where he is useful to you he will not establish his claim to a pleasant sinecure but rather lose it. (It is after all unthinkable that Lucanus should take a stand for R. against you in the matter.) If you are unable to get anywhere with Richthofen with such a trump in your hand, my negotiating with him would be all the more hopeless. In that case the immediate establishment of the post of Political Director and a telegraphic recall of Mumm would be indicated. But as I already said in the detailed exposition, R. will yield as soon as he realizes how serious the matter is. Mumm would have the advantage from your point of view that he would keep Ri. in order, or rather pass over him to the order of the day. I can't do that because my bureaucratic basis is too narrow. But R. must be kept in order, for he lacks the feeling for the essential consideration in official matters as well as a sense of duty. Yesterday I heard it said that recently he spent two whole successive afternoons chatting and drinking tea at Frau von Körner's,[1] while the Ministry was waiting.

[1] Probably the wife of the Director of the Economic Policy Division in the Foreign Ministry.

If, contrary to expectations, it should come to it that I leave, I shall have to console myself with the thought that apparently the future brings us little else than suffering for the mistakes previously committed by others.

Now farewell. For the time being I will sulk in my corner near the Kreuzberg awaiting further news from you, which more probably than not will bring the strike to an end. I shall then—*after* he has agreed to my signing the less important and, according to circumstances, urgent documents—be as free and easy with R. as possible, and I think that his most recent experiences will have had an educational effect on him.

If only for humanitarian reasons, could you also say something so that no one would have to wait any longer after 1 :30 p.m. and 7 p.m. You would make yourself popular with the whole Ministry that way. I personally don't care, I work later hours anyway and don't worry.

Please, remember me particularly warmly to the Countess and Donna Laura now that the tents are being struck. I remain with best regards

Your sincerely devoted

Holstein [...]

Richt. is weak and obstinate. I can only repeat again and again that *particularly if* you want to keep him because he is useful in a certain sort of way, you should tackle him firmly from time to time. His main defence whenever he is reprimanded for an oversight is to scream for a sinecure. There is method behind this, as behind his corrections watering down my drafts. But it should be possible to get him out of that habit. [...]

861.    Bernhard von Bülow to Holstein

Berlin, Monday morning,
17 October 1904

Dear Holstein,

[...] I had another and long conversation with R[ichthofen] immediately after my arrival.

The job of being State Secretary in the Foreign Ministry is not, *par les temps qui courent*, so pleasant as to make concern about losing this thorny post a particularly effective means of psychological pressure. I also have the impression that, if only for reasons of health, R. would give up his present post without feeling any pain. Finally R. knows that H.M. is in principle inclined to give sinecures to Ministers and State Secretaries who retire, especially if H.M. has stood in personal relations to them. Under these circumstances there is really not much that can be done by threats. But I did finally succeed in getting R. to agree that he would also meet your wishes in the question of signatures. But above all I succeeded in getting him to agree to co-operate with you *bona fide*. I am enclosing a letter,[1] which I received from him yesterday evening just before midnight.

[1] See enclosure.

Can you come to see me to-day at 6 o'clock? I would like to discuss your memorandum and the political situation in general. [...]

Your truly devoted

B.

Oswald von Richthofen to Bernhard von Bülow

16 October 1904

Your Excellency,

Supplementing what I said to-day I would like to emphasize especially that I for my part am readily prepared to do what I can to preserve the services of His Excellency von Holstein for you, the Ministry and myself. I am particularly quite ready and would in fact gladly bring it about, as it would ease my task in a welcome manner, that Holstein should be given the same full powers of signature for the Political Division (with the exception of the Personnel and Press Departments) as the Directors of Division II and III and the Head of Division IB now enjoy.

Hoping that this will help to achieve the desired end,

Most faithfully

Richthofen.[1]

862.    Memorandum by Holstein[2]

Berlin, 22 October 1904

For Prince Radolin's conversation with the Spanish Ambassador.

England is allowing certain warlike desires to become obvious. This is a new phenomenon in modern politics.

An unmistakable symptom of this desire is the tendency on the part of Japan to look for a quarrel among the European Powers under the pretext of a violation of neutrality. The Japanese Government, with Russia on its hands, would not be trying to fight a third party if it were not certain of English support. The Japanese Press is now taking a menacing tone towards Governments whose citizens have dared to furnish coal to the Russian Baltic Sea fleet. It is absurd, since the sale of English coal to the Japanese has not stopped since the beginning of the war. The

[1] Holstein wrote to his cousin Ida von Stülpn gel on 17 October: 'Two hours ago Bülow wrote me that Richthofen had accepted my conditions, the conflict thus being ended after having lasted four months.

'I had reached agreement with Bülow immediately during our first oral discussion, but Richthofen resisted when Bülow called him to Homburg, and talked of resigning. Yet I stood firm, and thus Bülow settled the matter at once after his return. Personally I am satisfied. But perhaps it would have been better if I had left now, for quite a number of things happen which I can't stop even if I am there! [...]

'Now that the conflict is over, I shall get together the documents connected with it and send them to you to keep. They might while away a rainy day for you—a study of life.' (Rogge, *Friedrich von Holstein*, p. 235.)

[2] The original copy of this document is in the Foreign Ministry files. It bears Bülow's initials and the note: 'Copy handed to Prince Radolin. H[olstein]. 23.10.' The original document is in French, with the exception of the third and fifth paragraphs, which are in German.

Japanese fleets are operating almost exclusively on coal from Cardiff. But in this question as in most international questions one risks making a miscalculation if one calculates with logic alone. What would be the ratio of forces? There is the important question. Now, it is obvious that Germany, which up to the present has no political treaty of any kind with the Russians, would make such an alliance in twenty-four hours if England or Japan wanted to lay down the law to her. Thus the alliance of 1895 would be reformed on a broader basis, because the Franco-Russian alliance is still in existence. The latter would come into force the moment the Russo-Japanese war was no longer localized but was extended to Europe.

In case the Spaniard expresses doubts as to whether France would abandon her neutrality:

The Franco-Russian treaty is still incontestably in force, and on land Germany and Russia together would always be powerful enough to make certain that it was carried out. France could not remain neutral.

To the further remark that France might then go over to the side of England:

Frankly, that is the secret hope—not of our Government, which wants peace—but of the military party. The military are always the same in every country. Only here they have no political influence. The march of events does not depend on them but on England, the Egeria of Japan. If the opposite side feels that such a poor pretext as that of coal is sufficient to justify a conflict, that would prove that they want a fight for its own sake, and that it would be useless for us to try to avoid it.

Holstein[1]

### 863. Holstein to Hugo von Radolin[2]

Berlin, 25 November 1904

Dear Radolin,

At the risk of repeating what you already know, I shall tell you something more of the dinner with the Kaiser.[3]

When I went to the conference, I met Schwartzkoppen[4] at the door who said to me: 'Your Excellency has been asked to dine to-day with His Majesty.' I replied: 'That is out of the question because I haven't got a dress suit.' After the conference I said to Bülow: 'I hear that you were

---

[1] Note by Radolin: 'I have in accordance with my instructions mentioned the contents of the memorandum of . . . , personally handed to me, in a conversation with the Spanish Ambassador, as my interpretation of the probable logical development of the situation.

'The Ambassador found my remarks to be so vitally important that he asked me whether I did not want to repeat them to M. Delcassé. I replied that I had not been instructed to do so. If I had spoken so openly to him, the Ambassador, it had been because I had special confidence in him as a friend.' (From the Radolin Papers.) In another memorandum of 22 October Holstein suggested that Radolin might touch on the same subject (minus the parts about the Franco-Russian treaty) with President Loubet.

[2] From the Radolin Papers.

[3] Holstein dined with the Kaiser on 12 November. (See also Holstein's letter to his cousin Ida von Stülpnagel of 26 November. Rogge, *Friedrich von Holstein*, pp. 236–7.)

[4] Erich von Schwartzkoppen, Bülow's adjutant.

so kind as to suggest my name to the Kaiser. I am very grateful, but can't come, I don't own a dress suit.' Bülow replied: 'That makes it very difficult for me. The Kaiser already said when I suggested you: "He won't come anyway." I shall write to the Kaiser: "Holstein would have been happy to come but he doesn't own a dress suit as he has lived for many years like a hermit." He won't worry at all about the dress suit.' That's how it turned out. When I returned from lunch, I was told H.M. had sent a message that I should come in a frock-coat.

The Kaiser was very kind to me, shook hands and made a joke about the dress suit. I replied: 'Yes, Your Majesty, in six hours I couldn't get one.' After dinner I kept at a distance, while Richthofen continually hung around H.M. When after standing for quite some time H.M. sat down, I was called. The others sitting with H.M. were the Chancellor and Tirpitz. This lasted about three quarters of an hour. H.M. did most of the talking, followed by myself. I also asked him questions repeatedly which he answered in detail. When he left he shook hands with Tirpitz and myself and made a bow to the others present. I do not believe that H.M. has got anything against me after the frank manner in which he behaved.

Naturally I did not come to Court. I won't change my way of life at the age of sixty-seven.

I now regard the incident of the summer as completely settled. It taught me quite a number of things in my old age. And I would like to thank you, dear friend, once again from the bottom of my heart.

The most interesting points on which you could report now, if you find out anything about them, are the conditions of peace and mediation efforts to achieve it.[1] It seems as if the Japanese have given the English to understand that they would welcome a good peace. The Japanese seem to be losing their breath, especially financially. It appears certain that London and Tokyo have been negotiating concerning peace terms acceptable to Japan. The English are trying to interest Washington and Paris in the matter.[2] We don't know what attitude Wash. and Paris are taking on the subject. In fact we only know the little I have just written. Perhaps you can find out something about France's attitude through the Spaniard,[3] Lardy[4] or the American.[5] You can use the above, rather meagre, information for this purpose. If you should speak to the Russian[6] you will have to avoid everything which might lead him to believe that you were trying to arouse suspicion of France. It would be best if to him you only spoke of the English-Japanese negotiations.

Are the Russians in Paris in favour of an early or of a glorious peace? The conclusion of peace will in any case be for Russia what the landing is after a balloon trip: the most dangerous moment. I would definitely

---

[1] In the Russo-Japanese War.

[2] See *Grosse Politik*, vol. XIXii, nos. 6168, 6172, 6271, pp. 388–9, 391–2, 545–6; *British Documents*, vol. IV, no. 57, pp. 64–6.

[3] F. Leon y Castillo.          [4] Swiss Minister in Paris, 1883–1917.

[5] Horace Porter. American Ambassador in Paris, 1897–1905.

[6] Alexander Nelidov.

doubt that they and Japan would be left alone. Doesn't [the Prince of] Monaco or his friend Cohn know anything?

Now farewell. [...]

Your

H.

### 864.   Hugo von Radolin to the Foreign Ministry[1]

TELEGRAM

Paris, 28 November 1904

At yesterday's *soirée* given by the Foreign Minister, the Spanish Ambassador addressed me with his characteristic impetuosity concerning Delcassé's categoric statement in the Chamber on the intention to uphold the Russian alliance.[2] He told me that this was a striking response to the warning which I had given him (the Ambassador) in confidence,[3] and which had made such a deep and lasting impression on Delcassé that he had repeatedly come back to what I had said. 'Your words put a flea in his ear', he remarked, 'he at once understood the gravity of the situation and that it was necessary to emphasize where he stood. This declaration won't please the English.'[4]

In the course of a lengthy conversation with Delcassé, I mentioned his speech in the Chamber and indicated that he had emphasized the Russian alliance. He replied that he always tried hard to ensure clarity and to speak the truth. [...] The American Ambassador yesterday told me in confidence that the English were apparently working for peace in the interests of Japan, and were sounding the ground in Washington in this sense. But there England was not trusted because she preferred to push others to the fore, and so reserve was being maintained. Regarding the possible settlement of hostilities, Delcassé dropped a remark in the course of our conversation to the effect that he would certainly take every care not even to create the impression that he wanted to act as mediator between the belligerents.

Radolin.

### 865.   Holstein to Alfred von Schlieffen[5]

Berlin, 29 November 1904

My dear Count,

Not until to-day did I see in the newspaper that the marriage of your

---

[1] From the Foreign Ministry files.

[2] On 26 November 1904 Delcassé stated in the Chamber of Deputies: 'Never has the utility [of the Franco-Russian alliance] been more evident, and never will we find a more opportune occasion to proclaim our loyalty and fidelity, for it powerfully protects the permanent interests of the two nations that concluded it.' (*Documents Diplomatiques Français*, Deuxième Série, vol. V, no. 460, p. 554.)

[3] See above, Holstein's memorandum of 22 October.          [4] In French in the original.

[5] From the Schlieffen Papers. The Schlieffen Papers otherwise contain only a few short notes from Holstein with a request to talk things over. (See Eberhard Kessel, editor, *Generalfeldmarschall Graf Alfred Schlieffen* (Göttingen, 1958), p. 54, note 1.) No letters from Schlieffen were found in the Holstein Papers. Schlieffen was Chief of the Army General Staff, 1891–1905.

314

daughter took place yesterday.[1] The event was of course widely known, but in my secluded life I had heard nothing about it.

First of all I hope that the consequent changes in your household will not be too painful for Your Excellency, and that the new situation will in the long run prove satisfactory and bring you joy. Next I suggest— since in the next few weeks you will perhaps be alone at home more than usual—that you will honour me perhaps tomorrow, Thursday, with a visit at the usual hour, between five and seven. I have a few things to tell you.

Your Excellency's very devoted

Holstein.

## 866.    Hugo von Radolin to Holstein

Paris, 8 December 1904

My dear friend,

I still have to thank you cordially for your kind and interesting letter of 25 November. You can imagine how pleased I was about the meeting. It is natural that it didn't please some of those who envy you. But I am really *very very happy* about it all. Bülow's *procédé* pleased me very much and proves how attached he is to you. He has captured my heart by what he did and I am as deeply grateful to *him* because of this act of friendship towards you as if he had rendered me an unforgettable service. And he can count on my absolute *dévouement* for the future.

I have sent a report on what I was able to find out about the mediation for peace.[2] According to that neither St Petersburg nor Paris wish to hear a word about it. And the English efforts in Washington were not, supposedly, successful either. [...]

But I do regret to have to see that the exaggerated consideration shown by Germany to Russia—the, so I am told, daily telegrams to the Tsar which are allegedly 'overwhelming' and annoying him—is creating the impression in *France* that Germany is trying to draw Russia away from France. This is naturally increasing the animosity felt here towards Germany. At the same time it is thought that the Russians are not only not feeling grateful for this wooing by Germany but are finding it troublesome, and that once the war is over and the Russians can breathe more easily they will turn against us with all the more animosity. To some extent the Russian character is like that. I am really afraid we are doing too much. Nobody ever likes the feeling of owing someone something. I did also want to mention this because it was pointed out to me by someone who merits attention how jealous the French were because of the consideration we have shown the Russians.

Excuse this hasty scrawl.

---

[1] On 29 November Schlieffen's daughter Elizabeth married Wilhelm von Hahnke, a major on the General Staff.

[2] Radolin had reported the same day that France did not feel inclined to support the English efforts to initiate peace negotiations. In Russian circles in Paris as well as in St Petersburg there was as yet no indication of a wish to make peace. (From the Foreign Ministry files.)

## 867.   Bernhard von Bülow to Holstein

[13 December 1904]

Dear friend,

I entirely agree that we should call Metternich over.[1] The decisive point is as always whether an agreement, alliance or treaty of any kind with Russia would increase or decrease the danger threatening from England. And not only towards us but also between Russia and England. For one thing is certain: while an agreement with Russia safeguarding the peace and raising our position in the world would be a great success for our foreign policy and would be welcomed in wide and in the best circles as a return to the traditions of Bismarckian policy, a bond with Russia which would in contrast to this draw England's hostility upon us would certainly be condemmed unanimously by the whole nation, by the German Princes first of all.

In recapitulating the course of our negotiations with Russia, I have the definite feeling—though I am not certain, for something like this is incapable of mathematical proof—that we would have secured a treaty with Russia if we had met the Russian wish for support during the peace negotiations more whole-heartedly.[2] You must not forget that the Russians are at least as mistrustful of us as we are of the Russians. Just as we are at least as much disliked abroad as we dislike foreigners. I still do not regard it as impossible to-day that an alliance with Russia could be achieved on some such basis as: Russia and Germany promise each other mutual support for a fixed period (for example five years with one year notice to be given) in case one of the two were attacked by a European Power. Secret article: Germany supports Russia during the peace negotiations. *Conditio sine qua non* would have to be that France should only be notified by Russia after the alliance between Germany and Russia had been signed. But I certainly grant you that it would be difficult for us to take the initiative, particularly as regards support for the Russians in their peace negotiations. H.M. will probably come to see me to-morrow morning. Is there something special I ought to tell him?

Most sincerely
Your
Bülow

## 868.   Holstein to Bernhard von Bülow
Copy

Berlin, 14 December 1904

Dear Bülow,

I have thought over your letter of yesterday evening and have reached the conclusion that a prior question must first of all be decided:

whether a defensive alliance between Germany and Russia would increase the danger of war which exists for Germany, i.e. whether it would increase the tendency of the English to go to war against Germany and Russia;

[1] Metternich was to be summoned from London in order to give his opinion on the effect a possible German treaty with Russia would have on Anglo-German relations.
[2] See *Grosse Politik*, vol. XIXii, chapter CXXXVII.

or whether a so-called neutrality agreement whereby Russia would cover us only in respect of the coaling and port questions would have a less irritating effect in England;

or thirdly, whether the danger of war can only be avoided by our not concluding an agreement at all and stopping our shipments of coal.[1]

Metternich will have to pronounce on the three parts of this question which was posed by Richthofen.[2] The terms of a possible German-Russian agreement should only be considered after that. As regards the terms, the following point of view is decisive.

(Our need for Russian support is determined solely by the coaling and port questions. But the only effective method to cover ourselves against possible consequences is by a simple defensive alliance. For if the cases when the alliance would become effective were specifically defined, they could easily be circumvented.)

The Russians must be told this quite calmly and frankly—under the heading 'terms'—just as it is set out here in the section enclosed in brackets.

Most sincerely<br>Your<br>Holstein.

Richthofen has just given me Schulenburg's memorandum.[3] The latter is known as an adherent of Eckardstein, i.e. a pessimist. This makes what he says about the effect of a Russian alliance all the more valuable.

H.

869.   Bernhard von Bülow to Holstein

15 December 1904

Dear friend,

I completely agree that the three prior questions you framed[4] should be submitted to Metternich who arrives here to-morrow morning. Given his nature, Metternich must be given time to think over his answers to these questions calmly. I would regard it as useful if Metternich were also asked on this occasion whether he regards the danger of an English attack to be as imminent and as inevitable as do Schulenburg[5] and Coerper.[6] How would it be if you also consulted other people with connections in London—e.g. Schwabach—on this last point?

Should we want to conclude an agreement with Russia, this would only be possible by working simultaneously on the Tsar and on Lamsdorff. We now have two good trumps in our hand, coal shipments and

---

[1] See *Grosse Politik*, vol. XIXi, chapter CXXXIII.

[2] See p. 316, note 1.

[3] Friedrich, Count von der Schulenburg. Military Attaché in London, 1902–6. The memorandum is dated 13 December. (*Grosse Politik*, vol. XIXii, no. 6154, pp. 359–66.)

[4] See above, Holstein's letter of 14 December, and *Grosse Politik*, vol. XIXi, no. 6139, pp. 331–2.

[5] See above, note 3.

[6] Naval Attaché in London 1904–7. Coerper's views were expressed in a memorandum of 18 November. (*Grosse Politik*, vol. XIXii, no. 6149, pp. 353–6.)

the forthcoming loan.[1] But a treaty secured by force *contre vents et marées* would, as you rightly emphasized the other day, be of relatively little value, not to mention the fact that by acting brusquely towards the Tsar we could lose all the ground which we have gained in St Petersburg in the last few years. H.M. would have to write to the Tsar somewhat as follows :

Thanks for the assurance concerning coaling.[2] The Far Eastern war has gradually rendered the general situation so insecure, that we must both be prepared at any time for some sort of incident, which could arise from causes other than the coal deliveries. Only by standing shoulder to shoulder will we be safe against suprises. Do you want a treaty with one year's notice for the duration of the war only, or for say five years? In the treaty we would guarantee each other mutual support in case during or after the war one of us were attacked by a third European Power, or if I were to be attacked by Japan. I would also gladly promise you my support in the peace negotiations. When we are both agreed, I leave it to you how you want to win over the French. Before that nothing must be allowed to get out at all about our negotiations.[3]

At the same time a similar dispatch would have to go to Alvensleben :

Our need for Russian support is due not only to the dangers arising out of the coal deliveries but also to the general situation in view of the attitude which we have adopted to the Far East conflict. We can take these dangers upon ourselves only if Russia assures us of her support. Otherwise, in view of the feeling in Japan and England, we cannot expose ourselves any further.[4]

The letter to the Tsar would have to be straightforward, loyal, friendly, and warm in tone, without any strong expressions; the dispatch to Alvensleben, calm, without unnecessary harshness, but firm.

In the light of Schulenburg's view of the situation in London we should here clarify amongst ourselves certain major questions. (1) In case of an English attack on us, is France also to be drawn into the war? The argument against this is that the General Staff thinks France is a very serious adversary, more so than in 1870, that a move against France could bring in Russia against us unless we had previously come to some sort of agreement with her; that perhaps even Italy might side with England and France. The argument in favour is that if the war remained confined to ourselves and England, we are practically powerless against England. By capturing our colonies and shipping, destroying our navy and trade and paralysing our industry, England could within a foreseeable time force us to a disadvantageous peace. But if France is involved, and particularly if we also bring in Belgium and Holland, we

---

[1] In January 1905 a loan of 231 million roubles at $4\frac{1}{2}\%$ was issued in Berlin at 94 and oversubscribed several times.

[2] Russia assured Germany of support in case Germany should become involved in difficulties arising from coaling the Russian fleet. (*Grosse Politik*, vol. XIXi, nos. 6136–7, pp. 328–9.)

[3] See the draft of the Kaiser's letter to the Tsar of 21 December. (*Grosse Politik*, vol. XIXi, no. 6141, pp. 340–1.)

[4] See Bülow's dispatch to Alvensleben of 21 December. (*Grosse Politik*, vol XIXi, no. 6142, p. 342.)

increase our risk, but we would at least have the chance of achieving military successes, obtaining guarantees and exercising pressure for our part. (2) What about Denmark? Would the disadvantage of a move in that direction, the resulting irritation of the Russians, be greater than the advantage of at least being able to protect the Baltic coast and affording our navy a better chance? (3) Is it advisable to prepare public opinion here and the German people gradually to the realization that a black cloud threatens us from the English quarter, so that we are not later on reproached with lack of foresight and irresponsibility?

Sincerely

Your

B.

## 870.  Holstein to Bernhard von Bülow
Draft

Berlin, 15 December 1904

Dear Bülow,

I have thought over your letter of two days ago thoroughly. It contains clear views, which, I believe, I can make my own. But—permit me to answer your confidence with confidence—what is lacking is the absolute firmness, which at a moment like the present one the Chancellor needs to achieve the desired end. Neither Richthofen nor Metternich nor I could take the responsibility before the Kaiser, the people, or world history, even if we wanted to. It is a good thing that you should listen to us, but the decision is yours alone.

The alliance question falls into two parts:

The question *whether*, and

the question *how*, i.e. the terms. That comes later.

I definitely advise that in the discussion of the question *whether*, Military Attaché Count Schulenburg should also take part, besides Metternich and Richthofen. I think it is hardly necessary for me to be called in since you are thoroughly familiar with my views; but naturally I am at your disposal. I would advise not to summon anyone else, for one thing because, as you will have noticed, it wouldn't really help, but mainly because the summoning of people who play no recognizable role in politics leaves outside observers with an impression of insecurity which can be exploited by the opposing side.

The telegram to Alvensleben stating that his instructions regarding the terms will come later leaves the question *how* open for us.[1] This telegram has saved the situation by giving us a little time for reflection.

Schulenburg may have gone to the country. It would therefore perhaps be best to invite him as soon as you know when Metternich is coming.

[1] Following up his telegram of 11 December (*Grosse Politik*, vol. XIXi, no. 6134, pp. 325–6), Alvensleben telegraphed on 12 December that Lamsdorff had asked to see him that day after his report to the Tsar. Alvensleben was immediately instructed to tell Lamsdorff that he was still waiting for his instructions regarding the terms of German-Russian co-operation. (From the Foreign Ministry files.)

I stayed at home this morning to think the matter through once again undisturbed before starting to write.

With best regards
Holstein.

871.    Holstein to Paul von Metternich
        Copy

Berlin, 16 December 1904

Dear Metternich,

It would be unforgivable if any possibly existing discord were to prevent us from working together for our country at a time when the problem is one of war and peace. Hence I am writing the following to you.

Two questions should be considered :

First : is the feeling in England such that it is possible or probable that England would use an opportunity that might arise, e.g. a Japanese appeal to the *casus foederis*, in order to make war on Germany ?

Secondly : would England's desire to make war on Germany be increased or diminished if she saw that Germany had concluded an agreement of a defensive nature with Russia ?

These two specific questions, which you, as the specialist on England, will have to consider, give rise to a third which lies equally within your official competence :

We have demanded from Russia that she should support us in any conflict which might result from the coal deliveries to the Baltic fleet.[1] Lamsdorff replied by way of a note, stating that Russia will stand with us *pour ce qui est de la question des charbons*.[2] Does that solve the problem ? Not necessarily. For Japan will not be so silly as to *specify* the *alliance stipulation* as the reason for war, but will seek and find some other reason. E.g. yesterday the Japanese Minister wrote to Richthofen in a most polite form : what about our treatment of Russian officers in Tsingtao ?[3] His Government had heard all sorts of stories about unjustified relaxations, the granting of leave, etc. This as a pretext for war would be as good as any other once the right moment had come. Therefore the Russian statement must not confine itself *specifically* to the coaling question as *casus foederis* if it is to cover us against complications arising out of this question. Probably the Russians will give us such a statement if they are really seriously interested in coal deliveries. But if they don't, we shall then be faced with a fourth question. Should we continue our deliveries at the risk of possible war without adequate assurances from the Russians, or should we stop them, thereby naturally annoying the Russian Government ? Naturally, I refrain from any attempt to influence your view on this question.

[1] *Grosse Politik*, vol. XIXi, no. 6129, pp. 320–1.
[2] *Grosse Politik*, vol. XIXi, nos. 6136–7, pp. 328–9.
[3] That is, Russian officers in neutral German territory who were now in German custody.

You will of course show this rough draft to the Chancellor.

Most sincerely<br>H.

I shall be happy to see you if you should find time to come and see me in my office.[1]

## 872.   Bernhard von Bülow to Holstein

[16 December 1904]

Dear Holstein,

Many thanks for your letters. It appears to me that the main point is that Metternich should produce a calm, completely objective and matter of fact statement of English conditions, feelings and intentions. That is why I have thoroughly informed him of the general situation, as you did—which pleased me greatly—while carefully avoiding influencing him in any way. I too did not submit any questions to Metternich concerning the situation outside his own field of action, e.g. on matters such as our relationship with Russia, the intentions of St Petersburg, or the possibility or impossibility of co-operation with France.

I would like to talk over the general situation with you to-day. Could you come and see me at 7 o'clock and then have a meal with me at 8? I am alone, as my wife wanted to inspect the Roland of Berlin, on the principle that one must look at everything, even things that one could not *a priori* approve of in view of Bayreuth. [...]

Most sincerely<br>Your<br>B.

## 873.   Bernhard von Bülow to Holstein

[25 December 1904]

Dear friend,

Lascelles is looking forward very much to seeing you to-morrow.[2] His last conversation with you[3] made a lasting impression on him. He was especially impressed by your remark that a certain group was at work to envenom relations between England and Germany. L. repeated this to Balfour. Both reached the conclusion that such tendencies did in fact exist. The two English statesmen naturally attributed them to Russia.

My remark that we still did not have an alliance with Russia though our relations were excellent, that we would be more than ready to conclude a defensive treaty with any Power, but would dislike signing any treaty of a different nature, made a great impression on L. though I had

---

[1] For Metternich's answer to these questions, see *Grosse Politik*, vol. XIXi, no. 6140, pp. 332–40.

[2] For Lascelles' account of his conversation with Holstein on 26 December, see *British Documents*, vol. III, no. 65b, pp. 58–9. Bülow's conversation with Lascelles took place, according to Lascelles, on 24 December (*British Documents*, vol. III, no. 65a, pp. 56–8), according to Bülow on 25 December (*Grosse Politik*, vol. XIXii, nos. 6157, 6178, pp. 372–4, 400–3).

[3] No record of this conversation has been found.

thrown it out lightly. Useful though my hint was, I still believe that we should not drill too deep in this direction nor slap on the colours too heavily.

What would seem very useful to me are repeated hints that it would be impossible for us to continue disregarding the unanimously hostile attitude of the English Press, especially in view of the latter's weight and political insight. L. agreed with me when I told him that I did regard the majority of the English people as too sensible not to realize that England's international position would not be improved but worsened if we were weakened and paralysed, just as we would only lose if England were paralysed. I told L. quite calmly that not only H.M. but also responsible naval and military authorities had believed that England intended to attack us suddenly in view of the hostile attitude of all major English publications and public opinion and the indifference of the English Government in the face of this hostility. By the nature of things English threats against us were more important than former Pan-German abuse of England, since everyone knew that our power of attacking England was very much less than *vice versa*.

Most sincerely

Your

B.

# 1905

874.    Holstein to Hugo von Radolin[1]

Berlin, Friday [13 January 1905]

Dear Radolin,

I am enclosing a copy of a memorandum by Hammann for the Chancellor.[2] In it there is mentioned a letter which I am supposed to have written to you giving you instructions regarding your reports in view of H.M. Perhaps this is a forgery. I remember that I advised you for example to visit the French provinces and report thereon in accordance with H.M.'s wishes. Have you lost such a letter? Please try and remember accurately and don't make a mistake in your reply. If I know beforehand what I shall have to meet, the matter isn't serious and can be dealt with. For I have never written anything treasonable to you. But I must *know* whether there is a possibility that some letter I wrote to you, even one of quite harmless content, might have been stolen or used.

Your

H.[3]

Please return the copy. [...]

875.    Bernhard von Bülow to Holstein

[15 January 1905][4]

III[5]

H.M. also asked me whether he should call on Lascelles and tell him that our fleet had never been mobilized. On this occasion H.M. wants to tell Lascelles for the King's information that Russia and France were trying to sow enmity between England and Germany. I replied that H.M. should above all avoid creating the impression on Lascelles and the King that he wanted to draw England from France's side and to sow enmity between England and Russia. In any case, would you consider it useful if H.M. did on occasion say something once again to Lascelles, and if so what?

I would be very grateful if you were to draft or have drafted for me a private letter to Metternich, thanking him for his information and re-

---

[1] From the Radolin Papers.   [2] Not found.

[3] Radolin replied on 14 January: 'Your letter surprised me very greatly. First of all you never wrote anything to me that could not have been justified officially and that did not lie in the official interest. [...] Until now *not one* of these letters could have gone astray as neither seals nor locks have been tampered with, as I have just checked for myself. Those letters which I haven't kept, I have burned.'

[4] The date on which the two reports mentioned below were returned to the Foreign Ministry. (From the Foreign Ministry files.)

[5] Only section III has been found.

warding him with some explanatory thoughts and reflections. His report no. 43 was the most informative.[1]

H.M.'s marginal comments on this report and on the copy of Radolin's[2] —s.p.r.—are enclosed for your purely personal and strictly confidential information.

Most sincerely your

B.

876.   Memorandum by Holstein

Berlin, 6 February 1905

[...] A diplomatic action by Germany to bring about an alliance with Denmark[3] would at this moment considerably heighten the already existing state of general insecurity. An alliance between powerful Germany and little Denmark would be generally regarded as a renunciation of her independence by Denmark and her incorporation in the German Empire. As far as can be seen at this distance, the old King[4] has a genuine affection for His Majesty the Kaiser. But the King cannot conclude an alliance without the co-operation of the constitutional institutions, and these latter in turn are dependent on public opinion. That the people are hostile to Germany can be taken as axiomatic. It is true that this feeling has died down over the past forty years, but the suspicion that Denmark was to be brought to a state of dependence on Germany would immediately awaken instinctive reactions which could not be influenced by diplomatic means. They would turn for help to England and Russia. By 'they' should be understood not only the Danish people and the Danish Press but also the Danish Government. For any Government which at such a moment did not take the national hyper-sensitivity into account would be immediately removed, and even the monarchy, whose German roots have never been completely forgiven, could under certain circumstances be endangered. The English would then be given an opportunity to pose as the defenders of Denmark's independence against a 'forced' alliance with Germany, either by themselves, or more probably together with other Powers. England's only aim in the Baltic is the maintenance of the status quo. The same is true

[1] In his report of 12 January Metternich had described a conversation with Count Mensdorff, who had told him of French efforts to sow discord between Austria and Italy, 'due in part to the desire to disrupt the Triple Alliance'. Wilhelm II commented in the margin: 'And Radolin is astounded that we are so irritated with France!!!! How naïve.' (*Grosse Politik*, vol. XXi, no. 6425, p. 93.)

[2] Of 7 January. Radolin reported that the Dogger Bank incident no longer represented a danger to peace, and that Delcassé was now inclined towards mediation between Russia and Japan. (From the Foreign Ministry files.)

[3] The following memorandum by Bülow of 6 February was found in the Foreign Ministry files: 'In connection with the English threats, H.M. again spoke of Denmark. He admitted that any threat against Denmark could have dangerous consequences, but did express his urgent desire for an alliance with Denmark in order to prevent thereby an English surprise attack on Kiel and the Baltic ports. If Schoen deserves the praise which I gave him, he should try to bring about such an alliance. Perhaps Schoen could be asked to discuss at some time the possibility of such an alliance (academically and without any reference).' (See the following document.)

[4] Christian IX, King of Denmark, 1863–1906.

of Russia. The plans of aggrandizement of both Powers concern the Far East, but they are not mutually exclusive; on the contrary, co-operation would only further them. M. Delcassé will take every care to prove to both that neither in the Baltic nor in the Far East are their interests opposed to an extent which would hamper their co-operation for the protection of Danish independence, but that such co-operation would actually provide the best possible stepping-stone towards achieving a community of interests in the Far East.

The plan of drawing Denmark within the outer ambit of the German Empire is a great idea of the future; but a condition for its realization is that either the English fleet should be otherwise engaged, or that the German fleet, either by itself or in conjunction with an ally, should be more or less equally strong. And a step in this direction to-day would be welcomed by the enemies of Germany and in particular those who are diplomatically working for a Franco-Russian-English Triplice. These three would thus be given the pretext for drawing together which they temporarily lost when the partition of China was prevented. And the worse their mood at the Chinese disappointment, the more keenly the opportunity would be seized to bring to life the new Triplice on account of Denmark. Once in existence, it would seek and find new tasks without any difficulty.

H.

## 877.   Wilhelm von Schoen to Holstein

Copenhagen, 11 February 1905

Your Excellency,

Isvolsky[1] is very happy at the now pretty certain prospect of Berlin[2] and highly flattered at the way in which this certainty has arisen. *Cela m'impose de grands devoirs moraux*, he said. Naturally he is now greatly interested in the time, a point on which he as yet lacks all information.

As regards Your Excellency's views on the question of an alliance with Denmark, I can express my most complete agreement with them. The time for it is not yet ripe, and the present time is as unfavourable as can be to take up this delicate question. For one thing the Danes themselves aren't ripe for it yet. They won't fall into our arms voluntarily and cheerfully at this time, no matter how embarrassed they may be about the problem of what they can do to fulfil their duties as a neutral and secure their independent existence. To purchase their goodwill by concessions in North Schleswig is out of the question. Should we use moral or even physical pressure there would be an awful row, both here and elsewhere. Here the gradually declining self-confidence would be brought to new and most unwelcome life, and abroad, East and West, people would not look on with great favour. Russia probably would never forgive us if we used its present difficulties to seize the key of the Baltic, and as regards the British, they would in their present mood

---

[1] Alexander Isvolsky. Russian Minister in Copenhagen, 1903–6; Foreign Minister, 1906–10.

[2] Of becoming Ambassador in Berlin, a prospect that failed to materialize.

hardly hesitate to accuse us of an unfriendly act and in this they would probably be supported by France. In short, it seems to me, as to Your Excellency, that the present moment is as unfavourable as could be in order to work for a goal which as such is certainly desirable and will be achieved in time, but very gradually. [...]

Respectfully as ever,

Your Excellency's most obedient

von Schoen

878.  Holstein to Bernhard von Bülow

Copy

Berlin, 20 February 1905

Should we offer to mediate? The question is what effect this would have in Russia? It certainly won't be a glorious peace for Russia. Lamsdorff will want to have the French as mediators, if there is to be any mediation at all. The only way we could mediate would be by getting Roosevelt to get the Japanese to tell him their lowest terms and at the same time put considerable pressure on them. According to Washington telegram no. 30,[1] he has already done so once. I am enclosing the telegram once again. One gets the impression that the President would like to co-operate with us in this matter. It would be a great boon for our position in the world and a great insult for England and France.

Before reaching a decision on this question, it would probably be best to await the Tsar's reply to H.M.'s letter, which I now strongly advise should be sent.[2]

879.  Memorandum by Holstein

[11 March 1905][3]

There are some views which are beyond discussion. I am therefore confining myself to specific objective points:

(1) In the Far East the Tsar can back down if he wants to, in the Balkans he cannot, for there he is being pushed, and the further he has backed down in the Far East, the harder he is pushed in the Balkans.

(2) It is improbable that peace will come about as the result of French and English mediation. Without a guarantee of execution, mediation is of no value to the Japanese. But the English will take care not to give such a guarantee alone with France, for the English would rightly fear that when it came to the point the French would leave them in the lurch. It would be quite different if Germany joined in the guarantee. The English would like that. Hence Rothschild's attempt to

---

[1] Of 17 February. (*Grosse Politik*, vol. XIXii, no. 6289, pp. 575–6.)

[2] The letter was sent on 21 February. Wilhelm II gave a detailed account of the view of Russian conditions which according to him was now generally held. He especially emphasized the unpopularity of the war in Russia, the danger to the dynasty which resulted from this, and the need for personal action by the Tsar to improve the situation. (*Briefe Wilhelms II an den Zaren*, pp. 361–9.) The Tsar telegraphed on 25 February: '*I thank you from the depth of my heart. Your long letter interested me greatly.*' (From the Foreign Ministry files.)

[3] See *Grosse Politik*, vol. XIXii, nos. 6187, 6189, pp. 411–12.

take soundings last week.[1] But as Germany won't join in the guarantee, the conflict will either be settled by Russian-Japanese negotiations or not at all.

(3) The settlement, if it is reached, will only be a provisional one. One can hardly assume that Russia will completely evacuate Manchuria, even withdrawing the railway guards. But that Russia should give up the game as permanently lost is out of the question. Both sides will continue to be on their guard.

(4) The idea that Russia could now join France and England in an attack on Germany is in complete contradiction to the facts. Germany, whose mere neutrality would prevent a number of Russia's opponents from getting at her, is the only Power with which Russia has no conflicting interests. It is futile to argue with anyone who to-day talks of the possibility of a Russian attack.

(5) It is certainly correct that we should not treat the Japanese as a *quantité négligeable*, and pay somewhat more attention to them in the diplomatic field. It would for example be quite useful if we made it clear to them that the difference in the course of events in 1895 and 1904 is explained by the fact that in the first instance Germany intervened, while to-day she is neutral.

880.    Holstein to Maximilian von Brandt[2]

Berlin, 26 March 1905

Your Excellency,

[...] Warlike and pacific tendencies are now fighting it out in St Petersburg. In Russian General Staff circles, as in ours, some people hold the view that time is working for Russia and that the war should therefore be continued. For even assuming that the Japanese were to capture Sakhalin and Vladivostok, their advance would be bound to come to a standstill somewhere in Eastern Siberia. They would then have to wait with shouldered arms until the Russians were once more ready to attack. And in the meantime the war would be more expensive for them than for the Russians, and it is not easy to raise the money, as the last loan showed. These considerations favour a continuation of the war, but against it speak Russia's creditors—an army which should not be under-estimated.

However, during the last few days the idea of a peace congress, to be convened in Paris, has made its appearance, as yet cautiously and discreetly. One can assume that this project originated in France. But it will not be easy to realize it. For already a few weeks ago it was reported through diplomatic channels that the Japanese, remembering Shimonoseki, were deeply suspicious of any grouping of the Powers and therefore did not want to hear anything of a congress or conference.

I would ask you not to mention the idea of a congress in Paris in the Press for the time being. It was confided to us in the very greatest

[1] Nothing was found on this in the Foreign Ministry files.
[2] From the Brandt Papers.

secrecy. We should rather wait until someone else does so. On the other hand I think that it would probably be useful if Your Excellency were to drop a hint in letters addressed to the Far East or to Orientals that the idea of a congress is once again current, and that this could hardly bring benefit to either China or Japan. For the more advisers, the more mouths there are to feed.

With best wishes for your health,

Your Excellency's ever sincerely devoted

Holstein.

## 881.  Bernhard von Bülow to Holstein

28 March [1905]

With reference to this evening's telegram addressed to me by His Majesty:[1]

(1)  We must immediately telegraph Tattenbach,[2] setting out the political situation as a whole, over my signature.[3]

(2)  I must telegraph H.M., quite calmly, making use of Kühlmann's[4] reports on the security measures and of the telegram re Delcassé which was held up this morning.[5] *Pejus eventum* we must think up a telegram in the event that H.M. should stay on board.

B.

## 882.  Holstein to Bernhard von Bülow
Copy

Berlin, 5 April 1905

Dear Bülow,

This morning too I have seen nothing in my newspapers regarding the collective responsibility of the Powers in accordance with treaty obliga-

---

[1] In the Anglo-French agreement of 8 April 1904, England had recognized France's interests in Morocco. Since the Germans had not been consulted about this agreement, they proposed to disregard French claims to a preponderant interest in Morocco. To demonstrate this disregard, the Kaiser was to land at the Moroccan port of Tangier and treat Morocco as a free and independent state, where all foreign Powers had equal rights. On 28 March the Kaiser had telegraphed from Lisbon: 'In Tangier hell has now broken loose. Yesterday an Englishman was almost murdered there, and I regard the matter [of landing there] as pretty doubtful after all. Since Tattenbach, who knows the situation well, also has doubts, I have given instructions for him to come along and have a look at things before I go ashore.' (*Grosse Politik*, vol. XXi, no. 6580, p. 279.)

[2] Christian, Count von Tattenbach. Minister in Tangier, 1889–95, in Lisbon, 1897–1908; temporary head of the Ministry in Tangier, 1905; Ambassador in Madrid, 1908–10.

[3] This telegram was sent on 29 March. (*Grosse Politik*, vol. XXi, no. 6581, pp. 279–80.)

[4] Richard von Kühlmann. First Secretary of Legation in Teheran, 1901–3; in Tangier, 1904–5, in The Hague, 1907; First Secretary of Embassy in London, 1908–14.

[5] Bülow telegraphed to Kaiser Wilhelm II on 29 March: 'I am very happy that Your Majesty is taking Tattenbach along to Tangier. He is well acquainted with local conditions. Delcassé is sweating blood because Your Majesty's visit to Tangier will upset his finely-spun plans. He had let it be stated in Fez that France was acting on behalf of all the European Powers, who all agreed to and wished for Morocco's subjection to France. If Your Majesty now appears in Tangier, received with jubilation by all the Mohammedans, fêted by all the non-French Europeans, and without taking any notice of the French, Delcassé will be in the soup. 'I have forwarded Kühlmann's detailed reports on the security measures taken in Tangier to Tattenbach.' (From the Foreign Ministry files. The telegram was drafted by Holstein. See also *Grosse Politik*, vol. XXi, no. 6582, pp. 280–1.)

tions concerning Morocco.[1] Thus until yesterday evening no hint in this direction was given. And yet how useful this would have been just before the question raised in the French Chamber. It would have given the Socialists one more argument against Delcassé. Contractual collectivity is a principle on which we can take a firm stand without ourselves appearing to harbour aggressive intentions. Moreover this idea has the advantage that while affecting French interests, it does not affect French pride, just as the collective victories of 1814 were not so great an insult to the French as the German victory, gained alone, in 1870. If France refuses the Conference, she puts herself in the wrong, shows that she has a bad conscience and evil intentions. If the Conference is held, it will, whatever the result, definitely not hand Morocco over to the French. These are the advantages of the Conference idea, unique in character. On Saturday I used my rather feeble strength in order to give expression to them in good time.[2] But the proposal was dropped.

I can understand that *Geheimrat* Hammann does not appreciate their scope. His talent lies more in the field of internal and police matters. I have found often enough in the past that dealing with foreign affairs can be a burden to him. But that you, who have grown grey dealing with major political questions, should not appreciate the importance of the concept of contractual collectivity, that I find discouraging. How is the Sultan, intimidated by France, to find the courage to propose a conference, if he sees that Germany is loath to embrace openly the idea of a Conference.

In any case under these circumstances I shall abstain ever after from making any suggestions regarding Press directives.

> With best wishes
> Your sincerely devoted
> Holstein.

883.   Holstein to Hugo von Radolin[3]

Berlin, Tuesday, 9 :30 a.m., [11 April 1905]

Dear Radolin,

At the time of writing this I do not know yet whether the telegram to you, which I dictated twenty-two hours ago, has been sent.[4] Illness[5] and the great distance have slowed down official processes; that is why I prefer to write you a letter rather than a dispatch. I do not know whether the latter would get through the official channels by to-night.

---

[1] Holstein is referring to the Madrid Convention of 3 July 1880, signed by Germany, Austria-Hungary, Belgium, Spain, the United States, France, Great Britain, Sweden, Norway, Italy, the Netherlands and Portugal, to protect the rights of the signatory states in Morocco. A trade treaty of 1 June 1890 had further clarified these rights.

[2] See Holstein's memoranda of 3 and 7 April 1905. (*Grosse Politik*, vol. XXii, nos. 6597, 6606, pp. 297–9, 308–9.)

[3] From the Radolin Papers.

[4] In this telegram, dated 11 April, Radolin was instructed to continue to maintain cool reserve towards the French about Morocco. The telegram closed with the Talleyrand quotation mentioned later in this letter. (From the Foreign Ministry files. See p. 331, note 7.)

[5] See below.

The fact that Tattenbach is being used shows that we want to pursue a firm policy.[1] Nothing else would be possible anyway after what the Kaiser said to Chérisey.[2] To retreat once one has taken up a position would have the same consequences as shirking a duel. One exposes oneself to further and greater humiliations.

French boasting concerning the English-Spanish-Italian grouping is enough to make one laugh. Fortis[3] has already stated that Italy has had enough with *one* Tunis. Spain—though the Government does not dare to say so—considers herself cheated and is beginning to fear that France wants to exploit Morocco all by herself. England will not play an active part if only because of America. The latter naturally has no intention of threatening force, but diplomatically she will express herself in favour of the open door and the convening of a Conference.

It therefore won't do any harm if, should the *Spaniard* start talking about Morocco, you were to remark to him casually : '*A Berlin on croit savoir que si la chose devenait sérieuse, la France resterait seule.*' Naturally you must not mention any of the above details, nor anything concerning America.

[4]( The Anglo-French treaty expressly provided for the maintenance of the status quo;[5] we therefore had no reason to take any action (at that time). We regard England's role in this treaty in this light : England was fully justified in disposing of English interests in Morocco. We regard it as out of the question that she also intended to dispose of the interests of other treaty Powers. England left the others to their own devices. We think that international law demands that these others must be consulted either singly or collectively if France takes steps to alter the status quo. The objection raised in the French Press that the earlier conferences and treaties did not deal with political changes but merely with questions relating to private interests is a debating point and not valid. A political change like the Tunisification of Morocco—which is

[1] In a telegram of 6 April Bülow asked the Kaiser whether Tattenbach, who was at that time in Tangier, could not take charge of the Legation there for the time being, because he believed 'that this would strengthen our diplomatic position in Morocco and not fail to have an effect on France'. ( *Grosse Politik*, vol. XXii, no. 6605, p. 308.)

[2] Third Secretary at the French Legation in Tangier. At the time of the landing in Tangier on 31 March 1905, Schoen had telegraphed to Berlin : 'All His Majesty's conversations were colourless with the exception of the following : '[Conversation] with the French Chargé d'Affaires at first also unimportant. But when the latter transmitted Delcassé's respects and regards and in effect welcomed His Majesty to Morocco in Delcassé's name, the reply was : the significance of the Imperial visit was that His Majesty claimed free trade and fully equal rights with other nations for Germany; when Count Chérisey generously prepared to admit this, His Majesty remarked that he would reach a direct understanding with the Sultan, who as a free ruler of an independent country enjoyed equal rights, that he would know how to give his ustified demands their due weight, and that he expected these to be fully respected also by France. Count Chérisey grew pale, wanted to reply, but was prevented from doing so by a curt dismissal, and went off with bowed head.' ( *Grosse Politik*, vol. XXi, no. 6589, pp. 286–287.)

[3] Alessandro Fortis. Italian Minister-President and Minister of the Interior, 28 March 1905–3 February 1906.

[4] Red bracket.

[5] See Article II of the Anglo-French treaty of 8 April 1904. ( *British Documents*, vol. II, no. 417, pp. 386–7.)

evidently planned now—naturally also touches the private interests of the non-French treaty Powers as a whole; a Conference would thus be more than ever indicated. Non-French economic interests have been wholly driven out of Tunis, as is well known.)[1]

I have just received the news that all my telegrams of yesterday were sent off: H.M.,[2] Rome,[3] Washington,[4] London,[5] Paris.[6] Rome was twelve pages, London eight pages in length. Yours was far and away the shortest. You must confine yourself to an attitude of serious reserve. Our whole attitude would suffer misrepresentation if you were to allow the Moroccan question to be treated as a topic for the tea-table in your house. But you must always remain polite and calm. Yesterday's quotation of Talleyrand was a marginal comment by the Chancellor.[7] He has heard that you can sometimes be a *mauvaise tête*.

Exceptionally and in strict confidence you can on occasion mention some of the things which I have enclosed in red brackets, *but not to Frenchmen*. If any mention of Morocco is made by the Russians, you will perhaps be able to drop the remark: 'In some ways I am glad that Russia never took part in any of the Moroccan conferences. Since she is not a treaty Power, she is not faced with the embarrassing necessity of having to choose between France and ourselves.'

Apart from Russia, all the Great Powers, the United States, Portugal, Holland, Belgium, and Sweden took part in the conferences. [...]

A week ago on Friday I could not raise myself upright in bed in the morning. When I tried to get up nevertheless, I had to support myself on the furniture and against the wall. Dizziness, nausea, a result of insufficient flow of blood to the head due to overwork. For two days I stayed in bed, absolutely quiet, then I had to do some work again, and in any case I was restless. But I haven't been to the Ministry yet. I am dictating the most important things here—yesterday I was dictating for over five hours—but at least I escape all the unimportant stuff which comes to the Ministry in stacks.

Now I am well again. But it was a warning, for I probably narrowly escaped a stroke. Fränkel,[8] when I had him called, immediately tried to determine whether I had any feeling in my toes and fingers. Everything was in order. I have spared myself to some extent until now only because of my weakness, but this is getting less. [...]

With a cordial handshake

Your

Holstein

[1] Red bracket.    [2] *Grosse Politik*, vol. XXii, no. 6614, pp. 320–1.

[3] *Grosse Politik*, vol. XXii, no. 6613, pp. 318–20.

[4] The telegram to Washington instructed the Ambassador to give the widest currency to the point of view of the German Government in the Moroccan question. (From the Foreign Ministry files.)

[5] *Grosse Politik*, vol. XXii, no. 6843, pp. 605–6.    [6] See above, p. 329, note 4.

[7] On Radolin's telegram of 9 April Bülow wrote: 'It is desirable that Radolin should remain completely calm *vis-à-vis* his *chers collègues*. Above all, no nervousness, no irritation, no rancour. *"Avec un front d'airain et le sourire sur les lèvres on passe partout"*, said Talleyrand, and Radolin is his great-nephew.' (*Grosse Politik*, vol. XXii, no. 6612, pp. 316–17.)

[8] Dr Bernhard Fränkel. *Geheimer Medizinalrat*.

Flotow,[1] for whom generally speaking I have a high regard, is too sensitive for difficult situations. That is the impression of the powers that be here. You must be all the more suave—neither irritable nor anxious.

884.    Josef Neven-Dumont[2] to Holstein

Cologne, 19 April 1905

Your Excellency,

With reference to our conversation yesterday I permit myself to submit the following:

( 1 ) Both the editor of the *Kölnische Zeitung* and Herr von Huhn, are quite prepared to stress the treaty point of view even more than hitherto when discussing the Moroccan affair in future, and to dispute the advisability of a separate agreement between Germany and France while pointing out repeatedly that the status quo in Morocco can only be altered with the participation of all the signatory Powers. In particular the convening of a conference is to be represented as entirely appropriate, as soon as this proposal is made public.

Should Your Excellency have any wishes regarding details—over and above these general considerations, it will also be possible to meet these as soon as they come to our knowledge.

( 2 ) Herr von Huhn has been editorially instructed by the *Kölnische Zeitung*—incidentally I contributed to this decision—to state that in case the Foreign Ministry should find it necessary to meet any French declaration with a refusal *a limine*, we should find it impossible to give any special support to such a policy. On the contrary we would have to leave the sole responsibility for such a step—whose effect seems to us incalculable—to the men conducting policy in Berlin. Naturally this would not be expressed in this form in the *Kölnische Zeitung*. In that case the paper would simply confine itself to reporting events as they took place. Herr von Huhn has repeatedly assured me that he too has only expressed himself in this sense, and that for all other contingencies he has proffered the effective co-operation of the *Kölnische Zeitung*.

( 3 ) When I talked with Herr von Huhn yesterday afternoon and questioned him on all the details I had discussed with you, he stated in particular:

( a ) that he had never intended in any way to pursue his own policy.

( b ) that he clearly remembered the circular note shown to him in which a conference was recommended, and that he had been quite prepared to support the policy outlined in it,

( c ) that the treatment of the Moroccan question had naturally been frequently discussed in the Foreign Ministry during the last few days. During these discussions the various possible solutions had been mentioned, including the question whether one should allow oneself to

---

[1] Hans von Flotow. Counsellor of Embassy in Paris, 1904–7; *Vortragender Rat* in the Foreign Ministry, 1907–10.

[2] Partner in the firm Neven-Schauberg; co-publisher of the *Kölnische Zeitung* and the *Strassburger Post*.

negotiate with France at all or whether all overtures were to be refused, by pointing to the fact that an alternative policy had already been adopted. In an endeavour to ensure unity of action between Berlin and Cologne, he had then discussed the various possibilities with Cologne, and had been instructed from there that Cologne was quite ready to support official policy in every way, but that they were worried in regard to a refusal *a limine* of French overtures, because such tactics would strengthen Delcassé's position in France and would be indefensible in the Press in Germany because of the incalculable consequences. Since, as Your Excellency stated to me, such a policy has never been intended, this reservation could not have been aimed at Your Excellency's policy.

(*d*) Nothing had been further from his mind than to pose an 'ultimatum'; he had merely emphasized the complete preparedness of the *Kölnische Zeitung* to support Government policy, whether the intention was to negotiate with Morocco alone or to choose the conference method. In the course of the conversation he had then also explained that agreement on this point had been reached with Cologne, and that Cologne and he too would support the Government's tactics.

(*e*) He (Huhn) would have submitted all this to Your Excellency in person if he had in the meantime had an opportunity to talk to Your Excellency; he was convinced that Your Excellency would have raised no objections to his explanations.

Herr von Huhn more than anyone regrets the misunderstandings which have arisen. He has the greatest respect for Your Excellency, and, in view of the long and trusting political collaboration, he confidently hopes that it will be possible to dispose of these misunderstandings in an open-hearted discussion. I would therefore ask Your Excellency to give him the opportunity for such a discussion as soon as possible, since I am convinced that the misunderstandings which have arisen will be removed thereby.

While expressing to Your Excellency my deep gratitude for your kind and understanding reception, I remain

With all respect<br>Your Excellency's devoted<br>Neven-Dumont.[1]

## 885. Holstein to Josef Neven-Dumont
Copy

Berlin, 20 April 1905

Personal and Secret

Dear *Herr Kommerzienrat*,

On Tuesday afternoon, the French Ambassador, on the basis of an

---

[1] Holstein replied on 21 April: 'I regret that I cannot grant your request that I should continue to receive Herr von Huhn. You will recently have had the opportunity to observe that diplomatic policy and Press policy are moving independently of each other in different directions. In these circumstances I for my part would regard it as inappropriate to furnish a newspaper with political guidance, thereby possibly creating confusion.' In a letter of 22 April Neven-Dumont defended Huhn and maintained that he had either heard of Holstein's intentions too late, or had not understood them properly.

*aide-mémoire* which however, he did not wish to give us, informed acting State Secretary Mühlberg of the following :

There appeared to be a misunderstanding between France and Germany over the Moroccan question. Should this be the case, why didn't Germany ask the necessary questions of M. Delcassé? Apart from this, the *aide-mémoire* merely repeated some of Delcassé's recent statements in the French Chamber.

Mühlberg replied : 'There was no misunderstanding on our side; in the Moroccan question we were not alone, but merely one of the signatories of the Madrid Convention. The reforms which were now being considered for Morocco might be of such a nature as to jeopardize all the interests of the non-French co-signatories. It seemed to us that the simplest and most natural means for the removal of the feeling of insecurity and mistrust which had become generally apparent in recent months was to bring about an exchange of views between all the co-signatories.'[1]

The above was sent on that very Tuesday night to our representatives in all the Treaty countries.[2] Naturally, Ambassador Bihourd[3] also telegraphed immediately, and so Delcassé must have been informed at the latest on Wednesday morning.[4] On Wednesday evening Radolin telegraphed : 'To-day's *Temps* carries a Berlin report, according to which it is not so much the Kaiser or the Chancellor but Herr von Holstein, long an official under Bismarck and a consistent enemy of France, who is behind the Press campaign concerning Morocco. His influence on the Kaiser was far greater than the Chancellor's.' Thus, a clumsy attempt to arouse mistrust of me in Bülow. This side of the question is of no concern to me, for Bülow knows very well how very solid his position with the Kaiser is, and how completely out of touch with His Majesty I am—incidentally entirely because of my own wishes.

But the attack is not without significance in other respects. It shows great dissatisfaction, not only in the Berlin correspondent of the *Temps* and those who fed him the material, but also at headquarters in Paris, otherwise the report would have been suppressed there. In view of the position of the *Temps*, I regard it as out of the question that this paper would have lent itself to such an extraordinary act of hostility without having previously asked Delcassé. But Delcassé, when he received this enquiry, already knew that Germany was quite prepared to negotiate, but not alone and in secret, but as a Treaty Power. The fact that he allowed the attack to be made shows that Germany's attitude did not suit the French Minister.

Such an attack would have been impossible if the *Norddeutsche Allgemeine* would have printed the short and straightforward sketch of a

---

[1] Mühlberg memorandum of 19 April 1905. (*Grosse Politik*, vol. XXii, no. 6623, pp. 332–3.)

[2] *Grosse Politik*, vol. XXii, no. 6624, pp. 333–4.

[3] Georges Bihourd. French Ambassador in Berlin, 1903–7.

[4] Bihourd's telegram arrived in Paris on Wednesday morning, 19 April. (*Documents Diplomatiques Français*, Deuxième Série, vol. VI, no. 314, pp. 377–9.)

programme (it is in the files!) which I dictated on my sick-bed on Saturday, 1 April.[1] The last sentence pointed out that a conference represented the simplest and most harmless method of solving the Moroccan complication. On Saturday evening I received a note from the Chancellor telling me that he was in full agreement with my Press memorandum and that he had suggested that it might appear in the *Norddeutsche*.

Instead the *Norddeutsche* printed a piece on Sunday, 2 April, saying exactly the opposite. For Germany's reserve in the Moroccan question was ascribed to the fact that we had been ignored in the conclusion of the Anglo-French agreement and that even now M. Delcassé seemed quite disinclined to approach us. Germany's position as a Treaty Power, which gives us our standing from the point of view of international law, was kept obstinately concealed from the eyes of the world both in that Press notice and also for quite some time after that in the counsels of our Press prophets. As for the public, they were left far longer than was advisable with the alternative : separate negotiations with France, or straight refusal of any French overture. Thus, the Press was working without any inherent connection with the diplomats. You know the diplomatic orientation, and especially the Chancellor's position regarding it. You were able to convince yourself that we have stood from the beginning for the collectivity of the Treaty Powers and that all the state papers drafted in accordance with this point of view—some of which because of illness I could not discuss even verbally—had been agreed to by the Chancellor. And it was the Chancellor who explained to the Kaiser that Germany would have to take its stand on the legally unassailable principle of the collectivity of the Treaty Powers. But the Press went its own way, and that is the reason why only last week the straight refusal of a French overture could be described to you as one possibility. Since I had informed Herr von Huhn on Friday of the circular dispatch to Vienna, Brussels, The Hague, Stockholm, and Lisbon, in which only the collectivity of the Treaty Powers was talked of, while the possibility of a straight refusal of the French advances was not even considered, Herr von Huhn might well have thought fit, in my opinion, to telephone and tell you that according to his latest information, a straight refusal was out of the question. But I have realized as a result of this incident that I lack the gift of clarifying things for Herr von Huhn. Herr von Huhn, who knows the correspondent of the *Temps*, will be better able than I to discover whence the correspondent derived the view that I am a longstanding enemy of France. This view is utterly mistaken. My standpoint is a very simple one. I do not for a moment believe in the possibility of drawing France closer to us in the foreseeable future by polite demonstrations. On the contrary, in this way we would delay a rapprochement, because we would further increase the natural self-esteem of the French and might even lead them to believe that we were afraid of them. If this latter eventuality were to materialize, the danger of war

[1] See Holstein's letter to Bülow of 5 April.

would, I think, be close, for the French would then take the first opportunity to step on our toes. On the other hand I have never, in spite of some disappointment, entirely lost my belief in the possibility of gradually bringing the two nations closer together again by the pursuit of common interest and co-operation in specific instances.

Count St Vallier,[1] before the Tunisian action, and Baron Courcel after the French defeat in Tonkin when General Négrier was wounded,[2] asked for Germany's good offices. In both cases these were forthcoming, and probably contributed more or less decisively to France's success, without however leading to any noticeable change of popular sentiment in France. These two actions, in whose execution I played a part, did not stop me from suggesting some time later a third attempt to achieve a practical improvement in German-French relations. A few days before the fall of Minister Hanotaux, Count Münster, acting on instructions, suggested to him that we might co-operate in certain South-West African colonial matters. The point at issue was to use an opportunity which might have presented itself should Portugal, because of great financial difficulties, have been led to a voluntary surrender of certain areas. This German-French collaboration would have been directed, though perhaps only tacitly, against England. M. Hanotaux received the German Ambassador's suggestion favourably and intended immediately to instruct the French Minister in Lisbon accordingly. But he stated that he could not come to any definite agreement with us before the existing French Ministerial crisis was at an end. But the Ministerial crisis had this outcome : eight days later Delcassé occupied Hanotaux's place. And since then all has been silence. The French Minister in Lisbon from that time on could not be brought to discuss the Portuguese colonial question with the German Minister, and when Richthofen went so far, a few months later, as to drop a hint to the Marquis de Noailles, the latter made it quite clear that in the obtaining situation he regarded the idea of German-French collaboration in specific instances as hopeless.[3]

During all the years that M. Delcassé has been a Minister he has never replied to this formal query by the German Ambassador. Only when M. Hanotaux, not so very long ago, criticized him in a magazine because of a missed opportunity for a rapprochement with Germany, M. Delcassé made an enquiry here : 'He had heard some vague stories; what was behind them, could we inform him ?[4] The object was to make us take the initiative a second time in a matter where failure would have been absolutely certain considering the state of Anglo-French relations at the time. In the same way, M. Delcassé has over the years repeatedly tried to place us in awkward situations by making overtures, usually directed against England, to one or other of our high-level official agencies through persons without any recognized position, whom he could disavow whenever he pleased. The overtures were never such as to compromise him, while he could use the reply of the German agency

---

[1] Charles, Count de St Vallier. French Ambassador in Berlin, 1877–81.
[2] On 28 March 1885.         [3] See *Memoirs*, chapter VI.
[4] See *Grosse Politik*, vol. XVIIIii, nos. 5884, 5885, pp. 797–800.

in question—Foreign Ministry or Paris Embassy—against us in England. Delcassé never took up our hint to take *official* steps—that is what diplomacy is for—and the official and completely positive suggestion by Count Münster has remained without an answer to the present day. This last fact by itself proves that M. Delcassé never honestly intended to draw closer to us, but that he merely wanted to use our overtures, if we had made any, in order to gain a higher standing in England. If a French Minister tries to be on good terms with England and furthermore tries to place Germany in awkward situations, he is only doing his job. But then he must not get cross with a German diplomat if the latter doesn't want to stick his head in the lion's maw.

If you should be interested in this subject, there is no lack of material which I can show you next time you come. But I believe that the above is quite sufficient to give you the general idea. I am not *at all* in favour of your mounting a big attack on Delcassé. That would only make him more interesting to the French. You should confine yourself, it seems to me, to saying that when Bülow made his speech last year a few days after the conclusion of the Anglo-French agreement (about which Delcassé always reminds him), Bülow was justified in assuming that France would not disregard the other Treaty Powers so completely in her Moroccan policy as has in fact happened for some considerable time.[1] Furthermore, that the Anglo-French agreement formally only foresaw the maintenance of the status quo, while now the Tunisification of Morocco, i.e. the elimination of all non-French interests, was in the air. You have had the opportunity of convincing yourself at first hand that the *diplomatic* policy which we are conducting over Morocco is the Chancellor's own policy. The attack on me in the *Temps* is an expression of bad temper by one or more of our contemporaries. It is complete nonsense and for that reason makes not the slightest impression on me. *I* am supposed to be conducting the Press campaign against France. You have seen with your own eyes that the Press is the one subject on which I have quarrelled with the Chancellor, because the Press directorate until the last few days ignored the Treaty principle and the collectivity of the Treaty Powers arising from it, leaving the public with the impression that the only alternatives were : separate negotiations with France, or a straight refusal of the French overtures. The sortie against me makes it quite obvious how unwelcome the refusal to pose this alternative and the emergence of the Treaty principle are, not only to the *Temps* correspondent here, but also for example to M. Delcassé. The Treaty principle puts France in the wrong at the very start of the affair. And, as you may have read recently, between nations right and wrong only lose their significance if the evil-doer is strong enough to overcome all resistance. France is certainly not in a situation to do so at present. A telegram from Metternich received to-day[2] shows that the English are moving very

---

[1] In his speech to the Reichstag of 12 April 1904, Bülow welcomed the Anglo-French entente as a contribution to world peace and expressed his conviction that German rights would not be disregarded.

[2] *Grosse Politik*, vol. XXii, no. 6845, pp. 608–9.

carefully—I am speaking of official and responsible circles—showing not the slightest inclination to quarrel with us over Morocco. In this connection I would like to repeat my urgent request to emphasize our relations with America as little as possible. There is another thing I would ask you not to mention and that is the anti-English proposal we once made to Hanotaux, for any reminder of this would immediately be used to annoy the English.

Now farewell. I want once again to tell you how sorry I am at having been responsible for spoiling your sons' Easter holiday. But I think you will agree with me that it was a good thing you came.

I am still sitting at home. With best wishes for Easter, dear *Herr Kommerzienrat*,

Your very devoted<br>Holstein.

P.S. Reading through this exposé, where the personal element takes second place to the historical one, I find I would do well to emphasize that *meo voto* the Berlin arrow of the *Temps* should best be left lying on the ground. If you see no grounds or more valid reason to take up the matter—I certainly don't. H.[1]

886.    Holstein to Hugo von Radolin[2]

Berlin, 1 May 1905

Dear Radolin,

From the dispatch arriving simultaneously with this letter[3] you will see that your attitude on Moroccan matters is fully appreciated here. You, for your part, can have no complaint on the score of insufficient or unclear instructions.

It was obvious that Delcassé was trying to put the blame on you and Richthofen, as if you two had either not understood the French statements, or else not passed them on properly. But we saw through their game, and therefore Mühlberg quickly decided to refuse Bihourd's offer to transmit to us 'complete' French memoranda on the conversations between yourself and Delcassé.

Delcassé's assertion that the Minister in Fez[4] had *not* introduced himself as the mandatory of the European Powers appears to be untrue.[5] When this finally becomes public, it will hardly render Delcassé's position stronger. How much simpler the matter would have been if Rouvier[6] had given you the information he gave you the other day a year

---

[1] On 22 April Neven-Dumont thanked Holstein for his letter, which gave him the basis for the correct appraisal of all situations that might arise, and enabled him to avoid or if necessary correct any mistakes in their representation in the Press. He assured Holstein once again that the *Kölnische Zeitung* would follow his policy toward France on Morocco 'in the conviction that it was the correct one'.

[2] From the Radolin Papers.

[3] Of 1 May. (*Grosse Politik*, vol. XXii, no. 6644, pp. 353–5.)

[4] Delcassé was referring to Georges Saint-René Taillandier, French Minister in Tangier, 1901–6. The French representative in Fez was Vice-Consul H. Gaillard.

[5] Radolin had telegraphed this statement of Delcassé's on 14 April. (*Grosse Politik*, vol. XXii, no. 6621, pp. 328–30.)

[6] Maurice Rouvier. French Finance Minister in the Combes Cabinet, 1902–5; Minister-President, Finance Minister, and (from 6 June 1905) Foreign Minister, 1905–6.

ago.[1] But Delcassé, leaning on the President's goodwill, has for years behaved like a dictator in matters of foreign policy. And he in turn has been pushed by the English. I myself hardly doubt—you might occasionally perhaps raise this idea with Rouvier in the form of a question—that the English hope to see a German-French conflict, I mean a real war, over Morocco, in order to have a free hand themselves somewhere else, perhaps in the Persian Gulf or in Abyssinia. One can quite understand that they think the moment ripe for action, now that Russia has been weakened by a severe blood-letting. France, however, unless otherwise engaged, would hardly let the English take Abyssinia, Yemen, or Muscat without protest. This I think is the reason why England is driving the French to speed up their Moroccan action as much as possible. On the other hand I definitely do not believe—and I have reasons for this—that in case of war the English Government would come to the aid of France arms in hand, for example with the intention of taking this opportunity to destroy the German fleet. Incidentally, M. Rouvier will be at least as well informed on this score as I am.

The Moroccan question, which as far as France and ourselves are concerned could have been solved easily and simply last year, has now become much more difficult and complicated because Delcassé made two mistakes: his disregard of, or shall we say dilatoriness towards, Germany, and on the other hand his unreasonable haste about Morocco. The latter, as I have said, may well have been suggested by England. With good will, both we and France will get out of this without any harm being done, I hope. But no unreasonable haste! First of all let Tattenbach get to Fez so that one can see clearly what the situation is and what Delcassé has so hastily stirred up there. His plan to treat Germany as *quantité négligeable* shows him up as an amateur in diplomacy.

With best regards
Your
Holstein.

887.   Holstein to Hugo von Radolin[2]

Berlin, 8 May 1905

Dear Radolin,

As regards Morocco, Delcassé evidently wants to arrange matters so that you are blamed for the misunderstanding. His intention becomes quite clear from the fact that he didn't say a single word about Morocco to you last Wednesday,[3] while at the same time approaches were made

---

[1] On the evening of 26 April Rouvier told Radolin that France would do everything in her power to live on good terms with Germany. 'We would do everything possible and give any explanation or satisfaction that might be desired.' (*Grosse Politik*, vol. XXii, no. 6635, pp. 344–5.)

[2] From the Radolin Papers.

[3] See Radolin's telegram to Bülow of 8 May. (*Grosse Politik*, vol. XXii, no. 6657, pp. 373–4.)

in Rome on his instructions.[1] It is up to you to show Rouvier the perfidiousness of this outflanking manoeuvre—directed against you, against Germany, which is to be duped, and *against Rouvier, the object being to achieve a success, thereby supplanting him in Loubet's confidence*—in its true light. Perhaps this could be done with less embarrassment through Betzold,[2] rather than directly. But the most important thing is that you should not become irritable. Countess Alvensleben has after all given you the reputation of being quarrelsome. [...]

Neither Delcassé, nor Barrère, nor Luzzati, will have even dreamed that we would inform Rouvier directly of the approach in Rome. This outflanking manoeuvre hasn't done any of those concerned, neither Delcassé nor Monts, any good with Bülow. On the contrary.

With Rouvier we must speak quite openly when the opportunity offers, both about the material and the personal issues.

Should Barrère visit you, I would be very polite, but only discuss the material issue—Germany's position towards the Morocco affair, and that only if he brings up the matter. If he touches upon the finessing manoeuvre, I would say, yes, I know that a démarche was made to my colleague in Rome and that my Government returned the same answer as in Paris.[3]

I would mention, as a general directive, that it is not of advantage either to Germany or to you, if Barrère were to interpose himself between you and Rouvier. Rouvier must continue to feel at all times that he can get full information only from you direct—or possibly from Betzold. I have nothing against the latter if you haven't.

As regards Delcassé, his power—at least for now—has been pretty well broken as a result of Rouvier's intervention and mistrust. But the time might come again when he would be strong enough, with Loubet's help, to remove Rouvier. That is why it would definitely be best for Rouvier to remove him now, by pointing to the difficulties he has raised for France with Japan because of the neutrality question.[4] You might perhaps discuss this point objectively and quite calmly with Betzold.

As regards Delcassé, I would give no cause for complaint in your dealings with him, but I would let him feel that as far as Germany is concerned he is mistrusted. Bourgeois would probably be the best successor for Delcassé from our point of view. Barrère and Cambon

---

[1] Monts had telegraphed on 2 May : 'Signor Luzzati, at Delcassé's request, made a démarche to me stating that France was prepared to grant His Majesty the Kaiser some striking satisfaction, desired and specified by us, in order to reach with us a solution to the Moroccan question in a manner not too greatly injurious to French honour. M. Barrère had been empowered to repeat this offer to me and to enter into discussions.' ( *Grosse Politik*, vol. XXii, no. 6648, p. 362.)

[2] French financier; an intimate of Rouvier. (See *Grosse Politik*, vol. XXii, no. 6646, pp. 357–9.)

[3] Bülow had replied that Germany, after having declared that she had taken her stand on the basis of the collectivity of the Treaty Powers, could not conclude a separate treaty with France at the first French offer without any change having taken place in the situation. ( *Grosse Politik*, vol. XXii, nos. 6649, 6650, pp. 363–7.)

[4] Japan had regarded it as a breach of neutrality when France allowed the Russian fleet sailing to the Far East to anchor off Madagascar and, later, off the coast of Indo-China.

(Madrid) are incalculable, because keen on action. But that is a tricky point, for the French will care little—or at least only in exceptional circumstances—whom we would like best.

With most obedient respects to the Princess,

Your old Holstein.

I am dealing with Morocco alone with Bülow, in the greatest harmony.

888.   Holstein to Hugo von Radolin[1]

Berlin, 22 May 1905

Dear Radolin,

[...] I find it striking that, according to a report from Tattenbach, Delcassé even most recently has continued to pursue a policy of intimidation and threats in Fez.[2] Also some of the semi-official articles which have been telegraphed here, for example a very pessimistic piece in the *Figaro*, are forcing me to ask providence whether Delcassé is trying to arouse public opinion in France in the hope that Germany would then back down. This idea doesn't originate with me. A prominent French journalist very recently said to a German, who then told it to Richthofen, that Delcassé's whole Moroccan policy was based on the conviction that when the psychological moment came the powers that be in Germany would not have the necessary 'guts'. A similar hint, though less obvious, was also dropped to Kühlmann in Tangier by a Paris journalist some time ago. If the French continue to believe that we will back down they will come a bad cropper. The Chancellor and, so I am told, the Kaiser see quite clearly that it would be more dangerous, particularly for Germany, to retreat than to stand firm. The war which would be avoided by giving in now would certainly be forced upon us after a short interval under some other pretext and worse conditions. But I do not believe in war at all because I doubt whether Delcassé is the man to carry the French with him. [...]

Until we see each other again shortly,

With best wishes
Your
Holstein.

889.   Holstein to Hugo von Radolin[3]

28 May [1905]

Dear Radolin,

In great haste only this one point. It seems to me the ideal solution if Miquel,[4] *on the Chancellor's instructions*, were to inform Rouvier and

---

[1] From the Radolin Papers.

[2] According to Tattenbach the French Minister had stated on Delcassé's instructions that no other Power had the right to interfere in Moroccan affairs. (*Grosse Politik*, vol. XXii, no. 6663, pp. 380–1.)

[3] From the Radolin Papers.

[4] Hans von Miquel. Second Secretary at the Paris Embassy, 1902–May 1905; First Secretary in St Petersburg, 1905–8; in Constantinople, 1908–12.

other persons directly of our *griefs* concerning Delcassé. This way you will be kept out of it.

Best regards

Your

Holstein.

The Chancellor agrees to this method of operation if you agree to it.[1]

## 890. Holstein to Hugo von Radolin[2]

7 June 1905

Dear friend,

Letter just received.[3] All right then, at half past five.[4] [...]

From what you have let me know just now I see that Rouvier wants to bargain. Unfortunately we are not in a position *to make concessions to him at once, overnight.*[5]

Your

## 891. Holstein to Hugo von Radolin[6]

Berlin, 14 June 1905

Dear Radolin,

What did H.M. say in his Döberitz speech in front of the foreign officers, or rather what did Hugo[7] tell you about this? We, the Chancellor and I, know nothing.[8] You must not risk getting a refusal from Hugo, but do write me what he has told you voluntarily. If you should wish it, I will keep what you tell me entirely to myself, but *pour ma gouverne personelle*, as the Chancellor's adviser, I must be informed. It seems to me that H.M. has a bad conscience, as he hasn't said anything to the Chancellor. Judging by the phlegmatic attitude which Rouvier adopted in the first conversation after your return,[9] I would assume that H.M. reassured the French regarding the danger of war. In this he could of course be mistaken, for sometimes events are more powerful than the human will, and England is doing everything she can to bring about a German-French war.

The reason why I telegraphed you yesterday not to speak with Rouvier until to-day was that Loubet in the course of yesterday probably received a direct telegraphic message from Roosevelt through the French Ambassador in Washington.[10] In it Roosevelt points out that in case of a war with Germany, England stands to gain a lot, France to lose

[1] See *Grosse Politik*, vol. XXii, no. 6674, pp. 393–7.

[2] From the Radolin Papers.

[3] Not found.

[4] Radolin had begun a short leave on 5 June in order to go to Berlin for the marriage of the German Crown Prince.

[5] Delcassé had fallen on 6 June. Rouvier had taken over direction of the French Foreign Ministry.

[6] From the Radolin Papers.

[7] Prussian Lieutenant-Colonel. Military Attaché in Paris.

[8] See Bülow's telegram to Radolin of 10 June 1905 (*Grosse Politik*, vol. XXii, no. 6704, pp. 429–30), and Holstein's letters of 15 September 1905 *et seq.*, below.

[9] See Radolin's telegram of 11 June. (*Grosse Politik*, vol. XXii, no. 6705, pp. 430–1.)

[10] J. J. Jusserand. French Ambassador in Washington, 1903–24.

a lot.[1] Naturally you must not mention to any one that you know anything about this. It was Roosevelt's own idea. Formerly he trusted England, but he has gradually become suspicious. But this step, which would otherwise certainly create an impression, will be largely neutralized if in the meanwhile Rouvier should have received from General Lacroix[2] the assurance that 'it is all bluff' as Delcassé said, and that H.M. loves France.[3] Yet in reality bad diplomatic incidents could occur should the Moroccan affair remain unresolved. With some good will France could meet us halfway. But if Rouvier simply sticks fast to the Delcassé programme and wants to realize it *right now*, I certainly think the future is black, and the English will be able to gloat.

Basically the problem between ourselves and France is now a matter of form; for we don't want to upset France's future.

In Monday's issue of the *Lokalanzeiger* I discovered yesterday the enclosed surprising piece.[4] I doubt that the Sultan would voluntarily make such a proposal, and against the Sultan's will Germany cannot partition Morocco, at least not now.

When Betzold was here, Rouvier stated through him: *Si l'Allemagne ne veut pas que nous allions au Maroc, nous n'irons pas, voilà tout.*

And what does Rouvier say to-day?

I for my part urgently desire that we should reach an understanding with France, if only to annoy the English. But how can it be done? I am curious what Rouvier will tell you in the second conversation.[5] I regret that he doesn't want to remain Foreign Minister, although Freycinet would probably also not be bad.

To-day there is nothing more to be said about Morocco until it is known what Rouvier will say. I wish I saw a decent way out, but the English are naturally agitating as much as they can and are probably also spending money on the Press. [...]

I am sending this letter to-day from Cologne through a post-office official. Please send me your answer through him. Either write it entirely for me alone, or else write a letter which I can submit, with a post-script for me alone. You can tell Rouvier and his confidants in all sincerity that we would very much like to get out of the impossible situation in which Delcassé has placed us and arrive at a better relationship with France, but Rouvier must show us a decent way out. We cannot violate the Sultan, partition against his will.

Please give my best regards to the Princess and destroy this letter within twenty-four hours.

Your
Holstein [...]

[1] See Speck von Sternburg's telegram of 12 June. (*Grosse Politik*, vol. XXii, no. 6707, pp. 433–4.)

[2] Henri de Lacroix. French representative at the marriage of the German Crown Prince, 1905

[3] See Lacroix's report on his conversation with the Kaiser. (*Documents Diplomatiques Français*, Deuxième Série, vol. VII, no. 334, pp. 403–6; see also Thimme, *Berliner Monatshefte* (1937), p. 873, note 31; H. O. Meisner, 'Gespräche und Briefe Holstein's 1907–1909', *Preussische Jahrbücher*, vol. 228, pp 8–9.)

[4] Not found.

[5] See Radolin's telegram of 14 June. (*Grosse Politik*, vol. XXii, no. 6710, pp. 438–9.)

892.   Holstein to Bernhard von Bülow
       Copy

Berlin, 17 June 1905

Dear Bülow,

I was pleased that you did not continue to discuss the subject of the Kaiser's comments after we were no longer alone. I shall now briefly and quite calmly set out my point of view.

The Kaiser has always tended to be critical, but recently the occasions on which his complaints have been of an insulting nature, apparently on purpose, have grown more frequent. It would not be difficult to collect quite a selection if this were necessary. The Foreign Ministry is doing its job and does not merit this degree of open disdain. It can definitely be said that over the last hundred years no King of Prussia has treated a department of the central government with such marked contempt for such unimportant reasons. It is obvious what a harmful effect it must have on the lower-ranking officials if they see how the Kaiser treats the department.

You said that the simple and discreet method by which I personally thought of removing myself from the ambit of these insults is in turn insulting to other people who are in a similar situation. As far as I can see there then remains only one remedy, and that is that the attention of His Majesty should be drawn to the bad effects resulting from the violent tone of his reprimands. I am quite prepared to expose myself personally in order to bring to an end a situation which I regard as undignified. For example, as the senior of the higher officials in the Foreign Ministry, I could make a submission to you destined for His Majesty, in which I briefly explained how and why I felt myself to be in a difficult situation as a member of the Foreign Ministry. The consequences which His Majesty might draw from such a complaint I would find more acceptable than the continuation of the present state of affairs with the repeated expressions of the Kaiser's contempt at shorter or longer intervals.

Your sincerely devoted
Holstein.


893.   Holstein to Bernhard von Bülow
       Copy

B[erlin], 18 June 1905

Dear Bülow,

From the memoranda I wrote to-day you will have seen that *je ne demande pas mieux* than to go on working. But your comparison with Montezuma is inaccurate. It is true that like Montezuma's companion I am lying on the gridiron, but alone. I cannot regard the matter as settled. In the verbal discussion which you intend to have I shall only be able to repeat that a continuation of the present situation without change would be unacceptable to me as I explained in my letter of yesterday.

Your sincerely devoted
H.

894.  Hugo von Radolin to Holstein[1]
Copy

Paris, 22 June 1905

My dear friend,

[...] But,[2] as a politician inexperienced in matters of foreign policy, Rouvier can be easily influenced. I hinted at this already some time ago. The last note[3] proves that he was terrorized by the 'Chinovniks' of the Foreign Ministry—Louis[4] is probably one of the most important ones— and also the 'colonial' fanatics, of whom Etienne,[5] the Minister of the Interior, is certainly one. Révoil,[6] Etienne's *âme damnée*, is actually supposed to have inspired the note if he did not write it himself. Incidentally I had the feeling (and I am not mistaken) that Rouvier was considerably embarrassed with me when he hurriedly read the note to me *par acquit de conscience*; for he realized well that the note was not in accord with the way in which we had discussed matters in detail, good-naturedly, at length and frequently. (More of this in the telegram I sent to-day).[7] The hint, in my telegram of Tuesday,[8] that Rouvier would probably try to squeeze out something more was correct. But he is going further than I thought he would. But I do feel that when he sees that he can do nothing else [than] to accept the conference and that *he will get no far-reaching concessions from us* (at the most, official confirmation of what I told him privately as my opinion about the reforms— French influence in the frontier region also as regards military matters), he will finally yield to the inevitable and formally accept the conference as desired.

I must therefore *urgently* ask for patience in order *not to bring matters to a break*. I shall come back to this *very coolly* with Rouvier, and hope that I will reach the goal, in spite of the strong pressures to which he may be subject. I shall continue to go on working in this sense directly with him and his confidants Léon[9] and Dupuy.[10] Betzold is very useful to me and Rouvier trusts him.

*Therefore, please, patience.* The note should perhaps not be taken too seriously. Its impression on me is that of a beautifully stylized but impractical elaboration, which contains many contradictions. Here really *nobody* wants war and that is something one can count on. But we

[1] From the Radolin Papers. Not found in the Holstein Papers.

[2] Radolin had written in the earlier part of the letter that a journalist by the name of Hansen had no influence on and no contact with Rouvier.

[3] Of 21 June. (*Documents Diplomatiques*; *Affaires du Maroc 1901–1905*, (Ministère des Affaires Etrangères, Paris, 1905), no. 272, pp. 235–8.)

[4] Georges Louis. Director of political affairs in the French Foreign Ministry.

[5] Eugène Etienne. French Minister of the Interior in the Rouvier Cabinet, 1905; Minister of War in the Rouvier and Sarrien Cabinets, 1905–6.

[6] Paul Révoil. French Governor-General of Algeria, 1901–3; delegate to the Algeciras Conference, 1906; Ambassador in Berne, 1906, in Madrid, 1907–10.

[7] *Grosse Politik*, vol. XXii, no. 6724, pp. 457–9.

[8] Probably Radolin's telegram of 21 June (Wednesday). (*Grosse Politik*, vol. XXii, no. 6720, pp. 452–3.)

[9] A financier in Paris, of Turkish nationality.

[10] Jean Dupuy, the former Prime Minister.

must not unnecessarily injure their national honour. *I* continue to stand very firmly for the demands of our policy, and when they see *that we do not want to insult them* they will finally accept the inevitable. [...]

The *Echo de Paris* carried violent articles of English origin.

Please, read these articles.

The French know very well that England is using a softer tone towards us. Rouvier has no illusion about perfidious Albion.

In haste<br>
Your cordially devoted<br>
Hugo.

### 895. Holstein to Bernhard von Bülow

23 June [1905]

Dear Bülow,

You can go ahead and resign, for—this is one of the differences between us—your resignation won't be accepted. At the most there would be talk of the whims and moods of His Excellency.

My case is different. As I've said, I shall now first of all wait till to-morrow.

H.

### 896. Holstein to Hugo von Radolin[1]

Berlin, 23 June 1905

Dear Radolin,

Yesterday His Majesty was informed of the unfavourable situation of the Moroccan question,[2] and right now, at seven o'clock in the evening, the Chancellor has received a long reply by telegram.[3] The Kaiser entirely shares the Chancellor's point of view and finds it inconceivable that Rouvier should have set himself the task of realizing Delcassé's programme, thus enhancing the latter's prestige. He told the Prince of Monaco what he thought of this in no uncertain terms. The Kaiser says that the Prince was completely overcome and intended to write at once to Rouvier. So this letter will probably arrive in two days' time in the morning. It will have been necessary if the theory of the two trends[4] is still current in Paris. The letter will kill it.

It is definitely a great weakness of Rouvier's and shows a lack of logical reflection that he has not realized how, by adopting the Delcassé programme, he is helping Delcassé back to his feet, the man who is now probably his worst enemy. Could you not exercise your influence through Léon or Dupuy so that Rouvier does not choose his advisers so exclusively from the Delcassé clan as seems to be the case now? Louis' removal would, I think, be a necessary pre-condition if Rouvier really wants to break with his predecessor's anti-German policy—though it doesn't look as if he does at the moment.

---

[1] From the Radolin Papers.
[2] *Grosse Politik*, vol. XXii, no. 6723, pp. 455–7.
[3] *Grosse Politik*, vol. XXii, no. 6730, pp. 465–6.
[4] That is, two trends in German foreign policy, the Kaiser's and the Foreign Ministry's.

I find the Onjda-affair[1] pretty sinister; I would regard the fall of Onjda as a real threat to German-French relations, because it would face Germany with the alternative of calmly accepting an *échec* (one could say disgrace) or of reacting sharply. I still have the hope that Rouvier will come to his senses before it is too late and adopt a reasonable policy again instead of wrapping himself in the prophet's cloak of Delcassé. That is why for the time being I still entirely agree with the patience you preach. But do make sure that nothing goes wrong in Onjda. The Chancellor read your last two letters and praised them very much; altogether he is very appreciative of your tactful yet firm stand up till now.

As ever

Your rather tired

Holstein.

## 897. Holstein to Hugo von Radolin[2]

Berlin, 28 June 1905

Dear Radolin,

[...] Morocco is not going very well. I am not disclosing a diplomatic secret when I say that we are not getting anywhere. I had hoped that our relations with France would improve after the settlement over Morocco, but at the moment it doesn't seem likely. Looked at objectively the proposals which Rouvier made to you[3] are identical with those contained in last week's exposé.[4] We will not agree to negotiations *before* the invitations to the Conference are in train. The Conference would thus not take place, and we shall remain, for we can do no other, with shouldered arms at the Sultan's side—a state of affairs which could lead to all sorts of complications. The French too seem to think so. Schlieffen to-day wrote to the Chancellor, who sent me the letter, that reservists had been called up for the frontier corps, while none were being released. Further that troops in the frontier garrisons had received combat uniforms and equipment and tinned rations for four days. For the time being the Chancellor wants to prevent counter-measures being taken—I think he is definitely right in this, because once that starts, both sides will drive each other further and further; but if the French continue with their preparations, it will not be possible to stop our military from taking steps here too, otherwise the responsibility becomes too great. Let us hope for the best.

I am pretty well up till now in spite of much work, because there is no trouble. The Chancellor agrees with H.M. on the one hand, on the other also with

Your old friend

H.

I submitted your letter which arrived yesterday[5] to the Chancellor.

[1] The region of Onjda on the Algerian border was the centre of a revolt by Bu Hamara, a pretender to the Sultanate of Morocco. Radolin had received information that the Pretender was receiving French support. (*Grosse Politik*, vol. XXii, no. 6724, pp. 457–9.)

[2] From the Radolin Papers.

[3] On 27 June. (See *Grosse Politik*, vol. XXii, no. 6746, pp. 485–7.)

[4] See p. 345, note 3.          [5] Not found.

898.    Holstein to Hugo von Radolin[1]

Berlin 1 July 1905

Dear Radolin,

I was somewhat surprised to learn from the newspapers that special plenipotentiaries are to negotiate in Paris concerning Morocco. That sounds almost funny, since we have kept on saying that we do not want such separate negotiations. To-day's dispatch[2] will probably put an end to this talk and bring the matter to a decision. If the French don't want to play, we shall negotiate with the Sultan and stand by his side with shouldered arms until the Conference convenes. I cannot imagine that such a state of armed peace, when any day there might be incidents on the frontier because of the Pretender, can be helpful to French business.

As regards the English alliance offers, I cannot easily be led to believe that such offers should again have been made recently. It would be pardonable for M. Dupuy to exaggerate somewhat for the sake of his cause.[3] But I certainly believe one thing quite firmly, that both Bertie and possibly Lansdowne would like to see France involved in war. England could then consider whether it seemed profitable to join in the war or not. In the latter case she could in the meantime take over the whole coast of the Persian Gulf with ease.

In to-day's dispatch neither Delcassé nor England are mentioned, but Rouvier will presumably be clever enough to mention, if not in the Chamber, at least in discussions with the party leaders, that Delcassé and not Rouvier is to blame for the present situation and also that and for what reason the English want to embroil the French with us.

On the memorandum which I drew up for the Chancellor for his conversation with Bihourd, the Chancellor marked those passages of which he made use. These I had copied afterwards. Therefore what you have got has actually been said.[4] There is no reason why you should not give it to Dupuy to read. But if he should ask for a copy, say that as a matter of form you cannot provide one without special authorization. If he wants to make notes, that is another matter. I do hope that the affair will after all be settled soon one way or another. The way in which the French keep changing their minds is gradually making the discussions appear undignified. One can see that a number of people are taking a hand in it.

I think the French believe us to be cleverer and sharper than we are. They expect us to come out with Heaven knows what far-reaching ideas. I for my part regard it as the main aim of the Moroccan action that we should demonstrate to the French *ad oculos* that it is better to treat us well rather than badly. Perhaps better official relations than hitherto would then develop on the basis of mutual respect.

[1] From the Radolin Papers.

[2] *Grosse Politik*, vol. XXii, no. 6753, pp. 495–8.

[3] Radolin had telegraphed on 30 June : 'Dupuy also confessed to me in confidence that the English Ambassador was trying to bring the alliance with France, drafted at England's request when Delcassé was in office, into effect. Rouvier was adopting a negative attitude.' ( *Grosse Politik*, vol. XXii, no. 6752, pp. 493–4. )

[4] See *Grosse Politik*, vol. XXii, no. 6753, enclosure, pp. 497–8.

If Hanotaux had remained in office, normal diplomatic relations between ourselves and France would have come into being long ago. Delcassé has deliberately and with perseverance hampered them.

I do wish the Conference had already convened, then I would be less worried than I am now, in fact not at all; for then any incidents which might still be provoked by that ghastly Pretender[1] would be of no more concern to us than to the other Treaty Powers. Now and until the Conference convenes we stand alone beside the Sultan.

For technical reasons it seems to me impossible or at any rate most impractical to hold the Conference anywhere but in Tangier. It stands to reason that a large number of important questions, for example the position and taxation of native agents of foreign Powers, etc. etc. can only be completely appraised and decided on the spot.

Who in Paris can have thought of Rosen?[2] Perhaps a French correspondent in Berlin.

With best regards
Your
Holstein.


899.    Holstein to Hugo von Radolin[3]

Berlin, 2 July 1905

Dear Radolin,

The Chancellor has just read to me your reports nos. 519[4] and 520[5] including the enclosure.

I hope the French will accept our minor alterations.[6] If not, then nothing will be settled, we shall have a state of *paix armée*, out of which, with English help, a war could easily develop. But I hope that common sense will prove victorious, for the alterations are such that the French can easily accept them.

I thank you cordially for the good opinion [of me] which was expressed in your letter.[7]

One more thing, absolutely secret. Bülow has read both the private telegrams I sent to-day.[8] He has initialled them and I have marked them *ad acta secreta*. The telegrams express Bülow's views.

In haste
Your
H.

[1] See p. 347, note 1.
[2] As special German plenipotentiary for the Moroccan question.
[3] From the Radolin Papers.
[4] *Grosse Politik*, vol. XXii, no. 6756, pp. 501–2.
[5] *Grosse Politik*, vol. XXii, no. 6754, p. 499.
[6] To Rouvier's drafts for a note exchange concerning the Moroccan Conference. (*Grosse Politik*, vol. XXii, no. 6755, pp. 499–501.) For the changes proposed by Germany, see *Grosse Politik*, vol. XXii, no. 6758, pp. 504–6.
[7] Not found.
[8] *Grosse Politik*, vol. XXii, no. 6757, pp. 502–3. The second telegram has not been found. See below, p. 350, note 2.

## 900.   Holstein to Hugo von Radolin[1]

5 July 1905

Dear Radolin,

Pardon the pencil. I have only a few minutes if the letter is to leave at noon to-day.

The Chancellor is impatiently awaiting your private answer to my private telegram of the day before yesterday.[2] How did Dupuy take the 'vision of the future'? What impression did you get? The programme outlined there would be in the best interests of France as of Germany, but it would run directly counter to the Delcassé programme, for he wanted to go *with* Spain and Italy *against* Germany. Delcassé's following will thus perhaps oppose the 'vision of the future'.

But there are many Frenchmen who regard collaboration between France and Germany as useful. Thus, for example, Capitaine Juinot Gambetta, a member of the French military mission in Morocco, said in Tangier just recently: 'France and Germany have to rely on each other to defend their Far Eastern interests.'

If only for this reason, the French will think carefully before allowing matters to come to a diplomatic break with us over Morocco.

I do not believe that the English agitation is dangerous. People now see through the English. But the French—that is the drift now—want to tie us down in advance to agree to everything that France will demand at the Conference. We cannot tie ourselves in advance in this way, certainly not as long as we are in the dark concerning France's later policy. Later —*on verra*.

Best regards, also to the Princess, from

Your
Holstein.

If your impression is that the *ballon d'essai* concerning future policy has fallen to earth it is your duty to say so openly. You are a sensitive observer and will surely have noticed all sorts of things during the exchange of views on the subject. If in the present circumstances it seems to you risky to speak of the 'vision of the future', *don't* do so without having consulted me beforehand. Please, do so either by private telegram or by private letter; or perhaps a telegram that a letter is on the way. The person who is bringing you this letter could bring back yours.[3]

---

[1] From the Radolin Papers.

[2] In his telegram of 2 July (see p. 349, note 8) Holstein had sketched his personal ideas on the future course of the Moroccan question; France should not make any attempt to seize Morocco at once, as Delcassé had intended; genuine efforts at reform should be made, but these would probably fail; Germany would then back French claims on Morocco, and possibly Germany would also seek a share; in any case third parties, specifically Spain, would be excluded from the spoils.

[3] Radolin replied in a private telegram of 7 July (*Grosse Politik*, vol. XXii, no. 6761, pp. 510–11) that Holstein's ideas were in complete accord with those of Dupuy, and that Rouvier, before he had taken over the Foreign Ministry, had expressed similar ideas.

## 901. Holstein to Hugo von Radolin[1]

Berlin, 9 July 1905

Dear Radolin,

I am very glad that at last the Conference is assured.[2] It was a trial of patience, and you will have seen from the telegrams I sent yesterday[3] that people here were beginning to get nervous. It seems the matter would hardly have been brought to a conclusion without Dupuy who appears to be a determined man who can think straight. Now that the needle has been threaded it will probably be possible to pull the thread through further. Hence I understand why the enemies of German-French collaboration did all they could to prevent the needle being threaded.

Now, in the discussions that lie ahead, the main point is that France should not try to get us to agree to special advantages for the French. An honest effort must be made to bring about the international reforms. There is no reason to suppose that these will succeed any better than in Turkey. In the meantime both France and Germany must conduct their policy in such a way that no new causes of conflict appear, so that when the psychological moment has come the two Governments can reach agreement without drawing in third parties. It will not be necessary to conclude any kind of treaty or agreement in advance, for the national interests of both countries point to a rapprochement. Although I am no optimist, I can see that feeling towards us in France is improving, and that men are really to be found there now who have the courage to say publicly that, given certain conditions, co-operation with Germany could be of benefit to France. On the other hand the anti-German element, men like Révoil, Louis, Cambon and their gang will regard it as their task to make proposals at the Conference which will drive a wedge between France and Germany. By that I mean proposals which involve French *mainmise* or else special advantages *right now*. In all decency we can't do that, not now.

It would be a good thing if you told Dupuy something about Tatten-bach, whom the French evidently regard as a 'bogey-man'. In his last telegram before leaving Tangier for Fez,[4] Tattenbach suggested that it might be more practical to reach an understanding with the French rather than with the Sultan; in the long run conditions in Morocco were untenable. He received the reply:[5] Agreement with France is not to be thought of now, but the future remains open. In fact there could be no question of such an agreement as long as Delcassé was in power. More-

[1] From the Radolin Papers.

[2] Radolin had telegraphed France's final acceptance on 8 July. (*Grosse Politik*, vol. XXii, no. 6766, p. 514.)

[3] On 7 July Radolin had telegraphed another French draft of the proposed note exchange. Holstein telegraphed on 8 July: 'Bülow said just now that you should not have accepted the French proposals, which arrived here to-day, or else handed them back after examination.' In a second telegram of 8 July Holstein said: 'The Chancellor also said just now: "Radolin must speak firmly. It is not apparent that he has done so in the last few days." Firmly, but calmly and with goodwill.' (From the Radolin Papers.)

[4] Of 29 April. (*Grosse Politik*, vol. XXii, no. 6642, pp. 350–2.)

[5] Of 30 April. (*Grosse Politik*, vol. XXii, no. 6643, p. 352.)

over we had at that time already taken our stand on the basis of the collectivity of the Treaty Powers, a stand which could not be abandoned at will. In Fez Tattenbach therefore pursued the policy, which he had been instructed to pursue, skilfully and successfully, although he personally rather favoured an understanding with France. I shall send you the relevant passage from that telegram of Tattenbach—if possible with the next courier, so that you can say to Dupuy that you yourself actually read it. I do believe strongly that honesty and truth are among the most useful political factors, because in the long run they make one's work much easier; but I fail to see any honesty in the proposals of Révoil and Co.[1] In my pretty wide experience I have hardly ever met with more sophistry than in their productions. And everything is constantly designed to make the Sultan believe that we have broken the treaty. This only makes the negotiations more difficult, for naturally we approach all these proposals with the greatest distrust. We just cannot drop the Sultan, now or in six months. M. Dupuy, who has the same part in this political drama as Desgenais in the plays by Dumas junior—the friend of the family with lots of common sense—should regard it as his special task to make this problem of decency clear to Rouvier.

The letter must go. Mühlberg, who was dining at Bülow's, was still there when your telegram 284[2] arrived. Bülow recognized fully the difficulties which you had to overcome.

I shake you cordially by the hand

Your

Holstein.

902.    Holstein to Hugo von Radolin[3]

Berlin, 13 July 1905

Dear Radolin,

I submitted your letter of the 11th[4] to the Chancellor, who incidentally, as I hear, repeatedly spoke highly of your work to a number of persons in the last few days. And he had every reason to do so. From your letter and also from your telegram 296[5] I gather that in the immediate future we must still be prepared for unacceptable French proposals. Supplementing the diplomatic reports by Press reports leads me to the assumption that the French will demand full freedom of action for their administration of Morocco on the basis of a mandate granted to them by the Treaty Powers. Again and again it is Delcassé's programme which re-emerges, slightly differently dressed up. Delcassé regarded the English treaty[6] by itself as a sufficient legal basis, whereas now the

---

[1] See *Grosse Politik*, vol. XXii, no. 6762, p. 512.    [2] See above, p. 351, note 2.

[3] From the Radolin Papers. A note by Radolin reads: 'Discussed with Dupuy, in part also with Rouvier.'

[4] Not found.

[5] Of 11 July. Radolin had reported that he had spoken to Dupuy along the lines of his instruction (*Grosse Politik*, vol. XXii, no. 6771, pp. 521–2). Dupuy would use his influence on Rouvier in the direction desired (elimination of hostile elements, in particular Révoil), but success was not to be expected overnight. (From the Foreign Ministry files.)

[6] Of 8 April 1904.

remaining Treaty Powers are to agree, but in both instances France is pursuing the identical objective which is to gain control over Morocco immediately. It seems to have been useless that we have stated again and again that we could not agree at this time to a French seizure of Morocco. M. Révoil, who drafted the French proposals, refuses to allow himself to be put off by that. Who knows, perhaps he would even prefer it if the affair ended in a row.

Altogether the French Government—by which, however, I don't mean Rouvier but Révoil and Co.—is working in a dishonest and malicious manner. Madrid has reported that an enquiry has been received whether Geneva would be acceptable as the meeting-place for the Conference. The intention thus is simply to ignore our proposal regarding Tangier. In reality Tangier is the only possible spot, because the majority of the questions to be discussed are primarily local problems—economic, financial, police and administrative matters cannot be judged from Geneva. They will require frequent reference to expert assessments by persons with local experience. It would be simply laughable to deal with such matters in Geneva. You will receive a telegram on this subject before this letter reaches you.[1]

It is important in the discussions that now lie ahead that you should always inform Dupuy well in advance of what will happen, and that you point out to him that from the beginning we have openly and honestly emphasized our point of view, to wit that at the moment both amputation and French seizure are *inadmissible*. Whoever is working to this end therefore is deliberately working against a German-French agreement and for Delcassé.

It seems to me that the above-mentioned statesman committed political suicide the day before yesterday.[2] He was faced with the unpleasant alternative of either admitting that he had been mistaken in the assumption that Germany would stand for anything, or else of justifying his policy by stating that France and England together would have been strong enough to have risked a war. Delcassé decided in favour of the latter, he preferred to appear foolhardy rather than stupid. But in doing so he does appear to have ruined his future, for it is evident that the great majority of the French people shares Rouvier's view that the English ships have no wheels. I suppose that Rouvier's position has been further strengthened by Delcassé's statement and that he will now find it easier than before—as soon as he wants to that is—to deprive Delcassé's following of any influence in the coming negotiations.

It seems to me very important that you should continue to remain in constant touch with Rouvier, perhaps through intermediaries rather than directly. Dupuy naturally is the chief mediator, but Léon and Betzold can perform useful services. You can only gain in authority with Rouvier

[1] *Grosse Politik*, vol. XXii, no. 6775, pp. 526–7, note *.
[2] In an interview published in the *Gaulois* on 12 July, Delcassé revealed that at the Cabinet meeting on 6 June he had advocated a firm alliance with England and outlined a programme based on this alliance. When his colleagues objected that this would provoke an attack by Germany, Delcassé declared that France would be in a position to reply.

if you always tell him in advance what is acceptable and what isn't. [...]

As a curious item of news I finally want to mention that Bihourd, according to his own testimony, is being starved of news by the Quai d'Orsay. He has repeatedly said to Bülow that he is being told nothing. That, of course, is due not to the Minister but to the *bureaux*, who will certainly already have a successor—Barrère possibly—*in petto*.

> With a cordial handshake
>
> Your
>
> Holstein.

903.　Holstein to Hugo von Radolin[1]

Berlin, 20 July 1905

Dear Radolin,

I read with special pleasure the article in the *Journal pour Rire*, describing Rouvier on the speaker's rostrum. But, as I've said, I don't believe in Rouvier's naïveté. He acts as if he were naïve and uses this naïveté to do business. On the other hand he is really a weak man and allows himself to be terrorized by the Delcassé group.

I was brought to write this letter when I read in the paper this morning that the Cabinet would shortly reach a decision on the place for the Conference. To please Germany a single session would perhaps be held in Tangier, and then the Conference would be convened somewhere else, possibly in Geneva. In this I again see the activity of the Delcassé group, which has still not given up the hope of finally bringing about the German-French conflict desired by Delcassé. In this connection I would like to say that it was of special interest to me to see from one of your reports that Delcassé now intends to remain silent and suffer all the attacks made against him. I see that as a sure sign that he hopes to come back. And why shouldn't he? After all, Rouvier is working directly for him by allowing Delcassé's following a free hand.

The location of the Conference, to which I now return, is of great significance. If the Conference meets anywhere except in Tangier, it will become a purely political one. For surely nobody can seriously assert that the economic and financial affairs of Morocco can be dealt with at The Hague or in Geneva. But if the Conference does assume a purely political character, it will again lead to an intensification of the German-French conflict. This final objective always becomes apparent in everything that Révoil proposes. That is why I expect that the French proposals for an agenda will be unacceptable—if he drafts them. There is a great difference between German and French policy in the Moroccan question. We have openly and honestly told the French how we think it ought to be dealt with, now and in the future. In verbal exchanges the French politicians show complete understanding for our ideas, but in the written exchanges and also in many items appearing in the inspired Press one or other point of the Delcassé programme always reappears; for example, the idea that has appeared in some papers that

---

[1] From the Radolin Papers.

France should receive a mandate from Europe to establish order in Morocco is identical with the point of view adopted by Taillandier on his arrival in Fez, when he regarded the mandate as having been given already. If Révoil really continues to control matters and goes on asking us to agree to Morocco's subordination to France in one form or another, or if he expects of the Treaty Powers that they should pass expert judgments on local Moroccan questions on the shores of Lake Geneva, my advice will be that we should not make ourselves a laughing-stock through endless palaver, but that we should let the negotiations with France rest and instead negotiate with the Sultan. Naturally this would immediately create a much more serious situation, a situation of in-security which might give rise to incidents. But it is not our fault. Right from the very beginning (dispatch 740)[1] we told M. Rouvier absolutely clearly how far we could go and what we could not do. We can*not* lend our hand to the immediate mediatization of the Sultan; if *that* is what Révoil asks of us, the negotiations will not lead to anything, and in that case Rouvier might fall. Whereas if he were now to let a moderate man work out moderate proposals, the overwhelming majority of the French people would be content, for they have long looked upon the Delcassé programme as something that was done away with at the same time as Delcassé. Up till now the defeat has been exclusively one of Delcassé. But if Rouvier were now to allow himself to be tempted by the perfidious insinuations of Delcassé's following into taking up again the main point of the programme, the mediatization or Tunisification of the Sultan, it would be he, Rouvier, not Delcassé, who would suffer the inevitable *échec*. In this connection Hanotaux's article in the *Journal* (of the 12th I think) which you submitted was very instructive, because there the elimination of the Delcassé programme is treated as something already achieved and a matter of course anyway.[2] That is why, in Rouvier's own interests, it would be disastrous if he now allowed himself to be talked into reviving this programme, which the French look on as dead and buried, by subscribing to it. I still hope that Dupuy will succeed in checkmating the plans of the Delcassé group and making it clear to Rouvier that his own interest demands that he should not rehabilitate the Delcassé programme, that he should make no effort in this direction and not lend his authority to such an effort.

It would be very helpful to both parties if Dupuy were to discuss the detailed proposals with you in advance. You are after all fully in the picture as to what is acceptable to [us] and what is not. And for you personally also it is better if no more proposals are sent here of which Bülow can say afterwards: 'These should have been fended off by Radolin.'[3]

If Révoil stays on, nothing sensible will be achieved. Couldn't

---

[1] Of 4 May 1905. (*Grosse Politik*, vol. XXii, no. 6650, pp. 364–7.)

[2] In this article in the *Journal* of 12 July Hanotaux had sharply criticized Delcassé's foreign policy, and had gone on to praise the skill with which Rouvier had freed France from a difficult situation.

[3] See p. 351, note 3.

Rouvier give him some nice diplomatic post somewhere to get rid of him? That should be possible. Do discuss this point also with Dupuy some time. Perhaps that would be the solution of the problem.

Please give my best wishes to the Princess. With best regards

Your gradually tiring

Holstein.

## 904. Memorandum by Holstein

Berlin, 31 July 1905

For the Chancellor.

England is thinking of presenting us with the bill for the Krüger Telegram, the Boer War episode, the naval drive and other items.

His Majesty the Kaiser has discussed the question of drawing Belgium and Denmark closer to Germany with the Kings of Belgium[1] and Denmark.[2] The English Government has authentic information on these plans and wants to prevent their fruition. As a counter-move it wants to inflict a naval or diplomatic defeat on us over the Moroccan question.

The Rouvier Cabinet doesn't want war, that is why it dropped Delcassé at a time when it thought a war possible. Delcassé actually didn't want a war either. But he was convinced that faced with England and France, Germany would retreat. His Ministerial colleagues didn't believe him at that time.

To-day the situation is different. After the cordial reception of the French military mission by His Majesty the Kaiser[3] the fear of war in France has come to an end. The papers told the public that His Majesty had said among other things that a war between France and Germany would be a civil war. Following up the francophil demonstrations by His Majesty, Delcassé's followers, strongly supported by the English, have been saying since then that Germany had probably never intended to do anything but to bluff. The term bluff has even been used in the French Press. The change of feeling became apparent immediately after the return of General Lacroix, and there has been no change since. Before that M. Rouvier had stated: '*Si l'Allemagne ne veut pas que nous allions au Maroc, nous n'irons pas, voilà tout.*' Now the French Minister in Fez is putting forward the same programme as in Delcassé's time, to wit a European or rather a German mandate for France. The French Government no longer sees a danger of war in this, and therefore sees no reason to moderate its demands. We must therefore expect that the French proposals which will be made shortly will not be very different from Delcassé's programme.

What will be the effect if, in the hope of improving French sentiment

---

[1] See the enclosure to this document.

[2] See *Grosse Politik*, vol. XIXi, chapter CXXIX. A telegram to Schoen of 28 July 1905 contained the following passage: 'The earlier German soundings already led at that time, as you discovered, to a Danish enquiry as to the shortest period of time within which the English fleet could reach Copenhagen. A renewed effort would probably not remain hidden from the English, just as the earlier effort did not, as King Christian does nothing without his Ministers.' (*Grosse Politik*, vol. XIXi, p. 89, note *.)

[3] See p. 343, note 3.

towards us, we show ourselves very conciliatory and abandon the point of view which His Majesty the Kaiser said was his on 31 March?[1] The public, both German and non-German, would regard this as a humiliation of the German Emperor and the first great practical success of the Franco-English *entente cordiale*. It would put an end to any doubts as to the usefulness of the entente for France, and France would not be drawn closer to Germany but rather driven further away. In the foreseeable future she would stand steadfastly and firmly by England.

That is the point at which we can expect Russian diplomacy to take a hand.

For inner-political reasons the liberal and revolutionary elements in Russia want to work together with republican France and liberal England against the quasi-autocratic German Emperor. Guided by the same inner-political reasons, the Tsar and his party desire the opposite, that is that France should not make common cause with England but draw closer to Germany. Even Count Lamsdorff, who is not very far-sighted, will perhaps realize now that a striking Franco-English success in the Moroccan question would strengthen the entente and bring French dependence on Russia, which existed hitherto, to an end. Thus the Tsar and his party have a very considerable interest in seeing that the Moroccan question should not end in a diplomatic defeat for Germany or in war.

How would the Tsar's diplomacy have to work in order to favour our cause?

Very simply. Lamsdorff and Nelidov would have to tell the French: 'If your aim is to humiliate Germany there will be war. But Russia will not be able to support you in a war which you are fighting in order to acquire, not to defend, territory. Therefore you'd better get on with Germany.'

That would be sufficient to make Rouvier see reason again. To-day neither he nor the rest of France believe in the possibility of war; moreover they all believe that Russia, in so far as she is able, will support France, initially by diplomatic means.

The Björkö meeting[2] has indicated that the Tsar and those who still stand by him have at last begun to realize what dangers the co-operation between France and England as well as co-operation *with* France and England would hold for Imperial Russia. For us to persuade the Tsar's diplomacy to work against England's counsel in Paris, exclusively directed towards war or Germany's humiliation, therefore appears to be an attainable objective. The best way for us to prepare such a diplomatic suggestion in St Petersburg would be if the Kaiser were to write to the Tsar; but the general and immediate political situation will have to be discussed by the German Ambassador with Count Lamsdorff. It seems doubtful whether Count Alvensleben would be up to this task. From a purely objective point of view Herr von Miquel would be particularly

---

[1] In his speech at Tangier. (See p. 330, note 2.)
[2] Between the Kaiser and the Tsar on 24 July. (See *Grosse Politik*, vol. XIXii, chapter CXXVIII.)

suitable. But I cannot judge whether Lamsdorff is the sort of man who would discuss a problem with a Chargé d'Affaires on a basis of equality. If not, Germany's interests demand a change of Ambassadors in the very near future.

I would recommend making an attempt with Miquel and sending Count Alvensleben on leave immediately. There is no time to be lost, for events are moving fast towards a decision.

Holstein.

ENCLOSURE
Memorandum[1]

Berlin, 30 December 1904

After yesterday's luncheon at the New Palace, to which I had been invited, His Imperial and Royal Majesty was gracious enough to inform me in a lengthy conversation of the reasons why he did not feel inclined to return the visit which His Majesty the King of the Belgians had paid him in January this year.[2]

His Majesty the Kaiser first of all referred to a report from the year 1889, in which the former Imperial Minister in Brussels, the present Ambassador in St Petersburg, Count Alvensleben, had warned against an Imperial visit to the Belgian capital in view of the presence there of a large number of unsafe French elements, which might possibly use His Majesty's presence in Brussels in order to stage anti-German demonstrations and insult the person of the Kaiser.

The main reason, however, why His Majesty did not at this time intend to pay a return visit to Belgium was the fact that King Leopold still owed His Majesty a reply to the question submitted to him in January, as to what attitude he, the King, intended to adopt in case an armed conflict should break out between Germany and France or Germany and England.

In explanation His Majesty told me in this connection that he had categorically demanded of the King during a lengthy conversation in January of this year, that he, the King, should give him a written declaration now in time of peace to the effect that in case of conflict Belgium would take her stand on our side, and that to this end the King should amongst other things guarantee to us the use of Belgian railways and fortified places. If the King of the Belgians did not do so, he—His Majesty the Kaiser—would not be able to give a guarantee for either his territory or the dynasty. We would then, if the case arose, immediately invade Belgium and the King would have to suffer all the—to him— harmful consequences. If on the other hand the King were to make the desired declaration at this stage, he—His Majesty the Kaiser—felt inclined, though he did not like doing so, to give him not only a guarantee regarding the continued existence of the Kingdom of Belgium in its

---

[1] From the Foreign Ministry files.

[2] In that part of Bülow's report to the Kaiser of 26 December 1904 not printed in the *Grosse Politik*, (vol. XIXii, nos. 6157, 6178, pp. 372–4, 400–3), he had advocated that Wilhelm II pay a visit to the Belgian Court. (See *Grosse Politik*, vol. XIXii, p. 403, note *.)

present form, but also to enlarge Belgium by granting it territory in Northern France—His Majesty at this point also used the term 'Old Burgundy'. King Leopold presumably realized clearly what he and the Belgian dynasty could expect from a victorious republican France.

His Majesty concluded these statements, made in a lively manner, by remarking that the King of the Belgians had now had a full year in which to consider the question; in spite of this long interval he had not given an answer yet, and he would have to wait for a return visit until he had done so in a manner satisfactory to H.M. the Kaiser.

H. A. von Bülow[1]
*Legationsrat*

## 905.  Holstein to Hugo von Radolin[2]

Berlin, 4 August 1905

Strictly secret
Dear Radolin,

I am still not as well as I would like to be. I hear that the French proposals[3] have arrived. But as yet I know of nothing. I have had to put off Betzold twice already. He had been told to come on Sunday at twelve.

I would like you to clear up one point for me which really belongs to the past. But it could perhaps become topical again—possibly.

Do you remember a private telegram described as a 'vision of the future'?[4] It contained one of the various solutions which the Moroccan question could receive: the solution by a direct agreement between Germany and France.

An amputation, that is a partition, is completely out of the question to-day or to-morrow, *but one could prepare for the future by establishing reform zones which could gradually become spheres of interest.*

Have Rouvier or Dupuy or anyone else of importance at any time dropped a hint that Germany might possibly get a sphere of interest in the future? We cannot make such a suggestion, for its refusal would place us in a most awkward situation. But it seems an obvious thought that if the French were prepared to let us have a sphere of interest in Morocco they would have dropped a hint to this effect some time. This sphere of interest couldn't be anywhere else except on the Atlantic coast, on its southern part.

Until now you have said nothing of such a French hint in your letters and reports. Please, telegraph immediately on receiving this letter, either: 'no such hint has been made to me up till now', or: 'it has been mentioned to me, details by letter.'[5]

The latter in case Dupuy or someone else has ever sounded you out as to whether we would accept territorial compensation.

[1] Hans Adolf von Bülow. First Secretary at the Legation in Brussels, 1899–1905.

[2] From the Radolin Papers.

[3] Sent by Radolin in a telegram of 2 August. (*Grosse Politik*, vol. XXII, no. 6783, pp. 532–3.)

[4] Of 2 July 1905. (See p. 350, note 2.)

[5] A telegram by Radolin has not been found. (See below, Radolin's letter of 5 August.)

I am posing the question at this time because the French are evidently trying to acquire some territory in the 'border zone' (no one knows what extent this will have.) The German public will then say: 'Why only the French? Either no one gets anything, or we get something too.'

A proper annexation is completely [im]possible now; our obligations to the Sultan prevent it. But a future annexation might perhaps be prepared by the creation of reform districts which would turn into spheres of interest later. The simplest way would be if the French said to us: 'We shall reform the border zone, do you want to reform the southern part of the Atlantic coastal area?' That was the 'vision of the future', that is how it was meant. But if no hint in this sense has ever been made to you, it must be assumed that the French don't want to give us anything. The English are probably advising them not to concede us anything.

You must therefore on no account ask direct questions which might later even be published in the Press. But please telegraph immediately to-morrow one of the two above versions, depending on whether hints have been dropped to you or not. Will you also write me via the person bringing you this letter whether in your personal opinion the French would prove receptive to such an idea, or whether, in view of everything you have heard, you consider this improbable. If such a solution appears out of the question, it would at the same time also relegate the dream of a direct agreement with France to the distant future. We must then fix things so that no one gets anything—and this could easily make for tension in our relations with France.

*We would be quite happy if no one were to get anything. We would be less happy if France dined while we looked on.*

So, please, a telegram to-morrow, Saturday, and a letter by this messenger. Be extremely careful.

With a handshake in friendship as ever

Your exhausted
Holstein.

906.   Hugo von Radolin to Holstein[1]
       Copy

Paris, 5 August 1905

My dear friend,

After five years the first attack of gout!! I am writing this in bed, and therefore please pardon the pencil. I was happy to hear that you are better and back at work again. Many thanks for the letter of the 4th which I have just received. I have carefully re-read your private telegram of 2 July regarding the 'vision of the future'. Immediately upon receiving it I talked over the contents, particularly that *one* part, with Dupuy—*conversando* and off-hand as my personal opinion, as instructed—and I found that he agreed completely with every part of the plan.

---

[1] From the Radolin Papers. Not found in the Holstein Papers.

With reference to the sentence: 'In the new situation which would result, Germany would support France's Moroccan [claims] against the claims of third parties', I added by the way: 'quitte à nous entendre à nous deux plus tard.' This also Dupuy seemed to appreciate. In accordance with the instructions given to me at the time, and especially as you did not seem to want to go into greater detail concerning the 'swindle in South-West Africa', I too did not want to venture *further* with Dupuy. I dropped no other hint to M. Dupuy. But that does not exclude my coming back to this point more openly and quite unobtrusively as soon as *Dupuy* returns, if you agree. I could possibly drop a confidential word in Reinach's[1] ear first. He is *very close* to Rouvier, and as I have discovered, discusses everything with him. I think I can assure you that it would not get into the newspapers. Incidentally, when I discussed this point (in the private telegram of 2 July) with Dupuy, I could hardly have expected him to take up the question in greater detail. For the main object of the conversation was to prevent any over-hasty solo plans, whether by France or others, and in particular to ensure that the idea of an *amputation* of the Sultan should not become current in the foreseeable future. I am sure that Rouvier and his friends in all honesty do not intend to get stuck in Morocco, but, as has often been said, to confine themselves to securing the frontier with Algeria. At the moment there is no indication that he *wants to annex* any frontier districts in the foreseeable future. That is why he (Rouvier) understands our point of view: *pas d'amputation.* But, naturally, this is based on the premise that no other Power wants *territorial* advantages either.

Naturally he has a difficult time with the colonial party on this point. *Reserver l'avenir* is an expression which Rouvier likes to use. I revert to this with him repeatedly, *'no premature grabbing.'* Incidentally this was carefully avoided in the last exposé.[2] I am convinced that if at some *later* stage—naturally *much later*, as you yourself have repeatedly emphasized—a partition to the benefit of one or another country were to be considered, they would understand here that *we* also should be given a territorial zone, even though, in accordance with the instructions I have received, we have hitherto stated again and again that (at least for the time being) we were seeking nothing except equal commercial rights. The newspapers on the other hand have already said on a number of occasions that it would be no more than fair for Germany to get *territorial* compensation. But this never took shape, as the occasion did not arise and because it was always stated: 'For the time being it is not intended that any of the Powers concerned should get *any* special advantages.' (There was no mention of any *territorial* gain.) Public opinion too was convinced of our good intentions and realized that there was no reason to mistrust us. At least it was not thought that it was intended to obtain any special advantages *before* the Conference. At this stage came the unfortunate incident of the alleged concessions in Fez, for

---

[1] Joseph Reinach. French writer; a Deputy.
[2] *Grosse Politik*, vol. XXii, no. 6783, pp. 532–3.

which Count Tattenbach was held responsible.[1] As you will have seen, the Press took an extraordinarily impassioned stand against these *premature* concessions. Unfortunately public opinion was thereby aroused into positive hostility. I am very happy about the *denial* which has produced a much calmer situation.[2] But it will not be possible overnight to kill the opinion held by the public that the intention is to secure special advantages through the over-eager Minister *before* the Conference. It would be regrettable if our conciliatory attitude towards France were to be endangered because of minor *local* advantages. [...][3]

You are quite right when you say why shouldn't *we* too get some territory if the *French* were to get some. But none of the leading politicians here are thinking of territorial gain right now; we made this point sufficiently clear to them. If you say that the French are talking of a *frontier zone* in which they are to get a mandate from the Conference Powers, this rests on the view expressed in Berlin telegram no. 133 of 16 June,[4] which states (not as a proposal, but as an objective deduction): 'The army and police would at first have to be organized on an *international* basis, in that (as M. Rouvier has rightly emphasized), the Conference would have to grant a mandate for the carrying out of the necessary reforms. Naturally, in so far as the area next to the Algerian border is concerned, this mandate could be given to France *alone*, thereby satisfying France's main wish (as far as can be seen from Rouvier's statements)'.

I also wanted to point out that in your letter of yesterday you said for the *first time*: 'Creation of *reform districts*, which would later become *spheres of interest*, to prepare for annexation at a later date.'

I believe the French would at a later date come to an understanding with us concerning the cession of some territory—later on when they *themselves* are thinking of taking something. But right now they are *not* thinking of it, if only because of the way we have emphasized the integrity of the Sherifian Empire, which the French intend to respect for the time being. As I immediately telegraphed yesterday,[5] Rouvier told me (see my report no. 253 of 27 June)[6]: 'The expression 'on the *Atlantic coast*', in accordance with telegram 133, could easily give rise to the belief that Germany wants to seize it.' I concluded from this that he wanted to avoid this expression, that is a *precise definition* of this expression so as not to provoke premature and unsuitable protests from the general public, as if Germany intended future annexations on the *Atlantic* shore. The repeated statements and assurances made by the

---

[1] The Sultan had offered Germany numerous economic and other concessions in Morocco. Bülow telegraphed to Tattenbach on 11 July: 'We regard the concessions offered to us by the Sultan as desirable advantages, but we shall be able to accept only if they do not run counter to the decisions to be expected from the Conference.' (*Grosse Politik*, vol. XXii, no. 6774, pp. 524–6; see also no. 6784, pp. 533–5.)

[2] *Grosse Politik*, vol. XXii, no. 6785, pp. 535–6.

[3] In the omitted part of this letter, Radolin warned Holstein against Count Tattenbach, about whom he had heard much unfavourable criticism from German as well as from many other sources.

[4] *Grosse Politik*, vol. XXii, no. 6711, pp. 439–41.

[5] Not found.          [6] *Grosse Politik*, vol. XXii, no. 6746, pp. 485–7.

Kaiser to the King of Spain that we had *no territorial* desires or interests, something that has also been said in all my instructions hitherto, fully justified Rouvier in his assumption that this was honestly meant. Hence he wanted to avoid the use of the expression 'Atlantic Ocean', so as not to furnish ammunition to those Frenchmen who assert—also in the Chamber—that Rouvier *a été roulé par l'Allemagne*. And actually it is being more and more widely said (though as yet in cautious terms) that 'Germany is in fact seeking a *pretext* to provoke France and end up by declaring war.' '*Not* content with bringing about the fall of Delcassé, Rouvier is being asked for things which cannot be accepted in the long run. He is being defrauded due to his gullibility and naïveté. Attempts were being made to foster belief in Germany's honest unselfishness, which wasn't as great as that. France had been prevented from gaining special advantages, while all sorts of concessions were being secretly obtained by the Minister *before* the Conference.' That is the feeling now, and Rouvier does not find it easy to calm down opinion and disprove these allegations. Hence he was greatly relieved by the circumstantial denial, which I transmitted to him immediately through his *chef de cabinet*,[1] whom I had summoned to my bed, to which I was already tied. Now my hope is that the French exposé will meet with approval in Berlin. In it Rouvier has tried to prejudice as little as possible any decision by the Conference by using the most general terms. Clemenceau's attacks—his influence is not to be under-estimated—are becoming very violent. I have sent in a selection of his articles. He is naturally working for *England*, and has found a welcome pretext in the alleged concessions. What a pity! The feeling was by and large favourable, there was on the whole agreement with Germany's policy, and then this regrettably exaggerated incident occurred and disturbed the peaceful development.

I close in haste, so that the post office official can leave again without delay.

With best wishes for a speedy and complete recovery. Johanna sends regards,

Your faithful<br>
Hugo [...]<br>
6 August 1905

P.S.

Finally, I want to say once again what I telegraphed yesterday. When discussing the 'vision of the future' with Dupuy, neither he nor anyone else of political importance dropped any hint to the effect that Germany might some time in the future claim or obtain a sphere of interest in Morocco. But I am firmly convinced that if a partition of the country or a division into spheres of interest were to take place, France would be considerate enough not to create any difficulties for us. All the politicians here believe, and say so out loud, that Germany's increasing population and her increasing trade must find and deserve to find some room for expansion; and therefore it is obvious that if Germany conducts

---

[1] M. Moreau.

such an active policy in Morocco, it does so in the long run not *pour les beaux yeux du Maroc ou de la France*, but in order to secure a position there, though she does not speak of this for the moment, claiming only commercial advantages and equal rights. That is why I would welcome it, if I were authorized to talk over Germany's *expectations discreetly* with *reliable people*, such as Dupuy or Reinach, particularly should France have similar ambitions. I would do so on the basis that these ideas were personal ones.

### 907.    Holstein to Hugo von Radolin[1]

Norderney, Villa Victoria,
22 August 1905

Dear Radolin,

[...] We will now, I hope, get the Conference and through it an understanding of a *general* nature with France. You can assure Dupuy quite definitely that Germany is not pursuing any plans involving territorial acquisitions in Morocco. If the Government were to do so, it would be disavowed by the Kaiser, who just now has a positive horror of Africa because of the revolts everywhere. The one respect in which the French must show some consideration for our situation is that they must not act *too fast*, so that the Kaiser isn't forced to disavow himself. *Voilà tout.* It would be a good thing if you were to discuss this thoroughly with Rouvier and also with Dupuy before your departure. The matter is important enough for Dupuy to come to Paris for a few days because of it. You might send him a message to this effect.

*The French need not worry themselves concerning Tangier as the location for the Conference. Our wish to reach an understanding with them will be shown there too.*[2]

Let us hope that Flotow will be able to control his extreme nervousness while he is acting as Chargé d'Affaires.

With best regards
Your
Holstein.

### 908.    Draft by Holstein[3]

[September 1905]

Dear Niky,

I did not want to omit telling you that Uncle Bertie[4] has invited my

---

[1] From the Radolin Papers.

[2] In another letter of 22 August 1905 Holstein wrote: 'Our demands will be twofold:
   (1) Equal rights in the economic sphere for *non-Frenchmen* (no special advantages for Germany).
   (2) Safeguarding the prestige of our Kaiser by not trying to force him to hand over the Sultan to the French for better or for worse six months after his speech in Tangier. I think the English would like to see the latter development in order to humiliate the Kaiser.' (From the Radolin Papers.)

[3] This draft was written early in September 1905. The Foreign Ministry files contain a memorandum by Holstein of 3 September 1905 suggesting a letter by the Kaiser to the Tsar whose contents with regard to Morocco tally closely with this draft. As far as can be seen from the files, the letter was not sent.

[4] King Edward VII.

Ambassador to Windsor, evidently with the intention of questioning him about our meeting at Björkö. Our uncle remarked that great mystery surrounded our meeting and that you had not even told Count Lamsdorff a single word about the contents of the conversation. Metternich wrote that the King had said (verbatim), that it was strange to leave one's own Foreign Minister in the dark concerning such important events, especially such an efficient and excellent Minister as Count Lamsdorff.[1]

This remark by the King shows that the English Ambassador questioned Count Lamsdorff and that the latter feigned ignorance. I esteem this reserve all the more highly, as, to speak quite frankly, I have hitherto suspected that Lamsdorff intended to draw you into a triple alliance with France and England. I have sometimes quietly wondered how a Russian Minister could get such an idea, for naturally France and England would always make common cause against you in this group, just as they did in the Crimean War and in all aspects of the Eastern question. But Lamsdorff's negative attitude in response to the Ambassador's soundings shows that Lamsdorff is in fact completely devoted to you and only thinks of your interests.

Uncle Bertie also talked to Metternich about the Moroccan question and complained of my Moroccan policy, which, he was convinced, had only one object; to disturb the Franco-English understanding (on one occasion the King even used the term *alliance*). But it would not succeed. The understanding between England and France rested in the very nature of things, because both nations believed in liberal and progressive principles.

In the face of the King's suspicion, which is directed against me, my justification is a very simple one. I am not tempted by the thought of acquiring a part of Morocco, and I said so already in the spring of 1904 to King Alfonso.[2] I therefore paid no attention to Morocco until February or March this year when the Sultan of Morocco informed me through diplomatic channels that the French Minister in Fez, acting on Delcassé's instructions, had told the Sultan that Germany also was one of the Powers which had given France a mandate to act as she thought fit in Morocco. Was that true? Whereupon I replied repeatedly and emphatically that I could not have given such a mandate since I regarded the Sultan as an independent sovereign. The conflict between my policy and the policy adopted by Delcassé then led to the Minister's resignation, as the rest of the French Cabinet, led by Rouvier, pronounced in favour of reaching an agreement with Germany. This occurred at the beginning of June. Delcassé's disappearance and the switch by the French Government to a pacific policy were a bitter disappointment to our English uncle, for he had wanted to use Delcassé as a tool in order to drive France into a war against me. If Russia were involved in a war against Japan at the same time as Germany was at war with France, England

[1] Metternich to Bülow, 14 August 1905. (*Grosse Politik*, vol. XXii, no. 6870, pp. 651–9.)

[2] The Kaiser had met King Alfonso XIII of Spain in Vigo during his Mediterranean cruise in the spring of 1904. (See *Grosse Politik*, vol. XVII, no. 5208, p. 363.)

would have had a free hand in the Persian Gulf and elsewhere, even if she was supporting France with a part of her fleet. Yet England's policy suffered no discouragement after Delcassé's fall. The King himself and his diplomats, supported by the English Press and numerous newspapers in all countries—which are bought by English money—have been constantly at work in the last two months with the object of driving the French Government into resuming Delcassé's aggressive policy. Their efforts have not been completely fruitless. This is shown by the fact that in its latest note[1] the French Government has again asked that it should be empowered to take what action it thinks fit in the whole of Morocco. That is exactly the same demand that Delcassé already made in March. This demand was completely dropped after Delcassé's fall and has been revived now only on English recommendation and because of the firm promise of English support.

As I've said, my interests in Morocco are not important, but I cannot —six months after having stated that I regard the Sultan of Morocco as an independent sovereign—make a contradictory statement now, by saying that in the capacity of a Moroccan treaty Power I empower and indeed charge France to act as she thinks fit in Morocco. And yet in this the consideration which I owe to my person and my imperial word take second place to another aspect, which is of very great importance not only to me but also to you. If we now allow France simply to seize Morocco, that is a victory for France, advised by England and backed by English naval demonstrations. As far as the French are concerned this will furnish proof that their correct policy is to work with England if they want to gain successes. The Franco-English *entente cordiale* would then change into a lasting alliance. This alliance is all the more dangerous because, as Lamsdorff will have told you, the Anglo-Japanese alliance was extended a few days ago on a more general basis.[2] This is being kept secret for the time being at the request of the English. The news came here from a Japanese source, and Alvensleben was instructed to inform Lamsdorff in confidence.[3] If now France were also to join this Anglo-Japanese grouping it would be equally disadvantageous to you and to me. In order to prevent this I see both in your as in my interest only one method, that is to stop France from gaining important advantages as the result of the common Franco-English advance at this stage. We must postpone the granting of more important concessions regarding Moroccan territory until such time as we, you and I, ask the French to go with us *à trois*. I think that a decision in our favour would be rendered much easier to the French by the prospects of Moroccan advantages. If you share my opinion we must give the French at the forthcoming conference only a small part of what, driven by England, they are asking for, in order that something is left which can be given to them

---

[1] Of 31 August. (*Affaires du Maroc 1901–05*, no. 330, pp. 290–2.)

[2] On 12 August. (*British Documents*, vol. IV, no. 155, pp. 164–9.)

[3] See *Grosse Politik*, vol. XIXii, no. 6338, pp. 635–6. Alvensleben was empowered on 16 August to inform Lamsdorff of the information contained therein. Alvensleben telegraphed on 17 August that he had carried out these instructions. (From the Foreign Ministry files.)

later. At the moment there are certain limits anyway regarding the concessions which can be made to France as far as I am concerned, in view of the statement I made to the Sultan six months ago. I can represent this as the main reason. But the real reason is that for everything they will get now the French will feel gratitude only towards the English, and will therefore all the more surely join the Anglo-Japanese group. Since, however, you are interested in keeping control over the French, and I am interested in changing our present correct relations with France into friendly ones, we must conduct our policy in such a manner that the French will have to thank not England but us for their Moroccan acquisitions. That is why we must postpone a settlement of the Moroccan question, or, as the diplomats say, treat the question dilatorily.

H.

### 909. Holstein to Hugo von Radolin[1]

Dammhaus bei Clausthal, Wednesday, 13 September 1905

Dear Radolin,

I was really sad to see from your letter,[2] that you feel insulted by Rosen's mission to Paris.[3] I was present when the decision was taken—at Richthofen's suggestion—and I know for certain that there was no intention of insulting you. Rosen was supposed to discuss points of detail, being a specialist on Morocco, and Kriege, who during the last eight weeks has been doing the paper-work on Morocco, was to accompany him. I think—although this was not actually said—that Bülow and Richthofen were guided by the consideration that neither of them, particularly not Richthofen, felt inclined to stay in Berlin during the coming weeks because of the Moroccan question. Since I *had* to leave, I am sure they wanted to shift the focal point of the negotiations to Paris by bringing all the specialists together there. Kriege appears to have gone on strike. He pulled a very sour face when I saw him and pointed out that he was senior to Rosen. For your sake I would have preferred it if two had gone, and therefore I strongly advised Kriege to go.

I can assure you absolutely that I was not given the least reason to

---

[1] From the Radolin Papers.    [2] Not found.

[3] While Holstein was on leave in the Harz, Princess Radolin had written to Frau von Lebbin to ask what she knew about the appointment of Rosen. Frau von Lebbin replied on 10 September: 'As far as I know, the proposal to send Herr Rosen and Herr Kriege originated with Richthofen and was supported by Holstein because it was regarded as a means of lessening Radolin's responsibility. H. thought this desirable since it was impossible to foresee how the matter would go. H. has said that Radolin was seeing things too much through French eyes; one proof of this was the French idea that Germany was planning a war. For the detailed negotiations specialists were necessary. Kriege knew the Moroccan question better than Holstein or anyone else in Germany. Germany really did wish to reach agreement with France, but faced with the sly manoeuvres by the French specialists, we too had to send specialists into action. Rosen, as Minister in Morocco, was leading the special mission. He was very conciliatory, whereas, as I've said, Kriege was chosen because of his thorough knowledge of the subject. It would cause us sincere regret if an agreement with France were not reached, for then certainly an unpleasant situation would arise. But Holstein is convinced that it will be possible to reach agreement provided some good will is shown by the French too, something that has only been the case to a small extent hitherto.' (From the Radolin Papers.)

suppose that anyone wants to get rid of you. That is why my advice is to accept the situation quite unconcernedly and to treat Rosen as a specialist, *as our Révoil*. When discussing the Morocco question with anyone in official circles or with Dupuy, I would hint that Germany wants nothing for herself, that the Kaiser took up a position in Tangier which only he is entitled to interpret, but that, from everything you have heard, H.M. is well-intentioned towards France also on this question. (That actually is the simple truth. H.M.'s speeches in Tangier fixed our policy in definite channels for the time being, but recently I have heard that he doesn't care about Morocco.) Obviously you must make sure that Rosen keeps you informed of all details.

I do not know the details of the Moroccan programme which we adopted when replying to the last French note,[1] but I presume that the reply was conciliatory, as the Chancellor has become convinced that H.M. too feels in a conciliatory mood.[2] I presume that you will give Rosen a Moroccan dinner; I would keep him on the lead through politeness and share the work with him when that is possible.

As I said, I am convinced that you have no reason to indulge in any black thoughts.

In haste<br>Your<br>H.

Naturally you will also continue to report on Morocco, whenever you think you should.

Richthofen was afraid of the responsibility of conducting the Moroccan negotiations in Berlin without me.

13 September 1905

P.S. I see no reason why you shouldn't confidentially express optimism towards Rouvier or Dupuy concerning the probable outcome of the negotiations, pointing to H.M.'s friendly attitude.

Sometimes it seems to me that you are too French, but lately I have come to believe that you know H.M.'s character and idiosyncracies better than I did. I *definitely* believe that you will be acting in accordance with H.M.'s wishes if you emphasize his conciliatory and friendly intentions in Paris.

But don't pick anyone indiscreet to make these statements to. For if Rosen hears of them, he *could* possibly write to Berlin: 'The Prince is making the French obstinate by what he is saying about H.M.'s conciliatory attitude.'

As I said, I regard it as useful that you should talk in this way, but in confidence and to reliable people (Rouvier, Dupuy).

910.   Bernhard von Bülow to Holstein

Baden Baden, 15 September 1905

Dear friend,

My wife and I were overjoyed to see from your letter of the 4th of this

---

[1] See p. 366, note 1.
[2] See *Grosse Politik*, vol. XXii, no. 6801, pp. 558–9.

month[1] that you could successfully undertake a long hike through the mountains. Few men of our age—especially men in official positions—can do as much, and I hope and believe that this is sure proof that you still have, and will continue to have for a long time, great physical powers of endurance. May your stay in the Harz do you a lot of good again, as so often in the past.

As regards the political exposition in your letter, I believe that this was not based on absolutely correct premises. At any rate I cannot find any analogy between the Rosen mission (the term 'mission' is too formal in this connection and not really apt) and the Haugwitz mission. Moreover, we cannot reproach H.M. with having made the treatment of the Moroccan question more difficult for us, or with having interfered in it. During your well-earned leave I want to spare you any painful incidents, but, in view of the confidence we have in each other, can do no other but to send you copies of the letters exchanged between Radolin and myself during the last few days, naturally for your own personal information only, and with the request that you treat them as secret.[2] I confess that this sudden attack by Radolin surprised me very much and hurt me deeply. There are no objective grounds for this sudden declaration of war directed against me. I have not merited this from Radolin, whom I held in St Petersburg only with great difficulty, and, when his situation there had become untenable, recommended him to H.M. for the fine post in Paris. After such a past I was not prepared for ingratitude. And I took Radolin to be more objective and a better official. But one learns as long as one lives. Who can have stirred him up, into what circles, hostile to me, can he have been drawn? You will agree with me that my reply was very calm and conciliatory. But I shall know how to uphold a Chancellor's authority, notwithstanding urbanity in matters of form. Not on my own account, but in the interests of the service and the country. Where would we get to if our representatives abroad were to ask for three days leave to go and complain about the Chancellor to His Majesty whenever they found a decision by the Chancellor inconvenient?!!! I have never seen anything like it during the eight years that I have conducted our foreign policy. I have not forgotten what the Holy Writ says about the fig-tree which is not to be felled and burned at once, and I have therefore replied to Radolin in such a manner as to leave

---

[1] Not found.

[2] In a letter to Bülow of 10 September Radolin had complained that Rosen and Kriege had been sent to Paris by the Foreign Ministry to negotiate independently of the Ambassador on the most important outstanding questions concerning Morocco. Radolin maintained that such a procedure was a heavy blow to the prestige of the Kaiser's Ambassador and requested that there should either be a change of plans or that he be granted three days leave to present the problem to the Kaiser. Bülow replied on 14 September that Rosen had been sent at his orders, with the approval of the Kaiser, because the negotiations on Morocco had reached a deadlock. It was hoped that Rosen's specialist knowledge would help to resolve the technical details which still blocked the way to an understanding. There had been no intention of lessening the Ambassador's prestige in any way. Bülow therefore refused the requested leave of absence, and should Radolin insist, would ask the Kaiser to choose between them. Bülow concluded by appealing to Radolin's patriotism to do everything in his power to help achieve an understanding with France over Morocco. (From the Radolin Papers.)

the way to an understanding open. But should he continue in his insubordination towards me, I would of course ask His Majesty to choose between his resignation and mine.[1]

We like it here, in spite of a lot of rain. My wife and Donna Laura have asked me to send you their very best regards. I am

Ever yours most sincerely

B.

### 911.  Holstein to Hugo von Radolin[2]

Dammhaus bei Clausthal, 15 September 1905

Dear Radolin,

Pay close attention to this letter, it is very important. Poor Betzold who died very recently, told Schwabach a few days before his death that he had heard news from Paris which had taken him aback. Someone (presumably Moreau or Léon) had written to him : 'One cannot understand the attitude of the German Government which creates difficulties over matters on which the French had long ago received promises from the Kaiser.'

This news is of a kind to clear up the situation. I do not think that the French are lying. The promises by the Kaiser of which they speak can have been given by him only to General Lacroix or possibly to the Prince of Monaco. At least until recently the Chancellor knew nothing about this, otherwise he would not have continued to defend the stand which the Kaiser took in his speech at Tangier on 31 March. The Chancellor not only signed, but also corrected and gave the exact shading to all the important instructions concerning Morocco which you received. The Chancellor therefore knew nothing at all of the 'Kaiser's promises'. For the Chancellor always prefers a settlement to a dispute, and the stand on the—improvised spontaneous—speeches by the Kaiser at Tangier was all the more unpleasant both for him and the Foreign Ministry because no future advantage could be discerned. If the Chancellor had dreamt that H.M. had made promises, he probably would have been greatly relieved. My explanation for the fact that H.M. said nothing about the promises to the Chancellor, with whom he is on good terms otherwise, is that they were separated from each other all through the summer, and really saw each other only an hour or so at a time. All

[1] Radolin also sent Holstein copies of his exchange of letters with the Chancellor, with two cover-letters of 16 September in which he commented at length on the Rosen-Kriege situation and complained bitterly of Bülow's letter. 'That is not the way to write to the second senior Ambassador of the Kaiser and a high dignitary who is sixty-five. His appeal to my patriotism does make it difficult for me to drop my task, and moreover it would, I think, be regrettable if there had to be a change at the Embassy right now. But my honour prevents me from simply accepting the slap in the face, and I therefore intend to place my post at His Majesty's disposal.'

Holstein replied on 20 September. 'Formally you have put yourself in the wrong by threatening the Chancellor with H.M. That wasn't clever. Too much temperament.

'You can be sure that I am not standing by with folded arms. First of all I must find out how the land lies. In the meantime please don't do anything without asking me first or before you have heard from me.' (From the Radolin Papers.)

[2] From the Radolin Papers.

the same the matter is vexing for the Chancellor, for he has been compromised vis-à-vis the French. They must surely have noticed long ago that the Chancellor knows nothing or they think we want to finesse; hence perhaps Rouvier's remark : Was it our intention to 'do' him?

My advice now is as follows :

Go and see Rouvier and tell him that Betzold received letters from Paris shortly before his death in which it was said that one couldn't understand the attitude of the German Government which created difficulties over matters on which the French had long ago received promises from the Kaiser. You were now coming to ask what sort of promises had been made by the Kaiser—possibly at the beginning of June to General de Lacroix. For surely they were hardly intended to remain a secret between the Kaiser and the French Government. If you had known of them earlier you would have been in a position to speed the negotiations very considerably. It was quite understandable that the Kaiser hadn't said anything about it to the Chancellor, for the Kaiser all through the summer was on his travels by sea and land and was thinking of all sorts of things. That should have made it all the more important to confide in you, just as Betzold had now been confided in. This omission was the only cause of the unpleasant obstruction and confusion which had obtained during the past months.

If Rouvier, as I would assume, then says something about the Kaiser's promises—I guess they'll be a few brief remarks in general terms and of considerable consequence—I would think it useful and proper if you were to inform the Chancellor of them by private letter. Not in an official report, because he will be very sensitive regarding the Kaiser's reserve towards him.

You can start the letter with Betzold's statements, whereupon you had asked Rouvier for information; or more briefly and better, you can start straightaway by saying Rouvier had now told you this and that about the Kaiser's promises. Naturally the letter must be written in such a way that it can if need be be submitted to H.M. without annoying him. My explanation for the promises is that H.M. took an interest in Morocco for a short time because he hated Delcassé, but soon lost interest. He only should have said so to the Chancellor. During the last days in Berlin, I had the impression that Bülow had heard something new which embarrassed him, but I was too unwell to worry much about it. But after they wrote to me here to tell me about Betzold's statements concerning the Kaiser's promises,[1] I believe that *that* was the reason for sending Rosen. The object was to change course *sans en avoir l'air*.

I regard it as all the more useful that you show that you are informed. But with complete objectivity and easily. You had chosen to report by private letter, because you could not judge to what extent those statements by H.M. had been understood correctly, and whether it would still serve any practical purpose to take them up again now. (And then finish.)

---

[1] No letter to this effect has been found.

That's how I envisage the matter at this distance. Judging by what I have heard of Rouvier's character, I think that's the right method. He must be brought to understand that it wasn't that you were put on ice by Berlin, but that the Chancellor too didn't know anything until very recently.

With a cordial handshake

Your

H.

### 912.   Hugo von Radolin to Holstein[1]

18 September 1905

[...][2] How does the Kaiser's remark 'that he would be happy to lead the fine troops which he has on the Rhine, and has just inspected, across the Rhine to the West' (his admirer, General Gallifet, told me this three days ago!!) accord with the view you expressed in your last letter[3] that H.M. desires the establishment of good relations with Paris and basically doesn't care about Morocco.

As regards your letter which arrived here this morning,[4] I shall go and see R[ouvier] immediately upon his return the day after to-morrow and put these specific questions to him. But I am convinced that were there any truth in Betzold's statement, that is if Rouvier had known of this alleged remark of the K[aiser] and the K[aiser] had in fact said something along those lines, I would surely have heard of it before now from Rouvier or Loubet or Moreau or Dupuy. Considering that I have been told again and again that I had given assurances about a *forthcoming attitude* by our Government and the Kaiser if Delcassé should fall and the Conference be accepted, and that my promises had not been fulfilled hitherto, it would only be natural for these gentlemen to tell me that the Kaiser himself had also spoken in a conciliatory vein. It would be an obvious argument. The fact that they have not done so proves to me that they knew nothing of such a statement, or rather that no such statement was made by the Kaiser. My belief would be that Betzold used the Kaiser's name vis-à-vis Schwabach in order to convey that the Kaiser's 'representative' had, following his instructions, spoken in such a conciliatory manner. But, as I've said, I shall call on Rouvier at once and raise the matter with him in the manner you have suggested. If there should be any truth in it, he will surely tell me so. [...][5]

Your

Hugo.

[1] From the Radolin Papers.

[2] The first part of Radolin's letter gave an account of the situation created by the Rosen-Kriege mission.

[3] Of 13 September.

[4] In a letter of 17 September Holstein wrote: 'Whatever may have happened, please ask Rouvier without losing any time what promises His Majesty has made to the French. Send the information you get first of all to me, so that we can consider what should be done with it. Don't ask questions and don't think it all out, but just follow my advice.

'If possible, write down the actual words used by Rouvier regarding the promises.' (From the Radolin Papers.)

[5] Holstein telegraphed on 18 September: 'Your speculations and guesses are of no use. You must try to find out what has been said by His Majesty. I need it in your interest.' (From the Radolin Papers.)

913.   Holstein to Bernhard von Bülow[1]
       Draft

Friedrichroda, Villa Lorenz, 19 September 1905

Dear Bülow,

Your letter of the 15th of this month, the kind intention of which I gratefully and sincerely appreciate, reached me at a moment when I was[2] trying to come to terms with a piece of news I had just received. A short time beforehand I had heard that Rouvier had had Betzold informed, a few days before the latter's death, that the Moroccan position which the German Government had been defending against France had been surrendered to the French long ago by the Kaiser, and that therefore the attitude of the German Government was incomprehensible to Paris. Betzold was completely astounded by this revelation. I received this news via a reliable intermediary, as my departure prevented a meeting with Betzold which he had wanted. It confirms a suspicion which I harboured for a time already in June,[3] and illustrates a state of affairs which I do not want to describe as normal. It happens often enough that a monarch who feels that he is absolute conducts his own policy. But it is something quite new in the history of diplomacy for a constitutional sovereign to keep secret from his own Government the concessions which he had made to a foreign Government, thus placing it in a situation where for a period of months it has to defend a position which the monarch surrendered long previously. You know better than anyone that we defended the Moroccan position not because we were out for acquisitions—under the obtaining circumstances, in particular England's attitude, the prospects of getting anything there were small— but merely in order to uphold His Majesty's prestige. I was still writing to you in this sense from Clausthal. But in the meantime His Majesty had yielded long ago. The French knew this, but we didn't. We were inexplicably faced with the fact that until General de Lacroix's return the French Government had been yielding and conciliatory, and afterwards became tough and self-confident. Now the reason for this sudden change has become apparent. The French had a direct promise from the Kaiser.

We must face the fact that this sort of thing may occur again. We must therefore count with the possibility of finding ourselves, without any means of preventing it, in impossible situations.

While I was reflecting on this, I received your communication concerning the incident with Radolin.[4] I completely condemn the form in which Radolin made his complaint—incidentally he himself has only informed me in a brief and summary manner hitherto. His letter is that of a lonely, touchy man acting under the stimulus of very great irritation, and formally he has thus placed himself in the wrong. But unfortunately

[1] This letter may never have been sent. See below, p. 374, note 1.
[2] At this point in the draft Holstein crossed out the words 'anyway already feeling in much the same mood as Radolin's, though for a different, not personal reason.'
[3] See above, Holstein's letter to Radolin of 14 June 1905.
[4] Of 15 September.

I cannot share the view that he had no grounds for his complaint. From your correspondence and also from the newspapers I see that Rosen is negotiating *on his own*, and not merely on one or the other technical points but on all aspects of the Moroccan question. If his instructions justify this complete elimination of Radolin—and Rosen, naturally, would not exceed his instructions—this is an open slap in the face for Radolin, who therefore assumes that he is being blamed for the lack of success in the negotiations hitherto. I never believed in the possibility that such instructions would be given, and would on no account have initialled them had I remained in Berlin. I merely thought that they would negotiate jointly. Now it is too late. Radolin wants to leave. His leaving on account of the Moroccan question would be a personal defeat for myself, for his instructions were based on my advice to you. It is not Radolin's fault that it proved impossible to carry them out.

The addition of this personal motive to the already existing objective one allows me no further hesitation: My official activity has come to an end. By the 15th of next month, when my leave expires, I shall have vacated my office in which I have worked for nineteen years. Shortly before that date I will submit my resignation in which I shall only mention my health.[1]

I wish you, dear friend, with all my heart good fortune both in the personal and official spheres. The latter would furnish proof that the German Empire too was not doing too badly.

Please give my very best regards to the Princess and Donna Laura.

As ever in friendship

Your

H.

I am enclosing a letter from Bussche,[2] which seems to show that Rouvier has been talking to representatives of third countries about German-French relations as if he were talking to us. The Government would like to—but public opinion.

Always the same old story which I have heard so often since 1885.

914.　Hugo von Radolin to Holstein

Paris, 23 September [1905]

My dear friend,

I put the question to M. Rouvier, referring to Betzold's letter.[3] He assured me, and I believe him, that he had at no time directly learnt of any statement by the Kaiser containing any sort of promise. And thus he could not have passed on such information to B. He repeated to me what the Kaiser had said to General L[acroi]x and the Prince of M[onaco]— which I already knew—and no promises of any kind were mentioned.

---

[1] Holstein carried his threat of resignation no further. (See below, his letter to Brandt of 23 December 1905, and his letter to Ida von Stülpnagel of 2 November 1905. (*Rogge, Friedrich von Holstein*, pp. 243–4.)

[2] Hilmar, Baron von dem Bussche-Haddenhausen. First Secretary at the Embassy in Washington, 1903–6; *Vortragender Rat* in the Foreign Ministry, 1907–10. Bussche's letter has not been found.

[3] See above, Holstein's letter to Radolin of 15 September.

If R. had heard of any such statements, even if he had done so in confidence, he would surely have told me. Incidentally he told me so in a frank and friendly way. So my view has been confirmed that B[etzold] got a vague letter from one of his friends, in which the general conciliatory remarks made by the Ambassador as the Kaiser's representative are attributed to the latter. In my opinion it is of no significance. [...][1]

Your
Hugo.

## 915.  Holstein to Maximilian von Brandt[2]

Berlin, 14 November 1905

Your Excellency,

[...] I have the impression that the French have been treated with too much kindness by us from up on high. As a result they are beginning to feel that since the entente with England they are masters of the situation. [...]

Rouvier too told us repeatedly during the Moroccan negotiations that he wanted nothing more than a rapprochement with Germany. But he told an Austrian Ambassador who called on him when passing through: 'I, Rouvier, would not feel disinclined towards a rapprochement with Germany, but French public opinion isn't ripe for it yet.' So once again it will have been Germany which alone and unilaterally showed the desire for conciliation. It is obvious that the relations between the two nations will not be improved in this way. The French Ambassador in Rome, Barrère, once dropped a remark to Monts in the spring: 'If sometimes a little less had been done from the German side it would have been more.'

It is certainly significant that ever since Delcassé's revelations conjuring up the prospect of English military and naval support,[3] the French have been talking more of rectifying 1870 than they have done for years. Now, the less they fear a German attack, the more they talk about it. I still continue to believe in only one danger of war, that is the danger arising from the belief that we shall yield to firm pressure. [...]

In sincere respect
Holstein.

[1] In the remainder of his letter, Radolin showed that his position vis-à-vis Rosen had become untenable. The important parts of the Holstein-Radolin correspondence on the Rosen issue, which was never settled to the satisfaction of the people involved, were published by Thimme, *Berliner Monatshefte* (1937). (See also Friedrich Rosen, *Aus einem diplomatischen Wanderleben*, 2 vols. (Berlin, 1931–2.) An agreement between Germany and France on the draft programme for the Morocco conference was reached on 28 September. (*Grosse Politik*, vol. XXii, no. 6832, p. 592.) Bülow sent Radolin a telegram of appreciation for his part in the Morocco negotiations, and congratulated him especially on his ability 'in making good use of the special technical knowledge of Minister Rosen and *Geheimrat* Kriege under your direction.' (Thimme, *Berliner Monatshefte* (1937), p. 890.) Radolin immediately sent a telegram to Frau von Lebbin, then at Friedrichsroda: 'Just received telegram of thanks from the Chancellor which pleases me very greatly.' (From the Radolin Papers.)

[2] From the Brandt Papers.

[3] On 15 October, 1905, the *Matin*, the organ of Delcassé, published revelations about an Anglo-French understanding directed against Germany, by which England promised to mobilize her fleet in case of a German attack on France, seize the Kaiser Wilhelm Canal, and land 100,000 men in Schleswig-Holstein.

916.   Hans von Flotow to Holstein

Paris, 8 December 1905

Dear *Herr Geheimer Rat*,

[...] In my opinion the Kühlmann information does not represent a move on the part of the Government here, but merely the speculations of a young Secretary of Legation who likes to be in on things.[1] Judging from my knowledge of the important people here, they would never have chosen this inappropriate and doubtful channel. Kühlmann filled out his speculation by conversations with myself, and I must say that I gathered the lowest possible opinion of his diplomatic tact from the way in which, in spite of my obvious and repeated attempts at evasion, he practically threatened me in order to get information from me, appealing to the fact that he was being kept informed by the Foreign Ministry. I would regret it if the German Government allowed itself to be persuaded to take any sort of action, for which in my opinion there is absolutely no basis. [...]

I have reported officially on the latest phase of the Moroccan affair, and it is a matter of extraordinary satisfaction to me that Your Excellency shares my point of view. I have already written to the Prince [Bülow] that in my opinion it is not advisable to turn the Conference into a farce and endanger our credit with the Conference Powers, which is as important in politics as it is in business, by agreements such as those being demanded here now.[2] On the other hand I regard the Conference itself as the psychological moment which will decide our relationship with France for a long time to come. But Your Excellency will recognize that better than I can. [...]

With profound respect and admiration I have the honour to remain, my dear *Herr Geheimer Rat*,

Your Excellency's most obedient

Flotow [...]

917.   Holstein to Maximilian von Brandt[3]

Berlin, 23 December 1905

Your Excellency,

[...] I have taken some leave over the holidays, until 3 January, partly in order to rest, partly in order to decide whether I should stay on or go now. I incline towards the latter.

In October 1900, Bülow tried hard for a solid hour to persuade me to accept the post of State Secretary. I refused because I had already refused any promotion ten years earlier, but also because my eyes—due to cataract—would have made the representative duties difficult for me.

---

[1] Kühlmann had reported that France was willing to conclude a pre-conference treaty on Morocco with Germany. (*Grosse Politik*, vol. XXIi, no. 6906, pp. 20–2; see Richard von Kühlmann, *Erinnerungen* (Heidelberg, 1948), pp. 246 *et seq.*)

[2] Concerning the mandate over the police in Western Morocco. (See *Grosse Politik*, vol. XXIi, nos. 6905, 6908, pp. 19–20, 23.)

[3] From the Brandt Papers. See also Holstein's letter to Brauer of 7 December. (Brauer, *Im Dienste Bismarcks*, pp. 410–13.)

Nevertheless I owed Bülow thanks, and so I have since helped him as best I could. But gradually England has come between us as a wedge. It is a misfortune for the German Reich that the Bülow family lost its home in 1864 because England dishonourably left the Danes to their fate. The present Chancellor was fifteen then. Since that time he has been unshakably convinced that anyone who has dealings with England comes to rue it later. That is not true. Without England the Japanese would not have won, since Delcassé would otherwise surely have come to Russia's assistance. And France for her part has significantly strengthened her position by the entente with England, while our position was weakened by the estrangement between ourselves and England, and until the change of Cabinet[1] was even threatened. Bülow's aim has been and remains to work with and draw closer to Russia. He refuses to realize that the old Russia, where we had to pay attention only to the Tsar and his Foreign Minister, has now gone for ever more. The new 'Russian Russia' is anti-German. In the Zemstvo and popular assemblies the war against Germany is described as 'unavoidable'. Events have made the programme 'with Russia and against England' completely ridiculous. The change of government in England is an unexpected stroke of luck for us which we should make use of. Metternich is urging us to do so with a solemnity which is quite unusual in him.[2] But the indications are, I fear, that Bülow is standing by his old prejudices. He wants to disregard England and reach an understanding with France. A childish plan. The French are sitting in a nice position between England and Russia, and are thinking more of the 'despoiled provinces' than they have done for a long time. In order to dampen French ardour, we must convince the English that we are not planning anything against them, i.e. the English. As soon as the English stop thinking of a war against Germany, the French too will lose their desire for war. But we should hurry and improve our relations to England in the next few years while the new Russia is still busy at home. But in this connection some things are being done which I disapprove of. In his speech of 6 December,[3] the Chancellor read out an instruction of mine to London of 11 April.[4] The guiding thought in this instruction was that France, which had acquired rights, should have consulted with the Treaty Powers, while England which had relinquished rights had no need to do so. But in the official stenographic report two short clauses in the instruction are *missing* which state that we are not holding England responsible for France's omissions. The whole sense of the instruction has thereby been completely changed. As a result of these omissions our reproaches are now directed just as much against England as against France. The important German papers, who had stenographers in the Reichstag, printed the complete instruction, but the foreign Press got the 'improved text', with

---

[1] On 5 December 1905 a Liberal Government under Sir Henry Campbell-Bannerman succeeded the Conservative Balfour Cabinet.

[2] See *Grosse Politik*, vol. XXii, nos. 6883, 6886, pp. 681–2, 685–90.

[3] In the Reichstag.

[4] *Grosse Politik*, vol. XXii, no. 6843, pp. 605–7.

the omission, from Wolff.[1]  The result was inevitable; the English took Bülow's whole speech to be anti-English.  It is obvious that such 'printing errors' don't make me happy in my work.  I would ask you, however, not to let anything be known of my intention until I have carried it out.

With a cordial handshake<br>
Your Excellency's sincerely devoted<br>
Holstein.

918.    Joseph Maria von Radowitz to the Foreign Ministry[2]

Madrid, 30 December 1905

I would like to add to my report on the statements made by M. Jules Cambon[3], that during a number of confidential conversations with me he did not drop any sort of hint along the lines of Kühlmann's report.[4]  He can thus hardly be assumed to have inspired these proposals.  Furthermore, I have talked with his brother, Paul Cambon, who is at present visiting him here, and similarly heard no reference to them from him. Both appear to think that the Conference will at least bring the controversy over Morocco to a standstill, thus calming down the excitement, which is very necessary now.  I have heard from Spaniards and from colleagues that the French are stating they definitely want a satisfactory outcome of the Conference, while the Englishman[5] is expressing himself doubtfully on this subject.

I reserve a further report on the attitude of the other representatives. In the meantime the majority probably feel that the living conditions in Algeciras will be pretty grim, and that it would therefore be desirable to reach an understanding as soon as possible and bring the matter to an end.

Radowitz

[1] The Wolff news agency.

[2] An official report which Holstein kept in his private archive.  No copy was found in the Foreign Ministry files.

[3] Of 27 December 1905.  (*Grosse Politik*, vol. XXIi, no. 6919, pp. 32–3.)

[4] See p. 376, note 1.

[5] Sir Arthur Nicolson.  English Minister in Tangier, 1895–1904; Ambassador in Madrid, 1905–6, in St Petersburg, 1906–10.

# 1906

919.   Holstein to Bernhard von Bülow
        Draft[1]

Berlin, January 1906

I regret to inform Your Highness that my political conscience no longer permits me to support your activity in foreign policy by my work. I feel in duty bound to justify my point of view by the following observations.

*The* diplomatic attention of Germany is at the present time focused on three main points : the Near East, Morocco, and Anglo-German relations.

In the *Near East* we have identified our policy for many years with that of Russia and Austria, we aided them in plaguing the Sultan and used our influence to force through dubious reforms. It cannot be demonstrated that any German interest was hereby served. On the contrary, German interests demand the protection of Islam. Other Governments have recognized the political significance of Islam correctly : England and Japan have arranged to guarantee Asiatic Turkey to the Sultan. Why, for whom, for what, should the German Government destroy sympathies which H.M. the Kaiser has won among the people of Islam by years of consistent effort? For more than a year I have raised this question with Your Highness, but in vain. Your Highness concedes every additional Austrian and Russian demand, even those made quite recently, when it has become very obvious that the increasing influence of anti-German Slavic groups had made any activity friendly to Germany almost impossible. With every new demand for our support, Russian and Austrian diplomats freely admit that without the participation of Germany nothing can be achieved with the Sultan. They have therefore tried to make Germany take the leading part in the diplomatic pressure on the Sultan in order to make us bear the odium.

The Kaiser has put an end to this, as I believe, erroneous policy by refusing to release a German ship for the fleet demonstration.[2] As a result of this imperial decision it was at last possible to secure Your

---

[1] This letter was never sent. (See below, Bülow's letter to Holstein of 7 January. See also Brauer, *Im Dienste Bismarcks*, p. 416.) An earlier, somewhat sharper, draft of this letter was also found in the Holstein Papers.

[2] In order to compel the Sultan to introduce a programme of reform in Macedonia, Austria-Hungary and Russia suggested a fleet demonstration by the Great Powers in Turkish waters. To Bülow's proposal of 13 November 1905 for German participation, the Kaiser commented : 'All such demonstrations are quite ridiculous and end in failure. Under the present tense circumstances, when we are standing almost *alone* against the formation of large and hostile coalitions, our *last trump* is *Islam and the Mohammedan world*. To arouse them too against us and to annoy them by taking part in this thoroughly miserable and ridiculous farce I absolutely refuse to do.' (*Grosse Politik*, vol. XXII, no. 7566, pp. 300–2.)

Highness' signature for a dispatch to Vienna which had previously been refused whereby we drew attention to the dubious nature of further reform nonsense and announced the fact of Germany's non-participation.[1] From that time on the other Powers adopted a milder attitude towards Turkey, the fleet demonstration came to an ineffectual end and the Sultan, who got off with fairly easy conditions, has only the personal intervention of H.M. the Kaiser to thank. This action has put Germany's Near Eastern policy back on the right track. Your Highness' previous Near Eastern policy would in the end have driven the Sultan into the arms of an England, which is imbued with new enterprising spirit by the alliance with Japan, and which for months has shown an inclination to resume her old role of the protector of Turkey.

In the Morocco question, H.M. the Kaiser has, I believe, defined German policy as follows:[2] *Germany* has no intention of making a settlement of the Morocco question more difficult by trying to secure special privileges; on the other hand, there is no reason to jettison legitimate economic interests, which Germany shares with other civilized nations in Morocco, by conceding a general mandate to France.[3]

H.M. the Kaiser is herewith remaining within the framework of his modest yet dignified policy which he announced in Vigo[4] and on 31 March 1905.[5] But the possibility of holding to this programme has now been made more difficult for us by certain inconsistencies in the attitude of Your Highness, especially your interviews last autumn with the French journalists.[6] The far reaching and up till now unreciprocated concessions that Your Highness at that time accorded to France is making it more difficult for us now to convince the French that the German Government really intends to hold on to anything. We must be prepared to face the fact that when the French at the Conference are informed of the point of view corresponding to the intentions of H.M. the Kaiser, they will counter by referring to Your Highness' interviews. I also regret that Your Highness has *completely* neglected to inform the Cabinets of Washington and London about the moderation, indeed the modesty, of our aims in Morocco. The silence of the German Govern-

---

[1] *Grosse Politik*, vol. XXII, no. 7585, pp. 317–18.

[2] In the earlier draft of this letter Holstein wrote: 'As far as Morocco is concerned, it seems to me that the directive sent to Your Highness in writing and communicated orally to Prince Radolin by H.M. the Kaiser in every respect summarizes the only correct point of view.' The directive to which Holstein refers was prepared early in December 1905, and was later considerably modified by Bülow. (*Grosse Politik*, vol. XXIi, no. 6922, pp. 38–45.) The Kaiser communicated his oral directives to Radolin on 29 December. (Vol. XXIi, no. 6917, p. 31.)

[3] In the earlier draft of this letter Holstein wrote: 'by conceding a general mandate to France, that is, by sacrificing Morocco to a process of Tunisification.'

[4] In a telegram to Bülow of 16 March 1904 about his talk in Vigo with King Alfonso XIII of Spain, the Kaiser said: 'We discussed Morocco. Have congratulated the King on his arrangement with France of which I approve and which I consider sensible. We want no *territorial acquisition* there. Free ports, railroad building concessions, and import rights. He was much relieved and pleased about this.' (*Grosse Politik*, vol. XVII, no. 5208, p. 363.)

[5] See above, p. 330, note 3.

[6] The first interview was held on 2 October 1905 with M. Douvier, a confidant of Dupuy, for *Le Parisien*; the second on 3 October with M. Tardieu of the *Temps*.

ment is conducive to exciting mistrust, which for example has recently been quite obvious in the attitude of President Roosevelt. In this way Your Highness has facilitated France's pre-Conference diplomatic preparations and a German failure at the Conference is now more imminent than was necessary.

I feel that Your Highness is making a mistake in your Morocco calculations by believing, at any rate until recently, in the possibility that the French could be compensated for Alsace-Lorraine with Morocco and that they would even owe us a debt of gratitude. In reality, if the French acquired Morocco under the present circumstances, they would simply regard it as a success of the Entente Cordiale, pay their thanks to England, and establish closer ties with her than ever—all this has been expressed countless times in the French Press.

Why should France, which has nourished the idea of *revanche* for thirty-five years, renounce it now? Her position is more favourable to-day than at any time since the Peace of Frankfurt, there is lively mistrust between Germany and England as each suspects the worst about the other. French democracy has more tastes and distastes in common with the newly awakened Russian national empire than with the absolutist Tsardom of former days. The old Russia, where one only asked about the opinion of the Tsar and his Foreign Minister, has sunk out of sight and the Russian people, who will in the future have more or less influence on policy, have already on repeated occasions given free rein to their hatred of the Germans. A war *à trois* against Germany is therefore one of the possibilities of the future. Only when this possibility has disappeared will France perhaps seek rapprochement with Germany, but not before.

During the next few years Russia will be primarily occupied with her own affairs. If our *relations to England* do not improve during this period of grace, if in the meantime England's connection with the Dual Alliance becomes even closer, then the German Reich faces a serious future. Three against one are heavy odds.

The fall of the embittered and anti-German Tory Government because of domestic complications makes the possibility of an Anglo-German rapprochement more easy. Efforts in this direction have even already been made by both sides.[1] All the more regrettable are any incidents that disturb this work of reconciliation.

Your Highness' Press Bureau must be blamed for the failure to devote sufficient attention to our English relations. Just to give one example: during the past weeks the humour magazine *Lustigen Blätter*, whose staff consists mainly of foreigners, once again published one or more of those futile pictures, which always arouse bitterness in England. Why did not the Press Bureau, which after all has close contacts with the Police, prevent such things once and for all by sending a timely threat of expulsion to the foreign culprits, and even by extraditing one or another of them? For years the *Lustigen Blätter* have made a speciality of un-

---

[1] See *Grosse Politik*, vol. XXii, nos. 6881–7, pp. 672–96.

flattering pictures of the King of England, so one should be prepared for a recurrence of the same. I am citing this particular case because it is one of the most recent.

Even greater blame attaches to the Press Bureau for the way it handled Your Highness' speech to the Reichstag of the sixth of last month.[1] In the official stenographic report, which is supervised by the Press Bureau, a sentence was left out of the dispatch to London of 11 April which Your Highness quoted : that we did not blame England for not informing us of the Morocco Treaty of 1904, for England had only given up her rights, and for that she did not need the agreement of third parties. By leaving out this sentence, the conciliatory nature of this dispatch towards England was transformed into exactly the opposite. This cut gave the dispatch a sharply anti-English tone, for the criticisms levelled at France now hit England as well. As a result Your Highness' entire speech was regarded in England as a hostile declaration against that country. To correct this interpretation all that would have been necessary was a correction of the text. It would have sufficed if there had been an official statement saying, as happens often enough : 'Owing to a printing error, a sentence in the Chancellor's speech of the day before yesterday was left out. The correct text is, etc.' But the Press Bureau did not feel obliged to issue a correction, and thus allowed the anti-English nature of Your Highness' speech, to which the English Press at once drew attention, to persist. Since I cannot assume that this attitude accords with the wishes of Your Highness, I can only regard the matter as, at the very least, serious negligence on the part of the Bureau. The Bureau must know that apart from this, a major impediment to improved Anglo-German relations is the person of Your Highness, for ever since Your Highness rejected Chamberlain's publicly announced offer of collaboration between England and Germany by your statement in the Reichstag,[2] you are commonly considered in England to be England's principal opponent. The outpourings of yellow journalism in England against the otherwise so popular personality of the closely related German Kaiser would fall on less fertile ground if there were not the conviction that the Kaiser too—since you are his adviser—wants an anti-English policy. Your Highness' speech of 6 December, in its cut version, will necessarily increase this suspicion, and that at a time when here as well as there an effort towards rapprochement had begun. As I said before, serious blame attaches to Your Highness' Press Bureau in this connection.

And precisely at this time Your Highness has given that same Bureau proof of unlimited confidence. Your Highness has ordered that a copy of every incoming coded telegram is to be sent at once to the head of the Press Bureau. Your Highness' order is not limited in any way, so that the Press Bureau will be informed of even our most secret affairs, and what is more, since the telegrams are to be sent to the Press Bureau directly, it will in many cases be informed first.

[1] See above, Holstein's letter to Brandt of 23 December 1905.
[2] On 11 December 1899. See above, p. 173, note 5.

I do not know of a case where such an order has ever been made before in a Foreign Ministry, either here or in other countries. I fear that under certain circumstances this order may threaten the security of our secrets and therewith the security of the Reich. The desire to withdraw from the responsibility of the possible consequences of the new administrative procedure has fixed my resolve to ask to be retired with pension as soon as possible, and I make that request herewith.

H.

## 920. Bernhard von Bülow to Holstein

Sunday noon, 7 January 1906

Dear Holstein,

To my great astonishment, I have just been presented with your resignation.[1] You are asking to be released without naming any reason. I sincerely hope that your health has not grown worse. I had hoped on the contrary that your Christmas leave would have done you good. I can certainly not accept any other reason for your resignation at this time. At any rate I would like to talk things over with you before I do anything more about your resignation. Tomorrow morning I have to see His Maj., tomorrow afternoon there is a meeting of the Ministry of State. Tuesday I will be at your disposal the entire day.

With old regard<br>Your very devoted<br>B.

## 921. Holstein to Bernhard von Bülow
Draft

11 January 1906

Dear Bülow,

To be spat on by the Kaiser, and for *that* reason, Kiaochow, was really unexpected.[2] But it shows me absolutely clearly what my position has

---

[1] Not found.

[2] On 8 January *Le Figaro* printed an article containing what purported to be Hohenlohe's evaluation of Bülow, as told to a friend. According to the article, Hohenlohe maintained that he had succeeded in curbing some of the extravagant projects of the Kaiser, especially his plans with regard to China, but he feared that Bülow would simply carry out the Kaiser's plans without daring to risk an occasional remonstrance. To this article the Kaiser commented: 'Hohenlohe was precisely the one who with vigour and dash aided and warmly supported me in the Kiaochow affair, and he was the *only* one who did so, while the Foreign Ministry had shat in its pants and Tirpitz stood aside and grumbled. Hohenlohe, Hollmann, and I! We worked in absolute agreement and unity, and we two were filled with admiration for the cool power of decision and the daring of the old man! Germany has him to thank for Kiaochow.' Holstein sent this article and the Kaiser's marginalia to Bülow on 11 January with a cover letter in which he said: 'I must consider myself involved in the disrespectful remark about the Foreign Ministry, all the more so since I also worked in the Kiaochow affair. Your Highness came to Berlin during the Kiaochow crisis and knows that until your arrival I alone prepared the plans and carried out the diplomatic campaign for which His Majesty at that time praised Hohenlohe, and is to-day doing so again. I never received or demanded recognition for myself, since I simply did my duty. But the serious affront to my honour by His

gradually become and confirms me in my resolve. I get all the work and the shit-filled pants, while others get the praise : that is a distribution of work that anyone will get sick of sooner or later. My willingness to work has lasted for years, but now the supply has been exhausted completely.

I now know what Hohenlohe meant when he told me with an expression of unmistakable embarrassment: 'The Kaiser was just here and made me eulogies about Kiaochow. Before I had a chance to explain to him that the praise did not belong to me, he snapped his cigarette case shut and was gone.'

So all that the Kaiser knows about me is that I am a member of the Foreign Ministry which at the time 'had shat in its pants'.

What I have a right to expect is a declaration of honour from the Kaiser, not an Order, which would prove nothing. I have been called a coward, whereas it was *my* activity—'the cool power of decision and the daring of the old man'—that the Kaiser was admiring. If such a declaration of honour cannot be obtained, then my recent resignation request will once again be valid. I need not explain further to a gentleman that I cannot act otherwise.

I am faced with a similar unavoidable necessity in the question of the Directorship.[1] The indefinite position I hold to-day has gradually become an ignoble one, for I am dependent on the good will of both superiors and colleagues. The expression 'ignoble' was used yesterday by a calm observer who has no direct interest in the matter. Another observation I made yesterday further confirms me in this opinion. I must therefore stand by my request to convert my Counsellorship into a Directorship, and that this be sent *immediately* through official channels— Treasury, Bundesrat, Reichstag—unconnected with the appointment of the new State Secretary.[2] If the Reichstag then says : 'What does this insatiable man mean by wanting so many advantages? He shall have nothing'. Then at least I will know where I stand, and I can only hope that a few authoritative journalists will take up my cause.

In case of delay, you would also have to reckon with the possibility that the new State Secretary, who might have no interest in strengthening *my* position, would declare himself against the change.

On both matters, the imperial declaration of honour and the *immediate* motion to change my position, I must stand firm. For me these are questions of honour and dignity. If you think that one or the other is unattainable, I will not blame you, my dear friend. But you cannot then blame me if I resign. I believe in your good intentions, but as things now stand these are not enough. I urgently advise you, if things fail to work out with me, to bring in the probable successor to Richthofen on a

Majesty is something I have not deserved and I must defend myself against it. I can expect that Your Highness, as my superior officer, will inform His Majesty about the real state of affairs and secure the rehabilitation of my honour.'

[1] Holstein wished to be made Director of the Political Division, and as such be placed in control of the Press Bureau. (See Rogge, *Friedrich von Holstein*, pp. 244–5.)

[2] State Secretary von Richthofen had suffered a severe stroke, from which he died on 17 January. His successor was Heinrich von Tschirschky.

provisional basis at once. A quick decision is desirable for your sake and mine, as well as for the sake of the work.

*Sans rancune*

Yours most sincerely

H.[1]

## 922. Bernhard von Bülow to Holstein

Berlin, 11 January 1906

Dear Holstein,

I received your letter[2] just after I had already sent to ask if you could see me to-day, because I had several important business and personal questions I wanted to discuss with you. I understand the feelings you expressed in your letter and will present the problem to His Majesty. But for special reasons I think it would be best to bring up this matter orally with His Majesty. I will bring it up with His Majesty at the same time as the Directorship question, with which, as I already told you, I am in complete agreement. There is no opposition to it in the Ministry nor is there any wounded susceptibility, as I convinced myself yesterday. I have a bad cold, and Renvers[3] insists that I stay in my room to-day and tomorrow. If you are able to go out tomorrow, you can find me at 12 o'clock.

With best wishes

Your sincerely devoted

B.

## 923. Holstein to Bernhard von Bülow

Copy

B[erlin], 14 January 1906

Dear Bülow,

I thank you for this proof of confidence. So in the end we two will together drain the dregs of the Morocco question, a dubious pleasure; however, what one doesn't want, one often gets.

I will devote this afternoon and tomorrow to some badly-needed reading up on the subject, and Tuesday I will be at your disposal for a report.

I leave it to your judgment to decide whether, for the sake of sweet

---

[1] A shorter draft of this letter carries the postscript: 'Just as I was going to send my letter off to you, I heard that you had sent for me. A pity that I did not know that earlier for I could have saved myself the trouble of writing the letter. Now I am too worn out and ask to be excused. I wish the matter were settled, one way or another. For good measure I have just re-read my note to St Petersburg of 21 November '97, which at the time was submitted in draft form to the Kaiser and which had his unreserved approval. And now this is what comes of it. I am a coward. H.' Holstein refers to the note printed in *Die Grosse Politik*, under the date of 22 November 1897 (vol XIVi, no. 3711, pp. 97–8). The Kaiser commented when Hohenlohe submitted the draft to him: 'My congratulations on a masterful note, written in a good German, with which I am in full agreement. That is the kind of tone I like in dealing with foreign countries. Wilhelm I.R.'

[2] Of 11 January.

[3] Dr Rudolph von Renvers. Doctor and personal friend of Prince Bülow.

peace, you feel it would be desirable in future to have reports presented jointly with the Head of the Ministry.

Now I am going out walking, as an aid against insomnia. This afternoon I will start the work.

With best wishes<br>Holstein.

The great victory of the English Liberals on the first day of voting is significant for the future. I have seen many elections and have always noticed that the English voter—not to mention the French—likes to be on the winning side.[1] I can only repeat what I said a few months ago: 'The Tories should have their noses rubbed in the 100,000 men for Schleswig-Holstein'.[2] If the Liberals, who have recently seriously damaged their chances by their position on *domestic* issues, home rule, etc., are nevertheless able to win a great victory at the polls, then this is a victory for the *party of peace*. But this cannot under any circumstances be said out loud and before the end of the elections, and hardly thereafter.

## 924. Holstein to Hugo von Radolin[3]

14 January 1906

My affair was regulated yesterday. The difficulty was that I had demanded that Hamm[ann] be subordinated to me, and he was fighting against it. But the order has now been given that I am to lead the *entire* Division. My position is shortly to be made definitive.

I do not yet know who is to succeed R[ichthofen], and do not think that B. B[ülow] knows yet himself. If it is to be Tsch[irschky], then M[ühlberg] and I will give it a try. I have no idea how long it would work, but look upon everything with the equanimity of an old campaigner.

*Küss die Hand!*

## 925. Holstein to Hermann Speck von Sternburg
Draft telegram

Berlin, 14 January 1906

Private

After a lapse of some time, I am once again taking over the leadership of the Political Division, and this time the Press Bureau is included insofar as its activity is concerned with foreign policy. It seems to me that it would have been useful to have entered into an exchange of views with Washington and also with London at the beginning of December, as soon as our instruction for the Conference had been prepared. Our silence may have aroused suspicion against us and thereby eased the pre-Conference diplomatic preparations of France. For my as yet incomplete orientation it would be valuable to me to receive Your Excellency's absolutely frank opinion as to how we should handle America diplomatically during the Conference. Since the time for preliminary conversations has expired, I would assume that it would be best to wait and see

---

[1] The Liberals did in fact win the January election by a large majority.
[2] See above, p. 375, note 3.    [3] From the Radolin Papers.

how affairs at the Conference develop and whether a suitable subject for discussion with Washington comes up. However you can probably see a great deal there that I have missed. Please send a frank, personal opinion, which I will treat as confidential.[1]

The beginnings of the English elections indicate a decisive victory for the peace party. As soon as France is no longer sure of having the English fleet at her side in case of war, she will preserve a peaceful attitude.

Holstein.

### 926. Holstein to Joseph Maria von Radowitz[2]

TELEGRAM

Berlin, 16 January 1906

Private. Also for Count Tattenbach

Many thanks for your letter.[3] After the lapse of some time (since the beginning of September) I have once again taken over the leadership of the entire Political Division, this time including the Press Bureau. I find that the following situation exists:

The Kaiser openly declares that a German war on account of Morocco is absurd, but at the same time he stands by the position he took on 31 March.[4] Yesterday His Majesty returned a report from Rome in which Monts said that if he had been allowed to negotiate with Barrère in April, Delcassé would probably have conceded us a large piece of Morocco in order to stay in office.[5] His Majesty commented:

(1) 'Why. We don't need it', and (2) 'He didn't have the slightest intention of doing so'. To the remark of the Ambassador that the people in Paris are demanding the Tunisification at Morocco with a cynical frankness, His Majesty commented: 'They have emphatically denied it'. To the repeated allusions of the Ambassador as to what should be done in case the Conference came to nothing, His Majesty remarked: 'Nothing would be lost. Then we will stand by the decisions of the Madrid Conference,' and at the second allusion: 'Then we will get the status quo of Madrid; France will then have to break through that.' Thus the Kaiser specifically poses the alternative between his point of view and that of 1880 (or one as similar as possible).

The Chancellor too wants to avoid war insofar as this can be done with honour, but he is clear about the fact that in case of a diplomatic defeat,

---

[1] On 16 January Sternburg telegraphed to Holstein: 'Our silence about the Morocco Conference has aroused suspicion against us not only in the White House but in Congress, and has given rise to a widespread belief that we are looking for a quarrel with France; this has strengthened the position of France with the President, Congress, and public opinion.' The Secretary of State, on the other hand, was convinced of Germany's integrity. Sternburg agreed with Holstein's suggestion to discuss matters with Washington when a suitable opportunity presented itself. (From the Foreign Ministry files.)

[2] From the Foreign Ministry files.

[3] Not found.

[4] See p. 330, note 3.

[5] Monts' report of 10 January. The opinion cited by Holstein was not that of Monts himself, but of Luzzatti, who expressed the idea in a conversation with Monts. (From the Foreign Ministry files.)

the blame would be placed not only on the delegates but also on himself.

The English elections should make it easier for us to get a favourable outcome of the Conference. Our London Embassy says that the devastating defeat of the Conservatives is in large measure due to the increase in taxes caused by the threat of war, and even that yellow journal the *Daily Mail* says that fear of war was one of the causes. After this rejection of the jingos by the voters, France can hardly hope for English military support for a war of aggression on account of Morocco.

The preceding is not a directive, but is for your information; I take full responsibility for its accuracy.

Holstein.[1]

### 927.   Holstein to Hugo von Radolin[2]

Berlin, 19 January 1906

Dear Radolin,

To-day I have good news to report. My own affair has been settled satisfactorily, my doubts and grievances have been completely removed. The most difficult thing, or rather the only difficult thing, was the question of the Press Bureau. I had demanded that this office too, insofar as it dealt with foreign policy, should be subordinated to me. The Bureau must have fought *mordicus* against it, because the matter was hanging in air for several days. But I remained firm, made it a question of either-or, and at last the order came that I was to take over the leadership of the *entire* Political Division. The Chancellor is apparently very pleased that the matter is settled. He told me: 'I will never let you go. You have always brought me luck and are still bringing me luck. In the few days that you have been back, everything is going better. But I must tell you one thing: I was damnably angry with your friend Radolin on account of his letter with the threat at the end.'[3]

I replied: 'I can understand that, because I too, when I read the letter, interpreted the threat as being directed against you. But when I discussed the matter with Radolin later, I was convinced that the thought of threatening you had not crossed his mind. He intended his threat to be directed exclusively against Rosen, whose conduct annoyed Radolin into dropping all the diplomatic proprieties.' (I then said a few things about Rosen.) 'Radolin was completely confounded when I finally succeeded in proving to him that, as he had written it, the threat was directed against you. I can assure you positively that this idea had not occurred to him when he wrote the letter.'

Bülow then said: 'I am very glad to hear it. Would you please write to Radolin that I regard the matter as closed and forgotten.'

I am carrying out this commission with pleasure and also believe that Bülow believes me. I am equally glad that you did so well with your

---

[1] For Radowitz' reply, see *Grosse Politik*, vol. XXIi, no. 6952, p. 96.
[2] From the Radolin Papers.            [3] See above, p. 369, note 2.

report to the Kaiser.[1] The Kaiser wrote in large letters at the head of the report: 'Radolin did that well'. This remark at that place means that it referred to the entire report. So we can say that all's well that ends well.

Now I would like to tell you confidentially about a delicate and difficult matter, without Bülow's knowing I told you. He told me, adding that I should say nothing to anyone, that he had received reports (I assume from the police) that we should be prepared for a campaign of sensationalism by the scandal newspapers against certain persons in high places—on account of pederasty. In the first line of attack was the French Secretary of Embassy, Lecomte, who formerly enjoyed the same reputation in Munich. (Perhaps your son-in-law has heard about it.) Now Bülow is quite nervous about the possibility of such a scandal at this time. He discussed the matter from every angle with me and what we could do to avoid it, but I have followed his wish and have said nothing at all about it here at the Ministry. A few years ago, before Bülow was here, another Secretary of Embassy at another Embassy was suspected of the same thing. The German Government thereupon gave a highly confidential hint to the Government in question (one of our allies) and the apple of discord was quietly removed. I must however agree with Bülow that our relations with France are such as to make a hint of this nature, from Government to Government, a dubious business. On the other hand I pointed out that afterwards the French Government can reproach us with: 'This scandal could easily have been avoided without annoyance to anyone if you had informed us in time. The most gentle sort of hint would have sufficed.'

Meanwhile I have not told him or indicated in any way that I would inform you about this matter. I did not do so in order to leave you a completely free hand as to whether to say something or not. It really depends on your personal contacts. If you think that the matter will really be handled discreetly, then a timely warning may be in order, but if you think that the warning itself would lead to a scandal, then leave it alone. It will not be pretty, of course, if Harden[2] begins to discuss a 'Franco-German rapprochement from the wrong way around' in his [...]³ I myself had up till now heard [...]³ nothing about Lecomte except that he takes every opportunity of talking against Bihourd and making propaganda for Barrère. But this in-fighting has always been customary in the French diplomatic missions.

*In case* you think it would be better to drop a hint, you would make it generally clear that *you had no orders*, you had only heard that the scandal

---

[1] Of 6 January. Radolin reported that, following the line of the Kaiser's directive (*Grosse Politik*, vol. XXIi, no. 6917, p. 31) he had made it clear to Rouvier that Germany was seeking no special advantages at the Algeciras Conference. But if France refused to accept the principle of the Open Door for Morocco, then the already serious situation would become more serious still. Germany wanted only a satisfactory and peaceful solution. Rouvier declared that he was in complete agreement with this point of view. (From the Foreign Ministry files.)

[2] Maximilian Harden. Founder, editor, and principal contributor of the political-literary weekly journal *Die Zukunft*.

³ The letter is torn at this point. One word illegible.

Press was mobilizing for a campaign of sensationalism in which a leading role seemed to be assigned to the said Lecomte. You would say that the authorities will try to avoid this scandal, like any other, but that there was very little they could do about it because such scandalous revelations were usually circulated from Switzerland and were only later taken up by the rest of the European Press. You had no doubt whatever that all the German Governments would do everything in their power to give the accused people an opportunity to clear themselves by initiating libel suits. But because of your good personal relationships and in order to avoid later reproach, you wanted to drop this hint now, because a rapid transfer of the threatened diplomat would break the back of the whole scandal campaign or at least—and this seemed to you to be the most important point—would rob it of its international character.

Decide this matter entirely according to your own sure sense of tact. Naturally you will not name the Chancellor or me. But if anything at all is to be done, there is probably no time to lose. I repeat, however, that I personally have no opinion whatever about this Lecomte and his inclinations, and that I can only hope that he will emerge from the libel suits that are to be expected with his name completely cleared.

If you expected to hear from me who is to be State Secretary, then I'm afraid I must disappoint you. I named three, two imperial ambassadors and one outsider, whose appointment would cause me to resign immediately. With all the rest I will try to establish a *modus vivendi*. Tschirschky belongs in this last category. Now that my position is clearly defined, I will wait and see how it will work. I regard all this with the calm of my age and solitude. I think Tschirschky is actually the most probable. The Chancellor thinks so too.

I place no particular value on the recent query of Kriege about a possible conversation with Dupuy,[1] because I do not think that France will so early spontaneously propose anything that would be acceptable to us. But I think that we will emerge from the Conference decently and honourably as a result of the English elections and the attitude of America. After all, we do not want to gain anything, only we do not want to lose anything either.

Please convey my deepest respects to the Princess, and a warm shake of the hand for yourself.

Yours
Holstein.

## 928. Hugo von Radolin to Holstein

28 January 1906

My dear friend,

In haste I am sending you confidentially a letter that Tschirschky wrote to me about his appointment, and his hope to be able to count on

[1] See Bülow's telegram to Radolin of 16 January 1906, drafted by Kriege. (*Grosse Politik*, vol. XXIi, no. 6936, p. 67.) Dupuy had suggested a provisional reform of the police system in Morocco, whereby the status quo would be maintained as far as possible.

your kind support.[1] I am sending it to you so that you can see his good intentions. I am furthermore convinced that he means it in all honesty.

Your faithful<br>Hugo

ENCLOSURE

Heinrich von Tschirschky to Hugo von Radolin

Hamburg, 26 January 1906

Honoured Prince.

First I would like to thank Your Highness warmly for your telegram of congratulation on my appointment. The real pleasures here on earth are rare, however, and my selection as State Secretary, by which I feel honoured in the highest degree, is certainly not one of them. You know me well enough to realize that I never wanted the post and that I certainly never did anything in order to receive it. On the contrary, if only for reasons of health I tried to avoid it. But now there was nothing I could do but to accept the post and I will work with all my strength to fill it to the satisfaction of the Kaiser and the Chancellor. I am well aware of the burden of work that awaits me and the difficulties I will encounter. I hope that Herr von Holstein will have the kindness to ease the burden of my new and difficult position. Ever since my early days in the civil service, when for almost a year I lunched with him daily at the Kaiserhof, I have preserved an unswerving attachment to him, and as long as I live I will not forget that it was he who saved me from returning to Persia and thus almost certainly preserved me from a mortal illness. In my official capacity I desire nothing more than to conduct a policy beneficial to Germany according to my knowledge and conscience. Perhaps Your Highness would have the kindness, in consideration of the close friendship between yourself and Herr von Holstein, to ask him to support me in my position, which I certainly did not pick out for myself. I hope that Algeciras will have removed much of the work from Paris so that Your Highness can have a little more peace and quiet. We are hoping to find better weather in Berlin; here it is really dreadful.

Please remember me to the Princess.

In old attachment and gratitude<br>v. Tschirschky

## 929.   Holstein to Hugo von Radolin[2]

Berlin, 31 January 1906

Dear Radolin,

[...] My reputation as the protagonist of a war policy dates from last spring and was the work of petty enemies here. Thank you very much for your friendly efforts, but let the people write whatever they please. That I am represented as the protagonist of the 'Big Stick' shows what a man can come to.

Warm greetings<br>Your<br>Holstein

[1] See Enclosure.          [2] From the Radolin Papers.

930.    Heinrich von Tschirschky to Holstein

Hamburg, 3 February 1906

Your Excellency's

friendly letter of yesterday gave me great pleasure. If I can have the benefit of Your Excellency's rich experience and friendly support, for which I had hoped and of which I am now assured, then I can face the future calmly. I am looking forward to having the opportunity of doing political work with you, all the more so since I agree with Your Excellency that there never have been and never will be fundamental differences in the way we look upon the big political questions. [...]

That the German Press last summer was [dominated] almost exclusively by Gallic-coloured reports of the German journalists in Paris was something I too noticed with regret. We must try to relieve the Press Bureau of the Foreign Ministry of as much work as possible that does not concern foreign policy, although, in contrast to what I am told about the activity at Richthofen, I intend to restrict my own activity exclusively to matters of foreign policy.

As Your Excellency also indicates, stricter official discipline in the Ministry and therewith calmer and better regulated working methods would also not do any harm. That the Colonial Division is to be made separate[1] is a great deliverance in my opinion and in that of the entire Ministry I am sure. I will manage to get along with Körner.[2]

Once again heartfelt thanks for your friendly letter. I will not be able to get to Berlin before the middle of the month, because I first have to make a journey to Mecklenburg, Lübeck, and Bremen. I will then look forward to starting my official work with Your Excellency, and to discussing with you all the important political questions of the contemporary scene.

In old attachment

Your Excellency's most obedient

von Tschirschky.


931.    Holstein to Hugo von Radolin[3]

7 February 1906

Dear Radolin,

Things are going well for us at Algeciras in that a great many neutrals are coming over to our side. Révoil refuses to budge, as usual. Well, whether the Conference has any result or whether we keep the status quo, we will still keep the peace.

His Majesty is telling everyone that he wants peace, and France will certainly not provoke a war.

---

[1] The ambiguous position of the Colonial Division, which was a section of the Foreign Ministry but at the same time an agency directly responsible to the Chancellor, had become increasingly awkward in recent years. A proposal for the establishment of a separate Reich Colonial Office was therefore submitted to the Reichstag in 1906. This proposal was rejected by the Reichstag on 26 May 1906 and failed to secure approval until May of the following year. The Reich Colonial Office was established by an imperial order of 17 May 1907.

[2] Director of the Economic Policy Division of the Foreign Ministry, 1899–1913.

[3] From the Radolin Papers.

It is difficult for us to negotiate *for this reason* : because H.M., with all his desire for peace, is holding fast to his well-known position of 31 March. He would take it very much amiss if we 'sold out the Sultan to France'. Under these circumstances, *if* Révoil holds to his old programme of French domination, it is hardly to be expected that the Conference will have any result. In *that* case—and this is something the French will have to consider carefully—we would no longer be bound by our concession about the border zone.[1]

I have reason to believe that the French have met with all sorts of disappointments in the Morocco question, for instance in St Petersburg. This highly confidentially.

With best wishes
Your
Holstein.

## 932. Hugo von Radolin to Holstein

Paris, 9 February 1906

My dear friend,

Dispatch no. 220[2] is in complete accord with my own views and with our previous policy. M. Tardieu[3] of the *Temps*, who has become too big for his boots and thinks he can get away with anything, has apparently deliberately tried to commit the Government on the issue of the Police in order to compel Rouvier to adopt this policy as his own.

Up till now I have no reason to believe that Rouvier's thinking differs from his ideas of last summer, e.g. that he will propose nothing to the Conference that would be rejected because of Germany's veto. Rouvier has told me repeatedly : 'I will certainly avoid making any proposition that would run the risk of a veto. I want to have nothing to do with Morocco. All I want is to guarantee the frontier. Naturally I cannot allow others to move into Morocco if France does not do so.'[4] Those were his words ever since negotiations began. In the meantime he is probably under pressure from Révoil (and Tardieu via the Press) to follow another line. He has *not* done so with me, and since my return last December he has never again spoken to me about that ticklish problem in the Morocco affair. Nor have I had any occasion to take the initiative. The statements made to me by Jean Dupuy (see report no. 16 of 10 January) allow me to assume that Rouvier has not permitted any change in his opinions of last summer.[5] Perhaps he also has a 'guilty conscience' towards me and for that reason is avoiding broaching the subject. He is known to be weak and open to influence. I also think that I am acting according to the ideas of the Chancellor and yourself if I

---

[1] In the agreements of 8 July 1905. (See *Grosse Politik*, vol. XXii, chapter CXLVIII.)

[2] In dispatch no. 220 of 7 February, Bülow wrote that the concession to France in the zone of Morocco bordering on French territory was dependent on the rest of the Morocco question being regulated with the agreement and according to the interests of all the treaty Powers. (*Grosse Politik*, vol. XXIi, no. 6988, pp. 146–7.)

[3] André Tardieu. French journalist.          [4] In French in the original.

[5] According to Dupuy, Rouvier wanted to maintain the principle : neither victors nor vanquished. (*Grosse Politik*, vol. XXIi, no. 6934, pp. 64–5.)

wait for M. Rouvier to take the initiative in order to speak to him along the lines of dispatch no. 220. Furthermore I believe that despite all friendship with England (the exaggerated friendliness to the London County Council is intended to underline this friendship still more) the French have the feeling that under the present regime in England they can no longer count so absolutely on these neighbours. I also think that conditions and sentiment in Russia are not such as to encourage the French to undertake any risky adventures. This makes the position of M. Tardieu and Révoil the more irresponsible. How right you were when last June you already expressed the fear that if people like Révoil, etc, remained as advisers in the Foreign Ministry, the policy of Delcassé would continue as before via the back door. I believe I told you at the time what the former Adjutant of the Prince of Monaco, Captain (Navy) Sauerwein, whom Jean Dupuy has just taken on at a high salary as editor of the *Petit Parisien*, told me *in confidence* : namely that Révoil had stated in Foreign Ministry circles (when he was conducting the negotiations with Rosen) that he wanted no understanding with Germany and that he intended to act accordingly. This now seems to be the case.

Incidentally I warned Rouvier at the time against influences *à la Révoil*. He would not then admit that these existed.

I am beginning to have my doubts about Rouvier's veracity. I still ascribe it more to weakness than to bad faith. Thus it struck me that he wrote in that dispatch to Bihourd (no. 284 in the Yellow Book)[1] : 'On several occasions I have told Prince Radolin, without his having let me suspect the least difficulty, that we counted on his Government having no objection to our views about the international mandate, which would mean that we would ask the Conference to delegate to us everything that involved military reforms, or, more specifically, *the police*.'[2]

I, at any rate, do *not* remember that he said any such thing, and would like to question his accuracy. But if he did say or hint something like that, it could *only* have referred to the principle of such reforms, and even then only to the *border districts* (long before these latter had been conceded to the French *without mandate*). But this cannot be seen in that dispatch to Bihourd, and can therefore be incorrectly interpreted. If he had said this to me at the time, I would have reported it.

Furthermore, there is a contradiction of this demand in a later dispatch to Bihourd (no. 348 of the Yellow Book)[3] which specifically states : 'The guarantee for Germany lies in the fact that the decisions of the Conference have to be unanimous, and only her opposition would be needed to prevent the general mandate from being delegated to us.'[2] Incidentally, Dupuy does not really know how he should formulate this provisional police business and told me at the time that he still had to think it over. Since he has not yet said anything further to me about it, I think it is decidedly better *not* to bring up the matter again until he does so.

[1] Of 9 July 1905. *Affaires du Maroc 1901–1905*, p. 249.
[2] In French in the original.
[3] Of 25 September 1905. *Affaires du Maroc 1901–1905*, pp. 305–6.

I must close. The post is going.
Johanna sends a thousand good wishes

Your faithful friend<br>Hugo

I regret the statement in no. 284 of the Yellow Book was not corrected at the time it was sent to the Foreign Ministry to be checked.[1]

### 933. Kaiser Wilhelm II to Bernhard von Bülow[2]

Berlin, 11 February 1906

My dear Bülow,

I have allowed what you told me about Algeciras to run through my head, and in doing so I have had an idea. According to your account, the King of Spain has heretofore always refused to tell us anything about the Franco-Spanish treaty on Morocco[3] because he has promised France to keep it secret. Such conduct *after* his reception here[4] is impolite and leads to the suspicion that it contains some dirty items at our expense. You also reported that Rome was being two-faced as usual, and that Visconti seems inclined to concede more and more French demands. One might call it a 'Latin Union' against the Teutons in Germany—supported by the Teutons in London. This 'Union' has probably already long ago divided up the entire Mediterranean littoral of Africa by mutual concessions and agreements—without us—and with the sanction of England, which could then drastically reduce its fleet at Malta, for a 'Mediterranean Question' in the old Nelsonian sense would then no longer exist. An Entente Cordiale between Paris and London—thereby releasing ships for the new *North Sea* fleet. The King of Spain expects me to visit him! But refuses me any kind of political concession. I suggest that Your Highness let Madrid know quite bluntly that if His Majesty does not inform me about the agreement with France over Morocco, and if Spain—by supporting France—helps to jettison the Conference, then I will not pay a visit to Madrid this year! I am so much older than that lout that he at least owes me that!

Wilhelm I.R.

### 934. Holstein to Johanna von Radolin[5]

Berlin, 12 February 1906

Most gracious Princess,

With sad feelings I read the words in your letter[6] 'until we meet again shortly in Berlin'. To-day it unfortunately does not look as though that this will soon happen. A journalist, not a German, who arrived here a few days ago from Algeciras, said that the opinion was fairly general among the journalists there that Révoil had come with the firm intention

---

[1] See Holstein's reply of 10 February 1906. (*Grosse Politik*, vol. XXIi, no. 6994, pp. 152–4.)

[2] Handwritten copy from the Holstein papers.

[3] Of 3 October 1904. (*Documents Diplomatiques Français*, Deuxième Série, vol. V, no. 358, pp. 428–32.)

[4] Autumn, 1905.     [5] From the Radolin Papers.     [6] Not printed.

of preventing the Conference from achieving any result. In this he will probably succeed, considering the demands that he is making. In that case I look forward to a restless, disagreeable period of Franco-German relations similar to the period between '66 and '70.

There is unfortunately no question that you can leave now, while things are in a state of flux. I can hardly hope that the business can be settled, for apparently Révoil dominates Rouvier, so who is there to preach reason?

However, who knows? Perhaps a few sensible people may yet be found in France.

With deep respect
Holstein

935.　Bernhard von Bülow to Holstein[1]

[February 1906]

I would receive Courcel if I were you.[2] It would be necessary to make clear to him that France can reach agreement with us on the two main points at issue if she will add more water to her wine; but that otherwise we can simply let the Conference break up. It might be useful to comment on the exaggerated tone of the *Temps*, on the intransigent attitude of the French negotiators, and the sudden somersaults of French policy.

B.

936.　Bernhard von Bülow to Holstein

[22 February 1906]

Yesterday and to-day I discussed in detail the position of the Conference negotiations and the general situation with His Majesty. H.M. is firm, and said as much yesterday evening to O[sten]-Sacken,[3] nor will he change his mind because of the letter of the Grand Duke of Baden.[4]

Everything depends on our seizing the right moment for an acceptable compromise. We cannot tolerate a humiliation. The failure of the Conference would be, no matter how one looked at it, a diplomatic set-

[1] From the Bülow Papers. Only a typewritten copy of this document was available to the editors.

[2] Baron Courcel had represented France at the funeral of King Christian IX of Denmark on 18 February. For his conversations with Holstein, see *Grosse Politik*, vol. XXIi, nos. 7034–5, pp. 206–9.

[3] The Russian Foreign Minister had instructed his Ambassador in Berlin to attend the Court Ball on the evening of 21 February in order to find some opportunity to present the French point of view to Bülow and if possible to the Kaiser himself. (*Documents Diplomatiques Français*, Deuxième Série, vol. IXi, nos. 239, 253, pp. 332–5, 346–7.)

[4] After Bülow had informed the Grand Duke of Baden of the most important documents on the Morocco question, the Grand Duke sent a letter to Wilhelm II warning him against a war with France, which, even if it were victorious, would severely injure German industry and would be unpopular with the German people. The aim of German policy should be to loosen France from England by a policy of conciliation. The draft reply by the Foreign Ministry which was approved by Wilhelm II explained that Germany was standing firmly by her treaty rights, and in view of the threatening attitude of the French Press could not relinquish them without creating doubts about Germany's motives. The Kaiser wanted nothing better than to improve relations with France, but this depended on France alone. (From the Foreign Ministry files; see Bülow, *Denkwürdigkeiten*, vol. II, p. 209.)

back for us. Neither public opinion, Parliament, Princes, or even the army will have anything to do with a war over Morocco. The test of the correctness of the position we have taken will be whether we will be able to find an acceptable way out of this impasse.

Most sincerely<br>B.

## 937.   Bernhard von Bülow to Holstein

23 February [1906]

Agree entirely that you shouldn't be burdened with the drafting of the letter to Witte in addition to your other great burdens of work.[1]   But I count on your checking the draft thoroughly, for besides the development of America's attitude, this is one of the most important cards in the present game.

B.

## 938.   Hugo von Radolin to Holstein

Paris, 24 February 1906

My dear friend,

Just as the diplomatic pouch was about to be closed, I found the enclosed article in the *Temps*, which I am sending to you.[2] According to that it would seem that a certain old campaign is about to start again. This will not bother you, but such an article makes me very angry.

I only saw Baron Courcel for a moment yesterday, he was in a great hurry. He had not yet been able to talk with Rouvier, who was very busy in the Chamber. Baron Courcel received the impression, so he told me, that they did not want to burn their bridges. He also told me that he would use his influence *here* as much as possible *in favour* of the proposals made to him in Berlin.[3] I fervently hope that he succeeds. I believe, however, from everything I hear, that the people here will not be able to make further concessions without bringing about the fall of the Ministry. The political world in general is standing by a *non possumus*, namely that

[1] During Witte's visit to the Kaiser at Rominten in the previous September it had been arranged that Witte should communicate with the Kaiser through Prince Philipp zu Eulenburg. (Haller, *Eulenburg*, p. 326; *The Memoirs of Count Witte*, ed. by Abraham Yarmolinsky, (New York, 1921), p. 424). On 20 February Witte had written to Eulenburg informing him of Russia's desperate need for a foreign loan, and that the successful negotiation of that loan depended on the settlement of the Morocco crisis. As the loan was needed to combat the forces of revolution in Russia, Witte appealed to Germany to make concessions in Morocco in the interests of monarchical solidarity and to further the prospects of a continental alliance. (*Grosse Politik*, vol. XXIi, no. 7027, pp. 194–7.) The German reply of 27 February, drafted in the Foreign Ministry, recommended that Witte induce the French to find a solution to the Morocco crisis acceptable to Germany. (*Grosse Politik*, vol. XXIi, no. 7030, pp. 202–4.)

[2] The article of the *Temps* of 24 February stated: 'The *Mittagszeitung* has published an interview with a Conservative who said: "Germany is heading towards a defeat at Algeciras." The reason for this is the direction given to the negotiations by M. de Holstein, head of the First Political Section of the Foreign Ministry, who has been the evil genius of the entire Morocco affair. But there are precursory signs that it will not be long before this influence will be eliminated by the Crown.'

[3] See p. 396, note 2.

German spiked helmets and police uniforms will not be tolerated. That is the *vox populi*. Rouvier has *never* mentioned this point to me, so I don't know what he thinks about it. But I do not think that he will have the power to force the proposal through if it is made. As soon as C. has seen the Minister-President, I hope to talk with the former.[1] Telegram no. 70 of 23 February contains questions that are difficult to answer.[2] I must at any rate have a little time, for I do not want to give a superficial answer.

I would like to tell you privately my personal opinion, however, that if Rouvier were to make concessions too damaging to France's *amour propre* (they say that he has virtually reached the limit of the possible), he would in all probability be overthrown even before the close of the election period (16 March). For him it would therefore seem to be more advantageous if the Conference dragged on beyond 16 March. He could then still go on quietly negotiating in Algeciras when the Chamber dissolves itself to adjourn until the new elections. When he is less under fire from heated Deputies, it is not impossible that he may be induced to make further concessions.

If, owing to the activity of another Power, the Conference were now to break up without result, in all probability this would not hurt the Rouvier Cabinet. They would be able to say here that Rouvier had stood up to the German demands, and rather than give in to the Germans he had allowed the Conference to break up. But considering the curious quality of public opinion here, it is just as possible that they will accuse him of having bungled the business and that they will use this opportunity to break his neck. Both possibilities exist and it is impossible to predict the public mood, it changes from one moment to the other.

The followers of Delcassé are growing more powerful all the time and are trying to overthrow Rouvier. One way or another. Besides foreign policy, there are also questions of domestic policy which can serve as points of attack against Rouvier. The principal danger, however, lies in the personal ambition of people who would like to supplant Rouvier. Should Rouvier fall, it is probable that the chauvenist group (Delcassé followers) would have more opportunities.

By his speech yesterday, Rouvier has *momentarily* been *strengthened*.[3]

If *we* draw the bow too tight, either Rouvier will fall at once if he gives in to us, or he is made *stronger* if he energetically resists us. That is my very hastily conceived opinion, which I may well modify or amplify after consideration in answering the questions put to me. The mood in France

---

[1] Courcel informed Radolin on 27 February 'that he had not yet been able to have a detailed conversation with the Minister President, but that his first impressions in the Ministry and in political circles were not favourable. The guiding thought seemed to be the fear of losing prestige by further internationalization.' (*Grosse Politik*, vol. XXIi, no. 7047, p. 225.)

[2] In this telegram Bülow asked Radolin's opinion on the question of 'what effect the failure of the Conference would have on the mood in France, the position of the Rouvier Cabinet, and the forthcoming elections'. (From the Foreign Ministry files.)

[3] On 23 February Rouvier had replied effectively in the Chamber to the attacks on France's Morocco policy by the Socialist Deputy Jaurès, who maintained that France's intransigent attitude was endangering the success of the Morocco Conference.

is very very antagonistic towards us. The break–up of the Conference will not improve it, particularly if we hold fast to our programme.

The break up of the Conference will in my opinion have only a passing effect on the elections. Admittedly, the Nationalists (and Delcassé's followers) will strike the iron against us as long as it is hot. But the main issue in the elections will be the battle between the extreme Left against the moderates over the separation of church and state, the financial question (*bouilleurs de cru*, old age insurance, etc.).

The French *amour propre*, supposedly violated by the Germans, is naturally always brought into play. No one thinks of going to war, but if it is forced on the French, they will offer a stout resistance.

I am writing in terrible haste and ask you not to hold me responsible for what I have written. I am writing as my ideas run into my pen and cannot even re-read it.

Best wishes from Johanna<br>
Your faithful<br>
Hugo.

## 939.   Holstein to Hugo von Radolin[1]

4 March 1906

Dear Radolin,

[...] Above all, see to it that you further a direct Franco-German understanding through Courcel.

The English, in constantly bringing up the idea of a German harbour on the west coast of Morocco,[2] make me very suspicious indeed. Apparently they want to come up with this suggestion at the very end, when everything else fails. Their purpose is obviously to create even more antagonism between France and ourselves. In that case I would prefer almost any direct Franco-German agreement. Only the French should not want to gobble up the whole of Morocco at once. In that respect, Courcel must preach reason.[3]

## 940.   Holstein to Hugo von Radolin[4]

TELEGRAM

Berlin, 7 March 1906

Private. To be decoded in person.

Phili[5] is at work here to make himself Ambassador in Paris. For that reason he would like to have Barrère, a friend from Munich days, here as Ambassador as soon as possible, presumably so that he can then tell the Kaiser that the appointment of Phili to Paris was an essential preliminary condition for the improvement of relations; Lecomte, an intimate of Phili, is active in furthering this intrigue in Paris. They have tried to spoil the chances of all other possible candidates with the Kaiser, especially Dupuy, whom they have represented as a mere journalist. The

---

[1] From the Radolin Papers.     [2] See *Grosse Politik*, vol. XXIi, no. 7022, pp. 187–8.
[3] Holstein expressed similar ideas in a telegram of the same day. (*Grosse Politik*, vol. XXIi, no. 7055, p. 237.)
[4] From the Radolin Papers.     [5] Philipp zu Eulenburg.

Chancellor has now corrected this notion. You might ask Courcel whom he considers to be the more suitable, Dupuy or Barrère. I think I know that Courcel dislikes Barrère for general patriotic reasons because he thinks Barrère is more concerned with the interests of himself than with those of his country. I therefore advise that you discuss the Berlin ambassadorial situation not only with the Prince of Monaco but also with Courcel, without delay. You can tell Courcel at the same time that Barrère, who had friends in Germany, was having them work in his favour in Berlin. But that you as well as I considered Barrère to be a dangerous visionary, and that you felt that Dupuy or Bourgeois would be better. If you find that Courcel has a similar opinion, then express the hope that he will use his influence in the matter. The Kaiser, to whom Phili has already pictured Barrère as a wonder man, has already spoken to the Prince of Monaco in favour of Barrère, but he will now write to Monaco that after careful consideration Barrère does not seem as suitable as Dupuy or Bourgeois. The Prince of M., who was to-day in [...][1] still thinks that Barrère would be *persona gratissima*.

Naturally you will not breathe a word about Phili, but you could perhaps hint to Baron Courcel that Lecomte seems to be working through Barrère.

Uncle Fritz

941. Bernhard von Bülow to Holstein

14 March 1906

Dear Holstein,

[...] For various reasons the failure of the Conference would be less unpleasant for us now than it would have been a few weeks ago. But the question will always remain embarrassing as to why we had been so anxious to have the Conference, and that question will be raised here immediately. What Th. Wolff[2] writes in to-day's *Berliner Tageblatt*, p. [ ][3], column 2 (at the top) is a prelude to the campaign we can then expect. This criticism would grow even more sharp if after the break-up of the Conference the Pretender should win, the Sultan be deposed, or some other change occur in that unfortunately quite unpredictable Morocco. I think you will agree with my suggestion that Tattenbach be asked to give us his candid opinion on the situation.

I have given the Press detailed instructions in this sense. Behind the French effort to exaggerate the importance of the Casablanca issue[4] there apparently lies the fear, which Courcel has repeatedly expressed, that we intend to smuggle our Trojan Horse into Morocco through this port, with all the ensuing consequences that the French imagination can conceive.

---

[1] The document is torn at this point. Two words missing. On the evening of 7 March the Prince of Monaco arrived in Paris after a visit to Germany. (*Grosse Politik*, vol. XXIi, no. 7080, pp. 265–6.)

[2] Theodor Wolff. Editor-in-Chief of the *Berliner Tageblatt*.

[3] The number is missing in the text.

[4] Germany wanted to put the police in Casablanca under international control. (See *Grosse Politik*, vol. XXIi, no. 7060, pp. 241–3.)

That Rouvier is the innocent angel that he tries to make Radolin think he is, is something I believe less and less. Does Bourgeois really have an interest in making his debut with the failure of the Conference ?[1] So far as I know, his relations with Radolin were always friendly. It would be interesting to know to what extent the *Temps* article yesterday was perfidy towards Bourgeois, or bluff.

Most sincerely

Yours

B.

## 942.   Bernhard von Bülow to Holstein

17 March [1906]

[...] I concede that you were right when you said yesterday that we can in the end hardly make a *conditio sine qua non* out of Casablanca. But we must insist on it until we receive compensation for this guarantee of internationalization in other guarantees such as supervision of the police force or the bank question.

If our Morocco policy is to end satisfactorily, the Conference must not fail, but neither can we allow ourselves to be obviously defeated. [...]

Most sincerely

Your

B.

## 943.   Holstein to Bernhard von Bülow
Draft

23 March [1906], 11:00 p.m.

Dear Bülow,

It seems to me that Lamsdorff's unfriendly gesture[2] has aroused public opinion here to some extent. A determined move, to show that we have no intention of being pushed around, would be understood and well received. For that reason I raise the question whether you will not let it come to a break in case France continues to make difficulties. Three days ago I did not advise doing so because the questions still in abeyance are not *in themselves* worth letting it come to a break. Now I advise it in the interests of the Reich and in your own. In all probability the French will then give in. If they do not do so it will be,[3] in the present situation, a defeat for French diplomacy, and for Russia—which will then get its

---

[1] Bourgeois had become Minister for Foreign Affairs in the Sarrien Cabinet on 13 March. The Rouvier Cabinet had fallen on 7 March over a domestic issue.

[2] On 21 March the French newspaper *Temps* published an alleged instruction from Count Lamsdorff to Russia's representative at the Conference of Algeciras in which he denied that Russia had advised France to accept Austria's mediation proposal about police reform, or that Russia considered the internationalization of the police in Casablanca acceptable. Russia would on the contrary never cease to be a loyal ally of France. On the following day Count Osten-Sacken informed the German Government officially of this instruction. Though his version was less brusque than that published in the *Temps*, the German Government nevertheless considered the instruction 'deplorable' for Russo-German relations. (See *Grosse Politik*, vol. XXIi, no. 7122, pp. 312–13.)

[3] At this point in his draft Holstein crossed out the words : 'a lesson for them and for Russia that they will remember. Of course, you must be certain that we do not give in by next week.'

loan under usurious terms—and a warning to treat us more politely in the future.

H.

944. Holstein to Bernhard von Bülow
Copy

8:00 a.m., Sunday, [25 March 1906]

Dear Bülow,

Now I am going for a walk, at half past five I will be at the office. When the reply comes from Algeciras,[1] I suggest that we first find out what Stein[2] has to say about it. In decisive moments one shouldn't bind oneself to any rigid plan. On the question that matters—the impression on the rest of the world and the attitude in Paris—Stein is more competent to judge than any of us. Yesterday he spoke in favour of standing firm. This view I share. That the points still in dispute are not very important I know very well and that is why I felt before that standing firm or giving in was 'six of one to half a dozen of the other'. But after that crude, even though harmless, Russian threat, the situation is changed. This threat is really a bit of luck for us, because it makes it possible for us to free ourselves without risk from the principal charge that we are giving in because of fear.

It is equally important for us in our ordinary relations with Russia that Witte should have to pay the bill for Lamsdorff's anti-German policy, which hurts him financially and makes him look bad.[3] An opportunity like this, when one thing can lead to another—and absolutely *sine ira et studio*, but for financial and technical reasons—will hardly come again. It is the only way we can get rid of Lamsdorff. But even if he stays he will have learned that Germany must be treated decently.

Holstein.

945. Holstein to Bernhard von Bülow
Draft

Berlin, 25 March [1906]

Dear Bülow,

You ask whether we should communicate anything further to Washington. In my opinion, no. A thorough understanding of the

[1] On 24 March Bülow telegraphed to Radowitz: 'Because of the publication of the Russian instruction [see p. 401, note 2], which can or could be interpreted as an attempt at exerting pressure, we are faced with the necessity of considering more carefully than before the definitive stand we should take on the individual points still at issue in order to preserve our prestige.' Bülow enumerated the points in question and asked Radowitz for an immediate opinion so that the Foreign Minister could send him instructions for the next plenary session of the Conference on Monday. (*Grosse Politik*, vol. XXIi, no. 7129, pp. 322–3.) Radowitz telegraphed his reply on 25 March. (*Grosse Politik*, vol. XXIi, no. 7131, pp. 324–6.)

[2] Probably August Stein, Berlin correspondent of the *Frankfurter Zeitung*.

[3] Negotiations for a Russian loan were being conducted between Witte and the Berlin banker Mendelssohn. The German Government used this opportunity to put pressure on Witte, through Mendelssohn, so that the Russian Government would persuade France to give in on the points at issue at the Conference. (From the Foreign Ministry files.)

problem is lacking there. Herr von Böhlendorff's[1] questions the day before yesterday make me suspect that the Reichstag intends to concern itself further with Morocco. I am too low in rank to appear before a plenary session, but perhaps I could be called upon to appear as an expert before a commission. As a man without a future, I could perhaps supplement my instructions by saying much that would be useful for the German Reich. For me personally this could mean, at the worst, a patriotic and satisfying close to my career. I would need about three days for preparation.

I hope we will not let the present opportunity to take a firm stand go by unused. Admittedly this does not depend on you alone.

I went out walking to-day for six hours, in part during a snow storm, but precisely that refreshes a man because one does it so seldom.

With a deep bow
Holstein.

## 946.    Bernhard von Bülow to Holstein

Berlin, 25 March 1906

Dear friend,

You are quite right about Washington. Only I don't want to disturb our relations there. A mixed Franco-Spanish occupation of Tangier, perhaps with another harbour, would in my opinion be all to the good.

Whether in a commission or in plenary session, you would certainly defend our Morocco policy with success! And it can be defended, because both politically and economically we achieved everything that mattered. It is still uncertain whether the matter will come up in the Reichstag before or after Easter.

I am glad you had such a good walk. I too always liked snowy weather and snow storms. Like snowflakes, so the fates of men and peoples swirl around each other.

Most sincerely
Yours
B.

## 947.    Holstein to Hugo von Radolin[2]

Berlin, 28 March 1906

Dear Radolin,

I am sorry that you too are now being dragged into the fight about personnel for which the Morocco affair is providing an excuse. It is probably because Paris is a much coveted post. I attach no importance to all these attacks, chiefly because the Kaiser's marginal comments never contain unfriendly criticism. Still, I was sorry that the Princess did not come to Berlin for the silver wedding.[3]

---

[1] Karl von Böhlendorff-Kölpin. German-Conservative Member of the Reichstag.

[2] From the Radolin Papers.

[3] The silver wedding of the Kaiser and Kaiserin was celebrated in Berlin from 25–27 February.

Algeciras is now over.[1] I think we would have gotten more if we had waited a little, for the neutrals not only need peace—which this time was not in danger—but complete calm for economic and financial reasons. However, it is all right as it is.

With a warm clasp of the hand

Yours

Holstein

## 948.   Memorandum by Holstein

Berlin, 29 March 1906

On 20 February the Kaiser wrote in reply to a telegram from Metternich in which he informed us of Lord Rothschild's remark that Rouvier, by giving way too much on the police question, might be overthrown and replaced by Delcassé: 'It doesn't matter. That would make the position all the clearer. It is better to have Delcassé conducting his own policy than to have Rouvier do it for him. I am standing firmly by my position.'[2]

On 23 February a report came in from Count Monts in which he described a conversation with Luzzatti and which he summed up with the idea that Luzzatti was fundamentally convinced that at the last moment Germany would give in on the Morocco question after all.[3] The Chancellor ordered that Monts be instructed to leave no doubt in the mind of Herr Luzzatti of Germany's fixity of purpose. This telegram stated: 'It is hoped that Germany will give in to the moral pressure of the majority and agree to a solution along the lines of the Franco-Spanish—actually the purely French—group. The opposite will be the case. We will refuse. . . . But perhaps Herr Rouvier still harbours the secret hope that the German nerve will yet break. This hope is an error and will not be fulfilled, etc.' The underlined sections were added by the Chancellor in his own hand. The telegram was sent off on 26 February.[4]

On Monday, 12 March, the Chancellor in a conference informed the State Secretary, Under State Secretary, *Geheimrat* Hammann, and me that it was necessary to give in. With the exception of Hammann, we all opposed giving in and pointed out that if we stood firm we could be certain of mediation by the neutrals because they—Russia, Italy, and even Liberal England,—badly needed not only peace but complete calm. *Geheimrat* Hammann said that the giving-in could probably be smoothed over. The State Secretary replied that he could not judge what public opinion or the Press might think, but the Cabinets would of course not be deceived about our giving in, if we really did give in.

---

[1] On 27 March agreement was reached on the main points at issue at the Conference of Algeciras. (*Grosse Politik*, vol. XXIi, no. 7136, p. 329.) The final agreements were signed on 7 April.

[2] *Grosse Politik*, vol. XXIi, no. 7023, p. 188.

[3] This report was dated 19 February. Holstein has summarized the contents accurately. (From the Foreign Ministry files.)

[4] This telegram, no. 48 of 26 February, was drafted by Holstein. (From the Foreign Ministry files.)

The Chancellor, however, ordered that we should give in, and dictated the main points to Under State Secretary Mühlberg.[1]

On 24 March Count Monts reported that the Minister, Count Guicciardini,[2] had said: 'That the Conference finally did show some results was solely due to our giving in and our love of peace. In the police question we had made concessions which in all optimism he would have thought impossible. For Spain was after all only the squire of France and not a really independent state.'[3] As a reply to this, the Chancellor wrote: 'We must definitely rid Count Monts of the idea that we did not actually achieve as much as we had intended at the beginning of our campaign. If for tactical purposes we had here and there demanded more, and if we made the "suggestions" we allowed to drop appear as a great concession, that does not alter the fact that we can be perfectly satisfied with the results as a whole, as for instance our gains on the bank and police questions.'[4] To the telegram that was drafted word for word on the basis of this order, I made the comment: it would be well to examine whether this order is consistent with earlier instructions, specifically with telegram no. 48; otherwise carrying out this order might give rise to embarrassing questions.

H.

949. Holstein to Bernhard von Bülow
Copy

30 March 1906

Dear Bülow,

The development of affairs has forced me to make a personal decision, and I leave it to you whether you would like to talk things over beforehand. In that case I ask you to make it not later than Monday at the latest. Any messages will reach me at home, because I am taking sick leave to-day and tomorrow.

With best wishes
Most sincerely
Your
Holstein.

950. Holstein to Bernhard von Bülow
Copy

31 March 1906

Dear Bülow,

I must decline with thanks your friendly invitation for Monday

[1] In an undated memorandum in which he drew together the same facts as in the memorandum printed here, Holstein wrote at this point: 'The next day the Chancellor asked me to see him and informed me in strict confidence that the Kaiser had ordered a letter to be written to him that we must give in because our artillery and our navy were not in any condition to fight a war. This letter was written under the impression created by the news that King Edward had invited Delcassé to lunch.' (See *Grosse Politik*, vol. XXIi, no. 7059, pp. 240–1.)
[2] Italian Foreign Minister in the Sonnino Cabinet, 8 February–17 May 1906.
[3] Report no. 111 of 24 March. (From the Foreign Ministry files.)
[4] Bülow's note actually stated: 'This idea is wrong. We can say this to foreigners, especially in Algeciras, and let them think so. In reality we achieved what we intended from

evening, because Monday morning—I will just have completed the quarter-year—I am handing in my resignation and am at the same time sending the news to the Press in order to burn all bridges. I am resigning not because of the incredible question and answer game in the newspapers, but because of my incredible treatment by Tschirschky. He has turned over the Foreign Ministry to Mühlberg, and is concerning himself only with the Political Division; he is dealing directly with the Counsellors and has frozen me out. He has appointed Assistant-Counsellors in the Division without consulting me. Such a thing has not happened for sixteen years. This would already have been enough to cause me to disappear quietly during the summer holidays. But now the following has occurred : Wednesday evening[1] I brought Tschirschky the instruction to Algeciras drafted by Kriege,[2] and read it to him. He then said merely, without any comment : 'Please leave it here. I will discuss it with Mühlberg.' Thinking that he intended to summon Mühlberg as a third, I remained standing. But Tschirschky gave me a quiet nod of farewell, to show that the audience was over. Then Mühlberg was summoned.

That I would some day be bowed out by Tschirschky was something I never dreamt would be possible. But the most unbelievable things happen.

Tschirschky would not dare to do all that if he didn't have the Kaiser behind him. This is the supplement of that 'Prosit, Holstein'. H.M. finds me inconvenient and now wants to make foreign policy himself, without contradiction from the professional bureaucracy. That is why he is using Morocco as an excuse to get rid of me. That is his right. But to have me jostled out by Tschirschky is a method I do not consider honourable. Why not tell me : 'H.M. wants to follow a new course with new people'? I am not clinging to the job. The correct word for such conduct is one I do not care to use. I am quite willing to assume the role of scapegoat that has been assigned me from so many sides, because to stay longer in this *misère* would disgust me.

I wanted to tell you all this personally, so as not to leave like a thief in the night and so that you would not say later on : 'If you had only told me in time, I would have arranged everything.' But unfortunately I know that you could have done nothing, even with the best of intentions, *au point où sont les choses*. At the moment Tschirschky is stronger because he is newer.

It is important for me, however, to inform you that I blame you for nothing, but understand that, for objective reasons too, you will let things take their course. If I saw any way out I would be glad to suggest it, but I see none. To call Tschirschky to order, that is to force him to recognize my position as Director, is impossible because he has the

the beginning.' Holstein is quoting from the telegram to Rome of 29 March that was drafted on the basis of Bülow's note. (From the Foreign Ministry files.)

[1] March 28.

[2] This was a telegram of 28 March concerning the Moroccan police question. (From the Foreign Ministry files.)

Kaiser behind him. To educate Tschirschky is also impossible. So I will go. To be, or seem to be, a scapegoat is by no means the worst thing that can happen to a man.

Finally I would like to express the hope that you will not have the unfortunate idea of expecting me to stay longer under these circumstances.

With best wishes<br>
Most sincerely yours<br>
Holstein.

### 951. Holstein to Bernhard von Bülow
Copy

2 April 1906

Dear Bülow,

Of course I will come to see you at half past six and withhold my resignation until then.[1] In it I am simply referring to my resignation of last January, which is still in abeyance, and to our agreement to let the matter rest until after the Conference. I will leave it to you to send the first announcement to the Press. Someone whose opinion I value highly thinks that would be more correct.

Always sincerely yours<br>
Holstein.

### 952. Holstein to Bernhard von Bülow[2]
Draft

Berlin, 3 April 1906

Dear Bülow,

Thank you for your letter.[3] In our conversation I had wanted to ask you earnestly and urgently not to propose anything to the Kaiser on my behalf. Things have now gone so far—in part because of the allegedly official article yesterday in the *Tageblatt*—that I can see no decent way out but to resign. Please do not postpone it any longer, otherwise there may yet be some added humiliation.[4]

Best of luck on your battles in Parliament is the sincere wish of

Your<br>
Holstein

### 953. Holstein to Bernhard von Bülow
Copy

Grossbeerenstrasse 40, 3 April 1906

Dear Bülow,

After mature consideration I came to the conclusion to send my resignation through official channels immediately, without further delay.

---

[1] See Holstein's letter to Ida von Stülpnagel of 4 April. (Rogge, *Friedrich von Holstein*, pp. 245–7.)

[2] This letter was probably never sent.

[3] Not found.

[4] At this point in his draft, Holstein crossed out the words: 'for instance, being passed over in the matter of a decoration. Once I am out, then I no longer count.'

I want to thank you again most warmly for the friendly interest you have shown me during these last days in office. In bringing matters to a close, I believe I am saving you from official difficulties and preserving my personal dignity in the best way possible.

Considering how many years we have worked together, it is a matter of course that I will always be at your disposal if you at some time should find it useful to ask my opinion about some particular matter.

I take my leave of you with a friendly clasp of the hand.

Your old fellow-worker
Holstein.

### 954. Bernhard von Bülow to Holstein[1]

Wednesday afternoon, 4 April 1906

Dear Holstein,

Please rest assured that, over and above my own wishes and interests, I will not compromise your honour. But I would like to present your resignation to His Majesty myself, which will not be possible until tomorrow or the day after. At the same time, however, it is very difficult for me to let you go, as you must realize. That our personal relationship will remain the same despite official changes is surely a matter of course for both of us.

With best wishes
Your sincerely devoted
Bülow

### 955. Otto Hammann to Heinrich von Tschirschky[2]

6 April [1906]

*Geheimrat* von Renvers told me: H[is] H[ighness][3] has agreed that you should submit the resignation[4] to H[is] M[ajesty]. Herr von Loebell will send it to Your Excellency. Renvers also told me that Ilberg, H.M.'s personal physician, informed H.M. yesterday, on the basis of the information provided by the doctors who took care of the Prince in the Reichstag before Renvers saw him, that it was a stroke.[5] H.M. then said that the appointment of a deputy was in order. Renvers told Ilberg yesterday and to-day that he had immediately asked his colleagues where they had found evidence of paralysis, and had refuted their opinion. Actually there could be no question of a stroke in this case because there had been no evidence of paralysis or of prolapses. He, Renvers, needed a few days to see how the illness would develop and what measures would be necessary for recovery. As things had gone up to now, he was still firmly convinced that all would be well.

H[ammann][6]

---

[1] From the Bülow Papers. Only a typewritten copy of this document was available to the editors. See below, Holstein's note to Tschirschky of 18 April 1906.

[2] From the Foreign Ministry files.      [3] Prince Bülow.      [4] Of Holstein.

[5] On the afternoon of 5 April Bülow had collapsed in the Reichstag during a debate on the Morocco Question.

[6] Note by Tschirschky: 'confirmed by his brother Carl Bülow.' (See below, no. 960.)

## 956. Holstein to Hugo von Radolin[1]

Grossbeerenstrasse 40, 7 April 1906

Dear Radolin,

*Geheimrat* Hirschfeld operated on my left eye very well at the time. For that reason I am asking you to help him in any way he may desire. I have handed in my resignation on account of *incompatibilité* with T[schirschky]. The petition has gone to the Chancellor and is now in his hands. To put pressure on him at this moment would be brutal.[2] I am therefore asking for leave until the matter is settled. [...]

I know nothing definite about how the poor Chancellor is. I visit his wife every day.

With best wishes

Yours

H.

## 957. Memorandum by Heinrich von Tschirschky[3]

Berlin, 8 April 1906

Top Secret!

I have heard from the Ambassadors Count Lanza and von Szögyényi the following strictly confidential information:

On the morning on which the Chancellor, myself, and almost all of the Counsellors of the Foreign Ministry were in the Reichstag for the debates concerning the Foreign Ministry budget, His Excellency von Holstein requested the English Ambassador, Sir Frank Lascelles, to come to see him at the Foreign Ministry.[4] His Exc. von Holstein informed the Engl. Ambassador that, because of inimical influences both inside the Foreign Ministry and out, he had been forced to hand in his resignation, which had already been approved. The Kaiser had been given to understand that he, Holstein, was chiefly responsible that Germany's relations with England had developed in such an unfortunate manner. The opposite was the case. It was certainly not his fault that there had been tensions in the mutual relations of Germany and England. Herr von Holstein then named certain people who had agitated against him the most, above all Herr Hammann and Ambassador Count Bernstorff.[5]

Sir Frank is supposed to have listened to Herr von Holstein's comments quietly, but to have emphasized that he knew nothing about Herr von Holstein's alleged role in the development of Anglo-German relations.

The conversation lasted over an hour and a half.

T.

10 April.

The above information was confirmed to-day by Sir Frank himself,

---

[1] From the Radolin Papers.      [2] See above, p. 408, note 5.

[3] From the Foreign Ministry files.

[4] On 5 April 1906. (See *British Documents*, vol. III, no. 398, pp. 332–4.)

[5] Johann, Count Bernstorff. First Secretary in the Embassy in London, 1902–6; Consul-General in Cairo, 1906–8; Ambassador in Washington, 1908–17.

who personally told me about his conversation with His Exc. von Holstein.

From another source I heard that before his departure from Marseilles, King Edward instructed the English Ambassador here by telegram to keep him informed about the Holstein crisis.

T.

## 958.   Heinrich von Tschirschky to Holstein[1]

Berlin, 9 April 1906

I have the honour to inform Your Excellency that His Majesty the Kaiser and King has graciously decided to bestow upon you the diamonds to the Order of the Red Eagle, First Class, on the occasion of the Morocco Conference. I am sending the insignia to Your Excellency with my sincere congratulations for this mark of imperial favour. At the same time may I ask you to confirm their receipt and to fill out the enclosed form?

The Chancellor
Acting Deputy, von Tschirschky.

## 959.   Holstein to Maximilian von Brandt[2]

Berlin, 10 April 1906

Your Excellency,

My very warm thanks for your letter of the 5th.[3] In the course of this month I will probably go either to the Upper Harz or to Frau Kley at Friedrichsroda, and am already looking forward to discussing with you the question of the past—Algeciras—and the questions of the near future.

In the Morocco question, the Chancellor, the State Secretary, the Under State Secretary, and I all took the point of view that we should wait calmly until the neutrals in need of money and peace—Russia, Italy, etc.—came up with mediation proposals. It would not have taken much longer. However, His Majesty ordered the retreat,[4] and thereby justified the prediction of King Edward and Luzzatti that Germany would lose her nerve. Out of this retreat there arises an indefinite danger of war, because the pressure method, which succeeded in Morocco, may be applied against us at the next opportunity.

Among the questions of the future, the most interesting is that of the fleet; I refer to the international limitations on armaments. Bourgeois, his friend d'Estournelles de Constant,[5] and many Englishmen are in favour: those who want war with us as well as those who want peace.

What will our position be if the question should one day be firmly pushed into the foreground? What can we achieve by continuing our naval armaments? Could we ever challenge *both* England and France at sea? Can we expect that England will ever separate herself from France

---

[1] From the Foreign Ministry files.          [2] From the Brandt Papers.
[3] Not found.          [4] See above, Holstein's Memorandum of 29 March.
[5] French Senator; Second Delegate to the Second Hague Peace Conference, 1907.

as long as there is the danger of a German invasion? Is a German fleet that is unable to cope with an Anglo-French fleet an asset in war or a liability? Would the fear of a German land army, no matter how strong, but *without* a fleet, be great enough to cause England to take part in a Franco-German or Francorussian-German war?

That is a bouquet of questions that we will have to savour together.

With deepest respect to the feminine part of the family, I remain, in the hope of seeing you soon and with friendly greetings

Your Excellency's very devoted

Holstein

It was intimated to me recently that Phili Eulenburg and Radowitz had been corresponding and that in this way letters from Radowitz reached His Majesty. That would of course explain the joint Black Eagle.[1]

My resignation-petition has been sent to Bülow. Since I cannot press the matter now, I have asked for and received leave until the matter is settled. That can take another eight to ten days.

### 960. Karl Ulrich von Bülow[2] to Heinrich von Tschirschky[3]

Berlin, 14 April 1906

Your Excellency,

I am taking the liberty of informing you that my brother asked me yesterday to request you to settle the matter of Herr von Holstein by a personal audience with His Majesty.

Professor von Renvers, whom I shortly thereafter asked for a professional opinion on the mental condition of my brother, informed me that he would vouch for the fact that my brother was in full possession of his mental faculties in this matter.

May I ask Your Excellency not to mention my name in connection with this completely confidential communication on a matter with which I otherwise have nothing whatever to do, unless it should be necessary to mention it to His Majesty.

Yours most obediently,

Karl Bülow

### 961. Heinrich von Tschirschky to Kaiser Wilhelm II[4]

Berlin, 14 April 1906

Your Imperial and Royal Majesty,

I respectfully request leave to report that *Wirklicher Geheimer Rat* von Holstein, a *Vortragender Rat* in the Political Division of the Foreign

---

[1] On 3 April 1906 both Philipp zu Eulenburg and Joseph Maria von Radowitz, the German delegate at the Algeciras Conference, were awarded the Order of the Black Eagle. With this award Holstein thought he saw his suspicions confirmed that Eulenburg was 'influencing policy behind the scenes'. (Holstein to Ida von Stülpnagel, 28 October 1907, Rogge, *Friedrich von Holstein*, pp. 293–4; see also Holstein's letter to Monts of 22 April 1906, *Erinnerungen und Gedanken des Botschafters Anton Graf Monts* (Berlin, 1932), pp. 358–60.)

[2] Aide-de-Camp; brother of Chancellor Bernhard von Bülow.

[3] From the Foreign Ministry files.      [4] From the Foreign Ministry files.

Ministry, has requested that Your Majesty be asked to grant him leave to go into retirement with the pension to which he is entitled by law.

Friedrich von Holstein, born on 24 April 1837 in Schwedt on the Oder, worked in the law courts of this city first as Apprentice and then as Junior Barrister, and in December 1860 entered the diplomatic service as Attaché at the Legation in St Petersburg. In 1863 he passed his diplomatic examinations with the mark of 'good', and was thereupon sent successively to the diplomatic missions in Rio de Janeiro, London, Washington, Stuttgart, Florence, and Copenhagen. At the end of a three-year period of leave, he was employed from mobilization-day to 12 August 1870 at Imperial Headquarters, then in the Political Division of the Foreign Ministry, and shortly thereafter he was transferred to the Chancellery of the Reich Chancellor at Imperial Headquarters. After the conclusion of peace he was assigned to the diplomatic mission in Paris, was made Second Secretary of Legation there in November 1871, and in May 1872 was promoted to *Legationsrat*. Recalled to the Political Division of the Foreign Ministry in April 1876, he was named *Wirklicher Legationsrat* and *Vortragender Rat* in 1878, *Geheimer Legationsrat* in 1880, and in 1886 he was made *Wirklicher Geheimer Legationsrat* with First Class rank.

On 31 December 1898, Your Imperial and Royal Majesty graciously conferred on him the rank of *Wirklicher Geheimer Rat* with the title of 'Excellency'; on Your Imperial Majesty's birthday in 1901 you conferred on him the Order of the Red Eagle, First Class, with the Garland of Oak Leaves, and a few days ago, on the 9th of this month, you conferred on him the Diamonds of this Order; on 1 February 1892 you graciously conferred on him the Star of the Order of the House of Hohenzollern.

Under the circumstances, the petition of *Wirklicher Geheimer Rat* von Holstein to be allowed to go into retirement could be granted, for he has already passed the legal retirement age (sixty-five). I therefore take the liberty, with the approval of His Highness the Chancellor, of humbly presenting in draft form the order for the retirement of *Wirklicher Geheimer Rat* von Holstein with the humble request for Your Imperial Majesty's ratification.

von Tschirschky

962. Kaiser Wilhelm II to Bernhard von Bülow[1]

Berlin, 16 April 1906

I hereby grant the petition of *Wirklicher Geheimer Rat* von Holstein, *Vortragender Rat* in the Foreign Ministry, to go into retirement with the award of his legal pension. I am herewith returning the order for his retirement, which has been ratified by me.

Wilhelm I.R.

(countersigned) von Tschirschky

[1] From the Foreign Ministry files.

963.    Heinrich von Tschirschky to Holstein[1]
        Draft

Berlin, 17 April 1906

Your Excellency

I have the honour to inform you that, after receiving orders from the Chancellor, Prince von Bülow, I sent His Majesty the Kaiser and King a report concerning your retirement petition.

His Majesty has graciously consented to grant your request by the enclosed certified copy of the Imperial Order of the 16th of this month and to ratify the enclosed honourable dismissal that has been drawn up for Your Excellency.

I herewith have the honour to inform Your Excellency of this decision of our Most Gracious Lord.

Would you have the kindness to confirm the receipt of this dispatch.

The Chancellor

By [Tschirschky]

964.    Holstein to Heinrich von Tschirschky
        Copy

Grossbeerenstrasse 40, 18 April 1906

I have received Your Excellency's message of 17 April[2] and the enclosed order for my retirement. The statement Your Excellency makes that the information about my retirement petition was sent to His Majesty by Your Excellency after the receipt of an order from the Chancellor is either a mistake or a misunderstanding. According to *Geheimrat* von Renvers, the Chancellor cannot have given orders of any kind since his illness. On the evening before he fell ill, on Wednesday, the 4th of this month, he sent me a handwritten note[2] in which he replied to my pressing request for immediate retirement with the words: 'Please rest assured that, over and above my own wishes and interests, I will not compromise your honour. But I would like to present your resignation to His Majesty myself, which will not be possible until tomorrow or the day after.'

Holstein.

965.    Paul von Schwabach to Holstein

Brandenburg a.H., 19 April 1906

Your Excellency!

At this time, when your departure from the Ministry has become a settled fact, I feel compelled to tell Your Excellency how deeply I feel the significance of this moment. It is only natural that leaving the scene of an activity of several decades cannot take place without a feeling of depression, which at first may outweigh the pleasure in the recovery of freedom and quiet. I deeply hope, however, that with the help of your friends, Your Excellency's life will prove to be comfortably pleasant and

[1] From the Foreign Ministry files. A note on the draft states: 'sent 17/4 p.m.'
[2] See above.

413

stimulating, and the memory of the period now closed will culminate in the consciousness of having devoted a man's full powers to the common good.

For me to give any estimate of the value of Your Excellency's official activity would hardly be proper, but this much I can state : you have ever served only the cause and the cause of the Fatherland, and have always judged people by their devotion to and value for this cause.

It is perhaps excusable if at this time I should also think of myself and remember the many conversations which I was allowed to have with you in your office at the Ministry. Eight years have passed since Your Excellency granted me the *petites* and *grandes entrées* to your room—at my age, a considerable time! My relations to Your Excellency have meant more to me than you can perhaps realize, and I think that I can hardly overestimate their significance. I will not deny that a certain amount of personal vanity was also involved and that I was flattered to be able to discuss the most important questions with Your Excellency. But I am also certain that I learned an enormous amount, not only from the actual facts about which you informed me, but from the way in which you brought every item into its general context in your frequently so detailed but at the same time comprehensive expositions of the political situation.

But most especially I am grateful for the confidence Your Excellency showed me, for this I must regard as the prerequisite to everything else. I have always been proud of it, and at the beginning of my independent business activity, when I saw all sorts of difficulties before me, nothing gave me such courage as the realization that I had won the confidence and good will of Your Excellency. My gratitude for what you gave me can never be extinguished and your name will always be cherished by me as that of a benevolent well-wisher.

I close with a request : that you will allow me in future, too, to knock at your door from time to time, for you always had time for me when you were still overloaded with work.

With the expression of deepest respect, I remain

In faithful attachment

Your Excellency's most devoted

Paul Schwabach.

## 966.   Holstein to Hugo von Radolin[1]

Grossbeerenstrasse 40, 23 April 1906

Dear Radolin,

Many thanks for your good wishes and those of the Princess.

The two who brought about my retirement were Hammann and Phili.[2] The former, who ever since April 1905 spread the news in all directions that I wanted war with France; and Phili, who brought this information to the attention of His Majesty. Tschirschky, who originally had wanted to get along with me, was only a tool. He stands well with

---

[1] From the Radolin Papers.     [2] Philipp zu Eulenburg.

the Kaiser, but badly with his health; his eyes cannot stand the strain. He has things read to him, for the most part. For that reason he will probably try to get an Embassy, preferably Rome, as soon as possible. Until then he will probably do what H.M. and Phili ask.

That Phili, with his impractical ideas of a continental alliance directed against England, should be the chief adviser of the Kaiser is something that will not benefit the German Reich. For in my opinion, which you have long known, we must get closer to England, even though the personal jealousies of the two monarchs will make that rather more difficult.

Well, time will bring its own solutions. Perhaps you will be able to see some practical method there.[1]

I hear that Phili came to Berlin the week before last to hurry up my dismissal, because one could never know whether it might not be obstructed in some way.

With best wishes
Your
Holstein

## 967.   Holstein to Pascal David[2]
Copy

Grossbeerenstrasse 40, Berlin[3]

My dear Sir!

Since you know about my relationship with Prince Hohenlohe, etc., you will understand how natural it is that I should have heard a great deal about you for years. But that you, from so far away, should have learned so much about me, and that you then should have dedicated such a splendid and moving article to a retiring official, all this came as a surprise to me. A friend sent me the article after it was published. It hardly corresponds to the official line of the Press Bureau, which ever since it began its campaign in April 1905, seems to have set itself the task to prove to the German public that I was expendable. The curious thing was that up till that time the German public knew nothing at all about me. Then, a week after I informed Herr Neven Dumont that I would no longer receive Herr von Huhn because of his lack of judgment,[4] the first news began to come from Paris at the beginning of April 1905 that I was an enemy of France and was pressing for war. I regard Hammann, Huhn, and Stein as the three agitators who for almost a year have hammered out this theme and who finally made my removal possible. When a great central agency takes such a line and holds to it, eventually the whole world believes it. If Fischer (Franz) and Paul

---

[1] Radolin was at this time in London.

[2] Editor-in-Chief of the *Strassburger Post*, a branch of the *Kölnische Zeitung*. Seven of Holstein's letters to Pascal David of the year 1906, found in the Pascal David Papers, were printed in 1919. ('Zur Kenntnis der Vorkriegszeit. Briefe des Geheimrats von Holstein', *Süddeutsche Monatshefte* (March, 1919), pp. 420–8.) Copies of these letters were found in the Holstein Papers. In addition to the above letter, Holstein's letters of 13 and 29 May, 16 and 29 August are being reprinted in this edition.

[3] The letter is undated.          [4] See above, p. 333, note 1.

Hatzfeldt had been alive, this campaign would have collapsed, but I stood alone.

I am too much the royalist to say that H.M. used these rumours of wars as an excuse. But that I have long been an embarrassment to him is something you know as well as I.

At the new year, because I complained about Hammann, Bülow gave a written order that Hammann was to be under my authority, whereas up to that time the Press Bureau had operated independently of the Political Division. Hammann's goal is said to be to become Director of a Press *Division*. My own point of view was summarized in the idea that the Press Bureau, in its present extended form in the Foreign Ministry, was similar to a swollen liver in the human body, and was a symptom of illness.

Because of the new year's order, Hammann and his friends have probably decided to make every effort in their power, and they have finally succeeded in their purpose.

Besides myself, there is still many a useful official in the imperial service. But the number of those who give their opinion even when it is unpopular will probably be lowered by the example of what was done to me—perhaps for that reason.

I for my part will not now begin a campaign in the Press, if only because I can hardly say anything to third persons without hurting the Chancellor, and this I do not wish to do. His position has hardly been improved by my dismissal—which was pushed through while he was confined in isolation.

If you should come to Berlin, come to see me in my little den near the Kreuzberg. Please inform me beforehand, so that I may be at home.

Once more my hearty thanks<br>Your sincerely devoted<br>Holstein.

968.    Theodor Schiemann to Holstein

Evening, 25 [April 1906]

Your Excellency,

Many thanks for your letter. I am in no position to judge how necessary the decision you have made may be, nor do I presume to influence your purpose. But the objections are many, and your position is the more difficult because your opponents can operate anonymously, without proof and on hearsay. You will have to prove everything you say, and in doing so your hands will be half bound by the need to preserve professional secrets. At any rate, the whole matter demands the most careful consideration. Just to mention one thing, Ph. Eulenburg told me, when he showed me his voluminous and exemplarily ordered archive, that in the course of his political life he had kept everything, including every scrap of paper. You will have to reckon with things like that. Before taking action I would, if I were you, examine whether the materials that come into consideration can be proved by the evidence I have at my disposal—and on principle touch nothing that cannot be proved. Although there is a saying: many enemies, much honour, nevertheless even a great man can be defeated by attacks that come simultaneously from the front, the sides, and from the rear. A Paris correspondent of the *Journal des Débats* presented the case correctly in saying that you had to leave in order to give T[schirschky] room to manoeuvre. What I have read in English newspapers is tolerable, and at bottom acknowledges the great role that must be accorded to you. If you feel that I should not visit you at this time, I will agree, with the reservation that I will always be ready to come at your call.

With best wishes

Your sincerely devoted

Schiemann

## 969.   Hermann Speck von Sternburg to Holstein

Washington, D.C., 26 April 1906

Your Excellency

Now that we have heard here that His Majesty the Kaiser has approved your resignation, I feel obliged to tell you how deeply I regret your leaving the Ministry.

The most interesting and most instructive moments of my diplomatic activity were those in which I had the honour and distinction of discussing current political problems in your room in the Wilhelmstrasse.

I regard these discussions as milestones in my diplomatic career, and your opinions have been the channels which have conducted me through every difficult situation.

At this time I do not want to fail to express my most sincere thanks for the goodwill and confidence Your Excellency has always shown me to such a marked degree.

With the expression of my highest regard, I have the honour to be

Your Excellency's sincerely devoted

Sternburg

## 970.   Holstein to Theodor Schiemann
Copy

Grossbeerenstrasse 40, 26 April 1906

My dear Professor,

Your letter[1] was psychologically interesting to me. It makes me suspect that Philipp Eulenburg is playing with the idea of threatening me. As soon as I am certain about his intention I will deal with him, or at any rate with the head of his house, directly. If you personally would like to know my view on this matter, I would be glad to present it to you in a leisurely fashion, and will tell you a good deal that will be new to you.

Saturday from half past eleven to half past one I can be at your disposal; please let me know beforehand.

Your sincerely devoted

Holstein.

[1] Of 25 April 1906.  See above.

971.   Theodor Schiemann to Holstein

27 April 1906

Your Excellency,

Unfortunately it is absolutely impossible for me to see you tomorrow at the time you indicated. I am committed to a meeting of our Aid Committee, which I must attend, and by a conference at the Ministry of Culture.

As for the matter itself, I can tell you with absolute certainty that you are making a mistake. The remark in question was made on the first day of my visit when we were looking over the archive, and there was no possibility of a reference to your affair, of which not a word was said. I just recalled the remark when I wrote to you, otherwise I would have told you about it earlier. Yesterday, by the way, I looked through all the newspapers at a café, and found nothing that referred to you.

With best wishes
Your sincerely devoted
Schiemann


972.   Holstein to Theodor Schiemann
       Copy

Berlin, 28 April 1906

My dear Professor,

From your earlier letter[1] I did not have the impression that all this was merely hypothetical. Nevertheless, I was unutterably astonished that somebody who had as much dirt sticking to him as Philipp Eulenburg, who is open to attack from any side you care to choose, should turn to threats. But such characters occasionally have moments of hysterical over-excitement; otherwise P.E. would surely have avoided the Stuttgart adventure that cost him—or somebody else—at least 60,000 marks in hush money.[2] On the old rule 'never write, never burn', Prince Phili probably only observes the latter part. Did Hohenlohe never tell you about the Stuttgart story? The last thing I heard about the matter was when the old gentleman sent me the copy of a letter from P.E.[3] dealing with the subject and apologetic in tone.[4] I know that, besides myself, the Prince informed several other people about the affair, and seem to remember that you were one of them.

After this aside, I return to my point of departure. About Phili, I will do whatever I please, and presume that he too will do whatever he considers useful for himself. This I do not say confidentially, but openly and in writing.

Now farewell. If we live longer, I hope we will some time meet again. *A propos* of living, I just remembered that the latest authentic explana-

---

[1] Of 25 April. See above.

[2] Holstein presumably refers to a bath-house blackmail affair in which Eulenburg was involved in Vienna, not Stuttgart. (See Haller, *Eulenburg*, pp. 339–41; Hans von Tresckow, *Von Fürsten und anderen Sterblichen* (Berlin, 1922), pp. 157–9.)

[3] Note by Holstein: 'I must have put it with another letter that dealt with the same thing. Unfortunately not in Berlin.'

[4] See above, no. 737, enclosure I.

tion for my dismissal—surely you have heard it?—is that I was too old. The first two explanations, Morocco and Tschirschky, do not seem to have had the desired effect.

So let us keep the future open.

Your sincerely devoted
Holstein.

### 973. Holstein to Philipp zu Eulenburg
Copy

Grossbeerenstrasse 40, Berlin, 1 May 1906

My Phili!

This greeting is no mark of esteem, for 'Phili' to-day among contemporaries signifies—nothing good.

Your aim of many years, my removal, has now at last been achieved. The filthy attacks against me are also supposed to be in accord with your wishes. Everything has its two sides. I am now free, I need exercise no restraint, and can treat you as one treats a contemptible person with your characteristics. I do so herewith and expect to do more. You for your part may do whatever will amuse you or that you think suitable. Each can then represent his own point of view.

Most sincerely
Holstein

### 974. Axel von Varnbüler to Holstein[1]
TELEGRAM

3 May 1906

May I ask Your Excellency to indicate a time and place where I can speak to you tomorrow on an urgent matter?

Freiherr von Varnbüler.

### 975. Otto von Mühlberg to Holstein

Berlin, 4 May 1906

Dear Herr von Holstein,

Enclosed please receive Prince Eulenburg's sworn statement which you desired.[2] In return, your statement has been sent to the Prince.[3]

Under the assumption that the matter is hereby closed, I remain

With best wishes
Your
Mühlberg.

[1] According to Eulenburg's Diary Entry of 1 May (Haller, *Eulenburg*, pp. 328–9) and Hugo von Reischach (*Unter drei Kaisern* (Berlin, 1925), pp. 76–9), Eulenburg asked his friend Varnbüler to send Holstein a challenge immediately after the receipt of Holstein's letter of 1 May. The above telegram makes it appear as though this were the first communication Varnbüler made to Holstein on this matter. If this was the case, it invalidates Eulenburg's testimony that he sent Holstein a challenge immediately upon the receipt of his letter, and supports Holstein's statement that he never received a challenge from Eulenburg. The incident seems to have been settled in the Foreign Ministry before Varnbüler ever saw Holstein on Eulenburg's behalf. (See below, Mühlberg's letter to Holstein of 4 May, with enclosures dated 3 May; Holstein's letter to Pascal David of 16 August 1906; and Holstein's letter to Ida von Stülpnagel of 7 June 1906, Rogge, *Friedrich von Holstein*, pp. 256–7.)

[2] See Enclosure I.  [3] See Enclosure II.

Statement of Philipp zu Eulenburg

Berlin, 3 May 1906

The letter sent to me by *Wirklicher Geheimer Rat* von Holstein on the first of this month[1] is based on erroneous presuppositions.

I declare herewith on my word of honour that I had nothing whatever to do with his dismissal, nor have I had anything to do with the attacks against him in the Press.

Prince zu Eulenburg-Hertefeld.

Statement of Holstein

Copy

Grossbeerenstrasse 40, 3 May 1906

After Prince zu Eulenburg has declared on his word of honour that he had nothing whatever to do with my dismissal nor with the attacks against me in the Press, I hereby withdraw the damaging remarks used in my letter to him of the first of this month.

Holstein.

976.   Hugo von Radolin to Holstein

Paris, 8 May 1906

My dear good friend,

I cannot tell you the impression your letter to England[2] made on us. It is absolutely unspeakable and infamous. What thanklessness for the unselfish work of such an irreplaceable official, who has handled everything and surveyed the situation with such superb comprehension; who has concerned himself only with the greatness of his country, and whose vision has been so sweeping. Even all the important Englishmen are of this opinion, and have told me that they cannot understand how we could oust such an important man.

Despite the widespread opinion in circles here that you are an enemy of France, sensible people here are of a different opinion when they, like Rouv[ier] and J[ean] Dup[uy], know that the 'Dream of the Future'[3] is an indication of goodwill towards France. Where are the regrets of the man who did not want to let you go!!! It is discouraging to see things like that.

We are thinking of you constantly, my dear friend, and hope that you will pay us a visit either here or in the country. If you came here, we could put you up comfortably. You would not have to see anyone, and could make interesting observations. Talk it over with our dear friend[4] and see if she will not also pay us a long-promised visit here. Incidentally, I would like to come home for a few days at the end of the month in

---

[1] See above.
[2] Of 23 April. See above.
[3] See above, p. 350, note 2.
[4] Frau Helene von Lebbin.

order to welcome Alfred,[1] who is returning from the Near East, and to convince myself about his health. I would also like to see a German doctor myself, although I feel well.

Only I am deeply depressed by what has happened, especially where you are concerned. What are your plans? Do you intend to stay there, where you have had so much vexation, or do you intend to settle elsewhere? All this concerns us deeply, for we two are loyally attached to you—very loyally attached. Let us hope you will do something to take care of your eyes, although you are in good health, thank goodness, and are said to look almost youthfully fit.

Uncle[2] used his time here to good advantage. Under the cover of making a 'private trip', he helped along many a serious treaty, although this is naturally kept secret.[3] I am certain, however, that he was not here for nothing. Naturally—I should say, unfortunately—I did not see him. He sent me his personal regrets about it. His sister and her husband were very well disposed towards us and our country, but thought that the first step towards a rapprochement should come from *us*. *Over there* I noticed nothing of animosity against Germany, and I think the agitation in the Press stems far more from us than from them. Only we should not boast so much that we do not care whether the whole world is against us, and that we are capable of fighting the entire world.

We are, after all, completely *isolated* in the world, and everybody hates us, even Austria, which is absolutely furious about the Goluchowski telegram.[4] The outlook is not a pretty one in my opinion.

Now farewell for to-day, my dear friend. Give my best wishes to our friend.

Your faithful<br>H.

Johanna sends you a thousand warm good wishes.


977.   Pascal David to Holstein

Strasbourg, 10 May 1906

Your Excellency,

Please receive the warmest and most sincere thanks of a lonely man for your exceedingly kind letter.[5] It gave me a great deal of pleasure, the kind of pleasure that is not exactly common in the life of a journalist who takes his profession seriously, who wants to serve the cause and help shape the future, and who attends to the saying: *Justitia est fundamentum regnorum.*

---

[1] The oldest son of Prince Radolin.

[2] King Edward VII of England, the uncle of Kaiser Wilhelm II.

[3] During his visit to Paris early in March 1906, the King actually only exchanged views with French statesmen. ( *British Documents*, vol. III, no. 327, pp. 284–5.)

[4] An open telegram sent by Kaiser Wilhelm II to Count Goluchowski on April 13, 1906, thanking him for Austrian support at the Conference of Algeciras. 'You have proved yourself to be a brilliant second on the duelling ground and can rest assured of a similar service from me upon a similar occasion.'

[5] See above, no. 967.

I am enclosing everything I have written about the matter;[1] apparently you have only seen my first article.

With a sad smile I read Your Excellency's remark that I should have 'learned so much from so far away'. Alas, my sources of information lie in the far distant past, and grass has long been growing over my informant. This was my unforgettable friend Franz Fischer, to whom I owe the ability to write those words. He used to visit me in Strasbourg every autumn and to stay with me for a week. Then I would take him behind the scenes of the politics of Alsace-Lorraine which I had been observing from my desk for almost twenty-five years. I used to sit down at that desk at seven every morning, and would work through—except for a break after lunch to take a walk with my wife—until midnight. In exchange for my information, Fischer taught me about the personalities and the situation in Berlin, and it was he who so often graphically portrayed the figure of Your Excellency with devoted reverence in the light of his understanding; it was this that allowed me to presume to retrace the firm outline that remained in my memory. Every year I am able to go to Paris once or several times, every few years I go to London, I was in America in 1893 and 1904, but I only rarely come to Berlin. Thus the information from my well-informed, clever, and honest friend was of the greatest value to me. I have him to thank that occasionally, at an important moment, I am able to write an article here that is described in the Berlin Press as 'obviously based on good authority' or even as 'obviously official'. For me too the death of Franz Fischer came too early. Since his death I feel very much alone, for, with the exception of Dr Esser in London, I am the oldest of the *Kölnische Zeitung* group. If my excellent editor, *Kommerzienrat* Dr Jos. Neven Dumont, had not always treated me as a friend, I would feel even more lonesome at this frontier post of Strasbourg. The terrain here is a strange one in this 'period of transition' that began in 1870 and will probably last another fifty years or more. Life is interesting, but not pleasant. One does not feel at home here; one always feels like part of a German colony in a foreign city. Whenever I return to Strasbourg from a trip, I never have the feeling : 'This is my city, my home', but the same cool sensation as when I get to Paris : 'Here is a city in which I know my way around extremely well.'

In the first decades of my work here I was encouraged by the consciousness that I was working for the Germanization of the country, for the amalgamation of the native and immigrant population, for the Kaiser and the Reich. But the older I grow, the more I realize that the only real instrument of Germanization is *Time*. Whether the Government or the Press operates with somewhat more skill or less is only of incidental importance. [...]

With an admiration that extends unchanged and unchangeable over several decades,

I am Your Excellency's sincerely devoted
Pascal David

[1] Not found.

978.    Holstein to Otto von Mühlberg
        Copy

Berlin, 11 May 1906

Dear Mühlberg,

Yesterday evening I was sent a copy of the *Roland von Berlin*. The lead article is one called 'Holstein'. More lies, one piled on the other. As long as these filthy articles remain in the publications of Wilke[1] and Leipziger,[2] they are of no importance. They only become disagreeable when by some clandestine influence they are smuggled into decent newspapers, which would otherwise have nothing to do with such dirt. Tschirschky can prevent smuggling of this kind if he gives Hammann the necessary orders with the necessary authority. In case this little game of mud-slinging goes on, I may find it necessary to challenge Tschirschky.

As a man of conciliatory character, I feel it is right to make my point of view known first in an academic way, which I do herewith. I do not want to trouble you, dear friend, with an answer, for I intend later on to be guided by facts in any case.

In old friendship
Your devoted
Holstein


979.    Otto von Mühlberg to Holstein

Berlin, 13 May 1906

Dear Herr von Holstein,

The article in the *Roland* which you mention in your letter of the 11th had never been heard of here until now, and I first had to get a copy. It dates back to the 26th of April! I hardly need to say that we have the same feelings about the article as you yourself. Tschirschky gave an order to do everything possible to prevent personal attacks on yourself from being widely circulated long before this article, which so far as I know has not been used in any other publication, appeared.

Furthermore you will have noticed that Wilke, in his *Neue Gesellschaftliche Korrespondenz*, is now keeping quiet. *Sans vanité*, I felt that his latest articles were directed more against my own insignificance than against yourself.

In the hope of seeing you again before I leave, I remain with best wishes

Your old
Mühlberg[3]

---

[1] Dr Adolf von Wilke. Editor of the *Neue Gesellschaftliche Korrespondenz*.
[2] Leo Leipziger. Editor of the Berlin weekly journal *Der Roland von Berlin*.
[3] Holstein replied on 14 May: 'It was very kind of you to take the trouble to answer my letter. Naturally it does not matter to me whether orders have been given, but whether they have been observed.'

980.   Holstein to Pascal David
        Copy

Grossbeerenstrasse 40, 13 May 1906

My dear Sir!

Once again I thank you most warmly for being almost the only man in Germany to make a stand against this systematic baiting. Now, however, I would like to exclude personal affairs and to discuss factual matters with you as I would have discussed them with Fischer.

The German Reich is on the brink of a period of danger and degradation and is perilously close to it. To throw down the gauntlet and then to retreat—before what was even an imaginary danger—cannot come to a good end. The Morocco question was not dangerous. Russia and Italy are both in need of complete peace for financial reasons, and Liberal England, which would like above all to disarm and for whom a victorious France would constitute the greatest possible danger—none of these would have allowed matters to go as far as a war. But all stood firm for the time being because they hoped, and they even made it fairly obvious, that Germany would lose her nerve. To-day they all realize that they were right. Therein lies the danger. This same method will be used again. Nobody wants war nowadays because every sensible politician realizes that the masses will not follow blindly. *Vide* Russia. But for several to band together to humiliate one '*par raison demonstrative sans aucun danger personnel*', corresponds to the spirit of the times. And we alone are that 'one'. This can be seen from the reception of the 'Seconding' telegram[1] and the way the Austrian and especially the Hungarian Press has treated the proposal of a visit to Vienna, which was assumed to be a demonstration against England and Italy. The Austrians are cool and politically reserved, the Hungarians are obviously actually hostile.

There is only one possibility of preventing the certain dangers of the future : *we must from now on firmly oppose gratuitous provocations of word and deed and criticize them as political stupidity*. And it is precisely the loyal Press that must say this. In the *Vorwärts* such a line would only influence the masses, but it would not have any effect where it should, namely on the Kaiser. For all provocations are either conceived by the Kaiser or are conceived to please him. As an example, I will mention a relatively unimportant case in point. Ballin, who has all sorts of dangerous ideas in order to make himself interesting in the eyes of the Kaiser, wants, in the near future, to run a few ships between Basra and the Persian Gulf. (N.B., perhaps this is still secret, so say nothing about it!) Now in my opinion, as soon as this business becomes known, the question should be openly raised as to whether the insignificant advantages from such a project are compensation for Germany's inserting herself as a buffer between the rough edges of England and Russia and thereby actually facilitating a rapprochement between these two. Criticism, in order to be effective, must be outspokenly directed against the Kaiser. Naturally every word must be weighed, but the Kaiser must

[1] See above, p. 421, note 4.

be made to realize that his prestige will suffer if he follows every impulse. This applies above all to the personal remarks of His Majesty. He systematically discourages contradiction among the few people who have access to him. Remarks are supposed to be made like: 'You astonish me. I thought you valued your position.'

A very suitable case on which to have dug in would have been the speech the Kaiser gave in Strasbourg last summer when he read a lecture to both the Russians and the Japanese as though he were a global schoolmaster.[1] With that speech he caused us untold harm, not only in Japan. H.M. demonstratively displayed his displeasure against a man in high position (not Bülow) who risked making a vigorous criticism.

To sum up: without criticism we are done for. But this criticism can only be exercised by the Press and by Parliament, and the Press, as the more impersonal instrument, will have to begin it, because there are few personal lives in this country that are completely independent, even in Parliament. Still, the Deputies will take courage sooner if the Press shows the way.

At the recent debate on the theatre, one of the Conservative Deputies, I think it was von Arnim, said approximately: 'This debate has shown that we will have to attend more closely to affairs than heretofore.' Do you not think that the feelings of the entire German nation are expressed in these cautious words? Not only abroad but in Germany the fear of personal rule is increasing. And rightly so. The Kaiser has a dramatic but not a political instinct, he considers the momentary effect but not the consequences, and is actually for the most part unpleasantly surprised by them. People are gradually beginning to notice this. Therefore it seems to me that the psychological moment has arrived when the respectable Press can and must support the responsible advisers of the Crown against irresponsible influences by a restrained yet firm criticism by simply *taking a position in line with sound common sense*—without necessarily contacting the Government on every individual case. Only in that way can the Press support the responsible advisers, even though the Press Bureau will be compelled to take and express an opposite line, no matter who is Chancellor or Head of the Press Bureau.

I would presume that the man who saw eye to eye with Franz Fischer holds opinions very similar to my own. But how will your publisher regard the matter? I had a few lengthy conversations with Neven Dumont, and on the basis of those I believe your favourable opinion is justified. But he has one fault: he has too little confidence in his political judgment, regards himself merely as a business man, whereas his forceful character and clear vision would probably lead him to the correct decisions, also in criticism. The problem would probably look like this

[1] According to an article in the *Strassburger Bürgerzeitung*, the Kaiser said in a speech on 8 May that the morale of the Russian army at Mukden had been undermined by immorality and alcoholism. Now that Russia had shown her weakness vis-à-vis the Yellow Peril, Germany might be called upon to oppose the further spread of this danger. The Kaiser's remarks were officially denied. (Johannes Penzler, *Die Reden Kaiser Wilhelms II*, Third part (Leipzig, 1907), pp. 252–3.

to him, as owner: will the material interests of the paper be helped or damaged if it gives more open expression than heretofore to the general anxiety of the nation?

What is your view on this point? On this I can form no opinion.

In addition I would now like to add a second question: do you see any other remedy besides a tactful and restrained criticism? I see none, and am certain that such criticism would in every concrete case greatly ease the task of any Chancellor and his Ministers, especially if the latter could truthfully say that criticism was independent of their own wishes and desires.

This letter was written for you alone—I have time enough—and I ask you to treat it as confidential. Perhaps you might tell me in a few lines whether you think this remedy, or some other, is practicable.

With a firm clasp of the hand
Your sincerely devoted
Holstein.

## 981.   Heinrich von Tschirschky to Karl von Eisendecher[1]

Berlin, 13 May 1906

My dear friend!

My sincere thanks for your friendly lines of the 11th of this month. Unofficial reports of this kind about our Most Gracious Majesty, his moods and activities, are of great value to me, and I am taking the liberty of asking you to keep me informed about your personal impressions in the future as well. I have heard the outburst against Holstein here, too, and wonder who could have stirred up H.M. so much against Holstein recently. It was of course a pity that Holstein's career had to come to an end, but Bülow was so convinced of the necessity of this step —after the experiences of the past year, when Holstein handed in his resignation not less than four times, each time with new demands—that after he fell ill, his first words were to give me an order to present the resignation to H.M. I have nothing whatever against Holstein personally. On the contrary, I am sorry for him. But the hour for departure finally strikes for every official, and he himself had handed in his resignation *thirteen* times. Fickle are the favours of the great. For you, I wish from the bottom of my heart that the sun of the Most Gracious goodwill will continue to shine on you! This year, unfortunately, I will not again have the pleasure of seeing you on board the *Meteor*, and of sharing with you the joys and sorrows of these journeys. You can imagine that I am prepared daily for a turnabout in the imperial feelings towards myself. The foreign relations of Germany are at the moment very complicated, and the prime requisite in such a situation—the ability to await developments with calm nerves—is not exactly to the taste of H.M.

Perhaps I will yet have the opportunity to come to Kiel for a few days. In all events, my wife will be in the *Viktoria Luise*, where she will have the pleasure of seeing your wife.

[1] From the Eisendecher Papers.

You see that in accordance with your wishes I have used the same mode of address at the beginning of this letter. I am very happy indeed that you addressed me as 'friend'. I heartily reciprocate this sentiment, and you may be sure that I will do everything and welcome any move which will allow the 'gentleman' to supplant the 'official'!

Please convey my greetings to your wife.

In sincere friendship
Your
von Tschirschky

## 982.  Marie von Bülow to Holstein

14 May 1906

Dear friend,

My husband and I would very much like to see you before our departure! Please give us the *great pleasure* of dining with us next Thursday, 17 May, at eight, *quite privately*. In this heat, the evening hours are the most agreeable.[1]

## 983.  Memorandum by Holstein

17 May 1906

A year ago the French, all of them, feared a war with Germany, although King Edward told them: 'My nephew will give in, etc.' King Edward proved to be right. In order to support the present regime (Clemenceau), the King remained in Paris over election day.[2] The King is probably anxious to further the *disarmament question*, Bourgeois, d'Estournelles. The Government Press is singing paeons to the idea of 'always and under all circumstances with England' (Cornély).[3] All of these people already believe that Germany will give in. Only the *Éclair* has sounded a note of warning, and although it acknowledges that Germany, pressed on all sides, did give in, it is thinking of the moment when Germany may be tired of giving in further and will reject a disarmament proposal. In that event, England might have to face an easy war at sea, but France would face a dangerous war on land.

After Germany gives in the next time, Judet[4] will probably be one of the first to demand a revision of the Peace of Frankfurt. The question is therefore how to preclude a further giving-in on the part of the Kaiser. He will probably not want to go to war against England and France. To give in before a clenched fist would have very serious consequences. Therefore the place at which to give in must be carefully prepared well in advance, with these two formulae in mind: (1) Can we ever, no matter how great our efforts, achieve naval parity with the combined fleets of England and France? In our own right? By alliance? (2) Will the sum total of German military strength be augmented or relatively

---

[1] Holstein replied that he would be glad to come, provided that no controversial subjects were raised.

[2] The elections of 6 May 1906. See above, p. 421, note 3.

[3] Jean Joseph Cornély. French journalist; editor of the *Siècle*.

[4] Ernest Judet. French journalist; director of the *Éclair*.

diminished by an extreme programme of fleet building? A restriction of our land forces, a cause for war. Land forces essential for defence, but not the fleet. We cannot conduct a war against England without allies. No allies in sight. Against Japan we might perhaps proceed with America. Our conflicts with all other Great Powers will be decided on land.

984.    Holstein to Anton von Monts
        Copy

Berlin, 19 May 1906

Dear Count,

To supplement our yesterday's conversation, I wanted to show you a number of documents, among others Tschirschky's cover-letter to my Order of Resignation. In that letter of 17 April[1] there is the statement that Tschirschky 'after receiving orders from the Chancellor, Prince von Bülow' sent His Majesty a report about my petition for resignation.

Already at that time I assumed, and to-day I know for certain, that the quoted statement did not correspond with the facts. I did nothing about it, however, for the end result, which freed me from the need to work any longer with Tschirschky, accorded with my own wishes.

You are free to use this information as you see fit. [...]

Yours very sincerely
Holstein.

985.    Holstein to Pascal David
        Copy

Berlin, 29 May 1906

My dear sir!

I am truly grateful for the detailed exposition by which you gave me the opportunity to gain a full understanding for your point of view.[2] You have to deal with a mixed group that sees and feels things differently from the old Germans in the old homeland. It seems to me that your position now takes on particular significance as a frontier post. The French, that is the French newspapers, have recently begun again to take an aggressive attitude, for the first time since 1870. Now that Germany has just backed down at Algeciras, the accusations that Germany is the general disturber of the peace make a strange impression. I see in this a prelude to disarmament proposals, and for making antimilitarism an international principle. Now that we have once backed down before a majority—this is how every foreign country must interpret it—perhaps the same method can be applied at the Hague on the disarmament question. If we should then lose our nerve again, the third test of strength might be made over a revision of the Peace of Frankfurt.

Do you not find that the tone of the French Press towards us has changed, approximately from the day when Clemenceau wrote in his newspaper: *Guillaume II—c'est un pacifique*? I will not go further into

---

[1] See above.        [2] This exposition has not been found.

the cause, but only enquire about the tone that actually prevails to-day. How does Alsace-Lorraine stand on the question of anti-militarism? Has France succeeded in introducing this sentiment? Of course we have it in Germany too; its main spokesman is the *Frankfurter Zeitung*. I think that in the next test of strength—the disarmament question, or the limitation of arms—we will be surprised at the amount of support this hostile concept will find in Germany. It was the same with the Morocco Question. People only saw Morocco, they did not see that—once the Kaiser had committed himself by his speech at Tangier (*not* by his landing there)—it was a question of German prestige and of a first retreat. This was the first blow to Germany's status, and the second will no doubt follow shortly. Whether some understanding can be reached on naval armaments, perhaps on the basis of our present naval law, is in my opinion an open question. We cannot in any case create a fleet that will be able to face both the English and the French. But to tamper with our land army, that would be the beginning of the end. Yet to stand firm on this question will be more dangerous than on Morocco—*simply because of the fact that people no longer believe we will do so.*

Please write to me again when you have the time and the inclination. Your views are most interesting.

Yours very sincerely
Holstein.

986.    Holstein to Otto Röse[1]
        Copy

Berlin, 18 June 1906

My dear Herr Röse!

In issue no. 414, the *Schlesische Zeitung* has printed a speech of the diplomat Raschdau on foreign affairs. What he says about our not being isolated is childish. Of course we are isolated, and we will remain isolated as long as France and England co-operate. Giolitti says that the friends who are most important are those with whom one has had the most traditional but at the same time the most active relations. For Italy, those friends are of course England and France. Goluchowski points out that Austrian mediation was just as much in the interests of France as of Germany. In short, in the present international atmosphere it seems to me that the correct and dignified thing to do would be to act like Russia after the Crimean War (*la Russie se recueille*) and calmly to withdraw into ourselves rather than cling to people *qui nous remettent à notre place*. On this last point the observer can make glosses which are not favourable to ourselves—cf. the *Temps* of the 15th of this month. However, Herr Raschdau is not to be particularly blamed for supporting the Triple Alliance rather than allowing it to fall into abeyance, because in doing so he is merely following the score of the Press Bureau, whose composers are no more professional diplomats than Raschdau is himself.

But it is absolutely detrimental at this particular time to underline the

---

[1] Editor-in-Chief of the *Schlesische Zeitung*.

concept that Germany must now begin to take steps in order to reopen the Morocco question in a few years under the most favourable circumstances possible. If an English journalist publishes these 'ideas of a German diplomat' in England, our opponents will find in them one more argument for further securing their own solidarity and our isolation. That appeal of Raschdau's to German public opinion is actually the opposite of that calm and objective policy which you advocate in the first paragraph of the same issue of your paper. In view of this contradiction between a calm and a noisy policy, which must perforce nullify our previous joint efforts, I am discontinuing my activity. But I do not want to fail to express my sincere thanks to you at this time for the friendly and understanding way in which you received my various suggestions.

I just read your article about modern cooking with much amusement.

I remain, dear sir,[1]

### 987. Holstein to [Guido von Henckel-Donnersmarck] Draft[2]

Your Highness,

In the *Neue Freie Presse*[3] and again in the *Zukunft* of the 22nd of this month,[4] Harden has concerned himself with my affairs, and in doing so he has also discussed my quarrels with Count Herbert Bismarck and with Your Highness. Meanwhile a rumour has cropped up among journalists that Harden is in touch with you. To me, the source of his information is a matter of indifference. He mentions particulars which were known to only a few people but which, in the interests of truth as well as my own, make a correction desirable. Up to the present I have neglected to do anything about it because of the trouble involved, but should these discussions of my person continue I will undertake the task of correction at the next opportunity, and will have my legal adviser bring the matter to the attention of the *Zukunft*. The protocol of the Herbert affair will show whether the Count really sent me about my business 'without ceremony'.[5] Of the documents dealing with my quarrel with Your Highness, I will publish verbatim or the context of those that can be published without the risk of a libel suit. To clarify the situation, no more would be needed than the letter you sent to Count Waldersee to initiate your rehabilitation at Court,[6] as a result of which I furnished the necessary declaration for your rehabilitation.[7]

---

[1] Röse replied on 20 June: 'I feel obliged to express my thanks to Your Excellency for several memorable hours, for one of the most gripping pieces of work that I have ever had the pleasure to read in my career, and for unusually valuable lessons, from which I unfortunately do not seem to have learned as much as Your Excellency expected.'

[2] The draft is undated.  [3] Of 3 June 1906.

[4] In the *Zukunft* of 23 June 1906. This was a reprint of the article in the *Neue Freie Presse*.

[5] Harden, in writing about the *Kladderadatsch* affair (see vol. III, p. 461 et seq.), said that Holstein had taken issue with Count Herbert von Bismarck. 'The latter declared without much ceremony that he knew nothing about the matter.' (*Zukunft*, vol. 55, p. 464.) For the protocol, see vol. III, no. 400.

[6] See above, the Holstein-Bissing correspondence of 1898; Waldersee, *Denkwürdigkeiten*, vol. II, pp. 416, 418–19.)

[7] See above, nos. 668–9.

I regard my present letter to Your Highness as an act of sensible consideration for both parties.

Most sincerely

Holstein

*Wirklicher Geheimer Rat*

A reply to this communication would in my opinion be useless, and I therefore ask you to desist from sending one.

## 988.    Holstein to Pascal David
Copy

Berlin, 16 August 1906

My dear *Herr Direktor*,

So you almost replaced Fischer? If that had happened I would probably still be in office. A representative of the *Kölnische Zeitung* who understood me would have replied to the lies about my 'war policy'. No more was necessary. I can imagine that Huhn sprang every mine in order to bring the inexperienced Bennigsen to Berlin rather than yourself.[1]

Tomorrow, as I believe, the *Zukunft* will print a long and restrained letter in which over my signature I refute the chief lies and the most ridiculous stories about me, and designate the publication of this letter as an act of equity.[2] Before doing so, I made long and careful enquiries in order to form an opinion as to whether Harden was an honest fanatic or whether he could be bought. People in whose judgment I have confidence informed me that Harden was honest. Thereupon I wrote.

How will Harden react?[3] In what way will Hammann's hooligans [sic] go on trying to spread their venom further? This I will await calmly. The art of anonymous slander has taken an upward turn in Germany in the last twenty years that would not have been suspected before, but I will not abandon the hope that honesty will yet prevail despite the enormous inequality between the contending forces. Since I am proceeding in my own name, I can in all justice expect that my opponents will do the same—but will this expectation be fulfilled? They will probably first send out second-rate or disreputable journalists (Penzler)[4] into the field.

The only possible way is the one I have chosen, unless one lets everything take its course. Our courts of law have no understanding for affairs of honour, see, for instance, the Tausch trial.[5] And a real slanderer does not let himself be manoeuvred to the duelling ground. A few months ago I proceeded in writing, in the sharpest possible manner, against a decidedly younger man—not the best man by any means—of whose ill-will and hostile activity I was convinced. Among other things

---

[1] As Berlin correspondent of the *Kölnische Zeitung*.

[2] Holstein's letter, dated 5 August, appeared in the *Zukunft* of 18 August, vol. 56, pp. 229–35.

[3] Harden's undated reply was published in the same issue, pp. 235–44.

[4] Holstein may be referring to Johannes Penzler, journalist and author of several books about the Bismarck family.

[5] See vol. III, p. 652; note 3.

I called him a contemptible person.[1] He reacted by sending a friend who simply informed my second that the man I had attacked was ready to declare on his word of honour that he had never said or done anything against me among the people in question![2] I demanded this statement *in his own hand and in writing*—and I got it.[3] *Voilà*.

Tomorrow morning with this letter in my pocket, I am going out to buy a copy of the *Zukunft*. If I see that my letter has been printed, I will put this letter at once into the post box.

With best wishes<br>Holstein.

### 989.  Pascal David to Holstein

Strasbourg, 20 August 1906

My dear Excellency,

[...] Upon my return Sunday evening, yesterday, I found Your Excellency's kind letter on my desk, for which I thank you most warmly; and then in the Sunday edition, no. 919 of the *Strassburger Post* which I enclose, I found a reprint of the letter.[4] The publication was not quite what I had hoped for, but *enfin*, if one is not there oneself, one has to put up with such things. The first thing I did to-day was to secure a copy of the *Zukunft*, because our copy had been cut up at the printer's. It was not easy to do, because Strasbourg is a provincial city, and not a political or literary one either, but philistine. However, in the end I succeeded. Now came the big question: what should I do? Should I print Harden's reply, with comments? Perhaps Fischer might have been able to do this, for he knew all the facts thoroughly of which I had only a second-hand knowledge. Besides, there was the added difficulty: would the reader maintain his interest in such a detailed exposition? Do other newspapers reprint things from such a long article? The answer to both questions seems doubtful. Therefore I finally restricted myself to comments, of which I enclose a proof-copy.[5] The newspaper will probably not be ready in time for me to enclose a regular copy. If not, I will send you one tomorrow.[6]

With sentiments of deep respect<br>I remain Your Excellency's sincerely devoted<br>P.D.

### 990.  Holstein to Pascal David
### Copy

Berlin, 29 August 1906

My dear *Herr Direktor*,

Stein's article of 26 August has been given a great deal of attention.[7]

---

[1] Holstein refers to his letter to Eulenburg of 1 May.

[2] See above, p. 419, note 1; Haller, *Eulenburg*, pp. 329–31.

[3] See above, Mühlberg's letter to Holstein of 4 May 1906 and enclosures.

[4] Holstein's letter in the *Zukunft* of 18 August.          [5] Not printed.

[6] Holstein replied on 25 August: 'Despite the barking of Hammann, I am satisfied with the effect of my letter. As you at once recognized, this is expressed more in conversations than in the Press.'

[7] An article by 'Irenaeus' (pseudonym for August Stein) entitled 'Regierende', published

Together with your letter,[1] I received one from Ambassador Monts[2] who drew my attention to the article from Dresden, where he is taking the waters. And to-day still another person wrote me about it.

The article seems to confirm what Harden published about Bülow's falseness towards myself.[3] I fully share your opinion. Hohenlohe may have expressed himself critically about one single piece of advice, but whatever else he is supposed to have said is in my opinion a lie. I do not think there was anyone in the course of my long life who was so indebted to me for advice, both in great and small matters, as was Hohenlohe during the almost thirty years of our association. I will give two examples. (1) What year was it when Hofmann and Mayr[4] bungled things so badly?[5]

The military people at the time wanted to use the opportunity to oust Hohenlohe, whose regime they considered slack. Waldersee came to see me in order to explain that Albedyll was the man for Strasbourg. He then left in a huff. I advised Hohenlohe to come to Berlin and asked: 'Can you reform your Ministry without having to consult anyone?' He replied: 'According to the Constitution, yes, but according to custom, no.' I said: 'Well, for the time being let's leave custom aside.' Two days later Hohenlohe went back with a complete Ministry, to the great disgust of Minister Puttkamer, who also wanted to get the Strasbourg job. I had recommended Studt, of whom my friend Lebbin[6] had always had a good opinion. Studt did not prove to be too effective there in the west, but with his appointment the crisis was over. The Princess wrote me a letter of thanks at that time in which she said that it was thanks to me that Hohenlohe was staying on.[7] Czapski has seen the letter.

(2) When in November 1897 the Kaiser gave orders for Kiaochow to be occupied, it was I who, alone with Hohenlohe, conducted the diplomatic campaign in the first difficult period against the very angry

in the *Frankfurter Zeitung* of 26 August. Stein wrote that Prince Chlodwig zu Hohenlohe had warned Bülow against trusting Holstein's political judgment.

[1] Pascal David had sent the above article to Holstein in a letter of 27 August in which he wrote: 'I should like to say on this matter that *to me* the deceased Prince Chlodwig always expressed himself about Your Excellency in the warmest possible way. He always used to say, for instance: "My friend Holstein." [...] Nevertheless, it is certainly conceivable that the old Prince may once have told Herr von Bülow: "*In this particular case* I followed the advice of Herr von Holstein, but it did not turn out well." In the newspapers this has now been quite inadmissibly generalized.'

[2] Of 27 August. Not printed.

[3] In his reply to Holstein's letter in the *Zukunft* of 18 August.

[4] Dr Georg von Mayr. Under State Secretary for Alsace-Lorraine.

[5] In 1887. On this incident, see *Diaries*, entries of 14 March and 5 April 1887; Hohenlohe, *Denkwürdigkeiten*, vol. II, p. 410 *et seq.*; Rogge, *Holstein und Hohenlohe*, p. 273 *et seq.*

[6] Hermann Friedrich Karl von Lebbin, the husband of Helene von Lebbin. Lebbin had been *Vortragender Rat* in charge of personnel in the Ministry of the Interior. He died on 17 November 1884.

[7] Princess Hohenlohe wrote on 5 April 1887: 'I cannot tell you how touched I was by the trouble you gave yourself in aiding and seconding the Prince during the difficult time he has gone through in Berlin. I cannot refrain from expressing my deep gratitude to you and regret only that I cannot do so in person. I hope you will be able to frustrate the intrigues that will continue to crop up, but whatever happens I will never forget your kindness to the Prince.' (In French in the original.)

Russians. I wrote everything, he signed. The Kaiser was delighted and, when everything was over, he came to thank the Chancellor and show him a sign of his favour. When I came to see the Chancellor immediately afterwards he said rather embarrassed : 'I had intended to tell the Kaiser about you, too, but before I knew it he had snapped his cigarette case shut and was gone.'

At the time I didn't care, but to-day I think it would have been better to have expressed the wish to have received some mark of appreciation as well.

That Hohenlohe should have warned against me in general terms after this assistance and other similar aid seems unthinkable to me, for he was a decent man. However, one makes the strangest discoveries after having worked for decades in the second rank. Credit for success goes to one's superiors, but failures are left to the underlings. Bülow, I know, has recently been telling the story as Stein wrote it. Hohenlohe is dead, and it is unfortunately notorious that Bülow does not take truth too seriously. Could you not at some time ask Alexander Hohenlohe for his opinion? To be sure, the poor fellow would not be too happy about correcting the Chancellor.

That the official Press is beginning to bestir itself after my letter to the *Zukunft*, I too have noticed from the leading article 'Pacemaker' in the *Schlesische Zeitung* of 28 August which Herold[1] has just informed me was an egg laid in the Wilhelmstrasse. Incidentally, the editor-in-chief, Röse, was recently in Norderney. It is indubitable that Bülow does *not* want an improvement in our relations with England because he is afraid that he may be slaughtered as a peace offering, for he knows that he personally is the *bête noire* of the English. Incidentally, a very acute observer who saw the Chancellor quite recently told me : he found he had become quite small, no longer anything Olympian about him. Tschirschky is handling foreign policy and especially personnel questions directly with the Kaiser.

Bülow has the burning desire to establish closer relations with France. I have the same desire, but do not think it can be achieved at this time. England does not want this rapprochement, and England, which safeguards France's East Asian possessions against Japan, is now more important to France than ever. Furthermore France has far more reason to hope for a 'frontier rectification' or a 'revision of the Peace of Frankfurt' from an isolated, intimidated German Kaiser than from an ally of France that feels confident of French friendship. One can see from the novel that Marcel Prévost is just publishing in the *Revue des deux Mondes* what a great role the Alsace-Lorraine question still plays in the French consciousness.[2] I fear that the Kaiser, in order to get to Paris, and Bülow, in order to get compensation for the alienation of England for which he is partially to blame, will evince a willingness to make concessions that, instead of hastening a rapprochement, will make it more difficult. On this matter it would be of the greatest value to me to hear your opinion.

[1] Hugo Herold. Editor of the *Echo*.
[2] The novel was *Monsieur et Madame Moloch*.

Surely nobody has been able to study the psychology of the French so thoroughly as yourself.

Last winter Ambassador Barrère said : 'Germany showed France too much kindness last winter. Less would have achieved more.'

But now this letter is really long enough.

With best wishes

Your sincerely devoted

Holstein.

## 991.    Maximilian Harden to Holstein[1]

Grunewald-Berlin, 30 August 1906

Your Excellency

had mentioned in our conversation that the question of the protection of private property on the high seas might shortly become important and might be useful for us. I have thought over this suggestion, but have not yet arrived at any useful conclusion because I am unfamiliar with the material and I have not yet found the pertinent literature. If Your Excellency still believes that something beneficial can be done for German policy by developing this point in the Press, perhaps you would have the kindness to help me along by giving me a more precise idea of the ultimate goal. I would be very grateful.

I have kept a large number of newspaper clippings that were sent to me from the office, just in case.[2] Presumably Your Excellency has seen most of them. Otherwise they are at your disposal. There is nothing important among them. And the tone is more unfavourable to the rejoinder than to the reply. *Je ne m'en plains pas.* But would still sometime like to say a few words about the whole way the business was treated. Augustus Irenaeus[3] kept silent, so far as I can see. On the other hand he was the *ministre plénipotentiare* of the Chancellor at the Sonnemann jubilee.[4] A *galopin* of *Herr Geheimrat* Hammann wrote me protesting that the noble man had been done a grave injustice.

With profound respect, I have the honour to be

Your Excellency's devoted

Harden[5]

[1] This is probably the first private letter exchanged between Holstein and Harden. According to evidence contained in a letter from Harden to Holstein of 17 July 1907 and Holstein's reply of 19 July 1907 (see below), Holstein and Harden met for the first time shortly after mid-August 1906, some two weeks after Holstein wrote his open letter to Harden of 5 August for publication in the *Zukunft*. See Harden's later account of their meeting in the *Zukunft*, vol. 67, pp. 415–16. For a full analysis of Holstein's relationship with Harden and the complete text of Holstein's letters to Harden, see Helmuth Rogge, *Holstein und Harden* (München, 1959).

[2] Newspaper clippings dealing with Holstein's open letter in the *Zukunft* and Harden's reply.

[3] August Stein, the author of the Irenaeus article. (See above, p. 432, note 7.)

[4] Leopold Sonnemann. Publisher of the *Frankfurter Zeitung*, which was just celebrating its fiftieth anniversary.

[5] Holstein replied on 1 September that it was still too early to discuss the question of sea law in the Press, but he set forth his ideas on the subject at some length. He refused Harden's offer to send him newspaper clippings on their exchange of letters in the *Zukunft*, saying that he had already seen enough to have formed the opinion that it had served to clear away the fog on the main issue. Now people were saying that he and Harden must have been in touch

## 992. Holstein to Pascal David
Copy

Berlin, 3 September 1906

My dear *Herr Direktor*.

The juxtaposition of these two articles in the *Täglicher Rundschau*[1] will I hope please you as much as it did me. Delbrück[2] had wanted to avenge himself because I would never receive him. A few years ago—before the Japanese war—he sent the Foreign Ministry an article called 'Political Dreams' in which he recommended, among other things, the annexation of the Baltic Provinces by Germany. I ordered that he be requested not to publish the article because it was untimely. But he published it anyway.[3] Since that time I have refused to have anything to do with Delbrück, and I also knew that he had been criticizing me for a long time already.

It is a very good thing that your article immediately follows that of Delbrück.

To my regret I have heard that it was really Bülow himself who told Stein the story about Hohenlohe's warning. *In this general context* the story is certainly a lie. [...]

As for Alex. Hohenlohe, I hear that he is on very close terms with Stein. The latter is probably his only source of Berlin news.

Now to close in haste.

*Bonne poignée de main*
Yours
Holstein

I would just like to point out: the [*Berliner*] *Tageblatt* and Delbrück, the two most violent critics, have been very careful not to print any part of my letter; but surely that would have been the best means of publicly exposing both me and my ignoble machinations.

These wretched pin-pricks do not deserve a reply.[4]

## 993. Maximilian Harden to Holstein

Grunewald, 3 September 1906

Your Excellency

Thank you so much for the friendly letter. [...]

with one another for some time, for this was the only way to explain the calm tone of their correspondence. This showed that people were trying to chalk up to his (Holstein's) account many of the previous attacks on the Kaiser and Chancellor made in the *Zukunft*. In a postscript to his letter, Holstein said it was obvious that his present letter was not intended for publication, and left it up to Harden whether he wished to make use of any ideas it contained. (Rogge, *Holstein und Harden*, pp. 82–4.)

[1] A reprint of an article by Delbrück attacking Holstein in the *Preussische Jahrbücher* (vol. 125, p. 563 *et seq.*) and Pascal David's reply.

[2] Dr Hans Delbrück. Professor of History at the University of Berlin; editor of the *Preussische Jahrbücher*.

[3] In the *Preussische Jahrbücher*, January, 1896.

[4] On 3 September Holstein wrote to Harden that he was very much moved that since the previous spring Pascal David had on several occasions taken his part against official attacks, but he asked Harden not to mention David's name because he might otherwise get into difficulties owing to his connection with the official *Kölnische Zeitung*. (Rogge, *Holstein und Harden*, pp. 86–8.)

Yesterday I was sent a copy of the new *Irenaeus*.[1] I thought I saw in it an indirect and not exactly courageous reply to Your Excellency's publication.[2] I can see no other purpose, because what was said about His Majesty was very similar to *crambe repetita*. It was perhaps intended to show what an important role Stein and Huhn play. And at the end there is a fairly clear answer to the question Your Excellency did not even publicly ask, namely why the Press Bureau did not co-operate during the Morocco crisis.

I have no doubt that Stein got the things he said about Your Excellency's attitude in this affair from the Chancellor and the State Secretary. That he has often been with Bülow recently, 'in an intimate circle' and alone, I know for a fact. Also that the Chancellor has expressed himself to others as though Tangier[3] and the note handed over by Herr von Flotow,[4] etc., was the result of the policy Your Excellency had recommended to H.M., and as though he had become exhausted in the task of softening this policy. And it was he, and no one else,—as his confidential agents have told me (who come to see me occasionally and who, *quand même*, tell me of His Highness' admiration for me)—who expressed the suspicion that you and I were in touch with each other.

In the Pod[bielski] affair[5] he seems to have climbed down after he was received in an unfriendly manner in Wilhelmshöhe and H.M. said: 'The law will decide if P. did something irregular. We cannot object to the business itself because we after all knew about the whole thing. Bülow of course thinks differently. He fears for his job.' This statement is undoubtedly authentic. I see in the cases of Miquel,[6] Möller,[7] Holstein, Podbielski, the same method used over and over. The same method by which he lavishes favours on every representative of a big newspaper. 'Your article was really quite masterful.' Praise from the Press, the highest aim. Hence Hammann more important than the most penetrating political mind. And the desire to oust anyone who is steadily attacked in the Press. The decisive factors in the Podbielski affair were after all the articles in the *Norddeutsche*,[8] and their *generatio* was not

[1] See above, p. 432, note 7.   [2] Holstein's *Zukunft* letter.
[3] The landing of the Kaiser at Tangier on 31 March 1905 and his public statement on Germany's attitude towards the independence of Morocco. (See p. 330, note 3.)
[4] The note informing the signatory Powers of the Madrid Convention that Germany had accepted the Sultan of Morocco's invitation to a Conference at Tangier and recommending that the other signatory Powers also accept the invitation. (*Grosse Politik*, vol. XXii, nos. 6786–7, pp. 413–15.)
[5] In July 1906, Major Fischer, an official in charge of a branch of the Imperial Commissary Department, was arrested and accused of accepting bribes from the firm of Tippelskirch, which provided the bulk of the supplies for the German troops in South-west Africa. The Prussian Minister of Agriculture, Viktor von Podbielski, who had close business connections with the Tippelskirch firm, was accused in the Press of being involved in the affair, and various newspapers were demanding his resignation. Podbielski did in fact resign in November.
[6] Dr Johannes von Miquel, the Prussian Minister of Finance, whom Bülow dropped in 1901 when he failed to secure the passage of the Canal Bill, a favourite project of the Kaiser.
[7] Theodor von Möller. Prussian Minister of Trade, May 1901–October 1905. Since his appointment, Möller had been the object of considerable criticism and ridicule in the Reichstag and the Press.
[8] An article of 18 August in the *Norddeutsche Allgemeine Zeitung* stated: 'The Chancellor,

*aequivoca.* Also the alleged 'warning' of Hohenlohe can only have been given to Irenaeus by B.[1] Otherwise Stein would not have dared to publish it. For the survivor would be able to deny it at once.

An agreement *seems* to have been reached on this basis: P[odbielski] is to be cleared, and will soon thereafter leave the service *cum laude.* The desire to turn over some of the functions of Herr von Lucanus to Hammann seems to be hopeless.

With profound respect I am
Your Excellency's devoted
Harden

### 994.   Anton von Monts to Holstein

Zillerthal-Erdmannsdorff, 11 September 1906

My dear Herr von Holstein.

My warmest thanks for your most interesting and kind letter.[2] [...]

In the opinion of others as well, you came out of the Harden affair very creditably. H. would probably like nothing better than to keep the ball rolling; he needs new sensations. I wonder whether the fellow only writes to make money; or whether he really feels badly about the wretched course of our policy?

I hardly think that B. B[ülow] will be able to stay in office much longer. The Pod[bielski] affair, in which he came out second-best, was really a serious defeat for him; that is, it would have been a fine opportunity for him to resign with honour. Incidentally I agree with you that the time has not yet come for a really firm Chancellor. Although H.M. is supposed to be saying to intimate confidants that the domestic situation has become impossible, he is still supposed to cherish illusions about foreign affairs. Also about the mood of the country, which is rotten.

In foreign affairs things would improve quickly enough if only we would keep quiet. The centre of gravity of 62 million people in the heart of Europe is after all sufficiently large so that it cannot be ignored. I agree that a rapprochement with France at the moment is out of the question. But there are nuances. In time the English and French will set to quarrelling again, and then we can see. My ideal is and always has been to bring about a rapprochement among all the Central Europeans, who represent the culture and the hope of humanity. Even though their interests may conflict at certain points, the world is large enough to allow Germans, Englishmen, and Frenchmen to develop peacefully beside each other and to foster their well-being. If the Central Europeans, including Austria, could only hold together on all extra-European questions there would be neither a yellow nor an American peril. It

while he was at Norderney, had already demanded that Podbielski, the Minister of Agriculture, make a statement about the involvement of the Minister in the affairs of the firm of Tippelskirch which had been the subject of so much recent comment. In reply Minister Podbielski made a full statement, at the end of which he requested that his resignation from the service of the state be submitted to the Kaiser.'

[1] See above, p.432, note 7.
[2] Of 30 August 1906. (Printed in Monts, *Erinnerungen*, pp. 360–3.)

is strange that this insight is frequently expressed among the people, but that the rulers give free play to their passions and hatreds. [...]

Our working men, who were driven into Social Democratic courses by the manifold mistakes of Bismarck and are being driven further along this course principally by H.M., must be steered into other channels. In the long run a country cannot be ruled without the working men, or against them, for, whether we like it or not, Germany has already become an industrial state. The principles of the old Prussian class state are no longer applicable, particularly when the ruling classes show so little political judgment. By a timely recognition of the signs of the times, much could have been saved that was good and vital. But why should a proletarian feel any sympathy for Crown or Altar when he sees daily that under these banners the most despicable egoism is simply seizing special advantages for itself? As you quite rightly say, B. B[ülow] sees the truth just as a pilot sees the North Star, but neither necessarily steers in that direction. The Chancellor certainly is not lacking in intelligence, only in character and willingness to face a fight. Therefore, despite his great talents, he will in the end have to leave the stage without honour. It seems to me that he is still full of illusions, especially about H.M., and believes that the old relationship still exists. I am very sorry about all this personally, but even if one wanted to give the Chancellor hints, he would not believe them. The ladies, especially Donna Laura, probably see things somewhat more clearly. The latter has gone through the ups and downs of a leading statesman with Minghetti and knows quite well that glory and honour last for only a brief span of time, and that every Minister gets used up. But what then? Some servile person will be found soon enough, I'm afraid, and then the journey downhill will go on even faster than before. But in the end a great nation finds ways and leaders, and our young people will I hope do a better job and in many respects have an easier time of it than we have had in this time of transition to new ways. For, as I just said, the class state and rule by the Grace of God are no longer tenable in the light of modern times. [...]

Your most devoted
A. Monts

995.   Maximilian Harden to Holstein

Grunewald-Berlin, 14 October 1906

Your Excellency,

[...] I hope to hear something about these matters in the next few days.[1] I then hope to have the pleasure of seeing Your Excellency again (at my house, on a walk, or in the city); I would be very much interested in finding out more about Your Excellency's political ideas. I say this

[1] Harden refers to the publication of the first two volumes of Prince Hohenlohe's memoirs (*Denkwürdigkeiten des Fürsten Chlodwig zu Hohenlohe-Schillingsfürst*) which were officially regarded as grave political indiscretions. Both Harden and Holstein suspected that the work might have been published for political reasons. But see above, Alexander Hohenlohe's letter to Holstein of 27 July 1901.

quite frankly, because I have no fear of being misunderstood after Your Excellency's kind offer.[1]

With kindest regards
I am Your Excellency's very devoted
Harden [...]

996.   Holstein to Maximilian Harden
       Draft[2]

21 October 1906

My dear Herr Harden,

The Press activity developing around Tschirschky is remarkable. Eight to ten days ago the *Neue Freie Presse* first published the news that Tsch. would shortly be going to Vienna to confer there with Wedel and Monts and perhaps also with Goluchowski about the Triple Alliance and Italy.[3] (Telegram in the *Lokalanzeiger*.)

That was the gist of it. The form of the article was unusual and at once excited comment. A second article : Tsch. has no political purpose, only hunting. Third article : he had arrived, is paying calls.

The same thing in Rome. First : a political event. Then modest explanation by Tsch. : I am only State Sect., the Chancellor alone makes policy. In contradiction to this is the way the Italian Press is treating this trip, drafting programmes and making conditions. (*Lokalanzeiger* of last night and to-day.) Tsch. is actually being treated as the leader of German policy; the cistern that always used to wait for rain from above now appears as the source. Under the circumstances the presence of Count Monts is comforting, for one can be confident that he thoroughly understands the situation. One does not therefore need to be afraid that Italian diplomacy will oblige Germany twice in the same year to make agreements which objective foreign observers can regard as German retreats.

If, as I suppose, the foregoing coincides with your views, make use of it as you see fit. At the same time I would like to repeat again that in my opinion every mention of myself, whether laudatory or critical, diverts the attention and prejudices the effect. The more solitary you stand, the more effective you are. I would leave Tschirschky alone, although he has not behaved well towards me, if I were not really afraid, in view of the fuss that is being made, that he wants to perform some deed no matter what the cost, and is therefore ready to make harmful concessions. This fear is prompted by the programme of the official Italian *Corriere della Sera* (one of the most serious Italian newspapers) from which last night's *Lokalanzeiger* printed a short extract.) It is unnecessary to explain how and why our prestige would suffer in a really dangerous way

[1] Holstein had written earlier that day that he would like to call on Harden on the following day to talk over the Hohenlohe publication. (Rogge, *Holstein und Harden*, p. 89.)

[2] This draft is almost identical with the final version of the letter sent to Harden. (See Rogge, *Holstein und Harden*, pp. 91–3.) Rogge also shows how Harden actually made use of the letter in his articles.

[3] On Tschirschky's trip to Vienna and Rome, see *Grosse Politik*, vol. XXIii, nos. 7160–1, pp. 376–9.

if the German Government once again gave in to pressure—no matter on what question.

Monts has a high regard for the *Zukunft*. So if for only that reason.

With best wishes

Your very devoted

Holstein.

P.S. While out walking, I had some further thoughts. If, as the Viennese and especially the Italian Press assume, the talks are concerned with the renewal of the Triple Alliance, then one must after all ask the question: why such haste? Why should the *German State Secretary* be the first to take the initiative? Will we never learn to sit still and calmly await developments? Even supposing that the Triple Alliance Treaty is more important for Germany than for Austria and Italy—the opposite would be closer to the facts of the case, but supposing Germany were most interested—it would hardly be desirable to rub this fact under the noses of the other Powers concerned. An objective reason for this excessive haste would be difficult to find. It is simply an effort to carve the name of Tschirschky on the tree of world history before the Reichstag convenes. Here is where the reassuring part about Monts might be fit in. This material would not be adequate for a big article, but perhaps for Moritz and Rina.[1]

Good night

H.

997.   Bernhard von Bülow to Holstein

Berlin, Wednesday morning, 24 October 1906

Dear Holstein,

After a long absence I am again in Berlin and would be truly pleased to see you and talk with you. I need hardly tell you that my mother-in-law and my wife would be very happy if you would dine with us. However, if an hour in the morning or afternoon would suit you better than the evening, please let me know. With best wishes, I remain in old friendship

Your sincerely devoted

Bülow

998.   Holstein to Bernhard von Bülow

Copy

Berlin, 24 October [1906]

Dear Bülow,

As I wrote you in April, my advice is always at your disposal. Not that I see any possibility at the moment of its being of any use, because in the German camp—not in the enemy's—the prerequisites are lacking for a systematic and steady policy. It is gradually becoming clear that the hunt is up against us. The beaters are coming in view one after the other, and the only doubt in the mind of the German hare is whether

---

[1] A fictitious correspondence in the *Zukunft*, occasionally used by Harden to present his ideas.

running away sooner or later is more in line with a hare's tradition. He does not seem to think of anything besides running away, or so I conclude from the cowardly trip to Rome.[1]

This makes advising hard. But I will not shirk the job, and therefore ask whether it would be convenient for you to receive me Saturday morning, and at what time.

Ever sincerely your<br>
Holstein.

### 999.   Holstein to Bernhard von Bülow
Copy

Berlin, 25 October 1906

Dear Bülow,

As you will have gathered from a sentence in my letter of yesterday, I have been informed that the idea of changing the Triple Alliance treaty to the benefit of Italy is 'current'. I also know that you are opposed to it, or at least you were opposed to it a fortnight ago. (I did not hear all this from the Foreign Ministry.)

It is my intention to advise you to stick to this opinion when I next see you. I think that to-day Italy's withdrawal from the Triple Alliance would be much less unfavourably received than would the purchase of her remaining in the Alliance by concessions which would tend to make the Triple Alliance ridiculous. Furthermore, I do not think that Italy has any intention whatever of withdrawing, and for once the *Temps* happens to be of the same opinion as myself. (See the section marked in red.) I will send the clipping right away. Who knows, it may be a question of twenty-four hours. I should imagine that Rome is now putting pressure on Potsdam and Berlin.

More than ever we are being subjected to bluff, but no one will push things to extremes. Not Italy; not Clemenceau, because the Republic cannot accomodate victorious generals; not King Edward, because the majority of his subjects want peace.

Therefore : be firm! In addition, I will tell you about a little plan.

Best wishes<br>
Holstein

### 1000.   Memorandum by Holstein[2]

Berlin, 27 October [1906]

At Algeciras Germany gave in before collective pressure. If she now allows concessions to be pressured out of her in the Triple Alliance question, then the pressure system will have proved its worth a second time, and will then be used more often and will lead us gradually step by step to a revision of the Peace of Frankfurt. King Edward and Clemenceau are probably already agreed about this final goal, but they want to reach it by peaceful means. A victorious French general would probably

---

[1] See above, p. 440, note 3.

[2] This memorandum was probably prepared for Holstein's talk with Bülow on 27 October. (See above, no. 998.)

bring the present French Republic to a rapid end. Clemenceau is clever enough to know that. And King Edward knows that his own people would only fight a war in the most extreme need and for their own preservation. *Menacer souvent, frapper rarement* was the advice Marshal Marmont regarded as correct for Russia eighty years ago. Clemenceau and the King are probably planning something similar now. We must be prepared for all kinds of bluff—they will be tried out one after the other to see how they work. The greatest possible sharply accentuated firmness will under these circumstances be less dangerous for us than flabbiness, which would only encourage the opposition to pressure further.

I consider the tone Clemenceau has recently used in dealing with Germany to be bluff. If he wanted to negotiate, he would say nothing until a suitable moment. But he is using threats because he expects the desired results from threats alone.

Every concession that Germany now makes in foreign affairs will encourage this bluff. To give in on the Triple Alliance question would have two-fold injurious consequences, for it would shift the relations within the Triple Alliance and provide general encouragement for our enemies.

Is the Triple Alliance still of any use whatever? When it was formed it was intended to cover Italy against France and against Austria. To-day the cover against France is no longer necessary, so for Italy the Triple Alliance only serves the purpose to cover her against Austria. Does Germany have any interest in the continuation of *this* situation? No.

If Italy no longer wishes to proceed against France, the reciprocity is removed for the protection we furnish Italy against Austria. What Italy's *diplomatic* support against France means, we have seen at Algeciras. The way in which France and Italy are proclaiming their tender relations makes the whole Triple Alliance ridiculous. On the other hand, the relations between Austria and Italy are made worse by the fact that Italy, both her King and her people, allows herself all kinds of discourtesies towards Austria in the conviction that Germany in the end will prevent a conflict among her allies.

After the abrogation of the Triple Alliance, Italy, in the knowledge that she will have to bail herself out of any consequences of her actions, will behave more carefully towards Austria.

If France moves in as the backer of Italy, that still would not make an offensive war like that of 1859 probable; for the Republic must avoid war in its own interests. But the fact that Italy's defence would be supported by France would be enough to cool the relations between Austria and France and on the other hand to bind Austria faster to ourselves. A German-Austrian alliance would be taken seriously both at home and abroad. Nobody can say that any longer about the Triple Alliance. The Austro-Hungarian monarchy, which is to-day crowded between Germany and Italy, would once again move into the front rank by the transformation of the Triple Alliance into a Dual Alliance; the question—for or against Austria—would once again be relevant, and might even bring about a difference of opinion between France and England. France, as the ally of Russia, is working to bring about the fall of the Dual Monarchy. Pichon[1] maintains close relations with the Hungarian independence party. In doing so, he is keeping up a French tradition of several hundred years. Louis XIV was even in the process of allying himself with the Turks against Vienna.

England on the other hand has shown that ever since Marlborough she will take an authoritative stand in the interests of preserving Austria. English sympathy for Austria was a guiding principle of Bismarck's Danish policy in 1864.

We know to-day from the reports of Sternburg, among others, that England and France are united in the idea that one of these days some parts of Austria may fall to Germany.[2]

German diplomacy might dig in at this point and enter into direct discussions with London about the future of Austria. We are in a position to furnish documentary evidence that—despite Chéradame—we are working to preserve the Austro-Hungarian monarchy.[3] Years ago we proposed a treaty of *désintéressement* in St Petersburg.[4] Lamsdorff agreed to the idea, but demanded that we present him with a finished German draft treaty. Alvensleben was ordered to prepare a draft, which by its very nature could only have been brief and simple, in conjunction with Lamsdorff, but Lamsdorff refused to help in any way. We could only interpret this as a desire on the part of the Russian Minister to preserve complete freedom of action so as to be able to advise the Tsar to reject the treaty. It therefore seemed advisable not to press the matter further. Nor did Count Lamsdorff bring up the subject again. The German standpoint to-day is still the same as it was at that time. We would be happy to sign a treaty whereby Russia and Germany would undertake not to exploit any possible internal conflicts for the purpose of securing territorial advantages or sovereign rights. Up till now the death of Kaiser Franz Joseph has been regarded as the psychological moment for the outbreak of such conflicts; because of this assumption, such a treaty, if it came to the knowledge of the monarch, would make a painful impression on him. The events of the past year have shown, however, that we must reckon with the possibility of conflicts and new combinations within the borders of Austria-Hungary even under the present regime. A treaty of *désintéressement* could therefore be justified by the situation without need to mention the question of a change of rulers.

In the ninety-one years that have passed since the Congress of Vienna, no Tsar has ever shown the inclination to annex Austrian territory,

[1] Stephen Jean-Marie Pichon. French Foreign Minister in the Cabinets of Clemenceau and Briand, 25 October 1906–1911.

[2] See *Grosse Politik*, vol. XIXii, no. 6304, pp. 597–8.

[3] Holstein refers to the thesis of the French writer André Chéradame that it was in the German interest and part of German policy to allow the Austro-Hungarian Empire to disintegrate so that Austria might be absorbed by Germany. (See *L'Europe et la Question d'Autriche au Seuil du XXe. Siècle* (Paris, 1906).)

[4] In the spring of 1905. *Grosse Politik*, vol. XXII, chapter CLIX.

although, for instance in 1849, there was a favourable opportunity to do so. Count Lamsdorff's reserve towards a declaration of disinterestedness can therefore only be explained by his concern not to give the leaders of Panslavism any possible material for attacks on his policy. The German Government too would expose itself to the attacks of Pan-Germans if the treaty became known. But this annoyance would be balanced by the advantage that this *désintéressement* on the part of Germany and Russia would encourage the loyal political parties within the Dual Monarchy and aid in the preservation of its internal stability. The preservation of the Dual Monarchy is possible, for the majority of the Hungarian leaders know within their hearts that the preconditions for the permanent independence of the Magyars do not exist. During the last conflict, so far as we know, Kaiser Franz Joseph did not give in to the Magyars but to the entreaties of Grand Duchess Valerie.

The question is whether England still takes the same interest in the preservation of the Austro-Hungarian monarchy. If the answer is yes, then a careful query in St Petersburg would not in any way disturb good Anglo-Russian relations. If the query were successful and a declaration of disinterestedness were brought about, one more danger of war for Europe would thereby be averted.

Whether a treaty of disinterestedness would meet with approval among the other neighbours of the Dual Monarchy, especially Italy and Serbia, is doubtful; but their accession would not seem to be of paramount importance, for they will hardly distrub the peace unless they are certain in advance of the support of at least one of the Great Powers.

## 1001. Maximilian Harden to Holstein

Grunewald, 27 October 1906

Your Excellency,

Thank you so much for the friendly and interesting letters.[1] I am pleased (and relieved) that I am able to agree in my judgment of events with the most experienced expert on international affairs. Doubly so, because we unfortunately judge past events so very differently. I too find what is going on now almost unbelievable. Only, *hélas*, it is after all in line with what has gone before. Herr von Speck performed similar gymnastics.[2] And I was not much less disgusted by the way the Chancellor paid court to that bicycle manufacturer Prinetti and to that Francophile Luzzatti. Italy is obviously the point on which B[ülow] loses what remains of his judgment; perhaps because it is a *point d'honour* of the Principessa Zoe Maria.[3]

But Tschirschky must surely have special orders from H.M. Otherwise he would not risk it, if only because he would run the danger of

---

[1] See above, Holstein letter of 21 October. In a letter of 26 October, Holstein made further criticisms of Tschirschky's trip to Rome. This made the Italians think their value had gone up, whereas their behaviour in the past months had made the Triple Alliance a laughing stock. (Rogge, *Holstein und Harden*, pp. 93–5.)

[2] In a letter of 27 October Holstein defended Speck von Sternburg, saying that he had often shown courage in carrying out his duty. (Rogge, *Holstein und Harden*, pp. 95–6.)

[3] Princess Bülow.

seriously wounding the (by no means small) vanity of his Chief. *Ceterum censeo*. . . . It is my sincere conviction, after considering the matter again and again : the personal policy of the Kaiser is at the root of all evil. He is a 'brilliant nature' (*tant pis pour un empereur*) but has no political talent. Not enough of a Coburger to drive a hard bargain, not enough of a Hohenzollern to maintain a dignified reserve, and, whenever necessary, to show himself brave and fearless. If this manner of conducting policy by impromptu inspirations, whose consequences are never thought through to their conclusion, does not cease, I can see no hope. And with all due consideration for the monarchy, I do not know whether a great, hard working people can to-day still be circumscribed by such characteristics of a single person. [...]

Your Excellency's assumption that our acquaintance is not unknown seems to be correct. Dernburg,[1] with whom I spent an evening recently, made an allusion. Objectively, I can see nothing prejudicial in that. The Consortium[2] may perhaps grow somewhat more fearful on that account. Your Excellency will be able to see how quickly things get about by the fact that a remark Your Excellency is supposed to have made about my Dernburg article[3] (plums out of my pudding) has already been repeated to me.[4]

With kindest regards I am
Your Excellency's very devoted
Harden

1002.    Holstein to Bernhard Bülow
       Copy

Berlin, 31 October 1906

Dear Bülow,

I am grateful that you took the time to write that letter to me.[5] To show my gratitude, I would like to emphasize once again the following points which we have already discussed.

*First* : The day before yesterday someone—an official—told me : 'I hear that Bülow no longer receives material on foreign policy.' This fact, which is being talked about in all official circles of Berlin, naturally harms your position. From now on, have them send you a suitable amount of material daily, and let Scheefer[6] pick out the most important for you. Who does the picking-out for you is nobody else's business.

*Second* : You must once again accustom people to submit foreign policy matters to you in writing, and to the fact that you can make the decisions

---

[1] Bernhard Dernburg. Director of the Bank of Darmstadt; Director of the Colonial Office, 1906–7; State Secretary of the Colonial Office, 1907–10.

[2] A reference to Prince Philipp zu Eulenburg and his friends.

[3] An article called 'Kolonialwaren', published in the *Zukunft* of 15 September 1906, vol. 56, pp. 391–406.

[4] In his letter to Harden of 27 October, cited above, Holstein denied that the 'plums out of my pudding' remark had originated with him. He had, in fact, thought that Harden had written the article at the request of Dernburg, certainly not to make his work more difficult.

[5] Not found.

[6] Prince Bülow's private secretary; *Geheimer Regierungsrat* in the Reich Chancellery.

even without consulting them. You must do this unless you want to become Chlodwig II.

*Third*: I advise that tomorrow already you instruct the Press to treat coolly Italy's demands on the Triple Alliance which have recently been voiced in the Italian Press. We were agreed on this matter, but so far this standpoint has not been expressed in the Press. This instruction to the Press could be made completely objective and impersonal if you give the order before Tschirschky returns; otherwise he might have other ideas and make objections.

With best wishes<br>H.

Bernstorff recently told someone that the ill-feeling between England and Germany was so great on both sides that an improvement could not be expected in the near future.

I hope that you will summon Metternich soon, at any rate before you talk to Aehrenthal. Things are not so bad if one handles them correctly.

## 1003.   Diary Entry

10 November [1906]

Tschirschky is running the Foreign Ministry quite independently of the Chancellor, and is even signing dispatches sent to the Kaiser.

During Tschirschky's conversation with the King of Italy, the Triple Alliance was not mentioned. The King spoke of the unjustified touchiness of Austria. (Demonstrations by the kindred peoples of Trieste, Imola.) Public opinion was decisive in determining Italy's foreign policy.[1] (Then why an alliance?)

## 1004.   Diary Entry

11 November [1906]

In letters from Ph.[2] to Ku.,[3] he[4] is referred to as 'Sweetheart'.

Lecomte was also invited for the visit the Kaiser is now making to Liebenberg.[5] The Press does not say who was there.[6] [...]

---

[1] Tschirschky wrote an undated memorandum about his conversation with the King of Italy that was placed in the Foreign Ministry files on 6 November. Holstein has accurately summarized the main points.

[2] Prince Philipp zu Eulenburg.

[3] Kuno, Count von Moltke. Aide-de-Camp of the Kaiser; General in command of the forces in the City of Berlin. A close friend of Eulenburg's.

[4] Kaiser Wilhelm II.

[5] Prince Eulenburg's estate.

[6] 'The thought that the Frenchman had been with the Kaiser in the most intimate type of circle drove little Harden [...] into an absolute frenzy', Holstein wrote to his cousin Ida von Stülpnagel almost a year later. (4 November 1907, Rogge, *Friedrich von Holstein*, p. 296.) It was this evidence of Eulenburg's political indiscretion that appears to have set off Harden's famous journalistic campaign in *Die Zukunft* against Eulenburg and his friends. On 17 November Harden published an article containing unmistakable hints about an unnatural quality in Eulenburg's male friendships, but above all the article attacked the political influence of Eulenburg and his friends on the Kaiser, and called for a removal of that influence 'by any possible means'. ('Praeludium', *Zukunft*, vol. 57, pp. 251–66.) Harden soon showed what means he intended to use when in a long article of 24 November he inserted a short dialogue between a 'Harpist' and a 'Sweetie' showing that he knew that Eulenburg and Count Kuno Moltke referred to the Kaiser among themselves as 'Sweetheart' [Liebchen]. ('Dies irae',

1005.   Holstein to Pascal David
        Copy

Berlin, 19 November 1906

My dear *Herr Direktor*,

How are you? Someone told me recently that you had written two articles on behalf of Alex. Hohenlohe. I would be grateful if you would send them to me. I would very much like to defend him, but do not quite see how it can be done.

The chief objection to the memoirs[1] is that one gets the impression from them of quite a different Chlodwig Hohenlohe than the wise and kindly man whom one thought to have known. To me this was a genuine disappointment.

The publication is said to have seriously injured the Hohenlohe family *tutti quanti* with the Kaiser. General Count Hülsen-Häseler[2] told one Hohenlohe: 'Believe me, the whole Hohenlohe family might as well bury itself.' But all that can change.

About domestic affairs you probably know more than I do, or at least as much, because after the Hohenlohe memoirs there have been all sorts of other publications, or rather revelations.

Publishers have approached me with really fantastic offers,[3] but I haven't the slightest intention of 'making revelations', certainly not now.

Furthermore, Fleischer[4] pressingly urged me[5] to write the monthly article on foreign policy in the place of Hugo Jacobi.[6] I declined because I know that Jacobi was 'official'. If I wrote at all I would want to preserve the calm independence of my own opinion. For instance, in contrast to the official line, I am firmly convinced that a German-Austrian dual alliance would enjoy greater respect in the world than a Triple

*Zukunft*, vol. 57, p. 291.) On the day this article was published Harden wrote to Holstein: 'There are undoubtedly moments when one must and can be content simply to warn people who are politically dangerous'. Harden's method worked, for shortly after the publication of these hints Baron Alfred von Berger, director of the Hamburg Theatre, came to see Harden on Eulenburg's behalf to persuade him to stop his attacks. This Harden agreed to do if Eulenburg promised to stay out of politics. On 14 December 1906 Harden wrote to Holstein: 'The Harpist [Eulenburg] has gone to the land of the lemon trees; has therefore kept his word. For how long?' Actually Eulenburg went to Territet on Lake Geneva. (*Zukunft*, vol. 61, pp. 179–80, 190, 196–7, 258; Haller *Eulenburg*, pp. 342; Bülow, *Denkwürdigkeiten*, vol. II, p. 292.)

[1] The memoirs of Prince Chlodwig zu Hohenlohe (see p. 439, note 1), whose publication had been authorized by Prince Chlodwig's son, Prince Alexander, and which were edited by Dr Friedrich Curtius.

[2] Dietrich, Count von Hülsen-Häseler.

[3] One of several offers was made by Albert Langen, a Munich publisher and founder of the *Simplicissimus*, a magazine of political satire. Langen offered to pay Holstein 60,000 marks upon delivery of the manuscript, and six marks for every copy sold. If Holstein's work sold 40,000 copies, as the Hohenlohe memoirs had done (and Langen was confident that it would), Holstein would receive a total of 240,000 marks. In addition he was to receive one-half of all payments made for newspaper or magazine rights, and two-thirds of all payments made for translation rights.

[4] Richard Fleischer. Owner of the *Deutsche Revue*.

[5] In a letter of 7 November. Not printed.

[6] Editor-in-Chief of the *Berliner Neuesten Nachrichten*.

Alliance made ridiculous by Italy. I told Bülow so, too, but with him Italy is a matter of sentiment.

I had two talks with Bülow, of two hours and of forty-five minutes. I was unable to see any particular changes in him, either mental or physical, but other people are of a different opinion. I am unable to estimate the solidity of his position or his health, but do not believe that a crisis is imminent.

Judging from a distance, I should say that in his impatience Philipp Eulenburg has ventured too far to the fore (they say he wants the Strasbourg job). By doing so he has made public opinion rebellious. Now they will have to wait until public opinion calms down before undertaking any big changes in personnel. Bülow even recently stated that so long as he is Chancellor, Phili will not get to Strasbourg. But Phili is very clever.

Members of Parliament, foreign diplomats, and officials are by now agreed on the complete inadequacy of Tschirschky. It seems to me that Tschirschky is gradually becoming a ridiculous figure. But my opinion of Tschirschky is not impartial. You will in good time be able to form your own considered opinion on this subject.

I hope, dear Herr Direktor, that you are in good health, for that is the wish of

Your sincerely devoted
Holstein.

## 1006.    Holstein to Maximilian von Brandt[1]

Berlin, 20 November 1906

My dear Excellency.

[...] I seem to remember that on the fleet question we were of one and the same opinion, namely

(1) The more we arm at sea, the more we push England into the arms of France;

(2) we cannot, even if we treble our taxes, build a fleet to match the Anglo-French fleet, or even the English fleet alone;

(3) in a war against France alone, as that of '70 showed, the fleet plays an insignificant role.

(4) it is a threat and a challenge to England to say openly—as the Navy League has for years, each time it makes new demands for the navy—that the armaments are directed *against* England.

Points 3 and 4—insignificance of fleet in Franco-German war, and German naval armament directed against England—were mentioned yesterday in the French Chamber of Deputies.

Marschall said to me last summer, after we had discussed all problems of foreign policy for an entire day: 'Yes, the fleet, there is the greatest danger.' The danger is increased by the fact that in ship building (armour plate, etc.) there is a profit of countless millions, far greater than in the colonies. Not everyone who clamours for ships is a selfless patriot.

[1] From the Brandt Papers.

Germany stands or falls with her army, and for that every sacrifice must be made. The fleet increases the number of our enemies, but will never be strong enough to vanquish them. We cannot hope, now or later, for an equal fight at sea. The land army must—as in '70—equalize the inequality of the naval forces.

It is *not* economic rivalry alone that has made England our enemy. This exists in her relations with America and Japan. What is frightening the English is our accelerated fleet building and the anti-English motivation behind it. We have actually stated, not once but several times—and by no means always by non-official authorities—that our naval armament is directed against England and that we should be mistress of the seas. By making statements of this kind, Germany is left to stand alone. We cannot complain if the English finally begin to take us seriously. Perhaps it would be more a matter for complaint if people no longer did take us seriously.

If, in commenting on the debate in the French Chamber which is being resumed to-day, you could write something along these lines, it might be very useful. But in doing so you will be poking into a wasp's nest. Furthermore, a good many papers would not even print it because the Navy League has surrounded itself with a false aura of patriotism. I recall that the *Schlesische Zeitung* printed an article last summer that closed with the words : 'Beside the Navy League stands the Navy Trust.' This article was inspired by me and created some furor in naval circles. Since that time the editor-in-chief, Herr Röse, is said to have received a decoration.[1] [...]

With best wishes for your good health

Your Excellency's sincerely devoted

Holstein.

I recently told Bülow my opinion about Italy and the Triple Alliance,[2] but for him Italy is a matter of sentiment.

### 1007.   Pascal David to Holstein

Strasbourg, 25 November 1906

My dear Excellency!

I want to make use of a quiet Sunday evening when I do not have to prepare the 'next issue' to thank you most warmly for your kind letter.[3] I am enclosing what I wrote about the Hohenlohe memoirs.[4] It was for me a difficult task, because the feeling of veneration and attachment for the deceased, who was always benevolent and kind to me, conflicted with many other sensations. Added to that was my sympathy for Prince Alexander, whose position, as I recognized at once, was doomed to collapse, and an even greater sympathy for the old governor,[5] whose position will certainly not be strengthened by this publication. I hear

---

[1] Holstein refers to the fact that Röse was now no longer following his (Holstein's) anti-navy line. (See no. 986.)

[2] See above, Holstein's memorandum of 27 October 1906.

[3] Of 19 November. See above.          [4] Not found.

[5] Hermann, Prince zu Hohenlohe-Langenburg.

from Berlin that H.M. said in conversation that one might after all have expected Uncle Hermann to have been able to exercise greater authority over his cousin—an official subordinate.[1] That would accord with the remark you mentioned of Count Hülsen-Häseler.

As regards Prince Chlodwig, in my opinion one should take into account the fact that he never had the intention of publishing his notes. Curtius himself says in the introduction that the Prince told him: 'Will you help me to *write* my memoirs?' Then followed the invitation to Schillingsfürst Castle. If I understand Prince Chlodwig correctly, he had a large-scale publication in mind: the life, activity, and personality of Prince Chlodwig Hohenlohe-Schillingsfürst, German Chancellor, Imperial Governor of Alsace-Lorraine, German Ambassador in Paris, Minister-President of Bavaria, etc. etc. To that end, the recollections—that is the notes—should only serve as raw material! A summary was to have been made of these, and at one point or another letters were to have been inserted *in extenso*. But I am certain that the Prince never had a verbatim publication in mind! No, a biography, which Curtius was to have *written* and for which the notes were to serve as source material which was to be used with care and discretion. These notes were to be *used, not simply published*! Prince Chlodwig had not envisaged so easy a task as that. His mistake was to choose Curtius, who is a literary and highly cultured man, but too removed from practical affairs to do a job that involved so many practical considerations. To be sure, he cut a very great deal. I am a good judge of that, because of many many important things that Prince Chlodwig discussed with me, I can find no trace. But he also left a great deal that a practical politician, who knew something of the world, life, and people, would never have left! Prince Alexander's big mistake was that he did not supervise the work with sufficient care—if at all! If he had read the proof copies with sufficient care, he would surely have seen at once that there were ten, twelve, fifteen places at which we would have been *forced* to say: 'That cannot stay in, otherwise there will be the devil to pay!' If he had crossed out, say fifteen sections, everything would have been all right and no one would have become excited. Now the business has cost him his job, which meant more to him than most people assumed. And—all the Hohenlohes are being involved. [...]

Yours respectfully<br>Pascal David

[1] Prince Alexander zu Hohenlohe, who had authorized the publication of his father's memoirs, was the nephew of Prince Hermann and Head of the Administration of Kolmar in Alsace.

# 1907

1008.    Maximilian Harden to Holstein

17 January 1907

Your Excellency,

[...] Phili-Filou[1] has come back from Territet[2] for the Eagle Chapter.[3] He suffered a great disaster with his daughter (secret elopement from home, etc.) and is said to be very run down.[4] The Group[5] is behaving as though it expects and desires a victory for Bülow;[6] expects it with certainty. I would not be surprised if we read one of these days of a meeting between E[ulenburg] and B[ülow]. So much for Phili's alleged *désintéressement* in everything political. [...]

With best wishes for Your Excellency's health

I am your very devoted
Harden.

1009.    Holstein to Bernhard von Bülow
Copy

Berlin, 8 February 1907

Dear Bülow,

To use the historic words of Delacroix: *je félicite votre majesté, je félicite la France*—I say to-day: I wish you and I wish Germany joy. You are a child of good fortune, and I am glad to see it.[7]

Though you and I did not, many others regarded the dissolution as a shift to the left. Many people hoped—and I was afraid—that the election would leave you no choice. This expectation was also clearly expressed in the Press. But things did not work out that way. The new Reichstag offers you a choice between majorities with or without the Centre Party. I hope you will decide to try first *with*, and presume that that is also your idea. Your final appeal to the voters—which was criticized by the radicals for that reason—pointed to the Socialists as the

---

[1] Prince Philipp zu Eulenburg.

[2] See above, p. 447, note 6.

[3] The annual meeting of the Chapter of the High Order of the Black Eagle, with which Eulenburg had recently been decorated. (See above, p. 411, note 1.) With the return of Eulenburg to Germany, Harden resumed his attacks on the Prince in the *Zukunft*.

[4] Eulenburg's third daughter, Augusta, had eloped with the Prince's private secretary, Edmund Jarolymek.

[5] A reference to Eulenburg and his friends.

[6] In the forthcoming Reichstag elections.

[7] In the Reichstag elections of January and February 1907, the 'national' Parties gained heavily at the expense of the Social Democrats.

sole enemy;[1] and the slogan 'without regard to differences of religion' in the Kaiser's speech to the people was surely also inspired by you.[2]

Since the new Reichstag is supposed to be more compliant than the last one, it is possible that H.M. and the various departments will come forward with increased demands. Therein now lies the main difficulty of your position. When I saw you the time before last, we already discussed possibilities of this kind and you said that in such a situation the attitude of the Reichstag and the Press would be decisive.

Now I think that the new Reichstag will also have no inclination to vote funds other than those that are strictly necessary. The expenditures for the army will be among these, for the French are supposed to have overtaken us on arms for the infantry and on guided balloons. The German Reich stands or falls with the army. But the navy is a different story. Large demands for fleet building would now be grist to the mills of our enemies, who are in the process of collecting material for dealing with the disarmament question at The Hague.[3] Therefore if new demands are made, you can hardly counter them more effectively than by stating—or by having someone else state in the Reichstag or the Press: first we will have to await the outcome of the Conference.

With best wishes for the forthcoming bracing of the spirits,

Your

p.a.e. H.

## 1010.   Diary Entry

17 February 1907

I told Bülow and wrote to him that a break with the Centre Party would be harmful, if only because of the Polish question.[4] A shift of the German Catholics to the side of the Poles would have incalculable results.

I further told him that the real reasons for the dissolution had never been expressed. That the Southwest had only been an excuse.[5] He said nothing.

I advised him to discuss the effect of the Centre Party issue on the Polish question with Bethmann,[6] if possible also with the Heads of the Administration of Posen[7] and Silesia,[8] before he made any final decision.

[1] In his speech of 19 January Bülow did in fact direct his chief attacks against the Social Democrats, but he also sharply criticized the Centre Party for supporting the Social Democrats for tactical reasons.

[2] On the night of 5 February the Kaiser told cheering crowds in Berlin that the German people could overcome any forces opposed to them 'if all classes and confessions stood firmly and solidly together'.

[3] For the Second Hague Peace Conference, which convened on 15 June 1907.

[4] See above, Holstein's letter to Bülow of 8 February. Holstein repeated his arguments in a letter to Bülow of 16 February. (Not printed.)

[5] The Reichstag had been dissolved on 13 December when a coalition of the Centre Party and the Social Democrats refused to vote additional funds for the prosecution of the war against guerillas in German Southwest Africa.

[6] Theobald von Bethmann Hollweg. Head of the Administration of Brandenburg, 1899–1905; Prussian Minister of the Interior, 1905–7; State Secretary of the Reich Ministry of the Interior, 1907–9; Chancellor of the German Reich, 1909–17.

[7] Wilhelm von Waldow. Head of the Administration of Posen, 1903–11.

[8] Robert, Count von Zedlitz-Trützschler.

It was after all remarkable that just at this time, when people were trying to stir up Bülow against the Centre, H.M. was showing marked friendliness to the Catholics. (Speech to the people : 'without regard to differences of religion'.[1] Speech at the reception of the Knights of Malta.[2]) Up till now Bülow's strength has lain in the fact that people believed he could get along with the Centre better than anyone else. In this he was considered a specialist. He will never become a specialist in liberalism; in fact, the Liberals would have more confidence in any other Chancellor, even a military man, than they do in Bülow.

Bülow was apparently strongly influenced by the left. Stein.

At the time of the dissolution, B's position with H.M. had become shaky. Perhaps a result of the Press Campaign against the 'personal rule'.[3] I told B. this. Phili [Eulenburg] has a great many connections. The Kaiser decided to wait until the main elections. The Navy League worked against the Centre Party, but the Kaiser said nothing and let the Chancellor take the lead. In case the elections had come out badly, Wedel (Vienna) is supposed to have been considered for the Chancellorship. Radowitz was a candidate immediately after Bülow's illness, but when he was here last month for the meeting of the Black Eagle Order, his friends joked about his candidacy. He himself was deeply hurt when he noticed that his candidacy was no longer being taken seriously.

Last week I was told that Phili's candidate now was General Goltz Pasha. Perhaps because Phili thinks that 'a strong man would secure him greater protection'.

The Kaiser told Bülow (on the morning of the popular demonstration before the palace[4]) : if Bülow had not recovered, H.M. would have chosen Radowitz. A diplomat was required so that people would not think that H.M. wanted to conduct policy himself with Tschirschky. Naturally he preferred to have Bülow stay. Bülow told me that yesterday. [...]

I also told Bülow yesterday that people were saying that he not only had his speeches prepared in advance, but places in the draft were marked : 'the following sentence should be read in a louder voice' or 'a sentimental gesture might be made here'. He denied all this. I told him that such stories originated because he hardly saw anybody but Hammann and Loebell. He should see his Ministers more often and get material for his speeches from memoranda prepared in the Ministries.

I also told Bülow that I had tried to persuade Harden to take a more favourable attitude towards him, but without notable success. When I

[1] See above, p. 453, note 2.

[2] On 12 February the Kaiser received a delegation of the Silesian and Rhenish-Westphalian chapter of the Order of the Knights of Malta, who presented the Kaiser with his Bull of Appointment as a member of the Order, together with the Great Cross and the insignia of an Honorary Marshal of the Order. On this occasion the Kaiser expressed satisfaction about his new relationship with this Catholic Order of Knighthood. 'Your vows also assure me', he said, 'that all of you will prove yourselves true knights of this Order in the battle against atheism and revolution.'

[3] The personal rule of the Kaiser.

[4] After the results of the Reichstag elections were announced on the night of 5 February, the Kaiser and Bülow were cheered by the people of Berlin.

pointed out that under the present circumstances and influences the next Chancellor would certainly have the same weaknesses as Bülow but not the same skill, Harden replied: it was precisely the skill to which he objected. Bülow patched up everything. His successor, less skilful, would bring things to a crack-up. Then improvement might be possible.

Bülow remarked: you can see from that that Harden is still working entirely according to Bismarck's programme. That part about the crack-up Bülow had heard many a time from Herbert.

I also said that Harden had told me that Herbert had broken off relations with Bülow because Bülow had refused to oust me. Bülow confirmed that. A lady who knew Herbert well had told him, Bülow, that Herbert would no longer support him if I remained in the Service.

My impression of the talk with Bülow was unclear. B.B. is apparently being strongly influenced by Stein and Co. [...]

## 1011.   Maximilian Harden to Holstein

Grunewald, 21 February 1907

Your Excellency,

[...] My warmest thanks for Your Excellency's kind letter of yesterday. Mr Whitman[1] is one of those people steeped in the spirit of Herbert [Bismarck].[2] *Inde illae irae.* I only now begin to see clearly that with Herbert the effort to connect every misfortune with the name of his old friend[3] had become an *idée fixe.* Thus for years he told me that Your Excellency's loathing for everything Russian would always prevent the establishment of good relations with St Petersburg. And when I once wrote a very puerile article about Wilhelmstrasse 77,[4] he praised the stuff to the skies, but wrote that the greater danger was at Wilhelmstrasse No. 76,[5] etc. The effect of things like that on a journalist like W. is easy to imagine. I incidentally always thought him mediocre. [...]

With the warmest wishes for Your Excellency's health

I am, your very devoted

Harden   [...]

## 1012.   Maximilian Harden to Holstein

Grunewald, 28 February 1907

Your Excellency,

[...] I have meanwhile studied the painful subject,[6] have read a good deal, have also talked with medical specialists. It will not be easy to find a way to present the matter; but a way must be found. The extent of the evil is frightful. Two Barons Fürstenberg, one Baron von Kurland,

---

[1] Sidney Whitman. English journalist.

[2] Holstein had written Harden on 20 February about how he had snubbed Whitman at a chance meeting. (Rogge, *Holstein und Harden*, p. 125.) Holstein had described the same incident to his cousin two days earlier. (Rogge, *Friedrich von Holstein*, p. 275.)

[3] Holstein.          [4] The Reich Chancellery.          [5] The Foreign Ministry.

[6] The problem of homosexuality in high Court and Government circles.

Egloffstein, Wedel[1] (formerly, I think, with the staff of Kaiserin Friedrich), a young Limburg-Stirum,[2] etc. Lynar[3] was betrayed by a fellow who demanded blackmail payments. Prince F.H.[4] was often followed by officials and had been warned by Borries.[5] He used to dress up as a groom and got particular satisfaction (stimulation) out of the fact that he demanded payment. . . . There has also been suspicion against the man who was supposed to become Master of the Order of the Knights of St John[6] (friendship with a Fürstenberg, who shot himself); though thank goodness nothing came out about it. Although the police are said to have been ordered to find out. Terrible. The homosexual specialists say that His Majesty knows nothing of the whole business, considers it a crime, has never heard of the extensive medical literature on the subject.

With best wishes for Your Excellency's health

I am your Excellency's very devoted

Harden

### 1013. Diary Entry

3 March 1907

[...] In a letter of 16 February,[7] an afterthought of our talk, I advised Bülow not to alienate the Centre Party permanently on account of the Polish question. He did not reply, and now with his speech of last Monday he has broken with the Centre.[8]

Those two speeches, against the Centre and against the Socialists,[9] pleased the Kaiser. [...]

On the disarmament question Aehrenthal is standing firm, but Mérey[10] is unsteady. Here, Tschirschky is unsteady, apparently because he has his doubts about the firmness of H.M.

The right thing would be to make a firm treaty with Austria beforehand. H.M. would probably stand firm if harnessed in pairs.

Marschall would be the most suitable delegate. Wedel would be wax in the hands of Kriege.

### 1014. Diary Entry

5 March 1907

No policy whatever is being formulated any longer in the Foreign

[1] Edgar, Count von Wedel. Master of Ceremonies and Chamberlain at the Court of Wilhelm II; formerly Chamberlain at the Court of Kaiserin Friedrich.

[2] Menno, the son of Count Friedrich von Limburg-Stirum.

[3] Johannes, Count von Lynar. Major in the fashionable Gardes du Corps regiment. On 23 January 1908 he was condemned by a military tribunal to fifteen months imprisonment for abusing his authority for homosexual practices.

[4] The reference is apparently (but see below) to Friedrich Heinrich, Prince of Prussia. Commander of the Schwedt Dragoons. He was dismissed from the army and forbidden the Court because of homosexual practices.

[5] Georg von Borries. Head of the Berlin Police since 1903.

[6] Friedrich Heinrich, Prince of Prussia.          [7] See above, p. 453, note 4.

[8] A speech in the Reichstag on 25 February.

[9] The speech against the Socialists was made in the Reichstag on 26 February.

[10] Senior Department Head in the Austro-Hungarian Foreign Ministry; First Delegate to the Second Hague Peace Conference, 1907; Ambassador in Rome, 1910–15.

Ministry.  The Ambassadors make conversation but make no proposals. Tschirschky wobbles back and forth, totally incompetent.

The Kaiser spoke with indignation about me, because of my reconciliation with Harden.  Bülow said that he too was suspect with the Kaiser because of his relations with me.

Right after Bülow's return I had advised him confidentially to bring up in London shortly the question of the preservation of the Austro-Hungarian monarchy after the death of Kaiser Franz Joseph;[1] to inform them that we had brought up the question in St Petersburg but had found no response; to have Metternich come here beforehand to ask him if England still felt an interest, as she had in the past two hundred years, in the preservation of the Danube monarchy.

Bülow seemed to agree with the idea, made notes, and was going to send Metternich to see me.

Now Metternich has been in Berlin, but he did not see me.  Perhaps Bülow advised him not to, so that I would not find out what he and Metternich had decided.  So far as Bülow is still allowed to do anything at all about foreign policy, he is probably holding his anti-English inclinations because he is afraid that a genuine rapprochement would bring about his removal.  The sending of the New Year's letter to Liebert,[2] the revelations by the *Bayerische Kurier* of the close connection between the Navy League and the German Government[3]—these are facts that may operate against us in England for years to come, as R[4] quite rightly remarked.

Lascelles told Derenthall that after Bülow fell ill he had talked with me about a possible successor, and that I had praised Monts.

I have often praised Monts.  But after Bülow's illness I never saw Lascelles again.[5]

Lascelles is an uncertain quantity, more the King's man than a servant of the Government.  It is significant that he only sees the fanatically anti-German Saunders[6] but none of the other English correspondents here.

Gradually one person after another here is beginning to regard our position vis-à-vis England and France as critical.

[1] See above, nos. 1000 and 1002.

[2] General Eduard von Liebert, the former Governor of German East Africa, was a member of the governing board of the Pan-German League and a keen supporter of the Navy League. The letter to which Holstein refers was sent by the Kaiser to Liebert in his capacity as head of the German League against Social Democracy, and gave as the slogan for the forthcoming Reichstag elections: 'For the honour and welfare of the nation, against Social Democrats, Poles, Guelphs, and Centrists.'

[3] On 9 February the ultramontane newspaper *Bayerische Kurier* had published a number of letters of General Keim, the head of the Navy League, which purported to show that the Chancellor had supported the activity of the Navy League in the recent elections with official funds, and that he had also collaborated in writing some of the League's propaganda pamphlets.

[4] The editors are uncertain to whom this initial refers.

[5] Holstein saw Lascelles immediately after Bülow's collapse in the Reichstag on 4 April 1906. Monts was not mentioned in Lascelles' account of their talk. (*British Documents*, vol. III, no. 398, pp. 332–4.)

[6] George Saunders. Correspondent of *The Times* in Berlin.

## 1015. Maximilian Harden to Holstein

14 March 1907

Your Excellency,

[...] Still no word from the Elbes.[1] Awkward, because I don't want to send anything in writing, not even a message that I want to speak to her. [...]

Your Excellency's very devoted
Harden.

## 1016. Adolph Marschall von Bieberstein to Holstein

Constantinople, 27 March 1907

Dear Holstein,

I am deeply grateful for your friendly letter of the 12th of this month. I was very glad to receive news of you again.

I am very happy about the mission to the Hague for which I am being considered. The material interests me, and I think there are many gaps in the field of international law that can be filled in a useful way. I know nothing about the details on the disarmament question. In my opinion it is a strong presumption on the part of the English Government, after it has just accepted the 'two power standard',[2] to expect other Powers now to call a halt on armaments. I have no fear that the matter will turn out badly for us. Not only do we have an ally in Austria-Hungary, which must keep up its armaments on account of Italy, but also, as the recent article in the *Temps* announced, in France, whose friendship to England is too new to allow her to follow the English line completely. [...]

In old friendship
Your most devoted
Marschall.

## 1017. Diary Entry

17 April 1907

Tittoni actually did make a 'mediation proposal' on the disarmament question to the Chancellor at Rapallo.[3] Germany was to join in the discussion of the problem, but certain limitations were to be agreed on beforehand. Tittoni telegraphed to St Petersburg that Bülow had congratulated him on his proposal. St Petersburg telegraphed this to Berlin.[4] Berlin, however, wired to St Petersburg, Vienna, and Rapallo that the Italian proposal was totally unacceptable.[5] This telegram crossed

---

[1] Frau Lili von Elbe was the divorced wife of Count Kuno Moltke, about whose unnatural friendship with Prince Eulenburg Harden had already made several broad references in his *Zukunft* articles. Harden had championed Frau von Elbe's cause at the time of her divorce from Count Moltke, and from her he had learned many details of Moltke's private life, in particular of his relations with Eulenburg.

[2] The standard that Britain's fleet should always be equal to the combined fleets of her two closest rivals in naval strength.

[3] See Bülow's telegram to the Foreign Ministry of 4 April 1907. (*Grosse Politik*, vol. XXIIIi, no. 7911, pp. 199–200.)

[4] The German Embassy in St Petersburg reported the Italian proposal, but said nothing about Bülow's congratulations to Tittoni. (*Grosse Politik*, vol. XXIIIi, no. 7912, pp. 200–1.)

[5] This was telegraphed to Vienna on 6 April. (*Grosse Politik*, vol. XXIIIi, no. 7912, pp. 200–1.)

with one in which the Chancellor said he had referred Tittoni and his proposal to the Foreign Ministry.[1]

H.M. is in favour of complete abstention from the disarmament question—up till now. For that reason Tschirschky's position is *as yet* firm.

The whole business is significant in showing up the position of Bülow. [...]

1018.    Alfred von Kiderlen-Wächter to Holstein

Bucharest, 20 April 1907

My dear Holstein,

With old feelings of sincere and loyal friendship, I am sending you my best wishes for the great day of the 24th.[2] I was particularly pleased to see you looking so vigorous and well on my last visit to Berlin, and I dearly hope that you will long be granted the ability to look back on your long life of honourable and meritorious service with your present vigour so as to survey everyday affairs with Olympian calm, and—without the cares and excitement of daily pettiness in office—to be able to intervene here and there with your valuable advice.

There is certainly no lack of interest or of exciting scenes in the present world theatre; and it is perhaps preferable to sit as a spectator in the boxes than to be an actor—without any definite influence on the stage management. [...]

Uncle Edward[3] seems to be trying very hard to inaugurate an era of perpetual peace by taking trips. And how mistaken one can be in one's humble vassal-mentality. I had thought that at The Hague it would be a question of political and diplomatic activity. But I was much relieved to see from our choice of delegates that they will only be dealing with legal questions. *Nous verrons.* But however things may turn out, I will be thinking of you very specially on the 24th, and I will toast you in a glass of the best my cellar has to offer in loyal memory of the great stimulus, advice, and support for which I have you to thank. Perhaps that will even help to persuade you to visit me in Sinaia. You would be treated well there, meaning above all that you would not be tormented as a 'guest'! As for the trip, I would be glad to meet you in Pest. Think it over.

With sincere wishes and loyal devotion

Always yours gratefully
Kiderlen.

1019.    Maximilian Harden to Holstein

21 April 1907

Your Excellency,

[...] To-day, just a few of the things I have heard. Exchange of sentiments between Bülow and Phili. *Pax.* They assured one another that they had never ceased having a high regard for each other, no

---

[1] Bülow had already done this in his telegram of 4 April. (See above, p. 458, note 3.)
[2] Holstein's birthday.                    [3] King Edward VII of England.

question of animosity, etc. Relationship to Carlino[1] characterized as 'absolutely first-rate' (not to me, but to one of the intimates of the Chancellor). He has no fault whatever to find with T[schirschky] and was in full agreement with him. Nor did Bülow, whom he very much regretted losing, have any quarrel with T.

This is absolutely reliable.

Phili is feeling very uncomfortable. The affair of his daughter[2] (which is not so simple or so unfavourable to Jarolymek as he is making out; perhaps some 'masculine' jealousy involved) and fear of the 'future'.[3] He feels the desire 'to talk things over' with me. Apparently he is already in Wiesbaden.

The *interlocuteur* conceded that Ph[ili] had already 'sent' General Leszczynski[4] to me, but it was after all easier to talk things over personally.[5] [...]

With best thanks for yesterday and most respectful greetings.

Your Excellency's very devoted
Harden

1020.   Maximilian Harden to Holstein

23 April 1907

A birthday present for Your Excellency :

Lecomte has been recalled, will not return to Berlin, is being given a Ministry.[6] (The Moor has done his work?)

I know about it from a letter of Phili's (from Wiesbaden!!) who is complaining bitterly, and which I will keep until I see you again.[7]

Please observe discretion. The letter incidentally shows an intimate connection with the Chancellor.

Work refuses to flow, despite all efforts.

*Gratulator iterum*

Very sincerely
Harden

[1] A nickname for State Secretary Tschirschky. (See *Zukunft*, vol. 59, p. 46.)

[2] See above, p. 452, note 4.

[3] A pun on the name of Harden's magazine *Die Zukunft*.

[4] Paul von Leszczynski. Veteran of Prussia's wars against Denmark, Austria and France. At the time of his retirement in 1891 he was the Commanding General of the 9th Army Corps. Leszczynski was an old friend of Prince Eulenburg and was also frequently in the entourage of the Kaiser.

[5] According to Holstein's letter to Ida von Stülpnagel of 4 November 1907, it was from Leszczynski that Harden first learned of the Eulenburg-Lecomte relationship. (Rogge, *Friedrich von Holstein*, p. 296.)

[6] The French Ambassador in Berlin informed the German Foreign Ministry that he had for some time been aware of the rumours about Lecomte's homosexual tendencies. Although he had no reason to believe these rumours, he had considered it advisable to persuade Lecomte to go on leave. Lecomte left Berlin permanently on 13 June. (Mühlberg telegram to the Paris Embassy, 13 June 1907. From the Foreign Ministry files.)

[7] In a letter of 28 April Harden expressed regret at not having been able to congratulate Holstein personally on his seventieth birthday. 'I will probably now have to return Ph's letter', he wrote. 'The only things worth mentioning were the wording and the section about Lecomte's future.'

## 1021. Bernhard von Bülow to Holstein

Berlin, 24 April 1907

Dear Holstein,

I just left the Grossbeerenstrasse, where I had hoped to wish you many happy returns of the day personally. Since I did not find you at home, I will have to let these lines convey my best wishes and warm thoughts. I summarize them all in the hope that you will continue to retain for many years that full physical and mental vigour which you possess, together with so many other qualities, in such rare abundance. I would be so happy to see you. Any time would be convenient.

> In loyal devotion
> Sincerely yours
> Bülow

## 1022. Holstein to Bernhard von Bülow
Copy

Berlin, 25 April 1907

Dear Bülow,

On my return yesterday evening I was surprised by the news that you had called. I am very grateful for this friendly attention, as well as for the invitation to visit you. Although, so far as my advice is concerned, it almost seems to me that it no longer fits into the present combination of events and people. But I will come just the same if you want to talk with me because I am always glad to see you. Naturally I want you to name a possible time, for my own can for the most part be arranged.

> Always your sincerely devoted
> H.

## 1023. Memorandum by Holstein

Berlin, 30 April 1907

For the Chancellor.

I altogether agree with the view that it would be useful to submit the report from Pera of 5 November 1901 to Baron Aehrenthal.[1] Of course the imperial marginalia on page 10 will have to disappear because of the expression 'to second'.[2] The situation has changed since the time when the report was written. The aggressive role which Russia at that time played in the Balkans has now been assumed by Italy. Montenegro, once a Russian frontier post, is now an Italian postern gate.

Apart from the periods when Crispi was Prime Minister, Italy has never ceased to subordinate her policy to French advice—or rather wishes. Thus in the alliance against Austria in 1866, thus again in 1878

---

[1] Aehrenthal was in Berlin from 30 April to 4 May. (*Grosse Politik*, vol. XXII, no. 7373, pp. 55–6.)

[2] The report from Pera to which Holstein refers is printed in *Grosse Politik* (vol. XVIIIi, no. 5460, pp. 149–57.) At the part in the report in which Marschall stressed the necessity of supporting and strengthening the Sultan, the Kaiser noted on the margin: 'That is *our* aim and that constitutes *our* task, and Austria would do well to second our efforts.' This note was erased and is barely legible. It was not printed in *Die Grosse Politik*. (From the Foreign Ministry files.)

in turning down the seizure of Tunis suggested by Bismarck and Andrássy.[1] Again following French advice (see the *Giornale d'Italia* of 3 January 1902, talk of Delcassé with Ojetti) Italy turned her attention away from Tripoli and—towards Albania. France would like to have North Africa, with the exception of Egypt, for herself. The various treaties France has made with England as well as Turkey, especially in getting the El Djanet oasis (gateway to the Sudan) and Bilma, admit of no doubts on this point. The *Giornale d'Italia* commented on this on 24 September 1906: 'Our claims for peaceful penetration are made ridiculous, a counterpart to the unhappy incident at San Mun.'[2] Italy, her Government and people, follows the line laid down by France and is trying by every means—consular agents, schools, shipping subsidies, outright pensions, commerce to draw Albania into the Italian sphere of influence. Baron Aehrenthal will be better informed about this than we are. Although they are not in a brilliant financial position, the Italians are spending a lot of money on Albania. The treaties Italy has made concerning the preservation of the status quo *constitute no obstacle for this Italian activity*. Apparently Italy is waiting for the day when, as is hoped, Austria and Hungary will separate, and then, when the two former sections of the Empire are regarding each other with distrust, Italy will bring to fruition her long and carefully prepared plan to take over Albania. Once Valona becomes an Italian naval base, the Adriatic will be closed to Austria as well as to Hungary, and Trieste and Fiume will be ruined.

To hasten this development as much as possible, France is also working for the separation of Hungary. (Pichon.) And the family of Minister-President Kossuth[3] will be drawn over to the side of Italy not only by sympathy but by self-interest.

For the foreign observer it is hard to understand why the Press in both halves of the Empire, but especially the Hungarian Press which is after all not altogether pro-Kossuth, does not draw attention to the fact— not once but again and again—that the consequences of separation would be the ruin of their maritime commerce and the closure of the Adriatic.

When Count Lamsdorff was still Minister we suggested in St Petersburg that Russia and Germany should engage not to seek territorial advantage from possible future internal conflicts in the Austro-Hungarian monarchy.[4] Even in the desirable event that there should be no serious internal conflicts, it seemed a good idea to eliminate the suspicion that is now being nourished by France and England (Chéradame, etc.)[5] that Russia and Germany are lying in wait for the collapse of Austria in order

---

[1] See *Memoirs*, p. 105.

[2] In 1899 an Italian proposal to lease the Chinese harbour and territory of San Mun was rejected by the Chinese Government.

[3] The reference is to Louis Kossuth, Minister-President of Hungary during the revolution against Austria in 1849. Kossuth died in 1894 in Turin, and the leadership of the Hungarian Independence Party passed to his son Franz, who was Hungarian Minister of Trade in the Wekerle Cabinet, April 1906–January 1910.

[4] In the spring of 1905. (*Grosse Politik*, vol. XXII, chapter CLIX.)

[5] See above, p. 444, note 3.

to enlarge themselves. Count Lamsdorff said he was in favour in principle, but then surprisingly turned down the German proposal that he should aid in drafting this short and simple treaty. Presumably he wanted to recommend to the Tsar that he reject the treaty as an act of consideration for His Majesty Kaiser Franz Joseph, but in reality it was probably because the Minister feared that he would otherwise definitively alienate the Panslav elements. We did not pursue the matter further after he refused his co-operation.

What would Baron Aehrenthal say to our discussing this matter confidentially with the English Government and suggesting that the English do as we were doing in bringing up the question in St Petersburg as honest brokers? In doing so one would emphasize that this was not only a question of the imminent collapse of Austria-Hungary, but of composing the fears of Europe by removing a baseless suspicion. Ever since the time of Marlborough, England has shown an interest in the preservation of the Danube monarchy. It would be useful to find out whether this interest still existed. Campbell-Bannerman would by his very nature probably be most receptive to a proposal that increased the chances for peace and made war more difficult. At the same time it would be possible to see whether the oft-repeated English suspicion about Germany's desire for Austrian territory is sincerely meant or only an excuse for agitation against us.

Our attitude towards the Triple Alliance can still be summarized in the words of Prince Bismarck: 'I do not expect much from the accession of Italy, but at least the threat at Austria's rear is removed for certain eventualities.' The Triple Alliance is no embarrassment to us, it involves no sacrifice on our part, and we will therefore continue to foster it as long as Austria considers it useful. *The question as to whether the Triple Alliance actually helps Italy to carry on her propaganda in the Balkans undisturbed and contributes to Hungary's lack of awareness of the Adriatic danger is one that lies within the competence of our Austrian ally, not in our own.*

H.

### 1024. Maximilian Harden to Holstein

3 May 1907

Your Excellency,

[...] Yes, Bülow. There lies the unbridgable chasm. So he not only has the Reichstag in his pocket, but also His Excellency Holstein. *Forever.* To me, his commissions, omissions, speeches, are little better than treason. And his latest speech.[1] . . . Just to think about it makes my temperature rise. But there is no combating such shifty unscrupulousness. Two years ago he was spreading the word: Herr von H[olstein] is

---

[1] Harden refers to Bülow's speech of 30 April in the Reichstag defining Germany's attitude towards the Hague Peace Conference and outlining the country's foreign policy. (See below, p. 465, note 1.) Holstein had written to Harden on 2 May that so far as he could see, Bülow's speech had made a good impression abroad. (Rogge, *Holstein und Harden*, p. 149.)

the author of all our difficulties. So that I heard it from two sources. To-day (through *Temps, Figaro,* Trachenberg,[1] etc., etc.) he is spreading the word : Herr v. H. is inspiring Harden, and thus we are being undermined by moles. Yet shows the most touching friendship for the *inspirator.* Perhaps the main reason for my suffering. *Enfin,* I am sick of the whole business. Trachenberg, Witting,[2] *Temps,* and other riff-raff only say what they have heard from B. and B's creatures. And if that were not the case, that *gentleman* would be obliged to contradict. I am absolutely convinced that he is also superficially *dans les meilleurs termes* with Phili and Tschirschky. Everything an imposture. The only sensible remark came from the Guelph.[3] Otherwise, this Reichstag is ready to applaude the crudest kind of high treason. Only a tempest can help us now. My campaign will have to stop for the time being, after a parting shaft. Otherwise it would look like La Mancha.[4] One cannot repeat the same things forever. I would prefer to write about Colorado beetles. Is Bülow an honest man and 'the best man we have' : *optime.* In my opinion he has caused more disaster to the country than ten Studts would have been able to do.

Furthermore, nine-tenths has been accomplished of what our opponents wanted. Austria the saviour, the leader of the Alliance!! Aehrenthal, who is being fawned upon as though he were a God, loves us as much as Cambon. His official Press writes that Austria is now, as always, 'in favour of equilibrium'. *Sapienti sat.* I am told that 50,000 men are ready to march in Congress Poland. Only they will not march. If they did, not a single Austrian gun would go off. I consider this Alliance quite as ludicrous as the Italian. One may well call it a League of Peace : because it would not survive the first shot.

Your Excellency probably considers all this exaggerated, dillettantish, too extreme. I'm afraid. Can't see it any other way. Otherwise why should I have devoted my small quota of energy to these battles? Surely not to poke needles into Bülow, Phili, or Carlino. And the concern that recently has so often filled Your Excellency, the greatest expert, cannot have been swept away by to-day's breezes of May. An about-face : that is and remains the solution. Two who are utterly faithless : *c'est trop.* They can even see this abroad. The Reichstag is being swindled : and is quite content to be so. The 'honourable friend', Oldenburg,[5] who used to attack the Chancellor, now wishes him a long life. Ditto Trachenberg. *Et le reste.*

[1] Hermann, Prince von Hatzfeldt, Duke of Trachenberg. Free-Conservative Member of the Reichstag, 1878–93, 1907–11; Head of the Administration of Silesia, 1894–1903.

[2] Harden is referring to his brother Richard, who, with the rest of Harden's family, changed his name from Witkowski to Witting. Richard Witting was Lord Mayor of Posen, 1891–1902, and later became President of the Berliner Nationalbank. Harden made unflattering comments about his political pretensions in a letter to Holstein of 11 September 1907. 'He claims to be on intimate terms with the Chancellor', Harden wrote.

[3] On 1 May the Guelph deputy, Götz von Olenhusen, sharply criticized the Chancellor on the Brunswick question in the Reichstag.

[4] Don Quixote de la Mancha.

[5] Elard von Oldenburg-Januschau. German-Conservative Member of the Prussian Chamber of Deputies, 1898–1910; of the Reichstag, 1902–12.

I did not even think the section on disarmament was good.[1] Neither sufficiently to the point nor serious. Irony towards Bassermann:[2] *va bene*; but not suitable towards England.

But why such a sermon? I certainly do not flatter myself on the ability to convert Your Excellency, after so much experience, to my point of view. [...]

That the Duke of Trachenberg thinks he is the coming man could be seen from [his] statement that all Germany wished to retain Bülow. Thanks by back-scratching. *Figaro ci, Figaro là.* When Herbert told him he must by all means get rid of Holstein, he readily agreed and said he was only waiting for the suitable opportunity. He must surely have curried Tschirschky with similar words. If he were foreign minister of the Grimaldis, I might praise such arts. H.M. is supposed to be furious because things are not going fast enough with France. His telegram to Monaco (excessive) was printed in the *Figaro*. The French Press (*Temps*, etc.) first made me a *bête noire*, second the confidant of M. de Holstein, and third raised me into the nobility. A lot at once.

Now I can do no more than beg indulgence for the miserable form of this letter. I am lying down almost all the time, and writing is difficult.

The content? I can do no other.

With respectful greetings<br>Your Excellency's most devoted<br>Harden

The 'discussion' of the budget of the Foreign Ministry was delicious. A bare ten minutes. 'I am in no sense a bureaucrat.' And with that, Wolff-Metternich at the counsel table.

## 1025.   Holstein to Bernhard von Bülow
Draft

Berlin, 3 May 1907

Dear Bülow,

My best wishes for this new epoch in your life.[3] May your burden be light.

To judge from the Press, the statements about disarmament which were discussed on Monday[4] were well received.

Now I want to advise once more that you drum into Aehrenthal the idea that 'Germany, which has no conflicting interests with Italy, will

---

[1] In his Reichstag speech of 30 April Bülow said that the German Government had been unable to find a formula for disarmament that would meet the needs of all nations, and he doubted whether other Governments would be more successful. 'When—I think it was in 1874—the question of international law in wartime was to be discussed at a Conference in Brussels, Lord Derby stated in the name of the British Government that the British Government could only participate in the Conference if the question of the right to seize ships on the high seas were not discussed either directly or indirectly. Gentlemen, we could have done the same thing at this time, and made our participation in the Hague Conference dependent on the condition that the disarmament question not be discussed. In consideration for the Russian plan we have not done so, but restrict ourselves to allowing those Powers that expect some success from the discussion to conduct the discussion without us.'

[2] Ernst Bassermann. Leader of the National Liberals in the Reichstag.

[3] The 3 May was Bülow's birthday.

[4] See above, note 1.

stand by the Triple Alliance as long as Austria considers this to be useful'. This is the central point, everything else is secondary.

If Aehrenthal leaves here with the belief that Italy is really dearest to you, and that Austria can rely more on H.M. than on yourself—a belief that is surely being fostered in many quarters—then the direct exchange of ideas between rulers, to the exclusion of the Chancellor, will become a regular custom.[1] That Archduke Franz Ferdinand has already acted in this manner is a fact whose significance must be considered if one intends to estimate the situation correctly.

Aehrenthal, the spokesman for the Archduke, did not come until the latter had received a clear and satisfactory answer from H.M. to his decisive question. The Archduke and the Minister will now compare notes about with whom it is easier to negotiate and who takes the firmer line, H.M. or yourself.

Always your sincerely devoted<br>Holstein.

Do you think that H.M., perhaps at the suggestion of Tschirschky, has discussed the question of a change in the succession and a new Pragmatic Sanction.[2] I am inclined to doubt it.[3]

## 1026.   Holstein to Maximilian Harden
Draft[4]

Berlin, 4 May 1907

My dear Herr Harden,

I noticed with regret from your letter of yesterday[5] that your physical suffering has been made even worse by your state of mind. If I understand you correctly, you are reproaching me for giving the Chancellor my political opinion when he asks for it. I consider that to be my duty. It is not a question of the person of the Chancellor, but of the Reich. I am not responsible if my advice is followed or not, but I become responsible if I refuse to offer my advice for reasons of personal irritation.

About Bülow you and I have always been of a different opinion. You regard his fall as a good thing under all circumstances, whereas I have asked: 'What kind of successor may we expect?' That is the way we still stand to-day.

The Reichstag has neglected to examine the mistakes of the past. But the mistake we might have faced in the near future, a concession in the disarmament question, has been countered by the Reichstag. Since it

---

[1] At this point in his draft Holstein crossed out the words: 'H.M. will certainly do nothing to discourage it.'

[2] The reference is to the efforts of Emperor Charles VI to secure acceptance by the Powers of a Pragmatic Sanction whereby the integrity of the Habsburg Empire would be recognized and the succession to the throne would be regulated.

[3] Bülow replied on the same day: 'Many thanks for your good wishes and also for the interesting comments that accompanied them. Can you come to see me on Monday afternoon? And would six o'clock suit you? If I do not hear from you, I will expect you at that time.'

[4] The draft corresponds closely to the text of the letter actually sent to Harden. (Rogge, *Holstein und Harden*, pp. 150–2.)

[5] See above, no. 1024.

was you who conducted this campaign, at first even single-handed, I ascribed this favourable result to your credit. The Chancellor first allowed himself to be influenced by the sentiment in the Reichstag, and then also spoke out against participation in the disarmament negotiations.[1] I *know* that other opinions were expressed in other quarters, and therefore felt that the outcome of the debate on disarmament was particularly gratifying. My estimate of our international position remains the same : I am not afraid of any exaggerated desire for action on the part of our enemies, but of our own possible weakness.

That our relationship was disquieting to a great many people was something we knew already. Therefore each of us is fed with material that seems likely to separate us. It is well enough known that the *Figaro* and the *Temps* are fed from Berlin by the same people who have written against me since the spring of 1905. And it is natural that the various organs of Phili should be operating unrestrainedly and skilfully towards the same end.

The most obvious means of countering this would be for us to give up our relationship. But would that do any good? People who are habitual liars themselves would only say this was nothing but a sham and a farce. Furthermore, this would constitute a backing-down. So at least the question has appeared to me on the frequent occasions when I have thought it over recently.

But one may be of a different opinion.

As for the general situation. Yes, it has improved, thanks to the King whose excessive activity has finally made the English refractory. I had long waited in vain for this repercussion, but it is there at last.

A second improvement is the increasing stability of the Russian Government at home. The number of Russians stationed in Poland can be a matter of indifference to us, for they will never march against us. The three Imperial Powers can and will probably co-operate in the various important concrete problems of the present day. I see no danger there. The danger I see—and which you see too—is in our unrequited affection that draws us to the West. That is why I sent you the *Tag* with the brusque negative statement of Saint Saëns,[2] which fully and completely confirms Count Kessler's[3] letter. Do you think *this* danger has been removed? I'm afraid the little 'breezes of May' will be ineffective against things like this.

You know what a very high opinion I have of the influence and power of the *Zukunft*. But in my opinion even the *Zukunft* cannot desert the solid ground of the given facts of the situation. These given facts are:

(1) That the Reichstag has forgotten the past and is dealing with the problems of the present.

(2) That all Parties have promised their support if the Government deals firmly with the big issues of the moment.

(3) That the Chancellor has promised this kind of firmness.

---

[1] See above, p. 465, note 1.
[2] The composer, who was strongly anti-German. (See *Die Zukunft*, vol. 59, p. 119.)
[3] Harry, Count von Kessler. Curator of the Weimar Museum.

(4) That the statements by the Reichstag and the Chancellor have made a predominantly favourable impression both at home and abroad.

(5) Over and against this favourable situation there are the irresponsible influences. Can these ever weigh as much as all the other governmental factors? This is the question Germany must pose to her destiny, to-day just as much as four or eight weeks ago. To direct a general mistrustful attention towards these influences would therefore certainly be timely.

There is no hope of success, however, for an attack that diffuses itself against the entire political world—Government, Parliament, *and* the irresponsibles.

That is how I see things.

However, the embattled Press may have certain tactical rules differing from those of diplomacy, though the general lines of attack and defence surely hold true for both.

With best wishes for your recovery, and the desire to be remembered to your wife, I remain, my dear Herr Harden

Your very devoted<br>H.

## 1027.   Maximilian Harden to Holstein

7 May 1907

Your Excellency,

Ever since Wednesday evening I have had a very painful relapse, or whatever you wish to call it. Then, because of the holiday, I had to prepare an issue earlier than usual. That explains why I have not replied until to-day.[1]

I had no intention of reproaching Your Excellency. (1) I have no right to do so, and I like to mind my own business. (2) I might have assumed, but could not know, that Your Excellency's advice was asked and given. (3) I too would by all means have offered my advice if it had been requested, even to a Herr Hammann, if the interests of the Reich were in question.

Your Excellency unjustly imputes to me the wish to overthrow the Chancellor (for which, unfortunately, I am not powerful enough). I consider the incumbent in this position to be totally without talent in matters of *foreign* policy; what he had when he came into office and what he has to-day—that leaves a balance to which the objective observer need add nothing. I consider him to be under the present circumstances the most dangerous type of propper-upper, whose entire care and not insignificant talent (*de fumiste*) is spent in preventing the German people from becoming aware of their actual and dangerous position, on whose authority and with whose aid everything is falsified and—. And finally, I would like to have a Chancellor whom I could respect as a man.

He is to blame that I wrote the article which curiously enough led to

---

[1] To Holstein's letter of 4 May.

our acquaintance;[1] that to-day everybody is talking about a Holstein-Harden alliance. He is faithless, petty, greedy for applause, greedy for money, and he cringes like Friedrich Haase[2] before every wretch who 'might write something about him'.

Your Excellency does not resent in him what you resent in Whitman. I cannot be the judge of that. But since last summer (Podbielsky, Kardorff, etc.) I have no more respect for the man. Whether he goes or stays is a matter of indifference to me. There is no reason whatever for me to exercise restraint.

Your Excellency forgets the personal because the possibility of giving a Chancellor a bit of good advice here and there seems more important to you. I can understand that and find it patriotic and noble. I am on the outside. Your Excellency too knows political personalities whom you judge harshly and without consideration; but see no reason for restraint just because you know them.

I cannot agree that the Chancellor 'allowed himself to be influenced by the sentiment in the Reichstag'. He had after all refused long before to take part in the debate.

Your Excellency has changed your opinion about the situation fundamentally. Unfortunately I cannot do the same. That bit of disarmament. Quite pretty, but not the world. A token for the Reichstag. A speech oiled with humanity that proclaims his mediocrity. And nine-tenths are enthusiastic for any kind of Suttnerism.[3] Even the dull-witted Campbell treated the matter absolutely correctly: with polite irony.[4] And has anything at all been settled?

If I regarded the situation as optimistically as Your Excellency, well of course I would never have written what I did write. In that case it would have been wicked. I see people who will not change. Their oscillations are meaningless. The frightful syndicate I predicted twelve years ago, after the 'loveliest' speeches, has now been formed. Now there is also Russia-Japan, France-Japan. This will block every further possibility of our development in the wide open spaces. And we are only 'relatively' satiated.

And I see that the old humbug has started again. The newspapers are full of it. 'Everything exaggerated.' The most infamous deceit of a grown-up creative people. It is a crying shame that I cannot believe in Social Democracy.

I do not feel that E[dward] VII has been 'excessively' active. By no means. He goes about his business quietly, sensibly, and makes arrangements for the future. Your Excellency feels the English are hostile to him.

[1] Harden refers to his bitter attack on Holstein in the *Neue Freie Presse* of 3 June 1906, reprinted in the *Zukunft* on 23 June 1906. It was to this attack that Holstein replied in his own letter to the *Zukunft* of 5 August 1906 (published on 18 August).

[2] A famous character actor of the period.

[3] Bertha, Baroness von Suttner, was the founder and head of the Austrian Peace Society, and Vice-President of the International Peace League.

[4] On 6 May Sir Henry Campbell-Bannerman stated in the House of Commons that the British Government, like the German, wanted to avoid all steps in the disarmament question that might cause inconvenience to other Powers.

They are delighted with him, so far as I can see (and I have many contacts there), and they say: a splendid fellow who conducts our affairs superbly. How could this uniquely political people think otherwise? (Everything to the contrary is made to seem so.) The three threats to Britain are bogged down for a long while. And those three, Russia, Germany, America, *can* no longer get together.

All these views Your Excellency believes to be wrong. Our position threatened only by a few fairies. *Sauf le respect*, I cannot go along with that.

*If* these people are as dangerous as Your Excellency supposes, then the danger does not lie in them but in others. And then the picture looks totally different. I have an uncommonly high opinion of the intellect and experience of Your Excellency. But I cannot persuade myself to make Phili the evil genius of Germany's destiny.

Your Excellency says: to write about *that* would still be useful.

But the extraordinary depth of depression into which I have been plunged since the receipt of Your Excellency's letter is caused by something else. I never thought it possible that it would happen that anyone, no matter who, would ever be able to say to me: 'I have wondered several times whether I should break off my relations with you.' Now it has happened. Throughout my whole life I have never given anyone the right to talk down to me; have built up my life piece by piece, all by myself, so as never to have colleagues or superiors. Now I am an old man, and Your Excellency announces in the sick room: 'I have wondered several times. . . .' Why?

Whoever even asks such a question *has* answered it. (At our age we no longer count on our fingers.) Whoever poses such a question to someone else can only have the intention of seriously offending him. Why? I am not in favour of The Hague. But declarations of war à la Port Arthur should after all surely only be *ultimae rationes*. War? All right! But this way?

Bismarck once told me under similar circumstances: 'I can understand how a man with your temperament must suffer from being considered to be so to speak under my patronage. I think however: in friendly relationships one does not long ask the question: which of us is bearing the brunt? Rather one allows the more pleasant aspects of the relationship to override the less pleasant.' Or words to that effect.

It seems to me that this could really be a matter of greater indifference to Your Excellency than to me. (I will not cite my reasons. Besides, am too exhausted.) Even so, the thought of giving up the relationship for that reason never occurred to me. It occurred to Your Excellency 'on several occasions recently'. And Your Excellency tells me so.

B[ismarck] once wrote from Frankfurt to a circle of the high (or highest) officials that he did not intend to come to Berlin: 'One is too badly treated if one is not an Excellency.' And in the same city another genial German wrote: 'Curious that human beings who can otherwise accomplish so much can be completely bound up by pettinesses.'

I do not feel that this personal humiliation has injured me. But it gave me the feeling of a bitter disappointment.

Your Excellency's devoted
Harden

## 1028.   Holstein to Maximilian Harden
Draft[1]

Berlin, 8 [May][2] 1907

Dear Herr Harden,

I just returned and found your letter of yesterday.[3] I have not yet had a chance to read it thoroughly, something I will do this evening. But now, *currente calamo*, I want to write a brief reply which should reach you before the end of the day. I intend to get to the Potsdam station by half past three.

Apparently you do not realize what a powerful impression your last letter[4] was bound to make. Towards the end, after a violent exposition, you say: 'The French Press has made me (1) a *bête noire* (2) a *confident de M. de H.* (3) raised me into the nobility. A lot at once.' And before that, *dans le corps de la lettre*, '*Enfin*, I am sick of the whole business.'

I read all that very carefully and could only say to myself: 'That *may* mean that one is beginning to feel the discomforts of the relationship and the consequences are being considered.'

The purport of my reply was: 'I too have already had all kinds of experiences of that kind, but have ignored them. Nevertheless I would understand it if you were to decide otherwise.'

With your vulcanic temperament one simply considers possibilities that one would not consider possible with other people. Since, however, you thought nothing of the kind, the idea I presented for possible use has no practical significance. I am very glad about that.

From your previous remarks there is no indication that you know that Hatzfeldt-Trach[enberg] is a political suckling of the *Frankfurter Zeitung* Stein. This is notorious and has been the case for years. Stein brags about it constantly. Trach. invites him frequently and lets him disgorge. The whole Reichstag knows it. Hence, too, the 'moles'.[5] Always in the same corner.

Trach. is Stein's candidate for the Chancellorship, and T's latest effort is regarded in the Reichstag as the speech of a candidate.

Did no one ever tell you about these relationships? Curious. It strengthens the mistrust I feel about certain of your informants—about whose identity I have not the faintest notion. But I do think that they try to keep the really serious candidates a strict secret, or would like to do so, at least from the two of us.

Incidentally, I heard to-day that all sorts of things are brewing,

[1] The draft corresponds closely to the text of the letter actually sent to Harden. (Rogge, *Holstein und Harden*, pp. 153–4.)

[2] Holstein's draft was misdated 8 April.     [3] See above.

[4] Of 3 May. See above.     [5] See above, p. 464.

though not on the Chancellor question.[1] I must close. So do not grow any grey hairs on my account. They will come anyway.

With best wishes

Your very devoted

H.

## 1029.  Maximilian Harden to Holstein

9 May 1907

Your Excellency

Many thanks for the friendly letter[2] that calmed me down somewhat.

Ennoblement, *bête noire,* and elevation to the *confident de M. de H.* are things I regard as compliments. Big Paris newspapers have said : let us hope that the Kaiser does not allow himself to be influenced by the violent talk of M. Harden. If this talk has had any effect in the polar regions, I would regard it as having performed some slight service for the future of Germany.

The 'being sick of the whole business' of course had nothing to do with this train of thought. But perhaps I should toe the line a little more in my letters. However Your Excellency has spoiled me. And for weeks I have been very ill. Still so weak and plagued with pains that writing is extremely difficult. Had to lie down again this noon.

No, I did not know about the Trachenberg-Stein relationship. I have always considered him to be a candidate; and have now challenged him so brusquely that Your Excellency may not condone it.[3] But I am really 'fed up' with *this* kind of suspicion.

I am depressed to think that Your Excellency believes me dependent on 'informants'. This is not the case. A little psychology, a little ability to put two and two together; *voilà mes informateurs.* [...]

I remain, Your Excellency,

With best wishes

Your very devoted

H.

## 1030.  Diary Entry

9 May 1907

The *Tsar* ordered that Bülow be thanked for his speech of 30 April,[4] especially for his discussion of disarmament (which he rejected) and for the considerate way he discussed the royal journeys. In Bülow's opinion, Nicholas II believes in the solidarity of monarchical interests. This was

---

[1] This sentence referred, as Holstein wrote to Harden on the following day, to the action taken by the Crown Prince on the Eulenburg question. 'Since everybody is talking about it, it may very well be true. It remains to be seen what effect it will have.' (Rogge, *Holstein und Harden*, pp. 158–9.) On 2 May the German Crown Prince had brought Harden's articles attacking Eulenburg and Moltke to the attention of the Kaiser. According to the Crown Prince, this was the first time the Kaiser had heard the rumours about homosexuality among members of his entourage. (*Erinnerungen des Kronprinzen Wilhelm* (Stuttgart and Berlin, 1922), p. 13.)

[2] Of 8 May. See above.      [3] In the *Zukunft* of 11 May, vol. 59, pp. 201–2.

[4] See above, p. 463, note 1.

not the case with Alexander III. When once, while Bülow was Counsellor of Embassy in St Petersburg (1885 or 86), Queen Olga of Greece said something nice about her uncle, King Georg of Hanover, the Tsar pounded his fist on the table and said: 'All these little kings right and left mean absolutely nothing to me.'[1]

*Aehrenthal*, in contrast to Goluchowski and Calice, is in favour of a conservative Austrian policy in the Balkan Peninsula.[2] He says that Italian agitation in Albania is not so much the work of the Italian Government and its agents as of the Catholic Church. A paradoxical ingratitude of the Catholic Church towards Austria to the benefit of Italy. Kaiser Franz Joseph was in favour of preserving the Triple Alliance if at all possible.

However, in this connection Aehrenthal's distrust of Bülow on account of his Italian relationships must be taken into account.

Therefore I told and wrote Bülow beforehand: 'The German people are suspicious of the disarmament question and of Italy. You must consider that in your speech. You must also be more forthcoming than you usually are with Aehrenthal, for you will probably have been pictured to him as "Italian".'

My belief that Aehrenthal was suspicious was later confirmed by Szögyényi. For when Bülow informed him of his intention to show him an interesting report from Marschall of 3 January 1901,[3] the Ambassador said: 'He has seen it already. You gave me the report some time ago and empowered me to show it to Aehrenthal, who was just passing through here on his way to St Petersburg. Aeh. read it and then said—I would like to tell you this quite confidentially: "I wonder what purpose Bülow had in mind in showing me this report." '[4]

After this remark of Szögyényi the report was not shown to him again. One can see with what thoughts Aehr. came here. Bülow thinks that Aehr's earlier suspicion has diminished as a result of this visit.

Following my advice, and actually going against his own convictions, Bülow took a firm stand in the Reichstag against disarmament, and in doing so won approval. He also told Aehrenthal that Italy had no actual anti-German interests, that we did not consider the Triple Alliance [un]fortunate although we had no illusions about the efficacy of the Italian effort—*le cas échéant*. Prince Bismarck had regarded the significance of Italy's entry into the alliance relationship in the fact that thereby under certain circumstances Austria would have her back free. We would therefore leave the decision up to Austria as to whether the Triple Alliance should continue or not.

The Minister replied to this that there was to be sure a party in Austria which regarded the continued existence of the Kingdom of Italy as a menace and the break-up of Italy as a patriotic duty. But he did

---

[1] In French in the original.  [2] See above, p. 461, note 1.

[3] Holstein refers to Marschall's report of 5 November 1901. (*Grosse Politik*, vol. XVIIIi, no. 5460, pp. 149–57.)

[4] On 6 December 1901 a copy of this report was given to the Austrian Ambassador. (From the Foreign Ministry files.)

not share this view and his All-Gracious Sovereign in particular was very much for the continuation of the Triple Alliance.

Bülow then spoke of the danger of the Adriatic question both for Austria and Hungary. Why was this question discussed in detail in the Press, especially in the Hungarian Press, for instance in the *Pester Lloyd*? Kossuth was an Italian railway director.

Aeh. replied only that he had not yet had time to devote his attention to the Press.

Aeh. showed himself to be conservative. He considered universal suffrage to be demoralizing for all peoples, because all Parties were thereby compelled to cater to the prejudices of the masses. All Parties— Liberals, Centre—were thereby pushed further to the left. Even the Conservatives could only survive in Germany with the aid of the demagogic Landowners' League.

Aehrenthal thinks Russia is very weak, the private soldier very good, the officer decadent. Therefore it is in the deepest interest of Russia to postpone the solution of the Near Eastern question as long as possible.

A high opinion of Stolypin,[1] a very poor one of Witte.

Aehrenthal made a favourable impression on Bülow, less favourable on Mühlberg. Carries himself well, hampered by short-sightedness. Streak of Jewish. Does not particularly inspire confidence.

The conservative Aeh. and the democratic Mühlberg did not get along well together; perhaps Aeh. was too high and mighty.

About the way Tschirschky is pushing himself, both B.B. and M. were of one opinion. Furthermore, everybody involved is agreed that Tschirschky is *below* average, that he himself quite fails to realize it, and is on the contrary very well pleased with himself.

1031.  Maximilian Harden to Holstein

Grunewald, 10 May 1907

Your Excellency

Our letters crossed in the mail. Many thanks. About the Crown Prince, I in my solitude still know nothing.[2] Noticed only the small number of birthday celebrations.[3]

Your Excellency must know that your visit is always welcome and always a pleasure. Perhaps you will come Saturday morning.

At Court they spoke of nothing but 'Roulette' for three days, as I heard from two credible sources.[4] A sensation. And a laughable sniffing about to find out whether I had 'much material'. Otherwise too, the business seems to have a good deal of effect, in so far as a stupid magazine article can.

[1] Peter Stolypin. Russian Minister-President, 1906–11.

[2] See above, p. 472, note 1.

[3] For the birthday of Crown Prince Wilhelm on 6 May.

[4] An article in the *Zukunft* of 27 April (vol. 59, pp. 117–30). Harden had written: 'Prince Friedrich Heinrich of Prussia, because he suffered from inherited sexual perversion, was compelled to relinquish the post of Grand Master of the Order of the Knights of St John. Does a less stern code apply to the Order of the Black Eagle? There is at least one member whose *vita sexualis* is no healthier than that of the outlawed Prince.'

But the cosmetics applied by the official Press!!
Still weak, but still

Very devoted<br>Harden. [...]

## 1032.    Maximilian Harden to Holstein

Grunewald, 12 May 1907

Your Excellency,

Many thanks for the visit and the letter.[1]

'One specific point brought up in the conversation with Your Honour remains to be settled : the consequences that would ensue in case to-day's statement were not deemed adequate. In that case it would not seem necessary to me to proceed to the course of a personal conflict. The institution of the duel has the purpose of expiating and settling an otherwise unatonable insult, and to settle the matter forever. The purpose of this institution, however, cannot and should not be to hinder the clarification of a certain issue. A duel would formally settle the disputed matter, but would make any further effort to establish the truth impossible. I could not be a party to that. For even though I have no reason to doubt the truth of the word of honour which was given to me with certain reservations, it may become a political duty for me, despite all delicate personal objections, to prove the existence of an abnormal (though perhaps idealistic) masculine friendship and the fact that it tends to transgress into the world of politics—something about which I have not the least doubt after a conscientious examination of authentic documents.'

This was preceded only by : 'May I ask Your Honour to regard the following as a supplement to my letter of to-day.'[2]

The letter was sent off at four o'clock yesterday, registered, to Count Otto M. I had also considered the possibility of a special delivery letter; but finally thought I should avoid the appearance of *trop de zèle*. Like Bülow's cook, *j'ai réfléchi 24 heures*; think, however, that I could not refuse that first rigidly qualified statement—at least it was not in my nature to do so. 'I ask you for the sake of the unsullied reputation of the family.' In this frightfully delicate matter, one should not do more than is absolutely necessary.

(1) If I question his word of honour (which I cannot really do in good

---

[1] The quotation that follows in the text is taken from a letter Harden had sent on 11 May to Count Otto von Moltke, the cousin of Count Kuno against whom many of Harden's attacks in the *Zukunft* had been directed. Count Otto had gone to see Harden at his house on behalf of his cousin to persuade Harden to stop his attacks. He offered Harden Count Kuno's word of honour that he had never had sexual relations of any kind with men. This word of honour Harden accepted in a written statement of 11 May, saying that he had no reason to doubt the Count's word. After Count Otto had left him Harden began to wonder whether he had acted correctly, for he wished to preserve his freedom of action in case Count Kuno Moltke and his friends persisted in remaining in the Kaiser's entourage. He thereupon wrote a second statement to Count Otto Moltke which is quoted in full in this letter to Holstein. The whole incident is described and both statements to Count Otto Moltke are printed in the *Zukunft* of 22 June 1907, vol. 59, pp. 405–25.

[2] Harden's first written statement of 11 May. See note 1 above.

conscience), then I must either give satisfaction on the duelling ground or—before the case is *fully* proved—be called an irresponsible calumniator (after this 'most loyal' method of mediation).

(2) The whole comedy *may* be a preparation for a law suit, in which my position would be very bad if I had to prove direct relations with men. The object of these people *may* have been to find out: has he proof of *that*? Otherwise we will bring suit. Now, after the tactics I used, my position seems better; word of honour accepted; and Count Otto is obliged to swear that I told him at once, honestly and without evasion (which he urgently offered), what I meant and why I had published it. Also that this word of honour did not plumb my own thoughts on the matter.

(3) In such filthy business, which can easily turn even well-disposed people against you, every possible concession must be made which does not affect the *cause*. It is really horrible for a house like the Moltkes' to be forced to see this blot brought out into the open.

(4) I think Your Excellency will agree with me that it would be better in *every* sense not to ruin those two completely, but only to hit them so as to render them harmless to the country. It is not pleasant to live with corpses on one's back; even Palézieux[1] has disturbed many an hour for me. Not Bötticher.[2] I consider him to be a basically false person, and he fell like rotted fruit.

It seems to me (pardon!) that Your Excellency perhaps overemphasizes that first letter.[3] The Th. Wolff business is after all child's play in contrast to these *causa*. Would Your Excellency have wanted a letter that said only: 'I have no reason to doubt the assurance given as a word of honour that His Excellency v. H. did not write a letter to Radolin: are you sending us false reports?' Everyone would say: of course one does not write like that. Your Excellency will excuse the comparison. In this case everyone must say: since Harden was certainly not called in to witness the *immissio in anum* (if such a thing happened at all), he would have to say what he said; nor could he have said less; and whoever is satisfied with that. . . .

I can say with good conscience that not for one second was my action determined by *fear*. (Of course Your Excellency does not have to believe it.) I asked: do you not have to do that (not what was requested *at first*) for your own sake, in order to be able to respect yourself. Answer:. . . .

I have never told Your Excellency about all the threats that have been used heretofore (for four months) because this involved delicate matters

[1] Falconnet von Palézieux. Chamberlain of the Grand Duke of Weimar. In the *Zukunft* of 29 December 1906 (vol. 57, pp. 505–10) Harden accused Palézieux of having intrigued for the post of German Ambassador to St Petersburg through influential friends in Berlin and of having forced the resignation of Count Harry Kessler, Curator of the Weimar Museum, in order to curry favour with the Berlin Court.

[2] Harden had for many years been a severe critic of Karl Heinrich von Bötticher, particularly of the role he had played at the time of Bismarck's dismissal. He summarized his views about Bötticher in an obituary article in the *Zukunft* of 16 March 1907 (vol. 58, pp. 387–99).

[3] Harden's first written statement of 11 May. See note 1, p. 475.

with which I felt I had no right to bother Your Excellency. These threats (which even came via Witting; Bülow then asked that I be told: 'as long as he had something to say about it, no such thing would be done to me because it was not nice') did not cause me to retreat an inch.

I intend to do no more after these two letters. And I do not think anyone can take it amiss if now, in my galley-slave days,[1] I do not receive the emissary.[2] [...]

H.M. is said to be angry with Ph[ili] and to have demanded that he and Kuno hurry up and clear themselves.[3] Kuno declared that he would 'bring an action against me'. From the remark of his cousin, I assume unequivocally that the Officers Corps has started some kind of action against him.[4]

Willi Hohenau has blackmailers on his back and does not dare to bring charges before the public prosecutor.[5] Compromised at Court.

Public prosecutor also getting soft towards others. New proceedings contra Chaplain Dasbach[6] (Paragraph 175) have been cancelled. The singer who accused Hülsen of being a fancy boy was consigned to the insanity ward at the Charité 'for observation'; may perhaps be declared insane; then of course no trial.[7] Which Hülsen could only have conducted with the courage of utter desperation. The tactics are transparent.

Stirum's son (9th dragoons)[8] paid up; then when he couldn't do so any longer, he filed a denunciation, swore he was not a homosexual, had nothing to do with blackmailers. He was sentenced to four years in the penetentiary (the offence calls for nine). Public prosecutor and presiding judge saw to it that Stirum's name was not mentioned.

None of this official, but from reliable source.

I don't like illusions, but think that the morass is no longer dangerous. And the stench is prevented from spreading too far.

A little too much talk. Your Excellency will forgive me. Am dead tired.

With the most respectful good wishes from the fiery furnace, I remain Your Excellency's very devoted

Harden.

[1] The days before the *Zukunft* went to press.
[2] Count Otto von Moltke.
[3] See Bülow, *Denkwürdigkeiten*, vol. II, pp. 311–13; Haller, *Eulenburg*, 345–7; Reinhold Muschler, *Philipp zu Eulenburg* (Leipzig, 1930), pp. 621–4; Tresckow, *Von Fürsten*, p. 164; Robert Zedlitz-Trützschler, *Zwölf Jahre am deutschen Kaiserhof* (Berlin and Leipzig, 1924), pp. 160–1.
[4] On 3 May Count Kuno Moltke had in fact been obliged to leave the army until he had cleared his name.
[5] Wilhelm, Count von Hohenau. Aide-de-Camp of the Kaiser; Commander of the First Cavalry Brigade of Guards. On 23 January 1908 he was acquitted by a guard tribunal of honour of the charge of having abused his position for homosexual purposes, but his innocence was not fully established and he was obliged to leave the army.
[6] Georg Dasbach. Member of the Reichstag (Centre Party.)
[7] Georg, Count von Hülsen-Häseler, the General Intendant of the Royal Theatre, brought suit against an opera singer named Frank, who had accused him of homosexuality. Frank was later declared insane and the suit against him was dropped.
[8] Should read: 4th dragoons.

1033.  Maximilian Harden to Holstein

13 May 1907

Your Excellency,
    Many thanks.
    The enclosed letter was received to-day.[1] If the conversation had been conducted in that tone, I would have broken it off.  Actually he was sweet as honey.
    I think I will reply by pointing out that I am not obliged to make a further declaration and that I never concerned myself with the 'purity'. But wanted to inform Your Excellency about the letter.  Perhaps a word should be said about the 'limits'.[2] [...]
    Very miserable, but Your Excellency's very devoted

Harden  [...]

1034.  Holstein to Maximilian von Brandt[3]

Berlin, 15 May 1907

My dear Excellency,
    Many thanks for the belated condolences.[4] Yes, one has to take things as they come.  Also in politics.  The 'sad satisfaction' that Your Excellency mentions, I have to be sure in full measure.  Now that the business is gradually being understood in wider circles.  I myself at the time did not fully comprehend the situation; above all I did not know that Lecomte, the French Counsellor of Embassy, went to Liebenberg every fortnight.  I was only struck by the fact that immediately after our retreat,[5] on the 2nd or 3rd of April, Phili was awarded the Black Eagle at the same time as Radowitz.  Thereupon I handed in my second resignation.
    We will hardly meet with a second Algeciras at The Hague.[6] Public opinion has expressed itself in the Reichstag too definitely against a retreat.  Further, in my opinion our opponents only wanted to bluff, not to bite.  [...]
    With the request to be remembered to your wife,

I am yours very sincerely
Holstein

1035.  Maximilian Harden to Holstein

Grunewald, Whitsun, [19 May] 1907, noon

Your Excellency,
    [...] A brother,[7] sixty years old, a provincial judge, clever, *désinter-*

---

    [1] A letter of 12 May from Count Otto Moltke, who declared that there had been no qualifications whatever attached to Count Kuno's word of honour concerning his sexual relationships, and demanded that Harden define what he meant by an 'unnatural idealistic masculine friendship'.  (*Zukunft*, vol. 59, p. 424.)
    [2] Harden replied to Count Moltke on 14 May that he felt there was no need to say more than he had said already.  (*Zukunft*, vol. 59, p. 424.)
    [3] From the Brandt Papers.
    [4] Brandt's letter to Holstein was not found in the Holstein Papers.
    [5] In the Morocco crisis, at the Algeciras Conference.
    [6] The Second Hague Peace Conference, which convened on 15 June 1907.
    [7] Harden probably refers to his own brother, Dr Julian Max Witting, a judge in Braunschweig.

*esse*, not very well-disposed towards me, came to see me; and I told him about the Moltke case. As a captain in the home guard, he found nothing to criticize in the conduct of the opponent.[1] As a criminologist he thinks in a case when the truth cannot be fully established before a specially selected criminal court, two years' imprisonment; and it could never be fully established. He himself had the impression from the material[2] that only Phili had been sharply attacked, not K[uno]. He believes: a court of honour will probably be the next step (unfortunately, in the case of generals, to be selected by His Majesty) which could summon me as a witness (though admittedly I do not have to appear). Then after the cleansing had taken place, I would have to face a duel because of my conduct, of which he therefore disapproves; and perhaps even, if K. still wanted it, face a court trial which would be even more unfavourable for me. He would therefore have advised a refusal *on principle*; perhaps too, to have done nothing after the first declaration but to have let the people come to me.[3] That first declaration ('I have no reason to doubt') meant nothing, cleared nobody, and gave me a relatively more favourable position, without curbing the campaign itself; showed only good intentions in not going so far as a denial of all personal honour.

*Refero*. I do not really consider this opinion to be the final word. I do not regard the chances at a trial as being so unfavourable. Although I no longer have any doubt (according to what I have heard recently) that the challenge, etc., was done by order of His Majesty; and from that quarter influence on legal proceedings would always be possible. The memory of people who would fear giving offence to H.M. is curiously capricious.

I did not ask the legal expert's opinion about publication because it was certain that he would be definitely against it. This affair certainly has its great problems and difficulties. I think that everyone would be against it for whom the political interest was not so great that it would outweigh everything else. Even clever people (I could see this in the legal expert, too) are inclined to believe that the importance of this affair is being exaggerated. [...]

With thanks and best wishes
I am Your Excellency's very devoted
Harden [...]

## 1036.  Maximilian Harden to Holstein

22 May 1907

Your Excellency,

*Entre un monsieur*, non-political, playwright. 'Just think, the day before yesterday I accidentally met Police Commissioner Krüger at a party. He is in charge of the homosexual department. A fine fellow.

---

[1] On 16 May Count Otto von Moltke sent Harden a challenge on behalf of his cousin Count Kuno with the demand that he receive an answer within twenty-four hours. Harden rejected the challenge on the following day, stating in his letter to Count Otto that he had already given his reasons for avoiding a duel. (*Zukunft*, vol. 59, pp. 424–5).

[2] Harden's articles in the *Zukunft*.          [3] See above, p. 475, note 1.

Extremely frank. Spoke a good deal about you. "H. opened up the whole business. Since then all hell has broken loose. Recently I had to go through the *Zukunft* from 1893. But nothing ever comes of it all. The Counts, etc., turn to us, and we see to it that everything is straightened out".' (In such cases I of course make no further enquiries.)

I simply take the liberty of putting this little detail on record. [...]

Your Excellency's very devoted

Harden

### 1037.   Maximilian Harden to Holstein

24 May 1907

Your Excellency

[...] The sewer business still overflowing everywhere. *On ne parle que de cela chez nous*, somebody at Court wrote me.

Yesterday evening Geheimrat Rathenau[1] called to take me for an automobile ride. Even he, who usually pays no attention to anything but his own affairs, talked to me about it and said the Kaiser was very excited about the whole business. It *seems* that H.M. talked about it while hunting at Madlitz (where R. was with him).

Kuno adopted a light tone in talking about it to Fräulein von Monbart (cousin of the Head of the Naval Cabinet[2]); it was a quite ridiculous rumour.

I am told I don't even begin to guess to what extent homosexual and other perverted activity has spread, especially in Potsdam.

May I request that you do not mention old Herr Rathenau, who worships H.M.? I told him a little about Lecomte and Morocco, in order to have him pass it along to Hollmann to-day.

In great haste, Your Excellency's

Very devoted

H. [...]

### 1038.   Maximilian Harden to Holstein

26 May 1907

Your Excellency

will have read to-day's *Lokalanzeiger*, third page of the supplement. Harden backs down; law suit; Kuno's lawyer, von Gordon (the best).[3] Special from the correspondent in the Reich capital; a Dr Horn. Never heard of him. The Chancellor's warning has thus done no good. I am sorry on the monarchy's account. [...]

I hear H.M. says he doesn't want to see Phili any more and intends to find new people with whom to associate.

People are saying *all over*: everything comes from Herr von Holstein. Even journalists. I wouldn't be surprised if we don't soon read about it.

---

[1] Emil Rathenau. Director of the Allgemeine Elektrizitäts-Gesellschaft (AEG); father of Walther Rathenau.

[2] Georg Alexander von Müller. Admiral; Head of the Imperial Naval Cabinet, 1906–18. Fräulein von Monbart was the sister-in-law of Admiral von Müller.

[3] Harden refers to Moltke's intention to institute legal proceedings against him.

I don't yet know whether I should reply *at once*; will think it over to-night. I am sorry for the monarchy. In this law suit I may be condemned, will probably be physically ruined. But in ruthlessness I will astound even my enemies. I didn't want to.

> 'With hesitant resolve and vacillating mood
> I drew my sword; against my will
> While it was mine to choose!
> The need is dire, all doubts are fled,
> I now fight for my honour and my head!'

There will be corpses. The loathsome practice on which this regime is based—the practice of hunting down any man who speaks his mind with every means, with prostitution of the law courts and intimidation at the point of a gun—this practice may yet again triumph. I will try to see to it that it will be for the last time. A noble assemblage will be brought before the bar.

Is this conduct of a Lieutenant-General[1] and an Abbot[2]—from the first visit of Berger[3] to this whitewash in the Press—is this the conduct of a nobleman? Can anybody wonder that so many honest and cultured people in this country are Social Democrats?

Enough. The Chancellor had the right instinct in at least wanting to spare us this disgrace.[4] Did he want to? Whether he was in earnest or whether he really wants to see an uncomfortable opponent[5] jailed and killed off: this will be seen from whether the public prosecutor takes up Moltke's suit or whether he is obliged to take up his suit in a private capacity. The 'public interest' is surely no longer involved, now that he has been dismissed. The Government, even if it cannot prohibit the trial, can at least order the public prosecutor to reject the suit.[6] [...]

> With sincere good wishes I am
> Your Excellency's very respectful
>
> H.

## 1039. Maximilian Harden to Holstein

1 June 1907

Your Excellency

[...] Someone 'close' to Count K[uno] M[oltke] (probably the Abbot) sent a letter to the *Tageblatt* that is going the rounds of the newspapers. Meritorious Officer, war veteran, very painful to be dismissed under such circumstances, will prove that he has no perverted inclinations; libel suit (no longer: suit through the public prosecutor) against M[aximilian] H[arden]; wants to prove 'from what source this

---

[1] Count Kuno von Moltke.  [2] Count Otto von Moltke.
[3] See above, p. 448, note 6.
[4] Bülow wrote (*Denkwürdigkeiten*, vol. II, pp. 292-3) that he had tried to prevent a trial and the inevitable public scandal, but that the military advisers of the Kaiser compelled Moltke to bring suit against Harden. See below, Harden's letter of 1 June.
[5] i.e., Harden himself.
[6] According to German law the public prosecutor could only take up a case if it lay in the public interest. Moltke's suit was in fact rejected by the public prosecutor, so that he was obliged to resort to a private suit.

information is emanating *in the last analysis'*. This leads one to believe that they are actually aiming at Your Excellency (or at the Chancellor?).

If only for that reason, Bülow's efforts to prevent the trial will probably be of no use. The *Figaro*: *MM. Harden et de Holstein triomphent sur toute la ligne*. As though it were all a Gallophobe intrigue, anger perhaps that the channel Lecomte–His Majesty has been cut.

Sad that, as I understand, the engagement of Hohenau's daughter has been broken off for that reason.[1]

The provincial judge-brother[2] writes that he considers a precise, factual presentation on my part to be absolutely necessary to counter the false reports and distorted presentations of the case. But now I have said once and for all: until official steps make a trial certain, I will make no move of any kind. A nasty position. The newspaper reports do not look very promising for *me*, I'm afraid. After all, however, why worry about myself? Here big interests are at stake. If it were not too quixotic and subject to misunderstanding, would write to His Majesty.

The matter stands at present thus, as I believe to know for a fact: *maison militaire* etc. is raving, wants to take away Kuno's uniform and Phili's Black Eagle; for that reason, as they believe themselves lost without 'purification', they intend to bring suit. BOTH OF THEM. (In order not to be witnesses and under oath?) The Government absolutely against a trial, but powerless.

I do not know whether the *epistola ad Rathenaum*[3] was not my twelfth of March.[4] The *Tägliche Rundschau* to-day: 'The *Zukunft* is silent'. Etc. [...]

With sincere regards
Your Excellency's very devoted
Harden

1040.   Maximilian Harden to Holstein

3 June 1907

Your Excellency,

Many thanks. The Court report almost unbelievable.[5] Found out about it from another source two hours after Your Excellency's kind news. *Journée des dupes*. To-day I feel as though my nerves could stand no more.

It is the first case I know of that a Court report has been false. Situation *unchanged*. His Majesty: they should confess their guilt or bring suit. That H.M. should have heard of my intention (to keep quiet for the time being) is in my opinion, after what I have heard, out of the

---

[1] See above, p. 477, note 5.          [2] See above, p. 478, note 7.

[3] Not found. Rathenau, on behalf of the Chancellor, had tried to persuade Harden to institute a law suit against Eulenburg, a proposal Harden rejected. (See Rogge, *Holstein und Harden*, pp. 166–7.)

[4] A reference to the date of German retreat in the Morocco question.

[5] Incorrect information about the personalities under attack in the report issued daily to the Press about the Kaiser and Court.

question. That the group[1] should ever regain influence is considered *at the top* to be impossible.

I believe (in the interests of the Reich I am obliged to say: I fear) that the preventive action will fail because no one dares to speak frankly; either to H.M. or to K[uno] M[oltke]. As soon as K. even initiates the libel suit the business can no longer be stopped, with all the consequences that will ensue. It seems to me that the Chancellor fails to take this into account. In my opinion he should, if he really wants to prevent it, either present the case frankly to H.M. (something that has *not* been done) or oblige K.M. for 'patriotic' reasons to do nothing for about a fortnight (which would not cause any surprise, because legal proceedings often drag on for a long time.) Otherwise we will have a situation in which *nobody* wants the trial, yet it will still have to be conducted— and then with the utmost ruthlessness.

Politically it seems, according to what I have heard, that the battle is undoubtedly won. A turnabout is considered to be absolutely unthinkable.

With sincere regards

I am Your Excellency's devoted

H.

## 1041.   Maximilian Harden to Holstein

5 June 1907

Your Excellency

Now the dreaded diversions are there after all.[2] What days! And what nights.

Now that I no longer am in control of the campaign, now that the Press has mobilized, I am no longer responsible. *La faute à l'ennemi.* Not a soul learned anything from *me.* [...]

With respectful regards

Yours very sincerely

Harden

## 1042.   Maximilian Harden to Holstein

15 June 1907

Your Excellency,

I was so very sorry, yesterday of all days. But it was not my fault.

The hearing was held to-day.[3] I hope I got through this enormous difficulty safely. (1) By hiding nothing. (2) Fulfilling my duty as a witness. (3) Giving away nothing. (4) Not undercutting the witnesses for the next trial[4] or banishing the terror in Liebenberg. I hope. This

---

[1] Eulenburg, Moltke, *et al.*

[2] Moltke's private libel suit against Harden.

[3] In order to clear his name, Prince Eulenburg, instead of initiating a law suit against Harden, requested the provincial public prosecutor in his own district of Prenzlau (where the Eulenburg family estate of Liebenburg was located) to investigate the records of his past life. In this investigation Harden was summoned as a witness and asked to produce evidence that Eulenburg was guilty of homosexual practices in the sense of Paragraph 175 of the law code.

[4] The forthcoming Moltke-Harden trial.

declaration, in which every word was weighed, cannot be presented to His Majesty as 'purification'.[1]

Phili is really wonderful. To butter me up, he inserted a compliment to me in the charge sent to the public prosecutor. 'A writer of MH's reputation'. Wonderful.

After this declaration he will have to bring suit or go under, I think.

The judge at the hearing, who behaved very well, said himself that this whole procedure was 'hokuspokus'.[2] And as we were conversing pleasantly went so far as to say that he did not really see where Moltke found anything libellous. He had the articles right there, and could find nothing.[3]

The Elbes are coming to Berlin to-day.[4] I don't know how long they will stay. [...]

The 'bag' is respectable : Willi[5] and Tütü[6] are out, Phili's resignation (handed in), will be accepted.[7] Lecomte gone and discredited,[8] everything savouring of Camarilla at least made much more difficult. (That is what I meant with the title 'Just a few words';[9] these did the trick in the end.) I think, however, that the position of the Chancellor has become very weak. After his diplomatic efforts (and the deceitfulness) I have observed in recent weeks, I cannot say that I regret it.

H.M. does not exactly approve of the praises of his oldest, I understand.[10] [...]

Carlino[11] still a long way out of range. [...]

To anticipate distortions by the Liebenberger, I at once sent my testimony (against a Press law) to the newspapers.

With sincere regards

I am Your Excellency's very devoted

Harden

1043.  Maximilian Harden to Holstein

20 June 1907

Your Excellency,

Many thanks for the friendly letter.

Even I have never heard anything comparable in the way of wild and

---

[1] In his statement Harden said he had never accused Eulenburg of practices actually punishable by law, and could himself not bear witness to such practices because he had never had occasion to observe them. Harden maintained that as a witness he was not legally required to present the evidence of those who might have more information to give about Eulenburg's life, or to reveal their names. (*Zukunft*, vol. 59, pp. 409–10).

[2] This was not the public prosecutor in Prenzlau, but a judge in Charlottenburg before whom Harden gave his testimony.

[3] The articles in the *Zukunft* about which Moltke was instituting his libel suit.

[4] See above, p. 458, note 1.

[5] Wilhelm von Hohenau. See above, p. 477, note 5.

[6] Kuno von Moltke.

[7] Bülow had already informed Eulenburg on 11 June that his resignation had been accepted.

[8] See above, p. 460, note 6.

[9] An article in the *Zukunft* of 15 June 1907 (vol. 59, pp. 367–74) in which Harden reviewed his motives for his attacks on the Eulenburg 'Camarilla'.

[10] The German Crown Prince was being widely commended for his courage in bringing Harden's attacks on the Eulenburg circle to the attention of his father.

[11] Tschirschky.

general abuse. The impression on me (the strongest) is after all a matter of indifference. But the cause itself is seriously endangered. *C'est à refaire.*

The official Press is sounding a warning. Exactly the same tactics as with Miquel, Podbielski, H.—excuse me, I forgot that Your Excellency doesn't permit such talk.

I could make a scandal that would rock the world (frightful material) and wanted to avoid it in the interests of the monarchy and the Reich. The Chancellor of the German Reich has allowed the scandal to be forced upon us. Because he, unintelligent as ever, had hoped that I was virtually unarmed and that he could use this occasion to get rid of the second inconvenient person also. Actually: the third.[1] Excuse me!

The French newspapers are *absolutely marvellous.* Actually proof enough of how far treason must have spread already.

For me it is an epoch in my life.

Your Excellency's very devoted

H.

### 1044.    Maximilian Harden to Holstein

8 July 1907

Your Excellency,

That the law courts will bring out the truth is in my opinion out of the question.[2] Never. Vide Leckert-Lützow, Tausch[3] (even then: Phili; Marschall was on the wrong track; the commissioner was partly in the livery of Liebenberg, partly in that of Waldersee), Peters.[4] A friend of mine, a clever man and politically akin to Your Excellency, *Reichsgerichtsrat* Mittelstädt, always used to say that a petty court [*Schöffengericht*] was the most unsuitable tribunal for handling such affairs.[5] Of course one must do everything possible. Nevertheless I believe that a bad outcome (for me) is very probable. Only one thing is certain: those people are out, besmirched, and can never be cleansed. That will have to be my consolation.

Rathenau went to see Bülow the night before last. *Niente.* The Chancellor considers the trial a misfortune, with regard to foreign opinion.

He told someone else that it was too bad Harden was so often so incorrectly informed. Quite objectively, I do not find this to be true on important matters. [...]

Your Excellency's very devoted

H.

---

[1] Harden refers to Eulenburg, himself, and Holstein.

[2] Holstein had stated this belief in a letter to Harden of the previous day. He had also noted that Harden was again being represented as the instrument of his vengeance, although Harden's campaign had been going on for over three years whereas their acquaintance was only eleven months old. (Rogge, *Holstein und Harden*, pp. 178–9.)

[3] See vol. III, p. 652, note 3.

[4] See vol. III, p. 295, note 1.

[5] The Moltke-Harden law suit was to come before such a court, which consisted of a judge and two lay jurors.

1045.  Maximilian Harden to Holstein

17 July 1907

Your Excellency

[...] Lucanus is supposed to have had some bad days since 3 May and to be already one foot out of a job.[1] That a Loebell clique is campaigning for the succession is something Your Excellency has known longer than I. On the other hand I know something that Your Excellency does not know : that our acquaintance is now exactly one year old, and that it would be pleasant if we could both recover our health so as to be able to celebrate this anniversary in the rococo of Potsdam.[2] But please don't be alarmed. The handwriting alone surely shows how far away I am from recovery. [...]

With best wishes for the health of Your Excellency

I am your very devoted

Harden [...]


1046.  Diary Entry

13 August 1907

Prince Bismarck again and again expressed the firm conviction that the Kaiser would never again sign an order for mobilization; he lacked the necessary courage. [...]

Advice given to Bülow for Swinemünde.[3]

Because the Russian Government cannot conclude an alliance with us both because of the antipathy of its people towards Germany and because of its constant dependence on the French money market, it must be fully reassured on this point. The era of alliance treaties may well be nearing its end. The long-term peace treaties backed up by heavy armaments were an invention of Bismarck. Before that, one concluded an alliance in order to go to war immediately. Germany-Italy, 1866. The Holy Alliance was directed more against revolution than against other states. Bismarck gave birth to the Triple Alliance, then came the Dual Alliance, and now the alliance bouquet of King Edward. But interests can bind even without a treaty of alliance. And a treaty without interests does not endure. King Edward makes alliances as a pastime. But he is now becoming more friendly towards Germany so as not to stand alone vis-à-vis English public opinion, which is becoming cool towards the whole business, to the advantage of Germany. The upper ten thousand in England hardly have any illusions that in case of war they would have to reckon with the possibility of surprises from India as well as from Ireland. This thought does not make war any more popular. As a keen observer, King Edward has kept his eye on the barometer.

[1] Because of his failure to inform the Kaiser about Harden attacks against members of his entourage, a task the Crown Prince undertook on 2 May. (See above, p. 472, note 1.)

[2] Two days later Holstein wrote : 'Incidentally, you miscalculate our jubilee by one month. A year ago to-day we regarded one another as *chiens de faïence*, that is, as "legendary creatures".' (Rogge, *Holstein und Harden*, pp. 182–3; see also, p. 485, note 2.)

[3] The Kaiser, accompanied by Prince Bülow, had met the Tsar for talks at Swinemünde from 3–6 August. (See Rogge, *Friedrich von Holstein*, p. 283.)

As for France, she has become more dangerous to her neighbours by her anti-militarism than by her militarism.

The Balkan situation to be discussed in the sense that it is both in the German and Russian interest to preserve the status quo as far as possible and to see that things go slowly there, for Russia can hardly wish to have the Straits question definitely settled before Russia has regained her full strength.

Bülow spoke along the above lines.[1] Found little change in the Tsar, optimistic about the internal situation, with conservative tendencies and the desire to be on good terms with Germany for reasons of monarchical solidarity.

Isvolsky, more frank and intelligent than that deceitful Lamsdorff, judges the internal situation rather more pessimistically, and for this reason alone was thoroughly anxious for peace.

Bülow also explained to the Minister and to the Tsar that the danger of a Japanese attack was very remote because the Japanese Government had to reckon with the possibility of a sudden rupture of its relations with America. Even if both Governments, Tokyo as well as Washington, were peacefully inclined, a massacre of Japanese in California might stir up passions and lead to a break.

After Swinemünde, Bülow wrote Aehrenthal a private letter in which he informed him of the sense in which Balkan questions had been discussed there.[2] This letter seemed very desirable to me. Bülow also wrote about the changed attitude of the King and English people, and also about the reasons for this change (Ireland, India) with a view to the forthcoming meeting of the Austrians and the English.[3] The latter will of course try to persuade the Austrian cabinet to adopt a policy of action in the Near East. [...]


1047.    Holstein to Bernhard von Bülow
         Copy

Berlin, 29 August 1907

Dear Bülow,

From the size of the paper you can see that I have the intention of being lengthy.

First of all I want to thank you very much for the letter I received yesterday[4] which I read carefully on the sunny sands of the Teltow Canal. I assumed as a matter of course that you proposed nothing to Cambon.[5] But His Majesty had most likely done so already with

[1] See *Grosse Politik*, vol. XXII, nos. 7375–9, pp. 57–72.
[2] Not found. See *Grosse Politik*, vol. XXII, p. 72, note *.
[3] Kaiser Franz Joseph and King Edward VII met at Ischl on 15 August. (See *Grosse Politik*, vol. XXII, no. 7380, pp. 72–6; Rogge, *Friedrich von Holstein*, pp. 285–7.)
[4] Of 27 August. Published in Rogge, *Friedrich von Holstein*, pp. 288–9.
[5] The French Ambassador had paid a visit to Bülow at Norderney on 24 August. (*Grosse Politik*, vol. XXIii, no. 7275, pp. 596–7; vol. XXIV, no. 8290, p. 234.)

Etienne.[1] (See enclosure.)[2] That Cambon for his part made no offers of a concrete nature proves that he and especially his Government are not concerned about Germany's attitude. As in June 1905, H.M. will have given away so much that there is nothing more left to give.[3] And always *à l'oeil*! That is his speciality. He will, even if he reigns for another twenty-five years, always let *la proie* get away and chase after *l'ombre*. His foreign policy is sterile, his naval policy is sterile, and neither one nor the other will have any practical result for both are built up on false principles.

He likes to begin his foreign policy with an attempt at intimidation, but retreats if the opposition does not at once give in. (Krüger Telegram, speech at Tangier.) This characteristic, which at first was recognized only by Uncle Edward, is by now common knowledge. For that reason it will be difficult to find anyone stupid enough to give in to us before H.M. has time to do so himself.

The naval policy is of benefit to the naval trust (armour-plating, etc.) and the promotion of naval officers. For the rest of Germany it is detrimental and an indubitable danger both in foreign and domestic affairs. The Kaiser's speeches about the fleet, the Navy League, and the convulsive naval armaments—these are the things that have consolidated an overwhelming naval superiority against us. At no time and under no circumstances can our navy hope to hold its own against this superiority. For that reason this naval policy is sterile. If it is nevertheless continued —Tirpitz is said to have demanded two men-of-war beyond his original programme—then this would fall into the category of dangerous playthings. The Liberal—or Radical—English Government made a start to reduce the strength of the English fleet. The opposition and Admiral Fisher[4] shattered this plan merely by pointing to the intentions of the Kaiser. This makes it possible to understand how the English Naval Attaché, Captain Dumas, could sing eulogies to the Kaiser in Kiel about 'the splendid fleet, which owed its existence entirely to the iron will of His Majesty'. But also the three dreadnoughts that are now being built in England owe their existence indirectly to the iron will of H.M., although Dumas will not have mentioned this.

It is childish to state that our navy will be able to face the combined forces of England and France. It is also childish diplomacy when Etienne or Radolin dangle before us the possibility of drawing France away from England over to our side. What can England offer the French, and what have we to offer? Overseas? And an attack along the Vosges no longer

---

[1] On the evening of 25 June 1907 the Prince of Monaco and M. Etienne, the former French Minister of the Interior and Minister of War, dined with the Kaiser. Etienne indicated that a 'beau geste' on the part of the Kaiser towards France in Morocco would make possible 'bon accord' between the two countries. According to the Kaiser's report to Bülow of the conversation, he had told Etienne that Germany had made enough gestures and that it was now up to France to give some solid evidence of her goodwill. He demanded a firm alliance with France first; then he would make concessions in Morocco. (*Grosse Politik*, vol. XXIii, no. 7257, pp. 571–4.)

[2] Not found.　　　　　　　　　　　　[3] See above, nos. 891 and 911.

[4] Sir John Arbuthnot Fisher. First Sea Lord, 1904–10.

has to be considered. Any worries that may have remained about *that* after Algeciras have been swept away by H.M. (Lacroix,[1] Monaco, Etienne, Mabilleau.[2])

In 1898 you and I brought up the idea in Paris of co-operation on specific issues. Delcassé let the matter drop after Hanotaux had given it favourable consideration.[3] In 1898 such co-operation might still have been quite useful to France under certain circumstances, for at that time there was as yet no entente with England. To-day the French no longer need us. Only the fear of a bad temper on the part of Germany would to-day induce them to make friendly advances to Germany. But H.M. regards it as his chief task to remove this fear. For that reason France, when sooner or later she consigns the Algeciras Treaty to the waste paper basket, will hardly make any concessions to us in exchange.

There is a remarkable difference at present between the policy of the three Imperial Powers and the policy of the three Western Powers.

(1) I see from the newspapers that the legal reforms sponsored by England are now to be forced upon the Sultan after all. This means a hastening of the break-up of Turkey, and therewith a blow to German as well as to Russian interests, not only for the future when Turkey no longer exists, but already for the present, because Islam is made aware that Germany is not a support, not even a parachute. It would have been better for us—not to mention Russia—if Aehrenthal had stuck to the 'conservative Balkan policy' which he explained to you.[4]

(2) The Italian-Austrian 'friendship demonstration' that we are now witnessing has in its exaggerations an unstable quality, not to say a dishonest one. I find that this is also the opinion expressed by well-known Austrian journalists. Romstedt, for instance, points to the difference between Tittoni's opinion and that of the sufficiently well-known instinct of the Italian people, and he warns against cherishing illusions.

Among the possibilities for suspicion, the most obvious is that Aehrenthal has not gained the impression that Germany will follow a definite policy in either the Turkish or the Italian question. For that reason even he is stressing a policy of 'conciliation', that is, a policy of giving in sooner or later. So far as I can see, that is now the foreign policy of the three Imperial Powers, whereas England and France are quite openly following a policy with definite aims, and Italy too is steadily pursuing her national aims, although she is not in a position to operate quite so frankly as England and France. The three western Powers did not commit themselves to this dynamic policy until they were confident that they did not have to fear a war with a Great Power. England, which for a time was considered bellicose, is suffering from internal disorders. The things I told you about this have since been thoroughly substantiated. The Radical Government has proclaimed a state of siege in Ireland

[1] See above, nos. 891 and 911.

[2] Léopold Mabilleau. President of the National Federation of the Mutualité Française. On 26 June 1907 Mabilleau had visited the Kaiser at Kiel in the company of the Prince of Monaco, and had promised to work for an alliance between Germany and France. (*Grosse Politik*, vol. XXIi, no. 7258, pp. 574–5.)

[3] See *Memoirs*, pp. 113–14.           [4] See above, p. 461, note 1.

and is arresting one Member of Parliament after another. From Calcutta 'serious disturbances' were reported a few days ago, although the English Press prefers to maintain a total silence about things like that. These symptoms show that England has a particularly great need for peace and that she would restrain France from a European war if there were any danger. But there is no danger, because they know that German policy is above all else following the lode star of conciliation towards the West. The Kaiser wanted and wants it that way.

The only danger I can see is the repercussion the Kaiser's sterile policy will inevitably have at home. This danger is a great one. When people once begin to see that the sacrifices that are being demanded *crescendo* for the navy are purposeless tomfoolery, then Hervéism[1] will develop to such an extent that a nervous character like H.M. will feel obliged to reckon with it. Then we will have reason to fear a *domestic* Algeciras, and that means—into the frying pan.

The naval question is complicated by the activity of Spahn which surely has a perfidious intent.[2] I hope I am wrong. Under the circumstances, I fail to see what you would be able to do to further the cause of sound common sense. You would only be able to influence the Reichstag and the Press through people who would be more reliable—or rather, more discreet—than those who were used last year in the memorable campaign. On that I have no opinion *in concreto*. But I cannot get rid of the feeling that the way H.M. is conducting affairs—always arming and always ignominiously backing down or running after somebody—that this cannot go on much longer. [...]

With best wishes,
Your sincerely devoted
Holstein.[3]

### 1048.   Maximilian Harden to Holstein

Grunewald, 11 September 1907

Your Excellency,

[...] I will not trouble Your Excellency with my anti-Bülowisms. I have no doubt whatever that he is talking as the H[annoverscher] C[ourier] reports (only of course more cautiously, more impersonally).[4]

---

[1] The policy of class warfare and opposition to compulsory military service advocated by Gustave Hervé, who was ejected from the bar in France on this account. He later became an ardent nationalist and patriot.

[2] At a public meeting in Rheinbach on 11 August, Spahn, the leader of the Centre Party in the Reichstag, declared that Germany should spend an additional 40 million marks a year on her navy. Bülow, in his reply to Holstein of 3 September, believed that Spahn was simply following the trend of German public opinion 'which strangely enough is more pro-fleet in the west and south than on the waterfront'. (Rogge, *Friedrich von Holstein*, p. 292.)

[3] In a letter to his cousin of 31 August Holstein wrote: 'The last two days have been filled with writing a long reply to Bülow. But it will hardly do any good. Bülow is thoroughly capable of seeing the right thing to do, but the Kaiser says and does what *he* wants, and Bülow is dragged along. [...] Here and there I can neutralize the small bad influences, but when the Kaiser has distorted ideas about foreign or naval policy—I am too weak to do anything about that.' (Rogge, *Friedrich von Holstein*, p. 287.)

[4] Harden refers to an article of 3 September attacking Holstein and various members of the present Foreign Ministry staff, especially Under State Secretary Mühlberg. Holstein wrote

The people who lay it on thick think they are doing him a favour. But don't dare to 'submit' such prickly matters. For one and a half years he has allowed a friend who has done a good deal for him to be abused by his *canaille* and to be blamed as the source of all our troubles. I have enough if I think of Miquel, Podbielski, Lucanus, Posadowsky, or even of Phili. Perhaps Herr von M[ühlberg] has become a little inconvenient recently.

Furthermore: from only one quarter as yet his *Geheimer Rat* Scheefer is suddenly being vehemently attacked as a homosexual, the Chancellor is said to have been involved in a similar blackmail affair, Scheefer is being called 'his better half', the Chancellor 'is in exactly the same position as Prince E.', his nephew lived with Jarolymek, etc.[1] This came out to-day. Obviously Liebenberg inspiration. 'The great unknown figure behind Harden behaved outrageously towards members of the Round Table.' Pretty. *Cela recommence.* The attack on Scheefer presented as though it were backed up by facts.[2]

The *HC* and the *Indépendance* so far absolutely silenced. French Press again raging against me. *Confident de M. de H[olstein].* Too much honour.

Things look bad, it seems to me. The reply to Pichon's note![3] As against that (after Casablanca), Olmütz[4] is nothing. The French definitely count on the peaceful revision of the Treaty of Frankfurt. Our Press, led by Bülow (who *only* thinks of himself) says nothing or chatters nonsense (for instance, that we should now get a harbour in Morocco as compensation for allowing Clemenceau a free hand!!) And England knows that H.M. is only concerned in forming a coalition against his uncle.[5] High seas fleet. Prince Heinrich 'the pride of the nation' (according to experts, absolutely unsuited for top command post). Germany the block of granite, the model for all others. Just like old

to Harden on 12 September that he accepted the attacks against himself with the indifference of a man of seventy who was 'finished' anyway; but he was disgusted that the Chancellor did nothing to defend hard-working men like Mühlberg against similar attacks. (Rogge, *Holstein und Harden*, pp. 205–10.)

[1] In his above-mentioned letter to Harden of 12 September, Holstein suspected Hammann of having inspired the rumours about Scheefer, who, as the confidant of Bülow, was regarded by Hammann as his most dangerous competitor.

[2] On 16 September Holstein wrote to Harden: 'As regards Bern. Bülow specifically, I don't know what he has done to offend the Round Table [i.e. the Eulenburg group]. Do you? If he tried to sever the Lecomte connection I can hardly blame him, although at the time I refused to tell you about Lecomte. [See Rogge, *Friedrich von Holstein*, p. 296.] I find it less admirable that he stands by and allows Delbrück to represent me as the chief instigator of the whole mess.' (Rogge, *Holstein und Harden*, p. 212.)

[3] During the disturbances in Casablanca on 31 July, a number of Europeans were killed and European property was damaged. On 5 August a French warship bombarded the city, and five thousand French and Spanish troops landed. Fighting between European troops and the native inhabitants continued throughout the month of August. In a note of 2 September the French Embassy notified Germany of France's intention to establish, with the support of Spain, provisional police in those treaty ports of Morocco where such action seemed necessary to maintain order. The German reply of 8 September acknowledged the necessity of the French move, but noted that the action was provisional. (*Grosse Politik*, vol. XXIV, no. 8295, p. 240.)

[4] See p. 248, note 4.                    [5] King Edward VII.

times. And not a soul stirs. 'Splendid speech.' November: entry of the vanquished into London.[1] [...]

Our position reminds one of that of France before Bonaparte picked up Britain's glove. Instead of that lame reply, Retreat No. 4, a polite communication to M. Cambon that within a week order must be established according to the articles on the Police of the Algeciras Treaty; otherwise steps may be taken. *As yet*, probably no one would have made a move. Six corps mobilized. This is a question of the last possibility of regaining former prestige and to see to it that the Crown Prince will still have a Reich. To do that, every means is justified, I think. A person who only lives in the newspapers and in the afterglow of last night's editions might be up to the job of *portecoton*, but not to that of Chancellor in times like these.

If one were only allowed to talk! To talk openly for twenty-four hours! Can such an institution be maintained? Can one allow a hard-working people to be defrauded so systematically? And is it reprehensible to attack an official who has been a 'master' in organizing this deceit? [...]

I am Your Excellency's very devoted
Harden.

### 1049.   Maximilian Harden to Holstein

Grunewald, 18 September 1907

Your Excellency,

I hope you are as well as may be assumed from your kind and most gratefully received letter. Then Your Excellency will have enjoyed those few nice days (here only three).

*Quant à moi*, I am either done for (*paralysé*) or temporarily sterile. Impossible to fill even a postcard with passionate phrases. Always a dull headache and the nerves of a weepy girl. Yet for a fortnight I have locked myself away from the world to be able to get on with the work. In vain. I will have to give up the *Zukunft* if things go on this way. A mad situation.

Of what can Your Excellency have been thinking when you spoke of important questions that I might perhaps deal with now?[2] I wracked my weary brain over it in vain (the fragments proved to be empty). Everything 'pending' has after all been dealt with, to the best of my ability. Morocco at the moment so uncertain (probably until the end of the week, when Regnault[3] will have finished;[4] until the next instalment) that it would not be advisable to write on Tuesday what will be read on Sunday. Besides, have written volumes about it already. Everything *frustra*. The artfulness (or, to express it less politely, the deceitfulness) of the people in power is so polished that from within and without

---

[1] Harden refers to the prospective visit of the German Kaiser to England. (See below, p. 509, note 4.)

[2] The letter to which Harden refers has not been found in the Harden Papers.

[3] French Minister in Tangier, 1906–12.

[4] Regnault had gone to Rabat to talk with the Sultan of Morocco.

nothing disquieting leaks through. Until it is too late. Within, a *bloc à la Clemenceau*, without, a *coiffure à la Louis Napoleon*. Until it is too late. What difference does it make to somebody who is only interested in himself?

Now everybody is 'satisfied'. Exemplary politics. Even the Agrarians (Oertel)[1] and the Pan-Germans are not railing about electoral rights, nor about Morocco; on the contrary: they find the compensation in Anatolia very seductive.[2] This slogan has become popular.

Can Your Excellency really assume that I am afraid of the RH (*Right Honourable, not* Reich Hound) Hammann and his gang? It almost sounds that way.[3] Hurt me. But I would be unable to defend myself against such a suspicion. 'I, whose cold wounds ache: and now to be nettled by a parrot.'

No, the situation is different. In the first place, I find the whole business really too *mesquin*. Petty [people], petty means. A vermin exterminator, not a hero is needed there; and even though I do not consider myself to be a hero, still I do not fancy myself as an exterminator of vermin. In the second place, to me the guilty one is not the servant but the master. The master, who always knows exactly what is going on. *Cui bono?* The servant rarely, the master always. If H[ammann] provokes attacks on Your Excellency, B[ülow] should step in. (It is after all notorious that HE unleashed the pack against me; H[ammann] would be glad if he had nothing to do with me—on account of the boiling oil on his head.) I do not think it right always to blame Herr von Holstein for Bülow's French policy; or, *si parva licet componere magnis*, to thrash H., the servant, for the dishonesty of his master; because the former is after all there to deal the cards as he is ordered. [...]

If B[ülow] wants Herr von M[ühlberg] as State Secretary, it is not because he is the most suitable (surely he was only that as head of the Economic Division), but because he is someone who could never become a rival with His Majesty. After the manner of Kleinflottbeck,[4] nothing statesmanlike about it. After all, a State Secretary should really be someone who has been an ambassador or could become one; the only exception would be the extraordinary talent and knowledge, the experience and authority of Your Excellency. Can I warm up to M. as St. S. if I am anxious to form an objective opinion?

The whole business would not be worth talking about if the Chancellor did his duty and protected his officials. If he told H[ammann] and St[ein]: I will no longer tolerate such filthy business. But I am by no means certain that officially he does not want to dispense with Herr von M[ühlberg] as he did with Herr von Holstein. Or whether he did not speak damned differently to Cambon, Etienne, Huret,[5] and Company than he did to Your Excellency.[6]

[1] Dr Georg Oertel. Editor-in-Chief of the *Deutsche Tageszeitung*.

[2] A reference to the Sultan of Turkey's concession to the German-controlled Anatolian Railway Company to build the Bagdad Railway.

[3] The letter to which Harden refers has not been found in the Harden Papers.

[4] Bülow's villa on the Elbe.          [5] Jules Huret. Editor of the *Figaro*.

[6] See Bülow's letter to Holstein of 27 August 1907. (Rogge, *Friedrich von Holstein*, pp. 288–9.)

If Your Excellency could look at what is going on without feelings of personal sympathy, you might perhaps think much the same. [...]

It is impossible to conduct a serious and effective policy with this Kaiser. The Chancellor sees to it that this does not penetrate to the general consciousness, and that each morning everything is freshly varnished. Also a system. But as compared to that, what difference does it make whether the Press Bureau whips up a lather out of dirty water? After all, His Highness [Bülow] does the shaving himself. I am trying in vain to express myself clearly. Am to-day a poor attorney. But, *ceterum censeo....* And it is not nervous fear that determines my attitude. Herr Hammann cannot frighten me. [...]

Your Excellency's very devoted

H.

## 1050.  Bernhard von Bülow to Holstein

Norderney, 22 September 1907

Dear Holstein,

[...] The Austro-Italian friendship has, as you once rightly said, something false and hence something unhealthy about it. Nor will this acorn ever grow into a great oak. It grew (1) out of the ever-increasing desire for peace and quiet on the part of the old Kaiser, who also wants 'no trouble' on his southern frontier. (2) out of Aehrenthal's desire to improve relations between Austria and Italy (as well as with Bulgaria and Serbia) which had been strained by the somewhat brusque manner of his predecessor.[1] The turn-about was probably facilitated by the fact that our poor Monts had made himself so unpopular in Rome that in contrast other antipathies faded into the background. That intelligent Stock,[2] who was here, told me that the Italians had been disappointed both economically and politically by the French, that Barrère was finished; England was and remained, if only for geographical reasons, the *carte forcée*; thus Italian policy turned out to be an egg-dance between England and ourselves. Here too the activity of the Pan-Germans is detrimental, for they have a gift for making us hated everywhere. When a Pan-German travel agency was attacked in the Latin sector of Tirol, a high source in Vienna dropped the remark that Austria should come to an understanding with Italy about this territory. That they should settle their old differences along the Adige alone, but that both forbade the interference of the Pan-Germans. Just as two schoolboys, who have long been accustomed to beat each other up during the recess, turn upon the busybody who noisily and clumsily mixes into their quarrel.

In Vienna, Archduke Franz Ferdinand seems to have gotten up on his hind legs against the Magyars. I do not think it at all impossible that the Archduke, once he comes to power, will bring the Magyars to reason. I do not think for a moment that the latter would seriously let it come to a fight with Austria, much less a secession. Only they are unutterably spoiled.

[1] Count Goluchowski.
[2] Head of the Chancellery at the German Embassy in Rome.

Hohenlohe-Langenburg will shortly resign. Wedel is to take his place. Tschirschky is going to Vienna, and I understand that he is more annoyed than delighted about it because in spite of everything he would have preferred to remain as State Secretary in the proximity of His Majesty, or perhaps would have preferred Paris. As his successor I have proposed Mühlberg as first choice and Kiderlen as second. H.M. could not decide in favour of the one or the other, but instead wants an acting ambassador, and as such Schoen has been selected. I hardly know Schoen; but I was not displeased by what I saw of him. He is independent, even towards the top; energetic, not unskilful. I hope he will work out all right, although I would personally have preferred Mühlberg or Kiderlen. How long Schoen will remain is of course another question. All the foregoing, of course, absolutely confidential!

Tirpitz impressed me as being quite sensible during his recent visit. He is convinced that we will never be able to have a fleet that could match the English, and in opposition to many other currents and despite various technical supplements and improvements, he is holding firmly to his Navy Bill which is designed gradually to build up a fleet that is only intended for defensive purposes. [...]

With kind regards and good wishes from myself and my wife,

Most sincerely, your
Bülow.

1051.　Holstein to Bernhard von Bülow
　　　　Copy

26 September 1907

Dear Bülow,

I was depressed by your letter,[1] received this morning. Once again you have subordinated your sound common sense to the decisions—or let us say the whims—of the Kaiser. Monts, of whose uselessness and even harmfulness no one is so sincerely convinced as yourself, remains at his post. Tschirschky is going to Vienna instead of to Rome (where he would be least bad): a schemer from Saxony with a Viennese wife out of the third or fourth drawer. Those two will receive social snubs, and the diplomatic reports *s'en ressentira*.

To Strasbourg they are sending a man with the Langensalza medal, who is perhaps even an Alsatian *home ruler*—the Catholic element is of no importance whatever—as the actual ruler.[2] How can you justify such a thing? The trouble is, to be sure, that these matters are not decided according to your ideas, but according to the by no means infallible political instinct of the Kaiser. In this basic pattern of our national life nowadays, which is becoming more and more evident, there is a national danger, not only from abroad but perhaps even more *at home*, because slowly but surely people will lose confidence in this manner of ruling. What that means in dealing with the destructive forces that are at work, no one needs to tell you.

[1] Of 22 September. See above.
[2] Karl, Count von Wedel, who had won the Langensalza medal while serving with the Hanoverian forces in 1866 in the war against Prussia.

You know, my dear Bülow, that my loyalty to you has undergone severe tests. I have stood by you, and for years, as long as my strength permitted, I have tried to help you under circumstances where nineteen out of twenty would have lost their confidence and their patience. I did not forget that in October 1900 you wanted to treat my nomination to the post of State Secretary as a Cabinet question. It would have been better for you, for me, and for many other reasons, if I had at that time tried to see how long I could have gotten along with His Majesty. But this did not happen, and this backward glance cannot totally blind me towards the present. By your present most recent system of *optima voluisse sat est*, that is, of simply letting things take their course, our country not only loses the advantages of your many and versatile talents, but in addition you become the cover for things for which you can hardly answer, or for which you should not answer. This opinion is unfortunately spreading, and to be honest, there are no facts at hand with which to contest it, even if one could contradict in good conscience.

If you ask me : 'All right, what practical steps do you suggest?' I can only answer with the counter-question : 'Can things still be changed?' If the answer is yes, then send Tschirschky to Rome and—if Köller is to be dismissed—put in his place a good honest pre-'66 Prussian, for instance Schorlemer.[1]

But that will probably no longer be possible, because the Kaiser has gradually become accustomed to Sultanesque methods of rulership. These cases are after all only two isolated needles in a large coral reef. I am therefore resigned to the fact that in this case as in countless others, my advice will go unheeded.

Please present my respects to the Princess.

With old feelings of sympathy and sincerity,

I remain, my dear Bülow
Your most depressed
Holstein.

### 1052.   Bernhard von Bülow to Holstein

Norderney, 29 September 1907

Dear Holstein,

Many thanks for your letter of the 26th which I received yesterday. My thanks are not the less sincere because our points of view diverge on certain (important) matters, although not fundamentally. Rest assured that contradiction and criticism from you do not offend me, because I know that these are occasioned not only by friendly feelings towards me, but by political experience and political acumen of a rare quality.

For Strasbourg, the most important thing seemed to me to be to send a governor there who did not from the beginning think it was his task to foster a policy of conciliation towards France from the banks of the Ill. I think that, among the candidates for the Strasbourg post, Hermann

---

[1] Klemens, Freiherr von Schorlemer-Lieser. Head of the Administration of the Province of the Rhine, 1905–10; later Prussian Minister of Agriculture.

Hatzfeldt and Radowitz would have been inclined to pursue such a course. Since Bethmann is indispensable here for the time being, I thought that for this reason the selection of a general was indicated. Certain characteristics of behaviour and a certain financial position are necessary in the Reich territories which are less important in the rest of Germany. Among the military men, only Hülsen, Plessen, Lindequist,[1] and Wedel came into consideration. His Majesty would not release Hülsen. Plessen and Lindequist are worn out physically and up till now have been primarily active in the service of the Court. I do not deny the drawbacks of Wedel. But he possesses a quality particularly appropriate for Strasbourg, he has dignity. He will not run after the French. He is too reserved to do that. Besides, I have a stronger influence on him, who may some day become Reich Chancellor but who *bona fide* does not aspire to the post, than I have on people who regard Strasbourg merely as a *stepping stone* to Berlin. I have advised Wedel to retain Köller. H.M. likes Köller. I hope Köller will remain until we find a suitable successor for him.

With regard to Vienna, I am sure I may, according to my old habits and confident of your discretion, tell you everything with complete frankness. Tschirschky was no more the candidate of His Maj. for Vienna than Wedel was for Strasbourg. The manner in which Tschirschky worked for a conciliation with France via Monaco during my Easter holiday predestined him for Paris, where he himself wanted to go.[2] He is of course not the ideal ambassador for Vienna, but as a Saxon he will be well received both by the Kaiser and by the heir to the throne. A member of the middle class has an easier time in Viennese society than a member of the North German nobility. Of course I would prefer to have him in Rome. But this was the one post he had made certain of not receiving by obtaining a medical certificate that his chronic intestinal catarrh could not stand the climate there.

I am truly sorry that I was unable to push through the appointment of Mühlberg or Kiderlen as State Secretary. You know how much I think of Mühlberg. Nor can one deny that Kiderlen has the best political mind in the Service. Although more or less indifferent to Strasbourg and Vienna, H.M. insisted on having an active ambassador as State Secretary. In this category I consider Schoen to be the best. Whether he will last long? If he should leave, I am thinking of him for Rome.

With Moltke, the Minister,[3] I have discussed the question of electoral reform with the idea that this action should be carried out by the Ministry of the Interior. Moltke did an excellent job in East Prussia. He is a true Holsteiner, slow, very circumspect, but with *common sense*. On the question of electoral reform, real triumphs are being scored by

---

[1] Friedrich von Lindequist. Governor of German Southwest Africa, 1905–7; Under State Secretary of the Reich Colonial Office, 1907–10; State Secretary, 1910–11.

[2] Bülow is implying here that he had spared the present German Ambassador in Paris, Holstein's friend Prince Radolin. (See below, Holstein's letter to Radolin of 15 October 1907.)

[3] Friedrich von Moltke. Head of the Administration of East Prussia, 1903–7; Prussian Minister of the Interior, 1907–10.

political cant. The Liberals are calling for the Reichstag franchise,[1] although they know that therewith they will be ground between the millstones of Social Democracy and the Centre; the Centre itself is holding back its wishes on this point in order not to antagonize the Conservatives. There is hardly a question that demands more careful handling. [...]

With kindest regards from my wife and once again thanks for your letter.

As always your faithfully devoted
B.

### 1053. Maximilian Harden to Holstein

3 October 1907

Your Excellency,

Thank you so much for the friendly letter. [...]

As regards Austria I am to be sure as pessimistic as possible.[2] She cannot fight for us, nor even wish us well. Her primary concern is to keep clear of Wilhelmish adventures. Russia, England, and thus also France are important to her. I could even imagine some arrangement with Italy; especially in case of an actual advance into Turkish territory. And has Austria given up all German aspirations? I do not think so. The Bavarian Commander-in-Chief is Franz Joseph's son-in-law,[3] three-quarters Austrian. I regret that I see these things in a different light than Your Excellency; but no one can go *contra naturam.*

A later publication of the *Zukunft* is impossible; thus the opposition will hold the field for at least nine days. It is hardly possible that everything will be over on the 23rd.[4] Newspaper lies and misrepresentations have begun again. The affair is terribly difficult, and it may be the end of me. Still I have the feeling that it was necessary. My attorney[5] who of course (like all the others) has not yet taken a single step, has telegraphed that he wants to talk things over; so I must race to Munich and back. In the coming weeks there will hardly be any opportunity to think of work; it is horrible; always to be plagued by these court matters; every day six false reports. I have no illusions about this matter.

Saturday will commemorate fifteen years of the *Zukunft.* All alone, maybe six times away for three or four days. No wonder that one is tired out. I have never felt so miserable as I do now.

It is not clever of Bülow to bring suit against Brand.[6] They will try to

[1] A demand for equal universal suffrage in voting for members of the Prussian Chamber of Deputies, a system that already applied in voting for members of the Reichstag.

[2] Holstein had written to Harden on 29 September that in one respect Harden resembled Bülow, for neither had any use for Austria. (Rogge, *Holstein und Harden*, pp. 217–20.)

[3] Leopold, Prince of Bavaria and head of the Bavarian army, was married to Gisela, the eldest daughter of Kaiser Franz Joseph.

[4] The date set for the Moltke-Harden trial.

[5] Max Bernstein, a Munich lawyer.

[6] A writer named Adolf Brand had accused Bülow of homosexual practices in his journal *Die Gemeinschaft der Eigenen* (The Community of Kindred Spirits). Bülow promptly sued Brand for libel, and in a brief trial on 6 November Brand was sentenced to eighteen months in prison.

ascertain what role he played in the Phili affair. And with all this hokus-pokus, my affair will only be discredited. *Enfin*, one should not undertake the impossible. [...]

*Soror Imperatoris*[1] is in Munich and wants to see me; I will unfortunately hardly have time.

With best wishes I remain

Your Excellency's devoted

Harden [...]

1054.   Holstein to Bernhard von Bülow
        Copy

Friedrichsroda, 4 October 1907

Dear Bülow,

My warmest thanks for your kindness in informing me about the Tschirschky case. Unfortunately I cannot with the best will in the world change my opinion, which is admittedly of no importance.

There is no unsuitable appointment about which one could not say that a still more unsuitable appointment might have been made. In Tschirschky's case this would not even have been easy, because in addition to his other drawbacks there is also the fact that Aehrenthal has become aware of his inferiority and up till now has always treated him accordingly. This was after all known in Berlin. But in this as in other cases it was not a question of finding a man for an important position, but a position for an important man. Tschirschky wanted to go to Vienna, and probably arranged the business with His Majesty. Now T. will, as a result of diplomatic and social ill-treatment, either sulk or, like other insignificant people, he will seek his salvation by subjugation to the wishes of the Government to which he is accredited. And the Viennese aristocracy will be less tolerant towards an obscure Viennese woman[2] than towards a foreigner—about that we can surely have no argument.

No, it is a disastrous choice. The only sensible thing would have been to give Tschirschky the opportunity to fight his way through the Reichstag this winter. If he had succeeded in this, he would then have more prestige as an ambassador than he has to-day, for his appointment can now be regarded in Vienna as a proof of the small value we place on Austria's friendship.

Is postponement no longer possible? I suppose not, for otherwise you would probably have done so. Then, my dear friend, I can do nothing but to repeat my deep regret about a choice that will be detrimental for the future and that will later on be charged to your account, even if perhaps unjustifiably.

Always your sincerely devoted

Holstein.

---

[1] Princess Charlotte of Saxe-Meiningen, to whom Harden had been introduced by Dr Schweninger and from whom Harden received information about affairs at Court.

[2] Tschirschky's wife, the daughter of a factory owner from Budapest. (See Bülow, *Denkwürdigkeiten*, vol. I, p. 406.)

### 1055.  Maximilian Harden to Holstein

13 October 1907

Your Excellency,

(1) I would like to propose further:[1] to omit the words 'under my signature'. Reason: the possibility of the malicious insinuation: he usually writes in the *Zukunft* without a signature. (Your Excellency will understand how I mean it.)[2]

(2) At the point where Your Excellency says: otherwise the instigator would have allowed less free play to his imagination,[3] I would, to strengthen the criticism, point out that the main facts in contradiction of the story in the *Post* were already *publici juris* (wrong term) through the August letter,[4] and that one can only assume *mala fides*, unless of course the instigator thinks the facts in the August letter were incorrect.

(1) seems advisable to me; (2) is not really essential. If I receive *no* word from you, I will omit the three words (under my signature) and leave the second paragraph *as it is*.

The change 'Foreign Ministry' still seems very good to me.[5] The whole, in its noble and convincing calm, excellent.

The *Wiener Allgemeine Zeitung* (official) is said to have greeted Tschirschky very rudely. I am trying to get a copy.

The danger of intervention in the trial seems to be removed for the present. His Majesty wants to hear absolutely nothing about it. Final word: 'M[oltke] to be either cleansed or stoned.' Betting among the friends at Court: M. is quite safe, H. will lose; but it will be a very short trial.

*Nous verrons.* But quarter will not be given. [...]

I am much concerned about the Lecomte business. If he comes and gives his oath, if Phili comes and gives his oath. . . .

'Your oath is my oath'. [...]

> With most respectful regards
> Your very devoted
> Harden.


### 1056.  Holstein to Hugo von Radolin[6]

Berlin, 15 October 1907

Dear Radolin,

Thank you very much for the kind intention of paying me a visit. Because of the fine weather, I stayed away until October.[7]

---

[1] Harden is commenting on the draft of an open letter which Holstein was preparing for publication in the *Zukunft*. Holstein's letter, dated 12 October 1907, was published in the *Zukunft* of 19 October, vol. 61, pp. 91–3.

[2] In his draft, Holstein had referred to the fact that he had written a previous open letter to the *Zukunft* under his own signature—an indirect reference to the many anonymous articles that had been written against him.

[3] Holstein wrote that the author of an anonymous attack on him in the *Post* had obviously not thought that he would reply, 'otherwise he would have allowed less free play to his imagination'.

[4] Holstein's earlier open letter to Harden of 5 August 1906.

[5] This was presumably a change discussed orally.

[6] From the Radolin Papers.          [7] In the Harz mountains.

Since my return I have not heard much, but still a few things.

Tschirschky insisted on going to Paris, and he would have been sent there but for the opposition of His Majesty. Altogether you can be certain that H.M. is your *only* support. All the other people in authority here are either indifferent or actual enemies and enviers. You must make your calculations on that basis. I advised you to do so when I disappeared from the scene, and it seems to me that the advice has proved sound.

Therefore it would also be useful if you would put in an appearance frequently, for instance at one or another of the Court ceremonies in January. But under no circumstances for the Kaiser's birthday, because on that occasion you would be expected to do something yourself.[1]

Flotow's influence is minimal. Hammann is the man at the controls, and he has his own candidates for every job. He wanted Lichnowsky as State Secretary and Rosen for Under State Secretary. He said so himself. I hear that Rosen sways back and forth politically, but has a marvellous gift for getting along with the Press.

Best wishes
H.

## 1057. Bernhard von Bülow to Kaiser Wilhelm II[2]

TELEGRAM

Kleinflottbeck, 26 October 1907

For His Majesty the Kaiser and King.

I beg most humbly to report to Your Imperial and Royal Majesty that I am arriving in Berlin tomorrow, Sunday evening, at a quarter past seven. I most humbly request permission to be allowed to report to Your Majesty on Monday in the forenoon.

The conduct of the Moltke-Harden trial is scandalous. I am all the more indignant because I tried to use my influence in every (legal) way to ensure that the presiding judge keep a firm rein on the proceedings. In accordance with the intentions of Your Majesty, it will be the task of the military authorities to cauterize *ferro et igni* such filthy abscesses wherever they may be discovered. The army is too healthy, and our people are too healthy at their inner core, so that the task of purification should be speedily completed. The scandalous revelations that are now occupying the thoughts of the sensation-hungry public can best be overcome by our pursuing a firm and dignified policy that will lift the nation out of this morass and guide it to great ends.

Most faithfully and obediently
Bülow.

On 29 October Harden was acquitted, a decision immediately appealed by Count Moltke. On the same day the Prussian Ministry of Justice revoked the verdict on a legal technicality, and instructed the public

[1] Holstein means that Radolin would be expected to hold a suitable celebration at the German Embassy in Paris.

[2] From the Foreign Ministry files.

prosecutor to take up the case which five months earlier the public prosecutor had rejected on the grounds that it did not affect the public interest. The indictment was published on 14 November, and Harden was given five days to reply. His efforts to avert a reopening of the case failed. The new trial was scheduled to begin on 16 December.

The Holstein Papers contain no letters from Harden to Holstein between 13 October and 17 November 1907.

1058.   Holstein to Dr Pusch[1]
  Copy

Berlin, 8 November 1907

Dear Sir,

Thank you very much for your letter, which I confess gave me great pleasure.[2]

I whiled away the long hours of waiting by thinking over what I might be asked and what I could reply. I wanted if at all possible to express myself about the attack which the French Secretary of Embassy, Lecomte, made against me in the Paris *Matin*.[3] He virtually said 'that I had avenged myself on him, the well-known friend of Prince Eulenburg, for the political changes that led to my retirement.'

The official Paris *Temps*[4] commented on this in a leading article that culminated in the final sentence: 'Herr von H. must have powerful protectors (or a powerful protector), since *ses agents* can permit themselves to drag the honour of a French diplomat into the mire.'

That was aimed at Bülow, and the *agents* can only have referred to Harden. The Berlin Press, and above all the papers that are in close contact with *Geheimrat* Hammann, at once treated these accusations as proved and fell upon me. At the age of seventy, with my life behind me, I am fairly indifferent to all this in so far as I personally am concerned. But in the interests of the Chancellor and for general reasons I would have liked to have refuted these accusations, and I also believed that Bülow had me summoned for that purpose. (Incidentally, I have not seen the Chancellor for months and have not corresponded with him since the beginning of October.) I made a futile attempt to talk with the public prosecutor. I wanted to tell him what I intended to do, and wanted to request to be allowed to speak as freely as possible.

The agitation against myself probably emanates from three sources.

Perhaps Harden's opponents in his trial found it useful to make him out to be the instrument of someone else's revenge. Perhaps. But I also know that Tschirschky, to further his own cause, told everybody who would listen to him, including the Kaiser: 'Everything that Harden is

---

[1] District judge.

[2] In a letter of 7 November Dr Pusch expressed his regret for not having provided a room for Holstein where he could sit while waiting to be summoned as a witness in Bülow's libel suit against Adolf Brand. (See above, p. 498, note 6.)

[3] On 28 October the *Matin* had published an interview with Lecomte.

[4] Of 31 October 1907.

writing now is inspired by Holstein.' Finally, I am justified in assuming that *Geheimrat* Hammann secretly continues to work against me. Purpose : to undermine my relations with the Wilhelmstrasse as far as possible. When, fifteen months ago, I made the acquaintance of Harden (whom I consider to be a passionate but thoroughly honourable person), he told me—before witnesses, I believe—that a little while ago, after Harden had just published a violent article against me, *Geheimrat* Hammann had let him know through a Press agent named René that 'if Harden would receive him, Hammann was in a position to give him further information about me'. Harden had refused to receive him. Bülow, of course, had no part in this; he was *procul negotiis* while convalescing on the shores of the Baltic. And to-day, fifteen months later, Hammann continues to work along the same lines. At any rate I must assume so, after I was told yesterday that the attack in the *Post*, to which I replied with a letter in the *Zukunft*,[1] emanated from René, whom Hammann this summer raised to the rank of *Geheimer Hofrat*. But proof —as a specialist you know how difficult this can be to establish, even on matters which the proverbial sparrows have known for ages. A week ago the Press Bureau informed me through the Editor-in-Chief of a big German newspaper (not a Berlin paper) of how much they disapproved of the attacks upon me. Herr Hammann in particular had said on reading that article in the *Post* : 'this is too stupid. To this Herr von H. must and will reply.' So I was informed, verbatim. I, who have worked for thirty years at No. 76, Wilhelmstrasse, am supposed to believe that the *Post, National Zeitung, Vossische Zeitung*, etc., would hack about on me for nineteen months without encouragement from the Press Bureau. But I could prove nothing. Of course, an oath is an oath. But the human memory is by nature like an electric sign, on again—off again, according to necessity.

I take it as certain that Hammann wants to get his own back on Harden for rejecting his advances of last year. I for my part sent my recent counter-attack letter to Harden, in the first place because he had been almost the only one to take my part, and then because Hammann's enormous latent influence would have prevented publication elsewhere. I did not wish to expose myself to the possibility of a rejection.

I had wanted to counter the most recent attacks, set off by the Lecomte interview, by declaring under oath :

(1) That Prince Bülow never expressed the wish or hinted that I should pass on incriminating material about Eulenburg or anyone else to Harden, as the *Temps* led one to believe.[2]

(2) That Harden told the truth when he stated in court that he had never received any information about Lecomte from me. Harden was

[1] See above, p. 500, note 1.

[2] Holstein wrote to his cousin Ida von Stülpnagel on 25 November 1907 : 'I *had* material, which I had received directly from Bülow by the way—, and I suspect he gave it to me so that I should pass it on to Harden. But I refused to play and gave him *nothing*. [...] For instance, Bülow told me the whole story of the relationship between Eulenburg and Lecomte, about which I knew nothing.' (Rogge, *Friedrich von Holstein*, p. 297.) See also above, Holstein's letter to Harden of 16 September 1907, p. 491, note 2.

mistaken, however, when he added that it was he who first informed me about Lecomte. This error arose because I had avoided talking about Lecomte with Harden or even mentioning his name. To have acted otherwise would in my opinion have been unseemly on my part, as a former diplomat, although to-day I no longer need have consideration for anyone.

Perhaps I would have added that the news that the French diplomat had spent days in closest association with His Maj. the Kaiser drove Harden into a veritable frenzy.

I would have been happy to have replied to M. Lecomte blow for blow with a statement like this one. When I first received the summons to appear in court—I received it towards midnight—I thought it would be fitting to state: 'When one has been accused, as I once was, of having been instrumental in the retirement of Prince Bismarck, one finds such an accusation difficult to bear. To be accused of having aided in getting rid of Prince Eulenburg—and Lecomte—would not trouble my conscience. But I do not want to assume more than is my due, therefore, etc.' In the light of dawn this arabesque had faded away and by the afternoon everything had faded away and I walked home in real disappointment.[1]

The statement I had intended to make was presented to the French Ambassador yesterday by Herr von Schoen,[2] but under oath and publicly would have been better.

With deepest respect I remain, my dear *Herr Gerichtsdirektor*

Your very devoted

H.

1059.    Holstein to Bernhard von Bülow
         Copy

Berlin, 11 November 1907

Dear Bülow,

I am grateful for your friendly invitation to visit you.[3] Meanwhile, all the newspapers that are supposed to be well informed continue to load everything on me that no one else wants to bear. This is a matter of indifference to me, and I do not in the least believe that you have ordered this ceaseless agitation. But since this shows that no regard is paid to your relationship with me, I think it is better not to visit you as long as the Wilhelmstrasse continues to picture me as the villain in the piece. I say the Wilhelmstrasse because I know that for instance the recent attack in the *Post*, to which I was finally compelled to reply in the *Zukunft*,[4] actually emanated from *Geheimer Hofrat* René. Nor will this game soon cease, for it amuses those who play it and no one risks anything in doing so. The only harm might possibly be done to you if the Press should once again spread the news that in spite of everything the pernicious and notorious Holstein still came to see you.

---

[1] Holstein was not called to the witness stand.
[2] No document to this effect has been found.
[3] An invitation of 10 November 1907. (Published in Rogge, *Friedrich von Holstein*, p. 299.)
[4] See above, p. 500, note 1.

Therefore I would like to postpone my visit until things are once again put in order.

Meanwhile my best wishes accompany you from afar.

Most sincerely
Your
Holstein.

## 1060.    Maximilian Harden to Holstein

17 November 1907

Your Excellency,

Thank you very much for the letter. I was very sorry that Your Excellency did not wish to be here last night.[1] I was not asked for to-day, and so could not come. Herr von E[ckardt][2] is a good, kind, and also intelligent person. There is nothing he can do about this affair. He also realized this. Expert legal opinions do not interest Herr Bülow and his jurists.

I am afraid that the Wilhelmstrasse may possibly yet come to believe that such feelers come from me.

Nor do I of course talk with Renvers (who wants to).[3] Indictment without a hearing, 5 (five!!) days grace for a reply, the first decision annulled, Moltke summoned as a WITNESS (Ph. E[ulenburg], *not* by the Public Prosecutor), the same trial twice in six weeks (which even a bull could not endure—and I am no bull): The Chancellor demands it.[4] Let him drink the dregs. Probably, almost certainly, I will be ruined in the process. But I will not be the only one. The word 'consideration' has been crossed out of my dictionary. He who has lived through what I have lived through for months will understand. And if His Highness [Bülow], that . . . ,[5] understands or not is a matter of indifference to me.

Perhaps this number, which I will have to prepare a day in advance owing to the day of repentance, will be the next to last issue of the *Zukunft*. No matter. I know that I have done what I had to do. And that Russia is a paradise of freedom compared to this Germany.

New 'atrocities' against the witness Bollhardt[6] (whose testimony was not considered in the verdict in any case). I do not find it so strange that a commoner, who was on terms of champagne and popo and Du and Du among Counts, should later on become a delinquent. Who degraded him?[7]

[1] In a letter of the same day (Sunday), Holstein said that Eckardt had advised him not to disturb Harden because he should be allowed to spend all his time with his legal advisers. (Rogge, *Holstein und Harden*, p. 243.)

[2] Felix von Eckardt. Editor-in-Chief of the *Hamburger Korrespondenz*.

[3] In a letter of 14 November, Holstein warned Harden that Renvers was on very good terms with Hammann, and wondered whether Renvers should be drawn into the matter. (Rogge, *Holstein und Harden*, pp. 241–2.)

[4] In his letter of 14 November, cited above, Holstein wrote: 'As for the Chancellor, he will be very cautious about interceding for you now that he has been publicly accused of having set you on. If I saw any possibility in that quarter, I would have spoken with him myself.'

[5] The dots are Harden's.

[6] A former cuirassier who stated in the first Moltke-Harden trial that he had been debauched by Prince Eulenburg in Count Lynar's house.

[7] Bollhardt's testimony was considered unreliable because of his police record.

I will probably not take Kleinholz for many reasons, among others because he uses the *Tageblatt* for 'notices'. It 'makes no difference'.[1]

With kindest regards and a wish for your very good health, I remain Your Excellency's

Very sincere<br>Harden

The Public Prosecutor has summoned about eight witnesses against Frau von E[lbe].

## 1061. Maximilian Harden to Holstein

Grunewald, 19 November 1907

Your Excellency,

Thank you very much for your kind sympathy and advice. But there is really no longer any point in weighing reasons and straining the mind. For the whole business has after all been arranged 'at the top'. One would have to have icewater in one's veins to remain calm in the face of such villainy.

I hope that Your Excellency spent much more pleasant days. It is too bad that Herr von E[ckhardt] took away my hour on Sunday.[2]

I just received Your Excellency's special delivery letter.[3] Many thanks. Unfortunately that is not the case. There is a precedent.

The third decision of the Supreme Court. NO DOUBT that the case will be reopened.[4] Isenbiel, the public prosecutor, is strongly urging haste. Has written twice to the court; and there nobody has any doubts. Everything settled.

With grateful regards<br>I remain Your Excellency's very devoted<br>Harden

## 1062. Maximilian Harden to Holstein

25 November 1907

Your Excellency,

[...] Kleinholz sick, Bernstein tied down this week by a gigantic case, the trial almost upon us; everything already settled. No, I am in no mood for throwing snowballs. The *Zukunft* will have to go under on 1 December. Finis.

With best wishes I am<br>Your Excellency's very devoted<br>H.

The remark of His Majesty ('No turning back until the fellow is in jail') is already in the newspapers and has been reported to me by letter from all over. I will not again make a speech in court.

---

[1] In his letter of 14 November, cited above, Holstein urgently recommended that Harden secure *Justizrat* Kleinholz for his defence because he, as the counsel for Frau von Elbe in her divorce suit agaist Count Moltke, would be in a better position than anyone else to defend the credibility of this key witness. 'If this [credibility] is preserved intact, you don't need much more evidence.' Harden did in fact engage Kleinholz for his defence.

[2] See above, p. 505, note 1.          [3] Not found.          [4] See above, p. 502.

## 1063.    Maximilian Harden to Holstein

7 December 1907

Your Excellency,

[...] I do not seem ever to have expressed myself sufficiently clearly in our conversations.[1] Illegal procedure, utmost pressure from Government and Press, for weeks a distortion of the facts : already practically hopeless. But TOTAL hopelessness has been attained by allowing the plaintiff to appear as an oath-taking witness. He will be summoned *first*, will categorically deny everything for himself and his friends, under oath : *causa finita*. Everything one might then try to influence opinion would be completely and absolutely in vain. In *such a case*, where a theft of silver spoons is not involved, nor even *demonstrable* deviations from subjective truth, EVERYTHING is lost if one gives the real accused the weapon of the oath and if he is fortified and supported in advance by the Chancellor, Minister of War, Press, etc.

'Do you mean to say that His Excellency is telling falsehoods here under oath ? Or what is it that you mean to prove ?'

It would be ridiculous to try to batter down a wall like that.

The lawyers are of course of the same opinion.

Deeply grateful for the sympathy of Your Excellency.

Very sincerely

H.


## 1064.    Holstein to Maximilian Harden
Copy[2]

Berlin, 8 December 1907

My dear Herr Harden,

I am very grateful indeed for your letter which gave me the comforting assurance that you were in agreement with your defence attorneys. Apart from those three men no one understands the situation sufficiently well to be able to judge the main question : namely, whether it is practical under the given circumstances to use or withhold certain evidence.

Among the general public, as I was told again to-day, the trend in your favour is said to be continuing because the suspicion is gaining ground that pressure has been exerted against you. In circles great and small the Harden case is being followed with excited attention, and every rumour and trend connected with it is weighed and discussed. In general people seem to expect a largish fine; this is considered to be more likely than acquittal, from the way things stand. I was told that there is a rumour that Mssrs. Kleinholz and Sello[3] are broaching the question of bringing about a legal *modus vivendi*. From quite another

---

[1] Holstein had written on 6 December : 'I heard yesterday that the belief was growing in the Wilhelmstrasse that your case would be handled "leniently". I need not repeat my own views.' (Rogge, *Holstein und Harden*, pp. 249–50.)

[2] The copy is identical with the text actually sent to Harden. (Rogge, *Holstein und Harden*, pp. 250–1.)

[3] Dr Erich Sello. Count Moltke's attorney in the second Harden trial, and in his divorce case against the present Frau von Elbe.

quarter attention was drawn to the high decoration of *Geheimrat* Goldberger[1] as a surreptitious and interesting indication.

The best thing I can now do for you is to preserve you from useless comments during the coming week, so that I do not disturb you in person or in writing from devoting full attention to your own interests. So, until I hear from you and see you again after the 16th—after Philippi—which does not mean that I expect a particularly bloody battlefield.

> With best wishes
> Your very devoted
> Holstein.

### 1065.   Maximilian Harden to Holstein

12 December 1907

Your Excellency,

Many thanks.  I too am constantly receiving these false reports.  I recognize the method from the fact that they are also being sent to Your Excellency.[2]  There is not a syllable of truth in them.  'Unfavourable' is an expression that does not come anywhere close to expressing the true state of affairs.  The court HAS already rejected everything, in such a shameless fashion that it is actually unbelievable and even the lawyers are dumbfounded.  I always expected it would be like that and am not surprised.  The remark by the familiar authority (the highest),[3] illegal procedure, worst possible court, the talk of B[ülow] and the Minister of War, rejection of ALL evidence that does not pertain to active pederasty on the part of M[oltke] (which was never indicated), highest sentence ('you can after all start over again after a year', [His] Excellency said) and complete triumph for Liebenberg.  Thus it was intended and thus it shall be.

I would never have thought to have lost eighteen years of ascetic, untiring effort through this petty, abject affair; to see my entire existence flounder on a matter of indifference to me.  Now this has come to pass after all.

With all good wishes for Your Excellency's health

> I remain, your very devoted
> H.

### 1066.   Maximilian Harden to Holstein

13 December 1907

Your Excellency,

Thank you so much for the friendly letter.[4]  I have only seen the lawyers twice and have only discussed details with them.  There is

---

[1] *Geheimer Kommerzienrat* Ludwig Goldberger, a liberal writer.

[2] Holstein had written on 10 December: 'I for my part still believe the position is not unfavourable—and not only because of ignorance, but for other reasons.' (Rogge, *Holstein und Harden*, p. 251.)

[3] The Kaiser's alleged remark: 'No turning back until the fellow is in jail.' (See above, Harden's letter of 25 November 1907.)

[4] Of 12 December. (Rogge, *Holstein und Harden*, p. 252.) A copy of this letter is in the Holstein Papers.

nothing that can be done about the business. It has been definitely lost ever since the court rejected five out of the six questions that were to be put to E[ulenburg]. ALL the important ones; the first is only *pro forma* and will be answered in the negative. The public prosecution has every reason to be pleased and confident. Whether the attorneys will still want to try a few little tricks of the trade I do not know; nor do I care. Personally I have no intention of taking *any* speaking part in this comedy. Whether it has for me become a tragedy : about that my dear fellow citizens do not of course ask.

The presiding magistrate[1] has already said : 'Into the jug with the fellow.' The most worthy expression of a German judge. And after M[oltke]'s oath of purification the business is finished. I hope from the bottom of my heart that E[ulenburg] and Co. will then triumph; they have earned it because they have been more clever, and the friends of their friends. Me, everyone has left in the lurch. No matter. If two defenceless women, mother and child,[2] were not left in a perilous situation, I would laugh about this Timon experience. The misery of those two twists my heart. And they too will be dragged into the mire, because insurmountable obstacles have heretofore made it impossible for me to give them legal security.

Your Excellency, farewell.
Very sincerely
H.

### 1067.   Diary Entry

14 December 1907

[...] The tension and mistrust the English feel towards Germany, and which now figure as important factors in the calculations of all the statesmen in the world, has naturally been increased still further by the Navy Bill and by the chauvenistic and anti-English conduct of the Navy League.[3] Can it really be coincidence that these two events took place at a time when the Kaiser was trying, by means of a lengthy visit to England and by countless acts of kindness to people and institutions, to improve German-English relations?[4] Because surely no one can be in any doubt—except perhaps the Kaiser himself—that these two events make all his kindnesses useless and meaningless, and even give them an air of fraud. Who has an interest in the continuation of Anglo–German tension? Prince Bülow, who clearly realizes that he would have to be sacrificed to any real German-English reconciliation. For the English leave no doubt that they regard the present Chancellor as an enemy and

---

[1] Judge Lehmann.                     [2] Harden's wife and daughter.

[3] On 16 November 1905 a Navy Bill which increased the provisions of the Navy Bill of 1900 was accepted by the Bundesrat. The Navy League then began to demand that the building programme be accelerated so that the new ships should be ready by 1912 instead of 1917.

[4] The official visit of the German Kaiser and Kaiserin to England took place from 10–18 November. Afterwards the Kaiser spent an additional three weeks at Highcliffe Castle opposite the Isle of Wight.

an unreliable character.[1] Add to that the fact that the Hammann-Stein group, which advises the Chancellor, has an interest in acerbating the relations between the Government and the Centre Party. Keim[2] is useful for this purpose, too; he acts as a watershed into foreign and domestic policy.

It is also characteristic of the situation—and of the means that are being used—that the English Secretary of Embassy, Count de Salis,[3] is said to have made enquiries recently as to whether it was really true that Holstein had once again regained decisive influence over the Chancellor. Apparently they were again trying, as they have so often done for years, to blame everything disagreeable on my advice. That this has been done recently, particularly with reference to the anti-English measures—whereas I, throughout my life, have worked for good relations with England—is in truth an irony of fate and bears testimony to the competence of Bülow's Press Bureau, in which in this case I also include Rosen. He has used his old relationship with Lascelles dating from their days in Persia together to stir up ill-will against me. [...]

## 1068. Diary Entry

17 December 1907

General Keim informed a reporter—as he has done several times already—that all the rumours about the resignation of Salm[4]-Keim were without foundation. The Kaiser would not interfere in this purely personal matter, the General Assembly[5] (29 December) alone must decide.[6]

If Keim made this statement, he must surely know already that the Kaiser and Chancellor are on his side. One hint from the Kaiser would remove an active general from the scene. On the other hand it is probable that the General Assembly will decide in favour of the loudest talker. Anti-English statements will certainly be made there. For the Kaiser, Keim represents a programme of unlimited fleet building, for Bülow he is an anti-English agitator and also an irritant to the Centre Party. Bülow is no longer able to reach a reconciliation with the Centre, hence he has the greatest interest in rendering a reconciliation between the Kaiser and the Centre impossible as well, for such a reconciliation might open the way for Prince von Fürstenberg.[7] At this moment, Keim shields Bülow against both possibilities most dangerous to Bülow personally: reconciliation of the Kaiser with England and with the

[1] See *Memoirs*, pp. 181–8.

[2] August Keim. Presiding officer of the German Navy League, 1900–8.

[3] John Francis Charles, Count de Salis. Secretary of Embassy in Berlin, 1906–11.

[4] Otto, Prince and Rheingraf zu Salm-Horstmar. President of the Navy League to 14 June 1908.

[5] The General Assembly of the Navy League, which was scheduled to meet at Frankfurt-am-Main.

[6] A telegram from the Kaiser to the Assembly disavowing the League's anti-English agitation led to the resignation of General Keim.

[7] Maximilian Egon, Prince zu Fürstenberg. Member of the Prussian House of Lords and one of the highest dignitaries of the Empire. A friend of Kaiser Wilhelm II.

Centre. Therefore Bülow will handle the affair so that Keim will stay on. Let us see what happens on the 29th.[1]

### 1069.  Bogdan von Hutten-Czapski to Holstein

Berlin, 17 December 1907, 11 p.m.

All efforts have been in vain. I no longer believe in the possibility of success. If there should be anything new to report, I will inform you.[2]

H.

### 1070.  Holstein to Maximilian Harden
Draft[3]

Berlin, 25 December 1907

Dear Herr Harden,

I can think of nothing but the fateful blow that threatens you.[4] My chief attention is directed chiefly to the fabrications of the Press that interpret your physical weariness and toneless voice as signs of a lack of courage. By this very means they are trying to work on the feelings of the public, even more than by dramatic legal moves.

I see from the encyclopaedia that you are only forty-six years old—a generation younger than I am. How much you may still experience and accomplish!

Remember how a few years ago the Italian Minister-President Giolitti was castigated. And he was really accused of serious things.[5]

---

[1] Holstein noted in his diary on the following day that the General Assembly was to meet instead in Kassel on 18 or 19 January. At this meeting the General Assembly did in fact express its confidence in the leadership of the Navy League, with the result that General Keim withdrew his resignation.

[2] In his memoirs (*Sechzig Jahre Politik und Gesellschaft*, vol. I, pp. 467–8) Count Hutten-Czapski stated that he played an indirect part in only one of the 'scandal trials' of this period, namely the Moltke-Harden trial. He fails to mention that there were two such trials, and altogether his facts and chronology are rather confused. It is nevertheless possible to assume from his above note to Holstein that Hutten-Czapski's memoirs refer to the second Moltke-Harden trial. According to these memoirs, Richard Witting on behalf of Harden, and Guido Henckel on behalf of Moltke appealed to Hutten-Czapski to mediate the case. Hutten-Czapski thereupon persuaded a legal expert, *Justizrat* Loewenfeld, to assist in the task of mediation. Loewenfeld went to see *Justizrat* Kleinholz (who was not Moltke's attorney, as Hutten-Czapski states, but Harden's attorney at the *second* trial) and between them Loewenfeld and Kleinholz drew up an agreement. The effort at mediation failed, Hutten-Czapski said, because Moltke's superior officers, especially General Hahnke, maintained that he could not suscribe to a compromise of any kind.

On 18 December, presumably immediately after receiving the above note from Hutten-Czapski, Holstein wrote to Frau Selma Harden that he too had hoped for a quick and peaceful conclusion to the whole business in view of the health of her husband, but the fact that news of the negotiations had leaked out prematurely had doomed them to failure. (Rogge, *Holstein und Harden*, p. 258.) In all probability Holstein refers here to Hutten-Czapski's mediation efforts and to the fact that these efforts became known to Moltke's superior officers before a definite compromise settlement had been arranged.

[3] The draft is almost identical with the letter actually sent to Harden. (Rogge, *Holstein und Harden*, pp. 259–60.)

[4] Holstein refers to the seeming hopelessness of Harden's case, which was not decided until 3 January 1908. At this point in his draft Holstein crossed out the words : 'The fact that I am hereby losing my only defender is of secondary importance.'

[5] Giolitti's Ministry fell in November 1893 over a scandal in the state banks. A parliamentary investigation committee later acquitted Giolitti of personal dishonesty, but he withdrew from public life for several years.

But he did not lose faith in himself, but issued a statement that culminated in a *sursum corda*, and it was not long before he was once again on top. Giolitti is almost twenty years older than you are, although admittedly in better health. Still, I do not give up hope that you will emulate him in a *sursum corda*. This may perhaps be of no use with the judges, though it cannot hurt either, and for the world, for Europe and beyond, which is tensely watching the progress and especially the conclusion of this trial, it would be of great importance for everyone to see that you believed in yourself till the end.

Your own good faith, that must be your citadel, from which no one can expel you. I assume that I am not alone among your friends to hold this opinion and also that my views jibe with your own instinct. But I will send off these lines nevertheless, because at a crisis like this it may be a comfort to you to know that your instinctive feelings are shared by someone else.

This sort of thing may be of no moment for the law courts, but for the world, and for life itself, it is the *sursum corda* that counts.

I would not write this if I were not firmly convinced that you were fully up to this difficult situation. I am confident that you have the ability to create a wonderful final effect, calm and dignified like the first time, but in accordance with the circumstances, much shorter. 'Few words.'

Hoping to see you soon. With best wishes.

Yours very sincerely<br>Holstein.

## 1071.   Maximilian Harden to Holstein

31 December 1907

Your Excellency,

Will you kindly tell me as quickly as possible the name of the Colonel who can testify to Hahnke's statement.[1] I think I can say that I have been discreet at the cost of my own existence. I can be so no longer. I request that Your Excellency be good enough to give me the names and addresses as soon as you can. It is EXTREMELY important, and otherwise I will be obliged to invite Your Excellency as a witness. That would be tomorrow noon. I ask you to excuse the impatience. It is a question of life and death. In such cases one cannot be conventional.

Your Excellency's very devoted<br>H.[2]

[1] According to Harden (*Zukunft*, vol. 62, p. 298) one of the most important and well known officers in the army had told a Colonel that it was a fortunate thing Harden had opened this abcess, and that it was inconceivable that he would be given more than a small monetary fine.

[2] No reply to this letter was found in the Harden Papers.

# 1908

On 3 January 1908 Harden was condemned to four months' imprisonment and was obliged to bear the cost of both the first and second trials. Moltke's name was cleared. Eulenburg, who had been summoned as a witness, had sworn under oath that he had never been guilty of homosexual practices punishable by law, and, when pressed by Harden's attorney, had also sworn that he had never been guilty of 'filthy' practices of any kind. Harden appealed the decision of the second Moltke-Harden trial to the German Supreme Court at Leipzig.

## 1072.    Holstein to Maximilian von Brandt[1]

Berlin, 3 January 1908

Your Excellency,

[...] One can also make a good many observations about the Harden trial. The rehabilitation campaign is said to have been planned not by the Prince[2] but by Count August Eulenburg, or so I was told the day before yesterday. In connection with that, it is thought that Bülow will not last much longer and will be replaced by Marschall, who has always been on good terms with the Eulenburgs. That he was always on excellent terms with Phili is something I have been able to observe at close quarters. In Marschall's time Phili still had a voice in the selection of personnel, but after Bülow's appointment as State Secretary he had one no longer. When in 1898 Pourtalès was sent to The Hague, where Phili allegedly wanted to send Varnbüler, Phili is supposed to have said: 'There was a time when such an appointment could not have been made without my having been consulted.'

I have frequently heard the question raised as to whether the present unceremonial manner of swearing-in is sufficient to impress upon the taker of the oath the seriousness of the procedure. There is a good deal of discussion back and forth about the oaths that have been given in the course of this trial.

From what I can tell of the opinion of educated people, the rehabilitation of Phili would be regarded primarily as a *coup de force* and would be used as an argument against the present method of government.[3]

---

[1] From the Brandt Papers.
[2] Philipp zu Eulenburg.
[3] According to Zedlitz-Trütschler (*Zwölf Jahre am deutschen Kaiserhof*, pp. 183-4) the Kaiser was very pleased about the outcome of the second Moltke-Harden trial and wanted to rehabilitate Moltke and Eulenburg 'on an unprecedented scale'. He was prevented from doing so by his advisers.

In the hope of hearing soon again from Your Excellency, I remain with best wishes.

Your very devoted
Holstein.

### 1073. Maximilian Harden to Holstein

8 January 1908

Your Excellency,

Many thanks for your visit and letter.[1]

The reply to Lord Eisenbeil[2] could not be framed differently, because he presented me with two questions that he knew would have to be answered in the negative. I was rude enough.[3]

In the other matter[4] there is the danger that witnesses will be 'softened up' at *Prenzlau, praesente reo*.[5] (Neither B[ernstein] nor I could be present at the hearings.) Then proceedings would not be initiated,[6] the Prince by the grace of God could sleep in peace, and in the (unlikely) event of success in Leipzig,[7] I would have witnesses who were already committed when my case was reopened. On the other hand: if I wait and Leipzig accepts the verdict, then in ten days the order will come to begin serving sentence; after that he would no longer be restrained by an examination of the oaths;[8] if one wants to be brutal. The decision is difficult; because it is no longer possible to count on 'justice'.

There is no need to fear that B[ernstein] will be angered. As I now know, he is no good for anything but an appeal anyway. [...]

I am again in very poor health. Hope Your Excellency is much better, despite storm and rain.

With profound regards

Very sincerely
H.

### 1074. Maximilian Harden to Holstein

3 March 1908

Your Excellency,

[...] I have decided meanwhile that as soon as I can go out I will go to see the public prosecutor[9] and tell him directly: I want to give evidence now, unless you can assure me that you will suspend the suit of Eulenburg against myself immediately. This examination may reveal a good deal.[10] It would be a good thing if this gentleman (who one way or

---

[1] Not found.    [2] A pun on the name of Isenbiel, the public prosecutor.

[3] Harden refers to his final statement at the second Moltke-Harden trial.

[4] A reference to Prince Eulenburg's request that the state institute legal proceedings against Harden and Bernstein on his own behalf.

[5] See p. 483, note 3.

[6] Harden means that the whole case might again be settled by the procedure Eulenburg had adopted in the previous June at Prenzlau.

[7] A successful appeal on the part of Harden to the Supreme Court at Leipzig.

[8] Eulenburg's oaths concerning his moral purity. (See above, p. 513.)

[9] Isenbiel.

[10] Harden may have been considering this as a means of bringing his evidence against Eulenburg to the attention of the public prosecutor. He was later to take a much more dramatic course. (See below, p. 528, note 1.)

another will be the victim of this case) does not always see and hear only E[ulenburg]. I will nevertheless keep this plan absolutely secret, as well as the other preparatory steps I have taken. [...]

With best wishes I am

Your Excellency's very devoted

Harden

1075.  Holstein to Bernhard von Bülow
Copy

6 March 1908

Dear Bülow,

As you can see, the use of a calm but firm German policy in the Balkans soon put an end to the Anglo-Isvolsky bluff.[1] On all sides they are protesting that there was no intention of taking forceful action against the Sultan.[2] France in particular is reluctant, on account of Morocco, to be drawn into other complications. The moment was thus favourable for Germany to assert herself politically.

From the newspapers it seems to me that the recall of Osten-Sacken is to be presented in advance as a *fait accompli*. It may of course be—although I know nothing about it—that his old Munich friendship with Phili has temporarily caused the old gentleman to take a pessimistic view of present conditions.

Is the rumour true that Isvolsky and especially his wife would be glad to exchange St Petersburg for an embassy, and soon? If yes, then perhaps Pourtalès could give the Minister to understand that there is still the same Chancellor and the same Kaiser in Berlin who formerly expressed the wish to have Isvolsky here. It seems to me that a hint might perhaps be useful, and could certainly do no harm. Charikov, who is said to have been brought to St Petersburg *cum spe succedendi*, is a well-known Panslavist, but is *alleged* to be an opponent of English policy. To us the most inconvenient Russians are the friends of England and Poland. No Russian loves *us*; in that respect there is no difference between them. Could you not find out—through Szögyényi—what Vienna thinks about Charikov? Could you not, in fact, invite the 'gypsy'[3] some time to discuss the Sanjak incident and to impress upon him once again the part Germany played in reassuring the Cabinets. This would make for an easy opportunity to get comparative estimates about Isvolsky and Charikov.

[1] On 27 January 1908 Aehrenthal announced the intention of the Austrian Government to build a railroad through the Sanjak of Novi Bazar. The Austrian move aroused much international opposition, particularly on the part of Isvolsky and the Russian Panslavists, who suspected that Germany was behind Austria. The Germans for their part suspected that England and France had done much to stir up Russian hostility. Official tension between Germany and Russia relaxed somewhat towards the end of February, and on 20 February Bülow and Isvolsky exchanged assurances of their mutual desire for friendly relations between their countries. (*Grosse Politik*, vol. XXVii, chapter CLXXXVII.)

[2] The Sanjak was a part of the Turkish Empire and thus under the suzerainty of the Sultan, whose consent Austria had obtained for the building of the railroad.

[3] Szögyényi.

If Charikov is outspokenly anti-Austrian, then he would be compelled by the force of circumstances to line up with England, no matter whether he loves or loathes the English.

The Russian Government has now given up its ridiculous ship building programme of four milliards—an idea the Tsar allegedly got from abroad—and is now contenting itself with 150–160 million roubles, distributed over four years.

That reminds me that the view is held in high naval circles here that the Kaiser—only he, personally—would be able to convince the English of the harmless nature of our naval construction. If anything were ever done along these lines it would only be detrimental, for the English would regard it as an effort to blind them to the facts by mere words. So long as we continue to build at the present rate, the mistrust of us will increase. But such outbreaks of the imperial 'ego' are elementary phenomena against which, in general, nothing can be done. And whether experience—the realization of the deplorable effects—has ever done any good in the past is something I very much doubt.

I come now to the tax on beer.[1] I find the taxation programme of the Bavarian Finance Minister most vexing. If one confronts the Bavarians with the alternative: 'Either beer or an indefinite increase in Bavarian payments to the Imperial treasury'; what would they do? I think they would give in.

Irritation that we allow ourselves to be so tyrannized by the Bavarians is after all quite widespread. The tax on beer would be considered as a great achievement on your part.

I envisage the tactics as follows: first you will have to get Sydow's[2] support. He will agree if he has His Majesty and you to back him up. He must then introduce the idea in Prussia and in other states. A large bloc of non-Prussian votes is essential. And I would consider it a good thing if the excessive friendship between Bavaria and the other middle-sized and small states were cooled off a bit in the process.

The first requisite is that Sydow is thoroughly in favour. Then if he forcefully sounds the slogan: Beer or increased contributions to the Imperial treasury—it would, I think, be most effective.[3]

I had intended to visit you, but think that this means of communication is easier for you.

Please do not answer.

Most sincerely
Your
H.

---

[1] Part of Bülow's tax reform programme.

[2] Reinhold Sydow. State Secretary in the Reich Finance Office, 1908–9.

[3] In a letter to Bülow of 7 March Holstein wrote on this point: 'I recommend the following formula for our federal allies: "I have banished the spectre of a Reich Finance Ministry. To keep it away permanently I ask you to grant me the funds to cover the necessary expenditures through the tax on beer; but I also ask you to support me in fighting against impossible or exaggerated demands by demanding that in every case you *first* discuss what such payments are supposed to cover." '

## 1076.    Maximilian Harden to Holstein

8 March 1908

Your Excellency,

The neighbour,[1] kind and clever as always, regards the situation *considerably* more pessimistically than I do.[2] *Everything* is against me. If I proceed with new accusations, there will be a 'storm of indignation' against me. Still, it had to be considered. But it would be wise to await the decision of the Supreme Court[3] (about which the neighbour is very sceptical indeed, after information he has received). He was good enough to promise to think it over and discuss the matter again. His view was of great interest to me, and I think it is correct. The thing has been accomplished.[4] If I live to experience the joy of seeing Bülow die on Phili's glory, then I will at least have vengeance on one. On him who has ruined everything. And *ultra posse.* . . .

But what is all that in comparison with the Tweedmouth letter?[5] A bagatelle. There lies the great crisis. Much much worse than the Krüger Telegram. And the sweet Press (Eckardt[6] too) twists everything around neatly by lying about it. *Doux pays.*

With most respectful greetings and good wishes I am Your Excellency's devoted.

Harden.

Nieberding[7] also seems to have a hand in the game. Isenbiel went to see him. Leipzig? And not a word is said about Hohenau.[8]

## 1077.    Holstein to Klara von Helldorf-Bedra[9]
Copy

Berlin, 15 March 1908

My dear Madame!

When your husband last visited me some time ago, there was nothing about him to suggest his passing shortly afterwards. However, we who are in our seventies must always be prepared to be called away at short notice.

[1] The reference is to Wilhelm Knappe, a neighbour of Harden's, formerly Consul-General in Shanghai and a Doctor of Jurisprudence. He was a friend of both Holstein and Harden, and had frequently offered his advice on legal problems in the past.

[2] Holstein replied on 9 March that he did not have the impression that the 'neighbour' was so pessimistic about the situation, but that Harden had only told him of two pieces of evidence. 'One of these *might* prove worthless, because up till now the witness had based his opinions only on a photographic resemblance and had not again seen the subject in person.' (Rogge, *Holstein und Harden*, p. 271.) Holstein may have been referring here to the evidence of Georg Riedl, who had identified Eulenburg from a picture in a newspaper. (See below, p. 528, note 1.)

[3] See above, p. 513.

[4] The rehabilitation of Moltke and Eulenburg.

[5] A letter from the Kaiser to Lord Tweedmouth, First Lord of the Admiralty, of 16 February 1908 in which he tried to reassure the English on the subject of German fleet building. (*Grosse Politik*, vol. XXIV, no. 8181, pp. 32–5.) The existence of the letter was revealed and the contents summarized in *The Times* of 6 March 1908.

[6] Felix von Eckardt.

[7] Rudolf Nieberding. State Secretary of the Reich Justice Department since 1893.

[8] See above, p. 477, note 5.

[9] Wife of Otto Heinrich von Helldorf-Bedra, the leader of the Conservatives in the Reichstag.

The death of this contemporary made all the more impression on me because it again recalled to mind how our paths crossed in our active lives. Once again the question occurred to me that I had already considered so often: what would have happened if Herr von Helldorf had taken over the Ministry of the Interior at the time when the Kaiser personally requested him to accept it? Herr von Helldorf declined primarily because he wanted to allow no one the opportunity to question the disinterestedness of his proposals. I understood his attitude completely, but many a diversion and much uncertainty would have been avoided for the country if he had accepted. The Minister of the Interior is a powerful figure, and the ability to give orders is more effective than trying to convince others to give them. That is for me, who behaved in my official capacity exactly like Herr von Helldorf, the result of the experience of many years. But both of us finally had the consolation of being able to tell ourselves that he who makes his decision to the best of his conscience and knowledge, without concern for his own interests, has no reason for self-reproach.

For you, my dear madame, there can hardly be any consolation at the present time. But there is the possibility that the pain may be somewhat relieved by the memory of how much you always meant to the deceased. Even I, from afar, could recognize that.

With the expression of my deep sympathy, I remain, dear madame,

Your most respectful servant
Holstein

### 1078.  Maximilian Harden to Holstein

16 March 1908

Your Excellency,

I wouldn't exactly call these swift impressions a 'character study'.[1] The man *will certainly do what is demanded of him*; but is somewhat ashamed, would, if possible, like to do the decent thing and feels that with me he is dealing with a decent person. That is after all something. Of all the people concerned, he is the only one who has tried to deal with me in a straightforward manner. And even if he were worse: I still don't think my tactics were wrong. On the other hand, everything I hear (also of conversations with His Majesty about the affair) confirms me in the opinion that Prince B[ülow] is going on with his double game. He wants to be rid of both.[2] Of the uncomfortable critic, too. This would be *de la bonne guerre* if he had not purposely misled me with *messages of love*.[3] And thereby (fatefully) also harmed his own cause. [...]

Among my visitors yesterday was a jurist from out of town who agrees entirely with my point of view. He said he had talked with a good many colleagues; unanimous agreement: no evidence in the world

---

[1] Harden is referring to his visit to Isenbiel, the public prosecutor (see above, Harden's letter to Holstein of 3 March 1908). Neither Harden's 'character study' of Isenbiel nor Holstein's comments about it have been found.

[2] That is, of both Eulenburg and Harden.

[3] In English in the original.

would make a law court of Prussia accuse a Prince E[ulenburg] of perjury. Then, I said, things are worse here than in the Balkans. Quite right, he replied. They will 'investigate', then state that there is no reason to open the case; and with that the glorification[1] would be complete. *Relato refero.*

I have just now found out that on the point where Berger was weak (negotiation 'on behalf' of His Highness[2]) before the second trial, he had been intimidated by Phili's second. All sorts of things about that. He knew, of course, that he would not only lose those two, but His Majesty as well, and that he will hardly be staying under Bülow's roof again.[3]

The main expert, Moll,[4] is said to be almost exactly the same type as Tütü.[5] *Hinc illae irae.* The trio Moll-Lehmann-Levy[6] arranged the affair.

Witting was in Breslau, where a general on active duty told him that nobody there had any doubts about Tütü's homosexuality. All sorts of details. But 'to prove it'? The general of course did not want to be named. That is what they all do. *Doux pays.* Nobody will stand up and be counted, and I should offer myself as a sacrificial victim in this affair, and on top of that let everyone abuse me. With this human material the French affair[7] would have been impossible. And here it is *for* the interests of the state, whereas there it was against. [...]

With the best wishes for Your Excellency's health,

Your very devoted

Harden [...]

1079.    Maximilian Harden to Holstein

Grunewald, 18 March 1908

Your Excellency,

[...] The decision against me is to be submitted to His Majesty.[8] (Just as in the divorce case,[9] when M[oltke] sent enquiries to the conference room from the New Palace.[10]) For that reason perhaps the special infamy in the motives, the 'purification' of E[ulenburg], and the remark to the Chancellor. Gradually I am forced to the conclusion that we all *under-*estimated E's criminality. I think that he simply made a *bande à part* with Lehmann and I[senbiel]. That would 'explain' the entire procedure.[11] Otherwise inexplicable. Basically: position and power of a

---

[1] Of Eulenburg.    [2] Prince Bülow.

[3] Harden presumably means that Berger would lose the patronage of Eulenburg and Bülow as well as the Kaiser, and that he could not count on Bülow's protection. Nothing more has been found about Berger's part in the second Moltke-Harden suit. The inference from the above letter is that he did nothing.

[4] Dr Albert Moll. An expert on sexual perversion and author of several books on the subject. He had been called upon for a medical opinion at the second Moltke-Harden trial, and had stated that he found no trace of homosexuality in Count Kuno Moltke.

[5] Count Kuno Moltke.

[6] Editor-in-Chief of the *Vossische Zeitung*.    [7] The Dreyfus case.

[8] Presumably the pending decision of the Supreme Court at Leipzig.

[9] Count Kuno Moltke's divorce from his wife Lili, the later Frau von Elbe.

[10] Moltke was at the Palace as Aide-de-Camp.

[11] Of the second Moltke-Harden trial, which Harden maintained had flaunted the legal principle 'ne bis in idem'.

mistress. Dispenses offices, titles, decorations. Kistler,[1] Laemmel,[2] Wendelstadt,[3] and up. Nothing official has any chance against that sort of thing. And no limit to his overweening sense of power. Oath? On anything. (I have just heard that Kistler is supposed to have had fainting fits in the corridor.) Renaissance of the favourites. *Règne des mignons.* Incalculable. Nothing to be done, I fear. [...]

With best wishes

H. [...]

### 1080. Maximilian Harden to Holstein

Grunewald, 26 March 1908

Your Excellency,

Isenbiel is considering (he returned the stenographic report[4] to me) whether to prosecute Bernstein (possibly B. and me). If he does, we would have the best solution for the time being: B. indicted, myself as witness, etc.[5] But they will try to persuade I. to drop the case because 'we don't want any further scandal'. He (I.) has undoubtedly been honest up to now, but has been convinced by Beseler,[6] E[ulenburg] and Co. that the Chancellor was Phili's friend and that the interests of state demanded indulgent treatment of E[ulenburg] who was sick and innocent. In my opinion the whole business would take a significant step forward if B. (the Chancellor) would see the public prosecutor soon. He would then have the (extraordinarily naïve) man wrapped up in three minutes. It is NOT a question of myself. The whole business would at once take on a different aspect and the battle against E. would become serious and offer some prospect of success if I. knew, and knew for certain, that Wilhelmstrasse No. 77[7] did not wish to hush the matter up. B. would have a very useful tool; for I. would at once understand that the big B.[8] is a good deal more important for him than the little B.[9] If the Chancellor does not care to do so (his mistrust [of Isenbiel] is totally unjustified, and is probably only a facade, considering his vastly superior skill) then I. will never be convinced that Court and Ministry are not completely for E. I need hardly discuss the consequences. Once I. has suspended the case in order to please all parties, especially E. whom he considers to be the 'friend of the Chancellor', then this path is closed and he cannot retrace his steps. He would also always treat my evidence with the prejudiced view that it concerned friends of the Chancellor. For the decisive battle, I consider this conference to be quite extraordinarily important.

[1] Eulenburg's private secretary, for whom the Prince secured the title of *Hofrat* when he retired from public life in 1902. (Haller, *Eulenburg*, p. 306.)

[2] A lawyer (*Geheimer Justizrat*) in Neu-Ruppin, and an old friend of Eulenburg's.

[3] Baron Wendelstadt had been a guest at Liebenberg at the time of the Kaiser's visit, 7–10 November 1906, when M. Lecomte, the French Secretary of Embassy, had also been present. (Haller, *Eulenburg*, p. 315.)

[4] Not found.

[5] Harden is here suggesting another possibility for bringing his evidence against Eulenburg into the law courts. (See above, p. 514, note 10.)

[6] Dr Maximilian Beseler. Prussian Minister of Justice, 1905–17.

[7] The Reich Chancellery.　　　　　　　　　　[8] Bülow.　　　　　　　　　　[9] Beseler.

He[1] has *completely* taken in Rheinbaben[2] (since a fortnight ago); a bagatelle with I.

Monday evening, very faint with lack of breath. Since then, worse.

I hope Your Excellency is quite well.

With my best compliments
Your very devoted
Harden.

1081.  Maximilian Harden to Holstein

30 March 1908

Your Excellency,

Hülsen-H[äseler][3] is said to be carrying on a latent conflict with His Majesty; told a friend: 'I can't go along with that; I will resign and tell the truth: that E[ulenburg] perjured himself; I want to be and must be summoned as a witness.' Source: a general on active duty who heard it from H's confidant. Would be manly, and in its way, great. The verdict on Hohenau by the Court of Honour has actually been annulled.[4] A new Court not yet appointed. Much bad blood about that, too, among *old* officers.

In the Isenbiel matter, I hope it will be brought into the right channels. *If* B[ülow] is not persuaded to change his mind. The official *in charge* of the matter, Rasch, the prosecuting attorney, is *very* predisposed to-wards E[ulenburg] and M[oltke]; has conducted the affair up to now, has probably been talked around and swears they are innocent. That is not the attitude with which one should approach the matter. I. should put an *impartial man in charge* (preferable Katz,[5] of course, who would stick to the facts and would really try to get at the truth), and *with him* he should question the witnesses *himself*, and he should do so *here* (not allow it to be done by pre-selected judges); then the truth could be brought to light in a short time.

Whether it would be possible to say this to I., I do not know. As soon as I. learns that the people on top want only a thorough clarification of the matter, I would have complete confidence in him if only the official who works over the material and submits it to him were no longer the gentleman who talked so much with His Highness [Bülow] in the law court and who believes that 'in this business one could easily get one's fingers burned'.[6] In that case I might fire away. [...]

If one could now at least bring down the E[ulenburg] clique, so that there was no longer the slightest doubt about it, then *something* would have been gained. Then I would be glad to suffer. But the Chancellor must risk something too. The impression on His Majesty would surely

---

[1] Bülow.

[2] Georg, Baron von Rheinbaben. Prussian Minister of the Interior, 1899–1901; Minister of Finance, 1901–10.

[3] Dietrich von Hülsen-Häseler.          [4] See above, p. 477, note 5.

[5] Leo Katz. A prosecuting attorney in the Public Prosecutor's Office.

[6] The reference is presumably to Rasch, the prosecuting attorney.

be a strong one. (He wanted to give Friedrich Heinrich[1] a brigade! Not yet totally eliminated.)

Please excuse this haste.

Your Excellency's very devoted

H.[2]

## 1082. Maximilian Harden to Holstein

Grunewald, 1 April 1908

Your Excellency

Many thanks for the friendly lines.[3] I must ask your pardon for having written so hastily. A great deal of personal irritation (Dernburg-Rathenau),[4] sickness, and the severe agitation about the Hill affair[5] (*Daily News*!!) all combined. So I must have expressed myself very unclearly. Because of course I did not have the intention of bringing the question about the official-in-charge before the highest authorities (for something like that, the unusual word 'snarling' would have taken away my appetite), but to inform Your Excellency, according to the information I received, about the personalities who may have given rise to that frequently-mentioned 'suspicion'. After we had talked about the matter so much, I thought I could allow myself to inform Your Excellency about this supplement to the existing picture. In doing so, I counted on the *possibility* that *at some time* these hints could be used to show that not the older gentleman[6] but the young assistant,[7] and quite *bona fide*, might prevent *la vérité en marche*. I am sincerely sorry that, just after receiving the news about H[ülsen]-H[äseler], I threw my words together in this way.

Such incidents painfully show me *how* sick I am. The slightest excitement knocks me over. For days. At one time I would not have believed it possible. Such powers of resistance and ability to work will never return. The three days were terrible.

I ask pardon once again, thank you for your kind advice about travel,[8] and hope to see Your Excellency on Saturday (or earlier).

[1] Friedrich Heinrich, Prince of Prussia. (See above, p. 456, note 4.)

[2] Holstein replied on 31 March that any effort to effect an intervention in the operations of the office in charge of the matter would be ineffectual and also dangerous. (Rogge, *Holstein und Harden*, p. 276.)

[3] The letter to which Harden seems to refer in the text below has not been found. (See Holstein's letter of 31 March, Rogge, *Holstein und Harden*, p. 276.)

[4] Both State Secretary Dernburg and Walther Rathenau had offered to act as mediators in the Moltke-Harden case. Harden resented the implications in the Press that he had come to Dernburg as a suppliant. (*Zukunft*, vol. 62, pp. 410–14.)

[5] Upon the resignation of Mr Charlemagne Tower from his post as Ambassador to Germany, the American Government named Mr David Hill, then Minister to the Netherlands, as his successor. This appointment was officially accepted by the German Government, but soon afterwards President Roosevelt was unofficially informed that Hill was not considered suitable for the Berlin post because his income was not sufficiently large. To calm the resulting anger of the Americans, the German Government was obliged to announce officially that there had never been any change in the Kaiser's attitude towards Hill or in his willingness to receive him in Berlin.

[6] Presumably Isenbiel.          [7] Presumably Rasch, the prosecuting attorney.

[8] In a letter of 30 March, Holstein had recommended the Channel Islands, the Isle of Wight, or the Italian lakes as possible vacation spots for Harden. (Rogge, *Holstein und Harden*, p. 276.)

May I add that I was and am convinced that I have not taken up the time of important men *in my interests*? But for a matter that is damned serious and important. I hear very curious things about how things are being done on the *other* side of the Wilhelmstrasse;[1] there a man who is actually hostile to me is in charge of things.[2] If anything is to be done about the matter: fine. If they want to strangle the truth: I have done my duty; and perhaps more than my duty. The possibility I indicated seemed to me to be the last (because the man in question[3] only needs a *prop* in order to conduct the matter conscientiously and fearlessly); if it is not considered significant, then things will simply stay as they are.

With the best wishes for the health of Your Excellency

Your very devoted
Harden

## 1083.  Holstein to Bernhard von Bülow
Copy

Berlin, [3] April 1908

Dear Bülow,

A communication I just received[4] makes me certain that the step you intended to take has as yet not been taken. I am permitting myself to remind you of it. For a reason which we may have discussed but which you can in any case guess, I wish you would now make it clear that you have a certain interest in an objective and correct procedure, in order thereby to cut off every possible excuse for later criticism, no matter from which side it might come.

With old regard
Your sincerely devoted
Holstein

## 1084.  Bernhard von Bülow to Holstein

Saturday morning, [4 April 1908]

Dear Holstein,

You are not quite correctly informed.[5] I feel it is my duty to arrange for an objective, correct, and just procedure in this matter too, but think that ill-considered and clumsy moves would achieve exactly the opposite result. If you can come to-day, I will be at your disposal at seven o'clock. Between the Reichstag and audiences, I am busier than usual, but I will at least keep a half hour open.

With best wishes

Your sincerely devoted.
Bülow.

[1] The Ministry of Justice at No. 65 Wilhelmstrasse, opposite the Reich Chancellery.
[2] Presumbly Rasch, the prosecuting attorney.
[3] Presumbly Isenbiel.
[4] See above, Harden's letter of 30 March. Holstein presumably discussed the problem with Harden before writing to Bülow. (See below, p. 524, note 1.)
[5] See above, Holstein's letter to Bülow of [3] April.

## 1085.   Maximilian Harden to Holstein

5 April 1908

Your Excellency,

Thank you very much for your friendly efforts.[1] I urgently hope that they succeed. It is high time. But I fear that other influences will make themselves felt. [...]

Herr von Tresckow[2] was in Liebenberg for two days; to 'make enquiries'.[3] Charmed by his reception, happy family life, etc. Phili told him it was bad luck that he was always being confused with his brother;[4] once, without suspecting anything, he went to a bath house of dubious repute. Otherwise: completely innocent. I find this manner of making police enquiries new and most significant. In this way they will surely never find anything but innocent people. The commissioner as guest of the ambassador, and fêted for days. The glories of Old Prussia!

When one realizes what resources these people have, one can hardly count on a good outcome. At any rate, everything possible should also be done by the other side. We will have to wait and see.

With the best wishes for your health

I remain Your Excellency's

Very devoted

H.

## 1086.   Maximilian Harden to Holstein

9 April 1908

Your Excellency,

Many thanks. The audience took place to-day at noon. Big B. did it through Little B., and said very little to the man from Moabit.[5] Both facts diminish the effect *a little*. Still, I am enormously pleased about it; and can only sincerely thank Your Excellency for your friendly efforts. It was decided yesterday in the Reichstag; then discussed with Beseler.

I want to mention briefly that, so far as I could find out, there was *no* encounter in the woods of Hubertusstock, and that sending the commissioner to the house of family happiness was a decision of the Alexanderplatz, not of Moabit.[6]

---

[1] See above, Holstein's letter to Bülow of [3] April. Holstein wrote to Harden on [4 April]. 'The letter went off last night. I don't expect a written reply. I did it because you wanted me to. But for me, Munich remains the main point.' (Rogge, *Holstein und Harden*, p. 277.) Holstein was referring to Harden's plan to bring out his evidence against Eulenburg in a Munich law court. (See below, p. 528, note 1.)

[2] Hans von Tresckow. Official of the Berlin Police in charge of blackmail cases.

[3] Tresckow had gone to Liebenberg on 31 January 1908 to ask Eulenburg about the rumours concerning his sexual life that had come to the attention of the Berlin Police. (See Tresckow, *Von Fürsten*, pp. 153–9.)

[4] Prince Philipp's brother, Friedrich Botho zu Eulenburg, had been obliged to leave the army in 1901 because of homosexual activities.

[5] Harden means that Bülow had asked Beseler to inform Isenbiel of the Government's attitude towards the Moltke-Eulenburg-Harden case.

[6] Harden means that Tresckow had been sent on his mission to Liebenberg (see above, note 3) by the Police, not by the Public Prosecutor's Office.

I am much looking forward to seeing Your Excellency tomorrow.
With most sincere good wishes, I remain

Very respectfully

H.

1087.　Memorandum by Holstein

29 April 1908

*Relations with Bülow*

In December 1906, after the appointment of Dernburg, pressure was brought to bear on Bülow from several sides to appoint other men who were not professional civil servants, also Semites, to high offices.

Dernburg had been proposed by Hammann and Loebell; behind both, the motivating force was Stubenrauch.[1] Some years ago Stubenrauch recommended his drinking companion, Hammann, to Caprivi, and succeeded in getting Caprivi, just before his departure, to appoint Hammann, who at one time had vainly tried to pass the first state law examination, to the title of *Wirklicher Legationsrat* and the office of *Vortragender Rat* in the Foreign Ministry. Then, when the position of Chief of the Reich Chancellery fell vacant, Hammann proposed Loebell, a relative of Stubenrauch's. And it was also Stubenrauch who later on pushed the appointment of Dernburg, because he was indebted to him for a favour. Dernburg, while he was Director of the Bank of Darmstadt, had succeeded in making a bankrupt brother of Frau von Stubenrauch, the African explorer von Eberstein, a director of a Breslau bank (I forget whether it was the *Diskonto* or *Kommerzbank*). Eberstein does not seem to have felt up to the job, because he took his own life within a year. But Stubenrauch remembered his indebtedness to Dernburg. When Dernburg's post with the Bank of Darmstadt became shaky as a result of an excessive spirit of enterprise, the grateful Stubenrauch saved him by a transfer to the Colonial Office, through Hammann and Loebell.

Besides consideration for Stubenrauch, Hammann was probably also motivated by the desire to bring in more non-professional civil servants, especially Semites. This is a central issue for Hammann's political Egeria, Dr Stein of the *Frankfurter Zeitung*. [...]

The appointment of Dernburg fit into Stein's view of things, insofar as it meant a break with the tradition of professional civil servants. To strike while the iron was hot, they now put pressure on Bülow to make other, similar, appointments. The use of respected parliamentarians and important bankers as Ministers and State Secretaries was recommended and considered. Dernburg himself, as I know from a reliable person, felt shortly before the dissolution of the Reichstag[2] that he had the power to dispense portfolios.

To me this was one of several signs that indicated that the clique of Hammann, Stein, and Co., looked upon the dissolution of the Reichstag

[1] Head of the Administration of the District of Teltow. (See Hammann, *Neue Kurs*, pp. 6–7.)

[2] In December 1906.

and the break with the Centre Party as a decided shift to the Left. So one day around Christmas time I talked to Bülow about it and asked him if he intended to make further appointments à la Dernburg. At the same time I advised him against it. The German people assume that a professional civil servant is decent and honest until there is proof to the contrary. The non-professional, especially the financier, has no claim to this assumption but must prove himself first. Added to this there is the further disadvantage of the official inexperience of the non-professional. Even Gneist,[1] whom one cannot accuse of narrow-minded prejudice against *self-government*, that is, against government by non-professionals, mentions that the dark side of the system of Justices of the Peace is that the real work, and with that the real power, slips into the hands of the non-responsible paid clerks. The same thing can be said, *mutatis mutandis*, of every office whose chief is inexperienced in that particular branch of administration. Under someone like that the officials of a central office who are counted upon to do the work—what are in France called *Les bureaux*—achieve a status of independence that is unthinkable under a chief who is a trained expert. Furthermore, it was just at this time that any deviation from the professional tradition was bound to make the Conservatives, already irritated by the break with the Centre, suspicious of the Chancellor.

In presenting my point of view I found that the Chancellor had in fact been under strong pressure to appoint parliamentary or financial people. He named several names. At the same time the fiasco with Möller, the Minister of Trade, was before him as a warning example. Bülow thought that even a professional Minister of small talent would not be treated so badly as Möller had been treated by Richter.[2] I cannot now say whether I convinced Bülow, but I did strengthen the views he held already. So up till now Dernburg has remained the only wedge. And my views are shown to be right by Dernburg's position within his own office.

In the beginning Dernburg shocked his subordinates by his rude behaviour. For instance, one day when an Under State Secretary or a Director made a suggestion before strangers : 'That would probably be the most impractical thing (his listeners felt that he had wanted to say "the most stupid thing") that one could do.' But this situation corrected itself. The officials soon noticed that Dernburg had neither the intention nor the ambition to master the material, but that he only attached importance to his position vis-à-vis Parliament and the Press. From that time on the officials were on top, and they made Dernburg feel his dependence. A short time ago an important entrepreneur who is involved in railroad construction in Africa came to one of the officials in

[1] Rudolf von Gneist. Professor of Law at the University of Berlin under whom Holstein himself had studied. He wrote a number of works on the English governmental system, which he greatly admired.

[2] Before his appointment as Minister of Trade, Möller had served in both the Prussian Chamber of Deputies and the Reichstag as a member of the National Liberal Party. Eugen Richter, the leader of the German Radical Party, had not only attacked Möller's policies in the Reichstag, but had subjected the Minister to ridicule. (See Bülow, *Denkwürdigkeiten*, vol. II, p. 91.)

the Colonial office and referred to the fact that the State Secretary had made him a definite promise. 'That may be,' said the official, 'The State Secretary may have done so. But I am the person who has to work out the plans, and whatever I work out, the State Secretary will then sign.' I hear, too, that when Dernburg now screams at his subordinates, they reply in the same manner. So the opinion has gradually been formed among Berlin officials that anarchic conditions prevail in the Colonial Division, even worse than in Stübel's time.

Over a year ago I advised Bülow to get rid of State Secretary Stengel[1] in a friendly way because, although otherwise an excellent and also capable man, he was dealing with the tax question too much from the Bavarian point of view. That Bülow left him in the position until the end of 1907 was probably done for the two-fold reason that he did not again want to offend the Centre Party, and because no suitable person could be found who was willing to take that horrible job. The Secretary of the Treasury was merely an appendage of the Prussian Ministry of Finance, for he had to act according to what was decided in the Prussian Ministry of State. For that reason I advised Bülow to make the new Secretary of the Treasury at the same time a Prussian Minister without portfolio, so that he could attend the meetings and defend himself. Only in this way would the position become at all acceptable.

Bülow thought this was the egg of Columbus. He would keep the plan a secret until it had been approved by the Kaiser. Because Rheinbaben might threaten to resign if he heard about it *beforehand*. *Afterwards*, when His Majesty had actually rendered a decision on the matter, Rheinbaben would give in. This was exactly what was done, and the appointment of Sydow created no difficulties. I did not risk naming a candidate owing to insufficient knowledge of personnel; I only repeated my opinion—shared by Bülow—that a professional civil servant would be better than a non-professional.

We also agreed that the new Secretary of the Treasury must be urged to secure the taxation of beer and tobacco. It seemed to me that the most practical means of exerting pressure would be to present the Bavarians with the alternative of a beer tax or indefinitely large contributions to the Imperial treasury.[2] Bülow shared this view and said that Rüger, the Finance Minister of Saxony, had told him that he was glad a Prussian was to be made Secretary of the Treasury, because the Reich had suffered under the Bavarian financial administration of recent years.

When I saw Bülow the next time he told me that the new Secretary of the Treasury was willing to give the question of the beer and tobacco tax detailed study. Yesterday's speech by Pfaff, the Finance Minister of Bavaria, leads me to believe that Sydow, who was in Munich recently, brought strong pressure to bear on him. Because Pfaff says:

No direct Imperial taxes (income or inheritance); no indefinite contributions to the Imperial treasury. Perhaps inheritance tax on

[1] Hermann, Baron von Stengel. State Secretary in the Reich Treasury, 1903–February 1908.
[2] See above, Holstein's letter to Bülow of 6 March 1908.

descendants. This last is so generally disliked that I think even the Bavarians will then regard the beer tax as the lesser evil. It would almost seem that this was the intention of Pfaff's speech.

## 1088.   Maximilian Harden to Holstein

1 May 1908

Your Excellency,

I have been summoned as a witness for Saturday, 2 May, eleven o'clock 'in the criminal proceedings against Prince E[ulenburg]-H[ertefeld] for perjury'.[1]

Since I was just summoned this evening, I will tell the judge in charge of the enquiry that I need more time, and will then hand everything in in writing. There is a vast amount of material. *Very* great consequences.

Heated exchange of telegrams, Wilhelmstrasse-Venice-Corfu.[2] *Perhaps* the most epoch-making event since 1890. Franz Joseph (I hear privately) had the Munich trial telephoned to him three times to Schönbrunn. Cannot bear him[3] either.

I am on the track of material that E[ulenburg] *influenced the Press* during the Morocco crisis. That too would be something. And would probably interest Your Excellency especially.

Please excuse me. From eight in the morning until late at night, long distance calls, telegrams, telephone. Half dead. But *La Verité est en marche.*

I hope I will have the pleasure of seeing Your Excellency Sunday morning. *Much* to tell. Also about tactics. Against Bernstein, the court 'suspended its decision'. That means he will not be prosecuted.[4]

In excitement and hope,

With respectful greetings

H.

[1] At the Bülow-Brand trial (see above, p. 498, note 6) and again at the second Moltke-Harden trial, Prince Eulenburg had stated under oath that he had not only never indulged in sexual practices punishable by law, but that he had never engaged in unnatural sexual behaviour of any kind. On 25 March 1908 a Munich editor named Anton Städele published an article in his newspaper, the *Neue Freie Volkszeitung*, stating that Harden had accepted a bribe of a million marks from his opponents to suppress the evidence he had against them. The article was a part of a prearranged plan for bringing out Harden's evidence against Eulenburg in a Bavarian law court. Harden sued Städele for libel, and the case was heard before a petty court (Schöffengericht) in Munich on 21 April 1908. To prove that he was not suppressing evidence, Harden summoned two witnesses, Georg Riedl and Jakob Ernst, who testified that they had engaged in homosexual practices with Eulenburg. On the basis of this evidence Eulenburg was arrested on the charge of perjury on 8 May. His trial began on 29 June.

Holstein appears to have had a clear idea of Harden's plans in setting up the Munich trial, for on 19 March he had advised Harden against writing to the Supreme Court at Leipzig. Munich was the place to concentrate his efforts. Harden should give intensive thought as to how this could be done. (Rogge, *Holstein und Harden*, p. 275.)

[2] At the end of April the Kaiser was in Corfu in the course of a trip through the Mediterranean, and Bülow was in Venice for talks with Minister-President Giolitti.

[3] Prince Eulenburg.

[4] After the second Moltke-Harden trial, Prince Eulenburg asked the State to institute proceedings against both Harden and Bernstein. (See above, p. 514, note 4.) Both cases were suspended after the Munich trial.

## 1089. Holstein to Bernhard von Bülow
### Draft

21 May 1908

Postscript to a letter to Bülow[1] about my *Matin* interview.[2]

It is of decisive importance for Germany's future that there should be no doubt about the Kaiser's attitude towards the Peace of Frankfurt which Etienne and other Frenchmen are trying to create. Stahl[3] used to teach in his lectures : 'The King is the natural expression of the nation.' That is to-day truer than ever. As long as His Majesty intends to remain Kaiser, he must subordinate any personal impulses to national necessity. And he will want to remain Kaiser, in spite of everything. His threat of abdication when you would not at once agree to Ballin's million mark contract with Russia[4] was a dramatic impulse, as we agreed in Homburg. Incidentally, the rumour is gaining ground in political circles, probably unjustly, that H.M. has big investments with Ballin as he does with Krupp. H.M. simply behaves incautiously, in this as in other matters. In his—that is, in the monarchial—interest, as well as in your own, for your position in history, you must compel him to stick more closely than he has done heretofore to the paths which we regard as normal and sensible; without regard for hysterical threats (by which I think first of the above-mentioned one of 1904). And supposing he carries it out? That would not be the worst thing that could happen. Under the *given* circumstances, your *first* task is to *lead* the Kaiser, and it is only your *secondary* task to protect him *if* he allows himself to be led.

I am talking so seriously after careful consideration and with reason. People are beginning to see things increasingly clearly and before the curtain is fully drawn you will at least have to establish a little order in the situation, otherwise it will be bad for the monarchy and good for Bebel and Co.

I chose the *Matin*—to return to *that* subject—because it is the French counterpart of *The Times* and is much reprinted in England. The threat of *famine, révoltes* is intended for England.

## 1090. Bernhard von Bülow to Holstein

Monday, 25 May 1908

Dear Holstein,

Many thanks for your friendly lines. I share your opinion that for official and personal reasons we will have to handle the Morocco question

---

[1] Not found.

[2] Holstein told the Berlin representative of the Paris *Matin* on 23 May that the hate between the French and the Germans was a costly luxury, and predicted the time would come when the people of both nations would realize it was a useless expenditure. Holstein at the same time warned the French not to interpret little attentions on the part of Germany as indications of a feeling that would lead to a revision of the Treaty of Frankfurt, for he believed the Kaiser was at one with the German people in defence of that treaty. (See below, Holstein's memorandum of 1 June 1908.)

[3] Friedrich Julius Stahl, Holstein's professor of Natural and Canon Law at the University of Berlin.

[4] In September 1904. (See *Grosse Politik*, vol. XIXi, nos. 6080–1, pp. 251–3.)

with care.[1] I also agree with you that Radolin is better as Ambassador in Paris than those who would like to take his place. As long as I remain in office, I think I can say that there will be no change in Paris. But just because I want Radolin to stay, I say: to retain him would be easier for me if he succeeded in making it clear to the French that it is in their interests too not to excite and offend our public opinion too much by their actions in Morocco. *Est modus in rebus.*

I ordered the Press Bureau to supervise carefully the translation of the *Matin*[2] for the *Norddeutsche Allgemeine Zeitung*. I had the article submitted to His Maj. in the original. '*Montrez ma tête au peuple, elle vaut bien la peine*', Danton said on the scaffold. To read this interview is also worth the trouble. The *Tag* is supposed to print it tomorrow; I am trying to get it into the *Kreuzzeitung*.

I have urged Radowitz to postpone his intention to retire until autumn. That would make it easier to fill the post suitably.

In haste and with best wishes,

Sincerely yours

B.

## 1091.   Maximilian Harden to Holstein

28 May 1908

Your Excellency,

From everything I have, very reliably, heard, the best thing to do next would be to *prevent* Beseler from carrying out his wish to make I[senbiel] the scapegoat, but instead to allow I. to *show* that he intends to do the right thing. And he will show just that if they give him time. He is very fascinated by His Highness (on the other side of the Wilhelmstrasse).[3]

Schmidt[4] on the other hand, who works very hard, is behaving rather strangely. As impossible as it sounds: he allowed one of E[ulenburg]'s attorneys to be present at all the Munich hearings[5] and allowed him to question the witnesses. That *never* happens otherwise, nor does legal procedure permit it. And with a man who has been imprisoned because of the danger of collusion,[6] this is trebly strange. He has summoned me to appear again on Saturday.

---

[1] In 1907 civil war had broken out in Morocco when Mulai Hafid, with considerable local support, made a bid to become Sultan of Morocco in place of his brother, Abdul Aziz. At the end of April 1908, Mulai Hafid, the pretender, sent emissaries to France, England, Spain, and Germany. The delegation of Mulai Hafid was received in Berlin on 15 May and aroused considerable suspicion in France about Germany's intentions. (See *Grosse Politik*, vol. XXIV, chapter CLXXIX.)

[2] Of Holstein's *Matin* interview. (See above, p. 529, note 2.)

[3] Bülow. (See above, p. 523, note 1.)

[4] Investigating magistrate in the State's case against Eulenburg for perjury.

[5] The investigation of witnesses by the State in Munich in the Eulenburg perjury case.

[6] It was feared that Prince Eulenburg might try to influence his former servant Jakob Ernst, who was the most incriminating witness against him. One of the reasons for this belief was the discovery of a letter from Eulenburg to Ernst of 22 December 1907, written during the second Moltke-Harden trial when Eulenburg seems to have believed Ernst would be called to the witness stand. In his letter Eulenburg said, 'The infamous slanderous gang wants to ruin

I have sent him about five more typewritten pages. [...]

> With the best wishes for your health,
> I am Your Excellency's
> Very devoted
> Harden

## 1092.    Maximilian Harden to Holstein

30 May 1908

Your Excellency,

To-day, too, I received a very good impression of the investigating magistrate.[1] Details later. To-day just the most important; just between ourselves, please, because I promised discretion. I am telling the following to *no one* at the moment; not to E.Z.[2] either, because of Your Excellency's distrust. But I have no objection if the Chancellor hears about it.

At my instigation, the investigating magistrate also took an interest in the point made by Holstein (political activity of E[ulenburg]; denied under oath). And in Liebenberg, *important* material relating to this matter has been confiscated; quite a lot, it seems.[3] According to that (he says), the matter is not *quite* as it has previously been pictured. 'The Holstein matter is connected with something else.' (Radolin letter?[4] Lecomte? Affair of honour?) Since I never ask a direct question in such cases, I decided in favour of the first. Still the matter appears to me to be of *outstanding* importance; *transcending the personal and offering insight into the entire complex of operations.* But how to get at it?

What I can do will be done. The rest must be done by the Chancellor —in the most effective way—and with Bismarckian ruthlessness. Namely: receive Isenbiel as soon as the investigation is completed and ask to have *the political documents* submitted to him *in the original.* He need only say at that time that he wants to see I., and when; I will see to it that I. *requests* permission at that time (a better way, because less obtrusive) in order to be able to supplement his previous report.[5] (Very simple and natural; if Beseler gets at the matter first, we will not be safe from manoeuvres.) And real proof of Holstein's point, and in general of Phili's backstairs political activity, must surely be of greatest importance

us after so many years and cover us with filth. Everything happened so long ago anyway, and besides you have nothing to say. All this is only being done to bring disgrace on you and me.' (Testimony presented in evidence at the Eulenburg trial, 9 July 1908. See Haller, *Eulenburg*, p. 366.)

[1] Probably Schmidt, though see above Harden's letter to Holstein of 28 May.

[2] Perhaps Eugen Zimmermann, head of the Scherl publishing house, whom Holstein suspected of maintaining close relations with Hammann.

[3] On 5 June 1942 the German Foreign Ministry tried to obtain the political correspondence mentioned above by Harden from the Ministry of Justice. The reply was that all the documents connected with the Eulenburg trial had been destroyed in 1932. (From the Foreign Ministry files.)

[4] Not identified.

[5] Probably Isenbiel's report of April 1908 on the Eulenburg case. (See below, Harden's letter to Holstein of 1 June 1908.)

to the Chancellor, too. All the more so since Paris is apparently impli-
cated, and in my opinion we are to-day closer to the danger of war than
at any time since '76.

This in a great hurry and with a wicked headache.

But also with best wishes.

Your Excellency's devoted

H.

All these confiscations unfortunately came a few weeks too late.

### 1093.  Maximilian Harden to Holstein

31 May 1908

Your Excellency,

I hope that the evening, for which I thank you very much, agreed with
you.

I forgot a small but characteristic point. Up till yesterday the police
had not yet given the presiding magistrate the memorandum of
Meerscheidt-Hüllesem which he had requested and which I recently
mentioned in the *Zukunft* and had named as evidence in my testimony as a
witness.[1] It is certain to contain important material. Apparently
Stubenrauch won't play. Saw Beseler yesterday. And am less doubtful
than ever that Beseler, who might be adequate as a provincial judge, is
not working in Bülow's interests. It is all the more important that we
have a man in Moabit who is open to persuasion. If only for inconvenient
questions to the witnesses.[2]

The statement of Bülow-Loebell that the Chancellor does not intend
to intervene in the pending M[oltke]-Harden case was in my opinion
superfluous, to say the least.

With best wishes I remain

Your Excellency's most devoted

H.

I have tried to avoid mentioning yesterday's chance colloquium, not to
B[ülow] either, and think that complete discretion is assured; otherwise
misunderstandings might arise, and B. might think he was being circumvented. The gentleman will keep silent. I am sure Your Excellency will
not quote the honest E.Z.[3] to B. He is useful and decent.

I have reasons, very pertinent and recent ones, to offer the modest
advice to treat B[ülow] *with caution*. Truth is not his strong point. Not
in his relations with friends, either. [...]

### 1094.  Maximilian Harden to Holstein

1 June 1908

Your Excellency,

I do not wish to be misunderstood about the last topic we discussed
to-day:

[1] A list of several hundred men suspected of homosexuality, prepared by Police Inspector
Meerscheidt-Hüllesem. (See Tresckow, *Von Fürsten*, pp. 115–16.)

[2] See below, Harden's letter of 1 June 1908.

[3] Perhaps Eugen Zimmermann, of whom Harden seems to have had a better opinion than
Holstein. (See above, p.531, note 2.)

Important political material confiscated; Beseler and Co., whom I do not trust at all (especially because at the moment so devoted to the Chancellor), could take it to the wrong place; if the Chancellor sees it, he will be able to see deep down into the witches' cauldron and may find names and facts that will interest him. He can only see it after the preliminary investigation is closed and *before* the documents have been turned over to the court by the public prosecution. It would be inconspicuous if I[senbiel] were given a hint through the usual channel that he would be allowed to report to the Chancellor to supplement the report he made last April.[1] It would be best if the Chancellor could indicate the day and the hour, so that I. could request an audience for that time. It is therefore a question of doing the Chancellor a favour which under certain circumstances might become useful for further investigation.

Further: it is important that I. keeps control of the matter, and that the Chancellor keeps control of I., because otherwise inconvenient questions might be put to the witness M[aximilian] H[arden], (who does not need to be summoned at all, and who would not be summoned by I.), and possibly also to other witnesses. For instance: 'What do you know about the intentions, feelings, etc., of the Chancellor?' And so forth. If Harden is not summoned as a witness by the public prosecutor, he need not be available at all during the period of the E[ulenburg] trial. The names of the 165 witnesses he knows, he has named long ago.

See my last letter.

I permit myself to recommend caution about B[ülow] *only* in the interests of the cause. I am never certain that he is not keeping a trump in his sleeve just in case. *Et qu'il me vend, pour se soulager.* Only for that reason am I interested in the historical circumstances of Your Excellency's dismissal. Conclusion by analogy. Miquel, Podbielsky, Holstein, are all certain that he did not do it.

In all haste, with best wishes

Your Excellency's very devoted

H. [...]

1095.   Memorandum by Holstein
       The Franco-German Rapprochement (Continued)[2]

1 June 1908

Recently the correspondent of the *Matin* here[3] informed me of various statements in French newspapers, especially in the official *Temps*, which explain the unsatisfactory attitude of Germany in the Morocco question by the fact that even to-day I was still influencing the Morocco policy of the German government. Actually, since my departure I have avoided as a matter of principle talking about Morocco with the Chancellor or any other official person. These lies are being spread chiefly by the representative of the *Temps* here, Roels, an Alsatian who is at the same

[1] Not found. See above, p. 531, note 3.
[2] The first part of Holstein's essay on the problem of a Franco-German rapprochement was printed in the *Memoirs*, chapter VI.
[3] M. Lionel Caro.

time an intimate of Hammann and Cambon. Roels, who is considered a fanatical Frenchman in Press circles here, was one of the first to start the rumour in April 1905 that I was the one who was urging war with France. The real source of this rumour was Hammann, who wanted to get rid of me, and who from the spring of 1905 always took the same view as France, also in the Morocco question. From the beginning of April 1905, until the 8 or 9 December 1905, when the Chancellor made his big Morocco speech in the Reichstag,[1] the Press Bureau did not write *one single* article to explain, or rather to defend, the Chancellor's personally-conducted Morocco policy. The German public and Press were obliged to turn for clarification to explanations of French and English origin. No wonder that the German public failed to understand German policy and regarded it with suspicion. When Bülow gave Hammann a nudge, the latter assured him that a stand in the official Press would only arouse opposition and make the problem more acute. Bülow contented himself with that, and may not have been sorry to see that meanwhile the chief responsibility for this increasingly unpopular question was gradually being loaded on me. In this way—I will not go into the Morocco question here—it was possible for the belief to spread everywhere that there was such a thing as a Holstein war policy. So if to-day, in the spring of 1908, the Press Bureau is spreading the lie that our Morocco policy is still being influenced by me, the purpose is absolutely clear: the Chancellor is to be made to see that his relations with me are detrimental by pointing out that these relations make his policy more difficult. Since I am considered a war-monger (even if unjustly), the suspicion that I am influencing his Morocco policy must make a large number of people suspicious of that policy as well.

I therefore decided to establish by a public statement that since my retirement I have had nothing to do with Moroccan affairs. It also seemed useful to me to say a few words about the Peace of Frankfurt and about the possibility of war. I wrote the whole interview, including the questions the correspondent was to put to me, in French and then dictated it to him word for word, with the stipulation that nothing be changed.[2]

I had said nothing beforehand to the Chancellor. When the telegram came that the interview was in the process of publication, I informed Bülow in writing about its contents and purpose. Bülow replied on Thursday, 21 May:

'Dear Holstein. I too think that an interview as outlined by you may be useful. In particular I fully share your opinion that the position not only of the Kaiser but of all patriotic Germans cannot be a subject of doubt. I will have the *Matin* article submitted to me tomorrow and have to-day already given instructions that the interview is not only to be discussed objectively but appreciatively.' etc. etc.[3]

On Sunday, 24 May, the article appeared. Even before that Bülow had

[1] Of 6 December 1905.
[2] This was Holstein's *Matin* interview of 23 May. (See above, p. 529, note 2.)
[3] Holstein's copy of Bülow's letter corresponds with the original in the Holstein Papers.

at my request ordered that it be published in the *Norddeutsche Allgemeine Zeitung*, and this was done. At the same time Hammann had a message sent to me by a round-about route : to convince me how erroneous my assumption was that he was working against me, he at once, as soon as he heard about the article, drafted a memorandum to the Chancellor recommending that it be published in the *Norddeutsche*!

In fact, as soon as Hammann heard about the interview he gave the word : 'No mention is to be made of Holstein's interview. Holstein is done for.' And this directive was actually followed more closely than Bülow's. The interview was only published in its entirety—apart from the *Norddeutsche*—in the *Kreuzzeitung*, under special pressure from Bülow. The other newspapers only printed a stunted version.

## 1096.   Maximilian Harden to Holstein

12 June 1908

Your Excellency,

[...] Since I cannot know what may become of the Eulenburg *causa* in the hands of our justice officials, I would like Your Excellency to read what *I*, after years of collecting, submitted to the court in the way of material. Just so that one person, whose opinion I value, should know what the situation is and what 'Harden actually had'. I ask you to be good enough to take this trouble, and *then to return the material to me*. Many thanks in advance. [...]

With sincerest good wishes I remain

Your Excellency's devoted
Harden.

## 1097.   Memorandum by Holstein

15 June 1908

[...] From Corfu, the Kaiser had Turkan Pasha[1] advise the Sultan to grant the concession for the transverse railroad from Serbia to Antivari which would circumvent Austrian territory and prejudice both the economic and political position of Austria-Hungary.[2] In doing so, His Majesty—spontaneously and gratuitously—aided the policy of the four Powers[3] to the detriment of our Austrian ally. To make the significance of this act even greater, and to serve notice that German policy was a personal, imperial policy, His Majesty sent a message to Baron Aehrenthal when he passed through Vienna recommending this transverse railroad, but this message was not sent through the German Ambassador or the German State Secretary, who were both at hand, but through Prince von Fürstenberg, as the confidential agent of the Kaiser.[4]

Our Kaiser has therefore, in the most unequivocal manner possible, shown the Cabinet of Vienna that in at least one important Balkan question it cannot count on German support; yes, and furthermore, that

[1] Turkish Minister; Ambassador in St Petersburg, August 1908–13.
[2] See *Grosse Politik*, vol. XXVii, no. 8746, p. 365.
[3] England, France, Russia, and Italy.
[4] See *Grosse Politik*, vol. XXVii, no. 8747, pp. 366–7.

H.M. has used his personal influence in Constantinople to put through anti-Austrian plans.

On this basis Austrian policy has no choice but to reach the best possible understanding with the other four Powers. The most difficult part of such an understanding—and also the factor that impelled Austria-Hungary to Germany—lies in the conflict between Austro-Hungarian and Italian interests. Italy is striving to get Albania, and thus might one day cut Austria-Hungary off from Saloniki and from the Mediterranean altogether. This difficulty would be removed with one stroke if Italy were to receive Tripoli instead of Albania in a division of the Turkish inheritance. We know that France, according to the programme of Cambon and Delcassé, wants all of North Africa including Tripoli, and has therefore done everything to encourage Italy's diversion towards Albania. England on the other hand would be glad to install Italy in Tripoli, between Egypt and French North Africa. During the last fifteen years English statesmen have repeatedly occupied and familiarized themselves with the idea that Syria would be France's share of the Turkish inheritance. If Syria becomes French and Tripoli becomes Italian, no stubborn opposition is to be expected from either of these satisfied Powers to Austria's getting Saloniki—at least not for the moment. All the less since France (Clemenceau) will have the not unreasonable hope that the five-Power group that carried through a partition of the Turkish Empire without a world war might do the same thing with the Peace of Frankfurt.

The only possibility I can see of preventing such a five-Power group would be if we gave the Cabinet at Vienna the certain assurance that it could count on German support for Austrian interests in the Balkans—and possibly even for which interests.

## 1098.   Maximilian Harden to Holstein

Tuesday, 16 June 1908

Your Excellency,

Many thanks for your kind effort.[1] At once did everything possible. Court summons fixed for 29 June. 5 arranged to-day. I[senbiel] wrote to his Minister he thought it necessary to conduct the business himself. Beseler left him completely in the lurch; *not one syllable* said about the Chancellor's friendly words (*gentleman*, etc.); treated like a scapegoat; what I. submitted in the way of political papers apparently *not* passed on (which was his duty after all), but said that political matters were to be returned to the Prince [Eulenburg] because they had nothing to do with the trial; and this has been done, to my great regret. B[eseler] left I.

[1] Harden had written on 15 June: 'The investigation of E[ulenburg] seems to be conducted energetically but unintelligently. It is certain that I[senbiel] submitted some documents about politics to the Ministry of Justice; if Bes[eler] failed to forward them [to the Chancellor] he has thereby shown how he understands his duties. I. could at any time be summoned to give a personal report. But I have the impression that the Chancellor doesn't want this sort of advice.' Holstein replied on the same evening, apparently after having seen Bülow: 'I[senbiel] *has* already been talked about, and he *will* be talked to, very soon I think.' (Rogge, *Holstein und Harden*, pp. 297–8.)

without directives in order, no matter what might happen, to be able to sacrifice him as the guilty party. Standard 'superior officer' tactics towards *minorum gentium*. But now I. wants to conduct the business himself, and I hope he will not be left without support. *He* did not summon me as a witness; it is doubtful whether the defence will do so, in order perhaps to draw out political matters and to ask about the Prince [Bülow], etc. One might get out of that by going on a journey, if necessary.

This in the usual Tuesday rush. Please excuse me.

Your Excellency's most respectful

H.

So 'what was said about I.' has been passed along.

### 1099.  Maximilian Harden to Holstein

Monday, [22 June 1908]

Your Excellency,

[...] For the time being, only the summons of Mayer[1] and Bernstein has been decided on. I myself am still doubtful. If it is *not* necessary, it would probably look more decent if I did not participate. (The stage director should not appear before the audience.) If it is necessary (E[ulenburg]'s clique is still acting as though it were 'certain of victory'), I can be summoned any day, even during the proceedings. (Which also leaves the difficulty that the presiding magistrate and the defence can summon me at any time.) After thinking it over for a long time, it seems advisable to me : *s'abstenir*; to wait and see if the scales still need this extra weight. If it were a matter of personal choice, I would use the opportunity to say a good deal. But is that wise? [...]

With best wishes for recovery

I remain Your Excellency's very devoted

Harden[2] [...]

### 1100.  Maximilian Harden to Holstein

27 June 1908

Your Excellency,

[...] I still hope that K.[3] will be well enough to go out by Monday.[4] We will be able to count on him. A question as to whether his chief on

---

[1] Wilhelm Mayer, the presiding judge at Harden's Munich trial. (See above, p. 528, note 1.)

[2] In a letter dated Thursday, probably of 25 June 1908, Holstein wrote that he was pleased that Bernstein would be questioned early in the Eulenburg trial. He could then decide whether or not Harden's appearance as a witness would still be necessary. 'I do not think that Riedl or Ernst will want to perjure themselves. And I think a detailed examination of Eulenburg is the correct procedure. He cannot then say: "I was muzzled".' Holstein believed that Isenbiel's desire to examine Eulenburg early in the trial was not an indication of another about-face on his part, but an effort to show that he was giving the accused every opportunity to defend himself. After the examination of Eulenburg would come the evidence of Riedl, Ernst, and Mayer. (From the Harden Papers.)

[3] The initial probably stands for Leo Katz, the prosecuting attorney.

[4] The Eulenburg trial was scheduled to begin on Monday, 29 June.

the other side of the Wilhelmstrasse[1] will not still allow himself to be influenced a little. I am not easy about it. It would be very very useful if on Monday an announcement could appear in the *Lokalanzeiger*, prosaic, without bite of any sort: he has been ordered to return the Black Eagle.[2] That would have a strong effect. Only crude weapons are of any use in Moabit.

If I think of the weapons used by the opposition, and what E[ulenburg] would do if he had any trumps at all!

But Your Excellency may perhaps wish this matter to be kept quiet; in that case we must get along without this particular trump card.[3] Mayer and Bernstein: probably it can still be repeated in time.[4] But there is the danger that they won't get their turn until the Munich people[5] *have* been summoned.

One needs a lot of patience and quiet nerves; a question on which one has worked for six years; and now no possibility to take a direct part.[6]

The 'preliminary reports' in the newspapers are once again pretty wretched.

But above all else, there is now the wish for Your Excellency's rapid and complete recovery.[7]

That is the wish of everyone in the little house in the woods.[8]

With sincere good wishes

H. [...]

1101.  Maximilian Harden to Holstein

Monday, [29 June 1908][9]

Your Excellency,

To-day E[ulenburg] of course denied everything; Ernst[10] must be bribed or sick; he (Eulbg.) had wracked his brains for weeks in vain;

[1] Chancellor Bülow.

[2] On 20 May Eulenburg had been ordered to place his Black Eagle decoration *ad depositum* because of his present inability to take proper care of it. Eulenburg returned the Black Eagle and all other decorations that had been awarded him on 22 May. (Haller, *Eulenburg*, pp. 421–3.)

[3] Holstein replied on 28 June that he was not certain why Eulenburg had been asked to return the decoration, and that it would be wisest to keep quiet. (Rogge, *Holstein und Harden*, p. 301.)

[4] Presumably the procedure at the Munich trial. (See above, p. 528, note 1.)

[5] Ernst and Riedl.

[6] In his letter of 28 June Holstein wrote that he still was doubtful about the wisdom of Harden's decision not to appear as a witness in the Eulenburg trial. 'I have already said that I would not care to express myself on the subject because I do not see all the ramifications of the affair so clearly as you do, and also because I, though to a lesser degree, appear to have a personal interest in the matter. Actually, the accusation of having participated in rendering E[ulenburg] harmless, though completely unjustified, would not disturb me in the least.'

[7] Holstein had been suffering from stomach haemorrhages, a disorder from which he died in the following year. He had been confined to his bed since 21 June. (See below, Holstein's letter to a journalist of 10 July 1908.)

[8] Harden's house in Grunewald.

[9] The first day of the Eulenburg trial.

[10] Jakob Ernst. The fisherman from Starnberg who had served as Eulenburg's personal servant and whose testimony at the Munich trial about his sexual relations with the Prince (see above, p. 528, note 1) was the most important evidence in the State's case against Eulenburg.

inexplicable; for Riedl[1] only a contemptuous gesture. Unimpressive. But skilfully presented; very calmly, like a novel. Factually, nil. Attempt to work on witnesses, (*a*) by a parade of the family, happiness, eight children, (*b*) democratic: 'made many enemies by never recognizing difference between Princes and commoners'. Factually, as I said, nil. Whether he still has tricks in reserve, *nescio*; from 'inside' I hear that to-day very favourable for me; even Kanzow[2] favourable. Most unusual procedure *outside*, however; if one thinks how accused prisoners are usually brought into the court room! He is said not to give the appearance of being ill at all. Very calm, collected; in the family circle. What must have happened in the Charité![3]

That even Kuno[4] turned up (with a beard!!) is surprising.

This in all haste after a terrible day. It *appears* that Bernstein and Mayer will be summoned tomorrow. No witness to-day yet.

Many thanks for the kind letter. With best wishes for your health I remain

Your Excellency's very devoted

H.

1102.  Maximilian Harden to Holstein

1 July 1908

Your Excellency,

I was pleased to hear, upon enquiry, that you are getting along well; or at least as well as could be expected.

What is happening in Moabit is so completely unheard of in the legal history of half-way civilized people that I must renounce the comforting pleasure of seeing Your Excellency, because I should not bring excitement into the sick room. Only: for three days, *toujours lui*, family vignettes, treated like a conquering hero; he chatters on, lies a blue streak, nobody contradicts, nobody can hear what he says, and he is working on the jury with a clever simulation of illness. Not *one* witness for the prosecution summoned so far, Bernstein and K[atz] not in the court room. Meanwhile they hope that the simple people from Starnberg[5] will get involved in brawls or with women in the big city; or something similar. No mortal would have survived a trial of more than five or six hours with this load of incriminating evidence against him. Then: three years' penal servitude; or five. Because the matter is clear as day. Here people are everywhere talking about acquittal. Also, the hero can, if things get uncomfortable, always break off proceedings because of illness.

Poor Prussia. This is the end. No honest man can support this 'order'.

---

[1] Georg Riedl. Another former fisherman from Starnberg who had given evidence about sexual relations with Eulenburg at the Munich trial. Riedl had drifted from job to job since leaving the Starnberg region and had been in jail several times. Most recently he had been a milk dealer.

[2] Presiding judge at the Eulenburg trial.

[3] The hospital where Eulenburg was confined while awaiting trial.

[4] Moltke.      [5] Ernst and Riedl.

It may yet crack up on this sort of thing. But nothing can blot out this disgrace.

With deep deep good wishes I remain

Your Excellency's very devoted

H.

## 1103.  Maximilian Harden to Holstein

3 July 1908

Your Excellency,

Thank you very much for your effort to write letters, which I hope has not been too much for you. Unfortunately I cannot allow myself the pleasure of a visit because to-day I have hardly a quarter of an hour to myself; also fear to bring along too much that would excite.

Obviously strict orders have been given; via Beseler. They do not want to. They do not dare to. Whether I will nevertheless succeed in getting justice is still doubtful. But the disgrace of these days can never be wiped out. Woe to the Minister of State who is responsible. Some day there will be fearful repercussions.

The interrogation of Bernstein will be continued to-day. For hours, the most irrelevant things. Orders have already been given that Bernstein and Mayer cannot be in the court room when Riedl and Ernst are interrogated. They want to 'handle' the poor Bavarian natives, who do not understand Prussian, without interference.

Not a single harsh word is addressed to the criminal.

I will have no part of the miserable farce, and am still determined not to appear unless I have to. Because I do not fit into this picture and would strike a tone that would be bound to lead to constant conflict.

The first three days, without Bernstein or any other control: that was it.[1] Incidentally, Bernstein too has been sworn to silence.[2] I would laugh in the face of anyone who expected me to do that. [...]

With the very warmest good wishes, I remain

Your Excellency's devoted

H. [...]

## 1104.  Maximilian Harden to Holstein

5 July 1908

Your Excellency,

I hope you are now as well as ever, if not better.

Incredibly run down; request indulgence. Norderney[3] should not be duped by the Press. *I* will vouch for I[senbiel]. He is the best, the only person who can now do anything. I have done much to-day. I. says that all four lawyers in the case think a verdict of guilty is absolutely certain, unless the twelve should directly contravene the law or unless Ernst retracts (impossible). He is handling him[4] with velvet gloves so that he

---

[1] The first three days of the trial were occupied with the interrogation of Eulenburg.

[2] The public had been excluded from the courtroom. Harden means that Bernstein had sworn not to reveal anything about the proceedings.

[3] Chancellor Bülow, who was at this time in Norderney.   [4] Prince Eulenburg.

does not become 'more sick' and the trial is derailed. He will allow no one to drive him from the path of justice, which is on the side of Harden, and he will bring full pressure to bear in his summing-up. I believe I can now vouch for him; in addition, Loebell or someone else (*reliable*) can speak a few friendly words to him: all the better to counter other influences. In that case it would be good if I knew about it beforehand.

The impression yesterday (Trost),[1] incredible. The best prelude for the Starnberger.[2] The decisive words of Phili to Trost: 'Do you masturbate or fuck each other.' Romantic! Up the Hohenzollern!! Manliness! The halo is gone. I. said there was not the slightest doubt about the credibility of the witness.

The letter of Dohna-Schlobitten[3] to Phili was published and sent by me to I.[4] Among other things: 'You are simply such a *liar* that it lies heavily on my conscience that I introduced such a *rascal* into the intimate society of our beloved and most gracious Kaiser.' etc.

I. is afraid that my testimony might arouse bitterness, because until yesterday the sympathy of jurors was with E. The question still *in suspenso*.

With best wishes<br>
I remain Your Excellency's devoted<br>
H. [...]

## 1105.   Maximilian Harden to Holstein

9 July 1908

Your Excellency,

[...] I wanted to try to come to-day for a brief half hour. But the visit of your colleague will certainly be more stimulating. Because I am totally at the end of my strength. Without the slightest help day and night. Doing everything alone; this cannot go on. And the shameless wickedness of the way those people are operating. The most insolent example of class justice that has ever existed. We are an object of ridicule abroad; and have deserved it. People are writing to me from a host of countries: you should be ashamed of yourselves! [...]

Wilke was just summoned as a witness by telephone. Knows nothing. A dozen witnesses of greatest importance: but Wilke is summoned. It is the *comble des combles*.

But all this won't help the wretch.

The campaign against Your Excellency at first was one against Bülow. Silesian grandees (Guido)[5] are running Trachenberg[6] as their candidate, and declare they can make B. impossible by remarks about His Majesty (also in writing, allegedly); apparently also want to inculpate him as being too intimate with Herr von H. (In this matter,

---

[1] A witness for the prosecution.   [2] Ernst and Riedl.

[3] Richard, Prince von Dohna-Schlobitten, at whose Prökelwitz estate the Kaiser often used to hunt, and where Eulenburg too was a frequent guest. (See Haller, *Eulenburg*, pp. 48–9.)

[4] A letter of December 1901. (See *Zukunft*, vol. 64, p. 132.)

[5] Guido, von Henckel-Donnersmarck.

[6] Hermann, Prince von Hatzfeldt, Duke of Trachenberg.

even *friends* of Your Excellency have spoken incautiously.) *Regierungs-rat* Martin[1] is said to be helping in the Press. An inactive diplomat being considered for the Foreign Ministry (Lichnowsky?).[2] The Silesian friends know young Pless[3] very well. The whole business to be attempted towards autumn, allegedly. As I hear confidentially. Anyway, Guido busy in every rat hole. B. will have to watch out and show that he is master. Also in the Eulenburg matter. I would have the *Norddeutsche Allegemeine Zeitung* say that any expression of doubt that the Prince could be treated differently from other accused persons *sui generis* was an insolent insult to German honour. Then B., as E.'s executioner and the defender of justice, will be impossible to remove. I fear he has a tender spot by way of his military brother,[4] which is known to E[ulenburg] and Einem;[5] this brother is highly suspect; à la Knesebeck.[6] [...]

Your Excellency's very devoted<br>H.[7] [...]

1106.   Holstein to a Journalist
        Copy

10 July 1908

Dear Sir,

From my sick bed I thank you for your objective discussion yesterday of my relations with the Chancellor.

As to the alleged 'conciliation' I should like to remark that on the day I handed in my resignation—2 April 1906—and then about six weeks later, before Bülow went to Norderney to convalesce, I dined with him, alone, although I otherwise never accept an invitation. This fact, *which is intended only for your personal information*, proves what my feelings were when I departed.

To be sure, people have tried assiduously and repeatedly to shift the responsibility for pushing me out to others and to create the belief—also in me—that it was precisely Prince Bülow who wanted to get rid of me. But my view of the value and purpose of this rumour has never varied.

With respectful regards

Your very devoted<br>Holstein

All sorts of things about my illness have now been said in the Press, most of them incorrect.

[1] Rudolf Martin, who in the following year published a book, *Fürst Bülow und Kaiser Wilhelm II*, blaming Bülow for most of the errors of German policy and exonerating the Kaiser. (See *Memoirs*, p. 190.)

[2] Karl Max, Prince von Lichnowsky, who had been a *Vortragender Rat* in the Foreign Ministry until 1904, and was to become Ambassador to London in 1912.

[3] Hans Heinrich, Prince of Pless, one of the Kaiser's closest friends.

[4] Karl Ulrich von Bülow.

[5] Karl von Einem. Prussian Minister of War, 1903–9.

[6] Bodo von dem Knesebeck. Court Chamberlain. He was said to have been blackmailed for many years by a tailor named Rode. His case never came before the law courts. (Tresckow, *Von Fürsten*, p. 119.)

[7] Compare this letter with Eugen Zimmermann's letter to the Chancellor of 11 July 1908. (Rogge, *Holstein und Harden*, pp. 309–10.)

Three weeks ago a small blood vessel in my stomach burst, a result of hardening of the arteries. Both the physician who is treating me, Dr Grünfeld, and *Geheimrat* Goldscheider, who was called in for consultation, declared that there was no danger but that particular care was necessary to prevent further bleeding. So during these past three weeks I have lain quiet and have lived on liquids, am very weak, but have some reason to expect that there will be steady improvement.

There has been no sign, thank goodness, of intestinal bleeding (which usually means cancer), and as I said, I am being treated by Dr Grünfeld.

These facts I put at your disposal in case you think it indicated to say more or to set the facts straight. I have no particular wish in this regard.

## 1107.  Maximilian Harden to Holstein

13 July 1908

Your Excellency,

[...] It is hardly worth the trouble to say anything more about Moabit. A crying disgrace. This *must* bring retribution some day, even though everyone is now philosophically silent. The questions and personal comments you hear from members of the jury are without exception favourable to the accused. Bernstein thinks acquittal is possible, that prison is unlikely, and says that in forty years of legal practice he has never seen anything that came even close to comparison with this. *Whatever* can be done, I am doing; I have never had so much work and worry as now. But I am all alone, without any help whatever. [...]

With the best wishes for Your Excellency's complete recovery,

I remain your devoted

H.

## 1108.  Maximilian Harden to Holstein

14 July 1908

Your Excellency,

[...] Moabit absolutely incredible. The farce goes on, every day at least three perjuries, and since guilt has long since been proved, they are only trying to attentuate the business and work on the sentimentality of the jury. In the newspapers, almost everything twisted. And I cannot go on. All alone!! Things are ripe. The Harden and Eulenburg trials could not happen in Russia, someone wrote to me to-day from London. I only hope now for a triumphal entry through the Brandenburg Gate. *E[ulenburg] triumphans.*

With sincere good wishes for your health (and the request to be kind enough to return the Einemiana)[1]

I remain Your Excellency's devoted

H.

[1] Presumably something written by or about General von Einem.

## 1109. Maximilian Harden to Holstein

17 July 1908

Your Excellency,

It seems to me that the most important thing now is to see to it that the weak man by the sea[1] is correctly informed as soon as possible so that he can inform His Majesty (for whom after all everything was intended) correctly. If there is a possibility to do that, I will be glad to co-operate. B[ülow] is to believe nothing that has not been examined by Your Excellency (about the proceedings *in foro*). Plessen, the representative of the Foreign Ministry, Kessel[2] and Co., are no reliable sources of information.[3]

I[senbiel] after all did everything that the authorities behind him allowed him to do, and I feel he should be kept *pro futuro*. But for what happened yesterday, the Kanzow circus would have gone on.[4] It seems to me to-day that we need I. and the presiding magistrate, but that we should keep them better informed.

I was sincerely pleased to see Your Excellency so well. If I could only sleep!!

With the request to be remembered to Frau von L[ebbin] I remain your warmly devoted.

H.

## 1110. Maximilian Harden to Holstein

20 July 1908

Your Excellency,

[...] 'Emigrate' : from three sides I get this advice. Quite right. The Government is after all to blame. The Chancellor knows exactly how things stand, but lacks the courage to say so, much less to intervene. And before the decisive battle, he runs away with his two cronies.

On the other side, the one stands up for the other, even in the most dire peril. I had to get through these terrible weeks without the smallest bit of help; and feel it in every limb : health and magazine are going to the devil; and if I break down tomorrow, all is lost. It was madness to begin under such circumstances. But now that I have done so, I must go on, as long as I can. How long will that be?

In all this horror, I am glad that Your Excellency is feeling better. If at all possible, I will come Thursday around three or six. Around five

[1] Chancellor Bülow in Norderney.

[2] General Gustav von Kessel, Commander of the Gardes-du-Corps, was rumoured to have homosexual tendencies. He was on Police Commissioner Meerscheidt-Hüllesem's list of suspects. (Tresckow, *Von Fürsten*, pp. 143–4.)

[3] Holstein replied on the following day that he had 'written' and had enclosed a copy of a leading article of last night's *Berliner Neuesten Nachrichten* which had called for a postponement of the trial. (Rogge, *Holstein und Harden*, p. 313.)

[4] Harden probably refers to Eulenburg's breakdown in the courtroom. On 17 July the trial was suspended because of the defendant's health. This meant that when Eulenburg would again be brought to trial the proceedings would have to begin all over again. Another trial was begun on 7 July 1909, almost a year later, but after only a few hours Eulenburg's health again broke down. The case did not come before the courts again and no legal decision was ever reached. Eulenburg died on 17 September 1921.

I will probably be in the vicinity to make a call in connection with the affair. Of course I will only come if I can be certain not to disturb. There is still a great deal to report.

With best wishes, also from mother and child, for the good health of Your Excellency,

I am your very devoted

H.

A very decent letter just came from the public prosecutor, who sends thanks for all the information during the trial, and who invites me to discuss the matter at his private house. *Pas trop de zèle surtout.* I will wait a few days.[1]

## 1111. Bernhard von Bülow to Holstein

Norderney, 20 July 1908

Dear Holstein,

[...] I neither wrote nor inspired, directly or indirectly, the article in the *Süddeutsche Korrespondenz*.[2] Nor did I give instructions that such an article, or a similar one, should appear. I have, however, said once and for all and most emphatically that the Press, in so far as it can be influenced, should speak of you only with the respect and dignity that is your due. That this is occasionally not done proves that there are people who are annoyed that we two have been good friends for a generation. *Habeant sibi.* This does not make me shy away from you, or you, I think, from me. [...]

What you say about our attitude in eastern affairs and specifically towards Austria is in my opinion absolutely correct. I have written in this sense (privately and confidentially) to Aehrenthal.[3]

Once again, the very warmest good wishes from me and my wife. Is it still hot in Berlin? I hope you are not suffering from the heat, and that you will soon be back in the open air and in your familiar rounds.

Always your most sincerely devoted

B.

## 1112. Bernhard von Bülow to Holstein

Norderney, 28 July 1908

Dear Holstein,

[...] Concerning the revolution in Turkey,[4] Helfferich,[5] who just returned from Constantinople, told me that especially in the Turkish

---

[1] Holstein replied on the same day that he understood completely how Harden felt, but thought this was largely an aftermath of his recent anxieties. 'For you have won.' He hoped Harden would come to see him before he saw Isenbiel, and expected him on the following Thursday afternoon (July 23). (Rogge, *Holstein und Harden*, p. 316.)

[2] See Rogge, *Holstein und Harden*, p. 310.

[3] Not found in the Foreign Ministry files. See Bülow's letter of 23 July 1908 in *Österreich-Ungarns Aussenpolitik von der bosnischen Krise 1908 bis zum Kriegsausbruch* (Vienna and Leipzig, 1930), vol. I, no. 18, pp. 14–15.

[4] On 24 July 1908, under the threat of revolution, Sultan Abdul Hamid announced the restoration of the Turkish Constitution of 1876 which in effect gave the Young Turk reform movement control of the government.

[5] Karl Helfferich. Member of the Colonial Division of the German Foreign Ministry, 1901–6; Director of the Anatolian Railroad (in Constantinople), 1906–8; from 1908 a member of the Board of Directors of the Deutsche Bank.

army all the good and decent elements regarded the change that had taken place as the last possibility for the recovery and maintenance of Turkey, which would have collapsed hopelessly under the scandalous administration of the Yildiz-Kiosk.[1] Helfferich thinks that the Sultan is clever enough to come to terms honestly with this new course in the realization that this, and only this, will save him, too. I too was struck by the article in the *Temps*. Do you not think that the co-operation of the English and the Russians will also be made more difficult by the revolution in Constantinople? In all countries they have sought to weaken or annex, the Russians have always taken the reactionary elements under their protection: in Poland and in Sweden, in the Balkan states and Turkey, where they have always protected the Old-Turks. The recent turnover in Turkey can hardly be welcome to the Russians; but an English Government can hardly oppose liberal and constitutional ideas in Turkey. I realize how misleading historical analogies can be, but find nevertheless that the events that have taken place in Constantinople are reminiscent of the eleventh-hour effort of the Poles with their constitution of 1791. May the Turks have better luck. I have just telegraphed to His Maj., completely in line with your ideas; stressed the effort that is being made to represent the Turkish constitution as an English victory and a German defeat, and, with an exposition of the historical and diplomatic significance of this turnover, said: that on Friday he should inform the Sultan through Kiderlen[2] of his good wishes and that he should express the expectation that this act of wise statecraft would contribute to the well-being and strength of the Turkish Empire.[3] The first news of the revolution in Turkey hardly aroused pleasure at the highest level.[4] I at once addressed myself by telegraph and by letter against this point of view which in my opinion was mistaken.[5] It was strange that the wish was at once expressed to send Marschall back, even before the end of his leave, although Kiderlen is again doing a good job.[6]

Tomorrow I am going via Berlin to Swinemünde. The day after tomorrow I will stay in Berlin only a few hours. On my return I will stay there over Sunday. I very much hope you will allow me to come to see you on Sunday, and I hope above all that I will find you well recovered and stronger. With warmest good wishes from my wife and myself

Your sincerely devoted<br>
Bülow [...]

[1] The country residence near Constantinople of Sultan Abdul Hamid II.

[2] While Marschall was on leave, Kiderlen was acting Ambassador in Constantinople.

[3] See Bülow's telegram to the Kaiser of 28 July 1908. (*Grosse Politik*, vol. XXVii, no. 8887, pp. 578–9.)

[4] On 25 July Bülow had telegraphed to the Foreign Ministry: 'His Majesty the Kaiser and King regards the measure taken by the Sultan in reestablishing the constitution as a sign of weakness that may well be exploited by the English in a most unfortunate way.' (From the Foreign Ministry files.)

[5] No such telegram or letter was found in the Foreign Ministry files.

[6] The Foreign Ministry advised against the recall of Marschall at this time on the grounds that such a step might create alarm and be generally misunderstood. (*Grosse Politik*, vol. XXVii, nos. 8878–9, pp. 564–5.)

1113.   Holstein to Bernhard von Bülow
        Copy

29 July 1908

Dear Bülow,

Many thanks for your letter.[1] How much I look forward to your coming on Sunday I need hardly tell you. I am not yet up to long walks or drives. I would be grateful if you could let me know tomorrow when you intend to come on Sunday, so that I can postpone the doctor who still comes every day, and possibly other visits.

I hope Kiderlen receives the instructions about which you write; these should also be published afterwards, here.

I am wondering about a further instruction that need not come from the Kaiser and need not be published either. Could you not have Kiderlen tell the Sultan the following: 'When in 1889 the Emperor of Japan granted a constitution, he borrowed two provisions from the Prussian, or rather the German, constitution.

(1) That Ministers are responsible to the Emperor, not to Parliament;

(2) That a Press law provides for severe punishment for insulting the head of the state.

Both provisions have thoroughly proved their worth in Japan, which has undergone many a storm in the past twenty years, and the authority of Emperor Mutsuhito is to-day a great one. The Sultan, who can judge conditions in Turkey much more accurately than I (Bülow) will be in a position to estimate whether it would not be wise to make use of these two points in his empire as well, in case he has not perhaps done so already.'

So much for the instruction for Kiderlen, who might also tell the Sultan that he must, with the aid and sanction of his order-loving subjects, hold the revolutionary elements within bounds, for these commonly abuse their freedom—such people exist in all countries.

I think that this commission would make an excellent impression on the Sultan. Perhaps on His Majesty, too, if you inform him, though I have no opinion on this.

Even if the matter becomes known it can do you no harm. The example of the success in Japan is your justification.

Incidentally I have also noticed recently that efforts are being made to represent Marschall as the only specialist able to cope with the situation.

Everything else can wait until Sunday.

Always yours most sincerely
Holstein.


1114.   Holstein to Bernhard von Bülow
        Copy

30 July 1908

Dear Bülow,

I still owe you my opinion about the Turkish revolution. Here it is:

[1] Of 28 July. See above.

It is difficult to compare the Turkish movement with any other because, with the possible exception of England under Cromwell, no revolution has ever rested on such a self-conscious and firm religious foundation as this one in Turkey. The Turk really believes in his religion (exceptions prove nothing), and the head of this religion is the Padishah. As a spiritual ruler he has more power than the Pope because there are hardly any unbelievers in Islam. Hence the Sultan, together with the priesthood whose interests are surely identical with his own, holds stronger reins than any other ruler, at least so far as Mohammedans are concerned.

The disrupting elements are the Christians. These, however, are divided by animosities, and logically the Mohammedan block should retain the upper hand against them. Their relative numbers, which are unfavourable to the Turks in Europe, are compensated for in Asia and Africa (Tripoli).

It would therefore be foolish for anyone—like Dr Wirth[1] to-day in the *Rote Tag*—to predict a definite unfavourable result. The future is, as usual, uncertain, but the Sultan as Padishah has significant odds on his side.

Sincerely and in haste

Your

Holstein

Ferid Pasha,[2] who is supposed to be in charge of the elections,[3] is an energetic and clever, and at the same time experienced, man; an Albanian.

## 1115.  Holstein to Bernhard von Bülow
   Draft

13 August 1908

Dear Bülow,

To-day I will and must touch on a theme that since 12 March 1906 has been avoided between us—Morocco. On that historic day Hammann said when you informed him of the Kaiser's demand that we give in: 'The affair can be handled in such a way that no one will notice that we are giving in.' As you know, this 'handling' has not been successful abroad, and it has so far only been partially successful at home because the people wanted peace and quiet. But the psychological moment is now approaching when the eyes of the Germans at home will be opened *nolens volens*.

From everything I see and hear, the French are giving us satisfactory assurances and are at the same time doing the exact opposite. Because they know that *Guillaume Pacifiste* will only talk and never act. Precisely there lies the danger. To-day foreigners talk about Wilhelm II as they used to talk about Friedrich Wilhelm IV after Olmütz.[4] And probably within a year, if things go on this way in Morocco, the Press,

---

[1] Dr Albrecht Wirth. Authority on the middle east, and author of numerous books and articles on history and politics.

[2] Turkish Grand Vizier, 1903–8.

[3] Elections provided for by the restored Constitution of 1876.          [4] See p. 248, note 4.

Parliament, and people of *Germany* will begin to judge Wilhelm the Second as do foreigners—unless, of course, H.M. succeeded in unloading the blame on you.

To leave Morocco in the lurch just at this time, when Mohammedanism is again becoming a power factor in Turkey, means driving the Turks into the arms of England. Furthermore, as long as our aggressive naval policy continues, England will go through thick and thin with France. We must therefore recognize that we will have England and France against us if we come to the defence of the Act of Algeciras. Even a more courageous man than the Kaiser would hesitate with his decision under such circumstances. But H.M. will not hesitate at all, but will at once repeat his statement: 'Now that Delcassé is out of the way, I will make no difficulties for you in Morocco.'

H.M. will probably also have been under pro-French influences in Kronberg—to ensure French neutrality in the event of a German-English conflict (for as long as that would be convenient to France!)[1] As soon as it is obvious that France is making game of us in Morocco, you, who will have to defend the Kaiser, will have to swallow a great deal from Parliament and Press.

How can that be avoided? So far as I can see, only by a change in our naval policy. As soon as England is freed from the anxiety of a second *Norman invasion*, she will begin to consider her own Moroccan interests; she will by no means immediately desert France, but will advise the French to moderation in Morocco, whereas to-day it can only be to the advantage of English policy that Germany should appear in the worst possible light before the entire world in Morocco—*avilir pour démolir*.

How would it be if you submitted simultaneously two reports to the Kaiser, one from Metternich, which would once again pull together all the important statements by English statesmen and the great newspapers about the threatening aspect of German armaments; and one from the Foreign Ministry showing that the French in Morocco *se moquent de nous*. To both you would then comment: England's fears are ridiculous, but it is impossible to argue about national susceptibilities. This fear exists, and as long as it exists England will[2] support France and may even allow France to push matters to a conflict with us. We will then be confronted by the choice of a humiliation for the Reich and for the Kaiser, or a fight against superior forces—at sea, anyway.

Whether and what practical use can be made of this, you will know better than I.

I feel nevertheless that things cannot go on much longer as they are now being run by the Kaiser without severe detriment for the Reich and for you.

With best wishes
Holstein.

[1] The Kaiser and the King of England met in Kronberg on 11 August 1908. (*Grosse Politik*, vol. XXIV, nos. 8223–6, pp. 122–9; *British Documents*, vol. VI, nos. 111–24, pp. 173–200.)

[2] At this point in his draft Holstein crossed out the words: 'go with France through thick and thin. H.M. can then draw his own conclusions.'

Just after I finished the letter I talked to Roberts,[1] who told me with pride and pleasure that you had given him the honour of inviting him to the Hill dinner.

R. recently had a long conversation about German naval policy with the English Naval Attaché, Captain Dumas. The latter said that the English were not so much concerned about the *present* naval programme as about the new demands that could certainly be expected.

This statement is interesting for you, since you are already getting ready to anticipate such new demands. Roberts hinted that the English believe war to be inevitable if this naval armament goes on as it has without limit. He thinks the King probably touched on the subject at Kronberg.[2]

1116.    Memorandum by Holstein

15 August 1908

Anglo-German Relations.
German Naval Policy.

Recently Metternich, who dislikes writing anything that would displease the Kaiser, could not avoid writing a private letter to the Chancellor in which he developed the idea that all efforts to bring about better relations with England would be fruitless as long as we continued our naval policy.[3] The English would always judge this by what we did, not by what we said.

The Chancellor submitted this letter to the Kaiser—which probably accorded with the intentions of the writer. The Kaiser annotated the letter with a series of angry commentaries that are obviously intended to prevent further expressions along these lines. Among other things, H.M. says he will send Metternich a rocket that will send him flying.

Nevertheless, Under Secretary of State Hardinge expressed himself in exactly the same way recently to Rücker-Jenisch[4] in Kronberg.[5]

It was impossible to hope for a change in English public opinion as long as Germany continued to build warships at this pace. The English people felt it was necessary to maintain their present naval superiority, and will accordingly make the necessary heavy monetary sacrifices. But these sacrifices and the ever-present danger of a life and death struggle with Germany can only have a harmful effect on their attitude.

Jenisch's replies are meaningless because they are not convincing.

[1] American journalist.

[2] The subject was discussed at length in the conversation between Sir Frank Lascelles and the Kaiser (*Grosse Politik*, vol. XXIV, no. 8223, pp. 122–4; *British Documents*, vol. VI, no. 112, pp. 175–6) and between Sir Charles Hardinge, Permanent Under Secretary of State for Foreign Affairs, and the Kaiser. (*Grosse Politik*, vol. XXIV, nos. 8225–6, pp. 125–9; *British Documents*, vol. VI, no. 117, pp. 184–90.)

[3] Letter of 1 August 1908. (*Grosse Politik*, vol. XXIV, no. 8219, pp. 107–16.)

[4] Martin, Baron von Rücker-Jenisch. Bülow's cousin; Prussian Minister to Darmstadt, 1906–13; on several occasions Foreign Ministry representative in the Kaiser's retinue.

[5] See Rücker-Jenisch's telegram to the Foreign Ministry of 12 August 1908. (*Grosse Politik*, vol. XXIV, no. 8227, pp. 129–31.)

But it would be interesting to know whether the King touched upon this subject with the Kaiser.[1]

It is also an interesting indication that within the last week the *Rote Tag* and the *Frankfurter Zeitung* have published articles naming the over-hasty German fleet building as the chief cause of the hostility between England and Germany. It remains to be seen whether this discussion will be continued or whether this question will be silenced, as it has been heretofore. Just as the other question has been silenced as to whether the almost exclusive construction of battleships is in Germany's interest, or whether—as Admiral Galster[2] has pointed out in his pamphlet[3] Germany should not prepare for a 'little war' at sea, with submarines, torpedo boats, fast cruisers.[4]

## 1117. Bernhard von Bülow to Holstein

Norderney, Sunday morning, 16 August 1908

Dear Holstein,

[...] According to what Jenisch writes me, Friedrichshof[5] did not go badly. The King in a friendly mood, very tactful, very quiet dignity *avec une pointe d'ironie pour notre agitation*. Hardinge emphasized the friendly intentions of Englishmen of all parties, and at the same time very cautiously raised the question of an armaments agreement. His Majesty explained to him with great energy that England was so very far ahead of us at sea that fears about a German invasion were untenable. On land, France could put more men under arms than we, in proportion to population. That is true. What the English fear, however, is that we, once our national financial reform[6] has been passed, will proceed to expand our present (relatively modest) naval programme with immense sums. If I am still Chancellor then, I will not permit any such Icarus flight. Not only for reasons of foreign policy, but for domestic policy as well. We cannot have both the greatest army and the biggest navy. We cannot weaken the army, for our destiny will be decided on land. The prerequisite for an agreement about the scope and tempo of our naval construction—a question raised by English newspapers with liberal tendencies—is of course that the English avoid everything that looks like a threat or a pressure. A German Minister who gave in to such pressure, above all in the fleet question, would come to an end à la Hannibal Fischer.[7] And the opponents of such a Minister would natur-

---

[1] There is no indication in the British or German documents that he did so.

[2] Vice Admiral Karl Galster (retired).

[3] *Welche Seekriegs-Rüstung braucht Deutschland?* (Berlin, 1907).

[4] See Heinrich Otto Meisner, 'Gespräche und Briefe Holsteins, 1907–1909,' *Preussische Jahrbücher*, vol. 229, pp. 165–74, 229–46.

[5] The visit of King Edward to Castle Friedrichshof at Kronberg. (See above, p. 549, note 1, and p. 550, notes 2 and 5.)

[6] Taxation reform bills to cover increased Government expenditure were introduced in the Prussian Landtag on 20 October and in the Reichstag on 19 November 1908.

[7] Head of the Administration of Oldenburg; Minister of Lippe. In 1852 he sold the fleet of the German Confederation.

ally tell the monarch that he need only oppose such proposals in order to take over *le beau rôle* and to become even more popular than Zeppelin.[1]

[...]

With kindest regards and good wishes

Most sincerely yours
Bülow

1118.　Holstein to Bernhard von Bülow
　　　　Copy

19 August 1908

Dear Bülow,

[...] We may now hope that the Kaiser will some day also become sensible about the fleet question.[2] Now he has spoken to Hardinge about the 'event of war'[3] because he knows very well that the present [British] Government will not go to war. He was singing another tune when Beit[4] warned him of the prospect of war at Christmas, 1905.[5] And the speech at the Arsenal![6] But now H.M. is on top of the world, says he must 'put a little backbone' into Metternich and the Ministers. He will stay that way as long as the matter is not serious; then comes the usual disaster.

If Metternich now gets a reprimand from H.M., he should say:

'I am only the sentinel who reports what he sees. In all other respects I carry out what I am ordered to do. But there is no one who could justify Germany's naval armaments to the English with so much knowledge of the facts as Admiral von Tirpitz. Could he not some time while on leave pay a visit to England as a private individual, and on that occasion explain the matter clearly to a few leading personalities? I (Metternich) would be glad to arrange the meetings. Or it could be arranged without me, if that were desired.'

People who have been close to H.M. assume that he has committed himself to Tirpitz and Müller—whom he cites repeatedly—just as in the anti-Hill campaign.[7] In that situation, too, H.M. cited those two. For that reason it would be useful if H.M. were to get the idea to send Tirpitz on ahead. Otherwise they will always say it was our weak-kneed diplomatic service that bungled the business.

Why not send a hint to Metternich about Tirpitz?[8] [...]

Farewell. Always your most sincerely

Holstein

[1] Ferdinand, Count von Zeppelin. Inventor of the rigid balloon-type airship.
[2] In the preceding unpublished paragraph Holstein had congratulated Bülow on persuading the Kaiser to adopt a benevolent attitude towards the Young Turk revolution, with the result that relations between Germany and Turkey had improved.
[3] See above, p. 550, note 2.
[4] Alfred Beit. English financier.
[5] See *Grosse Politik*, vol. XXii, no. 6887, pp. 690–6.
[6] A speech by the Kaiser to his officers on New Years Eve, 1906, in which he expressed himself very pessimistically about the international situation.
[7] See above, p. 522, note 5.
[8] See below, Bülow's letter to Holstein of 25 August 1908.

1119.  Holstein to Bernhard von Bülow
       Copy

21 August 1908

Dear Bülow,

Hardinge will have reported that every concession on the fleet question has been refused, even the very smallest, and so has every question of slowing down armaments.[1]

In consequence there will now be a gigantic request for appropriations in England.

In consequence, tariffs and abusive language.

In consequence, demands for an expansion of the German programme.

In consequence, general financial confusion in Germany.

And as a final consequence:

Danger of war against vast superiority of power.

I think that His Majesty now feels he can allow himself every liberty with the present English Government. But this Government is after all aware that if the people and the Press feel it has been too careless, it can be swept away overnight; like the peace-loving Aberdeen Cabinet which had to give way to a Palmerston Cabinet as a result of Sinope (Nov. or December 1853).[2] At that time, too, it was a naval question that stirred up the English people.

The present Government will not go to war so easily, but it will arm, and have to arm heavily, after H.M. brusquely refused every concession —though to be sure only *conversando*, so far.

Would it be possible while there is still time—that is, before on the one hand the Kaiser, and on the other the English Government and Parliament, have committed themselves, to make the Kaiser understand the disastrous consequences of his dramatic and intransigent words at Wilhelmshöhe?[3]

What Metternich can do on this matter, and with what means, is something I cannot judge from here.

Worry, real worry about the certainty of imminent war, or a *personal* humiliation—these are the only things that would have any effect on H.M., but their effect would be certain, as past experience has shown. Tirpitz too has very weak nerves as soon as *he* has to do the bailing. So, Tirpitz *to the front*!

Yours most sincerely
Holstein

1120.  Bernhard von Bülow to Holstein

Norderney, Sunday noon, 23 August 1908

Dear Holstein,

My sincere thanks for your friendly and intelligent letter. You are

[1] See above, p. 550, note 2.

[2] In November 1853 the Russians destroyed at Sinope a division of the Turkish fleet transporting troops to the Asiatic front during the Russo-Turkish war. The incident provoked great indignation in Britain, and was a factor in bringing Britain into the war against Russia. Aberdeen did not give way to Palmerston until January 1855, however.

[3] Nothing has been found on this point.

right in assuming that I used my influence to secure the pardon of the Captain of Köpenick.[1] Nor was it easy to secure this pardon in the face of pedantry and red tape. You forgot to add, however, that it was you who advised this pardon. You had an eager ally in my wife, who to be sure always wants to pardon everyone on principle, though in this case quite rightly. [...]

I had Metternich here with me for several days. I discussed the situation with him in detail. I prepared the ground for him myself in that I presented my view of the situation very frankly and very definitely in several letters to His Maj.[2] I stressed especially the following: that I (in contrast to many others) had not believed in the imminent danger of war when the English assembled their fleet in the Channel four years ago. That I now regarded the situation as serious. That the present concern in England could not be blamed on a few professional agitators, but went much deeper. That diplomacy could not be conducted if every friendly and as yet completely academic question about the possibility of removing this concern were treated as an affront and answered with demands. That English foreign policy differed from the continental by its great consistency, that Grey pursued approximately the same policy as Lansdowne, and that if he wanted to pursue another policy he would suffer the same fate as Aberdeen, whom the English people had considered too soft and too impressionable in dealing with Tsar Nicholas and which led to the Crimean War. That it was above all important on the one hand not to conduct an ostrich-like policy, and on the other not to bar the way for all time, completely and intransigently, to the possibility of an understanding about naval armaments. I drew attention to the fact that a break with England would not only draw France but also Russia into the fray, whereas it was very unlikely that the recently liberalized Turks, who conducted ovations before the British Embassy in Pera, should march against England, and that the hope of serious disturbances in India and Egypt was really most fragile. I advised Metternich to propose to H.M. that Tirpitz be sent to England to explain to the leading people there how exaggerated were their worries about the fleet (which in truth cannot be denied). We diplomats eagerly studied the *Nautikus*,[3] but after all Tirpitz knew much more than we about this field. Metternich would either pave the way for him or stand aside entirely, whatever he preferred.

During the past weeks I have spent a lot of time working on national financial reforms and the financial situation of the Reich. It is ever clearer to me that even the most thorough-going reform will be of no use and the most inclusive taxes will only be a drop on a hot stone unless we return to greater economy. In every sphere and every office we must

[1] In 1908 a cobbler named Wilhelm Voigt had disguised himself as an army captain and had ordered the arrest of the mayor of Köpenick on a fictitious charge. The incident provoked considerable amusement at the expense of the German army and bureaucracy, but Voigt himself was sentenced to a term in prison.

[2] Not found in the Foreign Ministry files. (See Bülow's letter of [26 August 1906], *Grosse Politik*, vol. XXIV, no. 8239, pp. 148–51.)

[3] The German naval handbook.

practice greater simplicity and economy. We cannot at the same time have the greatest army in the world—and on the shoulders of our army rests our future and our fate—, the most generous and expensive welfare policy in the world, and build and modernize a gigantic fleet. The less the English sound a threatening note, also in the Press, and the more they avoid tampering with their present programme which has been sanctioned by all civilian parties (but has been declared totally inadequate by naval enthusiasts), the easier it will be to allow common sense to come into its own and win the victory here.

You say nothing about how you are, my dear Holstein. I hope this is a good sign, and that these lines find you well recovered. With kindest regards and good wishes, also from my wife

Faithfully your

B.

## 1121. Holstein to Bernhard von Bülow
Copy

25 August 1908

Dear Bülow,

If I understood correctly that you criticized His Majesty for his bullying attitude in Kronberg,[1] then in my opinion you acted wisely and perceptively. Three months after the Krüger Telegram, when he saw the effect it had on the English, H.M. spoke of that 'unfortunate Krüger Telegram'. It would not surprise me if the same thing should happen with all this bravado about the fleet. The official English Sunday newspaper, *The Observer*, already carries the information that the Government intends to build thirty Dreadnoughts in the next four to five years at a cost of two million pounds each, and will demand a credit of sixty million pounds sterling for this purpose. I am curious to see what impression this news, if it turns out to be correct, will make in Germany. For the time being it is being treated as bluff in the papers of the Navy League. We will then see what armaments competition means. Anglo-German naval competition: that is as though your banker Hoefft wanted to compete with Rothschild.

With the Kaiser, the situation is pointing up to a competition of Bülow-Tirpitz or Tirpitz-Bülow; you will win in this if you keep calm and make use of the available opportunities, because sound common sense and a fearful pocket book are on your side.

But Tirpitz too is fighting with all available means. One of these means is the citizenship law. A limitless extension of citizenship to the Germans living abroad—living abroad permanently. In consequence of this, an endless increase in propaganda. Tirpitz says in his memorandum: 'The more propaganda, the more prestige for the Reich'. To protect such new and artificially created 'national interests' we of course need more ships. That is the heart of the matter.

So far as I know, the other Ministers are all *opposed* to the extension of citizenship demanded by Tirpitz and Bethmann, but they are holding

[1] See above, p. 549, note 1.

back because Loebell informed them that *you* had not yet made up your mind but were still considering the matter. In this, it seems to me, they are making unjust use of your name, because you expressed your objections to Bethmann long ago that this planned extension would result in an enormous increase of propaganda and—by annexing many hundreds of thousands of Germans in North and *South* America—would only increase the already active distrust of us by the Americans. The one like the other would augment the dangers of war for the Reich and would increase our isolation, without compensation.

Loebell, in writing, impressed on the various agencies the need for dealing quickly with the citizenship law. Why, I should like to know? *Rien ne presse.* I suspect that the real reason is so that Tirpitz and Co. can make their point before Schoen, who has taken, for him, an unusually firm stand on this matter, is back from leave. I should like to recommend that, to prevent this, you send a short note to the Ministry of State—now. Since you still seem to have confidence in the old drafting ability, I enclose a draft.

Draft

As Minister for Foreign Affairs I feel it is important that the objections which may be raised (or which have been raised) on the part of the Foreign Ministry with respect to the proposed extension of the citizenship should receive the consideration their significance merits. Therefore it is my desire that, although discussions of the matter can begin beforehand, the Ministry of State should not make any final decision until after the return of State Secretary von Schoen.

Please bring this request and the reasons on which it is based to the attention of the Ministers of State.

To the Chancellery, and for the information of the Foreign Ministry.

*    *    *    *    *

This statement can be made more forceful by making the objection more specific:

'Significant increase of causes for conflict and war as result of metamorphosis of permanent American citizens into pseudo-Germans. Incalculable increase in propaganda. Increase in American distrust.'

But this addition does not seem to me to be necessary. Even without this, the wishes of the Chancellor will be sufficient to keep the question open until Schoen's return—since almost all the Ministers feel dubious about the project anyway. [...]

It seems that France wants another *Morocco Conference* in order by this means to get out of her Morocco difficulties and perhaps to secure for France a favourable revision of the Act of Algeciras. Such a Conference would be a certain second defeat for Germany. For, with the way the fleet question stands at present, England would adhere to France more than ever. Russia needs a French loan of a billion. We know how Italy and Spain behave. And Austria is still angry with us about the 'Seconding' telegram.[1] The Ballplatz has just eluded a preliminary conference

[1] See above, p. 421, note 4.

to work out a programme for the London Conference on sea law in order to present the Austrian programme independently in London—which has already been done. At a new Morocco Conference, therefore, Germany would be more isolated than ever.

For that reason it would be advisable for the Chancellor to send an instruction along the following lines to Berlin, without delay, as a prophylactic measure :

'In case anyone should bring up the question of a new Morocco Conference, he should be told immediately that there is no reason whatever to hold one. Nothing has happened that might invalidate the Act of Algeciras, France has given assurances to abide by it, and as for the most pressing problems, it will be easier to reach an understanding about carrying out the provisions of the Act now that Morocco is ruled by one Sultan than when power was divided between two rulers.'[1]

If Germany were to-day to reach an agreement with Mulai Hafid and in conjunction with him were to initiate separate negotiations with France, these would undoubtedly have surprisingly good results both for Germany and the world. But one must reckon with the possibility that the Kaiser will interfere with those negotiations as he did the first time. That he has not forgotten the impressions he received in the time of Lecomte-Monaco can be seen once again in his policy of half-measures towards Alsace-Lorraine. ( Zorn-Bulach. )[2]

For that reason, only for that reason, I cannot take the moral responsibility of advising that we open a new chapter in the Morocco question in conjunction with Mulai Hafid. We should not forget that last autumn at the Hague a French negotiator said to a German negotiator : 'If you make difficulties for us here, the French Government will deal directly with the Kaiser and the question will then be settled at once.'

By bluff and flattery the French could make the Kaiser do anything. A tried and true method. King Edward would whisper as before : *mon neveu se calmera. Chien qui aboie ne mord pas.*

Furthermore, for three years German public opinion has been educated by Theodor Wolff and others here with similar ideas to the view that Morocco is not worth a single flutter on the stock exchange to Germany. Whether the Press, even the so-called official Press, would be willing to change its tune at a moment's notice is most doubtful. Therefore I would not risk another step, but confine myself to recommending the above-quoted instruction. That is absolutely fool-proof advice, for a new Conference would sanction a revision of the Act of Algeciras *in pejus*, and would probably simply sanction French domination of Morocco.

Many thanks for your enquiries about my health, etc., etc.,

Holstein [...]

---

[1] On 23 August 1908 Mulai Hafid, who had himself proclaimed Sultan in May 1907, decisively defeated the forces of his brother Abdul Aziz, Sultan of Morocco since 1894.

[2] Hugo Zorn von Bulach. Under State Secretary for Alsace-Lorraine, 1895–1909; State Secretary from 1909.

## 1122.  Holstein to Bernhard von Bülow
Copy

27 August 1908

Dear Bülow,

As a supplement to my letter of the day before yesterday I recommend to-day that you recognize Mulai Hafid now, without delay.[1] This is not a political *action* that the Kaiser might ruin, but a single *act* 'that looks well and costs nothing'. On the contrary, it will probably bring considerable benefit to German industry. When the Moroccans see that we do not wait for France's approval like French vassals, they will not place their orders so exclusively in France as France is striving to have them do.

As you will see from the *small* clipping,[2] France is negotiating with Russia about recognition. Also with England. Just recently the French Chargé d'Affaires[3] spoke about a *common accord*.[4] However, as I wrote the day before yesterday, in every joint action Germany will be isolated and pushed in a corner. So we should be on our guard against any joint action. We would play an undignified role in such an event.

Since the Sultanate question is not dealt with in the Act of Algeciras, we can take independent action as a Great Power. By an independent act of recognition *we neither break an obligation nor do we assume an obligation.* We simply recognize a fact.

The French are engaged in negotiating with Mulai Hafid and are making their recognition dependent upon his agreeing to French concessions—or rather monopolies—to the detriment of other Powers, especially Germany. We will disturb this game if Germany recognizes him. The Foreign Ministry too thinks that something should be done. But the nervous Klehmet would like to restrict himself to sending a consular representative to Fez, without a specific declaration. I advise against that because it is a step that betrays fear. Stemrich[5] agreed with my opinion. In the memorandum that is to be sent to you to-day, both possibilities are therefore being mentioned—semi and full recognition. I definitely advise against the semi, also in your personal interests. If there is anything that Germany has to avoid above all else, it is the appearance of being fearful.

And by out and out recognition we risk *nothing*, otherwise I would not advise it. This has also been well prepared by the official article in the *Süddeutsche Reichs-Korrespondenz* which I read last night in the *Berliner Neuesten Nachrichten*.

I would advise sending recognition *by telegraph* to Tangier, because at this moment Pichon and Révoil are considering what price they should demand of the Sultan for recognition 'by the Powers'.

etc. etc.

Holstein

---

[1] See *Grosse Politik*, vol. XXIV, chapter CLXXXI.
[2] Not found.     [3] Baron de Berckheim.
[4] See Stemrich's memorandum of 26 August 1908. (*Grosse Politik*, vol. XXIV, no. 8407, pp. 377–8.)
[5] Wilhelm von Stemrich. Under State Secretary in the Foreign Ministry, 1907–11.

1123.   Bernhard von Bülow to Holstein

Norderney, Sunday morning, 30 August 1908

Dear Holstein,

My sincere thanks for your friendly and very interesting letters. I understand very well the advantages the immediate and unilateral recognition of Mulai Hafid would have for me. But to agree to such a step would put me into an awkward position with His Majesty. Metternich has now once again told me and His Maj. that even the present English Cabinet would go through thick and thin with France on the Morocco question, and that even an agreement with us on naval armaments would not change that. All the English parties agree that France should at least be allowed to have Morocco as compensation for the great losses France has suffered to England for centuries in every part of the world. Co-operation with France on Morocco seemed to all Englishmen not only politically sound but actually a matter of honour. If we should suddenly recognize Mulai Hafid unilaterally, this would naturally anger the French and this anger would carry over to England. Now in these last weeks I have very seriously and emphatically pointed out to His Maj. that unlimited naval armaments will inevitably lead to war with England, and that such a war would find us confronted by an overpowering coalition. If this recognition-bomb were now to explode, H.M. would be told that it was not our naval programme but our Morocco policy that was to blame for the tension with England. For years the Navy office has maintained the thesis that not our ship building but the mistakes of our foreign policy, especially towards France, are to blame for our isolation and for the tension with England. Now above all I cannot expose a flank to such attacks. The enclosed denial in the *Norddeutsche Allgemeine Zeitung* was ordered five days ago by the Kaiser.[1] Wangenheim has opposed our unilateral recognition of Mulai Hafid.[2] I have therefore had the Foreign Ministry advise His Maj. to propose to the Powers that, in the interests of finally establishing peace and order in Morocco, they recognize the actual ruler of the country, Mulai Hafid; at the same time, Vassel[3] is being sent to Fez.[4] If the French treat our proposal dilatorily, the Moroccans will know where they stand with us, and the desire of the other Powers to go along with the French delaying tactics may be weakened. [...]

With all the best wishes, also from my wife.

Faithfully yours
Bülow.

---

[1] On 28 August the *Norddeutsche Allgemeine Zeitung* published an official denial of a newspaper report that the Kaiser had authorized his Minister in Tangier to recognize Mulai Hafid as soon as the latter accepted the Act of Algeciras.

[2] See his telegram of 29 August. (*Grosse Politik*, vol. XXIV, no. 8419, p. 390.)

[3] Acting Consul in Fez, 1904–8; regular Consul in Fez from 1909.

[4] The German Government took care to emphasize that the return of Dr Vassel to Fez after the victory of Mulai Hafid had no political purpose. (*Grosse Politik*, vol. XXIV, no. 8418, p. 389.)

## 1124. Maximilian Harden to Holstein

Grunewald, 2 September 1908

Your Excellency,

[...] Although word has come from the North Sea[1] that everything must be done to effect a settlement,[2] I don't think that anything will be done and must make a decision about further tactics—which is made more difficult by Bernstein's idyll at Sorrento. As soon as I am finished I will go off somewhere, because I can no longer bear it here. The first thing is the question as to whether I should completely block the way to a settlement. This way would be: entering a complaint, which would mean that the Supreme Court would *probably* drop its order of 12 November 1907 to suspend proceedings;[3] then the private lawsuit would continue and both the public prosecutor (after a hint) and the private complainant could withdraw their appeal. Since something *must* be done now (because Moltke's suit was considered valid by an interim court), the decision cannot be postponed. [...]

Your Excellency's very devoted

H.

## 1125. Holstein to Bernhard von Bülow

Copy

Dammhaus, 3 September 1908

Dear Bülow,

First I want to thank you very much for having again found time last Sunday to write a detailed letter.[4]

The denial of recognition by the Kaiser himself, that is indeed a 'coup'. This imperial *actus* confirms what Harden told me recently: 'I am receiving very unfavourable reports from the Reich territories. These are now being governed once more in the Frenchified Manteuffel manner, by the wish and command of the Kaiser. I can see from that that the impressions of the Phili-Lecomte era are still at work.'

As in the Reich territories, so in Morocco the German cause is suffering one *échec* after another, so as not to anger the French. And if people later on complain, it was not the Kaiser, but instead they will criticize 'the Government', i.e., yourself.

But I can see that, with the Kaiser's habits, it will be hard to do anything against his will. At least see to it, in the interests of your position before the German people and before history, that the interests and security of the Reich are preserved in the fleet question, so that madness does not win out in this sphere.

A preliminary weapon for Tirpitz is, as I have said, the extension of citizenship. If T. notices how little importance the Prussian bureaux attach to his and Bethmann's 'motives', he may, since he needs this bill

---

[1] From Chancellor Bülow at Norderney.
[2] Harden refers to the original private law suit of Count Moltke against himself. (See above, p. 481, notes 4 and 6.)
[3] The order to suspend the decision of the first, private, Moltke-Harden suit.
[4] See above, Bülow's letter of 30 August.

for his purposes, try to secure the aid of His Majesty. But there you will have a very strong position if you point out the American danger. The reports of Speck in the Foreign Ministry files will provide you with enough material. Hatzfeldt's letter[1] also clearly expressed the anxiety that if American distrust should ever be provided with an *élan*, the end could not be foreseen.

The Kaiser's last speech is somewhat naïve.[2] H.M. says : 'I will go on arming and cannot be talked out of it. But I have no evil intentions, so *you* do not have to arm.' H.M. hopes in this way to prevent the gigantic English navy bill, which seems sinister to him and to our navy people. And it is sinister. But the most sinister thing of all is that the English realize that they do not have adequate manpower to be able to man this gigantic fleet completely. Before they have reached the limit of their manpower, therefore, they will logically have to go to war. This psychological moment would have to come—since the naval construction programme is to be completed in four to five years—within the next two to five years, and then preferably with a change of Cabinets in England. Then the day will come when H.M. is presented with the choice of a dictated agreement or a fight against superior naval forces. Will his decision differ from that of 1906 ? And, if he gives in, will that not be a triumph for anti-monarchial and anti-military elements ?

I am looking forward to the English commentaries on the Kaiser's speech. To be sure, only the most innocuous will get by the censorship of the Wilhelmstrasse. King E. made his comment in advance when he said recently in Marienbad : 'England has nothing but peaceful intentions, *even if she is arming in accordance with circumstances.*' [...]

Always your sincerely devoted<br/>Holstein [...]

## 1126. Maximilian Harden to Holstein

5 September 1908

Your Excellency,

Many thanks for the good news that you are feeling better.[3] I have not been so pleased about anything for a long time.

I can't understand Bülow. I can understand that Herr Dr Rosen should boast about his 'success'.[4] But an experienced man like B. must realize that *to-day* he cannot recover lost ground with such means. England and France are foaming with rage about the note (Hafid) ;[5] and

---

[1] Hermann, Count von Hatzfeldt-Wildenburg, the son of Holstein's old friend Paul von Hatzfeldt. Count Hermann was at this time Secretary of Embassy in Washington. His letter has not been found.

[2] A speech in Strasbourg of 30 August, in which the Kaiser stated that the peace of Europe was guaranteed by the strength of the German armed forces on land and sea, and that Germany was determined to preserve the strength of those forces despite threats from abroad.

[3] Holstein had written on 3 September that on the whole there was no doubt that he was getting better. (Rogge, *Holstein und Harden*, pp. 323–5.)

[4] Concerning the recognition of Mulai Hafid. See note 5.

[5] The announcement of the German Government's proposal for the joint recognition by the Powers of Mulai Hafid as Sultan of Morocco. The order for this announcement was sent from Berlin on 31 August. (*Grosse Politik*, vol. XXIV, no. 8421, p. 392.) Holstein had written to

are justified in saying that nobody knows any more what we really want or what we intend to do. We have after all agreed to give the neighbouring Power the position of priority;[1] Rosen won't be able to free us from this *crux* (Lacroix).[2] We are becoming odious; nor can we demand such a hasty recognition before full clarification and guarantees.

The Hardinge business was in the *Täglicher Rundschau* the day before yesterday.[3] B[ülow] must have told Herr E[ugen] Z[immermann] about it too, and obviously differently; because the article in the *N[eue]* *G[esellschaftliche]* *C[orrespondenz]* is very aggressive. More so than I can condone. I have not seen E.Z. since his trip. What it amounts to is that Anglo-German relations are once again worse than they have been for a long time. I don't see how it will end, and don't see why an agreement in which both parties give in should be considered a humiliation.

That England will support France is obvious. But I also doubt that Austria (despite Tschirschky's visit[4] and Schoen's talk[5]) will again 'second us brilliantly'.[6] I am obliged to assume from news I received from private sources that Aehrenthal wants to 'mediate', not to support us. Mediation in this case means: to facilitate our retreat. Should one begin when one is certain to be left in a minority? Bülow forgets how much he is committed in Morocco problems, and with whom he is dealing.

Via Marienbad[7] I hear from private sources: His Majesty [the Kaiser] wanted French Military Attaché in Metz. Two dispatches. Clemenceau twice abruptly refused. *Hinc illae irae.* Which won't last.

To-day I am having trouble expressing myself (as the stylistic master will have long since noticed); but still wanted to say *one* thing to-day. This alone was the purpose of the letter.

Bülow is getting into an increasingly bad position vis-à-vis the western Powers *and* Russia. Personally. Everywhere the word is going 'round; the Kaiser wants to do the right thing, peace, a Europ-[ean] understanding; The Chancellor is to blame for the 'pin-prick' policy. Absurd. But I can see how this dualism is taken up and spotlighted, and see in this a serious danger to B. He is made the bogey man, and one who is not even feared but is simply a nuisance. Who is doing that? A successor of Phili or one of his allies? And does B. see through the game? I refuse to be convinced that His Majesty doesn't hate him and is hiding unfriendly intentions behind his bouquets.

Harden in his letter of 3 September that the dementi in the *Norddeutsche Allgemeine Zeitung* that the Kaiser had not recognized Mulai Hafid (see p. 559, note 1) showed that Germany was still trying to deal gently with France.

[1] Harden refers to Germany's concessions to France concerning Morocco.

[2] The concessions allegedly made by the Kaiser to General Lacroix, the French Military Attaché. (See above, p. 343, note 3 and no. 904.)

[3] Hardinge's talk with the Kaiser about the German fleet. (See above, p. 550, note 2.)

[4] Harden probably refers to Tschirschky's visit to Vienna in October, 1906, and his efforts to preserve the Triple Alliance. (See above, p. 440, note 3.) Tschirschky had been made Ambassador to Vienna in 1907.

[5] With Aehrenthal on 5 September. (*Grosse Politik*, vol. XXIV, no. 8242, p. 155.)

[6] See above, p. 421, note 4.

[7] Where the Kaiser and King Edward VII had recently met.

I should think that an honourable policy should not *now* try to change the status of the Morocco question that the Phili boys created for us.[1] That should be counted off as a loss. The personal ambition of Herr Rosen (who didn't see me but who saw Witting and enchanted him) should not be allowed to involve us. Meanwhile no one is making a move towards allowing himself to be hurried by our agitation. Why all the fuss?

Why the speech at Strasbourg?[2] It was enthusiastically received. As usual. It has always begun in this way. 'This we will never do.' And then we do it. If we *now* get an armaments agreement, *then* it will be a humiliation. And is it inconceivable?

Very possible that the French will bring up the fantasy of a Franco-German understanding via Zorn-Wedel.[3] If they succeed there will be nothing any more on which we can take a stand without danger; and the *entente cordiale* will be all the firmer.

In London and Paris they are making jokes about a second Krüger (Abdul Aziz);[4] unfortunately not without reason. First Tangier,[5] then the indecent hurry to recognize the brother[6]. . . .

It is unfortunate that the *Daily Graphic* ascribes the Hafid note[7] to Herr von Holstein, who during the absence of Bülow and Schoen is running affairs.[8] Even here this is found amusing.

Phili can receive visitors without hindrance and is writing uncensored letters in which he pictures himself as a martyr of slander and asks that this view be spread.[9] Never before has a prisoner on trial been treated like that. Leszczynski is said to have said some very strong things against E[ulenburg] in Gastein and to have broken with him completely. Curious, because in the trial he was after all summoned as a witness by E.

*März* and *Süddeutsche Monatshefte* contain vicious attacks on me.

The ridiculous statement in the papers that Ernst is insane is probably intended above all to have an effect on this unstable man.[10] Then a nice psychiatrist comes along and says that this evidence isn't really any

---

[1] Harden is here following Holstein's argument that Eulenburg was to blame for the failure of Germany's Morocco policy.

[2] See above, p. 561, note 2.

[3] Hugo, Zorn von Bulach, Under State Secretary for Alsace-Lorraine, and General Karl von Wedel, the Governor of Alsace-Lorraine, both of whom Harden considered too eager for friendly relations with France.

[4] Harden means that Germany's hasty move to recognize the deposition of Sultan Abdul Aziz of Morocco was comparable to the Kaiser's famous telegram to President Krüger of 3 January 1896.

[5] The landing of the Kaiser at Tangier on 31 March 1905 which marked the beginning of the Morocco crisis. (See above, p. 330, note 2.)

[6] Mulai Hafid, the brother of Sultan Abdul Aziz.

[7] See above, p. 561, note 5.

[8] See above, Holstein's letter to Bülow of 27 August 1908.

[9] After his physical breakdown at his trial, Prince Eulenburg was kept under police surveillance in the Charité hospital.

[10] In his letter to Harden of 3 September Holstein said he had written to Bülow on the previous day that if Ernst were really sent to an insane asylum, Harden would very probably call on other people to give evidence if the case continued.

*rocher*. If the poor fellow will now have to fear another Dr Frey,[1] he will of course lose what little stability he still has. All this would surely hardly be possible in Montenegro.

I still have no word from the law court. (And Eisenberg[2] says : get a vacation or collapse. It *seems* that the Supreme Court in a similar case invalidated the *procedure* that was adopted, and thus could also prevent such a procedure in my case and turn the case back to a private suit (with the assistance of the public prosecutor). In that case the public prosecutor *could* withdraw (upon instructions) and could (something he can't do now) withdraw the sentence demanded by the public prosecutor on M[oltke']s behalf.[3] Since it is no longer in the public interest, the public prosecutor would have grounds to let the gentleman fight for his cause by himself. But this won't happen. On the other side there is the possibility, if the old suit is renewed, that the law court (which would then *not* be the court of Lehmann[4]) would have the *legal* right to restrict evidence as it saw fit. That's what makes the decision so difficult. Especially since one doesn't know what they are brewing 'upstairs'. Whether they will have the—audacity to conduct the Moltke trial before and without E[ulenburg]?[5] The Ministry of Justice wants to scale this height.

Too much for someone who needs to convalesce! I ask pardon, won't do it again soon, and send warm wishes, also in the name of Maxe and her mother,[6] for your good health.

With best Sunday greetings
I am Your Excellency's very devoted
Harden

### 1127.   Maximilian Harden to Holstein

10 September, 1908

Your Excellency,

Many thanks for the kind letter.[7] I hope the health has continued to improve.

I do not think anything useful will be done in Norderney. Herr E[ugen] Z[immermann] was told that, as a patriot and Chancellor, he wanted to and had already taken an important step. A direct question by Z[immermann]: I cannot decide whether to do that. B[ülow] should *only* do what he thinks he should do for the *cause* and for his King. The same thing will happen as before. Indecisiveness until the last minute.

Quite the best thing to do would be for the Chancellor to have Dr Katz inform him quickly about the legal situation. This quiet, clever, reliable, and impartial man would give him a clearer picture in fifteen

[1] Dr Ludwig Frey, who did much to discredit the evidence furnished by Frau von Elbe in the second Moltke-Harden trial.

[2] Dr Max Eisenberg. Harden's physician.

[3] In the second Moltke-Harden trial. (See above, p. 513.)

[4] The Judge who had presided over the second Moltke-Harden trial.

[5] Before the conclusion of Eulenburg's trial for perjury, and without Eulenburg as a witness.

[6] Harden's daughter, Maximiliane, and his wife.          [7] Not found.

minutes than anybody else; also point out the right course to pursue. But B. won't want to, although it is quite 'safe'.

E[ulenburg] is preparing to get his release and has received Geritz,[1] an accomplice!! Quite unheard-of. Isenbiel returns from leave on the 15th. Then they will set a date for my trial and have a cosy time of it without E[ulenburg]. [...]

Radolin is supposed to be going *very soon*. Who is to succeed him, *nescio*. It is sad that B[ülow] was so completely dominated by Rosen's '*charme*'. The foreign Press is shameful. But we are already tacking.

The little house wishes you pleasant days.

With sincerest midnight greetings

I am Your Excellency's very devoted

Harden.[2]

## 1128.   Bernhard von Bülow to Holstein

Norderney, 11 September 1908

Dear Holstein,

[...] Did I already write you that I had a long and interesting conversation with the delegate of the Young Turk committee?[3] He made an excellent impression, not at all boastful, not filled with illusions, not doctrinaire. If only all radicals were like that! I put him in touch with Aehrenthal. The Austrians are a bit leery of the revolution in Constantinople because they fear for Bosnia. I feel it is useful to overcome this uneasiness and suspicion. My Young Turk told me that Young Turkey did not intend to disrupt the status quo either in Bosnia or in Egypt. In my opinion the Austrians favour the Turkish element and play it off against the southern Slav element in Bosnia. In the latter, that is in the Serbo-Croatian irredenta, lies the real future danger for Austria-Hungary.

I am up to my ears in Reich financial reform. It is growing increasingly clear to me what this reform of our finances will mean not only economically and militarily, but also purely diplomatically. The undiminished enormous influence of France, her unshakable prestige, is not only the result of her military strength nor even of her culture and language, but is to a great extent the product of her wealth of capital and its liquidity. That is the primary reason for French influence in Spain, Italy, Russia and many other countries. Now the French are trying to find a financial wedge in Hungary. That will emerge more clearly the longer we continue our miserable economic dependence on loans and contributions from the individual German states. We must have the courage to assume the new taxes ourselves, which we are actually now perfectly able to do. Last year a Frenchman who visited me here last year, Huret, told me that he had travelled all over America and Germany

[1] Eulenburg's steward, with whom he was supposed to have shared a hotel bedroom. (*Zukunft*, vol. 64, p. 228.)

[2] A copy of Holstein's reply of 12 September (Rogge, *Holstein und Harden*, pp. 326–8) was found in the Holstein Papers.

[3] Ahmed Risa. (See *Grosse Politik*, vol. XXVii, no. 8908, pp. 609–10.)

and had subjected both countries to a close economic inspection for some years. He was also well acquainted with many other countries. Together with the United States, we had made the most rapid and the greatest economic progress of any country in the world. Every year we consume three (I repeat, three) billions in beer, wine, and spirits. And with that we should not be able to stand new taxes! Behind the shouting about and against new taxes there is only party politics, pettiness, and brutal selfishness, the type of bullying egotism that only thinks of itself and its narrow interests. But I am also convinced that any new taxes will be useless without greater economy. We cannot provide for and maintain simultaneously the most powerful army, the most generous social welfare programme and a gigantic fleet. It is here that we have the road block to an unlimited fleet-building programme and the possibility of seeing the clouds that have been lowering over the land clear away.

I have summoned Schoen to Berlin so that he can back me up on the (very important) question of the extension of citizenship.[1] [...]

Always sincerely yours

B.

1129.  Holstein to Bernhard von Bülow
       Draft

Dammhaus, 13 September 1908

Dear Bülow,

Your letter of the 11th received.[2] I am grateful to you for having thought of me. Unfortunately you have had more trouble than pleasure in the last few days.

When I wrote last week, I only knew that you rejected the unilateral German recognition of the Mulai Hafid because of what Metternich had said about the irritation of the English, and also in order not to give Tirpitz an excuse to make trouble. This I could understand.

But I did not know that you had allowed yourself to be persuaded by Rosen to take a step against which I had urgently warned you, and with reason: I mean the proposal for joint recognition.[3] Did you think that this *acte d'une ambition honteuse* would *not* irritate the Entente Powers, or that it would *not* furnish the Tirpitz group with the means of making trouble? Those in favour of this diplomatic misstep must have thought so. Because when the French and English Press began to spit, they shrank back and declared officially—I read it with sorrow in the *Tag*—that there was no question of a note, that it was only an oral communication. First step towards a retreat. New proof that the German tail is good for nothing but to be drawn between the legs. Foreigners make game of us and complain more loudly than if we had taken an independent and self-assured action. For Germany itself the Press Bureau will gloss things over.

If we did not feel it was opportune to act independently, then we should have sat still. The attempt to take over the leadership of a hostile

---

[1] See above, no. 1121.  [2] See above.  [3] See above, p. 561, note 5.

majority was illogical and therefore a failure. I told you beforehand that Aehrenthal, warned by Golu[chowski]'s fate, would not co-operate. That is what happened. 'Austria-Hungary has no reason to take a position in the fight for precedence.'[1] We are now more isolated than ever. But the worst is that we have once again demonstrated a lack of seriousness of purpose, not to say of courage.

I had also predicted that we could undertake an isolated act, but not carry through a campaign because the Kaiser would undercut it. That too has happened. In his speech at Kolmar the day before yesterday, the Kaiser said so plainly that no one could have misunderstood him: 'Do not get excited, friends. All that is a lot of nonsense.' The French will accept that explanation.[2]

I am certain that you see all that to-day as clearly as I do. Rosen, Mr Malaprop, shares with the Kaiser the special talent of running the ship of state on the rocks.[3]

Besides the Morocco question, I was also worried about the fleet. Early in September the *Neue Gesellschaftliche Korrespondenz* printed a highly official article—which was generally recognized as such—which described the naval discussions at Kronberg very precisely and authoritatively.[4] Even before that both Sovereigns had said all sorts of things, the one in anger, the other bragging, that would best have been left unsaid. Here however it was clearly stated for the first time: 'Yes, you English have been told off; not by the Chancellor, whom you always unjustly distrust, but by the Kaiser, your dear relative. It is he who refuses to be talked out of these unlimited armaments.' The effect of this pronouncement can be seen in the tone of the English Press, to which it was directed.

This violent way of dealing with this topic can *only* be justified in case there is the intention of shortly declaring in the Reichstag in this connection: 'The Kaiser has been misunderstood. He has no intention whatever of unlimited arming.' But a statement must have a solid and positive core, for a simple denial and generalizations will not be enough.

A sensible statement, i.e. one that would take account of the financial position, especially the necessity for a sound evaluation of the technical problems before we risk hundreds of millions, would naturally be bitterly attacked by the fleet people—enthusiasts and vested interests. To be able to stand up against this, you will have to see to it that the Press

[1] The origin of the sentence quoted by Holstein has not been determined. On 1 September Brockdorff-Rantzau telegraphed from Vienna that Aehrenthal had informed him he had no desire to be involved in the internal problems of Morocco. (From the Foreign Ministry files.) On the other hand, Aehrenthal told Schoen on 5 September that he understood Germany's desire to hasten the recognition of Mulai Hafid and that this was a position worth supporting. (*Grosse Politik*, vol. XXIV, p. 420, note *.)

[2] The Kaiser had simply assured the citizens of Kolmar that their city could grow and develop in peace under the protection of the German eagle.

[3] Holstein commented further on this point in a letter to Harden of 14 September in which he stated that the present unfortunate international position of Germany was due to the Kaiser's interference in every diplomatic action. (Rogge, *Holstein und Harden*, pp. 334–5.)

[4] See above, p. 550, notes 2 and 5, and nos. 1119 and 1126.

prepares the terrain—more so than has heretofore been done, so far as I know. In my opinion, an excellent example of the type of thing that should be done is an article in the morning edition of the *Kreuzzeitung* of 4 September which deals with this theme. 'Is the army beginning to suffer because of the fleet?' *That* idea will be effective all over Prussia, and every Prussian who is not a Social Democrat will prick up his ears. Have them submit the article to you, *nisi factum*, and give orders that this particular theme—whether and in what way the army can be harmed by the fleet—should be brought up again and again from every possible point of view and in the newspapers of every political party; for instance also from the point of view of the more or less adequate tenets of the army officers. This will have effect on public opinion, not on the Kaiser. On him something else will have effect: namely fear of England. He will consider, despite his thoughtless frivolity, that once England has her great fleet, or only a part of it, and is certain that in a given moment she is 'one up' on us, she will make practical use of it either by deed or by threat. Therefore instruct Metternich—although that should be the task of the Naval Attaché—for his part to report as early and as fully as possible about everything he hears in connection with the great navy bill. Under the pressure of these reports—if they come soon enough—the Kaiser will probably allow you a freer hand in making a reassuring statement—really reassuring—in the Reichstag than he would otherwise do. And Tirpitz too has weak nerves, as we both know.

So, for people and Parliament, discuss the question: 'How can the damage to the army by the navy be prevented?' And for the Kaiser, the earliest possible information about the boomerang being prepared in England. Perhaps you can in this way bring about a *détente*. If you do not succeed, then as the danger increases our German tail will once more react in the customary manner because 'changes are not likely to occur', as they say in Roman law.

Harden, who has recently again received all sorts of information from Court (among other things that the Kaiser summoned the French Military Attaché to Metz but that Clemenceau refused permission)[1] has heard that Radolin is to be dismissed *very shortly*.[2] I will not argue for or against, but I am convinced of this: that Marschall would be dangerous for you in Paris, both personally and objectively; because if the Kaiser wants to have Marschall in Paris, it will probably be because of some fantastic scheme. Marschall is a talented man, but from what I have seen of him, he would lend himself to almost anything.

In that case Erni[3] would be better in Paris. After the colonial fiasco, the Kaiser will not so quickly make him Chancellor of the Reich.[4] It seems to me that the question for you becomes: is it easier to keep Radolin in Paris or to get Erni there?

[1] See above, Harden's letter of 5 September 1908.
[2] See above, Harden's letter of 10 September 1908.
[3] Prince Ernst zu Hohenlohe-Langenburg. Head of the Colonial Office, 1905–September 1906.
[4] While Head of the Colonial Office, Hohenlohe had been severely criticized in the Reichstag as an ineffective administrator.

To return to Harden: if you now go to Berlin, you should really concern yourself with the question as to whether the Moltke trial should actually be carried on despite the continued 'illness' and absence of Phili. I do not say this for Harden's sake. I have no fears for him, as things are going—but I am concerned about the enormous scandal that might occur if Harden, who up till now has really been quite restrained, should be obliged to summon a number of highly placed personages, even royal Princes, as witnesses. Something for which Kuno set the precedent in the first trial by referring to the testimony of the Kaiser.

I suggest that you *immediately* ask Isenbiel, or if he is on leave, *Staatsanwalt* Katz, to inform you about the matter, and that you then bring it up in the Ministry of State and explain clearly:

'The legal question as to whether or not it is possible or permissible to continue the Moltke trial without the participation of Prince Eul. is something I leave up to the lawyers. For me the political consideration is decisive, for with the elimination of Eul., Harden, to defend himself, will presumably call up persons whose involvement would in my opinion be highly undesirable, and I think that you will agree with me. So if the condition of Pr. Eul. seems to make it necessary—or possible—to exclude him from the proceedings, then surely legal reasons can be found to prevent the continuation of the Moltke trial. That this trial should have been prevented for political reasons is a point of view I have taken since it first began, as the Minister of Justice knows. The political objections that made me take this view one and a half years ago have in the course of the proceedings grown steadily greater.'[1] When the Ministers hear what is at stake, they will surely all be of the same opinion. Einem, too, and especially he, because the further the matter goes, the more he will be involved.[2] [...]

Always your sincerely devoted<br>Holstein

I do not want to get involved in tax questions, otherwise I would say,

(1) That I would be disgusted if Bavaria again prevented a tax on beer.

(2) Inheritance taxes on descendants means the end of estate owners and peasants. Do not under any circumstances make *that* tax a Cabinet question.

## 1130.   Maximilian Harden to Holstein

Westerland, 16 September 1908

Your Excellency

Has the frequent habit yourself of saying: 'I will never accustom myself to that.' And similar things. Is it then so inconceivable that I,

---

[1] At this point in his draft Holstein crossed out the sentence: 'I would advise that you completely by-pass the Minister of Justice, who from the beginning has not behaved correctly towards you in this matter, and go directly to the Ministry of State.'

[2] While Harden was on holiday in Westerland, Holstein wrote to Frau Harden on 16 September that he had expressed himself on the 'business matter', but that this could not replace the measures to be taken by Harden himself. (From the Harden Papers.)

also old, always alone, always obliged to rely on myself, should have difficulty in adjusting myself to the views of others in everyday life? May this not be the smallest injustice on the part of the kind adviser? And has Your Excellency not noticed how intensively and seriously I ponder over *everything* that you say or write?[1] [...]

E[ugen] Z[immermann]: there too I ask for justice. I *have* told him approximately just that.[2] But (1) he was only there[3] six days, has been back for ages; (2) he has *his* interests in mind; (3) I do not see through his latest intentions; (4) he is always 'peeved' when I think it is necessary to attack the Chancellor (as I did recently) on matters of policy; (5) the Chancellor cannot be allowed to assume that *I* want something from him; (6) it is always different when an intermediary speaks (poverty of our ability to express ourselves); and (7) I don't trust B[ülow], and can't after the experiences with E.Z. and Rathenau; nor can I expect that he should deal straightforwardly with me. His interview with Whitman shows at least that he has grasped the viewpoint of M. de Holstein: to be friendly towards England (*mais trop de zèle!*) and cold towards France. But I don't find it *very* good; though admittedly I only read excerpts here.[4] [...]

The Chancellor told EZ he had 'already taken important steps in the matter' (?) and was completely of the opinion that it must end.[5] Well, well. Z. thinks Hülsen-H[äseler] was in Norderney for that purpose. *Dubito.*[6] [...]

Deeply and sincerely grateful for kind interest

With best wishes for your health

Your very devoted

Harden

## 1131. Holstein to Bernhard von Bülow
Draft

17 September 1908

Dear Bülow,

After this statement by Lord Brassey[7] I take it as certain that there will be a great bill unless there is a *détente* soon. And not long after that there will be an ultimatum, because John Bull will not bear *that* tax burden indefinitely.

[1] Holstein had written with some pique on 12 September because Harden had ignored his advice on where to spend his holiday. (Rogge, *Holstein und Harden*, pp. 326–8.)

[2] In his letter of 12 September, Holstein had urged that Harden ask Eugen Zimmermann to present the potential dangers of a renewal of the Moltke-Harden trial to the Chancellor when Zimmermann visited him in Norderney.

[3] In Norderney.

[4] Bülow's interview with Sidney Whitman appeared in the *Standard* of 14 September.

[5] The Moltke-Harden case.

[6] Holstein replied on 18 September that he assumed that the Chancellor had intended to do something in the interests of the State, and it seemed plausible to him that Hülsen-Häseler should have been in Norderney for that purpose. Holstein then informed Harden of what he had written to Bülow about his case in his letter of 13 September. (Rogge, *Holstein und Harden*, pp. 336–7.)

[7] Lord Thomas Brassey. Lord Warden of the Cinque Ports and expert on British naval affairs.

Brassey is a thoughtful older man with no bluff in his make-up. When he speaks to the Union of the Chambers of Commerce of England as their president, it means something.

'Feverish armaments'. That means, therefore, that they believe in a German attack and will not allow it to come to fruition.

The best way for us to get out of this position—I at least can see no better way—would be for a Reichstag Commission to investigate the brief but definite technical objections raised by Galster[1] and for experts to be questioned on the subject before hundreds of millions are thrown into the water. But perhaps the Kaiser has another idea *in petto*. Perhaps he thinks: let us go on. The English will not take decisive action immediately. And if they do I will say: 'Bülow and Tirpitz misinformed me.'

And you, what do you think? I am afraid that you too believe in letting things run on.

Hence I sign myself as

Yours most fatalistically<br>Holstein

## 1132. Bernhard von Bülow to Holstein

Norderney, 25 September 1908

Dear Holstein,

[...] We are agreed in that, once we have cleaned up our financial situation, we cannot permit a fantastic Naval Bill, which would again disturb the economic balance—achieved with so much trouble at home—, and which would also mean trouble abroad. In my conversations with His Maj., with my Prussian colleagues, with the Ministers of the individual states, and with Deputies, I have tried to anticipate and prevent such a development. I do not even think it altogether out of the question that even while the present naval programme is in existence we may come to an understanding with England. The prerequisites for such an understanding depend partly on us, partly on others. It depends on us to see to it that Reich finances are not again upset by exorbitant shipbuilding costs, and if such a danger arises, that we draw timely attention to the danger and its consequences. It is up to us to prevent demands and expenditures for the fleet from overwhelming and engulfing the interests of the army, on whose shoulders our fate and future actually rest. I talked very seriously along these lines with the Chief of the General Staff. It is up to us to deal carefully with the Morocco question so as to keep open the possibility of an understanding with England. The mistakes made in this area have been pointed out by you with your usual perspicacity, and with justice. But, to a greater extent than you perhaps realize, I have to assume responsibility for what others have done out of ignorance or malice. Now things are so that if our differences with France over Morocco become accentuated, they will—*id est, rebus sic stantibus*—also become accentuated with England; in that case our fleet

---

[1] See above, p. 551, note 3.

Icaruses can always say that it was not our ship building but the clumsy handling of the Morocco affair by the Foreign Ministry and its inability to get on good terms with France that are to blame for the tension with England. What does not depend on us is that England should not resort to pressure and threats which would preclude the possibility of an agreement. I have heard from several sides that people would be only too glad to awaken the suspicion that the Foreign Ministry is behind Galster. If only for that reason I must be very very careful about how I bring up the points I raised above. But I know how sure I can be of your discretion. I have noticed, by the way, that Galster has been more read—and approved—than I had myself believed.

In domestic politics, Reich financial reform is of course in the foreground. The desire for greater economy and simplicity was very evident in the session of the Bundesrat. I like Sydow; he is no four-flusher, substance instead of appearance, a tremendous capacity for work, and at the same time equipped with good nerves and a sound sense of humour. The main thing in my opinion is that we do not demand too little; that we propose a few fundamental large-scale taxes rather than a lot of small unworkable ones; that we seriously take up the problem of paying off the national debt so as to avoid a reversion to our previous economic policy of borrowing; and that the Government shows energy, seriousness and firmness of purpose corresponding to the incredible importance of the whole matter.

The tension between Bulgaria and Turkey is disquieting to those who have an interest in Turkish credits, and also to disinterested friends of Turkey.[1] C[olmar] von der Goltz has summarized his most recent impressions about Turkey in the opinion that the Turkish army has deteriorated badly during the past thirty years of rotten government and that at the moment the Turkish army would hardly be on a par with the Bulgarian. Fortunately the Bulgarians are not supposed to be fully aware of their own military superiority. Aehrenthal is currying favour with the Bulgarians. He thinks that the ill-treatment Goluchowski accorded the Bulgarian heir to the throne since his re-baptism was a political mistake,[2] he regards the Bulgarians as a counterweight to the (for Austria more dangerous) Serbo-Croatians. I thought the way in which they provoked the Geschow case in Constantinople was clumsy. It was characteristic of our friend Marschall to have regarded this incident from the formal standpoint of international law, and to have established the formal legal justification for the Turkish move with great legal perspicacity in an endlessly long report.[3]

[1] There was much hard feeling in Bulgaria when Geschow, the Bulgarian diplomatic agent in Turkey, was not invited to an official banquet in honour of the Sultan's birthday because he was the representative of a Turkish vassalage. (See Marschall's telegram to the Foreign Ministry of 13 September 1908, *Grosse Politik*, vol. XXVIi, no. 8948, pp. 68–9.) On 24 September the Bulgarian Government took the opportunity of a railway strike to take over the railway lines going through Bulgarian territory. On 5 October Prince Ferdinand announced Bulgaria's complete independence from Turkey and proclaimed himself Tsar of Bulgaria.

[2] The conversion of Crown Prince Boris to the Orthodox faith in February 1896.

[3] Of 18 September. (From the Foreign Ministry files.)

You are absolutely right that the Moltke trial should not be resumed until the Eulenburg case has been settled. Every patriot must hope that, while fully upholding the law, the country may be spared new scandals for the sake of its prestige in the world. I have expressed myself very forcefully in this sense. The question is only what will happen if Eul. should die. They say and assume in Berlin that he will live only a few more months, perhaps only a few weeks. I am of the opinion that all in all Radolin is the best Ambassador for Paris. He knows the terrain, he had tact and skill, and is a *Grand Seigneur*. I can think of no one better. There is an enormous amount of intrigue against him. Besides Marschall and Lichnowsky, Hermann Hatzfeldt would above all like to go to Paris; he has in his cousin and intimate friend, Dolly Castellane, a zealous partisan there who is doing what she can against Radolin. His Maj. does not want to remove Marschall from Constantinople now under any circumstances. His Maj. is very down on poor Erni, especially after what Köller told him about the dynastic desires of the Hohenlohe family.

I see with horror that I am at the end of the fifth page and have to reach for a larger envelope. I close in sending once again the very best wishes and warmest regards from my wife and myself,

Your sincerely devoted<br>Bülow.

### 1133.  Maximilian Harden to Holstein

Westerland, 26 September 1908

Your Excellency,

[...] Here a week of superb sunshine. Not a ripple in the sea. Smooth as glass, warm land wind. That saps the energy terribly, and the nerves suffer. But nothing can compare with the Phili business. What an unparalleled disgrace and crime. What perfidy. What a desecration of Prussian justice. Free, without bail, at his castle, without supervision.[1] With Geritz and Co. Even disinterested people feel this is an inconceivable piece of villainy. This is the end. If I ever recover I will say a word or two to Mssrs. Bülow and Beseler the like of which they have never heard before. The Press says not a single word. And for weeks the Chancellor has been chattering the most hopeless nonsense to win indemnity in that quarter. Obviously promised to save La Pompadour. That man is the most amusing example of perfidious falseness that I know. But he's going to go under the knife. [...]

With the sincerest wishes for your good health

I am Your Excellency's very devoted<br>Harden[2]

---

[1] On 25 September Eulenburg had been released on bail. Harden based his above statement on incorrect rumours that Eulenburg would be released without bail.

[2] Holstein replied from the Harz on 27 September that he agreed with Harden's feelings about release without bail, but that release *with* bail was after all not so bad. He had reason to believe that steps had been taken to prevent a resumption of the Moltke trial before the end of the Eulenburg trial, and advised that Harden temporarily refrain from pulling all the stops on his organ. (Rogge, *Holstein und Harden*, pp. 339–40.)

### 1134. Maximilian Harden to Holstein

Westerland, 1 October 1908

Your Excellency

has, as I sincerely hope, arrived safely and in good health.[1] Many thanks for the letter which I received this morning.[2]

The Supreme Court is of course totally indifferent. A farce. Bülow, Bülow, Bülow: nothing more. Only he. Always. Every underhanded action was his doing. He must be pilloried and publicly disgraced as the man who consciously made a whore of justice. And if I die ten deaths: this I will accomplish. Every means is justified. He and his 'taking steps'!!!

He fears nothing any more, E[ulenburg] fears nothing any more, and I am to be slaughtered. The Supreme Court is of course in league with them. Hence have decided to have nothing to do with *any* 'charges'. I will no longer have any part of this infamous juridical farce. The juridical part of it is unimportant in any case. Eulenburg is a pure beam of light in comparison with B[ülow].

His head must fall. Everything else is unimportant. But of course other people will see all this and react differently. *On a toujours la force de supporter les maux d'autrui.* I have burned all my bridges, including of course the one to the public prosecutor's office, and will take the only path that is open to me. If that perfidious empty-headed fellow is stronger than I, then he is right. Amen.

With all good wishes I am

Your Excellency's devoted

H.

### 1135. Maximilian Harden to Holstein

Grunewald, 5 October 1908

Your Excellency,

Many thanks for the friendly letter. I do not think that I need assure Your Excellency how glad I would have been to see you immediately after my dismal return. Now I will have to look forward to Thursday.[3]

Immediately after the release and glorification of Prince Eulenburg, Herr Lehmann, in his delight about the elimination of this witness, set the date for Moltke vs. Harden for 24 November. (I heard about this *very confidentially*; it will not be made public until later, in a 'suitable' manner.) So: a trial without E[ulenburg] before a court presided over by Lehmann; which means: conviction of H[arden] no matter what happens. No need to consider steps, moves, in this affair. It would be childish to count on the use of evidence in this business after what we

---

[1] From his holiday in the Harz mountains.

[2] Holstein's letter of 27 September. (See above, p. 573, note 2.)

[3] Holstein had written on 4 October that he supposed Harden would want to avoid being disturbed, and perhaps also any discussion with reference to the Chancellor. (Rogge, *Holstein und Harden*, p. 341.)

went through with E.[1] Everything turned out to be even more incredible than I, 'the pessimist', had predicted.

E. undisturbed, can bribe and influence as he wishes; stands unbowed, as a martyr; and M[oltke] arrives without this witness before a 'fixed' tribunal and has had *a full year* to 'check' everything. Nothing has been done about Kistler.[2] All witnesses have seen by the example of Ernst and Riedl that it does not pay to give evidence against such gentlemen. Geritz conducts his beloved master in triumph to his castle. The directors of the (dependent) Charité hospital suddenly find they have no room for a prisoner under investigation. He is deathly ill, but can be moved in an auto.

With best wishes for your health, I am

Your Excellency's very devoted

H.

And at the same time the Chancellor maintains, as I know for a certainty, that in agreement with the Minister of Justice he has succeeded in arranging that there should be no proceedings against Harden before the conclusion of the E[ulenburg] trial.


1136.   Holstein to Maximilian Harden
        Copy[3]

5 October, evening, [1908]

My dear Herr Harden!

You can imagine what effect your news had on me. But this is not the time for figures of speech.

What I would do? I would have a reliable person inform the authority who maintained he had *succeeded* in arranging that the one trial not be resumed until the other had been concluded: 'The date [for the trial] *has* been fixed, for 24 November. What do you say to that?'

I think *the reply would under all circumstances furnish some clarification*, even if it were quite unclear. Above all it would clarify the question as to whether the particular authority had been betrayed by a subordinate. The way things stand now there is no longer any possibility of subterfuge. Until you have a reply, I would occupy myself with other problems. This would take a week. Whether it can be spared, I do not presume to judge. All-in-all, my thinking on this subject cannot claim any great consideration because of my incomplete knowledge of the situation.

So, until Thursday. [...]

Your very devoted
Holstein

[1] At the Eulenburg trial.

[2] Eulenburg's former private secretary, who had allegedly tried to persuade Ernst to keep silent about his relations with the Prince. (See above, p. 530, note 6.)

[3] The text is identical with the letter actually sent to Harden. (Rogge, *Holstein und Harden*, p. 342.)

## 1137. Holstein to Bernhard von Bülow
Draft

Berlin, 7 October 1908

Dear Bülow,

Since Mühlberg telegraphed from Norderney that he would come to see me yesterday at six, I thought that he had some message for me. According to circumstances, this could hardly have referred to anything but the Harden affair. Since there was no time to be lost, I brought up the subject at once. He said he had no instructions about this, but that you had in his presence twice firmly stated that you felt a resumption of the Moltke trial before the conclusion of the Eulenburg trial was out of the question. That if necessary you would summon the Minister of Justice and inform him that you would make the conclusion of the Eulenburg case *before* the Moltke case a Cabinet question. A quarter of an hour after receiving this information, I got into an auto in order to inform Harden. He heard what I had to say calmly and only said something like : he had already heard something similar.

When I asked : 'Yes, but what more needs to be done?' he replied : 'I have just, since my return, read a letter—not addressed to me—signed by Herr von Loebell and written on official stationery which stated that Herr von L., at the instruction of the Chancellor, had *succeeded in arranging* with the Minister of Justice that the case Moltke vs. Harden should not be resumed until the case vs. Eulenburg should be concluded. And now, a few days later, Herr Lehmann has set the date for the Moltke trial on 23 November,[1] and has also said that he will conduct the proceedings because he considers himself to be "impartial". What am I to think? How should I, how can I, regard this matter?' etc. etc.

I replied : 'This is certainly a contradiction, but it will undoubtedly be resolved. He, Harden, will surely wait to see *whether* the contradiction is resolved before he does any more about this aspect of the matter?'

Harden replied : 'Yes, of course.' That took a considerable weight off my chest.

Still, I am astonished that such a contradiction should occur officially, and in Prussia. Someone, perhaps Beseler, perhaps Lehmann, seems to have played a dubious role. Loebell's letter was quite correct and proper, need not fear the light of day, and might on the contrary have a favourable effect *provided* that it proves to be correct.

I only see few people, but those whom I have seen since my return were agreed that the general public was amazed about the release of Eulenburg. The opinion was expressed repeatedly that Eulenburg must have threatened to do something, otherwise the matter was inexplicable. The Berlin Press, anti-Harden, influenced from many sides and also permeated with homosexuals (so they say), has up till now gone its own way. Will it be able to hold this course in view of the feelings that are already becoming evident among the public and which would grow considerably if the law actually tried to condemn Harden while the main

---

[1] This date was announced on 7 October in the *Berliner Lokalanzeiger* and other newspapers.

witness, Eul[enburg], was staying at Liebenberg 'unable to appear'? A question I cannot judge. But of this I am certain: of the general desire for *peace and quiet*. Whoever provides peace and quiet will be the popular man.

With best wishes
Holstein.

### 1138.     Holstein to Bernhard von Bülow
Draft

Berlin, 8 October 1908

Dear Bülow,

The simultaneous move by Bulgaria and Austria[1] reminds one distantly of the co-operation of Prussia and Austria in '64. At that time Austria covered us against the western Powers, to-day Austria is covered by Bulgaria against Russia. Because a Russian move in favour of Turkey against Bulgaria would be impossible to explain to the Russian people. In my opinion Aehrenthal has so far handled the matter very skilfully. He is also, without intending to do so, representing our interests by excluding the *concert européen* from the whole business, or is at least trying to exclude it. In this we will naturally have to support him, because the *concert européen* is the English means of fabricating English hegemony in Europe. The *concert européen*, like every *societas*, is exploited to the advantage of the most powerful group, which is to-day England, France, Italy, who would be supported on most occasions by Russia if only in *revanche* for the Congress of Berlin and the Austrian successes of that period. Italy *has* to go along with the western Powers, even if she does not want to, and is now only exhibiting pro-Triple Alliance *airs* in order to lure Austria and ourselves before the tribunal of Europe, something Italy fervently wishes to do. Once they have us at the Congress conference table, the old grouping of Algeciras will once again take shape. England and France still have great obligations towards Italy for that.

The *concert européen* also has the characteristic of serving as a buffer between England and Russia. Without this buffer there might easily be friction with Russia, now that England is once again striving to play the leading rôle in Constantinople.

Therefore: *no Congress! Exclusion of the concert of Europe*. There is no longer anything to be won or lost in our position in Turkey. Turkey has been lost through no fault of ours. As a result of the move by Austria and Bulgaria, the Young Turks have been driven into the arms of England once and for all—much to our advantage. For an understanding between England and Russia is only conceivable if England is either indifferent or hostile to Turkey, which has been the case from the time of the Drummond Wolff treaty[2] until two months ago. The first

[1] On 5 October Bulgaria proclaimed her complete independence from Turkey, and on 6 October Austria announced the Austrian annexation of Bosnia and Herzegovina.

[2] Of 22 May 1887 between Britain and Turkey, by which Britain agreed to evacuate Egypt within three years unless internal unrest in Egypt obliged the British to remain. The Sultan, supported by France and Russia, refused to ratify the treaty.

public pronouncement of Sir Edward Grey yesterday in favour of Turkey is something I heartily welcome.[1] The friction with Russia will come, *nolens volens,* for instance in the question as to whether all ships of war or only those belonging to the Black Sea states should be allowed through the Straits. At a Congress, England would to be sure almost always be able to enforce its will about everything—by the power of attraction of the greatest weight. For that reason England wants to force a Congress.

I spoke in this sense to Stemrich in the last few days; he agreed with me in theory, but his feelings are on the side of Turkey, as are mine.

If a Congress is to decide about Bulgaria's future, Bulgaria will wish to take part—something the Turks will not desire. If Bulgaria takes part against the wishes of Turkey, then the participation of Greece (Crete) will also be proposed,[2] and then Serbia will not wish to be left out either as an interested or injured party. But if all these restless spirits explode at a Congress, the old rule will once again be proved correct that a Congress or Conference *before* a war never prevents a war. Peace can be preserved much better by an unimpassioned exchange of views among the Great Powers, Cabinet to Cabinet.

As usual, His Majesty made a false start.[3] He is against Austria and for the Turks, and thus is hitching himself to Uncle Edward's wagon. H.M. simply has no political flair, that is all there is to it. He is also capable of declaring himself in favour of an international guarantee of Macedonia to Turkey, by which the English will show themselves as the protectors of Turkey and will exclude Austria for all time from Saloniki —and probably he will do just that. My attention was already drawn to this effort on the part of England at the time of the Congress of Berlin.

I close as I began : Austria is fighting to-day—for egotistical reasons —*our* battle against the *concert européen,* alias English hegemony, alias encirclement.

With best wishes

Holstein

I almost forgot to mention Goltz Pasha.[4] The Young Turks— advised by England—would like to borrow him from us on the eve of mobilization. A nice idea—for an Englishman. Because by doing so we would encourage the Turks to go to war, make Russia *and* Austria angry with us, and would give the English the right to say : 'There, you see how Germany is instigating war.'

My grandfather Brünnow used to say : 'My child, the fool is not the person who demands something, but the person who does it.'

But H.M. will be inclined.

H.

---

[1] In a speech at Wooler, Northumberland, in which he defined the attitude of the British Government towards events in the Near East, Sir Edward Grey said it was desirable to lose no time in assuring Turkey that in any revision of the Treaty of Berlin her interests would receive full consideration, and that Britain would use her influence in this direction.

[2] Crete had proclaimed her union with Greece on 7 October.

[3] The Kaiser complained bitterly about not having been informed in advance of Austria's intention to annex Bosnia and Herzegovina, and of being forced into an anti-Turkish policy. ( *Grosse Politik,* vol. XXVIi, nos. 8939, 8992, pp. 50–4, 110–12. )

[4] The German General, Kolmar von der Goltz.

1139.   Holstein to Bernhard von Bülow
        Draft

Berlin, 10 October 1908

Dear Bülow,

(1)   The assurances Schoen gave the Turkish Ambassador, according to to-day's newspapers, are being generally regarded as a drawing-away from Austria and Bulgaria.[1] By this pusillanimity we discourage Austria, which as I said is fighting *our* battle against the *concert européen*. The Kaiser snorts at Szögyényi[2] and Schoen draws away from Austria—the combination will contribute significantly to weaken Aehrenthal's powers of resistance to the Congress. But the joint action of the Congress will contribute just as little to the honour of Germany as the joint action recommended by Rosen, Klehmet, Flotow (Wolff) on Morocco.[3] Germany has no foreign policy at all at the present time, and cannot have one in this constant back and forth and confusion unconfined. But the responsibility in the end will always fall on you.

Therefore I would in your place tell the foreign ambassadors immediately after you arrive in Berlin : 'It is not up to us to criticize Austria, but to ask ourselves whether, under the circumstances, we should support Austria? Yes, we should.' And you will ask His Majesty whether it is really his intention to come to the aid of Uncle Edward and the English hegemony of Europe.

The Straits question which was left unsettled by the Congress of Berlin is now coming up as a bone of contention between Russia and England. It would be much better if those two were to negotiate about it between themselves rather than at a Congress, so that Europe does not have to *guarantee* the solution they reach and support England against Russia, just in case Russia should accept this new treaty with the same bad grace as she did the Black Sea clause[4] and the Batum clause[5]—because *now* Isvolsky will make far-reaching concessions. That is why England is *now* demanding a Congress.

To sum up, a Turkish-Bulgarian war (with which the English are at present bluffing) would now be of greater advantage to Germany than a Congress. Because if the Bulgarians come out on the short end, Russia will have to protect them against a loss of territory. And England is obliged to protect Turkey against loss of territory according to the Cyprus treaty.[6] Do ask Szögyényi whether Austria will take it upon

---

[1] State Secretary Schoen had assured the Turkish Ambassador that there had been no previous agreement between Germany, Austria, and Russia for the action taken by Austria and Bulgaria. (*Grosse Politik*, vol. XXVIi, no. 8997, p. 116.)

[2] See Jenisch's telegram to the Foreign Ministry of 7 October. (*Grosse Politik*, vol. XXVIi, no. 8994, pp. 113–14.)

[3] See above, Holstein's letter to Bülow of 13 September 1908.

[4] Of the Treaty of Paris of 1856 by which Russia agreed to the neutralization of the Black Sea. Russia took advantage of the Franco-Prussian war of 1870–1 to abrogate the Black Sea clauses.

[5] Of the Treaty of Berlin of 1878 by which Russia was obliged to make Batum, recently acquired from the Turks, a free port. In 1886 Russia proceeded to fortify Batum despite the Treaty of Berlin.

[6] By the Anglo-Turkish Treaty of 4 June 1878 Britain was only obliged to defend Turkish territory in Asia.

herself to keep Serbia and Montenegro quiet; also ask him artlessly and objectively whether in Aehrenthal's opinion it would be easier to preserve Anglo-Russian unity with or without the buffer of Europe.

To leave England and Russia face to face in the Balkans, especially on the Straits question, *without* the buffer of Europe—that is in my opinion the correct policy at present both for Austria and for ourselves.

(2) Yesterday evening the pro-Eulenburg *Berliner Neuesten Nachrichten* carried an interview with Judge Lehmann in which he blandly declared that during the forthcoming Moltke trial Eulenburg could very well be summoned as a witness, although he could not be placed under oath.

The idea of summoning a person accused of and virtually condemned for perjury to be a witness—in his own cause!—before the end of his own trial is incredible, but shows that Lehmann and the people behind him will stop at nothing. In this business you will have to put your foot down very firmly. The Minister of Justice will at first assume that you will accept a rejection of your protests with the same Hohenlohe-like resignation as you did the first time. I am however convinced of the contrary now that I know about the letter which Loebell wrote at your instructions.[1] Simply ask Beseler whether he thinks that this protection of pederasty and perjury will remain unnoticed indefinitely, and against whom the effect will be directed.

His Majesty is—unfortunately—probably the biggest loser.

Best wishes from

Your sincerely devoted
Holstein

1140.    Bernhard von Bülow to Holstein

Norderney, 10 October 1908

Dear Holstein,

Many thanks for your friendly and valuable information.[2] The setting of the date [for the Moltke-Harden trial] was as great a surprise to me as it was to you and others. I took steps immediately and so emphatically that I have hopes of success. I will tell you orally how all this happened. This time the Ministry of Justice seems to have had nothing to do with it. But how is it possible for H[arden] to think that I am behind it! Do tell him the anecdote about King Friedrich Wilhelm III and the aide-de-camp von Malachowski. The entire country wants to have peace and quiet at last; that is also in the interests of the state which I am bound to defend, just as it is my duty to see that no injustice is done to anyone, not only *sub specie juris stricti* but also from the point of view of the *jus aequum*.

Your views on the political situation interested me in the highest degree. I will hold Tuesday open so that we can discuss it at our leisure. Will you come to see me Tuesday at six? I hope you are again quite

---

[1] See above, Holstein's letter to Bülow of 7 October 1908.
[2] See above, Holstein's letter of 7 October 1908.

well and cheerful (without the wasp-waist). If it is more convenient for you, I will come to you.

With best wishes, sincerely

Your

B.

### 1141. Holstein to Bernhard von Bülow
Draft

Berlin, 11 October 1908

Dear Bülow,

So far as I can see, His Majesty and the Foreign Ministry continue to draw away from Austria demonstratively, and just now when Austria is fighting our fight. Statements by Marschall are being published that would tend to give Franz Ferdinand and Aehrenthal serious doubts about our reliability. As in Morocco so in the Eastern Question. The very thing is usually done against which I advised. In my last two letters[1] I said what I wanted to say about the East.

To-day I would like to return to the Harden affair. In the time before the trial on 23 November, Harden intends to give a series of speeches before public gatherings in order to inform the general public about his case and the reasons for his actions. Ever since the surprise of having the date set for the trial, and especially since Lehmann's interview,[2] Harden believes that the law is not acting independently, that he cannot count on objectivity, and that he now has to defend himself by using every means. He says that the courts, and particularly the public prosecution, have only one legally correct standpoint to take, and that is to declare that the Moltke trial cannot be resumed so long as the position of the chief witness, Eulenburg, has not been made clear by the conclusion of *his* trial. 'That', says Harden, 'is the only correct thing to do. The procedure Lehmann is now trying to adopt is a warping of justice against which I shall fight with the utmost energy and ruthlessness—I can do no other. I have not heard that the Chancellor has taken steps with the Justice Department, and suspect that if such steps had been taken, the judges would not have proceeded so forcefully and arbitrarily. But now —six weeks before the trial—it is high time for me to inform the public about the actual state of affairs and the truth about what is happening. I do so unwillingly, but Lehmann's actions—in his interview he simply told barefaced lies—have convinced me that I am to be led to the slaughter.' In the foregoing I am telling you substantially, somewhat toned down, what Harden told me this morning when I visited him to see how the affair had been shaping up recently.[3]

[1] Of 8 and 10 October. See above.

[2] In the *Berliner Neuesten Nachrichten*. See above, Holstein's letter to Bülow of 10 October 1908.

[3] Harden had expressed similar ideas in a letter to Holstein of 10 October. 'It is a splendid coincidence that simultaneously on the international scene the entire stupid mendacity of our policy is breaking to pieces. I hope to live to see the day when Bülow has to flee by night. My situation is exactly as it was in December 1907; but I am determined this time to rage with Scythian ruthlessness against the coalition of that black gang of criminals.'

You and I have long ago agreed that the conduct of the various departments in this affair, especially the Justice Department, can only do great damage to the concept of the state and loyalty to the monarchy. How the public has recently regarded these things can be seen from the main picture in the latest *Kladderadatsch*;[1] I wonder if His Majesty has seen it?

For an old royalist it is a very sad thought that no one is drawing the Kaiser's attention to the danger that threatens him and his House. I have asked Harden by appealing to his patriotism to wait at least until the end of this week before giving his first lecture.[2]

Therefore whatever is yet to be done *must be done this week*. The Minister of Justice has only to order the public prosecutor—or rather, to permit him—to explain that in examining the documents again it is evident that the resumption of the Moltke trial without the participation of the main witness, Eulenburg,—that is, before the conclusion of the Eulenburg trial—is not possible. If the Minister of Justice refuses to do that, then he must have compelling reasons, or rather orders. Then there would be nothing left to do but to inform the Kaiser about what is at stake for his House.

I could have told you the foregoing tomorrow orally if I had urgently asked to see you. But I have no hesitation whatever in setting down in writing that I have done what I could to prevent serious trouble. How justified my warning was would only become obvious if the crash we both wish to avoid should, contrary to all our hopes, takes place.

I very much doubt that Harden could be influenced by anything but the cancellation of the date for the trial. He is disdainful of every kind of assurance.

With best wishes
Most sincerely your
Holstein[3]

## 1142.   Holstein to Bernhard von Bülow
Draft

Berlin, 13 October 1908. Sent at half past eight [a.m.]

Dear Bülow,

To-day there is the reception of ambassadors. I would like to suggest that, through Schoen, you deliver the following brief, calm statement:

'Whether we intend to participate in a Congress? We have no objections against doing so, provided that Austria-Hungary participates.

[1] The picture, entitled 'The End of Faustphili', shows Eulenburg in an armchair being carried to heaven by angels, while Isenbiel and the devil Harden gaze up in anger. The caption is a play on Goethe's *Faust*, part II, act V.

[2] At this point in his draft Holstein crossed out the words: 'which I suspect one [might regard] as the final break'.

[3] On 12 October Harden thanked Holstein for his latest information. 'That I am finally forced to believe that the Chancellor wants this kind of miscarriage of justice is not surprising. For one and a half years the opposite has always happened of what I was informed about his intention to see justice done.'

To take part in a partial Congress which would a priori be anti-Austrian would not be to Germany's interest.'[1]

We would make this statement as something perfectly natural and without immediately demanding a service in return from Austria—as some newspapers desire. In the first place, Austria is fighting *our* fight against the *concert européen* (the encirclement group), and secondly, in case Austria wants to pursue an active policy she will *always* need German support so badly that we can present our conditions later. It is above all important now not to frighten Austria away from the active policy she has just initiated (for Austria in her present two sections can never become *too* powerful for our purposes); and then it is important to show Austria that, despite the attitude of His Majesty,[2] she *can* count on us. Later she will also *have* to reckon *with* us.

I have heard Bismarck declare time and again that it was a serious mistake that Prussia insisted on participating at the Congress of Paris in 1856. By staying away she would have made her significance much more felt. If to-day Germany and Austria stay away, the whole Congress collapses. *Then* France (because of her holders of Turkish securities) and Russia (because of internal weakness) will bestir themselves to prevent a war in the Balkans; but not until they see that there will be no Congress. Meanwhile they participate in the bluff because they are counting on the buffer of Europe. At any rate, both would endeavour to localize a Balkan war. This would in any case be preferable for Germany and Austria than a Congress where conditions would be dictated to us, the defeated group.

Until this evening

Most sincerely your
Holstein.

Probably Isvolsky will express the hope that Germany will support Russia's Eastern policy, especially on the Dardanelles question.[3]

The reply to this would be :

'Germany will have to consider this question in connection with her general interests (or within the framework of all our interests). Russia has identified herself during the past few years with a group whose object it is to checkmate German policy. This was particularly obvious at Algeciras. It would be senseless for us to support this particular group by bringing pressure to bear on Turkey and to force these two friendly empires, or one of them, to make a decision which was regarded as contrary to their interests or their dignity.

[1] See Bülow's account of his talk with the Austrian Ambassador on 13 October (*Grosse Politik*, vol. XXVIi, no. 9033, pp. 160–2), and Schoen's presentation of the case to the Ambassadors in Berlin (vol. XXVIi, no. 9046, p. 177).

[2] See above, p. 578, note 3.

[3] On 16 September 1908 Isvolsky and Aehrenthal had come to an informal agreement at Buchlau whereby Russia was not to oppose Austria's annexation of Bosnia and Herzegovina, and Austria was not to oppose the opening of the Straits to Russian warships. When Austria occupied Bosnia and Herzegovina, Isvolsky demanded the convocation of a conference to consider the Austrian action, and sought support for his own Straits programme. He came to Berlin for this purpose 24–26 October. (See *Grosse Politik*, vol. XXVIi, nos. 8934–5, pp. 35–43; *Österreich-Ungarns Aussenpolitik*, vol. I, p. 80 *et seq.*).

'If, as a result of the incredible outside agitation, there should be a war in the Balkans, I think that it would probably be localized because I cannot see that any of the continental Powers would have any interest *de faire le jeu de la politique anglaise*. A war would be particularly unwelcome to Germany, which wants no territorial gains. But it might perhaps be better to risk a war at the side of Austria and perhaps other allies than to wait until the existing open or latent conflicts of interest should be resolved in a succession of wars, as in 1805, 1806, 1809 and 1812. The Prussian policy that conducted us to Jena will not be repeated as long as I am Chancellor.'

### 1143.   Memorandum by Holstein

18 October 1908

In my conversation with Mr Valentine Chirol,[1] I said absolutely everything I had to say about the fleet question. Chirol listened with interest, without however showing the animation he sometimes exhibits. He for his part told me how the Kaiser in Norway had made that much-discussed statement on board an American yacht: 'Germany and America had the same task of working together against England.' An English Secretary of Legation who was on board immediately copied down the statement and sent it to the Foreign Office.

I said that to be sure the family quarrel between uncle and nephew has strained the relations between the two Powers.

Chirol emphasized that a possible later improvement in Anglo-German relations would under no circumstances mean a cooling-off of relations between England and France. I replied that Germany would probably attach no great importance to that—the cooling-off. France in herself was no longer so important, she was in a state of decline.

He did not like to hear this. He believed that though the view of a decline of France was held by many, he did not share it.

He then brought up the Eastern Question and made it clear that this was the only thing he was really interested in at the moment. Animatedly, and sometimes passionately, he expressed the following three ideas:

(1) England was pursuing a pro-Turkish policy not on Turkey's account, but because of our own Mohammedans. For that reason we were trying to bolster Young Turkey.

(2) These efforts were being seriously endangered by the action of Austria. Austria had behaved shockingly badly; she should have asked permission beforehand. This was the policy of the heir to the throne[2] who might be suspected of aggressive plans.

(3) It is up to Germany to make it clear to the Cabinet at Vienna that the interests of all have to be considered, just as Germany did thirty years ago with proud Russia.

---

[1] According to internal evidence (see p. 585, note 1) this talk took place on 16 October. Chirol had another talk with Holstein on the morning of 19 October. (*British Documents*, vol. VI, no. 101, pp. 158–61.)

[2] Archduke Franz Ferdinand.

I replied that the agenda of the Congress had already been published the day before.[1] It had the appearance of a bill of indictment against Austria. The Austrian Press was united in rejecting it. It could hardly be assumed that Germany would participate in the indictment of Austria.

In my opinion Turkey would do better if, perhaps with English mediation, she reached a direct understanding with Bulgaria; the same thing was true about an understanding with Austria.

Turkey would suffer further losses at a Congress. I pointed out that if Italy agreed to exclusive passage [through the Straits] for the *stati rivoreschi*, i.e. for Russia, that she will surely have secured some advantage for herself beforehand. Chirol said that to be sure Russia and Italy had co-operated a good deal recently.

The outstanding point in Chirol's remarks was his statement that the resumption of the pro-Turkish attitude had been rendered necessary by England's colonial policy, so that this policy will not soon again be abandoned. But then it is not easy to see how England, if she wants to strengthen and bolster Young Turkey, can pull in the same harness with Russia, which wants to bring about Turkey's quick demise.

First the Anglophile Isvolsky must be brought down. If he is succeeded by the Panslav Charikov—as many believe he will be—the latter will probably be on bad terms with Austria (which would be no misfortune for us), but he would be on at least equally bad terms with England, the foster-mother of the Turks. Then gradually the encirclement-group will break up into its component parts.

In dealing with Turkey we should restrict ourselves to the assurance that we will bring no pressure to bear on the Straits question. And we should stick to that. Even if Austria should demand that we advise the Turks to give in on the Straits question, we should say that we will not encourage the Turks to resist, but that we could not assume *responsibility* for giving further advice.

To give the Turks *positive* assurances, even of the most innocent kind, would be to relieve the English of their responsibilities as protectors. If the Turks ask us for anything, we will refer them to England and only say that we will never support any move *against* them. If we follow this policy consistently and leave England and Russia alone together in the Near East as much as possible, only a miracle could prevent their running afoul of one another sooner or later.

H.


1144.   Bernhard von Bülow to Holstein

Tuesday evening [20 October 1908]

Absolutely Confidential!

Dear Holstein,

At the present time I am so frightfully run down between the Eastern

[1] By the Havas news agency on 15 October. (See *Grosse Politik*, vol. XXVIi, no. 9044, pp. 174–5.)

Question, Reich financial reform, Walhalla,[1] Landtag, and wedding celebrations[2] that I can only write you hurriedly and briefly. But I must thank you for your most significant letters about the present situation which I received here upon my return from Regensburg. What you say is (as usual) thought through and excellent. I have drawn upon this wealth of material for telegrams to various quarters. In particular I stressed to Marschall that the Turks need not be shy in their demands for English support and English protection now that England needs the Porte and Islam.[3] I have also drafted a programme for the talks with Isvolsky that will make it possible for me to conduct the conversation in a manner that will accord with our interests and the general situation.[4]

In the trial business, Isenbiel told Loebell yesterday that the trial would not be held on the 23rd of next month. He will in any case give the appropriate orders if these are at all necessary. I told Dr W. Rathenau[5] about this to-day. [...]

With very best wishes

Most sincerely your<br>Bülow

### 1145. Holstein to Bernhard von Bülow
Copy

Berlin, 21 October 1908

Dear Bülow,

Letter received with thanks.[6] France is conducting, without consideration for Russia or England, her own French policy, the policy of the holders of Turkish securities. As soon as the French Government saw that a Congress would compensate the Balkan states at the expense of Turkey, they published the agenda of the Congress to frighten away the Turks. Now Constans[7] is negotiating between the Turks and the Bulgars and the French Press says that a Congress (or rather a Conference) would serve no purpose. France is simply aware that she is indispensable. The French know that England (on account of Germany) and Russia (on account of new loans) need France badly, and so the French make no further effort to be accommodating.

It would be a great success for Isvolsky if he could save the Congress, which has been rendered doubtful by the *ami et allié*, with the help of Germany. He will assure you that in that case *vous supplanterez la France perfide dans le grand coeur russe*. Whoever believes it gets a china doll.

---

[1] On 19 October Bülow took part in a ceremony to unveil a bust of Bismarck in the Walhalla at Regensburg.

[2] Prince August Wilhelm of Prussia, the fourth son of the Kaiser, was to be married on 22 October to Princess Alexandra of Schleswig-Holstein.

[3] In a telegram to Marschall of 20 October. (*Grosse Politik*, vol. XXVIi, no. 9059, p. 200.)

[4] See above, p. 583, note 3.

[5] Walther Rathenau. Successor to his father Emil Rathenau as head of the Allgemeine Elektrizitäts Gesellschaft (AEG); Reich Minister of Reconstruction, May–October 1921; Foreign Minister, 1922; assassinated 24 June 1922.

[6] Bülow's letter of 20 October. See above.

[7] Jean Ernest Constans. French Ambassador in Constantinople, 1899–1909.

Your refusal is made more easy by the French action. 'At the advice of France, the Turks have begun to negotiate directly with Bulgaria and Austria. What would be the use of a Conference? To enlarge Serbia and Montenegro, whether at the expense of Austria or Turkey? Germany has no interest in either of those small Balkan states, whereas we are allied with Austria and stand on the best of terms with Turkey.

'The sanctity of the Treaty of Berlin? *Mais c'est la Russie qui a commencé par biffer l'article relatif à Batoum.*[1] Russia knows that we will not oppose her Straits policy. But that with the present grouping of the Powers we should be expected to support that policy, that we should use our pressure to compel our friends and allies to give in—that is asking too much. I could not be answerable to the Kaiser and people for such a policy. And since a Congress would presumably expect us to exercise such pressure, I am opposed to a Congress and Conference. I express my opinion frankly, but believe that France, which as your ally should feel some consideration for your wishes, has an even stronger desire than Germany to prevent Turkey from giving up any part of her full sovereignty either in the Sanjak or in the Straits. The French Government has not informed me of any secret projects, therefore I can tell you candidly that six or seven years ago, when the Triple Alliance was renewed, Prinetti, who makes no move without the advice of Barrère, wanted to include an article intended to keep Russia out of Constantinople.[2] I cannot believe that France's Eastern policy should have changed in these few years, all the less so since I see that to-day France is trying to obviate the need for a Congress. Because a Congress, just like the Berlin Congress thirty years ago, would naturally exercise its generosity at the expense of Turkey, and of Turkey only. France, as the ally of Russia, cannot express so frankly as Germany the reasons why she opposes a Congress.'

Thus, it seems to be, you should speak with Isvolsky, quite frankly, calmly, amicably, and fearlessly. Your case is so strong that you should be able to shake him off easily, despite his persistence—for you are his last hope, now that he has been dismissed with polite phrases in London and Paris.

And do not forget about Aehrenthal. France, in mediating with the Turks for recognition of the *fait accompli*, draws a big step closer to Austria. They will see eye to eye on the question of *maintaining the present situation in the Balkans*, and this may easily develop into a permanent understanding. Not only Kramarsch[3] and Klofač,[4] but other groups in Austria would much prefer to go along with France than with Germany. *Germany can, if she wants to, offer the Austro-Hungarian monarchy more than can France, but when the opportunity occurs—i.e. now—*

[1] See above, p. 579, note 5.

[2] See the negotiations for the renewal of the Triple Alliance in 1902. (*Grosse Politik*, vol. XVIIIii, chapter CXXII.)

[3] Dr Karl Kramarsch. Leader of the Czech party in the Austrian Chamber of Deputies.

[4] Václav Klofač. Editor of the journal *České Slovo*; member of the Austrian Chamber of Deputies.

*we must show that we really want to.* For the sake of our position among the peoples of Austria-Hungary, it is important that we should emphasize our willingness to support them more than we have done hitherto *in the Press.* The anti-German Press in Austria is still crawling with Marschall's remarks.[1] Could you not take the section of the Speech from the Throne in which mention is made of 'our ally'[2]—I was very pleased about this unusual inclusion in a speech to the Landtag—, and make some pro-Austria comments about it and have those comments printed in the Press review of the *Norddeutsche Allgemeine Zeitung*? In my opinion that would be a minimum. An *entrefilet* in the *Norddeutsche* would be better, but I do not consider that essential. I come back to this point constantly because its importance becomes clearer to me daily.

The communication for the Turks about which you write seems to me very skilful.[3] Let us hope that Marschall delivers it. Since he wants a Congress, or a Conference, he may not wish to add to Turkey's distrust of England. Do have Schoen make the same communication to the Turkish Ambassador[4] here.[5] At the same time Schoen could ask the Ambassador 'whether there was any reason to suspect that England, basing her claims on the Willcocks[6] concession, should use the opportunity of a Congress to propose the inclusion of Mesopotamia in the English sphere of interest.[7] We had heard this but could not really believe it.'

Someone told me this to-day who just returned from Constantinople. The Young Turks already suspected this. It can do no harm to increase this suspicion. I would not say a word about it to Isvolsky. It is not impossible that Russia would be glad to agree to this, and perhaps has agreed to it, as payment to England for the Straits.

*Summa summarum*, I remain of the opinion that if there is no Congress or Conference, if England and Russia are always obliged to seek a direct understanding, that without the buffer of Europe their good relations will be of uncertain duration.

For Germany this result would mean substantially more than a sour herring.[8] [...]

Wishing you the best of luck for the coming days,

Most sincerely your
Holstein.

[1] See Holstein's comments about these in his letter to Bülow of 11 October 1908.

[2] In the speech from the throne to open the Prussian Landtag on 20 October 1908 the Kaiser stated: 'The German Reich, in loyal collaboration with its allies, will work for a peaceful and just solution of the present difficulties.'

[3] See above, p. 586, note 3.

[4] Osman Nisami Pasha. Turkish Ambassador in Berlin, 16 October 1908–13.

[5] Whether such a communication on the part of Schoen was made to the Turkish Ambassador could not be determined from the Foreign Ministry files.

[6] Sir William Willcocks. Adviser to the Turkish Department of Public Works.

[7] Willcocks had been engaged by the Young Turk Government and sent to make extensive surveys in Mesopotamia with a view to carrying out large irrigation schemes in that area. (*British Documents*, vol. V, p. 256.)

[8] A reference to the quarrels between Germany, England and Russia over fishing rights.

## 1146.  Maximilian Harden to Holstein

Grunewald, 24 October 1908

Your Excellency,

[...] Rathenau told me a few things about a talk with the Chancellor. I[senbiel] has promised to do his best.[1] Even the Wilhelmstrasse doesn't seem to think it is at all certain; only probable. Nothing is known for certain in Moabit, either. It is really bad. Not quite four weeks yet.[2] Who knows when we may be told that the 'independent judges can't be influenced' etc.? Then we can do nothing more and the confederates can laugh. The trustworthy Sello,[3] who has talked with Lehmann, has spread the word that the trial will definitely be held; there was not the slightest reason to reject Lehmann; few witnesses; E[ulenburg] need at most testify out of court (in other words, on his little deathbed) about the one question: whether he knew anything about Tütü's[4] homosexuality; every other question should be rejected, etc.

Instinct, without any rational support, tells me that Hammann is about to go. I have thought about it a great deal and wish, little as I would like it personally, that Eugen Zimmermann would be asked to be his successor,[5] and that he would accept (despite the fact that his income now is of course far greater). It would be a piece of luck for the Chancellor, whom he is clever enough to like so much. The thing that persuades me is the conviction that no one else would be anywhere near as suitable for this job as this strangely talented man. Then something could really be accomplished with this apparatus. Which is so necessary precisely at this time. Also of great importance would be that Your Excellency could again put your invaluable experience to work on this important instrument. What could not be done in that field with a little intelligent thinking! But who knows whether H[ammann] won't stay on? And the journalists are spreading the rumour (inconceivable to me, *quand même*) that the Frankfurt Stein[6] was the coming man.

With warmest good wishes for Your Excellency's health (my cold refuses to give way and is seeping with Isvolskyish tenacity through the entire carcass) and in expectation of Sunday,

Very devoted

H.

## 1147.  Holstein to Bernhard von Bülow

Copy

Berlin, 28 October 1908, 5:00 a.m.

Dear Bülow,

Frau von Lebbin brought me your friendly message, and I thank you

[1] Presumably to prevent the renewal of the Moltke-Harden trial. In a letter to Harden of 24 October Holstein wrote that in his opinion the crux of the matter seemed to be whether Isenbiel would really do 'his best' and would actually be allowed a decisive voice in the affair. Harden should discuss this point with an expert, and then write a letter to his friend Rathenau which the latter could pass on without need for commentary. (Rogge, *Holstein und Harden*, pp. 355–6.)

[2] Until the date set for the trial.     [3] The reference to Moltke's attorney is of course ironic.

[4] Count Kuno von Moltke.     [5] As head of the Foreign Ministry's Press Bureau.

[6] August Stein of the *Frankfurter Zeitung*.

very much. But before I see you I would like to propose two things.

(1) The Press Bureau at Vienna is coolly spreading the lie that England's antagonism to Austria was solely the result of Kronberg[1] and was only directed against Austria because she was the ally of Germany. The real conflict was not an Anglo-Austrian over Bosnia, but an Anglo-German over who was to have the dominant influence in Constantinople.

Austria, as I saw from the beginning, is anxious to push us to the front and to step back herself. But under no circumstances a Press war with Vienna! Forbid this specifically before it is too late. *Make your reply along different lines*, namely: send every mediation proposal that is communicated to us, whether it comes from Russia, England, France, or from all three—such proposals are being mooted in the Press—*directly* to Vienna, with the explanation: 'Germany wished to avoid every appearance of exercising pressure on her ally. This appearance might be created even by acting as go-between.' Actually 'mediation' after all means that one advises partial backing-down. It is precisely this that we do *not* want. We will hold to the principle (without saying so) that for Germany's interest it is better if *all* the interests involved have to come to direct understandings with one another without a buffer of any kind, whether this be called Europe or Germany. We will declare only, in case they want to push us into the foreground as intermediary (like His Majesty with General de Lacroix[2]), that we will put no obstacles in anybody's way.

(2) 'The alleged proposal of England to offer the Turkish Government several hundred million francs to support the development of the Turkish state, and in addition to place an English squadron at Turkey's disposal as security against reactionary coups, would be something to fill every friend of Turkey with satisfaction if the proposal did not come from England. For, whether rightly or wrongly, England has for twenty years been suspected among European diplomats of having pushed every conflict in the Balkans to a crisis. This concern would not exist if France had participated in the English proposal. France is wealthy, a seapower, and a friend of England, so why should not the two have acted together? Europe would then be assured that they were trying to find a peaceful solution, because France with her three to four billions in Turkish securities has a definite interest in seeing to it that Turkey is not once again put in the position—as she was thirty-three years ago—of having to opt between preparation for war and payment of interest.'

I recommend the foregoing—not as a confidential communication to Cambon, for France wants no confidences with us—but as a subject of conversation for you and Schoen with *all* diplomats, great and small, English, French, Turkish, etc. I would very much like to suggest even to bring up these ideas in the Press, except that the Press always goes its own way anyway. We thereby show that peace is more important to us than our influence in Constantinople, which makes us suspect on every hand—by England as well as by Austria.

[1] See above, p. 549, note 1.    [2] See above, p. 343, note 3, and no. 904.

The idea of an Anglo-French partnership for building up Turkey will hardly be realized, for Clemenceau will not want to propose anything that will offend the English. And Russia would see in this co-operation a resumption of the policy of the Crimean War. But no one can blame you if, in the interests of peace, you innocently bring up this idea with diplomats and in the Press.

With best wishes

Holstein.

### 1148.   Maximilian Harden to Holstein

29 October 1908

Your Excellency,

The trial has been suspended.[1] For what reason I do not know. It is not to be given out. Whether for a short or longer period I do not yet know. Just heard about it by telephone from I[senbiel].

I refrained from making any proposal, because I[senbiel] had already made one and a decision had to be made on his proposal first.

I am completely overwhelmed by the unprecedented monstrosity of the *Daily Telegraph* interview.[2] *Finis.* Tuesday evening I received the first hint, and for that reason have written nothing and have been feverish ever since.[3]

With many thanks for the friendly letter, and with all good wishes for your health,

I am Your Excellency's very devoted

H.

### 1149.   Maximilian Harden to Holstein

30 October 1908

Your Excellency,

My sincere thanks.[4] But there is as yet no decision *in principle*[5] and, if the pederasts again begin to work in their usual haunts, we may in three weeks be back where we started. [...]

The big event:[6] on that I can only gag. I am convinced that something must be DONE. Talking does no good here. The shame cannot be wiped out in any other way. I have decided. If everyone does his little bit, then we may be saved. I do not value my own life at a farthing.

But Bülow stands (stood?) before the question as to whether, as a man, he can go on living with himself.

---

[1] The Moltke-Harden trial.

[2] On 28 October the *Daily Telegraph* published an interview with Kaiser Wilhelm II on Anglo-German relations. (See *Grosse Politik*, vol. XXIV, chapter CLXXVIII; *Memoirs*, pp. 171–4 and Appendix III, pp. 203–7, where the interview has been reprinted.) Holstein's letters to Bülow on the *Daily Telegraph* affair have been published by Rogge, *Holstein und Harden*, pp. 359–65.

[3] Holstein replied on the following day that what had made Harden so angry was indeed an exceptional performance, and he thought it would be a good thing if this were stated everywhere. For the chief actor—the Kaiser—it was a severe lesson, but would it do any good? (Rogge, *Holstein und Harden*, pp. 365–6.)

[4] Presumably for Holstein's letter of the same day. (See above, note 3.)

[5] On the Moltke-Harden case.          [6] The *Daily Telegraph* interview.

I will demand, *crûment*, immediate abdication.  Calmly and constantly.
My best wishes accompany Your Excellency

Very sincerely

H.

### 1150.  Maximilian Harden to Holstein

11 November 1908

Your Excellency,

[...] Bülow's miserable end ( ?) I deplore.  That he could make this speech,[1] in this way, every sentence against his better judgment, is of course perhaps a piece of heroism.  But doesn't he know *yet* where one gets with this partner in arms ?[2]  And there is after all such a thing as a sense of honour.  After the speech he was saying that all the party leaders had congratulated him.  *Poverino!*  There was just one opinion about the effect.  To-day he is said to have been terribly abused, and he said nothing.  Did he already hand in his resignation to-day ?  To die like that, to fall so falsely!  Yesterday I thought at first he wanted to become the Tutor-Chancellor.  Then everything would have been understandable.  Maybe.

Incidentally, I wrote nothing about him *personally*; indulgently, and only *objectively* severe.  It wasn't easy for me.  But he needs this to deal with His Majesty.  [...]

In a very painful mood
I am Your Excellency's devoted
Harden.

### 1151.  Maximilian Harden to Holstein

Grunewald, 15 November 1908

Your Excellency,

[...] How I have suffered and allowed myself to be pelted with mud to avoid a gigantic scandal!  I will not do so a second time.  Because now I am also quite sure that it is *pro patria*.

Incidentally: if Isenbiel (who has already been by-passed for Chief Public Prosecutor) is not made General Public Prosecutor, he will have to resign.  Then, under the No. 1 Public Prosecutor from Constantinople,[3] the united fairies can again take courage.  But they do not know what I know, and that is that I am firmly determined this time to protect no one.

I mention the 'affair' because it seems to me the fundamental cause of the present crisis.  Since then, complete loss of balance at the top.  One thing after another.  With that, mad anger of the homos against the Chancellor.  He knows, of that I am convinced, that his evaluation in history depends on his conduct during the present days.  But is perhaps making the mistake of thinking that the possibilities of intimidation by the Liebenberg party are the greater as long as my trump is held back.  I

---

[1] Bülow's speech of 10 November in the Reichstag on the *Daily Telegraph* incident.
[2] The Kaiser.  [3] Baron Marschall von Bieberstein.

no longer have any confidence in promises and reservations; this monarch will *never* change, and is simply in the hands of blackmailers. At best he can only rule as Hammann now does over the Press Bureau: agree to everything, because everybody has something on him. In England there are still a vast number of letters. In Highcliffe[1] *everything* was discussed, before journalists, and *everything* has been written down. A polite gentleman like Asquith would not have spoken as he spoke yesterday[2] unless they had already *decided* to draw the teeth of this Kaiser as they did Bonaparte's, only without bloodshed. To clear ourselves of shame and ridicule, we will *have* to go to war, soon, or face the sad necessity of making a change of imperial personnel on our own account, even if the strongest personal pressure had to be brought to bear. (Or I could say: even if we had to do things in 'Earnest'.[3]) Even Schulz, the Kaiser's personal aide, who has gone through some bad times, says that things cannot go on this way. And can a conscientious person expose Germany to further crises? I am not certain that if some morning the news arrived that our fleet had been sunk, Podewils[4] would not go to the Austrian Ambassador and discuss whether we should mobilize or. . . . History knows no definitives. And Wittelsbach[5] was never more Austrian than to-day.

There is still time. I am fundamentally opposed to false cures, promises, declarations: which leave everything the same while we slip into the abyss. Anybody would be a possibility, even Friedrich August,[6] even a child, after what has happened. Only not the one we have. 'He wasn't cut out for it,' Bismarck said to me; 'The Imperial programme is and will always be: everything must be set topsy-turvy.'

And can he, after everything that has now been said abroad and at home, think—seriously think—that he can again play the Kaiser and the highest authority?

This is the end; and the only question is whether we will have the courage to perform the operation, or whether we prefer the slow decomposition of the body of the Reich.

In sorrow and anger,

Your Excellency's very devoted

H.

## 1152.   Wilhelm Stemrich to Holstein

Siena, 15 November 1908

Your Excellency!

My sincere thanks for the friendly letter of the 9th of this month which was addressed to Stresa and with the slow forwarding of the Italian mails

---

[1] The estate of Colonel Stuart-Wortley, the British officer to whom the Kaiser expressed the opinions published in the *Daily Telegraph*. (See above, p. 591, note 2.)

[2] On the necessity for England to maintain naval superiority over the combined fleets of her two closest rivals. (The Two-Power standard.)

[3] A pun on the name of Jakob Ernst.

[4] Klemens, Count von Podewils. Minister-President and Foreign Minister of Bavaria, 1903–12.

[5] The Bavarian royal house.          [6] The King of Saxony.

did not reach me until the evening of the day before yesterday. I really do not know how I can thank you for the friendly interest you have shown in me, and am deeply moved. But does Your Excellency really think that I can stay on now that Klehmet—according to the newspapers—has been dismissed?[1] I am still of the opinion that both of us are innocent.[2] It has become my firm conviction that the Chancellor wanted to reserve his decision—if he had not already made it—about the suitability of publication and, in order to be able to have a competent judgment of the matter, had ordered copies of the two English documents with our factual corrections to be submitted to him. If this view was mistaken and he had also expected us to express ourselves about the suitability of publication—why then did not Herr von Müller[3] make a further enquiry? If one is not asked, then there can surely be no question of *tacens consentire videtur*.

But that is not how it turned out. Klehmet has been sacrificed. In my opinion I too must now believe this. How can I face Klehmet or the other members of the Foreign Ministry? How can I keep their confidence unless I acknowledge that I am just as guilty as Klehmet? And what will our own and foreign diplomats say? I am afraid they will point accusing fingers at me, and classify me as one who will stay on in office at the cost of a subordinate. These are my feelings, for which Your Excellency will surely have a certain sympathy. Tomorrow we are leaving here for Florence (Hotel de la Paix) and at the end of next week will return to Berlin *uno tenore*. I would be very grateful if I could then come to see you (even before the end of my leave of absence on the 25th). Perhaps I have a wrong conception of the case after all; I will make immediate enquiries about a possible visit.

    With deepest respect

Your Excellency's most obedient<br>Stemrich.

### 1153. Bernhard von Bülow to Holstein

Monday [16 November 1908]

Dear Holstein,

Only a word in a great hurry. You are quite right that everything must be avoided that has the appearance of pressure on His Majesty.[4] Not only because of the mood of His Maj. but also in view of the mood of the country. From hundreds of letters I can see that the mood of the country is different from that of the intellectuals in Berlin. The country

[1] Klehmet was the Foreign Ministry official to whom the *Daily Telegraph* interview had been submitted for an official check before the article was published. Klehmet was not dismissed, but was appointed Consul-General in Athens in the following year.

[2] Stemrich had been acting State Secretary when the *Daily Telegraph* article was submitted to the Foreign Ministry, and Klehmet's report on the article had been sent to Bülow under Stemrich's name. (*Grosse Politik*, vol. XXIV, no. 8251, pp. 169–74.)

[3] Felix von Müller. Minister to The Hague, 1908–15; temporarily serving as Foreign Ministry aide to the Chancellor at Norderney.

[4] The Kaiser had granted Bülow audience for the morning of 17 November to discuss the problems arising from the *Daily Telegraph* interview.

wants the Kaiser to change; but it does not want any harm to come to him. Above all, the country wants to have peace and quiet soon. The Germans lack the revolutionary streak of the Latins; they are not dramatically inclined.

Otherwise everything is still quite uncertain. The article in the *Konservative Korrespondenz* can be traced back to the fact that news had leaked through to the Conservatives that at Donaueschingen[1] it had definitely been decided to change over to a new course (*rectius die restitutio in integrum ante '90*). In the thought that personal rule by the monarch might be exercised through a 'Bismarckian' programme and personalities with a Bismarckian tinge, the Conservatives did not wish to miss the boat.

Now we for our part must above all avoid pushing matters too hard; this you have sensed with your usual perspicacity. Excessive pressure in the Press would produce the opposite of the desired effect.

Keep your fingers crossed for me tomorrow.

Faithfully your<br>Bülow

## 1154. Holstein to Bernhard von Bülow
### Draft

16 November 1908

Dear Bülow,

The curious change in the tone of your letter to-day[2] as compared with Saturday allows me to suspect that you received a friendly token from the Kaiser, directly or indirectly.

I for my part still regard the programme we agreed on after our conversation on Saturday as the minimum of what the country expects in view of the times and necessities of the moment. That the 'Berlin intellectuals' demand a great deal more you know yourself.

As a practical method of pushing through this programme, I would like to submit for your consideration the ideas developed in the letter I sent to-day by pneumatic tube.[3]

If you cut down the programme, the verdict about you will be: 'He was more concerned about the good opinion of the Kaiser than about the good of the country'—and you will have to suffer the consequences in Parliament within a few months.

I set no store by the 'hundreds of letters'. I too have talked to people and read letters, and only a few hours ago talked with an elderly noble *Landrat*, and believe that I too have some knowledge of the thinking and feeling of the country.

From your letter to-day I fear that for the sake of the Kaiser you want

---

[1] The Kaiser had spent 7–16 November in Donaueschingen on a visit to the Prince of Fürstenberg.

[2] See above.

[3] In his letter to Bülow, Holstein said that nothing could be accomplished with the Kaiser by an appeal to reason, but everything could be accomplished by an appeal to fear. (Printed in Rogge, *Holstein und Harden*, pp. 386–7.)

to make a false peace between the Kaiser and the people, nay, between the Kaiser and the Reich, and that within a few months you will be miserably ruined. For who will there then be to defend you?

I feel it is my duty to be so frank at this time.

As always, your sincerely devoted
Holstein

## 1155. Holstein to Bernhard von Bülow
### Draft

17 November 1908

Dear Bülow,

I am sending this letter through Frau Röber[1] by car, so that it arrives in time.[2]

Prittwitz[3] is of course the candidate of the Eulenburgs. Yesterday I heard from someone who was not involved that Beseler had said that the Moltke-Harden trial *must* be resumed. All this hangs together, this affair and the big affair.

Be firm, Bülow, do not let them pull the wool over your eyes. The Kaiser will think twice before he lets you go, at this time. But if the worst should happen, if he will not listen to reason, it would be better for you to go now, as a great man, than in a few months as a despised one. That you should sacrifice your person *and* your duty is something the Kaiser cannot expect.

Your old friend
Holstein

## 1156. Bernhard von Bülow to Holstein

[17 November 1908]

ABSOLUTELY SECRET!

Mood more irritated, opposition more stubborn, conversation more difficult than I had assumed from the information of Jenisch and Valentini[4] who had seen me beforehand.

I held firmly to all the demands listed in my notebook, without toning anything down. I left no doubt that I would otherwise resign at once.

The communiqué for the *Reichsanzeiger* (drafted by me[5]) I forced through in opposition to the idea of a manifesto or a Cabinet Order (which was again proposed!).

The rest depends on the attitude of the Parties—especially the Conservatives—in the Reichstag and the Landtag. To-day I am calling together the Ministers and the Bundesrat. Tomorrow I will personally talk with politicians and influential journalists. If I am supported by the Parliaments, there is the possibility that from now on there will be a different kind of rule, and a good many things can get better. If I do not

---

[1] Holstein's housekeeper.

[2] Before Bülow's audience with the Kaiser. (See above, p. 594, note 4.)

[3] Karl von Prittwitz und Gaffron. Chief Public Prosecutor in Naumburg.

[4] Rudolf Valentini. Head of the Secret Civil Cabinet, 1908–18.

[5] On the conversation between the Kaiser and Bülow. The draft of the communiqué is printed in *Grosse Politik*, vol. XXIV, no. 8266, pp. 191–2.

get support, then the many intriguers and office-seekers who are *novarum rerum cupidi* will soon have the pleasure of a change of Chancellors; for a time everyone will be happy and hopeful, and then everything will be the same again. Whatever happens,

Always your faithfully devoted<br>Bülow

### 1157.    Holstein to Bernhard von Bülow[1]

Berlin, 17 November 1908

Dear Bülow,

It seems to me that the hardest part is over! That the Parties—those, that is, you need to carry on your Government—should demand more than they have already achieved is in my opinion unlikely, because their expectations were modest from the beginning, and the Conservatives in particular want to vex His Majesty as little as possible.

Manifesto, Cabinet Order are acts of absolutism, and as such may be more welcome to extremists of the Right. But even for the Conservatives the memory of 'To my dear Berliners'[2] should be reason enough to reject such methods. Furthermore, this would mean that the person of the Kaiser would once again step into the foreground, something that must after all be avoided on principle.

I am naturally anxious to see how you worded it.[3] But I already congratulate you on the victory. I think you will have the people you need in a block on you side. Independents and Centre will be divided. The Bundesrat and the powers behind it will surely be on your side. For these will hardly wish to injure the monarchial principle.

I think it would be useful if you could to-day still give a few hints to Kiderlen. He is spending the evening with Buch,[4] Kröcher,[5] etc.

My happy congratulations

With best wishes<br>Holstein.

Incidentally, all power to Renvers for your having survived these gymnastics so well.

### 1158.    Holstein to Bernhard von Bülow
### Copy

26 November 1908

Dear Bülow,

[...] The Eastern problem is growing more acute. England realizes

---

[1] From the Bülow Papers. Only a typewritten copy of this document was available to the editors. (Printed in Rogge, *Holstein und Harden*, pp. 391–2.)

[2] The proclamation issued by Friedrich Wilhelm IV, King of Prussia, on 19 March 1848 during the revolutionary disturbances in Berlin.

[3] The communiqué for the *Reichsanzeiger* (see above, p. 596, note 5.) On the evening of the same day Holstein wrote to Bülow: 'The statement in the *Reichsanzeiger* is in my opinion very tactful and dignified. In this way the Reich and also the Kaiser get out of the business in the most decent way imaginable.' (From the Bülow Papers.)

[4] Leopold von Buch. Leader of the Conservatives in the Prussian House of Lords.

[5] Jordan von Kröcher. President of the Prussian Chamber of Deputies (Conservative Party).

that her recent pro-Turkish policy will *inevitably* involve her in quarrels with Russia; therefore the English Government is doing everything in its power to find other opponents for Russia. Turkey and the Slavic Balkan states are being encouraged to go to war against Austria, with the expectation that in that case Russia cannot remain neutral. The English know perfectly well that as soon as the army, above all the Guards, move towards the frontier, that the Tsarist regime will be swept away by revolution. '*Vive le Douma*', Campbell-Bannerman cried before he died, and his shrewd colleagues are acting accordingly.

The Tsar knows *nothing*—I heard this again quite recently—and Isvolsky lacks perspective, lives only for the moment, and hopes to frighten Austria and Germany by bluff. He will bluff until sometime he will not be able to back down. I think you should order Pourtalès to talk over the dangers of the situation with Isvolsky in a friendly way and to inform him again that no matter what happens, we will not bring pressure to bear on Austria. *À propos*, do have them send you the sharp article against Aehrenthal in the *Frankfurter Zeitung*. This separate policy of the official Press will probably not cease as long as the present topsy-turvy situation, which is becoming increasingly obvious, lasts. To counter this, even Raschdau would be a good thing.[1] He would at least follow a *German* policy—to the best of his ability.

The enclosed clipping from the *Berliner Neuesten Nachrichten*[2] reveals in a few words the obvious Anglo-Turkish war policy.

Most sincerely your
Holstein.

1159.   Holstein to Bernhard von Bülow
Copy

28 November 1908

Dear Bülow,

You are in my opinion obliged to submit the war article in the *Standard* 'Should we wait any longer?' (announced yesterday, though it will probably not come in until to-day) to the Kaiser, and then to ask the question of how Germany's position towards England would shape up in case of war. The navy will have to give an answer. Because it is not merely a question of the *Standard*. The movement set in motion by Roberts[3] must create a belligerent attitude, because people will say: 'The army is not much good anyway, but the *fleet* is to-day decidedly stronger, so—the sooner the better.'

Perhaps I will get more precise information from England in the next few days. I will inform you of anything that is of interest.

Would you not at the same time have His Majesty ask Tirpitz—or you ask Tirpitz in the presence of H.M.—what measures he would suggest (that accord with the honour of the Reich) to lessen or at least

---

[1] As State Secretary in the Foreign Ministry.     [2] Not found.
[3] After his retirement as Commander-in-Chief of the British Army in 1905, Roberts devoted his energies to rousing his countrymen to the need for improvements in the army and for general military training and service.

prevent further distrust on the part of England that is obviously created by our naval armaments. It seems to me that slowing down ship building because of technical reasons (the building of experimental ships, testing of certain points) would be a highly desirable step, but Tirpitz would have to suggest it himself. That would be better than if you were forced to do so by an interpellation in the Reichstag. Or do you think the latter would be better?

Something must be done. First, I think, you should submit the article in the *Standard* and see what H.M. has to say.

That he should allow a slight indisposition to interfere with a matter of such urgency seems to me improbable.

(2) It is also highly desirable that the Turks should have their eyes opened about the inevitable consequences of a war with Austria: 'It is inconceivable that Turkey, in the present state of her armaments and even with the aid of the small Balkan states, can assert herself militarily against Austria, for all the bravery of the Turks. Russia, despite her sympathy for Serbia and Montenegro, will be most hesitant to intervene militarily because of her internal situation and the danger that the parties of revolution, which are now urging war, will make use of the absence of the army for anti-dynastic purposes. Under no circumstances could the Tsarist Government allow this opportunity offered by war to go by without securing a guarantee from Turkey for free passage through the Straits, and the promise that at least the northern entrance to the Straits not be fortified. Once Turkey is in trouble militarily, she will have to concede these and every other demand, as in 1878. If she wants to secure herself against such amputations, she must secure a guarantee from England and Russia for the integrity of her present territory before the war, or at least get a promise that neither (England or Russia) shall demand territorial concessions from Turkey for themselves or for others either in the course of the war or at its conclusion.'

This idea should be brought up as quickly as possible:

(*a*) by Kiderlen, with the Turkish Ambassador here.

(*b*) by Marschall with the Foreign Minister[1] and with the Grand Vizier.[2]

(*c*) possibly also by Pourtalès with Turkan Pasha, who is a really clever diplomat and who was Chargé d'Affaires in Berlin at the time of the last war. This communication should be *left up to* Pourtalès.

I consider to-day's two suggestions to be very important.

Most sincerely your<br>Holstein.

1160.   Holstein to Bernhard von Bülow[3]
        Copy

December, 1908

Dear Bülow,

From the way Stemrich is being treated I can see that your own sense

---

[1] Tewfik Pasha.          [2] Kiamil Pasha.

[3] This letter was never sent. In a letter to Holstein of 1 December, Kiderlen, who was Acting State Secretary in place of Schoen until 2 December, wrote: 'I look upon the Stemrich

of decency and judgment are no longer decisive in determining your decisions, but rather those of your advisers. I herewith relinquish, not without deep regret, all further intercourse with you, in order not to be partly responsible for the final fiasco that seems inevitable with the present methods of conducting affairs.

## 1161.    Bernhard von Bülow to Holstein

Friday [4 December 1908]

Dear Holstein,

Many thanks for your friendly letters. Stemrich is going to stay on. [...]

Also, *secretum* and *secretissimum* : I have written officially to Tirpitz and, pointing in some detail to the fact that the growing agitation in England is entirely the result of our ship building, requested a reply to the question as to whether he thought Germany could contemplate a war with England calmly and confidently.[1]

My ladies were much pleased by your visit. Donna Laura, who has been able to see and judge the qualities of many men, thinks she has never encountered *une intelligence plus lucide, et une conversation plus nourrie* than your own. They—and I—are only sorry that you complained about your health! Can we not help you or be of service to you in some way? You know that we would do so gladly, and that it would come from the heart.

With sincere wishes and greetings

Your

B.

## 1162.    Holstein to Bernhard von Bülow

Copy

Berlin, 5 December 1908

Dear Bülow!

(1) Yesterday's letter received with thanks.[2] Now at least people will not be able to make anything of a Stemrich case.

(2) I have read that England, Russia, and France intend to exercise joint pressure on Austria. With that, and with the proceedings in the Italian Chamber, the Eastern Question enters a critical phase. Schoen, who quite rightly feels he is not up to the requirements of the situation, tried to persuade Kiderlen to remain here a while longer. K. naturally refused.[3] I would *urgently* recommend, however, that you order Kiderlen to continue to handle the Eastern Question with Zimmermann; the rest of the Foreign Ministry is no concern of Kiderlen's. If K. does not

business as settled after a talk I had with him this morning. I told Schoen I would arrange it tonight with the Chancellor. But I now hear that he has gone to see St. himself. Schoen will at any rate do everything to keep St. He told me he could not do the job without help and wanted to keep me here. I however excused myself, and now he will *have* to get together with St. More when I see you.'

[1] Letter of 30 November 1908. (*Grosse Politik*, vol. XXVIII, no. 10235, pp. 21–3.)

[2] See above.                              [3] See above, p. 599, note 3.

remain, the outlook is bleak. For you in your solitary heights now have to divide your attention between too many things, and I am too far away and too inadequately informed. Neither of us can carry the responsibility of seeing to it that nothing is neglected. *But that nothing should be* neglected can, at a time like the present, be a life and death matter for Germany, and thereby also be decisive for your position before history.

The best thing would be if Kiderlen were given my former room next to the State Secretary, because he must after all keep the latter informed. Kiderlen has heretofore always kept in touch with me, which will surely have accorded with your intentions. He has announced himself for to-day at ten in order to say good-bye, but if you want to keep him, there is no time to be lost.

I suspect that the purpose of this idea—in which I need not be mentioned—will be more obvious to Schoen than to Kiderlen, but that makes no difference; get your hands on Kiderlen. Nor can it matter at a time like this whether the Kaiser likes it or not. Now it is a question of the Reich and of you. They should not be able to accuse you of neglect.

Best wishes<br>
Your<br>
Holstein.

1163.   Bernhard von Bülow to Holstein

Monday, [7 December 1908]

Dear Holstein,

The Kiderlen business has been arranged.[1] I consider Kiderlen to be the best political mind in the service, and at the same time an indefatigable worker. I will hold to him.

The agitation against Aehrenthal by the encirclement Powers is going on merrily. I hope the old Kaiser will not lose his nerve. He tends to become impatient if difficulties are not solved overnight, because in the twilight of an unhappy life he above all wants peace and quiet. On the other hand it is obvious that to drop Aehrenthal now would be a blow both to the monarch and the monarchy. At our Court my 'friends' are said to be spreading the news that a year ago I had asked His Majesty to express himself in England in the sense of the *Daily Telegraph* article. H.M. had informed me that he had done so in a letter of twenty-four pages, and I had thanked him *chaleureusement* and in detail. Later on however, I had introduced the business into the Press myself—and then denied it—in the most perfidious way. *Elle est bien bonne.*

I will speak very clearly, very simply, very definitely to the Reichstag.[2] I cannot yet deal with the Conference question because this is at present in the background. The superb ideas you gave me on the subject I will use at the second reading.

With very best greetings and good wishes

Sincerely yours<br>
B. [...]

---

[1] See above, Holstein's letter of 5 December.   [2] See below, p. 603, note 1.

## 1164.    Holstein to Bernhard von Bülow
Copy

7 December 1908

Dear Bülow,

To-day's letter received with thanks.[1]

I hear that Sir Edgar Speyer hopes to be received by you, now that he has been received by Asquith.[2]

Ambassador Goschen said recently that he had talked with you for over an hour, but that he had not heard anything that was 'really reassuring'.[3]

If you are not in a position to say anything 'really reassuring' (naturally about fleet building) to Speyer, perhaps it would be better if you did not receive him at all. To be sure it must be remembered that even before the deflation that followed the present crisis, Tirpitz expressed himself to an English journalist along the lines of conciliation. And here he probably makes things sound even better, especially in tête-à-têtes.

If therefore Tirpitz talks in a conciliatory way to Speyer, while you stand firmly by the Naval Law, then Speyer will return to England with the impression: 'You can talk with the Secretary of the Navy, but you can do nothing with the Chancellor.' And the English will say again. 'Aha, Bülow, there is the enemy.'

It would still be something if you told Speyer: 'Perhaps the Reichstag will have technical objections and demand a more precise examination of the construction plans. That would slow up the rate of construction *ipso facto*. If the Reichstag has no objections, then we can do nothing about the naval plans which have been approved by every branch of the Government.'

When you confer next time with Parliamentary leaders, you would tell them about this talk with Speyer. If they then ask: 'What does Your Highness think?' I would reply: 'Since I do not keep up with technical developments, I can neither express nor remove doubts. Ask the Naval Ministry or other technical experts. I am confident that the plans of the Naval Ministry can be subjected to the examination of other experts.'

The Reichstag might perhaps understand this hint. Without such a hint, I am afraid they will find it impossible to keep up with that clever Tirpitz.

Most sincerely your
Holstein.

[1] See above.

[2] Speyer, an English banker, had been in Berlin in November and again in December, when he was in fact received by Bülow. (See *Grosse Politik*, vol. XXVIII, p. 37, note *.) There is no record of this conversation in the Foreign Ministry files.

[3] Holstein may be referring to a conversation of 13 November. (*British Documents*, vol. VI, no. 105, pp. 165–7.) There is no record of this conversation in the Foreign Ministry files.

**1165.** Holstein to Bernhard von Bülow
Copy

8 December 1908

Dear Bülow,

I cannot unfortunately compliment you on yesterday's speech.[1]

Leading from the idea that Aehrenthal must be protected, you intended to speak 'very briefly, very firmly,' then however did exactly the opposite and in particular did not support Aehrenthal. The uninitiated must say to himself that the basic purpose of the speech was probably to 'calm' the encirclement Powers, i.e. to encourage them, and to make Austria feel correspondingly insecure. I am anxious to see the practical effect of this speech on Austrian statesmen.

A parliamentarian—the only one to whom I spoke to-day—said : 'The Chancellor spoke in too soft a manner, almost fearfully. The public will say : "If the Kaiser is not to express himself any longer, then the Chancellor must take a firmer line, otherwise there will be a vacuum".' I quote word for word what I was told.

I regard this speech as a political misfortune for the Reich and also for you.

Most sincerely your
Holstein


**1166.** Bernhard von Bülow to Holstein

Wednesday, [9 December 1908]

Dear Holstein,

On my return from Potsdam I received your letter of yesterday.[2] You know how highly I value your opinion. I know how much you have my interests at heart. I also know that I am not guilty of thinking I always know everything better, but I am convinced that in this case I struck the right tone, especially with regard to Austria. The decisive influences in Austria, which I know well, are not afraid that we will desert them. They have no fears of this kind about me, above all. But they are concerned that we may expect more of Austria than Austria is able to perform. With that I do not mean to say that the Austrians think we may act perfidiously. It is far more the feelings of a rider who has had two dangerous falls towards a rider on a stronger horse who has not had such experiences. Aehrenthal himself has repeatedly requested me not to allow our Press to adopt 'too definite' a line (also *quoad* alliances like the Triple Alliance). In addition, and here I agree with Kiderlen, Aehrenthal is now making the mistake of treating Turkey and also Bulgaria and Rumania in too high-handed a fashion, as a Viennese nobleman treats a country bumpkin. This too I had to consider. I hope

---

[1] In his speech to the Reichstag of 7 December, Bülow said that Germany had important economic interests in the Balkans, but that she had no more occasion now than a generation ago to allow herself to be forced to take a leading role in the work of political reconstruction in that area. This was the task of Powers more closely concerned with Balkan affairs.

[2] See above.

you are over your cold! As soon as I am finished with the Reichstag, I will again announce myself. I have a good deal to tell you.

Warmest greetings

Your

B.

## 1167. Holstein to Bernhard von Bülow
Copy

14 December 1908

Dear Bülow,

The report from Hintze[1] offers an incomparable opportunity to give the Tsar a true picture of the Eastern Question. I have discussed every detail with Kiderlen.

Main points:

(1) Isvolsky was not deceived by Austria.[2] Austria promised—as compensation—not to oppose freedom of passage through the Straits, and has remained true to this promise up to the present. It was about England that Isvolsky was deceived. For twenty years England told everyone: 'The Straits are a matter of indifference to us.' But since the outbreak of the Turkish revolution, England is supporting Turkey. To be sure, a good many people in Constantinople believe in the possibility that England will demand Mesopotamia as the price of this support.

(2) England is now trying to turn the bitterness of Russia, which is the natural consequence of England's turn-about on the Straits question, against Austria, which was after all prepared for its part to leave the Straits to Russia. A Russian-Austrian war would be useful to England; this would also aid the revolutionary movement in Russia with which England sympathizes just as she does with the Turkish revolution.

(3) France has a great interest in preserving the Anglo-Russian friendship. Furthermore, the Franco-Russian alliance is a matter of life and death for France. Therefore it may be assumed that at Russia's request France would intercede in England for a solution to the Straits question in Russia's interest. Furthermore, it *is* much more important for England to preserve the Entente with France than to secure Mesopotamia.

To sum up: *Isvolsky was not deceived by Austria, but rather England deserted her former attitude.* And: *Russia should bring pressure to bear on France, France on England. This is how the Straits Question may be solved.*

Excuse the style. In flying haste

Most sincerely

Your

Holstein

[1] Paul von Hintze. Naval Captain; Naval Attaché in St Petersburg. In a report to the Kaiser, Hintze wrote: 'His Majesty the Tsar of Russia told me to-day: in yesterday's Note Austria had offered to free Batum from the restrictions of the Treaty of Berlin, a miserable compensation! The Tsar described his aim as free rights of passage through the Straits in accordance with the decision of a Conference, but not by a separate or secret treaty with the Turkish Empire. [...] The Tsar ordered me to report to Your Majesty that Your Majesty might have complete confidence in him, that he was master here.' (*Grosse Politik*, vol. XXVIi, no. 9180, p. 369.)

[2] At the Buchlau Conference. (See above, p. 583, note 3.)

604

## 1168.   Bernhard von Bülow to Holstein

Monday [14 December 1908]

Dear Holstein,

'Excuse the style' are the only three superfluous words in your letter.[1] The style was masterful, as usual, and the ideas were on the same pinnacle as the style. I am happy to be able to agree with you entirely on this question, as I am in the judgment on Monts' opinion.[2]

Many thanks for your friendly letter of Friday. I am very glad to hear that you are up and about again. As soon as I am somewhat less engaged I will come to see you. Tomorrow I want to talk with Szögyényi along the lines of the last dispatch to Vienna which Kiderlen probably showed you and with which you will certainly be in agreement.[3] *Il est dans votre ordre d'idées.*

With very best greetings and good wishes

Faithfully
Your
B.  [...]

## 1169.   Maximilian Harden to Holstein

15 December 1908

Your Excellency,

Many thanks for the friendly words.[4] But I don't want to disturb the Chancellor once again with this business.[5] He will probably be glad not to hear about it and not to have to do anything about it. It appears that the Minister[6] never gave orders in our sense, and that the M[oltke]-H[arden] business is now coming up after all.

I heartily hope that Your Excellency will be able to resume your walks before Christmas.

With sincerest holiday greetings

I am Your Excellency's
Very devoted
H.

## 1170.   Holstein to Bernhard von Bülow
Copy

18 December 1908

Dear Bülow,

[...] *Crown Prince*: The Crown Prince made the statement that he was going to inform the Kaiser about the 'Kiderlen Case' last Friday or

---

[1] Of 14 December. See above.

[2] In a report of 9 December Monts had reported that a number of Austrian statesmen were extremely critical of Aehrenthal and had described his policy as absolutely disastrous for the Austro-Hungarian Empire. (*Grosse Politik*, vol. XXVIi, p. 336, note *.)

[3] A dispatch of 12 December. (*Grosse Politik*, vol. XXVIii, no. 9295, pp. 516–18.)

[4] In a letter to Harden of 14 December, Holstein advised him not to burn his boats earlier than necessary, and offered to forward a letter to Bülow if Harden so desired. (Rogge, *Holstein und Harden*, p. 421.)

[5] In a letter to Holstein of 13 December, Harden had again expressed the fear that a date would be set for another Moltke-Harden trial before the Eulenburg case had been decided.

[6] Dr Beseler, the Minister of Justice.

Saturday.[1] You will therefore be able to decide whether the necessary enlightenment of the Prince has already taken place or whether it is still to be done. The Prince will probably be most impressed by the fact that Kiderlen's absolutely independent and well-to-do sister, the widowed Baroness Gemmingen, a friend of Duchess Vera von Württemberg, has stayed with Kiderlen on several occasions. About Frau Kiepke [sic] someone once said to me : 'One need only display her photograph to wipe out all suspicion.'

The situation seems to me to indicate that you should take the Crown Prince somewhat in hand personally. The man is now, as you say, under the influence of Upper Silesia.[2] And a week ago he even said : 'Bülow is after all done for.' That sounds like Trachenberg and Co. Considering the frivolous manner of the young gentleman, I attach no special importance to this statement. It only shows that you should take him up. I should think that as an experienced statesman you would talk with him seriously, calmly, not be too forthcoming, and somewhat authoritative.

It is my firm conviction that the Kaiser must now be *very* careful for his own sake, because the memory of Friedrich Wilhelm IV is spreading dangerously and the mere suspicion could be fateful.[3] [...][4]

1171.   Holstein to Bernhard von Bülow
         Draft

26 December 1908

Dear Bülow,

[...] Kiderlen thinks, or thought last Tuesday morning, that the maximum Austrian concessions should be certain economic ones—for instance, customs concessions and an Austrian guarantee to Turkey for a new loan. He was *opposed* to a redemption payment because that would make the Turks more presumptuous towards Bulgaria. He thought that the granting of redemption payments would be an unfriendly act on the part of Austria towards Bulgaria. I go a step further and even consider the guarantee to be *dangerous*.[5] What will Austria do for instance if, encouraged by Russia (as in 1875) the Turks declare when the first

---

[1] In a letter of 16 December, Holstein warned Bülow that the Crown Prince intended to play the same role against Kiderlen that he had played on 2 May 1907 against Eulenburg (see above, p. 472, note 1), that is, to 'enlighten' him about Kiderlen's relationship with his housekeeper Hedwig Kypke. (Bülow, *Denkwürdigkeiten*, vol. II, facing p. 416.)

[2] Prince Hermann Hatzfeldt-Trachenberg had formerly been Head of the Administration of Silesia. Holstein is referring to the whole coterie of great Silesian magnates, including Prince Guido Henckel.

[3] King Friedrich Wilhelm IV of Prussia, the Kaiser's great uncle, had died insane.

[4] The copy bears no formal ending.

[5] At this point in his draft Holstein crossed out the words: 'The Turks, encouraged by England, would say the second time the interest fell due: "We will make our other interest payments, but this new loan is such an excessive burden, *non possumus*." Then the guarantor will have the loan around his neck, to the jubilation of the encirclement Powers. In 1875 it was Russia that persuaded the Turks not to make interest payments. I therefore understand why Austria is cautious. I should like to recommend that *we* don't get involved in the details but merely say: "We will support your position as a Great Power." We know how far Aehrenthal will give in once he begins.'

interest payment falls due : 'We are just barely able to pay the interest on our old debts, but not on our new ones' ?

Austria would then simply be paying, and if Germany had encouraged the guarantee, the Austrian Press would make Germany morally responsible.

etc. etc.

Most sincerely
Your
Holstein.

1172.    Holstein to Bernhard von Bülow
       Draft

27 December 1908

Dear Bülow,

We have repeatedly discussed the urgent need for an understanding between Austria and Bulgaria. The immediate evacuation of the Sanjak and the delay in reaching an understanding with the Bulgars are the two big mistakes on the part of Aehrenthal. The success of Austria depends on the understanding with Bulgaria as well as on Germany's loyalty. *The one is as important as the other.* We should stress the significance of this understanding to the Austrians at every possible opportunity. Once again Austrian snobbery is responsible that this has not been done long since. Bismarck indicated the harmful nature of this quality in a dispatch intended for Haymerle in about 1880 or '81.[1]

Austria will lose unless she reaches an understanding with Bulgaria soon. Bulgaria may yet be seduced into joining Isvolsky's projected Balkan league. That would overthrow Aehrenthal and Austria would give in; whereas otherwise, as soon as an Austro-Bulgarian agreement has been reached, the question of the redemption payments for the Turks which have been demanded of them both would become less difficult because they could then work together on that question.

Therefore, my dear friend, I repeat—not for the first time—my urgent advice to recommend to Aehrenthal once again that he seek an understanding with Bulgaria as quickly as possible, now that Isvolsky's speech gives him the opportunity.[2] Let us hope it is not already too late and that Russian diplomacy has not already gained a firm position in Sofia.[3] That would in the end mean a defeat for us, not through *culpa nostra* but through *culpa alterius*, but it would be all the same thing to the world in general.

In your dispatch to Vienna[4] which should be worded so that it can be read aloud, point directly to the danger *that Russia, perhaps together with*

<hr>

[1] A dispatch of 17 May 1881. (*Grosse Politik*, vol. III, no. 530, pp. 172–3.)

[2] In a speech to the Duma of 25 December, Isvolsky declared Russia's political goal to be the union of Bulgaria, Serbia, Montenegro, and also Turkey, in the common aim of preserving their national and economic independence.

[3] At this point in his draft Holstein crossed out the sentence : 'The Russians are not likely to be as slow about it as the Austrians.'

[4] Of 28 December. (*Grosse Politik*, vol. XXVIii, no. 9298, pp. 520–2.)

*England, may offer her services to Bulgaria as a mediator in order to get
better terms in Constantinople, with the stipulation that Bulgaria join the
anti-Austrian bloc.* Vienna does not yet seem to have envisaged this very
distinct possibility.

But do not lose any time, dear friend.

Most sincerely
Your
Holstein.

### 1173.  Bernhard von Bülow to Holstein

Sunday, [27 December 1908]

Dear Holstein,

My very best thanks for your kind and interesting letter[1] which shows,
I am glad to see, that we agree in our estimate of the situation. The
central point of Isvolsky's speech is the idea of a Balkan League directed
against Austria.[2] Not until Russia succeeds in creating such a league will
Austria's position be really serious. The very benevolent tone Isvolsky
adopted towards Bulgaria proves that the Russians hope to join the
Turks and the Bulgarians in their prospective bloc. Austria must reach
an understanding with Bulgaria, and as quickly as possible, before the
Russians (English and French) snatch it from them. I too think it is not
impossible that the encirclement Powers may offer their *bons offices* to the
Bulgars in Constantinople with the stipulation that the Bulgars join the
anti-Austrian bloc.

For weeks I have again and again urgently advised Vienna to come to
an understanding with the Bulgars.[3] I asked Kiderlen to keep this very
point in the forefront, and he agreed with me about it. I also wrote in this
sense to Aehrenthal.[4] I discussed it in detail with Szögyényi.[5] In
commenting on Isvolsky's speech, which provides a first-rate *point de
départ*, I have just indicated the points for a dispatch to Vienna which will
follow our ideas and will be suitable to be read aloud.[6] I will talk to
Szögyényi again myself.

Aehrenthal has all the less reason to hesitate in reaching an agreement
with the Bulgarians—*without delay!*—because he is in a difficult position
with the Turks. The Austrian exporters are complaining because they
fear (exaggeratedly, in my opinion) a boycott that will exclude all
Austrian commerce from the Levant. The Hungarian Minister-
President who is at the same time Minister of Finance,[7] is protesting
against the monetary demands that Turkey has so far made a condition

[1] Of 27 December. See above.   [2] See above, p. 607, note 2.
[3] See *Grosse Politik*, vol. XXVIii, nos. 9292, 9295, pp. 513–15, 516–18.
[4] Not by private letter, but through a dispatch to Tschirschky of 12 December. Tschirschky
was empowered to read the dispatch to Aehrenthal. (*Grosse Politik*, vol. XXVIii, no. 9295,
pp. 516–18.)
[5] No memorandum of this discussion was found in the Foreign Ministry files. (See
*Österreich-Ungarns Aussenpolitik*, vol. I, no. 752, pp. 606–11.)
[6] See above, note 4.   [7] Dr Alexander Wekerle.

for an understanding. He has promised to balance the Hungarian budget, which was in difficulties because of the refusals to pay taxes, and Aehrenthal had promised him at the time that the annexation[1] would not cost anything. Along with this acute difficulty, there are the chronic troubles that every Austrian Minister has to face : the difficulties of the dual form of government, the nationality struggles in both halves of the empire, the infinite pettiness, especially of the Viennese. One has to have lived there to know *qu'Aehrenthal n'est pas sur un lit de roses*. All the more reason for him to do what is correct and *possible* to improve his position. How right you are in what you say about Austrian snobbery! *Il faut les avoir vu sur place, à Boucarest, à Athènes, partout, pour s'en rendre compte.* And the 'gentleman', for whom a person does not exist unless he has the rank of Baron, is opposed by the Russian Balkan diplomats who always meet the Balkan carpet baggers on their own level in the sewers and who immediately understand each other.

But their is no lack of more favourable signs. Kiamil Pasha, who sees everything from the English point of view, is beginning to excite the anger of the Young Turks. He did not even send a copy of the speech from the throne to his ministerial colleagues beforehand. The Young Turks are also wondering what lies behind his rude behaviour towards Austria (inspired by Lowther).[2] Furthermore, the Young Turks have noticed with displeasure that the Entente Powers, especially the French, are favourable to the annexation of Crete. The Young Turks say, not without justice : after Turkey's last victorious war and in view of the whole development of the Cretan question, the annexation of Crete is a far greater blow to Turkey's national feeling than the loss in peacetime of Bosnia and Herzegovina which were given up thirty years ago anyway.[3] Everything I hear from financial circles and from Russian friends indicates that the Russians neither want nor can allow it to come to a clash with Austria. Just yesterday a financier told me : if the Russian loan does not go through, Russia will be bankrupt by spring. In my opinion we should participate the less in this loan because the more Russian securities the French buy up, the more afraid they will be of war. An old Russian friend wrote me : '*Il parait qu'on croit en Europe qu'Isvolsky veut s'en aller en guerre comme feu Marlborough. Le pauvre Isvolsky! Il n'est que trop heureux si on le laisse en paix. Lui et faire la guerre!*'

If Austria backs down it is not our *culpa*, in that too you are right. I wonder whether they will stand firm? Szögyényi told me confidentially : 'It is a psychological question, a question of the inner feelings of an old and much-tried man on whom no one exercises any real influence, who works everything out himself, a noble character, a regent with a great sense of duty—but in need of peace and quiet, and when there are difficulties, easily impatient.' But Szögyényi hopes and thinks that the

[1] Of Bosnia and Herzegovina.
[2] Sir Gerald Augustus Lowther. British Ambassador in Constantinople, 1908–13.
[3] Austria-Hungary had been given a mandate to occupy (as opposed to annex) Bosnia and Herzegovina by the Treaty of Berlin in 1878.

Kaiser will remain firm this time in the realization that backing down after this onset would mean the end of Austria's policy and position as a Great Power for the foreseeable future.

Once again warmest thanks and best wishes from

Your sincerely devoted

B.

# 1909

1174.   Holstein to Bernhard von Bülow
        Copy

2 January 1909

Dear Bülow,

I do not see what should prevent you from suggesting that the Bulgarian compensation question[1] be decided at The Hague. The Hague was after all established for questions of this kind. If our bankers should oppose, they might be answered through the Press with: 'Aha, you wanted to use this opportunity to make a killing, that is why you object to The Hague.' That would quiet them immediately.

And the Bulgarians too would put themselves in the wrong before the world if they rejected The Hague. So the sooner this is proposed, the better.

The Bulgarian representative here[2] is not, I understand, a serious man of affairs. I therefore withdraw my suggestion that you discuss the reformation of Bulgaria's foreign relations with him and restrict myself to the second part of my proposal:[3] that you write Romberg[4] a *letter* that he can read out loud to the Prince. The letter might begin with the idea that one should have the railway question decided at The Hague to make room for the important political considerations necessitated by the present situation. Then would follow the points of view I recently developed.[5]

The present Bulgarian Cabinet is already wobbling again. The Prince is the stable pole there, and is a real statesman. I think he will use his influence *in favour of* The Hague. The slogan of the Russian Press 'Away with the Coburger' must be uncomfortable for him and must also arouse the desire to enter into closer political relations with us, as well as with Austria. The Balkan League would for him actually mean his dethronement, his mediatization.

[1] Compensation to Turkey for the Bulgarian Government's appropriation of railway lines running through the country at the time of Bulgaria's announcement of her complete independence from Turkey.

[2] N. P. Nikiphorov. Bulgarian diplomatic representative (Minister from 1909) in Berlin, 1904–10.

[3] Submitted in a letter of 1 January (not printed). In a fragment found with his letter of 1 January, Holstein maintained that Bulgaria's present aim should be independence without isolation. This goal, he believed, could only be reached through closer relations with Austria, and this in turn would mean closer Bulgarian relations with Germany, to the mutual benefit of both countries.

[4] German Consul-General, later Minister in Sofia, 1905–10.

[5] On 14 January Bülow sent a private letter to Baron von Romberg along the lines suggested by Holstein. ( *Grosse Politik*, vol. XXVIii, p. 527, note *.)

I advise that you send this letter to Romberg, which Kiderlen will probably draft, to Sofia by courier immediately.

Let us hope that Romberg is not on leave. Usually a person is away just when one needs him. As Goethe says : 'One needs what one has not, and what one has one needs not' (which cannot refer to Tschirschky, because Goethe never knew him).

The best thing would be to enclose a copy of the letter, which Romberg could leave with the Prince. Romberg can even ask directly whether the Prince wants a copy. This move would create a feeling of confidence and would thus be all the more appropriate. Nor is there anything in the letter that we cannot stand behind. The letter accords with German interests, and in Bismarck's opinion one can never blame anyone for standing up for his own interests. I should think that the Prince feels confidence in you because—when Below was still there[1]—you gave him some quite disinterested advice.

With best wishes<br>Holstein

## 1175.   Bernhard von Bülow to Holstein

Saturday evening, 2 January 1909

Dear Holstein,

Between a long conference with His Majesty, a visit from the (quite senile) Osten-Sacken who once again complained about Aehrenthal, another very long visit from Prince Heinrich (who is reasonable), and a great many things to write, I was very busy to-day. But I must thank you for your two letters[2] and the clever ideas about Bulgaria. *Rebus sic stantibus* I too consider a letter to Romberg better than a talk with the politically hopelessly inadequate (in contrast to his sovereign) Bulgarian representative here. Kiderlen is expected back tomorrow. I will discuss the important matter with him immediately. [...]

The Isvolsky-Aehrenthal duel is getting more heated all the time. Isvolsky has asked the Tsar to issue an order that in view of the Austrian revelations of past Russo-Austrian treaties,[3] confidential intercourse with the Austrian Embassy should cease.[4] Isvolsky sends this information in a very excited and verbose dispatch to Osten-Sacken with the request that we use our influence in Vienna.[5] Evidently Isvolsky fears further revelations from a more recent period that may be even more awkward

---

[1] Gustav von Below-Rutzau, the Prussian Minister in Stuttgart, had been German Consul-General in Sofia 1900–5.

[2] Of 1 January (not printed) and 2 January (see above).

[3] See *Grosse Politik*, vol. XXVIi, nos. 9055, 9166, pp. 186–95, 351.

[4] See *Grosse Politik*, vol. XXVIi, nos. 9170–2, pp. 356–9.

[5] In a dispatch to Vienna of 4 January, Bülow informed Tschirschky that Osten-Sacken had read him a dispatch from Isvolsky who stated that if Austria did not stop its revelations he would find himself obliged to publish the Russo-Austrian treaty of 28 September 1904 which was directed against Italy. (See *Grosse Politik*, vol. XXVIi, nos. 9170–2, pp. 356–9; *Österreich-Ungarns Aussenpolitik*, vol. I, no. 839, pp. 696–8.)

for him.  I have rejected this Russian demand in the coolest possible and even ironic manner.  [...]

Most sincerely
Your
B.  [...]

1176.    Holstein to Bernhard von Bülow
Draft

6 January 1909

Dear Bülow,

The Schlieffen article[1] and its adoption by the Kaiser is a very pointed reversion to the practices of the past; one could even call it a mockery of constitutional forces.  In its way clever.  The Kaiser can always appeal to the 'indiscretion' (which was of course part of the plan).[2]  In fact, it could not be more harmful.  Fearful, as at the time of Algeciras, discouraging for Austria (that is the worst of it), and encouraging for the encirclement Powers.  We again have two types of foreign policy: the policy of the bureaux that is for firmness, and the Kaiser's policy that considers firmness to be dangerous.  The enclosed[3] shows what people abroad think of all this.

If I were Chancellor, I would tomorrow calmly hand in my resignation and say to myself: 'Either it is accepted, and then I go out in triumph; or—5 to 1—it is not accepted, and then the Kaiser will have to behave and I will with one stroke have achieved the authoritative position in history that a Chancellor must possess in the interests of the Reich, *especially now.*'  Think this over.  But I do not want you to act merely on the advice of an outsider.[4]

Ask Kiderlen!  I have not discussed the matter with him, but think that if he considers it at all possible he will give you the most expedient advice for staying on.  In *my* opinion, depending on your decision, your position will either become appreciably greater, or become noticeably smaller.

With warmest greetings
Holstein.

1177.    Bernhard von Bülow to Holstein

Sunday, [10 January 1909]

Dear Holstein,

My very best thanks for your friendly, clever, and suggestive lines.[5]

[1] 'Der Krieg in der Gegenwart', *Deutsche Revue*, 1909, vol. I, pp. 13–24. The article was unsigned. (See *Memoirs*, pp. 159–67.)

[2] At the New Year's reception of the commanding generals the Kaiser, in addition to his usual discussion of the military situation, read aloud a part of the above article which also dealt with questions of foreign policy. The authorship of the article was revealed through an indiscretion. 'The question is urgent as to who committed the indiscretion', Holstein wrote to Bülow on 9 January. 'The suspicion of the political world is directed towards His Majesty. Perhaps. But it may also have been a politically-minded general who wants to upset your Eastern policy and you along with it. To the Turcophile Goltz, for instance, this policy must be a horror.'

[3] Not found.        [4] Holstein even prepared a draft for Bülow's resignation. (Not printed.)

[5] In addition to the above letter of 6 January, Holstein had written two letters to Bülow on 9 January on the same subject. (Not printed.)

I have thought the position over very carefully on a morning walk. As so often in life, I have to pick my way between two hazards. I must prevent that unbelievably foolish (or perfidious) article[1] from having too discouraging an effect on Austria; but I must also avoid offending the feelings of the army and the acute military sensibilities of the majority of the nation. What I told you a few days ago about the feelings and fears in Conservative circles has recently become even stronger as the result of certain events. As Chancellor (and Minister-President of Prussia) I have to take into account such feelings and deeply-rooted traditions.

I immediately set to work on the first problem. I think that what I told Szögyényi[2] and what I (with Kiderlen) wrote to Aehrenthal[3] will have a useful effect. As for the rest, I will of course not allow myself to be prevented from writing and saying to His Majesty whatever I consider to be my duty in the way of political counter-measures and the preservation of political order. I will also consider what to say about it to the Reichstag.

Let us hope that Aehrenthal now comes to an understanding with the Turks. I would like to see Isvolsky's face when that happens. Even Osten-Sacken spoke of Isvolsky and his Balkan league *avec une pointe d'ironie*.

I was so busy this morning—in part with dull internal problems—that I am quite tired. But I send you my hearty best wishes, and sincerely hope that your health will continue to improve.

Faithfully

Your

B.

### 1178.    Bernhard von Bülow to Holstein

Wednesday noon, 13 January 1909

Dear Holstein,

Many thanks for your friendly and suggestive lines.[4] Kiderlen has drafted a dispatch to Vienna for me that is entirely in line with your thinking:[5] we are not opposed to the Conference on principle, but think we are at one with the Imperial and Royal Government in the belief that only under very definite conditions would such a Conference not be a danger to the vital interests of the Central European Empire: participation of all the Powers; complete preliminary agreement on all the points of issue; holding of the Conference, which should be merely a *bureau d'enregistrement* and not an Areopagos, not in a capital, but in Venice, Florence, or Geneva. I find that we three—you, Kiderlen, and I—work

---

[1] See above, p. 613, note 1.

[2] No record of this talk was found in the Foreign Ministry files. (See *Grosse Politik*, vol. XXVIii, no. 9259, pp. 479–81.)

[3] In a letter of 8 January. (*Grosse Politik*, vol. XXVIi, no. 9173, pp. 359–60; vol. XXVIii, no. 9302, pp. 526–8, and p. 463, note **.)

[4] Not found.

[5] Of 12 January. (*Grosse Politik*, xol. XXVIi, no. 9175, pp. 361–2).

very well together. This refers also to my last letter to Aehrenthal,[1] from which I expect a useful effect. Meanwhile the Russian Press cannot conceal its annoyance about the Austrian-Turkish agreement.[2]

My brother Carl, who was in Vienna a few days in the course of a hunting trip, told me (confidentially) a good many things about his impressions there : the old Kaiser is very disturbed about the troubles that resulted from the annexation of Bosnia and Herzegovina; he thinks, however, that the dismissal of Aehrenthal would be a *capitis diminutio* for the monarchy. The heir to the throne is all for Aehrenthal. There is a great deal of talk against Aehrenthal in the salons; one of his chief opponents is Goluchowski. Also many of his subordinates are intriguing against him. The army is good and has regained confidence in itself. People are shaking their heads about the Schlieffen article. Our friends are precisely the ones who least understand such a lukewarm attitude. The Kaiser, the heir to the throne, Ministers, Generals, full of appreciation for me; that I should remain in office was more important than anything else. Marschall and Goltz are considered to be opponents of Aehrenthal's policy, Hatzfeldt a ridiculous figure; full sympathy for Wedel. Great indignation about the attacks of the Centrist Press against my policy. These are generally blamed on Oppersdorff,[3] who keeps in touch with the extremist Poles and who wants to adopt the methods in our eastern province by which Schwarzenberg,[4] Thun,[5] and Harrach[6] ruined the German cause in Bohemia.

I completely agree with your view that it is in the interests of the country to prevent new state legal cases. I cannot offer an opportunity for attack on legal questions, and will keep my eyes open. The further development of the domestic situation depends primarily on the attitude of the Conservatives. It is my *ceterum censeo* and my honest conviction that last November[7] I took into account the interests of the Crown as much as the interests of the country, and that I acted as a true royalist.

With best wishes, always most sincerely

Your

B.

## 1179.   Holstein to Bernhard von Bülow
Copy

20 January 1909

Dear Bülow,

Some months ago I wrote to you : 'Never make the inheritance tax a

---

[1] See above, p. 614, note 3.

[2] An agreement of 12 January by which Turkey recognized Austria-Hungary's annexation of Bosnia and Herzegovina in exchange for financial compensation.

[3] Hans Georg, Count von Oppersdorff. Member of the Reichstag, 1908–18. (Until 1912 a member of the Centre Party.)

[4] Felix, Prince von Schwarzenberg. Austrian Minister-President, 1848–52. In 1850 he imposed the 'Humiliation of Olmütz' on Prussia.

[5] Leo, Count Thun. As Governor of Bohemia in 1848 he refused to take orders from the Imperial Government and set up a sort of provisional government of Czechs and German moderates in Prague.

[6] Johann, Count von Harrach. Member of the Austrian Reichsrat, with pro-Czech sympathies.

[7] At the time of the *Daily Telegraph* crisis.

Cabinet question.' I hope that you have not done so, despite your yesterday's speech.[1] You are contradicting yourself, my dear friend. You talk like a Conservative, but with this inheritance tax you are actually putting the axe to the roots of the estates of the landed gentry and the peasantry. I have just heard that at the moment the Radicals are the most contented Party in both Parliaments, and they have reason to be because they hope for a change in ownership of landed property.

There are efforts being made to bring about an understanding between the National Liberals and the Centre Party with a view to a change of Chancellors.

What the Conservatives think you can see from the cool reception of your yesterday's speech.

That reminds me that someone once said to me about Caprivi: 'He now only has Rickert[2] and Co. on his side.' That was a few weeks before the end.

It is also being noticed that you are holding yourself aloof, that you have not discussed the situation recently with any Member of Parliament. People are concluding from that that you are giving up the game. If that is not the case, then in my opinion you should give up the aloofness and the inheritance tax. I do not fully trust my own judgment on this matter, but do talk to Kiderlen about it. He is not a specialist either, of course, but he has an instinct for what is possible to a high degree which most of your former advisers lack. He also has all sorts of connections. May everything yet turn out well.

N.B. To-day is Mother Spitzemberg's[3] birthday.

Your
Holstein

1180.   Bernhard von Bülow to Holstein

Wednesday, 20 January 1909

Dear Holstein,

Many thanks for your friendly letter.[4] Next to squaring the circle, a financial reform is probably the most difficult possible problem here. Reasons: (1) Lack of feeling of responsibility by party leaders, who do not count on the possibility of having to rule themselves in the foreseeable future, as in countries ruled by Parliaments, but who instead see almost everything (especially taxation questions) merely from the standpoint of the deputy who finds fault with everything and trembles before his voters. (2) Intensive dislike on the part of the voter of any diminution of his customary standard of living or of his previous income. The petty-bourgeois and philistine quality in our German

---

[1] On 19 January, during the budget debate in the Prussian Chamber of Deputies, Bülow spoke of the desirability of an inheritance tax. 'We cannot disregard this tax in our present time of need [...]. We cannot levy hundreds of millions on liquid assets and leave landed property completely free.'

[2] Heinrich Rickert. National-Liberal, later Radical Member of the Prussian Chamber of Deputies from 1870; Member of the Reichstag from 1874.

[3] Widow of the former Minister of Württemberg in Berlin.

[4] Of 20 January. See above.

character—the result of our historical development during and since the great blood-letting of the Thirty Years War—is particularly obvious here. (3) Overwhelming material considerations; these have increased greatly since our big successes of 1866 and '70. Hardly anywhere do vested interests parade the point of view of those interests more shamelessly. (4) The laxness within the Parties. The Centre is really the only one among them that knows what discipline means. (5) General tendency on the part of Press and public to do nothing but criticize and never act productively. In England the exact opposite is true.

I only decided to carry out the big financial reform because it could be postponed no longer. If it fails this time, it will only be back again next year under less favourable circumstances. This worm will not die. We will also always be faced with the necessity of proposing a tax on property in addition to the indirect taxes. Without this coating, no Reichstag will swallow the pill of consumer taxes amounting to several hundred million. The only possible property taxes are : a Reich property tax : would not be passed by the Bundesrat; quota payments by the federal states to the Reich treasury : would be the ruin of all the smaller states; indirect quota payments by the federal states : would amount *de facto* to a Reich property tax and mean the mediatization of the federal states. That leaves only the inheritance tax. If it fails this time—and the reform along with it—then it will be back as surely as the sun will rise in the east. Only probably under much more unfavourable circumstances and presuppositions for the property owner! The main thing now in my opinion is to make this clear to the Conservatives before they have to pay for it with their heads. Kiderlen must help in this. We must also try to go even further in toning down the inheritance tax in so far as it affects landed estates. Just during the past week I have seen a series of Members of Parliament, and next week the Parliamentary dinners begin.

Warmest greetings from your much harassed and faithfully devoted

Bülow

## 1181.　Holstein to Bernhard von Bülow
### Copy

27 January 1909

Dear Bülow,

Kiderlen was just here. It was a relief to hear from him that you are firmly decided not to intervene in either the Italian University Question[1] or in the Eastern Question. If too much is said about either of these problems, this can be easily remedied because the statements do not come from you.

The French are first trying to bring pressure on Austria through you. If you refuse, France will at last be forced to urge Russia to adopt a calm attitude. Naturally they do so unwillingly.

If we had held firm another few weeks three years ago, the Russians

---

[1] Holstein refers to Italian agitation for an Italian university in Trieste.

would have been compelled—for the sake of their loan—to advise France to give in. Now the opposite will probably occur, because France does not want a war in the east. But first they are trying their luck in Berlin.

With best wishes

Your

Holstein

1182.   Bernhard von Bülow to Holstein

Thursday, [28 January 1909]

Dear Holstein,

What you wrote about the dangers and disadvantages of intervention[1] accords so fully with my own views that I have used these arguments in a letter to His Majesty.[2] That France wants no war in the *east* can be seen not only in the French Press but in *every* word of Cambon. Szögyényi told me yesterday that the situation in Hungary seems to be clearing up.[3] The main argument now being used against Aehrenthal is the possibility that *I* may not be Chancellor much longer, and in that case Austria-Hungary would be *à la merci* of incalculable policy changes. I have calmed Szögyényi on this point and will not leave the field so easily. Although I have a cold, I have twelve Members of Parliament coming to dine, and before that a dull conference.

I hope you are feeling better

With best wishes from your most sincerely devoted

B.

1183.   Holstein to Bernhard von Bülow

Draft

29 January 1909

Dear Bülow,

To this Russian proposal, whereby Russia intends to play the dominant Power in the Balkans,[4] I would reply:

'Since the declarations by the responsible authorities both in Constantinople and in Sofia have already established the fact that none of the leading Governments has aggressive intentions;

'Since the collective move proposed by Russia might create the illusion that the Powers, or some of them, doubted the sincerity of this declaration;

'Since Germany at the moment sees no reason to doubt the sincerity of this Turk-Bulgarian declaration, therefore Germany sees no reason to make such a move which by its very nature will cause offence somewhere.'

[1] See above, Holstein's letter of 27 January.

[2] A letter of 29 January 1909. (*Grosse Politik*, vol. XXVIii, no. 9197, pp. 407–10.)

[3] No record of this conversation was found in the Foreign Ministry files.

[4] Schoen telegraphed to Vienna on 28 January: 'Russian Government has proposed here that all Great Powers immediately and simultaneously voice a protest in Constantinople and Sofia against the military measures being taken on the Turk-Bulgarian frontier, and that at the same time they express their opposition to the idea of a rectification of frontiers.' (*Grosse Politik*, vol.XXVIii, no. 9309, pp. 532–3.)

I would communicate this to Szögyényi at once, and also publish it.[1]

> In great haste, most sincerely
> > Your
> > Holstein

## 1184. Memorandum by Holstein

8 March 1909

The most interesting recent phenomenon in the field of German foreign policy is the increasingly evident contradiction between legitimate official policy and the policy of the Press Bureau. Last Friday the *Norddeutsche Allgemeine Zeitung* declared unreservedly that even if the Serbian troubles grew more acute, Austria-Hungary would enjoy the support of Germany. At the same time, however, the almost equally official *Kölnische Zeitung* carried a repentence sermon addressed to the Austrian Press warning of the need for consideration towards little Serbia. And now we have already received payment for this simultaneous move in two directions. For on Sunday a widely read Vienna newspaper said: We can hardly expect anything from Germany except articles in the *Norddeutsche Allgemeine Zeitung*, especially since the *Kölnische Zeitung* never ceases to molest Austria-Hungary with advice *which coincides with the hope expressed in Paris* that Austria will listen to reason.

Upon enquiry, I heard through Kiderlen and other people in the Political Division that the Press Division and Herr von Huhn have for some days expressed the urgent desire to castigate the Austrian Press for its excessively independent attitude. According to what he told me, Kiderlen had *rejected* this idea by explaining that even though the Austrian Press may here and there have adopted the wrong tone, still a *public* criticism on our part would be out of order and misunderstood.

But Herr von Huhn could not be restrained from expressing his criticism of the Austrian Press in unequivocal terms, and it seems, as the above article in the *Neues Wiener Journal* shows, that he has to some extent succeeded in making the statesmen of the Danubian monarchy doubtful about the faithfulness and reliability of their German ally. The blunt way the Vienna newspaper pointed to the fact that Herr von Huhn is following the line of French policy is worthy of notice. I have repeatedly drawn attention to the way the Press trio of Hammann, Huhn, and Stein are always in agreement with the point of view of French policy.

When Herr von Huhn was afterwards challenged by the Foreign Ministry for his latest achievement, he put the whole blame on the editors; they had 'perverted' the whole conclusion of his article. It requires a certain amount of audacity to think that the Political Division would believe that sort of thing. Because the latter is very familiar with the *metus reverentialis* of the Cologne editors towards the Wilhelmstrasse, and therefore knows that it is out of the question that the people in

---

[1] Contrary to Holstein's advice Bülow decided to let Germany join in the démarche proposed by Russia because Austria saw no objection to it. (*Grosse Politik*, vol. XXVIii, nos. 9310–2, pp. 533–4.)

Cologne would tamper with what appeared to be a highly official Berlin news item.

It is fortunate that Kiderlen, at my urgent advice, decided to emphasize our loyalty as an ally *very definitely*, and in the *Norddeutsche* at that. Because Huhn's article, if it had been left to stand by itself, would have appeared like a direct warning on the part of the German Government and would have had the effect of a bucket of cold water on the nervous Austrians. Not only in Vienna but all over Europe it would have raised doubts about the stability of German political leadership, with incalculable results. That the Huhn article was not without effect, despite the statement in the *Norddeutsche*, can be seen from the changed tone of the *Neue Freie Presse*. On Sunday this newspaper discussed the possibility 'that certain questions that do not affect the direct political and economic relations between Austria and Serbia should be submitted to a European Conference after agreement had been reached between the two abovementioned states.' This sounds considerably less confident than the statements of this same newspaper in the preceding days. Such symptoms allow me to believe that Austria may yet back down at the eleventh hour if the Press Bureau is allowed to maintain its ambiguous attitude until the decisive moment, i.e. until 31 March, when the Austro-Serbian economic treaty expires. There are also other indications that Germany's reliability is being questioned. Pourtalès reported recently that Nicolson, the English Ambassador, had advised the Russian Government to hold firmly to its position on the Serbian question. Because, if things did come to a crisis, Germany would again retreat and leave Austria to her own devices.[1] The English are using similar arguments in Belgrade, as the Foreign Ministry has discovered from a reliable source, in order to encourage Serbia to maintain a stubborn resistance.

It should be mentioned that so far as the stability of German policy in the Austro-Serbian question is concerned, there is the advantage that the Kaiser, for whom as we know the personal factor always predominates, has a strong prejudice against the Serbs as regicides.[2] It remains to be seen of course how much the Kaiser's feelings could change if the French began to exercise direct influence on him, for instance through a letter from the Prince of Monaco. The instinctive love of the Kaiser for France and the French will in my opinion always be a constant source of sudden difficulties and dangers for the German people. The next ten years will show whether I am not right about this.

1185. Holstein to Bernhard von Bülow

Copy

12 March [1909], Anniversary of the retreat over Morocco.
Dear Bülow,

The hour of decision for Austria has arrived.

---

[1] No report from Pourtalès exactly corresponding to the above statement of Holstein was found in the Foreign Ministry files. (See *Grosse Politik*, vol. XXVIii, nos. 9387, 9400-1, pp. 616-18, 631-2.)

[2] King Alexander I of Serbia had been assassinated on 10 June 1903.

Austria can only stand firm if she is absolutely certain that we will stand by her to the end. Therefore we must TO-DAY inform Aehrenthal through Tschirschky in Vienna and Szögyényi personally here that :

'The Serbian note does not in any way change the nature of the Austro-German alliance. This remains in force no matter what turn events may take as a result of Serbia's attitude.'[1]

The fact that Germany has made this statement in Vienna must be brought to the knowledge of the Ambassador here at once, even before the message is received in Vienna. This cold bucket of water should put a quick end to the most recent concentric bluff probably inspired by King Edward, because no one wants war. Since the above statement is only a confirmation of our previous policy, approved and even ordered by the Kaiser, you will probably in my opinion not need specific [permission] to send it, but if necessary you can probably get it without trouble by telephone, because the Kaiser is against Serbia and for Austria. The Kaiser has been in no way to blame for the ambiguity that has occasionally been observed in Germany's attitude; this was exclusively the fault of the German official Press.

If you fail to give this statement to the Cabinet in Vienna *now, at the psychological moment*, you will be responsible now and in history in case Austria finds herself forced into the path of concessions and thus gradually onto the side of the encirclement Powers. I feel myself obliged to tell you this.[2]

Most sincerely
Your
Holstein

## 1186.   Maximilian Harden to Holstein

Grunewald, 5 April 1909

Your Excellency,

My sincere thanks for the kind letter. I deeply regret that Your Excellency's health took a turn for the worse in the last few days. Though I was very pleased to hear that the night was bearable and that you feel better to-day. I have confident hopes that the spring air will restore your strength and again permit short walks.

Politically Your Excellency just had the pleasure of a strong and strengthening success.[3]

Nothing essentially new about the trial. I am holding to the position : if an *honourable* solution is possible on the basis of the 'statements' (about which even the chief public prosecutor says Harden hasn't conceded any-

---

[1] In a note of 10 March Serbia had referred the final solution of the Bosnian question to the signatory Powers of the Treaty of Berlin, a position that was not fully acceptable to the Austro-Hungarian Government. (See Kiderlen's memorandum of his talk with the Austrian Ambassador of 12 March. *Grosse Politik*, vol. XXVIii, no. 9425, pp. 652–3.)

[2] Germany declared her intention to stand by Austria-Hungary, but at the same time offered her mediatorship in the Bosnian crisis. (See *Grosse Politik*, vol. XXVIIii, nos. 9437–8, pp. 669–71.)

[3] On 31 March Serbia sent Austria another note recognizing the annexation of Bosnia and Herzegovina. (See *Grosse Politik*, vol. XXVIii, no. 9497, pp. 728–32.)

thing whatever in them), then I am willing;[1] if this is not possible, then there will be a fight without quarter. This second method of settlement would be better for me, worse for the Reich; and the patriotism to which one pays lip-service must also occasionally be demonstrated by sacrifices. I will not permit myself to be duped again.

Even Ballin wrote me: 'Every decent person would consider it monstrous if they proceeded against you while Herr Eulenburg is sitting in Liebenberg.' [...]

With the very best wishes from everyone in the little house,

I am Your Excellency's very devoted

H. [...]

### 1187.  Maximilian Harden to Holstein

Grunewald, 23 April 1909

Your Excellency,

I send very best wishes for your birthday in the sincere and confident hope that spring will find you as well as ever.

Nothing about myself to-day. It seems to me that the shame is not mine if I am constantly deceived and lied to by a German Chancellor. It costs me money and health; but this time things are so arranged that it will cost him his office and his reputation.[2]

But this nastiness shall not becloud the day on which all of us in the little house in the woods will be thinking most warmly of Your Excellency.

Affectionately and faithfully

Harden.

### 1188.  Maximilian Harden to Helene von Lebbin

8 May 1909

My dear Madam,

I think you know how deeply we feel with you the grievous loss which this evening has brought to your life.[3] It would be presumptuous to speak of myself to-day. Presumptuous too, to offer you what is generally called 'comfort'. Only the realization of having meant so much to so significant a person can bring you anything resembling comfort.

With full and painful sympathy and in reverence before your grief,

I am, my dear madame

Most sincerely

Harden

---

[1] Harden is referring to the possibility of a settlement of the Moltke-Harden suit by an exchange of statements, to avoid the necessity of another court trial. This procedure had in fact been adopted by the two principals, who signed a statement settling their differences and sent it to the public prosecutor on 22 March 1909. The public prosecutor, however, refused to recognize this settlement and insisted on proceeding with the case. A new trial was held, and on 20 April 1909 Harden was sentenced to pay a fine of six hundred marks and the cost of all three Moltke-Harden trials. According to Harden, he intended to appeal this decision but was persuaded to drop the case by Bülow, who empowered Ballin to offer Harden full reimbursement for the cost of the trials. Harden accepted this offer because on 12 June 1909 he received written statement from Count Moltke which he regarded as satisfactory. (*Zukunft*, 30 September 1922, vol. 113, pp. 246–52; *Köpfe*, vol. III, pp. 503–6.)

[2] Harden is again referring to Bülow's failure to prevent a resumption of the Moltke-Harden trial. (See above, note 1.)

[3] Friedrich von Holstein died on 8 May 1909.

# INDEX to vols. III and IV

[*Note.* biog. = biographical sketch]

Abaza, Alexander: **III** 256 biog. n. 2

Abbas Hilmi II, Khedive of Egypt (1892–1914): **III** 438 biog. n. 1, 438 n. 2

Abdul Aziz, Sultan of Turkey (1861–76): **III** 564 biog. n. 2

Abdul Aziz, Sultan of Morocco (1894–1908): **IV** 112 biog. n. 1, 329, 330 n. 2, 343, 347–9, 351–2, 355, 360–2, 364 n. 1, 365–7, 393, 400, 437 n. 4, 492 n. 4, 530 n. 1, 557 n. 1, 563

Abdul Hamid II, Sultan of Turkey (1876–1909): British negotiations, **III** 379, 385–6, 396, 398–9, 404, 407–8, 410–11, 430; **IV** 258–9, 262, 489, 515, 577; Armenian massacres, **III** 532–3, 544, 557–9, 563–7, 643; Crete, **IV** 26–7, 54; Young Turk Revolution, **IV** 545–8; miscellaneous, **III** 61–4, 68, 70, 153 n. 6, 162 n. 6, 172, 178, 193, 320, 391–2, 410–12, 414–15, 438 n. 2, 493; **IV** 6–7, 15, 69, 102, 116, 128, 149, 158–9, 164, 241, 251–2, 254, 266, 379–80, 461 n. 2, 493 n. 2, 535, 572 n.1

Abeken, Heinrich: **IV** 248 biog. n. 3

Aberdeen, Lord: **IV** 553–4

Abyssinia: **III** 206 n. 2, 309 n. 1, 318, 495 n. 1, 549, 553, 555, 597 n. 2, 599 n. 2; **IV** 65, 339

Adlerberg, Alexander, Count: **III** 179 biog. n. 9

Aehrenthal, Alois Lexa, Baron then Count von: **III** 286 biog. n. 1, 288, 450, 460; **IV** 137, 447, 456, 461, 463–6, 473–4, 487, 489, 494, 499, 515 n. 1, 535, 545, 562, 565, 567, 572, 577, 579, 581, 583 n. 3, 587, 598, 601, 603, 605 n. 1, 606 n. 5, 607–9, 612, 614–15, 618

Africa: **III** 121, 129–32, 136, 139 n. 4, 197, 244, 296, 339, 341–2, 344, 364 n. 3, 371–5, 410, 442, 474, 486, 494, 501, 547–8, 610–11, 644, 655; **IV** 71, 88 n. 3, 89, 160, 186 (*See also individual countries*)

Agliardi, Antonio, Cardinal: **III**, 184 biog. n. 2, 316 n. 5

Agrarians: **III** 500, 505–6, 519; **IV** 249, 266, 291, 493

Ahmed Risa: **IV** 565 biog. n. 3

Albania: **III** 202, 448, 564, 567, 588, 644; **IV** 38, 75, 103, 266, 284, 462, 536

Albedyll, General Emil von: **III** 125 biog. n. 2, 128–9, 159–60, 186 n. 8, 188–9, 190–1, 197, 218, 224, 267, 289, 291, 352; **IV** 433

Albert, King of Saxony (1873–1902): **III** 299 biog. n. 2, 356, 388, 475, 611–12, 627; **IV** 28

Albrecht, Archduke of Austria: **III** 210 biog. n. 1, 252, 312, 508 n. 2

Alexander I, Tsar of Russia (1801–25): **III** 553 n. 5; **IV** 116

Alexander II, Tsar of Russia (1855–81): **III** 43, 55 n. 2, 56, 195, 256, 294

Alexander III, Tsar of Russia (1881–94): Three Emperors' meeting, 1884 **III** 102–4, 123–4; Battenberg marriage, **III** 152–3, 174, 175 n. 4, 272; visit of Wilhelm II, 1888, **III** 280, 283–90, 293–4; trips, **III** 316 n. 5, 317 n. 4, 318–19, 326; miscellaneous, **III** 70, 81, 83–4, 88, 101 n. 4, 107, 109, 164, 165 n. 4, 169–70, 178, 194–6, 227, 228 n. 1, 238–9, 247–50, 256–7, 308–10, 316, 322, 326–8, 330–1, 349, 358 n. 1, 363–6, 387, 652 n. 3; **IV** 146, 473

Alexander I, King of Serbia (1889–1903): **III** 286 n. 2, 311

Alexander of Battenberg, Prince of Bulgaria (1879–86): **III** 88 biog. n. 2; marriage, **III** 147 n. 8, 149–54, 162, 166, 181, 188, 189–92, 215 n. 4, 271 n. 3, 272–3, 293; Bulgarian affairs, **III** 170–1, 192–3; Bulgaria's international role, **III** 158, 164–5, 167–8, 172 n. 2, 174–8

Alexander, Prince of Hesse: **III** 164 n. 2

Alexandra, Princess of Wales, then Queen of England: **III** 250, 292 biog. n. 2, 317, 659; **IV** 17

Alexandra Feodorovna, Tsarina of Russia, née Princess Alix of Hesse-Dramstadt: **III** 549 n. 2, 565; **IV** 1 n. 3

Alexei Alexandrovich, Grand Duke of Russia: **III** 284 biog. n. 2

Alexeiev, Admiral Eugene Ivanovich: **IV** 282 biog. n. 3, 283

Alfonso XII, King of Spain (1875–85): **III** 89–92, 154, 227

Alfonso XIII, King of Spain (1886–1931): **IV** 363, 365, 380 n. 4, 395

Algeria: **IV** 284, 347 n. 1, 361–2

Alsace-Lorraine: **III** 90–1, 99–100, 124–5, 146, 149, 197, 207, 226, 277, 368, 554; **IV** 381, 422, 428–9, 433–4, 495–7, 557, 563

Alten, General Karl von: **III** 129

Althoff, Friedrich: **III** 246 n. 3

Alvensleben, Friedrich Johann, Count von: **III** 67 n. 2, 332 biog. n. 6, 500; **IV** 288, 318–19, 357–8, 366, 444

Ampthill, Odo Russell, Lord: **III** 128 biog. n. 2

Ampthill, Lady Emily: **III** 223 biog. n. 4

Andrássy, Julius, Count: **III** 202 biog. n. 2, 212 n. 1, 308, 430; **IV** 462

Andrieux, Louis: **III** 73 biog. n. 5

Anethan, Baron von: **III** 488

Antoine, Jules Dominique: **III** 87 biog. n. 2

Aoki, Shuzo, Viscount: **IV** 202 biog. n. 2

Arabi, Ahmed: **III** 59 n. 4, 64

Arco-Valley, Emmerich, Count von und zu: **IV** 263 biog. n. 2

Arenberg, Franz Ludwig, Prince von: **III** 657 biog. n. 1; **IV** 272

Armenia: **III** 319, 410, 485 n. 1, 531–3, 534 n. 1, 535, 544, 549, 557–9, 563–7, 576, 580, 643–4, 655 n. 4

Arnim-Boitzenburg, Hermann, Count von: **III** 216 biog. n. 1; **IV** 270–1, 425

Arnim-Boitzenburg, Sofie Adelheid, Countess von: **III** 41 n. 7

Arnim-Kröchlendorff, Malwine von (née von Bismarck): **III** 41 biog. n. 6, 42, 45

Arnim-Suckow, Harry, Count von: **III** 30 biog. n. 2, 31–9, 41 n. 7 & 8, 44, 78, 456–8, 461–3, 466–74

Letter from, **III** 457–8

Arnim, Colonel: **III** 601, 610, 621

Ashburnham, Lord: **IV** 110

Ashinov: **III** 309

Asquith, Herbert Henry: **IV** 172 biog. n. 5, 593, 602

Auer, Ignaz: **IV** 190 biog. n. 6

Augusta, German Kaiserin (wife of Wilhelm I): **III** 191, 215–16

Auguste Victoria, German Kaiserin (wife of Wilhelm II): **III** 219 biog. n. 1, 317 n. 5, 319, 323, 661; **IV** 1 n. 3, 45 n. 1, 270

August Wilhelm, Prince of Prussia: **IV** 586 n. 2

Aumale, Henri, Duc d': **III** 269 biog. n. 3

Australia: **IV** 153, 156, 177

Austria-Hungary: breakup of, **IV** 445, 447, 461–3; Bosnian crisis, **IV** 577–9, 581–8, 590, 598–601, 603–9, 611–15, 617–19; Crete, **III** 632, 643; **IV** 17, 20, 35, 40, 54, 64–5; domestic affairs, **IV** 54–5, 101, 107, 445, 457, 609, 618; Eastern question, **III** 165–7, 171–7, 173, 176, 198, 269, 272–3, 285, 294, 321–2, 386, 426–30, 443, 447–50, 453, 459–60, 463–5, 468, 482–3, 486–7, 556–7, 559–60, 567, 580–2, 588–9, 591–2, 594, 665; **IV** 16, 48, 284, 379–80, 473–4, 489, 515, 535–6, 565; Far East, **III** 512; **IV** 57; France, **IV** 53; Germany, **III** 209–11, 233–6, 240–3, 246, 253–4, 298–9, 305, 308, 328, 338–9, 357–9, 364, 413 n. 2, 426–30, 478–9; **IV** 116, 118 n. 3, 248 n. 4, 421, 424, 438, 456–8, 464, 498, 556–7, 567, 581–3, 620–1; Great Britain, **III** 182, 187–8, 190, 192, 196, 404, 426–30, 447–65, 598, 617; **IV** 72–3, 77–8, 444–5, 457, 462–3, 487, 577; Hague Peace Conference, **IV** 124; Italy, **III** 62, 203, 252–3, 317, 319–20, 322 n. 3, 489, 572; **IV** 103–5, 221, 249–52, 276, 287, 324, 461, 494; Morocco, **IV** 329 n. 1, 401, 556–7, 562, 567; Portugal, **III** 367, 370; Russia, **III** 83–4, 93–4, 101, 109, 124, 132, 158, 166–8, 170, 192, 236, 239–43, 246–8, 293, 311–12, 378, 383–4, 452; **IV** 2–3, 8, 38–9, 54, 137, 278, 444–5; Three Emperors League, **III** 104, 124, 126–7, 312; Triple Alliance, **III** 62, 81, 198–204, 205–7, 373–6, 380, 573; **IV** 75, 251–2, 440–1, 443–5, 447, 464–6; miscellaneous, **III** 158, 194–6, 203, 245–6, 251–2, 254–5, 298 n. 2, 303–8, 312, 381–2, 535, 606; **IV** 5

Bacquehem, Olivier, Marquis von: **III** 303 biog. n. 1

Baden: **III** 314–16, 333, 345–6, 405, 627, 639; **IV** 11–12
Badeni, Kasimir Felix, Count von: **III** 579 biog. n. 1, 581–2; **IV** 55
Bagdad Railway: **IV** 174 n. 4, 175, 236
Baladzy: **IV** 267–8
Balfour, Arthur James, 1st Earl of: **IV** 65 biog. n. 5, 67–70, 73, 81, 84, 109, 111, 122, 128, 141, 142, 157, 169–71, 185–7, 206, 214, 256–7, 271, 274, 321, 377
Ballin, Albert: **IV** 234 biog. n. 3, 235, 424, 529, 622
Bánffy zu Losoncz, Desiderius, Count: **IV** 55 biog. n. 2
Barrère, Camille: **III** 132 biog. n. 4, 292; **IV** 246–7, 251–2, 259, 287, 340, 354, 375, 387, 389, 399–400, 435, 494, 587
Barrington, Sir Bernard: **IV** 231 biog. n. 3, 232
Barthélemy-Saint-Hilaire, Jules: **III** 55 biog. n. 3
Bassermann, Ernst: **IV** 465 biog. n. 2
Battenberg, Alexander: see Alexander, Prince of Bulgaria
Bavaria: **III** 53, 104, 163–4, 264–5, 271, 275–6, 314, 334–5, 339, 346, 361, 401, 406, 408, 477, 593, 595, 604 n. 3, 618 n. 1, 619–20, 622–3, 625–7, 629, 658; **IV** 11–12, 266 n. 14, 516, 527–8, 569
Bazaine, General: **III** 388 n. 1
Bear Island: **IV** 142–4
Beatrice, Princess: **III** 151 n. 1, 216 biog. n. 6, 217
Bebel, August: **IV** 190 biog. n. 4, 529
Beck-Rzikowsky, Friedrich, Baron von: **III** 233 biog. n. 4, 234–5, 245, 311–12, 580–2, 588, 591, 594
Beckmann, Albert: **III** 32 biog. n. 5, 34 n. 7, 35, 95–7, 123
Bedford, Francis Russell, 9th Duke of: **III** 63 biog. n. 3
Beit, Alfred: **IV** 552 biog. n. 4
Belgium: **III** 488; **IV** 160, 177, 318, 329 n. 1, 331, 356–8
Below-Rutzau, Gustav von: **IV** 612 biog. n. 1
Below-Schlatau, Paul von: **IV** 131 biog. n. 6
Benedek, General Ludwig August, Ritter von: **III** 248 biog. n. 2
Bennigsen (Journalist): **IV** 431
Benomar, Count: **III** 91 biog. n. 3

Berchem, Max, Count von: **III** 108 biog. n. 3, 145, 167, 169, 212–13, 314, 333, 346–7, 354, 401, 423 n. 3, 424; **IV** 96, 258
Berckheim, Baron de: **IV** 558
Beresford, Lord Charles: **IV** 115 biog. n. 5
Berger, Alfred, Baron von: **IV** 447 n. 6, 481, 519
Bergmann, Dr Ernst von: **III** 257–60, 262, 265–71
Berlepsch, Hans Hermann, Baron von: **III** 389 biog. n. 7
*Berliner Lokalanzeiger*: **IV** 289, 292, 343, 430, 480, 538, 576
*Berliner Neuste Nachrichten*: **III** 467–9, 623, 648, 650; **IV** 448, 544 n. 3, 558, 580, 581 n. 2, 598
*Berliner Tageblatt*: **III** 273; **IV** 400, 407, 436, 481, 506, 530, 566
Bernstein, Max: **IV** 498 biog. n. 5, 506, 514, 520, 528, 537–40, 543, 560
Bernstorff, August: **III** 12
Bernstorff, Johann, Count von: **IV** 409 biog. n. 5, 447
Bernuth: **III** 225 biog. n. 2
Berthelot, Marcelin: **III** 596 biog. n. 5
Bertie, Sir Francis: **IV** 93 biog. n. 1, 348
Bertole-Viale, Ettore: **III** 244 biog. n. 4
Beseler, Dr Maximilian von: **IV** 520 biog. n. 6, 524, 530–3, 540, 573, 576, 580, 582, 596, 605
Bethmann Hollweg, Theobald von; **IV** 453 biog. n. 6, 497, 555–6, 560
Betzold: **IV** 340 biog. n. 2, 343, 345, 353, 359, 370–4
Bihourd, Georges: **IV** 334 biog. n. 3, 338, 348, 354, 389, 394
Billot, Jean Baptiste: **III** 79 biog. n. 2, 82, 133
Bismarck-Schönhausen, Herbert, Count von: **III** ix, 26 biog. n. 2; career, **III** 108–9, 133–4, 143 n. 1, 146 n. 2, 155–6; Wilhelm II, **III** 298, 332; Friedrich III, **III** 258–60, 262, 265, 461; Battenberg marriage **III** 188–9, 191; St Petersburg trip, 1888, **III** 280, 282–8, 291–4; Holstein quarrel, **III** 333 n. 6, 461, 466, 467 n. 1, 469; after resignation, **III** 333, 337, 340–1, 345–6, 423 n. 2, 500, 506; Austria, **III** 204, 233–5, 241–2, 245, 253 n. 3, 298 n. 2, 304; Russia, **III** 214, 227–8, 237, 238 n. 1, 239 n. 2; Triple Alliance, **III** 200, 206–7; miscel-

laneous, **III** 27–8, 41, 43–4, 67, 90, 103, 106, 113, 115, 119–20, 125, 129, 130, 136–7, 140, 145, 150, 157, 166, 169 n. 3, 180, 193, 196, 211–14, 216–17, 225, 230, 232, 244, 246, 251, 261, 267–8, 270–1, 274–6, 278, 295–6, 299–301, 306, 320 n. 1, 326, 329 n. 3, 339, 413 n. 2, 491, 495, 505–6, 510, 519, 597; **IV** 1, 6, 20, 96, 103 n. 4, 129, 131 n. 4, 143, 156, 170, 175, 181, 269, 271, 430, 455

Letters to, **III** 70, 324–5, 333–4

Letters from, **III** 46–7, 49, 51–4, 56, 60–70, 72, 75–6, 85–7, 90–1, 101–4, 109, 113–14, 116–29, 131–2, 137–9, 143–4, 148–9, 161, 295–6, 300–1, 317–20, 334, 388

Bismarck-Schönhausen, Johanna, Princess von (née von Puttkamer) : **III** 8 biog. n. 1, 10, 17, 21–3, 41, 44, 51–2, 105, 114, 134–5, 143, 186, 215–16, 301

Letters from, **III** 103, 105, 106

Bismarck-Schönhausen, Marie, Countess von : see Rantzau

Bismarck-Schönhausen, Otto, Prince von : **III** biog. n. 1; Minister in St. Petersburg, **III** 3–13, 15, 17, 20–3, 29; character, **III** 40–3, 45–6; health, **III** 41, 46, 51–2, 255; relations with Holstein, **III** 48, 333–4, 337; Hatzfeldt, **III** 67–8, 91–2, 146, 155–8; Wilhelm I, **III** 51; Crown Prince and Princess, **III** 95, 147, 149, 159–61, 166, 179–81; Wilhelm II, **III** 169, 228–32, 299, 300–1, 313–15, 328–30, 332, 337; resignation, **III** 324–5, 328–30, 332–41, 343, 345, 347, 354; **IV** 476 n. 2, 502; after resignation, **III** 335, 346, 406, 413, 415, 423, 426–8, 434, 449, 478, 481, 485, 494, 497–8, 500–1, 503, 506, 508, 510, 519, 568, 573–5, 585, 589, 612, 650, 654–6, 660–1, 663–4; **IV** 10, 20, 72, 91, 271; attacks on regime of Wilhelm II, **III** 338, 341, 346 n. 1, 350, 379, 388, 402, 406, 413, 415, 419–21, 423, 449, 476, 500–1, 503, 514, 520, 656; Arnim case, **III** 31 n. 5, 32, 34–5, 36 n. 4, 37 n. 2, 38, 457, 461–2; Battenberg marriage, **III** 150–4, 181, 185–6, 188–92, 272–3; colonial policy, **III** 135; anti-revolutionary bill, **III** 477–8; Three Emperors meeting, 1884, **III** 102, 125–7, 132, 134–5; Triple Alliance, **III** 200–4, 206, 208; Austria, **III** 201, 203–4, 210, 233 n. 3,

234–5, 241, 253–5, 303–5, 312, 322, 392; Egypt, **III** 59–60, 64, 66, 68–9, 122–3, 139–40, 205; Great Britain, **III** 121, 172 n. 2; France, **III** 75–8, 85 n. 5, 86, 129, 190; Russia, **III** 55 n. 2, 56, 71–3, 85 n. 1, 86, 164, 165 n. 4, 167, 171 n. 3, 195–9, 210, 228, 237–9, 312, 316–17, 322, 326–8, 331, 338; Spain, **III** 91–2, 209; Switzerland, **III** 315–16; Press, **III** 389 n. 1, 477 n. 2, 589 n. 3, 650, 652 n. 2; miscellaneous, **III** 3, 50, 53–4, 83, 87, 89, 90–1, 99, 104–5, 107–8, 110, 113, 115, 117, 120, 125, 134–5, 141, 143, 147, 183–4, 188, 195, 207, 211–13, 216, 223–5, 244, 253, 255 n. 2, 260–8, 270–1, 273–6, 278–9, 286, 296, 301, 319, 335, 349, 353, 357, 373, 379, 387, 401, 459; **IV** 3, 96, 100, 103, 142–3, 167 n. 4, 187, 190, 248, 259, 276, 287, 439, 455, 462–3, 470, 473, 486, 583, 586 n. 1, 593, 607, 612;

Letters to, **III** 168, 186, 187

Letters from, **III** 164–5, 169–70, 187, 296–7

Bismarck-Schönhausen, Wilhelm, Count von (Bill) : **III** ix, 26 biog. n. 2, 27–8, 40–1, 43–4, 46, 102–4, 106, 126, 128, 137, 216, 333–4, 337, 339, 519, 520

Letters from, **III** 49, 118, 124, 125–6, 129–31, 133–5, 136–7, 139, 140, 212–13, 213–14, 224–5, 227–8, 329–30

Bissing, Moritz Ferdinand, Baron von : **III** 466, 467 n. 2, 468, 470 n. 4, 471 n. 1, 472 n. 1, 473; **IV** 89–90

Letters to, **III** 472; **IV** 94

Letters from, **III** 470–2; **IV** 90–1, 95

Björkö treaty : **IV** 357, 365

Blanc, Alberto, Baron di : **III** 208 biog. n. 4, 319, 320 n. 1, 459, 484, 485 n. 1, 486, 495, 543, 560, 572, 583 n. 3, 590, 600

Blaserna, Pietro : **III** 245 biog. n. 2, 298, 473; **IV** 48, 219

Letter to, **IV** 178–81

Letter from, **IV** 181–2

Blaze de Bury, Baroness : **III** 35 biog. n. 4

Bleichröder, Gerson : **III** x, 60 n. 2, 104 biog. n. 2, 105–7, 119, 128, 137, 142, 224, 313, 332, 458

Blokland, Beelaerts van : **IV** 13 biog. n. 4

Blowitz, Heinrich Opper von : **III** 78 biog. n. 5, 142

Blumenthal, General Leonhard von : **III** 355 biog. n. 2

Boer War : *see* South Africa
Böhlendorff-Kölpin, Karl von : **IV** 403
 biog. n. 1
Bojanowski : **III** 200 biog. n. 4
Bollhardt : **IV** 505 biog. n. 6
Borckenhagen, Captain : **III** 657
Boris, Crown Prince of Bulgaria : **III**
 591 n. 1; **IV** 572 n. 2
Borries, Georg von : **IV** 456 biog. n. 5
Bosnia : **III** 203, 312; **IV** 565, 577, 583,
 590, 609, 615, 621
Botha, General Louis : **IV** 266, 269
Bötticher, Karl Heinrich von : **III** 325
 biog. n. 7, 329, 330, 339, 418, 478,
 500, 561, 568, 573, 575, 621 n. 2, 623,
 653, 663; **IV** 42 n. 1, 43–5, 476
Boulanger, General Georges : **III** 226
 biog. n. 3, 251 n. 1, 276
Bourgeois, Léon : **III** 596 n. 1; **IV** 124
 biog. n. 5, 340, 400, 401, 410, 427
Bramann, Dr Fritz von : **III** 228 biog. n.
 2, 229–30, 258–60, 262, 266, 269
Brand, Adolf : **IV** 498 biog. n. 6, 502,
 528 n. 1
Brandenburg, Friedrich Wilhelm, Count
 von : **IV** 123 n. 3
Brandt, Maximilian von : **III** 42 biog. n.
 6, 511, 530, 531; **IV** 196, 214
 Letters to, **III** 362, 514, 516–17; **IV**
 176–8, 208, 327–8, 375, 376–8, 410–
 11, 449–50, 478, 513–14
 Letters from, **III** 514–15; **IV** 203–5
Brassey, Lord Thomas : **IV** 570 biog. n.
 7, 571
Bratianu, Joan : **III** 162 biog. n. 8, 321
Bray-Steinburg, Hippolyt, Count von :
 **III** 209 biog. n. 3
Brazza, Savorgnan de : **III** 79 biog.
 n. 8
Breteuil, Marquis de : **III** 250 biog. n. 2
Bright, John : **III** 63 biog. n. 1
Brincken, Egon, Baron von der : **III** x;
 **IV** 97 biog. n. 3
Brockdorff, Theresa, Countess von : **IV**
 229 biog. n. 3
Brockdorff-Rantzau, Ulrich, Count von :
 **IV** 567 n. 1
Broglie, Jacques, Duc de : **III** 98 biog.
 n. 1
Bronsart von Schellendorf, General
 Walter : **III** 492, 560 biog. n. 6, 561,
 568, 573, 575, 595, 610–11, 613–14,
 618, 620–22, 625, 627–8, 630, 633,
 635–6, 640–1, 645, 647–8, 653–4, 656
Bruck, Karl, Baron von : **III** 224 biog.
 n. 3, 244–5, 252–3, 318–19, 343, 397
 n. 1

Brühl, Hedwig, Countess von : **III** 218
 biog. n. 1, 223 n. 3, 258
 Letter from, **III** 218–19
Brunswick succession : **III** 73, 75, 262–
 3, 287, 292, 294
Bu Hamara : **IV** 347 n. 1, 349, 400
Buch, Leopold von : **IV** 597 biog. n. 4
Bucher, Lothar : **III** 41 biog. n. 3, 49,
 80–1
 Letter from, **III** 80
Bulgaria : **III** 86–9, 124 n. 2, 132, 150,
 152–4, 157 n. 4, 158, 162, 164–5, 167,
 170–8, 181–2, 184, 186–7, 192–5,
 199, 209, 239, 256, 269, 272–3, 285,
 293–4, 309, 319 n. 2, 320–1, 349, 450,
 453 n. 2, 557, 591, 594, 605, 644; **IV**
 38, 494, 572, 577–80, 585–7, 603,
 606–8, 611–12, 618
Bülow, Adolf von : **III** 113 biog. n. 1,
 115, 120, 148, 190, 473, 648
Bülow, Alfred von : **III** x, 83 biog. n. 1;
 **IV** 234
Bülow, Bernhard, Prince von : **III** x,
 xiv, 54 biog. n. 3; relations with
 Wilhelm II, **IV** 96–8, 183, 234–5,
 268–72, 370–1, 383 n. 2, 437–9,
 495, 594; Harden, **IV** 389–90, 452,
 455, 459, 464–5, 468–9, 477, 480–5,
 490–4, 498–9, 501–2, 505, 507, 509,
 513, 517–21, 524, 528, 530–3, 536–8,
 540–2, 544, 560–2, 564–5, 570, 573–
 5, 589, 591–2, 605, 622 n. 1; Holstein, **IV** 128–30, 178–81, 216, 244–8,
 269–71, 292–313, 315, 376–7, 379–
 85, 388, 405–9, 411–13, 416, 426,
 428, 433–4, 435 n. 5, 436–7, 440,
 447–9, 453–4, 466–7, 502–4, 525–8,
 533–5, 542, 545–6; Far East, **IV** 49–53,
 56, 59, 61 n. 3, 205, 213; France, **IV**
 268, 281–2, 286, 400; Great Britain, **IV**
 77, 80, 108, 114–18, 122, 148, 152–
 3, 155, 159 n. 2, 160–1, 167, 173,
 175, 215, 223, 232, 238, 244, 246–7,
 377–8, 457, 509–10, 550; Hague
 conferences, **IV** 126, n. 1, 127, 145;
 Morocco, **IV** 331, 334–5, 337, 340–2,
 346–50, 352, 355, 362 n. 1, 367–8,
 370–1, 375 n. 1, 376, 379–85, 393 n.
 3, 398, 404–5, 410; domestic affairs,
 **IV** 453–4, 456, 463, 467–8, 516, 525–
 6, 554–5, 565, 569; miscellaneous, **III**
 75–6, 119, 122–3, 148, 159, 179, 194–
 5, 288, 332, 384, 423 n. 3, 424, 448,
 455, 456 n. 1, 473 n. 1, 475, 483, 485,
 490 n. 1, 495, 500, 542, 551–2, 560,
 566 n. 1, 577–9, 582 n. 4, 583 n. 1,
 3, 4, 586 n. 5, 587, 598 n. 1, 618, 621

n. 2, 622 n. 1, 624, 629, 632 n. 1, 635, 642, 645, 649, 651; **IV** 42, 44–6, 68, 74, 76, 87, 90, 101, 123, 138, 140–1, 151, 184–5, 187–8, 194–5, 201, 203 n. 1, 206 n. 4, 208, 227–8, 249, 250, 267, 288 n. 3, 323, 386, 391, 435, 486–7

Letters to, **III** 479–80, 491–2, 496–7, 499–502, 548–50, 568, 573–4, 604–6; **IV** 13–14, 18–20, 37–9, 43, 66–7, 70–4, 96–8, 130–2, 134–5, 142–4, 189–91, 216–18, 234–7, 252–4, 275–7, 289–92, 299, 300, 305, 307–11, 316–17, 319–20, 326, 344, 346, 356–8, 373–4, 379–86, 395, 401–3, 405–8, 412, 441–2, 446–7, 452–3, 461, 465–6, 487–90, 495–6, 499, 504–5, 515–16, 523, 529, 547–50, 552–3, 555–8, 560–1, 566–9, 570–1, 576–84, 586–91, 595–600, 602–8, 613, 615–18, 620–1

Letters from, **III** 54–58, 74, 77–9, 81–3, 87, 93, 97–100, 106, 110–16, 119–20, 145–6, 236–40, 246–51, 255–7, 320–2, 432–3, 449–51, 458–61, 473, 490, 497, 508–9, 548, 550–4, 582–3, 586–7, 590, 598–9, 603–4, 617–18, 621–2, 631–2; **IV** 48, 56–8, 62–3, 65–6, 85, 130, 167–8, 170–1, 178, 182, 193, 201, 219, 224–5, 235–6, 260–2, 265–6, 274–5, 277, 291–2, 293, 300–2, 307–8, 310–11, 316–19, 321–4, 328, 368–70, 383, 385 396–7, 400, 403, 408, 441, 461, 494–8, 501, 523, 529–30, 545–6, 551, 553–5, 559, 565, 571–3, 580, 585–6, 591–5, 600–1, 603–5, 608–10, 613–18

Bülow, Bernhard Ernst von: **III** 31 biog. n..1, 42, 46, 67 n. 2, 68, 105; **IV** 259

Letters from, **III** 31, 36, 38–9

Bülow, Hans Adolf von: **IV** 359 biog. n. 1

Memorandum from, **IV** 358–9

Bülow, Karl Ulrich von: **IV** 408 n. 6, 411 biog. n. 2, 542, 615

Letter from, **IV** 411

Bülow, Marie von (née Princess Camporeale): **III** 111 biog. n. 1, 112–13, 115–16, 120, 148, 384, 432, 451, 473, 590; **IV** 14, 42, 48, 302, 306, 307, 321, 409, 439, 441, 445

Letters to, **IV** 292, 294–5

Letters from, **IV** 294, 427

Bülow, Otto von: **III** x, 34, 42, 67 n. 2, 70 biog. n. 1, 127, 310, 462

Letter from, **III** 84–5

Burian, Stefan von: **III** 285 biog. n. 3, 594

Busch, Klemens: **III** 48 biog. n. 1, 50, 54, 86, 87 n. 1, 104, 130 n. 4, 132, 136, 139, 144, 167

Letter to, **III** 48

Letters from, **III** 57, 59, 210

Bussche-Haddenhausen, Hilmar, Baron von dem: **IV** 374 biog. n. 3

Calice, Heinrich, Baron von: **III** 452 n. 1, 563 biog. n. 2, 564; **IV** 40, 473

Cambon, Jules: **I** 192 biog. n. 1; **IV** 265, 340, 351, 378, 464, 487–8, 492–3, 533, 536, 590, 618

Cambon, Paul: **III** 226 biog. n. 1, 394–5, 492; **IV** 233, 378

Cameron, Sir Ewen: **IV** 118 biog. n. 1

Camesasca: **III** 618 n. 1

Campbell-Bannerman, Sir Henry: **IV** 172 biog. n. 3, 377 n. 1, 463, 469, 598

Canovas de Castillo, Antonio: **III** 154 biog. n. 6

Caprivi, Leo, Count von: **III** 124 biog. n. 8; opinions of, **III** 333 , 335–6, 340, 342–3, 346–7, 352, 354, 359, 362, 383, 461–2; domestic policies, **III** 340, 357, 384, 402, 405–6, 408–9, 416–23; anti-revolutionary bill, **III** 475–6, 478–81, 498, 502, 508, 586, 598; resignation, **III** 473, 475–6, 478–81; Austria, **III** 338, 359, 382, 392, 450 n. 4; Britain, **III** 435; France **III** 387; Italy, **III** 342–3, 358–60, 380; Russia, **III** 358, 360; miscellaneous, **III** 53 n. 7, 126, 136–7, 203, 230, 261, 263–4, 267–8, 332, 333 n. 6, 337, 339, 348, 355–6, 361, 379, 388–9, 402 n. 2, 413 n. 2, 415, 423 n. 2, 429, 438–9, 455, 456 n. 3, 468, 473 n. 1; **IV** 127, 235 n. 1, 525, 616

Letters to, **III** 348–52, 419–20

Letters from, **III** 135–6, 399–400, 515

Carlos, Crown Prince, then King of Portugal (1889–1908): **III** 147 n. 7, 364

Carlos, Pretender to the Spanish throne: **IV** 110 biog. n. 3

Carnot, Sadi: **III** 385 biog. n. 2, 475 n. 1; **IV** 191

Caro, Lionel: **IV** 533

Carol I, Prince, then King of Rumania (1866–1914): **III** 162 n. 5, 320, 321

Carolath, Elizabeth, Princess (née Countess Hatzfeldt-Trachenberg): **III** 43 biog. n. 3

Caroline Islands: **III** 154, 183, 208, 342; **IV** 79 n. 6, 89, 115

Casimir-Périer, Jean Paul : **III** 474 biog. n. 2, 491 n. 6

Cassini, Count : **III** 524 biog. n. 3, 524 n. 2

Castell-Rüdenhausen :
Letter to, **IV** 103–6

Castellane, Dolly : **IV** 573

Catherine II, Tsarina of Russia (1762–96) : **III** 256, 553 n. 4

Catholic Church : **III** 33, 51, 57, 82, 111–12, 183–5, 238, 264 n. 3, 300–2, 572 ; **IV** 45–6, 249, 473, 495

Cavour, Camillo, Count di : **IV** 105 biog. n. 2

Centre Party : **III** 57, 58, 73, 93, 185, 324, 400–2, 405–6, 409, 422, 498–500, 503, 623, 654 ; **IV** 18, 27, 46–7, 167, 249, 266 n. 4, 271, 452–4, 456–7, 490 n. 2, 498, 509, 525–7, 615–17

Challemel-Lacour, Paul : **III** 81 biog. n. 2, 85, 96

Chamberlain, Joseph : **III** 63 biog. n. 2, 121, 136–7, 421–2, 599, 603–4, 617 ; **IV** 29–30, 64–5, 67–72, 75, 78–9, 83–4, 86, 109, 111, 113, 116–18, 120, 122, 139, 148–9, 151, 157–63, 165, 169–70, 173, 185, 187, 206, 214, 236–40, 243–4, 252–3, 256–7, 262–3, 269, 271, 273, 382
Letter from, **IV** 118
Letter to, **IV** 119

Chambers, Judge : **IV** 142 n. 2

Chambord, Count of : **III** 73 biog. n. 1, 75, 78, 82

Chaplin, Henry, Viscount : **III** 65 biog. n. 4 ; **IV** 87, 169

Charikov, N. W. : **IV** 7 biog. n. 3, 515–16, 585

Charlotte, Princess of Sachsen-Meiningen (née Princess of Prussia) : **III** 232 biog. n. 3, 233 ; **IV** 499

Charmes, Francis : **III** 98–100, 142

Chelius, Major Oskar von : **IV** 285 biog. n. 1

Chéradame, André : **IV** 444 biog. n. 3, 462

Cherevin : **III** 317 biog. n. 3, 326

Chérisey, Count : **IV** 330 biog. n. 2

China : Anglo-Russian railway agreement, 1899, **IV** 107, 115–17, 149 ; Boxer question, **IV** 187–9, 193–215, 217–24, 232 ; France, **III** 79, 81–2, 87, 95–8, 144, 226 ; German search for naval base, **IV** 4–5, 22–4, 33, 36–7, 48–53, 83, 88, 253, 262, 287 n. 3 ; Great Britain, **IV** 30, 64–5, 67, 71–3, 98, 107, 110, 115, 164, 257, 277 ;

Kiaochow, **IV** 55, 57–61, 64, 68–9, 99, 131, 144, 239, 245, 383, 433–4 ; rivalry of Powers, **IV** 255, 263–4, 271–2, 325 ; Russia, **IV** 32, 62, 78 n. 2, 138, 150, 184–6 ; Russo-Japanese war, **IV** 277–9, 282, 325–7, 340 n. 4 ; Sino-Japanese war and Chinese loan, **III** 495, 506–8, 510–33, 536–7, 539–41, 545–6 ; **IV** 105, 150, 204 ; United States, **IV** 92–3 ; miscellaneous, **III** 393 n. 2, 522–5, 547, 659, 662

Ching, Prince : **IV** 202 biog. n. 6, 204–5

Chirol, Valentine : **III** xiv, 421 biog. n. 4, 481–2 ; **IV** 160, 165, 257, 584–5
Letters to, **IV** 239–41
Letters from, **III** 421–2, 521–6 ; **IV** 237–8, 242–3, 246–7

Christian IX, King of Denmark (1863–1906) : **III** 340 n. 1 ; **IV** 324, 396 n. 2

Churchill, Lord Randolph : **III** 196, 206, 250, 341

Clarence, Albert Victor, Duke of : **III** 398 n. 4

Clemenceau, Georges : **III** 98 biog. n. 5, 142, 251, 488 ; **IV** 363, 427–8, 442–3, 491, 493, 536, 562, 568, 591

Clermont-Tonnerre, Count : **IV** 177

Coerper : **IV** 317 biog. n. 6

Cohen, Dr Eduard : **III** 51 biog. n. 2

Connaught, Arthur, Duke of : **III** 538 biog. n. 4 ; **IV** 119, 217

Conservatives (Germany) : **III** 54, 75, 131, 141, 324, 337, 357, 400, 402, 406, 409, 415–16, 423 n. 1, 500, 505, 656–7 ; **IV** 28, 266, 425, 498, 518, 526, 595–7, 614–17

Constans, Jean Ernest : **IV** 586 biog. n. 7

Constantine, Crown Prince of Greece : **III** 319 n. 3, 643

Constantine, Grand Duke of Russia : **IV** 7

Cornély, Jean Joseph : **IV** 427 biog. n. 3

Corti, Luigi, Count : **III** 204 biog. n. 3, 205 n. 1 ; **IV** 103

Costaki Anthropulo Pasha : **IV** 15 n. 4, 26

Courcel, Alphonse, Baron de : **III** 123 n. 1, 129–30, 544, 566, 596–7, 600, 601, 605–6, 617 ; **IV** 22, 26, 99, 141, 287, 336, 396–400

Cowper, Earl : **III** 62 biog. n. 3

Crailsheim, Christoph Krafft, Baron then Count von : **III** 264 biog. n. 4, 275, 335, 361, 402

Crete : **III** 320, 349, 414–15, 632, 643–4, 645 n. 1 ; **IV** 15–17, 22, 27, 32, 35, 37–41, 47, 54, 62–5, 67, 69, 578, 609

629

Crispi, Francesco : **III** 214, 224 biog. n. 2, 228, 244, 252–3, 300, 302, 317–20, 342–3, 348–51, 358–60, 362, 365, 448, 451, 459, 489, 549, 551, 583 n. 3, 590, 600; **IV** 103–5, 461

Cromer, Sir Evelyn Baring, Earl of : **III** 434 n. 2, 601 biog. n. 3, 607

Cronje, General Piet Arnoldus : **IV** 185

Croy-Dülmen, Georg, Prince von : **III** 12 biog. n. 1, 13, 15, 16, 20–2

Cucchi, Francesco : **IV** 103

Cumberland : see Ernst August, Duke of

Currie, Sir Philip : **III** 377, 426 biog. n. 1, 442, 443 n. 1, 444–5, 452–3, 482, 492, 562; **IV** 15, 109, 262

Curtius, Dr Friedrich : **IV** 448 n. 1, 451

Curzon, Lord : **IV** 128–9

*Daily Telegraph* affair : **IV** 591–5, 601, 615

Damiani : **III** 244 biog. n. 1, 318–19, 343

Dardanelles : **III** 203, 385–6, 424 n. 4, 425–30, 443, 447–53, 459–60, 463–5, 467 n. 3, 468, 482–7, 493, 547, 549–52, 555–60, 576, 580–2, 585, 588–92, 594, 605–6, 664–5; **IV** 9, 15, 32, 39, 71, 75, 116, 128, 136, 142, 144, 149, 161–2, 164, 267, 487, 579–80, 583, 585, 587–8, 599, 604

Dasbach, Georg : **IV** 477 biog. n. 6

David, Pascal : **IV** 415 biog. n. 2
   Letters to, **IV** 415–16, 424–6, 428–9, 431–2, 432–5, 436, 448–9
   Letters from, **IV** 421–2, 432, 450–1

Davis : **IV** 187

Decazes, Duc de : **III** 35 biog. n. 6

Deines, Major Adolf von : **III** 235 biog. n. 2, 236, 240, 242, 246, 254, 311, 389

Delagoa Bay : **III** 494 n. 1; **IV** 21–2, 24–5, 29, 33, 62, 88 n. 3, 98–9, 111, 158, 173–4, 184–5, 215. *See also* Transvaal

Delarey, General Jacobus Hercules : **IV** 269

Delbrück, Professor Dr Hans : **III** 473; **IV** 436 biog. n. 2

Delcassé, Théophile : **III** 474 biog. n. 4; German relations, **IV** 277, 312 n. 1, 325, 489, 536; Russia, **IV** 278, 314, 377; Morocco, **IV** 279, 328, 330 n. 2, 333–43, 346, 348, 350–6, 363, 365–6, 371–2, 375, 387, 394, 398, 549; miscellaneous, **IV** 147–9, 174, 184, 262–4, 266–7, 274, 404, 405 n. 1, 462

Delianov, Rudolf : **III** 256 biog. n. 1

Denmark : **III** 287, 291, 294–5, 317; **IV** 177, 283 n. 3, 288, 319, 325, 356, 377

Derby, Earl of : **III** 121 n. 3, 137 biog. n. 2

Derenthall, Eduard von : **III** x, 213 biog. n. 1; **IV** 96, 158, 457

Dernburg, Bernhard : **IV** 446 biog. n. 1, 522, 525–7

Déroulède, Paul : **III** 100 biog. n. 1, 368

Develle, Jules-Paul : **III** 440 biog. n. 3

Devonshire, Duke of : **III** 165 biog. n. 3; **IV** 122, 169–70, 206, 214, 220

Devonshire, Duchess of : **IV** 223

DeWet, General Christian Rudolf : **IV** 269

Deym, Franz, Count : **III** 404 biog. n. 3, 405, 459 n. 3, 460, 463–5, 556–8, 566–7, 572 n. 1, 597, 607, 664–5; **IV** 26, 79, 223

Diederichs, Admiral Otto von : **IV** 49, 51, 245

Diedrichs, Captain : **III** 603

Dietze-Barby, G. A. von : **III** 40 biog. n. 5

Dilke, Sir Charles : **III** 54 biog. n. 6, 61, 63–4, 68–9, 341, 460

Disarmament : **IV** 427, 429, 453, 456, 458, 465–7, 469, 472–3, 487, 553

Disraeli, Benjamin : **III** 61 biog. n. 5

Djevad Pasha : **III** 386 n. 2

Dockhorn : **III** 36 n. 4, 38–9

Dohme, Robert : **III** 232 biog. n. 4

Dohna-Schlobitten, Richard, Prince von : **IV** 541 biog. n. 3

Dokturov, General : **III** 247

Dolgoruki, Nicholas, Prince : **III** 102 biog. n. 2, 103–4, 107, 175–6, 238

Dönhoff, Countess Marie : see Marie von Bülow

Dönhoff-Friedrichstein, August, Count von : **III** 30 biog. n. 6, 461, 499

Douvier : **IV** 380 n. 6

Dragomirov, General Michael Ivanovich : **III** 247

Dreyfus, Captain Alfred : **III** 480, 488; **IV** 519

Duff, Alexander William George, Duke of Fife : **III** 341 biog. n. 2

Dufferin and Ava, Frederick Blackwood, Marquis of : **III** 64 biog. n. 4, 128, 378 n. 1, 390, 440, 585

Dumas, Captain : **IV** 488

Dunajewski, Dr J. von : **III** 303 biog. n. 2

Dupuy, Jean : **III** 474 biog. n. 6; **IV** 345–7, 350–3, 359–61, 363–4, 368, 372, 380 n. 6, 390, 393–4, 399–400, 420

Durnov, Marie: **III** 288 biog. n. 2
Durnovo, Ivan Nicholaievich: **III** 310 biog. n. 2

Eberstein: **IV** 525
Eckardstein, Hermann, Baron von: **IV** 113 biog. n. 4, 117, 147–8, 157–8, 160–2, 164, 183, 185–6, 216, 222–3, 225–30, 233, 245, 260, 262–3, 265, 269–70, 274–5, 317
Letters to, **IV** 118, 219
Letters from, **IV** 119, 146, 168–70, 171–4, 175, 219, 231–2
Eckardt, Felix von: **IV** 505 biog. n. 2, 506, 517
Edward, Prince of Wales, then King Edward VII of England (1901–10): **III** 65, 68, 119, 137, 219, 292, 317, 347, 398 n. 4, 538; **IV** 87, 129, 146–7, 160, 167–8, 195 n. 7, 196 n. 1, 212, 217–18, 227–31, 236, 240–1, 269, 271, 289 n. 3, 291–2, 323, 364–5, 382, 405 n. 1, 409–10, 421, 427, 442–3, 457, 459, 467, 469, 486, 488, 491, 549–51, 557, 561–2, 567, 578–9, 584, 621
Egloffstein: **IV** 456
Egypt: **III** 54, 59–66, 68–70, 74, 98–9, 119, 121–3, 129 n. 2, 130, 139, 140, 144, 182, 188, 190, 193, 197, 205 n. 2, 372–6, 386, 396–9, 404, 407, 410–12, 430, 434 n. 2, 438, 442, 549, 596, 599–603, 605–8, 615–16, 644, 664; **IV** 15, 30–1, 69, 75, 98, 100, 103, 141, 234, 284, 291, 462, 554, 565, 577 n. 2
Einem, General Karl von: **IV** 542 biog. n. 5, 543, 569
Eisenberg, Dr Max: **IV** 564 biog. n. 2
Eisendecher, Karl von: **III** 24 biog. n. 3, 313 n. 2, 314 n. 3, 315 n. 1, 316 n. 1 & 2, 664; **IV** 147
Letters to, **III** 24–6, 27–8, 30, 40–2, 43–5, 46–7, 49, 109, 313–16, 332, 337, 347–8; **IV** 426
Letters from, **III** 332–3, 345–6
Elbe, Lili von: **IV** 458 biog. n. 1, 484, 506, 507 n. 3, 519, 564
Elena, Queen of Italy: **IV** 38 n. 1
Elizabeth, Kaiserin of Austria: **III** 210
Engelbrecht, Karl von: **III** 245 biog. n. 1, 252, 362, 473, 599, 601; **IV** 44
Ephrussi, Mme: **III** 107
Erlanger, Baron Emil: **III** 35 biog. n. 5
Ernst, Jakob: **IV** 528 n. 1, 530 n. 6, 537 n. 2, 538 biog. n. 10, 539–41, 563, 575, 593
Ernst I, Duke of Sachsen-Altenburg (1853–1908): **III** 612 biog. n. 2

Ernst II, Duke of Sachsen-Altenburg (1908–11): **III** 612 n. 2
Ernst August, Duke of Cumberland and Brunswick: **III** 73 biog. n. 2, 75, 287, 292–4
Esternaux, Ernst: **IV** 234 biog. n. 4, 260
Estournelles de Constant: **IV** 410 biog. n. 5, 427
Etienne, Eugène: **IV** 345 biog. n. 5, 488–9, 493, 529
Euan-Smith, Sir Charles: **III** 375 biog. n. 1
Eulenburg, Alexandrine, Countess zu: **III** 487 biog. n. 1
Eulenburg, August, Count zu: **III** 157 biog. n. 2, 161, 271, 492, 506, 649, 652; **IV** 90, 513
Eulenburg, Botho, Count zu: **III** 53 biog. n. 7, 90, 225, 408–9, 421, 423, 475–6, 478–80, 506, 589, 621, 624, 629, 642, 645, 653; **IV** 12–13
Eulenburg, Friedrich Albert, Count zu: **III** 53 n. 7, 90
Eulenburg, Friedrich Botho zu: **IV** 74 n. 2, 524 biog. n. 4
Eulenburg, Philipp, Count, then Prince zu: **III** 163 biog. n. 1; Wilhelm II, **III** 300, 346–7, 468 n. 1, 476 n. 1 & 2, 646; **IV** 128, 242, 252, 255, 397, 411, 454, 560; Holstein, **III** 432, 456 n. 4, 469 n. 1 & 3, 470 n. 1 & 4; **IV** 181, 414–20, 432, 447, 449, 478, 502–4, 596; Harden, **IV** 446–7, 452, 458 n. 1, 459–60, 464, 467, 470, 472 n. 1, 477, 479–80, 482–4, 491, 499, 500, 505, 508–9, 513–14, 517–24, 528, 530–3, 535–44, 562–5, 569, 573–7, 580–2, 589, 592, 605, 622; Austria, **III** 449–50, 455, 461, 478–9, 482–3, 489 n. 3 & 4, 490–1, 510, 535, 542, 558 n. 4 & 5, 559, 572 n. 1, 567 n. 1, 592 n. 1; Far East, **III** 536–7; German domestic politics, **III** 497–8, 500, 568–70, 574, 583, 586, 589 n. 2, 590, 598–9, 603–4; military courts-martial question, **III** 609 n. 3, 613 n. 1, 614 n. 2 & 3, 615 n. 2 & 3, 617–18, 621–3, 626, 630 n. 2, 631–42, 645, 647 n. 1, 649; miscellaneous, **III** 264 n. 3, 352 n. 2, 361 n. 2 & 3, 389 n. 1, 400 n. 3 & 4, 405 n. 1, 417–19, 421 n. 2, 447, 451 n. 1, 462, 473, 480 n. 3, 487 n. 3, 531, 548, 550, 553–4, 566 n. 1, 582, 608 n. 6, 609 n. 3, 656 n. 1, 660 n. 1, 662 n. 4 & 5, 664 n. 3; **IV** 192
Letters to, **III** 468–9, 576–8, 592–4, 610–13, 624–6, 628–9, 647–8, 650,

651–60, 662–5; **IV** 9–13, 89–90, 193, 419

Letters from, **III** 163–4, 168, 251, 264–5, 271, 274–6, 307, 334–6, 338–40, 352–4, 361, 388–9, 400–3, 405–6, 408–9, 421–4, 469–70, 475–8, 487, 489, 490–1, 498–9, 502–6, 509–12, 541–2, 551–2, 568–75, 578–82, 587–92, 594–5, 608–10, 613–15, 618–21, 623–4, 627, 630, 642, 650–1; **IV** 2, 8–9, 14, 16, 20–1, 28, 42, 53–4, 74, 100–1, 107, 174, 192, 420

Eulenburg, Wendt, Count zu : **III** 41 n. 5

Fabrice, General Alfred, Baron then Count von : **III** 29

Fabrice, Oswald von : **III** 27 n. 2, 163

Fashoda incident : **IV** 99

Faure, Felix : **III** 511 biog. n. 2, 521, 524 n. 2; **IV** 47

Fehleisen, Konstantin von : **III** 7 biog. n. 1, 8, 17

Feldmann, General : **III** 247

Ferdinand, Prince, then King of Bulgaria (1887–1909) : **III** 269, 285, 319 n. 2, 321, 591 n. 1, 594; **IV** 572 n. 1, 611–12

Ferid Pasha : **IV** 548 biog. n. 2

Ferrero, General : **III** 543 biog. n. 3, 597, 600; **IV** 26

Ferry, Jules : **III** 79 biog. n. 5, 96, 98 122, 137–42, 226

Fischer, Dr Franz : **III** 334 biog. n. 2, 335, 475; **IV** 96, 244, 415, 422, 424–5, 431–2

Fisher, Sir John Arbuthnot : **IV** 488 biog. n. 4

Fleck : **III** 325 biog. n. 4

Fleet question : see Navy (German)

Fleischer, Dr Richard : **IV** 448 biog. n. 4

Floquet, Charles : **III** 251 biog. n. 1

Flotow, Hans von : **IV** 332 biog. n. 1, 364, 437, 501, 579

Letter from, **IV** 376

Forckenbeck, Max von : **III** 357 biog. n. 1, 360

Ford, Sir Francis Clare : **III** 407 biog. n. 2, 415

Formosa : **III** 508, 510 n. 4, 514, 525

Forster, William Edward : **III** 62 biog. n. 4

Forstner, Colonel von : **III** 245, 253

Fortis, Alessandro : **IV** 330 biog. n. 3

France : Africa, **III** 129–30; Armenia, **III** 563–4, 566; Bosnian crisis, **IV** 577, 583, 586–7, 590–1, 600, 604, 608–9, 617–18, 620; Catholic Church, **III** 82, 183–4; Crete, **III** 632; **IV** 17, 54, 64; domestic affairs, **III** 57, 73–9, 82, 87, 474, 480, 488, 596 n. 1; **IV** 329, 398–9; Eastern question, **III** 429, 467 n. 3, 484, 486, 560, 664–5; **IV** 14 n. 2, 39, 48, 116, 138, 266, 284, 535–6; Egypt, **III** 59–62, 64–6, 70, 74, 122, 130, 139, 144, 182, 188, 190, 193, 197, 411–12, 599–601, 605–7, 616; Far East, **III** 79, 81–2, 87, 95–8, 131, 144, 393, 434 n. 4, 435–7, 440, 443, 446; **IV** 57–9, 61, 194, 197, 202, 214, 221 n. 5, 224, 255, 279, 313, 315, 326; Germany, **III** 75–6, 85–6, 99–100, 122–3, 129, 131, 133–4, 137–8, 140–2, 187, 192, 196–7, 204, 210, 226, 276–7, 296, 344, 368–70, 384–5, 387, 474, 491–2, 543, 550; **IV** 3, 10, 26, 77, 89, 141, 150–1, 168, 198, 214, 232, 263–4, 267–8, 280–2, 284–6, 288–9, 306, 321, 323, 336–7, 377, 410–11, 420, 424, 427, 434, 438, 442–3, 457, 487–93, 496–7, 529–30, 533–4, 551, 565; Great Britain, **III** 60, 66, 70, 74, 81, 98–9, 133, 142, 171, 342, n. 2, 344, 390, 410, 425–6, 443, 445, 474, 544, 596; **IV** 15, 27, 29, 31–2, 41, 51, 56, 66, 69, 71, 72, 78, 79, 81, 92–3, 99, 110, 128, 138, 149, 169–71, 188, 223, 257–9, 261–5, 267, 274–6, 288, 291, 381, 444, 449, 490, 584; Hague Peace Conference, **IV** 124; Italy, **III** 253 n. 1, 318, 348–9, 474, 549; **IV** 103–6, 220–1, 246–52, 254, 256, 262, 266, 269, 324, 443, 461–2, 494, 498; Morocco, **IV** 274, 328–43, 345–76, 378, 380–1, 386–7, 390, 393–4, 398–401, 403, 405, 491, 515–16, 534, 548–9, 556–63, 566–7, 571–2; Portugal, **III** 365–7, 372–6; Russia, **III** 55–6, 81–2, 194–5, 238–9, 247, 249–51, 278, 306, 387, 423, 437–8, 443, 605–6, 655 n. 3; **IV** 23–4, 52–3, 62–3, 67, 75–6, 147, 161, 165–7, 184, 196, 199–200, 213, 217, 277–8, 280, 312, 314, 326–8, 486; Sino-Japanese war, **III** 495, 507, 510–18, 520–1, 523–31, 533, 535–6, 541, 545–6; Spain, **III** 91–2; Tuat, **III** 391–2, 394, 396–7; miscellaneous, **III** 54, 220, 300, 339, 342, 363, 532 n. 4, 553, 556, 583 n. 2, 585, 617; **IV** 9, 112, 177, 191

Fränkel, Dr Bernhard : **IV** 331 biog. n. 8

Frankfurt, Treaty of : **III** 368, 616; **IV** 1, 381, 427–8, 434, 442, 491, 529, 534, 536

*Frankfurter Zeitung:* **III** 461 n. 3; **IV** 77–8, 165, 402 n. 2, 429, 432 n. 7, 435 n. 4, 437 n. 1, 471, 525, 551, 589, n. 6, 598

Frantzius : **IV** 127

Franz Ferdinand, Archduke of Austria : **III** 210, 307 n. 1 308, 364; **IV** 466, 494, 581, 584

Franz Joseph, Kaiser of Austria (1848–1916) : Eastern question, **III** 450, 460, 556, 559, 579, 581–2; **IV** 601, 610, 615; domestic affairs, **IV** 2, 54–5, 101, 444–5, 457, 463; Russia, **III** 246, 252–4; **IV** 38 n. 3, 54; Three Emperors meetings, **III** 102–4, 109, 123–4, 149, 161, 210–12, 298 n. 2, 299, 303–5, 312, 322, 339, 357 n. 2, 359, 363, 413 n. 2, 450, 479, 503, 592 n. 1; Triple Alliance, **III** 199, 201–2, 204; **IV** 473–4, 494; Wilhelm II, **III** 169 n. 2, 170; miscellaneous, **IV** 487 n. 3, 497–8, 528

Fredericks, General : **III** 238 biog. n. 4

Frerichs, Dr Friedrich Theodor : **III** 12 biog. n. 6

Frey, Dr Ludwig : **IV** 564

Freycinet, Charles de : **III** 61 n. 1, 64 n. 7, 65 biog. n. 5, 66, 79, 82, 142, 183, 190, 193, 195; **IV** 343

Friedberg, Heinrich von : **III** 161 biog. n. 3, 260, 532

Friedrich **III**, German Crown Prince, then Kaiser (1888) : Battenberg marriage, **III** 154 n. 1, 162, 164–5, 168, 179–81, 189, 190–1, 271 n. 3, 272; health, **III** 147, 212–20, 227–30, 257–60, 262–5, 267–71, 275, 278 n. 2, 282; Seckendorff, **III** 218–19, 221–3; miscellaneous, **III** 90, 94–5, 102–3, 125, 136, 145, 147, 149, 155–6, 159–60, 192, 214–15, 231–2, 261, 266, 276, 286, 638; **IV** 83

Letter to, **III** 169–70

Friedrich, Kaiserin : see Victoria, German Crown Princess

Friedrich I, Grand Duke of Baden (1856–1907) : **III** 108 biog. n. 2; influence on Wilhelm II, **III** 313 n. 2, 333, 337, 339, 480 n. 2; miscellaneous, **III** 257, 314–15, 345–6, 348, 627, 639; **IV** 11, 396

Friedrich II, Grand Duke of Baden (1907–18) : **III** 346 biog. n. 2, 348

Friedrich August III, King of Saxony (1904–18) : **IV** 593

Friedrich Franz II, Grand Duke of Mecklenburg-Schwerin (1842–83) : **III** 345 biog. n. 3

Friedrich Heinrich, Prince of Prussia : **IV** 456 biog. n. 4, 522

Friedrich Wilhelm IV, King of Prussia (1840–61) : **III** 3 n. 6, 484 n. 1; **IV** 248 n. 4, 548, 597 n. 2, 606

Frommel, Emil : **III** 503 biog. n. 1

Fürstenberg, Maximilian Egon, Prince zu : **IV** 510 biog. n. 7, 535

Gabriel, Dr : **III** 418 biog. n. 1

Gaillard, H. : **IV** 338 biog. n. 4, 365

Galimberti, Luigi : **III** 238 biog. n. 5

Galitzin, Jean : **III** 284 biog. n. 4

Galliffet, Gaston, Marquis de : **III** 79 biog. n. 1; **IV** 372

Galster, Vice Admiral Karl : **IV** 551 biog. n. 2, 571–2

Gambetta, Captain Juinot : **IV** 350

Gambetta, Léon : **III** 54 biog. n. 4, 55–7, 60, 64 n. 7, 65, 75, 77, 79, 81, 98–9; **IV** 3, 9

Garashanin, Milutin : **III** 311 biog. n. 1

Gasnier : **III** 296 n. 3 & 4

Geffcken, Dr Heinrich : **III** 296 biog. n. 1, 297

Gemmingen, Baroness : **IV** 606

Georg, Prince, then King of Saxony (1902–1904) : **IV** 11

Georg, Duke of Mecklenburg-Strelitz : **III** 5 biog. n. 1, 17

George I, King of Greece (1863–1913) : **IV** 16–17

George, Prince of Greece : **IV** 16 n. 4

George V, King of Hanover (1851–66) : **III** 287 n. 2; **IV** 473

George, Prince of Wales, then King George V of England (1910–36) : **IV** 236

Gérard, August : **III** 524 biog. n. 1, 525

Geritz : **IV** 565 biog. n. 1, 573, 575

Gerlach, Leopold von : **III** 484 biog. n. 1

Germany : domestic affairs, general, **III** 324–5, 329, 335, 337, 346, 357, 362, 388–9, 400–2, 405–6, 415–20, 422–3, 475–6, 477–9, 481, 490, 496–506, 508, 568–71, 573, 575, 577–9, 586–7, 589, 590, 593, 595, 598, 601, 603–4, 610–15, 617–42, 645–60, 662–3; **IV** 11–12, 18–19, 27–8, 42–6, 96, 190–1, 235, 265–6, 270, 272, 291, 439, 452–6, 497–8, 516, 525–8, 551, 553, 555–6, 560, 565–7, 569, 571–2, 596–7, 602, 615–17; anti-revolutionary laws, **III** 324, 420, 475 n. 1, 4, 5, 477–8, 481, 499, 503, 586; **IV** 11–12, 19, 190–1; army, **III** 70–3, 85, 125–6, 128, 196, 233, 242, 245, 323, 344–5,

352–6, 561, 595, 610–11, 614 n. 3, 620, 657–8; army legislation, **III** 241, 291, 329, 383–4, 388–9, 418, 422–3, 499 n. 1, 618, 620; army courts martial question, **III** 560 n. 5, 561, 573, 575, 595, 609–15, 618, 620–30, 632–7, 639–42, 645–51; canal bill, **IV** 266; citizenship bill, **IV** 555–6, 560–1; electoral laws, **III** 475 n. 3, 476–7; **IV** 497–8; finances and taxes, **IV** 11–12, 18, 453, 516, 551, 553, 565–7, 569, 571–2, 586, 615–17; *Kulturkampf*, **III** 57 n. 3, 184; labour, **III** 329, 331, 335, 338 n. 4, 475 n. 1; **IV** 191; Lippe inheritance, **III** 610–12, 614, 621 n. 2, 631, 634–5; Press law, **III** 344; school bill, **III** 400–2, 405–6, 408; **IV** 266; tariffs, **IV** 265, 270–1, 291, 527–8, 553; *see also* Navy, Press; for foreign affairs, see under individual countries
Gersov: **III** 175
Gervais, Admiral: **III** 387 n. 3
Geschow: **IV** 572 biog. n. 1
Gianotti: **IV** 286
Giers, Nikolai Karlovich: **III** 85 biog. n. 2, 89, 101 n. 4, 108, 127, 145, 148 n. 4, 153, 165 n. 4, 169, 171 n. 3, 174, 179, 239, 250, 285–6, 294, 310 n. 3, 330, 358, 360, 505 n. 5, 550
Giolitti, Giovanni: **IV** 249 biog. n. 3, 285, 429, 511–12, 528 n. 2
Gladstone, William Ewart: **III** 54 biog. n. 5, 62–5, 67, 70, 98, 122–3, 130–1, 133, 138, 142, 165, 214, 414–15, 421, 425, 427, 429, 433, 435–7, 440–1, 443–4, 460; **IV** 116
Glinka, General: **III** 284, 289
Gneist, Rudolf von: **IV** 526 biog. n. 1
Godeffroy, Senator: **III** 35
Goerz: **IV** 148 biog. n. 5
Göhring: **IV** 117, 119
Goldberger, Ludwig: **IV** 508 biog. n. 1
Goldscheider, Professor Alfred: **IV** 543
Goltz, Karl August, Count von der: **III** 154 biog. n. 2, 299, 336
Goltz, General Kolmar, Baron von der: **III** 398 biog. n. 1; **IV** 454, 572, 578, 613 n. 2, 615
Goluchowski, Agenor, Count: **III** 535 biog. n. 1, 556, 558–9, 563, 566–7, 572–3, 576 n. 1, 579–82, 588–9, 591–2, 594, 606, 632, 643–4; **IV** 2–3, 8–9, 16, 20, 38–9, 48, 53–4, 64, 78, 242, 421, 429, 440, 473, 494, 567, 572, 615
Golz, General Gustav: **III** 325 biog. n. 8, 502

Gorchakov, Alexander, Prince: **III** 13 biog. n. 2, 15, 19, 43
Gordon, Adolf von: **IV** 480
Göring, Karl: **III** 406 n. 1, 408
Görz, Count: **III** 340
Goschen, Sir George: **IV** 123, 141, 157, 169, 602
Gossler, General Heinrich von: **III** 653 biog. n. 2, 654, 658; **IV** 11
Granville, George Leveson-Gower, 2nd Earl: **III** 60 biog. n. 4, 61, 63–7, 69–70, 128–31, 136–7
Great Britain: Africa, **III** 129–30, 443, 655; Anglo-Japanese alliance, **IV** 252, 366–7; Armenia, **III** 563–4, 566–7, 576, 580; Austria, **III** 182, 187–8, 190, 196, 208–9, 426–30; **IV** 78, 444–5, 457, 462–3, 487, 577; Bosnia, **IV** 577–80, 584–8, 590–1, 597–8, 604, 606–8, 620; Crete, **III** 632, 643–44; **IV** 15–18, 54, 62–3; domestic affairs, **III** 121, 157; **IV** 172, 191, 255–6, 386; Eastern question, **III** 158, 166, 171, 173–8, 188, 192, 269, 273, 385–6, 424 n. 4, 425–30, 443, 447–50, 452–3, 459–60, 463–5, 467 n. 2, 468, 482–7, 493, 549, 551–2, 555–7, 559, 580, 588–92, 664–5; **IV** 8–10, 19–20, 40, 48, 138, 162, 284, 379–80, 535–6, 546, 548, 554; Egypt, **III** 59–66, 68–70, 121–3, 130, 139, 144, 182, 188, 190, 205 n. 2, 386, 396–8, 399, 404, 407, 410–12, 430, 434 n. 2, 438, 442, 599–602, 604–8, 615–16; Far East, **III** 95, 97, 434 n. 4, 435, 437, 440, 443, 446; **IV** 5, 22, 36–7, 50–3, 57–9, 61, 64–5, 107, 186, 188–9, 195, 202–7, 255, 264, 271, 278–9, 282–3, 287 n. 3, 311–13, 315, 326; France, **III** 60, 65–6, 70, 98–9, 133, 142, 443, 445, 474, 596; **IV** 15, 27, 31–2, 56, 76, 79, 257–65, 274–6, 279, 288, 291, 314, 336–7, 339, 394, 427; Germany, **III** 119, 121, 128, 131, 136–8, 142, 165–7, 169, 172 n. 2, 214, 223, 341–342, 344, 426–30, 433–7, 439–42, 443, 451, 493–4, 537–9, 543, 547–8, 597–8, 655, 661–2, 664; **IV** 24–6, 29–33, 35, 41, 66, 68–73, 77–89, 92–4, 98–101, 108–29, 137, 140–4, 147–66, 168–77, 184–9, 193, 196–200, 206–9, 211–15, 217–19, 222–7, 231–2, 236–9, 242–7, 252–4, 256–63, 269–73, 274–5, 291–2, 306, 316–17, 320–6, 377–9, 381, 409–11, 415, 421, 424, 428–30, 434, 438, 442–5, 447, 449–50, 457, 469–70, 486–9, 491–2

509–10, 517, 529, 550–6, 561, 568, 570–2, 584–5, 591–3, 598–9, 600–2; Hague Peace Conferences, **IV** 126–7, 458, 465 n. 1, 469 n. 4, Ireland, **III** 62–3, 65, 68, 165, 378, 433; Italy, **III** 351–2, 404, 440, 446 n. 2, 451, 453, 495; **IV** 66, 103–6, 221, 250, 252, 267, 462, 494, 498, 536; Morocco, **IV** 328–31, 337–9, 342–3, 346, 348–350, 356–7, 360, 363, 365, 375, 386–388, 394–5; Portugal, **III** 364, 366–7, 370–7; Russia, **III** 67, 145, 148, 172, 238, 247, 293, 306, 316, 378, 424, n. 4, 425, 444, 534, 616; **IV** 30, 67, 75–6, 116, 128, 136, 139, 146, 217–18, 277–8, 318, 365, 515–16; Sino-Japanese war, **III** 495, 507–8, 510–13, 523–6, 528, 531–2, 541; South Africa, **III** 551 n. 3, 552, 554, 582–6, 597, 616–17; **IV** 22–5, 29, 36, 98, 139, 149, 156–7, 173; Tuat, **III** 390–4, 396–7; Turkey, **III** 220, 379, 414, 531–5; United States, **IV** 93, 173
Greece: **III** 320, 414–15, 465, 644; **IV** 16–18, 20, 26–7, 35, 37–41, 60, 62, 578
Grévy, Jules: **III** 98 biog. n. 3, 142
Grey, Sir Edward: **IV** 172 biog. n. 4 554, 578
Gries, Dr: **III** 260
Grünfeld, Dr Hermann: **IV** 543
Guicciardini, Count: **IV** 405 biog. n. 2
Gurko, General Joseph: **III** 255 biog. n. 3
Güssfeldt, Dr Paul: **III** 340 biog. n. 3, 343
Gutschmid, Felix Baron, von: **III** 511 n. 1, 516 biog. n. 9, 518–19, 528 n. 3, 529, 531; **IV** 23, 30, 45
Gyulai, Franz, Count: **III** 248 biog. n. 1

Hacke: **III** 521 biog. n. 4, 531
Hacke, Veronika, Countess von (née von Flemming): **III** 7 biog. n. 2
Haeseler, General Gottlieb von: **III** 355 biog. n. 1
Hague Peace Conference, 1899: **IV** 106–8, 123–7, 129–31, 135, 145, 513
Hague Peace Conference, 1907: **IV** 453, 458–9, 470, 478, 611
Hahnke, General Wilhelm von: **III** 332 biog. n. 3, 340, 344, 355–6, 561, 573 n. 1, 611, 615 n. 3, 635, 648; **IV** 511 n. 2, 512
Hahnke, Major Wilhelm von: **IV** 315 n. 1
*Hamburger Nachrichten:* **III** 478, 589, 623

Hammann, Otto: **IV** 244 biog. n. 4, 248, 257, 270, 289, 294, 297, 300–1, 303–4, 308, 329, 386, 404, 409, 414–16, 423, 431, 432 n. 6, 435, 437, 454, 468, 491 n. 1, 493–4, 501–3, 505 n. 3, 510, 525, 531 n. 2, 534, 548, 589, 593, 619
Letters to, **IV** 295, 297 n. 1
Letters from, **IV** 293, 297, 408
Hammerstein, Wilhelm von: **III** 480 n. 3
Hanotaux, Gabriel: **III** 474 biog. n. 3, 518, 527–8, 596, 606, 664; **IV** 14 n. 2, 22, 24, 27, 29, 51, 53–4, 57, 63–4, 336, 338, 349, 355, 489
Hansemann, Adolf von: **III** 514 biog. n. 5
Harcourt, Sir William: **IV** 172 biog. n. 6
Harden, Maximilian: **III** xiv, 457 n. 1, 502; **IV** 389 biog. n. 2; relations with Holstein, **IV** 430–3, 438, 457, 502–4, 511 n. 2, 568–9, 596; Eulenburg, **IV** 447 n. 6; Bülow, **IV** 454–5, 501, 576, 580–1; Moltke trials, **IV** 501–2, 511 n. 3, 513, 573, 576, 580, 581–2, 586
Letters to, **IV** 436 n. 4, 440–1, 466–8, 471–2, 507–8, 511–12, 575
Letters from, **IV** 435–6, 439–40, 445–6, 452, 455–6, 458–60, 463–5, 468–71, 474–86, 490–4, 498–500, 505–9, 512, 514–15, 517–25, 528, 530–33, 535–45, 560–5, 569–70, 573–5, 589, 591–3, 605, 621–2
Harden, Selma: **IV** 511 n. 2, 569 n. 2
Hardinge, Sir Charles: **III** 239; **IV** 550–3, 562
Harrach, Johann, Count von: **IV** 615 biog. n. 6
Harris, Walter B.: **IV** 265 biog. n. 1
Hartington, Marquis of: *see* Devonshire, Duke of
Hasse, Professor Ernst: **IV** 195 biog. n. 6, 270–1
Hatzfeldt-Trachenberg, Hermann, Prince von: **IV** 464 biog. n. 1, 465, 471–2, 497, 541, 606, 615
Hatzfeldt-Wildenburg, Helene, Countess von (née Moulton): **III** 30 biog. n. 5, 44, 110, 192; **IV** 229–31
Letters to, **IV** 182–3, 228–9
Hatzfeldt-Wildenburg, Hermann, Count von: **IV** 147, 155, 183, 228–31, 561, 573
Hatzfeldt-Wildenburg, Paul, Count von **III** ix, 13 biog. n. 1; Bismark relations, **III** 67–8, 105, 273; career,

**III** 120, 138, 155–6; Battenberg marriage, **III** 188, 273 n. 1; miscellaneous, **III** 30 n. 5, 44, 49, 70–1, 73, 87, 95, 104, 110, 119, 121, 123 n. 1, 128, 142, 176, 180–2, 204 n. 1, 218–20, 225, 317, 342, 348 n. 2, 377 n. 2, 385, 386 n. 1, 389, 393 n. 2 & 3, 397 n. 1, 398 n. 2, 399 n. 3, 408 n. 1, 424 n. 4, 425 n. 1, 434 n. 2, 435 n. 1 & 2, 438 n. 2, 443 n. 1, 446 n. 1 & 2, 450 n. 3, 460, 463 n. 6, 485 n. 2, 493 n. 5, 512 n. 1, 520–1, 527 n. 3, 534 n. 1, 537–8, 543 n. 4, 544 n. 2 & 3, 549, 551 n. 3, 552 n. 1, 554 n. 1, 558 n. 5, 559 n. 3, 560 n. 2, 565, 566 n. 1, 567 n. 2, 586 n. 4, 596, 604, 617 n. 2, 632 n. 2, 643 n. 1, 644 n. 1, 645 n. 1; **IV** 9 n. 5, 83, 99, 104, 118–19, 129, 133, 143, 170, 173, 193, 200, 202, 220, 231–2, 257, 259, 261, 416, 465; *see also* Great Britain
Letters to, **III** 154, 193–6, 373–4, 393, 414–15, 539, 547–8, 586, 643–5; **IV** 21, 27–8, 34–5, 48–53, 55–8, 62–6, 68–70, 75–7, 80–2, 85, 92, 101, 146, 155, 158–61, 164–7, 170–1, 195–7, 209, 213–14, 218, 227–8
Letters from, **III** 50, 89–92, 108, 146, 155, 156–8, 165–8, 171–2, 176–7, 204, 205, 274, 348–52, 365–7, 370–2, 376–80, 385–8, 390–9, 403–5, 413–16, 424–30, 433–4, 434–47, 451–3, 463–8, 480–7, 493–6, 506–8, 510–13, 530–5, 542–5, 547, 554–60, 565–8, 596–8, 600–1, 607–8, 616–17, 632–3, 661–2, 664–5; **IV** 15–17, 25–7, 29–33, 36–7, 39–42, 58–9, 64, 66–7, 70–4, 77–9, 84–9, 92–4, 108–23, 137–43, 147–58, 161–5, 167, 185–9, 198, 206–12, 214–15, 221–7, 229–31, 233
Haugwitz, Christian, Count von: **IV** 369
Haweis, Reverend Richard: **III** 409 n. 4
Hay, John: **IV** 92 biog. n. 6. 93, 111, 196, 278, 387 n. 1
Hayashi, Tadusa: **IV** 263 biog. n. 3
Haymerle, Heinrich, Baron von: **III** 202 biog. n. 1; **IV** 607
Heeremann von Zuydwyk. Klemens, Baron von; **IV** 18
Heinrich, Prince of Prussia: **III** 229 biog. n. 1, 230–1, 258, 260–1, 267–8, 270, 280, 288, 299, 300–2, 344, 616, 618 n. 1, 619; **IV** 24, 35, 251, 290, 491, 612
Letter to, **III** 262–4

Heinrich, Duke of Mecklenburg-Schwerin: **IV** 112 n. 2
Helfferich, Karl: **IV** 545 biog. n. 5, 546
Helldorff-Bedra, Klara von: **IV** 517 biog. n. 9
Letter to, **IV** 517–18
Helldorff-Bedra, Otto Heinrich von: **III** 323 biog. n. 3
Hellwig: **IV** 127
Henckel-Donnersmark, Guido, Count, then Prince von: **III** 35 biog. n. 2, 456–8, 467–73; **IV** 45, 89, 90–1, 94–5, 511 n. 2, 541–2, 606
Letters to, **III** 467; **IV** 430–1
Letters from, **III** 457–8
Henckel-Donnersmark, Leo von: **III** 458 biog. n. 2
Hengelmüller von Hengervár, Ladislaus, Baron von: **III** 209 biog. n. 2, 311
Henry, Prince of Battenberg: **III** 151, 193 n. 1
Herbette, Jules: **III** 190 biog. n. 7, 193
Herold, Hugo: **IV** 434 biog. n. 1
Herrfurth, Ernst Ludwig: **III** 389 biog. n. 6, 406
Hervé, Gustave: **IV** 490 biog. n. 1
Herzen, Alexander: **III** 553
Herzog, Eduard: **III** 183 biog. n. 3
Heuduck, General Wilhelm von: **III** 196 biog. n. 6, 197
Heyden-Rynsch: **III** 325 biog. n. 5
Heyking, Edmund, Baron von: **IV** 4 biog. n. 2
Letter from, **IV** 4–5
Hicks-Beach, Sir Michael Edward: **IV** 169 biog. n. 3
Hill, David: **IV** 522 biog. n. 5, 550, 552
Hintze, Admiral Paul von: **IV** 604 biog. n. 1
Hinzpeter, Georg Ernst: **III** 589 biog. n. 4 & n. 5; **IV** 191
Hirschfeld, Dr: **IV** 409
Hitrovo: **III** 88 biog. n. 4, 177 biog. n. 7, 322, 529
Hobrecht, Arthur: **III** 225 biog. n. 1
Hoefft: **IV** 555
Hoensbroech, Paul, Count von und zu: **III** 496 biog. n. 2, 497, 503
Hofmann, Karl von: **III** 91 biog. n. 1; **IV** 433
Hohenau, Wilhelm, Count von: **IV** 477 biog. n. 5, 482, 484, 517, 521
Hohenlohe-Langenburg, Ernst, Prince zu: **IV** 568 biog. n. 3, 577
Hohenlohe-Langenburg, Hermann, Prince zu: **IV** 96 biog. n. 3, 450–1, 495

Hohenlohe-Schillingsfürst, Alexander, Prince zu : **III** 480 n. 3, 487 biog. n. 2, *504, 532,* 613, 615, 618 n. 2, 646; **IV** 434, 436, 439 n. 1, 448, 450–1
Letters from, **IV** 233, 234

Hohenlohe-Schillingsfürst, Chlodwig, Prince zu : **III** 38 biog. n. 1; Holstein, **IV** 433–4, 436, 448, 450; Marschall, **III** 496–504, 508, 560–1, 568–71, *573–5, 578–9, 586–7, 589–90, 593–5, 598, 603–4, 608–10, 613–15, 617–18, 620–30, 632–7, 639–42, 645–50, 651–6*; changes in ministry, **III** 491, 494–505, 508, 568–71, 573–5, 577–9, 586–7, 589–90, 593–5, 601, 603, 610–15, 618, 620–3, 626–42, 645–55; Wilhelm II, **IV** 12–13, 19, 22, 34, 35, 42 n. 1, 43–4, 46–7, 96–7, 168, 383 n. 2, 384; foreign policy, **IV** 10–11, 29, 40, 51; Austria, **III** 489, 560 n. 1, 579, 581, 589 n. 1, 655 n. 4; China loan, **III** 530–1, 537 n. 4; miscellaneous, **III** 36 n. 4, 52, 56, 58, 74–5, 77 n. 1, 78 n. 1, 79, 81, 85 n. 5, 93, 97–9, 100, 113, 115, 120, 122, 137–42, 146, 149, 159, 246 n. 3, 310, 480 n. 2, 481–2, 487–8, 490 n. 3, 491–2, 509, 529, 548, 554 n. 2, 556, 560–1, 572, 577, 579, 595 n. 1, 598, 602 n. 1, 616, 619–20, 656, 659–60, 661 n. 1, 664; **IV** 8, 20 n. 2, 32, 43, 130, 165, 201, 229, 233–4, 415, 418, 432 n. 7, 439 n. 1, 447

**Letters to, III** 38–9, 96; **IV** 130
Letters from, **III** 53, 56, 73, 144, 146–7, 196–7, 207, 246, 273, 454, 466, 492, 519–20, 536–7, 633–4, 645; **IV** 61, 134, 191–5, 210

Hohenlohe-Schillingsfürst, Konstantin, Prince zu : **III** 595 n. 1

Hohenlohe-Schillingsfürst, Marie, Princess zu (née Sayn-Wittgenstein) : **III** 310 n. 1, 640, 646; **IV** 433

Hohenthal und Bergen, Wilhelm, Count von : **III** 658 biog. n. 2

Hoiningen-Hüne, Karl, Baron von : **III** 324 biog. n. 3

Holland, Sir Henry : **III** 341 biog. n. 1

Holleben, Theodor von : **III** 462 biog. n. 3; **IV** 45, 82, 92, 196, 200, 251

Hollmann, Admiral Friedrich von : **III** 358 biog. n. 3, 496, 502, 504, 603, 610, 623, 659; **IV** 11, 14, 18–19, 383 n. 2, 480

Holstein, August von :
Letters from, **III** 3–23

Holstein, Friedrich von :
Letters to Herbert Bismarck, **III** 70, 324–5, 333–4; to Bissing **III** 472; **IV** 94; to Blaserna, **IV** 178–81; to Brandt, **III** 362, 514, 516–17; **IV** 176–8, 208, 327–8, 375, 376–8, 410–11, 449–50, 478, 513–14; to Bernhard Bülow, **III** 479–80, 491–2, 496–7, 499–502, 548–50, 568, 573–4, 604–6; **IV** 13–14, 18–20, 37–9, 43, 96–7, 130–2, 134–5, 142–4, 189–91, 200, 216, 234–5, 254, 257, 275–7, 289–92, 297, 299–300, 305, 307–8, 309–10, 316–17, 319–20, 326, 344, 346, 373–4, 379–86, 401–3, 405–8, 441–2, 446–7, 452–3, 461, 465–6, 487–90, 495–6, 499, 504–5, 515–16, 523, 529, 547–50, 552–3, 555–8, 560–1, 566–9, 570–1, 576–80, 581–4, 586–8, 589–91, 595–6, 597–600, 600–8, 611–13, 615–18, 620–1; to Marie Bülow, **IV** 292, 294–5; to Klemens Busch, **III** 48; to Castell Rüdenhausen, **IV** 103–6; to Chirol, **IV** 239–41; to David, **IV** 415–16, 424–6, 428–9, 431–6, 448–9; to Eckardstein, **IV** 219; to Eisendecher, **III** 24, 27, 30, 40–5, 313–16, 332, 337, 347–8, 431; to Eulenburg, **III** 466–9, 576–8, 592–4, 610–13, 624–6, 628–9, 642–3, 650–60, 662–4; **IV** 9–13, 89–90, 193, 419, 420; to Hammann, **IV** 295–6; to Helene Hatzfeldt, **IV** 182–3, 228–9; to Paul Hatzfeldt, **III**, 193–6, 373–4, 447–8, 586, 643–5; **IV** 21–5, 27–8, 34–5, 48–53, 55–6, 63–4, 68–70, 75–7, 80–2, 85, 92, 101, 155, 158–61, 164, 165–7, 184–5, 195–7, 209, 213–14, 218, 227–8; to Harden, **IV** 440–1, 466–8, 471–2, 507–8, 511–12, 575; to Henckel-Donnersmark, **III** 467; **IV** 430–1; to Hohenlohe, **III** 494; **IV** 130; to Kiderlen-Wächter, **III**, 622–3, 648–50; to Lindenau, **III** 630–1, 634–42; to Marschall, **III** 479; to Metternich, **IV** 127–9, 135–6; to Mühlberg, **IV** 298, 299, 423; to Pourtalès, **IV** 301, 303; to Pusch, **IV** 502–4; to Radolin, **III** 110, 159–61, 170, 172, 174–8, 181–3, 187–93, 215–17, 222–3, 232–3, 268–9, 297, 316–17, 323, 360–1, 412–13, 466–7, 472–3, 481–2, 506, 513–21, 527–32, 555–6, 562, 569, 575–6, 584, 601–4, 615–16, 660–1; **IV** 1, 7–8, 34, 46–7, 106–7, 144–6, 189, 232, 241–2, 255, 266–8, 278–80, 282 n. 1, 298, 301, 306–

7, 338–43, 346–56, 359–60, 367–8, 370–2, 386, 388–91, 399–400, 403–4, 414–15, 500–1; to Johanna Radolin, **IV** 250–1, 303–4, 395–6; to Richthofen, **IV** 262–3, 287–8; to Röse, **IV** 429–30; to Schiemann, **IV** 417, 418; to Tiedemann, **III** 46; to Wilhelm II, **III** 403, 431–2; to a colleague, **III** 80–1; to a journalist, **IV** 543–4; memoranda, **III** 374–6, 448–9, 456–7; **IV** 98–100, 251–2, 263–5, 282–4, 288, 311–12, 324–5, 326–7, 356–8, 404–5, 427, 442–5, 461–3, 525–8, 533–6, 550–1, 619–20; diary entries, **IV** 244–8, 268–73, 447, 453, 456–9, 472–4, 509–11

For letters to Holstein, see names of correspondents

Holstein, Luise von: **III** 12 biog. n. 5

Holtzendorff, Dr: **III** 39 n. 1

Holtzendorff, Adele von: **III** 12 biog. n. 2, 22

Holtzendorff, Ida von: see Stülpnagel

Holtzendorff, Minna von: **III** 3, 12, 14, 18–19, 21, 23

Hompesch-Rurich, Alfred, Count von: **III** 652 biog. n. 1, 652 n. 2, 654

Horn, Dr: **IV** 480

Hovell, Dr Mark: **III** 262 biog. n. 1, 266

Hoyos, Countess Marguerite: **III** 413 n. 2

Hsii–ching–cheng: **III** 514 biog. n. 3, 515

Hudson, Sir Charles: **IV** 105

Huene: **III** 344 n. 3

Hugo, Colonel von: **IV** 342

Huhn, Arthur von: **IV** 332–3, 335, 415, 431, 437, 619–20
Letter from, **IV** 296–7

Hülsen-Haeseler, Dietrich, Count von: **III** 340 biog. n. 4; **IV** 2, 448, 451, 497, 521–2, 570

Hülsen-Haeseler, Georg, Count von: **IV** 477 biog. n. 7

Hungary: **III** 187, 210, 298 n. 2, 305, 308, 312, 382, 608 n. 6; **IV** 424, 445, 462, 474, 495, 565, 609, 618

Huret, Jules: **IV** 493 biog. n. 5, 565

Hüssen: **III** 325 biog. n. 6

Hutten-Czapski, Bogdan, Count von: **III** 560 biog. n. 3, 560 n. 5, 627–8, 634, 636, 639, 646; **IV** 433
Letters from, **III** 560–1; **IV** 511

Iddesleigh, Sir Stafford Northcote, Earl of: **III** 172 biog. n. 1, 178, 193

Ignatiev, Nikolai Pavlovich, Count: **III** 54 biog. n. 7, 66–7, 84, 211, 256

Ilberg, Dr von: **IV** 408

India: **III** 178, 373, 375–6, 424 n. 4, 425–6, 429, 485 n. 2; **IV** 39, 71, 128–9, 258, 486–7, 490, 554

Inouye, Katsunoske, Marquis: **IV** 202 biog. n. 3

Ireland: **III** 62, 65, 165, 422; **IV** 486–7, 489

Irene, Princess of Hesse: **III** 270 n. 1, 344

Isenbiel: **IV** 506, 514, 517–24, 530–1, 533, 536–7, 540–1, 544–5, 565, 569, 582 n. 1, 586, 589, 591–2, 622

Isvolsky, Alexander Petrovich: **IV** 325 biog. n. 1, 487, 515, 579, 583, 585–8, 598, 604, 607–9, 612, 614

Italy: Abyssinia, **III** 599, 602, 606–7; Armenia, **III** 566 n. 1, 576; Austria, **III** 252–3, 317, 319, 322 n. 3, 449–50, 489, 572; **IV** 276, 458, 462–3, 489, 494, 498, 535–6, 577, 585, 600, 612, 617; Crete, **III** 632, 644; **IV** 17, 35, 65; domestic affairs, **III** 214; **IV** 210–11; Eastern question, **III** 198, 269, 320, 426, 428–30, 443, 447–50, 451, 453, 460, 464, 551–2, 555, 560, 588; **IV** 461–3, 473–4; Far East, **III** 532; France, **III** 474–549; **IV** 266–7, 284–5, 288, 324, 350, 565; Germany, **III** 62, 196, 210, 299–302, 343, 348–51, 358–60; **IV** 48, 103–6, 220–1, 285–7, 289, 318, 424, 429, 486–7; Great Britain, **III** 204 n. 1, 208–9, 374–5, 390–2, 404, 435–6, 440, 446 n. 2, 447–8, 451, 453, 495, 544, 596–8, 617; **IV** 70, 72–3, 75, 77 n. 2, 79 n. 3, 137–8, 166, 252–3, 255–9, 261; Morocco, **IV** 329 n. 1, 330–1, 340, 395, 404, 410, 556; Portugal, **III** 363 n. 2, 365 n. 1, 397 n. 1; Triple Alliance, **III** 62, 81, 198–207, 373–6, 380, 573; **IV** 38, 66, 246–52, 254, 269, 440–5, 447, 449–50, 464–6; Tuat, **III** 390–2, 394, 396–7; miscellaneous, **III** 187, 193, 203, 224, 244–5, 318–19, 336, 338–9, 378, 459, 484–6, 512, 550, 553, 583 n. 2; **IV** 5, 20, 54, 57, 69

Ito, Marquis: **IV** 252 biog n. 5

Jacobi, Hugo: **IV** 448 biog. n. 6

Jacobini, Ludovico, Cardinal: **III** 57 n. 3

Jameson, Dr Leander Starr: **III** 582 n. 2

Jarolymek, Edmund: **IV** 452 n. 4

Japan: Chinese loan, **III** 514–21, 526–27, 529–33, 536–7, 539–41, 545–6; **IV** 150; Great Britain, **IV** 23, 66, 150,

170, 186, 188, 218–19, 224, 239, 252–3, 255, 263, 366–7, 377, 379–80, 434, 450; Russia, **IV** 196–7, 202, 274, 365, 487; Russo-Japanese war, **IV** 277–80, 282–3, 311–18, 320, 326–8, 436, 470; Sino-Japanese war, **III** 495–6, 506–8, 510–14, 522–5, 528, 544; **IV** 105, 204; miscellaneous, **III** 507, 510–11, 514, 516–21, 523, 528–31, 533–6, 540–1, 544–5; **IV** 57, 59, 264, 306, 340, 425, 428, 469, 547

Jaurès, Admiral Benjamin: **III** 82 biog. n. 1

Jaurès, Jean: **IV** 398 n. 3

Jenisch: see Rücker-Jenisch

Jeschke, Captain: **IV** 50

Jomini, Alexander, Baron: **III** 55 biog. n. 6, 101

Jonin: **III** 89 n. 2

Judet, Ernest: **IV** 427 biog. n. 4

Jusserand, J. J.: **IV** 342 biog. n. 10

Kállay, Benjamin von: **III** 209 biog. n. 4, 311

Kálnoky von Köröspatak, Gustav, Count **III** 109 biog. n. 2; Germany, **III** 392, 483, 489; Eastern question, **III** 311–12, 448, 450, 452–3, 459, 460, 463–5, 487, 580, 594; Italy, **III** 449, 489 n. 4, 572–3; Portugal, **III** 371; Russia, **III** 233–6, 241–3, 245–6, 252–5, 482, 486; Three Emperors League, **III** 123–4, 127, 132, 153, 166, 172 n. 2; Triple Alliance, **III** 198–201, 204, 206–7, 209, 380; miscellaneous, **III** 86 n. 4, 87 n. 1, 123–4, 161 n. 5, 187–8, 190, 202–3, 209, 211–12, 228, 240, 271–3, 298 n. 2, 304–5, 308, 319, 322 n. 3, 328, 338, 357, 359, 364, 392 n. 3, 404, 428, 447–8, 491 n. 6, 512

Kaltenborn-Stachau, General Hans von: **III** 356 biog. n. 2

Kanzow, Judge: **IV** 539 biog. n. 2

Kapnist, Dmitri, Count: **III** 141 biog. n. 5

Kapnist, Peter, Count: **III** 55 biog. n. 4, 141, 143, 589; **IV** 6, 7

Karavelov, Petko: **III** 175 biog. n. 2, 321

Kardorff, Wilhelm von: **III** 654 biog. n. 2; **IV** 469

Karl Ludwig, Archduke of Austria: **III** 307 n. 1

Károlyi, Alois, Count: **III** 190 biog. n. 6

Katargi, Laskar: **III** 322 biog. n. 2

Katkov, Michael: **III** 177 biog. n. 5, 211, 238

Katokatsy: **III** 249 biog. n. 4

Katz, Leo: **IV** 521 biog. n. 5, 537–9, 564, 569

Kaufmann: **IV** 266 n. 5

Kaulbars, General Alexander, Baron von: **III** 175 n. 4

Kayser, Paul: **III** 296 biog. n. 2, 313–314, 329 n. 3, 474, 501–2, 547, 610–11, 640
Letter from, **III** 329

Keim, General August: **IV** 457 biog. n. 3, 510

Kessel, General Bernhard von: **III** 45 biog. n. 5

Kessel, General Gustav von: **III** 161 biog. n. 2, 218, 220, 232, 269, 271; **IV** 544

Kessler, Harry, Count von: **IV** 467, 476 n. 1

Ketteler, Klemens, Baron von: **IV** 188 n. 1, 194, 205 biog. n. 2

Keudell, Robert von: **III** 44 biog. n. 2, 45, 48, 127, 129

Khevenhüller-Metsch, Rudolf, Count: **III** 124 biog. n. 3

Kiamil Pasha: **III** 386 n. 2, 564 biog. n. 4; **IV** 599, 609

Kiaochow: see China

Kiderlen-Wächter, Alfred von: **III** x, 83 biog. n. 2, 279 n. 5, 339, 340, 383 n. 1, 392 n. 3, 398, 424, 436, 455, 456 n. 4, 461–2, 466, 475–6, 544, 602 n. 3, 604, 623 n. 3, 624, 631 n. 2, 643, 645 n. 1, 647 n. 1, 662 n. 5; **IV** 34–5, 122 n. 5, 178–9, 495, 497, 546–7, 597, 599–601, 603, 605–6, 608, 612–14, 616–17, 619–20
Letters to, **III** 359, 622–3, 648–50
Letters from, **III** 83–4, 87–9, 279–92, 343–7, 354–60, 383–4, 416–19, 537–9, 602–3, 621, 647–8; **IV** 3–4, 34, 43–7, 459

Kimberley, John Wodehouse, Earl of: **III** 444 biog. n. 1, 493 n. 5, 506–7, 510, 547; **IV** 33

Kistler: **III** 541 biog. n. 1; **IV** 520 biog. n. 1, 575

Kitchener, General Horatio Herbert: **IV** 240

*Kladderadatsch*: **III** 456 n. 4, 461–3, 466–7, 662; **IV** 127, 430 n. 5, 582

Klehmet, Reinhold: **III** 516 biog. n. 6; **IV** 127, 193, 257, 272, 294, 298 n. 2, 558, 579, 594

Kleinholz: **IV** 506–7, 511 n. 2

Klepsch, Colonel: **III** 93, 241, 247–8
Klofač, Václav: **IV** 587 biog. n. 4
Knappe, Dr Wilhelm: **IV** 517 biog. n. 1
Knesebeck, Bodo von dem: **IV** 542 biog. n. 6
Knorr, Admiral Wilhelm von: **III** 496 biog. n. 3, 610, 662 n. 1
Koellner, Captain: **IV** 17 n. 4
Kojiro, Outchijama: **IV** 66 n. 1
Köller, Ernst Matthias von: **III** 561 biog. n. 2, 568, 570 n. 2, 571, 573, 575, 578, 587, 604, 652, 654; **IV** 46, 496–7, 573
Köller, Georg von: **III** 405 n. 1
*Kölnische Zeitung:* **III** 33, 75–6, 82, 123, 211, 214, 334 n. 2, 335, 388 n. 1, 450, 479 n. 5, 480 n. 3, 505; **IV** 296–7, 332–8, 415 n. 2, 422, 431, 436 n. 4, 619
Konrad, Dr von: **IV** 290 biog. n. 3
Köpenick, Captain of: see Voigt, Wilhelm
Korea: **III** 507, 516; **IV** 196, 202
Körner: **IV** 309 n. 1, 392 biog. n. 2
Kossuth, Franz: **IV** 462 n. 3, 474
Kossuth, Louis: **IV** 462 biog. n. 3
Kotsubey, Princess: **III** 194
Kramarsch, Dr Karl: **IV** 587 biog. n. 3
Krauel, Dr Friedrich: **III** 213 biog. n. 2, 295, 342; **IV** 45
Krause, Dr Hermann: **III** 227 biog. n. 3, 258–61
Kreutz, Countess: **III** 257
*Kreuzzeitung:* **IV** 290, 530, 535, 568
Kriege, Johannes: **IV** 305 biog. n. 1, 367, 369 n. 1, 370 n. 1, 372 n. 2, 375 n. 1, 390, 406, 456
Kröcher, Jordan von: **IV** 597 biog. n. 5
Krüger (Police Commissioner): **IV** 479–80
Krüger, Friedrich von: **IV** 76 biog. n. 2
Krüger, Paul: **III** 493 biog. n. 1, 584 n. 4, 605, 617; **IV** 33, 36, 111, 139, 148, 151, 172, 261
Krüger Telegram: **III** 584 n. 4, 605; **IV** 22–3, 29–31, 36, 80, 143, 160, 239, 247, 271, 356, 488, 517, 555, 563
Krupp, Friedrich Alfred: **III** 358 biog. n. 4; **IV** 529
Kühlmann, Richard von: **IV** 328 biog. n. 4, 341, 376, 378
Kuropatkin, General Alexei: **III** 247, 249; **IV** 194
Kurowski: **III** 45 biog. n. 4
Kusserow, Heinrich von: **III** 126 biog. n. 2

Kwang Hsü, Emperor of China (1875–1908): **III** 507; **IV** 203, 205
Kypke, Hedwig: **IV** 606

Laboulaye, Antoine de: **III** 195 biog. n. 2
LaCroix, General de: **IV** 343, 356, 370–1, 373–4, 489, 562, 590
Laemmel: **IV** 520 biog. n. 2
Lamezan, Ferdinand, Baron von: **III** 308 biog. n. 3
Lamsdorff, Vladimir Nicholaievich, Count: **IV** 7 biog. n. 2, 193–4, 317, 319 n. 1, 320, 326, 357–8, 365–6, 396 n. 3, 401–2, 444–5, 462–3, 487
Landsberg, Moritz: **III** 32 biog. n. 5, 33, 55, 95
Langen, Albert: **IV** 448 n. 3
Langenbuch, Dr: **III** 162 biog. n. 3, 186
Lansdowne, Henry Charles Keith Petty-Fitzmaurice, 5th Marquis of: **IV** 160 biog. n. 1, 169, 214–15, 218, 222–6, 229–32, 253, 255–8, 261–2, 265, 274, 291, 348, 554
Lanza di Busca, Carlo, Count: **III** 660 biog. n. 6; **IV** 192, 247–8, 250–2, 285–7, 409
Lardy: **IV** 313 biog. n. 4
Lascelles, Sir Frank Cavendish: **III** 175 biog. n. 5, 516, 542 n. 1, 586, 597, 602, 643, 655–6, 659, 661; **IV** 36, 80, 100, 150, 159, 196, 200, 215, 229 n. 4, 259, 261, 269, 271, 291, 321, 323, 409–10, 457, 510, 550 n. 2
Launay, Eduardo, Count di: **III** 205 biog. n. 6, 390–1, 396–7, 449; **IV** 38, 103–4
Lebbin, Helene von (née von Brandt): **III** ix, xiii, 42; **IV** 7, 281, 367 n. 3, 375 n. 1, 420, 544, 589
Letter to, **IV** 622
Lebbin, Hermann Friedrich Karl von: **IV** 433 biog. n. 6
Leckert, Heinrich: **III** 652 n. 3; **IV** 485
Lecomte, Raymond: **III** 511 biog. n. 3; **IV** 389–90, 399–400, 447, 460, 478, 480, 482, 484, 491 n. 2, 502–4, 520 n. 3, 531, 560
Lehmann, Judge: **IV** 509, 519, 564, 574, 576, 580–1, 589
Lehndorff, General Heinrich August, Count von: **III** 41 biog. n. 3, 45, 129, 461
Leipziger, Leo: **IV** 423 biog. n. 2
LeMaistre, Rudolf: **III** 320 biog. n. 5
Lemanski, Vladimir Ivanovich: **III** 256 biog. n. 4

Lenbach, Franz von : **III** 111

Leo XIII, Pope (1878–1903) : **III** 183–5, 299–302, 572; **IV** 103 n. 4

Léon : **IV** 345 biog. n. 9, 346, 353, 370

Leon y Castillo, Marquis del Muni : **IV** 232 biog. n. 3, 267, 313–14

Leontiev : **III** 549 n. 2, 553

Leopold II, King of the Belgians (1865–1909): **IV** 160, 358

Leopold, Prince of Bavaria : **III** 356, 627; **IV** 498 n. 3

Leopold, Prince of Hohenzollern : **III** 398, 409

Lerchenfeld-Koefering, Hugo, Count von : **III** 336 biog. n. 1, 346, 658

Leszczynski, General Paul von : **IV** 460 biog. n. 4, 563

Leuthold, Dr Rudolf von : **III** 282 biog. n. 2, 346, 353, 469

Leutwein, Major Theodor : **III** 610 biog. n. 2, 611

Levisohn : **III** 32 biog. n. 5, 33

Levy : **IV** 519 biog. n. 6

Leyden, Casimir, Count von : **III** 434 biog. n. 1 & 2, 441, 448

Leyds, Dr : **IV** 174 biog. n. 3

Li-hung-chang : **III** 507 biog. n. 1, 662; **IV** 202–5

Liberals : **III** 53, 75, 297, 400–2, 415, 627; **IV** 266, 454, 498

Lichnowsky, Karl Max, Prince von : **III** 450 biog. n. 7, 663; **IV** 180, 182, 248, 257, 259, 295, 304, 501, 542, 573

Liebenau, Eduard von : **III** 223 biog. n. 5, 347
Letter from, **III** 277

Lieber, Dr Ernst Maria : **III** 499 biog. n. 1, 623

Liebermann von Sonnenberg : **III** 655 biog. n. 1; **IV** 185, 244

Liebert, Eduard von : **III** 659 biog. n. 2; **IV** 457

Liebknecht, Wilhelm : **IV** 190 biog. n. 3

Liechtenstein, Franz von Paula, Prince von und zu : **III** 563 biog. n. 3; **IV** 137

Lignitz, Viktor von : **III** 72 biog. n. 3, 93, 109

Limburg, T. M. Roest van : **III** 28 biog. n. 1

Limburg-Stirum, Friedrich Wilhelm, Count von : **III** 49 biog. n. 4, 67 n. 2, 332, 491; **IV** 97, 171

Limburg-Stirum, Menno, Count zu : **IV** 456 biog. n. 2, 477

Lindau, Dr Rudolf : **III** 32 biog. n. 4, 38, 76, 260, 279, 333, 467

Lindenau, Karl von : **III** 359, 626 biog. n. 2, 633, 634 n. 1, 642 n. 2; **IV** 97, 180–1, 192, 194

Lindequist, Friedrich von : **IV** 497 biog. n. 1

Linevich, General : **IV** 201

Lippe inheritance : **III** 611–12, 631, 634–5

Lo-feng-luh : **IV** 203 biog. n. 2, 204, 208
Letter to, **IV** 205

Lobanov-Rostovski, Alexei, Prince : **III** 64 biog. n. 6, 211, 238, 243, 460, 505, 509 n. 2, 510–13, 515 n. 3, 518, 520–1, 526–31, 533–7, 539–41, 544 n. 2, 545, 549–50, 553, 555–6, 562–3, 565, 567, 573, 576, 584, 605–6, 616, 632; **IV** 6–7, 22, 61, 63, 136, 142

Loë, General Walther von : **III** 260 biog. n. 1, 261, 356, 589

Loebell, Friedrich Wilhelm von : **IV** 290 biog. n. 3, 454, 486, 525, 532, 541, 556, 576, 580, 586

Loën, General Leopold, Baron von : **III** 4 biog. n. 1, 5, 7–12, 16, 17, 20–1

Loewenfeld : **IV** 511 n. 2

Löhning : **IV** 266 biog. n. 2

Lonsdale, Hugh Cecil Lowther, Earl of : **IV** 275 biog. n. 3

Lottum, Moritz, Count : **III** 27 biog. n. 5

Loubet, Emile : **IV** 220 n. 1, 279 n. 5, 281 biog. n. 4, 283–5, 287, 312 n.1, 339–40, 342, 372

Louis, Georges : **IV** 345 biog. n. 4, 346, 351

Lowe, Charles : **III** 123 n. 3

Lowther, Sir Gerald Augustus : **IV** 609 biog. n. 2

Lozet, H : **III** 370

Lucanus, Hermann von : **III** 292 biog. n. 1, 357, 476, 492, 496–7, 506, 561, 571, 593, 611 n. 2, 621 n. 2, 647, 651; **IV** 43–6, 309, 486, 491

Lucius von Ballhausen, Robert, Baron : **III** 40 biog. n. 6

Lüderitz, Adolf : **III** 136 biog. n. 1

Ludwig, Prince of Bavaria : **III** 618–20

Luise, Queen of Denmark : **III** 287 biog. n. 1

Luitpold, Prince Regent of Bavaria (1886–1912) : **III** 335, 339, 388, 477, 658; **IV** 266 n. 4

Lumley, Sir John Savile : **III** 128 biog. n. 3

Lumsden, General Sir Peter : **III** 148 biog. n. 3

Lutz, Johann, Baron von: **III** 265 biog.
n. 2, 276, 314
Lützow, Karl von: **III** 652 n. 3, 660
n. 2; **IV** 485
Luzzati, Luigi: **IV** 248 biog. n. 1, 340,
387 n. 5, 404, 410, 445
Lynar, Alexander, Prince zu: **III** 30
biog. n. 4
Lynar, Johannes, Count von: **IV** 456
biog. n. 3, 505 n. 6
Lyncker, Moritz, Baron von: **III** 182
biog. n. 2, 218–19, 223, 232, 269, 619
Lytton, Edward Robert, Earl of: **III**
369 biog. n. 2

Mabilleau, Léopold: **IV** 489 biog. n. 2
MacDonald, Sir Claude: **IV** 202 biog.
n. 4
Macedonia: **III** 162, 203, 563, 567, 594
n. 1; **IV** 17, 379 n. 1, 578
Mackenzie, Dr Morell: **III** 212 biog.
n. 2, 213–15, 217–19, 227, 259–60,
262, 265–6, 269–70, 282
Mackinnon, Sir William: **III** 341 biog.
n. 5
Maclean, Sir Harry Kaid: **IV** 265 biog.
n. 3
Malet, Sir Edward: **III** 64 biog. n. 5,
175–8, 181, 190, 340, 413, 433 n. 2,
434, 441, 538, 551–2, 554 n. 1 & 2,
556
Malietoa, King of Samoa (1880–98):
**III** 342 n. 3
Maltzan-Gültz, August, Count von: **III**
40 biog. n. 4
Manchuria: **IV** 196–8, 201, 213, 282–3,
327
Manteuffel, General Edwin, Baron von:
**III** 46 biog. n. 4, 90–1, 125, 146 n. 3,
149, 225
Manteuffel, Otto von: **IV** 248 n. 4
Maple, Sir John Blundell: **IV** 117 n. 5,
226
Margaret, Queen of Italy: **III** 317 n. 5,
319, 336
Margarethe, Princess of Prussia: **III**
168, 185–6, 189
Maria Christina, Queen of Spain,
Regent (1885–1902): **III** 225 biog.
n. 5, 227, 367, 370
Maria Feodorovna, Tsarina of Russia:
**III** 250, 284 biog. n. 1, 287, 328, 363
n. 2, 505 n. 5, 518, 565, 632; **IV** 2, 4,
6, 60
Marschall von Bieberstein, Adolf Hermann, Baron: **III** 333 biog. n. 1;
domestic affairs, **III** 473 n. 1, 480,

491, 496, 498–506, 508, 569, 573,
575, 577, 579, 586–7, 590, 594, 601,
603–4, 609–12, 618, 621–5, 629–30,
633–5, 642, 651–5, 660, 663; anti-
revolutionary bill, **III** 475, 496–504,
508; military courts-martial question,
**III** 595, 598, 608–10, 613–15, 617–
18, 620–30, 632–7, 639–42, 645–50;
relations with Hohenlohe, **III** 560–1,
568–71, 573–5, 578–9, 586–7, 589–
90, 593–4, 603–4, 651–6; with
Wilhelm II, **IV** 34, 42 n. 1, 44–5,
546–7, 568; Austria, **III** 588, 591–2;
Great Britain, **III** 494 n. 1, 576;
Portugal, **III** 365 n. 1, 367, 371–2,
374; Russia, **III** 616; Turkey, **IV** 461
n. 2, 572–3, 581, 586, 588, 592, 599,
615; miscellaneous, **III** 337, 339–40,
342–3, 348, 354–5, 359–60, 363, 369,
380 n. 1, 389, 392 n. 3, 407, 424 n. 4,
434 n. 2, 438, 461, 479 n. 3, 488, 509,
514, 516–21, 529, 531, 551 n. 3, 559
n. 2, 560 n. 4, 566 n. 1, 576 n. 1, 578,
655 n. 3, 658, 659 n. 3, 661–2; **IV** 13,
14, 16, 19, 22, 25, 26 n. 1, 27–9, 46,
49, 259, 449, 456, 473, 485, 513, 573,
581
Letter to, **III** 479
Letters from, **IV** 59, 101–2, 458
Martens: **IV** 125
Martin, Rudolf: **IV** 542 biog. n. 1
Maybach, Albert von: **III** 157 biog. n. 1,
325
Mayer, Edmundo: **III** 318 biog. n. 4
Mayer, Wilhelm: **IV** 537 biog. n. 1,
538–40
Mayr, Dr Georg von: **IV** 433 biog.
n. 4
McKinley, William: **IV** 92 biog. n. 4,
110, 166
Mecklenburg, Helene, Princess von: **III**
73 n. 3, 86
Meerscheidt-Hüllesem: **IV** 532 biog.
n. 1, 544 n. 2
Meiningen: see Charlotte, Princess of
Mendelssohn: **III** 389 n. 5; **IV** 224 n. 3,
402 n. 3
Menelik II, Negus of Abyssinia (1889–
1914): **III** 318 biog. n. 2, 549
n. 2
Mensdorff, Count: **IV** 324 n. 1
Mentzingen, Friedrich, Baron von: **IV**
265 biog. n. 2
Mérey von Kapos-Mére, Baron: **IV** 456
biog. n. 10
Mesnil, Oskar, Baron de: **III** 25 biog.
n. 1

Metternich zur Gracht, Paul, Count von Wolff- : **III** 403 biog. n. 3, 407 n. 1, 410 n. 2, 411 n. 3 & 4, 414, 601, 607, 608 n. 1; **IV** 244–5, 257–60, 274–5, 291, 316–17, 319, 321, 323–4, 337, 365, 377, 404, 447, 457, 465, 549–50, 552–4, 559, 566, 568
Letters to, **IV** 127–9, 135–6, 183, 261–2, 320–1
Letters from, **III** 407–8, 410–12; **IV** 133, 217–18, 230, 236–7, 252–4
Meyer-Cohn : **III** 6 biog. n. 1, 7
Michael Nicholaivich, Grand Duke of Russia : **III** 565; **IV** 1 biog. n. 4, 7
Midhat Pasha : **III** 564 biog. n. 3
Milan I, Prince, then King of Serbia (1868–89) : **III** 285, 286 n. 2, 292, 311 n. 2; **IV** 148 n. 1
Militza, Princess of Montenegro : **III** 308 n. 4
Miliutin, Dimitri, Count : **III** 85 biog. n. 3
Minghetti, Donna Laura : **III** 111 n. 1, 473, 590; **IV** 14, 48, 219, 254, 307, 439, 441, 600
Minghetti, Marco : **III** 111 biog. n. 2; **IV** 439
Miquel, Hans von : **IV** 341 biog. n. 4, 357
Miquel, Dr Johannes von : **III** 388, 402, 475 biog. n. 6, 506, 642, 645; **IV** 18, 42, 44–6, 168, 437, 485, 491, 533
Mirbach-Sorquitten, Julius, Count von : **III** 423 n. 2, 653 biog. n. 3, 654
Mittnacht, Hermann, Baron von : **III** 356 biog. n. 1
Mohrenheim, Arthur, Baron von : **III** 195 biog. n. 1 & n. 3, 520–1, 599
Moll, Dr Albert : **IV** 519 biog. n. 4
Möller, Theodor von : **IV** 437 biog. n. 7, 526
Moltke, Friedrich von : **IV** 497 biog. n. 3
Moltke, General Helmuth von : **III** 72 biog. n. 2, 125–6, 128, 233, 234 n. 5, 236, 242, 253, 255, 264
Moltke, General Helmuth Johannes Ludwig von : **III** 545 biog. n. 1, 556; **IV** 571
Moltke, Kuno, Count von : **III** 469 biog. n. 5, 500, 601; **IV** 447, 458 n. 1, 472 n. 1, 475–84, 498, 500–2, 505–9, 511 n. 2, 513–14, 517, 519, 521–2, 524, 528 n. 1 & 4, 532, 539, 560, 564, 569–70, 572–6, 580–2, 586, 589, 591, 596, 605, 621–2
Moltke, Otto, Count von : **IV** 475–9, 481–2

Monaco, Albert, Prince of : **IV** 279 n. 5, 280–1, 314, 346, 370, 374, 400, 488 n. 1, 489, 497, 620
Monbart, Fräulein von : **IV** 480
Monson, Sir Edmund : **III** 320 biog. n. 2, 415
Montebello, Adrien, Count : **III** 423 biog. n. 4, 540
Montenegro : **III** 203, 209; **IV** 38, 461, 580, 587, 599, 607
Monts, Anton, Count von : **III** 183 biog. n. 2, 235, 246, 312, 500, 502, 504, 508, 577, 593, 658; **IV** 11, 288 n. 3, 340, 375, 387, 404–5, 433, 440–1, 457, 494, 605
Letter to, **IV** 428
Letters from, **III** 183–4, 302–4, 311–12, 380–3, 455, 542; **IV** 284, 438–9
Moreau : **IV** 363, 370, 372
Moret y Prendergast, Segismundo : **III** 208 biog. n. 1, 226
Morgen, Major : **IV** 136
Morier, Sir Robert : **III** 128 biog. n. 4, 137 n. 3, 174, 176, 238–9, 387–8
Morocco : **III** 129 n. 2, 226, 373, 375–7, 390–7, 410–12, 443, 531, 544; **IV** 9, 112, 114, 120–2, 129, 137–8, 140–1, 150, 165, 169, 184, 232–3, 250, 255, 257–9, 261–5, 274, 276, 279, 288, 293, 328–43, 345–76, 378, 380–2, 385–7, 389–407, 410–11, 424, 428, 430, 437, 442, 478, 480, 488, 491–3, 528–31, 533–4, 548–9, 556–63, 566–7, 571–2, 577, 579, 581, 583, 613, 620
Morphy : **III** 154
Morrison, G. E. : **IV** 205 biog. n. 3
Moser, Rudolf von : **III** 462 biog. n. 1
Mouy : **III** 253 biog. n. 2
Mozambique : **III** 493–4, 506
Mühlberg, Otto von : **III** 514 biog. n. 7, 529 n. 5, 530; **IV** 13, 180, 300, 309, 334, 338, 352, 386, 404–6, 410, 474, 490 n. 4, 493, 495, 497, 576
Letters to, **IV** 298, 299, 423
Letters from, **IV** 419, 423
Mulai Hafid, Sultan of Morocco (1908–1912) : **IV** 530 biog. n. 1, 557–9, 561–3, 566–7
Müller, Felix von : **IV** 234 n. 2, 494 biog. n. 3
Müller, Admiral Georg Alexander von : **IV** 480 biog. n. 2, 552
Mumm von Schwarzenstein, Alfons, Baron : **III** 516 biog. n. 3, 660; **IV** 46, 309
Munckel : **III** 39 n. 1

Münster, Georg Herbert, Count zu: **III**
60 biog. n. 3, 61, 63, 65–6, 68–70,
114, 121, 126–7, 129–30, 139, 141,
146, 148 n. 4, 155–6, 159, 195, 344,
385, 424, 474 n. 1, 511, 528, 584 n. 4,
596 n. 1 & 2, 604, 607; **IV** 71, 127–8,
131 n. 2, 135, 171–2, 174, 336–7
Letters from, **III** 340–2, 368–70,
409–10, 474, 480, 488, 517–18, 584–
85, 596, 599–600, 606–7; **IV** 107–8,
125–7
Murad V, Sultan of Turkey (1876): **IV**
241
Muraviev, Michael, Count: **III** 194
biog. n. 1, 357–8, 360; **IV** 1–8, 38
n. 3, 47, 48 n. 2, 50, 52–4, 57–8, 60–1,
64, 125, 136–7, 142–6, 149, 184
Muscat: **IV** 122, 339
Mutkurov: **III** 175 biog. n. 3

Napoleon III, President, then Emperor
of France (1848–70): **III** 19; **IV** 105,
177
Napoleon, Prince (Plon-Plon): **III** 78
biog. n. 4, 82
Natalie, Queen of Serbia: **III** 285–6,
292
National Liberals: **III** 402, 405, 423
n. 1, 656–7; **IV** 616
*National Zeitung*: 96–7, 106, 664
Navy (German): **III** 126, 137, 262,
264, 295, 344, 347, 358, 496, 505–6,
586, 589–90, 602–3, 623, 629, 635,
639, 641, 649, 657, 659, 664; **IV** 82,
284, 427–9, 449–50, 453, 488, 490–
1, 566–8; Kaiser's views, **IV** 5, 11,
14, 18–19, 23–4, 27–8, 45, 167–8,
488, 516–17, 552–3; relations with
Britain, **IV** 25, 261, 323, 325, 339,
356, 410, 457, 495, 509–10, 549–51,
552–6, 559–63, 570–2, 584–5, 593,
598–600, 602
Navy League: **IV** 449–50, 454, 457,
488, 509, 555
Négrier, General: **IV** 336
Nelidov, Alexander: **III** 492 biog. n. 3;
**IV** 6, 15, 40, 313, 357
Netherlands: **IV** 112–13, 138, 318, 329
n. 1, 330
*Neue Freie Presse*: **IV** 430, 440, 469
n. 1
*Neue Gesellschaftliche Korrespondenz*: **IV**
423, 562, 567
Neven-Dumont, Joseph: **IV** 415, 422,
425–6
Letter to, **IV** 333–8
Letter from, **IV** 332–3

Nicholas I, Tsar of Russia (1825–55):
**III** 250, 256, 553; **IV** 554
Nicholas II, Tsar of Russia (1894–
1917): **III** 116 n. 2, 168, 179, 289
biog. n. 1, 424 n. 1, 489, 505 n. 5,
509, 512, 517–18, 521, 524 n. 2, 526–
27, 530, 545, 549 n. 2, 556, 562, 565,
567 n. 1, 576, 580, 584 n. 3, 618 n. 1,
632, 634, 643, 652 n. 3, 653, 655 n. 3,
659–61, 663; **IV** 1, 4, 35, 49–50, 53,
54, 57, 60–1, 80, 82, 100, 106, 108,
125, 131, 136, 157, 186, 193–4, 196,
198 n. 3, 199–201, 207, 278, 282–3,
315, 317–19, 326, 357, 444, 463,
472–3, 486–7, 516, 598, 604, 612
Nicholas Michailovich, Grand Duke of
Russia: **III** 179 biog. n. 12, 180–1
Nicholas Nicholaievich, Grand Duke of
Russia: **III** 179 biog. n. 11, 180–1
Nicholas, Prince, then King of Montenegro (1860–1918): **III** 308 n. 4
Nicolson, Sir Arthur: **IV** 378 biog. n. 5,
620
Nieberding, Rudolf: **IV** 517 biog. n. 7
Nigra, Constantino, Count: **III** 200
biog. n. 1, 319, 453, 572, 590; **IV**
124, 286
Nikiphorov, N. P.: **IV** 611 biog. n. 2
Noailles, Marquis de: **IV** 233 biog. n. 1,
336
*Norddeutsche Allgemeine Zeitung*: **III**
129, 131, 185, 313, 316, 330; **IV** 47
n. 3, 266 n. 3, 269, 334–5, 437, 530,
535, 542, 559, 561 n. 5, 619
Normann, Karl von: **III** 95 biog. n. 1,
223
Novi Bazar, Sanjak of: **IV** 515, 587, 607

Obernitz: **III** 40 biog. n. 2, 45
Obrutshev, General Nicholas: **III** 109
biog. n. 5, 247; **IV** 52
O'Connor, Sir Nicholas: **III** 563 biog.
n. 4
Oertel, Dr Georg: **IV** 493 biog. n. 1
Ojetti: **IV** 266, 462
Oldenburg-Januschau, Elard von: **IV**
464 biog. n. 5
Olenhusen, Götz von: **IV** 464 biog.
n. 1
Olga, Queen of Greece: **III** 283, 288
biog. n. 1; **IV** 473
Oliphant: **III** 35
Olmütz, Punctuation of: **IV** 248, 491
Onou: **III** 70 biog. n. 3
Oppersdorff, Hans Georg, Count von:
**IV** 615 biog. n. 3
Orleanists: **III** 73–6, 78–9, 86, 92, 98

Orlov, Nicholas, Prince: **III** 102 biog. n. 5, 107
Orly, Admiral: **III** 309 n. 1
Ormond: **III** 258
Oskar II, King of Sweden (1872–1907): **III** 290 biog. n. 1, 340 n. 1
Oskar, Prince of Prussia: **III** 291
Osman Nisami Pasha: **IV** 588 biog. n. 4, 599
Osten-Sacken, Nicholas Dimitri, Count: **III** 509 biog. n. 2, 510, 517, 529–31, 537, 542, 660; **IV** 4, 8, 53, 128, 131, 136, 142–3, 221, 226, 396–7, 401 n. 2, 515, 612, 614

Paasche, Dr Hermann: **III** 654 biog. n. 3
Palézieux, Falconnet von: **IV** 476 biog. n. 1
Pallain: **III** 98–100, 142
Palmerston, Henry John Temple, Viscount: **III** 422; **IV** 177, 553
Parnell, Charles Stewart: **III** 62 n. 2, 63 biog. n. 4
Paul, Grand Duke of Russia: **III** 168 n. 4, 179
Pauncefote, Sir Julian: **IV** 124 biog. n. 3
Pecci, Countess: **III** 301–2
Penzler, Johannes: **IV** 431 biog. n. 4
Perpignan, Mlle: **III** 223 biog. n. 2
Persia: **III** 36, 563; **IV** 136, 138, 164, 175, 259, 339, 348, 366, 424
Persiani: **III** 285 biog. n. 2
Pescadores Islands: **III** 510 n. 4, 512 n. 1, 513, 519, 529 n. 1
Peter Nicholaievich, Grand Duke of Russia: **III** 308 n. 4
Peters, Dr Karl: **III** 295 biog. n. 1, 296; **IV** 485
Pfaff: **IV** 527–8
Pfeil, Count: **IV** 21 n. 4
Philippe, Comte de Paris: **III** 73 n. 3, 78–9, 86 biog. n. 1, 192
Philippine Islands: **IV** 76, 79 n. 6, 89, 110–11, 115
Pichon, Stephen Jean-Marie: **IV** 444 biog. n. 1, 491, 558
Pisani-Dossi, Alberto (Carlos Dossi): **III** 318 biog. n. 3
Pless, Hans Heinrich, Prince of: **IV** 542 biog. n. 3
Plessen, General Hans von: **III** 280 biog. n. 5, 283, 469, 471, 573, 619, 659–60; **IV** 45–6, 218, 245, 497, 544
Plessen, Ludwig, Baron von Scheel-: **III** 138 biog. n. 2

Pobedonoszev, Constantin: **III** 249 biog. n. 3, 256; **IV** 7
Podbielski, Viktor von: **IV** 291 biog. n. 1, 437–8, 469, 485, 491, 533
Podewils, Klemens, Count von: **IV** 593 biog. n. 4
Poincaré, Raymond: **III** 474 biog. n. 5
Poland: **III** 19, 23, 94, 237–8, 248, 255; **IV** 3, 240–1, 266 n. 3, 453, 456–7, 467, 515, 546
Polovzov: **III** 249–50, 520
Polstorff, Wilhelm: **III** 461 n. 3, 463
Porter, Horace: **IV** 313 biog. n. 5, 314
Portugal: **III** 363–7, 370–7, 380, 465; **IV** 22, 24–5, 33, 88–9, 93, 141, 184–7, 209, 215–16, 329 n. 1, 331, 336
Portuguese Colonies: **IV** 88, 98–9, 110–11, 154, 165, 173
Posadowsky-Wehner, Arthur, Count von: **III** 571 biog. n. 1; **IV** 45, 491
Poschinger, Heinrich, Ritter von: **III** 497 biog. n. 1
*Post*: **III** 75, 95, 97, 274, 296 n. 3, 421, 654
Pourtalès, Friedrich, Count von: **III** 278 biog. n. 1, 284, 288, 300, 360, 461, 467, 516; **IV** 45, 106, 306, 513, 515, 598–9, 620
   Letters to, **IV** 301, 303
   Letters from, **III** 278–9, 292–5, 306, 308–10, 325–8, 330–1; **IV** 302, 304–5
Press (British): **III** 169, 173, 178, 187, 385–6, 396, 496, 616; **IV** 30, 37, 70, 110, 160, 165, 171, 173, 185, 188, 256, 258, 265, 279, 563, 566; Germany, **IV** 81, 83, 236, 238–9, 253, 260–1, 269–70, 289, 551, 555, 570, 598–9, 602; *Daily Telegraph* affair, **IV** 591–5, 601
Press (German): Arnim affair, **III** 32–35; Bismarck Press, **III** 346, 389 n. 1, 449, 477–8, 589 n. 3; Official, **III** 38–9, 53, 55, 72, 74–6, 78, 82, 85–6, 95, 131, 242, 296 n. 4, 362, 505; **IV** 242, 260, 266, 270–1, 289, 292, 308, 377–8, 381–2, 392, 400, 404, 424–6, 452–3, 490–1, 526, 528, 530, 533–5, 557–8, 576, 588, 590, 601, 613–14, 619–20; attitude to Great Britain, **IV** 73–4, 109, 236, 238–9, 242–3, 246, 261, 271; Holstein, **III** 466–9, 473; **IV** 176–7, 332–8, 391, 415–17, 422–6, 428–9, 430–6, 448, 468, 502–4, 529–30, 533–4, 542–3, 545, 567–8, 584 (see also Harden-Holstein letters); miscellaneous, **III** 52, 95, 97, 106, 142, 188, 211, 255, 315

n. 1, 338, 346 n. 1, 413, 417, 420–
1, 530, 573, 601, 609, 623–4, 629,
632 n. 3, 636, 641, 652, 660 n. 4; **IV**
12–13, 57, 189, 199, 203, 503, 505
n. 2, 528 n. 1, 545, 548, 551, 558,
562–3, 573, 596–7, 619; *see also* under
names of leading newspapers.

Press Bureau (Foreign Ministry): **IV**
311, 381–2, 384–6, 388, 416, 425,
429, 437, 530, 534–5, 566, 619

Preysing-Lichtenegg-Moos, Konrad,
Count von: **III** 618 n. 1, 620 biog.
n. 1

Prinetti, Giulio, Marchese: **IV** 221
biog. n. 2, 246–8, 250–2, 254, 258–9,
267, 269, 445, 587

Prittwitz und Gaffron, General Karl
von: **IV** 596 biog. n. 3

Progressive Party: **III** 53, 128, 141,
251 n. 2, 297, 422

Pückler, Karl, Count von: **IV** 165 biog.
n. 4, 171

Pusch, Judge, **IV** 502 biog. n. 1
Letter to, **IV** 502–3

Puttkamer, Maximilian von: **III** 90
biog. n. 2; **IV** 433

Puttkamer, Robert von: **III** 90 biog.
n. 4, 128, 130

Rabe, Major von: **III** 227 biog. n. 2, 233
Radolin, Alfred von: **IV** 421
Radolin, Elizabeth von: **III** 569 biog.
n. 2

Radolin-Radolinski, Hugo Leszczyc,
Count, then Prince von Radolin: **III**
x, 110 biog. n. 1, 168, 169 n. 3 & 4,
216 n. 4, 218, 231, 277, 359, 414,
415, 423–4, 430, 438 n. 2, 452, 462,
511, 515 n. 3, 517 n. 3, 520 n. 2, 530,
536 n. 3 & 4, 537, 539 n. 3, 549, 569
n. 2 & 3, 600, 601 n. 1, 604; **IV** 48
n. 2, 50, 61, 131 n. 2, 142–3, 193–4,
197, 200, 202, 212, 324, 334, 369–70,
373–4, 380 n. 2, 387, 401, 476, 488,
497 n. 2, 530–1, 565, 568, 573
Letters to, **III** 110, 159–61, 164–5,
170, 172, 174–6, 181–3, 187–93,
215–16, 217, 220–3, 232–3, 268–9,
297, 316–17, 323, 412–13, 466–7,
472–3, 506, 513–21, 527–32, 562,
569, 575–6, 584, 601–4, 615–16,
660–1; **IV** 1, 7–8, 34, 46–7, 106–7,
144–6, 189, 232, 241–2, 255, 266–8,
278–80, 298, 301, 306–7, 308, 311–
14, 323, 329–31, 338–43, 346–56,
359–60, 364, 367–8, 370–2, 386,
388–95, 414–15, 500–1

Letters from, **III** 155–6, 168, 179–
82, 185–91, 214–22, 227–33 257–70,
384–5, 473, 492–3, 509, 526–7, 535–6,
539–41, 545–6; **IV** 5–7, 60, 136–9,
157–8, 198–9, 201, 274, 280–2, 314–
15, 345–6, 360–4, 372, 374–5, 390,
393–5, 397

Radolin, Johanna, Princess von (née
Countess Oppersdorff): **III** 413 n. 1,
467, 482, 519, 562, 569, 576; **IV** 306,
367 n. 3, 467
Letters to, **IV** 250–1, 303–4, 395

Radolin, Lucy Josephine Julie von
(Doudouce): **III** 110 n. 7, 268, 467,
541, 562, 576

Radowitz, Joseph Maria von: **III** 42
biog. n. 3, 44–5, 48, 67 n. 2, 87, 112,
116, 205, 386, 396, 398, 413–14, 462,
497, 500, 604, 653; **IV** 82, 110, 184,
287, 387, 402 n. 1, 411, 454, 478,
497, 536
Letter to, **IV** 378
Letter from, **IV** 387

Rampolla del Tindaro, Mariano, Cardinal: **III** 299 biog. n. 4, 300

Rantzau, Kuno, Count von: **III** 41 n. 4,
49 biog. n. 1, 51, 81, 104–5, 107,
117–18, 182–3, 264 n. 3, 271, 275,
300, 314 n. 3, 335–6, 361
Letter from, **III** 101

Rantzau, Marie, Countess (née Countess
Bismarck): **III** 41 biog. n. 4, 44, 105

Ras Alula: **III** 206 biog. n. 2

Rasch: **IV** 521–3

Raschdau, Ludwig: **III** 297 biog. n. 4,
348, 359, 441, 577, 611, 653; **IV** 45,
234 n. 2, 429–30, 598
Letter from, **III** 297–300

Rascón, Juan Antonio, Conde de: **IV** 78
biog. n. 3

Rathenau, Emil: **IV** 480 biog. n. 1

Rathenau, Walther: **IV** 480 n. 1, 482
n. 3, 485, 522, 570, 586 biog. n. 5,
589

Ratibor und Corvey, Max, Prince von:
**III** 382 biog. n. 1, 479 n. 2; **IV** 45
Letter from, **III** 478–9

Rauch, Major von: **III** 5

Redern, Wilhelm, Count von: **III** x, 55
biog. n. 4, 142 biog. n. 1, 192; **IV** 294
biog. n. 4

Regnault: **IV** 492 biog. n. 3

Reichstag: **III** 45, 128, 141, 143, 201,
207, 241, 280, 314, 324, 329, 332,
337, 384 n. 1, 389 n. 1, 402, 406, 422,
475–6, 499, 501, 504, 561, 586, 589
n. 2, 593, 601, 603, 609, 613, 618

646

n. 2 & 3, 622–3, 626–7, 629–30, 635, 639, 642, 645, 652–8; **IV** 11–12, 14, 18–19, 46, 170, 237, 272, 275, 403, 452–4, 456–7, 463, 465, 466–8, 471, 473, 490, 499, 516, 523, 525–6, 595–6, 602, 616–17

Reichenau, Lieutenant-Colonel von : **III** 381–2

Reinach, Joseph : **IV** 361 n. 1, 364

Reischach, Hugo, Baron von : **IV** 294 biog. n. 3, 419 n. 1

René, Karl : **IV** 503–4

Renvers, Dr Rudolph von : **IV** 385 biog. n. 3, 408, 411, 413, 505, 597

Reouf Pasha : **III** 531 biog. n. 3

Ressmann : **III** 474 biog. n. 7

Reuss, Henrich VII, Prince : **III** 127 biog. n. 2, 146, 161, 172 n. 2, 196, 212 n. 1, 233 n. 5, 234 n. 4, 235 n. 3, 312, 322 n. 3, 357 n. 2, 359, 364 n. 2, 380 n. 1, 382, 389, 405, 417, 421, 447 n. 3, 448, 450, 453 n. 2, 455, 456 n. 1 & 3, 459, 462, 479, 660, 663
Letters from, **III** 198–212, 233–6, 240–3, 245–6, 251–5, 271–4, 304–5, 307–8, 322, 328, 338, 340, 359, 363–5, 379–80, 453–4, 456, 471–2

Reuss, Princess (née Princess of Sachsen-Weimar-Eisenach) : **III** 455, 459, 663

Révoil, Paul : **IV** 345 biog. n. 6, 351–5, 368, 392–6, 558

Rex : **IV** 128 biog. n. 1

Rheinbaben, Georg, Baron von : **IV** 521 biog. n. 2, 527

Rhodes, Sir Cecil : **III** 493 biog. n. 4; **IV** 30, 33, 118, 160, 172, 184, 186–7

Ribot, Alexandre : **III** 369 biog. n. 3

Richter, Eugen : **III** 659 n. 3; **IV** 526 biog. n. 2

Richter, General : **III** 284 biog. n. 3; **IV** 7

Richter, *Ministerialrat* : **III** 246 n. 3

Richthofen, Oswald, Baron von : **III** 655 biog. n. 2; **IV** 96–8, 135, 143–4, 206 n. 4, 225, 244–5, 248, 251, 254 n. 1, 259, 269–70, 272, 289–90, 292–9, 303–5, 308–11, 313, 317, 319, 336, 338, 367–8, 384 n. 2, 386, 392, 410
Letters to, **IV** 262–3, 287–8
Letter from, **IV** 311

Rickert, Heinrich : **IV** 616 biog. n. 2

Riedl, Georg : **IV** 517 n. 2, 528 n. 1, 537 n. 2, 538, 539 biog. n. 1, 540–1, 575

Rifaat Pasha : **III** 564 biog. n. 5

Röber, Frau : **IV** 596 biog. n. 1

Roberts, Lord : **IV** 261 biog. n. 2, 598

Roberts, Elmer : **IV** 550

Robilant, Nicolis, Count di : **III** 198 biog. n. 3, 199–206, 209

Roels : **IV** 533

Romberg : **IV** 611 biog. n. 4, 612

Roosevelt, Theodore : **IV** 251 n. 1, 278 biog. n. 2, 326, 342–3, 381, 387 n. 1, 522 n. 5

Röse, Otto : **IV** 429 biog. n. 1, 434, 450
Letter to, **IV** 429–30
Letter from, **IV** 430 n. 1

Rosebery, Archibald Primrose, 5th Earl of : **III** 65 biog. n. 2; personality, **III** 433, 447; Egypt, **III** 430, 434 n. 2, 438 n. 2; France, **III** 443; Germany, **III** 439–42, 444, 446 n. 1 & 2; Mediterranean, **III** 447, 450 n. 3, 451, 453, 460, 464–5, 467 n. 3, 482, 487, 544; miscellaneous, **III** 165 n. 4, 341, 404–5, 414, 422, 425–7, 433 n. 2, 434–7, 441 n. 2, 444–6, 452, 483, 485 n. 2, 493 n. 5, 512, 533, 538; **IV** 83, 170–1, 175, 186

Rosen, Friedrich : **IV** 271, 287 n. 3, 294 biog. n. 2, 305, 349, 367–72, 374, 375 n. 1, 388, 394, 501, 510, 561–3, 565, 566–7, 579

Rosenberg, General Heinrich von : **III** 45 biog. n. 3

Rotenhan, Wolfram, Baron von : **III** 120 biog. n. 1, 138, 140–1, 385 n. 5, 441 n. 2, 537, 621–2, 640, 644, 647; **IV** 52, 92–3, 194
Letter from, **III** 140

Rothschild, Alfred de : **III** 515 biog. n. 1; **IV** 65 n. 1, 71, 116–17, 147, 160, 164, 173–4, 197, 206, 224, 257, 260, 275, 326, 404

Rothschild, Meyer Alphonse von : **III** 107, 303

Rothstein : **III** 529 biog. n. 6, 530 n. 2, 602; **IV** 138

Rottenburg, Dr Franz Johannes von : **III** ix, 102 biog. n. 1, 107, 119, 160, 224, 301, 313, 325

Rouvier, Maurice : **IV** 338 biog. n. 6, 339–43, 345–8, 350 n. 3, 352–7, 359, 361–5, 368, 371–5, 389 n. 1, 393–4, 396–8, 401, 404, 420

Rücker-Jenisch, Martin, Baron von : **IV** 550 biog. n. 4, 551, 596

Rudini, Antonio, Marchese di : **III** 378 biog. n. 1, 390–1, 396–7, 489 n. 4; **IV** 248, 250, 254

Rudolf, Archduke of Austria : **III** 214 and n. 2, 305, 307–8

Rüger : **IV** 527

Rumania : **III** 162, 165 n. 5, 167–8, 309, 320–2, 592; **IV** 603

Russia : Armenia, **III** 563–7, 576, 580; Austria, **III** 93–4, 101, 109, 132, 166, 172, 236, 239, 240–3, 246, 253, 278, 294, 311–12, 321, 363–4, 378, 389, 452, 573; **IV** 2–3, 38, 53, 78, 457, 462–3; Bosnia, **IV** 577–80, 583–8, 590–1, 598–600, 604, 606–9, 611–12, 615, 617–18; Bulgaria, **III** 86–9, 152–3, 158, 164–5, 171–8, 192, 194, 199–200, 239, 269, 272–3, 285, 294, 319–20; Crete, **III** 632, 643; **IV** 17–18, 35, 40, 54, 64; Eastern question, **III** 43, 157–8, 166, 188, 203, 319, 321–2, 349–50, 385–6, 424 n. 4, 425–30, 443, 447–50, 451, 453, 459–60, 467 n. 3, 482, 484–6, 493, 547, 549, 552, 555, 557, 560, 580–2, 588–92, 664–5; **IV** 6, 8–9, 14 n. 2, 15, 38–9, 48, 61, 128, 136, 138–9, 175, 236, 267, 276, 284, 379, 461, 474, 489, 535, 546, 553 n. 2, 554; Egypt, **III** 559–600, 602, 604–7, 615–16; Far East, **IV** 5, 36–7, 49–53, 57–61, 107, 188–9, 193–4, 196–202, 206 n. 4, 209, 217, 221 n. 5, 222–4, 253, 255, 469; France, **III** 55–6, 81–2, 88, 193–7, 226, 249, 278, 306, 387, 437–8, 443, 596, 605–6, 655 n. 3; **IV** 10, 23–4, 62–3, 66, 165–6, 184, 267, 356, 365, 394, 434, 444, 556, 565; Germany, **III** 56, 70–3, 84–5, 101, 107, 109, 164–70, 172 n. 2, 187, 201, 213–14, 228, 236–40, 246–7, 249, 278–9, 286, 290, 292–4, 306, 308, 313, 322, 326–8, 330–1, 340, 342, 345, 358, 360, 363, 389, 425, 509, 550, 562, 584, 604, 618–19, 652 n. 2, 659, 661; **IV** 1, 23, 26, 32, 68, 77, 80–5, 88, 99–100, 108, 116, 118 n. 3, 142–6, 151, 156–8, 167, 187, 196–8, 211–12, 217–18, 231, 240–1, 249, 252, 254, 268, 277, 288, 312, 316–21, 323–6, 356–7, 377, 381, 411, 424–5, 429, 444–5, 455, 486–7, 529, 554; Great Britain, **III** 145, 148, 172, 306, 317, 411–12, 429 n. 4, 425, 444, 534, 597, 616; **IV** 27, 30–1, 41, 66, 69, 71–3, 75–6, 92–3, 115, 129, 149, 150, 160–5, 169–71, 175, 209, 219, 222–3, 261–2, 274–5, 279, 339, 470, 515–16, 577–8; Hague Peace Conferences, **IV** 124–7, 131, 458, 465 n. 1; Morocco, **IV** 331, 356, 365–6, 397, 401–2, 404, 410, 556, 558, 562; Reinsurance Treaty, **III** 333 n. 6, 337 n. 5, 338,

340, 652 n. 2; **IV** 2, 38; Russo-Japanese war, **IV** 277–80, 282–3, 311–18, 320, 326–8, 340 n. 4; Portugal, **III** 363 n. 2, 366, 373; Sino-Japanese war and Chinese loan, **III** 495, 507, 510–21, 523–4, 526–33, 536–7, 539–41, 544–6; Three Emperors League, **III** 126–7; Triple Alliance, **III** 81; Turkey, **III** 43, 435, 532 n. 4

Rustem Pasha : **III** 386, 398–9, 404, 532

Rüte, Princess : **III** 136 biog. n. 2

Saburov, Peter : **III** 55 n. 2, 101 biog. n. 2, 102, 108

Sagasta, Praxides Mateo : **III** 154 biog. n. 7

Saigo, Marquis : **IV** 23 n. 2

Saint-Saëns, Camille : **IV** 467

Salis, John Francis Charles, Count de : **IV** 510 biog. n. 3

Salisbury, Robert Gascoyne-Cecil, 3rd Marquis of : **III** 61 biog. n. 2; Abyssinia, **III** 543, 555, 597; Crete, **III** 643–4, 664; domestic affairs, **III** 378; **IV** 169, 172, 186–7, 220, 255; Egypt, **III** 596, 599–600, 607; **IV** 15 n. 2; Far East, **III** 541; **IV** 37, 51–2 55–6, 65, 107, 185–6, 188, 200, 202, 206–8; France, **III** 391; **IV** 184; Germany, **III** 537–8, 543; **IV** 41, 67, 69–74, 81–9, 101 n. 4, 108–23, 128–9, 138–43, 148–62, 164–5, 168–71, 175, 183, 185, 187, 189, 206, 209–13, 219, 222, 224, 231–2, 253, 271; Greece, **IV** 16–18, 26–7, 40, 62–4; Morocco, **III** 411; **IV** 137, 250; Portugal, **III** 365 n. 1, 366–7, 370–7; South Africa, **III** 586; **IV** 29–33, 36, 98, 140, 148; Togo, **III** 547; Triple Alliance, **III** 534, 598; Tuat, **III** 390–4, 397, 404; Turkey, **III** 379, 386, 398, 407–8, 410–11, 413–14, 531–5, 544, 549, 555–60, 564, 566–7, 572 n. 1, 576, 632, 664; miscellaneous, **III** 62, 148, 157–8, 165–7, 171–2, 176–7, 188, 193, 204, 207, 220, 273, 340–2, 351–2, 377–8, 387–8, 390 n. 4, 393 n. 2, 396, 404 n. 4, 405, 427, 436, 444, 449, 452, 460, 483, 484, 486–7, 512, 528, 530, 542, 552, 554, 565, 617, 661, 664 n. 1; **IV** 9, 22, 25, 39, 104, 257, 259, 261–2

Letters from, **III** 393, 414–15, 539

Salm-Horstmar, Otto, Prince and Rheingraf zu : **IV** 510 biog. n. 4

Samoa: **III** 342, 378; **IV** 23, 33, 34, 79 n. 6, 109–13, 118 n. 3, 119–21, 132, 137–8, 140–1, 143 n. 2, 144, 152–65, 171, 176–7, 239, 271

Sanderson, Sir Thomas Henry: **III** 453 biog. n. 1, 510, 533, 566; **IV** 26, 30, 39, 109, 215–16, 222
Letter from, **IV** 17–18

Sarrien: **IV** 401 n. 1

Saucy: **III** 194

Sauerwein, Captain: **IV** 394

Saunders, George: **IV** 457 biog. n. 6

Saurma v. d. Jeltsch, Anton von: 59 biog. n. 1, 68–9, 403, 558 n. 2, 562, 564–5, 643; **IV** 15, 36, 38, 40 n. 1, 44, 123 n. 2
Letter from, **III** 557–8

Saxony: **III** 299, 622, 627, 629; **IV** 11–12

Say, Léon: **III** 82 biog. n. 2, 98

Sayn-Wittgenstein, Peter, Prince von: **III** 310 n. 1

Schäfer, Colonel: **IV** 54 biog. n. 1

Schaumburg-Lippe, Adolf, Prince zu: **III** 611 n. 1, 612; **IV** 96 biog. n. 4

Schauss, Friedrich von: **III** 53 biog. n. 3

Scheefer: **IV** 446 biog. n. 6, 491

Schele, Friedrich Rabod, Baron von: **III** 501 biog. n. 1, 502, 504, 601

Schenck zu Schweinsburg, Baron: **III** 525 biog. n. 1

Scheven: **III** 31 biog. n. 7, 35–6

Schiemann, Professor Theodor: **IV** 258 biog. n. 2
Letters to, **IV** 417–18
Letters from, **IV** 416–18

Schleinitz, Alexander, Baron, then Count von: **III** 12 n. 7

*Schlesische Zeitung*: **IV** 429, 434, 450

Schlieffen, General Alfred, Count von: **III** 364 n. 4, 382, 594; **IV** 347, 613–15
Letter to, **IV** 314

Schlözer, Karl von: **IV** 268 biog. n. 1, 309

Schlözer, Kurd von: **III** 4 biog. n. 3, 5, 8, 14, 22–3, 67 n. 2, 462; **IV** 127

Schmidt: **IV** 530 biog. n. 4, 531

Schnäbele, Guillaume: **III** 212 n. 1, 226 n. 2, 387

Schoen, Wilhelm von: **IV** 290 biog. n. 2, 292, 308, 324 n. 3, 330 n. 2, 495, 497, 504, 556, 562–3, 566, 567 n. 1, 579, 582, 588, 590, 599 n. 3, 600–1, 618 n. 4
Letter from, **IV** 325–6

Schönborn-Buchheim, Friedrich, Count von: **III** 302 biog. n. 3

Schorlemer-Lieser, Klemens, Baron von: **IV** 496 biog. n. 1

Schrader, Dr: **III** 259 biog. n. 2, 262

Schrötter, Dr Leopold: **III** 227 biog. n. 4

Schuckmann: **IV** 21 n. 5

Schulenburg, Friedrich, Count von der: **IV** 317 biog. n. 3, 318–19

Schulz: **IV** 593

Schumacher: **III** 316

Schwabach, Julius Leopold: **III** 514 biog. n. 6

Schwabach, Paul von: **III** xiii; **IV** 244, 257, 260, 291, 317, 370
Letter from, **IV** 413–14

Schwartzkoppen, Erich von: **IV** 312 biog. n. 4

Schwartzkoppen, Maximilian von: **III** 480 biog. n. 5

Schwarzenberg, Felix, Prince von: **IV** 615 biog. n. 4

Schwarzhoff, Colonel Gross von: **IV** 135 biog. n. 4

Schweinitz, Hans Lothar von: **III** 72 biog. n. 4, 73, 84–5, 101–2, 106, 108–9, 113–17, 125, 142, 145–6, 148 n. 4, 165, 195–6, 213, 283, 287–8, 290, 292, 310 n. 3, 328, 330–1, 361, 363–5, 394, 423, 532, 550, 568, 577

Schweninger, Dr Ernst: **III** 103 biog. n. 1, 105–6, 114, 213, 228, 663; **IV** 499

Scott, Sir Charles Stewart: **IV** 149 biog. n. 1, 189, 212

Seckendorff, Captain Albert, Baron von: **III** 230 biog. n. 2, 260–1, 267–8, 280–1, 283, 291
Letter from, **III** 262–4

Seckendorff, Götz, Count von: **III** x, 94 biog. n. 1, 110, 113, 115, 147, 171, 216–23, 230, 232–3, 260, 265–6, 317, 368–9; **IV** 275
Letter from, **III** 94–5

Sello, Dr Erich: **IV** 507 biog. n. 3, 589

Semon, Dr: **III** 638

Senden und Bibran, Admiral Gustav: **III** 343 biog. n. 2, 593, 610–11, 649, 657, 659–60, 664; **IV** 14, 19, 27, 45, 49–50, 147, 245

Serbia: **III** 124 n. 2, 132, 158 n. 1, 203, 209, 256, 284–5, 292–3, 311–12, 321, 349, 644; **IV** 38, 146, 445, 494, 572, 578, 580, 587, 599, 607, 619–21

Seymour, Sir Beauchamp: **III** 66 biog. n. 4, 69, 440 n. 1

Shakir Pasha: **III** 398 biog. n. 5, 399, 533

Shirshkin: **III** 545 biog. n. 4; **IV** 6

Shuvalov, Paul, Count: **III** 193–6, 330 biog. n. 3, 331, 363, 597, 661, 663; **IV** 6

Shuvalov, Peter, Count: **III** 102 biog. n. 4

Siam: **III** 435, 437, 440, 443; **IV** 83, 259, 262–3

Silvela y de la Vielleuze, Francisco: **IV** 110 biog. n. 4

Skobelev, General Michael: **III** 89 biog. n. 1

Smith: **IV** 110

Social Democrats: **III** 141, 251 n. 2, 324 n. 2, 335 n. 3, 402, 405, 420, 475 n. 1; **IV** 190–1, 241, 439, 452–3, 456–7, 469, 481, 498, 568

Solms-Sonnenwalde, Eberhard, Count zu: **III** 48 biog. n. 2, 90, 318 n. 2, 360, 378 n. 1, 390, 397, 448, 456 n. 1; **IV** 103 n. 4, 105
Letters from, **III** 154, 208, 224, 244–5, 252–3, 276–7, 301–2, 318–19, 336, 342–3

Solomon Islands: **IV** 152, 162

Sommerfeld, Gustav von: **III** 94 biog. n. 2, 147, 159–61, 216, 224
Letter from, **III** 147

Sonnemann, Leopold: **III** 491 n. 6; **IV** 435 biog. n. 4

Sophie, Princess of Prussia, then Queen of Greece: **III** 168, 189, 319 n. 3

South Africa: **III** 372, 374, 493; **IV** 22–5, 29, 31, 33, 51, 92, 98–9, 101, 139, 149, 151, 171; Boer War, **IV** 158, 172–4, 176–7, 185, 187–8, 213, 215, 220, 236–7, 239, 243, 244 n. 5, 246 n. 4, 250, 255, 265–6, 269, 271, 275, 356; *See also* Transvaal

Southwell, Lord: **III** 27 biog. n. 3, 42

Southwest Africa: **III** 136 n. 1, 610; **IV** 173, 283 n. 2, 336, 360, 437 n. 5, 453 n. 5

Soveral, Luis Marie Pinto, Marquis de: **III** 380 biog. n. 5; **IV** 184

Spahn, Peter: **IV** 272 biog. n. 1, 490

Spain: France, **III** 91–2, 226; **IV** 350, 565; Germany, **III** 89–92, 154, 183, 208, 342; Great Britain, **III** 208–9; **IV** 110, 137–8; Morocco, **IV** 329 n. 1, 330, 353, 378, 395, 403, 405, 491, 530, 556; Philippines, **IV** 76, 78, 89, 115; Portugal, **III** 363 n. 2, 365–7, 370–3, 375, 377 n. 2; Tuat **III** 390 n. 3, 391–6; miscellaneous, **III** 89–92,

154, 410, 465, 512, 514 n. 1; **IV** 112, 232–3, 250, 311

Speck von Sternburg, Hermann, Baron: **IV** 110 biog. n. 1, 204, 343 n. 1, 444–5, 561
Letter to, **IV** 386–7
Letter from, **IV** 417

Speyer, Sir Edgar: **IV** 602 biog. n. 2

Spitzemberg, Karl Hugo, Baron von; **III** 45 biog. n. 2

St. Vallier, Charles, Count de: **IV** 336 biog. n. 1

Staal, Baron: **IV** 26 biog. n. 6, 115, 124, 208

Städele, Anton: **IV** 528 n. 1

Stahl, Professor Friedrich Julius: **IV** 529 biog. n. 3

Stambulov, Stefan: **III** 175 biog. n. 1, 594

Stanley, Sir Henry: **III** 341 biog. n. 6

Stein, August: **IV** 402 biog. n. 2, 415, 432–8, 454–5, 471–2, 493, 510, 525, 589, 619

Steininger, Karl, Baron von: **III** 233 n. 3 & 6, 242 n. 1, biog. n. 3

Stemrich, Wilhelm: **IV** 558 biog. n. 5, 578, 599–600
Letter from, **IV** 593–4

Stengel, Hermann, Baron von: **IV** 527 biog. n. 1

Stengel, Karl, Baron von: **IV** 108 biog. n. 1

Sternenberg: **IV** 290 biog. n. 3

Stirum: *see* Limburg-Stirum

Stock: **IV** 494 biog. n. 2

Stöcker, Adolf: **III** 251 n. 2, 323, 356

Stolberg-Wernigerode, Otto, Prince zu: **III** 421 biog. n. 1

Stolypin, Peter: **IV** 474 biog. n. 1

Stosch, General Albrecht von: **III** 95 biog. n. 2, 126, 264

Straits: *see* Dardanelles

*Strassburger Post*: **IV** 415 n. 2, 432

Struck, Dr Heinrich: **III** 41 biog. n. 2

Stuart-Wortley, Colonel: **IV** 493 biog. n. 1

Stübel, Oskar Wilhelm: **IV** 220 biog. n. 1, 223, 527

Stubenrauch: **IV** 525 biog. n. 1, 532

Studt, Konrad von: **III** 571 biog. n. 2; **IV** 433, 464

Stülpnagel, Ida von (née Holtzendorff): **III** ix, 3 biog. n. 5, 12, 14, 18, 22, 44, 160 n. 1; **IV** 407 n. 1
Letters to, **IV** 311 n. 1, 447 n. 6, 503 n. 2

Stülpnagel (Military Attaché): **III** 45

Stumm, Ferdinand, Baron von : **III** x, 42
n. 4, 67 biog. n. 3, 69, 295, 366, 393
n. 4, 498
Letters from, **III** 67, 226–7
Stumm-Halberg, Karl Ferdinand, Baron
von : **III** 416 biog. n. 4, 475 n. 1
Sturdie, Captain : **IV** 114
Sturdza, Demeter : **III** 167 biog. n. 3,
255
Suttner, Bertha, Baroness von : **IV** 469
biog. n. 3
Swaine, Colonel Leopold : **III** 485 n. 2,
547 biog. n. 2, 554, 576–8
Letter from, **III** 547–8
Sweden : **III** 290–1; **IV** 329 n. 1, 331,
546
Switzerland : **III** 129 n. 2, 310 n. 3,
313–16; **IV** 41
Sydow, Reinhold : **IV** 516 biog. n. 2,
527, 572
Széchényi, Imre, Count : **II** 23 biog.
n. 2; **III** 197, 206–7, 212, 233–5, 242,
252–5, 304–5
Szécsen von Temerin, Nicholas, Count :
**III** 322 biog. n. 1
Szögyényi-Marich, Ladislaus, Count
von : **III** 201 biog. n. 3, 255, 311, 450
n. 4, 489, 556, 580, 588, 591, 663;
**IV** 2, 8–9, 20, 38, 64, 251–2, 409,
473, 515, 579, 593, 605, 608–9, 614,
618–19, 621

Taaffe, Eduard, Count von : **III** 298,
n. 2, 299 biog. n. 3, 302–5, 317
Taglioni : **III** 36 biog. n. 2
Taillandier, Georges Saint-René : **IV**
338 biog. n. 4, 355
Tamasese : **III** 342 n. 3
Tardieu, André : **IV** 380 n. 6, 393 biog.
n. 3, 394
Tattenbach, Christian, Count von : **IV**
328 biog. n. 2, 330, 339, 341, 351–2,
362, 387, 400
Tausch : **III** 652–3, 662, 664 n. 3; **IV**
12, 45, 431, 485
Tavera, Schmit, Ritter von : **III** 177
n. 1, 181 biog. n. 8, 194
Letter from, **III** 197
Tenterden, Lord : **III** 67 biog. n. 1
Tessendorf : **III** 36 biog. n. 3
Letter to, **III** 36
Letter from, **III** 37
Tetuan, Carlos O'Donnell y Abrey,
Duke of : **III** 393 n. 4, 394 biog.
n. 2
Tewfik Bey, Lieutenant-Colonel : **III**
404 biog. n. 2

Tewfik Pasha : **III** 398 biog. n. 3, 558;
**IV** 102, 599
Thibaudin, Jean : **III** 79 biog. n. 3
Thielau, Wilhelm Otto Florian von : **III**
44 biog. n. 1, 45
Thielen, Karl von : **III** 325 biog. n. 3
Thielmann, Max, Baron von : **III** x, 58
biog. n. 2, 77 n. 1; **IV** 46 n. 2
Thiers, Louis Adolphe : **III** 32 biog. n. 1,
33, 35, 98
Thile, Karl Hermann von : **III** 31 n. 5,
34 biog. n. 2
Thornton, Sir Edward : **III** 175 biog.
n. 6
Three Emperors League : **III** 102–4,
125–7, 132, 176, 186–7, 200, 512
Thun und Hohenstein, Franz, Count,
then Prince : **III** 305 biog. n. 3
Thun und Hohenstein, Leo, Count : **IV**
615 biog. n. 5
Thyra, Princess of Denmark : **III** 287
n. 3
Tiedemann, Christoph von : **III** 46 biog.
n. 1, 90
Letter to, **III** 46
Timachev : **III** 518
Timor : **IV** 92–3
Tirard, Pierre Emmanuel : **III** 79 biog.
n. 4
Tirpitz, Admiral Alfred von : **IV** 51
biog. n. 1, 53, 82, 161 n. 4, 162,
245, 277, 313, 383 n. 2, 488, 495,
552, 554–6, 560, 566, 568, 571, 598–
602
Tissot, Charles Joseph : **III** 60 biog.
n. 5, 61, 64 n. 9
Tisza, Kálmán : **III** 298 n. 2, 299 biog.
n. 3, 303–4, 308
Tisza, Ludwig : **III** 460
Tittoni, Tommaso : **IV** 284 n. 3, 285
biog. n. 7, 286–7, 458, 489
Togo : **III** 494, 506, 547, 566; **IV** 65,
68–9, 73
Tolstoy, Ivan, Count : **III** 13 biog. n. 3,
15
Tornielli Brusati di Vergano, Giuseppe,
Count : **III** 377 n. 2, 378 biog. n. 2,
390, 393, 396, 451
Tower, Charlemagne : **IV** 522 n. 5
Transvaal : **III** 494 n. 1, 551 n. 3, 552,
554, 582, 583 n. 2, 584–6, 597, 603–
4, 616–17; **IV** 13, 24, 29–33, 36–7,
51, 122, 149, 151, 156–9, 168, 172,
185, 187. *See also* South Africa
Tresckow, Hans von : **IV** 524
Tricoupis, Charilaos : **III** 320 biog. n. 3,
414–15

Triple Alliance : **III** 62, 81, 98–9, 176, 198–207, 209, 252–3, 318, 338, 349–50, 365–6, 373–6, 377, 379–80, 386, 425, 429, 433, 436, 448, 450 n. 4, 452, 464 n. 2, 467 n. 3, 483–5, 489 n. 3, 528, 533–5, 544, 548–51, 553–5, 562, 564, 573, 583 n. 2, 592, 594, 597 n. 2, 600–2, 606–7; **IV** 5, 20–1, 38, 66, 68, 72, 75, 78, 79 n. 3, 103–6, 214–15, 220, 222–5, 236, 246–8, 250–2, 256, 261, 269, 276, 284–7, 295, 429, 440–5, 447–50, 463–4, 486, 562 n. 4, 577, 603

Tripoli : **III** 193, 209; **IV** 251, 254, 258–9, 262, 462, 473–4, 536, 587

Trost, Dr : **III** 334–5

Trost : **IV** 541

Tschirschky und Bögendorff, Heinrich von : **IV** 131 biog. n. 5, 251, 298 n. 2, 306, 308–9, 384 n. 2, 386, 390, 404, 434, 445, 447, 454, 456–7, 459–60, 464–5, 466, 484, 495, 497, 500, 562, 609 n. 4, 621; relations with Holstein, **IV** 391, 406–7, 409, 414–15, 417, 419, 423, 428, 436, 440–1, 449, 474, 499, 501–2

    Letters to, **IV** 408, 413

    Letters from, **IV** 391–2, 409–13, 426–7

Tseng, Marquis : **III** 96 biog. n. 1, 97

Tuat : **III** 390–2, 398, 443

Tunis : **III** 54, 61, 244, 348–51; **IV** 103–5, 284, 330, 336, 462

Turban, Ludwig Karl Friedrich : **III** 316 n. 2

Turkan Pasha : **IV** 535 biog. n. 1, 599

Turkey : Armenia, **III** 563–5, 567; Bagdad Railway, **IV** 174 n. 4, 175, 236, 493 n. 2; Bosnia, **IV** 535–6, 572, 577–9, 583–5, 587–8, 590–1, 598–9, 603, 606–9, 611, 614–15, 618; domestic affairs, **IV** 101–2, 266, 351, 489; Egypt, **III** 61, 63–5, 68, 386, 396–8, 399, 404, 407, 410–12, 430, 438; Great Britain, **IV** 69–70, 75, 115–16, 150, 258–9, 262, 379–80, 489, 515–16, 549, 554, 577–8, 584–6, 604; Greece, **III** 320, 414–15; **IV** 37–41, 54; Russia, **III** 43, 170, 424 n. 4, 562; **IV** 2–3, 7–8, 136; Young Turks, **IV** 545–8, 552 n. 2, 565, 577–8, 584–5, 588 n. 7, 604, 609; miscellaneous, **III** 43 n. 2, 61, 64, 86 n. 5, 87 n. 1, 132, 158, 162 n. 6, 170, 171 n. 5, 175–8, 188, 193, 203, 209, 220, 269, 317, 329, 481, 493, 531–3, 534 n. 1, 535, 537, 544, 549, 551,

557–9, 588 n. 2, 606, 655 n. 3; **IV** 15–16, 26–7, 149, 251, 254, 462, 553 n. 2. *See also* Dardanelles

Tweedmouth, Lord : **IV** 517 biog. n. 5

Tyrrell, Mrs Julia : **III** 110 biog. n. 5, 260, 268, 576

Tzu Hsi (Chinese Empress mother) : **IV** 185, 188, 203, 205

Ultramontane activity : **III** 53, 82, 163, 314, 316, 354, 401, 405

Umberto I, King of Italy (1878–1900) : **III** 55 n. 1, 206 n. 2, 244, 302, 317 n. 5, 318, 336, 459, 490 n. 1, 602 n. 3; **IV** 34, 48 n. 1, 103, 190

United States : China, **IV** 83, 92–3, 98, 186, 188–9, 196–7, 202, 207, 217–19, 264, 282–3, 487; Germany, **IV** 270, 428, 438, 522, 552, 556, 561, 584; Great Britain, **IV** 98–9, 111–13, 159, 166, 169, 215, 277–8, 450, 470; Morocco, **IV** 329 n. 1, 330–1, 338–40, 380, 386–7, 390, 397, 402–3; Philippines, **IV** 76, 78, 89; Russo-Japanese war, **IV** 313, 315, 326; Samoa: **IV** 109–14, 121, 151, 176 n. 4; miscellaneous, **III** 129, 131–2, 495 n. 2, 585; **IV** 107, 191, 565

Üxküll, Baron : **III** 224 biog. n. 4, 238, 253

Valentini, Rudolf von : **IV** 596 biog. n. 4

Valerie, Grand Duchess of Austria : **IV** 445

Vannovski, General Peter : **III** 109 biog. n. 4, 247, 249

Varnbüler, Axel, Baron von : **III** 462 biog. n. 2, 500; **IV** 513

    Letter from, **IV** 419

Vassel : **IV** 559 biog. n. 3

Vatican : see Catholic Church

Venezuela : **III** 585 n. 2; **IV** 245–6

Vera, Duchess of Württemberg : **IV** 606

Verdy du Vernois, General Julius von : **III** 162 biog. n. 1, 236, 323, 346, 352, 356, 358, 384 n. 1

Versen, General Max von : **III** 340 biog. n. 2, 357

Victor Emanuel III, King of Italy (1900–1946) : **IV** 38 n. 1, 210–11, 221, 284 n. 3, 285 n. 2, 286–7, 443, 447

Victoria, Queen of England (1837–1901) : **III** 60, 151, 174–6, 179, 182, 204 n. 4, 214 n. 1, 216–19, 221–3, 271 n. 3, 222–3, 282, 369, 435 n. 1, 437–8, 537–9, 543, 585; **IV** 17, 35, 41, 74,

81, 83, 101 n. 4, 119, 122, 140, 146, 151, 160, 164, 217, 238, 243, 261
Letter to, **III** 222
Victoria, German Crown Princess, later Kaiserin Friedrich: Battenberg marriage, **III** 164–6, 168, 179–82, 185, 187, 189, 191; Crown Prince's health, **III** 213, 217–18, 227–8, 257, 259–62, 265, 267–70; Seckendorff, **III** 216–17, 220, 222–3, 233; Wilhelm I, **III** 277; Wilhelm II, **III** 228–32; as Kaiserin, **III** 317, 333, 384, 549, 655 n. 3; **IV** 81, 236, 271; French visit, **III** 368–70, 385; miscellaneous, **III** 94–5, 111–12, 147–9, 155–6, 192, 214–15, 265–9, 297
Letters to, **III** 221–2; **IV** 82–4
Letters from, **III** 186, 220–1; **IV** 85–6
Viktoria, Princess of Prussia: **III** 147 n. 7, 227, 150–4, 181, 188–9, 191, 215, 272
Villaume, General Karl von: **III** 247 biog. n. 1, 289, 291, 326, 659
Virchow, Professor Dr Rudolf: **III** 259 biog. n. 1
Visconti-Venosta, Emilio, Marquese di: **IV** 20 n. 5, 48, 64, 286–7, 395
Vishnegradsky, Ivan: **III** 249 biog. n. 2, 256, 309, 383
Vitzthum von Eckstedt, Friedrich, Count: 283 biog. n. 1, 292
Vladimir Alexandrovich, Grand Duke of Russia: **III** 196 biog. n. 2, 283–4, 289, 292, 306, 562, 655 n. 4; **IV** 1, 7, 196, 217
Vladislaev: **III** 249
Vlangaly: **III** 238 biog. n. 3
Voigt, Wilhelm: **IV** 554 biog. n. 1
Völk, Dr Joseph: **III** 53 biog. n. 2
Vollmar, Georg von: **IV** 190 biog. n. 5

Waddington, William Henry: **III** 61 biog. n. 3, 122 n. 1
Waldeck-Rousseau, Pierre: **III** 81 biog. n. 3, 82; **IV** 184
Waldersee, General Alfred, Count von: **III** 29 biog. n. 2, 70–3, 94, 117, 124, 126–9, 161, 233–5, 241, 253, 268, 317–18, 323, 338, 340, 347, 352–7, 362, 364, 467 n. 2, 468, 470, 473, 505–6, 568, 575, 624, 629, 642, 645, 653, 654 n. 1, 656; **IV** 1 n. 3, 90–1, 94–5, 193–5, 199, 200–2, 206–7, 212, 217, 234 n. 2, 430, 433, 485
Letters from, **III** 279, 295
Waldersee, Marie Esther, Countess von (née Lee): **III** 323, 356

Waldeyer, Dr Wilhelm: **III** 269 biog. n. 4, 270
Waldow, Wilhelm von: **IV** 453 biog. n. 7
Wallace, Sir Donald Mackenzie: **III** 486 biog. n. 1
Wallenberg, Marie von (née von Rochow): **III** 49 biog. n. 5, 215–16
Walter, Arthur Frazer: **IV** 123 biog. n. 1
Wangenheim, Hans, Baron von: **IV** 241 biog. n. 2
Wartensleben, General Hermann Wilhelm, Count von: **III** 128 biog. n. 7
Wedel, Edgar, Count von: **IV** 456 biog. n. 1
Wedel, Karl, Count, then Prince von: **III** 93 biog. n. 1, 202, 235–6, 339, 421, 424; **IV** 123 n. 2, 129, 246 n. 2, 254 n. 1, 269, 440, 454, 456, 495, 497, 563, 615
Letters from, **III** 93–4, 149–54, 312–13; **IV** 210–11, 220, 248–50
Wedel-Piesdorf, Wilhelm von: **III** 470 biog. n. 2, 472, 490 n. 3
Wegner, Dr: **III** 215 biog. n. 2
Wehren, Colonel von
Letter from, **III** 117–18
Weissenfeld, Count: **III** 611 n. 1
Wekerle, Alexander: **III** 460 biog. n. 2; **IV** 608
Welsersheimb, Rudolf, Count: **IV** 8 biog. n. 1, 125
Wendelstadt, Baron: **IV** 520 biog. n. 3
Wentzel, Richard: **IV** 291 biog. n. 2
Werder, Bernhard von: **III** 109 biog. n. 6, 114, 116–17, 532, 650
Werthern-Beichlingen, Georg, Baron, then Count von: **III** 163 biog. n. 4, 164, 264–5, 271
Werthern, Major von: **III** 291
Wesdehlen, Ludwig, Count von: **III** 36 biog. n. 1, 42, 415 n. 2
White, Andrew D.: **IV** 92 biog. n. 5, 93
White, Sir William: **III** 174 biog. n. 5, 175–8, 188, 379–80, 386
Whitman, Sidney: **IV** 455 biog. n. 1, 469, 570
Wichert, Ernst: **III** 462
Wichmann, Karl: **IV** 176 biog. n. 2
Wielopolski, Alexander, Marquis: **III** 19 n. 1
Wilhelm I, King of Prussia (1861–88) and German Kaiser (1871–88): **III** 38, 51, 55 n. 2, 67 n. 2, 70–2, 85, 87

n. 1, 90, 101 n. 3, 108–9, 114, 117, 123–5, 128, 135, 147, 149–51, 156–7, 161, 168–9, 180, 182–5, 188–91, 213–15, 225, 228–30, 234, 244, 263, 266–7, 271, 276 n. 1, 282, 401, 431, 600, 619 n. 2, 658 n. 1; **IV** 83, 268

Wilhelm II, Prince, Crown Prince (1888) then King of Prussia and German Kaiser (1888–1918): as Prince Wilhelm, **III** 90, 116–17, 148, 168–9, 178 n. 2, 214, 219, 223, 227–32, 251, 262, 264–8, 270–1, 273, 275–6; relations with parents, **III** 214, 227, 266, 277; as Kaiser, **III** 283, 287, 290–2, 294–7, 300–2, 307, 318–20, 326, 335–6, 338, 344, 357, 360–2, 364, 399–400, 403, 431, 438, 439, 445, 454, 462, 468 n. 1, 469, 483, 489, 491–2, 516, 521, 538 n. 3, 541–2, 544–5, 548, 579 n. 2, 583 n. 4, 589 n. 3, 592–3, 597, 656 n. 1, 660–1; **IV** 2–3, 48, 76–7, 102, 165, 211, 251, 287, 324 n. 1, 422, 448, 451, 515; health and personality, **III** 281–3, 288, 291, 293, 301, 322–3, 325, 343, 346, 353, 383–4, 403, 418, 470 n. 1, 577, 613, 636–8, 641, 655–6; trips, **III** 278, 280, 285, 292, 297 n. 5, 299 n. 5, 314 n. 1, 317 n. 2, 319 n. 3, 338 n. 3, 340 n. 1, 343 n. 1, 358 n. 1, 383 n. 1, 416 n. 1, 422 n. 1, 424 n. 2, 434 n. 2, 508 n. 2, 602 n. 3, 609, 614, 617 n. 4; visits to England, **III** 434–7, 439, 537–9, 542–3, 608; **IV** 48, 146, 151–2, 157, 164, 166–70, 217–18, 243, 261, 269–70, 272, 275, 292, 492, 509; Mediterranean cruise, **IV** 285, 287 n. 3, 288–9

Personal relations: Bismark, **III** 299, 301, 313–16, 324, 328–30, 332, 337–8, 340, 345, 346 n. 1, 350 n. 2, 402 n. 1, 413 n. 2, 481, 494, 505–6, 519 n. 4, 520, 573 n. 2, 575, 655, 661; **IV** 175; Bülow, **IV** 96–7, 234–5, 245–6, 260, 265, 269–73, 275, 293, 319, 370–1, 383 n. 2, 438, 447, 457, 466, 596–7, 612, 614; Eulenburg, **IV** 242, 399–400, 447 (*see also* Eulenburg, Philipp); Harden, **IV** 435 n. 7, 437, 446–7, 456, 472 n. 1, 477, 479–84, 491–4, 498, 504, 506, 509, 513 n. 3, 518–21, 528, 541, 544, 562, 564, 580, 582, 591–2; Hatzfeldt, **III** 437, 439, 483, 524, 597; **IV** 26–7, 35, 75, 165, 183, 227–9; Holstein, **III** 354; **IV** 8, 10–13, 19, 43, 46–7, 80, 90, 95, 127–9, 131, 133–5, 179, 191, 200, 271,

294, 298–300, 302, 306, 312–14, 323, 383–5, 406–14, 416–17, 424–7, 435 n. 7, 437, 457, 486–90, 495–6, 500, 502, 529, 566–7, 595–7; Waldersee, **III** 323, 347, 352–6, 362

Foreign affairs: Armenia, **III** 549, 643; Austria, **III** 298–9, 304, 312, 322 n. 3, 357, 382, 389, 556, 560 n. 4, 579–80, 582, 589 n. 1, 592 n. 1; **IV** 446, 535–6, 578–9, 581, 583, 588, 603–4, 613–14, 618, 620–1; Crete, **III** 643; Eastern question, **IV** 379–80, 546–7; Far East, **III** 531, 536, 539, 541, 662 n. 1; **IV** 49–53, 57, 60–1, 195–6, 199–200, 383 n. 2, 384–9, 433–4; France, **III** 339, 368; **IV** 10, 14, 279 n. 5, 280–2, 284–9, 434, 487–90, 529, 534; Great Britain, **III** 339, 386 n. 1, 435 n. 1, 437, 446 n. 1, 485 n. 2, 537–9, 543, 544 n. 3, 551 n. 3, 552, 554, 556–7, 576, 585, 597 n. 2, 602, 664; **IV** 13, 29, 31–2, 36, 41 n. 3, 48, 70–3, 75, 80–2, 87–8, 100–1, 108, 118 n. 3, 119–23, 140–1, 146–7, 148 n. 2, 150, 152–3, 155–6, 159–64, 167, 170–1, 185, 189, 239–40, 254, 258, 272–3, 291, 322, 356, 382, 516–17, 550–5, 567, 598; Greece, **IV** 20; Italy, **III** 339, 343, 350 n. 2, 351 n. 1; **IV** 445; Morocco, **IV** 328 n. 1, 330–1, 334–5, 340 n. 1, 341–3, 346–7, 356–9, 364–9, 370–5, 380, 387, 389, 392–3, 396, 410, 421, 548–9, 557–62, 566–7; Russia, **III** 278–9, 316–17, 326–8, 330–1, 350 n. 2, 389 n. 5, 562, 660; **IV** 1, 5, 106–7, 137, 142–5, 157, 209, 316, 318, 357, 604; South Africa, **III** 493 n. 2, 584 n. 3 & 4, 586, 601, 603, 605, 608 n. 3; Triple Alliance, **III** 350 n. 1, 564; Turkey, **III** 386 n. 1, 655 n. 3

Domestic affairs: **III** 313–15, 324–5, 327, 329, 331, 338 n. 4, 344 n. 3, 357, 384, 400–3, 405 n. 1, 406, 408–9, 416–18, 421, 490, 505 n. 1, 560–1, 577, 601, 623, 631 n. 2; **IV** 11, 34–5, 39, 46–7, 168, 190–1, 266, 439, 453–4, 518, 551; anti-revolutionary law, **III** 475–80, 499, 503; army bill, 1892, **III** 388–9, 422–3; *Daily Telegraph* affair, **IV** 591–5, 601, 615; Krüger Telegram, **III** 584 n. 4, 585, 605; **IV** 22–3, 31; naval policy, **III** 344, 347, 505 n. 3, 506, 589–90, 602–3, 623 n. 1, 649, 657, 659; **IV** 11–12, 18–19, 24, 27–8, 459, 510, 516–17, 551–6, 561, 566–7, 571, 584;

personnel questions, **III** 421 n. 2, 423–4, 455–6, 490, 495–504, 508, 568–74, 578–9, 583 n. 4, 586–7, 589–90, 595, 598, 603–4, 609–15, 618, 621–31, 633–7, 639–42, 645–7, 649–50, 652–4, 656–8, 660, 663; **IV** 42, 43–5, 129, 156, 192–3, 241–2, 260, 267–8, 290, 292, 294–6, 310, 344, 391, 399, 403, 434, 495, 497, 499, 527, 573, 601, 605–6; relations with German states, **III** 334–5, 618 n. 1, 620, 658 n. 1; **IV** 11–12, 19

Letters to, **IV** 54, 85–6, 134, 411–12, 501

Letters from, **IV** 82–4, 395, 412

Letter drafted by Holstein **IV** 364–7

Wilhelm, German Crown Prince (son of Kaiser Wilhelm II) : **III** 361; **IV** 332 n. 4, 343 n. 2, 472 n. 1, 474, 484, 492, 605–6

Wilhelm II, King of Württemberg (1891–1918) : **III** 356, 475 n. 3, 477

Wilhelm, Duke of Brunswick : **III** 287 n. 2

Wilhelmina, Queen of the Netherlands (1890–1948) : **IV** 112 n. 2, 113 n. 1

Wilke, Dr Adolf von : **IV** 423 biog. n. 1, 541

Wilke, Carl : **III** 31 biog. n. 2, 34, 36, 456–7

Letters to, **III** 31, 37

Willcocks, Sir William : **IV** 588 biog. n. 6

Willisch : **III** 135, 458; **IV** 81, 127, 135

Wilmowski, Karl, Baron von : **III** 224

Winterfeld, General Hugo von : **III** 218 biog. n. 3, 265

Wirth, Dr Albrecht : **IV** 548 biog. n. 1

Wissmann, Hermann von : **III** 341 biog. n. 3

Witte, Serge, Count : **III** 515 biog. n. 4, 516, 520, 526–7, 529–30, 532, 536, 539–40, 545–6, 565, 616; **IV** 39, 58–61, 116, 138, 144 n. 4, 196–7, 222, 224, 397, 402, 474

Wittich, General Hans Heinrich von : **III** 280 biog. n. 1, 291

Witting, Richard : **IV** 464 biog. n. 2, 477, 511 n. 2, 519, 563

Witting, Dr Julian Max : **IV** 478 biog. n. 7, 482

Witzleben, General Job von : **III** 11 biog. n. 1

Woermann, Adolf : **IV** 162 n. 1, 163 biog. n. 1

Wohlgemuth affair : **III** 310, 315 n. 1

Woldemar, Prince of Lippe-Detmold : **III** 611–12, 614, 621 n. 2, 631, 634–5

Wolff, Sir Henry Drummond Charles : **III** 354 n. 2; **IV** 69, 110 biog. n. 2, 577 n. 2

Wolff, Eugen : **IV** 195 biog. n. 5

Wolff, Theodor : **IV** 400 biog. n. 2, 476, 557

Wolkenstein-Trostburg, Anton, Count von : **III** 123 biog. n. 4, 187–8, 190, 240, 448, 450, 460; **IV** 14

Wolseley, Garnet Joseph, Viscount : **III** 538 biog. n. 2, 542–3, 599

Württemberg : **III** 335, 401, 405, 477, 622, 629

Yorck von Wartenburg, Maximilian, Count : **III** 241 biog. n. 2, 309

Zahn, Major : **III** 352 biog. n. 2

Zankov, Dragan : **III** 321 biog. n. 1

Zanzibar : **III** 126, 136 n. 2, 344, 372, 375; **IV** 32, 152, 170, 185

Zedlitz Trützschler, Robert, Count von : **III** 400 n. 3, 402 biog. n. 4, 406, 408 n. 3; **IV** 453, 513 n. 3

Zeppelin, Ferdinand, Count von : **IV** 552 biog. n. 1

Zimmermann, Alfred : **IV** 56 biog. n. 3, 245, 600

Zimmermann, Eugen : **IV** 531 biog. n. 2, 532, 562, 564, 570, 589

Zinoviev : **III** 88–9

Zorilla, Manuel Ruiz : **III** 87 biog. n. 3

Zorn, Professor Philipp : **IV** 108 biog. n. 2, 126–7

Letter from, **IV** 123–5

Zorn von Bulach, Hugo, Baron von : **IV** 557 biog. n. 2, 563

*Zukunft, Die* : **III** 457, 461, 502, 623; **IV** 389 n. 2, 430–2, 434–5, 440, 446 n. 3, 447 n. 6, 452 n. 3, 458 n. 1, 460 n. 1 & 3, 467, 469 n. 1, 474–80, 482, 484, 498, 500, 503–6, 512 n. 1, 522 n. 4, 532, 541 n. 3